Freud Evaluated

Freud Evaluated
The Completed Arc

Malcolm Macmillan

The MIT Press
Cambridge, Massachusetts
London, England

First MIT Press edition, 1997
© 1991 Elsevier Science B. V., Amsterdam, The Netherlands
Afterword © 1997 Malcolm Macmillan

Reprinted from *Advances in Psychology*, Volume 75, 1991. The MIT Press has exclusive license to sell this paperback book edition throughout the world.

This book was set in Times Roman by Asco Trade Typesetting Ltd., Hong Kong, and was printed and bound in the United States of America. This book was printed on recycled paper.

Library of Congress Cataloging-in-Publication Data

Macmillan, Malcolm, 1929–
  Freud evaluated : the completed arc / Malcolm Macmillan. — 1st
MIT Press ed.
    p. cm.
  Originally published: Amsterdam ; New York : North-Holland ; New
York, N.Y., U.S.A. : Distributors for the U.S. and Canada, Elsevier
Science, c1991.
  Includes bibliographical references and index.
  ISBN 0-262-63171-7 (pbk. : alk. paper)
  1. Psychoanalysis. 2. Personality. 3. Freud, Sigmund,
1856–1939. I. Title.
[BF173.M353   1996]
150.19′52—dc20   95-48931
                                                          CIP

Contents

Foreword

With the publication of this accessible new edition of *Freud Evaluated*, Malcolm Macmillan and The MIT Press have advanced the long debate over psychoanalysis to what may well be its decisive moment. By now, nearly everyone grants that the standing of Freud's ideas must be assessed without recourse to the hero worship that he so cunningly promoted and perpetuated. But should we be trying to salvage a core of indispensable insight from his increasingly troubled legacy, or must we admit that his "discoveries" were simply illusory? Does it suffice that later analysts disavowed many of his most vulnerable judgments, or do those successors remain attached to a fundamentally untrustworthy means of obtaining knowledge? This book, I believe, supplies the answers in a definitively authoritative form.

A product of twelve years of intensive labor, *Freud Evaluated* merits inclusion among the masterworks of revisionist scholarship on Freud and his movement. Indeed, its importance can be measured by what those predecessor books had left undone. Frank Sulloway's *Freud, Biologist of the Mind* (1979), for example, precisely because it revolutionized our idea of Freud's scientific affinities and habits, fostered an appetite for a study that would combine Sulloway's historical density with a rigorous epistemic critique of Freud's propositions. And though Adolf Grünbaum's *The Foundations of Psychoanalysis* (1984) brilliantly supplied just such a critique, it was confined largely to Freud's clinical theory, leaving his metapsychology aside. Moreover, history played little part in Grünbaum's argument, which, for the sake of maximum fairness to an object of criticism, took at face value Freud's after-the-fact professions of methodological sophistication. We must turn to *Freud Evaluated* if we want to recapture the actual logic or illogic that governed each of Freud's increasingly arcane formulations of his psychological system.

But why should we want to do so, except out of ordinary biographical curiosity? Isn't the "context of discovery" strictly irrelevant to the "context of justification"? That is what we were all once taught. Macmillan argues persuasively, however, that formal, ahistorical scrutiny can tell us at most whether or not a given theory passes muster; it does not show exactly where the theory went wrong or whether it ever rested on a genuine observational base. By reconstructing, at every juncture, both the climate of ideas in which the theorist ventured his postulates and the difficulties he faced because of his own earlier commitments, the historically informed evaluator can piece together the motivation behind choices that might otherwise appear baffling. Thereby we can come to know the thinker's intellectual style and progressively make out whether his theory tended to be responsive to recalcitrant facts and to the objections of skeptical colleagues.

This is what Macmillan accomplishes with admirable patience and clarity. First he introduces us to Freud's early mentors and idols, showing how the founder of psychoanalysis picked up ominously mistaken general notions from Meynert and Charcot, among others. Then he examines the a priori manner in which Freud arrived at sexual etiologies for the dubious "actual neuroses," and shows how those etiologies dictated his subsequent approach to hysteria, before, during, and after the debacle of the seduction theory. As the biographical skein unwinds and Freud's constructs become ever more byzantine, Macmillan reduces each new set of assumptions to its logical components, indicates the necessary evidential ground that Freud never supplies, draws forth telltale confusions and contradictions, and exposes the ad hoc, pseudoexplanatory character of each new posited energy, drive, and psychic agency. And in the bargain, he shows how Freud's fatal indifference to the contaminating factor of suggestion and his loyalty to an overreaching version of determinism guaranteed that he would misconstrue his clinical findings.

I hope I am not making *Freud Evaluated* appear more like a corpse-strewn battlefield than an engaging book. The truth is that a high drama awaits readers who can meet Macmillan on his demanding terms. There is indeed a struggle going on here, and a momentous one. Arrayed on one side are Freud's impulses toward closure and comprehensiveness; on the other, the usually tacit criteria that any well-formed theory must meet. We see from the outset that Freud possesses some awareness of the scruples that the scientific ethos entails; but we also watch him suppress that awareness at every turn in order to maintain his Faustian claims to privileged insight. Will he ever realize that he needs to resume contact with the realm of validated experience? The answer is that there can be no turning back from gnostic pretension; it can only be redoubled as new anomalies are heaped upon the old. Although the outcome—a system of thought that negates the very right of its adversaries to pass judgment on it—is thus foredoomed, the ingenuity of Freud's extended end game never ceases to be astonishing.

Not least among this book's virtues is its explicitness about the standards that normally govern scientific theory formation. That a theorist's terms should denote independently ascertainable entities or processes; that the theory should not rely for corroboration on "facts" of its own manufacture; that theoretical statements should possess unambiguous testable consequences; that a proposer of deterministic claims must attend to sufficient, not just necessary, causes; that guesses should not be rhetorically promoted to certainties—these and other requirements, some transparent and some quite technical, acquire a vivid life in Macmillan's pages. In addition to being a trenchant brief against psychoanalysis, *Freud Evaluated* can be read more generally as an object lesson in scientific accountability.

Unfortunately, those who could profit most from such a lesson are the least likely to heed it. For reasons that any reader of this book will come to appreciate, contemporary Freudians tend to feel antagonistic toward science and eager to recast psychoanalysis in soft-edged hermeneutic terms. Whatever the merits of such an effort, Macmillan joins Grünbaum in showing that it is contrary to the intentions of Freud, who thought he was fashioning a natural science like any other. And although that fact needn't deter a latter-day Freudian from reducing psychoanalysis to "narrative truth" or mere discourse, there remains Macmillan's demonstration that the concepts to be salvaged in ghostlier form were never warranted in the first place. After *Freud Evaluated*, the essentially fideistic nature of adherence to Freudian notions ought to be generally apparent.

In nearly every time and place, of course, faith has been able to rally more supporters than reason. There are always plenty of people "who sleepily insist," as Macmillan puts it in a rare polemical moment, "that it is better to have ideas that glow even feebly in the light of a thoroughly bad theory than admit complete ignorance." Nevertheless, the perennial appeal of sheer belief does not prevent particular faiths from running their course and dying out. We already know that the glory days of psychoanalysis are long gone; they departed with Freud's untenable boast of enormous explanatory and therapeutic power. Those who hope or fear that such days will return need look no farther than *Freud Evaluated* to be assured that, in this instance at least, it is the turn of reason to prevail.

Frederick Crews

Preface to the MIT Press Paperback Edition

This MIT Press paperback differs from the 1991 North-Holland printing in containing an original Foreword and an Afterword, the latter covering the literature between 1991 and 1995. In addition, alterations and corrections arising from copyediting the work have been included; the spelling in the text, together with some idiomatic expressions, has been Americanized; minor errors in reference citation and listing discovered in the 1991 edition have been corrected; and the Index has been substantially improved.

I have to thank Professor John Kihlstrom of Yale University for recommending publication to The MIT Press and Emeritus-Professor Fred Crews, University of California, Berkeley for both his support of that proposal and for his very fine Foreword. In helping me with the Afterword, either by providing guides to the recent literature, or reprints, or advanced copies of new work, or comments, my thanks are due to Dr. Mikkel Borch-Jacobsen, Professor Frank Cioffi, Professor Fred Crews, Professor Edward Erwin, Dr. Allen Esterson, Professor Clark Glymour, Professor Adolf Grünbaum, Dr. Philip Rubovits-Seitz, Dr. Russell Powell, Dr. Bruce Quinn, Dr. Ana-María Rizzuto, Dr. Rosemarie Sand, Dr. Max Scharnberg, Dr. Richard Skues, Dr. Anthony Stadlen, Dr. Frank Sulloway, Mr. Peter Swales, and Dr. Richard Webster. None of these is, of course, responsible for what I have done with their ideas and suggestions.

My special thanks go to Amy Pierce of The MIT Press for the enthusiasm with which she took up the proposal and Sarah Jeffries for the many suggestions that have improved the clarity of the text. I have also to thank the School of Psychology at Deakin University for providing me with such a congenial retirement home, especially for the various facilities needed to work on this corrected edition. I am much indebted to my friends Professor Nicholas Wade, for the imaginative cover design, and Mr. Vladimir Kohout, for the cover photograph. Finally, Dr. Edith Bavin of La Trobe University gave the North-Holland printing a very close reading and me much support during the preparation of this corrected printing.

Burwood and Box Hill
March 1996

Preface to the 1991 Edition

Freud Evaluated had its origins in a series of lectures to undergraduate students in the Department of Psychology at Monash University. In the beginning the lectures had dealt separately with the twin themes of psychoanalytic personality theory and the application of scientific method in psychology but, as the series developed, it became apparent that aspects of the evolution of the theory might be used to demonstrate some of the principles of scientific enquiry. Both the early version of *Freud Evaluated* and the present one reflect that aim.

Because the lectures relied so much on original sources it was hard to provide reading and suitable reference material. I attempted to meet that need by expanding my lecture notes into the manuscript of the first version of *Freud Evaluated.* The work was begun during some spare time I found during a sabbatical leave in 1972–73, in the Department of Physical Education–Women at the University of Wisconsin, Madison, and the final draft was completed in Melbourne during the summer vacation of 1973–74. Soon after its completion I found myself dissatisfied with what I had done and was tempted to undertake a revision. It was one occasion on which I should have resisted Oscar Wilde's advice because, having yielded to that temptation, I found myself gradually succumbing to another: to produce the most comprehensive critique of psychoanalytic personality theory I could. *Freud Evaluated* is therefore very different from a simple lecture supplement and is virtually a new work.

In the lectures I had avoided secondary sources and interpretative accounts as much as I could and wherever possible drew on the publications with which Freud was familiar, especially the works of Charcot, Bernheim, Janet, Meynert, Jackson, and Darwin. Much of the light that those works provided for illuminating Freud's thinking in the lectures and in *Freud Evaluated* was provided by the skilled translations of Lillias O'Dea, North Melbourne, Drs. P. J. Weir and Andrew Wood of Melbourne, and Dr. James W. Coleman, Department of German, University of San Francisco. Lillias's translations were especially important: her multilingual skills enabled me to compare, among other things, the original of Charcot and Bernheim with Freud's German translations and the various English translations. Most of the retranslations are also hers.

To display a serious critical interest in Freudian theory in Australia is, as elsewhere, to declare oneself a member of a special kind of minority: one whose numbers guarantee intellectual isolation. Having written *Freud Evaluated* in a virtual intellectual vacuum, I am therefore more than usually appreciative of the encouragement that several of my colleagues and friends gave me and of the critical reading which a number of them made of draft chapters. I am particularly indebted to Emeritus Professor William O'Neil, Professor Frank Cioffi, Professor Ross Day, and Dr. Dianne Bradley who each read all or almost all of them. The late Professor Oliver Zangwill, who read the whole manuscript and discussed much of the detail with me, was, of course, kindly and encouraging as well as penetrating and direct in his criticism. As Oliver did, Professor E. R. ("Jack") Hilgard of Stanford University and Professor Max Coltheart, then of Birkbeck College, and Professor John Kihlstrom, of the University of Arizona, were good enough to allow me to visit their departments, mainly to use nearby libraries, and they also arranged for me to give seminars. For helping make some of the drafts more literate, especially in improving my treatment of theoretically obscure points, I am much in the debt of Liz Gallois and Lindsay Image of Melbourne. I am also more than pleased to acknowledge much valuable information very generously provided by Peter Swales.

I have been helped a great deal by the clerical, professional, and technical staff of my own Department. *Freud Evaluated* could not have been completed had it not been for the typing, computer programming, electronic, and photographic skills shared by Lesley Anderson, Nan Appleby, John Dick, Mike Durham, Jan Gipps, the late Desi Green, Vladimir Kohout, Lola Pasieczny, Lynne Steele, and Pam Ward. Help from Graeme Askew and Graeme Ivey, of the Monash University Educational Technology Service, and James Meehan, of my own Department, made the camera-ready copy possible and Dr. Garry Thorpe provided most of the assistance for the index. Cathy Cook and Cheryl Roberts, Technical Officers in my Department, worked very hard at finding references and Cathy, who had also carefully checked so many of the drafts, worked just as cheerfully in the final stages at solving what threatened to become an endless series of problems.

I have also to thank various Libraries, Librarians, and Library Staff for the rapidity with which they were able to meet my requests. My special thanks go to the Librarians and staff of the Biomedical Library of Monash University, the Brownless Library of the University of Melbourne, the Australian Medical Association Library, Melbourne, the Middleton and Memorial Libraries of the University of Wisconsin, Madison, the Stanford and Lane Medical Libraries of Stanford University, Cambridge University Library, Birkbeck College Library of the University of London, and the British Library.

Finally, to two of my friends I am especially grateful. Professor Ross Day, the Chairman of my own Department provided encouragement and formidable critical advice as well as funds that defrayed the costs of research assistance and translation preparation not met by Grants from the Monash Special Research Fund. My very special thanks go to Leonie Ryder not only for an enormous amount of critical help but also for encouraging me to begin and, once having started, to persevere.

Box Hill and Clayton, Victoria
May 1990

Acknowledgments

For generously allowing the use of material contained in some of my previously published papers I thank the following:

The *Journal of the History of the Behavioral Sciences* for Beard's concept of neurasthenia and Freud's concept of the actual neuroses, 1976, 12, 376–390, and Delboeuf and Janet as influences in Freud's treatment of Emmy von N., 1979, 15, 299–309 (by permission of the editor);

The *Australian Journal of Psychology* for Freud's expectations and the childhood seduction theory, 1977, 29, 223–236 (courtesy of the Australian Psychological Society);

The *International Journal of Clinical and Experimental Hypnosis* for The cathartic method and the expectancies of Breuer and Anna O., 1977, 25, 106–118 (© Society for Clinical and Experimental Hypnosis, April, 1977);

The *International Review of Psychoanalysis* for Freud and Janet on organic and hysterical paralyses: A mystery solved?, 1990, 17, 189–203 (© Institute for Psycho-Analysis);

The *Psychoanalytic Review* for New answers to old questions: What the complete Freud-Fliess correspondence tells us, 1990, 77, 555–572 (by permission of the *Psychoanalytic Review* published by the National Psychological Association for Psychoanalysis);

Elsevier-North-Holland and the Freudian School of Melbourne for the use of earlier and shorter versions of New answers to old questions: What the complete Freud-Fliess correspondence tells us, in J. A. Keats, R. Taft, R. A. Heath, and S. H. Lovibond, eds., *Proceedings of the XXIV International Congress of Psychology* (vol. 4) (pp. 303–314), Amsterdam: North-Holland 1989, and Freud and Janet on organic and hysterical paralyses: A mystery solved? in O. Zentner, ed., *Papers of the Freudian School of Melbourne: Australian Psychoanalytic Writings* (pp. 11–31), Melbourne: the Freudian School of Melbourne, 1988, respectively.

The publishers and copyright holders of works by Sigmund Freud have permitted the use of extracts, reprints, or extensive quotation as follows:

The Standard Edition of the Complete Psychological Works of Sigmund Freud, translated and edited by James Strachey and published in London by Hogarth Press and in New York by Basic Books (permission of Sigmund Freud Copyrights, the International Psycho-Analytical Association, Hogarth Press, U.K., and Basic Books, U.S.A.);

Leonardo da Vinci and a Memory of His Childhood and *Totem and Taboo* (permission of Routledge, U.K.);

The Psychopathology of Everyday Life (generous permission of Mark Patterson Associates, U.K.);

The Interpretation of Dreams and *Introductory Lectures on Psycho-Analysis* (kind permission of Unwin Hyman Ltd., U.K.);

The Psychopathology of Everyday Life, translated by Alan Tyson, edited by James Strachey. Editorial matter © by James Strachey, translation © by Alan Tyson (U.S.A. and Canada); *Totem and Taboo*, translated by James Strachey, © 1950 by Routledge and Kegan Paul, Ltd., copyright renewed 1978 (U.S.A.); *Leonardo da Vinci and a Memory of His Childhood*, translated by Alan Tyson, first American edition 1964, all rights reserved, (U.S.A.) (permission of W. W. Norton & Company, Inc.);

Introductory Lectures on Psycho-Analysis, © 1966 by W. W. Norton & Company, Inc., © 1965, 1964, 1963 by James Strachey, 1920, 1935 by Edward Bernays (permission of Liveright Publishing Corporation).

Introduction

Alles Gescheite ist schon gedacht worden; man muss nur versuchen, es noch einmal zu denken.
—Goethe: Sprüche in Prosa. Maximen und Reflexionen, I.

Freud Evaluated: The Completed Arc is a critical evaluation of Freud's personality theory that, because it is historically based, provides an evaluation very different from most. What I do is to describe the observations that Freud made and set out the theoretical ideas he put forward for explaining them. I then try to judge the adequacy of his explanations against the logical and scientific standards of his own time. It is largely this historical basis that leads me to believe that this volume is a justified addition to what seems to be a veritable torrent of books on Freud. My hope is that the historical perspective will give the reader a sound basis on which to make a judgment about psychoanalysis as a method of investigation and a theory of personality, as well as a sense of what Freud was about from his own standpoint.

Freud in Context

I site Freud's endeavor, particularly the first twenty years of it, in the psychological and psychiatric context of the time. The period has not been given the critical attention it warrants, despite the important work of Andersson (1962), Stewart (1967), and Sulloway (1979). All of Freud's important assumptions and characteristic modes of thought are to be found in this formative period. Many of the tests of his theoretical propositions were also simpler then than they later became, and the sources of many of the current difficulties in psychoanalytic theory more readily identifiable.

By examining the early period, one sees more clearly the continuity of Freud's thought with that of his predecessors, especially with Charcot's—it was not until about 1900–1905 that he developed a theory radically different from any that had gone before. Bringing out these kinds of continuities is not meant to detract from Freud's originality. What I hope it does is allow his contributions to be seen as the development of already existing trends. To me, the specific characteristics of Freud's approach seem more distinct than when they are related only to a general intellectual context, as in Ernest Jones's (1953–1957) account, or to a general social context as in Ellenberger's (1970) history.

Placing Freud in the psychological and psychiatric context of his day also brings out more clearly the basis of a number of the unresolved problems of contemporary psychoanalytic theory. For example, Breuer's original notes on Anna O. show how he and Freud misinterpreted the significance of her treatment. Rather than being a specific if limited therapy for hysteria, it was a quite typical, patient-initiated and -directed treatment. Breuer's notes also confirm that the affective quality of early psychoanalytic treatments were actually retrospective reinterpretations. In the fullness of time, affect became libido, and Breuer's specific cathartic method became a more complicated but just as specific reliving transference therapy. Some of the basic problems about the role of libido and the essential features of therapy—problems that currently plague psychoanalytic theorists and clinicians—are the result, I argue, of Breuer's and Freud's misunderstanding their original case observations.

The Core Criticism

Although what I have said might suggest that *Freud Evaluated* is primarily a historical work, that is not the case. The core of the evaluation centers on Freud's basic method for gathering data—free association. The method is not much written about and hardly ever criticized. I believe what I have to say about it is new, and that my criticisms are much more substantial than the few that have been made. A very large amount of contemporary psychoanalytic literature is also examined to trace how various present-day theoretical difficulties have their roots in Freud's originally inadequate observations and methods, in the faulty framework he adopted for identifying causes, and in his poorly formulated theoretical concepts. So infrequently is methodological criticism of this kind made in works on psychoanalysis, that mine almost amounts to a novelty.

There are some genuine novelties, too. Of them, the most important relate to the deterministic assumptions on which the psychoanalytic method of observation is based. Delboeuf's experimental investigations of the hypnotic phenomena demonstrated by Charcot, which he observed practically at the same time as Freud, are used to establish Freud's naïveté about the determinants of psychological phenomena, a naïveté that was carried over to the method of free association. I also believe *Freud Evaluated* to be the first major work on the development of Freud's ideas to use Masson's edition of the complete Freud-Fliess correspondence. From the letters, I have been able to show that Freud began his search for the causes of hysteria with the explicit intention of extending his already formulated but incorrect hypothesis that sexual factors caused the actual neuroses.

Although *Freud Evaluated* is a critical work, I do not believe that any other appraisal allows Freud and his colleagues and followers to speak so directly for themselves. My method of working is largely responsible. For the most part my analyses of Freud's observations and theoretical concepts were made before I turned to the psychoanalytic literature. I have to say that I was more than a little surprised to find that so much of what I arrived at independently was stated explicitly there, although mostly in a fragmentary and unorganized way. However, the degree of dissatisfaction psychoanalysts have with the theoretical aspects of their discipline is not widely known outside it. This work lets the intelligent reader in on what is almost a professional secret and, I believe, does so comprehensively.

Psychoanalytic critical writings have three characteristics. First, as I have already noted, the criticisms tend to be isolated and not related to one another. One might find an absolutely devastating argument for doing away with Freud's concept of instinctual drive, for example, in which the effects of so abandoning it on hypothesized processes such as repression are not considered. Second, although many critiques begin with a summary of the earlier literature, particularly of Freud's own writings, they display little real historical sense. That concepts change is usually made very evident, but the reasons for the changes are not brought out so clearly. Third, the criticisms never probe the evidence very deeply. Occasionally, issues involving the interpretation of data are raised, as for example in the charge of a masculine bias to Freud's developmental theses, but the status of the data themselves and the method by which they were gathered are hardly ever questioned. Free association, having been immaculately conceived by Freud, is maintained in its virginally pure state by even the most thorough of psychoanalytic critics.

The Place of Historical Evaluation

Historical analyses, or even historically based analyses, are not common. In fact, combining historical and logical methods runs counter to one of the most influential modern arguments, which says that historical considerations are irrelevant for judging the validity of scientific theories. The argument derives from Popper (1959), who emphasized that theories should be tested through the logical consequences that can be derived from them. In his view, the test of a scientific theory is identical with testing the consequences of a deductive argument. A hypothesis can be regarded as the premise of an argument from which factual consequences may be derived. Just as the premise of a logical argument is rejected if its conclusions or logical consequences are false, so a hypothesis is rejected if the predicted factual consequences are at variance with observation. Popper believed science progressed through successive falsifications of its hypotheses. Sometimes the rejection of a single, crucial hypothesis was supposed to lead to the rejection of the theory from which it derived. More often though, a set of complex judgments about the relevance of a number of such disconfirmations were required to overthrow a theory (Popper 1970, p. 50). Whatever the complexities, theories were to be discarded because observation falsified their logical consequences.

For Popper, nonlogical considerations are irrelevant. It does not matter what the propounder of a theory intended, what motives led to the theory being formulated, or how it evolved. Only its present logical consequences allow it to be confirmed or rejected. All that matters are the consequences of the tests to which it can be put. Although the history of a theory may be interesting socially or in its own right, analyses from those points of view are quite different from scientific evaluations. Feigl sums up this position:

> It is one thing to retrace the historical origins, the psychological genesis and development, the social-political-economic conditions for the acceptance or rejection of scientific theories; and it is quite another thing to provide a logical reconstruction of the conceptual structures and the testing of scientific theories.   (Feigl 1970, p. 4)

At least since Kuhn (1962) reservations have been expressed about this conclusion. History shows that in reality, scientific theories are rarely accepted or rejected simply because of tests of their consequences (Lakatos 1970; Feyerabend 1970). Nor do scientists work by systematically trying to falsify their theories and by probing the possibilities of giving them up.

In fact, the two rather different disciplines of history and logic may complement each other. It is even possible that historical evaluation can help solve some of the problems that have so far defeated the logicians. A historically based evaluation sets the record straight and enables us to see what the relations between the empirical facts and the theoretical constructs really were. That clarification in itself assists the process of evaluation. For example, suppose the attempt to confirm a theory fails. By itself, the failure provides no guide as to where the fault lies. Perhaps the original facts were inaccurately described or the original theoretical terms inadequately formulated. Would it not be sensible to see how those terms or statements were arrived at? Was there a worthwhile theory to begin with? Until the relation between fact and construct is clarified, we cannot tell whether the theoretical ideas were required by observation alone, by theory alone, or by some combination of theory and observation. In brief, historically based evaluations help us establish what has to be explained and whether any explanatory effort is justified. We are also placed on more certain ground in deciding which kinds of evidence should count as confirmatory and which as disconfirmatory.

A third reason for undertaking a historical analysis is that it sometimes helps to solve two related problems in the conventional interpretation of Popper's falsification principle. Both have so far resisted logical solution. The first is that of determining whether a given negative observation or experimental result is really crucial. That is, does a particular failure to confirm an observation require the theory to be rejected?

The related problem is that of determining when the point has been reached at which successive disconfirmations require the theory to be abandoned. We certainly need help in making these decisions. No well-defined logical threshold separates good science from bad; by itself, Popper's principle does not even demarcate science from pseudoscience, as he thought.

An example may illustrate my points. At one stage, Freud's theory of neuroses required him to assume that certain childhood sexual experiences recalled by his patients had actually occurred. Later, after concluding that they were reporting false recollections, he formulated an alternative explanation based largely on the assumption that a sexual drive with quite specific characteristics existed in childhood. Since then, a number of observational and clinically based studies failed to confirm the existence of a drive having those qualities. Now, by themselves, these later disconfirmations did not (and could not) point to Freud's misrepresentations of the few observational data he did have, to the theory-driven nature of the original conceptualization and its internal contradictions, or to the restricted range of alternatives that had led him to his particular formulation. Nor did the failures illuminate just what it was that required explanation.

I would not want to overvalue the virtues of historically based enquiries even were I to succeed in demonstrating them. Not only is the history of each science unique, but empirical and theoretical factors may interact differently at different stages in the development of the one discipline. Consequently, it is not possible to make a statement about the value of historical evaluations that holds for scientific theories in general. One has only to think of the fate of Kuhn's thesis that scientific theories developed through the effects of revolutionary paradigm shifts on scientists' mundane puddling about in their normal work-a-day world. Without claiming great knowledge of the history of science, I have the distinct impression that few historians of science now believe that Kuhn did much more than describe very broadly *one* of the ways changes sometimes come about. Analogously, whatever it is that can be established about the value of an historical evaluation of psychoanalysis may not apply elsewhere.

Some psychoanalysts have made appreciations of the value of historical analyses not entirely inconsistent with mine. Thus, after discussing the effects of the separation of the historical sciences from the natural sciences on the methods of enquiry used by psychoanalysts, Klauber (1968) concluded that placing psychoanalytic theories in a historical context followed a mode of explanation that had been used impressively with other sciences. He also thought the historical method might be of value for assessing the significance of theoretical controversies in psychoanalysis. Even though they agree that historical analyses say nothing about the scientific status of a theory,

Ellman and Moskowitz (1980) point out two "extra-theoretical ... instructive" features of them. First, understanding the origins of a theory may help in determining whether an adherence to the analogies that theories tend to generate has been detrimental to the theory's own development. Second, historical analyses may aid in showing if a theory and its analogical model have become confused.

A Plan

The journey through *Freud Evaluated* is a long one. To make it as easy as possible, the book is divided into four parts. In part I, I try to establish what the initial assumptions were that Freud brought to his study of psychological phenomena and the neuroses. Because most of them are related directly or indirectly to the treatment of the patient known as Anna O., I begin with a detailed consideration of her case. The assumptions examined include those about the role of ideas and the importance of affect as determinants of symptoms, Freud's naïve deterministic views about the causes of hypnotic and hysterical phenomena, and the faulty framework he developed for gathering and evaluating data about the causes of neuroses. Although he did not develop the method of free association until much later, the assumptions underlying it also underlie the methods he did use, and I make the problems with it explicit.

Part II contains a description and an evaluation of Freud's first theoretical ideas and his applications of them. His claims for the mechanism of repression are compared with those of its rivals. No basis is found to choose his concepts in preference to the others. The sources of the theory of the neuroses Freud formulated with Breuer are traced and the theory itself formally set out and assessed. I find it to be based on concepts of nervous system functioning that were out of date even in Freud's day, not to have a genuine logical structure, and not to generate acceptable explanations. I argue that Freud's expectations about the causes of neuroses were incorrect and led him astray in investigating what he called psychoneuroses. The same expectations were also responsible for the childhood-seduction hypothesis and its collapse. From the evaluation of the new theories in part II, I conclude they do not explain dreams or symptoms or childhood sexuality and that they do not provide an adequate general theory of the mind or of sexuality.

The final synthesis that Freud arrived at is set out in part III. There I examine how Freud introduced the concepts of ego and ego-instinctual drives to his theory of the mind, and conclude that their introduction was a consequence of the earlier sexual theory. For a fragile childhood ego to control an instinctual childhood sexual drive, it had to be of similar strength, and only something like an ego-instinctual drive would be able to provide it with that kind of energy. My analysis brings out the general unsuitability of the notion of instinctual drive that Freud adopted and the fact that conceptually it was not able to power the ego's functions in the way he required. The introduction of the death instinct and the tripartite apparatus of id, ego, and superego are seen as somewhat more remote consequences. Difficulties with the ego-instinct laid the foundations for the death instinct. Because the death instinct could not be found a home in the earlier theory of the mind, Freud had to construct an id, an ego, and a superego to house it. However, the death instinct itself is inadequate conceptually, and he was forced into making inconsistent assumptions about it. Nor was he able to describe adequately how the mental structures form or how they carry out their functions.

I bring the preceding criticisms together in part IV. First there is a general evaluation of psychoanalysis as a personality theory. I pay particular attention to the constituents of the personality and their supposed origins, citing what empirical data bear on their validity. I try to clarify the relevance that the marginal effectiveness of psychoanalysis as a type of therapy has for judging its validity as a theory of personality. Evidence for the validity of the method of free association is then examined in detail, and the status of psychoanalysis as a science is discussed. My conclusion is that Freud's method is neither capable of yielding objective data about mental processes nor of potential value for those seeking to turn psychoanalysis into an acceptable historical or humanistic discipline. Because some may find it puzzling that such negative conclusions can be made about a putative science that is so widely believed in, I bring *Freud Evaluated* to an end with some speculations about the continuing appeal of Freud's ideas.

I believe the historical evaluation I have attempted shows where the major weaknesses of psychoanalytic personality theory lie and that it helps to clarify just what it is that requires explanation. I also think it complements the more usual methods of evaluation. Whether my judgment has more or less value than this can be assessed only by those who persevere to the end of chapter 16.

I BEGINNING ASSUMPTIONS

1 Anna O. and the Origins of Freud's Personality Theory

Sebastian: This is a strange repose, to be asleep
*   With eyes wide open . . .*
—Shakespeare: *The Tempest*, Act II, i.

During the night of July 17–18, 1880, a twenty-one-year-old girl anxiously awaited the arrival of the surgeon who was to operate on her seriously ill father. Sitting alone at the patient's bedside, her right arm over the back of her chair, she went into a state of mental *absence* and:

During this state she hallucinated black snakes that crawled out of the walls, and one, that crawled up toward her father, to kill him.
Her right arm had become anesthetic through its position and her fingers turned into little snakes with death's heads (the nails).
It seems probable that she tried to use her paralyzed right arm to drive off the snake. When the hallucination had vanished, she tried to pray in her terror, but language failed her, she could not speak any, until at last she thought of a saying in English and found herself able to think and pray in this language only. The whistle of the train, which was bringing the Prof., broke the spell.
The next day her listening for the arrival of the expected Professor reduced her to such a state of abstraction that he was finally in the room, without her having heard anything at all. . . .
as often as the hallucination of the "black snake" occurred evoked by an intensified state of anxiety [angst] or by some snake-like object, her right arm became extended and completely rigid. As often as she listened in an anxious and tense way, she became completely deaf again. (Hirschmüller 1978, p. 350; cf. Breuer and Freud 1895, pp. 38–39)

Described here, in a fairly literal translation I had made of the original case notes, is what purports to be the basis of one of the most famous and influential illnesses in history. It is the description penned by the Viennese physician Josef Breuer, friend of the much younger Sigmund Freud, at the end of his treatment of the pseudonymous Anna O. It sets out what he believed was the root cause of her hysteria (Hirschmüller 1978). Freud's interest in what came to be called the psychoneuroses was first aroused by this case, and it was his collaboration with Breuer on similar ones that decisively influenced the discipline he was to found. It is a good place with which to start a critical evaluation of Freud's personality theory.

In part I of this book I try to bring out the assumptions on which Freud based his study of this and other cases of neuroses. The problem he set himself was to explain how symptoms such as Anna O.'s hallucinations and paralyses were isolated from her normal consciousness; that is, how these symptoms were outside the patient's control. In discussing his explanations, I make explicit his views of what constituted the legitimate determinants of psychological phenomena, and I evaluate the methods on which he based his treatment and how he went about establishing causes. I argue that his views of determinism were wrong, and that his causal analyses led him to an incorrect identification of the causes of neuroses. Free association, Freud's basic method of treatment and of gathering data, is shown to be based on these faulty deterministic assumptions.

In this chapter I argue that the case of Anna O. provided the shakiest of foundations on which to build either a theory or a therapy of hysteria. Not only do the case notes tell us quite definitely that she was not cured, they reveal with special clarity that neither Breuer nor Freud understood the extent to which she shaped the treatment or the significance of her doing so.

My main reason for using the original case notes rather than the later published account (Breuer and Freud 1895) is that they throw doubt on the affective interpretation of Breuer's therapy. Breuer's early description of the treatment is significantly different from the later account in placing little or no emphasis on Anna O. expressing previously unexpressed emotions. There is, in other words, little indication that what Anna O. called her talking cure required her to abreact while she recalled and relived the emotionally charged circumstances under which she acquired her symptoms. My argument is that this affective interpretation of Breuer's cathartic method is a reinterpretation of the talking cure that originated with Freud some ten to twelve years later. By that time, as I argue in chapters 2 and 3, Freud had come to such a peculiar view of the determinants of psychological phenomena that he was unable to appreciate just how much he was contributing to what he was investigating and treating.

Breuer's Observations

Breuer first attended Anna O. in November 1880 for a nervous cough she developed during a general deterioration in physical health attributed to overzealous nursing of her very sick father. Although the snake hallucination is supposed to have occurred before Breuer's first visit, only minimal signs of disturbance were evident to her family. But, according to Breuer's original case notes, her peculiar behavior led him to diagnose her immediately as mentally ill (Hirschmüller 1978, p. 352). This peculiar behavior included strange sleeplike, autohypnotic states in the afternoons that were sometimes replaced by a heightened excitement, as well as momentary *absences* during which Anna O.

would stop in the middle of a sentence, repeat the last words only to continue talking again after a short pause.   (Hirschmüller 1978, p. 353; cf. Breuer and Freud 1895, p. 24)

She seemed only partly aware of the fact that an *absence* had occurred and she had no knowledge of what happened during it.

Much later, Breuer reconstructed the events of this *first phase*, which began in about mid-July 1880 and lasted until December 10 of that year. According to him, Anna O. again experienced the hallucination during the *absences*, and a second state of consciousness began to develop around it. Toward the end of the phase she rested more and more in the afternoons, "waking" in the evening to the sleeplike state that now usually preceded the excited condition. Breuer described this phase as one of latent incubation, remarking that, unlike most such phases, the events occurring in it were to become completely accessible to him. The original case notes also reported muscular twitches or jerks and a not unimportant facial neuralgia, but these symptoms are not described in any detail in the later account (Hirschmüller 1978, pp. 349–350; cf. Breuer and Freud 1895, pp. 21–41).

By December 11 Anna O. was so ill she became bedridden. The *second phase* of the illness then commenced immediately with what Breuer called apparently quite new symptoms (Hirschmüller 1978, p. 352; cf. Breuer and Freud 1895, p. 23). These included headaches, complex disturbances of vision, a convergent squint, paralysis of the neck muscles, and contractures and anesthesias of the arms and legs. Anna O. now complained of having

two selves, a real one and an evil one which forced her to behave badly and so on. More and more clearly it became evident that ... she had two entirely distinct states of consciousness which became all the more clearly distinctive, the longer her illness lasted. In the one state she recognized her surroundings, was melancholic and moody, but relatively normal, in the other state she hallucinated, was "naughty"; if after the lapse of this phase something had been changed in the room, or someone had entered or gone out, she would complain: of having lost some time and would remark upon the gap in her train of conscious thoughts....
These interruptions gradually increased till they reached the dimensions that have just been described, and during the climax of the illness ... she was almost never normal ... during the day. (Hirschmüller 1978, p. 353; cf. Breuer and Freud 1895, p. 24)

The second state of consciousness stabilized as the illness progressed and was essentially a prolongation of the *absences*.

A complex speech disturbance also manifested itself during this time. Anna O. gradually lost her speech. Initially she was unable to speak in grammatically correct German and later she was unable to speak at all for two weeks. Breuer hypothesized that the speech loss had come about after she had been "offended by her father and had decided not to ask after him any more." Breuer then "forced her to talk about him" and she regained her power of speech completely (Hirschmüller 1978, p. 354; cf. Breuer and Freud 1895, p. 25).

Breuer made a related observation about her mood changes:

[D]uring her *absences* in the day-time she moved around in a definite sphere of thought....
In the afternoon she lay as if somnolent and in the evening she complained: "torment, torment." At first accidentally, and later, when we learned to pay attention to it, on purpose,
someone would repeat ... a word which was connected with these thoughts, and soon she ...
began ... to tell a story in the style of Andersen's Picture-Book or a fairy-tale.... A few
moments after the end she then awoke, was obviously calmed down, or as she herself called it
"comfy" [*gehäglich*].... The stories were all tragic, some of them very charming, but mostly
dealt with the situation of a girl anxiously sitting by the bed-side of a sick man. (Hirschmüller
1978, p. 354; cf. Breuer and Freud 1895, pp. 28–29)

A degree of what can be called deliberateness now became apparent:

We noticed, e.g., that she would occasionally, during the day, speak such words as desert, when
I then gave her the cue-word "desert" in the evening, she would start a story about someone
lost in the desert etc. (Hirschmüller 1978, p. 354; cf. p. 357)

Or, as Breuer later said, during these daytime *absences*

she was obviously creating some situation or episode to which she gave a clue with a few
muttered words. It happened then—to begin with accidentally but later intentionally—that
someone near her repeated one of these phrases of hers while she was complaining about the
"tormenting." She at once joined in and began to paint some situation or tell some story.
(Breuer and Freud 1895, pp. 28–29)

Breuer encouraged her to tell the stories, as the comfortable or normal state that
ensued lasted until the next day. Concurrently her physical symptoms were somewhat
relieved.

After her father's death in April 1881, the *third phase* of Anna O.'s illness commenced. Not having been allowed to see her father during the previous two months,
she was totally unprepared for his death. Two days of stupor followed and she
developed more symptoms: all human beings looked waxlike, and she could not
differentiate one from another; she developed a pronounced negative instinct toward
her relatives; and she now lost the ability even to understand German. She did not
seem to see the famous psychiatrist Krafft-Ebing, who had been called in as a consul-
tant (Hirschmüller 1978, p. 357), and his forcible breaking down of this negative
hallucination by blowing smoke into her face caused her to fall to the ground unconscious. A severe anxiety attack then ensued. Breuer calmed her down with difficulty,
but on his next visit several days later he found

she had been abstaining from food the whole time, was full of feelings of anxiety, her *absences*
full of horror images, with death's-heads and skeletons. (Hirschmüller 1978, p. 357; cf.
Breuer and Freud 1895, p. 27)

Breuer now observed that if during her evening autohypnoses she could be persuaded to talk about her hallucinations, she would come out of that state

calm and cheerful, would sit down to work, and draw or write far into the night, completely rationally, she would go to bed around 4 o'clock and in the morning the same thing began again. It was a truly remarkable contrast, between the irresponsible patient in the day-time pursued by hallucinations and the completely clear-headed person at night. (Hirschmüller 1978, p. 357; cf. Breuer and Freud 1895, pp. 27–28)

Over the next six or seven weeks, as the two states of consciousness became more distinct, Breuer continued encouraging her to talk about her hallucinations. This resulted in a more tolerable state for at least a part of each day, but it had little other effect on the mental symptoms and none at all on the physical. In fact, Anna O.'s condition so deteriorated, with suicidal gestures becoming so very frequent, that she was forcibly transferred to the Inzersdorf Sanatorium outside of Vienna on June 7, 1881. She returned to Vienna only at the beginning of November.

With the exception of five weeks during July and August, Breuer saw her daily during this part of the third phase. After her return to Vienna she extended her talking to include some bizarre behaviors, not reported at all in the published account of the case, that Breuer referred to as *caprices*. The first *caprice* she talked about appears to have been stocking-wearing:

In the evening when she ... was put to bed, the patient had never allowed her stockings to be removed ... she woke up at 2 or 3 o'clock ... complaining about the slovenliness of letting her sleep with her stockings on. One evening she told a true story which had happened a long time ago, of how she used to sneak into her father's room, to listen (she was no longer allowed to do night duty at that time), which was why she slept in her stockings, and of how her brother had caught her once and so on. (Hirschmüller 1978, p. 360)

Since she left the stockings on during a different state of consciousness from that into which she woke, she naturally had no recollection of how she came to be wearing them. The *caprice* of stocking-wearing ceased after she told Breuer about its origin.

Talking about the origins of her temporary inability to drink had a similar effect:

For 6 weeks during the hottest time of the year, she did not drink a single drop and quenched her thirst with fruit and melons. At the same time of course she complained about her tormenting thirst, but when water was brought to her lips, she could not be persuaded to take a single drop, without giving any explanation. At last one evening she told how she had seen her lady-companion's small dog, which disgusted her, drink from a glass of water, and how she had said nothing, in order not to appear rude (many weeks ago). 5 minutes later she complained of thirst, drank 1/2 a bottle of water and from then on her inhibition about drinking disappeared. (Hirschmüller 1978, pp. 360–361; cf. Breuer and Freud 1895, pp. 34–35)

The disappearance of this minor symptom seems to have marked the end of the third phase of the illness and the beginning of the *fourth phase*.

Breuer was astonished at the removal of the stocking *caprice* and the inability to drink. He seems then systematically to have exploited Anna O.'s willingness to talk during her evening autohypnoses, concentrating on the origins of her contractures, paralyses, anesthesias, disturbances of hearing and vision, and her other symptoms. It is Anna O.'s talking about the origins of these major symptoms that properly constitutes what she named, in English, as the "talking cure," and its use defines the fourth phase.

During this phase a quite remarkable feature of the disorder appeared. In endeavoring to clear up the remaining symptoms, Breuer found that Anna O. spent a good deal of each day in living through the events of the same day exactly one year earlier. According to him, entries in her mother's diary confirmed the accuracy of the reenactments. Over a period of six months, from January to June 1882, Breuer had to contend with the 1881 memories as well as those of the corresponding day in 1882. Two independent sets of recollections were now required to reconstruct the complex chronology of each symptom. For, unless Anna O. talked about *each* of the many appearances of a symptom in a particular order, it was not removed. And that order had to be exactly the *reverse* of the order of its many manifestations. Because of this complexity, Breuer decided to hypnotize Anna O. and make up a list of each of the times on which a given symptom appeared:

I used to visit her in the morning and hypnotize her ... I would next ask her to concentrate her thoughts on the symptom we were treating at the moment and to tell me the occasions on which it had appeared. The patient would proceed to describe in rapid succession and under brief headings the external events concerned and these I would jot down. During her subsequent evening [auto] hypnosis she would then, with the help of my notes, give me a fairly detailed account of these circumstances.   (Breuer and Freud 1895, p. 36)

This induced hypnosis, which is not described in the case notes at all, provided an *aide mémoire*: Anna O.'s talking cure continued to take place only during the evening autohypnoses.

Even with the list, the work of recollection was laborious. For example, there had been some 300 times when she had failed to hear something said to her and these were classified into seven groups: 108 instances when she had not heard someone come into the room, 27 instances of not understanding when several people were talking, and so on. Each instance had to be classed correctly in its group, placed correctly in the sequence, and then talked about in reverse order. Central to these recollections was the hallucinatory image of the snake about to bite her father. Its reenactment ended the fourth phase of the illness. According to Breuer's 1895 account, "the whole illness was brought to a close" although "it was a considerable time before she regained her mental balance entirely" (pp. 40–41).

Psychoanalytic mythology tells a different story about the termination of treatment. Anna O. is supposed to have developed a pseudopregnancy in which she fantasised Breuer as the father of her child. However, as Ellenberger (1972) remarked long ago, neither of the original sets of case notes mentions the pseudopregnancy. Breuer, the mythology continues, calmed Anna O. down and left Vienna immediately with his wife for a second honeymoon, during which Breuer's second child was said to have been conceived. By the simple expedient of consulting the birth registry, Ellenberger (1970, p. 483) showed this child to have been born three months *before* the supposed pseudopregnancy.

Breuer himself was wrong in implying that Anna O. was cured. Although neither described in his published account nor referred to publicly by him or Freud, within five weeks of the close of treatment Anna O. had the first of four relapses. On July 12, 1882, she was admitted to the Sanatorium Bellevue, Kreuzlingen, Switzerland, where she remained until October 29, 1882 (Ellenberger 1972; Hirschmüller 1978, pp. 152–156, 362–364). Many symptoms remained: the hysterical features, speech disorders, alterations of consciousness, and the facial neuralgia. It was not surprising that she was described as criticizing "in an unfavourable manner the inadequacy of science in the face of her suffering" (Hirschmüller 1978, p. 364). Her symptoms seem not to have changed by the time she was discharged from Bellevue.

During the next five years Anna O. was retreated in the Inzersdorf Sanatorium on three occasions for a total of ten months (July 30, 1883–Jan. 17, 1884; March 4, 1885–July 2, 1885; and March 30, 1887–July 18, 1887). In the admissions book from which Hirschmüller derived these data, diagnoses were recorded only in general terms. For Anna O. it was "hysteria" each time. She was pronounced "better" on the second occasion and "cured" after the first and third. Binswanger wrote to Breuer on January 13, 1884, that she was "quite healthy, without pain, or anything else." But in January and May 1887, Freud's fiancee wrote to her mother that although Anna O. was apparently quite normal during the day, she still suffered from hallucinations as evening approached (E. Jones 1953–1957, vol. 2, p. 225).

No one knows how she was finally relieved of her symptoms, but some time before the end of the 1880s she was symptom free. She then commenced a quite notable career in social work, and is now regarded as the founder of the profession in Germany.

The Significance of the Talking Cure

Breuer, as we have said, believed Anna O.'s symptoms to be hysterical. Before going on to discuss what he made of her case, let us consider some alternative diagnoses. Her symptoms were, of course, quite severe and the immediate outcome of the treatment quite limited (E. Jones 1953–1957, vol. 1, p. 225; L. Freeman 1972), the degree of which became apparent only with work by Ellenberger (1972) and Hirschmüller (1978). Diagnoses other than hysteria therefore were suggested. First, several writers, mainly American psychoanalysts, proposed or implied the lack of success might have been because Anna O. was a schizophrenic or borderline psychotic (Goshen 1952; Reichard 1956; Karpe 1961; Bram 1965; Schur 1972, p. 38; Martorano 1984; Masterson 1984; Noshpitz 1984; Spotnitz 1984). The overuse of the diagnostic category schizophrenia in the United States, as well as the continuing confusion between it and multiple personality (Bliss 1980; Greaves 1980; Marmer 1980; M. Rosenbaum 1980; Boor 1982), is probably responsible for the retrospective diagnoses of schizophrenia. While a schizophrenia might not be inconsistent with the initial outcome, it is not consistent with her contemporaneous correspondence, which lacks any sign of schizophrenic thinking (e.g., Hirschmüller 1978, pp. 369–370, 379–380).

Nor does a schizophrenia or borderline condition fit well with Anna O.'s long-term features: the absence of cognitive or social impairment as well as the intellectually complex, demanding, and socially useful life she led in the struggle for women's rights, for relief for refugees and orphans, and against prostitution (Jensen 1970; L. Freeman 1972). For much the same reasons, "substituting the fashionable term 'borderline state' is not the answer," as M. Rosenbaum (1980) particularly warns. Another "mental illness" explanation is Pollock's (1972, 1973) proposal that Anna O. suffered from pathological mourning or melancholia. He assumed it took several years to clear up and implied that the diagnosis explained the partial remissions. However, he produced no facts, and what he presented as evidence consists of psychodynamic interpretations of doubtful validity.

More recently, Eysenck (1985/1986), Thornton (1986), and Orr-Andrawes (1987) argued that Anna O. suffered from some organic malady, either by itself or that her hysteria was based on such an illness. The difficulties in establishing any retrospective diagnosis with certainty are enormous, and it is worth noting first of all that none of these writers agree with one another. At best we have an organic pathology of an unspecified and indeterminate kind. Second, one finds that these opinions are based on very partial readings of Breuer's case notes. Thus Thornton claims that Anna O. had "fits." Now, the only convulsions Breuer observed occurred in the last few months of treatment, before the end of June 1882. Others were recorded among the withdrawal symptoms as she was treated for morphine addiction in the Bellevue Sanatorium, but only *after* Breuer's own therapy had ended (Hirschmüller 1978, pp. 367–369, 362–363). This late appearance, some eighteen months after the frank onset of the disorder, is not at all consistent with tubercular meningitis. Third, in arguing for Anna O. having tubercular meningitis, neither Thornton nor Eysenck seems to put much weight on Breuer's exclusion of the possibility (Hirschmüller 1978, p. 354). Given Breuer's medical skill, one may presume the exclusion to have been reasonably soundly based. Thornton practically dismisses Breuer's consideration of it altogether, claiming, quite incorrectly, that Breuer "recounts the entire case history from an entirely psychogenic basis" (Thornton 1986, p. 132).

In general, Thornton did not conduct her search for an organic pathology with much balance. She went so far as to describe one of Bernheim's hysterical young woman subjects as "i.e., a victim of epilepsy or other neurological disease" and therefore classified the negative hallucination induced in her by hypnosis as genuine. Thornton took its probable basis to be an epileptic discharge. In turn, these considerations led her to a similar interpretation of Anna O.'s negative hallucinations, particularly the one of Krafft-Ebing (Thornton 1986, pp. 138–139). Her equating the hypnotic trance with a psychomotor seizure is based on a similarly unbalanced view of the evidence (pp. 90–96).

Thornton also claimed it was the cough and "the introduction of the famous cathartic method" (1986, p. 139) that led Breuer to rule out meningitis. However, meningitis formed no part of Breuer's basis for his conclusion: he implicated the temporary disappearance of the aphasia after she woke from her afternoon sleep and all the other data on the variability of her symptoms (Hirschmüller 1978, p. 355). Anna O.'s story telling and letter writing rule out organic aphasia completely. What is relevant is neither the content of what she said nor its effect, but that she spoke and wrote at all. As is the case with some hysterical symptoms, her aphasia was quite variable.

Fourth, Anna O.'s later life, free as it was of symptoms of any kind, also ruled out most of these diagnoses as firmly as it disposed of the psychotic conditions. Finally, there is the independent confirmation of Breuer's diagnosis of hysteria in the records of her subsequent admissions to the Inzersdorf Sanatorium.

In opposition to these illness interpretations, Swales (1986a) suggested that the disorder was simulated. Although his argument has some merit, he seems not to appreciate the diagnostic significance of Breuer's observations that the paralyses and contractures were not diminished in intensity during sleep, which they would have been had they been simulations.

Were it the case that Anna O.'s symptoms had an organic basis in whole or in part, or that she was a simulator, the foundation she would then provide for psychoanalysis would be even shakier than I suggest. My main point is not that there is no serious challenge to Breuer's diagnosis. Rather it is that, although Breuer pictured Anna O. as the inventor of the talking cure, he failed to appreciate what lay behind her invention, domination, and direction of it. Freud, as well as most of the recent commentators, also missed its significance.

Ellenberger (1970, p. 484) seems to have been the first to point out that the direction Anna O. gave the treatment exactly parallels a number of classic eighteenth-century cases of what were undoubtedly hysterical illnesses in which, during either induced or autohypnosis, patients instructed those treating them about the causes of their symptoms and the methods of cure. Examples are the cases reported by Deleuze (1813) and Bertrand (1823), both cited by Dingwall (1967, pp. 16, 49).

The apparently absolute accuracy of Anna O.'s memory for the events of a year before and the intensity of the treatment also have their parallels in these and other cases mentioned by Ellenberger. More recently, van der Hart and van der Velden (1987) drew attention to the case of Rika van B., treated in 1851 by the Dutch physician Andries Hoek. Not only were the features of guidance of the treatment prominent—Rika van B. predicted various aspects of the course of her illness, including her recovery, and she instructed Hoek how to treat her—but in her regularly induced hypnotic state she recalled the circumstances under which her symptoms were acquired, reliving them with emotional expression in the later *waking* state.

Features such as these were regularly reported in the mesmeric press of the nineteenth century and were not confined to the early period (Dingwall 1967). In about 1900, Edgar Cayce, the American "medical clairvoyant," diagnosed the cause of his aphonia by "inspecting" his own vocal cords while hypnotized by another. Cayce then instructed his hypnotist to give him a suggestion to increase the circulation to the affected parts. When administered by the hypnotist, Cayce's self-prescription restored his voice. Of interest, his hypnotist knew of similar self-diagnoses from the work of de Puységur, the early mesmerist (Cerminara 1950).

As an aside, it is worth making the point that the literature contains a good deal of confusion regarding Breuer's use of hypnosis. Most of it centers around his induction of hypnosis, it being asserted or implied that he hypnotized Anna O. so that she might recall the symptom-producing events (Ferenczi 1908/1950; Freud 1893a, pp. 30–33; 1910a, pp. 12–13; 1925a, p. 20; Nichols and Zax 1977, p. 29). Breuer induced hypnosis only during the final stages of treatment (mainly in 1882), and then only in the mornings, and solely to obtain the list of topics to be dealt with during the subsequent evening autohypnosis. Even the context in which Breuer referred to his simple methods of hypnotic induction suggests they had not been in use before that time (Breuer and Freud 1895, p. 36). As if to emphasize this point, it is stated in the *Preliminary Communication* that the therapeutic observation of Anna O. "was made possible by spontaneous auto-hypnosis on the part of the patient" (Breuer and Freud 1893, p. 7) and, in summing up the case, Breuer speculated whether it was only possible

to discover the state of affairs in other patients by means of some such procedure as was provided in the case of Anna O. by her auto-hypnosis.   (Breuer and Freud 1895, p. 44)

Breuer's original case notes also only describe the talking cure as taking place in the evening somnolent, hypnotic, or "cloud"-hypnosis states.

The parallels between Anna O.'s case and the earlier ones of self-directed cures make it most unlikely that the talking cure could provide a firmer foundation for understanding hysteria. Anna O.'s contribution to her treatment therefore bears examination. Initially, she had spoken of the hurt done to her by her father and, from Breuer's later description, it can be seen it was actually she who played the crucial role in overcoming the speech inhibition, even though it was Breuer who forced her into speaking:

As *I knew*, she had felt very much offended over something and had determined not to speak about it. When *I guessed* this and *obliged* her to talk about it, the inhibition, which had made any other kind of utterance impossible as well, disappeared.   (Breuer and Freud 1895, p. 25. My emphasis)

Breuer's treatment strategy was based on the expectation that overcoming the specific suppression would result in a more general effect. But it was Anna O. who somehow communicated to Breuer both her feeling of offense and the deliberateness of her decision not to speak. His response to her communication set the train of therapeutic events into motion.

Breuer's response is too consistent with what Ellenberger (1966) called the concept of the "pathogenic secret" for it to have been merely idiosyncratic. From the earliest times and in many kinds of societies, illnesses of the most varied types have been seen as both the result of secrets and as being curable through their disclosure. By the time Breuer came to treat Anna O., the concept was well established in religion, literature, and criminology, as well as in the specialized literature on hypnosis and hysteria. Ellenberger specifically mentions recognition of the concept by the mesmerist de Puységur and its use by the Viennese physician Moritz Benedikt as the fundamental principle of his method of treating hysteria, a view of Benedikt's treatment already taken by Andersson (1962, pp. 114–116).

Breuer's first step in treating Anna O. was therefore consistent with a body of belief that her general speech function would be restored once her secret had been revealed. This would seem to be the significance of Breuer's later remark that it was through his observations of the speech inhibition that "for the first time the psychical mechanism of the disorder became clear" (Breuer and Freud 1895, p. 25). Anna O. may well have shared this belief about the role of secrets; it was not restricted to medical circles. In any case, she created a situation that demanded Breuer force her to reveal hers.

The second step in the treatment was Anna O.'s telling fairy talelike stories. Each story was based on a situation she had obviously created earlier during the day, and each elaboration required the presence of another person to repeat a word or some of the words from that earlier situation if her mood was to be made more comfortable afterward. A major influence on this step seems to have been a very widely accepted medical interpretation of Aristotle's doctrine of the essential role of catharsis in tragedy, one much discussed among Viennese intellectuals in the very year that Anna O.'s illness began. This medical interpretation came from Bernays (1857/1970) and generated enormous interest at the time of its original publication in 1857 and again on its republication in 1880. According to Lain Entralgo (1958/1970, p. 186) some 150 works were published soon after its first appearance, and Ellenberger (1970, p. 484) cited Dalma as showing similar enormous concern with the relation between catharsis and drama in Vienna after its republication. Coupled with the pronounced interest of Breuer and Anna O. in the theater, that relation could have created a set of beliefs in both of them about the likely effects of storytelling. And those effects would only have been to calm her general mood and not to alter her symptoms.[1]

Bernays (1857/1970) argued that the catharsis Aristotle mentioned in *Poetics* (VI) was the process by which the audience watching a tragedy were purged of the emotions of fear and pity. What Aristotle actually meant is totally opaque. It is difficult to know which parts of the brief clause in which the word catharsis is used relate to which other parts (Butcher 1902, p. 254, n. 1; Lain Entralgo 1958/1970, p. 195, n. 27) and this basic ambiguity also interferes with attempts to relate the clause to other passages in *Poetics*. As Else notes:

> The isolation and difficulty of the catharsis-clause are indeed notorious.... But critics and philologists are not the men to be daunted by lack of evidence: the mass of writing about [the clause] is almost in inverse proportion to the extent of visible material.   (Else 1963, p. 225; cf. Lain Entralgo 1958/1970, pp. 185–186)

The connection of this thought in *Poetics* with that in *Politics* is unclear, and uncertainty has always existed regarding where Aristotle's doctrine is to be placed in the corpus of other Greek writing on catharsis (Susemihl and Hicks 1894; Butcher 1902; Bywater 1909; Lain Entralgo 1958/1970; Else 1963; Hardison 1968). For what my opinion is worth, I am convinced the catharsis clause ought to be interpreted from within *Poetics* itself (Else 1963, p. 228). There is even something to be said for interpreting it to mean that catharsis purifies the emotions of pity and fear so that the audience can experience the same pleasure from the tragedy as from other dramatic forms and learn from the events portrayed in it in the same way (Hardison 1968, pp. 113–117).

Bernays' thesis was one in a very long line of medical and quasi-medical interpretations construing catharsis as removing fear and pity from the soul, much as a suitable medicine might purge the body of a disease (Bywater 1909, pp. 152–153, 361–365). What was novel about his idea was how he envisaged the mechanism of purgation. Most other commentators had been vague. Milton, one of the few to be explicit, thought of catharsis as a kind of homeopathic reduction. The effect of arousing pity and fear was

to temper and reduce them to just measure with a kind of delight, stirr'd up by reading or seeing those passions well imitated. Nor is Nature wanting in her own effects to make good [Aristotle's] assertion: for so in Physic things of melancholic hue and quality are us'd against melancholy, sowr against sowr, salt to remove salt humours. (Milton 1671, Preface to *Samson Agonistes*)

For Bernays, however, purging came about not because of a *reduction* of the emotions but because of their *discharge*:

The tragedy causes by (stimulation of) pity and fear the alleviating discharge of such (pitiful and fearful) emotions.
[*die Tragödie bewirkt durch (Erregung von) Mitleid und Furcht die erleichternde Entladung solcher (mitleidigen und furchtsamen) Gemüthsaffectionen*]. (Bernays 1857/1970, p. 16)

According to him, discharging pity and fear in this way expelled them or removed them from the soul, brought about short-term pleasure, and over a longer period, although not permanently, quieted the disturbing feelings.

Bernays' interpretation is open to grave objection. It is not really clear that Aristotle meant emotions were *discharged* (Susemihl and Hicks 1894, pp. 641–650; Else 1963, pp. 225 and n. 14, 227 and n. 18, 439–442). Nor do we really know what Bernays meant by an *alleviating* discharge. But, however construed, it does not seem to me to require the audience to *express* the emotions portrayed in the tragedy so much as to *experience* them. In chapter XIV of *Poetics* Aristotle even has pity and fear being calmed by merely listening to an account of a properly constructed tragedy. I believe the same would be true for Bernays; the passive spectator merely watching a tragedy would experience catharsis.

Whether or not Bernays's interpretation of Aristotle is correct is, of course, irrelevant. What matters is whether Breuer and Anna O. agreed with it, for it is, as Else (1963, p. 440) aptly describes it, "inherently and indefeasibly *therapeutic*." Bernays's was "the prevailing 'medical' interpretation" and continues to dominate "most thinking on catharsis" (p. 225, n. 14). Anna O.'s days were filled with hallucinatory fears and her evening stories with pity for a poor nursing girl in a fearful situation—precisely the emotions Aristotle incorporated into his definition of the tragedy. To someone interested in the theater it might not have seemed strange that telling stories involving precisely those emotions would benefit the teller's general emotional state. And Breuer was just such a person. Quite apart from Bernays's book or his own general cultural background, Breuer had a special and highly developed interest in the Greek drama (Meyer 1928) and could hardly have been ignorant of Aristotle's theory. Anna O.'s expectations would at least have matched his. She was a person of considerable culture (Jensen 1970), who conceivably knew of Bernays' book directly, and who had, on the evidence of her later writing, a pronounced theatrical talent. Long after her treatment with Breuer she wrote stories and plays in which pity for the central character was the dominant motif (Karpe 1961).

There is an additional more direct connection of Anna O.'s hysteria with the theater. In response to being restricted to an extremely monotonous life, she "wallowed" in

her highly developed poetic-imaginative talent. While everyone believed her to be mentally attentive, she lived through her fantasies, but when addressed was always mentally present immediately, so that no-one knew about this. This became, under the name of "private theatre" an established part of her mental life.   (Hirschmüller 1978, p. 349; cf. Breuer and Freud 1895, p. 22)

Anna O.'s repetition of the word "tormenting" was a hint that she be allowed to enact the situation or episode created during the daytime *absence*. Once the prompt of the cue word or words muttered during the *absence* was provided, she responded with the lines from her rehearsal. Breuer's expectations then allowed for the elaboration of a calming story that was little more than another performance in her private theater. This time, however, Breuer joined her in the audience to watch the melodrama of the pitiful girl fearfully nursing her sick father (Bram 1965). Ellenberger (1970, p. 256) also implicates the "theatrical and affected way of life" in Vienna during the 1880s as a cause of high prevalence of hysteria at that time, a thesis very plausibly supported by Bolkosky's (1982) analysis of the effects of problems of identity and communication on Viennese society and its citizens. True or not, it is at least the soil in which a cathartic method could grow.

The medical and other literature of the time devoted to altered states of consciousness might also have led Breuer to think of Anna O.'s two states of consciousness in theatrical terms and therefore as modifiable by catharsis. For although the number of cases of what would now be regarded as multiple personality reported by then was not more than five or six, the amount of discussion generated by them was considerable (Taylor and Martin 1944; Sutcliffe and Jones 1962). Nor was the discussion limited to the medical literature; in the nineteenth century such cases were thought to be especially relevant to questions about the nature of the self and the structure of the personality.

Taine, an enormously influential French philosopher, cultural historian, and literary critic, and one of the founders of French psychology, devoted a substantial part of *De L'Intelligence* to double consciousness and multiple personality. He used a striking theatrical metaphor to sum up the implications of these cases:

The human brain is a theatre where, on several planes, several different plays are staged simultaneously, but only one of which is illumined.   (Taine 1873, p. 16)

Of a case of mediumistic possession he concluded in similar vein:

Certainly one finds here a *doubling* of the self [*dédoublement du moi*], the simultaneous presence of two series of parallel and independent ideas, of two centres of action, two psychological persons juxtaposed in the same brain, each with a different mission, one at centre stage and the other in the wings.   (p. 17)

This metaphor was much quoted, and the paragraphs in which it appeared much referred to, for example, by Ribot (1884/1910, p. 122 n.), P. Janet (1886), and Binet (1889, 1892, 1892/1896). One may presume its central theatrical point was in even wider circulation, possibly being known to Breuer directly, as he was familiar with many other works by Taine (Meyer 1928). He must almost certainly have known of a similar metaphor used by his friend and colleague Ewald Hering, describing consciousness as a stage and ideas as actors (Hering 1870/1913, p. 8).

If talking about the hallucinations simply extended what had already happened in telling the fairy tales, no more than a general calming of mood would be expected. And that was what happened. As we have seen, Anna O.'s symptoms were not only unchanged, her condition so deteriorated that she was hospitalized. The talking cure proper began only when she began to talk about the *origins* of the *caprice* of stocking-wearing and her inability to drink. The expectation would then have been that talking would remove both the *caprice* and the inhibition of drinking, both being based on secrets—the secret listening, the suppressed remark to the lady companion. An alleviating discharge of emotion would result in a general, more comfortable mood. Again, that is exactly what happened. Ellenberger proposed Bernays's reading of Aristotle as a candidate for the therapy as a whole. On my reading of the case it can only be a candidate for the initial calming of Anna O.'s mood. Only one fact is not accounted for by this explanation: why did Anna O. take so long to bring about her final cure?

Anna O. continued to direct her treatment until the very end. She decided how and when it would terminate:

The patient herself had formed a strong determination that the whole treatment should be finished by the anniversary of the day on which she was moved into the country.... At the beginning of June, accordingly, she entered into the "talking cure" with the greatest energy. On the last day—by the help of rearranging the room so as to resemble her father's sickroom—she reproduced the terrifying hallucination ... which constituted the root of her whole illness. (Breuer and Freud 1895, p. 40)

In proposing this restaging (which is not mentioned explicitly in the original notes, although the hallucination itself is) Anna O. nominated the hallucination of the snake as the cause of her illness. Over the course of her illness she had combined features of two cases described some fifty years earlier by Colquhoun:

One of them announced repeatedly, several months previously, the day, the hour, and the minute of the access and of the return of epileptic fits. The other announced the period of his cure. Their previsions were realized with remarkable exactness.   (Colquhoun 1833/1970, p. 172)

We have already seen that the phenomena were known many years before these two cases (Dingwall 1967). What was novel about Anna O.'s prevision was how it directed Breuer to reconstruct the evolution of her illness.

If Breuer thought he had come upon a new and powerful method for treating hysteria, which Freud certainly thought he had, he was profoundly mistaken. Not only was Anna O. not cured, but she misled him about the cause of the temporary remission of her symptoms. How was she able to do this? At the time treatment began Breuer was a most distinguished general practitioner who had made two major and recognized contributions to scientific research. As a newly graduated physician he had undertaken original, basic physiological research into some of the regulatory mechanisms of respiration, and his conclusions had been communicated by Ewald Hering to the Academy of Sciences (Ullman 1970). Later he was proposed by Mach, Hering, and Exner for Corresponding Membership of the Academy, a distinction not often granted those lacking university titles or appointments (Meyer 1928). In between, and quite independent of Mach and Crum-Brown, he established the role of the semicircular canals in maintaining balance and discovered the function of the otoliths (Breuer 1923; Camis 1928/1930; Ullman 1970). Undertaken in a laboratory established in his own home, and maintained entirely at his own expense (Meyer 1928), his delicate surgical work contributed most to that discovery (Camis 1928/1930; Schlessinger, Gedo, Miller, Pollock, Sabshin, and Sadow 1967). The most eminent of Vienna's medical men were among the patients in his private practice (Breuer 1923).

Although Breuer had only the ordinary training of his day in psychiatry (Hirschmüller 1978, pp. 120–131) and lacked specialist experience in the treatment of neurotic disorders, his general scientific training and his extensive medical experience prepared him, almost as well as anyone in that era could have been prepared, to treat Anna O. Yet the talking cure was not, and could not be, a sovereign remedy for hysteria. Knowing little about the history of either hypnosis or hysteria, Breuer failed to see that Anna O.'s talking cure was simply one of many therapies that patients experiencing spontaneously occurring hypnotic states devise to instruct those caring for them to bring about their ephemeral "cures."

Breuer's Inferences

Having missed the main significance of the case, what then were the inferences Breuer drew from it? Unfortunately, they are not known in any detail from any contemporaneous source. The 1882 notes contain neither theoretical concepts nor empirical generalizations. In a letter to Forel some twenty-five years later Breuer wrote:

This much, however, I believe I can say: What follows immediately from the case of Anna O. is mine—that is to say, the aetiological significance of affective ideas, deprived of their normal reaction, which operate permanently like psychical foreign bodies; "retention hysteria"; the realization of the importance of hypnoid states in the development of hysteria; analytic therapy. (Cranefield 1958)

Breuer's recollection of the last three points may be accepted as they are, but the role he said he gave affective ideas requires analysis.

Analytic therapy, the process by which the memories of the various manifestations of the symptoms were classified, ordered, and connected to some root cause, had not been attempted previously. Retention hysteria, the generation of hysterical symptoms by withholding a response, was new. And, if one excludes Charcot, the role given "hypnoid states" was peculiarly Breuer's.

Breuer used the word hypnoid to refer to mental states resembling ordinary hypnosis. For him, hypnoid states ranged from reveries filled with emotion, such as daydreaming, through the fatigue after protracted emotion, such as after prolonged nursing of a loved relative, to the true autohypnoses. All of these varieties of hypnoid states were present in Anna O., her illness showing progression from the milder to the more marked forms. Just as in deliberately induced hypnosis, where it had been known for many years that there might be spontaneous amnesia in the waking state for the events of the trance (Chertok and Saussure 1973/1979, pp. 157–165), so Anna O.'s memories for the events taking place in her hypnoid states were lost. The absence of memory provided the starting point for Breuer's explanation.

Anna O.'s symptoms were based on sensations and perceptions first experienced in a hypnoid state. Her paralysis, for example, was an elaboration of her inability to move the arm that had gone to sleep; her hallucinations simply repeated what were originally false perceptions. However, she could not become aware of the causes of those symptoms because she could know nothing about what happened during the hypnoid condition. None of the memories arising in it could be assimilated into her normal consciousness. The creation of this split-off section of the mind, this second state of consciousness, was, in Breuer's view, the fundamental precondition for hysterical symptoms to form.

It is obvious that ideas played a major part in generating and removing Anna O.'s symptoms, but it is much less easy to accept the common interpretation of Breuer's claim that he recognized the etiological role of affective ideas "immediately." On the orthodox interpretation, Breuer required Anna O. to recall the memories of *emotionally charged events* and to give *full vent* to the previously unexpressed affect when she did so. Two things are wrong with this claim: it is quite inconsistent with what Breuer *described* as actually happening in the treatment, and, as will be seen later, it is also inconsistent with too many aspects of Freud's adoption of what he came to call Breuer's method.

Neither in the original case notes (Hirschmüller 1978, pp. 348–364) nor in the *descriptive* parts of the published account (Breuer and Freud 1895, pp. 21–41) did Breuer stress *emotional* expression. Rather, what he emphasized was *verbal* utterance. Some examples make this clear. Although all of the Andersen-like stories had sad or tragic themes, *emotional* arousal during the telling of them was nowhere mentioned. Indeed, some were described as very charming and like freely created poetical compositions, rather than as responses to the pressure of strong emotion (Hirschmüller 1978, p. 354; cf. Breuer and Freud 1895, p. 29). Breuer's later portrayal of Anna O. had her "shaking with fear and horror" as she reproduced and gave verbal utterance to the frightful images of the hallucinations that pursued her after her father's death (Breuer and Freud 1895, pp. 29–30), but in the original case notes, where the images are described as horror images, there is no mention of her talking about them at all. Nor are emotional reactions mentioned in the account of the removal of the stocking-wearing *caprice*. Perhaps of greater significance is their absence from the original description of Anna O.'s telling of the dog drinking out of the glass. In the later-published account we find that that emotional quality has actually *been added*.

Paragraph 1 of figure 1.1 is from Breuer's original case notes and paragraph 3 is from the published account. In paragraph 2 I have added the affective phrases from the published account to the original. From this it is clear Breuer uses the words "with every sign of disgust" to characterize Anna O.'s description of the scene before interpolating the phrase "after giving further energetic expression to the anger she had held back" between the end of the description and the request for water (Breuer and Freud 1895, pp. 34–35; cf. Hirschmüller 1978, pp. 360–361).

Breuer's original case notes make clear and direct reference to only a verbal mechanism by which Anna O. was relieved of the pathological stimuli with which she was burdened:

When ... everything *that had been added* during the five weeks of my absence had been *worked off* ... we achieved this good state. From all this it was clear that every product of her abnormal mental activity, whether it was a spontaneous product of her imagination or an event which had been interpreted by the pathological part of her psyche (*sentire*), affected her as a psychical

---

1. ... one evening she told how she had seen her lady-companion's small dog, which disgusted her, drink from a glass of water and how she had said nothing, in order not to appear rude (many weeks ago). 5 minutes later she complained of thirst, drank 1/2 a bottle of water ... (Hirschmüller, 1978, p.361)

2. ... one evening she told, *with every sign of disgust*, how she had seen her lady-companion's small dog, which disgusted her, drink from a glass of water and how she had said nothing, in order not to appear rude (many weeks ago). 5 minutes later, *after giving further energetic expression to the anger she had held back*, she complained of thirst, drank 1/2 a bottle of water ...

3. ... one day during hypnosis she grumbled about her English lady-companion whom she did not care for, and went on to describe, with every sign of disgust, how she had once gone into that lady's room and how her little dog - horrid creature - had drunk out of a glass there. The patient had said nothing, as she had wanted to be polite. After giving further energetic expression to the anger she had held back, she asked for something to drink ... (Breuer and Freud, 1895, pp.34-35)

Figure 1.1
Breuer's interpolations.

stimulus and persisted until *it had been narrated*, after which its effectiveness completely ceased to operate. (Hirschmüller 1978, p. 360; cf. p. 361. My emphasis)

Breuer's later reworking of the paragraph makes the point more clearly:

[E]very one of the spontaneous products of her imagination and every event which had been assimilated by the pathological part of her mind persisted as a psychical stimulus until it had been narrated in her hypnosis, after which it completely ceased to operate. (Breuer and Freud 1895, p. 32)

The overall mechanism described in the later account was also clearly a verbal one: "stimuli" accumulated in the mind during the secondary state of consciousness and had to be "removed," "disposed of," or "worked off" (Breuer and Freud 1895, pp. 29, 31, 32, 34, 35) by being given "verbal expression" or "narrated" (pp. 31, 32). Talking about these accumulated stimuli "relieved" or brought about their "unburdening" (pp. 30, 45).

Consistent with this, almost each time Breuer made specific mention of his systematic exploitation of the talking cure in the later account, he spoke of symptoms being removed by being "talked away" rather than by discharging the emotion associated with them (Breuer and Freud 1895, pp. 35–37). Again and again Breuer uses phrases appropriate to only a *verbal* process: narrate the hallucinations, talked herself out, verbal expression during hypnosis, giving regular verbal expression, calmed by verbal utterance, verbal utterance of her hallucinations, giving verbal utterance to her phantasies, brought to verbal utterance, and so on (pp. 27, 30, 31, 32, 34).

Nowhere in the original case notes or in the descriptive parts of the later account, then, is emotion nominated as that which is to be removed, disposed of, or worked off. In other words, the description of what Anna O. called her talking cure gives little indication of her being required to abreact the emotionally charged memories of the circumstances under which she acquired her symptoms.

Even had emotional expression been involved, modern opinion is very skeptical about its therapeutic value:

[C]linical experience tells us that catharsis and abreaction by themselves are effective in grief reactions and perhaps traumatic neuroses, and then merely to a limited extent. They are not usually effective *in treating hysterical symptoms*. (Hollender 1980. My emphasis)

Nichols and Zax (1977) express similar reservations about the value of catharsis. They emphasize the cognitive role of the verbal utterance, placing it even more centrally than emotional expression. Hollender (1980) also stresses the role of talking per se: utterance enabled Anna O. to translate the nonverbal message of her symptom "into verbal language."

These modern opinions confirm the conclusions of C. S. Myers (1920–1921) and McDougall (1920–1921) in their ancient debate with Brown (1920–1921a,b) on catharsis. All three used some type of cathartic method to treat victims of neuroses from the 1914–1918 War, Myers for longer than the others. Only Brown thought emotional expression to be central. Myers actually cured patients who, following his explicit instruction, revived the memory of the trauma *without* emotion. Although unable to compare this method with Brown's, he did not think its results to be inferior, an opinion with which Brown concurred. Naturally, Myers attributed more significance to the effect of reviving the affective and cognitive *experience* than to the effect of expressing the emotions. Brown allowed that some part of his results may have been due to "the faith which I had in psychocatharsis." Of interest here is that Hoek's report of the treatment of Rika van B. (van der Hart and van der Velden 1987) also emphasized her calmness during the hypnotic reliving. Only in the later waking state was emotion expressed. In this respect, her treatment falls somewhere between the methods of Brown and McDougall.

On the basis of his own psychoanalytic clinical experience, Marmor questioned the assumption that abreaction produced lasting therapeutic effects:

The dramatic evocation of anger or tears or a repressed memory may, it is true, leave [the patient] feeling transitorily calmer or more relaxed, but I have never seen it, in and of itself, produce the lasting personality changes which are the therapeutic objectives of the psychoanalytic process.   (Marmor 1962)

This is, of course, basically what we find in Breuer's description of the effects of the talking cure in Anna O.

Foreshadowing the detailed analysis in chapter 4 of Freud's adoption of Breuer's treatment method, it can be stated confidently that it was not until well after the end of 1889, possibly as late as the early part of 1893, that emotional expression during the reliving of traumatic episodes became the basis of his therapy. It will also be seen later, in chapter 7, that it could not have been until some time after the middle of 1891 that Freud arrived at the theoretical ideas that enabled him to give affect a role in the generation and removal of symptoms.

My view that the expectations of Breuer and Anna O. derived from a verbal utterance interpretation of Bernays's thesis is not, of course, inconsistent with the view that Freud's stressing of emotional expression dates from a later period. Although Bernays proposed that the alleviating discharge of emotion took place in the spectator, it would have been odd had he believed that, under the influence of the performance, the spectators in the audience would actually *express* the emotions of fear and pity. Attendance at almost any performance of a tragedy confirms this. Few in the audience express the emotions being portrayed—what they do is *experience* them. If an alleviating discharge takes place, it does so through the watching itself. Consequently, far from there being a discrepancy between a psychotherapy based on *verbal* utterance or *verbal* expression and Bernays's thesis of catharsis as an *alleviating* discharge, the two express the same idea. Talking about an event involving fear and pity discharges those emotions in exactly the same way as watching a play in which they are represented. Overt emotional expression is quite unnecessary.

What can be accepted is the importance Breuer placed on the accumulation of ideas in hypnoid states as the basis for the generation of hysterical symptoms and on the patient's talking about those ideas if the symptoms were to be modified. Breuer's caution in theorizing is also apparent. His major theoretical construct, the hypnoid state, went only a little way beyond the observable and was based on its fairly obvious resemblance to the true hypnotic states. Once it had been supposed there might also be amnesia for the experiences occurring in hypnoid states, the isolation of the symptoms followed. The hypnoid state made the pathological ideas unavailable to normal consciousness. Symptoms were due either to the reappearance of the hypnoid state in its entirety or to the intrusion of mental content from that state into normal consciousness. To the extent that verbal utterance rendered pathological ideas powerless, it was because it allowed them to be integrated with the primary consciousness.

Conclusion

Freud accepted what Breuer took to be the significance of his conclusions altogether too readily. He never seemed to have regarded the isolation of the symptom as other than the central problem in the neuroses, or talking about them as other than the central fact of therapy. Although his primary purpose in visiting Charcot in 1885 was to study neurological disorders, he soon became much more interested in Charcot's work on hypnosis and hysteria. Very probably this shift came about because Charcot, like Breuer, placed the transformation of ideas occurring in hypnosis-like states as central to the development and isolation of hysterical symptoms. Although Freud soon moved beyond Charcot's ideas about the causes of hysteria and the determinants of its symptoms, we will see that he never abandoned Charcot's quite incorrect view of the determinants of hypnotic and hysterical phenomena.

Note

1. Quite independent of me, Hollender (1980) arrived at a similar conclusion: "It is likely that Anna O. was introduced to catharsis as a method and then put it to use as a means of capturing and holding the attention of her scientifically minded physician." My argument goes further, of course.

2 Charcot, Hypnosis, and Determinism

Mangan: Don't you hypnotize me, though. Ive seen men made fools of by hypnotism.
Ellie: Be quiet. Ive seen men made fools of without hypnotism.
—Shaw: *Heartbreak House*, Act II.

Soon after his interest in neurological disorders had been aroused, Freud was introduced to the dispute between Jean-Martin Charcot and Hippolyte Bernheim on the nature of hypnosis. Freud was to become thoroughly familiar with the viewpoints of both. Although his attitudes toward the issues separating them reveal something of his thinking about psychological phenomena generally, their greatest importance is in revealing some of the more peculiar features of his assumptions about the lawful determination of mental processes. Those features were to persist and have far-reaching consequences for one of the most fundamental of Freud's concepts, that of psychic determinism. It is those assumptions that I consider in chapters 2 and 3.

During the last quarter of the nineteenth century it was the diametrically opposed views of Charcot and Bernheim that overshadowed most scientific inquiry into the subject. Charcot believed hypnosis to be governed by deterministic laws that produced, with strict regularity, well defined, physiologically based phenomena. Bernheim, on the other hand, proposed the different features of hypnosis simply reflected differing degrees of suggestibility; that is, the essence of hypnosis was to be found in a change in psychological functioning. Charcot thus held to what was characterized by Sutcliffe (1960) as a *credulous* position: he believed that the changes in behavior seemingly produced by the induction procedure reflected real alterations in the subject's physiology. Bernheim's view was what Sutcliffe termed *sceptical*: he demonstrated that many of the phenomena attributed to the hypnotic trance were to be observed in the waking condition. It was partly on these grounds that he concluded that the varied features of hypnosis reflected only different degrees of suggestibility.

Most of the particular issues over which Charcot and Bernheim argued derived from Mesmer's theory of animal magnetism or from the important developments stemming from it. Consequently, a discussion of Mesmer's work and what it led to provides an appropriate backdrop against which to consider Freud's views on the lawfulness of psychological phenomena.

Mesmer and Animal Magnetism

The beginnings of modern thinking about hypnosis derive from the work of Franz Anton Mesmer. Because of the similarities between Mesmer's ideas and those of others, his originality has always been doubted. However, his sources have usually been incorrectly identified. Even the knowledgeable Pierre Janet, for example, mistakenly believed Mesmer to have drawn primarily from the Scottish physician William Maxwell's compilation of the so-called wisdom of the ancients. According to Janet, Maxwell:

regarded all diseases as an outcome of the withdrawal of a vital fluid from our organs, and he believed that a proper balance could be reestablished by simply restoring the requisite amount of magnetic force.   (P. Janet 1919/1925, vol. 1, p. 30)

There is now no doubt whatever that Mesmer's ideas were almost all plagiarized from London physician Richard Mead (Pattie 1956). Mesmer's medical thesis of 1766 set out Mead's argument that tides in the atmosphere produced by movements of the sun and moon caused disease by disturbing the nervous fluid in the body. One of Mesmer's few original points seems to be a development of an idea of Newton's, proposing the disturbance might be mediated by the force of gravity rather than, as Mead suggested, through the air itself. By 1775 Mesmer referred to this force as either animal gravitation or animal magnetism (Pattie 1956, p. 285).

Mesmer's was clearly not a conventional astrological theory, as is sometimes said. In its final form, it held the whole of space to be filled with an invisible gas or fluid that, like a magnet, could both attract and repel. This medium was said to be disturbed by the movement of the planets, in which he included the sun and the moon. The human body was itself a magnet, divided into poles, one on each side, and illness was due to the planetary movements producing imbalances in the distribution of the magnetic fluid within the body. Because the fluid was subject to the influence of magnets, a proper balance of polarities could be reestablished by applying magnets to the body (Mesmer 1779/1970, pp. 54–56).

Mesmer's training was in medicine and his early medical practice was quite conventional (Goldsmith 1934; Walmsley 1967). In circumstances that are not entirely clear, the possibility of using magnets therapeutically occurred to him, and was at least reinforced, or even suggested, by the results of magnetic treatment achieved by an erstwhile friend, the astronomer to the Court of Vienna, the Jesuit Father Hell[1] (Binet and Féré 1887a/1887; Sarton 1944; Walmsley 1967). Increasing experience with magnets led Mesmer to devise his own highly individual method of treatment and to "discover" animal magnetism by simply dropping references to gravity from his theses. In 1779, shortly after his removal to Paris, he announced that in animal magnetism he had discovered a principle enabling all diseases to be cured.

The following descriptions give some idea of Mesmer's therapy and the response of the afflicted:

All the world wished to be magnetized, and the crowd was so great that Mesmer employed a *valet toucher* to magnetize in his place. This did not suffice; he invented the famous *baquet* or trough, round which more than 30 persons could be magnetized simultaneously. A circular, oaken case, about a foot high, was placed in the middle of a large hall, hung with thick curtains, through which only a soft and subdued light was allowed to penetrate; this was the *baquet*. At the bottom of the case, on a layer of powdered glass and iron filings, there lay full bottles, symmetrically arranged, so that the necks of all converged toward the center; other bottles were arranged in the opposite direction, with their necks toward the circumference. All these objects were immersed in water, but this condition was not absolutely necessary, and the *baquet* might be dry. The lid was pierced with a certain number of holes, whence there issued jointed and movable iron branches, which were to be held by the patients. Absolute silence was maintained. The patients were ranged in several rows round the *baquet* connected with each other by cords passed round their bodies, and by a second chain, formed by joining hands. As they waited a melodious air was heard, proceeding from a pianoforte, or harmonicon, placed in the adjoining room, and to this the human voice was sometimes added. Then, influenced by the magnetic effluvia issuing from the *baquet* curious phenomena were produced.   (Binet and Féré 1887a, pp. 8–9)

One eye witness described these curiosities in the following way:

Some patients remain calm, and experience nothing; others cough, spit, feel slight pain, a local or general heat, and fall into sweats, others are agitated and tormented by convulsions. These convulsions are remarkable for their number, duration, and force, and have been known to persist for more than three hours....
This convulsive state is termed the *crisis*. It has been observed that many women and few men are subject to such crises; that they are only established after the lapse of 2 or 3 hours, and that when one is established, others soon and successively begin.   (pp. 9–10)

Mesmer himself,

wearing a coat of lilac silk walked up and down amid this palpitating crowd, together with Deslon [d'Eslon] and his associates, whom he chose for their youth and comeliness. Mesmer carried a long iron wand, with which he touched the bodies of the patients and especially those parts which were diseased; often, laying aside the wand, he magnetized them with his eyes, fixing his gaze on theirs, or applying his hands to the hypochondriac region [i.e., upper abdomen] and to the lower part of the abdomen. This application was often continued for hours, and at other times the master made use of *passes*. He began by placing himself *en rapport* with his subject. Seated opposite to him, foot against foot, knee against knee, he laid his fingers on the hypochondriac region, and moved them to and fro, lightly touching the ribs. Magnetization with strong currents were substituted for these manipulations when more energetic results were to be produced.   (pp. 10–11)

Quoting from Figuier, Binet and Féré (1887a) added:

The master, erecting his fingers in a pyramid, passed his hands all over the patient's body, beginning with the head, and going down over the shoulders to the feet. He then returned again, to the head, both back and front, to the belly and the back; he renewed the process again and again, until the magnetized person was saturated with the healing fluid, and was transported with pain or pleasure, both sensations being equally salutary.   (p. 11)

The authors continued:

Young women were so much gratified by the crisis, that they begged to be thrown into it anew; they followed Mesmer through the hall, and confessed that it was impossible not to be warmly attached to the magnetizer's person.   (p. 11)

Mesmer's universal therapeutic principle was nothing more than reestablishing the magnetic balance by passes or by the use of the *baquet*.

Mesmer regarded the cures produced (or apparently produced) as proof of the correctness of his theory of the effects of the fluid on the body. Had he made only therapeutic claims, the validity of the theory would have been relatively easy to establish. But he went further: he claimed the all-pervasive magnetic fluid manifested itself *only* through its effects on the body, and that it was too subtle to be detected by any other means. Such subtlety did not seem surprising at the time. As Darnton showed in his analysis of the social role of mesmeric ideas in eighteenth-century France,

Science had captivated Mesmer's contemporaries by revealing to them that they were surrounded by wonderful, invisible forces: Newton's gravity, made intelligible by Voltaire; Franklin's electricity, popularized by a fad for lightning rods and by demonstrations in the fashionable lyceums and museums of Paris; and the miraculous gases of the Charlieres and Montgolfieres that astonished Europe by lifting man into the air for the first time in 1783. Mesmer's invisible fluid seemed no more miraculous.   (Darnton 1968, p. 10)

But it was precisely because of Mesmer's supposing the fluid to have its effects *only* on the body that it seemed more wonderful than any of these other forces. It was also precisely this that created a special problem for investigating the truth of the fluidic theory, and the solution to the problem marked the beginning of scientific enquiry into hypnosis.

Evaluating Mesmer's Theory

In the most important of the many controversies about animal magnetism that broke out soon after Mesmer's arrival in Paris, two central issues may be discerned. First, was the theory true? That is, did the all-pervading fluid actually exist? Second, were the behavioral changes, including the crises and cures, genuine? Initially, most interest attached to the investigation of the validity of Mesmer's theory. But, if the only effects of the fluid were to produce changes in the subjects, how could the investigation proceed? The first of the several Commissions of the French Academy of Sciences or the Royal Society of Medicine of Paris directed part of their enquiries to the *baquet*, the function of which was said to concentrate the magnetic fluid:

The commissioners in the progress of their examination discovered, by means of an electrometer and a needle of iron ... that the *baquet* contained no substance either electric or magnetic; and from ... the interior construction ... they cannot infer any physical agent, capable of contributing to the imputed effects of the magnetism.   (Bailly 1784, p. 86)

The Mesmerists, claiming the fluid to be too subtle to be measured with such crude devices as electrometers or magnetic needles, rejected this conclusion. The Commissioners were thus forced to find a method by which they could test the hypothesis that the fluid by itself produced the phenomena. What they did was to vary either the subject's belief about what was happening or the method of magnetization, and then observe the effects of those variations on the subject's behavior.

An experiment on the subject referred to as Mme. B____ illustrates the procedure. Mme. B____ fell into a magnetic crisis when, while her eyes were bandaged, she was told that d'Eslon was magnetizing her. In fact he was not. On a later occasion a magnetizer, concealed behind a screen, went through the motions of magnetizing her. Mme. B____ was initially unaware of his presence and no effects were produced. However, within minutes of being told she was to be magnetized from behind the screen the crisis came on. However, the magnetism was produced contrary to the rules said to govern it; in this instance, with a reversal of the magnetic polarity. As a consequence of many decisive experiments of this type, the Commissioners concluded that

the imagination without the magnetism produces convulsions, and that the magnetism without the imagination produces nothing,... They have concluded with a unanimous voice ... that the existence of the fluid is absolutely destitute of proof.   (Bailly 1784, p. 126)

These experiments of the Commissioners illustrate one of the principal features of scientific enquiry: the systematic variation of one kind of factor while its effects on another are observed. The subject's beliefs and the actions of the mesmerist were *independent variables*, manipulated at will by the experimenters; the behavior observed in the mesmerized subject was the *dependent variable*, being the consequence of the particular manipulations. Very probably these experiments are the earliest application of what we now think of as the scientific method to a psychological problem, and it was its application that enabled the Commissioners to answer so decisively the question of whether or not the theory was true. Indeed, for the Commissioners, the truth of the theory was the only question: "The animal magnetism may indeed exist without being useful, but it cannot be useful if it does not exist" (Bailly 1784).

Critics were quick to point out that the behavioral changes nevertheless required explanation: how could imagination and belief give rise to the profound physical changes of the crisis? And even if only some of the cures were genuine, how had they been produced? In the absence of definite answers to these questions, the theory of magnetic influence retained some credibility. Among Mesmer's followers this was bolstered by various criticisms of the Commission: they had preferred to investigate d'Eslon's practice rather than Mesmer's; they had been lax in their attendance at the demonstrations; they had failed to question the patients; and had made their observations too casually (Elliotson 1843/1970a, pp. 199–200, citing an 1825 summary).

One further aspect of scientific theorizing may be considered briefly here. Mesmer's theory was not criticized simply because Mesmer postulated a fluid that could not be sensed directly. Developed scientific theories typically include in their explanations of observable facts propositions about entities and processes that cannot be perceived directly. Take for example the observable fact of the sun traveling around the earth: the scientific theory about this is a restatement of the fact in terms of processes that not only cannot be directly observed but that are contrary to direct observation. Other examples spring readily to mind: the facts of the chemical combinations of elements are restated as theoretical propositions about valency-bonding processes, and the facts of illness are discussed in terms of submicroscopic entities such as viruses. However, when a theory contains unsensed processes and entities, it is proper to ask for evidence of them other than the very same facts the entities or processes were originally put forward to explain.

According to its protagonists, the truth of the theory was to be found in the relation between the facts of planetary motion, the facts of illness, and the effects of magnets or their equivalents. However, this same pattern of facts was also said to be explained by the fluid. Evidence was lacking for the existence of the fluid independent of those facts. Further, the validity of the theory could not being impugned by the failure to detect electrical or magnetic forces: the proposition that the fluid exerted only subtle influence blocked that line of enquiry. On the one hand the theory was an inference from certain facts, and on the other hand it was only those facts, and no others, that were "explained" by it. Nevertheless, the Commissioners were able to devise logically satisfactory tests. Had that not been possible, the theory would have been untestable—there would have been no way in principle through which its falseness could have been demonstrated. An important requirement of a scientific theory is that it be formulated in such a way that its disproof is possible.

Despite the entirely correct conclusion of the first Commission, criticisms of their work and the continued demonstration of mesmeric effects had the effect of keeping some form of the doctrine of animal magnetism alive. By default, the credulous view managed to survive its first sceptical scrutiny.

Hypnosis after Mesmer

Little progress was made toward understanding the basis of hypnosis after Mesmer. Few scientists of repute cared or dared to investigate it. If no contribution to a scientific theory of hypnosis could come from the orthodox, little could be expected from the odd assortment of suspect medical men, lay practitioners, charlatans, and quacks who maintained the interest. In the confusion of postmesmeric developments, three trends can be identified: the failure of Mesmer's direct followers to investigate or establish the properties of the fluid, the failure of those sceptical of the existence of the fluid to develop an alternative theory, and the inadequacy of the primitive physiological explanations that were proposed. Within each trend sceptical and credulous attitudes were mixed in varying proportions.

Among those whom Mesmer personally initiated into the practice of animal magnetism was Armond de Chastenet, the Marquis de Puységur. At the beginning of his mesmeric practice de Puységur's belief in the power of the fluid was conventional if somewhat extreme; he was so able to impregnate the trees on his estate with magnetic fluid that hundreds of people were cured of their illnesses simply by touching them. About Mesmer's demonstrations he seems to have been less enthusiastic:

From the first he viewed with dislike and suspicion the crisis attended with violent convulsions which he had witnessed at Mesmer's establishment.   (Podmore 1909, p. 71)

Although de Puységur used Mesmer's method of passes to magnetize his subjects, it did not produce the usual convulsive crises but, quite unexpectedly, according to Elliotson (1843/1970a, p. 200), a state resembling sleep in which conversation with the subject could be maintained. De Puységur's production of this condition of artificial somnambulism, or magnetic sleep as it was sometimes called, seems to have resulted as much from his aristocratic distaste for the crises as from his aristocratic status relative to his subjects. Elliotson observed that de Puységur's first three subjects were the daughter of his steward, the wife of his gamekeeper, and a female peasant from his estate. The passivity of these subjects in the sleeplike state may well have reflected the subordination of their menial, female selves to his aristocratic, male domination.

Ellenberger (1965) maintained this view analogously in discussing de Puységur's effect on his famous subject Victor. Victor was a young peasant from the estate who, like so many of the other subjects of that period when they passed into artificial somnambulism, seemed to become clairvoyant. To the existing problems of assessing the validity of the fluidic theory, which he himself eventually rejected, and the genuineness of the cures, de Puységur's work added the extra difficulty of establishing the truth of the claim that artificially somnambulistic subjects possessed parapsychological powers.

J. P. F. Deleuze, a follower of both Mesmer and de Puységur, went farther in the parapsychological aspects. His belief in the existence of the fluid was sustained in part by the claims of the somnambules that they could see the magnetizer shining with a brilliant glow (Dingwall 1967, p. 14). Deleuze did provide an important new defense of the fluidic theory; arguing that, however incredible the reported phenomena were, the very uniformity of the descriptions provided some proof they were real and not imaginary. This argument stood him in good stead when the effects of Perkins's metallic tractors (two pieces of metal, usually drawn lightly over the affected part of the body) were shown to be constant even when imitation metals were substituted. Since thousands of cures had been testified to, including, somewhat peculiarly, the saddle boils of horses, they must therefore have a real basis. Deleuze ruled out hopeful imagination on the part of the patient: first of all, imagination was too vague a concept to explain the effects; second, it was notoriously the case that hopeful patients were not always cured by orthodox physicians; third, it had been repeatedly observed that scoffers had been cured by magnetic practices (Dingwall 1967, pp. 16–20).

Baron Du Potet de Sennevoy (1834/1970) was the third of the great believers in the fluidic theory. He was the outstanding magnetizer of his day, being selected for study by the second commission of the French Academy of Science 1825–1831 (Colquhoun 1833/1970). Not only did he believe in the reality of the fluid, but he invented a "magic mirror" capable of producing convulsions in the user, and linked mesmerism with magic in other ways (Dingwall 1967, p. 54; Tinterow 1970, p. 175). His performances before the commission were sufficiently convincing for them to conclude that the phenomena of magnetism were real and not due to imagination. On a visit to England in 1837 he succeeded in reviving Elliotson's interest in mesmerism to such an extent that Elliotson introduced it into English medical and hospital practice (Elliotson 1843, 1843/1970a,b; G. Rosen 1946).

Elliotson was a medical innovator of some distinction, a Fellow of the Royal Society, President of the Royal Medical and Chirurgical Society, Censor (examiner) of the Royal College of Physicians, and Professor of the Practice of Medicine at

University College, London. Nevertheless, in his mesmeric work he was credulous enough not to have guarded against the effects of suggestion. He was continuously abused and harassed by his colleagues from the time that Wakley, then editor of *Lancet*, secretly substituted lead bars for the nickel ones used in one of his demonstrations, without thereby affecting the phenomena produced (Bramwell 1903, pp. 5–14; G. Rosen 1946). Elliotson founded a movement for popularizing mesmerism and developed reliable methods for using magnetic sleep as an anesthetic. Through that popularization, Esdaile (1846) was prompted to extend its application in a variety of surgical conditions, but with his death the more or less unmodified belief in the fluidic theory seems also to have died.

Whatever other positive contributions they may have made, and those of Elliotson and Esdaile to psychotherapy and surgery were particularly important, none of the believers advanced the understanding of mesmerism much beyond that of its founder. Characteristically, they were content to describe one unusual effect after another, and to attribute them, usually quite vaguely, to the imponderable fluid. They investigated neither the nature of the fluid nor its mode of action.

Curiously enough, the sceptical tradition that emerged while Mesmer was still alive was no more productive theoretically. A peripatetic Portuguese prior, the Abbé de Faria, was the first practitioner in this tradition. Initially an orthodox follower of Mesmer, he published in 1814 a work in which he denied the existence of the fluid and attributed mesmeric effects to the *impressionability* of the subject (Bramwell 1903, pp. 3, 280; Dingwall 1967, pp. 34–39). De Faria's skepticism was confined to the truth of the fluidic theory; he was quite credulous about some of the effects. For example, through some poorly contrived experiments he became convinced that mesmerized subjects acquired parapsychological powers enabling them to see and hear over vast distances and to transmit their thoughts. Credulity of this kind about the effects mixed with skepticism concerning the fluid also characterized the beliefs and work of other antifluidists of the period.

The work of Alexandre Bertrand is similar. Introduced to animal magnetism through a series of public lectures given by Deleuze in 1819 (Dingwall 1967, p. 46), he had produced within four years a cautiously approving text. Over the next three years he conducted a series of experiments, rather like those of the first commissioners, leading him to confirm their conclusion that most of the effects were due to the imagination (pp. 74–76). Bertrand was credulous about other things. He defended, for example, so-called eyeless vision—the apparent ability to see even though the eyes were bandaged. Effectively controlled experiments, even at that time, should have suggested more caution. He also believed patients could have prevision about their illnesses. His own patients as well as others announced in advance the time and duration of various modifications of the diseases from which they suffered, including when and how they were to be cured. Bertrand made no real effort to explain such unusual events; possibly this indefiniteness led the second commission to neglect his evidence. Thus de Faria's and Bertrand's skepticism had little impact on those wanting to believe; the fluidic theory was virtually unaffected by their work.

One of the early attempts to provide a physiological explanation of magnetic effects foundered similarly. Amédée Dupau, a physician of considerable repute who wrote at about the same time as de Faria and Bertrand, appears to have been the most consistently sceptical of all of the early writers. He restricted his consideration to normal effects, excluding the paranormal altogether, and he proposed a physiological explanation for them. Just before the second commission began its work, he published a critical analysis of previous experiments on the paranormal powers of the somnambules in which, again and again, he pointed to magnetists' failures to exclude normal sensory cues to the phenomena: experiments on eyeless vision had not always ensured the exclusion of the subject's normal vision by adequate (or any) bandages; in experiments on magnetization at a distance the conversations of others often served as cues to the presence of the allegedly unknown magnetizer; ordinary sources of knowledge were not excluded in experiments on thought transference, and so on.

Dupau accepted that diseases were often cured by magnetization, but his analysis led him to reject the claims that the somnambules had unerring powers of diagnosis and prescription. The diseases most readily cured were those nervous or chronic disorders (*affections nerveuses ou chroniques*) he knew from history and from his own experience to respond to all kinds of irrational procedures, including miracle healing (Dingwall 1967, pp. 58–74). Dupau's own theory seems not to have been spelled out in much detail. Analysis of the conditions for producing the magnetic state led him to implicate the superior social rank and knowledge of the magnetizer, the monotony of the induction procedure that caused the subject to lose interest in the external world, and the subject's temperamental susceptibility, often revealed by an imaginative constitution or the presence of spontaneous magnetic states. Once the magnetizer had set the imagination to work, physiological modifications to the nervous system took place, manifesting themselves in such physical symptoms as catalepsy and heightened sensory awareness, and such mental changes as greater suggestibility. In his view, the phenomena and physiology of magnetic sleep were simply extensions of normal sleep. No one wished to know this—at that time the fashion was for belief. Dupau's alternative explanation was then lost until it was unknowingly revived by James Braid.

Braid, who is rightly regarded as the father of the scientific study of hypnosis (Binet and Féré 1887a/1887; Waite 1899; Tinterow 1970), seemed to have established that all that was necessary to induce hypnosis was visual fixation producing muscle strain. Neither a magnetic fluid nor a personal or social relation with the hypnotist was involved. After observing a demonstration by Lafontaine in 1841 (Bramwell 1903, appendix A), Braid tentatively concluded that the inability of the subject to open her eyes after fixation was due to paralysis of the nervous centers controlling eye movements, caused by the induction procedure. His first three attempts at induction were carried out successively on a younger male friend, his own wife, and a male servant, and all succeeded. Each subject was instructed to fixate an object visually above and in front of the eyes, holding the head normally. Within minutes the eyes closed and a hypnotic state was produced.

It seemed to Braid that the changes in reflex function, respiration, and circulation that followed his induction procedure were consonant with a profound physiological change. Apparently he ruled out his personal qualities and the demands he created in his subjects as factors in producing hypnosis simply because the subjects did not anticipate the effects, and because his method of induction seemed a physiological one (Braid 1843/1970b). In these respects he was almost certainly incorrect. However, by denuding the induction procedure of its mystery, he provided a basis for scientific enquiry into the phenomena of hypnosis and maintained a running battle with Elliotson and the other mesmerists about this. More positively, Braid developed psychotherapeutic procedures and techniques of anesthesia. It was he who coined the term hypnotism (Braid 1842/1970a). His work directly influenced the formation of the two great French schools of hypnosis associated with the names of Bernheim and Charcot, respectively.

Whatever might have been the direction of Braid's later theorizing (Bramwell 1903, pp. 278–294), his earlier views show two important signs of credulity: the physiological explanation itself, and a supposed connection of Gall's phrenology with hypnosis. Braid considered it possible that pressure on some part of the skull of an hypnotized subject would bring about the activity that phrenologists had supposedly correlated with that part. For example, if the bump of musicality was pressed, the hypnotized subject would begin to sing. Frederick Engels, not usually first thought of in connection with hypnosis, provided an interesting and penetrating eye-witness account of a stage performance carried out by a man claiming to be one of Braid's disciples:

Now it happens that I also saw this Mr. Spencer-Hall in the winter of 1843–44 in Manchester. He was a very mediocre charlatan, who travelled the country under the patronage of some parsons and undertook magnetico-phrenological performances with a young woman in order to prove thereby the existence of God, the immortality of the soul, and the incorrectness of the materialism that was being preached at that time by the Owenites in all big towns. The lady was sent into a magnetic sleep and then, as soon as the operator touched any part of the skull corresponding to one of Gall's organs, she gave a bountiful display of theatrical, demonstrative gestures and poses representing the activity of the organ concerned; for instance, for the organ of philoprogenitiveness she fondled and kissed an imaginary baby, etc. Moreover, the good Mr. Hall had enriched Gall's geography of the skull with a new island of Barataria: right at the top of the skull he had discovered an organ of veneration, on touching which his hypnotic miss sank on to her knees, folded her hands in prayer, and depicted to the astonished, philistine audience an angel wrapt in veneration. That was the climax and conclusion of the exhibition. The existence of God had been proved.   (Engels 1898/1982, pp. 51–52)

Engels went on to describe his own experiments:

Apart from muscular rigidity and loss of sensation, which were easy to produce, we found also a state of complete passivity of the will bound up with a peculiar hypersensitivity of sensation. The patient, when aroused from his lethargy by external stimulus, exhibited very much greater liveliness than in the waking condition. There was no trace of any mysterious relation to the operator: anyone else could just as easily set the sleeper into activity. To put Gall's cranial organs into operation was a mere trifle for us; we went much further, we could not only exchange them for one another, or make their seat anywhere in the whole body, but we also fabricated any amount of other organs, organs of singing, whistling, piping, dancing, boxing, sewing, cobbling, tobacco-smoking, etc., and we could make their seat wherever we wanted. Wallace made his patients drunk on water, but we discovered in the great toe an organ of drunkenness which only had to be touched in order to cause the finest drunken comedy to be enacted. But it must be well understood, no organ showed a trace of action until the patient was given to understand what was expected of him; the boy soon perfected himself by practice to such an extent that the merest indication sufficed.   (p. 52)

If an amateur at the art could so easily make such shrewd observations, it is hardly necessary to enlarge upon Braid's failure to investigate the supposed phrenological aspects of the topic in a scientific manner. Although Braid was to complain that phrenological views had been wrongly attributed to him, and although he advanced possible alternative explanations for the behavior (Bramwell 1903, p. 290), he undertook no experimental program to dispel the earlier impression.

During his lifetime Braid's influence on the study of hypnosis was minimal. His work is important not for what it established, but for what it led to: the eventual disposal of the fluidic theory. And, even though he did not provide a scientifically acceptable alternative, his work showed how the phenomena of hypnosis might be encompassed within a scientific framework.

Two cautions emerge clearly from this brief survey of the early work on hypnosis— a methodological one about the conduct of experiments involving behavior, and a logical one about the drawing of theoretical and empirical conclusions. The best of the later work followed the experimental method proposed by the first commission. Facts established by it were eventually to show that the hypnotized subject had interesting but not especially unusual powers. However, little theoretical caution was observed by either the fluidists or the animists. For the former, the fluid somehow explained everything, whereas for many of the latter vaguely defined notions of imagination or suggestion were acceptable, all-pervasive explanatory principles. With some license, Charcot can be thought of as extending the fluidic tradition and Bernheim the animist.

Charcot and Bernheim on Hypnosis

By the last quarter of the nineteenth century, postmesmeric developments in France resulted in the emergence of two opposed schools of hypnosis, one at the Salpêtrière in Paris led by Jean-Martin Charcot and the other at Nancy acknowledging Hippolyte Bernheim as its leader. Charcot, the most eminent clinical neurologist of his day, had from about 1880 turned to the scientific study of hypnosis and hysteria. Initially he held a chair of pathological anatomy, and during that appointment he established the histopathology of amyotrophic lateral sclerosis, tabes dorsalis, poliomyelitis, multiple sclerosis, and the muscular dystrophies (McHenry 1969). In 1882 Charcot became the first person anywhere in the world to be appointed to a chair of neurology, and it can even be said that with him neurology was founded as a medical specialty. He established the first of the three outstanding groups of neurological investigators, the others being those of Erb and Oppenheim in Germany and Jackson and Gowers in London (McHenry 1969, pp. 270–271). His new interest in hypnosis was of fundamental importance. The various scandals associated with the Mesmerists, the critical exposures, and the opposition of orthodox medical men had left hypnosis largely to quacks, showmen, and charlatans. If it really were the case that only someone of considerable eminence could establish hypnosis as a respectable area of study, Charcot was the person to do it.

Social considerations also set the stage for Charcot (G. R. McGuire 1986a). During the late 1800s, the widespread sentiment that France was in a period of social decline led many intellectuals to become interested in what they saw as the basis of the decay: psychological dissolution in the individual. Social dissolution was to be understood through individual pathology. As well, normal processes were to approached through the abnormal. Hypnosis, hysteria, and the dissociated states observable in mediums as well as other spiritist phenomena were the exemplars *par excellence* of individual dissolution. Not only was Charcot eminent enough for the time, the time itself was ripe for him.

Charcot's entry into the area of hypnotic studies was preceded by a revival of interest among the orthodox. A reading of Braid's major work led Azam, a physician at Bordeaux, to conduct his own experiments and publish his conclusions. These findings were communicated to the Academie de Médecine by Velpeau in 1860 (Bramwell 1903, pp. 27, 30; cf. Chertok and Saussure 1973/1979, pp. 38–42). Broca, an important figure in the study of the cortical localization of speech, also read Braid at about the same time, and his outline of Braid's theory, together with a report on his own experiments, were communicated to the prestigious Academie de Sciences, which then set up a committee to report on the subject (Philips 1860/1970; Bramwell 1903, p. 27). Shortly afterward, Charles Richet, a young physiologist who was later to become famous in that field, began his work on hypnosis. Although Charcot's interest in mesmerism may then have already been aroused through his work evaluating Burq's metallotherapy (Harrington 1988), it was Richet's series of papers in well established journals that appears to have prompted Charcot into investigating the subject actively (Guillain 1955/1959; K. Levin 1978, p. 50 and n. 24; G. R. McGuire 1986a). By that time, hypnosis had also come to interest Taine, the philosophical inspirer of French psychology, and Ribot, the director of the first French psychological laboratory.

When supporting his candidacy for the Academie des Sciences, Charcot outlined how he had begun his work on hypnosis. Writing in the third person he said:

From the very beginning a prudent and conservative orientation was developed and applied to these investigations. This approach was only slightly influenced by the purely arbitrary skepticism practiced by those who, under the pretext of "purely scientific orientation," concealed a prejudice to see nothing and to hear nothing in these matters. At the same time every attempt was made to avoid being attracted by the esoteric or the extraordinary, a peril which in this scientifically unexplored field was encountered, so to speak, at every step of the way. Briefly, the method Charcot adopted for these intense physiologic, and neuropathologic studies can be summarised very simply; instead of allowing himself to be led into a pursuit of the unexpected and the mystic, he decided for the time being to attempt to analyze the meaning of the clinical signs and physiologic characteristics that can be identified among various conditions and phenomena caused by nervous reactions. He further decided to confine himself at first to an examination of the most simple and constant factors, the validity of which was the most easy to demonstrate, and only to investigate later and still with caution the more complex or evasive phenomena; and finally to omit studying systematically, except in a provisional way, those phenomena which are of a much more obscure nature and which for the moment do not appear to correlate with any known physiologic mechanisms. According to Charcot, it is largely because these very simple precautions have often been overlooked that studies of hypnotism as an experimental neurosis, which previously had been almost inaccessible, have not until now borne fruit to the extent anticipated and have not enjoyed everywhere the favorable reception that such studies should merit. Such studies, when properly prosecuted, are certainly destined to bring eventual light to a whole host of questions, not only from a pathologic standpoint but also from the standpoint of physiology and psychology. (Cited in Guillain 1955/1959, p. 167)

Charcot obviously believed his systematic, physiologically based method of inquiry would by itself guarantee that the errors of the past would be avoided.

Charcot began by systematizing existing observations about hypnosis, extending them where necessary by controlled experiments. From this work, which lasted over a number of years, he arrived at a description of various symptoms characterizing the states of hypnosis (cited in Binet and Féré 1887a, pp. 154–159). He distinguished three fundamental states:

1. *Catalepsy*, ordinarily produced by the subject visually fixating a given object. It might also be produced by opening the eyes while in the lethargic state. The major feature of the condition was that the limbs and other parts of the body would retain for a considerable period the position in which they were placed. Certain reflexes disappeared and anesthesia was pronounced, but some sensory functions were unimpaired.

2. *Lethargy*, produced by visual fixation or, if the subject was already in the cataleptic state, by closing the eyes. The main feature was a peculiarity of the musculature such that the limbs, after being raised and freed of support, dropped flaccidly back to their original positions. Reflexes were altered and the pupils were permanently contracted. Contractures of the limbs were exhibited on percussion of the tendons or on mechanical stimulation of the fibers innervating the muscles of those limbs.

3. *Artificial somnambulism*, produced by fixation of the gaze or by simple pressure or slight friction on the scalp while the subject was in the lethargic or cataleptic state. The main features were that although the subject appeared to be asleep, the limbs offered resistance to change, and the various methods for producing contracture were ineffective. Sensory functioning was often enhanced, with especially marked increases in visual and auditory acuity.

Charcot's physiological approach seemed well justified: the states were clearly separated, subjects passed from one to the other in a predictable manner, and the identifying features of each state were physiological. For example, hypnosis seemed to produce such a degree of muscular and nervous hyperesthesia that pressure on the muscles or nerves alone brought about the same contractions as direct electrical stimulation of them usually produced. As figure 2.1 illustrates, pressure on the cubital nerve of the forearm caused

the contracture of all fingers on the hand except the second and third, the same result as is given by electrical stimulation and which explains the distribution of nerves. (Charcot 1879–1880, p. 171)

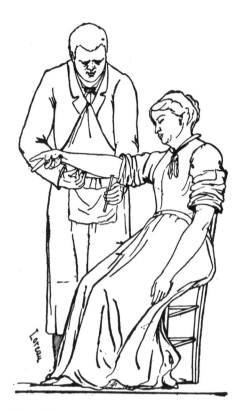

Figure 2.1
Mechanical stimulation under hypnosis of cubital nerve producing finger contractures identical to those produced by electrical stimulation in the waking state (Charcot 1879–1980, figure 7).

Similar contractures could be produced in the facial muscles, and even tetanization of the whole musculature was possible (pp. 171–173). These and other apparently regular changes in physiological functioning produced under hypnosis could be subsumed under a theory that the changes were based on alterations in neuromuscular excitability. Several other observations seemed consistent with this view. For example, Charcot noted his best hypnotic subjects were young hysterical women (1879–1880, pp. 162–163) and actually held that hypnosis was an artificial hysteria. Convinced that hysteria was a physiological disorder, it was then natural for him to make the further supposition that hypnosis was also physiologically based. His physiological theory thus had a degree of generality that linked hypnosis and hysteria with established neurological disorders.

Bernheim's view of hypnosis was very different. His introduction to the subject came from following up his criticism of the therapeutic work of an obscure Nancy physician, Ambroise Liébeault. Liébeault's own interest is often said to have begun two years before he graduated when, after reading a traditional book on animal magnetism and practicing the methods described, he found himself able to mesmerize others. Chertok and Saussure (1973/1979, p. 42), however, attributed Liébault's interest to the same paper of Velpeau's that eventually influenced Charcot. He incorporated hypnosis into his medical practice from the beginning, offering it as an alternative, free treatment to his predominantly peasant patients. In 1864 he retired from active fee-charging practice, devoting himself to writing a book (of which only one copy was sold!) and to the free clinic he established for the poor. His methods for inducing hypnosis were apparently those of the mesmerists, but he eschewed the fluidic theory. In his view, hypnosis came about because the subjects thought or concentrated their attention on sleep or the idea of sleep. After *rapport* had been established between the subject and the hypnotist, the hypnotist's direct or indirect suggestions produced the phenomena (Bramwell 1903, pp. 340–344). Liébeault's theory was, therefore, a psychological one.

Bernheim's approach differed only in minor details from Liébeault's. He distinguished various stages of hypnosis solely in terms of the degree to which suggestibility was increased: six stages for which there was memory in the waking state and three in which memory of things taking place under hypnosis was lost in the waking state. Suggestibility increased in stages 1 to 6, but it was not possible to suggest illusions or hallucinations. Stages 7 to 9 were marked by such increased suggestibility that the subject became susceptible to various types of hallucinations or other powerful suggestions. They were also distinguished by what Bernheim called somnambulism. Stage 7, for example, was somnambulism without susceptibility to hallucination and stage 9 was somnambulism with susceptibility to hallucination (Bernheim 1887/1888a, pp. 10–15).

Despite repeated attempts, Bernheim failed to confirm Charcot's observations concerning the progression through the states of lethargy, catalepsy, and artificial somnambulism. He also failed to repeat Charcot's observations of certain phenomena being invariably associated with the three states. Finally, he demonstrated the phenomena were not necessarily the result of changes in physiological functioning or neuromuscular hyperexcitability but were due entirely to suggestion. What accounts for the difference between the findings of Charcot and Bernheim?

It was clear to many contemporary observers, and not only to Bernheim, that the apparent lawfulness of the behavior of Charcot's subjects was brought about by a combination of the expectations of the experimenter with what the subjects believed was required of them ("demand characteristics," as Orne called them) and the effect of repeated practice. The functional changes characteristic of each stage resulted primarily from drilling the subject. Some rather more esoteric effects, such as the production of hemicatalepsy after only one eye was opened in the lethargic state, show quite clearly the effects of expectations, demand characteristics, and practice. Bernheim (1887/1888a, pp. 91–104) detailed many instances in which the phenomena were dependent on what subjects knew or thought they knew what was demanded of them. With respect to the Salpêtrière experiments using magnets to transfer sensibility from one part of the body to another, he warned:

It is well to add that many somnambulists possess extremely acute perception. The slightest indication guides them. Knowing that they should carry out the hypnotizer's thought, they make an effort to divine it. If the transfer experiments have been repeated many times with the same subject, he readily guesses that he should transfer such and such a phenomenon, and without anything being said before him, he can divine whether the transfer should occur or not, by the expectant attitude of the operator or by some other indication.   (p. 95)

He concluded his criticisms by saying that two things were necessary before valid conclusions could be drawn from experiments on hypnosis:

1st Take inexperienced subjects who have not been used in this kind of experiment, who have not assisted in such experiments made upon others and have not heard them talked about;
2d Make the experiment without speaking a single word before the subject, even in a low voice, because in all degrees of hypnotism he hears and notes everything with a sharpness of perception which is often quite remarkable.   (p. 104)

Charcot himself had seen that practice was necessary to produce some hypnotic effects, but he failed to attach significance to it. For example, of some of the stranger phenomena, he remarked they were "demonstrated well only by subjects who were already accustomed to hypnosis" (Charcot 1879–1880, pp. 176–177). It would be hard to imagine a clearer instance of a psychological set preventing the recognition of the obvious. As a neurologist, he interpreted the regularities as lawfully produced alterations in physiological functioning rather than as the consequence of psychological demands.

Charcot might also have been the victim of some deliberate deception. Dingwall (1967, pp. 256–257) cites the revelations of one of Charcot's former hypnotic subjects to the effect that she deliberately tried to fool Charcot with her performances. Even Guillain (1955/1959, p. 174, n. 11), to whom his own accusation of bias against Munthe's (1929/1945) similar charge can hardly apply, described how, six years after Charcot's death, he had seen Charcot's patients "if offered a slight pecuniary remuneration" imitate other allegedly physiologically determined conditions, the major hysterical crises.

Except for the completely credulous, almost all of the early workers in the field of hypnotism were aware of the need for methodological precautions of the kind Bernheim described. De Faria, Bertrand, and Dupau were quite conscious of these requirements and based their own criticisms of the fluidic view on them. So also was Braid, despite his credulity in other matters (Braid 1846). Even closer in time to Charcot were the warnings of the methodologically sophisticated André Morin (cited in Dingwall 1967, pp. 231–254). Disregard of these earlier cautions was the source of Charcot's errors.

The phenomena that Charcot so confidently asserted demonstrated the essential physiological basis of hypnosis were actually the same that had been demonstrated by Mesmer's descendants in the French traveling shows, music halls, and theaters. For example, because it seemed to be a physiological change, Charcot attributed special significance to hyperexcitability in the lethargic state. Altered excitability of this kind had already been observed by Braid when he produced paralyses and the like by mechanical pressure or by merely blowing air on selected parts of the body (Braid 1843/1970b, pp. 288–290), and it is more than possible he first saw these "symptoms" at Lafontaine's demonstration. Hyperexcitability may well have reached Charcot through Braid or others who inadvertently reproduced the same mesmeric phenomenon.

Much later, Charcot's favorite pupil, Pierre Janet, eventually analyzed the depths of Charcot's methodological failings and reconstructed the process by which he had been deceived. Charcot's assistants, rather than the man himself, hypnotized the subjects, and their instruction in the techniques of hypnosis were obtained from current practitioners of animal magnetism; some of the magnetizers even worked in Charcot's clinic![2] Janet further demonstrated that the various features of the states of hypnosis exhibited by Charcot's subjects were virtually identical with those described previously in the mesmeric literature. He concluded:

Is it not rather quaint to find that during the years 1878 to 1882 Charcot was presenting to the Academy of Sciences what he believed to be fresh physiological discoveries destined to discredit for ever the claims of the magnetisers, when in reality he was merely reproducing the century-old teaching of these same magnetisers?   (P. Janet 1919/1925, vol. 1, pp. 191–192)[3]

Toward the end of his life there is some evidence that Charcot's doubts about the defects of his work on hypnosis crystallized into certainty and that he proposed a complete revision of it (Guillain 1955/1959). It was barely begun before he died in 1893.

Delboeuf's Scepticism

In December 1885, at the very time Freud was at Charcot's clinic, the Belgian psychologist Delboeuf arrived to study transfer and polarization, the latest hypnotic phenomena to have been produced there. As Wolf (1973) so well brought out, a major controversy soon erupted between Delboeuf and the workers at the Salpêtrière. A series of experiments by Binet and Féré (1885a,b,c) seemed to show that perceptions and actions could be transferred from one side of the body to the other by use of magnets. For example, an image in the subject's right eye was transferred to the left when a magnet was placed near to the left side of the head. Polarization referred to a complex series of visual effects produced in complementary colors of hallucinatory colored images. Emotions could also be changed into their complements; for example, under the influence of the magnet, love would change into hate.

As Delboeuf described it later, he attempted to repeat the experiments, and being only partly successful, looked for reasons. He became convinced transfer took place only when subjects knew what was being demanded of them (Delboeuf 1886a). On his return to Liege, and in a somewhat more sceptical frame of mind, he attempted to reproduce Charcot's three hypnotic states as well as the phenomenon of transfer. His results, which were published only four to six months after Freud left Paris, were mixed: transfer could not be demonstrated when conditions were properly controlled, and the three states did not seem to be necessary components of hypnosis (Delboeuf 1886b,c).

Binet (1886) replied to Delboeuf's criticism by pointing to a number of procedural errors and defects in his understanding of the phenomena being investigated. Quite reasonably he argued that even if Delboeuf had produced all the phenomena in his subjects by suggestion alone, that demonstration did not preclude their production by physiological means as well. Although Delboeuf did not formally accept Binet's counter (Delboeuf 1886d), he did go on to make another and more careful attempt to produce the phenomena by suggestion (Delboeuf 1888–1889, 1889). To his own satisfaction and that of his colleagues, he was completely successful. Two years later Binet surrendered. In discussing multiple personality he said that Charcot's work on hypnosis presented

a host of causes of error, which very often falsify the results without the knowledge of the most careful and prudent experimenter.... One of the principal and constant causes of error ... is suggestion, that is, the influence of the operator by his words, gestures, attitudes and even silences, on the subtle and alert intelligence of the person whom he has put in the somnambulistic state.   (Binet 1892/1896, p. 76. Partly retranslated)

Although Binet (1892/1896, pp. 78–79, 300) was critical of the incompleteness of the explanation offered by Bernheim's suggestion theory, he went on to say that "all" that had been written about the physiological basis of hypnosis "seems to me to be fanciful" (p. 79). He wryly concluded that one had to be content with what were admittedly unsatisfactory psychological hypotheses because

all things considered, they are worth more than false notions, and we do not hesitate to prefer them to physiological hypotheses, which while seeming more exact are really much more hypothetical.   (p. 80)

So as to leave no doubt about the shift in his position, he added a footnote:

Readers of my earlier works will see that I have altered my view on this important point. (p. 80)

Delboeuf had taken just five years to force this admission of the correctness of his criticism from one of the leading representatives of the Charcot school. His doubts, first aroused within days of his arrival in 1885 at the Salpêtrière, turned him into a skeptic within a few months. Now it was accepted that the so regularly observed characteristics of hypnosis really were due to influences unconsciously transmitted by Charcot (cf. Apfelbaum and G. R. McGuire 1986).

Delboeuf's major conclusion about the role of suggestion was also consistent with many of the early observations made at Nancy. During a discussion of hypnotic phenomena demonstrated at the Nancy Medical Society in 1882 it was remarked that Charcot's three states of hypnosis could be produced by a variety of means (Hillman 1965). One year later Bernheim and Charpentier reported an experiment showing that the effect of a magnetic field on a hysterical patient's vision depended on the subject knowing whether or not the apparatus was switched on (Bernheim 1887/1888a, pp. 260–266; Hillman 1965).

Freud and the Charcot–Bernheim Controversy

Freud studied with Charcot at the Salpêtrière between mid-October 1885 and February 1886 (Freud 1886a). Soon after that he translated some of Charcot's *Lectures* into German (Charcot 1887/1886, 1888/1894) and defended Charcot's views at, as he saw it, some cost to his own reputation. Two years after his time with Charcot, Freud translated Bernheim's major work into German (Bernheim 1887, 1887/1888b) and visited Nancy in the summer of 1889. In 1892 he translated a second book of Bernheim's (Bernheim 1891, 1891/1892). He was therefore thoroughly familiar with the work of both men.

Some vacillation is evident in Freud's attitudes to the work of those two men (editorial note, *Standard Edition*, vol. 1, pp. 67–69). Bernheim's mastery of induction techniques and the varied types of disorders he treated impressed him a great deal. However, he remained critical of Bernheim's theory that hypnosis was only suggestion, and about this he was inclined to repeat Delboeuf's inference: "That being so, there is no such thing as hypnotism" (Breuer and Freud 1895, p. 101; cf. Delboeuf 1891). In Freud's view, Bernheim had simply replaced the undefined concept of hypnosis with the even more poorly defined concept of suggestion. Although at one time he had doubts about the comprehensiveness of Charcot's theory and clearly rejected the master's proscription of hypnotic therapy, like Deleuze, he just as clearly accepted that the uniformity and apparent lawfulness of the phenomena attested their validity. Freud discounted unconscious influences in producing the phenomena, and held with Charcot that the essential nature of hypnosis consisted of alterations in the excitability of the nervous system.

Freud's position derived from his particular view of determinism. Defined simply, determinism is the idea that all things and events have their determinants, or causes. Freud took this to mean, in part, that the causes of hypnosis had to be sought in the causes of those features of hypnosis that were invariably present. Suggestion would be incapable of producing uniform phenomena because suggestions from different hypnotists would vary. Systematic observation of the kind practiced by Charcot guaranteed the identification of the idiosyncratic characteristics defining hypnosis, and only a physiological theory provided a satisfactory basis for explaining hypnotic phenomena because only that kind of theory could invoke processes unaffected by suggestion.

Freud was not alone in taking that view of determinism. Ironically enough, Janet also once used this very argument for favoring Charcot's theory over Bernheim's. After describing himself at the 1889 International Congress on Hypnotism as adhering to a psychological viewpoint, Janet characterized Bernheim's opinions as dangerous because they would "lead to the suppression of all forms of determinism," and added:

[F]or my part I do not hesitate to affirm that these interpretations are anti-psychological, because psychology, like physiology, has laws which suggestion is incapable of bending. (Bérillon 1889, p. 109; cf. P. Janet 1895)

This rather curious view of determinism was hardly defensible at the time, and psychologists would now reject it entirely—the lawful determinants of many kinds of behaviors include suggestion. In any case, it led Freud as well as Charcot (and Janet at that time) to a totally incorrect concept of hypnosis. But, as Delboeuf's contemporaneous experience showed, that error could have been avoided by a little more skepticism.

Conclusion

From the beginning of its study, sharp observations and properly conducted experiments showed unconscious influences to play a major role in determining the phenomena of hypnosis. Investigations by Delboeuf and experiments at Nancy further confirmed what had long been established. Whereas Binet and Janet and others of the Charcot school came to accept that the phenomena resulted from the unconscious transmission of the experimenter's intentions to his subjects, Freud never did. In 1888 Freud was prepared to concede that some unspecified parts of the work of Binet and Féé might be methodologically suspect. But the physiological symptoms of hypnosis were "most definitely" not to be regarded as due to suggestion, and transfer in hysterical subjects was "indubitably a genuine process" (Freud 1888c, pp. 78–80). Except, perhaps, for an obscure hint in his obituary of Charcot (Freud 1893c, pp. 22–23), nowhere did he concede any other deficiencies in the Salpêtrière investigations. He never really modified his position and never recognized the extent to which investigators could unconsciously influence their subjects.

Freud's errors in his evaluation of Charcot's work become a little more comprehensible in the context of the other points of difference between the Salpêtrière and Nancy schools. Charcot's experiments convinced him that only hysterical subjects showed the three states of hypnosis, and that hypnosis was best regarded as artificial hysteria. Bernheim correctly rejected the experiments as having been poorly conducted. On the other hand, on the basis of equally bad experiments (which Charcot correctly rejected), Bernheim had concluded that serious crime could be induced under hypnosis. The frontier between the credulous and the sceptical was not clearly located between Paris and Nancy, nor was all scientific virtue only in the one place and all error in the other. A newcomer, such as Freud was to psychological exploration, especially using a compass as faulty as his in this admittedly confusingly mapped territory, might well have become lost.

Notes

1. The name is sometimes given as Hehl. In the interests of English-language humor at least it should be noted that the name, which derives from Holl, appears as Hell on the title pages of his astronomical works (Sarton 1944).

2. Harrington (1988) drew attention to an inaccuracy in this account of Charcot's involvement. She is able to cite an 1878 report of Gamgee, who visited the Salpêtrière and saw Charcot induce hypnosis.

3. Ellenberger (1970, p. 98) attributes Janet's criticism to a much earlier paper that is, in fact, almost entirely laudatory of Charcot (P. Janet 1895), and G. R. McGuire (1986b) cites Barrucand's *Historie de l'hypnose en France* for a date of 1923. However, the quotation shows that Janet's criticisms date from 1919.

3 Freud, Determinism, and Hysteria

Those voices from the past, which ... still resounded in the disturbed mind of that wretched old woman, were all that survived of the glory that had been Charcot's Salpêtrière.
—Ellenberger: *The Discovery of the Unconscious.*

It was only with the work of Charcot about 100 years ago that hysteria began to be understood. Charcot's essential point was that hysterical symptoms were based on lesions produced by the action of unconscious mental processes rather than on physical alterations to the nervous system. Part of the impact of his work on Freud seems to have been due to the similarity between his and Breuer's conceptions of how symptoms formed.

Hysteria itself had been known well before Charcot, of course. From the very beginning of medicine many attempts had been made to understand it (Veith 1965). The searchers had not lacked diligence. Diseases and misplacements of the womb, blasphemous demoniacal possession, and unbridled or frustrated sexual passions were all proposed as its cause. During those years hysteria was not even a disease for many investigators; rather it was deceitful malingering. When Charcot began his work, possession was no longer believed in, but all of the other causes were still clamoring for attention. Charcot's great merit was to take hysteria seriously and reject the view that it was malingering. He thought of it as a disease of the nervous system, and began a comprehensive program of clinical and experimental inquiry. What he brought to his study were detailed examinations of the symptoms, methodical comparisons of hysteria with other conditions, and, most important, a physiological theory that seemed to encompass its determinants. Freud accepted the theses completely, particularly the emphasis on the lawful way in which the phenomena of hysteria were governed.

Part of Charcot's impact on Freud came from the way his deterministic and physiological thinking, with its rejection of unconscious influences as determinants of psychological phenomena, matched Freud's own. In this chapter, I will show how the particular view of determinism the two men shared led them to make the most profound of errors. We will see that it is also the view of determinism that underlies Freud's later work.

Hysteria and Organic Disorders

In Charcot's time the term hysteria referred to a striking set of physical and mental symptoms that more or less successfully mimicked organically caused disorders but seemed not to be based on changes in the structure of the nervous system. Among the physical symptoms were convulsions, contractures, and paralyses, disorders of the special senses such as blindness and deafness, and disorders of sensations such as anesthesias and hyperesthesias. Mental symptoms included complete or partial loss of memory or consciousness, hallucinations, and the complex of behaviors referred to as multiple personality. Few patients exhibited all of these symptoms. In some the combination of symptoms was present permanently, and in others convulsions and hallucinations appeared episodically as hysterical attacks.

For Charcot, the first thing to be disposed of conceptually was the notion that hysterics were malingerers, able to produce their symptoms intentionally. He conducted many experiments to establish the differences between hysterical symptoms and their simulated equivalents. These seemed to show hysterics did not have to exert themselves to maintain their symptoms. For example, the respiration of a hysterical subject with a permanent contracture of the thumb to which force had been applied differed from that of a normal subject attempting to simulate the contraction. In figure 3.1 the simulator's respiration shows greater signs of effort than the patient's. Whatever else hysteria might be, it could not be an intentional simulation of organic disorder.

Not unnaturally, Charcot used the same method of studying hysteria that had been so successful in his study of organically based conditions: close systematic observation of the signs was combined with attempts to localize the site of the lesion in the nervous system. In this way the essential symptoms could be identified, related to one another, and characterized as fully as possible. Noting with great care the details of the permanent symptoms and the episodic attacks, Charcot convinced himself that hysterical symptoms reflected changes in the functions of the organs rather than in their anatomical structure.

His point may be illustrated with two of his patients known as Deb____ and Porcz____. Each had developed a paralysis and loss of sensation in an arm after an injury to the shoulder. Figure 3.2 is Charcot's representation of the anesthesias. In Deb____ the loss of function is exactly as expected from a rupture of the main nerve trunk in the arm carrying the motor and cutaneous nerve fibers. In Porcz____ the whole limb, excluding the fingers, is affected and cannot possibly be accounted for by the rupture of a major nerve supply (Charcot 1887/1889, pp. 262–273). Not only is it the case that the nerve fibers to the shoulder area do not have their endings so precisely distributed, but the nerve supply to the arm has a different origin from the shoulder girdle. Further, because the nerve supply to the arm includes the fibers terminating in the fingers, the arm *alone* cannot be affected; the fingers also would have to be involved. No single injury could give rise to the pattern of sensory loss shown by Porcz____. Neither could it cause the anesthesias that were almost pathognomonic of hysteria, those in which the boundaries of the sensory loss ran perpendicularly to the axis of the limb (Charcot and Marie 1892).

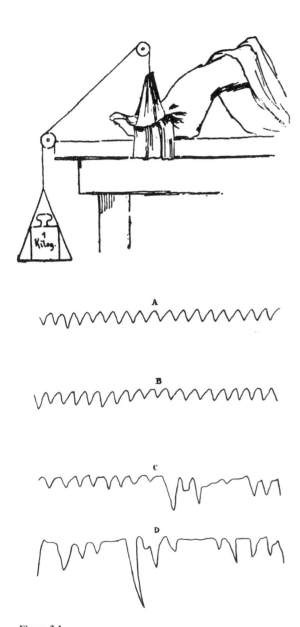

Figure 3.1
The drawing shows force being applied to a contracted thumb. Below are respiration recordings of a hysteric (A and B) and a simulator (C and D) (Charcot 1887/1889, figure 19, p. 96, figure 20, p. 97).

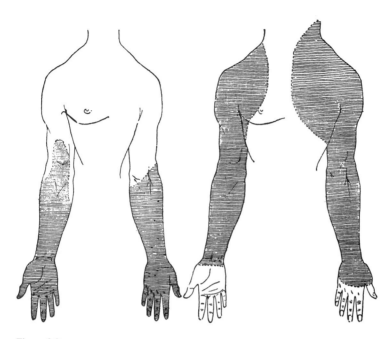

Figure 3.2
Left, organic anesthesia (Deb____) and right, hysterical anesthesia (Porcz____) (Charcot 1887/1889, figures 54 and 55 p. 268, and figures 56 and 57, p. 269 respectively).

Organic disorders were caused by alterations to the structure of some part of the nervous system—structural or anatomical lesions—occurring at any level up to and including the cerebral cortex. Charcot assumed that in hysteria there were similar lesions, but that they were always located in the cerebral cortex and were functional rather than structural. For example, in considering the details of an hysterical paralysis, he proposed:

There is without doubt a lesion of the nervous centres.... It is, I opine, in the grey matter of the cerebral hemisphere on the side opposite the paralysis, and more precisely in the motor zone of the arm.... we may believe ... it is not strictly limited to the motor zone, and that it extends behind the median convolution to the adjacent parts of the parietal lobe. But certainly it is not of the nature of a circumscribed organic lesion.... We have here unquestionably one of those lesions which escape our present means of anatomical investigation, and which, for want of a better term, we designate *dynamic* or *functional* lesions.   (1887/1889, p. 278)

Dynamic or functional lesions were clearly thought of as analogous to structural or anatomical lesions. But, although Charcot often alluded to dynamic lesions, he was unable to characterize them in any way, to spell out in any detail how they differed from the structural lesions they resembled, or to be very specific about how they were formed.

Major Hysteria

Charcot differentiated two types of hysteria: traumatic and major. Major hysteria was characterized by changes in consciousness and by convulsions. A typical attack proceeded through four successive stages:

1. The epileptoid or convulsive stage

2. Stage of clownism or major movements

3. *Attitudes passionelles* (hallucinatory stage)

4. *Decline terminal* (terminal confusion)

The spontaneous attack would frequently be signaled by some unusual sensation or aura, such as a constriction in the throat, a throbbing in the temple, or a ringing in the ears. It could also be triggered by pressure applied to certain parts of the body, what Charcot called the hysterogenic zones (figure 3.3). Oddly enough, pressure on these zones could sometimes also terminate a spontaneous attack once it had begun. In women an especially important hysterogenic zone was located on an area of the abdominal wall corresponding to the ovaries. So regularly did pressure there terminate attacks that some patients wore an "ovarian compressor" to inhibit them.

The characteristic features of what Charcot called major hysteria are well illustrated in case of Ly___ (Charcot 1887/1889, pp. 248–251). As was usually the case, Charcot examined this patient in front of his students, commented to them on the diverse features of the case, and went so far as to provoke a hysterical attack for them to see. Although all four of the stages were present, the ritual nonconvulsive movements of stage 2 were not marked. It is also of interest that Ly___ was male. Two hysterogenic zones were present, and:

Moderate pressure exercised on the last point immediately determines an attack, which we are thus able to study in all its details.

The attack is preceded by the characteristic aura—epigastric constriction, a feeling of a ball in the throat, &c. At this moment, and even before the patient loses consciousness, his tongue becomes stiffened, and is retracted in his mouth towards the left side. It is found by aid of the finger that its point is carried behind the molars of that side. The mouth, half opened, is likewise deviated towards the left side. All the left side of the face shares in the deviation. The head itself is strongly drawn toward the left. The patient then becomes unconscious. The upper extremities are extended, first the right and then the left. The lower extremities remain flaccid, or at least they are very little stiffened. The movement of torsion towards the left,

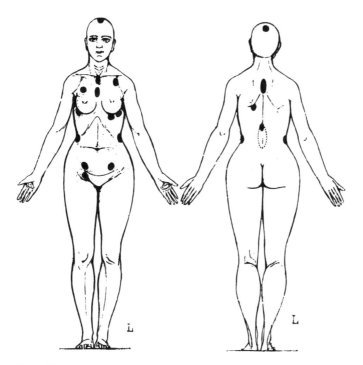

Figure 3.3
Hysterogenic zones in a female patient (Bourneville and Regnard 1876–1880, vol. III, pp. 48–49).

at first limited to the face, soon becomes general, and rolling over, the patient lies on his left side. Next, clonic convulsions replace the tonic spasm. The extremities are agitated by frequent vibrations, but of limited extent. The face is the seat of rapid tremblings, and then follows a stage of complete relaxation without stertor. But at this moment the patient seems tormented by horrible visions. He mentally sees again, without doubt, the scene of his quarrel ... and utters reproachful words: "Scoundrel ..., Prussian ..., struck with a stone, he is trying to kill me." The words are spoken in a perfectly distinct manner. Then, all of a sudden, he changes his attitude. Seated on his bed he is observed to pass his hand over one of his legs in such a manner as to disengage some reptile which encircles the limb, and during that time he mutters something about the worm. The scene at Sceaux comes back to him "I will kill you ..., a gun-shot ..., you will see." After that period, signalised by delirium and corresponding passionate attitudes, the epileptoid stage is spontaneously produced, thus inaugurating a new attack which can in no wise be distinguished from the first, and which may be followed by many others. Pressure on the hysterogenic points interrupts the evolution of the different phases. On wakening, Ly___ appears dazed and stupefied, and he states that he remembers nothing which has transpired.   (Charcot 1887/1889, pp. 249–250)

The content of the hallucinations seemed related to incidents dating from three years before:

[H]e was engaged in efforts to rid himself of a tapeworm, from which he suffered, and for which purpose he took pomegranate bark, which had the desired effect. At first, fragments of the worm were voided, and then the whole. The sight of the taenia in his excreta so struck him, that for several days he suffered from slight nervous complications, such as colics, pains and tremblings of the limbs, &c.
A year ago, while working at his trade at Sceaux, he witnessed one of his comrades violently strike his son. Ly——— desired to interpose, but his comrade turned furiously upon him, and while Ly——— was fleeing hurled a stone at him. Fortunately, the stone did not strike him; but the fright experienced by Ly——— was very severe. Immediately he was seized by trembling of the limbs.... He fancied every moment that he saw the tapeworm, or that he was again engaged in the strife with his comrade.   (1887/1889, pp. 248–249)

However, other data in the history were taken as evidence for the hysteria having a hereditary basis: hysterical attacks in the mother, alcoholism in the father, hysteria in the grandmother and aunts.

Note that Charcot fails to comment on the possible *causal* connection between the earlier incidents and the content of the hallucinations, even though he granted that, while hallucinating, the patient "mentally sees again . . . the scene of his quarrel." The failure is consistent with his estimate of external events as mere precipitators of major hysteria. Elsewhere he said the hallucinations showed how

the psychical element begins to play the first part in these morbid phenomena.

But then added that the

vivid impression or . . . emotion formerly experienced by the patient . . . often has played a part in the *explosion* of hysterical symptoms.   (Charcot and Marie 1892. My emphasis)

From this perspective, Ly——— would have developed hysterical attacks regardless of the action of external factors. His hereditary weakness would have seen to that.

Freud was to differ from Charcot about the causes of major hysteria. For him (and Breuer) it was to be explained in the same way as traumatic hysteria, the second type that Charcot distinguished.

Traumatic Hysteria

What Charcot called traumatic hysteria had a more definite onset than major hysteria. It usually followed a physical injury and had no physical basis. Its symptoms included paralyses, losses or augmentations of sensation (anesthesias or hyper-esthesias), and the special sense disturbances previously mentioned. Although some or all of these symptoms were also to be found in major hysteria, they were there not preceded by a definite trauma. These points become clearer in the following typical case:

The man named Le Log____[1] was born in a little village of Brittany, and he is now twenty-nine years of age.... By occupation he was formerly a cook's assistant, but lately, for want of better work, he went in to the service of a florist in the market.... every second or third day, he went to a horticulturist at St. Cloud to fetch plants. These he brought back on a little hand-barrow, which he drew, while his master's son, young Conr____, helped by pushing behind.

It was on returning from St. Cloud in this fashion on October 21st 1885, about 6 o'clock in the evening, that the accident happened which was the cause of all his troubles. On this evening, when it was very nearly dark, Le Log____ was dragging his barrow along the road beside the Seine. He had arrived at the top of the Pont des Invalides, when all of a sudden, a heavily laden laundryman's van, driven by some drunken men at railway speed, charged into him. The wheel of the hand-barrow was struck, and Le Log____ was violently thrown on to the footpath, from which he was picked up absolutely unconscious. The horse of the laundry-man's van did not touch Le Log____, and its wheels *did not pass over him*. There was no apparent wound, nor was any blood discovered about his person. Le Log____ was placed upon his own barrow and was taken in the first place to a chemist's shop, where he remained for about twenty minutes, and was then carried, still unconscious, to the Beaujon Hospital.

The preceding details were given by young Conr____, and confirmed, moreover, by a man named L____, a post-office official at the Palais de l'Industrie, who was present during the collision. The account which Le Log____ himself gives of the affair when he is questioned is a very different one. *He has made out a long history of the accident* in which he firmly believes, and of which the circumstances appear to him from time to time *in his dreams*. The laundry-man's van came charging along with much noise; the horse fell right upon him, and struck him in the breast with its head. He fell down, struck his head violently on the ground, and finally the heavy van *passed completely over his body, across the upper part of the thighs*. Generally, when his dream arrives at this point, the patient wakes up suddenly screaming. At the Hôtel Dieu, and here also at the Salpêtrière, he has often been heard to cry out "Stop! don't drive on, the horse is going to crush me."

As a matter of fact, the patient has completely lost all recollection of what passed at the moment of the accident. It is very probable that he was affected at the time by an *intense cerebral commotion*, followed by a form of amnesia which MM. Ribot and Azam have de-scribed under the name of *traumatic retrograde amnesia*.

He was transported to the Beaujon Hospital, where he remained during five or six days without consciousness.... When his consciousness returned he was very surprised to find himself in the hospital; he remembered absolutely nothing of what had taken place. It was only after he heard the history from those around, as he himself confesses, that the circumstances of the accident as he narrates them occurred to his mind.

Several facts relative to his state in the Beaujon Hospital are worthy of being mentioned. (1) *His lower extremities seemed to him as though they were dead*. At first he was unable to lift them from the bed, except with the aid of his hands, but at the end of a few days he was able to leave his bed, go out of the hospital, and walk part of the way home on foot. (2) He had several large bruises on the hip, the right groin, and over the lower abdomen. (3) He suffered with his head in the same way he does now.   (Charcot 1887/1889, pp. 374–376)

Le Log____'s anesthesia and hyperesthesia are represented in figure 3.4.

Two important features in Le Log____'s case history should be noted: the first is the interval between the traumatic event and the appearance of the symptoms, and the second is the marked discrepancy between what had actually happened and what he recalled as having happened. With respect to the interval Charcot hypothesized:

We have here a phenomenon of unconscious or sub-conscious cerebration, mentation or ideation. The patient, in a case of this sort, is aware of the result, but he does not preserve any recollection, or he only preserves it in a vague manner, of the different phases of the phenomenon.   (1887/1889, p. 387, n. 1)

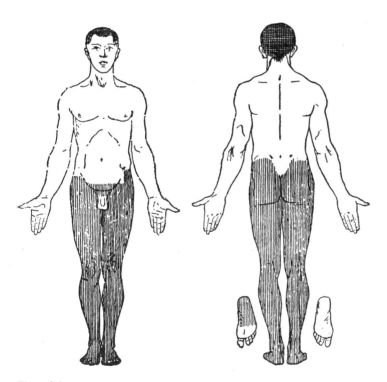

Figure 3.4
Distribution of anesthesia in Le Log____. A patch of hyperesthesia is on the head (Charcot 1887/1889, figure 84, p. 380).

The unconscious process took time—there was therefore a period of incubation before the symptoms appeared. In one respect Le Log____'s history was atypical: patients were not always unconscious between the trauma and the symptoms, even though they were always unaware of how their symptoms had been elaborated.

With respect to the discrepancy between the reality and his recollection, Le Log____'s history was very typical: his memory was of having been knocked down by the horse and run over by the van, whereas in reality neither had touched him. As Janet was to put it in some later comments, possibly about this very case,

Charcot, studying the paralyses, had shown that the disease is not produced by a real accident, but by the *idea* of this accident. It is not necessary that the carriage wheel should really have passed over the patient; it is enough if he has the idea that the wheel passed over his legs.   (P. Janet, 1920, p. 324. My emphasis)

Charcot's explanation was that the traumatic event gave rise to an idea that then overpowered the mind and realized or expressed itself in physical form as a symptom. *Realization* was the unconscious mental mechanism by which he believed ideas were turned into hysterical symptoms.

Charcot's explanation was based not only on the analysis of case histories: symptoms produced experimentally under hypnosis seemed also to implicate realization. Charcot showed that verbal suggestion under hypnosis could create the paralyses, the anesthesias, and the other sensory disabilities found in hysteria, and that these experimentally produced symptoms reproduced in minute detail the characteristics of hysterical symptoms. For example, the zones of anesthesia produced by hypnotic suggestion were separated from one another by the same well-defined boundaries as in hysteria, being arranged in the same geometrical segments. How striking the similarity was may be gauged in part by comparing Charcot's representation of hypnotically created anesthetic zones (figure 3.5) with Le Log____'s (figure 3.4). In neither instance did the zones correspond to the anatomical distribution of the nerve fibers.

That symptoms could be produced at all under hypnosis was due to the peculiar consequences of suggestion in that state. Under hypnosis it was possible, Charcot said,

to bring forth by suggestion or intimation, an idea, or a coherent group of associated ideas, which become lodged in the mind in the manner of a parasite, remaining isolated from all the rest and interpreted outwardly by corresponding motor phenomena. If such is the case one can conceive that an inculcated *idea* of paralysis, being of this type, results in an *actual* paralysis; and we shall see that in such cases it will frequently appear with as distinct clinical characteristics as a destructive lesion of the cerebral substance. (Charcot 1887/1889, p. 289. Retranslated, my emphasis)

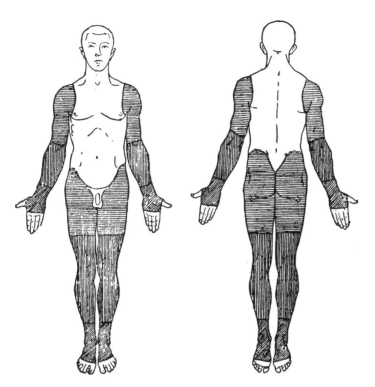

Figure 3.5
Distribution of anesthesia in a partial paralysis suggested in hypnosis (Charcot 1887/1889, figure 85, p. 381).

For an idea to be realized it had to be isolated from the rest of consciousness. Otherwise it and its symptom would have been modifiable by an act of will. But modifications of that type were demonstrably not possible—patients could not will their symptoms away. The isolated idea or group of ideas were

screened from the control of that large collection of personal ideas long accumulated and organized which constitute the conscience properly so-called, the *ego*. (1887/1889, p. 290. Retranslated)

Ideas were transformed into symptoms, that is, realized as symptoms, by unconscious mental processes outside of the control of the ego.

Further experiments seemed to identify a source of ideas even more relevant for understanding traumatic hysteria than direct verbal suggestion. Charcot sometimes hit some of his hypnotized subjects unexpectedly on the arm or leg thereby causing:

a total or partial paralysis of the lower limb. When partial paralysis of the movements of the joint ... occur the loss of motor power of that joint carries with it almost necessarily ... cutaneous and deep anaesthesia of the corresponding segment of the limb. (1887/1889, p. 382, n. 1; cf. pp. 304–305)

In a later *Dictionary* article he described the process very succinctly:

A man predisposed to hysteria has received a blow on the shoulder. This slight traumatism or local shock has sufficed to produce in this nervous individual a sense of numbness extending over the whole of the limb and a slight indication of paralysis; in consequence of this sensation the idea arises in the patient's mind that he might become paralysed; in one word, through autosuggestion, the rudimentary paralysis becomes real. In other words, the phenomenon is brought about in the cerebral cortex, the seat of all psychical operations.   (Charcot and Marie 1892)

The idea from which the hysterical symptom developed was the idea generated during the trauma, either in the manner supposed by Janet or through the sensations produced during the trauma itself.

Charcot's chain of reasoning also required there to be a similarity between the hypnotic and traumatic states. Speaking of two of his male patients he said:

Without doubt the two men were not at the moment of their fall in a hypnotic sleep, nor subsequently, when the paralysis was definitely established. But in this respect it may be inquired whether the mental condition occasioned by the emotion, by the Nervous Shock experienced at the moment of the accident and for some time after, is equivalent in a certain measure in predisposed subjects ... to the cerebral condition which is determined in "hysterics" by hypnotism. Upon the assumption of this hypothesis, the peculiar sensation ... which we may suppose to have been produced in ... our two male patients by a fall on the shoulder, that sensation, I say, may be considered as having originated, in the former as in the latter, the idea of motor paralysis of the member. But because of the annihilation of the *ego* produced by the hypnotism in the one case and ... by the nervous shock in the other, that idea once brought to the surface would become lodged in the brain of the patient, in that very place, be removed from every influence, be strengthened, and finally become powerful enough to realize itself objectively through a paralysis. In both cases, the sensation in question plays the part of a veritable *suggestion*.   (Charcot 1887/1889, p. 305. Partly retranslated)

In mental conditions such as hypnosis and nervous shock, ideas created unconsciously from the sensations experienced in the traumatic situation spread unchecked to produce symptoms.

Although realization was described vaguely, it seemed to Charcot to be consistent with other observations.[2] Reynolds (1869) had long since seen a paralysis develop in a patient seized by the idea that she *might* become paralyzed after a long and fatiguing walk. After becoming aware of a progressive weakness in her legs she was finally unable to walk at all. The idea of paralysis had been transformed into a real inability to move. Möbius (1888, cited in Decker 1977, p. 83) had similarly hypothesized that hysterical symptoms, formed when ideas arising in the void created in consciousness by strong affects, acted like hypnotic suggestions.

Experiments on the relation between emotional expression and posture or muscular activity seemed also to support the concept of realization. According to Binet and Féré, Braid had observed that the posture assumed by hypnotized subjects affected their emotional expression. For example, when a subject was placed in a posture expressing anger and the fists clenched, the person's face expressed menace (Binet and Féré 1887/1887a, p. 71).

After confirming that observation, Charcot and Richer (1883) went on to explore the contrary possibility that modifications of facial expression would produce changes in bodily attitudes or positions. Using mild electrical stimulation of the muscles of the face to produce a particular facial expression, they found the rest of the body took up an attitude consistent with it. For example, when stimulation of the occipitofrontal muscles produced the facial expression of astonishment (raised eyelids, wrinkled forehead, eye fixation, enlargement of the palpebral opening), the mouth also opened slightly and the arms raised themselves in semiflexion with the palms turned outward. Bodily attitudes expressive of aggression and defense, pain, fear, and laughter were also observed after stimulation of the appropriate facial muscles.

Charcot and Richer concluded that ideas operated unconsciously through the muscle sense; stimulation of the muscles suggested the corresponding posture to the appropriate centers of the brain. Other workers seemed to find that a given postural attitude produced an appropriate and real idea or emotion. Azam, for example, observed a hypnotized subject to be *thinking* of prayer after her arms and hands had been placed in a prayerful attitude (cited in Binet and Féré 1887/1887a, pp. 76–77). It seemed reasonable to conclude that a two-way connection existed between ideas or feelings and bodily attitudes or postures such that one could give rise to the other.

A two-way connection between ideas and postures was consistent with a then very influential theory according to which one had to have an idea of a movement before it could be carried out. Several other observations seemed to support it. Some neurological disorders were marked by patients' inability to discern the position of their limbs after their arms of legs had been moved passively. Although not lacking in muscle power, these patients were usually also unable to move their limbs voluntarily. It was argued that, lacking the idea of the existing position, the patients could not move their limbs to a new position; or, if they could, they were unable to judge when it had been reached.

Perhaps the strongest argument was the introspective observation advanced by William James (1890b) and others. When learning a new movement one had to have a more or less precise idea of it at first but, with repeated execution, it was performed automatically whenever willed. James pointed out that a person was aware only of the consequences of an act of will, not of the willing itself, and that the only consequences of willing were movements. Familiar everyday movements seemed also to be based on the unconscious transformation or realization of ideas.

Breuer and Charcot

According to Freud, Charcot reacted with reserve when he (Freud) told him (Charcot) about Breuer's treatment of Anna O. If Charcot did, it was probably not simply because he was skeptical about the possibility of treating hysteria. First, Freud could have said only that Breuer's talking cure produced a temporary remission. Freud must have known of the patient's relapses. He certainly knew that in mid-1883 Breuer regarded Anna O. as "quite unhinged" and even hoped she would die and "be released from her suffering." In addition, it is very difficult to imagine Freud being unaware of what his fiancée knew about Anna O. at the beginning of 1887 (E. Jones 1953–1957, vol. 1, p. 225). Given Charcot's extensive knowledge of the history of attempts to treat hysteria, it is unlikely Breuer's ephemeral success would have interested him much at all.

Second, had Freud described the classic magnetic-illness features of the case, especially the spontaneous somnambulistic state that allowed the therapy to take place, Charcot would have been justified in displaying even less interest. We have noted Ellenberger's (1970, pp. 121–123, 484; 1972) opinion that Anna O.'s history was too much like the earlier cases for late-nineteenth-century workers to take her treatment seriously as a model, and Charcot himself may certainly be included among those doubters (Charcot 1879–1880).

In getting us to react to his story of Charcot's disinterest as one of a great opportunity missed by the leading student of hysteria, Freud diverted our attention from something of rather more interest: the very considerable similarity between the theoretical ideas of Breuer and Charcot. According to Breuer, the memories of perceptions and sensations occurring in hypnoid states behaved like foreign bodies, connected with but dissociated from the normal consciousness. When those memories forcibly intruded into the normal consciousness they brought with them the original perceptions and sensations as symptoms. Patients had no control over their symptoms and could not understand where the disorders had come from because they had not experienced the events in a normal, primary consciousness. Freud was therefore more than a little justified in allowing himself the anachronistic expression that Breuer had *followed* Charcot in making assumptions about the hypnoid state (Freud 1896c, pp. 194–195).

By the time Breuer came to prepare Anna O.'s case for publication, dissociation theory, from which Charcot's notions formally derive, had been fully established by French workers in the field of psychopathology, mainly by Charcot's colleagues. Dissociation theory had developed from the study of the many cases of alternating states of consciousness and multiple personality reported between 1816, when the most famous of the early cases appeared (Mitchill 1816; Carlson 1984, 1989), and 1858 when Azam began his observations on Felida X. (Azam 1876; Taylor and Martin 1944). What makes Felida X. important is not only that in her primary state of consciousness she had no knowledge of what transpired in the secondary state: she was the first patient in whom symptoms that were present in one state were absent in the other. In her primary state, Felida X. was morose and afflicted with hysterical deliria, convulsions, paralyses, and contractures, but bright, affectionate, and symptom free in the second. Later workers such as Mesnet (1874, cited by Taine 1873), Dufay (1876), Camuset (1882), and Bourru and Burot (1885) showed how the different states could be brought about and demonstrated, just as in Anna O.'s case, that the symptoms displayed, or whether they were present at all, depended on which of the states was manifest.

Breuer further believed that the first hypnoid state acted as a focus: experiences occurring in other hypnoid states tended to become connected with it. In *Studies on Hysteria*, which contained the later published account of Anna O., Breuer used the French term *condition seconde* for the totality of this group of memories. Its fully developed form was a dual consciousness, or *double conscience*, and it was such a secondary consciousness that was the repository of all of Anna O.'s symptoms.

Breuer proposed that Anna O.'s habitual daydreaming and reveries were predisposing causes. By themselves neither they nor their contents were abnormal—the states were readily interrupted and there was no amnesia for their content. The illness proper began with the root cause of the snake hallucination and arm paralysis. Both were experienced in a hypnoid state and both recurred momentarily the next day when, in an *absence*, Anna O. saw a snakelike object. The same day she was in such a state of abstraction while waiting for the surgeon that she failed to perceive him entering the room. The reveries and day-dreams, the hallucination and paralysis, and the unresponsiveness to the surgeon, now formed a *condition seconde* and subsequent experiences incorporated into it. For example, her eyes filled with tears when her father had asked her the time. In trying to read the watch face, she brought it close to her eyes and produced an enlarged image and a convergent squint. These visual peculiarities were added to the *condition seconde*; when they recurred they produced a squint and a general tendency to see things as enlarged (macropsia). The strengthening of the secondary consciousness until it was permanently present, brought into being a set of more or less perfectly understandable daytime symptoms. Just as gradually as the complex secondary state of consciousness was elaborated, so also was a more complex set of symptoms. Not until December 1880 were anything other than the *absences* manifest, and initially they were so fleeting as to have been unnoticed. But by the time Anna O. was herself so fatigued she was confined to bed, the *condition seconde* was strong enough to be present during most of the day. Breuer, it will be remembered, emphasized that the newness of her symptoms was only apparent; according to him, they had been present soon after the original foundation hallucination.

Some of the other theoretical constructs on which Breuer drew were formulated originally by two of Charcot's close colleagues, Binet and Pierre Janet. Both had described a secondary consciousness forming from the remnants of experiences occurring in spontaneous somnambulistic states, and both had offered explanations of how it had come about. Although their major theoretical accounts were published relatively late (Binet 1889–1890, 1892; P. Janet 1889), most of the theory was contained in papers appearing shortly after 1886 (Binet and Féré 1887b; Binet 1889; P. Janet 1886, 1887, 1888).

That Breuer eventually came to owe the French school of psychopathologists an extensive theoretical debt is shown by comparing his original case notes on Anna O., which contain practically no theory, with his discussion of her in *Studies on Hysteria*. Nevertheless, even his initial conception of her hysteria was probably not far removed from that of Charcot and his school. In attributing the origins of symptoms to ideas arising in a state resembling hypnosis, and in characterizing them as psychical foreign bodies, Breuer's views were at one with the conclusions Charcot had drawn from his case analyses and from his experiments with hypnosis. We can take Freud's partial anachronism farther and say that in introducing the concept of hypnoid hysteria, Breuer extended the views of Charcot and his colleagues on the origins of traumatic hysteria and the mechanism of hysterical symptom formation. It is not surprising Freud responded so positively to Charcot's teachings or that, with Breuer, he would come to insist that what Charcot had termed traumatic hysteria should be the model for all hysteria (Breuer and Freud 1893, pp. 5–6; cf. Freud 1893a, pp. 30–31).

Charcot, Freud, and Determinism

Charcot's observations seemed to him to be consistent with hysterical symptoms being produced by lawful alterations in physiological functioning. The phenomena themselves, the pattern in the attacks of major hysteria, and the similarity of the symptoms across cultures and historical periods, all seemed to be part of such a precise determination that suggestion could be ruled out as a cause (Charcot 1887–1888, p. 305). Yet unconscious influences had undoubtedly contributed to the symptoms of Charcot's hysterical patients. Unconscious imitation of organic disorders was always a possibility. Who, even today, has not seen a spastic contracture, a poststroke paralysis or aphasia, or an epileptic or febrile convulsion?

The relatively poorer health services of an earlier era probably made such models even more readily available. Some patients learned the phenomena through unconscious imitation of other hysterical patients. This was especially so at the Salpêtrière. Practically nowhere else were stages of major hysteria observed that corresponded to those Charcot so meticulously described. Other patients learned by divining what the physicians wanted to see. For example, in Brouillet's well-known painting *Une leçon clinique à la Salpêtrière*, the hysterical patient Charcot is demonstrating is at the point of passing from the first stage of her attack into the stage of clownism, or major movements in which she will display the famous *arc de cercle*. Ellenberger pointed out her model. On the wall of the lecture theater, in full view of the patient and her audience, hangs the 1878 drawing by Charcot's colleague Paul Richer of another patient who has completed her arc (Ellenberger 1970, between pp. 330 and 331, caption to his reproduction of the painting). Charcot's patient can use that model to complete her own arc.

There is an important paradox in these kinds of unconscious learning. None is in opposition to Charcot's theses, each is actually consistent with them. *The idea* in the mind of *the patient* causes the symptom. Even when the idea originates with the experimenter or physician, it is the unconscious transformation of that idea *by the patient* that brings the symptom into being. Transformation may be accepted; indeed, it must be, even though Charcot's false physiological theory has to be rejected.

Another even stronger reason than these general considerations for including suggested ideas among the lawful determinants of hysterical symptoms is the implication that the detailed characteristics of symptoms are completely determined by them. I am not aware that this implication, which follows directly from an observation of Janet's reported in 1892, has been drawn previously. In that year, Janet began an over-all analysis of hysterical symptoms with a consideration of the peculiarities of hysterical anesthesias. Like Charcot, he was impressed by the impossibility of the pathology of the lesion corresponding with what was known from anatomy. A single whole finger might be anesthetic from its junction with the hand, or the whole hand below the wrist might have lost sensation just as if it had been covered by a glove. As Janet put it:

These distributions of anaesthesia obviously do not correspond to anatomical regions, it is not the region innervated by the cubital or the median nerve that is anaesthetic—it is *the* hand or *the* wrist. (P. Janet 1892a. My emphasis)

He then drew the following extraordinarily novel conclusion:

the localization is not anatomical, it is physiological, as M. Charcot rightly says. But I would like to add a word, this distribution corresponds to a very *crude*, very *common*, *physiology*. When an hysterical patient has her hand paralysed, where should the insensitive area be? On the muscles that are not functioning, that is on the forearm. And yet, the anaesthesia is nearly always confined to the hand itself and to the wrist. In hysterical blindness, anaesthesia bears not only on the retina, but on the conjunctiva, and even on the eyelids: the amaurotic hysterical has spectacles of anaesthesia on the face. She has *lost her eye*, not only in the physiological sense, but in the *popular sense* of the word, namely all that fills the orbit. It would seem that, even in these localized anaesthesias, the habitual associations of our sensations, *the ideas* we conceive *of our organs*, play an important role and determine these distributions. (P. Janet 1892a. My emphasis)

What was lost to normal consciousness was the idea of the organ or its function, as Le Log___'s feeling that his legs were dead illustrate.

From Charcot's discussion it is clear that he did not differentiate sharply between the idea of organ dysfunction and the idea of the organ itself (Charcot 1887/1889, pp. 254–256, 264–273, 297–302; Charcot and Marie 1892). What Janet was proposing, in effect, was that the latter gave rise to the former. The fact that the patient's ordinary, everyday idea of an organ or function was reflected in the symptom had another radical consequence:

hysterical anaesthesia is not for us an organic malady, it is a mental malady, a psychological malady. It exists not in the limbs, nor in the medulla, but is represented in the mind, if you like, in the cortical regions of the brain. (P. Janet 1892a)

Consequently, the understanding of hysterical anesthesia had to be based on what the psychologist could contribute about the effect of ideas, rather than on what the anatomist knew about the distribution of nerves or what the physiologist understood of physical function.

We now see, immediately as it were, why hysterical symptoms *have* to be uniform across cultures and historical epochs. To the extent that the ideas people have of their organs and their functions are uniform, so the hysterical symptoms those ideas generate will also be uniform. Had none of Charcot's hysterical patients ever seen an organic symptom or any other hysterical patient, or been present at his demonstrations, the details of their symptoms would have been exactly the same. The similarity of their ideas would have proved a more than adequate determinant.

Determinism in the formation of hysterical symptoms reveals itself in the lawfulness and regularity with which ideas cause symptoms, whatever their source, and especially in the lawful and regular way in which they determine the detailed characteristics of the symptoms. Consequently, it is irrelevant to object to Charcot's work, as Page, Babinski, and Hurst did (Hurst 1920, pp. 6–7), on the grounds that such pathognomonic signs of hysteria as hemianesthesia or restriction of the visual field are produced by the physician's examination of the patient. In supporting his objection, Hurst also showed that when even medical students were asked to indicate how organs would be affected were they to become anesthetic or paralyzed, they also drew on the crude, common, or popular physiology that Janet described (1920, pp. 8–11). When Hurst tended to dismiss hysterical symptoms as due to the imagination, he therefore did not see how his demonstration of Janet's point actually supported determinism.

Conclusion

As with hypnosis, Freud never saw that the role of unconscious influences in hysteria could be acknowledged within a deterministic framework. The key to his views is found in some comments he made on hypnosis and hysteria in the *Preface* to his translation of Bernheim's *De la Suggestion*:

If the supporters of the suggestion theory are right, all the observations made at the Salpêtrière are worthless; indeed, they become errors in observation. The hypnosis of hysterical patients would have no characteristics of its own; but every physician would be free to produce any symptomatology that he liked in the patients he hypnotised. We should not learn from the study of major hypnotism what alterations in excitability succeed one another in the nervous system of hysterical patients in response to certain kinds of interventions; we should merely learn what intentions Charcot suggested (in a manner of which he himself was unconscious) to the subjects of his experiments—a thing entirely irrelevant to our understanding alike of hypnosis and of hysteria. (Freud 1888c, pp. 77–78)

Freud was to be as wrong about hysteria as he was about hypnosis.

Suggestion can be given its proper role and the three most valid and important aspects of Charcot's theory accepted: the role of ideas in producing symptoms, the notion of an active but unconscious mental process elaborating the symptoms, and the concept of hysterical symptoms being maintained by a set of isolated or dissociated mental processes. What must be rejected is Charcot's narrow, mistaken view of determinism, the one adopted by Freud.

When Freud came to treat his own patients, he never accepted that influences transmitted unconsciously from him to them had important effects on what they claimed to recall about the origins of their symptoms. His view was that the important determinants of remembering were internal, part of the very fabric of the patient's thoughts, and as impervious to outside influence as the processes determining the phenomena of hypnosis and hysteria at the Salpêtrière were supposed to have been. Although it is true that his adaptation of Breuer's method for use in the waking state led him to develop a set of explanatory notions very different from the dissociation concepts Breuer and Charcot had favored, it did not cause him to give up his mistaken view of the determinants of psychological phenomena.

Notes

1. Le Log___ arrived at the Salpêtrière about a month after Freud had left Paris, and his case does not appear in Freud's translation of Charcot's *Lectures*. However, similar features had been described in a less concentrated form in other cases, especially in the case of Pin___, whom Freud probably did see (Chertok and Saussure 1973/1979, pp. 72–83), and similar theoretical comments made about them.

2. But not, as Havens (1966) suggested, in an otherwise excellent article, in a less formal and less organized manner than Charcot described the theoretical concepts used in his neurological work. Nor, as Havens implied, are these remarks of Charcot to be attributed to "the memory of a biographer or the footnotes to the appendices to his lectures." All of the theory is to be found in the translations he overlooked personally and, in condensed form, in the *Dictionary* article (Charcot and Marie 1892). Although Havens (1973) later seems to have withdrawn his charge, denigration and neglect of Charcot's theoretical contribution are very common (Veith 1965; J. A. Miller, Sabshin, Gedo, Pollock, Sadow, and Schlessinger 1969). Only Owen (1971) gives a reasonable account of it, although his appreciation is uncritical.

4 Freud's Adaptation of Breuer's Treatment Method

Macbeth: Can'st thou not Minister to a minde diseas'd, Plucke from the Memory a rooted Sorrow, Raze out the written troubles of the Braine.
—Shakespeare: *Macbeth*, Act V, iii.

Between 1886 and 1895, after returning to Vienna from the Salpêtrière, Freud devised a method for removing the symptoms of hysteria in the waking state. Important as this was in its own right, what was more fundamental was the complementary set of waking-state theoretical concepts by which he tried to explain how symptoms were acquired in normal consciousness. For him, symptoms were determined by the memories of affectively charged events of which patients could recall having consciously tried to rid themselves. As he came to see it, mental life largely reflected the difficulty the nervous system had in dealing with the effects of unpleasant emotion.

The focus of this chapter is the gradual emergence over the nine-year period of the new therapy, which was based on Freud's new method of retrieving memories in the waking-state, and the theoretical concepts that went with it. I take up the treatment methods and the more or less immediate conceptual issues to which they are related. I begin with Freud's use of Bernheim's method of direct hypnotic suggestion and the variant of it pioneered by Delboeuf and Janet, showing affect not to have been involved in either. Freud's dissatisfaction with hypnosis is seen as a preliminary to his developing a waking-state therapy, and I argue that consistency required him to explain how symptoms could also be acquired in the waking state. I demonstrate that it was through some concepts of Janet's and Hughlings Jackson's that affect first came into Freud's conceptualization of symptom formation, before tracing the very gradual emergence of his concepts of repression and conversion after he recognized it. Finally, I show how Freud then built up a model deriving from Meynert, Charcot, and Jackson, from which he explained how the memories recalled by the patient were related to the symptom. I examine the deterministic assumptions underlying the model and illustrate Freud's use of them in guiding his therapy.

Freud's Use of Hypnosis

As a preliminary to considering Freud's therapy, I would stress that in tracing how the most distinctive of the methods by which he treated psychoneurotic conditions developed, we have to be very clear what Breuer's method was. As Breuer practiced it with Anna O., it had three components: autohypnosis, the retrieval of the causal memory, and talking about the original event. A deliberately induced hypnosis and insistence on the expression of emotion during the verbal utterance were later components. Freud appears to have begun treating nervous disorders soon after he returned from Paris in 1886, but nearly seven years were to elapse before the expression of emotion became basic to his therapy. In the first six and a half years, Freud either used ordinary hypnotic suggestion or he used hypnosis to recover the causal memory before modifying it by direct hypnotic suggestion. Although he said he first used Breuer's method in mid-1889, all the evidence is against his version of the cathartic method then being one that required the patient to express the emotion associated with the causal event. Not until mid-1892 did affective concepts find their way into Freud's theory, and it was only after that that they came into his practice. Consequently, not until the end of that period could he begin to develop what is usually thought of as his most distinctive contribution to psychotherapy: abreaction of previously unexpressed emotion.

From the middle of 1885 Freud employed the traditional methods of deep and whole body massage for paralyses and contractures, baths for relaxation, and both baths and mild electrical stimulation for the restoration of lost sensibilities and functions (Masson 1985, Letters of Nov. 24, 1887, Feb. 4, 1888, and May 28, 1888; E. Jones 1953–1957, vol. 1, pp. 234–235). At the same time, he occasionally used direct hypnotic suggestion; Jones mentions, for example, its use in June 1886 (1953–1957, p. 235). But, as a letter to Fliess indicates, it was not until late in 1887 that he began using hypnosis in a systematic way, obtaining "all sorts of small but noteworthy successes" (Masson 1985, Letter of Dec. 28, 1887).

It was not to Charcot that Freud was indebted for the use of hypnosis in therapy. While he accepted and developed Charcot's propositions about traumatic hysteria, he disagreed with Charcot almost from the beginning on the usefulness of hypnotic suggestion as a therapy. Contrary to many assertions (e.g., Wollheim 1971, p. 24), Charcot was quite wary of using hypnosis for treating hysteria. The testimony of Charcot's colleagues (Freud 1892–1894, pp. 140–141; P. Janet 1919/1925, vol. 1, pp. 326–327) and the judgment of historians (Owen 1971, pp. 127–133; Schneck 1961; Veith 1965, p. 236) show Charcot made little therapeutic use of hypnosis.

A careful reading of Charcot's own works bears out his negative evaluation of the therapeutic use of hypnosis. However, he extols the virtues of hypnosis as a means of *studying* hysteria before remarking:

[F]rom a *therapeutical point of view*, for example, hypnotism has not so far given all the results that we were justified in expecting from it. Its scope of action is limited. Contrary to what might have been expected *à priori*, its action on . . . hysteria . . . is restricted.   (Charcot and de la Tourette 1892)

Again specifically about the treatment of hysteria:

Hypnotism may be of some service, but not so much as one might *à priori* expect; it may be employed against some local symptoms. Although it may be true that in hysteria as such hypnotism prudently applied has not any injurious effects, it is quite certain that in the majority of cases the inconsiderate use or abuse of hypnotism has been followed by very serious complications. *Suggestion* may be employed without hypnotism, and may be quite as effective as in hypnotic sleep.   (Charcot and Marie 1892)

Charcot largely restricted hypnosis to experiments and demonstrations.

Freud nevertheless added hypnotic suggestion to his treatment methods almost immediately after he returned to Vienna. The step was probably provoked by his reading Bernheim's book on hypnotic suggestion, which had appeared the year before. In the same letter to Fliess announcing his successes, he explained he was "already bound by a contract" to translate it (Masson 1985, Letter of Dec. 28, 1887).

Bernheim's influence is to be seen very clearly in Freud's use of the Nancy school procedures for inducing hypnosis. In Bum's *Lexicon* Freud described only two induction procedures: training subjects to imitate at a signal those other patients who had already been hypnotized, and techniques "which have in common the fact that they recall falling asleep through certain physical sensations" suggested directly to them (Freud 1891, pp. 107–108; cf. Freud 1890/1905c, p. 294). Freud recalled seeing the first procedure in Bernheim's clinic, whereas the second is, even down to the visual fixation on the fingers, the only method described at length in Bernheim's book (Bernheim 1887/1888a, pp. 1–4; cf. Liébeault cited in Chertok and Saussure 1973/1979, p. 42). Neither of these methods resembles those of Charcot, who required the hypnotizer to stare fixedly at the subject, to apply light pressure to the subject's closed eyes (Charcot 1879–1880, pp. 162–167), or to use Braid's method of inducing fatigue in the muscles of the eye (Charcot and de la Tourette 1892). Suggestions such as those used by Bernheim were rarely if ever employed at the Salpêtrière, and suggestion was not regarded as an important aspect of the induction. G. M. Robertson's (1892) contemporary account confirms these differences.

As for treatment, Freud quite specifically adopted the second of the two methods used by Bernheim, whose patients were either reassured they would be well on waking from their hypnotic sleep or given direct suggestions that their symptoms would disappear (Bernheim 1887/1888a, part II, chapter 1). In Villaret's *Handwörterbuch* Freud described the direct treatment of the psychological sources of hysterical symptoms as consisting of

giving the patient under hypnosis a suggestion which contains the removal of the disorder in question. Thus, for instance, we cure a *tussis nervosa hysterica* by pressing on the larynx of the hypnotized patient and assuring him that the stimulus to coughing has been removed.   (Freud 1888a, p. 56. Emphasis altered)

G. M. Robertson (1892) also mentioned how Bernheim similarly added to the verbal suggestion that sciatic pain would disappear by passing his hand along the patient's leg "to suggest that some active measures were being used."

Freud's other references to hypnotic treatment—the brief one in the review of Forel's *Hypnotism* (Freud 1889, p. 100), the somewhat longer discussions in the *Die Gesundheit* chapter written in 1890 (Freud 1890/1905c; cf. editor's introduction, *Standard Edition* 1, pp. 63–64), and Bum's *Lexicon* (Freud 1891b, pp. 111–112)—similarly stress the importance of removing the symptom by direct suggestion. Indeed, in Bum he went so far as to state:

The true therapeutic value of hypnosis lies in the *suggestions* made during it. These suggestions consist in an energetic denial of the ailments of which the patient has complained, or in an assurance that he can do something, or in a command to perform it.   (Freud 1891b, p. 111)

This whole-hearted endorsement of Bernheim's technique was also implicit in Freud's use of it in the first of the two treatments of the patient described in the paper on hysterical counterwill, a treatment that cannot have taken place later than mid-1890 (Freud 1892–1893, pp. 118–120). Furthermore, as late as April and May of 1892 Freud gave two expository lectures in which he again spoke of Bernheim's suggestion method rather than any other (Ellenberger 1970, pp. 443–444). It was also then that the counterwill patient probably had her last hypnotic suggestion session. Later in that year, in the autumn, Freud began treating Elisabeth von R. without using suggestion at all (Breuer and Freud 1895, p. 135).

Freud seems to have abandoned Bernheim's direct hypnotic suggestion during a short period late in the summer of 1892. Until then his therapy relied on it even when he first started to use Breuer's method or technique.

Adding Suggestion to Breuer's Technique

Freud was quite specific that he first drew on Breuer's technique with the patient known as Emmy von N. in May of 1889 (Breuer and Freud 1895, p. 48). Since then, Swales has advanced Freud's treatment of Frau Cäcilie, which he dates from the same period, as based on reliving emotionally charged memories under hypnosis (Swales 1986b). However, in neither case was any kind of cathartic method used.

Emmy von N.

Freud said it was because Emmy von N. was a hysteric who could easily be put into the somnambulistic state that he decided to use Breuer's method. We note, however, that he calls it a technique of "*investigation* under hypnosis" and not a *therapy* (Breuer and Freud 1895, p. 48. My emphasis). What he did use hypnosis with her for was to *locate* the incidents that seemed to have caused her symptoms, but his *treatment* did not emphasize either talking or emotional expression. We will see that although the therapy did have a new element to it, it was essentially a variant of Bernheim's technique of direct suggestion.

Freud differentiated three components in Emmy von N.'s treatment. The first was the usual Bernheim method of direct hypnotic suggestion. Freud suggested to her that "all her symptoms should get better" (Breuer and Freud 1895, p. 51), her gastric pains would disappear (p. 54), her menstruation would resume twenty-eight-day periodicity (p. 57), and so on.

The second component was an investigation under hypnosis of the origins of the symptoms, and then the use of suggestion to weaken or remove the pathogenic ideas on which they were based. That this was a variant of the method of direct hypnotic suggestion is clear from Freud's description. Thus his suggestions included wiping away or effacing the mental images "so that she is no longer able to see them before her" (p. 53), suggestions that the images "would only appear to her again indistinctly and without strength" (p. 55), and to remove "her whole recollection of them, as though they had never been present in her mind" (p. 61).

Freud used the variant in treating some of Emmy von N.'s motor symptoms that were based on incidents in which she had been frightened. For example, she frequently broke off her conversation, contorted her face into an expression of hatred and disgust, stretched out her hand, and exclaimed anxiously, "Keep still! Don't say anything! Don't touch me!"[1] Just as suddenly as she broke off her conversation, she would resume it (p. 49). When questioned under hypnosis about the origin of this symptom, she described four separate frightening events, widely separated in time, "in a single sentence and in such rapid succession that they might have been a single episode in four acts" (p. 57). Freud concluded that her "protective formula" defended her from the recurrence of the frightening experiences, but he restricted himself to using direct hypnotic suggestion to remove the anticipatory fear (p. 57). The traumatic memories sustaining other motor symptoms, a stammer and a vocal tic, were similarly modified (pp. 54, 57–58).

Emmy von N.'s talking about the traumatic events was the third component. About a week after the treatment began she seems to have calmed herself by recounting a series of frightening experiences:

At the end of each separate story she twitched all over and took on a look of fear and horror. At the end of the last one she opened her mouth wide and panted for breath. The words in which she described the terrifying subject-matter of her experience were pronounced with difficulty and between gasps. Afterwards her features became peaceful.   (Breuer and Freud 1895, p. 53)

Even so, more than talking was involved:

My therapy consists in wiping away these pictures, so that she is no longer able to see them before her. To give support to my suggestion I stroked her several times over the eyes. (p. 53)

Freud noted this meant that the effect of talking, especially of the emotional expression that accompanied it, could not be separated from that due to hypnotic suggestion (p. 53).

Frau Cäcilie

Swales (1986b) dates the beginning of the treatment of Frau Cäcilie (Anna von Lieben) as possibly in July of 1889 and describes it as involving recollection and emotional expression under hypnosis. By themselves those facts would run against my thesis, and would do so even more strongly if Masson's 1888 date is correct (Masson 1985, p. 20).

Freud mentions Frau Cäcilie in passing to illustrate his theses on the formation of false connections in consciousness, the way a premonition of an unconscious process might reveal itself in consciousness, the possibility of hysterical symptoms existing in the gifted, and the weakness Janet placed centrally as a consequence of the domination of unconscious ideas rather than a cause of them (Breuer and Freud 1895, pp. 67, n. 1, 76, n. 1, 103, 238). Freud classed the "several hundreds of ... cycles" he witnessed with Frau Cäcilie as providing him with the information that gave the direct impetus "to the publication of [the] 'Preliminary Communication'" (p. 178). Because by far the largest part of Freud's use of her case was to *illustrate* his views on the formation of symptoms by symbolization (pp. 175–181, p. 181, n. 1), I believe his reference is to that role rather than to the results of her treatment, which, according to Swales, was not successful.

Actually, neither Freud nor Breuer says very much about Frau Cäcilie's treatment. Freud treated her attacks of pain by laying "energetic prohibitions" on them under hypnosis, that is, by the usual Bernheim method (p. 177). About a year later he added to this therapy. Frau Cäcilie then began to have hysterical attacks in which the hallucinations pointed to an earlier causal experience:

I was sent for at the climax of the attack, induced a state of hypnosis, called up the reproduction of the traumatic experience and hastened the end of the attack by *artificial means*. (p. 178. My emphasis)

What were Freud's artificial means? Why does he not mention or allude to talking about origins either in this general description or when he discusses the treatment of those specific symptoms, such as facial neuralgia, heel pain, head pain, various miscellaneous pains, and *globus hystericus*, that did require her to reproduce the circumstances of their origin? (pp. 178–180).

Breuer does mention what seems to be a talking cure with emotional expression, but what he says is not without its peculiarities:

She would ... be relieved of the unconscious idea (the memory of a psychical trauma, *often* belonging to the remote past), *either* by the physician under hypnosis *or* by her suddenly describing the event in a state of agitation and to the accompaniment of a lively emotion. (p. 231. My emphasis)

Why does Breuer confine emotional expression to the effects of what seem to be Frau Cäcilie's spontaneous utterance and not include it as part of an active treatment? Was the physician's contribution simply one of removing the pathogenic idea under hypnosis?

As with Emmy von N., there were clearly different components to Frau Cäcilie's treatment. How did they evolve? Despite Swales's (usual) assiduous search, the record is silent. The one very important clue he does provide supports my thesis: Freud wrote to Minna Bernays in July of 1889 advising her to read Edward Bellamy's (1880/1969) novel *Dr. Heidenhoff's Process* if she wished to understand his treatment of Frau Cäcilie. The fictional doctor Heidenhoff invented a technique, which he called "thought extirpation," for wiping out troublesome memories. It involved passing a nonconvulsive electric current through the patient's head while the patient concentrated on the reminiscence. Because Heidenhoff recommended it for any kind of troublesome memory, not just for traumatic ones, and because neither narration nor emotional expression was required, Freud was alluding to no cathartic method. What Heidenhoff's process most resembles, indeed surprisingly so, as we will now see, is a variant of the method of suggestion apparently pioneered by Delboeuf and Janet. The difference is that Bellamy's character did it electrically, and Delboeuf and Janet did it hypnotically. Frau Cäcilie's treatment does not therefore conflict with my argument that Freud's therapy before 1892 or 1893 was based on direct hypnotic suggestion.

Freud and Janet's and Delboeuf's Methods of Therapy

When Freud summarized his treatment of Emmy von N. he brought out its three components very clearly:

As is *the usual practice* in hypnotic psychotherapy, I fought against the patient's pathological ideas by means of assurances and prohibitions, and by putting forward opposing ideas of every sort. *But I did not content myself with this*. I investigated the genesis of the individual symptoms so as to be able to combat the premises on which the pathological ideas were erected. In the course of such analysis it habitually happened that the patient gave verbal utterance with the most violent agitation to matters whose accompanying affect had hitherto only found outlet as a motor expression of emotion. I cannot say how much of the therapeutic success each time was due to my suggesting the symptom away *in statu nascendi* and how much to my resolving the affect.   (Breuer and Freud 1895, p. 101. Emphasis altered)

Freud's contrasting the second component in which he investigated the genesis of the symptom with the usual practice of direct suggestion tells us, I believe, that the hypnotic attack on the pathogenic memory was a new therapeutic tactic.

Where did the new technique come from? It was not part of Breuer's or Bernheim's repertoire. However, only a few months before Emmy von N.'s treatment began, both Delboeuf and Janet had used almost exactly the same method, which they described in almost the same words as Freud, to treat recurrent hallucinations similar to those exhibited by Emmy von N. Freud almost certainly knew of Delboeuf's use of the method, and probably knew of Janet's, before he applied it himself.

Delboeuf's Therapy

Early in 1888 Delboeuf visited Bernheim's clinic at Nancy. His long, four-part account of the visit was liberally illustrated with summary case descriptions and contained a comprehensive discussion of the theoretical differences between the Nancy and Salpêtrière schools (Delboeuf 1888–1889, parts 1–4). In the third installment of the paper Delboeuf described a case of his own in which the treatment clearly went far beyond the simple, direct suggestions and reassurances used by Bernheim:

Here is a poor mother. Her room was next to that of her son who was sick and dying. One day, about six in the morning, as she sleeps, she thinks she hears this cry: Mama! Half awake, she thinks she has been dreaming and falls asleep again. A half-hour later, she enters, as was her practice, the room of her son and finds him stretched out on the ground, dead and covered with the blood that had come out of his mouth. At the sight, her reason flees, she is assailed by remorse, and from that day, a cry resounds incessantly in her ears: Mama! This cry, she ends by producing it herself, both at home, in the presence of her family and in the presence of strangers, on the street, on the train, at every instant the bloody image of her son presents itself in front of her, and the cry: Mama! bursts from her breast.   (Delboeuf 1888–1889, part 3, pp. 8–9; cf. Delboeuf 1889, pp. 51–52)

The patient was brought to Delboeuf because her own doctor had not been able to hypnotize her:

She is put to sleep under his eyes after a few minutes. At my voice *the vision pales, effaces itself, disappears*. I dare defy her to see it. I go as far as making a dramatic description of the scene.

It is all over, no more bloody phantom arising unexpectedly, no more cry: the patient can smile.   (pp. 51–52. My emphasis)

An hour later she accidentally saw a dying dog and relapsed. A few more sessions of treatment spread over several weeks brought about a permanent cure.

Later in the same paper Delboeuf referred to the case in the context of the variability in susceptibility of patients to hypnotic suggestion. After proposing that susceptibility fluctuated throughout the day, and that the art of the hypnotist consisted in bringing about the moment of maximum susceptibility and prolonging it, Delboeuf added:

My observations lead me even further. They tend to make me believe that many nervous states or mental illnesses have as their origin a natural suggestion which acted as this special moment. Let us recall the case of the mother whose lamentable story I recounted above. Consequently one can understand how the hypnotist assists the cure. *He puts the subject back into the state in which his trouble manifested itself and combats with the spoken word the same trouble, but in a state of rebirth.* [Il remet le sujet dans l'état où le mal s'est manifeste et combat par la parole le même mal, mais renaissant.]   (Delboeuf 1888–1889, part 3, p. 28; cf. Delboeuf 1889, p. 71. My emphasis)

By suggesting the vision would pale and disappear, and by defying the patient to see it, Delboeuf was combating the premise on which the pathological fixed idea was erected; by returning the subject to the earlier state he was "suggesting the symptom away *in statu nascendi.*"

Janet's Therapy

Janet's patient Marie suffered from recurrent hysterical crises with deliria, hallucinations, and violent bodily contortions beginning two days after the onset of her menstrual periods. Concurrently with the attack, menstruation was suppressed. In the intervals between attacks, she had limited and variable contractures and anesthesias together with total blindness of the left eye. She sometimes experienced minor hallucinatory terror attacks, independent of the other two groups of symptoms. After seven months of unsuccessful conventional treatment Janet hypnotized her and asked her about her first menstruation. She recalled it to have been an entirely unexpected event when she was thirteen. Reacting with shame, she had tried to stop the menstrual flow by immersing herself in cold water. Menstruation ceased, but she then had a severe attack of shivering followed by several days of delirium. Menstruation did not recur until five years later. When it did, the symptoms present on her admission to hospital came with it. Janet decided to modify the memory of the immersion:

I tried to take away from the somnambulistic consciousness this fixed and absurd idea that menstruation had been arrested by a cold bath. I was unable to do this at the first attempt; the fixed idea persisted and the menstrual period which commenced two days later was almost the same as the preceding ones. But, with more time at my disposal, I tried once more: I was able to efface the idea only by *a singular means*. It was necessary to bring her back by suggestion to the age of thirteen years, to put her back *into the initial conditions* of the delirium, and then to convince her that her period had lasted three days and had not been interrupted by any unfortunate accident. Now, when this was done, the succeeding period arrived on the due date and lasted for three days, without bringing with it any pain, any convulsion nor any delirium.   (P. Janet 1889, pp. 438–439. My emphasis)

Janet treated two other groups of symptoms similarly. The minor hallucinatory attacks of terror were repetitions of feelings experienced when she had seen an old woman fall down some stairs and kill herself. After bringing Marie back

to the moment of the accident, I was able, not without difficulty, *to change the mental image*, to show her that the old woman had only stumbled and had not killed herself, and efface the terrifying idea: the attacks of terror did not recur.   (1889, p. 439)

Then he established that the left-sided facial anesthesia and left eye blindness appeared at the age of six years, after Marie was forced to sleep with another child who had impetigo on the whole of the left side of her face. Janet attempted a similar cure. Under hypnosis

I put her back with the child of whom she had had such horror, I make her believe the child is very nice and does not have impetigo, she is half convinced. After two repetitions of the scene, I get the best of it and she caresses the imaginary child without fear. The sensitivity of the left side reappears without difficulty and, when I wake her, Marie sees clearly with the left eye.   (1889, p. 440)

All three groups of symptoms were removed by modifying or effacing the mental images associated with their onset. Like Delboeuf, Janet returned the subject to the moment of maximum susceptibility, there combating the symptom as it was reborn.

Because Janet's treatment of L., or Lucie, was proposed by Ellenberger as the first instance of a cathartic cure (Ellenberger 1970, p. 413, n. 84), we might note how it differs from Marie's. Lucie's case is described in *L'Automatisme Psychologique* (P. Janet 1889), but Janet had reported it previously (P. Janet 1886, 1887, 1888). Clearly, it does not qualify for the distinction Ellenberger gives it. Lucie's hallucinatory terrors were traced to a sudden fright at the age of nine years; the symptoms reappeared with the emergence of a second personality, Adrienne, that had begun to form at the time. Janet described the treatment only briefly because it was to have been reported fully in another paper by himself and Powilewicz in *Revue Scientifique*

(P. Janet 1886). However, from my own search of the literature, as well as that of van der Hart and Braun (1986), it seems that Janet did not publish any more details.

What Janet did was to command the secondary personality not to have hallucinatory attacks. Lucie, the primary personality, was thereupon freed of the symptom. This treatment was clearly ordinary direct suggestion, as F. W. H. Myers' (1886–1887, p. 245) contemporaneous comment confirms. Although the explanation of the symptom is similar to that advanced by Breuer, the method of treatment has nothing in common with his or with what Janet did with Marie. F. W. H. Myers (pp. 240–241) saw clearly how it hinged on a direct suggestion to the secondary consciousness, as did William James (1890a,b, pp. 386–387) a little later. The only feature resembling Breuer's cathartic method is Janet's use of hypnosis to locate the memory of the original event.

Dating the Treatments

Direct hypnotic suggestion was Freud's usual practice and his attack on Emmy von N.'s pathogenic memories was novel. Delboeuf and Janet had also used the new therapy. Can the three uses be dated?

Freud and Emmy von N.   Freud gave May 1, 1889, as the date on which he began Emmy von N.'s treatment (Breuer and Freud 1895, p. 77) and, although the editors of the *Standard Edition* (vol. 2, pp. 307–309) suggested it began a year earlier and the problem of the chronology had to remain an open one, Andersson's investigations leave no doubt that Freud's dating is correct (Andersson 1962, p. 74, n. 1). The memoirs of Emmy von N.'s daughter confirm that treatment began in the spring of 1889 (Andersson 1979). Other unpublished documents collected by Andersson are, he tells me, consistent with that dating.

Delboeuf's Paper and Book   The date printed on the first part of Delboeuf's article in the volume of *Revue de Belgique* in which it appeared is November 15, 1888. The succeeding parts are dated December 15, 1888, January 15, 1889, and March 15, 1889. The four parts, virtually unchanged, were published almost immediately as a book (Delboeuf 1889). The book must have been in circulation by at least May of 1889, because it was listed as awaiting review in *Revue Philosophique* for June of that year (27: 651). Thus the crucial third part of Delboeuf's paper appeared well before Freud began treating Emmy von N., and the book itself appeared at about the time the treatment actually started. Delboeuf's description could well have been one of the influences leading Freud to the particular technique he used with Emmy von N.

In this connection it is worth noting that, although Delboeuf's general remarks on variations in susceptibility and the role of the hypnotist occupy less than 1 page of over 100 pages of text, they were regarded by G. C. Robertson, then editor of *Mind*, as sufficiently novel to single them out for special mention in his July 1889 review of Delboeuf's book (*Mind* 14: 470–471). One may assume other readers would have placed the same importance on them.

Janet's Thesis   The description of Marie's treatment first appeared in Janet's thesis, which, as the preface indicates, was completed by December 1888 and defended on June 21, 1889 (Ellenberger 1970, p. 339). Professor Henri Faure, Director of the Laboratoire de Psychologie Pathologique de la Sorbonne, tells me that Alcan's publication of the thesis as *L'Automatisme Psychologique* took place between Janet's completing it and April or early May 1889. On publication, twelve copies would have gone immediately to members of the jury, some would have been retained by Janet, and the rest would have been kept by the publisher. Of these, 100 would have been later deposited for distribution to university libraries and the remainder would have gone on sale immediately after the defense. Thus it is possible that printed copies of the thesis were in circulation even before the defense. Further, news of Janet's work was widespread before the defense. In England, for example, Myers knew of Janet's thesis before April 1889, since in a discussion of the then recent work on consciousness, memory, and alterations of personality he remarked that "Prof. Janet, of Havre, has a considerable book in preparation" (F. W. H. Myers 1889–1890, p. 63). Freud could have known of Janet's treatment of Marie before he began treating Emmy von N.

Origins   Two possibilities about the origins of the new treatment may be discounted because they are so unlikely. First, the method was developed by some unknown therapist and adopted almost simultaneously by Delboeuf, Janet, and Freud without any of them acknowledging the fact. Second, each arrived at the method independently. I think the evidence shows the more probable explanation to be that Freud adopted it after learning of its use by either Delboeuf or Janet. The dates leave us in no doubt that he could have known of Delboeuf's treatment before beginning his, and it is just possible that he could have known of Janet's.

An influence of Janet on Freud may be suggested by his using both "effacing" and "wiping out" to describe the alteration produced in the pathogenic memories. On the other hand, an influence of Delboeuf may be Freud's use of the word combat (*Kampfe*) to describe the attack on the pathogenic memory, and the belief that suggestion was to be directed to the birth or rebirth of the symptom (*in statu nascendi* v. *mais renaissant*). Neither of these quite central ideas is to be found in Janet's account.

There may be another clue in a curious feature of Breuer's and Freud's acknowledgment of Delboeuf's treatment. Breuer and Freud cited Janet as having produced a cure, presumably of Marie, by a method analogous to their own; however, Delboeuf was quoted, together with Binet, as having recognized only *the possibility* of such a therapy (Breuer and Freud 1893, p. 7, n. 1). Although this correctly represents Binet's proposal, it is obviously a totally incorrect account of what Delboeuf had done. Breuer's and Freud's quotation comes from precisely that part of Delboeuf's paper containing the speculation that cures were produced by returning the patient to the earlier state of susceptibility, and actually begins with the sentence that immediately *follows* the one in which Delboeuf asked his readers to "recall the case of the mother whose lamentable story I recounted above." That is, Delboeuf mentioned a specific cure—a cure, at that, in a case identical to Freud's earliest use of the same method—in the very sentence before the quotation that Breuer and Freud used to represent him as having seen only the possibility of a therapy. Does this oversight of Delboeuf's treatment while acknowledging Janet's signify a reversal of the real source of influence on the treatment of Emmy von N.?

Incidentally, if we assume that Emmy von N.'s talking and expressing emotion did have some effect, we seem to be faced with the problem of expectations. Why did Janet and Delboeuf not make observations similar to Freud's? Emmy von N. and Anna O. resembled each other in a number of important ways: both had recurrent and terrifying hallucinations intruding from a *condition seconde*, both had the ability to recall rapidly complete and complex sets of memories, and both had facility in describing traumatic events. These similarities became apparent almost immediately and could well have created in Freud the expectation that Emmy von N.'s talking about the origins of her symptoms would result in the same kind of emotional calm for her as it had for Anna O. Were he to have transmitted such an expectation to her early in the treatment, the fact that the effects occurred earlier with her than with Anna O. (if they occurred at all) would be accounted for. Janet and Delboeuf, of course, had no such expectation and could have had no observations to make about the effect of talking.

Freud's Therapy Between 1889 and 1892

Freud did not set talking about the origins of symptoms or expressing the original emotion as the *aim* of any part of Emmy von N.'s treatment. Indeed, as K. Levin (1978, p. 85) pointed out, Freud did not even expect with her "that the mere recollection of the relevant memories would induce a spontaneous cure." At this time his "tracing of hysterical symptoms to initiating events" was simply "a device for rendering hypnotic suggestion more effective" (p. 86). As for emotion, Nichols and Zax (1977, p. 32) noted that Freud's treatment of Emmy von N. actually seemed to *discourage* affective expression, and his descriptions read as if it were an afterthought. The same seems to be true of Frau Cäcilie.

If the role given affect in psychoanalysis does not come directly from the treatments of Emmy von N. and Frau Cäcilie (or Anna O.'s talking cure), what is its source? Is it in the observations Freud made in the therapy he practiced after those patients and before 1893? This seems unlikely. Whenever Freud does refer or allude to Breuer's method during that time, it is almost always conjoined with direct suggestion and never with emotion.

In the Villaret article of 1888, Freud described Bernheim's therapy as being more effective when combined with Breuer's method "and [leading] the patient under hypnosis back to the psychical prehistory of the ailment and [compelling] him to acknowledge the psychical occasion on which the disorder in question originated" (Freud 1888a, p. 56). Neither that acknowledgment nor the other features described by Freud correspond to talking or to reacting with emotion. A notable feature of the slightly later *Die Gesundheit* chapter is that it is confined to direct hypnotic suggestion and completely lacks even a hint of any version of Breuer's method (Freud 1890/1905c). What the editor of the *Standard Edition* (vol. 1, p. 100, n. 2) describes as "a probable reference to Breuer's technique" in Freud's review of Forel's *Hypnotism* is not. In the review Freud insisted that hypnosis satisfied all the requirements of a causal treatment for those hysterical disorders that were

the direct result of a pathogenic idea or the deposit of a shattering experience. *If that idea is got rid of or that memory weakened*—which is what suggestion brings about—the disorder too is usually overcome.   (Freud 1889, p. 100. My emphasis)

This description of the attack on the pathogenic memory exactly matches what Freud had done with Emmy von N. in the same year. The allusion, if it is one at all, is to the Delboeuf-Janet-Freud extension of the suggestion method and not to a technique based on provoking emotional reactions. Similarly, the allusion to Breuer's method in Bum's *Lexicon* is only in the possibility of obtaining "the most far-reaching psychical influence over [patients] by *questioning* them under hypnosis about their symptoms and the origin of these" (Freud 1891, p. 112. My emphasis). Although Freud referred or alluded to Breuer's method in his paper on hysterical counterwill, he said nothing at all there about emotion, and the treatment was not even based on modifying or altering the patient's memories (Freud 1892–1893, pp. 117–121). He was also quite explicit that what he could say about the origins of her symptoms was based on inference rather than on direct investigation under hypnosis (pp. 121–123).

On the other hand, where he did describe how strong emotion sometimes caused hysterical symptoms to vanish, he either did not link that fact closely to Breuer's method or made no connection with it at all. Thus, in Villaret emotion is mentioned only in passing (Freud 1888a, p. 56). In the *Die Gesundheit* chapter on "Psychical (or mental) treatment," which was probably written *after* the first seven-week phase of Emmy von N.'s treatment was concluded, Freud made much of the general effects of emotions on normal bodily states and their curative role in illnesses generally, but nowhere did he even hint at the possibility of emotional discharge as the basis for treating functional disorders such as hysteria (Freud 1890/1905c; cf. editor's introduction, *Standard Edition*, vol. 1, pp. 63–64).

During 1890–1891 Freud recommended using hypnosis as follows:

In a number of cases—namely where the symptoms are of purely psychical origin—hypnosis fulfils *all* the demands that can be made of a causal treatment, and in that case questioning and calming the patient in deep hypnosis is as a rule accompanied by the most brilliant success. (Freud 1891, p. 113. My emphasis)

As far as I can determine, this reference to calming is the only one he makes to emotion in his therapy prior to 1892.

It is clear therefore that until the spring of 1889 the only therapy Freud used was Bernheim's method of direct hypnotic suggestion. By that time he had had eighteen months' experience with it. If patients then came to him whose central symptoms and susceptibility to hypnosis were identical to those of a patient (or patients) recently described in the literature, what would have been more natural than for him to adopt the extension of the hypnotic suggestion method reported as successful with them? If he used Breuer's method before then it could have been only to investigate the *mechanism* of symptom formation and not as a therapy.

My dating is consistent with Freud's own. It was "during the early nineties" that he "confirmed Breuer's results in a considerable number of patients" (Freud 1924c, p. 194). For some time after 1889 his use of Breuer's method seems to have been limited to locating the memory of the traumatic event as a preliminary to modifying it by direct suggestion. Although this did focus on the role of the memory, nothing in what Freud wrote between then and 1891 expressed the view that hysterical patients had anything at all to remove or work off. Until he had adopted that view, it would have been impossible for him to have practiced a therapy based on the discharge of emotion.

Hypnotic Recall and the Pressure Method

By the end of 1892 Freud began to give up using hypnosis for locating symptom-producing memories and to modify them by suggestion. These steps toward developing new methods for investigating and treating hysteria are important because they formed the basis for an entirely new kind of theory of neuroses, one that did not draw on French concepts of psychopathology.

The chronology of Freud's abandoning direct suggestion under hypnosis is reasonably certain, but his reasons for giving it up are less certain. I begin with his references to his and his patients' dissatisfaction with the unreality created by hypnotic suggestions.

As early as 1891 Freud complained that

with hypnotic treatment both physician and patient grow tired far sooner, as a result of the contrast between the deliberately rosy colouring of the suggestions and the cheerless truth. (Freud 1891, p. 113)

Some time later, probably in the first half of 1893, he expanded on this sentiment. Commenting on some advice of Charcot's regarding the use of suggestion, Freud declared that Charcot's reservations about hypnotic therapy revealed

one of the greatest inconveniences with which the practical use of suggestion in the waking state and under light hypnosis has to reckon. In the long run neither the doctor nor the patient can tolerate the contradiction between the decided denial of the ailment in the suggestion and the necessary recognition of it outside the suggestion. (Freud 1892–1894, pp. 141–142, note to Charcot's p. 286)

It seems to me that this passage expresses more than dissatisfaction with the mere practical limitations of hypnotic suggestion. I believe it indicates the desirability of developing a treatment that could be used in the waking state.

Whether so or not, the immediate reason for Freud giving up hypnosis was the quite mundane one of encountering patients who could not be hypnotized. When he found such a patient he stopped the standard induction

and only asked for "concentration"; and I ordered the patient to lie down and deliberately shut his eyes as a means of achieving this "concentration." (Breuer and Freud 1895, p. 109)

Concentration produced, he believed, the deepest hypnosis of which the patient was capable. But was it deep enough?

Freud was at this time still so wedded to the belief that access to the memories of the *condition seconde* could be obtained only through hypnosis, he wondered if "I might be depriving myself of a precondition without which the cathartic method seemed unusable" (Breuer and Freud 1895, p. 109). Faced with this seemingly insoluble problem, he recalled Bernheim's demonstration of the relative nature of the subject's amnesia for the events of the hypnotic state and deduced a new technical procedure from it.

Like the older magnetists, who already knew that in the waking state subjects could be made to recall what had happened when they had been magnetized, Bernheim insisted his waking-state subjects could remember the events of the hypnotic trance (Ellenberger 1970, pp. 113–114). Bernheim placed his hand on his subjects' foreheads and, while exerting light pressure with it, urged them to recall what had happened while they had been hypnotized. The memories were eventually retrieved. Freud might have remembered Bernheim's actual demonstration, which may well have taken place during his 1889 visit to Nancy, but Binet's 1892 republication of it seems to me to be a more probable source.

Bernheim described a patient who had been given the posthypnotic suggestion that she would be unable to see him:

It was useless to tell her that I was there and that I was talking to her. She was convinced that they were simply making fun at her expense. I gazed at her obstinately and said: "You see me well enough, but you act as if you did not see me. You are a humbug, you are playing a part!" She did not stir and continued to talk to other people. I added, with a confident manner: "However, I know all about it. You can not deceive me! It is only two years since you had a child and you made away with it! Is that true? I have been told so." She did not move, her face remained peaceful ... I roughly raised her dress and skirt. Although naturally very modest, she allowed this without a blush. I pinched the calf of her leg and her thigh. She made absolutely no sign whatever.   (Bernheim 1888–1889, cf. Binet 1892/1896, pp. 307–308)

Bernheim induced hypnosis again and suggested that on awakening she would be able to see him. In the conversation that followed, she maintained she had not seen him. After challenging her denials, Bernheim went on:

"You remember everything that happened while I was not here—all that I said and did to you" ... I insisted; speaking seriously and looking her in the face I laid stress on every word: "It is true I was not there, but you remember just the same." I put my hand on her forehead and declared: "You remember everything, absolutely everything. There speak out! What did I say to you?" After a moment's concentrated thought she blushed and said. "Oh no, it is not possible you were not there. I must have dreamed it." "Very well; what did I say to you in this dream?" She was ashamed and did not want to say. I insisted. At last she said, "You said that I had had a child." "And what did I do to you?" "You pricked me with a pin." "And then?" After a few minutes she said: "Oh no, I would not have allowed you to do it; it is a dream." "What did you dream?" "That you exposed me."   (pp. 307–308)

The subject's inability to remember could be overcome by combining verbal insistence with physical pressure.

Elisabeth von R., whose treatment began "in the autumn of 1892," seems to have been the first patient with whom Freud used his new technique (Breuer and Freud 1895, pp. 110, n. 1, 135, 145). As Breuer had done with Anna O., Freud formed the opinion that her illness was due to some secret she deliberately concealed from him (pp. 138–139). He thought hypnosis would be necessary only to aid her recall at select points in her narrative. But, when it was called for, Freud found she could not be hypnotized. It was then that he seems to have recalled Bernheim's demonstration:

In this extremity the idea occurred to me of resorting to the device of applying pressure to the head.... I carried this out by instructing the patient to report to me faithfully whatever appeared before her inner eye or passed through her memory at the moment of pressure. She remained silent for a long time and then, on my insistence, admitted that she had thought of an evening... (p. 145)

The memory recovered was of an event linked by similar content to the memory Freud eventually held responsible for the symptoms. His repeated use of pressure recovered other seemingly relevant memories.

Hypnotically produced extensions of consciousness were therefore not preconditions for recovering traumatic memories. Nor was it the case that all memories could be retrieved. Freud noted several instances in which patients failed to recall therapeutically significant material, even when hypnotized quite profoundly (Breuer and Freud 1895, pp. 284–285). Furthermore, as early as Emmy von N.'s treatment, he found hypnosis was unable to assist in the recovery of temporarily forgotten and more or less trivial information (pp. 97–98). Hypnosis was no more omniscient than it was necessary.

A therapy based on a *condition seconde* rested partly on the assumption that the secondary consciousness could be fully studied only under hypnosis. Once Freud ceased to believe that hypnosis of any kind, even concentration, was required for recovering memories, he could move to a normal or waking-state treatment method. Despite the new modes of thought these observations presage, he was slow to abandon recall under hypnosis altogether. Elisabeth von R. was treated without hypnosis toward the end of 1892, as were Lucy R. at the end of that year and Katharina in August 1893 (Masson 1985, Letter of Aug. 20, 1893; Swales 1988), but the method was not given up completely until between January and March 1895. Concentration was still in use in the former month (Masson 1985, Draft H of Jan. 24, 1895) and was replaced with the waking-state pressure method only at the time the psychotherapy chapter for *Studies on Hysteria* was completed in the March (Letters of March 8 and 13, 1895; Breuer and Freud 1895, pp. 267–272).

Symptom Formation in the Waking State

Freud was not much quicker to move to a waking-state conceptualization of symptom formation than he had been to give up hypnosis-based therapy. For consistency with his therapy he had to abandon the idea that the innate tendency to form a *condition seconde* was the *sine qua non* for producing symptoms.

Freud considered two other mechanisms before arriving at repression, the one he finally settled on. Both were all but abandoned immediately. Because each was firmly based on a secondary consciousness, they illustrate the difficulties Freud had in making the theoretical move toward congruence. They were different in that the one called counterwill had no connection with emotion, whereas the other, associative inaccessibility, brought affect into Freud's theory for the first time through its interaction with the *condition seconde*.

Counterwill

By counterwill Freud referred to the temporary domination of the *opposite of* an intention or act of will the subject was trying to carry out. Thus a mother who intended to breastfeed her infant child had

a poor flow of milk, pains were brought on when the baby was put to the breast, the mother lost appetite and showed an alarming unwillingness to take nourishment, her nights were agitated and sleepless. (Freud 1892–1893, p. 118)

He hypothesized that the idea of every intention was accompanied by the idea of the intention not succeeding. Sometimes, as in the mother's case, the counterintention overwhelmed the primary intent. What Freud called counterwill was a collection of these "distressing antithetic ideas."

How Freud came upon this seemingly *ad hoc* concept of counterwill is a mystery. L. B. Ritvo (1972, pp. 249–254) pointed to Darwin's *The Expression of the Emotions in Man and Animals* as a possible source. Darwin (1872, chapter 2) explained what seemed to be the otherwise purposeless signs of affection in animals (e.g., the body crouch, lowered ears, and tail wagging of the dog, or the upright stance, erect tail, and arched back of the cat) as being movements and postures that were the antithesis of their aggressive, attacking behaviors. Heredity had linked purposeful signs of hostility with their purposeless opposites.

When introducing the concept of counterwill Freud did not acknowledge Darwin's principle of *antithesis*. It is of some interest, though, that when he did use another of Darwin's principles, that of the *overflow of excitation*, to explain some of Emmy von N.'s symptoms, he incorrectly cited Darwin as using it to explain tail-wagging. For

Darwin, tail-wagging was not overflow but antithesis. And, in the very next paragraph, Freud went on to say that some of Emmy von N.'s other symptoms were due to counterwill (Breuer and Freud 1895, pp. 91–92).

Counterintentions were stored at an unconscious level. They enjoyed

an unsuspected existence in a sort of shadow kingdom, till they emerge like bad spirits and take control of the body, which is as a rule under the orders of the predominant ego-consciousness. (Freud 1892–1893, p. 127)

Ordinarily the counterwill was suppressed and inhibited by normal consciousness. Each intention and counterintention had its separate physiological substrate in the nervous system. Under conditions of exhaustion, such as occurred in nursing, there could be a relatively greater exhaustion of

those elements of the nervous system which form the material foundation of the ideas associated with the primary consciousness; the ideas that are excluded from that chain of associations ... of the normal ego—the inhibited and suppressed ideas, are *not* exhausted, and they consequently predominate at the moment of disposition to hysteria.   (p. 126)

Once the substrate of the intention became relatively weak, the counterintention necessarily predominated. However, if there was present a

tendency to a *dissociation of consciousness* ... the distressing antithetic idea, which seems to be inhibited, is removed from association with the intention and continues to exist as a disconnected idea ... [which] can put itself into effect [realize itself] by innervation of the body just as easily as does a volitional idea under normal circumstances.   (p. 122)

Counterwill therefore required the same *sine qua non* as hypnoid hysteria.

Associative Inaccessibility

By *associative inaccessibility* Freud meant the way in which some of the ideas involved in the production of hysterical symptoms became inaccessible to normal consciousness. The concept resulted from his exploiting Janet's proposal that the details of hysterical symptoms were determined by the idea of the organ or its function. Freud's immediate use of Janet's concept was to solve a theoretical problem that had dogged him for years—the means by which hysterical and organic symptoms could be differentiated from one another—and we must begin with it.

Janet and Associative Inaccessibility   When Freud reported to the College of Professors in the Faculty of Medicine of the University of Vienna on his 1885–1886 visits to Paris and Berlin, he said his discussions and correspondence with Charcot

led to my preparing a paper which is to appear in the *Archive de Neurologie* and is entitled "Vergleichung der hysterischen mit der organischen Symptomatologie."   (Freud 1886a, p. 12)

As became clear later, however, at the time he wrote his report the paper did not exist.

Over the next two years Freud's letters to Fliess contain what seem to be references to his working on the paper, and in May 1888, two years after the report, the title Freud gave Fliess of the first draft implied he was making a rather more restricted comparison of hysterical and organic *paralyses* (Masson 1985, Letters of Dec. 28, 1887, Feb. 4, 1888, May 28, 1888, and Aug. 29, 1888). Later, in September of that year, in the preface to his translation of Bernheim's *Suggestion*, he publicly fore-shadowed that the paper was shortly to appear (Freud 1888c, p. 80). It did not. What Freud did publish in 1888 was an entry on hysteria for Villaret's *Handwörterbuch* in which he *described* the main symptoms of hysteria and only *partially compared* them with their organic counterparts. Five years later, when the paper proper did appear, it was confined to the paralyses and made only one point in addition to those made in Villaret: the lesion in hysteria was of the idea of the organ, and the intensity of the emotion accompanying it contributed to maintaining its isolation (Freud 1893b, pp. 169–172).

Freud's entry in the *Handwörterbuch* began with the assertion that

hysteria is based wholly and entirely on physiological modifications of the nervous system and its essence should be expressed in a formula which took account of the conditions of excitability in the different parts of the nervous system. (Freud 1888a, p. 41)

There being no such physiopathological formula,

we must be content ... to define the neurosis in a purely nosographical fashion by the totality of symptoms occurring in it. (p. 41)

After this apology Freud discussed convulsive attacks, hysterogenic zones, distur-bances of sensibility, disturbances of sensory activity, paralyses, and contractures. Except for the hysterogenic zones, he made some kind of comparison with the equivalent organic disorders. For convulsions and sensory disturbances the compari-sons were minimal, implicit even, but those for paralyses, contractures, and distur-bances of sensibility were quite explicit as well as detailed.

Charcot had pointed out that at least some of the individual symptoms of hysteria could be characterized negatively as, for example, in his discussion of Porcz____ (Charcot 1887/1889, pp. 265–273). Freud took this view farther by formulating slightly broader rules, although they were still negative:

Hysterical paralyses take no account of the anatomical structure of the nervous system which, as is well known, shows itself most unambiguously in the distribution of organic paralyses. (Freud 1888a, p. 46)

Thus, hysterical paralyses were almost always accompanied by anesthesia, and none resembled the peripheral facial, radial, and serratus paralyses in affecting groups of muscles or muscle and skin determined by common innervation. They were also different from the cortical paralyses, the only type with which they could otherwise be compared. In hysterical hemiplegia, for example, the arm and leg on one side were affected but not the facial muscles. Again, instead of a paralysis extending to a whole limb, only part of it might be affected, for example, the hand or shoulder. Furthermore, if the leg were paralyzed it was dragged along like a lifeless appendage rather than moved in a circular wheeling motion from the hip. Contractures were similarly "not explicable by the stimulation of particular nerve trunks" (p. 47).

When discussing hysterical symptoms more generally, Freud took his negative rule a little further:

they do not in any way present a copy of the anatomical conditions of the nervous system. It may be said that hysteria is as ignorant of the science of the structure of the nervous system as we ourselves before we have learnt it.   (pp. 48–49)

Expressed in almost the same words in the *Preface* to his translation of Bernheim's *Suggestion* (Freud 1888c, p. 80), this characterization of hysteria-as-ignorance marked the limit of his 1888 comparison.

The most noticeable feature of Freud's 1893 paper is that the first three of its four sections were probably completed within two years of his return from Paris. The central conclusion of those three sections had already been drawn in Charcot's own *Lectures*, and Freud himself had set them out (more systematically than Charcot, it is true) in the 1888 Villaret entry. Janet's thesis and Freud's elaboration of it are all that distinguish the long-delayed paper from the Villaret entry (cf. Freud 1893a; Charcot 1887/1889, lecture 21; Freud 1892–1894, p. 140, note to p. 268 of Freud's translation, and pp. 141–142, note to p. 368 of Freud's translation; editorial note, *Standard Edition*, vol. 1, pp. 158–159).

In the paper Freud argued that hysterical paralyses belonged to the group of cerebral paralyses rather than to the peripherospinal, even though they were much more precisely limited (e.g., to a single limb or muscle) and were more intense (e.g., complete losses of function rather than partial) than the organic cerebral forms. He then raised the problem of the nature of the lesion in hysteria. Although he accepted Charcot's characterization of it as dynamic, he rejected the possibility that it might be a transitory organic affection. Were it such, the characteristics of the two kinds of paralyses would be the same. Since they were not, an emphatic restatement of his 1888 "hysteria-as-ignorance" proposition was called for:

[T]he lesion in hysterical paralyses must be completely independent of the anatomy of the nervous system, since *in its paralyses and other manifestations hysteria behaves as though anatomy did not exist or as though it had no knowledge of it.* (Freud 1893a, p. 169)

Then, for the first time, he said that hysteria

takes the organs in the ordinary, popular sense of the names they bear: the leg is the leg as far up as its insertion into the hip, the arm is the upper limb as it is visible under the clothing. (p. 169)

Freud brought this section of the paper to a close by fully associating himself with Janet's views as they had been presented at the Salpêtrière, adding,

they are confirmed as much by hysterical paralyses as by anaesthesia and psychical symptoms. (p. 169)

As if echoing Janet's conclusion that hysterical anesthesia was a psychological malady, he began the next section of the paper by requesting the permission of his readers "to move on to psychological ground":

I follow M. Janet in saying that what is in question in hysterical paralysis, just as in anaesthesia, etc., is the everyday, popular conception of the organs and of the body in general. That conception is not founded on a deep knowledge of neuro-anatomy but on our tactile and above all our visual perceptions. (p. 170)

In the very next sentence he went on to say that if the popular concept

is what determines the characteristics of hysterical paralysis, the latter *must* naturally show itself ignorant and independent of any notion of the anatomy of the nervous system. (p. 170. My emphasis)

Freud thus explicitly explained his hysteria-as-ignorance characterization with Janet's thesis.

Freud's Use of Janet's Thesis   The major point of difference between the 1888 and 1893 works is in a new, fourth section in which Freud used Janet's thesis as the basis for a physiopathological formula to explain the isolation of the symptom. He began the 1893 paper by embracing the specificity of Janet's thesis. He then extended it with some emphasis:

[T]he paralysis of the arm consists in the fact that the conception of the arm cannot enter into association with the other ideas constituting the ego of which the subject's body forms an important part. The lesion would therefore be *the abolition of the associative accessibility of the conception of the arm.* (Freud 1893b, p. 170)

What caused the loss of accessibility? Freud called on analogies that seemed to show that people deliberately isolated those of their memories that were affectively charged. The analog could be comical, as with the man who refused to wash his hand because his king had touched it, or serious, as in the custom observed in some societies of burning the possessions of a dead chieftain along with his body. The function of the behavior was clear:

> The quota of affect which we attribute to the first association of an object has a repugnance to letting it enter into a new association with another object and consequently makes the idea of the object inaccessible to association.   (pp. 170–171)

Symptoms were "almost the identical thing":

> If the conception of the arm is involved in an association with a large quota of affect, it will be inaccessible to the free play of other associations.   (p. 171)

By using the quota of affect in this way to develop Janet's thesis into a physiopatho-logical formula, he brought affect into his explanation of symptom formation for the first time.

How could excessive affect prevent associations from forming? It had been held fairly generally in association psychology that the ease with which ideas formed and the extent to which they became conscious was proportional to the amount of accom-panying affect. What Freud did was to invoke a *subconscious* association between the memory of the event that had produced the symptom and the idea of the para-lyzed organ or lost function. The traumatic memory provided so large a quota of affect to this subconscious association that the associative affinity of the concept of the organ or function was saturated and could not form any more associations.

The lesion in hysterical paralysis was thus "the inaccessibility of the organ or function ... to the associations of the conscious ego," an inaccessibility caused by the fixation of the concept of that organ or function in its "subconscious association with the memory of the trauma" (1893b, p. 172). More generally, the lesion was of the idea of the organ, isolated from the ego by the emotional charge of the traumatic memory with which it was subconsciously associated.

Freud immediately emphasized the therapeutic aspects of this view:

> [T]he paralysed organ or the lost function is involved in a subconscious association which is provided with a large quota of affect *and it can be shown that the arm is liberated as soon as this quota is wiped out.* (1893b, p. 171. Emphasis altered)

It was in this way, again by developing Janet's thesis, that Freud first brought affect into an explanation of therapy. However, although we can see how he first used the concept, we have yet to find its source. I believe it to be the work of Hughlings Jackson, the eminent British neurologist whose papers on organic speech disorders Freud had read when preparing his own monograph on that subject (Freud 1891/1953).

Jackson, Affect, and Associative Inaccessibility   Since I set out a detailed argument about Jackson's influence on Freud in chapter 7, I confine myself here to a few of its points. Jackson argued that all actions, especially speech ejaculations and emotional reactions, resulted from the equilibrium of the nervous system being restored (Jackson 1879–1880a). Freud explicitly endorsed these ideas, and only after absorbing them did he begin to consider the possibility that the nervous system had the purpose of maintaining its quantity of excitation at a fixed level; that it achieved its aim by disposing of surplus excitation, especially increases brought about by emotion; and that symptoms were a consequence of abnormalities in the disposal of the excess. In the sketches for the *Preliminary Communication* he sent to Breuer in November 1892, Freud described the symptoms of hysteria as attempts to dispose of excess excitation. The physical were abnormal motor reactions and the mental were abnormal associations (Freud 1892, pp. 153–154). In the 1893 paper on paralyses he put these propositions more generally:

Every event is provided with a certain quota of affect of which the ego divests itself *either* by means of a motor reaction *or* by associative psychical activity. If the subject is unable or unwilling to get rid of this surplus, the memory of the impression attains the importance of a trauma.... The impossibility of elimination becomes evident when the impression remains in the subconscious.   (Freud 1893b, pp. 171–172. My emphasis)

Disposing of the affect through speech involved associations. Freud did not have this and the other concepts to which it is related before 1892. Jackson's theories therefore provided part of the basis for Freud emphasizing the real expression of emotion in the talking cure.

Jackson may have contributed more than the notions of equilibrium and discharge to Freud's concept of associative inaccessibility. He used words that strikingly foreshadowed Janet's to describe the language difficulties of aphasic patients. Thus, in speaking of the "dissassociation" of the objective "nervous arrangements" for words and actions from their subjective counterparts, he wrote:

[W]ere we *to use popular language*, and to say of a patient who "tries" to put out his tongue, and fails, or who tries to say "no" and fails that *he has lost part of his volition*, we should only mean that *he had lost ... the very objective actions [of speech] themselves*, their nervous arrangements being broken up; *he has lost a part of himself.* (Jackson 1879–1880b. My emphasis)

It does not seem to me to be unreasonable to suppose that Freud recalled these remarks when he read Janet's thesis and linked the two to form his own concept of associative inaccessibility.

The Significance of 1892   By returning to the Salpêtrière, we not only find out why Freud completed his paper when he did, but we learn why 1892 was such a turning point for his theorizing about affect. On March 11, 1892, at a regular clinical meeting there, Janet read the first of what was clearly to be a series of papers covering the major symptoms of hysteria. After dealing with hysterical anesthesia, he went on to cover hysterical amnesia on March 17 and suggestibility on April 1 (P. Janet 1892a,b,c; cf. Janet 1892d). It was in the first of these papers that he set out his thesis on the determination of hysterical anesthesias by ideas.

We have seen how Janet's thesis allowed Freud to lift what could be said about hysterical symptoms from the level of Charcot's basically descriptive and tentatively negative characterization and place it into a sophisticated theoretical framework. I believe we can reconstruct his reaction to Janet's thesis with some certainty. Within days of the public appearance of Janet's first paper, Freud suggested to Breuer they prepare their work on hysteria for publication. Then on June 28, 1892, Freud wrote to Fliess that Breuer had agreed to publish their "detailed theory of abreaction, and our other joint jokes [*Witze*] on hysteria" (Masson 1985, Letter of June 28, 1892. Translation modified, MBM). It is in this sentence that Freud uses the term "abreaction" for the first time. The next day, in a letter to Breuer, he formulated, also for the first time, the notion that the nervous system had something to dispose of. If this sequence of events is true, I believe it solves the puzzle of Freud's delay in developing a therapy based on affective discharge better than does Friedman's proposal (L. Friedman 1977, n. 2; cf. Andersson 1962, p. 90).

Freud outlined to Breuer two very slightly different explanations of how symptoms formed. In both theories, symptoms were due to sums of excitation that had been discharged along abnormal pathways. In the first version symptoms were attempts at reaction that had become hysterical because they persisted (Freud 1892, p. 148, n. 3); in the second, the one he settled on, they were attempted reactions that displaced otherwise unreleased sums of excitation (p. 148). For both versions he gave as the reason for the persistence of the reaction-displacement

the theorem which lays it down that the contents of different states of consciousness are not associated with one another.   (p. 147)

Dual consciousness and dissociation, rather than affect acting by itself, were therefore responsible for the isolation.

Here, as in the later *Preliminary Communication*, Freud's affectively based therapy remained within this dissociation framework:

It will be understood that our therapy consists in removing the results of the ideas which have not been abreacted, either by *reviving the trauma in a state of somnambulism*, and then abreacting and correcting it, or by *bringing it into normal consciousness under comparatively light hypnosis.* (1892, p. 150. My emphasis)

This genuflection toward normal waking-state processes by allowing them to occur in the hypnotic is also present in the published explanation (Breuer and Freud 1893, p. 17).

Until 1892, when Janet extended Charcot's theses on the role of ideas, Freud had had no conceptual framework from which to describe the peculiarities of hysterical symptoms, let alone explain them. Janet gave Freud exactly the positive characterization he needed. It allowed him to describe symptoms and move from description to explanation. Janet's thesis provoked him into seeking publication of the *Preliminary Communication* with Breuer and then allowed him to finish his paper. We can also surmise why Freud restricted himself to the paralyses: they were the most important of the symptoms *not* included in Janet's comprehensive discussion.[2]

It was not surprising that Freud's first explanations were couched in terms of dissociation and a secondary consciousness. In everything written between the second half of 1892 and 1894, subconsciousness was not due to the quota of affect itself but to the affectively charged event having been experienced in an elementary secondary consciousness. Freud thus indicated his continued debt to the French school of psychopathology, an indebtedness that also speaks to us from almost every other page of the sketches (Freud 1892, pp. 149–150, 153–154), from the finished *Preliminary Communication* with Breuer (Breuer and Freud 1893, pp. 11–17), and from his own public lecture on the new theory (Freud 1893a).

Dating Freud's Theoretical Shift

It took Freud about two years to move to his waking-state conceptions. In the *Preliminary Communication* of 1893 he and Breuer differentiated two groups of conditions in which hysterical symptoms were acquired. In the first, patients were not able to react to a trauma because the nature of the trauma excluded a reaction, or because circumstances precluded one, or because there was an intentional repression. In the second group, the lack of reaction was due to the presence of paralyzing affects, such as fright, or because of abnormal states, such as day-dreaming and autohypnoses. Here, the nature of the state made a reaction impossible. Both kinds of conditions could be present simultaneously. A trauma might take place during the presence of a paralyzing affect or a modified state of consciousness, and it could also produce an abnormal state that made a reaction impossible (Breuer and Freud 1893, pp. 10–11). We know that at this time Freud himself viewed hypnoid isolation as compatible with repression because he repeated the essence of these points in the lecture he delivered when the *Preliminary Communication* was published (Freud 1893a, p. 38).

Now, whether acquired by repression or in an hypnoid state, all symptoms were based on a split in consciousness:

[T]he *splitting of consciousness* which is so striking in the well-known classical cases under the form of *"double conscience"* is present to a rudimentary degree in every hysteria, and ... is *the basic phenomenon* of this neurosis. In these views we concur with Binet and the two Janets.   (Breuer and Freud 1893, p. 12. Emphasis altered, MBM)

Freud repeated this proposition in his own lecture (Freud 1893a, pp. 38–39).

Within a year of the *Preliminary Communication* he proposed the capacity for conversion as the basic predisposition to hysteria, although in a way that maintained a kind of compatibility with Breuer's view (Freud 1894, pp. 46–47, 50–51). But a year later, by the time of *Studies on Hysteria*, he denied that dissociation was fundamental and had come to view all so-called hypnoid symptoms as really caused by repression (Breuer and Freud 1895, pp. 285–286). Thus he paid off his indebtedness to Breuer and the French, and severed his conceptual ties to them.

Breuer's theoretical chapter in *Studies on Hysteria*, written two years later, shows practically no shift from this French mode of theorizing. True, Breuer did prefer to speak of a splitting of the mind rather than of consciousness (Breuer and Freud 1895, p. 225), but this distinction, or one very like it, was clear also to Binet, who nevertheless continued using words such as "split," "division," and "doubling" to describe alterations of *consciousness* (Breuer and Freud 1895, p. 225; Binet 1892/1896, pp. 90, 257–258). But Breuer's insistence that the tendency to splitting was basic to hysteria and that a rudimentary dual consciousness was present in every hysteria was unchanged (Breuer and Freud 1895, pp. 226–227).

The Scope of Freud's New Conceptualization

Freud's new theory went beyond hysteria. The older theories were so tied to concepts such as the *condition seconde* or the hypnoid state that they had little application to other neuroses. In contrast, repression and conversion could be easily generalized.

By the beginning of 1894 Freud made the first extension of his new theory. He had initially used the cathartic method simply to see how obsessional symptoms differed from the hysterical, but he found they had also been initiated by repression (Breuer and Freud 1895, p. 256). One patient provided direct evidence:

Something very disagreeable happened to me once and I tried very hard to put it away from me and not to think about it any more. I succeeded at last; but then I got this other thing, which I have not been able to get rid of since.   (Freud 1894, pp. 52–53)

And, from the less clear recollection of a patient whose attention was drawn directly to the cause of his obsession:

It can't come from that. I didn't think at all much about that. For a moment I was frightened, but I turned my mind away from it and I haven't been troubled by it since.   (p. 53)

Freud thought these "most unambiguous statements" proved the existence of defensive willing in obsessional neuroses (p. 52).[3]

It seemed to Freud that obsessional symptoms were formed when the unconscious process subsequent to the willing tore the affect from the incompatible idea and attached it to a previously innocuous idea. His analysis of one of his earliest obsessional patients provides an illustration:

A girl suffered from obsessional self-reproaches. If she read something in the papers about coiners, the thought would occur to her that she, too, had made counterfeit money; if a murder had been committed by an unknown person, she would ask herself anxiously whether it was not she who had done the deed. At the same time she was perfectly conscious of the absurdity of these obsessional reproaches.... Close questioning then revealed the source from which her sense of guilt arose. Stimulated by a chance voluptuous sensation, she had allowed herself to be led astray by a woman friend into masturbating, and had practised it for years, fully conscious of her wrong-doing and to the accompaniment of the most violent, but, as usual, ineffective self-reproaches.   (Freud 1894, p. 55)

A process, which at that time Freud called transposition or displacement, and similar to conversion, had attached the affect of self-reproach over masturbation to the idea of criminality.

At the beginning of 1894, therefore, Freud was ready to formulate his waking-state concepts, to extend his conceptualizations of symptom formation, and to lay the foundations of a unified theory of neuroses. By 1895 he had broken altogether with the traditional concepts derived from studies of hypnosis and hysteria.

Repression and Pathogenic Memories

The normal waking-state process Freud put forward as producing symptoms was *repression*. He supposed it to start with a defensive act of will by which patients attempted to forget thoughts having large quotas of affect associated with them and that were incompatible with their egos (Freud 1894, pp. 46–47). Emotion came into the process in a second way: repression had the unintended consequence of converting or channeling the affect into bodily processes, thereby producing such symptoms as paralyses, contractures, and anesthesias. At the same time the idea itself was forced into the unconscious (pp. 48–50).

The initial act of will that brought repression into operation was readily remembered:

[T]he most unambiguous statements by the patients give proof of the effort of will, the attempt at defence, upon which the theory lays emphasis.   (p. 52)

For example, Lucy R., seen at about the same time as Elisabeth von R., had said:

I wanted to drive it out of my head and not think of it again; and I believe latterly I have succeeded.   (Breuer and Freud 1895, p. 117)

Freud said his patients

had enjoyed good mental health up to the moment at which an *occurrence of incompatibility took place in their ideational life*—that is to say, until their ego was faced with an experience, an idea or a feeling which aroused such a distressing affect that the subject decided to forget about it ... patients can recollect as precisely as could be desired their efforts at defence, their intention of "pushing the thing away," of not thinking of it, of suppressing it.   (Freud 1894, p. 47)

Patients acted only to rid themselves of unwanted ideas; causing symptoms was not part of their intentions. Repressive processes therefore occurred

without consciousness. Their existence can only be presumed, but cannot be proved by any clinico-psychological analysis.   (p. 53)

Repression was thus partly inferred from the gap between the willing and the appearance of the symptom.

Freud conceived of repression as a psychological force because the pressure method had required him to insist repeatedly that his patients could retrieve memories of the causes of their symptoms:

[T]his insistence involved effort on my part and so suggested the idea that I had to overcome a resistance, the situation led me *at once* to the theory that by means of *my psychical work* I had to overcome *a psychical force* in the patients which was opposed to the pathogenic ideas becoming conscious (being remembered).   (Breuer and Freud 1895, p. 268. Emphasis altered)

These curious kinds of objectifications of subjective feelings were referred to as "logophania" by Ellenberger (1956), and although the term is not very satisfactory, I have adopted it because there seems to be no other.

Once Freud had made this logophanic transformation he said:

A new understanding seemed to open before my eyes when it occurred to me that this must no doubt be the same psychical force that had played a part in the generating of the hysterical symptom and had at that time prevented the pathogenic idea from becoming conscious. (Breuer and Freud 1895, p. 268)

Repression was therefore also partly an inference from the patient's resistance.

After observing that all the repressed ideas aroused distressing affects such as shame, self-reproaches, and feelings of being harmed, affects, in short, of a kind one would prefer not to have experienced and would rather forget:

From all this there arose, as it were automatically, the thought of *defence*. . . . The patient's ego had been approached by an idea which proved to be incompatible, which provoked on the part of the ego a repelling force of which the purpose was defence against this incompatible idea.   (p. 269)

The long time it took Freud to arrive at this conceptualization rather belies his use of "automatically."

Although forced out of consciousness, the idea had not been destroyed:

If I endeavoured to direct the patient's attention to it, I became aware, in the form of a *resistance*, of the same *force* as had shown itself in the form of a *repulsion* when the symptom was generated. . . . Thus a psychical *force*, aversion on the part of the ego, had originally driven the pathogenic idea out of association and was now opposing its return to memory.   (p. 269. Emphasis altered)

Concurrently with the increase in his use of the waking-state pressure method, Freud based more his theorizing on waking-state processes that were of a normal type. Even though conversion was as mysterious as any dissociation state concept, the defensive act of will antecedent to it was easily understood by analogy with the everyday experience of trying to forget unpleasant thoughts and feelings.

The Structure of Pathogenic Memories

In what we might call the simple view of symptom formation, each symptom was produced by a single memory. Separate acts of will were followed by discrete repressions, after which single conversions led to separate and single symptoms. Although Freud sometimes set out his expositions like this, it is clear he never held to the simple view in understanding actual patients (Freud 1893a, p. 32; 1894, pp. 49–50). Real symptom formation required repressed and nonrepressed events to interact with one another in much more complex ways, and he attempted to summarize those interactions in a causal model of the memory structure.

Breuer had observed that any one of Anna O.'s symptoms seemed to be related to whole sets of memories and that it was always the earliest in the set that seemed to be the most important. When Freud first used hypnosis to recover traumatic memories he also found that even a relatively simple symptom rarely had a single determinant. For example, when Emmy von N. was asked why she was so readily frightened, she recalled four separate sets of memories, in chronological order, containing an element of being frightened (Breuer and Freud 1895, pp. 52–55, 58–62).

Like Breuer, Freud found

the patient's communications are given in a reverse chronological order, beginning with the most recent and least important impressions and connections of thought and only at the end reaching the primary impression, which is in all probability the most important one causally.   (p. 75, n. 1)

A chronological ordering also seemed to be true of memories recovered by the pressure method. On its first use, Elisabeth von R. similarly produced a series of recollections rather than the memory of a single traumatic event (pp. 110, n. 1, 145).

In discussing this multiplicity of memories, Freud observed:

We must not expect to meet with a *single* traumatic memory and a *single* pathogenic idea as its nucleus; we must be prepared for *successions* of *partial* traumas and *concatenations* of pathogenic trains of thought.   (pp. 287–288)

To explain how the memories of these partial traumas succeeded one another and how the causal trains of thought were interconnected, he formulated one of his most important concepts, that of the pathogenic memory structure. Because the concept is essentially implicit in his work and commented on only infrequently, it requires explication.

Freud's Concept of Memory Structure

The *pathogenic memory structure* was built up around a nucleus of

memories of events or trains of thought in which the traumatic factor has culminated or the pathogenic idea had found its purest manifestation.   (Breuer and Freud 1895, p. 288)

The other memories were arranged around the nucleus in a three-dimensional way. The first dimension was chronological: memories closest to the nucleus were the earliest laid down, the later material being farthest away. A concentric stratification in terms of the degree of consciousness, or of resistance to retrieval, characterized the second dimension: memories nearest the nucleus were the most difficult to recover and recognize, those more peripherally organized were more readily recalled. The most important was the third dimension. It was an arrangement according to thought-content, the linkage made by a logical thread which reaches as far as the nucleus and tends to take an irregular and twisting path, different in every case. . . . The logical chain corresponds . . . to a ramifying system of lines and more particularly to a converging one. It contains nodal points at which two or more threads meet and thereafter proceed as one; and as a rule several threads which run independently, or which are connected at various points by side-paths, debouch into the nucleus.   (pp. 289–290)

In general, the logical chain ran from periphery to nucleus, but the actual pathway was much more complex: around the strata in terms of degree of consciousness, across them chronologically, and from surface to deeper layers and back.

Connecting Assumptions

In any given set of memories Freud found that some incidents, although not pushed out of mind, were followed by symptoms. Other incidents were repressed but did not seem to cause symptoms. Further, some symptoms seemed to manifest themselves only after a delay. Freud made three assumptions about the way in which these memories were connected to one another. First, at least one memory in a set had to have been repressed. Once repressed it served as a nucleus around which other ideas similar in content might be grouped even when they themselves had not been repressed. The second assumption was that affects from successively occurring traumas could summate, eventually becoming strong enough to be converted into a symptom. A given idea that lacked strong affect could produce a symptom because of its contribution to a pool of affect. The third was that an incubation period, of the type described by Charcot, might occur between the trauma and the symptom, even an intense trauma.

Freud's use of the first two assumptions is most clearly illustrated in his account of Lucy R. (Breuer and Freud 1895, pp. 106–124). This patient had complained of a smell of burned pudding being continuously present in her nostrils. She recovered memories of four events. The earliest was of a conversation in which she realized she was falling in love with her employer. The second occurred a little later when the employer criticized her severely for allowing a female guest to kiss the children for whom she was governess. She then felt her employer could never have loved her and she banished the memories of the earlier conversation and of her feelings of love, and the negative feelings she felt in response to his criticism. A third event almost repeated the second: her employer railed against a male guest for kissing the children. Cigar smoke had been in the air and she was troubled afterward by a persistent smell of cigar smoke; that is, a symptom had formed. The fourth and last event was one during which she received a letter that revived her thoughts of leaving her employment. The letter led to a game with the children and, in the distraction of the game, a pudding they had been cooking was burned. The presenting symptom was its odor.

The earliest event Lucy R. recalled was not repressed. Nor did it lead to a symptom. It was the second event that was repressed, and Freud thought it took the memory of the female guest with it. Together the two memories formed a nucleus to which the memory of the third scene, that of the male guest and the smell of cigar smoke, attached itself. The affect of that idea added to the pool, and the whole was converted into the mnemic symbol of a cigar smell. The memory of that scene then became unconscious even though it was not actively banished. Neither had Lucy R. tried to put the memory of the burned pudding of the fourth scene out of mind. Its disappearance, if it had disappeared at all, was due to its connection with the earliest repressed ideas. It produced the second symptom of the smell of burning because its affect also added to the pool.

Freud's assumption that symptoms might incubate is illustrated in the case of Katharina, from whom he recovered the memory of a traumatic incident that was followed three days later by prolonged vomiting (Breuer and Freud 1895, pp. 126–129). He believed the symptom resulted from a conversion of the affect of disgust that, after summing with the affects of similar previous incidents, required that time to incubate.

Together, the connecting assumptions allowed memories to be related even if they were not directly and explicitly connected to the symptom in time or in affective force or by intentional banishment. Rather than these kinds of observations being in conflict with Freud's theory, the assumptions maintained their consistency with his explanation of how repression converted affect into symptoms.

Every memory recovered could be given its place in the pathogenic structure through its direct connection to the symptom or its presumed connections to other memories, or through its connection to the pool of affect. Therefore Freud was able to argue that no memory recovered during treatment was unimportant:

It may be asserted that every single reminiscence which emerges during an analysis of this kind has significance. An intrusion of *irrelevant* mnemic images ... in fact never occurs. An exception which does not contradict this rule may be postulated for memories which, unimportant in themselves, are nevertheless indispensable as a bridge, in the sense that the association between two important memories can only be made through them.   (Breuer and Freud 1895, pp. 295–296)

Although this might have been true in the abstract, Freud's use of the connecting assumptions was to lead to dubious reconstructions of the ways in which the hysterias were supposed to develop.

Using the Structure

The relations among the nucleus, the other memories, and the symptoms defined more than an abstract organization from which only a history might be reconstructed or an intellectual understanding of the case be gained. One recollection led to another because of their causal contribution to the symptom, not just because they were related in content. Patients could be cured only by systematically working through the pathogenic structure and discharging the affect of the successive memories. Consequently, the concept of the structure and the assumptions about the connections between the memories and the symptom had the important practical use of guiding therapy.

In the case of Lucy R., for example, Freud rejected her first recollection as being the memory at the nucleus because it had not been intentionally repressed:

It all sounded highly plausible, but there was something that I missed, some adequate reason why these agitations and this conflict of affects should have led to hysteria rather than anything else. Why had not the whole thing remained on the level of normal psychical life? . . .
Now I already knew from the analysis of similar cases that before hysteria can be acquired for the first time one essential condition must be fulfilled: an idea must be *intentionally repressed from consciousness* and excluded from associative modification. . . .
I accordingly inferred . . . that among the determinants of the trauma there must have been one which she had sought intentionally to leave in obscurity and had made efforts to forget. (Breuer and Freud 1895, pp. 116–117)

From the assumption of an earlier repression and from his inferences about the content of the repressed memory, Freud made a guess about the memory, and her second recollection seemed to confirm it.

Other deficiencies could be similarly filled out. Critical examination of patients' accounts would "quite infallibly discover gaps and imperfections" such as inadequate explanations of interruptions to a train of thought or the attribution of feeble motivation to an action (Breuer and Freud 1895, p. 293). Because "the same demands for logical connection and sufficient motivation in a train of thought" (p. 293) could be made of the hysteric as of the normal, the patient was told,

You are mistaken; what you are putting forward can have nothing to do with the present subject. We must expect to come upon something else here, and this will occur to you. (p. 293)

Access to successively deeper layers of the pathogenic structure was gradually gained. Provided sufficient force was exerted, the therapist's insistence would make it possible to

penetrate by a main path straight to the nucleus of the pathogenic organization . . . now the patient helps us energetically. His resistance for the most part is broken.   (p. 295)

Despite the energetic direction Freud obviously gave to the search for the nucleus, he rejected the possibility he had influenced the content of the recollections:

we are not in a position to force anything on the patient about the things of which he is ostensibly ignorant or to influence the products of the analysis by arousing an expectation. I have never once succeeded, by foretelling something, in altering or falsifying the reproduction of memories or the connection of events. (p. 295. Emphasis removed)

Why did Freud believe that the memories recovered by the pressure method were always of events connected to the symptoms, that nothing accidental was ever brought to mind, and that it was not possible to force memories onto the patient by the method? The answers to these questions are found in other assumptions Freud made about the continuity of psychological processes and the relation between associations and symptoms.

Psychological Continuity

It seems to have been as a consequence of the pressure method that Freud came to assume mental processes were continuous. In essence, he believed that gaps in a sequence of conscious mental processes marked changes of psychological state. Gaps were simply points at which conscious processes became unconscious. The processes nevertheless remained psychological and had not become or turned into physiological processes. In other words, he rejected the equation of unconscious with physiological.

Freud did not always hold that psychological processes were continuous in this way. As Hering's lecture on memory and the famous debate between Mill and Hamilton show, the better-established tradition was that "conscious" was equivalent to "psychical," and "unconscious" to "physiological" (Hering 1870/1913, p. 10; Mill 1878, pp. 354–358). Originally Freud also adopted it. For example, at the end of the *Preface* to his translation of Bernheim, he assumed that gaps in a chain of conscious psychical processes were bridged by physical processes (Freud 1888c, pp. 84–85). But, by the time of *Studies on Hysteria*, he saw no need to continue with it, impressed as he then was by the way the lost memories retrieved by the pressure method eventually filled the gaps in the patient's account of the illness.

Freud explicitly based his assumption of the continuity of psychological processes on Jackson's version of psychophysical parallelism. Jackson argued strongly that physiological processes and their dependent psychical processes should not be confused with each other, warning especially against

the fallacy that what are physical states in lower centres fine away *into* psychical states in higher centres; that, for example, vibrations of sensory nerves *become* sensations, or that somehow or another an idea produces a movement. (J. H. Jackson 1878–1879)

Freud first used Jackson's thesis in 1891, in his *On Aphasia*, as a basis for his attack on the localizationist views of Meynert and Wernicke (Freud 1891/1953, pp. 54–56).

Although in his adaptation of Jackson's position he made the mental a *dependent* concomitant of the physical (and not just a concomitant), that change made his position somewhat stronger than Jackson's.

Freud described how he could follow a train of thought from

the conscious into the unconscious (i.e. into something that is absolutely not recognized as a memory), ... we can trace it from there for some distance through consciousness once more and ... we can see it terminate in the unconscious again, without this alteration of "psychical illumination" making any change in the train of thought itself, in its logical consistency and in the interconnection between its various parts. Once this train of thought was before me as a whole I should not be able to guess which part of it was recognized by the patient as a memory and which was not. I only, as it were, see the peaks of the train of thought dipping down into the unconscious—the reverse of what has been asserted of our normal processes. (Breuer and Freud 1895, pp. 300–301; cf. pp. 269, 293)

It was precisely the gaps in the patient's account of his or her symptoms that indicated the presence of "secret motives"; it was there that Freud looked for the connecting threads (p. 293). Toward the end of the treatment, he said later, the facts given by the patient enabled the construction of an "intelligible, consistent, and unbroken case history" (Freud 1905a, pp. 17–18).

The assumption of continuity was central. Eventually he was to say of the observations he made while filling the gaps that they became "*the determining factor of his entire theory*" (Freud 1904, p. 251. My emphasis). He held to this position until the very end:

We make our observations ... precisely with the help of the breaks in the sequence of "psychical" events: we fill in what is omitted by making plausible inferences and translating it into conscious material. In this way we construct, as it were, a sequence of conscious events complementary to the unconscious psychical processes. (Freud 1940a, p. 159)

For him, the only alternative to assuming that conscious processes were not unbroken sequences, complete in themselves, remained that of the concomitant "physical or somatic processes" being more complete than the psychological (1940a, p. 157).

Symptoms as Associations

In *Studies on Hysteria* both Breuer and Freud proposed associations between an intense affect and a simultaneously occurring pattern of muscular or sensory innervation as the most important immediate basis for the formation of symptoms. For example, Anna O.'s convergent squint formed when an intense emotional upset about her father coincided with the pattern of innervation of the extraocular muscles produced as she moved a watch closer to her eyes, thereby resulting in a real squint (Breuer and Freud 1895, pp. 39–40, p. 208). Elisabeth von R.'s leg pains resulted from the association between her erotic feelings for her brother-in-law and the real leg pains she was presumed to be experiencing simultaneously (p. 165). An association between a real olfactory sensation and a simultaneous feeling of love for her employer was said to explain the peculiarities of Lucy R.'s disturbed sense of smell (pp. 118–119). Associations might also create symbolic symptoms. For example, Cäcilie M.'s facial neuralgia was said to symbolize self-reproach because insults experienced figuratively as slaps in the face supposedly occurred at the same time as a slight toothache or facial pains (pp. 176–179). More extreme forms of symbolism were also observed. For example, Cäcilie M.'s penetrating forehead pains formed when she received a suspicious look she experienced as penetrating at the very time she was afraid (pp. 179–180).

Meynert's Physiological Associationism

There can be little doubt that it was Meynert's particular brand of physiological associationism on which Breuer and Freud drew. In 1865 Meynert published a paper that he claimed for the first time established a physiological basis for the formation of associations (Meynert 1884/1885, p. 153). According to him, an association was a linkage between the cells of the cortex in which the neural representations of the elements of the association were stored.

Meynert and his work were well known to Breuer and Freud. He was Professor of Psychiatry at the University of Vienna and author of a widely read textbook on psychiatry. It was in his laboratory that Freud worked for some years on brain anatomy. Even though Freud himself rejected a number of Meynert's anatomical and functional concepts (Freud 1891/1953, pp. 44–54), he, as well as Breuer, drew on other aspects of Meynert's work. For example, Freud fully accepted Meynert's associationism in referring to the associational pathways in the same terms (Meynert 1884/1885, p. 154). Again, when Breuer explained some symptoms as associations formed by simultaneity, he illustrated how one element of such an association recalled the other with what was obviously Meynert's example of the formation and revival of the association between the sight and sound of a lamb (although he called it a sheep) (Breuer and Freud 1895, p. 208; cf. Meynert 1884/1885, p. 154).

Induction, Cause, and Association

Breuer and Freud also accepted Meynert's view of an identity between an association, a logical relation, and a causal connection. Meynert argued:

Inferring one attribute of a phenomenon from the presentation of another attribute, constitutes an induction; it is a recognition *in the direction of causality*, for the bleating sound is taken to be the result of the presence of the lamb.   (Meynert 1884/1885, p. 154. My emphasis)

He added:

The anatomy of the cerebral structure, and the proof of the presence everywhere in the brain of an induction apparatus, render it highly probable that all perceptions received simultaneously or in continuous succession become correlated with one other. Such connections explain the relations of successively and separately received impressions to one another. Our methods of thought and of speech have designated this relation as one of causality; but this is a purely cerebral function, for there need be no bond in the outside world corresponding to these cerebral relations of causality.   (p. 177)

However:

as soon as the subjective bond of causality represents an actual union of things, the reoccurrence of external stimuli will establish a permanent association within the brain. Thus by the renewal of perception, such *associations* are turned into the elements of *inductive logical thought*.   (p. 177. My emphasis)

In Meynert's view then, an association was a logical induction from which causal relations could be inferred.

Freud implicitly equated the logical dimension of his pathogenic memory structure with a set of associations: he described the dimension as "an arrangement of memories according to *thought-content*, the linkage made by a *logical thread* that reaches as far as the nucleus" (Breuer and Freud 1895, p. 289. My emphasis). Both the arrangement of associations and the logical thread were causal connections, for it was in the nucleus that the causal "traumatic factor ... culminated or the pathogenic idea ... found its purest expression" (p. 288). Freud also used these ideas when describing chains of associations: interruptions were breaks in the thread (pp. 271–272), and ideas "closely linked in thought," that is, in content, led to the pathogenic idea, that is, the causal idea (p. 276). Only by formally identifying associations with logical relations and causal connections were these descriptions possible, and only then was Freud justified in using the connecting thread to guide therapy. Following a train of associations in this way was equivalent to unraveling a chain of causes and so revealing the internal logic of hysteria.

Determinism and Trains of Associations

Although Meynert's conception of the revival of one element of an association by another was a physiological one, past experience controlled the revival of both single associations and whole trains of thought, and completely determined which associations could be revived:

> certain obstacles which impede the excitation of cells in full repose are *very much lessened* after a single, and particularly after repeated, identical excitations of association-bundles uniting the cells of two distinct areas of the cortex; while the transmission of such stimuli to association-tracts, which have been called upon to unite other, previously established groups of associations, *becomes well nigh impossible.*   (Meynert 1884/1885, p. 155. My emphasis)

A pathway between two cortical images was provided by association tracts excited by both:

> A train of thought starts from a residual image in the cortex. All the associations connected with this image are, as it were, ready for action.   (p. 253)

The associations available were those experienced previously. When two images were present

> the associations connecting these two images are under double attraction, and will consequently be more intensely excited than any others.   (p. 253)

Common associations provided the pathways that allowed thinking to move from one image to another:

> The orderly evolution of any one thought implies a starting-point and a goal between which it runs its course. The two images are at either end of this course; and through a strict observance of this course a firm union is established between them. Just as a marksman, in spite of numberless objects around him, establishes a direct relation between his finger on the trigger and the bull's-eye which he is to hit, so a similar relation is established between the two terminal images, which controls the direction of the play of association.   (p. 253)

This bulletlike determinism meant that a train of thought could terminate only in an idea that shared experiences and pathways with the starting idea.

Freud's specific acceptance of the importance Meynert placed on common experience is evident in the 1888 article on the brain he wrote for Villaret's *Handwörterbuch* (Freud 1888d) in which, as Amacher (1965, pp. 58–59) pointed out, he also alluded to the lamb. Later, in the unpublished *Project*, written not long after *Studies on Hysteria*, Freud included the pleasurable and unpleasurable affects of earlier experiences among the factors determining noncritical, reproductive thought along with inborn pathways of transmission and facilitations due to previous common excitation (Freud 1950/1954, *Project*, part I, section 16, part III, section 1). Other than by helping the patient to overcome the resistance caused by unpleasurable affects, no action of Freud's could influence the recollective process. Once begun, recall determined its own paths.

Of course, in Freud's view the pathway between the symptom and the memory of the traumatic event was not single. Numerous pathways intersected in complex ways before coming together to join the pathogenic nucleus. Nevertheless, they were only laid down from sets of associations common to adjacent elements, and it was still only past experience that guided the present train to its end.

Freud's concept of a pathogenic memory structure and related assumptions had been arrived at before *Studies on Hysteria* was written. The concept later came to fruition as the primary method of psychoanalysis, that of free association. Although discussion of the rule takes us out of the historical period, it is appropriate to examine it here because it is based on essentially the same deterministic assumptions as the pathogenic memory structure.

The Primary Method of Psychoanalysis

The basic method by which psychological phenomena are investigated in psychoanalysis is *free association*. It is also the basis of psychoanalytic therapy. Free association consists of adjuring the patient to follow what Freud termed *the fundamental rule of psychoanalysis*: while focusing attention on the symptom, the dream, or the parapraxis (a faulty action such as a slip of the tongue) being analyzed, the patient has to suspend his or her critical attitude and report all the ideas that then come to mind. More correctly, given the meaning of the German *Einfall*,[4] the patient has to report those ideas that suddenly and involuntarily irrupt into consciousness.

Freud believed the ideas reported under the rule were no more random than those that came to mind in response to the pressure method. The various inadequacies in the patient's account so revealed were met with a demand for connection and motivation "even if [the train of thought] extends into the unconscious" (Breuer and Freud 1895, p. 293). When successfully met, the indistinct recollections became clearer, the effect of the mutilated manner in which the scenes emerged was overcome, and the elements missing from the broken connections were filled in. Similarly with the rule, despite the gaps, the confused order, and the broken causal connections, trains of complete associations could be followed to their causes. The "fundamental rule" was obviously implied in *Studies on Hysteria* and was much used before Freud gave it that name in 1912, in "The dynamics of transference" (Breuer and Freud 1895, pp. 270–272, 276, 280–281, 293–296; Freud 1912a, p. 107 and n. 2; cf. Freud 1896c, pp. 198–199; 1900, pp. 101, 523; 1901b, pp. 9, 80; 1904, pp. 251–252; 1910a, pp. 33, 35; 1916–1917, p. 287 and n. 1; 1925a, pp. 40–42).

The "fundamental rule" was largely a consequence of Freud's belief in psychic determinism. Ideas reported under it were determined or caused by the chains of ideas to which they were connected, and the chains themselves were also completely determined. Application of the rule depended on the twin notions of a train of thought being continuous and of it being guided by an unconscious idea. Freud assumed that ideas produced during free association were under the guidance of an unconscious idea connected with the one being focused on. The thesis was proposed explicitly by von Hartmann, although Freud came across it much later than when preparing *The Interpretation of Dreams*, where he first mentioned von Hartmann (Freud 1900, p. 528, n. 1 of 1914). It was also close to a concept of Meynert's.

According to Meynert, a train of thought beginning from a residual image in the cortex led inevitably to another with which it had previously been connected. Because he allowed that the connections of this initiatory image might be unconscious, in the sense of not being stimulated sufficiently to rise above the threshold for consciousness, a train of associations could occur even when all of the linkages were unconscious (Meynert 1884/1885, pp. 246–247, 252–253). Von Hartmann also had an idea evoking a train of thought, but in his case it was a motive or a special interest. Ordinarily the motive or interest was a conscious purpose but, "if one in appearance completely abandons his train of thought to accident," some other but unconscious special motive then directed "the train of thought to its particular goal" (E. von Hartmann 1882/1931, vol. 1, section B, chapter 5, pp. 283–284; cf. Freud 1900, p. 528, n. 1 of 1914). Freud put it the same way in one of his earliest implicit references to the rule, it was "demonstrably untrue" that trains of thought were purposeless; when conscious purposive ideas were abandoned, unconscious ones simply took their place (Freud 1900, pp. 526–529). The train of thought remained psychically determined.

What, then, did Freud mean by psychic determinism? Simply psychic causation. No idea became conscious unless it was logically connected with another, and ideas came or went from consciousness because of the kinds of causal links or associations they had with other ideas. These are the psychological assumptions underlying the pathogenic memory structure and the use of the pressure method. Free association stood in the same relation to psychic determinism as had the pressure method. As Brill (1938–1939) put it, free association was used "to find the origins of symptoms," a search that was "equivalent to a search for ... determinants."

Meynert's speculative physiological associationism provided Freud with the basis for treating associations as causal connections. If unconscious purposive ideas or motives set the train of associations in motion, and if only ideas already present in the mind could be incorporated into it, as von Hartmann and Meynert assumed, associations evoked by the starting idea could not but be other than causes or links in a causal chain that had to terminate with the purposeful, causal idea (E. von Hartmann 1882/1931, vol. 1, section B, chapter 5, pp. 276–277).

Freud clearly believed the pressure method, based as it was on robust deterministic assumptions, to be strong enough to resist his attempts to force memories onto his patients. However, the only mode of influence he considered, and rejected, was the same one he had previously considered and naively rejected in relation to Charcot, that of direct suggestion from therapist to patient (Breuer and Freud 1893, p. 7; 1895, p. 295).[5] Obviously he believed that in ruling out direct influence he could be sure that the memories would always be of events that had actually happened to the patient. Similarly, the fundamental rule guaranteed "to a great extent . . . that nothing will be introduced into [the structure of the neurosis] by the expectations of the analyst" (Freud 1925a, p. 41).

Reconstructing Hysteria

Freud used the assumptions underlying the pathogenic memory structure as an aid in reconstructing the way symptoms developed. Thus, with Lucy R., he not only assumed an earlier event; he guessed at its content and suggested to her she was in love with her employer before she revealed that fact. It was the discussion of those feelings that led to the recollection of unrequited love. Here he evidently guessed correctly.

In other cases the matter is not so clear. Freud supposed Katharina felt disgust before she vomited. Her rather reflective response to that suggestion is not very compelling: "Yes, I'm sure I felt disgusted, but disgusted at what?" (Breuer and Freud 1895, p. 129). Later he suggested directly what it was that had disgusted her but she replied only, "It may well be that that was what I was disgusted at and that that was what I thought" (p. 131). Despite the lack of conviction conveyed by these rejoinders, Freud made an incident in which she experienced disgust central to his reconstruction of the history of her vomiting.

In the case of Elisabeth von R. it is very evident that Freud used the assumptions to create a *plausible* account of the development of her symptoms rather than to recreate a *real* history, plausibility achieved in part by disregarding observations conflicting with the assumptions. It is also evident in that case that he preferred the plausible reconstruction to the observable or ascertainable facts. Elisabeth von R. developed severe hysterical leg pains two years after the death of her father whom she nursed for the last eighteen months of his illness (Breuer and Freud 1895, pp. 140–141). While nursing him she was persuaded to go to a party where she met a man of whom she was fond and stayed later than she had intended. Her father's condition being much worse on her return, she reproached herself for having enjoyed herself so much. This pattern of events suggested to Freud that he "could look for the causes of her first hysterical pains" in her relation with the young man and the conversion of the affect of the "erotic" ideas aroused by meeting him (p. 146). However, the pains had not commenced "at the moment of her return home," or even at about that time, and he was unable to identify "any psychical cause" for them (p. 147). Freud thereupon *assumed* a pain had been produced but that it "was certainly not perceived at the time in question or remembered afterwards" (p. 148).

In bringing the case history to a close, he summarized what was supposed to have happened as follows:

> While she was nursing her father, *as we have seen*, she for the first time developed a hysterical symptom—a pain in a particular area of her right thigh. . . . It happened at a moment when the circle of ideas embracing her duties to her sick father came into conflict with the content of the erotic desire she was feeling at the time. Under the pressure of lively self-reproaches she decided in favour of the former, and in doing so *brought about her hysterical pain.* (p. 164. My emphasis)

Freud acknowledged the conflict between his suppositional reconstruction and the patient's recollection:

> On the evidence of the analysis, I *assumed* that a first conversion took place while the patient was nursing her father. . . .
> But it appeared from the patient's account that while . . . nursing . . . and during the time that followed . . . *she had no pains whatever and no locomotor weakness. . .*
> the patient had behaved differently in reality from what she seemed to indicate in the analysis. (p. 168. Emphasis altered)

He then drew on the connecting assumptions to suppose that a second event, occurring two years later and really involving leg pains, converted the affect belonging to the first memory (p. 168). He concluded:

> Stated in terms of the conversion theory, this incontrovertible fact of the summation of traumas and of the preliminary latency of symptoms tells us that conversion can result equally from fresh affects and from recollected ones.   (pp. 173–174)[6]

Summations of traumas and the latency or incubation of symptoms are never facts, of course. They can only ever be implications from the assumptions about the ways in which symptoms, traumas, and affects might be connected. In Elisabeth von R.'s case, the "fact" of a delayed conversion of the affect of the first memory was nothing more than an implication of the way Freud's assumptions *demanded* the memories be connected. Freud's acceptance here of his reconstruction over what he was told shows a rather ominous preference for the plausible but theoretically neat over the factually uncomfortable.

Conclusions

Although Freud initially accepted splitting, hypnoid states, and secondary consciousness as fundamental to symptom formation, his observation that some symptoms could be removed in the waking state led him to the view that they could also be acquired in it. While the intermediate mechanisms of counterwill and associative inaccessibility show only too clearly the burden of the earlier heritage, he eventually overcame the inconsistency of being able to remove symptoms in a state different from that in which he previously assumed they were formed. Abnormalities in mental life resulted from the difficulty that psychological forces in the ego had in coping with the affect that accompanied an idea incompatible with it. An affectively based cathartic method was now central to his therapy, and with his new concepts he was able to suggest how symptoms other than those of hysteria were acquired.

Some of the psychological forces Freud described were familiar from everyday mental life. For example, the act with which repression began was like any other attempt to fend off an unwanted idea, and the continuous pressure confining the repressed idea to its unconscious exile was similar to other prolonged attempts to forget unpleasantly toned memories, and so on. Nothing at all resembling this view of psychological processes was to be found in the theories of his predecessors in the fields of philosophy, psychiatry, or abnormal psychology.

Freud's contention that trains of association had their own internal determinants, and could not be influenced directly, extended but did not go beyond the view of determinism he first expressed in relation to Charcot's work. Freud believed the ideas recovered by his patients were no more influenced by his expectations or suggestions than the phenomena at the Salpêtrière. Apart from helping to overcome temporary resistances, the therapist could not influence the process leading from one idea to another.

Freud insisted that nothing without significance appeared in the patient's consciousness—everything had a place in the pathogenic memory structure. Together with the three assumptions about interconnection, the structure purported to allow an accurate reconstruction of the history of the symptom. Freud's method of memory retrieval was objective and his assumptions about the structure supposedly wove each memory correctly into the tapestry of causal relations.

Although Freud thought his method of determining the causes of symptoms was as objective as any other scientific technique, his connecting assumptions meant that more or less direct tests of his causal hypotheses and explanations were not possible. Complex reconstructions are needed only if symptoms do not manifest themselves fairly soon after banishing the incompatible idea. On the simple view of symptom formation, anyone mastering the pressure technique or the method of free association could test Freud's explanations for themselves. It would then have been as reasonable for Freud to demand that his critics adopt his techniques as was for Galileo to demand his look through his telescope. Indeed, in the simple view, any such demand would have actually been more reasonable. Evaluating the causal significance of a single remembered idea did not rest on even as complex a web of theoretical presuppositions as did Galileo's use of the telescope (Lakatos 1970, p. 98).

Freud's assumptions put paid to the reasonableness of any demand that others repeat his observations. His hypotheses and explanations were soon made even more difficult to test. He allowed that the patient might even not remember the act of will. There was then nothing to which the appearance of the symptom could be related. This scope for apparently contradictory observations to be explained away and for plausible reconstructions to be preferred to fact meant that, almost from its beginning, a very heavy burden was placed on psychoanalysis in establishing the adequacy of its method and its theory.

A Note on Priority

Nearly thirty years after 1892, in *An Autobiographical Study*, Freud denied Janet any credit at all for the notion that the popular idea of the organ determined the details of hysterical symptoms affecting it:

Before leaving Paris I discussed with [Charcot] a plan for a comparative study of hysterical and organic paralyses. I wished to establish the thesis that in hysteria paralyses and anaesthesias of the various parts of the body are demarcated according to the popular idea of their limits and not according to anatomical facts.   (Freud 1925a, pp. 13–14)

No contemporaneous evidence exists of such a discussion. About six months after returning from the Salpêtrière, Freud presented a case of hysterical hemianesthesia to the Vienna Society of Medicine in which the limits and the distribution of the anesthesia could have been most usefully summarized with that concept, but he did not even hint at it (Freud 1886b).

How Freud conceptualized the paralyses at that time is revealed with special clarity in the footnote he appended to that part of his translation of *Leçons du Mardi*, in which Charcot distinguished between organic and hysterical aphasias. Charcot drew attention to the intense or absolute nature of hysterical aphasia—usually all speech was lost—and its precise delimitation or isolation—it affected spoken language only, the patient still being able to understand and use language in reading and writing (Charcot 1887, pp. 362–363). In his footnote, Freud described how Charcot had set him the task of comparing organic and hysterical paralyses, but said only that its outcome was "a further extension of the thesis laid down here by Charcot"; that is, hysterical paralyses were like the aphasias in being characterized by intensity and isolation. He made no reference at all to the "popular concept" (Freud 1892–1894, p. 140, note to p. 268 of Freud's translation). Unfortunately the footnote cannot be dated accurately, but it probably was written before June 1892 (editor's note, *Standard Edition*, vol. 1, p. 131).

The validity of Freud's 1925 claim to originality seems not to have been much discussed. Ernest Jones (1953–1957, vol. III, pp. 233–234) appears to accept it, but he clearly mixes Freud's propositions of 1888 with Janet's of 1892, and others have followed him. Thus K. Levin (1978, p. 76) discussed Freud's characterization of hysterical aphasia that appeared in another of Freud's (1888b, p. 89) contributions to Villaret in a context in which he interprets Freud's 1888 hysteria-as-ignorant thesis as if it included Janet's of 1892 on ideas. However, in the companion piece in Villaret Freud only *described* hysterical aphasia and said nothing about its relation to anatomy. Levin therefore conveys the quite incorrect impression that Freud explicitly proposed the loss of the common-sense notion of speech as the basis of hysterical aphasia.

One can make similar objection to the argument of Chertok and Saussure (1973/ 1979, pp. 76–77) that Freud had no need to acknowledge Janet at all. According to them, the essential points of Janet's 1892 concept are summed up in Freud's two 1888 propositions about hysterical disorders not copying anatomical conditions and their ignorance of the structure of the nervous system. However, neither of those propositions is as positive and specific as Janet's. And, as we have seen, even with them, Freud was unable to finish his paper.

More recently, Masson (1985, p. 22, n. 2) said Charcot marked his own copy of the journal in which Freud's paper appeared at exactly the point where Freud states the 1893 version of the hysteria-as-ignorance view. Since Masson's discussion is also in a context that represents Freud as the originator of Janet's thesis, he thereby implies Charcot's recognition of Freud's originality. Charcot's markings cannot have that significance. Charcot himself stated the ignorance view, at least in part, and Freud set it out formally in 1888. For Charcot to have recognized Freud's originality, he would have had to have marked the passages where Freud extended and transformed Janet's well-known thesis.

Notes

1. Pappenheim (1980) claimed that Emmy von N. suffered from Gilles de la Tourette syndrome, but the changes in the symptoms are not consistent with that organic condition. In any case, Pappenheim did not make a detailed enough comparison of Emmy von N.'s symptoms with their alleged organic counterparts.

2. See also the note on Freud's claim to priority on page 114.

3. Statements like these, which are among many, and which are exactly the same as those of the patients with hysterical symptoms already quoted, also show very plainly that patients consciously attempted to rid themselves of unwanted ideas. They therefore contradict the editorial note to *Studies on Hysteria*, which argues that *both* the intention and the repression were unconscious (Breuer and Freud 1895, p. 10).

4. For the considerable difficulties in translating the German *Einfall* and the expression *freier Einfall*, difficulties that are compounded by Freud sometimes using the latter as synonymous with *freie Assoziation* ("free association") and sometimes not, see the discussions by the editor of the *Standard Edition* (vol. 11, p. 29, n. 1; vol. 15, p. 47, n. 1).

5. The reports of Breuer's defense of Freud's views on the causes of hysteria in October 1895 show that Breuer also considered only direct suggestion (Sulloway 1979, appendix A).

6. Not as the *Standard Edition* has it, "fresh symptoms." Compare Freud's *Gesammelte Werke*, vol. 1, p. 242.

5 Causes and the Actual Neuroses

Why did Freud think that the symptoms of hysteria were caused by memories? For the most part, he and Breuer first implicated them because symptoms were removed by bringing the memory into normal consciousness: "Remove the cause and the effect will cease." We have also seen that as time went on the way the core memory could be placed in the pathogenic structure also became important. But a more sophisticated method of establishing and evaluating causes was required. In this chapter I show how the method that Freud developed waited on his work on neurasthenia and anxiety neurosis.

The main relevance of my evaluation of Freud's causal analysis is for his conclusion that hysteria had an exclusive sexual etiology. In neither the *Preliminary Communication* with Breuer nor in his own contemporaneous lecture on hysteria did Freud describe the repressed incompatible idea as having any particular content, let alone that it was sexual (Breuer and Freud 1893; Freud 1893a). Moreover, in the *Preliminary Communication*, the conclusions from the patients who were to be reported on in more detail in *Studies on Hysteria* were summarized without sexual factors being singled out. However, by the time the latter was written, both Breuer and Freud had come to believe that in most instances the idea was a sexual one. As Breuer put it: "The most numerous and important of the ideas that are fended off and converted have a sexual content" (Breuer and Freud 1895, p. 245; cf. Freud 1894, pp. 47, 52). Freud's investigations over the next few months convinced him that repression in obsessional neuroses was always of a sexual idea, and he was soon to extend that conviction publicly to hysteria (Freud 1895c, p. 75, 1896a,b).

Were simple observations, untrammeled by theoretical considerations or other expectations, responsible for Freud's adopting this exclusively sexual etiology? My answer is "no." For the most part it resulted from expectations generated by his false conclusion that the causes of neurasthenia and anxiety neurosis were also sexual. That is why in this chapter I concentrate on the inadequacies of Freud's methods of evaluating data about presumptive causes.

I begin by showing neurasthenia to have been the most important of the wide range of nervous diseases and disorders Freud investigated and treated at the beginning of his medical practice. It was largely through a faulty adaptation of Koch's postulates for determining whether a particular bacterium was the cause of a given disease that Freud concluded that neurasthenia, together with the entity of anxiety neurosis he detached from it, had an exclusively sexual etiology. This mistaken conclusion was well established by the time he started his extensive studies of hysteria, and from the first, he consciously attempted to establish a sexual etiology for it. When he did so, he used the same faulty principles for weighing the evidence as he had for neurasthenia and anxiety neurosis.

The Precedence of Neurasthenia

Freud himself tells us that neurasthenia and not hysteria was the most important of the wide range of nervous diseases and disorders he saw in the first years of his medical practice between 1886 and 1892 (Freud 1887, 1892–1893). We also knew that during that period he wrote to Fliess about only two cases of neuroses. One patient, a neurasthenic, was discussed in some detail but the other, a hysteric, although very important, was mentioned only in passing (Masson 1985, Letters of Nov. 24, 1887, Feb. 4, 1888, May 28, 1888, July 12, 1892; Swales 1986b). Furthermore, in the extensive discussions about neuroses that he initiated with Fliess at the end of 1892, Freud mentioned hysteria only in passing, and then in a fairly elementary way. What dominated his correspondence until the end of 1893 were neurasthenia and anxiety neurosis, what he came to call the actual neuroses.[1]

It is also clear from the correspondence that it was for neurasthenia, not hysteria, that Freud first proposed an exclusively sexual etiology. He had attempted to construct a general theory of the neuroses on a sexual basis from at least early 1894, possibly from as early as twelve to eighteen months before that. Thus, the potential causes of neurasthenia he listed at the end of 1892 were all sexual, and by February 1893 he appears to have concluded that this indeed was the case. In May he remarked that his explanation of anxiety attacks in virginal females was capable "of filling yet another gap in the sexual etiology of the neuroses," and a little later he spoke as if his sexual "etiological formula" was firmly established. Hysteria is barely mentioned in passing in the correspondence (Masson 1985, Draft A, possibly of Dec. 1892, Draft B of Feb. 8, 1893, Draft C of between Feb. and May 1893, and Letter of May 30, 1893).

Establishing Causes

Freud's conclusion that each of the actual neuroses resulted from a specific sexual practice is a statement of an invariant connection between the sexual practice as cause and the neurosis as effect. Generalizations of this kind set out either the necessary or the sufficient condition of some effect. When an effect Y is observed and a presumed cause X is also always present, then X is said to be necessary to cause Y or to be a necessary condition of Y. On the other hand, if when X is present Y also always occurs, then X is said to suffice to cause Y or to be a sufficient cause or condition of it. In other words, for a factor or set of factors to be the sufficient cause of some effect, it must be the case that when it or they occur(s) the effect always follows.

Analyzing Causes

Despite the many analyses of causality made between Aristotle's and more recent times (e.g., H. L. A. Hart and Honoré 1985), it has not proved possible to arrive at a universally valid definition of cause or to schematize *the* relation between cause and effect. Nevertheless, the view that cause and effect are easily defined and stand in rigid antithesis to one another is extremely plausible. As Engels noted in the preliminaries to his critique of Duhring's total revolution in philosophy, it is plausible because it is "the mode of thought of so-called sound commonsense." But, he went on:

[S]ound commonsense, respectable fellow that he is within the homely precincts of his own four walls, has most wonderful adventures as soon as he ventures out into the wide world of scientific research.   (Engels 1894/1947, p. 37)

In science, Engels explained, the extent to which any rigid opposition between categories of thought, such as cause and effect, can be maintained varies with the domain and object of investigation. Sooner or later, he argued, those oppositions reach a point beyond which they become one sided and limited, and have validity only in a particular case:

[B]ut when we consider the particular case in its general connection ... they merge and dissolve in the conception of universal interaction, in which causes and effects are constantly changing places, and what is now or here an effect becomes there and then a cause, and *vice versa.* (p. 38)

It is universal interaction that makes universally valid definitions impossible and, on the other hand, the relatively circumscribed domain that makes establishing the cause of disease possible.

Germ Theory, Koch's Postulates, and Causality

According to the germ theory proposed by Pasteur and Koch, diseases came about through infection by bacteria. The particular or specific organism responsible for a given disease could be identified by the three procedures enshrined in Koch's postulates. First, the suspect bacterium had to be different from any other by taking up staining material in a unique or specific way. Second, it had to be found in every instance of the given disease and not in any other. Third, inoculation of a culture from it had to produce the disease experimentally. Koch argued that only if all three conditions were satisfied could it be concluded that the bacterium was the specific cause of the disease.

When Koch's postulates are compared with the distinction between necessary and sufficient conditions, we see that the reaction to staining and the presence of the specific bacterium in every case of the disease but not in others identifies the necessary condition of that disease. Producing the disease in healthy but susceptible animals by inoculation with culture from the specific bacterium identifies the sufficient. Koch's postulates thus translate the distinction between necessary and sufficient conditions into precepts guiding research into causes.

Freud, Germ Theory, and Koch's Postulates

We know how much importance Freud put on Koch's postulates from his discussion of them in two articles he contributed to the American medical literature some twelve years before his papers on the actual neuroses (Grinstein 1971). The first, written early in 1883, evaluated some work questioning Koch's discovery of the tubercle bacillus. Freud summarized Koch's arguments as follows:

By applying a new method of coloring, he succeeded in detecting what he believes to be a new specific organism, and sought to establish its relation to tubercular disease by two important facts. First, this organism—bacillus—is nowhere found but in tubercular material, from which it is never absent; and, second, when cultivated and inoculated upon hitherto healthy animals, it causes well-characterized tubercular disease.   (Freud 1883, cited in Grinstein 1971)

The reaction to coloring (staining) distinguished among bacteria and thereby established if the one under investigation was specific to the disease. The first of the important facts described by Freud is, of course, none other than that which established the bacillus as a necessary condition: it was found only "in tubercular material." The second was the evidence for it being part of the sufficient conditions: it "cause[d]" the disease. (In the necessarily brief article Freud omitted discussing the other part, the precondition of susceptibility).

Freud's second article, written some twenty months after the first, evaluated the significance of a report that another bacterium had been found nowhere but in syphilitic tissues. The question was whether it was the cause of syphilis:

The results of further experiments on the cultivation of the new bacillus, and on infection of animals by subsequent cultures of it, and further microscopical investigation, are to be expected before the last word on the new bacillus can be said.   (Freud 1884, cited in Grinstein 1971)

Freud recognized quite clearly that the disease had to be produced by inoculation before it could be concluded that the sufficient condition or specific cause of syphilis had been established.

The causal framework Freud used to establish the causes of the actual neuroses was a revolutionary adaptation of Koch's postulates. Before this, no one had set out any kind of logical system by which the factors causing neuroses could be judged, and no one had applied principles from physical medicine to identify their specific causes. Carter (1980) was the first to show in detail that Freud derived his methods for evaluating the causes of neuroses from germ theory, although the indebtedness to Koch had been noted earlier (e.g., Macmillan 1976). Although Carter is undoubtedly correct in regarding it as a major attempt to bring some logic to the investigation of the causes of neuroses, he is wrong in thinking Freud's initial application of the precepts was to hysteria.[2]

We now consider Beard's concept of neurasthenia and his analysis of its basis and causes before examining Freud's use of Koch's postulates in his evaluation of its cause.

Beard's Neurasthenia

About fifteen years before Freud began his practice as a neurologist, the American neurologist George Miller Beard described a new clinical entity he called neurasthenia. In the absence of anemia or organic disease, neurasthenia was to be diagnosed by the following symptoms:

[G]eneral malaise, debility of all the functions, poor appetite, abiding weakness in the back and spine, fugitive neuralgic pains, hysteria, insomnia, hypochondriases, disinclination for consecutive mental labor, severe and weakening attacks of sick headache, and other analogous symptoms. (Beard 1869)

For Beard, "neurasthenia" retained its literal meaning of a weakness of the nerves.

Neither the term nor the belief that neurasthenia was a disease was original with Beard. The concept actually has a very long history in medicine (Arndt 1892b; López Piñero 1963/1983) and the word itself was in such common use in the second quarter of the nineteenth century that it is to be found in a number of medical dictionaries of that period. López Piñero (1963/1983, p. 73) cites two such entries from the 1830s, and Bunker (1944, p. 214, n. 54) has one for 1856. For a time neurasthenia was used to describe individual symptoms, but gradually it evolved into a name for a disorder or disease. The first person to so use it seems to have been Van Deusen in 1867, who also provided the first outline of a method of treatment (Van Deusen 1868–1869; cf. Bunker 1944, n. 54; Wiener 1956, n. 5).

Beard was unable to demonstrate any organic or physiological basis for the condition, although he did think there was a dephosphorizing of the nervous system, or a loss of other solid constituents, with, perhaps, slight changes in chemical structure. He was led to this essentially functional view by inference, or as he put it, it was "rendered logically probable," by Du Bois-Reymond's experimental production of analogous changes in the nervous system. He added:

We know that the intelligence of men and animals is proportioned to the quantity of the cerebral contents, that the proportions of water, of phosphorus, of fat, and of the other solid constituents of the central nervous system vary more or less with age, and with the intellectual and moral capacity, and that all forms of insanity are dependent on *some* central morbid condition. (Beard 1869)

From these "facts" it followed that any disturbance in the amount or quality of the constituents of the nervous system would create in it the morbid condition of neurasthenia.

The Causes of Neurasthenia

Beard distinguished two classes of causal factors: predisposing causes of hereditary descent and various precipitating or special exciting causes. He adduced no particular evidence for heredity and referred to familial tendencies in only a very general way. His clinical judgment provided the evidence for the precipitating or special exciting causes that included

the pressure of bereavement, business and family cares, parturition and abortion, sexual excesses, the abuse of stimulants and narcotics, and civilized starvation such as is sometimes observed even among the wealthy order of society, and sudden retirement from business. (Beard 1869)

In a somewhat obscure passage, Beard foreshadowed his later and better known thesis that the disorder had a social basis:

From statistics that I compiled and arranged a few years since, it appears that the expectation of human life or average longevity has at no time been greater than in the present century; that in no country is it so favourable as in our own, and that no class, on the whole, live longer than our leading brain workers, who are, of course, peculiarly liable to be affected with chronic neurasthenia. (op. cit.)

In short, by increasing life expectancy, improved social conditions increased the prevalence of neurasthenia.

Beard (1880, 1881) later announced significant alterations to his theory. By then the number of symptoms had grown enormously; even to list them in his table of contents took more than a page (Beard 1881). More important, he placed much greater emphasis on the overexpenditure of the vital force, or nerve force, than on changes in the nervous system, and the loss of phosphorus and other solids was barely mentioned. He assumed a hereditarily determined limit to the quantity of nerve force. The special exciting causes reduced even further an initially limited supply of nerve force already dangerously depleted by the pace of modern living. Neurasthenia was an *American* nervousness. American society was so advanced technologically and socially that the expenditure of nerve force required to adapt to it was beyond the capacity of many to restore. Any excess in life, for example, too much work, too much worry, too much alcohol, or too frequent sexual intercourse, added to the difficulties of adapting.

Treatment

Beard's treatment followed from his inferences about the causal process. The nervous system had to be supplied with tonics that would replace the lost solids or otherwise reverse the changes. The tonics included

air, sunlight, water, food, rest, diversion, muscular exercise, and the internal administration of those remedies, such as strychnine, phosphorus, arsenic, & etc., which directly affect the central nervous system.   (Beard 1869)

The application of mild electric current to the whole body, especially to the head and spine—what he called general electrization—had a special place in his treatment:

[I]t increases the appetite, promotes sleep, and develops the size and weight of the muscles—thus preparing the way for the *digestion of food*, which is itself one of the very best of tonics; for *rest*, which is really food for the nerves; for muscular exercise, which, in its turn, prepares the way for air and sunlight.
In this capacity of general electrization for marshalling to its aid other tonic influences, lies, I think, the secret of its power.   (op. cit.)

Beard believed that electrization might also "directly improve the quantity and quality of the vital force, in accordance with the theory of the correlation and conservation of forces" (op. cit.).

Beard's Assumptions

Rosenberg (1962) made explicit the three central ideas on which Beard's explanatory theory rested: the law of conservation of energy, the reflex theory of illness, and the electrical nature of the nervous impulse. Like physical energy, nervous energy (nerve force) was limited both in amount and distribution; when used in one activity, little or none was available for another. According to the reflex theory, reflex connections between different parts of the body enabled disease or malfunction originating at one bodily site to have pathological effects at another. The electrical nature of the nervous impulse provided a plausible analogy between the individual's store of nerve force and the limited capacity of a battery. The electrical analogy in turn justified the use of general electrization in treatment, because when it was allied with the law of conservation of energy, it could be supposed to restore the nerve force in much the same way that the charge of a battery could be restored.

Rosenberg may be slightly incorrect in attributing such a definite recharging notion to Beard. It is true that in the early version of Beard's and Rockwell's (1867) *The Medical Use of Electricity* and in Rockwell's edition of Beard's (1894) *Practical Treatise*, the discussion of the effects of electrization is reasonably consistent with this attribution. Nevertheless, in the last edition of Beard's and Rockwell's (1891) *On the Medical and Surgical Uses of Electricity*, also edited by Rockwell, they seem to repudiate the recharging analogy in that they question whether general electrization "has any direct influence on the quantity or quality of the nervous force" (pp. 217–225; cf. Beard and Rockwell 1867, pp. 16–17; Beard 1894, pp. 203–204).

Beard's (1884) analysis of sexual problems in *Sexual Neurasthenia* aptly illustrates the use to which he put these ideas. For him, sexual neurasthenia included sexual problems of all kinds: impotence, premature ejaculation, frigidity, uncontrolled sexual drive, and so on. He suggested that excessive expenditure of nerve force at any one of the three main centers of reflex activity—the brain, the digestive system, and the sexual system—would deplete the amount of nerve force available at the other two. Sexual neurasthenia could therefore be caused by nonsexual as well as by sexual excesses. Conversely, the general or nonsexual form could be caused by sexual excess. What symptoms were produced depended more on the reflex connections evoked than on the particular kind of excess.

Evidence for Causes

Beard's evidence that excess caused either the general or the sexual kind of neurasthenia was not very convincing. For the most part, he simply described patients in whom he believed the presumed causal factor was present. In few instances did he attempt to analyze the conditions under which the symptoms first appeared or give an account of how they developed. Nowhere did he essay a causal analysis in which the sufficient conditions were differentiated from the necessary. At the very most, Beard's evidence allowed only the conclusion that neurasthenia *might* develop in response to stresses of various kinds. And, when he claimed hereditary descent to be present, he did not go beyond enumerating other members of the family with the tendency. He was, of course, quite unable to express how strongly it was present in any particular individual.

The central mechanism proposed by Beard is also open to objection. If neurasthenia was due to loss of nerve force, what was that force? How was it produced? What was involved in its use and destruction? The later theory makes scant mention of these matters, and the earlier theory is not much more illuminating. There the functioning of the nervous system was said to depend on the quantity and quality of the chemical constituents of the brain. Although that might have been true, the theory gave no account of how the constituents were related to nerve force or how the force was used by the nervous system. Similarly, while it might have been true that the loss of constituents caused malfunction, the theory failed to say how the creation of nerve force was thereby impeded. Beard's concept of nerve force had only pseudo-physiological referents, and the mechanism he proposed was an empty one. Nothing could be said about a basis for neurasthenia in disturbed nervous system functioning.

Beard's social theorizing also rested on very few facts. No data demonstrated neurasthenia to be more prevalent in America than elsewhere; he simply asserted it to be so. He assumed the distinguishing feature of American society was its technology, and simply claimed it was twenty-five years ahead in steam power, the press, the telegraph, the sciences, and the mental activity of women (Beard 1881, p. vi). When examined, these indexes of superiority have the same arbitrariness as the earlier lists of causes and remedies; whatever might have been meant by the "mental activity of women," for example, it is obviously different from that indexed by steam power or the telegraph. Beard based his social theory on little more than unsupported assertions, and he gave no detailed account of how social pressures caused neurasthenia. At every point he simply inferred causal connections from mere conjunctions.

The odd nationalism, together with the fact that so many patients did complain of the symptoms, probably explains the amount of generally favorable attention given the theory in the United States; however, there were some critics. Despite Beard's deserved eminence in neurological and psychiatric circles, some of his colleagues referred to him as a kind of Barnum of American medicine. Spitzka, a neuroanatomist of considerable standing, opined of *American Nervousness* as "not worth the ink with which it is printed, much less the paper on which this was done" (cited in Rosenberg 1962).

Although the disorder became a medical fashion for a time, its importance gradually declined and it is now not thought to be of any great interest. Some years ago, in a series of papers devoted to a comprehensive evaluation of the concept of neurasthenia, few had a good word for it. Carlson (1970–1971) called it an archaic term, Chatel and Peele (1970–1971) estimated that the disease had been diagnosed in fewer than 50 of 102,000 patients admitted to their hospital over 114 years. Chrzanowski (1970–1971) went so far as to entitle his contribution "An obsolete diagnosis," and Mora (1970–1971), after noting that it had remained in the American Psychiatric Association's diagnostic guide until the 1951 revision, thought neurasthenia was best thought of as kind of precursor to modern conceptions of neurosis.

It is difficult to explain the demise of neurasthenia. Many psychiatrists, including Freud, recognized that the disorder was not confined to the United States, a fact that alone must have detracted somewhat from Beard's nationalistic explanatory schema. And even if we accept new terms for the symptoms originally described by Beard, or for subsets of them, none of the causal factors identified by Beard are peculiarly associated with them. What do not appear among the reasons for the disappearance of discussions of neurasthenia from the medical literature are the facts that Beard merely described instances of the disease, that he had not undertaken a proper causal analysis, that his central concept was vacuous, and that his theory could generate only pseudoexplanations. Until now, none of these aspects of Beard's concept seem to have been scrutinized.

Freud's Neurasthenia

Beard's description of the new clinical entity generated enormous interest. By the middle 1880s a very sizable literature of several hundred books and papers had accumulated (K. Levin 1978, p. 128), especially in German, including translations of Beard's own works (Morton 1883; Beard 1884, pp. 20–22). According to López Piñero, the "decisive period in the evolution of neurasthenia" was ushered in by Charcot, mainly in his *Leçons du Mardi*. Using the same approach as he had in studying hysteria, Charcot "legitimized neurasthenia as a major neurosis, comparable only to hysteria" (López Piñero 1963/1983, p. 74).

We can be certain Freud knew of Charcot's work on neurasthenia, but we cannot date either the time he became aware of it or when he translated that part of the *Leçons* to which López Piñero refers in which it was set out. Freud at least knew of Charcot's opinions of Beard's work as well as of Beard's work itself by the middle 1880s, since Charcot cited one of Beard's publications and discussed neurasthenia in the *Lectures* Freud translated in 1886 (Charcot 1886/1887, p. 218). In that same period, Freud became familiar with the condition itself. He referred to neurasthenia as "the commonest of all the diseases in our society" (Freud 1887), and a few years later remarked he had "come across [it] repeatedly every year in my medical practice" (Freud 1892–1893, p. 118).

Beard's Influence on Freud

The evidence that Freud was directly influenced by Beard's work is rather meager, amounting to his accepting some of the incidental opinions expressed in *Sexual Neurasthenia* that antedated Freud's own. Of this evidence, the strongest is Freud's repetition of Beard's assertion that agoraphobia had a sexual cause. Beard speculated that agoraphobia might be under the influence of the genital system (Beard 1884, p. 189), and what is probably Freud's earliest comment on the disorder echoes this completely: "The more frequent cause of agoraphobia as well as of most other phobias lies ... in abnormalities of sexual life" (Freud 1892–1894, p. 139). Positing this not immediately obvious relation between sexuality and phobia is the only evidence of any direct influence of Beard.

It is more likely that Beard's claim of a relation between sexual factors and neurasthenia provided the starting point for Freud's own theses, than that his work had a direct influence. When discussing "excessively frequent" seminal emissions, Beard said they "may be both results and causes of disease, indicating an abnormal, usually an exhausted state of the nervous system, and in turn reacting on the nervous system, increasing the very exhaustion that causes it." He then added:

Chronic neurasthenia is often accompanied, as one of its symptoms, by seminal emissions.... In almost all cases of long-standing nervous exhaustion, the reproductive system necessarily participates, sooner or later, either as cause or effect, or both. In very many cases, local disease consequent on abuse of these parts is a prominent exciting cause of general nervousness. (Beard 1894, pp. 100–101)

Although Beard cited four cases of general neurasthenia and one case (of seven) of sexual neurasthenia, none of which had an obvious sexual basis, in support of this opinion (Beard and Rockwell 1891, pp. 426–430, 584–591), Freud was to assert that, even in cases such as these, the causes were in the patients' sexual life.

Symptoms

Which symptoms Freud first included in neurasthenia is now difficult to establish. Between late 1887 and late 1894 he mentioned the following in various letters and drafts to Fliess: feelings of tiredness, weakness, and sadness; attacks of giddiness and weakness, paresthesias, sensations of pressure on the head and of drawing or pressing on the muscles; loss of appetite and weight, attacks of indigestion, dyspepsia, and constipation; neuralgias of all types; and loss of male potency (Masson 1985, Letter of Nov. 24, 1887, Draft B of Feb. 8, 1893). In his first paper devoted to the condition, Freud argued the time had come to restrict the term to such typical symptoms as intracranial pressure, spinal irritation, and dyspepsia with flatulence, and constipation (Freud 1895a). He did not mention fatigue and sexual weakness until later (Freud 1896a, p. 150).

What Freud meant by intracranial pressure and spinal irritation, especially the first, is not clear to the modern reader. López Piñero's (1963/1983) discussion does not clarify the matter: in the nineteenth century the term had many different meanings. Beard's (1894, p. 80) last description of spinal irritation was that it was a "tenderness either of the whole length of the spine, or, more likely, at certain points, as the nape of the neck, and between the shoulder-blades, and on the middle lumbar vertebrae." He added that "crawling, creeping, and burning sensations often accompany this tenderness." Ferenczi (1926/1955b), however, observed it to be "a condition varying in degree between an unpleasant sensation and a violent pain in the back."

Freud included fewer symptoms under neurasthenia than Beard. However, he presented no arguments for his selection or for his characterization of them as typical. Unlike Arndt (1892b) for example, who attempted a logical derivation of the symptoms from a supposed "fatigued or degenerating nerve," Freud made no attempt to account for either the origin of the symptoms or for their range.

Causes

The most obvious difference between Beard's and Freud's approaches to neurasthenia is the etiological role they gave to sexual factors. For Beard, sexual excess was only one of a number of factors that produced neurasthenia, whereas for Freud it was the only one.

We can be fairly certain Freud arrived at his view between the middle and end of 1892. During 1887 and 1888, in several letters to Fliess, he mentioned a patient with neurasthenia in whom the sexual agent he later proposed as cause was present, but he did not pay any particular attention to it (Masson 1985, Letters of Nov. 24, 1887, Dec. 28, 1887, Feb. 4, 1888, and May 28, 1888). Furthermore, in the paper on hysterical counterwill, probably written near the end of 1892, when discussing whether his patient's hereditary disposition was indexed by her brother's neurasthenia, Freud (1892–1893) wrote that he was "not certain whether it is not possible not to *acquire* this form of neurasthenia" without, again, laying stress on the sexual factors he mentioned in the brother's history. A schematic outline, probably sent to Fliess at the end of 1892, contains the first proposal of a sexual etiology for neurasthenia (Masson 1985, Draft A, possibly of Dec. 1892). A footnote to his translation of Charcot's *Tuesday Lectures* does make the same point but, although it may be earlier than the draft, it cannot be dated with any precision (Freud 1892–1894, p. 142, note to Charcot's p. 399).

Freud's very early remarks do not specify the nature of the sexual factor. Abnormal gratification (e.g., masturbation), inhibition of the sexual function (e.g., coitus interruptus), "affects accompanying these practices," and early sexual trauma all seem to have been thought of as contributing equally (Masson 1985, Draft A, possibly of Dec. 1892). By early 1893 he had narrowed the field. He argued that, singly or jointly, masturbation and incomplete coitus always produced neurasthenia. In males the two factors were typically held to operate at different periods:

Neurasthenia in males is acquired at puberty and becomes manifest when the man is in his twenties. Its source is masturbation. . . .
The second noxa, which affects men at a later age, makes its impact on a nervous system which is either intact or which has been predisposed . . . through masturbation. . . . This . . . is *onanismus conjugalis*—incomplete intercourse in order to prevent conception.   (Masson 1985, Draft B, Feb. 8, 1893)

Freud said that the various forms of incomplete coitus varied in severity: *coitus interruptus* was considered "the main noxa," being able to produce its effects even in "an individual who is not predisposed." Different severities of incomplete coitus, combined with different degrees of innate or acquired predisposition, resulted in different latencies with which neurasthenia was produced. Masturbation in the female produced neurasthenia in the same way as in the male, but it might also be a consequence of sexual relations with a neurasthenic male. How this consequence resulted Freud did not specify, although he implied that incomplete coitus practiced by the male was responsible (Draft B of Feb. 8, 1893).

Freud adduced four observations as evidence for his contentions. First, he claimed it was "a recognized fact" that neurasthenia was "a frequent consequence" of an abnormal sexual life. His view simply extended the scope of that factor. Second, the frequency of male neurasthenia matched the frequency of masturbation in men. Third, observations among his acquaintances proved to him that men "who have been seduced by women at an early age have escaped neurasthenia." Finally, he claimed "that the sexual neurasthenic is always a general neurasthenic at the same time."

None of this is very strong evidence. The "recognized fact" is buttressed by the editors of the Fliess papers—but not by those of the *Standard Edition* or by Masson —with a footnote of their own to a paper by Peyer (incorrectly given as Preyer) dealing only with the *sexual* form of neurasthenia (K. Levin 1978, p. 132). Freud's own two references to Peyer show him to have judged his work as barely relevant to the sexual etiology of the neuroses (Masson 1985, Draft C of Feb. or May 1893; Freud 1895a, p. 98). Masson adds to the confusion by incorrectly implicating another totally irrelevant Preyer, Wilhelm Thierry Preyer, the author of *Die Seele des Kindes*, in his notes to Freud's next draft, Draft C, written between February and May of 1893. The only author with a name like this relevant to what Freud had to say about sexual factors *in the actual neuroses* has to be Alexander Peyer, who wrote on *Congresses interruptus and onanismus conjugalis* as causes of sexual neurasthenia (K. Levin 1978, p. 132, n. 35). Where Freud does cite Masson's candidate, Wilhelm Thierry Preyer, it is as one of a group of writers on child psychology who had *nothing* to say about "the erotic life of children" (Freud 1905b, p. 173, n. 2).

If Beard's case summaries are typical, it is not at all obvious that sexual factors were frequently associated with the general form of neurasthenia. As he said, well before Freud made his bid:

In regard to the relation of neurasthenia to the genital function ... two errors have prevailed: that the genital organs have nothing to do with the causation of neurasthenia and allied affections, and that they are the exclusive causes ...

Without dispute ... there are some cases ... that depend entirely on genital irritation ... and entirely recover with the removal of the irritation; there are others that depend in part on irritation from this source; there are others that arise independently of all irritation of that kind. (Beard 1880, pp. 127–128)

The medical literature of the period is also best summarized as supporting the view that what Beard termed the general form of neurasthenia was only sometimes and not even frequently a consequence of an abnormal sexual life (Erb 1878, cited in K. Levin 1978, p. 129; Arndt 1892b). The situation was rather different for sexual neurasthenia in which, not surprisingly, masturbation and *coitus interruptus* were very frequently implicated. Levin, for example, cites Krafft-Ebing and Loewenfeld in addition to Peyer as supporting this conclusion (K. Levin 1978, pp. 130–132).

As to the relation between the prevalence of neurasthenia and masturbation, Freud seems to have been implying that the different frequencies of male and female neurasthenia matched the differences in male and female masturbatory habits. But in Freud's time there were no valid prevalence figures for masturbation in general, and it was almost certainly underestimated in females. With masturbation among females far more common than Freud assumed, neurasthenia should have been very much more common among them.

Neither are the casual observations by Freud of his acquaintances of much significance, although such data from more extensive inquiries would have been extremely important. He did propose collecting 100 case reports of male and female neurasthenics for study (Masson 1985, Draft B of Feb. 8, 1893), but this collection seems not to have been made. Although his subsequent letters and papers reported several cases of the related disorder of anxiety neurosis, some of which seem to be classified and numbered, neurasthenic cases were mentioned only infrequently and never numbered.

Finally, if, as may be supposed, Freud included under sexual neurasthenia such symptoms as impotence or premature ejaculation, it was simply not true these were always present with the symptoms of general neurasthenia.

Freud's Anxiety Neurosis

During the same period as he was codifying the symptoms he thought to be typical of neurasthenia, Freud proposed that a subset of them should be recognized as forming an independent clinical entity. He suggested the term anxiety neurosis, and first appears to have used that term late in 1892 or early 1893 (Freud 1895a; cf. Masson 1985, Draft A, possibly of Dec. 1892).

Symptoms

By the beginning of 1893 Freud recognized three distinct forms of anxiety neurosis: anxiety attacks, the symptoms of which he did not describe further; the chronic state of anxiety, in which hypochondriasis, phobias relating to the body, and anxiety relating to decisions and memory were the defining symptoms; and periodic depression, the symptoms of which were like those of melancholia. He began a collection of cases from which he eventually arrived at the following diagnostic criteria: general irritability, with especially marked auditory sensitivity; anxious expectation, in which the patient interpreted everyday events as presaging personal calamity; the overwhelming feeling of anxiety, with or without such physical symptoms as sweating and trembling; fearful night waking; vertigo; phobias and obsessions; digestive system disorders such as vomiting or diarrhea; and paresthesias (Freud 1895a).

Causes

Whereas Freud initially associated neurasthenia with a variety of sexual factors, from the very beginning he apparently linked anxiety neurosis with only one, which he called the inhibition of sexual function (Masson 1985, Draft A, possibly of Dec. 1892). In February 1893 he identified the inhibition as incomplete coition, most often coitus interruptus, a sexual practice he then assumed to produce neurasthenia also (Draft B of Feb. 8, 1893). His initial evidence implicating coitus interruptus is difficult to discern, but it seems to have been the occurrence of the symptoms in conjunction with the sexual practice or just after it. He noticed, for example, that the number and/or intensity of attacks diminished during pregnancy, when normal intercourse was possible, only to rise again after pregnancy, when withdrawal or similar contraceptive practices were readopted (Freud 1895a, pp. 103–104).

The Source of the Anxiety

At first Freud seems also to have been as much concerned with identifying the source of the anxiety as with establishing the sexual practice with which it was associated. He saw that the anxiety might be either a prolongation of anxiety over the conception the incomplete gratification had been designed to prevent or, somehow, a direct result of the incomplete gratification itself. By October 1893 he had seen at least one patient with anxiety neurosis, although she had not been at all worried about becoming pregnant (Masson 1985, Letter of Oct. 6, 1893, case 1). He later said the same was true of others (Draft E possibly of June 6, 1894). Freud concluded that anxiety about a possible pregnancy could not be the source of the anxiety in the attack. At the end of 1893 he also observed an anxiety neurosis in a "totally frigid" woman (Letter of Nov. 27, 1893). Since she experienced no sensations during intercourse, that meant those sensations could not be the source of anxiety either.

Having ruled out worries over the possibility of pregnancy and the sensations themselves, Freud concluded that the anxiety was *solely* a consequence of physiological aspects of the sexual act. By not being allowed a natural termination in orgasmic discharge, the *physical* excitation accompanying intercourse was diverted into the autonomic nervous system, and the anxiety was nothing more than the physiological reactions produced by it. From that point of view, he regarded the symptoms as substitutes or surrogates for the physiological reactions that should have taken place during orgasm.

The Actual Neuroses

About two years after his first paper on anxiety neurosis and neurasthenia was published Freud introduced the term actual neurosis to designate both conditions (Freud 1898a, p. 279). The name conveyed his belief that they had their origins in current or present-day (*aktuelle*) sexual problems, unlike psychoneuroses such as hysteria, obsessions, and phobias that originated from sexual traumas in the relatively distant past. Because of their different origins, the treatments differed: the former required only some adjustment to the patient's current sexual life, but the latter required that repressed sexual memories be rendered ineffective.

Freud's Causal Analysis

It seemed to Freud (1895b, pp. 135–138) that four different kinds of factors, or as he termed them, causes, acted together to produce the actual neuroses: precipitating causes, concurrent (or auxiliary) causes, preconditions, and specific causes. Precipitating causes were those that occurred last in the sequence of factors and immediately preceded the appearance of the neurosis. Concurrent causes were not present every time, and by themselves were unable to produce the neurosis. Preconditions were those whose presence was necessary, but by themselves could not bring it about. Specific causes were present in every instance and required only the additional presence of the preconditions to produce the neurosis. A specific cause could be distinguished from a precondition by being found only in one disorder. For example, because it was the specific cause of neurasthenia, masturbation could not also cause anxiety neurosis or hysteria. Specific causes were distinguished further from preconditions in that the latter tended to be of a general nature, varying little from one neurosis to another, and stable in having only slight apparent effect until the specific cause acted.

Freud set out an "etiological equation" or "etiological formula" to represent the relation between the factors. In the equation the several causes were regarded as terms that had to be satisfied if the neurosis, as the effect, were to occur. When the specific cause seemed not to produce a neurosis, Freud believed more effort had to be made to assess the contribution of the preconditions and the concurrent causes. If all the causes were present, they might not be at a sufficiently intense level; for example, a concurrent cause might be required to potentiate the effect of the other two.

Applied to anxiety neurosis, for example, the etiological equation identified a libidinal weakness, usually of a hereditary kind, as the precondition. Emotional stress, physical illness, or others of what he called the "stock noxae," might be concurrent causes. However, anxiety neurosis would only come about if its specific cause of incomplete sexual gratification was also present. Depending on which acted last, the illness could be precipitated by either the specific or the concurrent cause. Because precipitating causes were defined only by the time at which they acted, Freud eventually dropped them as a separate class (Freud 1896a, pp. 146–149).

Freud could hardly parallel exactly Koch's requirement of producing disease through inoculation. The logical equivalent can be established, however, by actively searching for instances in which the presumed cause is present but does not produce its effect. Only if systematic and exhaustive inquiries of nonneurotic individuals show the presumptive preconditions and specific causes to be absent from their histories and sexual practices does the presence of those factors in cases of neuroses allow them to be classed as sufficing for the neuroses.

Freud made no such inquiries. He maintained instead that all that was required to confirm his causal hypotheses was for the appropriate specific sexual factor to be present in the history of each patient (Freud 1895b, pp. 135–139). He represented himself as following established principles of medical logic. He noted, for example, that, although not everyone infected by the bacillus suspected of being the specific cause of tuberculosis actually developed the illness, that fact did not detract from its causal significance. The plausibility of these arguments conceals two very important weaknesses: what Freud described as the sufficient conditions are only the necessary, and the etiological equation was pseudomathematical.

Freud said the preconditions and specific causes of the actual neuroses were "among the '*necessary causes*'" (his emphasis), but clearly believed that together they defined the sufficient conditions, because he actually went on to say of the specific cause that it

suffices, if present in the required quantity or intensity, to achieve the effect, provided only that the preconditions are also fulfilled.   (Freud 1895b, p. 136. My emphasis)

Accepting for the moment that he represented his case reports accurately, all he had done was to show the presence of precondition and the specific sexual factor in each case. All that meant was that they were among the necessary conditions. Nowhere had he demonstrated that by *always* causing the neurosis, the specific factor and the preconditions were the sufficient conditions.

Freud did not bother with an equivalent of Koch's inoculation condition by conducting a systematic search for cases in which the presumed cause might be present but its effects absent. That is, he did not examine normal subjects—controls, if you wish—to see whether the presumed cause was at work in them (figure 5.1). He held

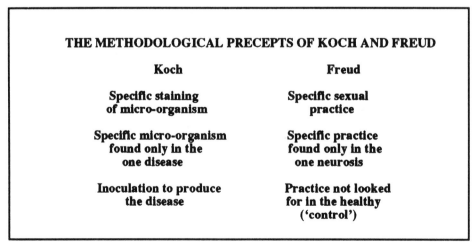

THE METHODOLOGICAL PRECEPTS OF KOCH AND FREUD

Koch	Freud
Specific staining of micro-organism	**Specific sexual practice**
Specific micro-organism found only in the one disease	**Specific practice found only in the one neurosis**
Inoculation to produce the disease	**Practice not looked for in the healthy ('control')**

Figure 5.1
Freud's adaptation of Koch's postulates.

the specific cause of anxiety neurosis to be incomplete sexual gratification primarily because he claimed it was present in every instance. Naturally, nothing solely identified in this way could be a specific cause. Freud knew this was not the right way to establish the sufficient conditions of the actual neuroses. He actually proposed studying "Men and women who have remained healthy" (Masson 1985, Draft A, possibly of Dec. 1892) and in Draft B of Feb. 8, 1893 he specified *non*neurotics as a necessary counterpart or complement to his investigations (my emphasis), but there is no evidence of any such study being conducted. He seems to have contented himself with a casual observation:

in the circle of one's acquaintances that ... those individuals who have been seduced by women at an early age have escaped neurasthenia.   (Draft B, Feb. 8, 1893)

Presumably, what this meant was that Freud never found masturbation among this group of nonneurasthenics. These observations appear to constitute his only evidence having a bearing on whether the presumed causes might be present in the healthy. Without more evidence it mattered little how many cases of neurosis were collected—the information critical for determining the sufficient conditions was not to be found in their histories. Kris (Freud 1950/1954, p. 64, n. 1) defends Freud by arguing that to conduct such a study "obviously would be impossible without collaborators." It is a very poor excuse. Although difficult for one person to conduct, the study was obviously absolutely necessary to Freud's thesis—and he knew it. We will see in chapter 8 that Freud had a collaborator in Felix Gattel, who spent some months investigating his causal hypotheses in a setting where he had ready access to nonneurotics.

Freud did not argue, of course, that an actual neurosis was caused by a single factor. After all, his etiological equation purported to show how the different classes of causes were related to one another. However, without procedures for identifying the factors or for measuring their strengths independent of each other, the relative contribution of each cannot be established. For example, suppose incomplete gratification failed to produce anxiety neurosis. Any one of the following meanings can be attributed to that fact: the specific cause might not be intense enough, the preconditions might be of insufficient intensity, or the concurrent cause might have failed to act sufficiently strongly. Because the strengths of the factors cannot be measured, there is no way of deciding among the various possibilities. And other problems arose. For example, where the precondition was hereditary, Freud could adduce only the fact of neurotic illness in the patient's relatives. However good an index of the presence of a hereditary predisposition such a fact might be, it cannot provide a measure of the *intensity* with which it operates. The equation is pseudomathematical in that it implies the factors can be measured, when that is clearly not the case. Stewart, the only psychoanalytic writer to have considered Freud's formulation in a critical way, notes that

Although it involves an equation with a variety of theoretical variables, none of these variables can be quantified or even distinguished except on theoretical grounds: *each is independently variable and only subjectively and post hoc estimatable.* (Stewart 1967, p. 35. My emphasis)

As a contribution to clarifying the role of the presumed causal factors, Freud's analysis, for all its apparent sophistication, is not really different from Beard's simple enumeration.

Stewart also drew attention to similar deficiencies in Freud's more general summary statement about the relations between the terms of the etiological equation. Freud had concluded

(1) Whether a neurotic illness *occurs at all* depends upon a quantitative factor—upon the total load on the nervous system as compared with the latter's capacity for resistance. Everything which can keep this quantitative factor below a certain threshold-value, or can bring it back to that level, has a therapeutic effect, since by so doing it keeps the aetiological equation unsatisfied.

What is to be understood by the "total load" and by the "capacity for resistance" of the nervous system, could no doubt be more clearly explained on the basis of certain hypotheses regarding the function of the nerves.

(2) What *dimensions* the neurosis attains depends in the first instance on the amount of the hereditary taint. Heredity acts like a multiplier introduced into an electric circuit, which increases the deviation of the needle many times over.

(3) But what *form* the neurosis assumes—what direction the deviation takes—is solely determined by the specific aetiological factor arising from sexual life. (Freud 1895b, pp. 138–139)

Freud's own comments recognized the vagueness of the concepts of total load and resistance, but Stewart points out there is no way they could ever be quantified:

Since none of the individual components of the load, or the total load, or the resistance, could be measured, the "equation" was from this point of view *worthless.* (Stewart 1967, p. 36. My emphasis)

And, since Freud's hypotheses that might have given meaning to these concepts are nowhere set out or defended, his summary version of his etiological argument was as worthless as the original.

In light of what is actually required to establish the cause of a neurosis, the inadequacy of reversing the *cessante causa cessat effectus* dictum is now apparent. In no field is the observation that modifying a phenomenon significantly by removing its presumed cause ever more than marginally relevant to the confirmation of the causal presumption. In particular, the history of placebo effects in medicine and psycho-pathology shows that symptoms of quite serious illness, not just minor psychological irritations, can be removed by procedures having little if anything to do with their real causes (A. K. Shapiro 1960; A. K. Shapiro and Morris 1978; Grünbaum 1984; Macmillan 1986).

Establishing how a particular therapy brings about its effects requires an analysis at least as complex as that implied in Koch's methods of identifying causes. Breuer and Freud did not do this. Largely because the symptoms of hysteria were removed by abreaction, they ruled out expectations and suggestion as the basis of their results and concluded they were due to catharsis (Breuer and Freud 1893, p. 7; 1895, pp. 255–256). Freud seems to have done no more in evaluating his treatment of the actual neuroses. He apparently to have believed that his advice to adopt more normal sexual practices was therapeutically effective, and that that outcome went toward proving he had correctly identified the causes of the actual neuroses. For the most part, as we will see in chapter 8, his followers did not believe in his causal scheme, and they had nothing like his degree of therapeutic success.

Conclusions

Despite the apparent sophistication of Freud's method of assessing the roles of the factors presumed to cause the actual neuroses, he no more stepped outside of the realm of case material than had Beard. Both used basically the same methods to identify and evaluate causal factors, and both committed the error of assuming that all that was necessary to identify a cause was to extract the features common to a group of similar cases. Neither investigated whether those features might be present where the neurosis was absent. Although Freud took a different view of the impor-tance of sexual factors, he disagreed with little in Beard's approach.

Freud had not established excessive masturbation and incomplete gratification as the specific causes of the actual neuroses, and in chapter 8 we will see that he did not even establish that they were among the necessary conditions. The real outcome of his work consisted of a misleading expectation that all neuroses might be caused by sexual factors.

Previously I argued Freud did not begin investigating the causes of hysteria sys-tematically until late 1893. Two letters among those made public for the first time in Masson's edition of the Freud-Fliess correspondence confirm this dating. More important, they also show Freud began his work on hysteria by attempting to extend the sexual etiology he thought he had already established for the actual neuroses.

In the first letter, written in May 1893, Freud said of his work on neurasthenia and anxiety neurosis:

The neuroses are somewhat at a standstill, am working more on hysteria. (Masson 1985, Letter of May 15, 1893)

In September, nearly five months later, and using the term *sexualia* to refer to his hypothesis that neurasthenia and anxiety neurosis had sexual causes, he wrote:

I happen to have very few new sexualia. I shall soon start tackling hysteria. (Letter of Sept. 29, 1893)

Given this expectation and his other assumptions, it was not surprising that he found sexual factors at work in hysteria, and given the defects of his sexualia, it was also not surprising that he again confused necessary with sufficient conditions.

By mid-1896 Freud concluded that hysteria was caused by sexual trauma in childhood. By that time too, the defective causal analysis was very much in evidence:

It does not matter if many people experience ... sexual scenes without becoming hysterics, provided only that all the people who become hysterics have experienced scenes of that kind.... Not everyone who touches or comes near a smallpox patient develops smallpox; nevertheless infection from a smallpox patient is almost the only known aetiology of the disease. (Freud 1896c, p. 209)

In bringing part I to an end, I do not think the wide-ranging effects of this and the other of Freud's defective methodological precepts and assumptions we have examined require additional comment. We must expect to find that these various deficiencies have a profound impact on the first of Freud's independent attempts to account for hysteria, as well as on his more comprehensive theory of the mental apparatus. It is the examination of those effects that makes up part II.

Notes

1. Peter Swales suggested to me that some caution should be exercised in so interpreting this peculiarity of the Freud-Fliess correspondence. He thinks it possible that Freud divided his interest in the neuroses between Fliess and Breuer, restricting his ideas about the actual neuroses to the former and sharing his ideas about hysteria only with the latter. This could have been the case, but I believe the detailed analyses of Freud's early theoretical concepts about hysteria in the last chapter show them not to be consonant with an exclusively sexual etiology either.

2. The influence of germ theory may be even more extensive than Carter (1980) suggests. Arlow pointed out, possibly without knowing Carter's paper, that Freud's whole conception of the cause of a neurosis as a pathogenic foreign body "drawing about itself the memory of contiguous events and of associated recollections ... is not unlike the organized tissue reaction surrounding the necrotic core of a tubercle in response to the toxin of the tubercle bacillus." Arlow also draws the further parallel between catharsis and "the extrusion or ejection of the noxious foreign body" (Arlow 1981; cf. Arlow 1959; Waelder 1967a).

II FIRST THEORIES AND APPLICATIONS

6 Mechanisms of Symptom Formation

Erskine: If you had been sent to Cambridge to study science . . . you would know that a hypothesis that explains everything is a certainty.
—Wilde: *The Portrait of Mr. W. H.*

In part II I attempt three things: first, to evaluate Freud's theoretical ideas as they stood at about the end of 1895; second, to examine some of the difficulties that arose in 1896 to 1897 when Freud tried to apply them; and third, to assess the modifications he made to his theory in response to those difficulties, which he published between 1900 and 1905.

The year 1895 is important because it marks the end of the first distinguishable phase of Freud's work. By that time Freud had extended the sexual etiology he first proposed for the actual neuroses to include the psychoneuroses, he had postulated mechanisms to explain both kinds of symptoms, and he had constructed his first explanatory theory.

Part II begins with an evaluation of the mechanisms by which Freud attempted to explain how symptoms form. His first and more general theory of psychopathology of which they were a part is then considered. Within a few months of the end of 1896 Freud's applications of these theoretical ideas led to the hypothesis that hysteria was caused by perverse sexual seduction in childhood, and I discuss the decision he eventually made that the seduction hypothesis was incorrect. The difficulties in Freud's explanations of the actual neuroses are also considered. The section concludes with an outline and evaluation of the considerable alterations Freud then made to his theory and that resulted in a general psychological theory applicable to normal and abnormal behavior. Although the differences between this much modified theory and the original one are quite marked, I believe certain defects in Freud's pre-1895 work were carried over into it.

I begin by focusing in this chapter on the status of the mechanisms Freud proposed for explaining how neurotic symptoms form. I compare his explanations with those of Charcot, Breuer, and Janet, and try to make explicit the bases on which choices among these explanations should be made.

A Reality for Explanatory Mechanisms?

The relations between observable causes and observable effects are usually explained in terms of processes or entities that cannot be sensed in any direct way. Freud supposed, for example, that repression of incompatible ideas caused symptoms of hysteria and that deflection of somatic sexual excitation caused symptoms of anxiety neurosis. Repression and deflection are hypothetical processes, and unlike the idea, the excitation, or the symptom, cannot be sensed or observed directly. The problem I consider here is whether and how these underlying processes or entities "exist" or are "real". Clearly some confirmation of psychoanalytic theory would come from showing that repression and deflection, unsensed as they are, actually existed.

It can be argued that to ask about the reality of explanatory mechanisms is to ask erroneously: mechanisms or entities are postulated or hypothesized precisely because the reality is unknown. Once the real processes linking causes with effects become known, real knowledge replaces hypothesis. In this view, to ask if mechanisms of repression and deflection really exist is to confuse a hypothetical process with the reality it tries to describe. Although this argument undoubtedly has appeal, it also undoubtedly should be disregarded. Galileo and his inquisitors both thought there was a difference between asking whether the earth's movement was only a hypothesis or if it really did move. So in our own time it seems make sense to inquire if there really are genes, quarks, or any of the other unsensed entities postulated in the modern sciences. Obviously a hypothetical mechanism or entity that refers to a real process is not itself that process, but recognizing its hypothetical nature does not preclude asking how well it depicts the underlying reality it reflects.[1]

Hypothetical and Other Constructs

During the 1940s a good deal of discussion centered on the status of the unsensed entities and processes, such as repression, that were incorporated into psychological theories. Eventually, MacCorquodale and Meehl (1948) admitted two processes into the corpus of psychological theorizing: intervening variables and hypothetical constructs. Does either of these notions describe the mechanisms hypothesized to cause symptoms?

Reflecting the fashionable positivism of the day, intervening variables and hypothetical constructs were limited to relating things that could be directly observed. An intervening variable stood for a relation that was otherwise expressed in a quantitative empirical law. For MacCorquodale and Meehl the correctness of an intervening variable was a function of the validity of the law expressing it. For example, in his studies of motivation and learning, Hull used the concept of "drive" to relate, among other things, observed performance on various learning tasks to a preceding condition of food deprivation (Hull 1943, pp. 57, 66). MacCorquodale's and Meehl's standards had it that drive was a correct intervening variable to the extent that a valid law expressed how quantitative variations in food intake were related to time taken to learn a task. In their usage, drive simply became an economical expression for a set of relatively complex experimentally determined relations. They could remain good positivists and make no reference to the bogey of nonobservable processes or entities.

On the other hand, a hypothetical construct was not reducible to a quantitative law, and its truth could not therefore be indexed by it. Because hypothetical constructs seemed to express more than empirical relations MacCorquodale and Meehl said they had surplus meaning. The character trait anxiousness illustrates the point. The term anxiety may be used to relate certain stressful conditions to sweating or accelerated heart rate, even though empirical laws relating the conditions to the behaviors cannot be expressed precisely. But a trait such as anxiousness is thought of as a more or less permanent disposition, existing in the individual apart from any particular empirical relation. Anxiousness cannot be sensed in the same way as anxiety, and is therefore said to have surplus meaning.

It is clear that the various symptom-producing mechanisms are neither intervening variables nor hypothetical constructs. First, none expresses more than a relation between *apparent* observables. Typically, they connect two unobservable psychological states, or an unobservable state and a symptom. Charcot's mechanism of realization, for example, relates an unobservable idea to an observed symptom, and Freud's repression expresses the difference between the original affect-laden percept of the traumatic situation and its memory. Second, in attempting to *explain* symptom formation, the mechanisms do more than *express* a relation. Maze (1954) long ago demonstrated that intervening variables cannot have an explanatory role: the very production of an effect requires the variable to do more than express a relation with its cause. A third reason ruling out symptom-producing mechanisms as intervening variables is that quantitative laws do not apply. If the criteria proposed by MacCorquodale and Meehl for judging the truth or correctness of intervening variables and hypothetical constructs do not apply to the mechanisms supposed to produce symptoms, can our question be answered at all?

Theoretical Terms

A starting point for an alternative to the MacCorquodale and Meehl view is provided by O'Neil's (1953) proposal that different hypothetical entities or processes might be classed according to the ways properties or qualities are attributed to them, or, as he put it, the ways in which they are characterized. I would extend his proposal with the suggestion that it is those theoretical terms whose characteristics or attributed properties can be investigated that have the potential for referring to real processes. A term has a real referent when investigation shows that those properties or qualities exist.[2]

O'Neil distinguished between hypothetical relations and hypothetical terms. By the former he meant concepts that expressed lawful relations between two classes of conditions, usually observable. His hypothetical relation was broadly equivalent to an intervening variable. A hypothetical term, on the other hand, was a term in the logical sense of being either the subject or predicate of a logical proposition. It was also characterized by having various qualities or properties attributed to it, and it was from these that explanations could be generated.

As an example, O'Neil discussed various ways in which a hypothetical term such as "memory trace" might be characterized. Were it assumed to be a relatively persisting mental image of a word that was not ordinarily conscious, qualities or characteristics would have been attributed to it, asserting, as O'Neil put it, what the trace was as well as what it did. It was a characterized theoretical term (O'Neil 1962, p. 96). On the other hand, to say that a memory trace was a relatively persisting alteration of mind said nothing, and he proposed calling such terms uncharacterized. They had only the virtue of pointing to what had yet to be explained. An uncharacterized entity or process told one only what the entity or process did, not what it was.

For my purposes, this proposal requires extending. A more adequate description of characterization is needed, as is a method for judging the correctness of a given characterization. The first step in characterization is to attribute properties to the term that logically entail the facts expressed in the relation. Characterizing memory traces as mental images of words, for example, attributes all the properties of word images to memory traces. The ways in which memory traces change over time, are consolidated or forgotten, interfere with one another, and so on, are explained by whatever produces changes in the images of words. Once logically suitable qualities like these have been proposed, the question of the correctness of the characterization reduces to the questions of whether memory traces do indeed resemble images of words, and whether the facts to be explained can still be arrived at from the qualities the traces are shown to possess. The process to which the hypothetical term refers exists to the extent that the characteristics exist. Characterization thus provides a basis for establishing the reality of proposed explanatory mechanisms.

Ellman and Moskowitz (1980) note a difficulty in the requirement that an independently characterized term has to enter into explanatory statements about at least two qualitatively different phenomena. They ask, what constitutes a qualitative difference? They are among the very few authors I have found in the psychological literature, and the only ones in the psychoanalytic, to discuss the question of whether theories or the nonlogical terms (entities) they contain may be judged true or false, that is, as having real referents or not.

Sometimes simple observation confirms or disconfirms the reality of a hypothetical term. When this happens, the characterization usually is of a single property having the potential to be observed directly. An illustration is provided by Harvey's use of the theoretical term "pore" in explaining the circulation of blood. On the basis of his observations of the anatomy and functioning of the heart, lungs, and blood vessels, Harvey concluded the heart pumped a fixed amount of blood through the body. He had then to assume that an exchange took place between the arteries and veins, and proposed this occurred through minute openings, or pores, too small to be seen. A logical implication of this characterization was that the pores would be visible through microscopes more powerful than those available in his own day. Some years after his death, minute vessels were observed, and the status of the pores changed. Postulated or assumed pores had been transformed into real capillaries; a theoretical term had become a fact.

Harvey's concept possessed the most essential attribute of a well-characterized theoretical term: genuine explanatory power. It allowed him to deduce how the heart could maintain the continuous circulation of a fixed quantity of blood. The explanation was also genuine, not the pseudoexplanation that would have resulted had he postulated the existence of pores so small and subtle they could never be seen even by the most powerful microscopes. Although in Harvey's day no observational test of the reality of the pores was possible, there was nothing in principle to prevent it. In principle testing of the factual consequences of the properties attributed to the term is the testability of the term.

What I maintain, therefore, is that the essential features of well-characterized terms—explanatory power and testability—derive from the hypotheses that can be generated from the properties attributed to them. Therefore the other features of well-formulated hypotheses considered by O'Neil (1962)—consistency of assumptions about the properties, clarity of definition, a small number of assumptions, and the greatest compatibility with other known or assumed processes—should also hold for well-characterized terms. I turn to the importance of these additional requirements.

Consistency in the properties attributed to a theoretical term corresponds to consistency in the assumptions of a hypothesis. Obviously it is quite essential, because properties inconsistent with one another lead to pseudoexplanations and reduced or absent testability. This is true even of simple theoretical terms. For example, although Mesmer's fluid was said to be imponderable, it was also said to be disturbed by the movement of the planets. Phlogiston, a substance once thought to be released during combustion, had negative weight attributed to it after it was found that elements burned in oxygen actually increased in weight.

In practice, the most useful hypotheses are those that are based on the most clearly defined assumptions, that involve the smallest number of assumptions, and that have the greatest compatibility with other known or assumed processes. Although these requirements are worth meeting, it should be stressed that they are not logical necessities but practical guides. The need for clear definition of qualities might seem self-evident; however, concepts are often required to represent processes that are only partly or imperfectly understood. Under those circumstances, the attribution of vaguely defined properties may be justified; all that can be asked is that definitions be as clear as the stage of investigation allows. The requirement of the smallest number of assumptions applies more properly to assumptions underlying explanations than to theoretical terms proper. It derives from the nominalist philosopher William of Ockham (or Occam) who argued that the fewer assumptions made in an explanation the better.[3]

Ockham used his principle to counter a then prevalent tendency for philosophers to propose unnecessary explanations for natural and supernatural events. The principle of parsimony, or Ockham's razor as it came to be called, is a useful guide even though it does not have the force of logical necessity. Similarly, the history of scientific concepts shows many valid theoretical terms are incompatible with other processes. The concept of dual consciousness used by the French psychopathologists was, as Binet noted, completely at variance with traditional associationist concepts (Binet 1892, pp. 269–270, 350–352). Freud's concept of an unconscious mind containing repressed ideas was similarly at variance with every one of the many other concepts of unconscious mental functioning in vogue in his time. In one sense, it must always be the case that new theoretical terms require the attribution of qualities of variance with those characterizing other terms. Were it not so, progressively deeper understanding of reality would not be possible.

Theoretical terms should not be discarded just because they fail to meet these practical rules of thumb of compatibility, parsimony, and definitional clarity. Being logically necessary, explanatory power, testability, and consistency of assumptions are more important.

Hysterical Symptoms

Having clarified the standards according to which theoretical terms ought to be evaluated, we may now examine how the mechanisms of hysterical symptom formation proposed by Charcot, Janet, Breuer, and Freud meet them.

Realization

Charcot supposed that, because normal ego control was lacking during traumatic events, the sensations generated in such events called up ideas that manifested themselves as symptoms. The properties he attributed to the mechanism of realization were essentially those required by the theory of ideomotor action. What marked the difference between normal and abnormal realization were the kinds of ideas involved and the presence or absence of ego control. What explanatory power Charcot's mechanism of realization possessed derived from the more general theory of which it appeared to be a special case.

The theory of ideomotor action postulated that a voluntary movement was always preceded by the idea or mental image of the movement (James 1890b, vol. 2, pp. 522–528). The evidence supposedly consistent with the theory was of very doubtful validity: James's summary of it shows it to be, in almost equal proportions, a mixture of speculation, dubious clinical observation, and introspection. Just after the turn of the century, when the experiments were conducted and the developmental observations coordinated, it became apparent that neither kinesthetic nor other images were among the precursors of movement (Bair 1901; Woodworth 1903, 1906). Especially important for this conclusion were investigations of subjects whose muscles were stimulated electrically to give them the kinesthetic sensations involved in movements. These subjects gained voluntary control only slightly faster than those subjects who were not stimulated. Many of the diseases in which patients were unable to sense or control the position of their limbs were not adequately described, and, if as appears to have been the case, a large proportion of these disorders were hysterical, the clinical observations were of doubtful value.

Further, as Woodworth (1906) observed, the sensations giving information about "the present condition of the member about to be moved" were not at all the same thing as the kinesthetic or sensory image of the impending movement. Indeed, the two were frequently opposed. For example, in alternate flexion and extension of the forearm, the sensations of extension evoke the ensuing flexion, and vice versa. The relevance of the clinical observations was thus based on a confusion between the roles attributed to sensations in maintaining and initiating movement. Finally, the introspective argument assumed little more than that willing was based on the idea of the desired consequence, and that the only effect of willing of which one became aware was an action. James himself believed the only reason why the theory was not self-evidently true was that ideas did not invariably cause movements. When no movement resulted, James believed one could detect on the fringe of consciousness an idea of an inhibiting action, counterposed to the original intention (1890b, vol. 2, pp. 525–527).

When Woodworth (1906) investigated the role of imagery directly, he used subjects well trained in introspection who had various types of imagery of various strengths. He obtained only a minority of reports in which the type of imagery was related adequately to the subsequent movement, and in nearly half of the reports there was no imagery at all. In his 1903 studies Woodworth tried to isolate the extension and flexion of his great toe from the others. He observed that attempts to prevent the others from moving were "a good means of insuring that they did move." Many of Bair's subjects had similarly noted the ineffectiveness of the idea of the inhibiting action to control the primary act. Woodworth concluded:

I infer from the results of Bair, combined with my own, that even in first getting control over a particular movement, at least in the case of adults, the kinesthetic image of that movement is neither a necessary nor a sufficient condition.   (Woodworth 1906)

Consequently, in Charcot's day, the evidence consistent with the theory of ideomotor action was not very strong, and the evidence gathered soon after was decidedly negative. Charcot's adaptation of the theory involved yet another difficulty and a rather special one at that. He assumed that the idea of the absence of a movement was equivalent to the idea of a movement:

The idea of movement, in the course of being executed, is already movement; the idea of absence of movement, if strong, is already the realisation of motor-paralysis; all this is entirely in conformity with the laws of psychology.   (Charcot and Marie 1892)

However, the assumption that the idea of movement produces an action does not logically entail a paralysis as a consequence of the idea of an absence of movement. As a result, even if the theory of ideomotor action was acceptable, Charcot's adaptation of it was not.

Like the mechanism that transformed normal ideas into actions, the mechanism of realization proposed by Charcot is also uncharacterized. It therefore lacks explanatory power, and because it has no properties or qualities of its own, it cannot be tested. Nevertheless, several investigations do suggest themselves. Modifications of sensory input by chemically induced anesthesias and paralyses ought to modify the experimental production of symptoms under hypnosis. Different degrees of hypnotic trance also ought to be associated with different degrees of realization and with variations in the relation between emotion and bodily expression. Investigating realization in these ways is not inconsistent with its uncharacterized status when it is recognized that the investigations do not concern the properties of the mechanism per se, but only the effect of altering the sensations the mechanism is supposed to transform.

What Charcot referred to as the absence of the normal control of the ego is also a completely uncharacterized process. Although it is implied that absence of control is a state opposite to that in which the controlling ego is present, the state in which control is present is not defined at all. Quite simply, what role the ego normally plays in controlling the transformation of an idea into an act is unknown. So too is what happens when those controls are in abeyance. Consequently, to the extent that the concept of normal ego control lacks explanatory power, so does its opposite.

Because Charcot does not always use it, some difficulty also exists about the centrality of the notion of the absence of ego control. For example, in the last quotation we see that he derived symptoms directly from the idea of the absence of action and not from any peculiarity in the ego's control. However, in a number of other places the absence of control seems central. If it is not central, the lack of characterization poses no problem in evaluating realization; the weakness of the ideomotor theory itself and the lack of characterization within it of the mechanism of realization become the bases for rejection. On the other hand, if absence of ego control is central, its own lack of characterization adds further to the lack of explanatory power of realization.

The assumption that a hereditary predisposition is necessary for hysteria provides one definite point at which Charcot's theory is open to test. However, heredity seems to have been given different emphases in different phases of Charcot's work. Even quite late he proposed heredity was only a dominant factor:

The dominant idea for us in the aetiology of hysteria is, therefore (in the widest sense), that of hereditary predisposition; although some individuals seem to be hysterical from their birth by reason of direct heredity, the *greater number* ... are simply born susceptible. (Charcot and Marie 1892. Emphasis altered)

Elsewhere, for example, in the role he gave the number of affected relatives in his discussion of Le Log____'s traumatic hysteria, Charcot seemed to imply the necessity of a hereditary predisposition in every case. Freud later objected that this kind of evidence often confused hereditary and nonhereditary diseases, that it did not exclude the possibility that the disease had nevertheless been acquired, and that the predisposition was not present in a number of his own patients (Freud 1896a). To the extent that the concept of predisposition was central to Charcot's explanations of hysteria, Breuer's and Freud's arguments and observations disproved them.

Finally, many inconsistencies were present between Charcot's theory and the evidence he took to support it. For example, whereas it was true that electrical stimulation of the facial muscles could produce the bodily attitude appropriate to the emotion so expressed, it failed to do so unless the stimulation was repeated many times (Charcot and Richer 1883). Although Charcot and Richer interpreted the fact differently, presumably the real function of the repetitions was to give the subject the opportunity of divining the experimenter's intentions. Charcot's conclusion that realization took place automatically, merely because the idea was called up by the muscle sense, was a rash conclusion for its own time and is not consistent with present knowledge of hypnosis.

Restriction of Consciousness

According to Janet, a consequence of the stimulation of the sense organs was the production of the corresponding elementary psychological processes in the mind he called sensations. More than one modality was usually excited and a large number of different sensations generated. These sensations Janet regarded as subconscious phenomena "isolated, without intervention of the idea of personality" (P. Janet 1892a; cf. 1892d, p. 36). Usually these elementary phenomena were synthesized into perceptions, and that unity might be assimilated into the previously existing concept of personality. "It is only after this sort of *assimilation* that we can truly say 'I feel'" (1892a,d, p. 36). To distinguish this type of perception from the recognition of external objects, Janet proposed the term "personal perception." Personal perception led to a more complete consciousness than the isolated elementary sensations could produce, but it did not necessarily assimilate all the sensations that were actually present. What Janet called the extent of the field of consciousness was simply not wide enough to allow all the sensations to be taken in.

Ordinarily this deficiency was overcome by directing attention successively to different aspects of the stimulus. But suppose a permanent narrowing of the field. Sensations from one or other modality would not be assimilated. The patient

neglects to perceive the tactile and muscular sensations, thinking he can do without them.... One fine day the patient, for he has truly become one now, is examined by the physician. He pinches his left arm and asks him if he feels it, and the patient, to his great surprise, affirms that he can no longer, if I can put it this way, recall as part of his personal perception the sensations so long neglected: he has become *anaesthetic*.   (P. Janet 1892a; cf. 1892d, pp. 39–40)

The sudden development of symptoms and the development of symptoms other than anesthesia could be readily accounted for. Janet proposed that traumatic situations produced a narrowing of consciousness such that all ideas occurring outside of it were cut off from the dominant consciousness. These split-off ideas then formed a second consciousness that manifested itself in the primary consciousness as symptoms. The tendency to a narrowing of the field of consciousness was permanent. It was based on a "psychical insufficiency," a hereditarily determined incapacity to attend to a wide enough range of stimuli.

Although restriction of consciousness plausibly leads to defective synthesis and assimilation and to deficits that produce symptoms, the processes themselves are quite uncharacterized. While Charcot tried to derive the mechanism of realization from the widely accepted and very plausible theory of ideomotor action, Janet's proposals had no such link. Janet's account of normal sensation and perception was quite novel, but it rested on nothing more than his own powers of description.

He cited no experimental, clinical, or other findings. In synthesis and assimilation he offered two uncharacterized theoretical terms completely lacking in explanatory power. Symptoms resulting from abnormalities in the processes were similarly not explained.

In any case, what explanatory power restriction might have had was weakened by its dependence on other poorly characterized concepts. Psychological weakness, or psychological insufficiency, was supposed to produce the narrowing of consciousness in which normal synthesis and assimilation failed. On the evidence for insufficiency, Freud noted about Emmy von N.:

> I must confess, too, that I can see no sign ... of the "psychical inefficiency" to which Janet attributes the genesis of hysteria. According to him the hysterical disposition consists in an abnormal restriction of the field of consciousness (due to hereditary degeneracy) which results in a disregard of whole groups of ideas.... If this were so, what remains of the ego after the withdrawal of the hysterically-organized psychical groups would necessarily also be less efficient than a normal ego.... Janet, I think, has made the mistake here of promoting what are after-effects of changes in consciousness due to hysteria to the rank of primary determinants of hysteria.... in Frau von N. there was no sign of any such inefficiency. During the times of her worst states she was and remained capable of playing her part in the management of a large industrial business, of keeping a constant eye on the education of her children, of carrying on her correspondence with prominent people in the intellectual world—in short, of fulfilling her obligations well enough for the fact of her illness to remain concealed. (Breuer and Freud 1895, p. 104)

Leaving to one side his strange translation of Janet's term, Freud's representation of Janet's emphasis on heredity is disputed. According to Laplanche and Pontalis (1967/1973, p. 194), Janet did not believe the insufficiency to be innate. Van der Hart and Horst (1986) accept that Janet's concept of a tendency to dissociate was a congenital one, but assert that for him the development of a frank dissociative disorder such as hysteria depended on an interaction of the tendency with the effects of inebriation, physical illness, and "vehement emotions."

Janet thought insufficiency was evidenced by such signs of physiological malfunctioning as variability in heart rate, blushing, and sweating, as well as by such psychological states as inability to concentrate, and feelings of depression and fatigue. He believed these signs varied with the patient's condition, being present when the symptoms were exacerbated and absent when the patient was well. However, he produced little evidence of the signs being present before the onset of the illness. More important logically is the fact that the signs from which he inferred insufficiency were the same as those from which failures in assimilation and synthesis were inferred.

Even if the mechanism proposed by Janet were genuinely explanatory, it would be difficult to test. Under what circumstances does personal perception fail? Modifications to sensory input might lead to different symptoms, but that would not differentiate restriction from realization. Janet gives a plausible account of the symptoms of hysteria, but it is clear the mechanism he proposed is almost completely uncharacterized and generates only pseudoexplanations.

Hypnoid Isolation

Breuer assumed the symptom was a manifestation of an idea that properly belonged to a secondary consciousness. When the secondary consciousness appeared, the ideas belonging to it came also. Some of these ideas would be symptoms. When the secondary consciousness manifested itself intermittently, like the occasional hallucinations of Anna O., the symptoms also appeared only intermittently. If the secondary consciousness coexisted with the primary state, the symptom was present permanently, appearing to belong to the primary state. In either case, the primary consciousness had no access to the ideas of the second state and no knowledge of the causes of the symptoms or how to control them.

The explanatory power of the mechanism of hypnoid isolation derived from the well-known properties of hypnotic states. Although hypnosis itself is not fully explicable even now, it was known then that the hypnotized subject's behavior was marked by increased suggestibility, amnesia for the events of the hypnotic state, and the ability to carry out posthypnotic suggestions. That symptoms might result from ideas arising in a special state, that they might exist apart from normal consciousness without the patient's awareness, and that they might continue to have effects long after the original experience, could be derived from the hypnoid state once it was assumed, as Breuer did, that the hypnoid state had properties similar to those of the hypnotic.

What Breuer did not explain so successfully was how the hypnoid state, the bearer of the symptoms, was revived. He described two very different kinds of revival. In the first, the hypnoid state reappeared as a consequence of a later experience having some similarity with one first experienced in the hypnoid state. For example, Anna O.'s hallucinations and paralysis first recurred as she reached, with arm outstretched, toward a bent stick resembling the hallucinatory snake she had tried to ward off the evening before (Breuer and Freud 1895, pp. 216–217). The appeal of this explanation is to associationism of an intuitive kind for, as we have already said, Binet (1892) pointed out that associationist psychology proper is quite unable to account for such connections between two different states of consciousness.

The second kind of revival Breuer described was when the memories of the *condition seconde* became strong enough to appear as a totality, as a *double conscience* (Breuer and Freud 1895, pp. 42–43). The difficulty of this explanation is that strengthening is not defined independent of the appearance of the secondary consciousness. Strengthening *is* the reappearance of the hypnoid state. At best, what it involves can be understood by reference to similar cases of double consciousness and multiple personality, the coherence of whose secondary states had frequently been remarked upon in the literature. The gradual strengthening in Anna O.'s case was but another instance of this well-known fact.

Breuer explained how symptoms might be present permanently in an otherwise normal state by supposing that the *condition seconde*, which contained the symptoms, was able to coexist with the normal state (Breuer and Freud 1895, p. 217). Experimental work by Binet and the two Janet's demonstrated how simultaneous communication with the two states of consciousness was possible. One might converse with the subject verbally on one topic while at the same time conducting inquiry into other matters through automatic writing. Neither mode of communication would influence the other. Typically, the subject spoken to showed extreme puzzlement on seeing the written communication (P. Janet 1886; J. Janet 1888; Binet 1889). Although the two states of consciousness were separate, they must nevertheless have been active at the same time for the two communications to have been possible. Given those demonstrations, the appearance of the symptom in Anna O.'s normal state was no more inexplicable.

This interpretation stands even if we allow, as Bernheim's demonstration suggests, that there is not an absolute lack of communication between the primary and secondary states. Nemiah (1974, 1985), who advocated the revival of Janet's theory, and Hilgard (1977), who actually revived dissociationist thinking, both suggested ways of resolving the apparent contradiction. Van der Hart and Braun (1986) also made some comparisons with Hilgard's neodissociation theory.

Although Breuer proposed no methods by which the mechanism of hypnoid isolation might be tested, the virtual identity of the hypnoid and hypnotic states indicates that hypnotic experiments could be used to test it. The kinds of experiments Charcot conducted, and those like Luria's (1932) done since in inducing conflict under hypnosis, although not without their problems (Reyher 1962; Sheehan 1969), go some way to testing the value of Breuer's supposition.

The major weakness of Breuer's explanation is its inability to account for symptoms that are not reproductions of hypnoid experiences. Some of Anna O.'s symptoms, including the paralytic contractures of the left extremities and the paresis of the neck muscles, were of this kind. No real explanation was proposed for them:

they never came up in the hypnotic analyses and were not traced back to emotional or imaginative sources. I am therefore inclined to think that their appearance was not due to the same psychical process as was that of the other symptoms, but is to be attributed to a secondary extension of that unknown condition which constitutes the somatic foundation of hysterical phenomena.   (Breuer and Freud 1895, pp. 44–45)

A similar problem exists when the symptom symbolizes an experience, for example, when hysterical vomiting symbolizes moral disgust. Although this mechanism was not observed in Anna O., it was sufficiently common in other patients for Breuer and Freud to note it in the *Preliminary Communication* (p. 5). Something other than simple isolation is required to explain how an experience is transformed into a symbol.

We have already noted how Breuer's later insistence that only affect-laden ideas could produce symptoms is inconsistent with certain of the facts about Anna O. Given that the hypnoid origin of the symptom explained the isolation from normal consciousness, it also seems unnecessary. Anna O.'s *caprices* had no affect directly associated with them. Neither the *caprices* nor Breuer's general explanation limited the power to produce symptoms to affect-laden ideas. Breuer may have thought the role of abreaction in removing symptoms required this recognition of the role of emotion in their formation. The surmise that only affect-laden ideas caused symptoms may have been necessary to explain the results of treatment, but it is not at all necessary to explain symptom formation.

Counterwill and Associative Inaccessibility

Quite apart from whether the histories of hysterics always show the presence of hypnoid states, the mechanism of hypnoid isolation is of limited generality. Similar problems are found with the intermediate mechanisms of counterwill and associative inaccessibility. The explanations deriving from both are limited to fairly circumscribed situations—exhaustion in the case of counterwill and excess affect for associative inaccessibility—and both depend on an undefined tendency to dissociation.

Counterwill poses another problem. The exhaustion has to be one capable of weakening the substrate of the intention without affecting (or perhaps not affecting as much) the substrate of the counterintention. No process of *general* exhaustion can produce a *selective* emergence of some of the host of counterintentions—the supposition defies all logic. Freud was forced to postulate the equally unsatisfactory idea of a partial or selective exhaustion. Later, in *Studies on Hysteria*, where counterwill is treated as a kind of supplementary mechanism, he seems to assume general exhaustion (Breuer and Freud 1895, pp. 91–93).

With associative inaccessibility there was also the half-voiced but very doubtful implication that excessive affect alone somehow prevented associations from forming. The idea was not unknown in the psychological literature of the period. Maudsley (1867, pp. 119–120) determined that by itself, strong emotion prevented "the free course of varied associations." In his view, strong emotion was a persisting tension of the energy of a nerve cell. And, "in proportion to the degree of persistent tension must be the retardation of, or hindrance to, the process of association." Although it is not known if Freud was aware of this particular proposition of Maudsley's, he did know of the work in which it appeared, if only because it had been cited by Charcot (Charcot 1887/1889, p. 308, n. 2). Janet certainly knew of it as he cited it in 1903 in *Les Obsessions et la Psychasthénie*. But Maudsley cited no evidence and advanced no argument to support the idea. Two years later Freud asserted the more usual proposition: "In general ... the part played in association by an idea increases in proportion to the amount of its affect" (Breuer and Freud 1895, pp. 165) but, oddly enough, in the unpublished *Project* of about the same period he appealed to a self-observation in support of his original notion (Freud 1950/1954, chapter II, section 6).

Although the concept of an affectively charged memory linked in a subconscious association could explain the isolation of the symptom, a *condition seconde* had to be present or to form with it. In that respect, associative inaccessibility had no advantage over hypnoid isolation.

Repression

According to Freud, the mechanism of repression began when an idea incompatible with the individual's normal standards presented itself to consciousness. It was then pushed out by a deliberate act of will and lost to consciousness when repression stripped the idea of its affect. In hysteria the affect was converted into a bodily symptom, and in the obsessions and phobias it was attached to another idea.

As Breuer indicated, repression was difficult to understand:

We cannot, it is true, understand how an idea can be deliberately repressed from consciousness. But we are perfectly familiar with the corresponding positive process, that of concentrating attention on an idea, and we are just as unable to say how we effect *that*.   (Breuer and Freud 1895, p. 214)

The difficulty arises because repression is uncharacterized and only expresses a relation. We know what it *does* but we do not know what it *is*.

Patients initially recall nothing of the origin of their symptoms. After resistances have been overcome, memories of traumatic events are recovered, each with its quota of affect intact. From those recovered memories the original perception of the traumatic event is reconstructed. Repression is an inference from the difference between the reconstructed, affect-laden percept and the presumed unconscious affectless ideas. The essence of repression lies in the detachment of the affect from the idea. As observed before, it is more correct to say that that detachment *is* repression. What Freud does not tell us is how it comes about.

As discussed in chapter 4, when Freud first described repression he placed considerable emphasis on its connections with observable behavior. For example, patients described the act of will, the symptom appeared afterward, and it disappeared after abreaction. As Freud's theory developed, these links became less important; patients might be unaware of their acts of will or even that they had once had an unwanted idea. Similar simple observational links were lost when it was proposed that affects might have to summate or a symptom might not appear immediately after a given trauma. The change made it very difficult to say when repression took place, to specify the conditions under which it occurred, or even to know if it had taken place at all.

Repression is quite different from any of the other mechanisms. Charcot and Janet proposed that symptoms formed as a consequence of a deficiency in a normal process, and Breuer invoked the similarity of hypnosis with hypnoid states. In contrast, and apart from the fact that its resemblance to everyday processes were themselves not understood, repression did not resemble or derive from any other process. Its explanatory power cannot be evaluated by evaluating anything else. This is not to say that repression is not consistent with any other theory. Certain of the characteristics of the memory of the traumatic event are in fact consistent with association psychology. From that theory it might be expected an idea lacking affect is neither distinguishable from other ideas in consciousness nor able to form associations with them. Depriving an idea of its affect would then account for its unconsciousness and isolation. The affect itself, lacking normal pathways of discharge, persists, rather than being forgotten in the ordinary manner, and is more vivid and forceful when recalled than in the normally forgotten, nonrepressed idea. Some of the qualities of the traumatic memory are thus consistent with the affect having been detached from its idea, but that tells us little about whether or not repression really takes place.

Although repression is consistent with some associationist notions, there is actually a fatal inconsistency. For an affect to be converted and for its idea to become unconscious, the separation of the two has to be complete or nearly complete. For abreaction to take place, however, the idea has to be recovered with its affect still attached. Symptom formation thus requires repression to separate the idea from its feeling, but symptom removal requires that they remain attached. The inconsistency remains whether the affect is supposed to be converted into a permanent somatic innervation or displaced onto another idea. It is also most improbable that the idea is stored as an unchanging, permanent trace (Loftus and Loftus 1980). However, if it is synthesized anew on each recollection, how is it, or how does it seem to be, exactly like the original?

What the mechanism of repression does seem to possess is generality. A single principle seems to explain not only the different kinds of hysterical symptoms, but the symptoms of other psychoneuroses as well. But, to explain how they came about, Freud had to invoke dispositional concepts that were as uncharacterized as repression itself. He was completely vague about how the tendency to form a *condition seconde* manifested itself other than through hysterical symptoms. The capacity for conversion was also uncharacterized, a point clear to Storring in 1900 (cited in Decker 1977, pp. 237–238, n. 4). A similar dispositional concept, one for displacing affect, was proposed to explain obsessions. None had definable properties. Each capacity or tendency was a post hoc inference from the fact that different patients undergoing similar experiences developed different symptoms. The very generality of the mechanism of repression derives in part from the completely uncharacterized dispositions on which Freud supposed it to operate.

The Symptoms of the Actual Neuroses

Freud derived his explanations of the symptoms of the actual neuroses from inadequacies or abnormalities in the discharge of somatic (i.e., physical) sexual excitation. He supposed that somatic sexual excitation arising in the sexual organs ordinarily formed linkages with the person's ideas of sexuality—what he called the psychosexual group of ideas—thereby creating libido and initiating sexual activity. In the absence of normal avenues of discharge, the somatic sexual excitation was deflected from the psychosexual group of ideas into the autonomic nervous system to produce there the physiological concomitants of orgasm, such as accelerated breathing, heart palpitations, and sweating, that were experienced as anxiety. In neurasthenia, although linkage took place, the threshold for discharging somatic sexual excitation was so low that it occurred too frequently. Neurasthenic symptoms, particularly the central symptom of weakness, were the result of the draining away of somatic sexual excitation.

The mechanisms have an attractive simplicity and plausibility. Each neurosis had its own cause: incomplete gratification caused anxiety neurosis, and masturbation or spontaneous emission produced neurasthenia. The general irritability in anxiety neurosis and its periodicity seemed adequately explained. Undischarged somatic excitation produced an irritability that waxed and waned with it. The characteristic circumstances under which anxiety neurosis developed also seemed to be explained; for example, in deliberate, prolonged, abstinence, the excitation simply built up to intolerable levels, finally exhibiting itself in the attack; in virginal anxiety, on the other hand, the linkage could not take place because the psychosexual group of ideas were too immature; again, neurasthenia in the male caused anxiety in the female because the male was unable to provide complete gratification for his partner. The reported loss of libido was also accounted for. Excitation was so regularly deflected that the normal linkage could not be reinforced by the pleasurable sensations accompanying orgasm. Gradually the link was broken, the libido declined and eventually disappeared completely. The lowered threshold for discharge appeared to explain one of the more puzzling features of neurasthenia: the excessive frequency of masturbation and spontaneous emission. Too little somatic excitation had to build up before there was a demand for another discharge—an automatic tendency to repetition had been created.

However, for each of the actual neuroses the explanations of symptom formation are inadequate and contradictory. Freud seems only to have implied a parallel between normal postintercourse tiredness and neurasthenic weakness, and that the latter generated the former (Masson 1985, Draft B of Feb. 28, 1893). That hint, rather than an analysis, gives the only indication of how the central symptom formed. Although it might have been possible to sustain an argument of the type Ferenczi (1912/1952b) proposed much later, neurasthenic weakness as the cumulation of successively produced feelings of tiredness, the other symptoms are not accounted for. How could digestive system upsets or sensations of pressure on the head derive from postorgasmic feelings of weakness or tiredness? Freud does not even hint at how such symptoms are produced. As a result, neither the major nor the minor symptoms of neurasthenia are explained.

Examination of the proposal that masturbation or spontaneous emission lowers the threshold for discharge of excitation reveals a similar explanatory hiatus (Masson 1985, Drafts E, possibly of June 6, 1894, and G, possibly of Jan. 7, 1895; Freud 1895a, pp. 108–109). Too frequent discharge was said to be the consequence of a lowered threshold, but unless it can be shown how this occurs, the concept of a lowered threshold adds nothing to the explanation. What Freud assumed required explanation. Finally, the claim that the symptoms of *both* neurasthenia and anxiety neurosis might result from coitus interruptus involves a major contradiction between the two explanatory mechanisms. In neurasthenia, little or no excitation was supposed to be available for discharge. How could any anxiety be produced? On the other hand, the abnormal discharge of excitation in anxiety neurosis did not predicate either too frequent discharge or a lowered threshold.

The major inadequacy of the theory of anxiety neurosis, and one Freud recognized, is that it is not apparent why anxiety, rather than some other emotion, should be experienced. Freud supposed the internal, somatic excitation was perceived by the ego as an external threat. Anxiety was the emotion appropriate to a threat (Freud 1895a, p. 112). Because the somatic sexual excitation is not perceived by the patient, the explanation requires that it be intense enough to register as a danger but not intense enough to become conscious when forming its linkage with the ideas located in the ego. Although such a selective mechanism might be consistent with anxiety attacks during abstinence, when sexual ideas might not be being attended to, it is hardly consistent with the attention consciously directed to sexual ideas during coitus interruptus. The latency of the anxiety attack poses another problem. One would expect the attack to occur when the somatic sexual excitation was maximally intense, at intercourse or soon after, rather than forty-eight hours later.

An important but frequently overlooked modification to the above explanation, made within months of its publication, may be construed as Freud's attempt to overcome the failure to find a source for the anxiety. Freud now proposed that anxiety arose from the deflection, not of somatic sexual excitation, but *psychical* sexual excitation, that is, of libido itself:

In my short paper intended to introduce anxiety neurosis I put forward the formula that anxiety is always libido which has been deflected from its [normal] employment. (Freud 1898a, p. 268)

This is not the original formula at all, but it does overcome part of the difficulty of the earlier explanation. No bodily or somatic process has to be transformed into a psychological state; both the cause and its effect are psychological. But the gain is illusory; even graver problems are created. First, if the mental effects are now accounted for, the physical accompaniments are not. As will be seen later, Freud recognized this problem by supposing that incomplete gratification led to the build-up of toxic substances in the blood, which then produced the physiological responses of anxiety. Second, as Oerlemans (1949) realized, the mentalistic explanation blurs the distinction between anxiety neurosis and hysteria, perhaps making it impossible to distinguish between them. Compton goes further, arguing that once

the differentiation between psychic and somatic libido is, in effect, lost, the whole concept of neurasthenia and anxiety neurosis requires re-evaluation. Freud did not do so. (Compton 1972a)

In addition, the new explanation is achieved at the expense of the very observations that led Freud to propose a nonmental basis for the anxiety, namely, the cases of anxiety neuroses in the sexually anesthetic. Perhaps it is not surprising that, in the paper reporting the modification, such cases were not mentioned at all and that, twenty years later, Freud said coitus interruptus plays a far smaller part in such instances (Freud 1916–1917, p. 402). It is difficult to resist the conclusion that the problem caused Freud to evaluate his case material in a somewhat arbitrary way. To this observation we might add Compton's (1972a) claim that Freud's "inference about the anesthetic women is obviously incorrect, and without that inference there is nothing to require the assumption of anxiety without psychic mechanism."

Both mechanisms are deficient in explanatory power, in testability, and in the consistency of their assumptions. The central all-pervading weakness of neurasthenia cannot be derived from too frequent discharge of somatic sexual excitation. In anxiety neurosis this may be the source of either the physical or the mental symptoms, but not both. Requiring sexual excitation to be intense enough to be perceived as a threat is inconsistent with assuming it would not then be intense enough to form a linkage. It is difficult to see how the mechanisms might have been tested. Even were it the case that the production of somatic sexual excitation and libido could be established physiologically, the core concepts of a lowered threshold and deflection would not thereby be tested.

Conclusions

In the sense that no mechanism has the potential for reflecting real processes, there is little to choose among those Charcot, Breuer, Janet, and Freud proposed. Hypnoid isolation has the greatest explanatory power, is the most readily testable, and has greatest consistency in its assumptions, but it is of extremely limited generality. Realization also explains only a limited number of symptoms, and those not very satisfactorily. Even had it been possible to characterize realization by the theory of ideomotor action, its fatal inconsistency is being based on the idea of an action being equivalent to the idea of no action. Restriction of consciousness involves no inconsistencies in assumptions but, being linked with an uncharacterized theory of perception, lacks testability and generates only pseudoexplanations. Repression resembles realization and restriction of consciousness in being uncharacterized and, to that extent, also untestable and nonexplanatory. Like realization, it is based on an inconsistency: it requires the assumption that affect can be detached from an idea but somehow remain linked to it. Hypnoid isolation, counterwill, and associative inaccessibility can all be rejected because they explain such a limited number of cases, but there is no real basis for rational choice among the other mechanisms.

Charcot and Janet did assume the presence of a hereditary predisposition that Breuer and Freud demonstrated was not present in their own cases. That demonstration led to the rejection of Charcot's and Janet's proposals and it also rather illogically led to the acceptance of the equally defective mechanisms of repression and hypnoid isolation. What seems to have been overlooked is that the tendencies to the splitting of consciousness and the capacity for conversion required by Breuer and Freud were undefined predisposing factors having exactly the same logical status as hereditary disposition.

Freud's descriptions of psychological forces did seem close to everyday experience, and the characteristics of the recovered memories also seemed to be consistent with some of the tenets of association psychology. However, the fact that the explanations given by repression of a wider range of symptoms were really pseudoexplanations seems not to have been appreciated.

The mechanisms Freud proposed for explaining the symptoms of actual neuroses similarly lack testability and are based on inconsistent assumptions. With respect to explanatory power, there are differences between the actual and the psychoneuroses. The symptoms of neurasthenia are not explained at all and the central symptom of the anxiety attack only partly so, and repression "explains" too much.

Repression is an uncharacterized theoretical term that has been substituted for the relation Freud wanted to explain. It tells us only what the repression is supposed to do, not what it is, and it has no potential for referring to real processes. Consequently, we should not be surprised to find that its main role has been to add to the difficulties of testing psychoanalytic theory.

Notes

1. The argument is strengthened rather than weakened by recent reports of the visualization of genes, the DNA helix, and the atom.

2. I had thought my extension of O'Neil's proposal to be unique, however, Williams (1989) described Ampère's understanding of theoretical entities in a similar way. The view attributed to Ampère does not have to derive from Kant or be tied to a religious view of the world.

3. Ockham does not seem to have formulated this principle as "entities are not to be multiplied without necessity."

7 A Theory of the Neuroses

... to calm the perturbations of the mind and set the affections in right tune.
—Milton: *The Reason of Church Government*

In this chapter I examine the theory of which the mechanisms considered in chapter 6 are part. It is Breuer's and Freud's theory of neuroses as it existed in 1895, and I concentrate on the ability the theory gave Freud to explain the facts of neuroses.

Ordinarily, of course, we speak of facts and theories as opposites. A fact is something that can be seen, or at least agreed on, but a theory refers to something less certain, often being equated with mere speculation. Usually, theories are cast in terms that do not refer to things in the visible world and about which ready agreement is not possible. Therefore they tend to be dismissed as having little if anything to do with their more robust antipodean relations. Properly regarded, however, theories exist to explain facts. We develop them to understand facts and to guide us in our relationship to them.

A theory may explain its facts in different ways. Arnoult (1972) brought together a number of threads from discussions that began in the last century and suggested that theories may be classified as abstract, reductionist, analogical, or metaphorical. A theory is abstract if it is expressed in terms of processes, things, or events that cannot be sensed directly. The most abstract theories are expressed solely in mathematical and logical terms. To the extent that any theory includes unsensed processes among its propositions, however, it has a degree of abstractness. Further, the manner in which a theory is expressed may be more or less congruent with its subject matter as, for example, when a psychological theory draws on such concepts as habit, attitude, and motive, or when a physical theory uses such concepts as particle, mass, or acceleration. If a theory described these concepts at what was believed to be a more basic level Arnoult classified it as reductionist. In this category he would include theories of perception or learning set out in neurophysiological terms.

Finally, if the theory bears only a figurative relation to the subject matter, it is analogical or metaphorical. An analogical theory retains some of the essential properties of the subject matter, especially the proportionality among different components, whereas a metaphorical theory does not. A description of the transfer of excitation within the nervous system as a moving current draws on an electrical analogy, as it assumes the same direction, regulation, and intensity in the current flow as in the neural process itself. Freud's characterization of counterintentions as demons inhabiting an underworld is clearly metaphorical.

Breuer's and Freud's theory purports to be psychological but it is actually a mixture of analogical and reductionist. The apparently neurophysiological terms it uses to describe psychological phenomena are the conventional analogues of electrical processes of the time. However, of greater importance than the type of theory of which Breuer's and Freud's instantiates is the logical relation between the facts and the statements of which the theory consists. In this chapter I will argue that only if the facts can be deduced from the fundamental statements of the theory can we say that they are explained by it. A logical connection must therefore exist between the assumptions and the facts. Without that link, and however it is expressed, the theory will lack explanatory power. This point is true for all domains of inquiry, holding equally for the mathematical, physical, biological, social, historical, and human sciences.

The central assumption of Breuer's and Freud's theory was that the nervous system was governed by a tendency to minimize its level of excitation. The essence of their explanations was that neuroses resulted from abnormalities in the disposal of surplus excitation. I begin this chapter by examining the nature and origins of Freud's ideas about excitation within the nervous system, how Freud thought the disposal of the surplus was brought about, and how he related these notions to his ideas about emotions. The theory itself is then outlined, its logical structure exposed, and its status evaluated.

Excitation and Its Reduction

Freud's earliest theoretical remarks on hypnosis and hysteria in the *Preface* to his translation of Bernheim's *Suggestion* (Freud 1888c) and in the contemporaneous contribution to Villaret's *Handwörterbuch* (Freud 1888a) had it that both hypnosis and hysteria were based on changes in the excitability of the nervous system. Fragmentary as these remarks are, they are worth examining because the concept of changes in excitability blossomed into two central theoretical ideas: that of psychic energy and the principle of constancy.

In his *Preface* to Bernheim, Freud said Charcot's approach to hypnosis was based upon the supposition that

the mechanism of some at least of the manifestations of hypnotism is based upon physiological changes—that is, upon displacements of excitability in the nervous system, occurring without the participation of those parts of it which operate with consciousness.   (Freud 1888c, p. 77)

Here Freud appears to have been referring to the changes in reflex action, the contractures produced by mechanical pressure and the other signs of neuromuscular excitability. But even the less florid responses to suggestion were also based on physiological processes. The blows Charcot had given his subjects were suggestions containing an objective factor, independent of the physician's will, and they reveal a connection between various conditions of innervation or excitation in the nervous system.   (p. 83)

In Villaret, Freud argued that the explanation of hysteria should be similarly based

wholly and entirely on physiological modifications of the nervous system and its essence should be expressed in a formula which took account of the conditions of excitability in the different parts of the nervous system.   (Freud 1888a, p. 41)

He specifically mentioned such mental symptoms as the strange associations of ideas, the inhibitions of the will, and the characteristic emotional expressiveness as requiring physiological explanation. He emphasized that all the symptoms showed

changes in the normal distribution over the nervous system of the stable amounts of excitation. (p. 49)

Freud did not define what he meant by a normal distribution or stable amount of excitation, but his later discussion of the increased influence of psychological processes on the physiological in hysteria gave a clue:

hysterical patients work with a surplus of excitation in the nervous system—a surplus which manifests itself, now as an inhibitor, now as an irritant, and is displaced within the nervous system with great freedom.   (pp. 49–50)

Although, as K. Levin (1978, p. 65) says, Freud's concept of surplus is vague and broad (as is that of its distribution), it can be seen that Freud was thinking of normal psychological life carried out by relatively fixed or stable amounts of excitation that are apportioned among such functions as willing, forming associations, and expressing emotions. Given the embryonic quality of these ideas, however, Green (1977) is clearly mistaken in thinking that Freud was at this time using the very specific and theoretically more advanced concept of a quota of affect. As I showed in chapter 4, the formulation of that concept was inextricably bound up with Freud's completion of his paper on the organic and hysterical paralyses. In 1888 Freud spoke only about surplus excitation, not surplus affect, and claimed that the surplus in the hysteric inhibited or exaggerated those functions. In any case, Green cites nothing to support his claim.

At the end of his Villaret contribution, Freud introduced the notion that the distribution of the surplus was controlled by ideas:

we may say that hysteria is an anomaly of the nervous system which is based on a different distribution of excitations, probably accompanied by a surplus of stimuli in the organ of the mind. Its symptomatology shows that this surplus is distributed by means of conscious or unconscious ideas. Anything that alters the distribution of the excitations in the nervous system may cure hysterical disorders: such effects are in part of a physical and in part of a directly psychical nature. (Freud 1888a, p. 57)

In his *Preface* to Bernheim, he gave ideas a rather more complex role than the relatively simple one Charcot had given them. In analyzing the action of the ideas used in inducing hypnosis, Freud began by supposing that closing the eyes led to sleep because eye closure was linked through connections inherent in the nervous system to the idea of sleep. Once the eyes were closed, sleep could occur only if there were present

changes in the excitability of the relevant portions of the brain, in the innervation of the vasomotor centers, etc. (Freud 1888c, pp. 83–84)

Excitation could be transmitted in both directions. The idea of sleep led to feelings of fatigue in the eye muscles and to changes in the excitability of the relevant parts of the brain. A hypnotic suggestion had its effects, then, because the idea suggested by the hypnotist produced alterations in excitability appropriate to it. The redistribution of excitation was thus effected through ideas and, as the phenomena of hypnosis and sleep showed, this was done unconsciously.

Three important notions of Freud's can be extracted from these remarks. First, psychological processes such as willing and the formation of associations could be described in physiological terms. Second, the manifestations of hypnosis and hysteria were based on changes in the distribution of excitation. Third, echoing Breuer and Charcot, hysterical symptoms could be conceptualized as due to a surplus of stimuli or excitation that was disposed of by unconscious ideas. I turn now to an examination of the details of these three notions and their sources.

Physiological Theorizing

A marked tendency to try to explain mental events in physiological terms can be discerned in the physiological and psychiatric literature of the second half of the nineteenth century. The particular form this tendency took in Germany, which provided the basis for Freud's thought, arose in opposition to the vitalist philosophy of the eminent physiologist Johannes Müller. Helmholtz, du Bois-Reymond, Brücke, and Ludwig, who were Müller's most distinguished pupils, formulated a distinctly materialist approach to physiological phenomena that could hardly have contrasted more with the outlook of their master (Bernfeld 1944; Cranefield 1957, 1966). Müller believed no continuity existed between the inorganic and the organic worlds: organic and inorganic substances differed in material composition, in the phenomena they exhibited, and in the forces on which they depended (Galaty 1974). The alternative position proposed by Müller's pupils was one of continuity, that all living phenomena were to be explained by physical or chemical forces or, were that not possible, by forces "equal in dignity," that is, equally material (Du Bois-Reymond cited in Galaty 1974; cf. Bernfeld 1944).

By the time Freud began to study medicine, this new biophysics movement, as it was called by Cranefield (1966, n. 5) in opposition to the misleading term "school of Helmholtz" coined by Bernfeld (1944), was well established. For some years Freud worked under Brücke, one of its cofounders, of whom he was to say some fifty years later that he "carried more weight with me than anyone else in my whole life" (Freud 1926b, p. 253). Brücke's field was the physiology of the nervous system, and his explanation of mental events was the opposite of Müller's. For example, Müller believed voluntary acts were the result of the "spontaneous and conscious direction of the nervous principle" to the appropriate part of the brain (Müller, cited in Amacher 1965, p. 17). Brücke, on the other hand, regarded all movement as due to reflexes; if consciousness was involved it was simply because the pathways conducting the nervous impulse went through the brain. As a causal agent, the mind could be eliminated from consideration (Amacher 1965, p. 18).

According to Amacher, Brücke himself devoted little time to psychological matters, regarding that topic as the province of his colleague, Meynert, the brain anatomist and psychiatrist. When Brücke did discuss mental events "he assumed that they were simultaneously paralleled by physical phenomena" (p. 16). Brücke's view, which he held in common with Meynert, allowed a process to be discussed partly in physiological and partly in psychological terms. Because he also worked with Meynert for some years, Freud was exposed to a double dose of this particular form of materialist philosophy. His own description of psychological processes in physiological terms is best seen as a direct influence of the biophysics movement (pp. 58–59).

The ways Brücke and Meynert conceived of reflexes and associations are especially important for understanding Freud's theory of hysteria. Brücke's major contribution was to extend the reflex doctrine, then recently clarified by Marshall Hall's work on spinal reflexes and endorsed by Müller, to all nervous action (Müller 1833–1840/ 1833–1842). Brücke accepted the results of recent histological studies of the brain as showing that the nervous system consisted of only two elements: nerve centers and nerve fibers. Some fibers connected sensory receptors to the nerve centers and others linked the centers to the muscles. Reflex action was produced when nervous excitation in the receptors was transmitted through the fibers to the centers and from there to the muscles. Because the system contained just the two elements, Brücke maintained that a reflex mode of functioning was the only one possible (Amacher 1965).

Meynert added his concept of the cortical reflex to Brücke's schema to explain how new connections or associations were formed. Laycock (1845) and Sechenov (1863) made similar proposals at about the same time, and although Meynert very probably knew of Sechenov's formulation, we do not know if he knew of Laycock's (Amacher 1965, p. 18, n. 12). Brücke followed Marshall Hall in supposing that most reflex elements were located below the level of the cortex. But, because direct electrical stimulation of certain areas of the cortex produced movements, Meynert went on to suppose that some permanent trace of the images of the sensations and perceptions involved in reflex movement were laid down in the cortex. Projection bundles of white matter linked the cortical cells in which the traces were registered to the subcortical centers and to the receptor and motor systems. Electrical stimulation of the cortical cells revived the trace, and excitation was transmitted to the muscles to initiate movement (Meynert 1884/1885, p. 144).

Meynert also supposed it was the association bundles in the white matter that connected the traces in the different cortical cells with one another (p. 150). In his opinion, these anatomical and physiological facts provided the whole basis for mental life. Images were brought into association with one another through the association bundles, and those associations provided the basis for the formation of new concepts and for inductive reasoning itself, which Meynert, like Wundt, regarded as the fundamental logical function. As early as 1865 Meynert claimed that his analysis of the anatomical structure of the brain provided a material basis for traditional associationist psychology (p. 153).

More than an anatomical structure was required, of course. Some means of activating it was necessary. The transmission of excitation through the nervous system was thought to fill that need. In the late 1840s du Bois-Reymond demonstrated that the propagation of the nervous impulse was accompanied by detectable electrical phenomena. Bernstein's investigations in the late 1860s showed it was most probable the nerve impulse was propagated by successive local depolarizations rather than by a direct transmission or transfer of physical energy. And when Helmholtz measured the velocity of the neural impulse in 1880, it turned out to be too slow for it to be an electric current. Nevertheless, excitation of the elements of the nervous system and the transmission of excitation within it tended to be thought of as analogous to electrical processes. Some kind of electricity was thought to energize the anatomical structures that Brücke and Meynert regarded as fundamental to behavior and to mental life.

Possibly because a unitary kind of excitation and a single mode of action provided little room for any vitalist principle, Brücke assumed the nervous system had only one type of excitation, and that only reflexes were elicited as it was transmitted from receptor to effector. For him, excitation was transmitted along preformed pathways, but Meynert used the same idea to account for the opening up of new ones. He proposed that when two cortical cells were simultaneously excited, the excitation was transmitted from one to the other along the association fibers connecting them. For example, if an animal was simultaneously seen and heard, images were simultaneously registered in cells in the visual and auditory areas of the cortex. Subsequent excitation of either type of cell caused excitation from it to be transmitted to the other and reexcite it. Thus, when only the sound of the animal was heard, excitation was transmitted along the previous pathway from the auditory cells to the cells in the visual area, where it revived and brought to consciousness the sight of the animal.

Meynert extended his physiological associationism to provide an alternative to Müller's vitalist explanation of voluntary movement. When the limbs were first moved, innervations from the muscles were registered cortically and associations were formed with other simultaneously present cortical images. At some later time, the excitation of the images reexcited the motor registrations. Excitation was then transmitted through the subcortical centers to the muscles (Meynert 1884/1885, pp. 153–161). Meynert believed that he had provided a physiological foundation for memory, inductive thinking, association by simultaneity, and voluntary movements.

Excitability and Hysteria

Benedikt's *Elektrotherapie* of 1868, Oppenheim's analysis of the role of ideas in hysteria (both cited in K. Levin 1978, pp. 48, 67), and Donkin's article in Tuke's *Dictionary* show the approach of Brücke and Meynert to mental activity to be consistent with a well-established mode of theorizing about hysteria, one that moved easily between psychological and physiological levels of descriptions. According to Donkin, the cardinal mental characteristic of the hysteric was

an exaggerated self-consciousness dependent on undue prominence of feelings uncontrolled by intellect—that is to say, on the physical side, an undue preponderance of general widely diffused, undirected nervous discharges, and an undue lack of determination of such discharges into definite channels. (Donkin 1892)

Like those of Brücke and Meynert, Donkin's particular suppositions were different from Freud's, but this mixture of the physiological and psychological was basic. The hypnosis literature contained a similar tendency to physiological theorizing. Even Bernheim, who advocated a psychological explanation of hypnosis, could discuss the concentration of attention as

the fixing of the nervous force upon the phenomenon,—the idea or image suggested,—is what appears to dominate. (Bernheim 1887/1888a, p. 153)

Freud's theorizing was therefore grounded in a well-established tradition.

Freud also seems to have built on some ideas that Charcot derived from the use of electricity in the treatment and diagnosis of nervous system disorders. From about the middle of the 1700s electricity was used to treat hysteriform disorders, and in about 1850, after du Bois-Reymond's investigations of the electrical nature of the nervous impulse, the method became quite popular. Electrical stimulation was recommended to restore sensibility, to overcome paralyses, and to reduce excitability (Arndt 1892a). Although it is very probable that observations of diagnostic value were made in the course of these treatments, it was Duchenne's experiments that provided electrical diagnosis with a systematic basis. In 1849 Duchenne (de Boulogne) distinguished the paralyses according to the response of the muscles to electrical stimulation. Hysterical paralyses were among those in which stimulation caused muscular contraction but in which sensation was either abolished or diminished (Stainbrook 1948).

Charcot brought the observations of muscular function made by Duchenne and the related therapeutic applications of electricity by Vigouroux (both at the Salpêtrière) together into a systematic method for exploring muscular and sensory function. He claimed to have coined the term "electrodiagnosis" (Charcot 1875–1877/1877, p. 30). He used the method to characterize the level and type of excitability of disease-affected muscles and nerves, combining that information with the results of traditional neurological examination. For example, he said some permanent muscle contractures were due to continuous and above normal levels of stimulation coming from a lesion in the spinal center that normally produced muscle tone (Charcot 1876–1880/1883, p. 268). He interpreted the symptoms of another type of spinal lesion as showing "a sort of inertia or stupor of the electrical elements of the nervous system" (Charcot 1887/1889, p. 28). Another example is his implication of a type of hyperexcitability of the cortical motor cells in a number of organically based conditions (pp. 37–38). Stable neurological symptoms were the result of stable, organically based alterations in the excitability of the nervous system. Hysterical symptoms could therefore be described as exhibiting their own stable patterns of changed excitability (pp. 87–89) and could also be presumed to be based on stable changes in the excitability of the nervous system.

Freud himself used electrical methods of treatment even before he visited Charcot's clinic (Bernfeld 1951), and probably used electrodiagnosis to examine his first independently studied patient with hysteria (Freud 1886b). But the influence of Charcot and the biophysics movement was more important to his theorizing about the means by which surplus excitation was disposed of by the nervous system.

Surplus Excitation and Its Removal

Freud's view that the hysteric attempted to dispose of a surplus of excitation had its basis in the physiological schemata of Brücke and Meynert, in the neurological theories of Hughlings Jackson, and possibly also in the semimystical speculations of Fechner.

According to Ellenberger (1956), Fechner was fortunate enough to have had revealed to him a number of the laws and principles according to which the universe functioned. One was that mental energy obeyed the general law of the conservation of energy and could neither be created nor destroyed. Mental energy, however, could be augmented, but only at the expense of physical energy. Fechner also formulated a principle of stability that he believed showed that mental activity was directed toward establishing stability. If mental energy increased, some activity had to occur to restore the original stable state.

Once the hysteric was thought of as having a surplus of excitation, the need to dispose of the surplus could be deduced from this "law" of Fechner's. However, although Freud was to acknowledge the contribution of Fechner to some of his ideas, the stability principle seems not to have been among them (K. Levin 1978, p. 89 and n.60). Nevertheless, Fechner's ideas were so well known it would have been impossible for Freud not to be familiar with them. And, in a part of Meynert's work that was clearly known to Freud, Meynert used Fechner's conservation law to explain, among other things, the supposed inhibition of cerebral blood flow during directed thinking (Meynert 1884/1885, pp. 248–252). This explanation is, of course, consistent with the notion that physical movement reduces the level of mental energy associated with thinking.

Brücke's and Meynert's descriptions of the way in which the nervous system worked could also be subsumed under a principle that required surplus excitation to be reduced. Brücke believed that successive excitations from repeated stimulation might have to summate before a particular reflex was elicited. The theory was common. James (1890b, vol. 1, chapter 3) cites a large number of authors who from 1873 on put forward a similar concept of summation and discharge. For Brücke, food might lodge in the esophagus for some time but produce only an occasional swallowing movement. The presence of the food

creates a constant stimulus. It lasts a long enough time during which the stimuli are summed so that it can release a reflex movement.   (Brücke 1876, cited in Amacher 1965, p. 14)

Summation of stimuli can be viewed as a local accumulation of a surplus of excitation, and the reflex swallowing movements as an attempt to dispose of it. In this view also, even the simple law of nervous conduction from receptor to center to muscles, which Meynert (1884/1885, p. 138) supposed to be all that was required to account for central nervous system activity, could be regarded as a means for disposing of the local surplus of excitation created by stimulation of the receptors. Now, neither Brücke nor Meynert attributed a purpose of any kind to reflex movements. That step was Freud's, and it is this that most distinguishes his approach from those of his predecessors.

As Sulloway suggests, Breuer may have been an influence in Freud's attributing purpose to reflex action. He claims that the Hering-Breuer reflex was "one of the first biological feedback mechanisms to be documented in mammals" (Sulloway 1979, pp. 51–52). It is now notorious how easy it is to interpret inhibitory control mechanisms as showing purpose and being directed toward teleological goals. Perhaps, as Sulloway suggests, Breuer's understanding of how the vagus nerve is involved in the self-regulation of breathing also was reflected in the ease with which he and Freud adopted the constancy principle (pp. 64–65). It should be noted, however, as Mancia (1983) points out, that Freud's own models lack a real inhibitory component. K. Levin (1978, pp. 89–93), of course, observed that the constancy principle owes nothing to these kinds of "physiological considerations." He was able to do so by classing Freud's *Project* as a clear "exception to Freud's pattern of emphasizing psychological interpretations" (p. 7), rather than as a work that "contains within itself the nucleus of a great part of Freud's later psychological theories" and that throws light "on some of the more obscure of Freud's fundamental hypotheses" (editorial introduction to Freud 1950/1954, *Standard Edition* 1, p. 290).

I intimated in chapter 4 that the work of Hughlings Jackson, the eminent British neurologist, seemed to me to be the greatest of all the influences that caused Freud to consider the possibility that the nervous system was guided by the purpose of disposing of excessive quantities of excitation. Freud read Jackson's works when preparing his own monograph, *On Aphasia* (Freud 1891/1953). Jackson argued that speech ejaculations:

are all parts of emotional language; their utterance by healthy people is on the physical side a process during which the equilibrium of a *greatly* disturbed nervous system is restored, as are also ordinary emotional manifestations.   (J. H. Jackson 1879–1880a)

He continued:

All actions are in one sense results of restoration of nervous equilibrium by expenditure of energy. (ibid. My emphasis)

These excerpts come from the part of Jackson's paper devoted to a topic of special interest to Freud, the so-called recurrent utterances or uncontrollable remnants of speech sometimes left to an otherwise speechless patient. We know Freud read this paper because he quoted from it, referred to case material contained in it, and endorsed Jackson's opinion that the ejaculations were all part of emotional language (J. H. Jackson 1878–1879, 1879–1880a,b; cf. Freud 1891/1953, pp. 56, 61).

Freud first indicated his belief that the nervous system acted to reduce excitation within twelve months of reading Jackson's paper. As we have seen, up to the first half of 1891, when *On Aphasia* appeared, he only spoke of hysteria as being based on an abnormal distribution of a surplus of excitation. The addition of a purpose, his characterizing the nervous system as acting to reduce its level of excitation, was first mentioned in the letter to Breuer on June 29, 1892. After referring to "our theorem of the constancy of the sum of excitation" he set out the proposition that

The chronic symptoms [of hysteria] would seem to correspond to a normal mechanism. They are displacements in part along an abnormal path ... of sums of excitation which have not been released. *Reason* for the displacement: attempt at reaction.   (Freud 1892, p. 148. My emphasis)

A few months later, in November 1892, when the theorem was spelled out in a little more detail, Freud not only expressed this reason or purpose more clearly, he made explicit a quite new feature that allowed him to explain mental symptoms:

The nervous system endeavors to keep constant something in its functional relations that we may describe as the "sum of excitation." It puts this precondition of health into effect *by disposing associatively of every sensible accretion of excitation* or by discharging it by an appropriate motor reaction.   (pp. 153–154. Emphasis altered)

In one sense it was easy to understand the physical symptoms. They were conversions of motor reactions that had gone awry. Only if associations were put on the same footing as movements could mental symptoms also be seen as the result of an abnormal disposal of excitation.

Association by simultaneity and symbolization were the two associative methods Freud thought could go wrong in disposing of increases in excitation (Breuer and Freud 1895, pp. 176–180). An innervation present simultaneously with excitation caused by a trauma could become directly associated with it (conversion). Symbolization occurred when the innervation came to stand in a verbal sense for an essential feature of the trauma. An insult might bring about a hysterical pain if the insult was experienced as a slap in the face at the time the patient was suffering from a trigeminal neuralgia. A physical basis as direct as this was not always necessary, however. A piercing look directed at a patient could result in penetrating head pains.

Sandler (1967) seems to be the only psychoanalyst to have noticed this subtle change in Freud's thinking. He did not appreciate its significance, however, remarking only that disposing of excitation by associative reaction "goes rather further" than motor reactions. But only by this associative generalization of his reflex model could Freud allow for the formation of associations to be as effective as movements in disposing of surplus excitation.

Although it may have been Breuer's and Freud's observations on Frau Cäcilie's symbolic symptoms that gave impetus to their publishing the *Preliminary Communication*, it is Jackson who apparently was the source of the theoretical underpinning. On the very page on which Jackson wrote of speech ejaculations restoring an equilibrium, he quoted the opinion of an unknown author that swearing had value as a safety valve for feelings and as a substitute for aggressive muscular action. Jackson then quoted another anonymous view that "he who was the first to abuse his fellowman instead of knocking out his brains without a word, laid thereby the basis of civilization" (J. H. Jackson 1879–1880a). Freud repeated both of Jackson's points exactly in the lecture he gave on his and Breuer's new theory of hysteria (Freud 1893a).

Unlike Forrester (1980, pp. 18–21), I do not think the parallel between Freud's conceptualization of the isolation of the hysterical symptom and Jackson's of the isolation of the recurrent utterances of the aphasic was the sole or even important influence in directing Freud's attention to the role of affect in isolating the symptom. Jackson hypothesized that the content of some of these recurrent utterances was determined by what was about to be spoken at the time the patient was taken ill. He believed a discharge of nervous arrangements formed the material substratum of speech, its physical basis, and from his observations on speech and memory he went on to infer that after one had finished speaking the

nervous arrangements just discharged remain for a short time in a state of slight independent organization.   (J. H. Jackson 1879–1880b)

In the aphasic, the nervous arrangements were kept in a state of greater readiness to discharge, later becoming fixed by the very repetition consequent on their being the patient's only speech (J. H. Jackson 1879–1880a, 1879–1880b). Where the utterance was jargon, Jackson supposed it to consist of elements of the real words the patient had been trying to put together prior to uttering. Strong emotion accompanying the onset of the cerebral insult caused the elements to be too hurriedly assembled so that, instead of saying, "Pity me" or "Come, pity me," the patient formed such sound combinations as "pittymy" or "committymy" that could not be broken down further. These nervous arrangements for speech remained "permanently in a state of dischargability far above normal."

Forrester interprets Jackson's remarks about recurrent utterances to mean that the nervous arrangements retain their high level of undischarged energy in a now *permanently closed* and *permanently activated* circuit, separated off from the other nervous elements.   (Forrester 1980, p. 18. My emphasis, MBM)

He is then able to draw what I believe is a quite specious implication that functionally isolated aphasic utterances parallel affectively isolated hysterical symptoms.

Freud concluded his remarks on recurrent utterances by offering an explanation of his own for their isolation:

I am inclined to explain the persistence of these ... modifications by their intensity if they happen at a moment of great inner excitement.   (Freud 1891/1953, p. 62)

He was correct to imply that Jackson had no explanation. Although Jackson concluded that the nervous arrangements for normal speech went out of function soon after speaking had finished, and that in the aphasic there remained "lines of less resistance than before," he was able to speak of the arrangements only as having "*somehow* achieved a degree of independent organization" (J. H. Jackson 1879–1880b. My emphasis).

Jackson later tried to connect the fixity of the recurrent utterance to what he saw as the closely related problems of the persisting memory of the last position of an amputated hand (phantom limb), of epileptic automatisms, and of repetitive actions carried out by unconscious head-injured patients. He grouped these phenomena together to

make a basis for the discovery of the reason why there is a fixation of states, which are normally temporary, upon the sudden occurrence of lesions of the nervous system.   (J. H. Jackson 1889)

But, apart from showing how the cases illustrated his doctrine of evolution and dissolution, he did not achieve his goal. Indeed, he had to admit of a man whose hand had been blown off while holding a glass, but whose phantom hand "retained" that position:

The persisting memory, so to call it, of the last position of the lost hand implies a persisting state in the highest centers. Why that state remained permanently, *it is impossible for me to say*. (ibid. My emphasis)

Therefore we must look elsewhere than to these ideas of Jackson's for an explanation of isolation of symptoms.

Having said that, Freud's shift to an emotional explanation may nevertheless owe something to Jackson. Not only did his own explanation involve excitement, but Jackson several times implicated strong emotion as contributing to the form as well as to the content of recurrent utterances. He also came close to suggesting that emotion contributed to their isolation as, for example, when he proposed that "strong emotion tends to more automatic, inferior, utterance" (J. H. Jackson 1879–1880b). And we must remember the way in which Jackson's reference to popular language in discussing aphasic incapacity could well have resonated with Freud's, so evocative is it of Charcot and Janet. As we saw in chapter 4, in both of the slightly different explanations Freud sketched of associative inaccessibility, the connection of his concepts about isolation with those of Charcot and Janet is very clear. It was not simply because ideas were invested with an excessive quota of affect that different ideas could not be associated with one another; it was because they occurred in different states of consciousness. However, once Janet proposed that ideas determined the characteristic features of hysterical symptoms, Freud could incorporate Jackson's notions of affect and of nervous system functioning into his pathophysiological formula.

Freud's proposal that associations were as potent as movements in disposing of excitation provided an affective basis for explaining catharsis as well as the formation of mental and physical symptoms. The *talking* cure could be reinterpreted as a *cathartic* method, emphasizing the expression of real emotion rather than mere narrative. It is precisely because Freud did not make this proposal until 1892 that I maintained in chapters 1 and 4 that if Breuer's method were based on discharge at all, it was really working off by utterance.

Giving the reflex the purpose of disposing of excitation explained symptom formation and removal. None of Freud's colleagues or predecessors found it necessary to formulate a purpose for the reflex, probably because what they had to explain gained nothing from it. For example, although Brücke declared that when a reflex was released by virtue of the summation of stimuli "the previous state of rest is reestablished" (Brücke 1876, cited in Amacher 1965, p. 14), he did not propose the recreation of that state to be the purpose of the action. A superordinate principle of that kind would have added only a scientifically undesirable vitalist purpose, or at least a teleological goal, to his otherwise materialist explanation. The Brücke and Meynert models had movements as their sole consequences and required nothing to explain them. But if it could be assumed that all the functions of the nervous system were guided by a tendency to dispose of surplus excitation, the reflex reaction could be regarded as only one of the means by which that end was achieved, and others might achieve the same goal. All behavior, normal as well as abnormal, could well be brought under the rubric of this inbuilt purpose.

Freud referred to his new found canon variously as the theorem, the theory, or the principle of constancy. It became the starting point for his general theory of behavior as well as for that of the neuroses. The same proposition, or one very like it, is at the core of modern psychoanalytic theory.

Emotional Expression and Symptom Formation

Toward the end of the nineteenth century the work on emotion that stood above all others was Charles Darwin's *The Expression of the Emotions in Man and Animals* (1872). Given that Freud's theory of hysteria held in part that hysterics suffered from abnormalities of emotional expression, it was not surprising that Freud should have adopted some of Darwin's ideas. What Darwin provided, however, was rather more than a few isolated theoretical constructs. His conceptualization of emotional reactions as being caused by the disposal of surplus amounts of nerve force or excitation matched Freud's ideas almost exactly. Because their basic concepts fit so well, Darwin's influence on Freud was rather greater than the two slight references to *Expression of Emotions* in *Studies on Hysteria* suggest. In fact, once Freud had adopted Darwin's theory, all he had to account for was how the abnormal expression of an emotion was transformed into a symptom.

Freud had the opportunity of knowing Darwin's work simply because he lived at a time when it created considerable interest, and he said that he was strongly attracted to Darwin's theories when he enrolled in the *Gymnasium* (Freud 1925a, p. 8). We know also that his first independent scientific work was conducted under Carl Claus, the eminent German Darwinist (L. B. Ritvo, 1972), and that he had owned a copy of Darwin's *Expression of Emotions* probably since 1881 (pp. 235–236). Ritvo also mentions Meynert as a more direct but little noted source that may have drawn Freud's attention to Darwin's book.

Over a number of years Meynert had been in profound theoretical disagreement with Darwin about the role of inheritance in expressive movements. Meynert's lengthy appendix to *Psychiatry* (1884/1885) contained an argument that the movements through which the emotions were expressed resulted from inbuilt connections within the nervous system having nothing at all to do with inheritance. Although he rejected Darwin's thesis on the inheritance of modes of emotional expression, Meynert appears to have accepted the central proposition that some of the movements were activated by excess nervous excitation. It was this that was to have the greatest impact on Freud.

Darwin began by supposing that nerve force selectively activated the various groups of muscles involved in emotional expression. He then drew very heavily on Herbert Spencer's essay, "The physiology of laughter" (1860), to support his contention that emotions increased the amount of nerve force, and that it was the flow of nerve force to the various parts of the musculature through which an emotion was expressed. Darwin quoted and endorsed Spencer's principle:

As Mr. Herbert Spencer remarks, it may be received as an "unquestionable truth that, at any moment, the existing quantity of liberated nerve-force, which in an inscrutable way produces in us the state we call feeling, *must* expend itself in some direction—*must* generate an equivalent manifestation of force somewhere." (Darwin 1872, p. 71)

He added that

when the cerebrospinal system is highly excited and nerve-force is liberated in excess, it may be expended in intense sensations, active thought, violent movements, or increased activity of the glands. (p. 71)

Darwin went on to accept a second of Spencer's principles:

Mr. Spencer further maintains that "an overflow of nerve-force, undirected by any motive, will manifestly take the most habitual routes; and, if these do not suffice, will next overflow into less habitual ones." (p. 71)

Darwin used Spencer's two principles to account for normal and abnormal expression of emotions. Normal expression occurred when emotional states of moderate intensity activated the habitual routes or pathways laid down by selective inheritance. The actual expression was comprehensible because those pathways were either currently appropriate (as when one ran in fear) or they had been appropriate at some previous evolutionary stage. Abnormal emotional expression resulted from intense emotions or frustrated moderate emotions causing nerve force to flow into channels not normally used. For example, jumping for joy was an abnormal expression of happiness, the result of overflow into motor channels.

The Accumulation and Transfer of Excitation

Little wit is required to see how readily Darwin's theory can be integrated with Freud's thought. First, both Darwin and Spencer took a quantitative view of the distribution of nerve force—a surplus had somehow to be disposed of. Second, consistent with Jackson's remarks on the effects of action, and possibly with Brücke's on the effects of release after summation, their suppositions at least implied that a state of rest would be reestablished, if not that the purpose of nervous functioning was to maintain a state of rest. It is consistent with this implication that Spencer was to place this purpose centrally in *Principles of Psychology* (1873).

Amacher, among others, maintained that the analogy between the flow of a liquid and the mode of transmission of the nervous impulse, so readily apparent in Darwin and Spencer, is also present in the conceptualizations of Freud and his predecessors (Amacher 1965). Were this so, Darwin and Spencer could be thought of as reinforcing a mode of thought already familiar to Freud, perhaps even causing him to adopt it. However, careful consideration of Amacher's quotations from Brücke and a detailed examination of Meynert's *Psychiatry* fail to support Amacher's contention. In fact, in one of the few places where Meynert discusses nerve force (in a comment on Darwin's use of the phrase "the excess of nerve force"), he seems to reject the hydraulic analogy because he redescribes transmission in then conventional physiological terms (Meynert 1884/1885, p. 275).

Nor is it the case that a fluidic model is to be found in the *Outline of a Physiological Explanation of Psychological Phenomena* by Freud's colleague Exner (1894), even though the mode of transmission considered by Exner is different from that described by Brücke and Meynert. By the time Exner's book was written, Cajal's histological studies had been reasonably widely accepted as showing that the elements of which the central nervous system was composed were not connected to each other structurally. Between the elements were discernible spaces; there was discontinuity rather than continuity. As a consequence, the propagation of the nervous impulse also had to be discontinuous.

The new view of nervous system structure, or neuron theory as Waldeyer's hypothesis of 1891 came to be called, put paid to hydraulic and electrical models of neural transmission. Neither a fluid nor a current in the crude electrical analogy could flow across the gaps. Even if the nerve impulse were electrical, it could not be transmitted through a discontinuous system in the same way as a current might pass through a network of connected wires. Neuronal transmission could, however, be pictured as involving the accumulation and transfer of quantities of some kind of energy. For example, from the facts of summation at nervous centers described by Brücke, Exner inferred that successive stimulation caused excitation to accumulate in the neuron until it reached a level at which it was transferred across the gap to the next one. His view was that when two neurons were simultaneously charged with excitation, an "intercellular tetanus" was established between them, and a quantity of excitation moved from one to the other.

A quantitative account of neural transmission in Exner's interpretation of the neuron theory was still possible, at least in principle. Spencer's and Darwin's ideas could also be adapted to an accumulator-transfer model—a name I prefer to Rosenblatt's and Thickstun's (1970) accumulator-discharge—even though that model was neither hydraulic nor electrical.

Freud seems to have developed his version of the accumulator-transfer model as part of his preliminary theorizing about the actual neuroses and psychoneuroses. Until then there is no strong evidence of any such thinking. It was probably not tied to the neuron theory, as Freud not only did not foreshadow Waldeyer's hypothesis, as claimed by Brun, Jeliffe, Jones, Spehlmann, Ellenberger, and Sulloway, he was actually a very late convert to it (Koppe 1983). However, shortly after Freud's basic approach to the two kinds of neuroses crystallized, the accumulator-transfer model appeared explicitly in the speculative neurophysiological essay known as the *Project*, the first part of which he wrote in September 1895, and the ideas for which had been germinating over at least the previous five months (Freud 1950/1954, part I; Masson 1985, Letter of Apr. 27, 1895).

An accumulation-transfer model of the kind proposed by Exner provided plausible solutions to three problems that were by then very much in the forefront of Freud's thinking and that could not be accommodated in the older neurophysiological theories. First, in hysteria, the detachment of the emotion or affect from the idea and its conversion into a bodily innervation could be thought of as a quantity of excitation redistributed to some other part of the mental structures in much the same way as a charge of static electricity might be redistributed:

in mental functions something is to be distinguished—a quota of affect or a sum of excitation—which possesses all the characteristics of a quantity ... which is capable of increase, diminution, displacement and discharge, *and which is spread over the memory-traces of ideas somewhat as an electric charge is spread over the surface of a body.* (Freud 1894, p. 60. My emphasis)

Freud went on to remark that this hypothesis (or model) underlay the theory of abreaction, describing it with a hydraulic analogy involving the "flow of electric fluid" (p. 61). This description did not mean, of course, that Freud was adopting a hydraulic model; he was simply using a conventional analogy.

The second of Freud's problems was the way in which the separate traumas of the psychoneuroses sometimes seemed to summate before producing their final result. In the accumulation-transfer conception, the affects of the traumas could be thought of as building up in a common store rather as a battery might be charged. After reaching a certain level, the total could be diverted onto another idea or into some part of the body. An accumulator model was also helpful in solving the third problem of the way somatic sexual excitation seemed to build up before being discharged. Here too, Freud used a hydraulic analogy to describe how excitation in neurasthenia was impoverished; it was as if the store of somatic sexual excitation had been "pumped empty" (Masson 1985, Draft G, possibly of Jan. 7, 1895).

Meynert pointed out that Darwin's explanation of emotions required little or no real knowledge of the nervous system. Nerve force, whatever that was, flowed along vaguely defined channels or pathways. Darwin's hydraulic model therefore overcame gaps in scientific knowledge about real anatomical pathways, real nervous impulses, and real ways in which excitation was propagated. Freud's accumulator-transfer model has the same characteristics. Solomon (1974) and Mancia (1983) noted that Freud's quantum of energy in motion is a mechanical analogy, the latter adding that, like most of his other neurophysiological concepts, it is

unacceptable or at least highly questionable, not only in the light of present-day knowledge of neurophysiology, *but even of knowledge in Freud's own time.*   (Mancia 1983. My emphasis)

Why did Freud hold to a view that was so at variance with the then known facts of the nerve impulse being propagated by local depolarization? I believe it was because he had the same need as Spencer and Darwin to overcome the lack of real knowledge of the physiology of the nervous system and its processes.

Precisely because it was analogical, Freud's accumulator-transfer model was able to describe the formation of complex associations like those in the pathogenic memory structure. In Meynert's theory, only those sensory components registered cortically and connected by association fibers could form associations. Little more than simple associations between the sight and sound of an animal or those between a stimulus and an approach or withdrawal movement could be built up. Associations of a more general and complex kind were not possible, especially those between memories of events having similar content or emotional quality and occurring with long intervals between them. A conception of energy accumulating in neurons before it was transferred overcame this limitation. Exner had already supposed the first transfer made subsequent transfers easier: it established what he called a *bahnung* ("pathway") or facilitation between neurons. The more frequently transfers took place and the greater the quantity of excitation transferred, the easier the facilitation. Contiguous neurons could thus be linked together; two neurons had only to be excited simultaneously for an association to be formed. The more often this happened, the stronger was the association and its tendency to be repeated (Exner 1894, cited in Amacher 1965, pp. 43–47).

Freud adopted Exner's view of facilitation and the formation of associations in his *Project* (Freud 1950/1954, part I, section 3). It had two advantages over the Meynert view: it enabled one to suppose that channels that had not been or could not be specified anatomically might link neurons in any of the ways required by the theory, and it allowed one to postulate ways for quantities of excitation to be dealt with other than by motor discharge.

As well as using a version of Exner's notions to explain facilitation and the formation of associations, a version Koppe (1983) shows clearly was an adaptation, not an adoption, and an idiosyncratic one at that, Breuer and Freud drew on them in several other ways (Breuer and Freud 1895, pp. 193, 195, 241). They supposed that Exner's concept of "intercellular tetanus" between adjacent neurons held for all conduction pathways, and that the total amount of this excitation defined the general level of excitation, or "intracerebral tonic excitation." Typically, this was distributed uniformly throughout the brain, but it varied with emotional state, with physiological need, and, as Exner also thought, with attention. The principle of constancy discharged and redistributed this excitation to keep it low in amount and even in distribution.

Freud's theory of symptom formation drew on these ideas by supposing that emotions or affects always increased intracerebral excitation in a nonuniform way. As Breuer put it:

It may be taken as self-evident that all the disturbances of mental equilibrium which we call acute affects go along with an increase of excitation.   (Breuer and Freud 1895, p. 201)

Broadly speaking, one of three things happened to the increased excitation: it found discharge in action, it found substitute discharge in speech (which involved motor innervations in any case), or it could "wear away" in the effort involved in forming associations with other ideas or otherwise level out. As Freud stated with respect to the suppressed reaction to an insult:

a healthy psychical mechanism has other methods of dealing with the affect of a psychical trauma even if motor reaction and reaction by words are denied to it—namely by working it over associatively and by producing contrasting ideas. Even if the person who has been insulted neither hits back nor replies with abuse, he can nevertheless reduce the affect attaching to the insult by calling up such contrasting ideas as those of his own worthiness, of his enemy's worthlessness, and so on ... finally the recollection, having lost its affect, falls a victim to forgetfulness and the process of wearing-away.   (Freud 1893a, p. 37; cf. Freud 1950/1954, part III, sections 1 and 3)

Breuer also apparently believed that in those cases of fear and anxiety when motor and associative reactions were not possible the increased excitation disappeared "by a gradual leveling out" (Breuer and Freud 1895, p. 202). However:

If ... the affect can find no discharge of excitation of any kind along these lines.... The intracerebral excitation is powerfully increased, but is employed neither in associative nor in motor activity. In normal people the disturbance is gradually levelled out. But in some, abnormal reactions appear.   (pp. 202–203)

Abnormal reactions led to "the passage of cerebral excitation to the vegetative organs" or it flowed off "in primitive movements" because excessive excitation bypassed or broke through "the coordinative centers" (p. 204).

The essential characteristics of hysteria were not abnormal patterns of emotional expression, however. These lay in the vicissitudes of the original affect. An intentional failure to discharge the affective excitation along adequate pathways provided the primary motive for the formation of symptoms. Symptoms began to form only when a tendency was created for subsequent discharge to follow the same abnormal pathway. Anything threatening to revive the original affect, such as an attempt to recollect the original trauma, would lead to a discharge like the first. Through repetition, this tendency to abnormal discharge would be strengthened. Finally, the affect would be discharged before the idea with which it was first associated could be remembered. Any stimulus tending to revive the original idea now produced only the abnormal reaction. The affect had been converted into a pattern of discharge. At the same time, the idea, being now deprived of all affect, would be indistinguishable from other affectless ideas. In other words, it would be unconscious. A similar process produced obsessions and phobias. There the separation was followed by the affect attaching itself to another idea and being discharged through the recurrence of the second idea. The first idea had, of course, become unconscious too.

Actual neuroses were also the result of abnormal responses to increases in excitation, and the theory applying to the psychoneuroses was consonant with them. All that had to be recognized was that the excitation resulted from a continuously operating, endogenous physical process rather than from an occasionally experienced affect. The physical process was assumed to produce pressure on the walls of the seminal vesicles and stimulate nerve endings there. Periodically that nervous excitation, or somatic sexual excitation, exceeded a threshold level and was transmitted to that part of the cerebral cortex where the ideas of sexuality were registered. By becoming connected to or forming a linkage with this psychical sexual group of ideas, somatic sexual excitation charged them with energy and created psychical sexual tension or libido that raised the level of intracerebral excitation. The principle of constancy then brought a tendency for the libido to be discharged. In the mature adult, discharge was through a specific or adequate action leading to the complex spinal reflex involved in orgasm. Discharge through orgasm relieved the pressure on the seminal vesicles, removed the whole of the previously existing somatic sexual excitation, and thereby reduced the level of psychical tension or libido. The theory obviously applied to males, but Freud believed it also applied to females, even though he recognized that women had no corresponding site where somatic sexual excitation was produced (Freud 1895a, p. 109).

The various kinds of incomplete gratification inhibited sexual function and resulted in somatic sexual excitation being deflected from the psychical sexual group of ideas. As was noted in chapter 5, psychical tension or libido was then not created and normal discharge was not initiated. Somatic sexual excitation spilled over into the autonomic nervous system to produce the physiological symptoms of anxiety. The

increase in excitation was concurrently sensed as a threat to the organism and generated the psychological feeling of anxiety (Freud 1895a). In the neurasthenic, masturbation produced lowered thresholds for linkage and discharge. Since excitation was
produced continuously, discharge took place too frequently. The result was that
sexual substances were depleted and the symptoms of neurasthenia ensued.

According to Darwin's theory, emotional expression resulted from increased nerve
force flowing into normally used pathways or into ones not usually available. Freud's
theory was similar. Increases in cortical excitation were followed by attempts to
reduce the level of excitation, but symptoms might result if unusual pathways were
innervated. Concurrent excitation of the muscular and sensory apparatus, often
present fortuitously, created a strong tendency for pathways of discharge to be
opened up to them, and resulted in the stable patterns of sensory and motor innervation that were the physical symptoms of hysteria. If the pathways to action were
unavailable or weak, some substitute figurative or symbolic expression of the affect
would result. Finally, if there was little or no discharge, the affect persisted in consciousness as a state of feeling (Breuer and Freud 1895, pp. 85–90, 164–169, 173–175,
180–181). The essential difference between Freud's theory and Darwin's was that
Freud had to explain how a transient abnormal emotional reaction could develop
into a permanent symptom.

The Theory

Critical evaluation of Freud's theory of abnormal psychology requires a more formal
account than I have so far provided. For this purpose I have arranged statements
constituting the theory according to content. They cover three topics: the creation
and disposal of excitation within the nervous system, affects and the consequences of
their expression, and the discharge of sexual excitation. After outlining the theory I
attempt to evaluate its logic.

The statements themselves are paraphrases of what appear to be the essential
propositions set out by Breuer and/or Freud. However, the second part of proposition 1.3 is not in Breuer's theoretical section of the *Studies*, although it is clearly
implied in his discussion (Breuer and Freud 1895, pp. 198–200). Except for proposition 7.9, which is also implied in Breuer's discussion (pp. 200–201), the whole of the
third section is Freud's. It is based substantially on his first paper on the anxiety
neuroses (Freud 1895a), although I have made some use of his correspondence with
Fliess (Masson 1985). For the sake of completeness, I have added the notion that
depletion of sexual substances and sexual weakness caused neurasthenia.

1. Excitation within the Nervous System

1.1   In the waking state the conduction and connection pathways of the brain are in a condition of *tonic intracerebral excitation.*

1.2   The level of this excitation is increased by stimuli impinging on the organism from within and without.

1.3   Excitation arising from within the organism has a somatic *source* and tends to be of a periodic, recurring nature.

1.4   A tendency exists within the nervous system to maintain the level of excitation at a constant, uniformly distributed optimum.

1.5   The maintenance of excitation at this optimum level is achieved either by neural discharge to the motor system or by redistribution into other associational structures within the brain.

1.6   Neural discharge tends to take place along preformed pathways. When such a discharge is complete, an *adequate reaction* is said to have occurred.

1.7   Discharge of excitation within the nervous system is controlled by resistances between its component parts. A particularly strong resistance prevents discharge through the autonomic nervous system to the organs of circulation and digestion.

1.8   The strength of these resistances varies from one individual to another depending on innate disposition, or because of long-standing states of excitation having existed previously in some part of the system, for example, as a consequence of illness.

2. Affects and the Discharge of Excitation

2.1   The psychological side of an affect is a disturbance of the dynamic equilibrium of the nervous system. Acute affects in particular always increase with increases in excitation.

2.2   The adequate reaction to affectively produced increases in excitation may be preformed, reflex patterns of motor activity, substitute speech reactions, or the activation of associations representing ideas. Any of these reactions restores equilibrium in the nervous system.

2.3   The strength of recollected affects in memory is a function of the adequacy of the original motor discharge or of its *abreaction* in words.

2.4   When the individual fails to react intentionally, affectively produced increases of excitation may not be dischargeable through normal motor, speech, or associative activity. In some individuals the failure leads merely to an *abnormal expression of emotion*, but in those with disposition to conversion, hysterical symptoms result.

2.5   Abnormal emotional expression occurs when weak internal resistances fail to prevent discharge into the autonomic nervous system and the circulatory and digestive systems are disturbed.

2.6   Symptoms of hysterical convulsion result from the excitation overwhelming or bypassing the centers coordinating motor behavior; bodily symptoms result from the excitation being *converted* into a pattern of muscular and sensory innervation; mental symptoms are the continuation of the original affect.

2.7   In hysteria the selection of one pattern of discharge rather than another is determined by such factors as the strength of the resistances involved, the presence of simultaneous excitation elsewhere in the body (i.e., the law of association by simultaneity), and figurative or symbolic modes of expression.

2.8   The recollection of an affect originally discharged in an abnormal way causes a repetition of the abnormal pattern of discharge. Excitation is then said to be converted into somatic phenomena, that is, to have brought about a hysterical symptom.

2.9   Frequent repetition of such abnormal patterns of discharge reduces the excitation of the affect such that the idea associated with it enters consciousness deprived of affect. Conversion is then said to be complete.

2.10   In those with the appropriate disposition, failure of affective discharge may lead to the attachment of its quota of affect to another idea. In this case the affect remains in consciousness and is experienced as an obsession.

3. Sex and the Discharge of Excitation

3.1   The accumulation of *sexual substances* within the sexual organs produces physical or *somatic sexual excitation*.

3.2   When the level of somatic sexual excitation increases above a certain threshold value it is represented in the brain as a *psychical stimulus*, and the *psychical sexual group* of ideas (concerned with sexuality) are *supplied*, *invested*, or *cathected* with energy.

3.3   Cathection of the psychical sexual group of ideas by somatic sexual excitation creates *libido*, or psychical libidinal tension.

3.4   The *adequate* or *specific* action that reduces this excitation is the normal sexual act culminating in orgasm.

3.5   Masturbation lowers the threshold for the discharge of somatic sexual excitation.

3.6   The continuous production of somatic sexual excitation and a lowered threshold for discharge cause frequent discharge at low levels of libidinal tension.

3.7   Too frequent discharge depletes the sexual substances and causes sexual weakness and fatigue.

3.8   Sexual weakness and fatigue cause the typical symptoms of neurasthenia: intracranial pressure, spinal irritation, and dyspepsia with flatulence and constipation.

3.9   Somatic sexual excitation may be *deflected* from the psychical sexual group of ideas. When this happens libido does not form.

3.10   Somatic sexual excitation unable to form libido may be discharged into the autonomic nervous system, producing there alterations in heart rate, breathing, and sweat gland activity. Those alterations are the physical signs of the anxiety attack and are surrogates for orgasm.

3.11   The ego perceives undischarged tension as a threat, and perceived threat produces the affect of anxiety.

3.12   Undischarged somatic sexual excitation consequently produces the subjective signs of the anxiety attack.

The Logic of the Theory

When I set Freud's theory out, it was appropriate to group the statements according to their content. In evaluation proper, the logical structure has to take precedence. Its starting point is provided by the three very general propositions about constancy, affects, and sexual excitation. The other statements are either about the regulation of the discharge of excitation in the nervous system or about the psychological and physiological processes required to derive the explanations of the symptoms. Some of these latter are not particularly limited to the neuroses.

The most general of all of the propositions [1.4] expresses the principle of constancy without which the nervous system cannot function. When it is linked with any other proposition stating that the level of intracerebral excitation has increased, it necessarily follows that an attempt will be made to reduce the level of excitation. For example, if physiological needs such as hunger and sex increase excitation, they must result in an action designed to reduce the excitation.

A general proposition such as constancy may be empirical or theoretical. Acceptable explanations may begin from either. However, if the proposition is empirical, it is evident that a theory based on it cannot claim to explain the observations from which it was itself inferred. Breuer and Freud make claims of precisely this kind. Among the kinds of behavior from which they infer the principle of constancy are the need for mental activity after intellectual inactivity (when the level of excitation was presumed to rise), the similar need for movement after motor quiescence, the "torment of boredom" resulting from reduced sensory stimulation, and the various actions performed to satisfy needs. Each was said to be preceded by an increase in excitation that was experienced as unpleasure. Breuer then argued:

Since these feelings disappear when the surplus quantity of energy which has been liberated is employed functionally, we may conclude that the removal of such surplus excitation is *a need* of the organism. And here for the first time we meet the fact that there exists in the organism a "tendency to keep intracerebral excitation constant." (Breuer and Freud 1895, p. 197. Original emphasis altered)

In the same discussion this newly formulated principle is used to explain such behaviors as purposeless motor activity, individual differences in the ability to tolerate mental and physical inactivity, the uncoordinated motor behavior of the infant in response to need, and the convulsions of the epileptic and the hysteric. Most of these behaviors are similar to the ones from which the principle was inferred and some are actually identical to them. The explanations generated from the principle are tautological.

Two kinds of observations would allow the principle of constancy to provide an acceptable explanatory starting point: neurophysiological measures of the level of cortical excitation, and independent behavioral changes directly correlated with them. Only observations of that kind could index the level of excitation before and after discharge and independent of motor activity or rest.

The second general proposition is that affects increase the level of intracerebral excitation [2.1]. When combined with the principle of constancy, it logically entails that emotional states will be followed by attempts to reduce the extra excitation. This entailment carries weight only to the extent that it can be shown, either directly or indirectly, that emotions actually produce increases in excitation. This is just what Breuer and Freud failed to do. Indeed, Breuer regarded the increase as self-evident (p. 201). Rather unnecessarily, then, he cited some behavioral evidence. But the behaviors (jumping for joy, crying with grief) were again of the very type requiring explanation.

The need to index the increases in intracerebral excitation caused by somatic sexual excitation [3.2] is also clear. Neither the general restlessness consequent to sexual deprivation nor the quiescence after orgasm, which Breuer cited as indexing the extremes of intracerebral excitation, can be so used. It is precisely those behaviors the changed levels of excitation are supposed to explain. The point applies most forcefully to general restlessness, because that is one of the symptoms of anxiety neurosis the theory should account for.

The lack of evidence for these three propositions independent of the behaviors to be explained by them is fatal to the theory. Breuer and Freud did not adduce acceptable independent evidence of a behavioral or neurophysiological kind for any of the propositions. Nor can that evidence be found today.

Defects in explanatory power resulting from the lack of independent evidence are just as marked when the propositions about the regulation of the discharge of excitation in the nervous system are considered (e.g., 1.4–1.8, 2.2, 2.4–2.7, 3.4–3.5, 3.9–3.10). The propositions about discrete pathways of discharge, resistances between sections of the nervous system, preformed actions capable of bringing discharge about, and associational structures capable of disposing of excitation are all used in conjunction with one or other of the three general propositions to explain the direction of discharge. For example, given an increase in somatic sexual excitation, knowledge that linkage was unavailable and resistance of the autonomic pathway was weak would explain why the discharge produced the physiological responses characteristic of anxiety. However, none of the concepts referred to in the propositions were defined other than by the gross behaviors that they were supposed to explain. Thus the autonomic reactions occurring in the anxiety attack were the sole indicators of weak resistance.

Similarly, even though the absence of an adequate motor response might be inferred from the patient's recollection of the traumatic event, failure of an associative reaction to occur was actually indexed by the conversion itself. Again, whereas hysterical convulsions were said to result from excitation breaking through the resistances surrounding the motor coordinating center, the presence in the convulsions of so-called primitive movements was the sole basis for inferring that the resistances had been broken (Breuer and Freud 1895, p. 204). The lowered threshold for the discharge of somatic sexual excitation in neurasthenia was also inferred from the very increased frequency the changed threshold was invoked to explain. In addition to nonindependence, the many concepts incorporated into this group of propositions that seem to refer to physiological processes are actually pseudocharacterized terms. Their referents are the very relations they are supposed to explain.

In contrast, the remaining propositions are capable of independent investigation and would, if true, add to the completeness and power of the explanations. Thus, if it were true that the strength of an affectively toned memory was a function of the adequacy of the original affective discharge [2.3], explanations of the formation of hysterical symptoms by conversion through successively repeated abnormal discharges would be strengthened. Again, if depletion of sexual substances did cause sexual weakness and fatigue [3.7], neurasthenic symptoms would be explicable. However, even though it is possible to investigate these propositions without any commitment to Freud's methods, or even to the study of abnormal conditions, it is not in fact known if they are true or false.

The following schematic outlines of the explanations of hysteria and the actual neuroses show the explanations generated by Freud's theory to consist of assumption piled on assumption rather than a linked set of propositions entailing the facts. They lack genuine logic.

The assumption that the nervous system operates according to the principle of constancy, together with the presumed regulating structures, implies that if increases in intracerebral excitation occur, the disposal of that excitation will be regulated by the structures. Assuming now that emotions raise the level of excitation, it follows of necessity that those structures will similarly regulate discharge consequent on emotional experience. By further assuming that particular types of regulatory defects, such as unavailability of a motor response or normal associative connections, direct excitation to the muscles of the body concurrently excited, hysterical symptoms such as paralysis and contractures are initiated. Two further assumptions account for the formation of permanent symptoms: attempted revivals of the idea originally associated with the affective experience repeating the abnormal discharge, and the frequent repetition of such discharge leading to the idea being completely deprived of its affect.

The actual neuroses are "explained" similarly. Assume that as sexual substances accumulate they produce increases in somatic sexual excitation. Assume the excitation has to reach an optimum intensity before its assumed connection with the psychical sexual group of ideas results in adequate discharge of excitation. Assume that masturbation lowers the threshold for discharge, that repeated discharge at low levels of intensity depletes the sexual substances, and that those consequences cause the symptoms of neurasthenia. It then follows that masturbation causes neurasthenia. Again, assume that somatic sexual excitation not discharged by linkage and orgasm is directed into the autonomic nervous system, assume that such discharge produces physical signs of anxiety and that the undischarged excitation is perceived as a threat, and assume that perceptions of threat generate the affect of anxiety. It then follows that deflected excitation causes the objective and subjective symptoms of anxiety neurosis.

Stated like this, the weaknesses of the explanations are almost self-evident. Assumptions are simply piled on top of one another until a pseudological chain has been constructed between the starting propositions and the clinical facts. If the worth of a theory is proportional to the evidence supporting its assumptions, Freud's theory is very unsatisfactory indeed. It is quite unable to explain either psychoneuroses or actual neuroses. It is not so much that the propositions are incorrect or that they lack direct or indirect empirical support. Rather the inadequacies arise because, for too many of the propositions, it is impossible to imagine what sort of evidence could show them to be correct or incorrect.

The Freud-Breuer Difference

Before concluding, I must defend my characterization of the particular combination I have presented here of Breuer's theoretical chapter of the *Studies* and Freud's theory of the actual neuroses as Freud's theory. Freud wholly dissociated himself from Breuer's chapter (Masson 1985, Letter of June 22, 1894), but it has not been possible until recently to say why he so sharply separated it from his own contribution.

Differences did exist over the relevance of the French concepts of psychopathology. By 1895 Freud had abandoned all notions that symptoms formed in other than the waking state or that treatment ought to be carried out other than in it, and his theoretical concepts changed accordingly. Breuer's theorizing had not at all kept pace (K. Levin 1978, p. 111). But the discussions in *Studies on Hysteria* show it was possible to reconcile the two approaches (Freud 1893a; cf. K. Levin 1978, p. 117).

A second source of disagreement was Breuer's fairly conservative theorizing as compared with Freud's tendencies to speculation. Even before the *Preliminary Communication* was published, Freud complained to Fliess:

My hysteria has, in Breuer's hands, become transformed, broadened, restricted, and in the process has partially evaporated.   (Masson 1985, Letter of July 12, 1892)

The difference hinted at here became marked by the time of the *Studies*. For a start, and although he believed hysterical symptoms were built on a physiological foundation, Breuer attempted a purely psychological mode to explain them. As he put it at the beginning of his theoretical chapter:

In what follows little mention will be made of the brain and none whatever of molecules. Psychical processes will be dealt with in the language of psychology; and, indeed, it cannot possibly be otherwise. If instead of "idea" we chose to speak of "excitation of the cortex," the latter term would only have any meaning for us in so far as we recognized an old friend under that cloak and tacitly reinstated the "idea." For while ideas are ... familiar to us ... "cortical excitations" are on the contrary rather in the nature of a postulate, objects which we hope to be able to identify in the future.... Accordingly, I may perhaps be forgiven if I make almost exclusive use of psychological terms.   (Breuer and Freud 1895, p. 185)

At almost the same time as Breuer was refusing to speculate, Freud was attempting just the opposite. Nothing could contrast more with Breuer's stance than the physiological and reductionist position with which Freud began his *Project*:

The intention is to furnish a psychology that shall be a natural science: that is, *to represent psychical processes as quantitatively determinate states of specifiable material particles.*   (Freud 1950/1954, part I, introduction. My emphasis)

Given the ignorance of neural processes at the time, Breuer warned against exactly this line of approach:

The substitution of one term for another would seem to be no more than a pointless disguise. (Breuer and Freud 1895, p. 185)

Freud was prepared to risk that result but Breuer was not.

Breuer largely restricted himself to such descriptive physiological terms from the contemporary scientific vocabulary as excitation, transmission, and resistance, without trying to explain or characterize them further. Thus, precisely while he was restricting his use of these physiological terms, treating them as givens, Freud began his speculative and pseudoquantitative characterization of them. His effort was to prove as unsuccessful as Breuer's comments implied it would be (Solomon 1974; Mancia 1983; Koppe 1983).[1]

In his introduction to *Studies on Hysteria*, the editor concludes that Breuer's theoretical chapter shows the same neurological bias as Freud's *Project* (*Standard Edition*, 2, pp. xxiii–xxv). If this were so, the above argument, which is based on the proposition that precisely this bias was a major point of disagreement between Breuer and Freud, would have to be rejected. What the editor seems not to have appreciated is that Breuer simply used neurological terms in a conventional and almost descriptive way, whereas Freud was attempting a further speculative characterization of them.

It has also been argued that Freud was the conservative theorist and that it was Breuer who possessed the truly speculative mind (Gedo, Sabshin, Sadow, and Schlessinger 1964; Schlessinger, Gedo, Miller, Pollock, Sabshin, and Sadow 1967). Breuer is therefore supposed to have been the one who made unwarranted leaps from concrete observation to remote theoretical construct. The argument is based on a comparison of statements by Breuer and Freud in *Studies on Hysteria* and judgments about the magnitude of the gap between the empirical and theoretical levels those statements reveal. The conclusion of Gedo et al. and Schlessinger et al. cannot be accepted. It is based on a number of methodological deficiencies of which the most gross concerns the material compared. Breuer's one case observation and the single theoretical chapter are contrasted with Freud's four case observations and his chapter on psychotherapy, which contains almost no theory. Breuer had virtually unlimited opportunity to theorize, but Freud was quite restricted. It would be surprising had the analysis shown a difference other than the one Gedo et al. and Schlessinger et al. report.

Before it can be concluded that one was more speculative than the other, equivalent kinds of materials from Breuer and Freud have to be compared. Either the case history material alone from the *Studies* ought to be analyzed or, since the interest is in how theoretical statements are used, Breuer's theoretical chapter should be contrasted with Freud's *Project*. If that were done there is no doubt whatever Freud was the more speculative of the two, an opinion Friedman (1977) also holds, although on somewhat different grounds. But, at the time the *Studies* was begun, the difference was not marked.

By maintaining that hysterical symptoms were intrusions from a secondary consciousness, Breuer also avoided completely Freud's concept of an unconscious mind as a kind of repository for repressed ideas. He clearly disapproved of thinking of unconscious processes in a way that gave them substantive properties (Breuer and Freud 1895, pp. 227–228). Possibly this is why he placed the phrase "in the unconscious" in quotation marks when he introduced that concept to his theoretical chapter in the *Studies* (p. 45, n. 1). Among a number of psychoanalytic writers, Abrams (1971a) especially noted how Breuer's conception of mental life was fundamentally different from Freud's.

Third, it has frequently been remarked that disagreements about sexual factors per se were not responsible for Freud's disapproval. At the time of the *Studies* Breuer seems to have been prepared to place at least as much stress as Freud on sexual factors (Breuer and Freud 1895, pp. 245–247; cf. Sulloway 1979, chapter 3, appendix A). However, an important difference in the way they thought about them recently came to light. In my view it explains two things: why Freud dissociated himself so strongly from Breuer's chapter, and Freud's puzzling later characterization of Breuer's hypnoid explanation as based on "a theory which was to some extent still physiological" (Freud 1914a, p. 11).

For Breuer, psychologically determined symptoms were erected on the foundation of "an idiosyncracy of the whole nervous system." It was, he emphasized, "a building of *several stories*" (*es ist ein mehrstöckiges Gebäude*). Developing the analogy, he went on:

Just as it is only possible to understand the structure of such a building if we distinguish the different plans of the different floors (*Stockwerke*), it is, I think, necessary ... for us to pay attention to the various kinds of complication in the causation of symptoms. If we disregard them and try to carry through an explanation by employing a single causal nexus, we shall always find a very large residue of unexplained phenomena. (Breuer and Freud 1895, pp. 244–245)

Hysterical stigmata and nervous symptoms such as some pains and vasomotor phenomena, even perhaps pure motor convulsions, "were not caused by ideas" but resulted from the fundamental abnormality of the nervous system. To try to attribute them to psychological causes was, he concluded,

just as though we tried to insert the different rooms of a many-storied house into the plan of a single story (*eines mehrstöckigen Hauses auf dem Grundrisse eines Stockwerkes eintragen*). (pp. 244–245)

Now, the most interesting thing about Breuer's argument is its placement. It occurs half-way into the very last section of his theoretical chapter, just after his discussion of those symptoms and characteristics he saw as resulting from innate and abnormal excitability, and just before his discussion and endorsement of sexual factors as "the most numerous and important of the ideas that are fended off and converted."

We can be fairly certain what Freud thought of Breuer's attack on single-nexus causation. From a previously unpublished portion of a letter to Fliess we learn that one of Freud's case histories was not to be

included in the collection with Breuer because the second level (*Stockwerkes*) that of the sexual factor, is not supposed to be disclosed there. (Masson 1985, letter of May 21, 1894)

Hence, although both agreed on the importance of the nexus of sexual factors, Breuer's interpolation clearly showed his unwillingness to derive all the symptoms from them.

Even with these two last very considerable differences, it is nevertheless possible to accept the theory Breuer outlined in the *Studies* as reflecting his own and Freud's views before Freud's speculative theoretical tendencies became prominent. Many years ago Bernfeld concluded from his analysis that the theory presented by Breuer "is conceived in the spirit of the 'physicalist' physiology, in complete accordance with Freud's earlier thinking, and represents Freud's ideas at the time of his collaboration with Breuer.... It is Freud's as well as Breuer's" (Bernfeld 1944). Nothing in the *Project* or the correspondence with Fliess, neither of which was known to Bernfeld, requires this conclusion to be modified (Amacher 1974; Waelder 1956b). Freud's own much later praise and endorsement of Breuer's theoretical contribution to *Studies* may even support it (Freud 1923a, p. 236; 1925e, p. 280).

Conclusion

My evaluation has concentrated on the formal or logical characteristics of Breuer's and Freud's early theory rather than on its content. In this respect it is unlike the assessments made by Thompson (1957) and Stewart (1967). In the final analysis, it is the logic of the relations between the propositions and between the propositions and the facts that determines whether a theory is worthwhile or not. Only when a theory implies its facts can it be said to explain them, and only when factual consequences can be deduced from a theory can it be said to be testable (Nagel 1959; O'Neil 1969, pp. 67–84). Unless the logical structure is present, to carry the content as it were, the content can have only limited meaning. This is why the language in which a theory is expressed is of such little moment. Ever since Braithwaite's (1953, pp. 88–114; 1960/1962) analysis of the relation between a theory and its model, it has been clear that, regardless of its type, a model can be adequate for its theory only if it has an identical logical structure. The types of models are defined by their content; it follows that the logical structure is a more important component of the theory than its content.

Many models are of a visual kind and, although visual imagery may be useful in thinking about structures and processes that cannot be seen, whether or not a structure or process resembles some picture of it visually or not is not the issue, as Ellman and Moskowitz (1980) point out. Sometimes it turns out that there is a resemblance, as with Harvey's pores. As often as not, however, as with subatomic particles or multidimensional space, for example, it does not make sense even to ask about the similarity. What does make sense is to make explicit the conceptual link between what we cannot see and the model. This means arriving at an independent characterization of what we cannot see. To take Ellman's and Moskowitz's example, the link between the DNA molecule and the picture of it as a double helix is given by its characterization "in purely geometric terms, without reference to its visual appearance" (1980).

An equally important reason for concentrating on the logical structure of Freud's early theory is that the logical deficiencies revealed in it are very like those of the later theory (Nagel 1959). Deficiencies such as lack of explanatory power and testability, use of assumptions having no empirical referents, and reliance on uncharacterized theoretical terms seem to reflect Freud's *style* of theory construction as much as the *standards* by which he judged the adequacy of his explanations. A connection of this sort between his early and late theories would not have been revealed if content had been the main consideration. We expect, of course, that these deficiencies will also show up in the applications of the theory to be considered in chapter 8 and in the later alterations to it outlined and evaluated in chapters 9 and 10.

Note

1. Pribram is one of the few neurophysiologists who states that the concepts of the *Project* relate positively to modern neurophysiology (Pribram 1962, 1965; Pribram and Gill 1976). I find his argument unconvincing. Not only is the central notion of cathexis not at all like the graded electrotonic excitations with which he identifies it (Swanson 1977), but neural transmission does not involve transfer of anything like the quanta of energy Freud postulated (Grenell 1977). Neither does Pribram mention the lacuna of an inhibitory process. I would add further that Pribram's thesis that the *Project* is based on a binary model of processing (from which he argues for Freud's anticipating modern information theory) is simply not supported by anything Freud wrote in the *Project* or elsewhere.

8 Expectations, Actual Neuroses, and Childhood Seduction

Miss Prism: Memory, my dear Cecily, is the diary we all carry about with us.
Cecily: Yes, but it usually chronicles the things that have never happened, and couldn't possibly have happened.
—Wilde: *The Importance of Being Earnest*, Act II

In this chapter I examine Freud's investigations of hysteria and the actual neuroses. For both disorders I will bring out how Freud's expectations about the kinds of causes likely to be at work created his clinical "facts" and how his explanations misinterpreted them. The context of the discussion is provided partly by evaluation of the theoretical ideas considered in chapters 6 and 7, and partly by analyses of the etiological equation and the assumptions underlying the pathogenic memory structure in part I. It will become apparent that Freud's approaches to understanding the causes of hysteria and the causes of the actual neuroses were identical.

It is well known that Freud's first attempt at explaining hysteria independent of Breuer and Charcot collapsed over a relatively short and clearly defined period. After gradually building up a thesis that hysteria was caused by parental seduction, he suddenly made an about-face. That his theory of actual neuroses was also abandoned is much less commonly remarked. In part the reason is that it subsided gradually, rather as an old balloon gradually shrivels and deflates. For the psychoneuroses, the alternative explanation that he found appeared to overcome the deficiencies of the earlier theory, and it was eventually easy for Freud to acknowledge that his seduction explanation really had been incorrect. Without a happy outcome of that kind, the theory of the actual neuroses eked out an existence of sorts in a shadow world, being neither definitely accepted nor rejected. Despite a number of modifications, it never became satisfactory, and toward the end, Freud virtually granted that the actual neuroses could not be explained. A number of his co-workers went even farther: they doubted there were or ever had been any such disorders.

Because it is evident that the expectations generated about the actual neuroses were simply transferred to hysteria, I begin with the former before considering the seduction theory.

The Actual Neuroses

I deal successively with the problems of Freud's theory of the actual neuroses by discussing his causal analysis, his explanations of the symptoms of neurasthenia and anxiety, and the role suggestion played in his gathering facts and in his treatment.

The Specific Causes

Freud consistently maintained it was easy to show that coitus interruptus and masturbation caused anxiety neurosis and neurasthenia, respectively. At about the time he first began to attract pupils and followers, he stressed that his initial discovery had been "easy to make and could be confirmed as often as one liked" (Freud 1906a, p. 272). Some eight years later he described the cause-effect relations as

a crude fact that springs to the observer's eyes.... I have no doubt that I could repeat the same observations to-day if similar pathological material were still at my disposal.   (Freud 1916–1917, pp. 385–386)

Ten years later he again said, "The observations which I made at the time still hold good" (Freud 1926a, p. 110).

Freud's certainty was echoed by Ernest Jones (1911a) who, after his extensive review of the mainly German evidence, concluded that incomplete sexual satisfaction, especially coitus interruptus, was clearly established as the cause of anxiety neurosis and that that conclusion was "not a matter of psychoanalysis ... it can at any time be tested by means of direct clinical investigation" (Jones 1911a). Despite this confidence, few psychoanalysts since about 1950 have agreed with Freud and Jones. Blau (1952), who attempted to resurrect the clinical concept of an actual anxiety neurosis, side-stepped the issue of sexual etiology and cited a number of patients in whom sexual factors could not be found. Even more equivocality was expressed by Gediman (1984). After accepting that there was a clinical entity entitled to be called actual neurosis, he implicitly rejected the sexual etiology, saying that it was due to factors in "the broader arena of excitability and frustration in the face of *any kind* of internal and external stimulation of traumatic intensity."

Brenner found no evidence of a relation between anxiety and abnormalities of sexual life. He also observed that most authors who had written on the subject assumed that there was a relation "without offering any independent evidence ... to corroborate it" (Brenner 1953). Among the notable psychoanalytic personalities to whom Brenner directed this reproof were Fenichel and W. Reich. It would seem also to apply to Ikonen and Rechardt (1978), who cite no observations to support their view that deficiently bound libido is the cause of anxiety in actual neurosis. Zetzel (1955a), Rangell (1955), and Waelder (1967b) are among other psychoanalysts who failed to confirm incomplete sexual gratification as a cause. Concentrating on anxiety neurosis but speaking of actual neurosis generally, Compton concluded the basis of the whole concept "was spurious to begin with," and that "no good evidence" existed for the existence of the actual neuroses as a clinical entity (Compton 1972b). Holt remarked, "Today very few clinicians indeed can be found whose experience confirms the etiological sequences Freud thought he saw" (Holt 1965). He also wondered "whether the whole concept was not based on the coincidence of a few chance clinical observations." We will see that these failures to confirm Freud's observations have rather more methodological significance than Holt allows.

Neurasthenia was a similar failure. Stekel seems to have been one of the first of Freud's pupils to disagree with his master on this matter, and denied completely any connection between it and masturbation (cited by Federn 1930 and by Lampl-de Groot 1950). He took the view that if masturbation was harmful at all it was because of the guilt feelings engendered by social disapproval. During the 1910 and 1912 discussions arranged by the Vienna Psychoanalytical Society, a substantial number of contributors took the same view or one very like it (Ferenczi 1912/1952b; Tausk 1912/1951). Freud himself acknowledged "significant uncertainties" among the participants about the causal role of masturbation (Freud 1912b). A little later, Brill (1916), one of Freud's earliest translators and his pioneer and major publicist in North America, concluded that his own clinical impression had been confirmed by several investigations showing the physical effects of masturbation to be minimal, even among young children.

Neither has later psychoanalytic opinion supported Freud. Federn (1930) was prepared to confirm what he called Freud's view that cumulative masturbation played a role in the great majority of cases, but claimed neurasthenia could also have other "exhausting moments" as causes. A. Stern (1930), Fenichel (1945b, p. 188), Frankley (1950), Lampl-de Groot (1950), A. Reich (1951), and Hojer-Pedersen (1956) all denied a direct or simple causal link or claimed it was yet to be proved. Psychoanalytic thought had at last caught up with the doubts expressed earlier by such nonanalysts as Edes (1904), Meagher (1924, 1936, pp. 99–103, 139), and MacCurdy (1923), all of whom had been sympathetic to Freud's views (the last two especially so), but none of whom was convinced by his arguments about neurasthenia.

Two reasons account for the conflict between Freud and his followers. The first is the indeterminacy of the etiological equation. There were no methods for measuring the strengths of any of the factors in the equation; disagreements were bound to occur, especially when the factors were present at low levels of intensity and had to sum with one another to have an effect. Given the widespread prevalence in the community of the specific factors of masturbation and coitus interruptus, of the stock noxae, and, presumably, of any precondition produced by masturbation, agreement must have been even less. The etiological equation virtually guaranteed dissension among those using it.

Second, not only did Freud's causal analysis confuse sufficient and necessary conditions, but it is doubtful he even identified correctly the necessary conditions of either form of the neurosis. Scrutinizing what has survived of his case material shows that at least some of the directness and simplicity of his initial causal formulations was based on the exclusion of cases running counter to the causal rule. Between late 1893 and mid-1894 Freud twice mentioned or implied that incomplete coition could be a cause of neurasthenia or a closely related condition in which there was also no anxiety (Masson 1985, Letter of Oct. 6, 1893, case 4, Draft F of Aug. 18 and 23, 1894, case 2). In the 1895 paper that relation was denied. It is true that Freud did refer to coitus interruptus as always producing in men an admixture of anxiety neurosis with neurasthenia, but unfortunately, that particular qualification overlooked at least one of his male patients with pure anxiety neurosis, that is, one without neurasthenic symptoms (Freud 1895a, pp. 113–114; cf. Masson 1985, Letter of Oct. 6, 1893, case 3).

Much the same point can be made about E. Jones's (1911a) review: he overlooked important papers, such as that by Booth (1906), who implicated coitus interruptus as causing neurasthenia. As K. Levin's (1978, pp. 131–132) discussion indicates, several of the authorities Jones cited, including Loewenfeld and Krafft-Ebing, had only gone as far as claiming incomplete gratification sometimes led to anxiety attacks (cf. Decker 1977, pp. 136–139 for further consideration of Loewenfeld's and other similar views). Since the causal scheme never was fully congruent with the case material, it is hardly surprising that later workers were unable to confirm it.

The Central Symptom of Neurasthenia

Disagreement also existed about how neurasthenic symptoms were produced. Ferenczi (1908/1950) seems to have accepted implicitly the inadequacy of Freud's explanation in his attributing the effects to the strain successful masturbation put on the sources of neuropsychic energy: "It is comprehensible that such a willed gratification requires a greater consumption of energy than the almost unconscious act of coitus" (ibid.). Weakness after masturbation was thus to be expected. Ferenczi also noted that the weakness was sometimes most marked the day after masturbation, and thought a summation of that weakness with others that were produced earlier had occurred. Were the process to be continued over a long enough period, a chronic weakness would result (Ferenczi 1912/1952b). The symptoms of general irritability, paresthesias, and other sensitivities were accounted for by supposing masturbation did not discharge all the excitation, and what was left behind kept the nervous system in a state of heightened excitability. Ingenious as this explanation was, it was bound to fail. Freud did not restrict the effects to "excessive onanism mostly continued long after puberty" as Ferenczi (1908/1950) did, and as A. Stern (1930) noted, Ferenczi did not define what was to be meant by excessive. Neither did Freud propose that neurasthenia was to be found only in those currently practicing masturbation, which was all Ferenczi's explanation really accounted for. Finally, the notion that the effects of repeated masturbation somehow summed to cause neurasthenia merely described what had to be explained.

Among the "significant uncertainties" that he saw as having emerged from the 1912 symposium, Freud included the manner in which masturbation produced its effects and its etiological relation to the actual neuroses. He concluded that the mechanism by which it produced organic damage was "unknown" (Freud 1912b, pp. 246, 251). In the years that followed he never returned to the problem and left it unsolved.

The Sources of Anxiety

We have already commented that Freud revised his ideas about the source of the anxiety in anxiety neurosis almost as soon as he put forward his original explanation. That revision was but the first of three. According to the first, psychical sexual excitation, or libido, rather than somatic sexual excitation was the source of anxiety. We have seen that the only advantage of this mentalistic reconceptualization was to enable an explanation in principle of the psychological symptoms, and that it was less successful with the physical symptoms. Proposing psychological causes for both psychoneuroses and actual neuroses also blurs one of the previously important distinctions between them. A partial solution to some of these difficulties, one that Freud apparently considered, is to think of anxiety and libido having quite different sources and being quite different from each other.

During the late 1890s Freud tried hard to work into his theory the concept that repression was based on an organic process capable of producing repression automatically, without the subject's awareness. He thought this might occur if an attempted revival of the memory of an abandoned childhood sexual activity produced a feeling of disgust rather than the original pleasurable libidinal affect. Disgust would then prevent the memory of the activity from becoming conscious. The mechanism required a strong associative connection to exist between libido and disgust. Freud thought the link lay in the phylogenetic history of mankind: after man adopted the erect posture, the pleasures of seeing and smelling the sex and excretory organs of the opposite sex were not as readily obtainable, and disgust was substituted. Toward the end of 1897 Freud therefore wrote to Fliess:

I have resolved, then, henceforth to regard as separate factors what causes libido and what causes anxiety. (Masson 1985, Letter of Nov. 14, 1897)

Because most of the rest of this letter deals with the organic basis of repression, Freud's proposal is hardly without any apparent connection with it, as the editor's introduction to *Inhibitions, Symptoms and Anxiety* states (Freud 1926a, p. 79).

In fact, to explain some of the symptoms of the hysterical patient known as Dora, Freud very soon went on to postulate a connection between libido and disgust that did not involve anxiety. Dora had reacted to an adolescent sexual experience with disgust. Freud assumed the experience began to revive the memory of a childhood sexual activity she had given up, and the attempted revival produced the disgust (Freud 1905a, pp. 28–32, 46–55, 85–86). But in the letter to Fliess, he complained of an essential obscurity "in the nature of the change by which the internal sensation of need becomes the sensation of disgust." We will see in chapters 9 and 10 that this continuing obscurity in the concept prevented him from pursuing the idea fully and applying it, at least in that form, to patients other than Dora.

Freud's second revision was based on the supposition that anxiety was produced by the build-up of toxic substances in the blood stream. It tended to be directed toward explaining the physical symptoms of the anxiety attack rather than the mental. Chemical substances distributed throughout the body were assumed to decompose and produce libido when the individual was sexually aroused. When libidinal discharge through orgasm was inadequate, the decomposed substances acted as toxins. Anxiety was now not a psychical transformation of libido, as the original and first revision held, but a poisoning brought about by a faulty metabolism of the chemical elements of sexual life.

Although this second revision was developed between 1900 and 1906, the basic ideas on which it was based were expressed in the correspondence with Fliess during much of 1896 (Masson 1985, Letters of Mar. 1, Apr. 2, June 30, Dec. 6, and Dec. 17, 1896). Taken together, the correspondence reveals that Freud "always conceived of the processes in anxiety neuroses, as in the neuroses in general, as an intoxication"; that he believed the differences between the symptoms of anxiety neurosis and neurasthenia required the postulation of two different toxic substances; and that the two hypothetical substances proposed by Fliess to explain the periodicities of male and female sexuality might be what he was searching for. The comparison of the neuroses with autointoxications then lapsed until 1905. Freud then made it public in the course of a theoretical digression about Dora:

No one, probably, will be inclined to deny the sexual function the character of an organic factor, and it is the sexual function that I look upon as the foundation of hysteria and of the psychoneuroses in general. No theory of sexual life will, I suspect, be able to avoid assuming the existence of some definite sexual substances having an excitant action. Indeed, of all the clinical pictures which we meet with in clinical medicine, it is the phenomena of intoxication and abstinence in connection with the use of certain chronic poisons that most closely resemble the genuine psychoneuroses.   (Freud 1905a, p. 113)

This rather cryptic remark, which may date from 1901, the year in which a manuscript about Dora was prepared, was expanded in the general theory of sexuality outlined in the first edition of *Three Essays*:

It may be supposed that, as a result of an appropriate stimulation of erotogenic zones, or in other circumstances that are accompanied by an onset of sexual excitation, some substance that is disseminated generally throughout the organism becomes decomposed and the products of its decomposition give rise to a specific stimulus which acts on the reproductive organs or upon a spinal centre related to them. (We are already familiar with the fact that other toxic substances, introduced into the body from outside, can bring about a similar transformation of a toxic condition into a stimulus acting on a particular organ.) The question of what interplay arises in the course of the sexual processes between the effects of purely toxic stimuli and of physiological ones cannot be treated, even hypothetically, in the present state of our knowledge. I may add that I attach no importance to this particular hypothesis and should be ready to abandon it at once in favour of another, provided that its fundamental nature remained unchanged—that is, the emphasis which it lays upon sexual chemistry. For this apparently arbitrary supposition is supported by a fact which has received little attention but deserves the closest consideration. The neuroses, which can be derived only from disturbances of sexual life, show the greatest clinical similarity to the phenomena of intoxication and abstinence that arise from the habitual use of toxic, pleasure-producing substances (alkaloids). (Freud 1905b, p. 216, n. 1. This passage is a reconstruction of the one that appeared in the first edition)

A subtle change to the role attributed to sexual discharge was now required, and Freud made it without hesitation.

In a discussion of the actual neuroses contemporaneous with this chemical theory of sexuality, Freud repeated that specific sexual practices were associated with the two neuroses, but modified their supposed effects by saying they resulted in "insufficient discharge of the libido" (Freud 1906a, p. 272). This idea was quite new. It is, of course, a necessary consequence of regarding libido as the product of the breakdown of sexual chemicals. Were all the libido discharged, no by-products would be left behind to act as toxins. This new process contradicts the thesis that masturbation caused neurasthenia by discharging the libido too fully. But, for neither neurosis was empirical evidence available as to the effectiveness of the discharge.

Another quite unsatisfactory aspect of Freud's revision is the alleged similarity among neuroses, autointoxications, and states of alkaloid withdrawal. By the end of the last century experimental physiological work had established the role of the thyroid gland, and it appeared to support the view that Basedow's disease, or thyrotoxicosis, was due to excessive secretion of thyroid toxins (K. Levin 1978, pp. 184–189). However, Freud's parallel between Basedow's disease and the neuroses was based on a superficial resemblance of the psychological symptoms of fatigue, irritability, and emotionality found in the two conditions. And whereas the substances in Basedow's disease were identifiable, the two sexual substances Freud's revision required were, are, and probably forever will remain entirely hypothetical.

Freud's third revision formed part of a more general rethinking of the relation between anxiety and repression. Its major consequence was to declare the matter a nonproblem. Originally, he supposed that when repression was unsuccessful and the impulse attempted reentry to consciousness, the attempt would be accompanied by the affect of anxiety. What he now proposed was a reversal of this relation: repression was the attempt to do away with the affect of anxiety that had been produced by feelings of helplessness, excessive libidinal tension, and like threats to the ego. After announcing the new theory Freud remarked:

It is still an undeniable fact that in sexual abstinence, in improper interference with the course of sexual excitation or if the latter is diverted from being worked over psychically, anxiety arises directly out of libido; in other words, that the ego is reduced to a state of helplessness in the face of an excessive tension due to need ... *though the matter is of little importance*, it is very possible that what finds discharge in the generating of anxiety is precisely the surplus of unutilized libido.   (Freud 1926a, p. 141. My emphasis)

Some years later, in his final comments on anxiety neurosis, Freud reaffirmed this point: "the question of what the material is out of which anxiety is made loses interest" (Freud 1933b, p. 85).

After having formed part of a very central topic for over thirty years, one of consuming theoretical interest, he finally left the source of anxiety unexplained. Further, he remarked, "we now understand the apparently complicated cases of the generation of anxiety better than those [like anxiety neurosis] which were considered simple" (p. 85). Perhaps better than any other single remark, this extraordinary conclusion reflects the problems anxiety posed for Freud's theory.

No better summing up can be given than Kaplan's pithy comment. Freud's work on the actual neuroses

began in certainty but went on to become elusive to observation and something of a trial to theory.   (D. M. Kaplan 1984)

Eventually it expired, becoming,

one might say, a ghost of its former self, a haunting rather than a palpable concern about which it no longer seems necessary to have views.   (op. cit.)

Another point should be added to Kaplan's *Decline and Fall*. Freud neither investigated nor treated any patients with actual neuroses after about 1900 (Freud 1925a, pp. 25–26). New clinical observations on the disorders formed no part of the basis for the second and third revisions: they resulted from changed interpretations of the original stock of facts and were motivated by attempts to produce consistency, either between the explanations of the two neuroses, or between the mechanisms of the actual neuroses and the psychoneuroses.

Suggestion, Facts, and Treatment

Clear evidence shows that suggestion played a major role in Freud's identifying sexual practices as the causes of neurasthenia. He put his neurasthenic patients under a good deal of pressure to admit to masturbation:

Having diagnosed a case of neurasthenic neurosis with certainty and having classified its symptoms correctly, we are in a position to translate the symptomatology into aetiology; and we may then *boldly demand confirmation* of our suspicions from the patient. We must not be led astray by initial denials. If we keep firmly to what we have inferred, we shall in the end *conquer every resistance* by emphasizing the *unshakeable* nature of our *convictions*. (Freud 1898a, p. 269. My emphasis)

He rejected the possibility of so obtaining false information:

Moreover, the idea that one might, by one's insistence, cause a patient who is psychically normal to accuse himself falsely of sexual misdemeanours—such an idea may safely be disregarded as an imaginary danger. If one proceeds in this manner with one's patients, one also gains the conviction that, so far as the theory of the sexual aetiology of neurasthenia is concerned, there are *no negative cases*. (p. 269. My emphasis)

His own colleagues as well as many nonanalysts had no such success—they found plenty of negative cases. What Freud called false accusation readily accounts for the discrepancy.

It is also possible that Freud misinterpreted the disappearance of symptoms after the patient adopted a normal sexual life. He simply took it to be a natural consequence of the removal of the cause. Against this Oerlemans (1949, pp. 23–24) argued that the failure of other analysts to obtain cures using the same therapy is consistent with Freud's cures having been produced by suggestion. Freud's authority and conviction played a much greater role in the investigation and treatment of neurasthenia than he was prepared to grant, and very probably the same was true of anxiety neurosis.

Childhood Seduction and Psychoneuroses

During 1896 Freud put forward a causal hypothesis that, together with its associated concepts, became known as the theory of childhood seduction. According to it, the trauma causing psychoneurotic symptoms were always sexual, always occurred in childhood, and always involved perverse sexual activities, usually forced on the child by an adult (Freud 1896c). In private correspondence to Fliess, he frequently implicated the patient's father as the seducer (Masson 1985, Letters of Dec. 6, 1896, and Jan. 3, Jan. 12, Jan. 24, 1897), including his own father (Letter of Feb. 8, 1897), eventually going so far as to speak directly of a "paternal etiology" for hysteria (Letters of Apr. 28, May 2, May 31, and June 22, 1897) and of his own father as "one of these perverts" (Letter of Apr. 28, 1897). The theory had a short life. By August, Freud was tormented by grave doubts (Letter of Aug. 14, 1897) and, terming the theory his neurotica, he wrote to Fliess five weeks later:

And now I want to confide in you immediately the great secret that has been slowly dawning on me in the last few months. I no longer believe in my *neurotica*.   (letter of Sept. 21, 1897)

The first reason he gave Fliess for doubting that the memories were of real events was that even when all the memories had been recovered and abreacted, it was not possible to bring "a single analysis" to a definite and successful conclusion (letter of Sept. 21, 1897). The second reason was that a specific causal factor needing the cooperation of preconditions for its effect had to be more widespread than those effects themselves. Therefore there would have to be very many more cases of childhood seduction than of hysteria, a fact that would hardly have escaped public notice. Freud's third reason was that the unconscious contained no indication of reality. In mistook the recollection for the memory of a real event. The fourth reason was that even in the uncontrolled thinking of the most severely psychotic patients, when the mechanism of repression was assumed to be in abeyance, no traces of seduction memories were found.

Although the patient's associations led to the origins of the neurosis, to what Freud referred to metaphorically as a veritable source of the Nile, the memories were false. No seduction had taken place at all, let alone by a sexually perverse father.

In the years after the collapse of the seduction theory, Freud came to the view that the seduction memory had not been derived from the experiences of the child in the external world, and he eventually placed its origins within the child. He supposed that what was recalled was a fantasy expressing the wish for the satisfaction of a perverse childhood sexual impulse. With this emphasis on the role of inner impulses and wished for gratifications he broke with *all* of his predecessors who had sought the origins of symptoms in the real experiences of the patient.

The step is such a momentous one that it is appropriate to consider whether it was justified. Did Freud completely exclude the possibility that the fantasy had an external basis? As with the actual neuroses, there is little point in appealing to the facts. Levin observes that three of Freud's four reasons for giving up the theory

could have been cited months earlier, while the fourth bears no relation to any comments previously made ... and is not pursued in subsequent discussions so that there is no clear indication of why the rejection of the seduction theory came at this particular time.   (K. Levin 1978, p. 200)

It is pretty obvious, as M. I. Klein (1981) comments, that Freud was merely reinterpreting the data he already had.

It is important to note that what was recalled from childhood appeared to be the memory of a real *sexual* experience, not mere erotic feeling or pleasurable sensation. What the child seemed to remember was sexual and perverse. Each of the three papers in which some part of the seduction theory was outlined used phrases such as "stimulation of the genitals, coitus-like acts, and so on" (Freud 1896c, p. 206; cf. 1896a, p. 152, 1896b, p. 163). The first two papers implied the activity was perverse, using terms such as "repulsive," "brute abuse," and "positively revolting" to characterize it. The last of the papers was quite explicit. The acts included

all the abuses known to debauched and impotent persons, among whom the buccal cavity and the rectum are misused for sexual purposes.   (Freud 1896c, p. 214)

Within the twelve months after this paper Freud claimed perverse sexual activity initiated by the patient's father was always involved.

How he came to attribute the role of seducer to the father is not at all clear. His published evidence does not support the thesis. In the first two papers, seven of the thirteen seductions reported were of *children by children* (Freud 1896a, p. 152; 1896b, p. 164). Most of the remainder were said to have been initiated by *adults unrelated to the child*: servants, tutors, governesses, and nursemaids. About four months later, in the third paper, *adults, including close relatives*, were said to make up "the much more numerous" group of seducers (Freud 1896c, p. 208). Since the sample reported on in the third paper was the original thirteen cases together with five new ones, the number of adult seducers could not have totaled more than eleven of the eighteen cases, even if an adult had been involved in all five of the new ones. A theoretical maximum of eleven adult seducers compared with seven child-child seductions hardly warrants referring to them as much more numerous.

Within about the next twelve months the early cases must have been reinterpreted or treated further for Freud to have been able to write to Fliess about the paternal etiology of the condition. In telling Fliess of the collapse of the theory, he remarked that his patients had blamed their fathers "in all cases" (Masson 1985, Letter of Sept. 21, 1897). Like his conclusions about the causes of actual neuroses, he retained this impression, at least about hysterical women patients, for many years (Freud 1925a, pp. 33–34; 1933b, p. 120). That successive transformations occurred of children into adults unrelated to them, of those adults into relatives, and of those relatives into fathers seemed to have been forgotten. Only the image of the fantastic seducer father remained, a transformation that raises serious questions about the accuracy of Freud's reporting (Cioffi 1974; Schimek 1987).

When publicly announcing the childhood seduction theory, Freud considered and rejected the possibility that he had influenced the recollections of his patients:

It is less easy to refute the idea that the doctor forces reminiscences of this sort on the patient, that he influences him by suggestion to imagine and reproduce them. Nevertheless it appears to me ... untenable. I have never yet succeeded in forcing on a patient a scene I was expecting to find, in such a way that he seemed to be living through it with all the appropriate feelings. (Freud 1896c, pp. 204–205)

Here he was repeating the essence of the claim, previously made in *Studies*, that the content of the recollections could not be influenced (Breuer and Freud 1895, p. 295). And, as in that instance, it can be seen the only mode of influence he considered was direct suggestion. He seems not to have thought indirect, unconscious suggestive influences might be important.

Freud's failure to consider these subtle unconscious factors is, of course, consistent with his view of determinism and, as we will see, with his notion of a neurosis having a logical and associative structure. The concept of a logical and associative structure is a development of the pathogenic memory structure considered in chapter 4. Like the earlier concept, it too is based firmly on Meynert's physiological associationism.

Although Freud nowhere formally defined or described what he meant by the logical and associative structure of a neurosis, his usage makes it clear it encompassed the totality of associations between the symptoms and the causal memories. He appears to have used the concept first when describing the memories of childhood seduction as being represented in the cases of hysteria by

a host of symptoms and of special features which could be accounted for in no other way; it is peremptorily called for [governed] by the subtle but solid interconnections of the intrinsic structure of the neurosis.   (Freud 1896a, p. 153)

The solid interconnections were associations, that is, connections of content, because in

> the relationship of the infantile scenes to the content of the whole of the rest of the case history ... the contents of the infantile scenes turn out to be indispensable supplements to the associative and logical framework of the neurosis.   (Freud 1896c, p. 205)

Again the interconnections were also causal connections:

> the aetiological pretensions of the infantile scenes rest ... above all, on the evidence of there being associative and logical ties between those scenes and the hysterical symptoms.   (p. 210)

Subtle peculiarities of the content of the symptoms were explained by the content of the infantile memories demanded by the intrinsic structure. That content completed the logical and associative structure, and the causal role of the memory was inferred from its logical and associative ties with the symptom.

Of the memories in the logical structure, the most important was the one at the nucleus. Freud described it as having two attributes: suitable determining quality and appropriate traumatic force. Neither was defined clearly or positively. An unsuitable determinant was one having a content bearing no relation to the nature of the symptom, and traumatic force was defined negatively, as the opposite of "an impression which is normally innocuous and incapable as a rule of producing any effect" (Freud 1896c, p. 194). Freud gave a hypothetical example that expanded on these definitions only by implication:

> Let us suppose that the symptom under consideration is hysterical vomiting; in that case we shall feel that we have been able to understand its causation (except for a certain residue) if the analysis traces the symptom back to an experience which *justifiably produced a high amount of disgust*—for instance, the sight of a decomposing dead body. But if, instead of this, the analysis shows us that the vomiting arose from a great fright, e.g., from a railway accident, we shall feel dissatisfied and will have to ask ourselves how it is that the fright has led to the particular symptom of vomiting. This derivation lacks *suitability as a determinant*. We shall have another instance of an insufficient explanation if the vomiting is supposed to have arisen from, let us say, eating a fruit which had partly gone bad. Here, it is true, the vomiting *is* determined by disgust, but we cannot understand how, in this instance, the disgust could have become so powerful as to be perpetuated in a hysterical symptom; the experience lacks *traumatic force*. (pp. 193–194)

The difference in traumatic force between eating a bad apple and viewing a decomposing corpse is readily sensed even if it cannot be expressed with any precision.

Similarly, the determining quality is quite apparent: seeing a decomposing corpse might well produce a tendency to vomit that could be perpetuated as a symptom. Freud's use of this resemblance in content to index the determining quality of the scene, that is, its causal relevance, is a development of the point implicit in Charcot that the sensory content of the symptom is based on and reflects the sensations experienced in the trauma. It is also based entirely on the formal identity of an association and a causal connection.

In summary, Freud used the concept of the logical and associative structure of a neurosis to refer to the complex of associational pathways running from the symptom to the memory of the core trauma to related memories. Since any one idea in the pathway implied the presence of another with which it had been previously experienced, the associative paths revealed the logical relations between the ideas and the symptoms and between the ideas themselves. In turn, the logical relations revealed the causal or deterministic connections. Associating to the ideas generated by the symptom necessarily led to the traumatic memory at the core of the structure where the memory was recognizable by its traumatic force and determining quality. The process leading from one idea to another had its own determinants and could not be influenced by the therapist (apart from helping to overcome resistances temporarily impeding the process). The memories recovered during treatment necessarily allowed an authentic reconstruction of the development of the neurosis. If a memory of a childhood seduction was at the core of the memory structure, a real seduction must have occurred (cf. Jacobsen and Steele 1979).

Unintentional Influences in Psychotherapy

Experimental and observational evidence about psychotherapy shows that the therapist can unintentionally influence the extent to which the patient talks, the extent to which emotional topics will be explored, the kinds of problems discussed, and the content of any memories recalled. This is consistent with Freud having unconsciously influenced the recollections of his patients and that influence creating the "memories" of a seduction in childhood.

The work of Matarazzo and colleagues, usefully summarized in Matarazzo (1962), shows that the formal characteristics of psychotherapeutic interviews are determined by the interviewer. These characteristics, which include whether subjects say anything or not and, if they do, the length of their remarks, are functions of the verbalizations of the interviewer. Matarazzo devised a standardized interview in which subjects were free to talk about anything they chose, but in which interviewers varied their remarks according to a prearranged schedule. During one part of the interview they always responded to the subject's remarks, in another they remained silent, and in yet another they interrupted. Across all groups of normal and abnormal subjects studied, interviewer silence increased the subject's silence and decreased the average length of each remark for all but those with schizophrenia. The decrease in length of remarks was greater in the interruption period than in the silent period. These findings are highly reliable.

Colby (1960, 1961) showed much the same effects even when the subject is only free associating: how much activity takes place and what its content is, is a function of the mere presence and sex of the experimenter. In their study of the psychotherapeutic interview Lennard and Bernstein (1960) stress the contribution the patient makes to the pattern of interaction that develops with the therapist, but their findings are generally consistent with those of Matarazzo—the formal aspects of psychotherapy are very much a function of the therapist.

The patient's behavior also may be directed by the therapist responding differently to different aspects of it. In an experimental analogue of a client-centered interview, Truax and Carkhuff (1965) demonstrated that the therapist could control the extent to which the patient explored his own problems. In the middle third of the interview the therapist simply refrained from making whatever was the best response dictated by the therapeutic rules, and within that period the patient's self-exploration declined. Truax (1968) later analyzed tape recordings of group psychotherapy sessions and showed that self-exploration increased when the therapist differentially responded to it. K. S. Isaacs and Haggard (1966) similarly noted that the extent to which patients discuss an affect-laden topic increases when therapists comment affectively on the verbalizations. Compared with nonaffective comments, patients' subsequent verbalizations were more affective and contained many more references to factors presumed to have influenced their lives and to have caused their problems. What is especially important is that delayed returns to the topics mentioned by the interviewer, although small in number, were much greater when those mentions were affective. Consequently, the patient's discussion of some topics appeared spontaneous and unconnected with the therapist's intervention. The more the therapist encourages self-exploration and the discussion of affective topics, the more probable it is that topics of the kind Freud regarded as traumatic will come to dominate the therapeutic interchange.

Particular kinds of content can also be emphasized by the therapist. The early work of Greenspoon (1955) on what came to be called verbal conditioning shows how it may be given. His experiments required the subject to utter single words over a fifty-minute period. During the first twenty-five minutes each plural noun was reinforced by the experimenter murmuring "mmm-hmm." Compared with the second half, in which the experimenter remained silent, the first period produced many more plural nouns. The narrow class of plural nouns rather than the wide class of nonplurals was more easily influenced. The simplicity of Greenspoon's findings are deceptive. Later work, reviewed extensively by Krasner (1958), Salzinger (1959), Greenspoon (1962), and Kanfer (1968), showed the extent of the influence to depend on such complex conditions as the social setting of the experiment, the personality characteristics of subject and experimenter, the expectations and awareness of the subject, and the particular response made by the experimenter. Nevertheless, the fact of influence is reliably established.

Verbal content may be similarly influenced in clinical-like settings. Beginning with the work of Fahmy (1953, cited in Greenspoon 1962), several studies have shown that responses equivalent to "mmm-hmm" influence the names given ink blot shapes and the content of stories the subject makes up in response to pictures. Subtle influences from the therapist may thus determine the content of several types of simple verbal responses given by patients.

Although these effects on simple responses are of interest, it is more important to know if they can occur with more complex psychological functions in clinical and quasi-clinical settings. Quay (1959) demonstrated that the content of recalled childhood memories could be influenced by the experimenter's verbalizations. Two groups of subjects were seen for two half-hour periods during which each subject was asked to recall events from childhood. In the first ten minutes of the first half-hour the experimenter said nothing. Then, for one group, he murmured "uh-huh" each time a subject recollected an event involving his or her family. For the other group, the verbalization was made after each recollection that did not involve the subject's family. Compared with the first ten-minute period, both groups increased the number of memories of the type that was followed by the experimenter's "uh-huh." The proportion of memories for family events was, however, higher in the first group than in the second.

In many verbal conditioning experiments as well as in other investigations I have mentioned, subjects appeared either to be unaware that cues from the experimenter or interviewer shaped their responses or, if they became aware, they rarely detected the direction the cues were meant to give. To them, their verbal productions seemed spontaneous. It was also noted by Matarazzo that the observers of his standardized interview were unable to detect fairly gross changes in interviewers' behavior.

Therapists themselves may not realize they are guiding the patient's thoughts in a particular direction. E. J. Murray (1956) and Truax (1966) separately analyzed individual therapy sessions conducted by Carl Rogers, the founder of the client-centered method of therapy, who believes therapists should neither approve nor disapprove of the topics the client (patient) raises. Both Murray and Truax found that Rogers exerted considerable selective influence without his apparently being aware of it. Murray categorized Rogers's statements in response to the client's remarks as approval, disapproval, or neutral. The proportions of these responses for each of the four main categories of problems first mentioned by the patient (sex, affection, dependence, independence) were then examined. Rather than the responses being equally represented for each problem, Murray found that Rogers disapproved of nearly all the sexual discussion and approved all of that in which the patient indicated his need for independence. As therapy progressed, sexual matters were raised less frequently and moves toward independence more frequently. Other problem areas were affected similarly: those eliciting Rogers's approval were discussed more frequently than those of which he disapproved.

Truax examined a random selection of verbal interactions between Rogers and another client. Each interaction consisted of a therapist statement followed by a client statement and a second therapist statement. Rogers's statements were evaluated according to the degree to which they possessed the qualities regarded by Rogers himself as facilitating therapeutic progress: empathic understanding, acceptance, and nondirectiveness. For seven of the nine classes of patient behavior studied, changes in the predicted direction were brought about by Rogers's selective responding. Thus the clarity of the client's expression and the similarity of his style of expression to that of Rogers, the degree of insight he showed, and the extent to which he discriminated among his earlier experiences and feelings were functions of differences in Rogers's responses. Rogers's qualities, functioned, therefore, as reinforcers. From these two studies it is clear that what patients talk about, how they talk about it, and the degree of understanding that develops are functions of therapists' differential responsiveness, even when therapists are unaware of responding differently.

The possibility that the differential responsiveness of the therapist is conditioned by the characteristics of the patient may be ruled out. Truax's and Mitchell's (1971) review shows the therapist, not the patient, to be the primary determinant of therapeutic interactions. One of the strongest lines of evidence is that therapists are remarkably consistent in their behavior from one patient to another and do not modify their behavior as patient characteristics vary. Although experimental investigations do show that pseudoclients can manipulate the behaviors of therapists, the effects are less marked on experienced and skilled therapists.

Another important type of evidence is suggested by Cartwright's (1966) study comparing patient changes in client-centered and psychoanalytic therapy. One member of each of two matched pairs of patients was treated by client-centered methods, the others by psychoanalytic or psychoanalytically oriented methods. If patients determined the therapeutic interactions, one would expect to find similar interactions for the matched patients in the two different treatments. In fact, with the partial exception of some behaviors of the psychoanalytically oriented therapist who actually used some client-centered methods as well, the therapists behaved according to the tenets of their schools. And so did the patients. Patients thus behave differently according to the different influences to which they are exposed. Although Cartwright's study is frequently cited as showing little or no difference in the patients' behaviors, it is clear that if data from a single ad hoc and unvalidated scale are disregarded, the patients behaved as their therapists would have wished them to.

Heine's (1953) earlier and more extensive comparison of psychoanalytic, client-centered, and Adlerian therapists also showed the patient's experiencing of therapy to be based on the therapist's orientation. Clearly the therapist, not the client, is the primary influence on the therapeutic process. Similarly, the psychoanalyst Marmor remarked of the depth psychology therapies that,

depending upon the point of view of the analyst, the patients of each school seem to bring up precisely the kind of phenomenological data which confirm the theories and interpretations of their analysts! Thus each theory tends to be self-validating. Freudians elicit material about the Oedipus Complex and castration anxiety, Jungians about archetypes, Rankians about separation anxiety, Adlerians about masculine strivings and feelings of inferiority, Horneyites about idealised images, Sullivanians about disturbed inter-personal relationships, etc.... What the analyst shows interest in, the kinds of questions he asks, the kind of data he chooses to react to or ignore, and the interpretations he makes, all exert a subtle but significant suggestive impact upon the patient to bring forth certain kinds of data in preference to others. (Marmor 1962)

However, this important psychoanalytic opinion and the supporting research evidence do not go as far as showing that the impact results in new creations such as fabricated or pseudomemories.

Fortunately, some instances are known of cases not unlike those of psychotherapy in which false memories have been created by the dominant partner. Perhaps the best documented is that of Virginia Tighe, who recalled a number of incidents in her previous incarnation as one Bridey Murphy, an Irish colleen. The recollections were fabricated during sessions with an amateur hypnotist who attempted to get her to recall the earliest possible events in her life (M. Bernstein 1956). The false recollections were based on events in her own childhood, such as her training in Irish dancing and "stage-Irish" monologues, and on her elementary knowledge of some events in Irish history (W. White, Hartzell, and Smith 1956). At Bernstein's insistence, the memories of these real events were worked up into pseudomemories of a previous incarnation. Although the content of the pseudomemories was old, its elaboration was as recent as Bernstein's hypnosis.

How subtle the process can be was shown by Kampman's and Hirvenoja's (1978) study of two people who hypnotically recalled earlier incarnations. Seven years after the incarnation stories, the subjects were rehypnotized and details known only to the "incarnate" personae were traced to information acquired in the subjects' actual childhoods. Much of the acquisition was casual or incidental. For example, one subject had learned the melody and modernized medieval English words of a song while ruffling through the pages of book in a library.

Memories of real past events are not the only sources of false recollections. For example, in the "auditing" or treatment offered in the pseudoscience of scientology the subject produces "memories" that draw on a content not known before the contact with scientology. Beginners are treated by those more knowledgeable. Adepts believe the individual has a continuous spiritual existence over [US] seventy trillion years and to be currently inhabiting a body that is the end result of a long biological evolutionary process. During auditing, certain traumatic memories are recalled, some of events that happened to the individual as a spiritual being, and others to the precursors of the body in which the spirit now resides. Among the former are unusual, extreme, and quite specific forms of electronic torture, and among the latter are life as an atom, a unicellular organism, a clam, an ape, a Piltdown man [sic], other human beings in previous lives, and a prenatal being. Scientologists expect the recollection of these events to relieve various problems and complaints. After many hours of auditing, neophytes characteristically recall having had just these experiences, at similar periods, and in the same way (Hubbard 1952a,b). The very peculiar content of the experiences speaks against their having been known beforehand. They are recent elaborations of newly acquired content.

Bridey Murphy and scientology illustrate two different modes of action of demand characteristics. Virginia Tighe had to discern what was required of her from the not-very-well-disguised expectations contained in Bernstein's suggestions. The neophyte scientologist's task is easier, for it is probable that the auditors do not disguise their expectations at all. In addition, through study of scientological doctrines, subjects have direct knowledge of what the recollections should be. Once they learn what is demanded of them, they adapt their "recollections" accordingly.

Freud's treatment has some important similarities with these two schemes. All three involve a subject's emotional and intellectual dependence on a mentor, and an interaction allowing the transmission of the beliefs and expectations of the investigator. Like Bernstein and the scientology auditors, Freud had expectations about the content of the memories to be recovered and the way they were related to one another. There is no reason why the content acquired from these expectations could not have been elaborated into pseudomemories and integrated with existing memories of real events. Although Mrs. Tighe's memories were not particularly vivid, well structured, or tightly integrated with her real memories, this is not so with the memories fabricated in scientology auditing, which are of complexly elaborated events, recalled in extremely vivid detail. They are also integrated with each other and with the subject's real memories. Although it may not be possible to explain how this happens, it obviously occurs. It is also evident that an essential precondition for integration is that the subject divine the investigator's expectations.

Freud's Expectations and the Causes of Hysteria

Only at the end of the period that began in late 1892 and ended in late 1896 did Freud's patients come to report their nuclear traumatic memories as being of sexual seductions in childhood. At the beginning of the period Freud had three specific expectations: first, all neuroses might be caused by sexual factors; second, a given disorder would always be caused by the one specific factor; third, a traumatic memory would be recognizable by the effects of its abreaction. These expectations affected the recollections of his patients in different ways. The first determined the type of content the memory of a traumatic event had to have, while the second and third set the standards by which the relevance of a given memory was judged.

I have already shown in chapter 5 how, before he began work on hysteria, Freud was convinced that he had established an exclusively sexual etiology for the actual neuroses. That work was so methodologically defective, however, it resulted only in an unjustified expectation that all neuroses would have sexual causes. Although Freud several times denied he expected the memories of trauma in hysteria to be of sexual experiences (e.g., Freud 1896c, p. 199), it is clear from the correspondence with Fliess cited in chapter 5 that he had been attempting to construct a general theory of the neuroses on a sexual basis from at least early 1894 and possibly from as early as twelve to eighteen months before. During the same period he considered the possibility that the psychoneuroses might also have sexual causes. For example, the fact that hysteria sometimes occurred together with neurasthenia was attributed to suppression of accompanying sexual affects (Masson 1985, Drafts A and B).

That Freud expected similar kinds of phenomena to have similar causes is apparent in his 1888 defense of Charcot against the imputation that the phenomena of hypnosis and hysteria produced at the Salpêtrière resulted from unconscious suggestion. Unconscious influences necessarily varied from one investigator to another and could produce only variable phenomena (Freud 1888c, pp. 77–80). Freud's argument is the obverse of the deterministic view that all things and events are the regular and lawful consequence of their causes or determinants. His search for the causes of the actual neuroses was clearly based on this same deterministic view: the two kinds of symptoms required two specific causes (Freud 1895a, pp. 91, 106, 109, 113). One of his later discussions of the causes of hysteria is consistent with his also looking for uniform causes of it from the beginning. He asked where the chains of associations terminated:

Do they perhaps lead to experiences which are in some way alike, either in their content or the time of life at which they occur, so that we may discern *in these universally similar factors* the aetiology of hysteria of which we are in search? (Freud 1896c, pp. 197–198. My emphasis)

As early as January 1894 Freud had concluded that the chief causes of hysteria and the only causes of obsessions were sexual traumas (Freud 1894, pp. 47, 52), and by May he had listed "the thesis of specificity" [of etiology] as a topic in the outline of a projected major work that was to cover all the neuroses (Masson 1985, Draft D, possibly of May 21, 1894). From the beginning he may well have expected similarities in the content and/or time of occurrence of the sexual traumas reported by his patients.

Freud's expectation that the effect of the abreaction of a given memory might be used to assess its contribution to the symptom also appears to have developed early and to have grown out of the conviction that the abreaction of a memory would always remove any symptom it maintained. Already, in the case of Anna O. Breuer revealed that whenever the accumulated stimuli were given verbal utterance the symptom disappeared. Breuer and Freud (1893, pp. 6–7) claimed the symptom would be untouched if the recollection was without affect. Freud's earliest lecture on hysteria endorsed this view (Freud 1893a, p. 35). About a year later (Freud 1894, p. 47), and again in the opening paragraphs of his chapter on psychotherapy in *Studies on Hysteria*, he quoted those parts of the *Preliminary Communication* that stressed the effectiveness of abreaction (Breuer and Freud 1895, p. 255). Later in the chapter he placed various qualifications on the scope of the cathartic method (pp. 261–265, 301–304), but since these were of an essentially practical nature, the patient being too resistant, or the phase of the illness being too acute, for example, they confirmed his assertion the method was "as a matter of theory ... very well able to get rid of any hysterical symptom" (p. 261).

Only a small step separates the belief that abreaction can remove any symptom from the practice of using the effect of abreaction to index the contribution of a given memory to it. When Freud took that step is not known. It was implied in one of the criteria he used for the differential diagnosis of actual neurosis: if the therapeutic results of abreaction were scanty, the disorder was probably an actual neurosis. Conversely, a therapeutic effect tended to indicate a psychoneurosis (Breuer and Freud 1895, pp. 256–259). Since the actual neuroses predominated among the patients Freud treated early in his medical career, it is possible he developed this differential diagnostic criterion fairly soon after he began investigating hysteria. He assumed that, rightly used, abreaction would always succeed. It is not at all unfair to say this expectation was based on the presumption that abreactive therapy was infallible.

With these three expectations Freud therefore had a mental set to search for memories of a uniformly sexual kind, the abreaction of which would relieve the patient's symptoms.

Guiding the Recovery of Causal Memories

According to the concept of the logical and associative structure of the neurosis, there had to be associative linkages between the ideas recalled in treatment and the symptom. The linkages or logical threads had to be followed if important traumatic memories were to be found. In *Studies on Hysteria*, Freud described how, in using the model of the pathogenic memory structure to guide his work, he had had to persevere with the connections suggested by the content of associations. In recovering the childhood seduction scenes he described the same practice:

Travelling backwards into the patient's past, step by step, and always guided by the organic train of symptoms and of memories and thoughts aroused, I finally reached the starting-point of the pathological process.   (Freud 1896a, p. 151)

This starting point was not reached automatically. Usually the first memories were of fairly recent traumatic events. Freud argued these could not be the causes because they varied

in their intensity and nature, from actual sexual violation to mere sexual overtures or the witnessing of sexual acts in other people, or receiving information about sexual processes. (Freud 1896b, p. 166)

These later traumas also lacked determining quality and traumatic force (Freud 1896c, p. 193). Nor was there therapeutic gain

If the memory which we have uncovered does not answer our expectations, it may be that we ought to pursue the same path a little further; perhaps behind the first traumatic scene there may be concealed the memory of a second, which satisfies our requirements better and whose reproduction has a greater therapeutic effect.   (p. 195)

Insistence might then be increased

If the first-discovered scene is unsatisfactory, we tell our patient that this experience explains nothing, but behind it there must be hidden a more significant, earlier, experience. (pp. 195–196)

Patients treated after 1893 were thus put under pressure similar to that to which Lucy R., Katharina, and Elisabeth von R. had been exposed. Each of them was also told that various of their memories did not explain their symptoms, and each was forced to try again.

The first consequence of Freud's insistence was that the chains of associations were pushed back from recent events to things supposed to have happened in puberty. But the sexual experiences recalled from that time also differed from one another in kind and in importance, for example, among an obscene answer to a riddle, an attempted rape, and surreptitious hand stroking combined with knee pressing. Serious and trifling events seemed to be involved equally. One further deficiency was evident: the content of the experiences had no sensory connection with the symptoms; that is, they lacked determining quality. Symptoms such as painful genital sensations, for example, could hardly have been produced by surreptitious caresses or answers to riddles. Freud extended the search:

I was unable to find indications that they had been determined either by the scenes at puberty or by later scenes ... It seemed an obvious thing, then, to say to ourselves that we must look for the determinants of these symptoms in yet other experiences, in experiences which went still further back—and that we must, for the second time, follow the saving notion which had earlier led us from the first traumatic scenes to the chains of memories behind them. In doing so ... we arrive at the period of earliest childhood ... and here we find the fulfilment of all the claims and expectations upon which we have so far insisted. (Freud 1896c, pp. 201–202)

The three expectations were met: the experience was sexual, it always had the same content and time of occurrence, and its abreaction seemed to produce a cure.

Within the logical structure, the childhood memory served as a focus for drawing other memories to it in the same way as the repressed memory in the pathogenic memory structure:

All the events subsequent to puberty ... are ... only concurrent causes ... they enjoy a pathogenic influence for hysteria only owing to their faculty for awakening the unconscious psychical trace of the childhood event. It is also thanks to their connection with the primary pathogenic impression ... that their memories will become unconscious in their turn and will be able to assist in the growth of a psychical activity withdrawn from the power of the conscious functions. (Freud 1896a, pp. 154–155; cf. Freud 1896b, pp. 165–166)

This connecting principle supplanted or incorporated the previous principle of the summation of trauma and also explained the latency of the effect of the childhood experience. Through it, all the memories recovered in treatment could be linked with one another and to the symptom.

So well did the various aspects of the theory fit together that Freud proposed coherence itself as "another and stronger proof" of the reality of the infantile memories. The proof was

furnished by the relationship of the infantile scenes to the content of the whole of the rest of the case history. It is exactly like putting together a child's picture-puzzle: after many attempts, we become absolutely certain in the end which piece belongs in the empty gap; for only that one piece fills out the picture and at the same time allows its irregular edges to be fitted into the edges of the other pieces in such a manner as to leave no free space and to entail no over-lapping. In the same way, the contents of the infantile scenes turn out to be indispensable supplements to the associative and logical framework of the neurosis, whose insertion makes its course of development for the first time evident, or even, as we might often say, self-evident. (Freud 1896c, p. 205)

What Freud is proposing here, as a standard by which the reality of the recalled event can be judged, is his subjective feeling of certainty about the suitability of patient's recollection.

Were these standards to be used in an ambiguous situation, we can be sure that any hint from Freud about his expectations would have potent effects. But, although some of his expectations were transmitted indirectly, as when the subject was led back to an earlier period by being told that a particular memory explained nothing, others were transmitted very directly. There is no doubt that before and during treatment Freud gave explicit information about the content of the memory being sought:

Before they come for analysis the patients know nothing about these scenes [of childhood seduction]. They are indignant as a rule *if we warn them* that such scenes are going to emerge. (Freud 1896c, p. 204. My emphasis)

Patients' recollections were guided from the nonsignificant late traumas to the sexual traumas of puberty by Freud's informing them of the required linking content. When telling the patient to try again, Freud would

direct his attention . . . to *the associative thread* which connects the two memories—the one that has been discovered and the one that has still to be discovered. A continuation of the analysis then leads in every instance to the reproduction of new scenes of the character we expect. (p. 196. My emphasis)

Guidance could hardly have been more specific. There was also a lot of it because at about this time Freud told Fliess he was "almost hoarse" from working at full pressure ten to eleven hours a day (Masson 1985, Letter of Dec. 6, 1896). Over at least the next two years his therapy continued in the same way: it gave him "occasion enough" for talking (Letter of June 18, 1897), he was "speechless" from too much therapeutic work (Letter of Oct. 9, 1898), and he was incapable of writing "after ten hours of talking" (Letter of Jan. 16, 1899).

Should Freud's patients have adapted their recollections to his demands their nuclear memories would have lacked reality. And that was what Freud found. Telling of their childhood seductions, patients would

suffer under the most violent sensations, of which they are ashamed and which they try to conceal; and, even after they have gone through them once more in such a convincing manner, they still attempt to withhold belief from them, by emphasizing the fact that, unlike what happens in the case of other forgotten material, *they have no feeling of remembering the scenes.* (Freud 1896c, p. 204. My emphasis)

Freud took this inability to remember as evidence of how basic and real the memory was, rather than that it might be false.

Here, in effect, Freud was repeating an argument first put forward in *Studies* about the memory in the nucleus, which was not, of course, a memory of childhood seduction. There he noted the patient might never remember the events "although he admits that the context calls for them inexorably" (Breuer and Freud 1895, p. 272). Those patients needed the specific hypothesis:

Not at all infrequently the patient begins by saying: "It's possible that I thought this, but I can't remember having done so." And it is not until he has been familiar with the hypothesis for some time that he comes to recognize it as well; he remembers—and confirms the fact, too, by subsidiary links—that he really did once have the thought.   (p. 299)

But when treatment ended there might still be no recollection:

Even when everything is finished and the patients have been overborne by the force of logic and have been convinced by the therapeutic effect accompanying the emergence of precisely these ideas—when, I say, the patients themselves accept the fact that they thought this or that, they often add: "But *I can't remember* having thought it." It is easy to come to terms with them by telling them that *the thoughts were unconscious.*   (p. 300. My emphasis)

Why should Freud not have put this same argument to patients who could not remember their seductions? What was recalled, or indeed whether anything was recalled at all, did not matter—the inexorable demands of context, that is, the need to arrive at a plausible reconstruction of the patient's past, took precedence (Cioffi 1972; Schimek 1987).

Whatever logical and theoretical implications the concept of a totally unconscious memory might have, one practical implication is obvious: allowing that a recollection was not necessary at all made it that much easier for Freud to believe in his theory and for his patients to fall in with his demands. I speak, of course, as if most of

Freud's patients really did recall a memory of seduction, and that where they did not, they eventually came around to accepting one that he believed they ought to have. The detailed reanalysis by Schimek (1987) establishes, fairly conclusively in my view, that most of the patients did not so report seduction memories. What Freud really describes is his foisting his reconstructions onto them, a fact that, when added to those I have so far considered, makes the rise and fall of the seduction theory even more comprehensible.

Each of Freud's reasons for giving up the theory had the happy consequence of letting him continue to believe that the psychoneuroses were caused by uniformly operating sexual factors and that the process of recollection was unaffected by unconscious influences. Freud's failure to bring any analysis to a conclusion did not question the infallibility of the cathartic method; the most that could be doubted was whether it had been used with suitable material. He could grant the logical point of a specific sexual factor having to be more prevalent than its effects without questioning the omnipresence of sexual factors themselves. By making the unconscious responsible for being unable to tell whether a memory was of a real event or not, he absolved himself (and his patients) from any error of judgment. Although when viewed in retrospect the fourth reason (Freud's failure to observe seduction memories in psychoses) is not without its peculiarities, it did not require him to abandon or alter his expectations; one would really have anticipated the fantasies he later proposed as substitutes for the pseudomemories to have been present. In essence Freud treats the failure as if it were irrelevant.

Freud could therefore continue to believe that the process of recollection was uninfluenced by his expectations and suggestions. In fact as time went on, he recommended giving

the patient the conscious anticipatory idea [the idea of what he may expect to find] and he then finds the repressed unconscious idea in himself on the basis of its similarity to the anticipatory one. (Freud 1910c, p. 142)

One could even unfold "the reconstruction of the genesis of his disorder as deduced from material brought up in [the first phase] of the analysis" before reaching the phase in which patients began recalling what repressed memories they could (Freud 1920b, p. 152).

Other Accounts of the Collapse

The seduction theory seems better accounted for by Freud's expectations than in any other way. Here I consider only those alternatives most relevant to my argument. A completely comprehensive analysis was made by Vetter (1988).

The Pressure Method—Schusdek

The seduction theory is most unlikely to have been the simple consequence of the pressure technique, according to Schusdek (1966). Schusdek contends that the error of mistaking a fantasy for reality would not have occurred had the memories been obtained by the method of free association. The contention must be rejected. Free association is based on the same assumptions about the determinants of the associational train as is the pressure technique. It would have led Freud and his patients just as readily to a pseudomemory of a childhood seduction.

Nonrepressed Memories—Klein and Tribich

On the basis of a very idiosyncratic reading of Freud's letter to Fliess, M. I. Klein and Tribich (1982a,b) posit that the reason Freud gave up the theory was the *failure* of his patients to report seduction memories or, if they did, that those memories had not been repressed. They interpret Freud's failure to complete any analysis as really meaning that he was not able to recover those memories. The absence of memories in deliria is similarly interpreted: they make it refer to Freud's failure to retrieve memories during treatment rather than to his failure to observe their spontaneous occurrence during the deliria themselves. Then, while they attribute Freud's third reason—lack of differentiation between truth and fiction in the unconscious—to the forcefulness of his technique, they also maintain that, despite that same forcefulness, Freud did not retrieve memories in enough of his patients.

Freud's Lack of Courage—Masson

Masson concluded that the seduction theory was abandoned because of "a personal failure of courage" (Masson 1984, p. 189) on Freud's part in refusing to face the very unpleasant consequences of Fliess's near-fatal carelessness in leaving half a meter of surgical gauze in a patient's nasal cavity during an operation. The victim, Emma Eckstein, was also a patient of Freud's who was at the same time conducting psychoanalyses of her own. Freud referred her to Fliess because of her stomach and menstrual pains. Under the influence of his nasal-reflex theory, Fliess was treating patients with similar complaints, probably quite successfully (Sulloway 1979, p. 152, and n. 13), by cocainization and cauterization of particular areas on the turbinate bones of the nose. With Emma Eckstein, he apparently experimented with a more radical procedure in which he removed part of the bone. The operation was performed in February 1895. The carelessness over the gauze then produced a major focus of infection, a near bleeding to death, a prolonged convalescence, and the permanent facial disfigurement of a lively and attractive young single woman.

Fliess's reputation was at stake, and Freud, undoubtedly feeling very guilty about the whole incident, came to his colleague's defense. During the convalescence Emma had repeated episodes of bleeding from the nose and she seems not to have recovered properly until late in May, almost four months after the operation. About a year later Fliess seems to have suggested to Freud that the episodic hemorrhaging was hysterical.[1] Freud quickly agreed (Masson 1985, Letters of Apr. 16, Apr. 26–28, May 4, and June 4, 1896). Emma, he claimed, had a history of nosebleeds and headaches, the latter thought to be due to malingering. She also had had erotic thoughts about a young doctor whom she wanted to treat her nosebleeds. Thus she welcomed her severe and painful menstruation as showing to others that she really was ill. Freud was present when the gauze was discovered, and when the near-fatal hemorrhage began he fainted. According to him, Emma experienced his reaction "as the realization of an old wish to be loved in her illness" (Masson 1985, Letter of May 4, 1896), an interpretation that he held to despite not being able to get the dates of the hemorrhages "because they were not recorded at the sanatorium" (Letter of June 4, 1896). Emma's bleeding was thus caused by sexual longing rather than by the trauma of the operation and the gauze.

Masson argues that by the middle of 1896 Freud was in a conflict:

On the one hand, his patients told him their memories of traumas from their childhood; these he had no reason to disbelieve ... On the other hand, one of the patients ... had been severely injured by an operation that Freud had recommended and which was carried out by his closest personal friend and scientific colleague. The tension between these two sets of events ... was bound to reach a breaking point. Freud would be forced to make a choice   (Masson 1984, p. 100)

Masson has it that Freud chose Fliess and fantasy over Eckstein and experience.

What is critical to Masson's argument is whether Freud really had no reason to think the seduction stories were of other than real events. According to Masson, during Freud's visit to Paris in 1885–1886, when he frequently attended lectures and forensic postmortems conducted by Brouardel at the morgue, he became all too well aware of the frequency of sexual assaults on children. His own investigations into the nucleus of hysteria pointed, Masson claims, to the same brutal and perverse acts. From these two facts Masson concludes that Freud should have believed his patients. He nowhere considers the arguments actually proposed by Freud in announcing the collapse of the theory. He simply dismisses them as "the very objections" raised earlier by Freud's own critics to Freud's belief "in the reality of childhood seduction" (p. 110) and more than adequately answered by Freud at that time.

Now, it is just not the case that Freud's arguments were ever aired in public. The points were made by no one other than Freud, and, at that time, in no place other than the letter to Fliess. That is, the objections about psychotic thinking, about not bringing any treatment to a real end, about the lack of reality in the unconscious, and about the prevalence of a specific cause that had to cooperate with a precondition were Freud's own, and not those of his critics. True, Freud discussed this last methodological requirement in public, but not as an objection. His discussion was positive, so to speak, aiming to explain how the prevalence of childhood seductions had to be greater than the prevalence of hysteria. All that he did in public in anticipating objections was to advance his theses about the determining quality and traumatic force of the scenes, to stress the coherence of the scenes with the logical structure, to point to the uniformity of the material apparently recalled, and to claim he had independent evidence that seduction had taken place in one or two instances. Whether the private or public arguments are considered, we might note M. I. Klein's (1981) view that Freud had little scientific reason for so reinterpreting his data.

Holt (1982), in his review of Balmary's *Freud and the Hidden Fault of the Father*, says that Balmary has Freud pulling back from the seduction theory because it "would have implicated his [Freud's] father as a child molester." If this is what she says, it is a reason similar to Masson's lack of courage. However, it conflicts with Freud twice so accusing his father (Masson 1985, Letters of Feb. 8, 1897, and Sept. 21, 1887).

Critics such as Masson, Balmary, and Klein and Tribich confuse the issue. Vetter (1988) tellingly brought out that the question is not whether seductions really occur in childhood. Nor, I would add, is it whether they cause hysteria. The issue is whether there are seductions of the type that cause the kinds of symptoms Freud wanted to explain.

Critics from within psychoanalysis are unable to view the psychoanalytic method of investigation as other than objective. Because they have to leave free association untouched, they can offer only the most simplistic of choices: real seduction versus perverse fantasy. If Masson, for example, were right, all that had happened in the Eckstein case was that Freud deliberately disregarded some of the facts revealed by the method. For Masson and his cocritics, the facts obtained by free association are not affected by the analyst's expectations or preconceptions. Those who do not hold the method sacrosanct and are able to doubt the objectivity of data gathered in psychoanalytical treatment have three choices, not two. The third is that the memories are fabricated during the course of treatment (cf. Cioffi 1972, 1974). Preexisting fantasies and real seductions both have to be ruled out by the failure to observe seduction memories during psychotic deliria. Real seductions may also be dismissed because of the strength of Freud's own methodological point about prevalence.

Gattel's Data on Prevalence—Sulloway

Sulloway observed that data on prevalence did exist and, what is more, they were gathered specifically for Freud (Sulloway 1979, pp. 513–515). During the second half of 1897, Felix Gattel, one of Freud's earliest pupils and followers, worked at Krafft-Ebing's Psychiatric Clinic at the Vienna General Hospital investigating the role of sexual factors in the actual neuroses. Gattel (1898) collected data on 100 consecutive outpatients with neurasthenia or anxiety neurosis. Although he initially excluded patients with severe hysterical symptoms, on closer examination he found 4 with pure hysteria among the 100. Because the sample included thirty patients with pure neurasthenia, the number of hysterics was about thirteen percent of that of the neurasthenics. Sulloway concluded that if we accept Gattel's claim to have established masturbation as the specific cause of neurasthenia in his thirty patients, and if we assume that seduction had taken place in all four of the hysterics, it followed that paternal seduction had to have a prevalence of at least about one-eighth that of masturbation. Gattel also found patients in whom symptoms of hysteria were present in other disorders, as well as some in whom neurasthenic symptoms were mixed with others. The ratio of all the hysterias, pure as well as mixed, to all the neurasthenias was 17:30. On that basis, it followed that seduction had to be even more widespread, having a prevalence of about half that of masturbation.

Sulloway suggested this improbably high upper limit helped undermine Freud's seduction etiology (Sulloway 1979, p. 515). Too high a prevalence of seduction was among the reasons Freud gave Fliess for giving up the hypothesis. Sulloway also observed that Gattel probably collected at least half his data before interrupting his work to join the Freud family for three weeks in Italy, early in September 1897, and that Freud's letter announcing his suspicions about the seduction theory was written almost immediately when he returned to Vienna, on September 21. It was also then, as we find from a previously suppressed passage in that same letter, that Freud's attitude to Gattel underwent a significant change. Gattel, Freud wrote,

is something of a disappointment. Very gifted and clever, he must nevertheless, owing to his own nervousness and several unfavorable character traits, be described as unpalatable. (Masson 1985, Letter of Sept. 21, 1887)

Although his previous references mentioned Gattel's neurotic traits, Freud was rather more positive overall: Gattel "greatly pleases me," he "is becoming much attached to me and my theories," and Freud even considered he might have the potential to work as Fliess's neurological assistant (Letters of June 18, 1887 and July 7, 1887). I am very tempted to think that the data Gattel gathered were partly responsible for Freud's change of heart.

Making Gattel's work partly responsible for the collapse of the seduction theory gives a chronology that is more pleasing than Masson's. Rather than having the theory abandoned as the result of developments that took place within a period of a few months, developments that perhaps culminated with Gattel's findings, Masson first has to assume that it took about a year for Fliess's and Freud's thinking about the unfortunate consequences of the operation on Emma Eckstein to generate the hypothesis of bleeding as a form of sexual longing, and then for Freud to take a further twelve months to decide against real seduction.

Conclusion

The theory of the actual neuroses was abandoned because no satisfactory explanation of the symptoms could be formulated and because the empirical generalizations on which it was based could not be confirmed. Neither Freud nor his colleagues ever arrived at a satisfactory explanation of the central symptoms of neurasthenia. Freud persisted for a long time in trying to account for anxiety attacks, making three distinct revisions of his theory before giving up altogether. The curious thing about these explanations was that there was really nothing to explain: excessive masturbation and incomplete gratification are not among the necessary conditions of neurasthenia and anxiety neurosis, let alone their specific causes. Neither the explanations nor the mechanisms were required. With regard to treatment, few of Freud's colleagues found that the actual neuroses responded to his simple therapeutic maneuvers. Here Freud appears to have underestimated the power his suggestions had both to produce therapeutic effects and to elicit the kind of evidence he sought.

The relatively sudden collapse of the childhood seduction theory was not due to any disconfirming observation or conflict with the facts. The answer I have given to the question of why Freud came to believe that hysteria was caused by perverse sexual seductions in childhood is the very substantial influence of his three expectations that sexual factors were all-important, that the causes of neuroses were uniform, and that abreaction adequately indexed the importance of a memory. Freud's concept of psychic determinism effectively prevented him from considering how his conscious suggestions and unconscious influences determined the content of the pseudomemories of the events his patients reported as having had or agreed with him they must have had. The pressure exerted on patients, subjective standards, and an elastic criterion by which total failure to recall was allowed to count as a memory all helped create the false recollections.

Freud's proposal that the recollections were of fantasies had several consequences. One was to reduce the importance of the cathartic method. Abreaction might still be used to reduce the effect of traumatic memories that had become linked with the fantasy. But it no longer had a role in identifying significant memories and it could not be central to therapy. Indeed, within ten years Ferenczi (1908/1950) classed the "old Breuer-Freud 'catharsis' or 'abreaction'" with such simple methods as suggestion and reassurance.

It might also be thought that another consequence of Freud's abandoning the seduction theory would be for him to neglect the effects of real trauma in favor of the analyses of fantasies. In fact, this alleged outcome was discussed by a number of different writers (M. I. Klein and Tribich 1982a,b; Masson 1984). Apart from some points I will make shortly, I would say that whereas it is true that Freud did come to place the primary emphasis on psychic reality—what was real for the patient—the analysis of Dora as well as analyses I have not so far considered (Little Hans, Wolf Man, Rat Man) show that this supposed neglect was far from total.

Even though the seduction theory was gone, Freud retained his expectations virtually intact, now incorporated into the concept of the logical and associative structure of the neurosis. All he had to do was to give a new account of the origins of the seduction pseudomemory. But that required explaining how sexual wishes created fantasies in childhood as well as how memories were laid down, how some of them were repressed, and how all of them retained some potential to become conscious. In short, what Freud needed was a comprehensive theory of the mind, one concerned with the relation of drives to mental processes generally, and not simply with the regulation and discharge of excess excitation. This new theory was largely set out in *The Interpretation of Dreams* and *Three Essays on the Theory of Sexuality*, and it is to those works we now turn. However, we can anticipate difficulties for the new theory to the extent that it invokes omnipresent sexual factors, is based on facts gathered and evaluated by a defective method, and is framed in such a way that the explanations it generates are similar to the earlier ones.

It is, of course, impossible to distinguish expectations from hypotheses in an absolute way. Both serve equally well or badly in guiding an investigation. A hypothesis usually has the advantage over an expectation because it most often is consciously formulated and carefully scrutinized. It is because the ideas on which Freud based his work were not so dissected that they are better designated as expectations than hypotheses. For example, Freud's expecting the causes of all neuroses to be sexual could be regarded as a hypothesis only if one were to overlook the fact that it was not established for actual neuroses. Again, it is reasonable to search for uniformity in causes, but to think that the causes of hysteria might be discovered without influencing the trains of associations is not. Although the belief is most obviously false, it is the one that has persisted longest in psychoanalytic theory and practice.

Note

1. As to responsibility for the longing explanation, my reading of the correspondence leads me to conclude that the first explanation was formulated by Freud in terms of Fliess's periodicity theory. I think Fliess then questioned his interpretation and proposed the alternative of bleeding as sexual longing. Then, in so far as Freud could check any facts, he did so and, after taking them as confirmation, he accepted Fliess's thesis. As evidence, consider the following points. First, Freud wrote on April 16, 1896, that he had "a completely surprising explanation of Eckstein's hemorrhages—*which will give you much pleasure.*" I take this to mean that Freud's explanation drew on Fliess's periodicity theory. Second, on April 26–28, 1896, Freud clearly attributed the longing thesis to Fliess, saying, "I shall be able to prove to you that *you were right*, that her episodes of bleeding were hysterical, were occasioned by longing, and probably occurred at the sexually relevant times" (my emphasis). He then indicated he was seeking more data, and a week later, on May 4, 1896, said he knew "only that she bled out of longing" before summarizing what he found. A month later again, on June 4, 1896, he wrote that, although the dates could not be obtained from the sanatorium, the story "is becoming even clearer; there is no doubt that her hemorrhages were due to wishes," and concluded with an unmistakable acknowledgment of Fliess as source: "Your nose has again smelled things correctly."

9 Dreams and Symptoms

... the fingers ... beat gently ... as if her memory had set them going mechanically with the remembrance of a favourite tune.
—Collins: *The Woman in White*, Gilmore's story

In forming his new theory of the mind, Freud brought together two reasonably independent lines of thinking about symptoms and dreams. He proposed that both were produced by similar kinds of repressed wishes coming into conflict with the same regulatory process. Because his explanation was not limited to symptoms and dreams, he saw it as a general psychology, or at least as providing the basis for one. Before setting out the theory itself and evaluating it, I give an account of the two strands of thought and how Freud united them.

Why Freud first evinced an interest in dreams, which he did over a number of years, is not entirely clear. At the time he began his work on hysteria his attention was directed to the manner in which the dream was constructed. Not long after that he identified a motive behind the apparently meaningless facade of the dream: each dream was caused by the attempt to fulfill a wish. Approximately two years later again Freud came to believe symptoms had a similar origin: the same forces that created the dream transformed wishes into symptoms. His theorizing also appeared to undergo a change, seeming to be cast in purely psychological terms; however, the earlier pseudophysiological mode of thought was still present.

Structure and Motive in Dreams

Well before becoming interested in the psychoneuroses Freud attempted to understand dreams. As a medical student he kept notebooks of his own dreams, and his letters to his fiancée refer to some of them and his attempts to interpret them. By 1882 he anticipated a basic feature of his later view on the structure of dreams:

I never dream about matters that have occupied me during the day, only of such themes as were touched on once in the course of the day and then broken off. (Letter of June 30, 1882, to Martha Bernays, cited in E. Jones 1953–1957, vol. 1, p. 351; cf. Sulloway 1979, pp. 321–329)

When he translated Charcot's *Leçons du Mardi* Freud noted a similar thing about hysterical deliria:

There emerges in hysterical deliria material in the shape of ideas and impulses to action which the subject in his healthy state has rejected and inhibited.... Something similar holds good of a number of dreams, which spin out further associations which have been rejected or broken off. (Freud 1892–1894, p. 138, note to Charcot's p. 137)

This footnote appears to be Freud's earliest published remark on the dream and shows his interest in the fact the dream developed from the trains of associations broken off, rather than in the *content* of the rejected impulses. That is, the interest is a *structural* one. Other remarks of this period clearly have the same focus:

> For several weeks I found myself obliged to exchange my usual bed for a harder one, in which I had more numerous or more vivid dreams, or in which, it may be, I was unable to reach the normal depth of sleep. In the first quarter of an hour after waking I remembered all the dreams I had had during the night, and I took the trouble to write them down and try to solve them. I succeeded in tracing all these dreams back to two factors (1) to the necessity for working out any ideas which I had only dwelt upon cursorily during the day—which had only been touched upon and not finally dealt with; and (2) to the compulsion to link together any ideas that might be present in the same state of consciousness. The senseless and contradictory character of the dreams could be traced back to the uncontrolled ascendancy of this latter factor.   (Breuer and Freud 1895, p. 67, n. 1)

This comment may be dated as belonging to the first half of 1894 (editorial note, *Standard Edition*, vol. 4, p. xv) and makes it quite clear Freud's interest was in the cursory day ideation, which provided the starting point, and the compulsion to link ideas together, which gave the dream its structure. He already recognized symbolism in dreams, but placed no special emphasis on it. For example, he and Breuer (1893) noted that a symbolic relation "such as healthy people form in dreams" sometimes connected the causal trauma and the symptom (p. 5). Nevertheless, almost two more years elapsed before he really paid attention to the content of dreams.

On March 4, 1895, Freud wrote to Fliess about what he called a small analogy to a dream psychosis (about which we unfortunately know nothing) of Emma Eckstein's:

> Rudi Kaufmann, a very intelligent nephew of Breuer's and also a medical man, is a late riser. He has his maidservant wake him, and then is very reluctant to obey her. One morning she woke him again and, since he did not want to listen to her, called him by his name, "Mr. Rudi". Thereupon the sleeper hallucinated a hospital chart [cf. *Rudolfinerhaus*] with the name "Rudolf Kaufmann" on it and said to himself, "So R.K. is already in the hospital; then I do not need to go there," and went on sleeping!   (Masson 1985)

Although Freud did not comment that the dream "allowed" Rudi to stay asleep while "being" at the hospital, I think we can agree with Schur (1966b) that the wish-fulfillment hypothesis had already been formulated. The single image of Rudi-in-a-hospital-bed could be construed as expressing simultaneously the conflicting wishes to wake and go to the hospital, and to continue sleeping.

The earliest unambiguous contemporary reference to the wishful character of dreams is a single sentence in a letter to Fliess of September 23, 1895. Quite abruptly and without further elaboration, Freud wrote, "A dream the day before yesterday yielded the funniest confirmation of the conception that dreams are motivated by wish fulfillment" (Masson 1985). It is quite difficult to determine when Freud formulated this hypothesis. During the night of July 23–24, 1895, we know he had a dream that he claimed in 1914 to be the first he ever submitted to detailed interpretation (Freud 1900, p. 106, n. 1 of 1914) and through which he grasped the general principle (Masson 1985, letter of June 18, 1900). However, no contemporary reference to the motives or impulses expressed in this dream, known as the dream of Irma's injection, has survived. Neither Schur (1966b, p. 48) nor Grinstein (1968, p. 46) accepts Freud's claim that it was the source of the wish-fulfillment hypothesis, even though at the end of the first part of the *Project* some elements of it were discussed in a context where the purpose and meaning of dreams was explicitly said to be wish fulfillment. Because the first part of the *Project* was completed between September 4 and October 8, 1895 (editorial note, *Standard Edition* 1, pp. 284–285), about the same time as the abrupt announcement of the hypothesis to Fliess, it seems more likely that Freud did not place wish fulfillment central to his method of interpretation until about September 1895 rather than July.

Actually, the earliest contemporaneous record of a dream explicitly interpreted as a wish fulfillment is the following report headed "Another Wish-Dream" (which implies there had been at least one earlier similar interpretation) that Freud recorded about eighteen months later:

"I suppose that this is a wishful dream," said E. "I dreamed that, just as I arrived at my house with a lady, I was arrested by a policeman, who requested me to get into a carriage. I demanded more time to put my affairs in order, and so on. It was in the morning, after I had spent the night with this lady."—"Were you horrified?"—"No."—"Do you know what you were charged with?"—"Yes. With having killed a child."—"Has that any connection with reality?"—"I was once responsible for the abortion of a child resulting from an affair. I dislike thinking about it."—"Well, had nothing happened on the morning before the dream?"—"Yes, I woke up and had intercourse."—"But you took precautions?"—"Yes. By withdrawing."—"Then you were afraid you might have made a child, and the dream shows you the fulfillment of your wish that nothing should happen, that you nipped the child in the bud. You made use of the feeling of anxiety that arises after a coitus of that kind as material for your dream." (Masson 1985, Draft L of May 2, 1897)

Freud seemed to have shown the meaningless elements of the dream were associated with a second set of meaningful ideas. Anxiety about pregnancy was so elaborated that the dreamer need not worry.

Freud had moved from being interested in the determinants of the structure of dreams to being concerned with their content. But if dreams were to be interpreted as fulfilling wishes, how was their typically senseless appearance to be explained?

The Construction of the Dream

In explaining the devious expression of wishes in dreams, Freud distinguished three aspects of the dream: its manifest content, its latent content, and the dream work. Put oversimply, the latent content provided the wish, the dream work disguised it, and the manifest content reflected its altered form. The disguise was brought about by the censorship, a function that endeavored to keep the wish out of consciousness altogether.

The Manifest Content

The manifest content is the dream as it is remembered. It includes visual images, contradictory impressions, lack of apparent structure, and so on. Although it is unimportant in the practical sense, being a mere starting point for interpretation, it is of the greatest importance theoretically. The dream theory has to account for the construction of the manifest content out of the latent content.

The Latent Content

The latent content includes all the components of which the dream is built: repressed infantile wishes, mostly of a sexual nature; partly conscious current preoccupations, arising either from conscious experiences during the previous day or from unconscious wishes themselves; and sensory excitations from somatic sources, for example, those of hunger, thirst, or sex. Of these components, Freud regarded unconscious infantile sexual wishes as making the greatest contribution.

The latent content could not be experienced directly: its presence was inferred from analysis of the associations to the elements of the manifest content. In reaching the latent content the dreamer was required to adopt a particular attitude of mind. The process of association had to be attended to without any judgment being passed on the content of the associations. Every thought, no matter how unimportant or objectionable it might seem, had to be allowed into consciousness. When the dreamer put his or her own critical attitude to one side, Freud believed the trains of thought that began with the manifest element necessarily ended at the unconscious ideas from which they had sprung.

The Dream Work

Four main processes transformed the meaningful latent content into the less comprehensible manifest content: condensation, displacement, representability, and secondary revision.

Condensation   Condensation referred to the difference between the meager manifest content and the vastness of the latent content, as well as to the process by which several distinct waking-life images or ideas fused to form a single image or idea. Condensation is well illustrated by part of an important dream of Freud's, that of Irma's injection:

A large hall—numerous guests, whom we were receiving.—Among them was Irma. I at once took her on one side, as though to answer her letter and to reproach her for not having accepted my "solution" yet. I said to her: "If you still get pains, it's really only your fault." She replied: "If you only knew what pains I've got now in my throat and stomach and abdomen—it's choking me"—I was alarmed and looked at her. She looked pale and puffy. I thought to myself that after all I must be missing some organic trouble. I took her to the window and looked down her throat, and she showed signs of recalcitrance, like women with artificial dentures.   (Freud 1900, p. 107)

Associations to the three elements of the complaints of stomach and throat pains, the examination by the window, and the pale, puffy appearance brought to mind three different people. One was another patient who had the same symptoms as Irma had in the dream; the second was another patient who had actually been examined beside a window; the third was Freud's wife who had looked puffy and pale during one of her pregnancies. The single dream image condensed the features of these different people who had in common their recalcitrance to one or another form of treatment.

Displacement   Displacement was either the replacement of one latent idea by another remote from it or a shift of emphasis from an important to an unimportant idea. Freud's dream of a botanical monograph illustrates the second type:

I had written a monograph on a certain plant. The book lay before me and I was at the moment turning over a folded colored plate. Bound up in each copy there was a dried specimen of the plant, as though it had been taken from a herbarium.   (Freud 1900, p. 169)

Freud thought the important ideas in the latent content concerned complications and conflicts in his relations with his colleagues, as well as the charge that he was not serious enough and pursued his hobbies too energetically. The botanical thoughts connecting these two important trains of thought with each other were themselves relatively unimportant. The central manifest image of the monograph was due to a displacement of emphasis from the two important trains to a less important, single visual image.

Representation   Representation of the latent ideas produced a further and quite characteristic distortion. Ideas were typically represented visually, a change necessitating the concrete representation of abstract ideas, the use of symbols, and peculiar portrayals of logical relations. For example, the logical relation of simultaneity was pictured by simultaneously present visual images of each thought; causal connections were temporal sequences of images or successive dreams on the one night; logical alternatives such as either-or appeared together, without contradiction; negations were disregarded, and so on. The logic of the dream was completely at variance with that of waking life.

Freud also believed that many dream symbols represented sexual ideas and impulses directly, as in the following dream related by what he described as an innocent lady dreamer:

She was putting a candle into a candlestick; but the candle broke so that it wouldn't stand up properly. The girls at her school said she was clumsy; but the mistress said it was not her fault.   (Freud 1900, p. 186)

A ribald student song about female masturbation was what the patient associated to the element of the candle. Partly because of this, Freud inferred the candle was a symbol of the penis.

Secondary Revision   The fourth component of the dream work ordered and structured all the elements, arranging the otherwise loosely and irrationally connected dream thoughts so they seemed more intelligible. Secondary revision was different from the other three components in that it usually added no elements of its own. Rather, it selected, rearranged, and emphasized what was already there. Secondary revision is, of course, a descendant of the compulsion to link ideas together that Freud remarked on much earlier. In some translations of Freud's works on dreams the concept is rendered as "secondary elaboration," a phrase conveying more accurately the capacity of a revision to produce its own distortions.

Censorship

Censorship attempted to block the direct representation in consciousness of the repressed unconscious wishes. Although in *The Interpretation of Dreams* Freud did not explicitly relate the mechanism of repression to censorship, his later writings make it clear that dream censorship was an aspect of repression.

He introduced the concept of censorship in explaining a dream manifestly expressing an exaggerated affection toward his friend R. At first he said he had been resistant to interpreting the dream because it contained a thought he did not want to accept:

When I had completed the interpretation I learnt what it was that I had been struggling against—namely, the assertion that R. was a simpleton. The affection that I felt for R. could not be derived from the latent dream-thoughts; but no doubt it originated from this struggle of mine. If my dream was distorted in this respect from its latent content—and distorted into its opposite,—then the affection that was manifest in the dream served the purpose of this distortion. In other words, distortion was shown in this case to be deliberate and to be a means of *dissimulation.* (Freud 1900, p. 141)

The basis for his conceptualization of the dream censorship was an analogy with the social dissimulation and the verbal disguises that critics of the political and social order had to adopt. Indeed, Freud thought that dream distortion and political censorship corresponded in such detail that the presumption of a similar causation was justified:

dreams are given their shape ... by the operation of two psychical forces (or we may describe them as currents or systems); and ... one of these forces constructs the wish which is expressed by the dream, while the other exercises a censorship upon this dream-wish. (p. 144)

The peculiarities of the manifest content, the dissimulation and disguise, were due to the opposition of censorship to the unconscious wish.

Symptoms as Compromises

In *Studies on Hysteria* and other early work, Freud derived the content of the symptom from sensory and muscular innervations present at the time the symptom formed, either directly or by way of symbolization. He otherwise advanced no particular reasons for a patient developing one symptom rather than another, or for the particular symbols that formed; and for a whole class of hysterical symptoms, the so-called stigmata, no reasons at all were given. From about the middle of 1896 he seems to have begun viewing symptoms as representing wishes, but it was nearly two and a half years before this idea was to be expressed as a theory.

At the beginning of 1896, in the draft of a paper as well as in the paper itself, Freud analyzed the processes by which he believed a number of symptoms formed, but did not imply that any of them represented either wishes or compromises between different wishes (Masson 1985, Draft K of Jan. 1, 1896; Freud 1896b). Obsessional ideas and affects were said to be only "a compromise between the repressed *ideas* and the repressing ones" (Freud 1896b, p. 170. Emphasis altered). Not until a letter of May 30, 1896, do we find the germ of Freud's later view: there almost all symptoms were said to be compromise formations reflecting an opposition between *uninhibited* mental processes and the *inhibitory* force of thought (Masson 1985). At the end of that year, in a letter of December 17, Freud reported his first example of a symptom as a compromise: according to his analysis a fear of falling out of a window represented a compromise between the unconscious impulse of going to the window to beckon to a man "as prostitutes do," that is, with sexual intent, and its rejection because of the anxiety it caused. By the middle of the following year, Freud said a symptom was the result of a libidinal *impulse* summating with a later *wish* for the impulse to be punished: "symptoms, like dreams, are *the fulfillment of a wish*" (Draft N of May 31, 1897). Only about two months later, when the childhood seduction theory was banished, it seems to have taken this new explanation of symptoms and the parallel with dreams with it. Not until the beginning of 1899 was the wish-compromise view of symptoms again referred to, even though Freud's correspondence with Fliess over the same period contains many references to wishes in *dreams* (Letters of Oct. 31, 1897, and Dec. 3, 1897).

Then, at the beginning of 1899, Freud quite suddenly announced the solution to the origin of the seduction fantasies of the neurotic to which, of course, the symptoms were related. The most recent traumatic experiences were linked by associations, or as he put it, projected back, to the germs of a sexual impulse already existing in childhood. He discerned some connection with dream formation, although its precise nature escaped him:

I want to reveal to you only that the dream schema is capable of the most general application, that the key to hysteria as well really lies in dreams.... If I wait a little longer, I shall be able to present the psychic process in dreams in such a way that it also includes the process in the formation of hysterical symptoms. So let us wait.   (Letters of Jan. 3 and 4, 1899)

The end of the period of waiting, and the time at which Freud finally came to equate symptom formation with dream production, can be dated exactly. Seven weeks later he wrote:

My last generalization has held good and seems inclined to grow.... Not only dreams are wish fulfillments, so are hysterical attacks. This is true of hysterical symptoms, but probably applies to every product of neurosis.... A symptom arises where the repressed and the repressing thought can come together in the fulfillment of a wish. The symptom is the wish fulfillment of the repressing thought, for example, in the form of a punishment....
This key opens many doors. Do you know, for instance, why X.Y. suffers from hysterical vomiting? Because in fantasy she is pregnant, because she is so insatiable that she cannot bear being deprived of having a baby by her last fantasy lover as well. But she also allows herself to vomit, because then she will be starved and emaciated, will lose her beauty and no longer be attractive to anyone. Thus the meaning of the symptom is a contradictory pair of wish fulfillments.   (Letter of Feb. 19, 1899)

This formulation of the mechanism of symptom formation is virtually the same as that put forward in *The Interpretation of Dreams*:

A symptom is not merely the expression of a realized unconscious wish; a wish from the preconscious which is fulfilled by the same symptom must also be present. So that the symptom will have *at least* two determinants, one arising from each of the systems involved in the conflict.... The determinant which does not arise from the *Ucs.* [the unconscious] is invariably, so far as I know, a train of thought reacting against the unconscious wish—a self-punishment, for instance. I can therefore make the quite general assertion that *a hysterical symptom develops only where the fulfillment's of two opposing wishes, arising each from a different psychical system, are able to converge in a single expression.*   (Freud 1900, p. 569)

Sexual impulses originally arising in infancy but later repressed provided the first wish (Freud 1900, pp. 605–606). Much later again, when this unconscious wish was revived, it became linked with an opposing preconscious wish. A successful modification by the preconscious system might allow the compromise structure so formed to enter consciousness (pp. 562–563).

Just how successful Freud thought these compromises could be is illustrated in the following case note:

I was called in to a consultation last year to examine an intelligent and unembarrassed-looking girl. She was most surprisingly dressed. For though as a rule a woman's clothes are carefully considered down to the last detail, she was wearing one of her stockings hanging down and two of the buttons on her blouse were undone. She complained of having pains in her leg and, without being asked, exposed her calf. But what she principally complained of was, to use her own words, that she had a feeling in her body as though there was something "stuck into it" which was "moving backwards and forwards" and was "shaking" her through and through: sometimes it made her whole body feel "stiff". My medical colleague, who was present at the examination, looked at me; he found no difficulty in understanding the meaning of her complaint.... The girl herself had no notion of the bearing of her remarks; for if she had, she would never have given voice to them. In this case it had been possible to hoodwink the censorship into allowing a phantasy which would normally have been kept in the preconscious to emerge into consciousness under the innocent disguise of making a complaint. (Freud 1900, p. 618)

The most cursory consideration of the mechanisms illustrated in this case note shows how closely Freud had come to model symptom formation on dream production. In *The Interpretation of Dreams* he tried to provide a theory explaining both.

A Theory of the Mind

Freud proposed thinking of the mental apparatus as a number of different systems, or groups of psychological processes, related to one another by the fixed temporal sequence in which they normally operated. This did not necessarily imply that the systems had locations in specific parts of the brain or mind, but Freud spoke of them as being spatially extended and later referred to them as making up a topographic model of the mind.

The Systems of the Mental Apparatus

The systems were explicitly conceived of as components of a reflex mechanism:

the psychical apparatus must be constructed like a reflex apparatus. Reflex processes remain
the model of every psychical function.   (Freud 1900, p. 538)

Although Bricke and Meynert were continuing to influence Freud's thinking, there
was the characteristic teleological addition:

at first the apparatus's efforts were directed towards keeping itself so far as possible free from
stimuli; consequently its first structure followed the plan of a reflex apparatus, so that any
sensory excitation impinging on it could be promptly discharged along a motor path.   (p. 565)

Psychical processes were said to begin with a perception at the sensory end of the
apparatus and to terminate typically in a motor response. Figure 9.1, which is based
on Freud's own diagrams, shows how excitation created by stimulation of the perceptual system, symbolized by the abbreviation *Pcpt.*, flowed through the apparatus to
be discharged by the motor system, or *M*. At this point, it should be noted the
model is very much a physiological one: a reflex apparatus with sensory and motor
components activated by a flow of excitation. Indeed, over many years it has been
apparent to philosophers, psychiatrists, and psychologists alike that the model simply
extends that set out in the *Project* (MacIntyre 1958, pp. 22–23; Wollheim 1971,
p. 63; MacCarley and Hobson 1977; Hobson and MacCarley 1977).

Repeated stimulation of the *Pcpt.* led to the uncoordinated motor responses of the
infant being replaced by the purposive behavior of the adult. This obvious effect of
experience seemed to Freud to require assuming that distinct memory traces of each
experience had been laid down, and that adult behavior was effective to the extent it
drew on them. Following a suggestion of Breuer's, Freud argued in the *Studies* that
the memory traces were not produced and retained in *Pcpt.*, and he now repeated the
point:

there are obvious difficulties involved in supposing that one and the same system can accurately retain modifications of its elements and yet remain perpetually open to the reception of
fresh occasions for modification.   (Freud 1900, p. 538)

Freud concluded that the memories were stored separately from *Pcpt.* He supposed,
as is also illustrated in figure 9.1, there to be several systems of memory traces
immediately following *Pcpt.*, which he symbolized by *Mnem.*, *Mnem.'* *Mnem."*, and
so on. *Mnem.* contained the memory traces of perceptions that occurred simultaneously, *Mnem.'* had the same traces organized with respect to similarity, and *Mnem."*
and the other systems had the material organized around other kinds of logical

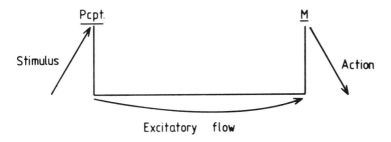

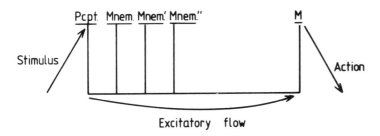

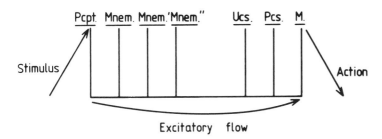

Figure 9.1
Freud's reflex-based mental apparatus (Freud 1900, pp. 537–541).

relation. Since an association was a linkage of simultaneous perceptions, its basis was to be found in the *Mnem.* systems:

Association would thus consist in the fact that, as a result of a diminution in resistances and of the laying down of facilitating paths, an excitation is transmitted from a given *Mnem.* element more readily to one *Mnem.* element than to another.   (Freud 1900, p. 539)

Again, even though no physiological processes were supposedly being referred to, Freud clearly retained Meynert's and Exner's ideas about associations and facilitation. However, in one very important respect, the memory store is conceived of differently: instead of one system of memories, there were several, containing, as they moved away from *Pcpt.*, progressively more abstract organizations of traces. Different levels of conceptual thought drew on different stores of traces or, perhaps, the same traces organized in different ways.

The unconscious and preconscious systems, symbolized as *Ucs.* and *Pcs.* respectively, were held to be the two psychical agencies mainly responsible for dreams and symptoms. *Pcs.* was characterized as having the critical function of determining the admissibility of thoughts to consciousness. Mental processes occurring within *Pcs.* would become conscious provided they were of sufficient intensity and were attended to. *Pcs.* was also the agency that directed waking life, and since this was mainly through voluntary, conscious action, Freud located *Pcs.* adjacent to *M*. He placed *Ucs.* on the sensory side of *Pcs.*, because whatever the intensity of processes in *Ucs.*, they could become conscious only after modification by *Pcs.*, as figure 9.1 indicates. Censorship, which is clearly a *Pcs.* function, was said to be located between *Pcs.* and *Ucs.* although it is not so pictured on the diagram. With this addition of *Ucs.* and *Pcs.* the model of the mental apparatus was complete.

Dream production began with excitation generated by the wishes stored in *Ucs.*, but dreams were actually fashioned out of modifications to that excitation as it passed through the various systems. At night, the wish caused a preliminary movement of excitation along the normal path leading toward *Pcs.* On the border of *Ucs.* and *Pcs.* the censorship forced the flow of excitation away from *M*. In any case, *M*. could not be activated because of sleep. The excitation now commenced a regressive journey toward the sensory end of the apparatus where, in cathecting *Pcpt.*, it produced the hallucinatory sensory images typical of the dream. To reach *Pcpt.* the excitation had to traverse the various systems of *Mnem.* in a reverse order of that in which they were laid down. Normal conceptual thought based on the logical relations stored in the more recent *Mnem.* systems therefore disappeared and was replaced with the logically more primitive thinking based on the relations stored in the older systems. Primitive relations of simultaneity, similarity, and contrast, for example, would be the last to be recathected before the visual metamorphoses of the dream thought. As Freud emphasized:

In regression the fabric of the dream-thoughts is resolved into its raw material.   (Freud 1900, p. 543)

Given the mental apparatus to be structured as Freud supposed, and given the various systems successively modified the train of thought cathected by the excitatory process, the regressive movement of excitation through the apparatus seems to account for the peculiar logic and imagery of the dream. What then accounts for regression?

Infantile Wishes and Infantile Thought

Freud believed that the regressive tendency of the dream was largely accounted for by supposing the basic wishes to be infantile, and that the dream revived their infantile mode of satisfaction. He proposed that infantile mental life was governed by the primary process, that is, a tendency toward the free discharge of the quantities of excitation accumulated within the apparatus. According to the principle of constancy, excitation from outside impinging on the sensory end of the reflex apparatus was discharged along motor pathways. Although even the uncoordinated movements of the infant could remove a source of external stimulation, it was otherwise with excitation arising within the apparatus. Major somatic needs could not be satisfied by reflex motor discharge, for all that caused was screaming and helpless kicking. Only an experience of satisfaction—nourishment in the case of a hungry baby—could discharge the increased excitation. Since Freud also assumed that accumulations of excitation were experienced as unpleasure and discharge as pleasure, the experience of satisfaction generated pleasure. Consequently, future unpleasurable accumulations of excitation produced by the particular need would set the apparatus in motion to repeat the experience of satisfaction, diminish the level of excitation, and so produce pleasure.

A wish was a movement of excitation that started with unpleasure and aimed at pleasure. Because of the infant's inability to control its circumstances, the attempted fulfillment of the wish was not through the re-creation of the actual experience of satisfaction; rather the infant hallucinated the percept of the satisfying object. Freud supposed the mnemic image of the perception concomitant with the experience of satisfaction had become associated with the memory trace of the excitation produced by the need, and that the association was strengthened with each subsequent experience of satisfaction. Later, when the need again arose, its excitation would recathect the image of the satisfying object, thereby producing a hallucination in the perceptual system. Infantile wishes directed excitation denied access to *Pcs.* into *Pcpt.*, because it was in that system that the objects satisfying the wishes were found in the past. The free discharge of energy of the primary process created a mode of thought necessarily dominated by inner need and hallucinated objects. In the adult, therefore,

Dreaming is a piece of infantile mental life that has been superseded.   (Freud 1900, p. 567)

The questions that now arise are what is it that supersedes primary process thinking, and why is it not available during dreaming?

Secondary Process Thought

During development Freud supposed that a more realistic secondary process gradually replaced the earlier, primitive primary process. By itself the primary process could not satisfy internal needs. Hallucinated breasts do not feed hungry babies. If a real object were to be found, the structure of the apparatus demanded that excitation had to reach *M.* where it could initiate action. Realistic thinking had also to be based on the availability of a large number of mnemic images of the various needs and their modes of satisfaction. Freud envisaged secondary process thought as the sending out of small amounts of excitation to memory traces that were likely to prove relevant, the successive scrutiny of those traces, the successive withdrawal of cathexes from those unlikely to lead to a realistic solution, and the eventual finding of a path of action likely to satisfy the particular need. Not all the mnemic images had to be cathected at any one time, but free access to the whole of them was necessary.

Because realistic thinking required only small numbers of traces to be cathected at any one time, Freud supposed only small amounts of excitation would be required to be expended. If a strong need was present during this tentative thought activity, the secondary process could draw on the rest of its energy to prevent or inhibit the free discharge of the excitation of the need. Secondary process realistic thinking was therefore quite different from infantile thinking because its

excitation is governed by quite different mechanical conditions from those in force under the dominion of the first system. When once the second system has concluded its exploratory thought-activity, it releases the inhibition and damming-up of the excitations [of the first system] and allows them to discharge themselves in movement.   (Freud 1900, pp. 599–600)

Freud attributed secondary process thinking to *Pcs.* and primary process thinking to *Ucs.* Sleep reduced the availability of the *Pcs.* mechanism, with the consequence that primary process thinking could be used to fulfill unconscious, infantile wishes. Infantile mental life, usually superseded in daytime, was reinstated at night.

Dreams gained part of their singularity from the impress of the primary process on the trains of thought occurring in them. Mobilized for free discharge, the quantities of excitation cathecting each component of the train distorted the thoughts. Freud thought that mobilization was effected in four different ways:

1. Excitation of individual ideas could be accumulated in a single element of the train to produce an *en bloc* discharge. This was the process of condensation.

2. Excitation could be transferred to ideas of intermediate significance rather than to important ideas; that is, displacement of emphasis from the central thoughts would occur and the formation of compromise structures would result.

3. Excitation could be transferred along normally little-used associational pathways to link ideas by homonyms and verbal similarities, thus giving rise to the strangeness of dream associations.

4. Excitation of one idea would not be accompanied by the inhibition of its opposite, as happened in normal thought. Mutually contradictory ideas could exist side by side or be expressed in the form of a single idea, as if there were no contradiction between them.

The peculiarities of the dream work, its complete contrast with secondary process thinking, derived from the greater mobility to which excitation was subjected once dream thoughts entered *Ucs.*

Dream Wishes

Freud supposed the major role of the residues of daytime thinking, which he invariably found in dreams, was to provide a point of entry for the admission of *Ucs.* wishes into *Pcs.* The unconscious wish transferred its excitation onto the day residue and created or reinforced a preconscious dream wish. When the day residue was a worry or, more frequently, an indifferent or affectless idea, the transfer formed a new *Pcs.* dream wish. If the residue was a thought that had been suppressed during the day, the transfer of the unconscious excitation reinforced it. In both instances the residue gained a new impetus to press toward consciousness. However, neither the new *Pcs.* dream wish nor the old *Ucs.* wish reinforcing it was admissible to consciousness. Both came up against the censorship of *Pcs.* that then initiated the dream work. Trains of thought subject to the dream work thus had their beginnings, but not their motives, in *Pcs.*

Some distortion of the *Ucs.* wish took place with this first censorship. The distortion was made the more readily because the unconscious wish was already generally attached to an indifferent or nonwishful day residue. Were it not for *Pcs.*, the initial distortion would have moved further toward consciousness. Denied that passage, the combined train of thought, consisting of the *Pcs.* residues and the *Ucs.* wish, now moved back to *Ucs.*, where it was subjected to the inevitable distortion of the primary process. Infantile wishful experiences or the fantasies based on them might then pull the combined *Ucs.* and *Pcs.* thoughts farther along the regressive pathway. Chronologically earlier than the unconscious wish instigating the dream, these infantile wishes had their memory traces closer to *Pcpt.* than those of the instigating wish. The train of thought therefore tended to be drawn toward the sensorily strong images of infantile wishes or fantasies. Regression was thus a two-sided process. It was

in all probability . . . an effect of a resistance opposing the progress of a thought into consciousness along the normal path, and of a simultaneous attraction exercised upon the thought by the presence of memories possessing great sensory force.   (Freud 1900, p. 547)

The regressive movement of the train of thought toward *Pcpt.* by *Ucs.* or, more correctly, the movement of the quantities of excitation cathecting the elements of the train, was thus doubly determined by the push or resistance of *Pcs.* censorship coupled with the pull or attraction of the infantile wishful experience or fantasy.

To complete the theory, Freud had to account for the indestructibility of infantile wishes and the function of the censorship. He based his explanation of these two central features of the theory on the development of the secondary process out of the primary and on the role of unpleasure in causing repression.

Repression and Dreams

Freud proposed that a prototype of repression occurred in the primitive psychical apparatus even before the secondary process developed. Any perceptual stimulus producing painful excitation would create a trace associating the memory of the stimulus with the pain. Realistic or hallucinatory attempts to recathect the memory trace of the stimulus would necessarily tend to revive the memory of pain. But, since the primary process operated according to the pleasure principle, the attempted recathexis would fail. What Freud described as an "effortless and regular avoidance" of a distressing memory was a necessary part of primary process functioning, and the prototype and first example of repression.

One consequence of this concept of prototypal repression is that memories of unpleasant experiences can never be available to secondary process thinking even if those memories are necessary to arrive at a realistic need satisfaction. Freud therefore gave the second system the power to inhibit the unpleasurable discharge at the very instant the painful memory was cathected. He emphasized this supposition as "the key to the whole theory of repression":

the second system can only cathect an idea if it is in a position to inhibit any development of unpleasure that may proceed from it.   (Freud 1900, p. 601)

How did this power not do away with prototypal repression itself? During development the pleasurable affect of some of the infantile wishes was transformed into unpleasure. As Freud emphasized, attempts to cathect the mnemic image would now only generate unpleasure, so

it is precisely this transformation of affect which constitutes the essence of what we term "repression."   (p. 604)

Preconscious thoughts onto which a repressed unconscious wish transferred its excitation shared the unpleasurable affect. By withdrawing its cathexis from the transference thoughts, *Pcs.* would now avoid the *Ucs.* train of thoughts and repress them.

Freud considered repression had one of three outcomes: success, symptom formation, or the production of a dream. Complete repression meant that little trace of the unconscious wish would be found in waking life. However, if the unconscious wish received what he called an organic reinforcement that was passed on in turn to the transference thoughts, those vehicles of the unconscious wish would seek admission to consciousness without the usual cathexis from *Pcs.* But the *Pcs.* trend originally withdrawing the cathexes would also have its opposition reinforced. A symptom would form as a compromise between the repressed unconscious wish and the preconscious trend opposing it. The third outcome, which presumably occurred when organic reinforcement was not provided, was the dream:

from the moment at which the repressed thoughts are strongly cathected by the unconscious wishful impulse and, on the other hand, abandoned by the preconscious cathexis, they become subject to the primary psychical process and their one aim is motor discharge or, if the path is open, hallucinatory revival of the desired perceptual identity.   (p. 605)

Because the unpleasure the train of thoughts now conveyed could not be inhibited, withdrawal of preconscious cathexis from transference thoughts acted as a push.

Although Freud does not say so directly, it is clear that censorship and repression were being equated, an equation already implicit in his earlier discussion of the representation and suppression of affects in dreams. There, in the dreams of the death of a loved relative

We can thus plainly see the purpose for which the censorship exercises its office and brings about the distortion of dreams: it does *so in order to prevent the generation of anxiety or other forms of distressing affect.*   (p. 267; cf. pp. 246, 460–462, 467, 488–489)

The mechanism of censorship-repression was central to the explanation of the dream. Censorship demanded distortion, as it were, and set the distorting mechanisms into action by the regression it compelled.

The Immutability of Unconscious Wishes

Freud derived the indestructibility of infantile wishes from the later development of the secondary process:

In consequence of the belated appearance of the secondary processes, the core of our being, consisting of unconscious wishful impulses, remains inaccessible to the understanding and inhibition of the preconscious; the part played by the latter is restricted once and for all to directing along the most expedient paths the wishful impulses that arise from the unconscious.   (Freud 1900, p. 603)

These early wishes were developmentally inaccessible; they could be neither inhibited nor understood; at most their energy could be directed or diverted toward higher aims. The wishes themselves could not be destroyed. Those wishes generating unpleasure if now revived were as inaccessible as the others and the affect attaching to them just as uninhibitable. But because of the affective transformation, they would now be experienced at the preconscious level as unpleasurable. Consequently, *Pcs.* would withdraw its cathexis from them, no transference of their energy would be possible, and they would not be diverted. Lacking the preconscious cathexis, they fell back unaltered into *Ucs.* Once embedded in memory, infantile wishes would, to turn Freud's metaphor, prance each night upon the dream stage. Only death called a halt to their noctambulations.

My comparison shows how closely dreams and symptoms resembled each other (cf. Ellenberger 1970, p. 491; and Sulloway 1979, pp. 345–346). By affixing their cathexes onto preconscious day residues, unconscious infantile sexual wishes initiated a progressive movement of excitation toward *Pcs.* Enough unpleasure was generated by this initial foray for preconscious cathexis to be withdrawn and a consequent reversal of the movement of excitation initiated. Earlier modes of need satisfaction stored in *Ucs.* now attracted the excitation and, in the regressive movement so maintained, the train of thought was subjected to the distortions of the primary process. The more ready discharge of energy in the unconscious produced condensation, displacement, and disregard of normal logical relations.

If organic reinforcement strengthened the train of thought, the production of dream and symptom diverged. Without the reinforcement, dream impulses began a third movement in the opposite direction, toward the perceptual system and hallucinatory expression. Only the wish to sleep then opposed that form of admission to consciousness. With the reinforcement, a third progressive movement toward the preconscious commenced, and if this new foray was successful, the wishful trend combined with an opposing preconscious impulse to gain admission to consciousness as a compromise. Dynamically and energetically, dreams and symptoms were otherwise equivalent structures. At only two points was the resemblance between dream production and symptom formation not quite complete: the final point of entry to consciousness and the final opposition to that entry were different.

The Theory Applied to the Case of Dora

Within a year of the appearance of the first copies of *The Interpretation of Dreams*, on November 4, 1899 (Masson 1985, Letter of Nov. 5, 1899), Freud began treating a hysterical patient known as Dora (Freud 1905a; Masson 1985, Letter of Oct. 14, 1900). His account of the case emphasized the importance of the interpretation of two of her dreams, and his explanation of her symptoms was based on the theory of mental functioning just outlined. Dora's case accordingly provides an eminently suitable starting point for a critical evaluation of Freud's theory.

"Only her father's authority" had forced Dora to come to Freud; she herself was quite resistant to the idea of treatment (Freud 1905a). "A slight passage of words" between her and her father had been followed by loss of consciousness, possibly with convulsions and deliria, for which she was amnesic. Other problems were soon revealed. From the age of eight years she had had laborious, difficult breathing (chronic dyspnea) that was occasionally exacerbated. At about twelve years of age she developed unilateral migrainous headaches that were invariably followed by severe coughing attacks. As time went on, these two symptoms separated, with migraines ceasing at sixteen years of age and coughing becoming worse. Typically, coughing attacks lasted from between three and five weeks—although one lasted several months—during which she frequently lost her voice (aphonia). In addition, she was low in spirits, dissatisfied with herself and her family, plagued by fatigue and lack of concentration, and unfriendly toward her mother, especially toward her mother's attempts to involve her in housework. Dora had contemplated suicide, perhaps not very seriously. She was then not quite eighteen.

Dora was "most tenderly" attached to her father, an affection increased by his many illnesses: when she was six years old he had tuberculosis and required considerable nursing; when she was ten he had a detached retina; and when she was twelve he developed a paralysis and mental disturbance after a confusional attack, all of which were the late result of a syphilitic infection. Dora's mother was occupied all day with narrow domestic affairs, especially house cleaning, and she had no understanding of Dora's more active interests. Dora withdrew completely from her mother's influence, looking down on her and criticizing her "mercilessly."[1] On the other hand, she was extravagantly fond of Frau K., a "young and beautiful woman" who, while nursing Dora's tubercular father, had begun an affair with him. A partial basis for the affair was probably provided by the fact, as Dora's father put it, "I get nothing out of my own wife." Dora, who knew of the affair for some time, nevertheless frequently visited the K.'s in company with her father. At such times she took "the greatest care" of the K.'s two children, being "almost a mother to them." Herr K., in his turn, was "most kind" to Dora; he frequently gave her "valuable presents"—once having flowers delivered daily—and often accompanied her on walks.

According to Dora, two years before treatment began, when she was sixteen, Herr K. made some kind of advance or proposition to her. Whether or not it was of marriage was unclear, for Dora interrupted him by slapping his face. After returning from the lakeside walk where the incident occurred, Dora insisted on cutting her visit short and returning home with her father. Two weeks later she told her mother of Herr K.'s advances, knowing the story would be passed on to her father, and insisted that the family, especially her father, break off relations with the K.'s. Confronted by Dora's father, Herr K. denied Dora's story, even suggesting that the whole thing was a fantasy stimulated by too much reading on sexual topics. Dora's father accepted that explanation, believing that Dora's irritability, depression, and suicidal gesture derived from his rejection of her pressure to stop seeing the K.'s.

Dora was full of reproaches against her father: she accused him of not wanting to consider Herr K.'s behavior too closely because it would disturb his own relation to Frau K., and she believed he used his ill health as a pretext to continue the affair; that is, he was malingering. But, "None of her father's actions seemed to have embittered her so much" as his willingness to accept Herr K.'s story that his advances had never taken place. These reproachful thoughts, which had a basis in fact, were nevertheless of obsessional intensity: Dora admitted they were not fully justified but, even so, she could not put them out of mind: "'I can think of nothing else,' she complained again and again" (Freud 1905a, p. 54). Freud regarded the intensity as pathological and "reflected" that the reproaches served to cover a similar *self*-reproach:

this excessively intense train of thought must owe its reinforcement to the unconscious. It cannot be resolved ... either because it ... reaches ... down into unconscious, repressed material, or because another unconscious thought lies concealed behind it ... Contrary thoughts are always closely connected ... and are often paired off ... such ... that *the one thought is excessively intensely conscious while its counterpart is repressed and unconscious*. (Freud 1905a, pp. 54–55)

This newly formulated principle allowed him to guess at the content of Dora's self-reproaches:

Her behaviour obviously went far beyond what would have been appropriate to filial concern. She felt and acted more like a jealous wife ... She was ... identifying herself both with the woman her father had once loved and with the woman he loved now. The inference is obvious ... she was in love with him.   (p. 56)

If unconscious love for her father provided reinforcement for the reproaches she directed at him, Freud asked why the affection was so recently revived. After all, until Herr K. made his proposition, Dora had been on the most friendly of terms with Frau K., virtually acting as an accomplice in the affair with Dora's father. Freud supposed Dora was also in love with Herr K., but that something about his advances to her so aroused her opposition that her feeling became distressing. She was then obliged

to summon up her infantile affection for her father and to exaggerate it, in order to protect herself against the feelings of love which were constantly pressing forward into consciousness.   (p. 58)

Dora's emphatic denial of this interpretation was taken by Freud to signify its correctness, which in his view was further confirmed by such things as her dejected reaction to not having received a birthday present from Herr K., and the observation of a relative that seeing Herr K. accidentally had caused Dora to go "as white as a sheet."

Dora's reproaches against her father served more than the purpose of suppressing her love for Herr K. The previous intimacy of her relations with Frau K., her references to Frau K.'s "adorable white body," and her anger that Frau K. had betrayed her by supporting her husband's story that the scene at the lakeside had never taken place suggested to Freud that those reproaches also suppressed her more deeply unconscious love for Frau K.:

She told herself incessantly that her father had sacrificed her to this woman, and made noisy demonstrations to show that she grudged her the possession of her father.... The jealous emotions of a woman were linked in the unconscious with a jealousy such as might have been felt by a man.   (p. 63)

It was against this pattern of feelings that Freud thought he detected in the analysis of her pathological reproaches that he commenced his interpretation of Dora's symptoms and two of her important dreams.

The first dream recurred periodically in exactly the same way. Dora had had it some nights before she told Freud of it:

A house was on fire. My father was standing beside my bed and woke me up. I dressed quickly. Mother wanted to stop and save her jewel-case; but Father said: "I refuse to let myself and my two children be burnt for the sake of your jewel-case." We hurried downstairs, and as soon as I was outside I woke up.   (p. 64. Emphasis removed)

She first had the dream on the night of the day after Herr K.'s advances. It recurred on each of the next three nights and ceased on her returning home.

On arriving at the house where the K.s were holidaying, Dora's father expressed concern about the possibility of fire; that concern was part of the day residue incorporated into the dream's formation. Recent discussions at home revived the topic of fire danger just before the dream's latest reappearance. The dream element of her father standing by the bed led to the recollection that, as she woke from her afternoon sleep after Herr K.'s proposition, she found Herr K. standing beside her. She then obtained a key to lock her room, but it was missing when she went to use it the next afternoon:

It was then that I made up my mind not to stop on with the K.'s without Father. On the subsequent mornings I could not help feeling afraid that Herr K. would surprise me while I was dressing: *so I always dressed very quickly.*   (p. 67)

Freud believed the dream corresponded to Dora's conscious intention to flee Herr K.'s attentions. He thought it was as if she said to herself she had to leave the house. In the dream the intention was represented by its opposite: Dora actually woke up after dreaming she had been able to get out of the house. The dream was repeated until the intent was realized through returning home with her father.

The theory required more than a conscious intent to form a dream. Questions to Dora about the element of the jewel case retrieved two memories that led to another motivating source, this time an unconscious one. One memory was of a dispute between her parents: her mother wanted a present of pearl drops, but her father gave his wife a bracelet. The second memory, also from the period before the first dream, was of an expensive jewel case Herr K. had given her. Freud interpreted the element "jewel-case" to stand for the female genitals, and supposed Dora thought to herself that Herr K. was persecuting her, that he wanted to force his way into her room, that her "jewel-case" was in danger, and that, if anything happened, it would be her father's fault. The dream expressed the opposite of the latter thought and represented Dora's father in the role of savior. The combination of that presumed inversion with Dora's inability to recall whether she would have liked the pearl drops herself (which Freud believed indicated Dora's repression of the thought) suggested to Freud that the rest of the train of thought also ought to be inverted. Dora was prepared to *give* to her father the sexual favors her mother *withheld* from him. Herr K.'s present of the jewel case provided the starting point of a parallel line of thought: Dora could also give to Herr K. what *his* wife also *withheld*. This latter thought was the repressed wish motivating the dream. As Freud explained:

The dream confirms once more what I had already told you before you dreamt it—that you are summoning up your old love for your father in order to protect yourself against your love for Herr K.... In short, these efforts prove once more how deeply you loved him.   (p. 70)

When Dora did not accept this interpretation Freud tried another line of argument that he hoped would convince her.

Freud's dream theory required an infantile wish to be represented in the dream. Where was that wish? He proposed that two trains of thought led off from the element "fire." One went to the idea of love through the symbolic meaning of fire. The second also led there, but through water as the opposite of fire. Because the genitals were wetted by drops of semen during intercourse, this second train built on the recollection of the pearl drops Dora's mother wanted from her husband. It then led to thoughts and memories of childhood enuresis Dora recalled as having started in her seventh or eighth year. The dream fulfilled an infantile wish about bedwetting.

Freud seems to assume that because children were often awakened at night to prevent them from wetting the bed, Dora's father woke her for the same reason. He further supposed Dora must have awakened to find her father standing by her bed and that he had "perhaps" woken her with a kiss (pp. 72, 86). The "essence" of the dream (oddly tucked away in a footnote) could be represented as Dora's thinking:

The temptation is so strong. Dear Father, protect me again as you used to in my childhood, and prevent my bed from being wetted!   (p. 73, n. 2)

The image of her father could appear in the dream as a substitute and cover for the image of Herr K., who the day before the dream first occurred similarly stood by her as she woke, perhaps also with the intention of kissing her. Since Freud believed bedwetting with a late onset, such as Dora's, was caused by masturbation, the appearance of her father in the dream also rescued her from sexual temptation. Reinforcement of the adolescent appeal for her father's aid against Herr. K.'s sexual temptation came from the memory of her father's actions in guarding her against similar infantile temptations. This was the infantile wish reinforcing the unconscious source revealed by the associations to the "jewel-case."

Even in this very condensed summary of the interpretation of Dora's dream, features typical of Freud's description of dream formation may be discerned. Freud would have assumed that the day residues about fire became linked with a repressed unconscious wish to yield to Herr K. This wish was not represented directly because the movement of excitation toward *Pcs.* was turned back until, gaining reinforcement from the infantile wishes about bedwetting and masturbation, it was represented as fulfilled through the revival of the memory image of the savior father. Condensation and displacement are shown by the multifarious connections of the elements of "fire" and "jewel-case" that also divert attention from immediate and past concerns. The revival of primitive modes of thought may be seen in the representation of the thought of giving through its contrary of withholding.

I will use Freud's analysis of some of Dora's minor symptoms, which entail a shorter examination than do the more complex ones, to reveal the same kinds of mechanisms at work there. Four years before Freud saw her, when she was fourteen, Dora was surprised by Herr K. unexpectedly embracing and kissing her. Her reaction was one of disgust, and after freeing herself she ran away. Apart from a slight loss of appetite, the disgust did not seem to produce any permanent symptom. However "a sensory hallucination" of the pressure of Herr K.'s embrace on the upper part of her body recurred from time to time, and she was unwilling, four years later, to walk past "any man whom she saw engaged in eager or affectionate conversation with a lady" (Freud 1905a, p. 29).

Freud began by asserting that Herr K.'s embrace

was surely just the situation to call up a distinct feeling of sexual excitement in a girl of fourteen who had never before been approached.   (p. 28)

He then said Dora's reaction of disgust was typical of the hysteric:

I should without question consider a person hysterical in whom an occasion for sexual excitement elicited feelings that were preponderantly or exclusively unpleasurable; and I should do so whether or no the person were capable of producing somatic symptoms.   (p. 28)

According to theory, the reversal of affect was a sign that repressed sexual ideas were already in existence, and it was from these that the disgust partly derived. Displacement also played a part:

Instead of the genital sensation which would certainly have been felt by a healthy girl in such circumstances, Dora was overcome by the unpleasurable feeling which is proper to the tract of mucous membrane at the entrance to the alimentary canal—that is by disgust.   (p. 29)

Freud then applied certain of what he called "rules of symptom formation" (which he did not spell out) to the sensory hallucination and the compulsive avoidance behavior. He supposed that, during the kiss, Dora had felt Herr K.'s erect penis pressing against her, and further supposed that there was excitation of her clitoris. The sequence of events was:

This perception was revolting to her; it was dismissed from her memory, repressed, and replaced by the innocent sensation of pressure upon her thorax, which in turn derived an excessive intensity from its repressed source. (p. 30)

Displaced clitoral excitation maintained the innervation of the sensation of pressure on the thorax. Freud assumed Dora thought men talking affectionately to ladies were likely to be sexually excited. Her avoidance thus prevented her from seeing the "somatic sign" of the erect penis.

Freud speculated that Dora's disgust at sexual excitement had a partly developmental basis. He believed disgust first arose in the child as a response to the smell and sight of excrement. Because of the excretory functions performed near the genitals, disgust was transferred to sexuality itself. Another more personal determinant of the reaction came from Dora's leukorrhea, a vaginal discharge she had from some uncertain but presumably early period. In Freud's view, the leukorrhea was caused by masturbation, and we have already seen that he also assumed masturbation had produced her bedwetting. Dora's mother suffered from a similar discharge, or catarrh, that Dora believed to have been transmitted to her mother by her father. As early as age ten years Dora associated her father's detached retina with "improper subjects," and two years later heard syphilis mentioned as a cause of his confusional attack. Dora's last governess, who had been in love with Dora's father, warned her that all men were frivolous and untrustworthy. Freud supposed that

To Dora that must mean that all men were like her father. But she thought her father suffered from venereal disease.... She might therefore have imagined to herself that all men suffered from venereal disease, and naturally her conception of venereal disease was modelled on her one experience of it—a personal one at that. To suffer from venereal disease, therefore, meant for her to be afflicted with a disgusting discharge. (p. 84)

Masturbation, the earliest sexual enjoyment she could have experienced, led to the disgusting leukorrhea. Herr K.'s revival of her sexual feeling not only revived the developmentally caused disgust, but also this more personal association with disgust.

Dora's infantile sexual wishes were repressed because they were associated with disgust. The kiss, the embrace, and the pressure revived the wishes, but disgust rather than pleasure was experienced. *Pcs.* cathexis were withdrawn from this unpleasant intruder from *Ucs.* and excitation flowed back into *Ucs.*, where it presumably was reinforced. On return to *Pcs.*, the compromise of the sensory hallucination was formed and allowed into consciousness. By maintaining part of the pattern of sensory innervation present during the kiss, the compromise satisfied both the old and new sexual wishes; by suppressing the sexual excitement producing the disgust, the demands of censorship were met.

Critique of the Clinical Application

Freud's explanations of Dora's symptoms and dreams were supposed to be based on the associations provided by *her* to the details of the symptoms and the elements of the dreams. His central methodological proposition, now familiar to us, was that it was

demonstrably untrue that we are being carried along a purposeless stream of ideas when, in the process of interpreting a dream, we abandon reflection and allow involuntary ideas to emerge. It can be shown that all that we can ever get rid of are purposive ideas that are *known* to us; as soon as we have done this, *unknown*—or, as we inaccurately say, "unconscious"—purposive ideas take charge and thereafter determine the course of the involuntary ideas.   (Freud 1900, p. 528)

Again,

when conscious purposive ideas are abandoned, concealed purposive ideas assume control of the current of ideas.   (p. 531)

However, details of the analyses of Dora's dream and symptoms show that only a very small proportion of the explanatory concepts derive from anything that can reasonably be described as *her* concealed purposive ideas. Freud's own background assumptions, his ad hoc explanatory principles, and *his* personal associations contribute considerably more than Dora's.

The most important of Freud's assumptions is that Dora ought to have been sexually excited by Herr K.'s kiss. Her disgust is Freud's essential evidence for a once strong but now repressed sexuality. No association of hers points in that direction. It is also an assumption that masturbation in childhood caused Dora's leukorrhea as well as her late-onset enuresis. The mere presence of those two conditions is Freud's *only* evidence of childhood sexual feelings. Dora herself had no recollection of having masturbated. Moreover, although she recalled she had been enuretic in her seventh and eighth years, she could not place the onset of her leukorrhea. That failure has two consequences: it weakens the already purely circumstantial case of her ever having masturbated (Freud 1905a, p. 78), and it makes it impossible to corroborate Freud's surmise that the "repression" of her sexuality, which the "ending" of "masturbation" was supposed to signify, actually preceded the attack of dyspnea (p. 79).

Dora's most direct contribution to the evidence for her childhood masturbation was a so-called symptomatic act that Freud *interpreted* as a symbol of masturbation. After analyzing part of Dora's self-reproaches, Freud concluded that she had once been a masturbator. She rejected that suggestion when he put it to her. But, a few days later, when he observed Dora opening a small reticule she was wearing, putting her finger into it, shutting it, and so on, he took the action to stand for genital manipulation. Dora's reaction to his interpretation is not reported, and it is possible Freud may not have even put it to her. If that is so, he must have regarded the mere possibility of the interpretation as confirming his supposition that she had masturbated.

A clitoral sensation produced by the pressure of the erect penis is necessary to explain the sensory hallucination and the avoidance behavior. But the only associations to the kiss contributing to that explanation are Freud's, not Dora's. To his question whether she knew that arousal in the male was accompanied by penile erection, Dora gave a "prompt and frank" reply that she did not. Freud seems to have believed her. But, without that knowledge, the mechanism proposed for the phobia could not be verified. It also makes it unlikely that Dora had had a clitoral sensation to reinforce the sensation of pressure on the thorax.

Sand is the only psychoanalyst to have provided an evaluation of Freud's treatment of Dora that matches mine. Her conclusions are as damning. She sets out ten claims that Freud makes in his report of the case and, after examining the evidence for eight of them, notes that

In each instance but one, the evidence provided for the contention was ... either flawed or scanty. (Sand 1983)

She concludes:

the case cannot serve as a demonstration of Freud's general thesis, that the aetiology of hysteria is psychosexual, nor of his several related specific theses regarding the role of trauma and repressed affect in the production of symptoms and dreams. (op. cit.)

Among the claims she investigated were that the symptoms were caused by and represented a repressed affect; that childhood experiences of thumbsucking, bed-wetting, and masturbation contributed to the symptoms and did so through "somatic compliance"; and that the dreams, especially the first, were related to the symptoms.

As Flowerman (1954) did before her, Sand impugns Freud's use of negative instances as confirmatory, and criticizes his use of his own associations rather than Dora's, and his extraordinary reliance on fitting together the jigsaw puzzle pieces to form a plausible logical and associative structure—a concept that, naturally enough, Sand does not call by that name. She does this without assessing the value of Freud's evidence that a recent sexual experience led to repression. Freud provided absolutely no evidence that the embrace gave rise to a genital sensation and an orally based disgust that, after repressing the affect, created the symptom through an oral somatic compliance.

Rieff (1959, p. 81), a nonanalyst, thought that "Dora could have turned down Herr K. for several good reasons. . . . Possibly she did not find him attractive." Erikson (1962) went so far as to question his master by wondering "how many of us can follow today without protest Freud's assertion that a healthy girl of fourteen would, under such circumstances, have considered Mr. K.'s advances 'neither tactless nor offensive.'" Scharfman (1980, p. 53) considered it "rather questionable that one would expect such a response in a girl that age when approached by a man who is her father's friend," a view shared by M. I. Klein and Tribich (1982a).

Much more important to the assessment of his explanation is the reasonableness of his assumption that Herr K.'s embrace and kiss had succeeded in arousing Dora genitally. For, without the pressure of Herr K.'s erect penis inducing genital excitation, the whole explanation of the symptoms fails: no repressed sexuality could have been revived, no feeling of disgust could be produced, no excitation could have been available for displacement on to the thorax, and no eyes need be averted from gallants in conversation. The same conclusion holds rather more strongly, perhaps, if one accepts Lewin's fundamental reinterpretation of Dora's sexuality: "her sexual objects were women, and only women" (Lewin 1973–1974). If, as he concludes, "men did not turn Dora on," Herr K.'s kiss could have had no sexually exciting effect at all.

Ad hoc principles are most evident in the two bases proposed by Freud for his analysis of Dora's reproaches. That a string of reproaches might cover a similar string of self-reproaches was said by Freud to be something that "soon becomes evident" (Freud 1905a, p. 35). In addition, the idea that excessively intense reproaches might be reinforced by an unconscious trend of thought was suggested to him by "reflection" (pp. 54–55). No other justification is provided for these principles. Neither appears to have been discussed elsewhere in Freud's writings, although they do bear some resemblance to his views on counterwill. From his assumption that reproaches simply cloaked the self-reproaches, he deduced Dora was in love with Herr K., and the unconscious reinforcement of the reproach was identified as her infantile love for her father. These two ad hoc principles, almost by themselves and without too much confirmatory evidence from Dora, seem to have provided Freud with the basis for characterizing what he took to be two of the three most important emotional currents in her life. For within what was probably two weeks of first seeing Dora, he wrote to Fliess that her case "has smoothly opened to the existing collection of picklocks" (Masson 1985, Letter of Oct. 14, 1900), and it is certainly true that he made his characterization before Dora had the first dream (Freud 1905a, p. 70).

Whatever the truth of these principles and their application, it is evident they have a degree of arbitrariness. Lewin (1973–1974), in the first extensive reconsideration of the case, concluded that Freud's picture of Dora's sexuality was basically incorrect.

According to his analysis of the reproaches, Dora was really in love with her own mother. What appeared to Freud to be love for her father was really Dora's masculine identification that enabled her to retain her mother as her sexual object. Her love for Herr K. was a similarly motivated expression of feeling for Frau K. as a mother surrogate. Among other things, this homosexual current explained her disgust with Herr K.'s kiss. On the other hand, Krohn and Krohn (1982) have it that Dora turned to Herr K. as a compromise for her repressed infantile and incestuous love for her father. Glenn (1980, p. 29), however, pictured Dora as struggling against Herr K. because he was an unacceptable substitute for her father. Lewin (1973–1974), as one might expect, thought she was attracted to Herr K. as a secondary consequence of her unhappy love affair with her mother. That any of these reanalyses appears as plausible as Freud's is due largely to the slimly evidenced ad hoc principles and personal associations on which they all rest.

The influence of Freud's personal associations is just as marked in his interpretation of Dora's dream. That the dream element of being saved by her father represented the latent thought that it was her father who actually exposed her to the danger of seduction was a speculation of Freud's, not an association of Dora's. Once having inverted this piece of the manifest content, Freud then, again on his own account, reversed the meanings of the dream thought concerning the present of the bracelet. In turn, that inversion generated his association of water as the opposite of fire and provided the links to thoughts of bedwetting and childhood sexuality. Each of the reversed-meaning interpretations came from Freud's associations—not one was provided by Dora. Freud actually presented Dora with those interpretations of the dream before establishing whether or not she shared those associations with him (Freud 1905a, pp. 68–73). His conviction that his associations reflected the structure of her thoughts took precedence over her denials, uncertainties, and evasions.

All such responses by Dora to Freud's questions and interpretations were regarded as the fruits of repression and, therefore, as confirming the applicability of his associations. For example, Dora denied knowing that children were warned not to play with fire because they might wet the bed. Nor had she noticed a large match-stand freshly placed on Freud's table. Because of both these denials Freud assumed she was aware of the fire-water-bedwetting linkage he discerned in her dream (pp. 71–72). Similarly, her inability to recall whether she would have been pleased to receive the bracelet her mother rejected was taken to mean she was confessing to a repressed thought (p. 69). Freud took the same line over the sexual allusion he recognized in the words "jewel-case"—Dora's evasiveness as to whether she knew of its slang meaning confirmed she really did know, but repressed the knowledge (p. 69, n. 4). Finally, her uncertainty about the time of the first occurrence of the dream was accepted as positive evidence that it actually followed Herr K.'s proposal (pp. 65–66). Consequently, the preconscious intent of the dream, the bedwetting allusions that led to the latent thought of masturbation, the sexual association of the jewel case, and the theme of a sexual love represented by the dream thought of the bracelet were all supplied by Freud in opposition to Dora's contrary associations or lack of them.

Much of Freud's analysis of the symptoms shows the same characteristic preference for his associations over hers. Apart from those mentioned earlier, one might note that Dora's inability to recall whether she had masturbated as a child was taken in conjunction with symptomatic play with the reticule "as a further step towards the confession" Freud was seeking. Although in the end Dora remembered nothing, her failure to deny Freud's supposition was taken by him as confirming that she had masturbated (Freud 1905a, pp. 76, 79). Some modern analytic reinterpretations lead me to question the masturbatory symbolism. Glenn (1980, p. 30) interprets the play with the reticule as a seductive gesture directed at Freud, but Krohn and Krohn (1982) see it as the sexual penetration of another woman. Either interpretation severs the link with the masturbation Freud's reconstruction demanded.

It also ought to be noted that associations were obtained to only about one-half of the elements of the dream's manifest content. None of the following elements were inquired into with sufficient persistence to trace their supposed unconscious roots: "My mother wanted to stop," "Father said: 'I refuse to let my children be burnt for the sake of your jewel-case,'" and "We hurried downstairs." The element "A house was on fire" gave rise to some associations, but was not itself traced to Dora's experiences or feelings. Some selection from the dream elements was clearly made, a fact also pointed out by Langs (1980, p. 65) about Freud's failure to examine a number of specific day residues, and by Kanzer (1980, p. 76) who noted Freud's definite and positive reaction to the residue relating to the brother's being locked in at night.

Although not based on as detailed an analysis, a considerable body of opinion, mainly psychoanalytic, supports my conclusions, or at the very least, is consistent with them. Rieff probably was the first to advert to Freud's domination of the treatment:

Freud applauds his own persistence; he speaks of using facts against the patient and he reports how he overwhelmed Dora with interpretations, pounding away at her argument, until "Dora disputed the facts no longer."   (Rieff 1959, p. 82)

Kanzer noted that Dora

was constantly pressured to confirm the analyst's interpretations and had little opportunity to freely bring forward her own associations, fantasies and ideas.   (Kanzer 1980, p. 75; cf. p. 79)

Perhaps this was because, as I. Bernstein (1980, p. 86) observed,

Freud knew too much about Dora before the analysis started. It led Freud to make a number of formulations and to anticipate matters to an extent where he was relying less on material as it came from Dora than on the information he had already obtained outside the analysis.

Whether this was so or not, there is no doubt about the

uncharacteristic tenacity with which he [Freud] defends his interpretations to Dora and to his readers. (Krohn and Krohn 1982; cf. S. Fisher and Greenberg 1977, pp. 366–367)

And, with equally characteristic Lacanian ambiguity, Kohon describes Freud engaged in

a persistent search for truth—although we do not know whether it is Dora's truth or Freud's. (Kohon 1984)

Begel (1982) even raises the possibility that Freud's interpretation of Dora's smelling smoke when she woke from the dream as a transference onto him of Dora's desire for a kiss from Herr K. was based as much on Freud's wish as Dora's. Although expressed more politely than Rieff, these psychoanalytic opinions are just as damning of Freud's objectivity as his.

Various theoretical problems that plagued Freud at the time have been proposed as accounting for his behavior. Maddi was early to point out that Freud was

ecstatic about Dora because he regarded her case as the clearest and most decisive evidence for his formulations.   (Maddi 1974)

Many psychoanalysts have subsequently accepted this point. Krohn and Krohn (1982) spoke of Freud's heavy narcissistic involvement "in looking for a case that would demonstrate and justify his emerging theories." Much the same thing was said by Langs (1980, p. 63), and Scharfman (1980, pp. 54–55) went so far as to conclude that in view of these larger aims, the treatment was really of secondary importance. But, of course, none of these psychoanalytic critics do what their criticisms really demand. Not one of them fundamentally rejects Freud's basis for interpreting the case. Each is wedded to what he thinks of as basic and reliable "facts" about Dora. Despite their criticisms of Freud's unrelenting influence, most of them nevertheless seem to believe that the resulting associations, even if they were, at the very least, obviously contaminated by Freud, provide valid information about Dora's symptoms and dreams.

Psychoanalysts most frequently use these criticisms to explain why Dora broke off treatment. What is most often stressed is Freud's sexualization of it. Freud himself would undoubtedly have acknowledged the sexuality of his imagery: it opened to his collection of picklocks, Dora's dream stood on two legs, and so on (Maddi 1974; Scharfman 1980, pp. 49–50; Kanzer 1980, pp. 78–79; Kohon 1984; Glenn 1986). Whether one accepts this Damoclean flight of psychoanalytic fancy or not, there can be no doubt that what have been called Freud's repetitive sexual interpretations erotocized Dora's relation to Freud (Scharfman 1980, p. 50; cf. Langs 1980, pp. 63–65; Kanzer 1980, p. 79; Gill, in Reppen 1982). Blos, speaking specifically of Dora's adolescence, said:

the consolidation of her neurotic condition had been short-circuited by the fact that her analysis was being conducted as if an adult neurosis already existed. As a consequence, the adolescent ego became overwhelmed by interpretations it was unable to integrate, and it simply took to flight. If there is one thing adolescent analysis has taught us, it is that ill-timed [sexual] interpretations are unconsciously experienced by the adolescent as a parental—that is, incestuous, seduction.   (Blos 1973)

Glenn (1980, 1986) and Kohon (1984) endorsed this conclusion, the former pointing to an important further consequence:

Freud's premature interpretations of Dora's symptomatic acts and their masturbatory significance must have convinced her that he was a dangerous adult trying to seduce her.   (Glenn 1980, p. 36)

In line with this, Glenn emends Freud's interpretation of the dream to include Dora's fantasy "that she was once more in danger sexually in her analysis with Freud as she had previously been with Herr K." (p. 65). He contends that Freud's interest in her sexuality caused *Freud* to appear in Dora's dream as seducer as well as protector. One cannot go this far, of course—Dora had had the dream *before* the treatment began!

Muslin and Gill (1978) believe part of the difficulties Freud had with Dora were due to a very strong *positive* countertransference he had to her (cf. Begel 1982). Showing a little more insight than most psychoanalysts, they say of their interpretations of other of Dora's behavior, "Of course, we recognize the speculative element in our suggestions and that, with ingenuity, anyone could make many more" (Muslin and Gill 1978). Just as well. As they themselves report, but do not comment on, Marcus (1984) had already argued that Freud's handling of the case was impeded by his strong *negative* countertransference to Dora, an interpretation later also preferred by Possick (1984; cf. Decker 1982; J. L. Jennings 1986). Whether or not the relationship was sexualized, there can be no doubt that Freud's interest in a sexual etiology contributed materially to the sexual content of Dora's so-called free associations.

We should also note that subsequent reinterpretations of Dora's dream have the same arbitrariness as Freud's original. For slightly different reasons, Lewin (1973–1974) and Krohn and Krohn (1982) claimed that fire represented destructiveness and aggression. On the other hand, Kanzer (1980, p. 73) said the rescue from the fire by the father was a birth fantasy, an interpretation he took to be confirmed by the fire-water dichotomy (which was, of course, Freud's!). Opposed to all of these is Erikson's characteristically equivocal addendum:

in Dora's first dream the *house* and the *jewel case*, besides being symbols of the female body and its contents, represent the adolescent quandary: if there is a fire in "our house" (that is, in our family), then what "valuables" (that is, values) shall be saved first? And indeed, Freud's interpretation, although psychosexual and oedipal in emphasis, assigns to the father standing by the girl's bed not the role of a wished-for seducer, but that of a hoped-for protector of his daughter's inviolacy.   (Erikson 1962)

Slipp (1977) and Decker (1981), admittedly in somewhat different ways, placed so much stress on the social and interpersonal factors operating in Dora's family that intrapersonal psychodynamic interpretations and formulations hardly seem necessary to explain the case (cf. Decker 1982).

Whether or not the somewhat contradictory interpretations of the Dora case can be reconciled, the most important point to emerge from our analysis is that, whatever might have been said in the abstract about the subject's unconscious purposive ideas generating the associations, most of them actually came from Freud's quite conscious and purposive ideas.

Critique of the Theory of the Mind

Two things distinguish Freud's theory of the mind from those of the philosophers, psychologists, and psychiatrists who before him gave credence to unconscious mentation. In his theory, mental contents are unconscious, preconscious, or conscious because they belong to the systems *Ucs.*, *Pcs.*, or *Cs.* Most other theorists, such as Fechner (cited in Meynert 1884/1885, p. 214), proposed that conscious ideas were distinguished from unconscious ideas only by being more intense (Whyte 1960). For Freud, no matter how intense an idea was, it could not become conscious unless it made itself admissible to the system *Cs.* His adaptation of the reflex model of mental functioning was also different from that of his immediate predecessors—Brücke, Meynert, and Exner—in that it could be activated by stored *psychological* needs. None of his colleagues or teachers were much concerned to explain psychological wishes, especially those in dreams, so that it had not been necessary to think of them being stored in a permanent repository. Meynert's model, for example, allowed that the infant might suck in its dreams, but it is clear that he thought this was the effect of the revival of cortical motor images of sucking by an actually present hunger (Meynert 1884/1885, p. 170).

Once it is granted that a regressive flow of excitation can occur within the apparatus, and that the flow activates the functions and contents of each of the systems within it, Freud's model of the mind allows immediate deduction of many important features of the dream. The placement of *Ucs.* and *Pcs.* toward the motor end of the apparatus defines the point at which the regressive flow of excitation is initiated, and the primary process of *Ucs.* modifies the flow such that the wish is disguised before appearing at *Pcpt.* The instigation by unconscious wishes, the incorporation of day residues from *Pcs.*, the effects of censorship, the consequences of the primary process in condensation and displacement, the revival of primitive modes of thought, and the hallucinatory visual imagery of the end product are the necessary consequences of the order in which the systems are successively energized. Closer examination of the model shows, however, significant deficiencies in the explanations of certain of the properties of dreams, of one of the important groups of symptoms, and of a number of aspects of normal mental function. Freud's account of the relations between the primary and secondary processes is similarly unsound. Repression and organic reinforcement, the two concepts most crucial to understanding dreams and symptoms, are uncharacterized theoretical terms and nonexplanatory.

Most of the defects of the model itself arise either from the very assumption of a fixed temporal sequence in its working, or from ambiguities in the way in which consciousness was thought to arise. Before considering these criticisms, it is worth stressing that the model is no theoretical fiction, assembled for mere convenience of thinking about the dream, as was positivistically implied by Gedo and Goldberg (1973, pp. 3–5, 48–59). Freud thought his theory was an approximation to the real state of affairs, and if it were to be replaced, it should be only by a theory that corresponded better to reality (Freud 1900, pp. 610–611). His basic assumption was that a given psychological process resulted from the particular order in which the systems operated. He thought the minimum premise entailing that outcome was the supposition that excitation appropriate to a given process passed through the systems in a particular temporal sequence (p. 537). This premise, said Freud,

does no more than fulfil a requirement with which we have long been familiar, namely that the psychical apparatus *must* be constructed like a reflex apparatus. Reflex processes *remain* the model of every psychical function.   (p. 538. My emphasis)

No mere analogy with a reflex was meant, as Arlow and Brenner (1964, p. 46) proposed. Nor was it a "crude analogy" that originated with Breuer, as Wollheim (1971, p. 63) seems to imply. The reflex conception of the mental apparatus, and the fixed order with which the systems within it functioned, were the two central givens of Freud's theory.

Normally the movement of excitation is from the sensory to the motor end of the apparatus, but under special circumstances, the direction of the flow can be reversed. Two points should be made. First, Garma (1969) noted "it is rather difficult to see how the reverse journey along the nervous reflex arc could be accomplished." This part of the theory seems to be based on inconsistent assumptions, whether or not its reflex basis is meant to be taken seriously. Second, apart from a somewhat ambiguous reference to "a simultaneous exploring of one path and another, a swinging of the excitation now this way and now that" (Freud 1900, p. 576), Freud does not seem to have allowed for the simultaneous flow of excitation in opposite directions.

Yet certain classes of hysterical symptoms and children's reactions to the frustration of their needs conflict with the assumption of a unidirectional excitatory flow. When the infant is most hungry, and presumably hallucinating the object that would satisfy its need, it is also most generally restless, often making sucking movements and crying. The hallucination requires a flow of excitation from $Ucs.$ to $Pcpt.$, but the motor activity and the crying requires a simultaneous flow to $M.$ Similarly, hysterical symptoms in which a motor response coincides with a hallucination, like some of those of Anna O. or Emmy von N., require a simultaneous activation of both $Pcpt.$ and $M.$ Although the hallucinations can be readily conceptualized as regressive products similar to the visual images of dreams, situating the motor system toward the output end of the apparatus makes it impossible to account for motor symptoms to be present at the same time. The path to $M.$ is progressive and the path to $Pcpt.$ is regressive.

Freud believed $Cs.$ to be a kind of double-sided sense organ. One side of it is directed to $Pcpt.$ where it senses the existence of perceptual qualities. Attention cathexes disposed on excitations within $Pcpt.$ make those qualities conscious as the perceptions of particular sensory modalities. The other side of the sense organ is directed to "the interior of the apparatus itself" (Freud 1900, p. 616), where in $Pcs.$ it senses the qualities of pleasure and unpleasure resulting from variation in the quantities of excitation. Kanzer (1981) finds the work of Lipps, the Munich psychologist, to be the source of this particular idea about consciousness. When outlining the systems in *The Interpretation of Dreams*, Freud did not at first indicate the relation of consciousness to them. Some thirty pages later he introduced the double-sided sense organ notion, expanding on it only in the very last section of the book, by which time it was clear that $Cs.$ was directed to $Pcpt.$ and to $Pcs.$ A footnote of 1919 to the outline of the systems located consciousness in "the system next beyond the $Pcs.$" and followed this with the non sequitur "in other words, that $Pcpt. = Cs.$" Freud had made his intention clear even if the argument was faulty (cf. Freud 1900, pp. 541, n. 1, 574–575, 615–616).

What this dual-sided concept entails is that consciousness can arise at only two places in the apparatus: *Pcpt.* and *Pcs.* Combined with the assumption of a fixed temporal sequence or direction to the flow of excitation, this limited access to *Cs.* makes for problems in explaining thinking in dreams and in normal life.

According to the regressive plan, the products of the dream work can become conscious only through *Pcpt.* However much a dream thought may be modified on its journey from *Pcs.* to *Mnem.*, it has to be transformed further into sensory images before being represented in the manifest content. Thus, in chapter 7 of *The Interpretation of Dreams*, where the theory of the mental apparatus is outlined, the discussion of the transformation by the primary process of a train of thought originating in *Pcs.* is entirely in terms of thoughts being prepared for perceptual representation (Freud 1900, pp. 592–597). Because direct access to *Cs.* from *Mnem.* is not provided for, there is no way in which dream thoughts can appear in the dream as thoughts per se. Consequently, the presence of dream thoughts in the dream as other than perceptual images contradicts a most fundamental feature of Freud's theory.

Arlow and Brenner drew much the same conclusion, although the force of their point is weakened by their incorrect assumption that the theory requires the regression undergone by the dream thoughts to be both uniform and complete (Arlow and Brenner 1964, pp. 118–119). If by complete they meant all thoughts have to be in sensory form, their criticism may be accepted. But in insisting on the uniformity of regression, they apparently overlooked some quite compelling reasons Freud advanced for supposing that the primary process affects dream thought differentially: the associative closeness of a thought to the repressed idea, the number of associations a dream thought had with others, the intensity of the thought, and its capacity for visual representation. Each of these factors determines the degree of regression possible or necessary (Freud 1900, pp. 284, 295, 306–307, 340, 344, 544).

Freud is sometimes able to explain how thoughts per se can be incorporated into the manifest content of the dream without contradicting the requirement of sensory representation. For example, if the censorship was unable to prevent the manifest content from causing anxiety, he assumed the censorship itself might add the thought, "This is only a dream," to reduce the importance of the manifest content. Although the judgment is a genuine intellectual act, its origins are in a still active portion of consciousness and it is not produced by dream work. Thoughts such as these, added to the dream after the manifest content is nearly completed, need not appear in sensory form. However, not all thoughts occurring in the manifest content are like these *Pcs.* judgments. From Freud's own descriptions it is obvious some are part of the very fabric of the latent content. For example, regarding his dream of Irma's injection, he observed, "I thought to myself that after all I must be missing some organic trouble," and "I thought to myself that there was really no need for her to do that" (Freud 1900, p. 107). When his analysis of these thoughts is examined, they are obviously an integral part of a latent content otherwise represented visually. Although they may have originated in *Pcs.* while Freud was awake, and although they might not have been much distorted, it is impossible to regard them as simple *Pcs.* additions to an almost completed manifest content. The closeness of their links to other latent thoughts requires they should have sensory representation.

Freud does recognize that intellectual activity in the dream also poses the problem of how such an apparently *rational product* can result from *irrational dream work*. This is, of course, a different problem from the representation of thought. It is a problem of where the rational ideas come from. Freud's solution is again that the thinking is only apparently produced by the primary process: dream thoughts are once more actually in existence before the dream begins, mostly as *Pcs.* thoughts left incomplete during the day, and are simply fitted into the dream with greater or lesser distortion (Freud 1900, pp. 445–459).

Had the model of the mental apparatus provided for direct access from *Mnem.* to *Cs.* without them going through *Pcs.*, dream thoughts other than sensory images could appear directly in the manifest content. Such a pathway would also allow for a more adequate explanation of normal recollective thought. In Freud's view, normal recollective thought required access to the raw material of the memory traces without perceptual hallucinations being produced. His explanation is that such thinking is initiated by a conscious process producing a regression only as far as *Mnem.*, but that stops short of reactivating *Pcpt.* (pp. 542–543). Even were it not just a description, for two other reasons it is a total failure as an explanation: first, since access to memories associated with nonrepressed ideas is also possible only through *Ucs.*, the distortion the primary process should produce in them is avoided by some quite unspecified means and, second, the method by which the regressive process is halted at *Mnem.* is unexplained. If mechanisms located in *Cs.* or *Pcs.* are supposed to be responsible, it is difficult to see how they have direct access to either *Ucs.* or *Mnem.* contents.

Arlow and Brenner (1964), Holt (1967), and Gill (1963) are among the psycho-analytic theorists who have drawn attention to the many inconsistencies with which Freud characterizes the systems and functions of the mental apparatus. Although several of the arguments advanced by these workers are accepted in the evaluation that follows, it is necessary to point out that some of Gill's critique is based on fairly gross misunderstandings of Freud's theory. Thus he (1963, pp. 33–34) virtually identifies the primary process, which is the mode of functioning of *Ucs.* and cannot become conscious, with the dream itself, which is conscious. The dream is formed by the primary process at the behest of the censorship, and must meet its requirements before becoming conscious. It is precisely because some aspects of the dream do derive from the censorship that they are admissible to consciousness. Gill's confusion is made worse by his belief that Freud attributes the function of censorship to the primary process (Gill 1963, pp. 98–101). Reading Gill's quotations from Freud carefully, and in context, shows Gill to be incorrect.

Censorship also poses a problem in that there are inconsistencies in its location, in its mode of operation, and its relation to the dream work. Freud variously places the censorship in *Pcs.* or on the border between *Pcs.* and *Ucs.*, while also proposing a further censorship between *Pcpt.* and *Cs.* But wherever the function is located, it is conceived of as exerting some continuous control over the distortion brought about by the dream work. It is almost as if the distortion is continuously tested to see if it has gone far enough. At a number of places in *The Interpretation of Dreams* the different locations of the censorships are discussed (Freud 1900, pp. 235–236, 553, 567–568, 615–618), and Arlow and Brenner (1964, chapter 2, pp. 133–135), Abrams (1971a), and Gill (1963, chapters 1 and 5) set out most of the problems caused by them. In essence, the difficulties reduce to the fact that, wherever it is located, the censorship has to exercise functions inconsistent with that location. For example, if the censorship is thought of as being a *Pcs.* function, it has to be regarded as a part of the secondary process; how then does it gain access to and exercise continuous control over primary processes going on in *Ucs*? Sandler and Sandler (1983) explored this particular inconsistency of Freud's in some detail. Their conclusion is that it is not possible to restore the second censorship either to this or to Freud's later theory of the mental agencies. McIntosh bravely resolves the problem of the second censor by declaring it to be purely terminological. He rejects the criteria of the relation to consciousness and the primary-secondary processes for dividing the psyche. For him the basic division is between linguistic and nonlinguistic activity, and it is not then difficult for him to say "it is simply a misnomer to call the two systems the conscious-preconscious and the unconscious" (McIntosh 1986).

An additional complication, to which less attention seems to have been paid, is the matter of whether or not censorship is required after dream thoughts have been transformed into sensory images. Freud's most direct remark was that consciousness would follow

when the content of the dream-process has become perceptual, by that fact it has, as it were, found a way of evading the obstacle put in its way by the censorship and the state of sleep in the *Pcs.* It succeeds in drawing attention to itself and in being noticed by consciousness. (Freud 1900, p. 574)

Censorship between *Pcpt.* and *Cs.* here seems specifically excluded. On the other hand Freud describes an attentional cathexis from *Pcs.* being directed on to the dream "after it has become perceptual" (p. 578). One imagines this attentional function as involving censorship. And, then again, in describing the excitation of *Pcpt.* produced by normal stimulation of the sense organs, Freud remarks the image is "probably submitted to a fresh revision before it becomes a conscious sensation" (p. 616). If external stimulation of *Pcpt.* provokes the censorship, the same ought to be true when the stimulation comes from within. Dream images are vivid enough to be mistaken for real images, and no basis can exist therefore for the censorship differentiating between the internal and the external excitation of *Pcpt.* If the externally produced image is subject to censorship, the same would have to be true of the internally produced image.

A final confusion over the placement of the censorship is to be seen in an implication of the 1919 footnote equating *Pcpt.* with *Cs.* (Freud 1900, p. 541, n. 1). If those two systems are identical, there can hardly be a censorship between them; and, according to the footnote, the identity of *Pcpt.* with *Cs.* is implicit in the original theory. Of course, in the case of normal stimulation, Freud might have meant only that, because all such stimulation begins at *Pcpt.*, the excitation to which it gives rise must pass through *Mnem.* and *Ucs.* before meeting the censorship at the border of *Pcs.* and *Ucs.* or in *Pcs.* But that proposal has its own difficulties: it is unlikely that Freud could have maintained consistently that all mental contents had to pass through the system *Ucs.* before becoming conscious.

Censorship is also related to condensation and displacement in an inconsistent way. Both processes form part of the dream work, seemingly contributing equally to dream distortion (pp. 307–308). Both also reflect primary-process thinking, having as their more intimate mechanism the free discharge of energy (pp. 595–596), a basis said to enable displacements of energy to facilitate condensation (p. 339). Yet only displacement was said to be a function of the censorship (pp. 308, 507, 533) [although Freud did at least once attribute both processes to the same motive (p. 482)]. Some years after *The Interpretation of Dreams* appeared he remarked,

> although condensation makes dreams obscure, it does not give one the impression of being an effect of the dream-censorship. It seems traceable rather *to some mechanical or economic factor*, but in any case the censorship profits by it.   (Freud 1916–1917, p. 173. My emphasis)

He once again added that displacement was "entirely the work of the dream-censorship" (p. 174). What the inconsistency reflects is Freud's difficulty in reconciling an explanation of dreams in terms of a regressive flow of excitation, where distortions are produced automatically, with an explanation in terms of wishes, psychological forces, and counterforces. I return briefly to this conflict in the next section.

The concept of secondary revision suffers from the same kinds of obscurities as censorship. Freud's description of it as forming part of the dream work has the consequence of it creating coherence despite its being part of a disorganizing primary process. Although Gill (1967) noted that the difficulty of attributing judgment in dreams to secondary revision was removed by Freud's later supposition that it was not part of the dream work (Freud 1923a, p. 241), to think of it then as a *Pcs.* function entails the further inconsistency of allowing *Pcs.* direct access to the primary process. Breznitz (1971) drew attention to the fact that Freud describes secondary revision in *The Interpretation of Dreams* as taking place at three distinctly different times: during the dream work, during sleeping but after the dream work has been completed, and during the attempted recollection of the dream. No function belonging to any one system can operate at the different levels these different times imply. Heynick brought out very clearly how Freud's attempt to make it do so in allowing for speech to be incorporated in dreams created "a theoretical problem less amenable to a satisfying solution" (Heynick 1981). As we have noted, secondary revision is obviously the direct descendant of "the compulsion to link together any ideas that might be present in the same state of consciousness." Freud tries to put it to work across three different states. But, in his model, no one function can so operate.

The characteristics of the systems *Ucs.* and *Pcs.* and those of the associated primary and secondary processes are inconsistent with one another in a number of important respects. The inconsistencies may be conveniently considered developmentally and in relation to the functions exercised by each system. Holt (1967) provided a number of weighty reasons for supposing Freud's characterization of primary process functioning to be such that secondary process thought, and *Pcs.* as a system, can never have developed from it. On the basis of experimental findings and direct observations, he argued it is most unlikely that an infant's memories are sufficiently veridical for it to discriminate between real and hallucinatory images. On general grounds he also maintained that repeated frustration after "barren hallucinatory attempts at immediate gratification" is unlikely to lead to adaptive, secondary process methods of need satisfaction. What is known from child development studies and the psychology of learning is, broadly speaking, consistent with this view. Holt's most telling point (curiously relegated to a footnote) is that the infant would be unable to differentiate real and hallucinated objects: both would be present simultaneously as the need is satisfied. No dynamic capable of urging the infant toward the real world can then be created. Thus, although it remains true that a hallucinated breast cannot feed a hungry baby, the infant's inability to differentiate the synchronously proffered, perceptually identical, real breast that can, would simply not allow the secondary process to develop.

Steele and Jacobsen (1977), who believe that Freud's proposition that the primary process precedes the secondary is mere assumption, and a problematical one at that, also contend that the problem of the emergence of the secondary function is not how the change takes place but that there is any change at all. They further point out that, before a hallucinatory wish-fulfilling object can be conjured up, it must have been experienced first. Finally, they state that it is difficult to see how there could ever be any observational proof of a hallucinatory stage. On the grounds that the degree of cognitive differentiation required contradicts "all the available evidence on cognitive development," Wolff (in Schafer 1965) challenged the assumption that the first instance of ideation could be hallucinatory wish fulfillment. Of Provence's view that a theory of infant development within the framework of psychoanalysis is possible, he also said it was "more our hope than our achievement."

Of the inconsistent characterization of the properties and functions attributed to *Ucs.*, the most important is that the unconscious supposedly can store highly structured repressed fantasies. According to the description of the primary process, the free discharge of energy prevents the development or storage of structured thoughts. Yet analysis of dreams and symptoms supposedly reveals the existence of well organized but unconscious fantasies. Fifteen years after completing *The Interpretation of Dreams* Freud himself acknowledged this logical difficulty, which has also been commented on in more recent times by a number of psychoanalytic theorists (Freud 1915c; cf. Gill 1963, 1967; Arlow and Brenner 1964; Arlow 1975). Although it is well recognized that Freud eventually made profound alterations to his theory in attempting to overcome this inconsistency, one important implication of the initial formulation seems never to have been drawn. It is that Freud's explanations of the formation of symptoms and of some types of dreams require the existence of a class of fantasies that the theory of the mind says cannot exist. Repressed fantasies cannot exist in *Ucs.* and cannot therefore be incorporated into dreams. Dreams incorporating such fantasies disprove the theory. Furthermore, because fantasies well enough structured to resemble real memories of childhood seduction cannot exist in *Ucs.*, they cannot explain hysterical symptoms.

Finally, three important deficiencies are discernible in Freud's explanation of the indestructibility of the infantile unconscious wishes. First, the mere lateness of the development of the secondary process does not entail the inability of that process to gain control over the earlier wishes. Freud's account of the development of the secondary process out of the primary is a description rather than an explanation. Second, an important inconsistency in Freud's description of the transformation of affect in repression is relevant to the creation of the reservoir of repressed infantile wishes. Freud believed the transformation could be inferred to have taken place when children were observed to react with disgust to activities they previously found pleasurable. He hinted that the alteration was "related to the activity of the secondary system" (Freud 1900, p. 604). If he is thus ascribing the transformation to the secondary system, he has assumed the secondary process has enough access to the affect of the unconscious memories to turn it into its opposite. As we saw, elsewhere he proposed that the second system was unable to alter those memories or to do more than direct their excitation into realistic channels. Consequently, this part of the theory makes inconsistent assumptions.

Third, organic reinforcement, the force enabling the repressed wish to gain access to *Pcs.*, is not only uncharacterized, it is undefined. In *The Interpretation of Dreams* it is mentioned only once, and then only in the context of the revival of the permanently repressed wish (pp. 604–605). In line with this is Brenner's (1979) observation that drives themselves are not explicitly included in the theory of the mind set out in *The Interpretation of Dreams*. Even in Dora's history, where the theory is mentioned frequently, it is quite inadequately described. Freud's account of the immutability of infantile wishes is thus a mixture of description, assumptions, and uncharacterized theoretical terms masquerading as an explanation. He advanced no compelling reasons for supposing repressed unconscious wishes from infancy remain unchanged over time and continue to influence the production of adult dreams and symptoms.

Perhaps there were no such reasons. According to Hartmann, Freud can be read as arguing for two outcomes of repression, "mere repression and the true disappearance of an old desire or impulse" (H. Hartmann 1952). That is, the repressed impulse may be so changed as to disappear. Loewenstein also said that Freud once actually did acknowledge that psychoanalytic treatment caused repressed unconscious wishes to lose their effects after they were raised to consciousness and correlated with reality (Arlow 1958). I take it that Freud held that treatment enables previously repressed unconscious mental contents to become accessible to consciousness or, to anticipate his later famous slogan, where *Ucs.* was, there *Cs.* will be. However, E. Kris (1956), M. H. Stein (1965), Malcolm (1982, pp. 161–162), and A. L. Rosenbaum (1983) all cite instances of patients who retained no knowledge at all of the dynamic processes allegedly revealed to them in their successful treatment.

Two not unimportant general consequences may be deduced from the preceding criticisms: explanations using the concept of repression or censorship, its coyly disguised relative, will be limited because of the uncharacterized nature of those terms. A similar restriction applies to the use of the concept of organic reinforcement. At a basic level then, Freud's explanations of many phenomena, and not just of symptom formation or dream production, are rather less than adequate.

A "Theory" of Wish Fulfillment?

Two different kinds of theories may be discerned in *The Interpretation of Dreams*. The first is cast in terms of mental structures and the regressive flow of excitation from one structure to another, and the other draws on such concepts as drives and wishes, and mental forces that, like the censorship, oppose them and force them into disguise. According to the first theory, the peculiarities of the dream arise because unpleasure, which the arrival of a repressed dream thought from *Ucs.* would cause if it entered *Pcs.*, forces the thought away from *M*. Passing through the primitive *Mnem.* systems it is further distorted by being prepared for representation as a visual image in *Pcpt.* This theory is a structural and economic (energy) one. By itself it accounts, as Freud noted, for the characteristically distorted manifest content (Freud 1900, p. 543). In the second theory, referred to by some psychoanalysts as the clinical theory, an unacceptable infantile wish, forced out of consciousness and kept out by a repressive force, seeks readmission, but can succeed only if its disguise bypasses or hoodwinks the repressive censorship. Dream distortion is forced on the latent dream thought by demands of the censorship.

Because Freud regarded the theory of the mental apparatus as so much disposable conceptual scaffolding (p. 536), it might be said that at least some of the criticisms I have set out in this chapter can be met by noting that they are largely irrelevant to the second theory. Many psychoanalysts have done so, most recently G. S. Klein (1975, 1976, chapter 3), Schafer (1976), and Stolorow and Atwood (1982). Even without a reflex theory of the mental apparatus it would still be possible to think of repressed wishes as the source of dreams, to regard their peculiarities as a result of condensation and displacement carried out at the behest of the censorship, and so on. All that would be lost, if it may be so put, is the general theory explaining dream production at other than this fairly immediate psychological level.

Three summary points from among many may be made about this argument. First, it concedes Freud was no theorist. Second, in what sense does a set of statements based on the proposition that dreams are wish fulfillments constitute a *theory* of dreaming? Third, if such a theory is possible, how might it be tested?

Let us leave the first point for later elaboration and begin with the second. Whether the wish principle was arrived at by Freud analyzing his own dreams, as contemporary evidence suggests, or whether it was based primarily on the dreams of his patients, as Freud's later accounts imply (Freud 1900, pp. 100–101; 1916–1917, p. 83; 1932, pp. 219–220), an impression is conveyed, as Fancher (1971) comments, of the principle resulting from strictly empirical and inductive inquiry. Freud also claims:

In most dreams it is possible to detect a central point which is marked by peculiar sensory intensity ... [which] is as a rule *the direct representation of the wish-fulfilment*   (Freud 1900, p. 561. My emphasis)

If this quality can be detected so readily—although Freud neither defines it nor gives examples—the wish-fulfillment proposition must be empirical. Now, many of the facts about dreams are explained with similar empirical propositions. Suppose, for example, it were true that direct wish-fulfilling dreams occur less frequently among adults than among children.[2] Explaining that fact requires the central wish proposition and two ancillary propositions, one of which assumes that realistic thinking replaces wishful childish thinking during development, and the other that during adult dreaming some realistic thought is still present. Both of these propositions are empirical. That being the case, it is possible that the theory is not a theory at all but a collection of empirical statements. I believe this point holds even if the principle of wish fulfillment does, as Fancher says, emerge "rather suddenly as a logical deduction from the assumptions [of the *Project*]," which is the central thesis of Fancher's (1971) paper, that emergence is not at all inconsistent with the principle having been arrived at empirically before the *Project* was written.

   Third, whether the wish-fulfillment theory can be tested at all seems to have been doubted by Freud himself. About a month after *The Interpretation of Dreams* appeared, while investigating his theory with a willing philosopher-subject, he wrote to Fliess, "There is too much that is new and unbelievable, and too little strict proof. I did not even succeed in convincing my philosopher, though he was providing me with the most brilliant confirmatory material"; he added, ad hominem, "it is easy for a philosopher to transform inner resistance into logical refutation" (Masson 1985, Letter of Dec. 9–14, 1899). He also said the proposition that dreams were wish fulfillments was an "assertion" or "assumption" that could neither be proved nor disproved:

we have constructed our theory of dreams on the assumption that the dream-wish which provides the motive power invariably originates from the unconscious—an assumption which, as I myself am ready to admit, cannot be proved to hold generally, though neither can it be disproved.   (Freud 1900, p. 598)

And, in a slightly different way:

this assertion cannot be proved to hold universally; but it can be proved to hold frequently, even in unsuspected cases, and it cannot be contradicted as a general proposition.   (p. 554. Emphasis removed)

Freud's reference to the impossibility of establishing the universality of the proposition is very likely an allusion to the problem of trying to establish the truth of such propositions inductively. Even if every dream ever dreamed were analyzed and found to confirm the wish principle, that demonstration would not guarantee it would hold for the next one.

In any case, a successful demonstration might not carry much weight. According to R. M. Jones (1970/1978, pp. 120–122), who is generally quite sympathetic to Freud's dream theory, wish fulfillment is a "consequence" of dreaming, not its "cause." Unconscious wishes, in his view, can only be incorporated into dreams and not instigate them. Making a related but somewhat stronger point, Foulkes (1978, p. 45, and n. 4) argued that the wish-fulfillment hypothesis is not empirical but "the only possible outcome" of using free association within the framework set by Freud's other theoretical ideas.

Freud's claim that the wish-fulfillment proposition cannot be "disproved" or "contradicted" may involve an even more serious objection. If it means anything other than that the theory is completely impervious to empirical test, it must refer to some difficulty in the method of analysis itself, perhaps the indeterminacy of the result:

Dreams frequently seem to have more than one meaning. Not only . . . may they include several wish-fulfilments one alongside the other; but a succession of meanings or wish-fulfilments may be superimposed on one another, the bottom one being the fulfilment of a wish dating from earliest childhood.   (Freud 1900, p. 219)

Elsewhere he said "it is in fact never possible to be sure that a dream has been completely interpreted" (p. 279). Sulloway described how virtually none of the early reviewers of *The Interpretation of Dreams*,

even the most friendly and respectful, failed to point out the questionable and unprovable nature of many of Freud's dream analyses.   (Sulloway 1979, p. 347; cf. Kiell 1988)

Sulloway also drew attention to the role played by what he terms "the methodological difficulties entailed in the objective application of [Freud's] technique" (1979, p. 347). In *The Interpretation of Dreams*, Freud did not set out any rules by which dreams were to be interpreted. His failure was criticized at the time and he conceded the fact (Decker 1977, p. 173). Writing as a psychoanalyst, Spanjaard was explicitly critical. He could find

nowhere in Freud's writings . . . an exact formulation of [the] procedure for conducting interpretations.   (Spanjaard 1969)

And Spanjaard cited many other analytic complainants. Over eighty years after Freud's main work on dreams, Grinstein (1983) eventually came to the rescue with his "systematic presentation of basic rules" of interpretation.

Even where there are rules they are readily denied. Thus Palombo denied the neutrality of the day residue: it "is always the point of access to an associative network of emotionally significant recent events." (Palombo 1984). Unlike some of the recent commentators, however, he did not deny the role of the repressed childhood wish, largely because he wanted to use characteristics of the manifest content to identify the associational pathway leading to it. Consequently, there is uncertainty about the task of interpretation, as well as questions about its complexity. Both provide plausible reasons for Freud's conclusion that the wish-fulfillment proposition could be neither proved nor disproved.

Another difficulty is that the basic wish represented in a dream had to be an infantile one (Freud 1900, p. 553). But it is noticeable this proposition was not established for important dreams such as those of Irma's injection or the botanical monograph. Eleven years later Freud added to the short essay *On Dreams* the proposition that "repressed infantile *sexual* wishes provide the most frequent and strongest motive-forces for the construction of dreams" (Freud 1901a, p. 682. My emphasis). But he hardly ever demonstrated that there was any infantile wish, let alone that it was sexual. Jones, who also remarked on the absence of evidence for infantile repressed wishes, says in fact that there almost never is a way of testing for their presence (R. M. Jones 1970/1978, pp. 12–13, 123; cf. Foulkes 1978, pp. 37, 57–58). Freud asserts but does not prove.

In any case, Steele and Jacobsen contend that the match between the interpreted manifest dream, which is supposed to be the latent dream, and the latent dream itself is always uncertain, and conclude, "In no way do associations show the childhood scene as a cause of the manifest dream" (Steele and Jacobsen 1977). They declare Freud's contrary conclusion to be a simple post hoc explanation. In addition, he relied explicitly on the "copious and intertwined associative links" provided by the dreamer, that is, on the dream equivalent of the logical and associative structure, but in so far as he said he suppressed the relevant material from his own dreams, he passed "beyond the bounds of acceptable evidence." After noting that the wish in the Irma dream was a preconscious one, Erikson (1954) attempted to find the infantile sexual wish behind it. That he actually used his own associations rather than Freud's is sufficient evidence that the rules for interpretation are too generously framed for the real role of infantile sexual wishes to be established.

This basic indeterminacy in the interpretative process has generated the many attempts to revise the wish-fulfillment theory so as to do away with unconscious wishes, censors, and disguises altogether. As early as 1937 Lorand stressed the clinical utility of direct interpretation of the manifest content, an approach that although criticized then, always appealed (Babcock 1966), being reendorsed recently by

Eckardt (1982) and Pulver (1987). This is due in part to Freud's own example. According to Spanjaard (1969), Freud incorporated the manifest reproaches he directed against Irma as a "very essential element" in his interpretation, and in the Dora dream, the manifest content was identical with the interpretation. Again, Greenberg and Pearlman (1978) used Schur's (1966b) material concerning Emma Eckstein's operation to reinterpret the Irma dream. To them, the manifest content portrays, in a way but little disguised, Freud's then current waking concerns. Although Emma was not Irma, as those authors suppose (Masson 1984, pp. 205–206), at Freud's request, Fliess examined Irma to rule out nasal pathology (Freud 1900, p. 117), and it is reasonable to suppose Freud's anxieties about Irma and Emma were linked. Greenberg and Pearlman accept Schur's contention that Freud repressed the Emma episode, and as a consequence, they emphasize the meaning of the dream as "a mere effort to disguise an unacceptable wish pressing for discharge." They do not see the concepts of drive discharge and dream censorship as any longer "necessary to our understanding of dream formation," a conclusion apparently shared by Eckardt (1982).

Although Greenberg's and Pearlman's argument about the Dora dream is plausible, it is not without difficulties. First, how does the wish that Freud seemed to uncover fit the drive discharge model? Second, neither they nor Schur considers a much more likely interpretation than Freud's repressing the Emma incident. Freud, unwilling to have Fliess's negligence paraded in public again, prepared an interpretation for the book in which reproaches about his own carelessness, rather than Fliess', were laid to rest. The central point of Greenberg's and Pearlman's interpretation is plausibly convincing nevertheless: Freud's conscious worry about Emma is directly reflected in the manifest content. In fact, they go farther and cite the analyses by Schorske (1975) of some of Freud's other dreams that show the manifest content to have derived from important waking experiences rather than from the indifferent ones his theory postulated. Palombo also points out that, although Freud thought the relations between the elements of the manifest content, particularly the coherent ones, should be disregarded as illusory, he also routinely broke his own rule:

The meaning of the dream as a whole is often both plainly visible and clearly related to the meanings that emerge from associations to its individual elements. To see this we have to look no further than the most interpreted of all of Freud's dreams, *the dream of Irma's injection.* (Palombo 1984. My emphasis)

This reliance on the manifest content has led to such absurdities as Hartman's (1983) outline of eight very different "themes" discerned by psychoanalysts in Freud's Irma dream, to which he then adds his own and those of Elms (1980) and Blum (1981).

Since then, Langs (1984) counted nine equally different interpretations, also made by other psychoanalysts, before he too added his own (cf. McLaughlin 1981).

Nonanalytic approaches seem equally as valid as the analytic. Using a structuralist approach developed for the study of myth, Kuper and Stone arrive at an interpretation similar to that of Greenberg and Pearlman (1978), but that is in some respects more comprehensive and seemingly correct. Yet their method is so fundamentally different from the psychoanalytic that, as they say, free association and "the entire distinction between the manifest and the latent dream is put into question" (Kuper and Stone 1982). Much the same thing can be said about Spence's (1981) use of Freud's waking concerns to interpret the botanical monograph dream. Applying his own quite specific and nonpsychoanalytic rules, Spence thinks independent judges could generate a dream similar to Freud's merely from "a description of the dream day and its three key events" (Spence 1981). Alongside prediction like this, post-diction interpretation would be child's play. The wish-fulfillment "theory" would require neither confirmation nor disproof because it would simply not be necessary.

As we have seen, shortly after *The Interpretation of Dreams* appeared, a "victim" offered himself to Freud as a subject through whose dreams the dream theory might be tested. He was the Viennese philosopher Heinrich Gomperz. After six months the pair gave up. As Gomperz wrote:

The experiment proved a complete failure. All the "dreadful" things which he suggested I might have concealed from myself and "suppressed" I could honestly assure him had always been clearly and consciously present in my mind.   (Cited in Masson 1985, p. 388)

After nearly ninety years, psychoanalytic and critical thinking about dream interpretation seems to have confirmed Gomperz's conclusion.

The Sources of the Difficulties

Decker (1975/1977, pp. 288–289) referred to a well-defined trend among the contemporary responses to *The Interpretation of Dreams* in which the ingenuity and plausibility of Freud's explanations were acknowledged at the same time as obvious but unclearly formulated doubts about their validity were expressed. For example, in what Decker described as "one of the most appreciative discussions," Sokal wrote:

In the analysis of … particular examples … Freud shows himself to be a true master of psychological observation, though just this virtuosity of his interpretive artistry may arouse in some a doubt as to the scientific worth of the theory.   (p. 289)

Decker took the phrase "interpretive artistry" to be a damning indictment of Freud. Laplanche was even more condemnatory:

The arguments are off the mark, and often the logic which is used is the famous logic of the "cauldron"[3] or indeed, to take another image, that of the famous bent rifle, which enables one to shoot round corners   (Laplanche 1981)

He illustrates his point by saying that Freud's arguments in support of the wish-fulfillment thesis show

inadequate examples, inappropriate reasoning, recourse to the pseudo-certainties of the manifest content ... [and] the contradictory revisions in the successive editions of the book.   (ibid.)

Yet Laplanche is insistent about the theory: "it works"! For him, as for most psychoanalysts, Freud's theses win out over the logic or the facts.

My analysis has identified the explanatory flaws that provide the bases for these misgivings. Partly they follow from the assumptions of the theory itself and partly they come from Freud's not specifying the rules for interpreting dreams and symptoms (and we will see in chapter 15 that it will never be possible to specify them). Even were we prepared to apply the theory to Freud's associations rather than to Dora's, such explanatory gaps are revealed that Freud's interpretations and speculative reconstructions cannot be taken seriously.

Over and above those issues is the matter of the control that Freud's own ideas exerted over the associations and interpretations generated during application of the theory. We have found no reason to suppose, as ought to be the case with a scientific theory, that the personal beliefs of the observer are likely to be irrelevant to tests of the theory. Freud believed any one observer ought to be able to uncover the same unconscious wish as any other. As early as 1909 the American psychologist Morton Prince, whose attitude toward Freud's theory was then reserved but not unsympathetic, confirmed some aspects of the dream theory but not, despite reasonably intensive inquiry, the roles of wishes, processes such as censorship and repression, or compromise formations (Prince 1910a; cf. E. Jones 1910; Prince 1910b). Prince's findings are virtually at one with those contemporary psychoanalysts who find it unnecessary to draw on either Freud's drive-discharge theory or the concepts of wish fulfillment, censorship-repression, and the disguise of dream thoughts.

It is, of course, commonplace that dream interpretations are similar within schools of psychotherapy using it, but different among them. Here the six discrepant interpretations of a set of dreams gathered together by Fosshage and Loew (1978) from a single patient are of interest. The interpreters had no direct knowledge of the patient or of her associations, so the data provide a less than complete test of the commonplace. But hardly anything is shared in the interpretations. Of special importance is the grossness of the discrepancies between the two psychoanalysts, one (Garma) more or less adopting a classical approach, and the other (Padel) the revisionist object-relations standpoint. Even Freud's hard and fast symbols were given quite different meanings.

A well-documented instance throws similar doubt on the objectivity with which symptoms are analyzed. During the 1920s Otto Rank, a close colleague of Freud's, announced he had been able to trace symptoms back to recollections of the trauma of birth. In discussing the role of suggestion in therapy, Edward Glover, a leading British psychoanalyst, remarked on

the rapidity with which some analysts were able to discover "birth traumas" in all their patients for some time after Rank first published his book on the *Trauma of Birth*, and *before it was officially exploded.* (Glover 1931b. My emphasis)

Glover here implicitly acknowledges that at least some of the clinically discovered "facts" of psychoanalysis depend on the preconceptions of the analyst. It is more than curious that a science should have something that can be described, even flippantly, as an official view of its facts. His description raises the possibility that the official view is based on the particular set of preconceptions held by the dominant members of a given school of analysis.

Conclusions

Many features of the dream may be deduced if the mental apparatus has the structure Freud supposed it to have and if the flow of excitation within it during dreaming is predominately regressive. In relation to symptoms, the main weakness is that the flow of excitation at any one time is assumed to be unidirectional, so the theory is unable to account for the simultaneous occurrence of hallucinations and motor activity. Inconsistencies in the placement of the censorship make it hard to see how that function is exercised, and limited access of the systems to consciousness makes it impossible to explain how preconscious thoughts can be incorporated into the fabric of the dream as thoughts, or how normal recollective thinking takes place.

Characterization of the systems of the apparatus, particularly the unconscious and preconscious systems and their related primary and secondary processes, is inadequate and inconsistent. Consequently, the theory cannot explain how infantile wishes and other mental contents come to be unconscious, repressed, or indestructible. Neither can the theory account for the formation of the structured and unconscious fantasies basic to the explanation of hysteria and other psychoneuroses.

Of course, the further problem is that what is called the theory of dream formation may not be a theory at all. If it is, it is either one that does not involve processes different from those of waking thought, and so does not require special testing, or it is quite untestable in any ordinary way.

Leaving these problems aside and looking at the theory from Freud's point of view, we find a most noticeable gap in that the repressed infantile sexual wishes supposed to be basic to dream formation are treated as givens. Freud makes no attempt to characterize them or to probe their origins. In a sense the theory is too mentalistic. It is a theory of a mental apparatus without a bodily or organic core. The theory of childhood sexuality to be examined in chapter 10 fills the gap by providing what purports to be a biological basis for infantile sexual wishes.

Notes

1. From Rogow's (1979) expansion of Freud's description of Dora's mother, Dora's reaction to her is quite understandable. Along similar lines, some writers have used Dora's case as an instance of Freud's neglect of real events as contributors to psychopathology after he gave up the seduction theory (M. I. Klein and Tribich 1982a,b).

2. As far as I can determine, it is very doubtful that children's dreams are all that transparent. On the basis of his many studies, Foulkes (1978, p. 44) concludes that children's dreams "seldom" have an obvious wish-fulfilling character. All that Ablon and Mack (1980) could be sure of was that they were based on "what matters most deeply to the child." They also issued a caution about the value of such concepts as "the working through of traumatic experiences" or "mastery" in relation to children's frightening dreams.

3. Laplanche so alludes to the irrational, primary process mode of thought of the unconscious as Freud conceived it.

10 A Theory of Sexuality

Holmes: The individual represents in his development the whole procession of his ancestors, and ... a sudden turn to good or evil stands for some strong influence which came into the line of his pedigree.
—Conan Doyle: *The Return of Sherlock Holmes*

Before 1900 Freud emphasized the role of sexual motives in normal and abnormal behavior, but it was not until *Three Essays on the Theory of Sexuality* of 1905 that the systematic attention he gave to the nature of sexual behavior per se resulted in a formal theory of sexuality. The central problem was that his interpretations and reconstructions of the sexuality of the psychoneurotic, especially the hysteric, seemed to show that it had been dominated from early childhood by perverse impulses. It was not surprising, then, that his consideration of sexuality was based equally on an examination of the sexual practices of the sexually deviant and the manifestations of sexuality in childhood.

I begin chapter 10 with an attempt to determine the origins of Freud's concept of an instinctual sexual drive. I argue that its characteristics owe more to the picture of human sexuality he drew in the actual neuroses and to the explanatory problems created by the collapse of the childhood seduction theory than to the biological and psychiatric literature of his day. After summarizing his basic arguments and concepts concerning perverse and infantile sexuality, I make two critical evaluations. One is of the concept of the sexual instinctual drive itself, where I argue that Freud's earlier work provided him with an inappropriate model for the new concept. The other is of the theory of sexual development, where my point is that, rather than providing an explanation of how adult sexual life emerged, Freud gave only a description, and an inaccurate one at that.

The Seduction Theory and the Sexual Drive

After the seduction theory collapsed, Freud gradually came to the view that the patient had recalled a fantasy. As we will see, various theoretical and logical requirements virtually forced him to postulate some internal cause for the perverse sexual content of the fantasies, for the ways in which the fantasies were connected to the symptoms, and for the ways in which what were undoubtedly memories of other real events became linked with both.

Already in the four to six months before the end of the theory Freud had given a reasonable amount of consideration to neurotic fantasies (Masson 1985, Letters of Apr. 6, 1897, May 2, 1897, and Draft L, letter of May 16, 1897, Draft M of May 25, 1897, and Draft N of May 31, 1897). The content of these fantasies was not of childhood seduction, of course, and Freud thought of them as having a different place among the determinants of symptoms. His first and rather rapid conclusion was that, although these other fantasies were based on early memories, they actually formed in later childhood and were "psychic facades produced in order to bar access to these memories" (Draft L of May 2, 1897). The kinds of fantasies he mentioned in this connection were those of worthlessness in female patients, which he regarded as based on identification with servant girls who had been involved in liaisons with the patients' fathers or brothers (Draft L), fantasies of being illegitimate (Draft M), and, possibly, death wish fantasies directed toward the parent of the same sex (Draft N).

Memories of real events, often the primal scene of the seduction, gave rise to fantasies and impulses that in turn determined the symptoms (Draft M). The memories bifurcated, one part being put aside and replaced by fantasies, and another accessible part leading directly to the impulses. The fantasies were primary; Freud even wondered if later on the impulses themselves derived from the fantasies (Draft N). Although he mentioned only the hostile death wish toward the parent of the opposite sex as an example of such an impulse, he described the impulses as perverse, usually in contexts implying they were always so. However, impulses deriving from specifically sexual experiences were first mentioned in the letter of May 2, 1897, where they were described as appearing in a distorted form as the symptoms of obsessional neuroses. Then, only two weeks before the collapse of the seduction theory, Freud linked the symptoms, the memories, the fantasies, and the perverse impulses together by stating that, as well as causing symptoms, memories gave rise to the fantasies and to the impulses. When both of these were repressed, "the higher determinations of the symptoms already following from the memories make their appearance" (Masson 1985, Letter of July 7, 1897).

An Alternative Source

With the end of the seduction theory it was not only necessary to find another source for the symptoms, the interconnection of perverse impulses and fantasies with the symptoms also had to be explained. The more specific questions with which Freud was faced were why was the false memory one of a perverse sexual experience?, what was the nature of perverse sexual activity in general?, and what was the nature of perverse sexual activity in childhood? The thesis he eventually arrived at was that perverse impulses existing in childhood gave rise to both the fantasies and the symptoms. Thus, instead of pathways from the primal scenes of seduction bifurcating and leading to the impulses and fantasies that reunited at the symptoms, the impulses were now the original forces and led by way of the fantasies to the symptoms.

Well before he abandoned the theory, however, Freud proposed that most of the basic hysterical symptoms, as well as some "exceedingly common" others, reproduced the sensations present in the victim's mouth, anus, and genitals during the seduction experience (Freud 1896c, pp. 214–215). Only those sensations had the right determining quality for the resultant symptoms. Similarly, in the search for sexual satisfaction, perverse adults repeated the most minute details of the act into which they had been seduced, once again experiencing the same sensations (Masson 1985, Letters of Dec. 17, 1896, Jan. 3, 1897, Jan. 11, 1897, Jan. 12, 1897, Jan. 24, 1897). Clearly an explanatory substitute for the "memory" of a real seduction experience had also to account for these particular details.

When Freud commented to Fliess on the consequences of the demise of the seduction theory, he said, "It seems once again arguable that only later experiences give the impetus to fantasies, which [then] hark back to childhood" (Masson 1985, Letter of Sept. 21, 1897). One of the difficulties with this view of the origin of fantasies was its failure to explain how *all* patients incorporated into their fantasies "horrible perverse details which often are as remote from their experience as from their knowledge" (Letter of Oct. 3–4, 1897). This explanatory problem, a result of the assumption of uniform causation, seems to have been why Freud continued to believe in a real sexual experience in childhood, a belief he maintained for some considerable time, if inconsistently (Masson 1985, Letters Oct. 3–4, 1897, Oct. 15, 1897, Oct. 31, 1897, Nov. 14, 1897, Dec. 12, 1897, Dec. 22, 1897, Jan. 16, 1898, Jan. 30, 1898, Mar. 10, 1898, Apr. 27, 1898, June 20, 1898, Sept. 27, 1898, Dec. 21, 1899, and Jan. 8, 1900; editorial notes to *Standard Edition*, vol. 1, pp. 260–261).

Although Sulloway (1979, pp. 207–210) expertly demolishes the myth that Freud's self-analysis was the reason for his abandoning the seduction theory and postulating the theory of infantile sexuality, it should not be overlooked that it was through his self-analysis that Freud came to regard the fantasies as normal psychological products rather than as pathognomonic of neurosis. Only about eight to ten weeks after his analysis began he seems to have noticed in himself the same feelings and fantasies he had previously seen only in his patients (Masson 1985, Letters of Aug. 14, 1897, Oct. 3–4, 1897, and Oct. 15, 1897). His immediate conclusion was that the parentage fantasies he observed in paranoiacs, and the combination of sexual feelings toward the mother and jealousy of the father of the hysteric, were universal events of early childhood. Once everyone had been "a budding Oedipus in fantasy" (Letter of Oct. 15, 1897).

Perversion and Repression

That the germ of this newly discovered universal sexual feeling was perverse in its object was plain enough, but rather more was required to explain the sensory content of the horrible perverse details that came to be incorporated into neurotic fantasies, and presumably into normal ones as well. A solution was provided by the line of thinking about repression Freud had been pursuing before he let go of the seduction theory and that was more or less independent of the inquiry into the origins of fantasies. As we have seen, at the beginning of 1896 Freud proposed that repression came about because the quantity of unpleasure released by premature sexual stimulation in childhood was vastly increased if an attempt was made to revive the memory after puberty. The difficulty with the theory was "the origin of the unpleasure" (Draft K of Jan. 1, 1896). Had Freud been able to identify the source, the tendencies of the mental apparatus to reduce quantities of excitation and avoid unpleasure, tendencies governed by the principle of constancy and the pleasure principle, would have brought about repression automatically.

By the beginning of 1897 Freud concluded that perverse sexuality in the adult came about because of some kind of failure of repression. In discussing the nature of the defense against memories, he asked how analogous seductions sometimes gave rise to perversions instead of hysteria, or obsessions, or one form of paranoia, or acute hallucinatory amentia (Draft K of Jan. 1, 1896). His eventual answer was that for perversion to result there was either no defense at all or the defense took place before the (unspecified) psychic apparatus had been completed (Masson 1985, Letter of Dec. 6, 1896). From this point of view, hysteria was *repudiated perversion* and not merely *repudiated sexuality* (Letter of Dec. 6, 1896), or, as he put it a few weeks later, it was the *negative* of the perversions (Letter of Jan. 24, 1897).

Although the formula focused attention on repression, it was not until Freud postulated an automatic basis for it that he was able to solve some of the problems of introducing a childhood sexual impulse into his theory. Significantly enough, the first hint was in the context of explaining how the same childhood sexual experience sometimes resulted in neurosis and sometimes in perversion. Freud supposed pleasurable "sexual release" was obtained during childhood from the stimulation of a number of different parts of the body, or erogenous zones, but at a later time their stimulation released a substance that generated anxiety and so brought about repression automatically (Letter of Dec. 6, 1896).

The date of Freud's letter rules out Moll's (1897, 1933) extension of the notion of erogenous zones as the main source of Freud's idea, as Sulloway (1979, p. 518) seems to imply. Chambard (1881), a pupil of Charcot, observed that orgasm could be produced in some somnambulistic hysterics by simply touching the inner side of the thigh, the groin, nipples, neck, and palms of the hands. He called these especially sensitive parts of the body *centres érogènes*. By analogy with Charcot's hysterogenic zones, for the areas did not overlap, Féré renamed them *zones érogènes* (Féré, cited in Binet and Féré 1887/1887a, p. 152). Krafft-Ebing (1898, 1965) adopted and popularized the concept, but it was Moll who first publicly extended it to include many other areas of the body and proposed that their stimulation produced sexual excitation physiologically, "without any primary and direct psychical activity" (Moll 1897, p. 93, 1933, p. 126).

Freud's conceptualization of repression as an automatic process seems not to have been developed further until about a month after he concluded that his own Oedipal feelings were universal. Suddenly, he then attempted to use what he saw as an important difference between human and animal sexuality to explain how the zones changed their function and released only unpleasure. For animals, the sight of the zones was always sexually exciting, and internal sensations arising from their stimulation contributed to the animals' own libido "the way the sexual organs proper do." In adult humans, on the other hand, the appearance and stimulation of the zones, even the idea of it, produced repellent sensations and unpleasure.

Freud supposed the difference had arisen during phylogenetic development when man's adoption of an upright carriage changed the role of smell now causing, as he put it, "formerly interesting [nasal] sensations attached to the earth" to arouse disgust (Masson 1985, Letter of Nov. 14, 1897; cf. Letter of Jan. 11, 1897). Because of his general adherence to the biogenetic law of recapitulation (Sulloway 1979), as well as the influence of Moll (1897, 1933; Masson 1985, Masson 1985, Letter of Nov. 14, 1897), and possibly also precipitated by the influence of James Mark Baldwin's views on phylogeny and ontogeny, about which he had read only a few days before (Masson 1985, Letter of Nov. 5, 1897; cf. Broughton 1981), Freud supposed that a similar change had taken place during the ontogenetic development of the child. Stimulation of the erotogenic zones in the child produced "something that is analogous to the later release of sexuality" (Letter of Nov. 18, 1897). During development the zones lost this capacity, and the revival of earlier memories involving their stimulation caused "an internal sensation analogous to disgust" (Letter of Nov. 14, 1897). From this postpubertal release of unpleasure, repression followed automatically. Freud found the organic origin of the unpleasure necessary for automatic repression in an ontogenetic recapitulation of a phylogenetically changed function.

There was, if I can so put it, a bonus: the areas of the body once able to release sexuality—the anus, mouth, and throat—were precisely the areas that seemed to have been involved in the childhood seduction "experiences." Stimulation of those zones in childhood was now a necessary condition for later neurotic repression and symptom formation, and it was that particular form of stimulation that provided the "horrible perverse" details. Memories of childhood genital stimulation also released more sexuality on revival than originally, but a nonneurotic compulsion was the result. Normality, in the sense of freedom from repression or compulsion, was thus dependent on all the erotogenic zones having escaped stimulation in childhood. Perversions were due to failures to abandon the zones of the mouth and the anus, failures inherent, it was implied, in the developmental process itself. Here we might note Compton's observation that Freud had to formulate "some concept of sexuality that could encompass not only the normal sexual behavior of adults—genital union in the service of reproduction—but also aberrant sexual behavior, childhood sexual manifestations, and the warded-off sexual impulses of neurotics" (Compton 1981a). Even with it, the automatic organic mechanism of repression still required some real experience to have occurred, and we have noted that Freud continued to search for an external source for some time. Then, quite late (and again quite suddenly), his self-analysis seemed to provide a solution:

fantasies are products of later periods and are projected back from what was then the present into earliest childhood; the manner in which this occurs also emerged—once again by a verbal link.   (Masson 1985, Letter of Jan. 3, 1899)

Freud's answer to the rhetorical question he asked next was to be of the utmost significance to the development of his theory generally and to his concept of instinctual drive in particular:

To the question "What happened in earliest childhood?" the answer is, "Nothing, but the germ of a sexual impulse existed."   (Letter of Jan. 3, 1899)

Because the sensory content of the symptom had to reproduce that of the cause, there had to have been sexual sensations and they had to have arisen in the mouth and anus. But, if by "nothing" Freud meant that those sensations had not been aroused by external stimulation, it followed that they had to be the result of the child's own activities and, if the tendency of the organism to avoid unpleasure was not to be violated, those activities had to generate pleasure in the zones (Masson 1985, Draft K of Jan 1, 1896; Freud 1950/1954, part III, section 11).

   Further, if the sexual content of symptoms and perversions was to be explained, infantile self-stimulation had to produce not merely pleasurable sensations but sexual sensations, if not actual sexual satisfaction. Consequently, the "germ" of the sexual impulse had to be autoerotic, had to use the child's own body as its object, and had to be capable of generating sexual sensations in the anus, mouth, and throat. Once Freud concluded that nothing had happened, his expectation about the relation between the sensory content of symptom and cause, his assumptions about the ubiquity of the pleasure principle, and possibly, as Amacher (1974) suggested, the logical demands of the reflex model itself, forced the further conclusion that the child had a sexual life consisting of autoerotic activities, some of which were of a non-genital kind.

Freud's self-analysis is usually cited as the source of his concept of an infantile sexual drive, but it seems to me very unlikely that he could have recalled any sexual sensations from his early childhood. Nor does it seem likely that he could have made any observations during his self-analysis that led in any direct way to the conclusion that fantasies were projections back to childhood. What I see as a more likely source of this new view was his sudden realization that his different expectations and theoretical requirements could be met by postulating autoerotic impulses in the early period of life. As soon as that view was adopted, it became possible to consider that "nothing" need have happened in childhood.

Child vs Adult Sexuality

Having decided that a sexual impulse existed in childhood, Freud then had to consider whether or not it resembled the adult drive. If he adopted the view that the immature and mature forms of the drive were essentially the same, he had to explain how the childhood behavior came to be replaced. Why would there be any change? On the other hand, if he took the view that adult and infantile sexuality were different, he had two other problems: in what sense was childhood sexuality actually sexual?, and how did the two forms come to be related as they did in perverse adult sexuality?

Some evidence shows that Freud hesitated between these two conceptualizations. Certainly he found the formulation of what he came to call "a sexual theory" very difficult. Almost a year after announcing to Fliess that he was considering developing such a theory as an immediate successor to *The Interpretation of Dreams* (Masson 1985, Letter of Oct. 11, 1899), his letters are full of such complaints as that he was "waiting for a spark to set the accumulated material on fire" he had been collecting on sexuality (Letter of Feb. 26, 1900; cf. Letters of Oct. 27, 1899, Nov. 5, 1899, Nov. 7, 1899, Nov. 9, 1899, Nov. 19, 1899, Nov. 26, 1899, Dec. 9, 1899, Dec. 24, 1899, and July 10, 1900). This prolonged gestation is of considerable interest because the solution Freud eventually adopted was already present in his correspondence with Fliess almost two years earlier. This is especially true of the letter of November 14, 1897, containing the idea of an initial release of sexuality being later replaced by unpleasure.

Examination of some aspects of the case of Dora throws further light on Freud's hesitation in placing the functions of the erotogenic zones in a concept of a childhood sexuality that was essentially the same as adult sexuality. He hesitated about the publishing itself. Although his analysis of the case was accepted for publication in January 1901, he withdrew it for some four to five months before resubmitting it, only to withdraw it again before he finally allowed it to appear after about another four years (editorial note, *Standard Edition*, vol. 7, pp. 3–4, 322). It seems to me to be very probable that Rogow (1978) is correct in pointing to Freud's break with Fliess as contributing substantially to his hesitation. The differences between the two cannot be dated with certainty, but they had become overt by August 1900. Dora was initially seen in the next month, and Freud completed the first draft of his paper by the end of January 1901. When describing to Fliess the framework he intended to use, he drew on ideas that were either Fliess's in their entirety, such as the conflict between female and male tendencies and the notion of bisexuality, or, like the erotogenic zones, theories to which Fliess had made a major contribution. It is precisely these concepts that are attenuated or missing altogether in the published account of 1905.

Hence it is of the greatest interest that while Freud told Fliess that Dora's symptoms would be "traced back to the character of the child's sucking" (Masson 1985, Letter of Jan. 30, 1901), his tracing did not involve the idea that stimulation of the oral erotogenic zone produced sexual excitation. Despite his conviction that the adult Dora entertained an oral sexual fantasy, he described her intense childhood oral stimulation as creating only a "somatic compliance," by which he meant a mere channel through which displaced adult sexual excitation might be expressed. However, as his remarks on somatic compliance reveal (and as his earlier use of the as-then-unnamed concept confirms) the process by which compliance was produced did not have to be sexual. For example, such a decidedly nonsexual event as rheumatic disease could, as with Elisabeth von R., leave behind a channel of expression that could be used for the realization of an unconscious mental conflict (Breuer and Freud 1895, p. 147; Freud 1905a, pp. 29–32, 40–42, 51–52).

I find it curious that Freud's explanation of Dora's symptoms makes no use of the most characteristic propositions of his later theory: the autoerotic nature of childhood sexuality and its expression through a number of independent instinctual drives, each with its own aim and object. Indeed, even though Dora's sucking was central, Freud did not describe it as autoerotic. There is a similarly curious quality in Freud's treatment of the feeling of disgust he thought to index and repress Dora's oral sexual activity. Before treating Dora, Freud had proposed that disgust originated in the altered role of the sense of smell. But, when actually discussing Dora's disgust, he emphasized the anatomical proximity of the organs of excretion with the genitals. However, later, in the *Three Essays*, he was inclined, as he was some nine years earlier, to assess that association as of minor importance (Masson 1985, Draft K of Jan. 1, 1896; Freud 1905a, pp. 31–32, 1905b, p. 152). Despite a number of similarities, the sexual theory implicit in his analysis of Dora is not the one found in the *Three Essays*. What is more important, it appears to be a theory based on a *qualitative* difference between childhood and adult sexuality.

In the *Three Essays* Freud adopted the alternative view: childhood and adult sexuality were essentially the same. Each erotogenic zone was the organ of a component sexual drive, and stimulation of it produced most of the drive's excitation. Other component drives, such as looking, were not located in the same kinds of erotogenic zones, but they also generated sexual excitation. Consequently, Freud's descriptions of the effects of stimulation stressed the frankly sexual outcomes. For example, sensual sucking, the exemplar of childhood sexual activity, had obvious sexual consequences in an orgasmlike reaction. A good deal of the evaluation of Freud's concept of an infantile sexual drive revolves around the sense in which the childhood behavior was sexual.

The Sexual Impulse

Freud began the first of the *Three Essays* with a conceptual analysis of the sexual instinctual drive. He distinguished among the libido, sexual objects, and sexual aims. *Libido* referred to the sexual instinctual drive in much the same way *hunger* referred to the nutritional instinctual drive. Libido was not characterized explicitly, however; Freud used only a hydraulic analogy; describing it as being diverted from one activity to another (Freud 1905b, pp. 156–157), as flowing like a blocked stream into collateral channels (pp. 170, 232), and as accumulating as a store of energy that could be used for other than sexual purposes (p. 232). Nine years later, when he defined libido formally as the psychical energy of the sexual instinctual drive (Freud 1914b), he was only making explicit the energetic conception already implicit in the *Three Essays* (Freud 1905b, p. 163). By *sexual object* Freud meant that from which sexual attraction proceeded, normally from an adult of the opposite sex. *Sexual aim* referred to the act toward which the instinctual drive tended and through which it was satisfied. Normally the aim was

the union of the genitals in the act known as copulation, which leads to a release of the sexual tension and a temporary extinction of the sexual instinct—a satisfaction analogous to the sating of hunger.   (p. 149)

For both aim and object the standard of normality was biological.

Essay I—Perverse Sexuality

Perversions were deviations of either sexual aim or object. Inversion, as Freud called homosexuality, showed that libido could be directed toward persons of the same sex. Some of the facts about homosexuality suggested to Freud that it resulted from a developmental disturbance and that "a bisexual disposition [was] somehow concerned" (Freud 1905b, p. 143). Both male and female inverts had, he thought, a

tendency to choose *feminine* sexual objects. In contrast, their sexual aims were likely
to be much more variable and range from simple, emotionally intense friendships to
sexual contacts of many different kinds. At the least, inversion showed that the
connection between the drive and the object was less intimate than might usually be
thought. In fact, they were "merely soldered together" (p. 148). The origins of the
sexual instinctual drive seemed to be independent of the object's attractions. Freud
thought these tentative conclusions were consistent with deviations in which the
sexually immature or animals were chosen as objects.

Ordinarily, more than just the genitals of the sexual object were, as Freud put it,
"valued" or judged positively. Indeed, the tendency was to *overvalue* the whole of the
body of the object, which helped turn activities connected with parts of the body
other than the genitals into sexual aims. From the fact that feelings of disgust were so
frequently aroused by oral-genital and anal-genital contacts, Freud concluded that
disgust was a "mental force" that restricted the sexual aim to genital activity. However, in some "normal" sexual acts as well as in perverse ones the drive was strong
enough to override disgust. Overvaluation of the object could also be strong enough
to extend to anything associated with the object, such as a part of the body like the
hair or an article of clothing, however inappropriate that thing, or fetish, might
otherwise be. In the perversion of fetishism, longing for the fetish took the place of
the object itself, and the normal aim was abandoned completely.

The preliminaries to genital union could become perversions if fixation on them
produced aims that replaced the normal. For example, looking at the sexual object
was normally sexually exciting, but it became perverse when only the genitals were
looked at, or when it overcame disgust and excretion was looked at (voyeurism) and
supplanted sexual union altogether. Freud added shame as a second mental force that
had to be overridden for perversions of looking to come into being.

Sadism and masochism were brought about by the relative weakness of a third
mental force. Freud took the two to be the active and passive forms of a single
condition. Sadism was based on the aggressive element of male sexuality sometimes
used in overcoming the resistance of the sexual object. Masochism had its roots in the
sexual overvaluation of the object that gave rise to the need for humiliation and
subjection. The capacity for pity at the painful suffering of another had to be overcome for sadism to be possible, and pain itself had to be overridden if masochism
were to develop. Pain, the third mental force, ordinarily prevented both.

From his analysis of the perversions Freud concluded that mental forces such as
shame, disgust, and pain acted as resistances to libidinal expression. In normal
development the sexual instinctual drive had to struggle against them. He also supposed these forces gave direction to the libido's development. He claimed to have

shown that perversions were based on "the convergence of several motive forces" (Freud 1905b, p. 162), and that they were of a composite nature. For him, the sexual instinctual drive was not simple, but was made up of various components.

Freud then claimed his analyses showed that the energy of the sexual instinctual drive was the only constant source of energy in the psychoneuroses, that the sexual life of neurotics was expressed in the symptoms of neurotics, and that the symptoms actually constituted the sexual activity of neurotics. This last claim was based specifically on the analysis of Dora's symptoms (p. 163). Because of the intensification of the mental forces of shame, disgust, and morality, the hysteric's sexual life was said to combine an excessive aversion to sexuality with an excessive craving for it. Drawing on the ideas expressed much earlier to Fliess, Freud claimed that psychoanalyses had revealed that the sexual drives of psychoneurotics were always perverse:

symptoms are formed in part at the cost of *abnormal* sexuality; *neuroses are, so to say, the negative of perversions.*   (p. 165)

Without exception, he maintained, the unconscious mental life of neurotics showed inverted impulses and tendencies toward every kind of perversion, especially those assigning a genital role to the mouth and the anus. The aims involved in looking, exhibiting, sadism, and masochism were motivated by "component" instinctual drives that he claimed played an especially prominent part in the formation of symptoms (p. 166). Masochistic impulses were essential to understanding why neurotic symptoms involved suffering, whereas a claimed connection between libido and cruelty accounted for the transformation of love into hate. Freud stressed that whenever an impulse having two forms was found in the unconscious of the neurotic, it would always be accompanied by the other: in the unconscious the exhibitionist was at the same time a voyeur. He also claimed that isolated perverse impulses were hardly ever found in the neurotic; usually there would be "a considerable number and as a rule traces of them all" (p. 167).

Freud then proposed that perversions as well as neuroses could be traced back to a number of component instinctual drives. The organs capable of receiving stimuli that contributed to the component impulses were called "erotogenic zones," and in perversions involving the mouth and anus they clearly functioned as substitutes for the genitals. The same was true of less obvious cases: in perversions of looking, the eye could be an erotogenic zone, and in sadism and masochism the whole body surface had that role.

The perverse sexuality of the psychoneurotic could be due to a constitutional tendency, but another factor might also be present. When neuroses were precipitated by repression or a failure of normal sexual satisfaction, the libido behaved like a stream whose main bed has become blocked. It proceeds to fill up collateral channels which may hitherto have been empty. Thus ... what appears to be the strong tendency (though, it is true, a negative one) of psychoneurotics to perversion may be collaterally determined, and must, in any case, be collaterally intensified.   (p. 170)

Neurotic patients drew differentially on their perverse dispositions and on the various internal and external factors that blocked libidinal expression.

Freud concluded the first of the *Three Essays* by arguing that because perverse impulses were to be found in the psychoneuroses, and because "an unbroken chain bridges the gap" between the neurotic and the normal, the disposition to perversion "must form a part of what passes as the normal constitution" (p. 171). A constitutional disposition of this sort ought to be observable in children. By foreshadowing that it might also be the case that the sexuality of the neurotic remained in or returned to an infantile state, he foreshadowed the main subject matter of the second essay. Attention should be directed, he said, to the sexual life of children, seeking there the influences governing the development of "perversion, neurosis or normal sexual life" (p. 172).

Essay II—Childhood Sexuality

Freud began the second essay by observing that the study of sexual activity in early childhood had been neglected. He supposed this was due partly to infantile amnesia, that is, to the general tendency for people to be unable to recall other than fragmentary impressions of their life before age six to seven years. But, because psychological examination showed experiences from that period had left "the deepest traces" (Freud 1905b, p. 175), it followed that those early impressions were not abolished. In fact, infantile amnesia resembled the amnesia of the neurotic for traumatic events. After asserting that infantile amnesia was due to repression, Freud noted that its existence provided a further resemblance between the mental states of children and neurotics, the first being the infantile nature of neurotic sexuality. He then asked:

Can it be, after all, that infantile amnesia, too, is to be brought into relation with the sexual impulses of childhood?   (p. 175)

He proposed that later hysterical repression was made possible by a store of repressed early childhood memories.

From the frequent reports of sexual impulses in early childhood, and from the nature of the childhood memories of the neurotic, Freud concluded that germs of sexual impulses were present at birth. They developed for a time, were overcome by a process of suppression, and reappeared at puberty. From what he said elsewhere in the *Three Essays*, the efflorescence of childhood sexual activity was between the third and fifth years. A period of latency then set and lasted until the beginning of adolescence. During the latency period the "dams" of disgust, shame, and aesthetic and moral ideas built up to restrict the flow of the sexual instinctual drive. Although it might seem that the dams were products of education

in reality this development is organically determined and fixed by heredity, and it can occasionally occur without any help at all from education.   (pp. 177–178)

Because of this organic determination, education should limit itself

to following the lines which have already been laid down organically and to impressing them somewhat more clearly and deeply.   (p. 178)

The dams were actually constructed from the sexual impulses themselves. At the beginning of the latency period the sexual drive was diverted into new, nonsexual aims; that is, it was sublimated. Freud averred that all historians of civilization had observed sublimation in the development of culture itself; "accordingly," the same thing happened in the development of the individual. Sublimation was based partly on the nonreproductive character of the childhood impulses and partly on their perversity, "which, in view of the direction of the subject's development, can only arouse unpleasurable feelings" (p. 178). The unpleasure evoked opposing mental forces that built up the mental dams of shame, disgust, and morality in order to suppress the unpleasure. Freud first called these forces "reacting impulses," but two years later he gave them their final name of reaction formations (Freud 1907b, p. 124).

He then took as an exemplar of childhood sexual activity what he called "sensual sucking" and examined it in detail. By this term he meant the evidently pleasurable, nonnutritive sucking by the infant, usually of the thumb, but sometimes of other parts of the body. Basing himself largely on the observations of Lindner, a Hungarian pediatrician who reported one of the few systematic studies of sucking, Freud claimed sensual sucking seemed to absorb the attention completely and to lead either to sleep or to "a motor reaction in the nature of an orgasm" (Freud 1905b, p. 180). He stated that "no observer had felt any doubt as to the sexual nature of this activity" (p. 180). Because it was directed toward the infant's own body rather than toward other people, the aim of sensual sucking was autoerotic, and the lips were an erotogenic zone. Thus it seemed clear this sensual sucking was sexual and that it was determined by a search for the pleasure first experienced when sucking at the mother's breast:

No one who has seen a baby sinking back satiated from the breast and falling asleep with flushed cheeks and a blissful smile can escape the reflection that this picture persists as a prototype of the expression of sexual satisfaction in later life.   (p. 182)

The pleasure provided by sensual sucking was not secondary to the satisfaction of hunger. Nutritive sucking expressed the instinct of self-preservation and sensual sucking the sexual impulse. Freud put it later that the sexual drive at first attached itself to or leaned on the nutritive activity, only later becoming independent of it.

Sensual sucking had the two essential characteristics of infantile sexual activity: it was autoerotic and its aim was dominated by an erotogenic zone. Although any part of the body could serve as an erotogenic zone, it was those parts most richly endowed with sensitive nerve endings and in which rhythmic stimuli evoked "a feeling of pleasure possessing a particular quality" that were often adopted (p. 183). In all erotogenic zones the aim was the same: to obtain satisfaction through stimulation. Freud supposed that during sucking a pleasurable sensation, due "no doubt [to] stimulation by the warm flow of milk," was first experienced during feeding (p. 181). Later remembrance of that pleasure created a need that he said revealed itself

by a peculiar feeling of tension, possessing, rather, the character of unpleasure, and by a sensation of itching or stimulation which is centrally conditioned and projected on to the peripheral erotogenic zone. (p. 184)

The aim attempted to replace

the projected sensation of stimulation in the erotogenic zone by an external stimulus which removes that sensation by producing a feeling of satisfaction. This external stimulus will usually consist in some kind of manipulation that is analogous to the sucking. (p. 184)

Sucking on the thumb or with the lips brought about a feeling of satisfaction by reproducing the pattern of stimulation caused originally by the warm flow of milk. The same mechanism held for the other zones: pleasurable sensations first experienced in the anus or the genitals later gave rise to a feeling of tension and a centrally conditioned sensation of itching that, when disposed of by "appropriate stimulation," brought about satisfaction (pp. 186–188).

Freud noted how intense excitation of the anal zone was virtually ensured by various intestinal disorders of early life. Children who held back their feces to produce "violent muscular contractions" and "powerful stimulation" of the anal mucosa were using the fecal mass as a masturbatory stimulus. Holding back the bowel contents "must no doubt cause not only painful but also highly pleasurable sensations" (p. 186). The child's refusal to defecate on request was, he said, "one of the roots of the constipation which is so common among neuropaths" (p. 187). He also claimed that most neurotics had special and secret scatological practices and ceremonies. The anus was therefore an erotogenic zone and its stimulation gave sexual pleasure.

The anatomical position of the genitals, their natural secretions, and their cleansing all combined to ensure that their potential for producing pleasurable feeling was realized early. Genital stimulation in infancy laid the foundation for the eventual primacy of the genital zone over the other erotogenic zones as well as for infantile masturbation itself. In Freud's opinion, infantile masturbation began and disappeared early. Revived before the fourth year, it persisted for a time until it was once more suppressed. The revival was either through a centrally determined tickling sensation leading to masturbation proper or through nocturnal enuresis that imitated nocturnal emission. Although external influences were not necessary to bring about the reappearance of sexual activity, seduction into sexual activity by an adult or another child he considered of "great and lasting importance" (p. 190).

Freud believed that many different forms of perverse sexual activity could be developed in the child who had been prematurely seduced, that is, seduction could make the child polymorphously perverse. From this he concluded that children had, "innately present in their disposition," an aptitude for all kinds of sexual irregularities. Thus children were like the "average, uncultivated," sexually inexperienced woman who could be led on by a clever seducer to adopt every sort of perversion. As Gilman (1981) pointed out, he now echoed some of Weininger's ideas about prostitution and constitutional tendencies:

considering the immense number of women who are prostitutes or who must be supposed to have an aptitude for prostitution without becoming engaged in it, it becomes impossible not to recognize that this same disposition to perversions of every kind is a general and fundamental human characteristic.   (Freud 1905b, p. 191; cf. Weininger 1903/1906; Masson 1985, Letters of July 20, 1904, July 23, 1904, July 26, 1904, and July 27, 1904)

The disposition to perverse sexuality was not only realized through the erotogenic zones. The component instinctual drives of looking (scopophilia), exhibitionism, and cruelty also contributed. Unlike the autoerotic activity of the erotogenic zones, the activities induced by these component drives were initially relatively independent of sexual satisfaction and "from the very first involve other people as sexual objects" (Freud 1905b, p. 192). Early seduction could draw attention to the genitals and create an interest in looking at the genitals of others. Because that interest was likely to be satisfied only when the child was watching someone else micturate or defecate, adult voyeurism would result. If the scopophilic impulse was repressed, the individual would become a compulsive viewer of the genitals of others. Children who were especially cruel were, Freud believed, justly suspected of precocious sexuality, and in them, no barrier of pity for the other halted the impulse of cruelty. The absence of that barrier might also lead to unbreakable connections being established between painful stimulation of the subject's own body and erotogenic sensations, with resultant masochism.

At this stage of his argument Freud thought he had shown that sexual excitation arose in three different ways: through the reproduction of organic need satisfactions, peripheral stimulation of erotogenic zones, and component instincts. In common with other writers of the period (Moll 1897, 1933; Krafft-Ebing 1898, 1965), he recognized other sources, in his case five, all of which involved stimulation of a rather general type: thermal stimulation from warm baths, mechanical excitation from such passive movements such as rocking and swinging, muscular activity of the kind involved in wrestling and romping, intense emotional excitement (pleasurable or unpleasurable), and intellectual strain. His evidence that these kinds of stimuli produced pleasurable sensations consisted of such facts as that children insisted on the incessant repetition of games of swinging and being thrown into the air, and that rocking was used habitually to induce sleep in restless children. Calling these pleasurable sensations "sexual" required an identification of "satisfaction" with "sexual excitation," and Freud therefore proposed those terms could be used "without distinction" (Freud 1905b, p. 201). He also stated that frankly sexual excitation sometimes followed such general stimulation.

From what he now referred to as his "tentative suggestions" about the sources of sexual excitation, Freud concluded with "more or less certainty" (p. 204) that sexual excitation was initiated in a more or less direct fashion by stimulation of the sensory surfaces, especially of the erotogenic zones. A great number of internal processes also produced excitation as a concomitant effect once their intensity passed beyond certain limits. The component instinctual drives were

either derived directly from these internal sources or are composed of elements both from those sources and from the erotogenic zones.   (p. 205)

He also thought it likely that variations in the contribution to sexual excitation from these indirect sources contributed to the "multiplicity of innate sexual constitutions" (p. 205). Finally, he voiced the suspicion that all the pathways leading from other bodily functions to the sexual were traversable in the reverse direction, and the existence of these reverse pathways explained how disorders of sexual function caused nonsexual conditions. For example, if sexual satisfaction arose during feeding, a reverse connection explained how nutritional disorders came about when sexuality was disturbed. Reverse pathways along which the sexual disturbances "trenched" on other somatic functions could also serve as channels for sublimation in the healthy.

Essay III—Sexual Development

Freud began the last of the three essays by describing the developmental changes that had to take place if the infantile sexuality he postulated were to be transformed into normal adult sexuality. First, the activities of the component drives had to combine to achieve pleasure in the genital zone, and the other erotogenic zones had similarly to become subordinate to the genitals. Second, the predominantly autoerotic sexual instinctual drive had to be directed toward an object. Third, what he called an "affectionate current" had to converge with the sexual current on the sexual object and the sexual aim.

What he described as the "primacy of the genital zone" (Freud 1905b, p. 207) came about because of changes in the effects of stimulation of the other zones. Stimulating them at puberty produced sexual excitement in the genitals as well as their own particular kind of infantile pleasure. Genital sexual excitation was marked by physical changes in the genitals and a psychological state of "a peculiar feeling of tension of an extremely compelling character" (p. 208). Primarily because the tension was accompanied by an impulse to change, Freud insisted that the tension had to be experienced as unpleasure. Were pleasure felt there would have been no tendency to change. Nevertheless there was a contradiction:

> If, however, the tension of sexual excitement is counted as an unpleasurable feeling, we are at once brought up against the fact that it is also undoubtedly felt as pleasurable. In every case in which tension is produced by sexual processes it is accompanied by pleasure; even in the preparatory changes in the genitals.   (p. 209)

Freud attempted to solve this problem by reanalyzing the contribution of the erotogenic zones to sexual excitation. Erotogenic zone stimulation in the adult clearly caused both pleasure and an increase in genital sexual excitement. With continued stimulation, the excitement built up to the point at which sexual substances were discharged in orgasm, an act accompanied by pleasure of "the highest" intensity (p. 210). He distinguished the pleasure due to stimulation of the zones from the tension of sexual excitation proper and from the pleasure due to discharge. He called the former "fore-pleasure" and the latter "end-pleasure." Fore-pleasure was "the same pleasure" already produced on a smaller scale in infancy. Its new function was to contribute to end-pleasure by increasing the level of sexual tension and so eventually producing "the greater pleasure of satisfaction" (p. 211).

Freud believed he had solved the problem of how pleasure from stimulation of the erotogenic zones gave rise to the need for the greater pleasure of orgasm, and also that he had explained deviations of sexual aim. In them an imbalance was produced between the slight amount of sexual tension compared with the considerable amount of fore-pleasure:

> The motive for proceeding further with the sexual process then disappears, the whole path is cut short, and the preparatory act in question takes the place of the normal sexual aim. (p. 211)

If during childhood the erotogenic zone or the component instinct contributed "an unusual amount of pleasure," and if "further factors" then brought about "a fixation," it would become difficult for the old fore-pleasure to become subordinate to the normal adult aim. Many perversions were based on this mechanism of "lingering over the preparatory acts of the sexual process" (p. 211).

Sexual excitation itself could not be treated "even hypothetically, in the present state of our knowledge" (p. 215). Because of his insistence that tension could not be felt as pleasurable, Freud had to have pleasure and tension "connected [only] in an indirect manner" (p. 212). The internal organs and the production of chemical substances were involved but, apart from outlining a chemical basis for the theory of sexuality that we have already considered in discussing the revisions to the theory of anxiety, he had to leave the basis of sexual excitation unspecified.

Sharp distinctions were also established at puberty between the masculine and the feminine characters. Before puberty there were differences in the development of inhibitions that took place earlier in girls than boys; in the expression of the component instincts, which tended to take the passive form in females; and in repression, which tended to be greater in females. Otherwise the differences were minimal. Indeed the autoerotic activity was so similar between the sexes that Freud believed libido was "invariably and necessarily of a masculine nature" and that the sexuality of little girls was "wholly masculine" (p. 219). Puberty induced two quite different processes. Boys experienced a great accession of libido, but girls "a fresh wave of repression" (p. 220). The repression was precisely of the girl's clitoral, that is, masculine sexuality. Stimulation of the clitoris now had to produce excitation of the vagina if the vagina was to supplant the clitoris as the predominant zone. Repression of the girl's masculine sexuality thus prepared the way for the full development of female sexuality. Because females had to change their leading erotogenic zone and males did not, they were more prone to neuroses, especially to hysteria.

Having explained how the genital zone had achieved primacy and how the new sexual aim had been adopted, Freud now turned to the process of explaining how the adult sexual object was found at puberty. He described the period of earliest infancy in which the sexual instinctual drive was linked to nourishment as one in which the mother's breast had been a sexual object. Autoerotism began with the loss of the breast and the subsequent redirection of the sexual impulse to the subject's own body. When autoerotism ceased at puberty, the direction taken by the sexual impulse was once again toward the breast:

There are thus good reasons why a child sucking at his mother's breast has become the prototype of every relation of love. The finding of an object is in fact a refinding of it.   (p. 222)

Throughout the whole time of the child's dependence on others, "even after sexual activity has become detached from the taking of nourishment," children learned to feel love for those who helped them and who satisfied their needs. Freud believed this love to be modeled on the suckling's relation. The sexual character of the child's dependence on others was to be seen in the anxiety of children, "originally nothing other" than a feeling they had lost the person whom they loved:

In this respect a child, by turning his libido into anxiety when he cannot satisfy it, behaves like an adult. On the other hand an adult who has become neurotic owing to his libido being unsatisfied behaves in his anxiety like a child: he begins to be frightened when he is alone. (p. 224)

Why, then, did male and female adults not both choose the mothers?—after all, both had had her breast as their first object.

Adult object-choice was, he said, first of all guided by the exclusion of blood relatives from consideration. In the human child the postponement of sexual maturation meant an incest barrier could be erected. Freud believed that pubertal fantasies, based as they were on infantile tendencies now strengthened by somatic pressure, showed the direction of the child's sexual impulse to be toward the parent of the opposite sex. When the fantasies were repudiated, a process of detachment from parental authority could take place and an object other than the parent he chosen. Failure of detachment occurred most often in girls who, if they retained their fathers as objects, would be sexually anesthetic and cold toward their husbands. Because the psychoneurotic had repudiated sexuality generally, the activity of finding an object remained unconscious. A characteristic combination of an exaggerated need for affection with an equally exaggerated horror of sexuality developed as a consequence. Freud claimed psychoanalyses showed that in neurotic females this characteristic resulted from incestuous object-choices. But even when no such abnormal consequence ensued, he believed the incestuous choices of infancy had long-lasting effects:

There can be no doubt that every object-choice whatever is based, though less closely, on these prototypes. A man, especially, looks for someone who can represent his picture of his mother, as it has dominated his mind from his earliest childhood.   (p. 228)

Although he said that "other starting points" from infancy might affect adult object-choice, he did not specify them.

Guidance of the adult choice also had to prevent inversion. An adult of the opposite sex had to be chosen. Freud thought the strongest factor was the attraction "opposing sexual characters exercise upon one another" (p. 229), the same factor responsible for sexual differentiation in the fantasies of puberty (p. 227). He was unable to indicate the basis of this attraction, and supposed further that by itself it was insufficiently strong to determine an opposite-sex choice. Reinforcement by social prohibitions against inversion was necessary because:

Where inversion is not regarded as a crime it will be found that it answers fully to the sexual inclinations of no small number of people.   (p. 229)

Freud presumed that a further powerful contribution to the choice of female objects by men came from the man's recollection of the affection shown him in childhood by his mother and other women who cared for him. In women the development of impulses of rivalry toward other females were thought to "play a part," as well as the sexual repression at puberty in discouraging them from choosing among their own sex (p. 229, n. 3).

Although much condensed, the best summary of Freud's theory is the one he made only a year after the *Three Essays* were published:

normality is a result of the repression of certain component instincts and constituents of the infantile disposition and of the subordination of the remaining constituents under the primacy of the genital zones in the service of the reproductive function ... *perversions* correspond to disturbances of this coalescence owing to the overpowering and compulsive development of certain of the component instincts, ... *neuroses* can be traced back to an excessive repression of the libidinal trends.   (Freud 1906a, p. 277)

I now turn to the evaluation of this developmental theory and the basic concepts of which it is constituted.

The Genesis of the Concept of Instinctual Drive

It is quite easy to show that Freud's 1905 concept of instinctual drive is quite different from those of instinct and drive current around the turn of the century. No one else used the word libido in quite the same way, distinguished so clearly between aims and objects of the instinctual drive, or, of special importance, stressed its internal sources. *Libido*, although not well defined at first, encompassed the sexual drive in the same way *hunger* took in the nutritional drive. *Aim* referred to the act toward which the drive tended and through which it was satisfied. Normally this was the union of the genitals in intercourse. *Object* meant that from which sexual attraction emanated, ordinarily an adult of the opposite sex. *Source* was not well defined at first but clearly referred to the internal processes that determined the drive.

Instinct, Drive, and Source   The literature of the late 1900s on the concept of instinct and the judgments of historians shows the German term *Instinkt* (and its English equivalent "instinct") was ordinarily used to describe simple reflexlike behaviors that were relatively invariant in form, unmodifiable by experience, and elicited by external stimuli (Preyer 1882, 1893a,b; James 1890b; Sully 1892; Morgan 1896; Groos 1899, 1901; McDougall 1905; H. S. Jennings 1906; Drever 1917; Bernard 1924; Wilm 1925). Although some kinds of instinctive behaviors, such as mating and nest building, were recognized as depending on internal conditions, those conditions were not emphasized. As Fletcher put it about Darwin, Morgan, James, and McDougall:

Whilst these writers were well aware of the existence and importance of these features, the state of knowledge at their time precluded any detailed positive statement as to their nature. (Fletcher 1957, p. 69; cf. Morgan 1896, pp. 8, 207)

Hence, the existing emphasis placed on external causes in discussions of the factors that elicited behavior could only be reinforced by this ignorance. It is not surprising, then, that McDougall noted:

Some writers have given ... organic conditions an undue prominence while neglecting the essential part played by sense-impressions.   (McDougall 1908, p. 23, n. 1)

On the other hand, the internal condition signified by the term *Trieb*, then most commonly rendered as impulse rather than as drive (as it is nowadays), had a connotation stressing the motor element to the detriment of the goal of the behavior, so giving it the meaning of a blind impulse (Morgan 1896, p. 140). Sully, who recognized that certain kinds of motor activity were prompted to some degree by *Trieb*, determined that that term was

commonly confined to those innate promptings of activity in which there is no clear representation of a pleasure, and consequently no distinct desire. Here the active element is greatly in excess of the intellectual.   (Sully 1892, p. 580)

When discussing why he had chosen to use *Trieb* in his work on play, Groos summed up the dilemma as follows:

We lack a comprehensive and yet specific term for those unacquired tendencies which are grounded in our psycho-physical organism as such. The word instinct does not cover the ground with its commonly accepted definition as inherited association between stimuli and particular bodily reactions. Even the imitative impulse which is responsible for the important group of imitative plays is not easily included in this idea, because no specific reaction characterizes it. It is safer, therefore, to speak of such play as the product of "natural or hereditary impulse" although even that is not entirely satisfactory, since many psychologists connect the idea of impulse [*Trieb*] with a tendency to movement.   (Groos 1899, p. 1, 1901, p. 2)

In a footnote he admitted he had modified his former view that the traditional concept of instinct was adequate to encompass variations in imitative play, and elaborated the point later (Groos 1899, pp. 364–372; 1901, pp. 284–290). The importance of his point is twofold: his discussion of instinct and drive is one of the few attempted in the nineteenth century, and his work was well known to Freud, who read it some time before completing the *Three Essays* (Freud 1905b, p. 173, n. 2).

If the discussions of Sully (1892), McDougall (1905, 1908), and H. S. Jennings (1906) reflect contemporary thought accurately, it was not usual for the internal drive tendencies alluded to by Groos (those "grounded in our psycho-physical organism") to be formally incorporated into concepts of instinct. Fletcher (1957, p. 6) asserted the contrary. According to him, most of the early writers believed instinctive behavior to be elicited only when the appropriate internal state was also present (Fletcher 1957, p. 6). However, Wilm's description of the situation seems to me to be more accurate. He observed that all that existed toward the end of the nineteenth century was only a tendency, although a growing one, to think of instincts as depending on internal states. When neurophysiological or mental antecedents of the behavior were referred to it was as

a vague restlessness or craving, as in hunger, migration, or sex, due to a condition of unstable equilibrium ... usually evoked by *an external stimulus*, but often occurring spontaneously, leading to an action which results in the relief of the restlessness by the attainment of the object of the conation, and to temporary satiation.   (Wilm 1925, pp. 145–146. My emphasis)

Wilm's very general descriptions of the relation between instinct and drive and of the instinct being elicited by external factors are well removed from the quite specific assertion of Fletcher. Indeed, so rarely was it proposed that instincts were *motivated* by drives, that Lorenz (1937/1957) insisted, apparently without challenge, on Craig's (1918) priority in formulating such a connection.

Lorenz is almost certainly wrong in his claim. Drever (1917; cf. Fairbairn 1939–1941) had already examined a number of similar formulations before Craig's relatively little-known paper appeared. Dugald Stewart's concept of "appetite" as it related to instinct, a concept well known in the early part of the nineteenth century, is a clear precursor of later motivational concepts of drive. Appetites originated in bodily states, were periodic rather than constant, and were accompanied by a feeling of unease. Stewart recognized three appetites of hunger, thirst, and sex and believed the impulses to which they gave rise were directed toward their respective objects, such as food, and so on. Of some interest to the later criticisms of Freud's concept (and to the collapse of Lorenz's) was Drever's identification of the fundamental inadequacy of these motivational formulations: whole classes of instinctive behaviors are quite unrelated to drive states. Drever (1917, pp. 247–249) mentioned fear and anger as examples of instinctive reactions to which the internal state merely predisposed the organism to react; he might well have added avoidance behaviors generally are hardly ever so motivated.

Aim and Object   The characteristics of aim and object clearly differentiate Freud's concept of instinctual drive from that of a *Trieb*-like impulse lacking direction. The characteristic of source (which he came to define as a continuously active physiological process) distinguishes the concept just as clearly from stimulus-elicited concepts of instinct. Freud's thinking was in line with the tendency described by Wilm, but it had a number of novel features. Although he used many apparently new terms in the turn-of-the-century literature on sexuality (Burnham 1974), the essentials of his concept are not to be discerned there. For example, Burnham is correct in claiming Krafft-Ebing used the term drive (*Trieb*) and recognized self-preservation and sexual drives, but Krafft-Ebing's definition of the drive construct was far removed from Freud's: he made no distinction between aim and object (indeed, his use of the latter term seems to be entirely descriptive) and he spoke of a drive as having "organic sensations" as its instigator rather than a source. Even though he recognized the distention of the seminal vesicles, he did not propose it as the source of a sexual drive. His concept of drive was "psychophysiologically" composed of ideas that could be awakened either centrally or peripherally, and the pleasurable feelings associated with them (Krafft-Ebing 1898, 1965). Consistent with this difference from Freud is Krafft-Ebing's view of homosexuality as involving an opposite sexual *feeling*, rather than an opposite object and an altered aim, and of the perversions without specific reference to either aim or object. In these respects, there is little correspondence between Freud's concept and those of the other writers mentioned by Burnham, namely Bloch (1907, 1908), Havelock Ellis (1900–1901/1897–1899, 1903), Eulenberg (1902, 1902/1934), and Kraepelin (1889, 1899, 1904, 1903/1907). With the exception of Moll, this is also true as far as I can determine of the many other writers on sexuality mentioned by Sulloway (1979, chapter 8). Moll's (1897, pp. 88–93, 1933, pp. 121–126) picture of sexuality resembled Freud's mainly in the emphasis placed on the impelling role of physical pressure in the seminal vesicles. Freud's threefold characterization of the sexual instinctual drive is quite original.

Component Drives The other main characteristic of Freud's concept, that of being composed of a number of separate component instinctual drives, is definitely not to be found in the works of other writers of the period even though, as Sulloway observed, it is foreshadowed by some of Moll's views. Moll proposed that the sexual drive consisted of two component drives: one to approach, touch, fondle, and kiss a person of the opposite sex and the other to bring about orgasm. These two impulses could be "sundered" (*Auseinanderfallen*), and Moll concluded that their tie might not necessarily be a close one (Moll 1897, pp. 8–11, 24; 1933, pp. 28–30, 48). He made rather more use than most other writers of the idea that stimulation of various parts of the body, for which he used the French *zones érogènes*, could generate sexual excitation. He also based a good deal of what he had to say on comparisons between the activity of the child and that of the perverse adult.

Freud's Concept Several of the crucial elements of Freud's first concept of instinctual drive, some in a reasonably developed form, are found in his correspondence with Fliess, especially in Draft D, possibly of May 21, 1894, Draft E, possibly of June 6, 1894, and Draft G, possibly of January 7, 1895 (Masson 1985), in the *Project* of September–October 1895 (*Standard Edition*, vol. 1) and in the first paper on the actual neuroses (Freud 1895a). Generally speaking, Compton confirms my opinion in saying that "sexuality . . . was first acknowledged to be important at a theoretical level by Freud in his concept of the actual neuroses" (Compton 1981a). From the sources we have mentioned, the elements of what Freud called his "schematic picture of sexuality" are as follows:

1. A *terminal organ* in which a recurrent physiological process gave rise to mechanical pressure on the nerve endings situated there (e.g., the seminal vesicles).

2. *Physical sexual excitation*, sometimes called somatic sexual excitation, arising in the nervous system as a result of pressure in the terminal organ.

3. A *psychosexual group of ideas*, that is, a group of ideas concerned with sexuality, to which physical sexual excitation could become linked after it exceeded some threshold value.

4. *Psychical tension*, later called *libido*, that resulted from the linkage of physical excitation with the psychosexual group of ideas.

5. A *specific action* and *specific reaction*, which obtained an object capable of discharging the excitation and placed it in a favorable position for the transmission of sensations to a spinal center.[1]

6. A *reflex action*, controlled by a spinal center, that discharged the substances in the

terminal organ, eliminated the pressure there, and reduced physical excitation and associated libido.

7. *Voluptuous feelings* (? or sensations) proportional to the quantity of excitation discharged, conducted from the terminal organ after discharge to the psychosexual group for the mode of discharge to be repeated when the tension recurred.

Although certain aspects of the picture obviously applied more to men than to women, Freud believed it could be extended in principle to women and, as we have seen, he used it to explain actual neuroses in women.

In Drafts D and E, apparently for the first time, Freud distinguished between two kinds of excitation affecting the psyche: external excitation, which had transient effects, and internal excitation, which had constant effects. In Draft E, sources of excitation external to the individual (*Erregungsquelle*) were said to give rise to a quantity of exogenous excitation that could be disposed of by any reaction reducing the excitation by the same amount. Hunger, thirst, and the sexual instinctual drive (*Sexualtrieb*) were mentioned as three types of internal source (*Quelle*) giving rise to endogenous tension that could be dealt with only by a specific reaction (*Spezifische Reaktionen*) that prevented the further production of excitation. The term specific reaction approximates that of aim in that such reactions are activities that eventually prevent the further production of excitation and satisfy the drive by lowering the level of tension. Furthermore, elsewhere in Draft E Freud appears to equate the term aim (*Ziel*) with the working over of physical tension generated by the sexual drive, and he may even have equated aim with what he called the physicosexual act (*physisch-sexualem Akt*), by which he seems to have meant copulation. His later remarks in the *Project* definitely equate specific action with aim, for he there distinguishes more clearly between the specific actions as the means by which the sexual objects (*Sexualobjektes*) are brought to the subject, and the "reflex contrivances," or reflex mechanisms, that remove the endogenous stimulation. So regarded, the specific action (or reaction) is thus the activity through which the drive is satisfied and to that extent is equivalent to aim (cf. the discussion of normal processes in part III of the *Project*). The term for sexual object, the last element in the concept of sexual drive, was first used in the schematic picture of sexuality in Draft G (Compton 1986c), where it was placed externally to the psychic. In the *Project* the usage was entirely consistent; there it was an exact equivalent of the food that satisfied the hunger drive.

Consequently, Freud's use of the terms source and object, and possibly aim, in his early correspondence with Fliess is reasonably similar to that in *Three Essays*. As we will see, it is much the same as in the later "Instincts and Their Vicissitudes"; however, three differences should be noted. First, the sexual instinctual drive in the

Three Essays actually consists of a number of different drives; the early concept does not even hint at such separation. As Sulloway (1979, pp. 299–305, 310–311) suggested, this difference may well be due to the influence of Moll's (1897, 1933) concept of component drives. Second, in the *Three Essays*, both aim and object are described as variable with respect to the drive, object more than aim, but this variability is not mentioned in Freud's earlier discussion. Again, Moll's view that the components might be sundered may be an influence. Third, in "Instincts and Their Vicissitudes" a drive is described as *having* a source, whereas earlier it was said to *be* a source. These three differences also most clearly distinguish Freud's concept from those of all of his contemporaries, even from those of Moll's I have just mentioned and those of Krafft-Ebing (1879–1880, 1898, 1904, 1965). As we have just seen, the origins of the most characteristic features are found in the explanatory tasks set by the failure of the childhood seduction theory.

Evaluation of the Concept of Sexual Drive

At first sight the changes Freud made to his picture of human sexuality in the *Three Essays* are considerable. However, each of the new drives is modeled almost exactly on the earlier conception of the adult drive. Most of the difficulties with his theory of infantile sexuality result directly from the adoption of this model.

The concept was based on an especially intimate relation between erotogenic zones and component drives on the one hand, and sexual excitation on the other. Stimulating a zone or eliciting a component produced two kinds of excitation: sexual, and that appropriate to the zone or drive itself. For example, when visual sensations were produced by the eye being stimulated, a "specifically sexual" excitation was produced in addition to the purely visual excitation. It was this that lent the component drive, here scopophilia, "a sexual character" (Freud 1905b, p. 168, n. 1). Erotogenic zones such as the mouth and the anus could become

the seat of new sensations and of changes in innervation ... in just the same way as do the actual genitalia under the excitations of the normal sexual processes.   (p. 169)

Consequently, the erotogenic zones and the organs associated with the component drives did not simply produce sexual excitation, they were also terminal organs (p. 168).

Somatic sexual excitation or something analogous to it was produced at each of the erotogenic zones and by each of the component drives as well as in the genitals. Each zone and organ of a component drive was also a terminal organ, capable of generating sexual excitation that, by energizing ideas, initiated a specific action that in turn brought about a state of satisfaction. Of course, in Freud's new picture the linkage had to be with a group of ideas different from those making up the adult's psychosexual group, but that change was only minor. Similarly, rather than the object of the sexual drive being pictured as something external to the individual, the childhood object of each drive had to be named as the individual. The specific actions had to be appropriate to the newly designated terminal organs and objects but, like the aim of the adult drive, it also had to bring about a reduction of physical and psychical excitation.

Sexual Excitation?

The first problem with the concept of sexual instinctual drive is the inadequacy of the explanation it generates of the production of sexual excitation. In the *Three Essays* this problem is that of how the need for repeating the stimulation of an erotogenic zone is created. Superficial, everyday experience seems consonant with Freud's premise that the remembered pleasure of an act may lead to a tendency to its repetition. However, any such need must have other and more important determinants. In Freud's early picture of human sexuality, a connection between the voluptuous feelings of satisfaction and the psychosexual group of ideas contributed to the tendency to repeat the act, and a similar mechanism had been included in the model of need satisfaction set out in chapter 7 of *The Interpretation of Dreams* (cf. Masson 1985, Draft G, possibly of Jan. 7, 1895; Freud 1900, pp. 564–567, 598–603). But in these discussions of satisfaction, the pleasurable memory is a mere creature of a need independent of and anterior to it. Freud's account of the primary process postulated that a change in the continuous impact of a need such as hunger came about only through satisfaction ending the internal stimulus. Once that happened, associations were formed between the memory image of the nourishment bringing the satisfaction and the memory trace of the excitation produced by the need. Then:

As a result of the link that has thus been established, *next time* this need arises a psychical impulse will at once emerge which will seek to recathect the mnemic image of the perception and to reevoke the perception itself, that is to say, to *reestablish the situation of the original satisfaction.* (Freud 1900, pp. 565–566. My emphasis)

Feelings of satisfaction are remembered only when a need revives them. Both in the hallucinatory context and when satisfaction is real, it is the need that reanimates the memory of the pleasure of satisfaction, not the reverse. The same conclusion follows, perhaps more evidently, from Freud's discussion of the experience of satisfaction in the *Project* (part I, section 11). Because of the way in which he conceptualized memories, that must be so: he sees memory traces as inert records requiring to be suffused with energy (cathexis) before they can be recollected as memories. Like the filaments of an electric light bulb, they are not allowed the luxury of a spontaneous glow. Remembered pleasures must be determined by something other than the association between the memories of the satisfactions and the acts that brought them about.

At two places in the discussion in the *Three Essays* one can sense the presence of an undefined, probably physiological process lying behind the need for repetition of the stimulation. First, Freud says of the projected sensation of itching that it is "centrally conditioned," an allusion that I believe applies only to a central drive state. Second, he counted a "feeling of tension" as one of the indicators of the need for repeating the stimulation, a feeling much more consistent with the presence of an unsatisfied, organically based need than with the memory of a pleasurable satisfaction. In fact, because he equated unpleasure with tension, and pleasure with tension *reduction*, it is quite impossible for the recollection of a *pleasurable* satisfaction to reveal itself as a tension. Continuously active physiological processes, such as those underlying hunger or the adult sexual drive, would produce tension, revive the memory of the mode of previous satisfaction, and so initiate action. Only a conceptualization of this type is fully consistent with the discussion of needs and satisfaction in *The Interpretation of Dreams* and that outlined earlier in both the *Project* and works on the actual neuroses. Needs conceived of in the way described in the *Three Essays* can motivate nothing. For a satisfying act to be initiated, the simple association proposed by Freud had, as it were, to be pushed by a central need state behind it.

In "Instincts and Their Vicissitudes," Freud's first substantial discussion of instinctual drive theory after *Three Essays*, the process we have discerned behind the need for repetition of stimulation was made quite explicit. *All* instinctual drives were described as having a source (*Quelle*) in a physiological activity exerting a constant force in the mind (Freud 1915a, pp. 118–119). Of the sexual instinctual drives he said:

They are numerous, emanate from a great variety of organic sources, act in the first instance independently of one another and only achieve a more or less complete synthesis at a late [? later] stage.   (p. 125)

The need for repetition of erotogenic zone stimulation could thenceforth be referred to the organic source of its associated component drive.

Freud found it easy to incorporate this addendum into the framework of the *Three Essays*. A 1915 amendment to that work described an instinctual drive as "the psychical representative of an endosomatic, continuously flowing [? welling up] source of stimulation" and Freud went on to say:

What distinguishes the instincts from one another and endows them with specific qualities is their relation to their somatic sources and to their aims. The source of an instinct is a process of excitation occurring in an organ and the immediate aim of the instinct lies in the removal [? cessation] of this organic stimulus.   (Freud 1905b, p. 168, and n. 1)

Each of the drives originally mentioned in the *Three Essays* was encompassed by the new definition. Each now had its own organic source as well as an aim and an object. In addition, whether they arose in a zone or, like looking, were not so located, they were now all called components of the sexual instinctual drive (Freud 1915a, pp. 125–126).

The new sources were entirely hypothetical, of course, and it was this lack of reference to even an imaginary physiological process that marked no real advance over the simple association originally postulated for explaining sexual excitation. Consider, for example, the eye as the organ of the sexual component drive of scopophilia or sexual curiosity. What recurrent physiological process within the visual system of the child could produce sexual excitation as a precursor to psychical tension or libido? Or, once nonnutritive sucking has become independent of feeding, what continuous chemical and biological processes determine that oral activity? In no way can these and similar questions about the other component drives be answered. Freud's modeling of the component drives more fully on his older picture of adult sexuality had not explained sexual excitation in childhood. The physiological processes on which the drives depended were nothing more than mere physiological figments, or, more correctly, pseudophysiological characterizations.

Sexuality in Childhood?

The second problem with the concept of the infantile sexual drive is the description of its aims and excitation as sexual. Studied objectively, most childhood activity of the kind Freud took to be motivated by component drives altogether lacks the distinguishing marks of sexuality and, as absurd as it may sound, much the same can be said about perverse adult activity. Considered subjectively, the data provided by clinical-therapeutic investigation are not only too much influenced by expectations, they are too fragile to bear the weight of the sexual interpretation Freud gave them.

First of all, although Moll (1909/1912, pp. 172–173) raised doubts about Freud's sexual interpretation of the observations on sucking made by Lindner, only recently has it become apparent how grossly Freud misrepresented them to support his view that sucking had a sexual aim. Bieber, who arranged a partial (and inadequate) translation of Lindner's (1879–1880, 1975/1879–1880) paper, pointed out some of Freud's "inaccuracies" (Bieber 1975). My comments on the complete translation are not constrained by any kind of identification with psychoanalysis and are rather stronger (Macmillan 1980; Lindner 1980/1879–1880). Of the 500 children studied, only 69 exhibited what Lindner called "pleasure-sucking" (*Wonnesaugen*). Lindner nowhere "clearly recognized" its sexual nature, as Freud (1905b, p. 180) claimed. Rubbing of the genitals or breast in conjunction with sucking took place in only five of the pleasure suckers, and every time in only two of them. Sucking was associated with masturbation proper in only four children, although Lindner conceded there may have been more: he "did not consider it socially proper to inquire or investigate more deeply" (Lindner 1980/1879–1880).

Freud was also quite incorrect in claiming a resemblance between orgasm and the motor reaction Lindner observed in four children. Lindner called these four children "exultant" (*exaltirt*) suckers and described how their sucking movements became more forceful, how the sucked object was pushed farther into the mouth, and how any associated rubbing movements became more intense. The exultant sucker would then

reach a state of rapture [*Verzucküng*] by shaking his head up and down, his spine as in an emprosthotonous writhing forwards, his feet stamping up and down, or if he is lying, jerking. This is the stage at which the exultants draw their own blood, pull out their hair, or stop up their organs of smell and hearing.... Sometimes he is so completely engrossed ... that he will pay no attention to threats and will be deaf to kind words.   (Lindner 1980/1879–1880)

No postsucking relaxation was described. It was certainly not true, as Freud (1905b, p. 180) implied, that Lindner depicted orgasm or even sleep as the outcome of exultant or any other form of sucking. Lindner's observations were that all but occasional suckers sucked at any time, wherever they might be. He actually added, "they prefer this pleasure most of all shortly before going to sleep, soon after waking up, and after a bath." This lack of connection between the orgasmic reaction and sleep, especially the failure of sleep to follow, detracts considerably from Freud's interpretation of pleasure sucking as sexual.

Further, signs such as flushed cheeks and blissful smile on the infant who falls asleep after feeding are equivocal indicators of sexual satisfaction. Freud's definite inference was warranted only if such expressive and bodily responses were found in what are incontestably states of sexual satisfaction and only in them. Ordinary observation contradicts: similar reactions result from the satisfaction of many different needs. Freud's observation was of doubtful relevance for another reason. During feeding, both the hunger and the sucking impulses are satisfied at the same time, and therefore all he could have concluded was that satisfaction of one or the other, or both, of those needs produced similar expressions of contentment. He later portrayed the blissful state as if it occurred independent of nourishment, after "sensual sucking has in itself brought ... satisfaction" (Freud 1916–1917, p. 313). Even this cavalier redescription does not count as evidence if it is true that nonsexual satisfaction may be just as blissful.

Freud provided much less evidence for interpreting the other activities as sexual. Anal stimulation gave sexual enjoyment because the infant's sensations during delayed defecation were "no doubt" highly pleasurable. Childish exhibitionism was sexual because children "show unmistakable satisfaction in exposing their bodies, with especial emphasis on the sexual parts." Children who are especially cruel "usually gave rise to a just suspicion of an intense and precocious sexual activity" (Freud 1905b, pp. 186, 192, 193). A similar lack of relevance marks most of his observations on the effects of mechanical excitation, muscular activity, extreme emotion, and intellectual effort. Particular difficulties stand in the way of accepting as sexual the undoubted pleasure resulting from such generalized forms of stimulation as rocking and swinging. At first Freud simply asserted that "sexual excitation" was so produced, equating it with both sexual satisfaction and pleasurable sensations. He then said these concepts "can to a great extent be used without distinction" (p. 201). But an explicit reservation about the nature of the "extraordinary pleasure" children appeared to obtain from satisfying their need for muscular activity shows he had some doubts:

Whether this pleasure has any connection with sexuality, whether it itself comprises sexual satisfaction or whether it can become the occasion of sexual excitation—all of this is open to critical questioning, which may indeed also be directed against the view ... that the pleasure derived from sensations of *passive* movement is of a sexual nature or may produce sexual excitation. (p. 202)

Freud attempted to justify his equating of sexual with pleasurable on the grounds that, from late childhood onward, nongenital stimulation produced sexual excitation in the genitals in addition to the pleasure of satisfaction appropriate to nongenital stimulation itself (p. 212). What this argument reduces to is the ascription of the almost mature form of the relation between genital and nongenital satisfaction to the earlier, immature period. Once again Freud assumed what had to be proved, namely, that these childhood pleasures are sexual and that they give sexual satisfaction. His final attempt at resolving the difficulty is in a later discussion of the relation between nongenital forepleasure and genital end pleasure and is considered in the next section.

Not only is it difficult to accept Freud's interpretation of component drive pleasure as sexual, but none of the activities typically follows a pattern of building up to a climax followed by relaxation. Lindner's description of exultant sucking does not include a definite ending of the activity. The same is true of Levy's (1927) observations of less intense forms of sucking, and Wolff (cited in Dahl 1968) remarked "nonnutritive sucking seems to be inexhaustible." Ozturk and Ozturk (1977) showed that children who are left to fall asleep alone after feeding tend to become thumb suckers. They suggest that if thumb sucking is followed by sleeping it may be through a simple reversal of this causal connection.

Except as it may be associated with defecation, anal stimulation seems on its own not to follow the typical pattern. Indeed, if the observations of Spitz and Wolf (1949) represent the real state of affairs, external stimulation of the anus hardly ever occurs in childhood: they saw it in only 16 of 384 infants. Playing with feces is the main mode of anal activity, although some doubt is thrown even on this by Heimann's (1962) observation that infants dislike their feces.

With genital stimulation the matter is less clear. It has long been known that direct manipulation may induce orgasm or orgasmlike reactions in little girls and to a lesser extent in little boys, but it does not seem to be a frequent consequence (Moll 1909/ 1912, pp. 57–59). Spitz and Wolf did not often see even self-absorption and withdrawal in children manipulating their genitals. In the absence of some type of external intervention, what appears to happen is that genital play is terminated by the child simply passing on to another activity. Kleeman's conclusion from one mother's detailed observations of her young son's reaction to discovering his penis is consistent with these points. After describing the child's penile manipulation as deliberate and accompanied by erections and expressions of pleasure, she drew attention to two of the qualities characterizing erotic activity as an "absorption of the attention by it and a mounting excitation" (Kleeman 1965) and concluded:

Mild pleasure rather than the prominence of these other two qualities marked William's tactile stimulation of his genitals in the first year.

Kleeman cited eight other psychoanalysts who made the same observations. As Moll concluded long ago, despite the frequency of genital manipulation in children, orgasm and orgasmlike reactions are rare.

Part of the reason that activity supposedly motivated by component drives does not follow the pattern of mounting excitement and relaxation is that it lacks a consumatory segment that brings the activity to a close. For the organic drives, Freud thought a "feeling of satisfaction" was brought about when a specific or consumatory reaction discharged the tension of the drive. Thus, the ingestion of food satisfied the hunger drive and the voiding of sexual products relieved adult sexual tension. But Moll (1909/1912, p. 58) observed that it was precisely the "voluptuous acme" that was "wanting" in the child. More generally, no such discharge mechanism was or could be described for either infantile or adult component drives. Pleasurable sensations from sucking, anal stimulation, or genital manipulation would have to be produced continuously, without coming to a definite end, which is exactly what is found. And, in relation to Freud's model of need satisfaction, that consequence is quite untoward, and makes his component drive thesis very doubtful. A consumatory reaction capable of terminating component activity with a degree of definiteness ought to characterize every instinctual drive.

Sexuality in the Perverse?

At the other end of the developmental spectrum, characterization of the behavior of the perverse adult was similarly problematical. In perversions based on fixations of the sexual preliminaries, Freud concluded that what occurred was a transformation "into new sexual aims that ... take the place of the normal one," that is, they provided sexual gratification (Freud 1905b, p. 156). Longing for the fetish, exhibiting one's self, and satisfying sexual curiosity became perversions once they took the place of the normal aim (pp. 154, 157). Furthermore, in perversions based on anatomical extensions, the mouth and anus were said to "behave in every respect like a portion of the sexual apparatus" (p. 169). In hysteria these same zones underwent changes in innervation and became capable of producing genital-like sensations. Perverse adult activity thus had a definite sexual aim and led directly to orgasmic sexual satisfaction.

However, in the literature on perversion Freud studied before writing the *Three Essays*, and especially in the case histories reported by Bloch, Havelock Ellis, Eulenberg, Kraepelin, and Krafft-Ebing, the perverse act was hardly ever described as bringing about orgasm and relieving tension by itself. Psychoanalytic writers on perversion also generally agree that preparatory acts do not supplant the normal sexual aim. What they do do is give rise to sexual excitement that must then be satisfied genitally. Balint (1936/1938), who referred to similar and much earlier remarks en passant by Ferenczi and Sadger, observed the perverse activity produced only excitement, relief being obtained only from subsequent coitus or masturbation. He added that this observation "applies equally to active and passive scopophilia, fetishism, sadism, masochism or whatever form the perversion may take." He repeated this view unchanged some twenty years later (Balint 1956), during which time it was endorsed implicitly by Bemporad (1975) and explicitly by no less an authority than Fenichel (1945b, p. 325). A similarly authoritative contradiction of Freud comes from the 1974 study group on perversion established by the American Psychoanalytical Association:

The cases considered by the group revealed that perverse behavior is usually terminated with genital orgasm no matter where the stimulus was applied. Though the major source of gratification lay in the extragenital stimulation genital orgasm seemed to constitute the "final common path" of sexual discharge.   (Ostow 1974, p. 4)

Prudently, the group qualified this generalization by saying that is was "of course, uncertain whether the sexual excitement *always* finds a genital outlet" (p. 4. My emphasis). If genital satisfaction is so intimate a part of the perverse act, if the perversion is only an "indirect way to genital end-pleasure" as Balint (1936/1938) put it, it cannot be the case in perversion that the normal aim has been replaced.

If adult perverse activity neither brings orgasm about directly nor provides a substitute for genital satisfaction, and especially if, by itself, it does not terminate with obvious signs of tension discharge, the curious and seemingly nonsensical question arises as to the way in which perversions are sexual. Should perversions turn out not to be sexual, what kinds of behavior ever could be? This question is undoubtedly the same that Compton calls the larger problem in Freud's theory:

How does one tell reliably what are sexual manifestations? What concepts are needed to state criteria for sexual manifestations in general? And for sexual manifestations in children in particular? (Compton 1981a)

Perversions clearly are sexual, but just as obviously, their sexuality must be rather different from Freud's view of them. And, if they are sexual and Freud's theory is to hold, childhood behaviors must be sexual in the same way.

Nor is Freud's slogan of neurosis as the negative of perversion now thought ever to have been true. Some of those who characterize it as elegantly simple and powerful simultaneously criticize it severely (Compton 1986a). To the extent that the slogan has been modified, the changes are not due to the accumulation of new clinical data, as Compton claims. They are alternative perspectives about what is already supposed to be known. Gillespie (1952), for example, sees *similarities* between perverse activity and the neuroses at the unconscious level. As he says, it is no wonder that psychoanalysts find it difficult to place the perversions in a developmental sequence. Does it not follow that this must also be true of childhood sexual activity generally?

Body as Sexual Object?

The third problem with Freud's concept of sexual instinctual drive lies with the claim that the subject's own body is the sexual object. As has been seen, well before the *Three Essays* were written, Freud came to view the essence of adult perversions as childhood behaviors that had escaped repression. Consequently, if he were to maintain this view after characterizing the childhood activity as autoerotic, adult perversions also had to be without object. And that is how he represented them, but the characterization had contradictions. After having first characterized sensual sucking as objectless (Freud 1905b, pp. 181–183), Freud then nominated the mother's breast as the child's first object (p. 222). He did not draw attention to the fact that if sucking was to be regarded as a substitute for sucking at the breast, it was nevertheless directed toward an object ("a refinding of it"). Furthermore, if the loss of the mother's breast really caused the drive to become autoerotic and if it remained so until puberty, the child's sexually based love for others during latency could hardly be regarded as an object-love based on the suckling's relation (pp. 222–223). And, although Freud granted such component instinctual drives as scopophilia, exhibitionism, and cruelty involved other people "from the very first" (pp. 191–192), he did not remark on the ensuing contradiction of his conceptualization of the other erotogenic zones—which did not, of course, involve objects—giving a sexual coloration to the component drives (pp. 167–168).

In the second edition of the *Three Essays*, published in 1910, Freud insisted that the separation in time between the stages of autoerotism and object-love was an artifact resulting from his deliberate use of mode of exposition that heightened the conceptual distinction between them (p. 193, n. 2). Because this lamentable excuse does nothing to resolve the conceptual confusion between the two modes of satisfaction, it appears to have been (justifiably) ignored by most psychoanalytic writers on libido theory. Even were it acceptable, it would not affect the basic criticisms.

One has to agree with Compton that Freud seems to imply

that the sexual drives proceed *simultaneously* along autoerotic and object-directed developmental pathways.   (Compton 1981a. My emphasis)

One also must agree that "It would be difficult not to acknowledge that there is some confusion here." Freud's claims about objectless childhood sexual drives have been judged incorrect by a number of other psychoanalytic writers. It ought to be pointed out, however, that, like Compton's, their verdicts tend to notice only the contradictory descriptions of infantile sexuality in the *Three Essays*.

Freud's own modifications to the theory of psychosexual development emphasized the relation of the drives to objects at the expense of their autoerotic proclivities. Except as a synonym for genital masturbation, he ceased to use the term autoerotism. In "Instincts and Their Vicissitudes" autoerotism was dropped as a developmental phase (Spruiell 1979) and, in Freud's last works infantile sexuality is not even described as autoerotic (cf. Kanzer 1964).

Many quite different psychoanalytic writers have asserted that the infant is dependent on sexual objects from the beginning and that autoerotism is a secondary development. According to Zetzel (1955b), among them are Ferenczi, Balint, Melanie Klein, and Fairbairn. Fairbairn (1941, 1952, 1956) especially criticized Freud's view that the libido sought only pleasure at the erotogenic zones:

The libido theory is based ... upon the conception of erotogenic zones. It must be recognized, however, that in the first instance erotogenic zones are simply channels through which the libido flows, and that a zone only becomes erotogenic when libido flows through it. The ultimate goal of the libido is the object.   (Fairbairn 1941)

He later qualified this formulation by observing it was the individual in his libidinal capacity, rather than the libido itself, who was object seeking, but continued to stress

it is implicit in the libido-theory that the object only becomes significant in so far as it is found to provide a means of forwarding the pleasure-seeking aim.   (Fairbairn 1956)

Fairbairn's revision places object-seeking propensities more centrally than Freud did in the *Three Essays*, and his basic criticism has been accepted by many other psychoanalysts even though his particular theory has not. Some ego-psychologists like the Blancks even take their reforming zeal seriously enough to suggest "disposing of the psychosexual stages of libidinal development" altogether (M. I. Klein 1983).

Many analysts, among them Fenichel (1945b, pp. 324–366) and Gillespie (1956b/1965), criticized Freud's view that perverse adult activity does not involve objects. Gillespie specifically rejected Freud's portrayal, adopting as a basis for his own approach the 1923 interpretation of perversions by Sachs, who insisted that component drives generally appear in perversions only *after* they become attached to objects. According to Sachs, component drives underwent this transformation as they passed through the Oedipal situation. Sachs used as the starting point for his argument the modification Freud himself made in "A Child Is Being Beaten" (Freud 1919a), published some fourteen years after the *Three Essays*. Freud did not take his argument to its logical conclusion. When Sachs did so, he totally demolished Freud's original thesis (Sachs 1923/1986; cf. Compton 1986a,b). Psychoanalyses of real perverse activities do not show them to be without objects, as Freud thought. Perversions cannot be more or less direct manifestations of objectless component drives that have evaded repression. In the course of discussing Limentani's views, Arlow (in Jaffe and Naiman 1978) reiterated that not until 1919 did Freud put forward a more complex view of perversions. Arlow specifically criticized Limentani's concept of perversion as "essentially a restatement of the thesis that perversion ... represent[s] total discharge and very early instinctual representations." I take this formulation to be identical with Freud's in the *Three Essays* (cf. Balint 1956; Gillespie 1952, 1956a, 1956b/1965, 1964; Jaffe and Naiman 1978).

Observation vs Clinical Analysis

It might be reasonably objected that the above points place too much weight on direct observations of behavior, especially of childhood behavior, and not enough on the clinical analysis and interpretation of symptoms. After all, Freud himself insisted repeatedly on the equal or even greater importance to his theory of data obtained in therapeutic investigations (Freud 1905b, pp. 163, 169, 192, 201), actually going so far as to say in the 1920 preface to the fourth edition of the *Three Essays*:

If mankind had been able to learn from a direct observation of children, these three essays could have remained unwritten.   (p. 133)

He believed that the difficult question of "the general characteristic which enables us to recognize the sexual manifestations of children" was answered by "the concatenation of phenomena into which we have been given an insight by psycho-analytic investigation" (p. 180). Or, as he said later, he called

the dubious and indefinable pleasurable activities of earliest childhood sexual because, in the course of analysis, we arrive at them from the symptoms after passing through indisputably sexual material.   (Freud 1916–1917, p. 324)

For example, clinical-therapeutic investigations of cases such as Dora's provided the main evidence for characterizing thumb sucking as sexual. Dora's childhood thumb sucking was thought of as creating a somatic compliance in the oral zone through which later sexual excitation found expression (Freud 1905a, pp. 51–52). Herr K.'s kiss aroused disgust because the sexual excitation supposedly produced in Dora by the pressure of his penis against her genitals had supposedly been displaced upward onto a now abandoned erotogenic zone. Because the sensory content of a symptom had to repeat that of its precursor, the earlier activity had to be sexual. Genital excitation, the one kind that was undoubtedly sexual, could find reflection in only those organs compliant enough with the demands of the sexual instinctual drive to have been sexually excited in the past. It is this purely theoretical requirement that Freud "arrives at" in the course of analyzing the symptoms.

Freud also argued against the hypothesis that the childhood behaviors originally produced an indifferent organ pleasure that became sexual only during development. A biological analogy suggested itself to him. He asked his readers to consider the problem posed by the very different bean and apple tree having originated from similar looking seedlings:

Am I then to suppose that they are really alike, and that the specific difference between an apple-tree and a bean is only introduced into the plants later? Or is it biologically more correct to believe that this difference is already there in the seedling?   (Freud 1916–1917, p. 325)

He then claimed it was

the same thing when we call the pleasure in the activities of an infant-in-arms a sexual one. (p. 325)

Abnormal adult sexual pleasure, albeit in repressed form, seemed always to have been foreshadowed by a childhood pleasure in the same zone. From the analogy, the earlier pleasure also had to be sexual.

Three things may be said about the privileged status Freud accorded his clinical-therapeutic data. First, although much of my criticism is based on data gathered by direct observation, a preference for clinical-therapeutic data cannot be used to dismiss them. They are, in fact, precisely the kinds of direct observations used by Freud himself to support the sexual characterization in the *Three Essays*. If they are unimportant to my arguments about sexual characterization, they must also be unimportant to Freud's. Why then did he cite them at all and apparently lay such stress on them?

Second, it is extremely doubtful if the sexuality of childhood activities can be established satisfactorily through analysis and interpretation of symptoms. To the extent that Freud's reconstruction of the history of Dora's symptoms rested on the sensory content expectation, and it does seem to have been its fundamental basis, the sexuality of her thumb sucking was pure supposition, incapable of empirical confirmation. All that clinical data can reveal is whether or not one kind of adult symptom or activity is regularly anticipated by a particular type of activity in childhood. They cannot illuminate the psychological content of what the child does. This point leaves aside, of course, Freud's use of his associations rather than Dora's, his doubtful interpretations of her behavior, and the inconsistencies in his piecing together the fragments of her developmental history, as well as the question of whether the method of free association is uninfluenced by expectations.

Third, Freud's plausible garden analogy misses the point as much as does his concluding assertion. It is rather like arguing that because the ear is involved in both activities, the child's pleasure at hearing the bird calls of Leopold Mozart's *Toy Symphony* is the same as that of the adult listening to Bach's *Suites for Solo Cello*. And, simply because oral stimulation is involved in both, is it to be claimed seriously that the pleasure derived from nonnutritive sucking is the same as that of concluding an ample dinner with a good vintage port? Adult characteristics may well develop from an earlier stage without being prefigured in their childhood precursors.

In some measure the preceding arguments are consistent with one of the main points made by Wolff in summarizing and endorsing Chodoff's (1966) criticism of Freud's theory of infantile sexuality:

apparent similarities between the sexual perversions of adults … and childhood preoccupations with specific body processes and anatomical orifices, are in no sense evidence for the psychosexual life of infants. What appears [sic] to be similarities on the surface, are nothing more than analogies of form from which we can infer nothing about meaning or erotic content of the young infant's psychological reality.   (Wolff 1967)

To turn the rather old epigram revived by Chodoff, Freud seems to have been in considerable error in supposing that infants enjoy themselves in infancy in the same way as do adults in their adultery. I have gone farther than either Chodoff or Wolff, of course. The similarities between what Freud took to be sexual activity in childhood and adult sexuality in its perverse and normal variants are not even analogies of form. Only by what amounts to a systematic misrepresentation can the childhood activities be pictured as sexual in any way at all.

Evaluation of the Theory of Sexual Development

In the last section it was evident that Freud described correctly neither the perverse sexual activities of the adult nor their supposed infantile counterparts. Even if the infantile drives and the predisposition had been described with perfect accuracy, Freud's theory of sexual development was still unable to explain how these elements could be assembled into the pattern of normal and abnormal adult functioning. This failure of the theory is best approached through successive analyses of the accounts of object-choice, the establishment of genital primacy, and the scope of the mechanism of repression.

Object Choice

One of the main deficiencies of Freud's account of object-choice is that it does not explain how the female comes to choose an object of the opposite sex. The basis of the deficiency lies in the assumptions that the object of importance to the child of either sex is the mother's breast, that the breast is the first object, and that the suckling's relation with the mother is the prototype of all other prepubertal relations. On these assumptions the male child was provided with a female object from the beginning. At puberty he had only to erect the barrier against incest by taking "up into himself the moral precepts" (Freud, 1905b, p. 225) expressly excluding the choice of his mother or someone in the circle of his immediate relatives.

Something more than this mechanism was required to ensure an opposite sex choice in the female, for were she simply to undergo the same development as the male, she would still be left with female objects. To overcome this problem Freud proposed that at puberty repression transformed the sexuality of the female from its masculine, infantile form into its feminine, adult form. Once the basic sexuality of the female had been so changed, it appeared to be simply a matter of the attraction of opposites coming into operation, a mechanism he described as "the strongest force working against a permanent inversion of the sexual object" (Freud 1905b, p. 229).

Both steps in this process were made necessary by the assumption that the important object had been the mother's breast. But neither the first and crucial step, the replacement of masculine sexuality by feminine sexuality, nor the second, choosing a male adult, was explained adequately.

Because Freud assumed that the little girl's sexuality was masculine, he had also to explain how it changed into feminine sexuality. Changes at puberty that supposedly increased libido in the male were supposed to produce a fresh wave of repression in the female. Nothing else in the theory presupposed such an outcome, except perhaps the circularly based and equally ad hoc assumption that in females "the tendency to sexual repression seems in general to be greater" (p. 219). What this repression had to produce was the exchange of the excitability of the clitoris for that of the vagina. What Freud described was a selective inhibitory process that put an end to the capacity of the clitoris to respond to manipulation in the old way, but which somehow allowed it to become excited enough during the normal sexual act for clitoral excitability to be transferred to the vagina (K. R. Eissler 1977, n. 15).

It was the *male's* sexual drive, aroused by the very repression of libido in the female, that actually created the new female response:

The intensification of the brake upon sexuality brought about by pubertal repression in women serves as a stimulus to the libido *in men* and causes an increase of its activity. Along with this heightening of [male] libido there is also an increase of sexual over-valuation [by the male] which only emerges ... in relation to a woman who holds herself back and who denies her sexuality. *When at last the sexual act is permitted and the clitoris itself becomes excited, it still retains a function: the task, namely, of transmitting the excitation to the adjacent female sexual parts.* (Freud 1905b, p. 221. My emphasis)

Consequently, although pubertal repression was supposed to inhibit clitoral excitability, it did so with very strange selectivity: the inhibition lasted only until heightened male sexuality incited the normal sexual act. The reexcitation of the previously restrained but now disinhibited clitoris then sparked off vaginal responsiveness rather than its own orgasm. No real explanation of the change in the sexuality of the female was being offered. Freud merely described what he needed to explain.

With respect to the choice of an adult male as the female object, Freud's explanation broke down completely. First, even if repression accounted for the change in the leading erotogenic zone, that change together with the attraction of opposite sexual characters did not account for the repudiation of the mother. In any case, Freud described the repudiation only for the male. The female was described as repudiating the *father* (pp. 225–227), although the theory not only had not provided her with such an object, but her relation to the father as object was not even mentioned. Nor was male homosexual object choice touched on.

We must note that the *Three Essays* at least contains and may even be built on a paradox: although it was the unconscious perverse tendencies of the psychoneurotic female that posed the original problem, Freud's theory was written almost completely from the point of view of male sexuality (Montgrain 1983). By this I do not refer to the quite trivial point of the masculine linguistic forms with which his ideas are expressed, but to such things as the male model implicit in Freud's accounts of the suckling's relation to the mother, the mother's role in teaching the child how to love, the role of the male in awakening normal female sexual responsiveness, and the discharge of sexual substances in relieving sexual tension, to name just a few. In chapter 14, the inability of the theory to portray female psychosexual development with any consistency, especially female object-choice, is shown to stem partly from this male orientation.

Genital Primacy

Of genital primacy it can be said that the deficiencies of Freud's account of its establishment undoubtedly reflect inherent contradictions in his characterization of infantile and adult sexuality. On the one hand, certain aspects of the theory required both forms to give rise to the same kinds of sexual satisfactions. On the other, the very idea that genital primacy existed in the adult implied infantile sexuality to be different in some way. Freud's descriptions of how genital primacy was attained reveal two different and equally unsatisfactory explanatory mechanisms. I call his first explanation "the changed role" solution. In it he proposed that the nongenital zones gradually lost their capacity to give specifically sexual satisfaction over the same period that the genitals acquired it. I call the second explanation "the augmentation" solution. According to it, the nongenital erotogenic zones had always been able to contribute to sexual excitement in the genitals at the same time that they produced their own particular pleasurable satisfaction. As the child grew older, all that happened was that this effect became more marked, or was augmented.

In the changed role explanation a sharp distinction was made between the end pleasure of sexual satisfaction and the fore pleasure preceding it. In childhood, all zones had been equal in the kind of pleasure they produced. On maturation, stimulation of the nongenital zones produced genital sexual tension as well as their own particular pleasure. Because Freud gave no reasons for this change in the role of the zones, the most that can be said is he described the change rather than explained it.

The augmentation solution proposed that stimulation of the nongenital zones in childhood produced sexual excitement and slight amounts of sexual tension in the genitals themselves. During development this effect stabilized, the quantity of genital excitation became greater, and finally the adult form of the relation between fore pleasure and end pleasure emerged. Freud described the embryonic form of the relation only in the second half of childhood, from about eight years of age until puberty, but it is clear he presumed it to be present also in the first half. As was mentioned earlier, his equating of sexual satisfaction, sexual excitement, and pleasurable sensations, when he discussed the effects of passive and active movements, is based on that presumption (Freud 1905b, pp. 208–233).

The augmentation solution has the advantage over the changed role solution in having to account only for the growth or development of an already existing function rather than explain how the more radical change is effected. Although that growth would itself have to be explained, the solution does have the potential for coordination with general development processes. Pubertal sexual development makes sexual excitation and sexual satisfaction possible for the first time. If it were better accounted for, that fact alone would remove some of the mystery of the relation among pleasure, excitation, and satisfaction.

However, were the augmentation solution to be adopted, it would become impossible to regard adult perversions as infantile activities simply carried over into adult life and as independent of genital sensibility. Freud's suggestion that perversions developed when genital excitation was weak compared with nongenital pleasure was consistent with the augmentation solution, of course. But he could specify the conditions of that developmental anomaly only very vaguely. All he could say was that the zone or component involved in the adult perversion "contributed an unusual amount of pleasure" in childhood and that further factors, which he did not name, produced a fixation (p. 211).

Consequently, if pleasurable satisfaction and sexual excitement were independent to begin with, the perversions were comprehensible, but the mechanism of genital primacy was not. Alternatively, if satisfaction and excitement were linked from the beginning, genital primacy was explicable, but not the perversions. Even if Feldman's claim were true that genitality is strong enough in the pregenital phase to give "the erotogenic zones an orgiastic potentiality" (Feldman 1956), the problem is not thereby solved. In brief, adoption of the augmentation solution would require such marked changes in the conceptualization of infantile and perverse adult sexuality, and such equally radical alterations in the explanation of psychosexual development, it is doubtful if Freud's sexual theory could survive. Freud, of course adopted neither solution. Nor did he resolve the difficulties it might have overcome. In the concluding summary of the *Three Essays* he conceded the recalcitrance of the problems associated with genital primacy, end-pleasure, and fore-pleasure:

We were reluctantly obliged to admit that we could not satisfactorily explain the relation between sexual satisfaction and sexual excitation, or that between the activity of the genital zone and the activity of the other sources of sexuality.   (p. 233; cf. Compton 1981a)

This concession, which seems to have been overlooked by most of those interested in psychoanalytic theory, trenches so deeply into the foundations of Freud's infantile sexual theory as to undermine it altogether.

Repression

Finally we turn to repression. We begin by observing that Freud does not define repression in any way in the *Three Essays*. We discern that he thought of it as producing a reversal of affect rather than as stripping the affect from an idea. Thus, if repression of the oral zone took place, the individual would "feel disgust at food and will produce hysterical vomiting" (Freud 1905b, p. 182). Again, since the pleasurable sensations derived from passive movement could create a compulsive linkage with sexuality, repression, "which turns so many childish preferences into their opposite," would create feelings of nausea if the adult or adolescent was swung or rocked (p. 202). Finally, the psychoneuroses were said to result from infantile perverse activity when "a reversal due to repression" took place (p. 238). So conceptualizing repression was a necessary complement to the characterization of infantile sexuality as pleasurably autoerotic. Unless reversal took place, infantile modes of satisfaction would never be given up. But what was the source of the unpleasure that supplanted the original pleasure? When he still believed in the seduction theory, Freud supposed that sexual experiences were unpleasant in themselves (hysteria) or were linked with a later unpleasantness (obsessions). The stimulation of the supposed memories of these unpleasant experiences simply released fresh unpleasure (Freud 1896b, p. 166, n. 2; Masson 1985, Draft K of Jan. 1, 1896). Obviously this thesis could not be maintained after the demise of the seduction theory.

The organic mechanism of automatic repression eventually replaced the original stripping of affect. Now, one of the difficulties with the organic explanation was that, in not knowing how the evolutionary change from "interesting" to "disgusting" sensations had come about, the uncharacterized process was simply transferred from the individual to the species. There was the additional difficulty that the implicit recapitulation assumption made a completely uncharacterized biological process responsible for sexual development. This biological process is implicitly present, of course, in the *Three Essays* and may be detected in at least three places. First, Freud said the reversal of affect brought about by repression was due to "internal causes" (Freud 1905b, p. 238). Second, the order in which the component instinctual impulses appeared, as well as the length of time before they succumbed "to the effects of some freshly emerging instinctual impulse or to some typical repression," was "phylogenetically determined" (p. 241). Third, the building of the dams of disgust, shame, and morality was said to be organically determined and fixed by heredity (pp. 177–178). And although Freud's phrasing of the relation between repression, reaction formation, and the dams is markedly inconsistent, there is little doubt that organic repression was the builder of the dams (pp. 178, 232). In a 1915 footnote to the *Three Essays* he made the point explicitly:

these forces which act like dams upon sexual development.- disgust, shame and morality.- must also be regarded as historical precipitates of the external inhibitions to which the sexual instinct has been subjected during the psychogenesis of the human race. We can observe the way in which, in the development of individuals, they arise at the appropriate moment, as though spontaneously, when upbringing and external influence give the signal.   (p. 162, n. 2)

The editor's introduction to the *Three Essays* formally identifies disgust, shame, and morality as "the repressive forces" (Freud 1905b, p. 127). The formulation is inaccurate: in Freud's view repression *created* the forces.

All that could ever be observed were facts about the appearance of shame, disgust, and morality, observations by themselves of little relevance to either recapitulation or the presumed hereditary nature of the process. Perhaps this is why Freud's conceptualization of these mental forces as part of a phylogenetically determined process are never given much attention in the psychoanalytic literature. If their instinctual aspects are mentioned at all, it is to reject their instinctual determination (cf. Kinston 1983; Spero 1984; S. B. Miller 1986).

In the theory of psychosexual development, repression was no more than an uncharacterized component of a mysterious biological unfolding. And, to the extent the assumptions on which it rested were inconsistent with the evidence on the inheritance of acquired characteristics, it was most unlikely that it had any explanatory power at all.

Not only was repression uncharacterized. Neither its results nor the conditions under which it operated could be described with any definiteness. Thus, Freud assumed the abandoned activity could be resumed once again if the mental forces were overridden by sufficiently strong libido, without seeming to see this qualification contradicted almost everything else he had recently written about it. In chapter 7 of *The Interpretation of Dreams*, for example, activities similar to those involved in restimulating old erotogenic zones were supposed to produce an unpleasure incapable of being inhibited. Yet Freud also explained the occurrence of "perverse" sexual activity in normal people, and the readiness with which the "average uncultivated woman" could be led toward a perverse sexual life by strong libidinal demands overriding the unpleasure. If repression were responsible for the permanent renunciation of the zones, not even the amatory skills of a Casanova should have been able to coax pleasure from them again.

One resolution of this contradiction would have been to differentiate "normal" from "pathological" repression and to suppose that libidinal urgings could overcome the former but not the latter. At several places Freud implied that such a distinction could be made, but nowhere indicated what the difference between the two kinds of repression might be, nor the conditions giving rise to each (Masson 1985, Letters of May 30, 1896, Dec. 6, 1896, and Nov. 14, 1897). However, something like normal repression was necessary to account for normal sexuality. Perversions were due to failures of repression, and the repression that caused hysteria resulted in excessive sexual cravings and aversions. Normal repression had to cause the erotogenic zones to be abandoned, but sometimes allow libidinal urgings to overcome the repressive forces as well as attenuating cravings and aversions. Repression of a quite different type or magnitude from that causing neuroses must have been involved, but Freud neither defined the nature of the difference nor specified the conditions under which the outcome was normal or pathological. In this respect also his developmental theory is without explanatory power.

Finally, the mechanism of repression seems too limited to explain object-choice. The main modifications to the infantile disposition were the replacement of auto-erotism by object-love and the creation of a genital aim. Freud's summary statement explicitly attributed the new aim to repression (Freud 1905b, pp. 237–238), but it was not at all evident what brought about the change in object. A very strong case can be made for repression being thought to be responsible. The prohibition against an incestuous object-choice was described as a barrier (p. 225), a term otherwise used only for the repressive mental force opposing cruelty (p. 193). That usage matched the connotation of the obstacles and dams opposing autoerotic libidinal aims. Incestuous pubertal fantasies given up before the final choice was made were described as being repudiated (p. 227), and Dora's heterosexual libido was similarly said to have been energetically suppressed (Freud 1905a, p. 60). All these terms are consistent with an appeal to repression as the determinant of object-choice. Certainly, if repression was not responsible, that whole process was left without a directing influence. If repression was the reversal of the affective quality of *sensations* produced in abandoned erotogenic zones, it was hard to see how that could change objects. Only if objects somehow shared in the afterglow of the sexual sensations produced in the zones could they or the tendencies toward choosing them have been repressed. Not only did Freud not propose such a connection, erotogenic zone activity was auto-erotic, lacking objects with which the sensual pleasure could be shared. By linking repression so closely to the erotogenic zones, he effectively prevented himself from explaining object-choice.

Biological Determinism and Sensory Content

When Freud set out for Fliess his reasons for rejecting the childhood seduction theory, he confessed he had been so greatly influenced by them he had been "ready to give up two things: the complete resolution of a neurosis and the certain knowledge of its etiology in childhood" (Masson 1985, Letter of Sept. 21, 1897). The theory set out in the *Three Essays* saves these two basic features. Proposing that germs of a sexual impulse were to be found in infancy and that they consisted of component drives seeking autoerotic satisfactions allowed Freud to continue to link the sensory content of the symptom to an earlier experience, albeit an autoerotic one, with similar content. Because of this retention of the deterministic ideas embedded in the concept of the logical and associative structure of the neurosis, "complete resolution" was still possible. And with that proposal, as Freud foresaw, "the factor of a hereditary disposition regains a sphere of influence from which I had made it my task to dislodge it" (Letter of Sept. 21, 1897). This resurgence of hereditary influence involved more than a simple predisposition: the order in which the component drives appeared, the length of time for which they were manifest, the construction of the dams restricting the sexual impulse, and the very mechanism of repression itself all had a hereditary basis. As Laplanche and Pontalis put it:

The sexual development of the child ... is defined as endogenous and determined by sexual constitution.   (Laplanche and Pontalis 1968)

Whether thought of as influences of an organic-constitutional kind or as characteristics acquired through the action of external influences during human evolution, these instinctual determinants are simply a necessary consequence of the deterministic views to which Freud continued to adhere after the collapse of the seduction theory. If the neuroses were not the consequences of seduction experiences, and if expectation and unconscious suggestion were to be rejected as influencing patients' recollections, only uniform hereditary influences could have been responsible for the clinical uniformities he had to explain.

His pseudobiology provides so good a screen for his inadequate logic that it is rarely pierced even when the "biology" is criticized as, for example, by Jacobsen and Steele (1979). When he went about "constructing an infantile past," as Jacobsen and Steele put it, it was not merely to provide a basis from which any particular causal explanation of abberrant adult sexuality could be derived. The resulting construction had to meet his *particular* deterministic ideas.

Conclusion

Freud's concept of a sexual instinctual drive filled the gap left by the collapse of the seduction theory and provided his mentalistic theory with an organic base. The drive was the most important and constant source of energy of the wishes that had to be repressed and, therefore, for the creation of fantasies and dreams as well as for the maintenance of neurotic symptoms. It was clearly of equal importance in motivating the perversions, infantile sexuality, normal character formation, and, through sublimation, the development of civilization itself.

The most telling evidence for an infantile sexuality having the characteristics Freud ascribed to it was not that obtained from direct observations of childhood but from his reconstructions of the histories of adult symptoms. Perhaps he was wise to give his clinical analyses such privileged status, because not only did his own and Lindner's observations fail to substantiate the characterization, but none have been found since.

Putting these difficulties aside, and granting the novelty of Freud's concept of a sexual instinctual drive, its field of action was one sided. It had no role other than as the main component of the new biologically oriented theory of sexuality. In fact, it was not until 1915, in the third edition of the *Three Essays*, that he offered a reasonably complete definition of the drive and described something of the wider significance of its energy (Freud 1905b, pp. 168, 217–219; cf. Compton 1981b). Even then it was next to impossible to see how aggression arose other than through some kind of frustration of the libidinal drive. As characterized by Freud, the pleasure-seeking drive could no better explain the supposed intimate connection between libido and cruelty than other theories. Furthermore, the mental forces of shame, disgust, and morality were pictured as constructed from the very libidinal material they were supposed to control.

These explanatory discontinuities result from the theory being based on a single instinctual drive. They would be removed by opposing sexuality with an ego-instinctual drive having mental and biological attributes resembling those of the sexual drive. Energy from such an ego drive could fuel aggressive behavior and give strength to the repressive forces and other ego functions. An ego-instinctual drive of this kind did provide the basis for the final changes Freud made to his theory. It is set out and examined in part III.

Note

1. These concepts of Freud's have no relation to the similarly designated ethological concepts.

III THE FINAL SYNTHESIS

11 The Ego and the Ego-Instinctual Drive

Shotover: A man's interest in the world is only an overflow from his interest in himself.
—Shaw: *Heartbreak House*, Act II

In part III, I examine the origins and validity of some of the central components of the final version of Freud's personality theory: the instinctual drives and the structures of the mind, what Freud called the mental apparatus, that regulated them. My analysis reveals that the important factor that led Freud to alter his conception of the mental apparatus from one consisting of conscious, preconscious, and unconscious systems to one made up of an ego, a superego, and an id, was the instinctual drives.

Were I mounting an argument, rather than describing and evaluating what happened, its general line would be that Freud's introduction of instinctual drives in the *Three Essays* actually *necessitated* the final version of his personality theory. We will see in chapter 11 that once he postulated an infantile sexual drive that was regulated by an automatic, organically based repression, he had to propose another instinctual drive as a counter to it, and the reintroduction of the concept of the ego is part of that counter. Freud then attempted to resolve the several problems associated with this conceptualization with the death instinct, which I examine in chapter 12. The ego-superego-id model of the mind, which I consider in chapter 13, was in turn required because of the need to find a home for the death instinct.

What I describe and evaluate in this chapter is Freud's conceptualization of mental life as a conflict between sexuality and the ego. Particular attention is paid to the means by which Freud thought the ego-instinctual drive gave its energy to the standards of the ego, because the real conflict took place between them and the demands of sexuality.

Conflict Between Instinctual Drives

Freud expanded the role given instinctual motive forces five years after the *Three Essays* when he briefly but formally described the concepts of ego and ego-instinctual drives for the first time. This paper, "The Psycho-analytic View of Psychogenic Disturbance of Vision" (Freud 1910e) began with a kind of return to Janet: hysterical blindness was due to certain ideas connected with the act of seeing being cut off from consciousness. Freud now asserted that to understand this dissociation

we must ... assume that these ideas have come into opposition to other, more powerful ones, for which we use the collective concept of the "ego" ... and have for that reason come under repression. (p. 213)

He then asked:

But what can be the origin of this opposition, which makes for repression, between the ego and various groups of ideas? ... Our attention has been drawn to the importance of the instincts in ideational life. We have discovered that every instinct tries to make itself effective by activating ideas that are in keeping with its aims. These instincts are not always compatible with one another; their interests often come into conflict. *Opposition between ideas is only an expression of struggles between the various instincts.* (pp. 213–214. My emphasis)

The notion that instincts activated ideas in keeping with their aims was, of course, a lineal descendant of the notion that somatic excitation linked up with the group of psychosexual ideas and invested or cathected them with energy. But if the sexual instinctual drive cathected sexual ideas, what was the drive that invested the set of ideas constituting the ego with energy and that opposed sexuality? An answer to that question was provided by the concept of ego-instinctual drives:

From the point of view of our attempted explanation, a quite specially important part is played by the undeniable opposition between the instincts which subserve sexuality, the attainment of sexual pleasure, and those other instincts, which have as their aim the self-preservation of the individual—the ego-instincts. (p. 214)

Mental life was henceforth to be seen as expressing a fundamental conflict between two biologically based drives. Freud persisted with the ego versus sexual drive concept until 1923, when he replaced it with the variant biological thesis that a death instinct, which he named Thanatos, provided the opposition to a poetically named Eros, or life instinct.

Origins of Ego and Ego-Instinct Concepts

We have seen that as early as *Studies on Hysteria* Freud thought of the repression of incompatible ideas as due to a force located within the ego:

The patient's ego had been approached by an idea which proved to be incompatible, which provoked on the part of the ego a *repelling force* of which the purpose was defence against this incompatible idea. (Breuer and Freud 1895, p. 269. My emphasis)

The psychical repelling force continued to be active. Precisely at the moment when the patient tried to recall the incompatible idea, Freud became aware

of *resistance*, of the same force as had shown itself in the form of *repulsion* when the symptom was generated.... Thus a psychical force, aversion on the part of the ego, had originally driven the pathogenic idea out of association and was now opposing its return to memory. (p. 269)

Although both the ego and the force that it deployed were extraordinarily central concepts, neither was characterized further. In *Studies on Hysteria*, the term "ego" was given some kind of meaning in that it was treated as a synonym for "self," "person," or "consciousness" (Rapaport 1959; Laplanche and Pontalis 1967/1973, pp. 132–135). The ego of *The Interpretation of Dreams* was "a poorly delineated shadow represented chiefly in the form of the censorship" (Pumpian-Mindlin 1958–1959). Neither work contained any characterization of the force that drove it. Some fifteen years were to pass before that indeterminacy changed.

Why did Freud not develop the concepts of ego and ego-force for such a long time? The first reason in perhaps that they were not at all necessary to the organic hypothesis of automatic repression that was in the forefront of his thought until about 1905. The hypothesis was that automatic repression came about when the role of smell changed as humans assumed the upright carriage. Children went through a similar developmental sequence, with the result that in adult life the revival of a memory of the stimulation of those zones also produced disgust:

To put it crudely, the memory actually stinks just as in the present the object stinks; and in the same manner as we turn away our sense organ (the head and nose) in disgust, the preconscious and the sense of consciousness turn away from the memory.   (Masson 1985, Letter of Nov. 14, 1897)

Erotogenic zones were not mentioned in *The Interpretation of Dreams*, but what Freud there described as "the essence" of repression was exactly the transformation of affect supposedly produced by organic repression (Freud 1900, pp. 600–605). The mechanism of repression mentioned in *Three Essays*, published five years later, was also based on a similar transformation of affect. As Hoenig (1976) puts it about this period of Freud's theorizing, "the repressive forces like disgust and morality are conceived as largely constitutionally given." An organically based automatic avoidance of unpleasurable memories rendered a force to push unpleasant memories out of consciousness and deny them reentry unnecessary. Neither a structure like an ego nor a force to motivate it was required.

I believe it is significant that whenever Freud spoke of repression subsequent to the *Three Essays*, he almost always described it as resulting from a psychological force rather than from an automatic process. For example, in his analysis of the German writer Jensen's story *Gradiva*, the force repressing the instinctual eroticism was mentioned frequently and always in contexts that were psychological (Freud 1907a, pp. 68–69, 90–93). With one possible exception, this purely psychological characterization seems to be true of every one of Freud's descriptions and discussions of repression over the period 1906–1909. For example, in trying to assess the effects of socially enforced standards of sexual behavior (what he termed " 'civilized' sexual morality") on mental illness, he spoke repeatedly of the repressive and suppressive effects that the "demands of civilization" made on the sexual instinctual drive (Freud 1908c, pp. 188–190, 200). Similarly, in the lectures on psychoanalysis delivered at Clark University in 1909, he declared the repressive forces to be "the subject's ethical and other standards," while the unpleasure that preceded repression resulted from "acceptance of the incompatible wishful impulse or a prolongation of the conflict" over it (Freud 1910a, p. 24). Instead of education limping along in the tracks of some organically determined processes that created the dams of shame, disgust, and morality, those mental forces were now said to be brought into being "under the influence of education" (p. 45).

If by 1910 Freud was picturing repression as due to forces that denied consciousness to ideas incompatible with the individual's ethical and moral standards, what are we to make of his earlier portraying of repression as due to an automatic tendency to avoid the unpleasure of restimulated, abandoned, erotogenic zones? Is it simply another inconsistency of formulation? Or, does it mean that between 1905 and 1910 he abandoned a biological conceptualization and replaced it with a psychological one? Neither. The two kinds of repression were brought into relation with each other by making one the precursor of the other: organic, automatic repression became "primal repression" and the ego-force caused "repression proper" or "after-pressure." The first operated in childhood and provided a nucleus or point of fixation around which later memories pushed out of consciousness by repression proper could adhere.

Both the ego-instinctual drive responsible for repression proper and the two-stage process of repression were introduced into the theory within a twelve-month period (Freud 1910e, 1911a). With them Freud arrived at a more plausible theoretical synthesis. First, a conception of mental life as resulting from opposed forces demands that the second force be of "equal dignity" to the first, in this case in having a similar biological basis. As Compton (1981c) has said:

The construct of ego drives ... represented an effort to give "the ego" some theoretical status comparable to that of the sexual drives: conflict cannot occur between forces which cannot meet on the same plane.

Even a developing ego able to draw upon the energy of a self-preservative instinct might be considered as possessing enough strength to match that of the sexual instinctual drive. An independent but related point is that once repression proper was conceived of as due to an ego-instinctual drive, the inconsistency was overcome of proposing that forces deriving from the subject's ethical and moral standards could repress the sexual drive when such standards were weak.

Something like an inconsistency of this sort was present, of course, in the supposition of *The Interpretation of Dreams* that repression could be carried out by the embryonic developing secondary process of *Pcs.* (Freud 1900, pp. 605–606). The same point applies to the proposal in *On Dreams* (Freud 1901a, pp. 678–679) that the ego was responsible for repression—how could a weak structure initiate repression? If emergent ethical and moral standards were to counter an adult type of sexual drive, the ego in which they were located had to be supplied with a considerable source of energy from the very beginning of its formation. Only an inherent or instinctual source met that requirement. Third, although it is possible to see how disgust, shame, and pity might be related to an erotogenic zone being abandoned, it is much more difficult to accept that kind of explanation for the appearance and function of ethical and moral standards themselves ("morality"). Although he did not acknowledge this difficulty, Freud eventually turned to a developmental process in which the ego-instinctual drives were central to account for the emergence of a set of standards in the ego.

It should be noted that nothing like these reasons were put forward by Freud when he introduced the concept of ego-instincts. However, it is of interest that in the several works that preceded the paper on visual disturbances, he did draw attention to the very large amounts of energy that the ego required to exercise its repressive function (Freud 1910a, pp. 53–54, 1910c, p. 146).

I now consider the one possible exception to the characterization of repression as a psychological force in the publications between 1905 and 1910. In a paper on hysterical fantasies Freud stated

Hysterical symptoms arise as a compromise between two opposite affective and instinctual impulses, of which one is attempting to bring to expression a component instinct or a constituent of the sexual constitution, and the other is attempting to suppress it. (Freud 1908a, p. 164)

Some aspects of the passage are very obscure—one instinctual impulse is described as bringing "a component instinct" or a "constituent" to expression—and harks back to the *Three Essays*. But it seems to me better construed as looking forward to the paper on vision, foreshadowing the argument that opposed one kind of instinctual energy to another. For this reason I quarrel with H. Hartmann (1952), who says the early neglect of the ego was due to the "impact of the theory of instincts." On my reading, it was not until instinctual forces were extended into the ego that the ego itself became important.

The main reason put forward by psychoanalysts for Freud's introduction of the concepts of ego and ego-instinctual drives is that it was not until the period 1905–

1910 that the concepts of self and ego became important for psychoanalytic explanations of homosexuality, schizophrenia, and paranoia. In this view, the concepts followed from clinical observations. However, that is only part of the story.

Freud first emphasized self and ego in his interpretation of a sexual perversion in which the individual gained sexual satisfaction from fondling his own body. In these cases and in homosexuality, or sexual inversion as he called it, he supposed that the self had been chosen as a love-object, an interpretation that naturally drew attention to the self as a concept. To refer to the tendency to self-love, Freud adopted the word "narcissism" from Nacke and Havelock Ellis—Narcissus being the Greek youth of legend who fell in love with his reflection. His first published use of the new term was in a 1910 footnote to the second edition of *Three Essays*, where he offered the following explanation of inversion:

In all the cases we have examined we have established the fact that the future inverts, in the earliest years of their childhood, pass through a phase of very intense but short-lived fixation to a woman (usually their mother), and that, after leaving this behind, they identify themselves with a woman and take *themselves* as their sexual object. That is to say, they proceed from a narcissistic basis, and look for a young man who resembles themselves and whom *they* may love as their mother loved *them*.   (Freud 1905b, p. 144, n. 1)

At about the same time as this footnote was written, Freud undertook a biographical study of Leonardo da Vinci. In it he argued Leonardo had marked sublimated homosexual tendencies having their basis in a similar family constellation (Freud 1910b, pp. 99–100). After repeating the conclusion of the footnote, but qualifying it by saying that it was based on only "a small number" of patients, he added that some of the women who cared for the children were "masculine ... able to push the father out of his proper place," but that in other cases the father actually was absent during the boy's childhood (p. 99). Both situations led to a "very intense erotic attachment" that could not continue consciously:

The boy represses his love for his mother: he puts himself in her place, identifies himself with her, and takes his own person as a model in whose likeness he chooses the new objects of his love. In this way he has become a homosexual.... He finds the objects of his love along the path of *narcissism*. (p. 100)

By so drawing attention to the self as a sexual object, the concept of narcissism virtually forced the ego back into Freud's theory. Later, when narcissism was thought to be a phase through which *all* individuals passed, the status of the ego was confirmed.

Freud's concepts of ego and ego-instinctual drives are best seen as drawing together three threads: one requiring him to postulate an instinctual source of energy responsible for the force causing repression proper, the second requiring an agency or set of ideas through which the instinct could operate, and the last requiring recognition of the self as an object that could be loved.

Narcissism as a Developmental Stage

Through a complex analysis of the connection between narcissism and homosexuality that he believed he had discerned in schizophrenia and paranoia, Freud attempted to characterize the ego rather more fully than he had in the paper on disturbances of vision. Redefinitions of narcissism and fixation were central to this analysis. Narcissism was now to be thought of as a developmental stage, inherently connected with homosexuality and in which erotically tinged social drives were created out of sublimations of the sexual drive. Fixation was now failure to pass through a stage completely and, in the narcissistic stage, the failure produced a disposition toward a later frank resexualization of these social drives. Paranoia was marked, Freud thought, by the patient's struggle to prevent these sublimations from being undone.

The subject of Freud's analysis was Daniel Paul Schreber, a prosecuting judge of a higher court district in Dresden who developed a paranoid illness shortly after being promoted to that position. Schreber had come to believe that God had directly inspired him to redeem the world and restore mankind to a lost state of bliss. God had first to destroy the world, then transform Schreber into a woman, and create a new race by breeding with him. Schreber seems to have believed that his transformation into a woman, or its possibility, made him the object of persecution and sexual abuse by the staff of the hospital in which he was confined. After some years of hospitalization, he made a considerable recovery, becoming, apart from his delusions, normal in almost every respect, able to participate fully in everyday social and intellectual life and to manage his own affairs. He then wrote an account of his illness and commenced what proved to be a completely successful legal campaign, in which he represented himself, for his discharge. After release from the hospital he found a publisher for his story. It was because of the minute detail with which Schreber recorded his particularly florid combination of megalomania and paranoid persecutory delusions that Freud was able to use Schreber's *Memoirs of My Nervous Illness* (1903/1955) for his analysis.

Almost at the very beginning of his study of the Schreber *Memoirs* Freud focused on the relation between narcissism and homosexuality. Citing his own study of Leonardo and some clinically based conclusions of Sadger, he contended that narcissism was a *stage* of development that began when the individual unified his separate sexual instincts (which have hitherto been engaged in auto-erotic activities) in order to obtain a love-object; and he begins by taking himself, his own body, as his love-object, and only subsequently proceeds from this to the choice of some person other than himself as his object. (Freud 1911a, pp. 60–61)

Speculating that this newly described stage "may perhaps be indispensable normally," Freud claimed that many people lingered in it long enough for adult homosexuality to arise:

What is of chief importance in the subject's self thus chosen ... may already be the genitals. The line of development then leads on to the choice of an external object with similar genitals —that is, to homosexual object-choice.   (p. 61)

So placed between autoerotism and object-love, narcissism was the immediate developmental precursor of homosexual object-choice.

Social drives arose at this stage, Freud asserted, because, even after a heterosexual choice, homosexual tendencies were not done away with. In sublimated form they combined with the ego-instincts to form social drives such as friendship, comradeship, esprit de corps, and love of humanity in general. All these drives had a strong erotic component. Freud now drew on what he called the "opinion" he had expressed in the *Three Essays* that infantile fixations provided a basis for a decomposition of the sexual instinctual drive (Freud 1905b, p. 235), and asserted that those fixations created dispositional points around which later illnesses formed. A backward or regressive flow of libido to one of these points expressed itself in a form appropriate to the earlier fixation. Freud implicitly assumed that the social humiliations and slights about which paranoics complained were attempts to prevent a regressive resexualization of their social drives:

People who have not freed themselves completely from the stage of narcissism—who, that is to say, have at that point a fixation which may operate as a disposition to a later illness—are exposed to the danger that some unusually intense wave of libido, finding no other outlet, may lead to a sexualization of their social instincts and so undo the sublimations which they had achieved in the course of their development.   (Freud 1911a, p. 62)

Here he drew on Karl Abraham's interpretation of the related condition of schizophrenia, or dementia praecox as it was then called. Abraham (1908/1927a) maintained that when schizophrenics withdrew from the world, they experienced a loss of the feelings that arose from sublimations of the libido, including the "finer social sublimations" and the sublimations (*sic*) producing "shame, disgust, moral feelings, pity, etc."

Having so used the fixation-disposition-regression hypothesis to explain the paranoic's complaints, Freud drew a more general conclusion:

Since our analyses show that paranoics endeavour to protect themselves against any such sexualization of their social instinctual cathexes, *we are driven to suppose* that the weak spot in their development is to be looked for somewhere between the stages of auto-erotism, narcissism and homosexuality, and that their disposition to illness ... must be located in that region. (Freud 1911a, p. 62. Original emphasis altered)

Here the connection between narcissism and homosexuality is attributed to their joint fixation in a normal developmental stage, rather than, as in the case of Leonardo, because of the repression of a strong incestuous object-choice.

Freud also used the hypothesis of a regression to a fixation-produced disposition to explain the magnitude and frankly sexual content of Schreber's delusions of persecution. Schreber's illness was preceded by dreams that an earlier mental illness had returned. One morning, while partly awake, he also had the feeling "that it really must be rather pleasant to be a woman succumbing to intercourse," an idea he said he would have rejected had he been fully awake (Schreber 1903/1955, p. 63). Freud described this idea or feeling as a dream and interpreted it as the revival of a homosexual wishful fantasy directed toward the psychiatrist who successfully treated Schreber for the earlier, less serious illness (Freud 1911a, pp. 33, 59). Shortly after the idea or feeling had occurred to him, Schreber's wife went away for four days. During that time he had "a quite unusual number of pollutions (perhaps half a dozen)" in the one night, that he blamed as the cause of the immediately ensuing breakdown (Schreber 1903/1955, p. 68). Freud interpreted this sequence of events to mean that "the basis of Schreber's illness was the outburst of a homosexual impulse" directed toward the psychiatrist (Freud 1911a, p. 45). Repression of the wish was achieved through the withdrawal or detachment of libido from the psychiatrist-as-object. However, the wish returned in the form of a delusion in which it was projected onto the psychiatrist—it was not Schreber who had homosexual longings for the psychiatrist but the psychiatrist who desired Schreber.

Freud also drew on K. Abraham's ideas to explain Schreber's megalomania or delusions of grandeur. Abraham proposed that the schizophrenic's well-known lack of interest in people and the external world was due to a destruction of the capacity for object-love, to the patient's libido having turned away from animate and inanimate things:

The mental patient transfers on to himself alone as his only sexual object the whole of the libido which the healthy person turns upon all living and inanimate objects in his environment, and accordingly his sexual over-estimation is directed to himself alone and assumes enormous dimensions. For he is his whole world. (K. Abraham 1908/1927a; cf. H. C. Abraham and Freud 1965, especially Letters of July 26, 1907, Freud to K. Abraham, and of Aug. 9, 1907, K. Abraham to Freud).

Freud endorsed this idea completely: after Schreber withdrew his libido from the psychiatrist, he withdrew it more generally, redirecting it onto his ego. Schreber was great because he was his whole world, Schreber was persecuted because others had homosexual desires for him.

Freud had been able to derive the main features of Schreber's illness—megalomania, sexualization of his social drives, and homosexual persecutory delusions—from the supposition that there had been a regression to a narcissistic stage located immediately before the stage of homosexual object-choice.

Narcissism, Omnipotent Thought, and Reality

More was involved in narcissism than the choice of self as the object of the sexual instinctual drive. Once chosen, the functions of the self were decisively altered by their being sexualized. Freud believed the change could be shown by comparing the beliefs and practices of so-called primitive peoples with those of children and obsessional neurotics. From his comparison in *Totem and Taboo* (1912–1913), he concluded that all three overvalued thought; that is, they all put more value on thinking than on reality. He paid particular attention to the magical practices of those who believed in animism, the view that all things in the world were alive, most often animated by the spirits of departed relatives. Believers in animism used magic as a technique for gaining control over the spirits inhabiting their worlds (p. 78). Some magic seemed to be based on an association of ideas by similarity, as when peasants had intercourse in the fields to encourage their crops to grow. Others were based on a real or imagined association by contiguity, as when the hair or nails of an intended victim were treated in a hostile manner. Such magical acts showed "the domination of the association of ideas" (p. 83), that is, of thinking, but Freud believed associations by themselves were insufficient to explain magic. Magical acts had to be motivated by wishes, and one had to have an "immense belief" in their power (p. 83). Thus when children satisfied their wishes in an hallucinatory way, they shared this "belief," and Freud concluded that childish play and animistic magic were based on valuing thinking too highly:

an attitude towards the world ... which, in view of our knowledge of the relation between reality and thought, cannot fail to strike *us* as an overvaluation of the latter. Things become less important than ideas of things: whatever is done to the latter will inevitably also occur to the former.   (p. 85)

Well before writing *Totem and Taboo* Freud observed a similar overestimation of the power of thinking in one of his obsessional patients. On one occasion, not long after the patient had been irritated by something done to him by a complete stranger, the stranger died. The patient described this power as showing the omnipotence of his wishes (Freud 1909b, pp. 226, 233). In *Totem and Taboo* Freud described this omnipotence as showing an "overvaluation of mental processes as compared with reality" (Freud 1912–1913, p. 87). The belief was peculiar to neither that patient nor to obsessional neurotics generally. All neurotics displayed omnipotence in that they granted greater reality to thought than to experience.

Freud linked omnipotence to the modes of thought of the child and the animist through libido theory and narcissism. Narcissism was now described as a *substage of autoerotism* in which the unified sexual impulses cathected the subject's own ego that was itself now said to be "constituted at about this same time" (pp. 88–89). Omnipotence was due to the thought processes of the ego becoming sexualized:

Primitive men and neurotics, as we have seen, attach a high valuation—in our eyes an *over-valuation*—to psychical acts. This attitude may plausibly be brought into relation with narcissism and regarded as an essential component of it. It may be said that in primitive men the process of thinking is still to a great extent sexualized.   (p. 89)

A considerable part of this primitive attitude was said to have survived in the neurotic, where it was enhanced by repression and presumably involved some degree of regression. In both the neurotic and the so-called primitive

The psychological results must be the same ... whether the libidinal hypercathexis of thinking is an original one or has been produced by regression: intellectual narcissism and the omnipotence of thoughts.   (pp. 89–90)

Freud then used his recapitulation notion to relate the development of the human's view of the world to the libidinal development of the individual. Historically speaking, animism had given way to the religious view that in turn was superseded by the scientific world view. In the child, narcissism corresponded to animism with respect to both chronology and content, religion to the choice of parents as objects, and science to the stage

at which an individual has reached maturity, has renounced the pleasure principle, adjusted himself to reality and turned to the external world for the object of his desires.   (p. 90)

The child's view of reality developed through the same stages as humans' own world view.

Notice how Freud subtly extended the conception of narcissism from that of a simple cathection of the ego by the libido, which merely turned the whole ego into a sexual object, to a more complex form where the *functions* of the ego themselves were modified by being sexualized.

Ego-Instincts and Reality

Freud regarded one of Schreber's symptoms as very characteristic of paranoia. His interpretation of it seemed to throw further light on the way in which the ego built up a picture of reality. The symptom was Schreber's belief that he was the sole survivor of catastrophic events that brought the world to an end. He subsequently came to feel that people in the world about him were unreal, they were fleetingly improvised beings (or "miracled up, cursorily improvised," to use the translation of the *Standard Edition*). Again following Abraham, Freud explained:

The patient has withdrawn from the people in his environment and from the external world generally the libidinal cathexis which he has hitherto directed on to them. Thus everything has become indifferent and irrelevant to him, and has to be explained by means of a secondary rationalization as being "miracled up, cursorily improvised." The end of the world is the projection of this internal catastrophe; his subjective world has come to an end since his withdrawal of his love from it.   (Freud 1911a, p. 70)

He answered the question of how any contact with the objects of the paranoic's world was now possible by attributing that contact to the ego-instincts. Instead of libidinal cathexes maintaining the paranoic's picture of the external world, "cathexes" of the ego-instinctual energy, what Freud termed "interest," now had that role:

It cannot be asserted that a paranoic ... withdraws his interest from the external world completely.... The paranoic perceives the external world and takes into account any alterations that may happen in it, and the effect it makes upon him stimulates him to invent explanatory theories (such as Schreber's "cursorily improvised men").   (p. 75)

By so attributing to the paranoid ego the functions of maintaining relations with reality and building up some sort of picture of it, Freud seems also to have assumed that these functions were exercised by the normal ego.

As seen in his correspondence with Jung, at the time he was completing the Schreber paper he was also working on another describing how the normal ego came to acquire its functions, especially those that enabled it to construct a realistic picture of the world. Eventually entitled "Formulations on Two Principles of Mental Functioning" (Freud 1911b), this paper seems to have been originally conceived of as a part of the Schreber study. Freud wrote to Jung:

My Schreber is finished, a short supplement or rather preface formulating the two principles, is being put in final shape today.   (W. McGuire 1974, Letter 225F of Dec. 18, 1910)

No such preface appeared. Whether the physical connection between the Schreber analysis and the "Formulations" was as close as the letter suggests, there can be no doubt about the close conceptual relation between them.

The main proposition of the "Formulations" was that knowledge of reality was the function of a *reality-ego*. Freud began his argument by reviving the notions of the primary process and the model of need satisfaction originally outlined in *The Interpretation of Dreams*. Unconscious mental processes were "the older, primary processes, the residues of a phase of development in which they were the only kind of mental process" (Freud 1911b, p. 219). Governed by the pleasure principle, unconscious processes strove for pleasure and withdrew from unpleasure.[1] Internal needs interrupted the primal state of psychical rest, but eventually, there was disappointment with the hallucinated object of need satisfaction, and the hallucinatory mode of thought was abandoned:

Instead of it, the psychical apparatus had to decide to form a conception of the real circumstances in the external world and to endeavor to make a real alteration in them. (p. 219)

What was then introduced into the mind was what was real, even if it happened to be disagreeable. No longer was the mind confined to pleasurable activities. What Freud called the "reality principle" now governed mental life.

Only the ego-instinctual drives sought realistic modes of satisfaction from objects in the external world, and it was only through them that consciousness, attention, memory, judgment, action, and thinking were produced (pp. 220–221). Consciousness, which came from the increased importance of external reality, was based on an appreciation of the differences among various kinds of sensory input or "sensory qualities," and not merely on the distinction between unpleasure and pleasure. The function of attention developed from the search for realistic modes of need satisfaction. Memory resulted from laying down a record of the results of the periodic searches. Judgment replaced repression when decisions were made if a given idea was true or not, that is, whether it was in accord with the memory traces of reality. Mere motor discharge was converted into action directed toward altering external reality. Thinking also delayed motor discharge until the memory of an appropriate action was found. Freud thought of this as a type of experimental action in which small amounts of cathexis were successively displaced onto the memory traces until the right ones were found. For this purpose the conversion of freely displaceable cathexes into "bound" cathexes was necessary, and this was brought about by "the level of the whole cathectic process" being raised (p. 221). Freud also supposed that all thinking had originally been unconscious. Only when thinking involved the cathexis of word-representations was it perceptible to consciousness.

Sexual instinctual drives played no part in producing these ego functions. Being autoerotic and incapable of frustration, they could not initiate development. Indeed, were there only sexual impulses, their autoerotic aims would have prevented development altogether, or at least have retarded it until some other process, an internal change, for example, forced the first steps toward object choice.

Just as ego functions resulted from ego-instincts and could be attributed to a reality-ego, so the functions involved in maintaining the autoerotic satisfactions of the sexual instincts were attributed to an earlier *pleasure-ego*. If the former was governed by the reality principle, the latter was under the sway of the pleasure principle. Hence the contrast:

the pleasure-ego can do nothing but *wish*, work for a yield of pleasure, and avoid unpleasure, so the reality-ego need do nothing but strive for what is *useful*. (Freud 1911b, p. 223)

In the "Formulations," Freud made a wholesale transfer to the two new "egos" of the principles of mental functioning he first described in *The Interpretation of Dreams*. The primary process of the system *Ucs.* now belonged to the pleasure-ego, and the secondary, from *Pcs.* and *Cs.*, were given to the reality-ego. The new functions were executants of a process motivated by the ego-instinctual drives that resulted in a realistic world view as long as the drives maintained their independence of the sexual drives originally attached to them. Sexual influence was an ever-present danger. At any time a "weak spot" might give way and allow the libido access to the functions of the reality-ego. As it had done in Schreber's case, this influence of the reemergent sexual drive could result in a fantastic world view dominated by the pleasure principle.

Although it is possible to see the above extensions of Freud's theory as the result of clinical observations on narcissism, homosexuality, and the psychoses, they are better regarded as the not too remote consequences of his introducing the concept of a sexual instinctual drive and supplementing the organic theory of automatic repression. I have already proposed that the concepts of ego and ego-instinctual drive were the first fruits of these two alterations. As soon as narcissism and the symptoms of psychoses were interpreted within a fixation-repression framework it was fairly easy to make the ego responsible for the sense of reality. Once the energy of the sexual drive was withdrawn from the world and the subject's ego was recathected, only the energy of the ego-instinct was left with which contact could be made. Abnormalities resulting from regression to a previous fixation point implied that the world of the normal was also constructed by an ego motivated by the energy of an ego-instinctual drive. The *Cs.*, *Pcs.*, and *Ucs.* components of the model of the mental apparatus previously described for normals and neurotics could be rearranged to form the two new structures of the pleasure- and reality-egos, and their primary and secondary processes redescribed as falling under the governance of the reality and pleasure principles.

Repression, Standards, and Conscience

So far Freud's analysis provided only an outline of how the ego developed. He had said nothing about where the standards necessary for repression proper came from. It was also in *Totem and Taboo* that he tried to account for them from his analysis of the irrational taboos of so-called primitive peoples and the similarly baffling rituals of the obsessional neurotic.

Freud thought that taboos were based on a particular combination of love and hate, what he called "emotional ambivalence." In three of the major classes of taboo objects that he considered—those of one's dead relatives, one's dead enemies, and one's rulers—unconscious hostility was projected outward:

The hostility, of which the survivors know nothing ... is ejected from internal perception into the external world, and thus detached from them and pushed on to someone else. It is no longer true that they are rejoicing to be rid of the dead man; on the contrary, they are mourning for him; but, strange to say, *he* has turned into a wicked demon ready to gloat over their misfortunes and eager to kill them. It then becomes necessary for them, the survivors, to defend themselves against this evil enemy; they are relieved of pressure from within, but have only exchanged it for oppression from without. (Freud 1912–1913, pp. 62–63)

Ambivalence was essential to this projection-based belief that the souls of the dead were transformed into persecutory demons (pp. 64–65) and to the animistic view that the world was inhabited by "innumerable spiritual beings both benevolent and malignant" (pp. 75–76).

From the resemblances between taboos and conscience, Freud argued that ambivalence was also involved in conscience. Conscience kept one of two opposing feelings unconscious, repressing it by a compulsive dominance. From that standpoint

it seems probable that conscience too arose, on a basis of emotional ambivalence, from quite specific human relations to which this ambivalence was attached. (p. 68)

He now had to show how conscience was linked to the standards of behavior involved in repression. He tried to do this some five years later, when some of his ideas about the ego had crystallized, and he posited a direct relation between the standards and repression:

Repression, we have said, proceeds from the ego; we might say with greater precision that it proceeds from the self-respect of the ego. The same impressions, experiences, impulses and desires that one man indulges ... will be rejected with the utmost indignation by another.... The difference ... can easily be expressed in terms which enable it to be explained by the libido theory. We can say that the one man has set up an *ideal* in himself by which he measures his actual ego, while the other has formed no such ideal. For the ego the formation of an ideal would be the conditioning factor of repression. (Freud 1914b, pp. 93–94)

By adulthood it was the ego-ideal rather than the ego that acquired the cathexes of the ego-libido, and it was this sexualized or cathected ego-ideal, rather than the ego itself, that provided the standards for initiating repression.

As Freud pictured it, the concept of the ego-ideal brought with it a new ego function, one that scrutinized the actual ego, measuring it against the standards of the ego-ideal, and by that means ensuring that narcissistic satisfaction was maintained (p. 95). It was through the conscience that this new ego function was exercised, and that the paranoic's delusions of being watched or noticed could also be understood. Freud said that many paranoid patients complained that

all their thoughts are known and their actions watched and supervised; they are informed of the functioning of this agency by voices which characteristically speak to them in the third person ("Now she's thinking of that again," "now he's going out"). This complaint is justified; it describes the truth. A power of this kind, watching, discovering and criticizing all our intentions, does really exist. Indeed, it exists in every one of us in normal life.   (p. 95)

Interpreting the voices as regressive manifestations allowed him to attribute the genesis of the ego-ideal to "the critical influence" (p. 96) of parents and other authority figures. Conscience, the watchman of the ego-ideal, was at bottom also an embodiment of parental and social criticism.

Freud said previously that the emotional ambivalence at the basis of the individual's view of reality was generated by criticism from parents and others whom the individual loved. Now he held ambivalence responsible for the formation and scrutiny of the social standards that governed the relations between individuals and their social world.

Narcissism, Love, and Hate

Notwithstanding the detail with which Freud explored Schreber's world, or the potentially universal sphere of action that the two principles of mental functioning opened up, and the role given the ego-instinctual drive, he had not provided much more than an outline of the way in which the development from narcissism occurred. Only in "Instincts and Their Vicissitudes" (Freud 1915a) was he able to integrate his ideas into a more or less comprehensive developmental theory.

He began his developmental account by arguing that the organism's capacity for distinguishing between a stimulus and an instinctual drive provided it with a means of differentiating the external world from the internal. Stimuli arose from the external world and tended to have only a momentary impact on the organism. On the other hand, instinctual drives impinged on the organism from within and tended to act as constantly applied forces. As a consequence, the organism could respond to or dispose of stimuli by a single motor response, typically one of flight, or at least one that removed the organism from their presence. Instinctual drives had to be responded to quite differently: removal or flight was impossible, only the provision of a satisfaction that altered the internal source of the drive could end its operation. Even a helpless living organism was therefore able to distinguish external from internal: "external" could be ascribed to those stimuli that motor responses would bring to an end, and "internal" to those where such action was of no avail (Freud 1915a, pp. 118–119). This "sound objective criterion" enabled what Freud now rather confusingly called "the original 'reality-ego'" (p. 136) to distinguish between its internal and external environments. The birth of the ego and its reality-sensing function derived from the differences in the responses to instinctual drives and to stimuli.

After so setting out the differences between stimuli and instincts, Freud drastically modified his concepts of narcissism and autoerotism:

Originally, at the very beginning of mental life, the ego is cathected with instincts and is to some extent capable of satisfying them on itself. We call this condition "narcissism" and this way of obtaining satisfaction "auto-erotic." (p. 134)

Narcissism was no longer a type of object choice taking place *after* autoerotism, nor was it a subdivision of the autoerotic stage. It was now a *primal state* present from the beginning of mental life, and autoerotism was the mode of instinctual satisfaction practiced in it.

The new definition of narcissism heightened the problem of how development from such a primal state of bliss could occur. For this purpose Freud made use of "the most important" of his postulates—the principle of constancy—now reformulated as follows:

the nervous system is an apparatus which has the function of getting rid of the stimuli that reach it, or of reducing them to the lowest possible level; or which, if it were feasible, would maintain itself in an altogether unstimulated condition. (p. 120)

In a further return to the basic ideas of the *Project*, he stated that it was consistent with the principle that simple movements "mastered" stimuli by withdrawing the organism from them. Instinctual pressure, on the other hand, forced the nervous system into "involved and interconnected" activities that so changed the external world that objects of satisfaction could be wrested from it. Instincts were the "true motive forces" behind the development of the nervous system and the picture of reality that its activities built up. The pleasure principle was also involved:

the activity of even the most highly developed mental apparatus is subject to the pleasure principle, i.e. is automatically regulated by feelings belonging to the pleasure-unpleasure series, [so that] we can hardly reject the further hypothesis that these feelings reflect the manner in which the process of mastering stimuli takes place. (p. 120)

Adding to the two principles the "working hypothesis" that the ego- and sexual instincts were the only kinds of drive allowed Freud to generate an explanation for narcissism being abandoned. Ego-instinctual drives were necessarily directed to the outer world of objects. Needs such as hunger and thirst had to be satisfied by external objects if the ego was to continue to glow with sexual libidinal light. Self-preservation drives forced the bliss of primal narcissism to be given up.

   The end of narcissism was not the only thing brought about by the difference in modes of satisfaction of the two classes of instinctual drives: from it Freud derived the development of the ego and the opposition that he needed between the ego and sexual instincts if repression was to take place. During the narcissistic phase he supposed the external world to be indifferent for the purposes of satisfaction and not to be cathected with the interest of the ego-instinctual drives. The ego itself, the ego-subject, corresponded to what was indifferent or even unpleasurable. The ego necessarily acquired objects from the external world and, in so far as those objects were sources of pleasure, they were incorporated into it, or to use Ferenczi's (1909/1952a) term, "introjected." On the other hand, anything within the ego that produced unpleasure, such as an unsatisfied instinctual drive, was expelled and projected on to the external world (Freud 1915a, pp. 135–136). Through introjection and projection the original reality-ego was purified and transmuted into a pleasure-ego that divided the external world and itself into two parts:

a part that is pleasurable, which it has incorporated into itself, and a remainder which is extraneous to it. It has separated off a part of its own self, which it projects into the external world and feels as hostile. (p. 136)

After this transmutation the ego as subject corresponded with pleasure and the external world with unpleasure.

   A further consequence of the appearance of the object was the development of the emotion of hate. According to Freud,

hating, too, originally characterized the relation of the ego to the alien external world with the stimuli it introduces.... At the very beginning ... the external world, objects, and what is hated are identical. (p. 136)

Objects that satisfied needs were loved and incorporated into the ego. After incorporation, any remaining objects "coincide with what is extraneous and hated" (p. 136). Hatred for that which caused unpleasure came to be associated with the ego-instinctual drives, and love of that which gave pleasure became linked with the sexual drive. As the ego developed out of the narcissistic stage, pleasure and unpleasure began to be reflected in the ego's relations to its objects. An object that was a source of pleasurable feelings would generate a motor urge to bring it close to the ego and incorporate it. Such an object was loved. On the other hand, if the object caused unpleasure, the motor response would repeat the original attempt at avoidance by increasing the distance between the ego and the object. Such an object was hated. The hatred might become intense enough to initiate an aggressive action designed to destroy the object. Love and hate thus reflected the relations of the whole ego to its objects.

Freud noted that in ordinary language it was not usual to speak of a love for the objects of the ego or self-preservative instinctual drives; rather one spoke of "needing" them. The word "love" tended to be restricted to sexual objects in the narrower sense, being used properly only after the component drives were unified and directed toward reproductive ends. The use of the word "hate" showed

no such intimate connection with sexual pleasure and the sexual function. . . . The relation of *unpleasure* seems to be the sole decisive one. The ego hates, abhors and pursues with intent to destroy all objects which are a source of unpleasurable feeling for it, without taking into account whether they mean a frustration of sexual satisfaction or [a frustration] of the satisfaction of self-preservative needs.   (Freud 1915a, p. 138)

Freud thus derived hate from the ego's struggle to maintain and preserve itself independent of the external world. Because of its origins, hatred was always to be found in most intimate relation with the self-preservation drives; love, of course, remained in intimate connection with sexual pleasure. Freud therefore proposed that the antithesis between love and hate repeated itself in the opposition of the ego to sexuality. Ego came into conflict with sexuality, eventually to repudiate sexuality completely.

To summarize: the object orientation of the self-preservation drives (1) was behind the movement away from primal narcissism; (2) forced the ego to make finer differentiations than those between internal and external, thereby creating a reality-oriented ego; (3) developed the latent opposition between ego and sexuality necessary for repression; and (4) created the hatred necessary for the feeling of ambivalence that contributed to both the animistic world view and the function of conscience.

The Conflict between the Ego and Sexuality

The proposition of Freud's most central to the theorizing I have considered in this chapter is that a basic conflict exists between the ego-instinctual and sexual-instinctual drives. Evaluating this proposition is complex because detours must first be made to evaluate four independent but related matters. The first detour relates to the concept of ego-instinctual drive itself: how adequate is Freud's concept and of what value is his picture of the relations among the drive, the ego, and the various functions assigned it? Second is the serviceability of Freud's explanation of homosexuality. The relevance, of course, is because it is partly with respect to inversion that the concept of narcissism was first introduced into the theory of personality development. The third of the preliminaries requiring scrutiny is the thesis that dispositional points are caused by infantile fixations, and that subsequent regression to them is the source of apparently new psychological characteristics. Finally there is the problem of how primal narcissism is abandoned, for it was from that process that the conflict between ego and sexuality was supposed to have developed.

Detour 1

Ego-instinctual drives share the four characteristics distinguished by Freud in "Instincts and Their Vicissitudes" (1915a): pressure (*Drang*), source (*Quelle*), aim (*Ziel*), and object (*Objekt*). That these attributes are possessed by only a small number of the component sexual drives was evident in the last chapter. They apply to an even smaller number of the ego-instinctual drives. For example, consider pressure, which Freud took to mean the amount of force or the measure of the demand for work expressed through action that the drive represented. "The characteristic of exercising pressure is common to all instincts; it is in fact their very essence" (Freud 1915a, p. 122). But, how meaningful is it to speak of the pressure of the ego-instinctual drives for mastery, for example? Similarly, Freud took the source of an instinctual drive to be "the somatic process" whose stimuli were represented in the mind as a drive. Now, although it may just possible to comprehend the sources of the nutritional drives in this way, it is much less easy to see what meaning attaches to the notion of a somatic process as the source of nonbiological ego-instinctual drives. Loewenstein long ago remarked that Freud's

> arrangement of the characteristics of instinct fits in very well with the sexual instincts and with those of hunger and thirst. But as far as I know no one has ever tried to apply it to the other manifestations of instinctual life, such as those, for instance, which spring from the instinct of self-preservation.   (Lowenstein 1940)

Neither has the more than fifty-five years since Loewenstein wrote seen any such application. In one of the classical statements of psychoanalytic instinct theory, E. Bibring inadvertently drew attention to the reason:

The criterion of source which had been used for the classification of the sexual instincts was carried over to the ego instincts, of which the nutritional instincts served as the typical example. They too could be linked with organs of origin and termination, once more with the help of hypothetical chemico-physiological processes.   (E. Bibring 1936/1941)

But for almost all the ego drives other than hunger or thirst, it is as inappropriate to speak of sources as it is of organs of origin and termination, and quite bizarre to think of them as having a chemicophysiological basis like that of the sexual drive.

Freud's conceptualization of instinctual drives is so tied to the hunger-sexual model that extension to other drives is impossible. Although other reasons are usually given, it is not difficult to see that it is precisely this "organic" conceptualization of all instinctual drives that is responsible for the well-known difficulty that psychoanalytic theory has in understanding ego-instinctual drives. Freud himself admitted that little could be said positively or definitely about these drives, but attributed this to the relative ease with which sexual drives were observable in the psychoneuroses, compared with the difficulty of observing ego drives in the paranoid and schizophrenic disorders (Freud 1915a, pp. 124–125). However, if the causes of what we might call "ego-behavior" are different in their very nature from those satisfying sexual and hunger needs, no amount of psychoanalytic observation of neurotics or psychotics could ever throw any light on the ego drives.

Freud did argue that knowledge of instinctual sources was "not invariably necessary" in psychology because sources could sometimes be *inferred from aims* (p. 123). His argument must be regarded with considerable caution if not rejected completely. By definition, behavior always involves a motor factor, or a demand for work, and the individual often seems to feel a quality of pressure in behavior. Further, much behavior can be described as directed toward a goal and terminating once that goal is achieved. Almost all behavior therefore possesses three of the four attributes that Freud used to characterize behavior motivated by instinctual drives. The *only* feature distinguishing the latter from behavior in general lies in its having a source in an internal somatic process. Inferring sources from aims therefore effectively reduces the number of defining characteristics to three and blurs the distinction between instinctual and noninstinctual behavior. Indeed, if it is true, as Bibring (1936/1941) claimed, that "the idea of source was the most important" of the criteria for classifying instinctual drives, it is improper, logically speaking, to infer the source from the aim.

Freud also seems to have believed that behaviors were motivated by instinctual drives because they led to the same pattern of satisfaction. For example, in the *Three Essays*, childhood exhibitionism was regarded as motivated by a sexual drive, partly because small children showed "an unmistakable satisfaction" in exhibiting themselves naked. Naturally, only if this satisfaction is identical with the satisfaction of an instinctual drive, and no other, can the similarity be taken as unequivocal evidence for instinctual drive motivation. Self-observation readily reveals many obviously nonorganically based needs associated with increased levels of tension from which pleasurable satisfaction in tension relief is obtained. Ranging from the drive to catch a bus to the gambler's compulsive placement of his bet, these needs also possess attributes that Freud regarded as instinctual. They therefore reduce the evidential value of the resemblance.

Several commentators have remarked on a peculiar vagueness in Freud's use of the concept of ego-instinctual drive. E. Bibring (1936/1941) drew attention to Freud's virtual equating of the constructs of ego and ego instincts: "the ego instincts stood for an ego." Hartmann (1948) noted that important components of the ego-instinctual drive, such as the tendency to master the environment, "which show a definite relation to self-preservation had a rather indefinite position in the system." Novey (1957) went so far as to claim that Freud was "plagued by the need to assign some substantial role to the ego instincts" and that he failed to do so. Sjoback (1973, p. 14) observed that Freud's discussions of ego-instinctual drives "are not very detailed and hardly give us a more tangible picture of the dynamics of conflict than the one to be found in his earlier writings." More recently, Compton (1981b) remarked on a set of problems created by Freud's failure to define both ego and ego-instinctual drive. An ambiguity inherent in the very conceptualization of instinctual drive is responsible for this incorporeality. It leads in turn to an inability to specify the relation between ego drives and ego functions. All of these critical considerations apply, at least in part, to recent attempts to revive the concept of an ego-instinctual drive (Khantzian and Mack 1983), including even those like Plaut's (1984), based on the assertion that the drive is characterized by a source, an aim, and an object.

The ambiguity of the concept of instinctual drive is discussed in the editorial note to "Instincts and Their Vicissitudes" (Freud 1915a, pp. 111–116), where it is observed that the inconsistencies in Freud's usage make it difficult to arrive at a single definition. The editors differentiate between two contradictory meanings of the term, meanings that I will call *representational* and *cathectional*. Representational meaning is found in most of the pre-1915 definitions and takes an instinctual drive to be "the psychical representative of somatic forces" (p. 112). Here an instinctual drive is equated with a mental representation, which presumably is an idea of a physiological process. The second meaning, the one that predominates after 1915, distinguishes sharply between the drive and the representative. The drive is a nonpsychical some-thing, presumably a bodily process, that supplies energy to or cathects an instinctual representative (p. 113). Our first difficulty is not knowing, even vaguely, what Freud might have meant by an idea being the mental representative of a drive. It cannot be the case that the ideas are as distinct as those of, say, the objects of the drive or that they are the conscious sensations Applegarth (1971) takes them to be. It seems to me that the hunger drive, for example, is probably to be thought of as represented by ideas and sensations that cause us to say we are hungry, rather than by an idea as definite as the food that would satisfy it. But one cannot be sure.

Our second problem is that neither meaning is consistent with the *use* to which the concept is put in the works considered in this chapter, where an instinctual drive is said to provide energy to, or activate ideas "in keeping with its aims" (Freud 1910a). An instinctual drive that *is* a psychical representative cannot cathect anything for, plainly, one idea cannot cathect another. Cathection for Freud is always *of* an idea by energy, or more correctly, of the neural traces of the idea. Activation of ego functions and cathection of the ego require a supply of energy rather than a mere connection with the inert traces of other ideas. On the other hand, the cathectional definition clearly requires the instinctual representative to be cathected *permanently* (Freud 1915b, p. 148), a requirement that makes it impossible to see how the drive can remain the same while it cathects other ideas. For example, if the sexual instinctual drive is the process that supplies energy to the ideas representing it, how can other, nonsexual ideas be cathected by it and the drive be still considered sexual? Although not without their own difficulties, the concepts of libido in the second of Freud's explanations of anxiety neurosis and of the quota of affect in *Studies on Hysteria*, posit a psychological energy having an endogenous source that is linked to or associated with a particular idea or groups of ideas that may also be diverted to other ideas. This implicit definition is consistent with the ways in which Freud *uses* the concepts of cathexes and instinctual drives before and after 1915, although it contradicts both of the formal definitions.

This ambiguity is reflected in Freud's failure to specify the relation between ego drives and ego functions. From his view of drive it is, at best, possible to imagine only how functions that are groups of ideas, such as the ego-ideal or the conscience, might be enlivened by an instinctual drive. Functions such as attention and the laying down of memory traces are not exercised by groups of ideas, and however well they might be described in terms of energy, it is impossible to see how instinctual energy cathects the executive part of such functions. For example, fluctuations in attention can be plausibly described as reflecting fluctuations in the quantities of energy bestowed on the ideas being attended to, but it is not at all easy to see how the executive or controlling mechanism acquires libidinal energy or applies cathexes to the ideas. Even more acute is the problem of functions such as consciousness and judgment: Freud simply does not provide enough information about them to begin imagining how they are related to energy. Although some of his descriptions of ego functions in terms of cathexes have a certain plausibility, there is a decided vagueness in his specification of the relation between the ideas constituting the ego functions and the energy said to cathect them.

Because the ego-instinctual drive was first evoked to explain repression, it is ironical that the hiatus between ego functions and ego drive is to be seen so clearly in that mechanism. Two aspects of the point may be distinguished: first, the source of the standards from which repression proceeds and, second, the nature of the force responsible in the three stage process of repression, originally described in the Schreber analysis. Let us accept some kind of opposition between the sexual and ego-drives, and that the former is held in check by the latter. How do activities motivated by ego-instinctual drives lead to standards of behavior being established? Freud is silent on the matter. Parental and other criticisms are involved, but what have they to do with ego-drives?

As to the second point, the newly described process of repression virtually makes the ego unnecessary. Freud proposed that repression be divided into the three phases of fixation, repression proper or after-pressure, and the return of the repressed (Freud 1911a, pp. 67–68). Fixation first created a "libidinal current" that behaved like one belonging to *Ucs.*, that is, like one that was repressed and that attracted other trends to it. In the second phase ("repression proper") "the more highly developed systems of the ego" forced the psychical derivatives of the fixated libidinal impulse and other trends that came into conflict with the ego out of consciousness. The third phase, "the return of the repressed," occurred when impulses deriving from fixation and repression proper manifested themselves in consciousness as symptoms. Freud does not describe the mechanism of fixation or primal repression at all. One is left to assume that it either results from the heightened pleasure of some component activity, because only that mechanism, mentioned in passing in the *Three Essays*, was ever suggested, or that it is the automatic organic mechanism in another guise. Either way, no reference need be made to ego or ego drive. Further, ideas fixated under primal repression were kept out of consciousness by a *Pcs.* counterforce or anticathexis. Freud speculated:

It is very possible that it is precisely the cathexis which is withdrawn from the idea that is used for anti-cathexis.   (Freud 1915c, p. 181)

Nunberg (1932/1955, pp. 243–245, 251, 281), H. Hartmann (1950), Parkin (1983), and Plaut (1984) *seem* to accept that Freud means the source of *Pcs.* anticathexes is the libidinal cathexis of the repressed idea itself. My doubt is whether some of these judgments are not based on a retrospective view through spectacles provided by Freud's later theory in which ego-instinctual drives had a different place (cf.

Applegarth 1971). However, if anticathexes are formed from the libidinal energy detached from the repressed idea, it is not necessary to postulate a repressive force based on another form of energy. The conclusion follows that the ego-instinctual drive does not explain how standards form, and that, even if it did, neither primal repression nor repression proper need draw on its energy.

The first detour is now complete. Summarizing: the concept of an ego-instinctual drive is inadequate in itself, and the relation between the drive and the structures and functions that it services is too vaguely stated to have genuine explanatory value.

Detour 2

Turning to the second of the preliminaries, homosexuality and narcissism, it must be said that even before the 1910 footnote to the *Three Essays* Freud advanced an explanation of homosexuality having very little to do with narcissism. Set out in "On the Sexual Theories of Children" (Freud 1908d) and in the "Analysis of a Phobia in a Five-Year-Old-Boy" (Freud 1909a), this prenarcissism theory proposed that in childhood the future male homosexual chose a woman as object and held to that choice

> so long as he assumes that they too possess what in his eyes is an indispensable part of the body; when he becomes convinced that women have deceived him in this particular, they cease to be acceptable to him as a sexual object. He cannot forgo a penis in any one who is to attract him to sexual intercourse; and if circumstances are favourable he will fix his libido upon the "woman with a penis," a youth of feminine appearance. Homosexuals, then, are persons who, owing to the erotogenic importance of their own genitals, cannot do without a similar feature in their sexual object.   (Freud 1909a, p. 109; cf. 1908d, p. 216)

He added that the homosexual remained fixated at a point between autoerotism and object love but, unlike the equivocality of the reference to the overvaluation of the genitals, that proposition had nothing to do with the later concept of narcissism. "Between autoerotism and object love" meant a stage before *normal* object love, not that there had been no object-choice at all. I call this explanation of homosexuality the disappointment-substitution hypothesis. Freud summarily indicated the evidence for it:

> As my expectations led me to suppose, and as Sadger's observations have shown, all such people pass through an amphigenic phase in childhood.   (p. 109, n. 1)

If by "amphigenic" is meant "amphigonic," all that Sadger could have shown is that the later invert passed through a phase of bisexuality—a rather more general point than the particularity of the disappointment-substitution hypothesis—and but little advance on the vagueness of Freud's conclusion in the *Three Essays* that "a bisexual disposition is somehow concerned in inversion" (Freud 1905b, pp. 143–144).

Freud's second explanation of male homosexuality was the first to involve some concept of narcissism and appeared in the *Three Essays* and the *Leonardo* study. According to it, homosexuality was based on the repression of an overly strong incestuous desire for the mother, a quite different basis from disappointment with her. In fact, according to this explanation, the child was so little disappointed that he identified with her after the repression, then selecting as his objects young men whom he could love as his mother had once loved him. It is at this point that Freud brought narcissism into the explanation. Homosexuals were said to "identify themselves with a woman and take *themselves* as their sexual object" and their new object-choices to "proceed from a narcissistic basis" (Freud 1905b, p. 144, n. 1; cf. 1910b, pp. 99–100). As in the perversion that Nacke had described, Freud here used the term narcissism as a synonym for self-loving behavior and hardly as a concept at all. This second explanation, which I call the repression-identification hypothesis, has only in common with the disappointment-substitution hypothesis the choice of object being made well past the autoerotic stage. However, it was again the analyses of "a small number" of homosexuals by Sadger, supplemented, it is true, by some conducted by Freud himself (Freud 1910b, p. 99 and n. 1; cf. 1905b, p. 144, n. 1 of 1910), that provided the evidence.

Not until the analysis of Schreber's *Memoirs*, when he advanced a third and very different explanation of homosexuality, did Freud transform narcissism from a method by which an object was chosen to a stage in a developmental process. According to the Schreber analysis, homosexuality resulted from the individual's failure to abandon sufficiently quickly his own body, especially his genitals, as a libidinal object. Later in life his choice was therefore of a person with genitals similar to his own. The fixation was supposed to be at a stage before *any* external object was chosen, when the autoerotic components, groping toward unified expression, selected the individual himself as a love object. I call this third explanation the narcissistic-fixation hypothesis (Freud 1911a, pp. 60–61).

Although the difference between this third explanation and the other two is obvious, the main evidence for it is exactly the same—Freud's and Sadger's analyses (cf. Freud 1905b, p. 135, n. 1, 1910b, p. 99, n. 1, 1911a, p. 60, n. 1). No new clinical observations could have led to the changes. Freud's use of the same evidence to support three quite different explanations shows his theorizing to be based on a rather more flexible conception of the relation between observations and conclusions than is usually the case in scientific inquiry. For this reason alone, judgment must be suspended on the adequacy of his derivation of inversion from a narcissistic fixation and also, as a consequence, on his proposition that development begins from an original narcissistic bliss.

Detour 3

As we embark on the third of the detours, we note that it was in the Schreber analysis that Freud first applied the supposition that fixations caused dispositions to illness that manifested themselves in later regressions. The *Three Essays* contains the earliest extensive use of the notion of fixation and, whereas two fairly distinct meanings of that term may be discerned, *neither* is related to the concept of regression. One meaning, broadly speaking, relates to the aim of the sexual impulse and the other to the effect of the early choice of object. In both instances, fixation is used to explain how aspects of childhood mental life come to be carried over into adulthood: aims fixated in childhood appeared in the adult as perverse aims and objects fixated in childhood appeared in the neurotic as repressed incestuous object-choices. In contrast, not only is the term regression not used at all in the *Three Essays*, there is only one rather special circumstances in which it is even implied:

In cases in which someone who has previously been healthy falls ill *after an unhappy experience in love* it is also possible to show with certainty that the mechanism of his illness consists in a turning-back of his libido on to those whom he preferred in his infancy. (Freud 1905b, p. 228. My emphasis)

Freud did not posit a closer relation between fixation and regression until the *Five Lectures on Psycho-Analysis* he delivered in 1909 (Freud 1910a). There he outlined the thesis that fixations create dispositions to later illness in the form of points to which the libido can later regress.

There is no doubt that the consideration given by Freud and others to dementia praecox and paranoia was the source of the new view of the relation among fixations, dispositional points, and regression. Among the ideas that Freud passed on to Abraham in mid-1907 was the possibility that some paranoics had "only inadequately completed the path from auto-erotism to object love," a developmental failure that created a "predisposition" and a point to which regression later took place. Despite Freud's contrary assertion, Abraham did not develop the suggestion. It seems to have been Freud himself who developed it in his study of the Schreber *Memoirs* (H. C. Abraham and Freud 1965; Letter of Aug. 9, 1907, K. Abraham to Freud; cf. K. Abraham 1908/1927a; Freud 1911a, p. 41, n. 1). At the end of September 1910, three months before the Schreber study was finished, Freud mentioned to Jung that in that work he had taken "quite a step forward in explaining the mechanism of the choice of neurosis" (W. McGuire 1974, Letter 212F of Sept. 24, 1910). As we know from his later work, that choice is determined precisely by fixation, disposition, and regression.

In the Schreber analysis Freud developed the fixation-disposition-regression hypothesis by first citing his and Sadger's work in support of a proposed narcissistic stage between autoerotism and object love (Freud 1911a, pp. 59–62). He then asserted that fixation during the narcissistic stage caused the sublimated homosexual feelings that contributed to the social drives. He advanced his "opinion" from the *Three Essays* that fixations produced dispositional points. Fixation in the narcissistic stage was then said to create a disposition that led to the resexualization of the social drives should regression occur. Freud then claimed that psychoanalyses showed that paranoics struggled against this resexualization. He was "driven to suppose" (p. 62) that there was a fixation somewhere between the stages of autoerotism, narcissism, and homosexuality. He next asserted that his evidence and his proposition had "shown" that fixations caused dispositions to subsequent illness (p. 67), a conclusion he used to explain the delusions, the megalomania, and the difference between paranoia and dementia praecox. For example, the attachment of libido on to the ego in megalomania was made possible by a previous fixation of the same kind in the earlier stage of narcissism (p. 72). Freud said that dementia praecox showed a more marked withdrawal from the external world than did paranoia, a difference now attributable to a more complete regression of libido. He therefore located the fixation point in dementia praecox in the stage of autoerotism, farther back than in paranoia (pp. 76–77).

Neither the observational nor the logical bases of Freud's arguments stand scrutiny. The psychoanalyses by Sadger and himself were originally cited to support quite different views of narcissism, and nowhere in the *Three Essays* was fixation described as producing a disposition around which symptoms might later form. Although Freud had argued that persecutory delusions were based on a repressed homosexual wish, he put forward no such argument for the sexual interpretation of the slights and humiliations about which the paranoic complained.

Freud's estimation of the role of homosexual impulses has also been disputed. Struck by the similarity between Schreber's delusional symptoms and the very real peculiarities of his upbringing, a number of psychoanalysts almost suggest that he had no disorder at all (Niederland 1951, 1959a,b, 1960, 1974; Schatzman 1971, 1973; Breger 1978; M. I. Klein and Tribich 1982a,b; Lyons 1982). Many others, according to Frosch (1981), put constructions on unconscious homosexuality so significantly different from Freud's that there has almost been a "denigration" of his thesis. Of those Frosch cites, most deny or ignore the role of homosexual tendencies altogether except to refer to them as "pseudo manifestations" or "pseudo phenomena." An author not discussed by Frosch goes even further by having homosexuality as a defense against paranoia! (Juni 1979). Frosch (1981) also notes a number of attempts to place the fixation point elsewhere. Of the more radical, the first to pay any attention to Schreber's relation to his mother, is R. B. White's (1961) interpretation of the disorder as an oral one in which the "unmanning" is a regressive attachment to the mother rather than castration.

Strong objections are made to the even more basic notions of regression and detachment of libido. Pao (1977) does away with fixation and regression altogether, asserting that "it does not explain the data" (cf. Ogden 1980). Freud's very basic propositions about the schizophrenic's withdrawal of libido have also been abandoned. T. Freeman (1977) began his paper by saying "for many years now there has been a continuing and sustained criticism" of Freud's hypothesis that the basic disorder in schizophrenia is a decathexis of object representations. He says that some patients with delusional ideas maintain their object cathexes, and others, the persecutory group, experience a decathexis followed by a return to the love object. Katan (1979) seems to agree. Here modern psychoanalysts prefer Jung over Freud. Within a few months of the publication of Freud's study of Schreber, Jung wrote to Freud that the loss of the reality function "cannot be reduced to repression [i.e., detachment] of libido"; he said he had had difficulties "throughout the years" in attempting to apply this aspect of libido theory to schizophrenia (W. McGuire 1974, Letter 287J of Dec. 11, 1911). (As became evident later, this theoretical difference was one of the main reasons for the break between Freud and Jung.)

Within the set of Freud's propositions it is as difficult to distinguish premises from conclusions as it is facts from assertions. What it was that "drove" him to suppose a fixation between autoerotism, narcissism, and homosexuality was not the force of a logical argument. Rather it was that that supposition made it possible to relate the mental content and psychological processes evident in Schreber's symptoms to a supposed earlier period in which the same processes and content could be assumed to have been present. Only that supposition explained to Freud the narcissistic processes and the content of the symptoms. And, being a supposition, Freud's claim that by being "driven" to it, he had "shown" that fixations created a disposition to a subsequent illness, is hardly justified. Nor did he establish that conclusion in such a way that it could be used to explain megalomania or the difference between dementia praecox and paranoia. The supposition is best thought of as an extension to the psychoses of the expectation that at the core of the neuroses there had to be a sensory content similar to that in the symptom.

Detour 4

Our fourth detour is made necessary by a certain obscurity in the way in which the relations between autoerotism, narcissism, and the ego are conceived. The question at issue is whether all three coexist from the first or whether some kind of developmental sequence links them. When first discussing autoerotism and narcissism Freud said:

we are bound to suppose that a unity comparable to the ego cannot exist in the individual from the start; the ego has to be developed. The auto-erotic instincts ... are there from the very first; so there must be something added to auto-erotism—a new psychical action—in order to bring about narcissism.   (Freud 1914b, pp. 76–77)

The new psychical action, or "operation in the mind," as it is elsewhere translated, is the development of the ego (Novey 1957; Laplanche and Pontalis 1967/1973, pp. 255–257). Consequently, Freud's first view was that autoerotism existed before either the ego or narcissism. However, according to a slightly later description:

Originally, at the very beginning of mental life, the ego is cathected with instincts and is to some extent capable of satisfying them on itself. We call this condition "narcissism" and this way of obtaining satisfaction "auto-erotic."   (Freud 1915a, p. 134)

Here he seems to say that ego and narcissism are present from the start.

The question of whether or not the ego is present from the beginning of mental life depends on the meanings of "ego" and "mental life." If the instinctual drives that motivate autoerotic activities are "mental" representations of somatic forces, it follows that mental life of some kind must commence as soon as the somatic sources begin producing endogenous excitation. And, because the sexual instinctual drive so brought into being is without object, autoerotic activity must also start then. Thus, only if the mental life provided by the mere presence of mental representatives is equated with ego activity can there be autoerotic cathection of an ego and also, therefore, the presence of a narcissistic state from the very first. On the other hand, if narcissism involves some concept of self, however primitive, mental life must take time to develop and cannot be present at the very beginning.

After examining Freud's different formulations of the concepts of autoerotism and narcissism, Kanzer (1964) concluded that Freud really meant autoerotism to be "a mode of pleasure to be obtained from one's own body, more specifically the erogenous zones, at any time of life," and that narcissism was an "ego-organization that functions from the beginning of mental life." He endorsed the view that auto-erotism, ego, and narcissism were born together, but seems not to have noticed that mental life had then to begin immediately. Neither did he understand that once the distinction between autoerotism and narcissism is so abolished "it is difficult to see just *what* is supposed to be cathected" as Laplanche and Pontalis (1967/1973, pp. 337–338) have observed. It is difficult not to conclude that the proposition that ego, narcissism, and mental life are all present from the start overlooks the mental nature of instinctual drives and the relatively long time the ego takes to develop.

The last detour may be completed by considering how the description of auto-erotism as the mode of instinctual satisfaction in the narcissistic state undermined the thesis that dementia praecox and paranoia had separate dispositional bases. Freud's original argument was that, however frequently paranoia seemed to be complicated by symptoms of dementia praecox, it was essential to maintain it as an independent clinical entity (Freud 1911a, p. 76). Schizophrenia had a different dispositional fixation:

> The regression extends not merely to narcissism ... but to a complete abandonment of object-love and a return to infantile auto-erotism. The dispositional fixation must therefore be situated further back than in paranoia, and must lie somewhere at the beginning of the course of development from auto-erotism to object-love.   (p. 77)

He was certain enough of this difference to propose that the term "paraphrenia" be used as a substitute for "dementia praecox" and "schizophrenia," then both in somewhat confusing use. His term suggested some relation with paranoia but distinguished what had been called schizophrenia or dementia praecox from it.

Clearly Freud's distinction and the new name made sense only as long as auto-erotism and narcissism were thought of as separate stages in a developmental sequence. As soon as they were considered components of a single primitive state, there could no longer be two dispositional points and two disorders corresponding to them. Freud made this change. In "On Narcissism" he still maintained some difference between paranoia and schizophrenia, but, because in that work autoerotism and narcissism were linked more closely than previously, he *extended* the term paraphrenia to cover *both* disorders. Hedging his bets, however, he continued to use the term "paraphrenia proper" to refer to schizophrenia (Freud 1914b, pp. 82, 86–87). After "Instincts and Their Vicissitudes," in which the developmental sequence was abolished altogether, the effective distinction between the two disorders also disappeared. Eventually Freud gave up the term paraphrenia completely (cf. editor's note to Freud 1911a, p. 76, n. 1).

Despite his advocacy, it is quite understandable why Freud's term paraphrenia never achieved wide circulation: it was a single name for two disorders that most psychiatrists (and psychoanalysts) saw as reasonably distinct. Of no great moment in itself, what the change does reflect is Freud's altered conception of the relation between autoerotism and narcissism. To that extent the change is consistent with the view that both were present at the beginning of life.

The Conflict

Having completed the four detours, we turn to the problem of the opposition between the ego and sexuality. Two related issues must be considered: first, what motivates the development from primary narcissism and, second, how the opposition itself grows.

Three Paths from Narcissism   Freud offers three contradictory explanations for narcissism being abandoned. In "On Narcissism" he posed the question of:

what makes it necessary at all for our mental life to pass beyond the limits of narcissism and to attach the libido to objects. The answer ... would ... be that this necessity arises when the cathexis of the ego with libido exceeds a certain amount.   (Freud 1914b, p. 85)

Note that this overcathection of the libido, curiously thought of as a damming *within* the ego rather than *by* it, is not pictured as a consequence of a failure of the libido to find satisfying objects. What is proposed involves no objects at all. It is, as it were, a completely internal motive, drawing in no way on the external world.

However, Freud's second reason for the movement away from narcissism makes a veiled reference to the external world:

The development of the ego consists in a departure from primary narcissism and gives rise to a vigorous attempt to recover that state. This departure is brought about by means of the displacement of libido on to an ego ideal imposed from without.   (p. 100)

Objects in the external world provide the basis for the ego-ideal and, to that extent, the second motive drew on some of the effects of that world. The motive is quite different from the first and is inconsistent with a chronology of ego development that places the formation of the ego-ideal at all late in childhood. The third motive was the one that found a permanent place in the developmental theory:

Those sexual instincts which from the outset require an object, and the needs of the ego-instincts, which are never capable of auto-erotic satisfaction, naturally disturb this state ... and so pave the way for an advance from it.   (Freud 1915a, p. 134, n. 2)

This is the same basis that was suggested in "Formulations" (Freud 1911b, pp. 222–223), and is similar to that implied in "On narcissism" (Freud 1914b, pp. 87–88). Although his description is straightforward enough, the cooperation here pictured between the ego and sexual drives poses problems for the opposition he later wanted to establish. Three so very different starting points for the movement away from narcissism may also seem an explanatory extravagance. However, they do make handsome provision for saving hypotheses.

Ego v. Sexuality   As to the opposition between sexuality and the ego, the essence of Freud's derivation is that love and hate become intimately associated with the sexual and ego-instinctual drives, respectively, repeating the fundamental antithesis of those feelings in their own relation. The plausibility of the derivation rests on ambiguities in the concepts of object and object incorporation, and on Freud's overlooking significant positive connections between the two kinds of drive.

Restricting consideration to "Instincts and Their Vicissitudes," the main thrust of Freud's argument is easy enough to follow: the impact of a stimulating, object-providing external world on a primitive organism that is concerned only to maintain its internal constancy causes the organism to hate that world. Opposition between ego and sexuality is a consequence of the ego-drives because, in seeking out objects, the latter disturb the autoerotically self-sufficient state of primal narcissism. Although Freud's starting point is fully consistent with the end point to which he was striving, two problems arise with his thesis that the external world is the source of unpleasure: the inexorable demands of internal instinctual drive states are far from pleasant, and it is actually objects coming from outside that bring pleasurable satisfactions. He deals with these hindrances peremptorily—need-satisfying objects are incorporated in the ego, thus ceasing to be a part of the external world; whereas instinctual demands are transferred from the internal to the external world by projection. The arbitrariness of these solutions becomes apparent when the postulated mechanisms are analyzed.

Although modeled on the analogy of eating, object incorporation does not mean that the thing in the external world becomes a physical part of the individual. Incorporation is rather the establishment of functional associations between the mnemic traces of the object and the network of associations constituting the ego. The ego seeks pleasure, the object gives pleasure, ergo the two sets of associations become linked. But it would be just as consistent to say that these functional connections ought to modify the ego's elementary picture of the external world so that it interprets the world as a source of pleasure and as something that should be loved. Dominance of the pleasure principle is an equivocal basis for hatred being maintained after incorporation. With equal logic it allows *either* love *or* hate to result from the impress of external objects.

Of the two things that can be said about projection, the first virtually repeats the point about introjection. Unsatisfied needs are undoubtedly unpleasurable, but the prolonged dependence of the infant means, as Freud made clear in other contexts, that the need-satisfying objects from the outside world are provided especially readily. Does not the model of need satisfaction predict, just as readily, that the unsatisfied need will be intimately linked with the image of the externally produced satisfying object? And would not those associations counter the tendency to project the unpleasure outward? The second point is that if it is true to say that unsatisfied need states provide the basis for discriminating the internal world from the external, it is surely inconsistent also to claim that unsatisfied needs fuse the two worlds by projecting the one onto the other. Introjection and projection are virtually the only functions of the pleasure-ego, and their abrupt introduction into the theory as the purifiers of the original reality-ego is as logically satisfying as the appearance of a deus ex machina in a morality play.

Freud's argument also overlooks the effect of the initial close, anaclitic attachment of the sexual-instinctual drives to the ego-drives. When sucking and hunger needs are satisfied by a single activity, how can a closer association form between hatred and ego than between hatred and the sexual-instinctual drive? And ought not the assumption that some of the sexual-component drives require objects "from the outset," a point relegated to a footnote along with other crucial inconsistencies (Freud 1915a, p. 134, n. 2), lead to the search for those objects associating sexuality and hatred at least as strongly?

A final peculiarity of the explanation of the ego's relation to hated objects should be mentioned. The converse of the motor urge to bring pleasure-giving objects closer and to incorporate them was said to be a motor urge that

> endeavours to increase the distance between the object and the ego and to repeat in relation to the object the original attempt at flight from the external world with its emission of stimuli. (p. 137)

Repulsion from the object was felt as hate, and could intensify to the point of creating an intention to destroy the object. With that intensification, Freud had conveniently transformed the motor urge to *avoid* the object into an urge to *pursue* it (p. 138).

Freud here assumed what had to be demonstrated. On commonsense grounds, the feeling appropriate to the avoidance of an avoidable unpleasant object is annoyance, not hatred. In supposing that unpleasure can be intensified to the point of hatred and that, at the same time, the motor urge to avoid was turned into its opposite of pursuit, Freud filled the very gaps with which his argument had to deal. That we do learn to love and hate what may be termed objects, and that we do sometimes avoid and sometimes pursue them is self-evident; what Freud cannot do consistently is explain how these emotions and actions are related to each other.

Objects and the Cathexes of Objects   Part of the difficulty in Freud's derivation of the love-hate opposition arises from the ambiguity of the concept of object. Although not much discussed, it is evident that the way object is used indicates little agreement about its meaning (Green 1977; Compton 1986c). Compton distinguishes five fundamental object concepts (Compton 1986c) and three others less central (Compton 1986d) in Freud's own writings. All these meanings are foreshadowed, as Boesky (1983) has shown, in Freud's use of the term object presentation in *On Aphasia* to refer to a complex of perceptual associations.

Compton (1986d) links Freud's different usages to the evolution of what he sees as Freud's two models of excitation reduction. In Freud's very early instinctual drive theory an object is the *sexual object* and, as such, both the source of excitation and a means to its relief. In the second model the object is the *perceptual object* that becomes incidentally associated with need satisfaction. Compton concludes that the discrepancies are not innocuous because, "What is buried in the ambiguous usage is one of the most fundamental problems of psychology: How does anything become mental?" (Compton 1986d). Putting it more specifically, he asks: "How does the likeness on which identification is based become mental and how does the mental alteration ... occur?" (Compton 1985a).

In the belated discussion in the recent psychoanalytical literature, the essence of the object as the mental representation of a real object has been remarked frequently (Compton 1985a, 1986d; Rangell 1985; Abend and Rangell, in Goldberg 1985). To my knowledge, no one makes the point that the cathexis of an object or its introjection or projection requires connections to be formed between the "traces" or "mnemic residues" constituting a structure like the ego and those making up the representation of the object itself. I take this to be the essence of the answer to the question of how anything becomes mental and how an alteration occurs. Here we have to be clear about what object cathexis entails. Years ago, Bellak expressed it succinctly:

it only appears that cathexes are really placed on external objects. Actually, the investment of libido is made in the (internal) object representations.   (Bellak 1959)

Although he uses the term "mental representation" rather than object, Arlow (1980) takes the same position.

My discussion of this basic idea of cathexis in relation to identification, projection, and incorporation indicates the magnitude of the problems involved. Ornston (1978) observes that even Freud "did not try to describe projection metapsychologically. Other analysts, who have tried, have had great difficulty" Is the immensity of this problem partly responsible for Boesky's (1983, and in Goldberg 1985) proposal to do away with the concept of mental representation as a structure? If that were done, what would become of the various internalization processes? What is evident is how little attention is paid to the mechanism even in contexts where it might be expected. Thus, although Arlow (1980) discusses the mental representations of pleasurable and unpleasurable objects in the context of the pleasure- and reality-egos, he does not extend his consideration to what projection and introjection involve. Similarly, Rangell (1985), who endorses the mental representation notion of cathexis, discusses internalization—but not projection—without mentioning how ego and object representations are brought together. Meissner (1980), it seems to me, comes closest to seeing that the problem is how "properties and characteristics of the external object ... are ... processed so that they become an inherent part of the subject's self." He also discusses a number of internalization processes, but he omits projection, a fact possibly related to shyness in recognizing that the basis of all these processes must lie in the association and dissociation of memory traces. Where mechanisms of internalization are discussed without examining the means by which object representations are linked to or disconnected from the representations constituting the ego, as in Ornston's (1978) analysis, little or no difference will be found between projection and introjection.

As a last point, if Freud's whimsical fancy of the bad external world shattering the dreamlike self-sufficiency of the child is to be maintained, autoerotism *has* to be the mode of satisfaction in it. And maintained it was. Freud thought that only a basic difference between autoerotism and object-seeking tendencies provided a suitable basis for deriving the opposition between ego and sexual drives. Broadly speaking, these arbitrary notions are necessary if a fundamental antithesis between the two kinds of drive is to be arrived at: pleasure-giving objects must be incorporated into the ego without changing the ego's feelings toward the external world, and sexual objects have to have effects different from the objects of the ego drive. It is difficult to escape the conclusion that much of Freud's arbitrariness and inconsistency was motivated by this theoretical requirement. Certainly the antithesis was not required by any facts he adduced.

The Basis of the Conceptual Inadequacy

One of the minor puzzles about the concepts of ego and ego-instincts is the unexpectedness of their introduction into Freud's theorizing. The editor's note to "Instincts and Their Vicissitudes" remarks that although the sexual instinctual drive had been introduced in the *Three Essays* and that the related concepts of sexuality and libido were present much earlier, "The other party to the conflict, 'the ego,' remained undefined for much longer" (Freud 1915a, p. 114). Self-preservation drives "had scarcely ever been referred to" and there seemed no reason for relating them to the ego's repressive function (which itself had not been much mentioned either). Then, in the paper on visual disturbances,

with apparent suddenness ... Freud introduced the term "ego-instincts" and identified these on the one hand with the self-preservative instincts and on the other with the repressive function. (p. 115)

I pointed out in the second section of this chapter how well these new concepts fit in with organic automatic repression being restricted to causing primal repression, and how well they met the requirement for a counter to the sexual drive to be instinctual. The new concepts derived solely from the need to provide a basis for a concept of repression consistent with the rest of the theory rather than from new observations. Because that need arose suddenly, their introduction into the theory also had to be sudden.

Freud's expediency in theorizing about the ego and its drive may be measured by his rather offhand remark that what was left over from the sexual component of neurotic conflict could be "brought together under the rubric of ego instincts" (Nunberg and Federn 1962–1975, vol. 4, Minute 168 of Mar. 27, 1912). It is not at all remarkable, therefore, that "ego" was not clearly differentiated from "ego-instincts" (E. Bibring 1936/1941) or that both concepts were so inadequately characterized. Even though ego was provided with functions in "Formulations," that provision is achieved by little more than a transfer of primary process functions from *Ucs.* to the pleasure-ego and the secondary from *Pcs./Cs.* to the reality-ego. Devised for other purposes, these older functions could not be brought into close relation with the energy provided by the newly proposed instinctual drive. Whatever the other virtues of the studies of Leonardo, of Schreber, and of *Totem and Taboo*, the discussions of the ego in them contribute little or nothing to the resolution of the obscurity of the relation between ego function and ego drive. The primary role of those works was to bring into the theory the ego as sexual object, and not to throw light on the ego drive and its functions.

Much of the difficulty with the new instinctual drive theory results from deficiencies in Freud's use of sexual and hunger drives as models. Paradoxically, it is precisely because the sources of the sex and hunger drives fit (or seemed to fit) his persuasive pseudophysiology that they are so inappropriate as models for the ego-instinctual drives and most of the component sexual drives. Although each instinctual drive was eventually described as having a source, for most of them those sources were uncharacterized, lacking even pseudophysiological referents. Even for the elementary scientific operation of classification, the theory was not viable. By adopting sex and hunger as models, Freud trapped himself completely in Schiller's poetic fancy that the world might be turned by hunger and love.

As an aside, we might note that Freud's appeal to Schiller is marvelously ironical. The theme of *Die Weltweisen* is that until the real forces driving the world are understood, its movement might as well be attributed to hunger and love! Furthermore, Schiller did not restrict instinctual forces to the two Freud considered. Freud transmuted the fancy into three theoretical dogmas: first, that "as the poet has said, all the organic instincts ... may be classified as 'hunger' or 'love,'" second, that love and hunger are equivalent to sexual and self-preservation drives, respectively, and last, that there was an "undeniable opposition" between the two kinds of drive (Freud 1910b, pp. 214–215). Nothing in "On Narcissism" or "Instincts and Their Vicissitudes" takes our understanding beyond this combination of the poetic and the dogmatic.

Provided one goes no farther than generalizing an opposition between ego and sexual drives, Freud's thesis has a degree of plausibility. Because of the superficial similarity between repression proper and the conscious and deliberate attempt to thrust unpleasant or repugnant ideas out of mind, it does not seem unreasonable to describe repression as resulting from an incompatibility between the ego's standards and a sexual idea. What Freud does not show, or makes little attempt to show, is how the ego-instinct acts in repression. Ego-instinctual energy plays no role in repression caused by the transformation of affect from an abandoned erotogenic zone. Neither does it have a role if the fixation of primal repression is due to an excessive pleasure. As for the anticathexis provided by *Pcs.*, if it is responsible for maintaining primal repression and initiating repression proper (Freud 1915c, pp. 180–181), Freud nowhere describes how *Pcs.* acquires its energy or why it should draw on the ego drives. Consequently, either the relation among *Pcs.*, anticathexes, and ego-instinctual drives is quite unspecified—in which case the proposed mechanism has little more explanatory power than Freud's interpretation of Schiller—or the anticathexes derive from the libido—in which case Freud has given up the poetic dogma—and the ego-instinctual drives are simply not involved in repression at all.

Vagueness about the relation between the sexual and ego-instinctual drives is also reflected in certain peculiarities of the effects of the sexual drive on the ego, in the inadequacies of the account of the movement away from primal narcissism, and in the tortuous explanation of the subsequent opposition between the two drives. Although it may be uncertain what it was that was cathected in narcissism, the cathexis resulted in sexual energy being located *within* the ego itself (E. Jones 1935–1936; E. Bibring 1936/1941). Ernest Jones described "On Narcissism" as "a disturbing essay" because this store of libido in the ego tended to obliterate the distinction between the ego-drives and the sexual drives. Freud nevertheless defended the separate identity of the drives. Biologically they were different and opposed, and the analyses of hysteria and obsessional neuroses "compelled" him to keep to the distinction: "I only know that all attempts to account for these phenomena by other means have been completely unsuccessful" (Freud 1914b, pp. 77–78). Neither argument is compelling. The point about the psychoneuroses is nothing other than that he used repression to explain them. The biological grounds are little more than an extension of Schiller's poesy.

One effect of the narcissistic ego being cathected was what Freud called the sexualization of thought. Yet the notion that thought in narcissism was sexualized is not required by the argument, nor is it justified by the evidence. Ferenczi (1913/1952c) showed that omnipotence of thought can be derived solely from a continuation of the hallucinatory wish-fulfilling thinking of the infant. Any object, whether of the sexual instinctual drive or not, can be conjured up by wishing its presence. The evidential basis is just as shaky. Freud himself seems to have first applied the phrase "sexualization of thought" to the tendency of obsessional patients to brood over their ideas. The brooding was seen as a regression from action to thought, a regression made possible in part by the intensity of the instinctual drive for sexual knowledge in the patient's childhood. Obsessional brooding was a regressive manifestation in which "the sexual pleasure which is normally attached to the *content* of thought becomes shifted on to the *act* of thinking itself" (Freud 1909b, p. 245. My emphasis). In *Totem and Taboo* sexualization had a rather different effect: it produced omnipotence of thought through an overvaluation of the *consequences* of thinking, rather than the sexual pleasure of a mere *act* of thought (Freud 1912–1913, pp. 88–90). Freud's "evidence" cannot justify both of these meanings. Once again, the vagueness of what exactly happened when the ego was cathected made both equally plausible.

Theoretical consistency also required that during the development from the primal narcissistic state associations be generated between sexuality and love on the one hand and ego and hatred on the other. Otherwise the two drives could neither develop nor maintain an antithesis. The mechanism Freud finally chose from the three he put forward—the ego drive's search for objects—was the easiest to adapt. But his adaptation was at the cost of having to make arbitrary assumptions about the effects of introjection and projection. Only if pleasure-giving sexual objects were introjected and unpleasant need states projected could he maintain that the ego drives were directed solely toward hated, external objects. He also had to overlook the effects of those sexual drives that seek objects from the external world, and to assume that when both drives were satisfied on the same object there was a dissociation between the effects of satisfaction; otherwise pleasure would accrue to both drives equally.

The difficulties in explaining hatred may be put another way. Basic to the theory is opposition between two types of drive, both of which seek pleasurable satisfactions; that fact alone makes it difficult to imagine how, other than through drive frustration, emotions other than love can arise. Indifference, or perhaps annoyance, might be thought of as resulting from the continued impact of unsought stimuli, but nothing else. It should now be obvious that Freud would have severe difficulty in explaining masochistic behavior. And he does.

If masochism and sadism are found together, it is economical to derive them either from a common source or from one another. The pleasure principle rules out primary masochism: one cannot assume that an organism would inflict pain upon itself. But, hatred and aggressiveness had to be devoid of sexual content; their status as ego-instinctual drives saw to that. So they provided no basis for the infliction of pain. These constraints virtually forced Freud into assuming a primary sadistic drive, having as its aim to master and humiliate the object rather than to inflict pain:

Psycho-analysis would appear to show that the infliction of pain plays no part among the original purposive actions of the instinct [of mastery]. A sadistic child takes no account of whether or not he inflicts pains, nor does he intend to do so.   (Freud 1915a, p. 128)

Freud went on to argue that once children experienced the effects of painful stimulation themselves, this originally active primary sadistic drive turned back on them and changed into a passive form. Masochism proper developed when painful stimuli generated sexual excitation and the individual sought others on whom to inflict pain. Another turning around of the drive then took place. Directed to the individual's objects in an active way it thus generated sadism proper.

Now, psychoanalysis had not "shown" that there was no primary masochism; indeed, within a very few years, Freud made primary masochism one of his most central propositions. The only thing that had been "shown" was the logical inconsistency of assuming a primary masochistic drive in an organism devoted solely to the pursuit of pleasure and the avoidance of pain.

Conclusion

The most important general conclusion is that the deficiencies of Freud's new theory of the ego, its functions, and its drives result from constraints imposed by other parts of the theory. All the elements of the theory were in existence well before the paper on vision, and it could almost have been made up from them without any new facts. *Studies on Hysteria* provided the idea of an ego and a repressing force located in it, *The Interpretation of Dreams* described the primary ego functions and those that developed from them, and the *Three Essays* adumbrated the concept of instinctual drive. The concept of an ego that was the object of the sexual drive, and the supposition that fixations produced dispositions to later regressions were the only really new elements. Although observations of perversion and psychosis contributed, they were not related in a consistent and convincing manner to the supporting evidence. There were also constraints on the ways in which the components could fit together, constraints imposed by the requirements that all instinctual life be governed by the principles of constancy and pleasure, and for there to be two opposed sets of instinctual drives. A real theoretical synthesis of these elements escaped Freud. At almost every point he retreated into vagueness or made arbitrary assumptions that created additional inconsistencies.

In chapters 12 and 13 we will see how he tried to escape these constraints by moving beyond the notion of a pleasure principle, by modifying much of his thinking about instinctual drives, and by making very considerable alterations to his model of the mind.

Note

1. Freud introduced this term for the first time in "Formulations." Previously the principle was known as the unpleasure principle. I use the later term, pleasure principle, throughout.

12 The Instinct Theory Finalized

Now, whom doth it not concerne to learn, both the danger, and benefit of death?
—Anonymous Introduction to Donne's *Deaths Duell*

In 1920 Freud announced a major revision of his conceptualization of instinctual drives and of the conflict between them. The battle was no longer between ego and sexuality. Those two old antagonists were fused together in a new life drive named Eros, and the force of death itself, surely the most weighty of all contenders, matched in struggle against it. Partly as a result, the model of the mind outlined in *The Interpretation of Dreams* also had to be revised. In this chapter I examine the new conceptualization of instinctual drives, and in chapter 13 consider Freud's new theory of the mental structures.

Although the stages through which Freud's thinking passed as he revised the instinctual drive concept are almost impossible to reconstruct, two distinct lines of thought can be differentiated: on the one hand, he brought together the sexual and ego-drives under the aegis of Eros, and on the other, he selected death as the opponent. We do not know which of these ideas came first.

Several writers have traced the concept of the death instinct back to the impression that the massive cruelty, destructiveness, and devastation revealed in the First World War made on Freud. One cannot doubt the depth of Freud's disillusionment, or the extent to which he believed that primitive instinctual passions had been unleashed (Freud 1915d). The war, he said,

destroyed not only the beauty of the countrysides through which it passed and the works of art which it met with on its path but it also shattered our pride in the achievements of our civilization, our admiration for many philosophers and artists and our hopes of a final triumph over the differences between nations and races. It tarnished the lofty impartiality of our science, *it revealed our instincts in all their nakedness and let loose the evil spirits within us* which we thought had been tamed for ever by centuries of continuous education by the noblest minds.   (Freud 1916a, p. 307. My emphasis)

Similarly, in his lectures, he asked his students to

consider the Great War which is still laying Europe waste. Think of the vast amount of brutality, cruelty and lies which are able to spread over the civilized world. Do you really believe that a handful of ambitious and deluding men without conscience could have succeeded in unleashing all these evil spirits *if their millions of followers did not share their guilt*? Do you venture, in such circumstances, to break a lance on behalf of the exclusion of *evil from the mental constitution of mankind*?   (Freud 1916–1917, p. 146. My emphasis)

His impeaching of instinctual forces is quite definite; however, he did not immediately alter his views on the sources of aggression. Nor need he: destructiveness, brutality, and cruelty resulted from the aggressiveness and hatred that he derived from the ego-instinctual drives. Indeed, he made that derivation in the very same weeks in which he so forcefully expressed his dismay at the results of the war (editorial introduction to Freud 1915a, p. 111 and 1915d, p. 274). Consequently, it is not surprising that he used the ego-instincts to explain the instinctual basis of wartime destructiveness (Freud 1915d, pp. 280–283).

We may also note that when Freud first intimated that there were instincts other than the sexual and ego-drives, he did so in a context in which he failed to mention either aggressiveness in general or the war in particular (Freud 1919d). The same point holds for *Beyond the Pleasure Principle* in which the death instinct was formally introduced into psychoanalytic theory (Freud 1920a). As the editors of the *Standard Edition* (vol. 19, p. 157, n. 2) remark, it was only from 1930 on that Freud turned his attention more to the outward direction of the death instinct, to aggressiveness and destructiveness. The impact of the war seems neither to have forced him to reconsider the origins of hatred and aggression nor to have contributed directly to his concept of a death instinct.

On the other hand, some writers traced the revised instinct theory, or at least that part of it that fused the sexual and ego-drives, to a theoretical difficulty created by the concept of narcissism. Narcissism required that the ego retain some of the original store of libido, and that retention either masked the independent energy ("interest") that the ego drive possessed, or it did away with an independent ego energy altogether. In this view, Freud's revision of the instinct theory resulted from his bowing to the theoretical need to dispose of a superfluous concept. Although in one sense this is correct, it has to be pointed out that over quite a long period Freud vigorously defended his separation of the two classes of drive (Freud 1914b, pp. 76–81, 1915a, pp. 123–125, 1916b, pp. 316–318, 1916–1917, pp. 350–357, 412–430, 1917b, pp. 137–139, 1919c, pp. 208–210). Usually he argued that the transference neuroses— hysteria and obsessional neuroses—were otherwise impossible to understand. The conflict between the demands of sexuality and the standards of the ego was absolutely critical to their explanation. Separation of the drives was also defended in terms of the very different sources from which they arose. Sometimes Freud made the additional point that to abolish the distinction would make concessions to the then recent Jungian and Adlerian heresies. Jung proposed that there was only one kind of mental energy and that it was nonsexual; by so doing, he posed an immediate challenge to the central position of sexuality in Freud's theory. Adler's challenge was as strong, as he wanted to make what was to Freud essentially an ego drive the sole or main force motivating behavior. What Jung and Adler both abandoned was sexuality and, with it, the notion of a conflict between ego and sexuality.

A limitation to the argument from narcissism stands out: only the bringing together of sexual and ego-instinctual drives is explained. There seems no necessity for the new drive to be a death instinct. Yet in a sense it is precisely the reconciliation of ego with sexuality that determines the attributes of the new opponent. This sense is provided by Freud's characteristic mode of thinking that always limited conflict to two parties. Either he thought this way because he could not otherwise explain mental conflict to himself, as his own writings and the opinion of Fairbairn (1939–1941) suggest, or because he had a predilection for casting explanations in terms of two opposing processes, sometimes called, rather confusingly, his dualism (E. Jones 1935–1936, 1953–1957, vol. 2, p. 320, vol. 3, pp. 266–267; Arlow 1959; E. Bibring 1936/1941; Loewenstein 1940; Flugel 1953). Certainly no logical requirement existed for only two instincts. As Gillespie (1971) noted, the essential bipolarity (as he correctly calls it) of Freud's theory was "not a necessary deduction from conflict." More recently, Holt (1975a) convincingly pointed out that psychoanalytic facts about conflict do not necessitate the assumption that "all motives may be reduced to any two." Nor, as Satinover (1986) shows, did the explanation of transference neuroses really depend on the conflict being between libidinal and ego energies.

However, once Freud decided to remain within the two-motive framework, the rest was decided. First, the opponent had to be able to counter an instinctual drive, ergo it had itself to be instinctual. Second, the behavioral manifestations of the new drive had to be muted, otherwise it would not have been so long overlooked. For the same reason, the new drive had to have its source in some not readily identifiable bodily process. Finally, since both the sexual and ego-drives were governed by the pleasure principle (the former in its pure version, the latter in the modified form of the reality principle), the new antagonist had to be independent of the pleasure principle and beyond it.

Where then was the evidence of an instinctual force opposed to Eros and governed by something other than the pleasure principle? And where was its source? To Freud it seemed that a substantial part of the answer to the first question was provided by behaviors that showed a compulsive tendency to repeat unpleasant experiences. What he called the "demonic character" of such repetitions directly suggested that the compulsion proceeded from

the instinctual impulses and probably inherent in the very nature of the instincts—a compulsion powerful enough to overrule the pleasure principle, lending to certain aspects of the mind their demonic character.   (Freud 1919d, p. 238)

In *Beyond the Pleasure Principle* he expanded on this assertion in three ways: he attempted to demonstrate that the behaviors did in fact violate the pleasure principle, he argued that all instinctual drives were repetitive and had been acquired in specific historical circumstances, and he interpreted the compulsion to repeat as a manifestation of an instinctual drive having death as its aim. Death was now the opponent for

Eros. Freud conceived of the drive as having both inwardly and outwardly directed forms, forms that allowed a ready derivation of masochism, sadism, and aggressiveness and so filled an important gap in psychoanalytical theory.

I begin this chapter with summaries of Freud's clinical and theoretical arguments for recognizing a compulsion to repeat and for deriving a death instinct. This is followed by an evaluation of the logical and evidential bases of his theses. Answers are sought to a number of specific questions, including the following: were the behaviors beyond the pleasure principle? was the compulsion to repeat instinctual? did instinctual drives have the characteristics Freud attributed to them? why did organisms die? what were the mechanisms by which the individual coped with trauma? how were the various principles and tendencies that regulated or governed mental processes related to one another? I claim that the proper answers to these questions contradict Freud's theses. Psychoanalytic alternatives to Freud's death instinct-based explanations of the compulsion to repeat, of sadism and masochism, and of aggressiveness are considered briefly before the final summary conclusion.

The Clinical Bases of Repetition

Freud thought three behaviors were governed by something other than the pleasure principle. They were the transference of some of the patient's feelings onto the analyst, the repetition of terrifying dreams in traumatic neuroses, especially war neuroses, and a particular type of children's play. I begin with Freud's analyses of these before considering his attributing them to the compulsion to repeat. After that I consider the claim that the compulsion had its basis in an instinctual death drive.

Transference

Freud began his discussion of repetition and transference by drawing attention to the problem of obliging the patient "to confirm the analyst's construction [of what had happened] from his own memory" (Freud 1920a, p. 18). Resistance often prevented unconscious ideas being brought to consciousness in this way. The patient could not remember the repressed material and acquired "no sense of conviction of the correctness of the construction that has been communicated to him" (p. 18). Instead of accepting the interpretation, the patient repeated in action some version of the repressed ideas. What was reenacted was always some part of the patient's infantile sexual life that brought with it

no possibility of pleasure, and which can never, even long ago, have brought satisfaction even to instinctual impulses which have since been repressed.   (p. 20)

Of necessity, the child's sexual activity had to end in failure and the loss of parental love. It could never be satisfied in actuality. Scorning the child's sexual love might result in the child developing some persistent but vain expectation of satisfaction from the parent. Or, unable to procreate or solve the mystery of where babies come from, the child might come to feel quite unable to accomplish anything. Neither remembered nor acknowledged in treatment,

Patients repeat all of these unwanted situations and painful emotions.... They seek to bring about the interruption of the treatment while it is still incomplete; they contrive once more to feel themselves scorned, to oblige the physician to speak severely to them and to treat them coldly; they discover appropriate objects for their jealousy; instead of the passionately desired baby of their childhood, they produce a plan or a promise of some grand present—which turns out as a rule to be no less unreal.   (p. 21)

Freud stressed that:

None of these things can have produced pleasure in the past.... In spite of that, they are repeated under pressure of a compulsion.   (p. 21)

A year later, in 1921, he added a sentence to emphasize the point even further: Although the childhood activities were motivated by instinctual drives "intended to lead to satisfaction," no lesson seemed to have been learned from the fact that each past attempt at satisfaction had led "only to unpleasure" (p. 21).

Freud also thought the lives of some essentially normal people were directed by a similar compulsion to repeat. Among the many examples he cited were the lover whose successive affairs always passed through the same stages before reaching the same unsatisfactory termination, the individual whose friendships were successively betrayed by his friends, and the benefactor who was abandoned in turn by each of his protégés and who seemed forever doomed "to taste all the bitterness of ingratitude" (p. 22). All such people seemed pursued by a malignant fate that compelled them to repeat the same mistake over and over again.

Traumatic Neuroses

A similar tendency for a repetition of the unpleasurable manifested itself in the traumatic neuroses when, as Charcot's patient Le Log____ had done, the patient relived the traumatic event or some derivative of it in his dreams. Freud asserted that such repetitions astonished people far too little:

They think the fact that the traumatic experience is constantly forcing itself upon the patient even in his sleep is a proof of the strength of that experience: the patient is, one might say, fixated to his trauma.   (p. 13)

Fixations of this kind could not explain why the memories intruded at night but not at all during the daytime, and why the wish-fulfilling function of dreams did not prevent the reappearance of the memories. If the wish-fulfillment function were to be saved, it followed that in some way it had to have been upset or diverted from its purpose.

Play

Freud observed his grandson playing in a way that seemed to illustrate the compulsion to repeat (Freud 1900, p. 461, n. 1. of 1919). At age one and a half years the child displayed few overt signs of distress when his mother left him, even though he was much attached to her. However, he did have

an occasional disturbing habit of taking any small objects he could get hold of and throwing them away from him into a corner, under the bed, and so on, so that hunting for his toys and picking them up was often quite a business. As he did this, he gave vent to a loud, long-drawn-out "o-o-o-o," accompanied by an expression of interest and satisfaction ... this was not a mere interjection but represented the German word "*fort*" ["gone"].   (Freud 1920a, pp. 14–15)

Other observations confirmed the meaning of the vocalization: the boy repeatedly threw a toy on a string out of sight while saying "o-o-o-o," but hailed his retrieval of it "with a joyful '*da*' ['there']," and he used "o-o-o-o" to accompany the crouching by which he made his image in a mirror disappear (p. 15 and n. 1). Freud eventually realized that the toy throwing was a game, that the only use the child made of any of his toys was to play "gone" with them, and that throwing them away, rather than recovering them, was the game's essential feature (pp. 14–15). He interpreted the game as compensation for the boy's lack of reaction to his mother's going away, but it was the unpleasant part of that experience that was being reenacted, not her return.

Alternative interpretations of the play were possible. Freud distinguished five. First, because the child was in a passive situation that overwhelmed him, he was actively repeating the experience in play in an attempt to master it. Instead of a compulsion to repeat, the behavior might be motivated by "an instinct for mastery ... acting independently of whether the memory was in itself pleasurable or not" (p. 16). It was also possible that the child was satisfying a hostile impulse, avenging himself on his mother for leaving him. Some of his later behavior was consistent with this explanation (p. 16). Third, Freud noted that children often tended to repeat "everything that has made a great impression on them in real life"; another motive for the repetition might therefore be an attempt to master the situation by abreacting the considerable affect associated with it (pp. 16–17). A fourth motive was suggested by the prevalence in childhood of "the wish to be grown up and to be able to do what grown-up people do" (pp. 16–17). Finally, in reenacting an unpleasant experience a child frequently handed on "the disagreeable experience to one of his playmates and in this way revenges himself on a substitute" (pp. 16–17). Because all five of these alternative motives yielded pleasure as their final outcome, the repetitive behavior could still be subsumed under the pleasure principle. None required the supposition of "tendencies *beyond* the pleasure principle, that is, of tendencies more primitive than it and independent of it" (pp. 16–17).

Some of the other repetitive behaviors were similarly ambiguous. Transference repetition might be due to the ego, "clinging as it does to the pleasure principle," calling on the compulsion to repeat so that repression would be maintained (p. 23, n. 1). Rational factors might explain why people repeated the same errors through-out their lives, and there might be "no necessity to call in a new and mysterious motive force" (p. 23). Freud concluded that the least doubtful instance was the repetition of the traumatic dream.

Quite suddenly he interrupted these considerations to assert that

on maturer reflection we shall be forced to admit that even in the other instances the whole ground is not covered by the operation of the familiar motive forces. Enough is left un-explained to justify the hypothesis of a compulsion to repeat—something that seems more primitive, more elementary, more instinctual than the pleasure principle which it over-rides. (p. 23)

If this primitive instinctual force did exist, one had to learn

what function it corresponds to, under what conditions it can emerge and what its relation is to the pleasure principle—to which, after all, we have hitherto ascribed dominance over the course of the processes of excitation in mental life.   (p. 23)

These concluding remarks thus tentatively characterize the force responsible for the compulsion to repeat. Freud now left his clinical evidence and turned to a theoretical analysis in which he tried to show that the compulsion had an instinctual basis.

The Theoretical Basis of Repetition

Even were it true that the compulsion to repeat overruled the pleasure principle, that fact alone did not show it arose from an instinctual drive. Freud's theoretical analysis attempted to meet the problem in two ways: first he tried to show how a repetitive tendency for coping with trauma might have evolved, and he then attempted to establish that the very essence of instinctual drives was that they were conservative, historically acquired, and directed toward reestablishing or repeating an earlier state of affairs. These analyses were conducted within the constraints of his conflict model: there would be two classes of drive in opposition, one of which would incorporate the sexual drive.

Trauma and Repetition

It seemed to Freud that the very factors that caused the evolution of the system *Pcpt.-Cs.* explained how a mechanism for dealing with trauma that overrode the pleasure principle was acquired. Consciousness, which arose in *Pcpt.-Cs.*, consisted of two things: perceptions of excitations originating in the outside world, and feelings of pleasure and unpleasure arising from within. *Pcpt.-Cs.* therefore had to be thought of as lying between the inside and the outside of the organism. Basing himself on Breuer's proposition from *Studies on Hysteria*, Freud then argued that if a system were permanently modified by successive excitations it would lose the capacity for responding to new stimulation. Responsiveness and modifiability were thus mutually exclusive.

So great was the intensity of stimuli impinging on the primitive organism from the external world that the transmission of excitation through its outer cortical layer was completely facilitated, and memory traces could not be laid down there. Consciousness would arise instead. Further, precisely because it was adjacent to the powerful stimuli from the external world, Freud concluded that *Pcpt.-Cs.* could not be further modified. Using what he claimed was Breuer's distinction between two kinds of energy, he described its elements as being able to carry only energy capable of free discharge and not to retain or bind it.

Energy arising from the external world had a second effect. Internally undifferentiated organisms, with only the capacity to respond to stimuli, developed a protective shield that absorbed most of the external energy before passing it on in less intense and nondestructive quantities to the deeper layers. Special modifications of the outer layer capable of taking in small quantities of this attenuated excitation and sensing its nature and direction were located immediately beneath the shield. These were the sense organs. Energy from the external world had thus created a protective shield having a primitive *Pcpt.-Cs.* system behind it. The protective function was paramount:

> *Protection against* stimuli is an almost more important function for the living organism than the *reception* of stimuli. (Freud 1920a, p. 27)

Protection was generally not required from internal drive stimuli—their magnitudes were "more commensurate with the system's method of working." Because they were not attenuated, the feelings of pleasure and unpleasure they generated came to predominate. Therein lay the importance of the pleasure principle. However, should internal stimuli become too intense, they too were treated as if they originated in the outside world and the mechanism of the protective shield used to reduce them. Such was the basis of the process of projection (p. 29).

How then could the pleasure principle be overruled? The traumatic situation itself suggested the answer. Traumatic excitations arose externally and were strong enough to break through the protective shield, flood in toward the interior of the organism, and there cause a profound disturbance in the distribution of energy. The organism was faced with the task of

mastering the amounts of stimulus which have broken in and of binding them, in the psychical sense, so that they can then be disposed of.   (p. 30)

Cathectic energy, mobilized from throughout the organism, was used to construct an anticathexis "on a grand scale" to effect the binding. Freud then inferred that

a system which is itself highly cathected is capable of taking up an additional stream of fresh inflowing energy and converting it into quiescent cathexis, that is of binding it psychically. The higher the system's own quiescent cathexis, the greater seems to be its binding force; conversely, *therefore*, the lower its cathexis, the less capacity will it have for taking up inflowing energy.   (p. 30. My emphasis)

The last part of this conclusion harks back, of course, to the Meynert-Exner mechanism of facilitation, both as Breuer used it in the theory of *Studies on Hysteria* and as Freud adapted it for the *Project*.

Traumatic neuroses came about when the protective shield was breached unexpectedly. Freud regarded the individual's unpreparedness for the danger as equivalent to a lack of cathexis in the first of the systems reached by the incoming stimuli, and as a necessary condition for the development of the neurosis. When the danger was expected, the anticipatory cathexis (or "hypercathexis") of these systems enabled binding to take place. Thereupon "a preparedness for anxiety" arose. Without the hypercathexis, the alien stimuli could not be bound in the first systems and continued to flood in until the hastily prepared anticathexis was able to stop them. Repetitive dreams were not so much attempting to fulfill a wish as

helping to carry out another task, which must be accomplished before the domination of the pleasure principle can even begin. These dreams are endeavouring to master the stimulus retrospectively, by developing the anxiety whose omission was the cause of the traumatic neurosis.   (p. 32)

Retrospective binding was attempted without reference to the pleasure principle. In view of the ultimate aim of his argument, it was perhaps surprising that, although

Freud described binding as independent of and more primitive than the pleasure principle, he also stressed that it was not in contradiction with it (p. 32).

Instinctual drives could sometimes produce changes in the distribution of energy matching those produced by external trauma. Instinctual impulses were not attenuated by the protective shield, and their point of contact with the mental apparatus was the system *Ucs*. Consequently they were subject to the laws of the primary process, and their freely mobile energy pressed strongly for discharge. Freud now claimed that it was easy to identify the primary process

with Breuer's freely mobile cathexis and the secondary process with changes in his bound or tonic cathexis. If so, it would be the task of the higher strata of the mental apparatus to bind the instinctual excitation reaching the primary process.   (pp. 34–35)

A disturbance analogous to a traumatic neurosis was produced when these higher strata failed. Again, only after binding or mastery had taken place was the pleasure principle able to dominate mental life. Freud reiterated that this repetition was also independent of the pleasure principle, rather than opposed to it (p. 35).

Repetition and Instinctual Drives

Suddenly Freud altered the thrust of his argument to assert that the manifestations of the compulsion to repeat in children's play and in transference were highly instinctual. Indeed, so striking was this characteristic that "some 'demonic' force" seemed to be at work (Freud 1920a, p. 35). Here he harked back to the paper, published a few months before, in which he first described the compulsion and where he maintained that what required recognition was that the basis of the repetitions was "inherent in the very nature of the instincts" (Freud 1919d, p. 238). In *Beyond the Pleasure Principle*, he said that it was precisely this demonic quality that led him to this hitherto unrecognized or insufficiently stressed aspect of instinctual life. He now concluded:

It seems, then, that an instinct is an urge inherent in organic life to restore an earlier state of things which the living entity has been obliged to abandon under the pressure of external disturbing forces; that is, it is a kind of organic elasticity, or, to put it another way, the expression of the inertia inherent in organic life.   (Freud 1920a, p. 36)

He acknowledged that this interpretation of the demonic instinctual force was the very opposite of the popular view. Most frequently, instinctual drives were thought of as vehicles of change. To support his interpretation, he cited the view of "many biologists" that instinctively governed migrations of fish and birds were due to those animals seeking out the localities in which their species had once resided, but from which they had become accidentally separated. However, "the most impressive proofs" came from heredity and embryology, where it was shown that the developing organism always recapitulated the structures and forms from which its own species evolved (p. 37).

A Deathly Argument Having thus established the possibility that some instinctual drives might have the restoration of an earlier state as their aim, Freud tried to prove that it was universally true. Because of the disorder of issues that he raised, it is not at all obvious that his intention was to do this through a formal deductive argument. He said he wished "to pursue to its logical conclusion" the following hypothesis:

all the organic instincts are conservative, are acquired historically and tend towards the restoration of an earlier state of things. (pp. 37–38)

But this hypothesis turns out to be Freud's first premise. To it he conjoined a second: everything that died naturally did so only for internal reasons. Coupling the premises compelled the conclusion:

"*the aim of all life is death*" and, looking backwards, that "*inanimate things existed before living ones.*" (p. 38.)

For the conclusion to carry any weight, it had to be shown that both premises were true. A ready proof that instincts were conservative seemed to be available for the first premise. If it were true, it followed, Freud believed, that organic development was due to changes in the external world being impressed on elementary living entities. A changeless world prevented the organism from changing because

if conditions remained the same, it would do no more than constantly repeat the same course of life. (p. 38)

Variations in external circumstance modified the organism and were stored up to be repeated as acquired instinctual dispositions. Instincts were therefore conservative. Freud also pointed out that it was inconsistent to maintain that the goal of an instinctual striving could be a state not previously experienced.

As for the historical component of the first premise, he described inanimate matter as being converted into living substance by the action of an external force generating tension in it. The tension necessarily sought to cancel itself out, and in so doing brought the first instinctual drive into being. Its aim, of course, was to return the newly created living substance to its previous inanimate and tensionless state. Paradoxically enough, in the very historical circumstance from which life evolved, Freud seemed to have found an instinctual drive aimed at destroying that life. Even present-day life could be viewed as a manifestation of the death drive. After life was created, the repetition of successively acquired instinctual dispositions prevented the organism from dying as easily as it was first able to. The phenomena of life were thus nothing more than manifestations of the circuitous paths to death that newly acquired and conservative instincts forced upon the living organism. Because their real function was to ensure that the organism died in its own way, self-preservation drives were thus fundamentally conservative. Indeed, they were mere creatures of the death instinct.

The Generality of Conservation   Freud now had to show that all the other instinctual drives were similarly conservative. He began by considering the sexual drives. Present-day elementary organisms were, he thought, probably much like their primeval ancestors, and the same could be said of the germ cells of multicellular organisms. The latter retained their original structure and their dispositions even though they had become separated from the organism as a whole. When, in the present, the germ cells began their development, they repeated the act to which they owed their own existence. One portion developed fully and the other became a new germ cell. Because sexual instinctual drives guided the destinies of the germ cells, it followed that they were also conservative in bringing back "earlier states of living substance" (Freud 1920a, p. 40). They were additionally conservative in that they were resistant to external influences. They preserved life for long periods, and Freud concluded that they were "the true life instincts" (p. 40). Because they acted against the other death-seeking instinctual drives, it could be concluded that an opposition was present between the sexual and other drives, an opposition "long ago recognized by the theory of the neuroses" (p. 40).

Freud next considered whether any drives existed that did not seek to restore an earlier state. Did any drives aim at goals never before achieved? (p. 41). It did not appear to him that there was a universal drive toward higher development in the animal world. Nor was there an untiring impulsion toward perfection in human life. To the extent that the latter seemed to be present, it was due to instinctual repression in a minority of leaders whose drives never ceased

to strive for complete satisfaction, which would consist in the repetition of a primary experience of satisfaction.   (p. 42)

Taken together, the death drive, the sexual drives, and all of the other instinctual drives could be considered as conservative. Not only did none of them aim at the new and unknown; all were directed toward restoring the conditions that had existed immediately before their own coming into being. Freud thought that this established the truth of the first premise.

Sexuality and the First Premise   A problem remained with the sexual instinctual drive. Although Freud drew a sharp distinction between it and the death drive, he was unable to attribute to it a really "conservative or rather retrograde, character corresponding to a compulsion to repeat" (p. 44). Although sexual drives did reproduce primitive states:

what they are clearly aiming at by every possible means is the coalescence of two germ-cells. . . . If this union is not effected, the germ-cell dies along with all the other elements of the multicellular organism. It is only on this condition that the sexual function can prolong the cell's life and lend it the appearance of immortality.   (p. 44)

However, he was quite unable to say what

important event in the development of living substance [was] being repeated in sexual reproduction, or in its forerunner, the conjugation of two protista [protozoa].   (p. 44)

The three parts of the initial premise did not, after all, seem to apply fully to the sexual instinctual drives.

The Second Premise   Freud went on to test the validity of the second premise, that of natural death being due solely to internal causes. He noted little agreement among biologists on the subject; however, he discerned an important analogy with Weismann's influential biological theory: the germ plasm, which was concerned with reproduction, was immortal, whereas the soma, virtually the rest of the body, was mortal. The distinction seemed to Freud to be a morphological corollary to his differentiation of the two classes of drives. True, in two significant respects the analogy was incomplete. Weismann's distinction applied only to multicellular organisms and not to the unicellular, in which the individual was both germ plasm and soma. Death could therefore appear only with the development of multicellular organisms and not, as Freud's theory required, at the very beginning of life. Second, whereas Weismann did hold that the multicellular organism died for internal reasons, the types of causes he proposed, such as imperfect metabolism or defective differentiation, lacked the iron necessity that Freud sought. The death of multicellular organisms was therefore "of no interest."

It was the alleged immortality of unicellular organisms that seemed more relevant. Some workers had kept ciliate infusoria alive for over 3,000 generations, but others observed signs of senescence well before that time. Two things seemed to postpone senescence and eventual death. If aging individuals were allowed to conjugate, both were rejuvenated, and it was only if each successive generation was provided with fresh nutrient medium that the infusorian become immortal. Infusoria died if the nutrient was not changed. Experiments showed the infusorian's own metabolic products to be fatal. Freud concluded:

An infusorian, therefore, if it is left to itself, dies a natural death *owing to its incomplete voidance of the products of its own metabolism.* (p. 48. My emphasis)

For at least some unicellular organisms it seemed to Freud that internal causes brought about a natural death. Even were that not so, Freud argued that the validity of the second premise could be maintained by distinguishing between overt and covert processes. The very primitiveness of protozoan organization might hide those internal processes that found visible morphological expression in more advanced organisms. The death drives might be so completely hidden "it may very be hard to find any direct evidence of their presence." From what Freud called his dynamic standpoint, as opposed to the morphological, it was "a matter of complete indifference" whether or not natural death occurred in protozoa. Further, he interpreted the generation experiments with protozoa as supporting the conclusion that they died for internal reasons, but the qualification could still be made that even if protozoa

turned out to be immortal in Weismann's sense, his assertion that death is a late acquisition would apply only to its *manifest* phenomena and would not make impossible the assumption of processes *tending* towards it. (p. 49)

So interpreted, Freud did not think biology flatly contradicted his "recognition of death instincts." Consequently, he felt "at liberty" to continue to entertain their possibility, an attitude that was again reinforced by the "striking similarity" of the distinction between the life and death instincts and Weismann's separation of germ plasm from soma. Freud also noted that his conceptualization was in accord with Hering's thesis that two opposed processes of anabolism and catabolism were at work in living tissue. Perhaps they too were guided by instincts.

A Death Instinct Manifest?   Were there any instinctual drives that did not belong to either of the new classes? Granting that the original instinctual polarity had "proved to be inadequate" (Freud 1920a, p. 52), Freud pointed out that ego drives could readily be fused with sexual drives and brought under the rubric of a life instinct. After all, narcissism required the recognition of a portion of the ego instincts as libidinal. But, he went on:

The difficulty remains that psychoanalysis has not enabled us hitherto to point to any instincts other than the libidinal ones. That, however, is no reason for our falling in with the conclusion that no others in fact exist. (p. 53)[1]

Taking sadism as a possible representative of the death instinct, admittedly "a displaced one," he reconsidered the polarity of love and hate in object love. Sadism could be thought of as the force motivating hatred and therefore as the sought-for manifestation of the death instinct. However, this rethinking required a modification of the thesis proposed in "Instincts and Their Vicissitudes" that sadism was primary. Sadism had had to be transformed into masochism by being turned around upon the ego before it could be deflected onto objects as secondary sadism. What Freud now proposed was a primary masochism. Once this masochistic drive fused with the life instincts, it was turned away from the ego and onto objects as sadism, although it could return as secondary masochism. If this reanalysis were accepted, a new polarity of life versus death could replace the older one of sexuality versus ego.

From within the framework provided by this polarity, Freud reinterpreted the evidence about conjugation. Conjugation prevented senescence because the exchange introduced new substances into each member of the pair. Cell division in the eggs of the sea urchin was similar. The process normally took place after fertilization, but could be initiated by introducing chemicals into the animal's environment. Both changes were the result of the influx of fresh amounts of stimulus, a view that

tallies well with the hypothesis that the life process of the individual leads for internal reasons to an abolition of chemical tensions, that is to say, to death, whereas union with the living substance of a different individual increases those tensions, introducing what might be described as fresh "vital differences" which must then be lived off.   (p. 55)

Freud now put forward the most astonishing of his paradoxes:

The dominating tendency of all mental life, and perhaps of nervous life in general, is the effort to reduce, to keep constant or to remove internal tension due to stimuli ... a tendency which finds expression in the pleasure principle; and *our recognition of that fact is one of our strongest reasons for believing in the existence of death instincts.*   (pp. 55–56. My emphasis)

The pleasure principle turned out to be entirely in the service of the death instincts! Life instincts introduced unpleasurable tensions—pleasurable relief was caused as the tensions were eliminated by the death instincts. Freud did not seem to notice that the conclusion had two very untoward consequences: the *life* instincts were immediately removed from the domain of the pleasure principle, and it was unclear in what sense the various repetitions were *beyond* the pleasure principle.

Despite his advocacy, Freud had shown only the death instinct had the character of a compulsion to repeat. That attribute was not possessed by the sexual instinctual drive. True, the two germ cells involved in sexual reproduction could be thought of as reenacting the beginning of organic life, but the "essence" of sexual life was a coalescence of two cell bodies that did not repeat an earlier event (p. 56). In whatever way the tendency to coalesce had come about, for example, along Darwinian lines following a first-chance conjugation, the life instincts must have already been in existence by the time it happened. Freud therefore recognized that he retained the death instinct hypothesis at the cost of admitting the life instincts had been present from the beginning (pp. 56–57).

At best he found equivocal support in biology for the complete applicability of his initial premise. He consequently turned to philosophy, there finding a legend that attributed sexual drives to the need to restore an earlier state. In Plato's *Symposium*, Aristophanes was made to tell a story of how homosexual and heterosexual forms of attraction had arisen. Originally there were three types of living creatures: men, women, and a union of the two. Each of these united creatures was doubled, possessing two heads, two sets of limbs, and so on. One day Zeus cut these primeval beings in two, whereupon each half came to desire reunion—one half-man with its other half, one half-woman with its counterpart, and each now single man or woman with its mate. Freud asked whether or not one should follow the lead given by Plato:

and venture upon the hypothesis that living substance at the time of its coming to life was torn apart into small particles, which have ever since endeavoured to reunite through the sexual instincts? that these instincts, in which the chemical affinity of inanimate matter persisted, gradually succeeded, as they developed through the kingdom of the [protozoa] in overcoming the difficulties put in the way of that endeavour by an environment charged with dangerous stimuli—stimuli which compelled them to form a protective cortical layer? that these splintered fragments of living substance in this way attained a multicellular condition and finally transferred the instinct for reuniting, in the most highly concentrated form, to the germ-cells? (p. 58)

At this point Freud broke off his speculations about what it was that the sexual drive sought to restore.

The Grand Thesis Although following Plato's hint might not be thought worth taking seriously, it leads to two things of considerable importance. In the first place, it enables Freud to incorporate into a single thesis all of the developmental events he thought relevant: the historical acquisition of death and life instincts having conservative and restorative aims, the differentiation of the protective shield in elementary organisms, the formation of multicellular creatures, and the specialization of germ cells and soma. It also makes explicit another constraint: sexual instinctual drives could only appear simultaneously with the appearance of the first living organism, and their aim had to be to restore an original unified state. Only a tension created by some catastrophic event that had wrenched them from a larger just-living whole could give them that aim. It was not enough that germ cells "repeat the performance to which they owe their existence," or even that they soberly repeat a "chance conjugation." Neither of these actions could generate the tension required by an instinctual drive; rather, they supposed such tension to exist already.

Freud began his summary of *Beyond the Pleasure Principle* by remarking that if the restoration of an earlier state was a universal characteristic of all instinctual drives, it was not a matter over which the pleasure principle at first had any control. Neither did it follow that restoration and the pleasure principle were opposed. He conceded that he had still to solve the problem of the relation between instinctual repetition and the dominance of the pleasure principle. Adverting to the opening section of his theoretical analysis, he said that he had found that

one of the earliest and most important functions of the mental apparatus is to bind the instinctual impulses which impinge on it, to replace the primary process prevailing in them by the secondary process and convert their freely mobile cathectic energy into a mainly quiescent (tonic) cathexis. While this transformation is taking place no attention can be paid to the development of unpleasure; but this *does not* imply the suspension of the pleasure principle. On the contrary, the transformation occurs *on behalf of* the pleasure principle; *the binding in a preparatory act which introduces and assures the dominance of the pleasure principle.* (Freud 1920a, p. 62. Emphasis altered)

Here the pleasure principle appears to refer to tension reduction or discharge because, after describing how the subjective experience of the sexual act, "the greatest pleasure attainable by us," was "associated with a momentary extinction of a highly intensified excitation," Freud concluded,

The binding of an instinctual impulse would be a preliminary function designed to prepare the excitation for its final elimination in the pleasure of discharge. (p. 62)

He had failed to clarify the relationships between the principles.

Freud's Theses Evaluated

Evaluating Freud's attempt to establish the existence of a death instinct capable of being the opponent of a fused sexual and ego-instinctual drive requires finding the answers to the following seven questions:

1. Were there classes of behavior that lay in some sense beyond the pleasure principle and were they manifestations of a compulsion to repeat?

2. Did the compulsion to repeat have an instinctual basis?

3. Were all instinctual drives historically acquired and conservative, and did they aim to restore an earlier state of affairs?

4. Did organisms die for internal reasons only?

5. What were binding and mastery? How were they related to instinctual processes?

6. What did it mean to say that the activities of the death instinct were *beyond* the pleasure principle?

7. How were the principles such as those of pleasure and constancy related to each other?

Beyond Pleasure?

Freud's classifying repetitions in transference, traumatic neuroses, and children's play as violations of the pleasure principle was based on an entirely subjective clinical judgment. The subjectivity can be seen directly in his dismissal of the "familiar motive forces" yielding pleasure, and indirectly through a comparison of his earlier and later explanations of traumatic and transference repetitions. We have seen that just where the arguments about the alternative explanations in *Beyond the Pleasure Principle* seem most evenly balanced, if not actually against the need to postulate a new motive, Freud announced that his "maturer reflection" required the rejection of pleasure explanations and justified the hypothesis of a compulsion to repeat that overrode the pleasure principle (Freud 1920a, p. 23). No logical grounds are given for the choice, and we can only conclude that it was determined by the subjective weighing of the attractiveness of the new against the plausibility of the old.

Transference repetition, in the sense with which we are concerned, was introduced in the discussion of Dora's case, where it referred to her transference onto Freud of feelings that she had first felt toward important people in her immediate past (Freud 1905a, pp. 116–120). Freud believed, for example, that during Dora's treatment her feelings of being sexually tempted by Herr K. had been revived and transferred onto him. Frightened that she might succumb in the same way that she had unconsciously wished to yield to Herr K., Dora then broke off the treatment (pp. 70 and n. 2, 74, 118–119). Because she had not expressed her feelings directly, Freud described her as having "*acted out* an essential part of her recollections and phantasies instead of reproducing it in the treatment" (p. 119). Transferences of this kind occurred inevitably and had to be detected and overcome because of the obstacles they raised to treatment; only after the transference was resolved would the patient accept the analyst's account of the symptoms or, as Freud put it, arrive at "a sense of conviction of the validity of the connections which have been constructed during the analysis" (p. 117).

Over the next few years he came to consider that the most significant figures in transference were the immediate members of the patient's family, especially the parents (Freud 1912a, p. 100). At the same time he placed more and more emphasis on the substitute function of acting out, that of its replacing supposed memories, emphasis that had the consequence of bringing the repetitive quality of the patient's actions more to the fore. Thus he noted that

the patient does not *remember* anything of what he has forgotten and repressed, but *acts* it out. He reproduced it not as a memory but as an action; he *repeats* it, without, of course, knowing that he is repeating it.   (Freud 1914c, p. 150)

The examples he then gave were the same or very similar to those he cited later in *Beyond the Pleasure Principle*: the defiant child who became the defiant patient, the patient who complained that he could not succeed and who originally felt hopeless in his infantile sexual researches, and so on (p. 150). The compulsive quality of these substitutes for remembering was also noted:

As long as the patient is in the treatment he cannot escape from this *compulsion to repeat*; and in the end we understand that this is his way of remembering.   (p. 150. My emphasis)

Freud did not consider here that the pleasure principle had been overthrown. Quite the opposite. His explanation was based on the *demands* of the pleasure principle:

If someone's need for love is not entirely satisfied by reality, he is bound to approach every new person whom he meets with libidinal anticipatory ideas.... Thus it is a perfectly normal and intelligible thing that the libidinal cathexis of someone who is partly unsatisfied, a cathexis which is held ready in anticipation, should be directed as well to the figure of the doctor. (Freud 1912a, p. 100)

Repetition in the transference was due to these unsatisfied instinctual demands once again asserting themselves, a renaissance not only not at all inconsistent with the pleasure principle but positively demanded by it.

In *Beyond the Pleasure Principle* Freud did not even refer to this original explanation. What he did was redescribe the infantile sexual impulses in a way that made a pleasure-governed explanation virtually impossible. He now said that in the past the child's sexual impulses "could never, even long ago, have brought satisfaction" from the parent. Hence, those drives, having learned "no lesson" from their repeated lack of gratification, produced only unpleasure on revival (Freud 1920a, pp. 20, 21). Is this description of the infantile impulses consistent with the rest of the theory? Do some of the sexual impulses never achieve satisfaction of any sort? It seems unlikely. From the moment of feeding on, at least some of the needs are satisfied fully, others partially. The impulse involving the genitals, such as it is, must share in this satisfaction in some way, if only, for example, through a linkage to the parental imagos concerned in the gratification of the other component drives. Without even partial satisfaction, there would be no occasion for that repression of infantile incestuous wishes that Freud supposed to mark the end of active infantile sexual life. And, once repressed, of course, the wishes were immutable, able to learn nothing; forming part of the system *Ucs.*, "time does not change them in any way" (p. 28). Experiences of an unsatisfying kind could have no effect. Hope always triumphed over experience. To postulate that these infantile drives never produced pleasure before their repression, or that the search for pleasure did not guide their adult strivings, is inconsistent with the theses on infantile sexual satisfactions contained in *The Interpretation of Dreams* and the *Three Essays*, and with some of the early remarks in *Beyond the Pleasure Principle* itself.

Freud at least discussed an alternative explanation for repetition in the traumatic neuroses in *Beyond the Pleasure Principle* before dismissing it, but he glossed over the fact that it was actually an older explanation *of his very own* that he was rejecting. When originally discussing the similarities and differences between traumatic neuroses of war and ordinary psychoneuroses, he explained traumatic repetition by the mechanism of fixation. He said the war neuroses gave

a clear indication that a fixation to the moment of the traumatic accident lies at their root. These patients regularly repeat the traumatic situation in their dreams; where hysteriform attacks occur that admit of an analysis, we find that the attack corresponds to a complete transplanting of the patient into the traumatic situation.   (Freud 1916–1917, pp. 274–275)

As we have seen, he later rejected this mechanism of fixation because he believed it did not explain why the trauma did not occupy the patient's mind during the daytime, its nightly intrusion thereby conflicting with the thesis that dreams attempted to fulfill wishes (Freud 1920a, pp. 13–14).

Absence of a daytime preoccupation is a strange argument. It could be as readily asked why the hysteric's day was not similarly taken up with reminiscences. However, according to Freud, traumatic memories are repressed in the hysteric precisely because their revival would generate unpleasure. As long as the repression is intact, the memories can only manifest themselves as symptoms. A similarly based explanation holds for the traumatic neuroses of war: only during sleep, when repression-censorship is lowered, will the repressed memory of the trauma return. But to say that is to admit that the repressed consists of other than pleasure-seeking drives, a fundamental although implicit assumption of *The Interpretation of Dreams* and the *Three Essays*. Even though Freud says that a fixation-based explanation of the repetition of the trauma shows a misunderstanding of "the nature of dreams" (Freud 1920a, p. 13), it is clear that what he is really asserting is merely the assumption that only pleasure-seeking impulses can be repressed. And that is to assume, of course, what ought to be proved. Otherwise a fixation explanation is perfectly acceptable. The revival of the trauma would generate unpleasure, and only during the nighttime relaxation of repression could it enter consciousness as a dream. We might also note the failure of the explanation that the repetition was a retrospective attempt at mastery. Why should mastery be attempted only in the dream? Here, as with the familiar motives, little or nothing in the logical sense is available to guide one in choosing between explanations based on the pleasure principle and those based on the compulsion to repeat.

Instinctual Repetition?

Freud's attributing an instinctual basis to the compulsion to repeat is based on a similar subjective standpoint. The compulsion, he asserted, proceeds "from the instinctual impulses ... probably inherent in the very nature of the instincts" (Freud 1919d, p. 238) and its manifestations "exhibit to a high degree an instinctual character" (Freud 1920a, p. 35). Any attempted justification of this characterization through an appeal to the demonic quality of the manifestations of the compulsion (that might, if the demonic quality were clearly defined, provide a reasonable argument) founders on the fact that that "quality" is nothing more than another description of the capacity of the compulsion to override the pleasure principle: "The manifestations ... when they act in opposition to the pleasure principle, give the appearance of some 'demonic' force at work" (Freud 1920a, p. 35; cf. 1919d, p. 238). And, of course, the whole attribution simply assumed the repetitions were not governed by the pleasure principle.

Something about the behaviors impressed Freud enough for him to suppose they had an instinctual basis, but what it was we cannot be sure. Clearly it involved a subjective and possibly a very personal reaction rather than logical analysis. When he first introduced the compulsion to repeat in his essay "The Uncanny," he at once linked it to instinctual processes. What that essay contained was not an analysis of instinct but descriptions of different kinds of repetitive phenomena, all of which allegedly created a feeling of uncanniness. In writing about dictionary meanings of the word uncanny he mentioned its equivalence to demonic in both Arabic and Hebrew (Freud 1919d, p. 221). Could it have been through his further equating of demonic with instinctual that uncanny repetitive behaviors came to be characterized as instinctual? Several times Freud expresses an opinion consonant with an equation of this sort; for example, in his picturing of the relation between the ego and the instinctual drives as a rider guiding his horse in the direction in which the horse wanted to go (Masson 1985, Letter of July 7, 1898; cf. Freud 1923b, p. 25, 1933b,

p. 77). But probably the most famous instance is his adoption of Groddeck's view that the mind contains a repository of impersonal forces, an "it," through which we are lived. He adds, "We have all had impressions of the same kind" (Freud 1923b, p. 23, n. 3).

Suppose, nevertheless, that we accept Freud's judgments and assertions, and grant that the repetitions are instinctually based. A problem remains of the sense here of the word instinctual. Certainly the instinctual character of the compulsion to repeat is very different from the instinctual processes defined in "Instincts and Their Vicissitudes." In no way does Freud maintain that repetition of this kind results from the mental representative of some somatic process exerting pressure on the mental apparatus, and having its aim of reducing tensions created continuously within the source of the drive. The compulsion to repeat, it is true, aims at eliminating an excess of excitation, but it does not, as did the earlier defined instinctual drives, generate that tension itself. It operates on the tension caused by external trauma or threatening internal demands. Only in one respect, then, is the compulsion "instinctual."

Death as an Instinctual Drive   The intimate mechanism of the death drive shares this deficiency of aim with the compulsion to repeat. Psychoanalytic critics have made much of the point when drawing attention to the fact that the death instinct and the outwardly directed aggressive drive, which some take to be independent of it, lack one or more of the defining attributes of source aim, object, and impetus or pressure (Fenichel 1935/1954b; E. Bibring 1936/1941; Loewenstein 1940, in Lussier 1972; Simmel 1944; Cohen, cited in Ostow 1957; Pratt 1958; Arlow 1959; Brenner 1971; Holt 1975a, in Dahl 1968; Hanly 1978; Fayek 1980; Lowental 1983; Downey 1984).

Claiming that the source was relatively easy to identify, Gillespie (1971) partly dissented, although his description of it as "the entire body" even if correct, is a little vague. Nevertheless, along with H. Hartmann, Kris, and Loewenstein (1949), Cohen (in Ostow 1957), and Arlow (1959), Gillespie specifically rejected the musculature as the source of an independent aggressive drive. Obviously the musculature can only ever be the *instrument* of a Freudian-type drive.

An aim has occasionally been allowed, usually some kind of tension reduction (Simmel 1944; Arlow 1959; Pleune 1961; Lebovici and Diatkine 1972), but beyond this it is said to be very difficult to specify (H. Hartmann, Kris, and Loewenstein 1949; Cohen, in Ostow 1957). It is generally agreed that the aggressive drive results in pleasurable satisfaction quite independent of any libidinal component with which it might be fused (H. Hartmann, Kris, and Loewenstein 1949; Brenner 1971; Sandler and Joffe 1966; cf. Slap 1967), especially if there is feedback for successful completion of the act (Sandler, in Lussier 1972). Cohen (in Ostow 1957), however, questioned whether, as with libidinal satisfaction, the outcome is pleasurable.

The mechanism of aggressive pleasure is not at all clear. Experimental and other evidence summarized by Holt (1975a) shows the tension-reduction model to fit the aggressive drive even less satisfactorily than sexual and hunger drives. Hanly (1978) also observes that while aggression involves a readiness to respond with a demand for action, it is a reflexlike reaction to an external releasing stimulus lacking the spontaneous and periodic quality of sexuality. Even those who, like Anna Freud (1972), defend the proposition that the earlier criteria of instinctual drive apply to the death instinct and the aggressive drive, nevertheless concede that very little is known about how they apply. Overall, a "considerable gap" exists between the clinical phenomena and the hypothetical source of the death instinct (Lowental 1983).

These limitations, as E. Bibring (1936/1941) pointed out, reflect an essentially changed concept of instinctual drive. In *Beyond the Pleasure Principle* there is no longer a definite process the aim of which is to remove a state of excitation in the organ from which it originated. This has to be, of course. Freud saw the death instinct as acting only to remove the tensions introduced by other drives, a view that has the necessary consequence of preventing the instinct from having a source like those of the life drives. What is true of the death instinct must also be true of its outwardly directed aggressive manifestations. An aggressive drive deriving from the death instinct can have neither source nor aim. One even inclines to the view that the shadow of Freud's changed conceptualization falls very darkly on most of the aggressive drives that have been proposed as alternatives because they also differ markedly from Freud's original concept. If, however, the death drive were to be based on some active process within the organism, as the interpretation of the poisoning of the infusoria and the vague parallel with catabolism begin to suggest, one would have created the not inconsiderable conceptual difficulty of having one active process abolishing a set of tensions by introducing another.

Trauma and Pleasure   At this point we must return to consider the assumption that the repetitions are not governed by the pleasure principle. Trauma, whether arising from external events or from inner demands, causes an excess of stimuli to flood into the mental apparatus where it has to be mastered by being bound. Binding *is* the conversion of freely mobile cathectic energy into mainly quiescent tonic cathexis (Freud 1920a, pp. 31, 62). While it is being accomplished, "no attention can be paid to the development of unpleasure" (p. 62). Traumatic dreams are repeated because binding requires the development of the anxiety not present at the time of the unexpected, original traumatic incident (p. 32). Repetition is also required to master or bind the excessive, freely mobile excitation belonging to the memory traces involved in transference repetition and in children's play (pp. 34–36). Bound energy is finally eliminated "in the pleasure of discharge" (p. 62), an end result reflecting the dominance of the pleasure principle. But must not this be equally true of the preliminary to discharge, the act of binding itself? Freud remarked that there seemed to be "no doubt" that unbound processes caused more intense feelings "in both directions" than their bound counterparts (p. 63).

Although binding of the traumatically produced excitation would raise the level of tonic excitation, the overall level would necessarily be reduced and, with it, unpleasure would also be reduced. Clearly the transformation would be governed by the pleasure principle. The reduction would then have the consequence of placing the compulsion to repeat in the service of the pleasure principle—in fact it would not be necessary to formulate a separate mechanism to explain the repetitions at all. We will see in the next section that many of the criticisms of the compulsion to repeat are based on a view rather like this, although the critics do not support it with any explicit or convincing argument. At least it can be said that they have capitalized on Freud's failure to establish an instinctual basis for the compulsion to repeat.

The superficial identity of the earlier and later meanings of the term instinctual, given by the incorporation into both of a tendency to reduce tension, seems to be *the* reason for Freud's thesis that all instinctual drives seek to restore an earlier state having any plausibility. Elimination of tension necessarily, and in this case trivially, restores the pretension state. Because the death instinct, the compulsion to repeat, Eros, and the instinctual drives as defined earlier are all pictured as eliminating a tension, they all *seem* to share the goal of restoration. But, once again, this is only appearance: in *Beyond the Pleasure Principle* it is only the death instinct and the compulsion to repeat that eliminate tension. Unlike the earlier instinctual drives, even the actions motivated by Eros cannot dispose of its excitation. If the death drive and the compulsion to repeat (as well as Eros, for that matter) are "instinctual," it must be in a manner quite different from other instinctual drives. The vagueness of this difference is the real meaning of E. Bibring's (1936/1941) comment that Freud's revised concept of instinctual drive was that of "a directive or directed 'something' which guided the life processes in a certain direction." Introducing a "something" hardly suggests greater precision, and leaves quite obscure the sense in which the compulsion is related to the death instinct.

Before turning to the third of our questions, I should say that I will not discuss the problems posed by the apparent lack of difference between the conservative and restorative tendencies. Freud must have meant these tendencies to be different—the dictionary meanings alone tell us that they are—yet he gave no instances of conservation that were not, at the same time, attempts to restore an earlier state.

When the instinctual drives are considered on Freud's own terms, the hypothesis that they have been acquired historically, are conservative, and act to restore an earlier state, does not hold for all of them. Freud himself was dissatisfied with his attempt to show how the sexual component of Eros was acquired, which meant also that he could not identify any state that it sought to restore. It is worth noting that the same failures are seen in his account of the ego drives fused within Eros. In fact, when pursuing the logical conclusions of his first premise, he made no attempt at all to inquire whether the ego-drives were covered by it. On the positive side, he did feel it held for the death instinct, although the only concrete example of a drive based on it that he could produce was, as he put it, a displaced one. On logical grounds, even this very limited validation can be disputed.

Freud's argument was that at the very instant that the life-creating tension was introduced into inanimate matter, a countertendency attempting to cancel that tension was also created (Freud 1920a, p. 38). Here he clearly assumed that something like Newton's law of action and reaction applied in the organic sphere. But this assumed what had to be proved. First, why should the force that created living matter behave in the same way as a physical force in the inanimate realm, or a tension "introduced" into an already existing organism? But, suppose there were a countertendency. Freud had to make the further assumption that it was *stronger* than the very force that created it. If death were to predominate over life, the movement to cancel new internal tensions had to be greater than those tensions themselves. Equivalent force and counterforce result only in balanced life and death instincts. This is, of course, another version of the problem of the mechanism of the death instinct: if that drive acts merely by canceling the tensions introduced by Eros, how does it come to be the stronger? To ensure that death was the more powerful, that it did win out eventually, Freud had to assume, unlike Newton, a convenient asymmetry of action and reaction. Even for the death instinct, then, his arguments are not especially convincing.

Historical Acquisition?

Freud's failures to show what the instinctual drives repeated are consonant with the lack of evidence of a more general trend for such biologically determined phenomena as migration, heredity, and embryological development to manifest repetitions of earlier stages. According to Ernest Jones (1953–1957, vol. 3, p. 277), Brun's 1926 review of the biological literature failed to reveal support for the death instinct, and the repetition theme was one of those he considered. Over thirty years later, Pratt (1958) cited devastating refutations, many of them dating from the 1900s, of the recapitulation "law" Freud used in this aspect of his theorizing. In calling on this same "law" to support his thesis that Eros tried to reestablish an earlier herma-phroditic state, Needles (1962) seems to have been unaware of its total rejection by modern biologists.

An Internal Death?

Neither are Freud's arguments in favor of an internal death any more compelling. Indeed, his interpretation of the experiments on the successive generations of pro-tozoa contains a quite fatal error. By attributing to internal factors the deaths of single-cell organisms kept in nutrient admixed with their own waste products, Freud implicitly redefined the organism to include part of its environment. The redefinition subtly shifted attention from processes internal to the organism to those mediating its interaction with the outside world. What were once external factors were necessarily transformed into internal ones. The absurd consequence of this redefinition is, as Silberer (1921) immediately pointed out, that one would have to attribute the death of a deep-sea diver suffocated by his own carbon dioxide in a malfunctioning diving bell to internal factors. If it is illogical to conclude that protozoa died for internal reasons, the observation that conjugation prevents senescence becomes irrelevant, both in itself and as it purports to bear on the thesis that new substances introduced into the organism create tensions capable of countering the death instinct.

About Freud's preparedness to contend that even if protozoa were immortal they might be such simple organisms that any manifestations in them of the death instinct could be hidden by the life instincts, we first note that it is an "arbitrary application to biology," as Silberer (1921) called it, of the latent-manifest distinction of the dream theory. More important, it indicates an unseemly willingness to adopt a position impervious to empirical test. On this point Laplanche observed that just when the reader has "the impression that an examination of the various theses would end up refuting the existence of an *internal* tendency towards death" (1970/1976, p. 110) Freud breaks off his argument to invoke a hidden metaphysical process consistent with his wished-for conclusion. Thus it is not quite true to say, as Pieper and Muslin (1961) did, that Freud simply denied Weismann's conclusions; rather he put himself in a position from which none of the observations on protozoa could have any relevance at all. Szasz's (1952) interpretation of Carrel's experiments on the immor-tality of chicken fibroblasts could be disposed of in the same way. Nor would any-thing come from observations of multicell organisms. As we have seen, to avoid the clear but unwanted conclusion that death was a *late* acquisition, Freud was just as ready to apply the manifest-hidden distinction to them. Only by misconstruing what little evidence there was could he claim that biological fact did not contradict a natural death, and only by retreating to an empirically impervious position could he maintain even the possibility that his second premise held. Here, as elsewhere, it is hard not to agree with Simenauer (1985) that "the stance in which Freud put his arguments" about the death instinct suggests that he was "defending a doubtful proposition."

Finally, it is worth remarking that the validity of neither premise is altered by it being true that inanimate things existed before living ones or even that the aim of life is death. First, in no sense can it be held that these conclusions follow from the premises. Second, even if there were a logical connection, the conclusions are not entailed uniquely. Inanimate matter may be prior and death may be the "aim" of life without there being any commitment to the theses that death is internally caused or that instinctual drives are acquired, conservative, and restorative.

Instinctual Binding and Mastery?

Turning now to the fifth question, it is not at all clear what Freud meant by "binding" and "mastery," the two processes most central to his conceptualization of the consequences of trauma (Wilbur 1941; Flugel 1953; Holt 1962). Were *Beyond the Pleasure Principle* the only thing to go on, binding and mastery would have to be classed as uncharacterized theoretical terms, and Freud's explanations drawing on them would have to be dismissed. Little enlightenment is to be obtained from Freud's other psychological works: neither term is defined explicitly, and their meanings have to be inferred from the relatively few places where they are used. However, using this method of contextual definition, even with the assistance of Holt's (1962) discussion of the distinction between bound and free cathexes, and of the relevant sections of Laplanche and Pontalis (1967/1973), only profound ambiguities result. It might seem possible to clarify the posttraumatic processes through consideration of the ostensibly neurophysiological concepts of the *Project*, but what is illuminated by that work is a contradiction so complete as to defy the possibility of an internally consistent explanation. The difficulty revolves around the question of binding: what is its mechanism, and by which mental system is it carried out?

According to the *Project*, neuronal activity was governed by the principle of neuronal inertia; that is, neurons ordinarily divest themselves of excitation as soon as they are charged with it. When they did retain some or all of the charge they were said to be cathected, and the energy so stored was described as being bound, as having been transformed from a freely mobile state into a quiescent one, and as no longer pressing for discharge. A cathected neuron inhibited the transfer of excitation between other neurons because its own charge of energy attracted to itself the energy passing between the others. The greater its charge, the greater the tendency to diversion. Diversion through such a side cathexis, as Freud called it, minimized or even inhibited transfer completely. What was true for a single neuron also held for a complete system of well-facilitated neurons possessing a more or less permanent store of energy, such as Freud believed the ego to be. The ego formed out of those neurons connected with the sources of endogenous excitation. By repeatedly supplying energy to them, the instinctual sources created the facilitations and provided the store of energy for the secondary process function of inhibition-by-diversion. The primary process tendency to press for free discharge was thus prevented or attenuated by the cathexis of the nucleus of neurons of the ego attracting incoming excitation to itself and binding it there (Freud 1950/1954, *Project*, part I, sections 14 and 15).

Although by the time *Beyond the Pleasure Principle* was written Freud had long since overtly discarded his purportedly neurophysiological mode of theorizing, it is clear that he thought similar mechanisms to be active in the binding that followed a traumatic event. However, what is missing from his account of the traumatic event are even moderately intelligible descriptions of the stemming of the incoming flood of excitation, of the mechanism of binding, of the mental systems in which it occurs, and of the eventual disposal of the excess excitation.

Binding as Damming   Consider first the halting of the flow of traumatically produced excitation. Freud nowhere says that a countercathectic "dam" is created to stop this flood of traumatic excitation. What he does do, in the paragraph immediately preceding the one on traumatic neuroses, is outline such a mechanism for coping with physical pain. One therefore has the impression that he means it to apply to trauma also.

Let us assume that he means that something resembling the pain countercathexis is constructed in the traumatic neuroses. If a dam made by charging the components of the mental apparatus lying in the path of the excitation with a higher level of energy were to bind the excitation, what need would there be for the dream repetition of the trauma? Freud's answer could not be that the excitation would be gradually disposed of by successive repetitive discharge, because for him repetition preceded binding. Repetition generated the anxiety that allowed binding to take place.

A comparison of the bases of the excitation in traumatic neuroses, children's play, and transference repetitions leads to a more reasonable answer. In transference and children's play, instinctual sources were supposed to cause excitation to well up continuously. In both instances, what was virtually a permanent quantity would demand to be bound. In traumatic neuroses, however, the trauma acted only the once, not even leaving behind the kinds of tissue and other changes that in pain continue to generate excitation in the absence of the stimulus itself. A store of excitation has to be created in traumatic neuroses equivalent to the instinctual sources in the other repetitions. Binding in these disorders is therefore best thought of as being of two kinds: the creation of a dam by an improvised countercathexis to stem the flood of excitation, and a later binding through repetitive discharge. Clearly, binding of the first kind does not require explanation by either the compulsion to repeat or the death instinct.

Binding by Repetition It is only for this second kind of binding that new principles have even to be considered. How, then, is it carried out? Freud's description is so vague that it is possible to read it, as Holt (1962) does to some extent, as implying that it is somehow effected through an anticathectic energy. The use of the terms binding and cathection elsewhere oblige us to assume, however, that energy is supplied to some part of the mental apparatus that does the binding. Fleshing out the bones of *Beyond the Pleasure Principle* with some of the ideas from the *Project* suggests how this might be done. According to the *Project*, binding is initiated by the ego when external or internal excitation seeks to recathect the memory traces of an experience whose revival would cause unpleasure. The attempt liberates a small quantity of unpleasure that, after being experienced by the ego as anxiety, signals the ego to cathect or hypercathect those systems able to provide a side cathexis. The ego takes the threatening cathexis into itself and, by so preventing its transfer to the memory traces, avoids unpleasure (Freud 1950/1954, *Project*, part I, sections 14 and 18, part III, section 3).

If a store of excitation were "dammed up" in traumatic neuroses its effects, although not periodic, would be like those of an ordinary instinctual source, but more intense. Excitation attempting to escape the control of the countercathexis would seek to recathect the memory of the traumatic event. The attempt would generate anxiety and the ego would act to reestablish control. During the day, when the ego was fully cathected, one would suppose this mode of defense to succeed each time. Only with the normal withdrawal of the ego's cathexes during sleep would the traumatic memory be recathected completely. Considerable anxiety would be generated, the hallucinating sleeper would wake, and the discharge would be terminated. Any excitation taken up by the ego in the process would necessarily be small in quantity and readily disposed of in associative activity. What this mechanism seems to explain admirably is that the memory is reexperienced, that the repetition occurs during sleep, and that those repeated partial discharges eventually result in the dream disappearing altogether. Traumatic dreams do have some tendency to fade in this way, a fact that has led some psychoanalysts to interpret dream repetition as attempted self-cure.

Provided that one makes a number of other rather doubtful assumptions, this outline explanation can be readily extended to the repetition of children's play and transference. First, one has to assume that what is being repeated in those activities will also generate unpleasure. If we make that assumption, we account for Freud's insisting, against all the sense of his previous writing, that the attempted libidinal gratification of his patients had never produced pleasure in childhood. Second, one has to assume that special features about the transference promote behavioral, day-time repetition. Third, it has to be assumed that, although it is unpleasant, the child's repetitive play is not experienced as such. Whereas the first of these assumptions may be only cavalier and not unreasonable, the second is clearly ad hoc, and the last flies in the face of observation.

My point applies to the explanation of all three repetitions. There is no conceptual gap to be filled by a compulsion to repeat. True, the repetitions are of unpleasant experiences, but they are nevertheless motivated by attempts at reducing an excess of excitation, reductions that have to be thought of as guided by the pleasure principle. The attempted recathection of the memory trace of the unpleasant experience succeeds only in the peculiar circumstance of the ego being weakened, caught off guard so to speak, and even then the discharge is only a limited one. Repetition is thus brought about by the ego's interference with the more or less continuous pressure for discharge. Repetition indicates that all is well with the ego and that the pleasure principle is still able to ensure that binding is carried out. What I criticize here is not what Freud said, of course, but what it seems reasonable to suppose that he meant. Should it be shown that my criticisms have been directed at a dam of straw, it must be remembered that Freud actually says nothing coherent about binding, mastery, or disposal. Either the compulsion to repeat is not at all necessary or we do not know how it fits into his pseudoexplanations.

Death beyond Pleasure?

In one sense our sixth question, that about the relation of the death instinct to the pleasure principle, is quickly answered: Freud began *Beyond the Pleasure Principle* by affirming an absolute opposition between them but ended it by placing the principle in the service of the instinct. Although this change in meaning is complex enough, he added complexity by later reviving the opposition but finally leaving the question unresolved. It is necessary, therefore, to consider in some detail the shifts in his argument. Establishing what he really meant in this connection is no trifling semantic exercise. What is at issue is the very basis of the revised instinct theory, as well as a good deal of the structural theory that follows it.

Freud begins by arguing that the pleasure principle is violated by the repetition of certain unpleasant experiences, experiences that reveal tendencies beyond the principle, tendencies "more primitive than it, and independent of it" (Freud 1920a, p. 17). Here one naturally takes him to mean that the tendencies really do oppose the pleasure principle, or at least set it to one side. His further remarks justify this supposition. He asks us to take courage and assume that the behaviors could be governed by such a mechanism (p. 22), which, he goes on to hypothesize, would seem more primitive, elementary, and instinctual than the principle "which it over-rides" (p. 23). "Beyond" here means "in opposition to."

Our understanding is soon shaken. Repetitive dreams reveal the presence of a function that, although independent of and more primitive than the pleasure principle, does not contradict it (p. 32) or even oppose it, but simply disregards it and then only "to some extent" (p. 35). Freud introduces another qualification, one we noted elsewhere, by saying that it is only when the compulsion acts against the pleasure principle that its demonic quality is manifest (p. 35). The phrasing implies that under some circumstances there is no opposition. Transference phenomena are not so qualified; there the compulsion evidently disregards the pleasure principle "in every way" (p. 36). But when Freud discusses binding, the opposition is completely obliterated. Whether in connection with a traumatic event or the instinctual impulses in play and transference, binding is a preliminary act that *introduces* the pleasure principle to ensure its dominance (p. 62). At the end of his search, Freud found nothing beyond the pleasure principle. Indeed, it was even *in the service of* the death instinct. Opposition to it by either the compulsion to repeat or the mechanism of binding could only be appearance, not reality.

Freud did not adhere closely to this identification of death with the pleasure principle. In "The Economic Problem of Masochism" (Freud 1924b), he seemed to revive a qualified opposition. There he distinguished three principles governing mental life: the reality principle, the pleasure principle, and the Nirvana principle. The first was unchanged in meaning, the second was considerably modified, and the last was new. The term Nirvana principle was adopted from Barbara Low (1920, p. 75), who used it to describe the desire of the newborn to return to its mother's womb, where all its wishes had been fulfilled. Freud gave it an altogether different meaning. It was the psychological equivalent of the principle of neuronal inertia, the tendency of the mental apparatus to reduce to nothing or to keep as low as possible the quantities of excitation flowing in on it (Freud 1924b, p. 159). He explicitly aligned the Nirvana principle with the death instinct, and the pleasure principle with the libido. Although, according to the revised instinct theory, the death instinct and Eros had to be in real opposition, the conflict between the principles expressing them was muted. The reality and pleasure principles were but modifications of the Nirvana principle: the former brought about by the demands of reality, the latter because the life instincts seized on a share in the regulation of the processes of life. These origins meant that

None of these three principles is actually put out of action by another. As a rule they are able to tolerate one another, although conflicts are bound to arise occasionally from the fact of the differing aims that are set for each.   (Freud 1924b, p. 161)

In the two other places where he mentioned the matter explicitly, an antagonistic relation is again portrayed, and rather more strongly (Freud 1923c, pp. 117–118, 1933b, p. 106). However, in his very last remarks, he again left the question open:

The consideration that the pleasure principle demands a reduction, at bottom the extinction perhaps, of the tensions of instinctual needs (that is, *Nirvana*) leads to *the still unassessed relations between the pleasure principle and the two primal forces, Eros and the death instinct.* (Freud 1940a, p. 198. Last emphasis mine)

Ultimately the sense in which the activities of the death instinct were beyond the pleasure principle was not clear. This is obvious despite the glib description by Ducey and Galinsky (1973) of Freud's position in "The Economic Problem of Masochism" as one from which he never deviated.

Principled Relations?

When trying to understand how the principles of pleasure, constancy, and inertia are related to one another, and so answering our last question, the first thing to note is the fundamental contradiction in all of Freud's formulations of the dominant tendency of mental life. Consider, for example, how it was stated toward the end of *Beyond the Pleasure Principle*:

The dominating tendency of mental life, and perhaps of nervous life in general, is the effort *to reduce, to keep constant* or *to remove* internal tension due to stimuli.   (Freud 1920a, pp. 55–56. My emphasis)

Reducing excitation, keeping it constant, and removing it are not synonymous, but, when treated here and elsewhere as if they were, the pleasure principle, which corresponds to the reduction of stimulation, is necessarily equated with two different principles, one that maintains a constant level of excitation and one that removes the excitation completely. Once the principles have been equated it is impossible to derive oppositions between them. Nor can it be the case that the instinctual tendencies expressed by the principles are different from one another.

Neural Confusion

How had this conceptual impasse, if that is what it is, been reached? And does it have a wider significance? I believe that Freud's first step, an imperceptible one at the time, was taken in the *Project* when he severed the tension-reduction function from the maintenance of a low level of excitation, thereby transforming the reduction function into a primary tendency that now tried to dispose of excitation completely. He took the second step in "Formulations on Two Principles of Mental Functioning" when, as a consequence of the introduction of the concept of narcissism, the sphere of influence of the pleasure principle was extended to regulate excitation arising from *external* as well as internal sources. Little distinction could thenceforth be made between the principles of pleasure and inertia. The impasse was reached in "Beyond the Pleasure Principle," where the restriction of the death instinct to removing tensions introduced by other drives necessarily equated the aim of the death drive with those of the two principles. I will now examine these three steps in some detail. In doing so, I have explicitly adopted a vocabulary that equates the pleasure principle with reductions in momentary increases in excitation, the constancy principle with the maintenance of some level of excitation, and the principle of inertia or Nirvana with the elimination of excitation altogether. Although this does some small violence to Freud's usage, it allows for considerable clarification of the issues.

In chapter 7 I pointed out that by 1888 Freud had analyzed hysterical symptoms in terms of increases in the stable amounts of excitation distributed over the nervous system. By the end of 1892, in his correspondence with Breuer and the sketches for the *Preliminary Communication*, he envisaged the nervous system as maintaining some more or less constant level of excitation by reducing or disposing of those quantities of excitation that increased that level:

The nervous system endeavours to keep constant something in its functional relations that we may describe as the "sum of excitation." It puts this precondition of health into effect by disposing associatively of every sensible accretion of excitation or by discharging it. (Freud 1892, pp. 153–154. Emphasis altered)

Although this self-regulating view of the nervous system is set out most explicitly by Breuer in his contribution to *Studies on Hysteria* (Breuer and Freud 1895, pp. 198–201), it obviously also underlies Freud's lecture of January 1893 (Freud 1893a, pp. 36–37) and several other of his works. From the paper comparing organic and hysterical paralyses, as well as from the synoptic statement of the mechanism of the neuroses contained in Draft D of the Fliess correspondence, and the discussion of the effects of exogenous excitation in Draft E, it is clear that throughout 1893 and the first half of 1894 Freud continued to hold the view that neuroses were disturbances of equilibrium brought about by surplus quantities of excitation that could not be dealt with by the normal mechanism of reducing the excitation to its previous level (Freud 1893b, pp. 171–172; Masson 1985, Draft D, possibly of May 1894, Draft E, possibly of June 1894). But, during the five and a half years beginning about mid-1894, the particular self-regulatory model implied in these later sources disappears almost completely from Freud's writings. What replaces it is only partly compatible with the older view of the nervous system.

It is in Freud's *Project* that we first find the rather different conception of the nervous system. From the Fliess correspondence it is evident that from April to September 1895 Freud was consumed with developing a theory of mental functioning based on quantitative considerations, "a sort of economics of nerve forces" (Masson 1985, Letter of May 25, 1895; cf. Letters of Apr. 27, 1895, June 12, 1895, Aug. 6, 1895, Aug. 16, 1895). His aim was to represent psychological processes as determinate states of specifiable material particles. The particles were to be the neurons, and a quantity of some kind subject to the general laws of motion was to distinguish the system's activity from rest (Freud 1950/1954, *Project*, part I, section 1). He first focused attention on the movement of excitation within the nervous system. "Processes such as stimulus, substitution, conversion, and discharge directly suggested the conception of neuronal excitation as quantity in a state of flow." The movement of quantity was explained by assuming that each neuronal element of the system had a tendency to divest itself of the quantities of energy that impinged on it. This principle of inertia, as Freud called it, explained movement within the system as a whole by movement within each of the system's components. The first conclusion he drew was that the principle of inertia made the reflex intelligible: "the principle provides the motive for reflex movement." The difference between this conception and Breuer's is obvious. No longer was the reflex a simple mediator of the organism's relation with its environment, as it was with breathing and thermoregulation. Removal of excitation was now the primary aim: "this discharge represents the primary function of the nervous system."

A further or secondary function was also assumed, one from which Freud tried to explain how the specific actions leading to drive satisfaction were selected. This secondary function obliged the nervous system "to abandon its original trend to inertia (that is, to bringing the level [of quantity] to zero)" and to maintain a store of quantity. Nevertheless, the original trend persisted:

modified into an endeavour at least to keep the [quantity] as low as possible and to guard against any increase of it—that is, to keep it constant. (Freud 1950/1954, *Project*, part I, section 1)

partial consequence of the eclipse of the first theory of instinctual drives. No longer was it necessary to derive opposition between love and hate. That had become a primary fact in the new theory, and the role of the pleasure principle could be correspondingly diminished in importance. With inertia placed more centrally, Freud could now allow constancy and pleasure to resume something like the roles they were given in the *Project* and *The Interpretation of Dreams*. Indeed, the term "principle of constancy" was brought out of storage for the first time in over twenty-five years; once more it was responsible for maintaining some degree of tension; once more it endeavored "to keep the quantity of excitation present ... as low as possible or at least to keep it constant" (Freud 1920a, p. 9); and once more the pleasure principle had the role of regulating the course of mental events. Invariably these were set in motion by an unpleasurable tension, but the direction given them resulted in a final outcome of lowered tension—unpleasure was thus avoided and pleasure produced (p. 7). But, unlike the references in "Formulations" and the *Introductory Lectures*, the pleasure principle was not described here as a governing or main tendency of mental life.

Although Freud set out the principles of constancy and pleasure on the first three pages of *Beyond the Pleasure Principle*, he delayed reintroducing that of inertia until some eight or nine pages from the end, after he closed the argument for the death instinct. I think it is not an accident that the precise point of its reappearance is immediately after he interpreted conjugation as introducing new tensions and so countering the tendency of the death instinct to cancel all tensions (pp. 55–56). The way the principle was reintroduced is also worth examining: it is part of a redefinition of what Freud called "the dominating tendency of mental life, and perhaps of nervous life in general" (pp. 55–56), but a definition that makes no explicit reference to the pleasure principle. The tendency consisted of the efforts "to reduce, to keep constant or to *remove internal tension due to stimuli*" (pp. 55–56. My emphasis). Elimination of excitation (removal) was now included beside the maintenance and reduction functions. Nor could Freud have done it in any other way. This tendency to remove tension was not quite the same as the original. Had it been, the other two principles might have been deduced from it in the same relatively uncomplicated way as in the *Project* and *The Interpretation of Dreams*. However, the new concept of instinctual drive made those derivations impossible. Elimination of excitation was now much more than a simple expression of inertia—it was *the* mode of action of the death instinct.

Further, because the death instinct acted only in this way, and because the pleasure principle regulated the reduction of tension, it followed that the pleasure principle had no control over the libido, but regulated only the activities of the death instinct.

Freud was therefore practically driven to the paradoxical conclusion that one of his "strongest reasons" for believing in the death instinct was that inertia expressed itself in the pleasure principle (pp. 55–56), and even the pleasure of orgasm could be interpreted as coming under the death instinct. "The greatest pleasure attainable by us," as he described it, was associated with "a momentary extinction of a highly intensified excitation" that reflected the "final elimination" of that tension "in the pleasure of discharge" (p. 62). Freud was thus forced to conclude that the pleasure principle was a tendency operating in the service of a function concerned with "the most universal endeavor of all living substance—namely to return to the quiescence of the inorganic world" (p. 62).

In "The Economic Problem of Masochism" he rejected this "unhesitating" identification of the principle of inertia with a pleasure principle that allowed Eros to escape its control: "such a view cannot be correct" (Freud 1924b, p. 160). But his belated correction was at an enormous theoretical cost. First, he had to jettison one of his oldest assumptions, namely, that increases and decreases in quantities of excitation caused feelings of pleasure and unpleasure. While still claiming that such quantitative variation had "a great deal" to do with those feelings, pleasure and unpleasure really depended on some other unknown characteristic "which we can only describe as a qualitative one" (p. 160). Second, Freud tried vainly to align the principle of inertia with the death instinct and the pleasure principle with the life instincts. The life instincts were assigned the role of modifying the principle of inertia, now properly called the Nirvana principle, into the pleasure principle. They had "seized upon a share in the regulation of the processes of life" (p. 160). What that seizure consisted of, and how it brought about the modification, was no more described than were the qualitative peculiarities in the variation of excitation that were now supposed to produce pleasure and unpleasure. The correction placed completely uncharacterized processes at the center of the theory. Explanations drawing on the pleasure-unpleasure relation or that involved the differential regulation of Eros and the death instinct could be nothing more than shadows of explanations.

Solution by Reformulation?

Is a way out of the impasse provided by adopting one or other of the reformulations of the principles, the instincts, or the relations between them suggested by other psychoanalytic theorists? For example, is anything to be gained by separating the instincts from the principles? Although we found no particularly close connection, Loewenstein (1940) said Freud's formulations of the regulative principles were "hampered" by too close an association with the instincts. Two attempts, although only partial, were made to prise them apart. Simmel (1944) distinguished Nirvana from the state produced by the destructive impulse, and Katan (1966) similarly separated it from death but retained the connection of pleasure with sexuality. Ernest Jones's (1935–1936) very peculiar proposition had the compulsion to repeat damping down external stimuli and the pleasure principle attenuating internal instinctual drives. He did not accept the death instinct, of course, but if his suggestion were to be applied to a context including it, the effect would not only be to do away with the evidence for something beyond the pleasure principle, but would make it difficult to conceptualize the internal processes involved in destructiveness. Apart from completely rewriting the theory of instinctual drives, Simmel's and Katan's revisions simply do not go far enough for one to estimate what their more limited consequences would be. The programmatic statement of Wolfenstein (1985) needs little consideration. He says he wants to argue for aggression and the Nirvana principle as derivatives of the clash between the pleasure and reality principles, but I find nothing in his paper that constitutes more than assertion.

Reformulations of the three principles themselves have also been suggested, although obviously not for the reasons adduced above. Usually on the grounds that the phenomenology of the two affects differ (Jacobson 1953), it has been proposed to differentiate a pleasure principle from an unpleasure principle (Eidelberg 1960, 1962; Kanzer and Eidelberg 1960; Schur 1966a, pp. 125–152, in Gifford 1964; Schur and Ritvo 1970) and the need for the differentiation is at least implicit in the acknowledged facts that the physiological mechanisms of the two states are distinct, involving rather more than increases or decreases in the amount of excitation or some rhythmical quality of it (Brunswick 1960; Needles 1964, 1969; Rangell 1967; Dahl 1968). Although this suggestion would probably resolve the Nirvana-death instinct difficulty, it would also require a fundamental recasting of the whole of Freudian theory. Every process logically dependent on the notion of tension reduction, including that of the wish as it is currently formulated, would have to be thought out afresh (G. S. Klein 1967; Holt 1975a). Obviously any such recasting of the theory would have to dispose of Freud's abiological characterization of the principle of inertia, both in itself and in relation to his picture of the primitive organism. This abiological trend has frequently come under attack. H. Hartmann (1948), for example, indicted the tendency to reduce excitation to a minimal level, and what he called the principle of constancy, as creating nonadaptive equilibria. Followed through, this judgment requires both principles to be given up. Needles (1969) went part of the way along this path in separating the tendency of "the psychic apparatus ... to avoid excitation of all sorts" (which he called constancy) from the pleasure principle and abandoning the former.

Against this has to be weighed the attempts made by such writers as Alexander (cited in E. Jones 1953–1957, vol. 3, p. 276), Ostow (1958), and Saul (1958) to bolster the concepts of a death instinct and a principle of inertia by appeals to the second law of thermodynamics. The appeals seem to be quite misguided because they are similarly abiological. According to the law, the entropy of a system, usually expressed as a ratio of the quantity of heat in the system to its temperature, tends to increase with time. Entropy increases as energy redistributes itself within the system as an equilibrium is reached, and would increase when living organism died. However, the death instinct interpretation of the second law must be rejected. It rests on too odd a set of assumptions, including that the organism together with its environment constitutes a closed system rather than an open one, that mental energy is homologous with physical energy, and that either or both of Freud's Nirvana and Fechner's state of absolute stability is equivalent to a state of zero entropy (Penrose 1931; Kapp 1931; Spring 1934; Szasz 1952; Laplanche and Pontalis 1967/1973, pp. 341–347). As Penrose (1931) concluded, "Taking all these things into consideration it must be regarded as very doubtful whether the assertion that in the living organism entropy tends to increase is true, or even has any meaning at all."

Brenner (1979) has since argued that simply because psychic energy is a derivative of a drive it cannot be treated as physical energy. The belief that it can be "leads to such absurdities as trying to apply the law of entropy to psychology or to questioning whether the mind is what physicists call an open energy system or a closed energy system." Were these problems to be overcome, there is, from Freud's point of view, a disastrous and unpleasant theoretical consequence, that Bernfeld and Feitelberg (1931) identified in their generally sympathetic discussion of the death instinct and the second law. A death instinct deducible from the second law leaves no place for a counterforce such as Eros: "The theory of energy has no cognizance of any partner, rival or opponent where the law of entropy is concerned." A successful appeal to the second law thus saves one instinct and one principle at the cost of having to discard all the others (cf. Adrian 1923).

We may note in passing that this is not to say that some of Fechner's ideas about the different kinds of stability might not be consistent with the second law—after all he was a physicist. However, his views on living systems were a good deal more complex than Freud's. Complete permanent immobility was only *one* of the four grades of stability that Fechner recognized; he did *not* believe that it applied to the biological realm; nor does it seem to have been the state to which processes governed by his version of the pleasure principle tended (Penrose 1931; Flugel 1953; Wilbur 1941; Ellenberger 1956; Laplanche and Pontalis 1967/1973, pp. 322–325). Consequently Foxe's (1943) rather curious analysis of the relation between Freud's and Fechner's principles may be disregarded: it rests on the proposition that Fechner proposed only one state of stability. We may similarly dismiss Needles's (1962, 1964) attribution to Fechner of a constancy principle in which stimulus tension was equated with unpleasure and stimulus extinction with pleasure.

Returning to my main theme, I believe that the most powerful of the critiques of the principles and their relation to the instincts can be extracted from the thesis of Laplanche and Pontalis (1967/1973, pp. 341–349) and later expanded by Laplanche (1970/1976, pp. 112–126). According to them, the problems result from Freud's faulty translation of psychological observations into biological terms. They observe that the first theoretical antithesis in Freud's work is between conscious and unconscious processes. Characteristics of the latter—stimulus, substitution, conversion, discharge, and, according to the authors, displacement—suggested excitation as quantity in a state of flow, a conception that in turn suggested, or was explained just as directly by, the principle of neuronal inertia (Freud 1950/1954, part I, section 1). Secondary processes were determined by modifications to the first principle that allowed for a store of excitation to be built up and maintained at a constant level. Discharge was thereby delayed. On the one side, then, is the principle of neuronal inertia, primary process, and freely mobile energy pressing for immediate discharge, and on the other is the principle of constancy, secondary process, and bound energy. According to these authors this fundamental antithesis finds expression as successive moments or syntheses as the basic contradiction works itself out during the development of Freud's theory: conscious versus unconscious, repressed versus nonrepressed, ego versus sexuality, and life versus death.[2]

While some of the inconsistencies in Freud's theoretical statements reflect the very real difficulty of conceptualizing such a complex dialectical process, there is also a real contradiction in the concepts themselves. Neuronal inertia, Laplanche and Pontalis maintain, is an abiological concept totally at variance with the requirements of any living system, and quite unsuited as a foundation stone for a general theory of psychology. No doubt motivated by the common nineteenth-century tendency to extend the principles of physics as widely as possible, it is based on the faulty method of translating behavioral data directly into physiological terms. For example, displacement of ideas in dreams is called displacement of quantities of neural excitation, and these are further translated into the physical terms of displacement of cathexes of physical energy.

Once critical attention is focused on this method of translation and the developmental sequence of Freud's thought, it is possible to resolve the problem of the principles in relation to the instincts. Regulation of the life instincts is to be attributed to the principle of constancy and the death instinct to the pleasure principle. Pleasure, Nirvana, and neuronal inertia all require the reduction of internal tension to zero. Resolution of the more fundamental contradiction requires abandoning those parts of Freud's theory that simply renamed psychological processes as physiological, and rejecting the whole tendency to infer the purported biological characteristics of organisms from clinical observations of patients.

The Primitive Organism

One thing that would certainly not be missed, were the latter suggestions adopted, is Freud's theoretical fiction of the primitive organism being brought into existence by energies impinging from outside. It is not necessary to argue, as A. J. Levin (1951) and Holbrook (1971, pp. 71–72) have done, that Freud's picture of the primitive organism surrounded on all sides by powerful and threatening energies reflects some personal peculiarity, perhaps even Freud's basic fear of the world. Support for the slogan that protection from stimuli is more important than their reception (and its corollary of the organism's tendency to avoid stimuli) is found in views common among late nineteenth-century writers on child psychology. Bernfeld (1925/1929) was to make this view central to his psychoanalytic account of the developmental process. Of course, at no time was it fully consonant with any wide range of observations on infants and children.

Today, in the light of the many studies documenting the active tendency of very young infants to seek out stimulation, it merely seems quaint. Although Bernfeld, and Fenichel (1935/1954b) later, reconciled, but not without difficulty, this craving for stimulus with Freud's principles, most analysts and nonanalysts alike saw it as quite contrary to the organism's supposed tendency to avoid stimulation (Nuttin 1956; Needles 1962, 1964, 1969; Holt 1975a). Even the nervous system does not act to divest itself of excitation—it is spontaneously active almost all the time, and its activity is modulated by external and internal stimulation (Holt 1975a; MacCarley and Hobson 1977). No resolution of this matter is possible along the lines suggested by Shapiro (1981): "The concept of the stimulus barrier must also be complemented by knowledge about the infant's stimulus seeking propensity." Shapiro seems not to see that the mere recognition of that propensity is a fatal blow to Freud's basic premise.

What is demanded by these largely psychoanalytical criticisms of the principles and the life and death instincts is nothing less than a complete revision of the whole of Freud's theory. The only other way is to return to the earlier definition of instinctual drive and find a source, aim, and object for the destructive impulses, so allowing them to introduce tensions of their own that challenge the tensions generated by Eros. And that conceptualization itself contradicts the most central thesis of *Beyond the Pleasure Principle*, which sought to find destructiveness in the very force that created life out of inanimate matter.

Alternatives to Death Instinct Explanations

Three questions have to be answered by those who reject the revised instinctual drive theory: what causes the repetition of unpleasurable behavior? what are the sources of sadism and masochism? and what is the basis of aggressiveness? The answers are relevant in different ways. Formally adequate alternative accounts of sadism, masochism, and aggressiveness do not challenge the death instinct. They simply restrict its explanatory scope. On the other hand, denying that the repetitions are peculiar questions the evidential base of the death instinct completely and so strikes at the heart of Freud's theory. The alternatives are also worth examining because of the possibility that they resolve the conceptual difficulties we have so far encountered.

Alternative Causes of Repetition

The psychoanalytic literature contains two outstanding features on the compulsion to repeat. The first is its one-sidedness—either some kind of more or less positive regulatory role is placed in the foreground or the more negative, even maladaptive, compulsive qualities are concentrated on. Rarely are both aspects considered in relation to each other. The second is that theoretical positions on the compulsion to repeat are relatively independent of the role given the pleasure principle or even whether or not the theorist accepts the death instinct. Two responses to Freud's new concepts may serve as illustrations.

Within a few years of the publication of *Beyond the Pleasure Principle*, Alexander (1925) interpreted the compulsive quality as revealing a fixation on methods of tension reduction and mastery. Although at that time he accepted the death instinct, he virtually dissociated repetition from it. It was not "in the strict sense of the term a repetition" but more a protracted attempt "to master stimuli or instinct-excitations." Reich's discussion was from the other position. Skeptical about the death instinct, he saw the compulsion as reflecting the adhesiveness of the libido, that is, its degree of attachment to previously encountered fixation points, and as expressing itself through the pleasure principle (W. Reich 1926, 1932/1950).

Ego Mastery or Fixation?   Ambiguities in the formulation of the role of the ego, in characterizing the pressure of instinctual drive and traumatic stimuli, and in describing binding and mastery make these peculiarities possible. Where the emphasis is placed on pressure from the drive or the trauma, the fixated and conservative, usually instinctual, qualities tend to be given prominence. On the other hand, where the ego's role is stressed, the compulsion is seen as aiming at mastery through binding and abreaction. There is also a shadowy middle ground in which pressure and regulation are uneasily combined.

Two papers by Waelder define the ends of the continuum. In the first he suggested that all psychic phenomena resulted from the combination of a *vis à tergo* of the instinctual forces with a pull from the ego. He found it difficult to decide how much each contributed to the repetitions; the two forces could be separated "only by abstraction" (Waelder 1930/1936). The difficulty may have been the reason for his failing to analyze the two processes further in his later paper (Waelder 1932/1933). The result was that the middle ground, which he himself took up, provided only a vague stage on which the other more one-sided interpretations figured.

Take as an example E. Bibring's (1943) very influential analysis. After identifying the two components in much the same way as Waelder, Bibring found some role for the ego, although he concluded by adopting a fixation view. The seeds of this outcome were laid in an earlier paper in which E. Bibring (1936/1941) classed all of Freud's clinical examples of repetition as instances of what he called a tendency to abreaction in fractional amounts. It is rather strange that he identified this tendency with a regulatory principle that arrested and bound stimulus energies by bringing them from a state of activity to a state of rest. Bibring implied that the ego worked according to this same regulative principle. In his second paper he distinguished two main meanings of the repetition compulsion. The first was "the expression of the 'inertia' of living matter, of the conservative trend to maintain and repeat intensive experiences" and the second was "a regulating mechanism with the task of discharging tensions caused by traumatic experiences after they have been bound, in fractional amounts" (E. Bibring 1943). He related only the repetitive or reproductive tendency to Freud's examples and then only to acting out in transference. None of the remainder of Freud's repetitions fell under it. Neither did they illustrate the second type of repetition, that devoted to the restitution or reestablishing of the pretraumatic situation. In words reminiscent of Charcot, Janet, and Breuer, Bibring described countercathexis as "a foreign body ... placed in the psychic organism." The imprisoned excitation periodically broke through the countercathexis and was then successively discharged in fractional amounts until complete restitution had been achieved.

Although Bibring inextricably linked the repetitive or reproductive function with the restitutive, he was unable to develop his idea. He thought that what he called the mechanical trend toward abreaction was not consistent with active attempts at mastery and repetition and those attempts did not always lead to tension reduction. He concluded that the compulsion was a property of the instinctual drives themselves that tended to fixate pleasurable and unpleasurable experiences alike. Fixation was a facilitation between the instinctual drive and the impressions occurring in association with it. Whenever the drive built up the tendency existed for the memory trace to be revived. The compulsion was thus "an instinctual automatism," and its only significant role was in maintaining impressive experiences regardless of their pleasurable or unpleasurable qualities. The ego's role was restitutive. Its task was to find ways in which the compulsion could be managed. With the responsibility so allotted, Bibring proposed dropping the phrase "restitutive tendency" altogether. Because he did not see that the ordinary ego function of inhibition was all that was required for the fractional discharge of the restrained traumatic excitation, his analysis ended in a complete separation of the two aspects of the function.

Fixation   In slightly different ways, Hendrick (1934, p. 300), French (1933, 1937), and Nunberg (1932, 1951, 1932/1955), who all took very different positions on the death instinct, also emphasized that compulsion resulted from a previous fixation or facilitation. Indeed, French (1937) claimed that its more familiar manifestations were "best understood in terms of the conditioned reflex principle." Fenichel's explanation of transference repetitions also belongs here. Unpleasurable repetitions were due to a discharge or binding tendency that was "stronger than the pleasure principle" (Fenichel 1935/1954b). The individual strove again and again for satisfaction but "again and again the ego responds to this striving ... which at a former time caused anxiety" (Fenichel 1938/1941b, p. 69). Loewald (1971) similarly described the unconscious determinants of passive repetition as "automatic and autonomous."

Ego Mastery   By the middle 1930s the trend represented by Alexander's position, that repetition enabled the individual to gain some kind of mastery, gained momentum. Denying any kind of "mechanical association" or "mechanical repetition," Schilder (1938, pp. 86–87) claimed the repetitions of his patients were revivals of situations in which they previously felt threatened. Kubie's critique was even more emphatic. After a detailed analysis of Freud's examples he concluded that:

there is neither any need nor any evidence for a "repetition compulsion"—and that the phrase itself has become a mere descriptive epithet, a psychoanalytic version of the word habit. (Kubie 1939)

He believed the concept lacked any kind of explanatory power, and saw the repetitions as attempted solutions to earlier injuries. Without making reference to either Kubie or Schilder, both Wilbur (1941) and Lowenfeld (1941) adopted the mastery view to some degree.

Two papers by Hendrick, together with his letter in response to criticism of them, extended the mastery type of explanation by making an ego-instinctual drive for mastery responsible for the repetition of traumatic situations. Mature mastery skills broke down under frustration and anxiety and had to be relearned by repetitive practice (Hendrick 1942, 1943a,b). Lagache (1953), M. M. Stern (1957), Pratt (1958), Waelder (1967a), Brenner (1971), and Downey (1984) did not adopt this thesis, although each endorsed the repetitions as belated efforts to master needs or satisfy earlier unresolved tensions. Stern and Pratt specifically promoted the ego as the vehicle of these efforts, a concept soon taken farther by Kanzer (in Gifford 1964), Malev (1969), and Siegel (1969). This view can be aligned with Fenichel's (1945b, pp. 42–46, 120–121) analysis of repetitions in children's play and traumatic neuroses, which also implicated the ego. Embarrassingly enough, Kasanin (1944) then implicitly embraced this interpretation for transference. Zetzel's (1956) review of concepts of transference recognized the same mechanism there, as did Loewald (1971) some years later. Krystal (1978) seems to hold to a mastery view in proposing that the repetition of intense affects is motivated by the need to regain comfort in having them. Similarly, Rothstein (1979a) represents the child's play as anything but neurotic or motivated by the death instinct. According to him, the child "joyfully repeats his successful functioning" in controlling and presumably mastering the (symbolized) appearance and disappearance of the mother. But also within the framework of a mastery interpretation is Moses's (1978) very different conclusion that repetition has part of its basis in the *warding off* of earlier painful experiences.

The whole ego-mastery trend was aptly summed up in Loewenstein's (1969) conclusion to his review of the literature of the previous fifty years on transference. The urge to remember, to master, to undo was, he said, "a powerful ego factor quite independent of the instinctual motivations to which we have been wont to ascribe repetition, reliving, reenactment in the transference." Fourteen years later Juda began his review by saying:

We no longer need to construe the repetition of earlier trauma as some sort of "daemonic" manifestation of the psychic apparatus, nor as a vicissitude of our "wish" to return to an organic state. (Juda 1983)

Basing himself on a mixture of Kohut's concept of cohesive self and Piaget's schema, which he substituted for protective shield, Juda added:

once confronted with new, unassimilated and unaccommodated experience, the human being must relive this experience again and again *ad nauseam* until he has developed a new schema with which to understand it.

Naturally he disagreed with Silverberg's characterization of the compulsion as an "enduring monument of man's profound rebellion against reality and his stubborn persistence in the ways of immaturity." It would, Juda said, be "more fruitful to reconstrue the repetition compulsion as *primarily* a healthy function of the cohesive self."

We must note that the mastery positions are not without difficulties of their own. Dorey (1986) differentiates distinct meanings of the two German words that have been translated by the one word "mastery." Mastery-domination (*Bemächtigung*) means dominating or even destroying another, whereas mastery-assimilation (*Bewältigung*) places the emphasis on the assimilation of excitation through binding. Even so, when Freud uses the concept of an instinctual drive for mastery:

> On the one hand, Freud considers this instinct, having the aim of mastery-domination, as a transformation of the death instinct, and hence of destructive trends.... On the other hand, ... he invokes [it] as the driving force behind children's play, as "the impulse to work over ... some overpowering experience" ... whereas, as few chapters further on, he describes this task of the psychic apparatus by the word [mastery-assimilation].   (Dorey 1986)

Dorey suggests that Freud's "highly ambiguous" use of the concept results from his "desire to link mastery-domination to the action of a single instinct—specifically, the death instinct."

A similar ambiguity is found in much contemporary psychoanalytic thinking. Thus Plaut (1984) believes Freud's dual-instinct theory cannot account for mastery, and contends that direct observations and clinical considerations make it necessary to recognize a *third* class of ego-instinctual drives that does. Distinct from the libidinal and aggressive drives, the new class meet the criteria of having a source in the perceptual motor system, an aim of directed motor activity, and an object in parts of the body. Plaut offers neither evidence nor argument for the existence of these essential defining characteristics. His one sentence listing them is mere assertion, as is his claim that H. Hartmann and his colleagues came close to a similar postulation.

Lipin (1963) showed that the concept was flexible enough for even instinctual formulations to be brought into line with the mastery view. He regarded compulsion as one of a number of instinctual drive representatives that, regulated by the principles of constancy and pleasure, produced maturational unfolding according to an innate genetic timetable. Repetitions of the kind considered by Freud were inhibitions and distortions of the activity of the compulsion. As Valenstein commented in the American Psychoanalytical Association panel discussion of Lipin's theses (in Gifford 1964), this made the compulsion favor progression as well as regression. Gifford added: "Ironically the repetition compulsion Freud considered such important evidence for a death instinct has been transformed by Lipin into a phenomenon that has some characteristics of a life instinct." Although Cohen (1980) rejects the death instinct and locates the repetition compulsion outside the pleasure principle, he approaches Lipin's position as he views the compulsion as an analogue of the pleasure principle operating at a lower level of organization: one of need rather than wish, and one involving the primary process of the id rather than the secondary process of the ego. Greenacre's (1967) concept is similar in that repetition compulsion results from a positive motivational factor.

Schur   Schur's (1966a) analysis is mentioned separately because it is the most comprehensive attempt at clarification since E. Bibring's (1943) of nearly 25 years earlier. Originally Schur (1953) took a kind of fixation view: automatic reflexlike responses developed in the ego under the impact of danger and anxiety. Seven years later he stressed the instinctual aspects by calling the repetitions manifestations of instinctive behavior patterns released when the executive apparatuses are or become passive in relation to the drives (Schur 1960). In slightly later panel discussions he implied that his concepts remained to be validated (Schur, in Gifford 1964), and he separated drive-based from defensive repetition, maintaining that if the compulsion was extended to the ego it might be given an adaptive-mastery role (Schur, in Blum 1966).

In his major work, Schur (1966a, pp. 129–145) brought these points to fruition by distinguishing between an unpleasure principle as a tendency to withdraw from excessive stimulation and a pleasure principle as a need to recreate situations of satisfaction by approaches to objects of gratification. Denying that concern over trauma was confined to night dreams, he claimed that when such dreams did occur they represented the ego's unconscious wish to undo the trauma; this required a reenactment that necessarily generated anxiety (pp. 177–178). The dream also served to repair the breach in the unpleasure principle caused by the original failure to withdraw from the stimulus. Traumatic dream repetition was not only not beyond the pleasure principle, it had absolutely no bearing on the death instinct (pp. 181–182). Nor were transference repetitions manifestations of the compulsion to repeat. Logically and historically it was impossible for the wishes behind them never to have brought pleasure and they remained attempts at satisfaction (pp. 182–184). Children's play also was a bad example because Freud was clearly "of two minds" about it (pp. 189–190). Overall Schur concluded:

none of Freud's psychological adductions used to substantiate his hypothesis of "beyond the pleasure principle" and the concepts of the death instinct are valid ... all the examples cited by Freud—certain types of children's play; the reproduction of unpleasurable experiences in the analytic situation and in acting out; and, above all, traumatic dreams—can be explained within the framework of the pleasure and unpleasure principles.   (pp. 192–193)

He reached the same conclusion nearly forty years after Symons: the compulsion to repeat fell within the sphere of the pleasure principle (Symons 1927).

Wallace (1982) subsequently endorsed the essence of Schur's conclusion. Granting that Freud "correctly divined" the repetitive nature of the phenomena he cited, Wallace believed he had built "a very shaky edifice" on them. Instead, the "correct explanation" of repetition was to be found in the "indestructibility" of unconscious wishes. Repetition was caused by their "incessant striving" that, as Schur observed, was entirely compatible with the pleasure principle and therefore not at all demonic.

Another approach bringing the repetitions within the purview of the pleasure principle returns to an early view of Freud's and interprets them as nothing more nor less than symptoms of frank neurosis: "All neurotic unpleasure is ... pleasure which cannot be felt as such" (Freud 1920a, p. 11). This trend seems to have begun with Kubie's (1941a) second paper on the compulsion and was extended by Joseph (1959) and Ferreira (1965). Here the ego was necessarily involved through its contribution to the compromise of the symptom. Of all the "neurotic" interpretations of the compulsion to repeat, the unkindest must surely be Weissman's (1956) strong prima facie case for the play of Freud's grandson being a neurotic, compulsively patterned activity, prototypal of adult obsessive-compulsive symptoms, and therefore governed by the pleasure principle.

To summarize on repetitions in play, the play that so impressed Freud is completely explicable within the framework of pre-1920 psychoanalytic theory. Neither as a neurotic symptom nor as a belated attempt at mastery does it violate the pleasure principle. Nor does it support a death instinct or a principle of inertia. Hendrick's thesis requires a more radical modification of instinct theory. Not only would the death instinct be done away with, but an independent instinctual drive to mastery would somehow have to be placed alongside other ego drives. Would it have an aim, object, and source? Or would it be a different kind of drive altogether?

Dream and Transference Repetition

Turning now to repetitive dreams, we find three common views among psychoanalysts. Dreams are repeated in traumatic neuroses because they are ego attempts to master the traumatic situation, or because they affirm infantile omnipotence (M. H. Stein 1956), or because they are driven, as Symons (1927) said, by powerful unabreacted affect. The first two interpretations do not violate the pleasure principle, do not require the postulation of anything lying beyond it, and result in no major modification to the pre-1920 theory. The third interpretation necessitates accepting that there are exceptions to the wish-fulfillment function of dreams, which Freud granted later for other dreams anyway, and that powerful unpleasurable affects arising externally pose exactly the same problems for the mental apparatus as do the more familiar, internally arising, pleasurable kind.

However, any such recognition would require a complete recasting of the relations between the principles, if not the development of entirely new ones. This would be so especially if the self-limiting properties of some of the symptoms of traumatic war neuroses (including the gradual fading of the repetitive dreams) were to be given adequate consideration (MacCurdy 1918, pp. 29–30; Rivers 1918, 1923, p. 27; Lowenfeld 1941; Grinker and Spiegel 1943, pp. 32–39). These properties are utterly at variance with a self-destructive motivation. This is true even if one accepts the later claim of Grinker and Spiegel (1945, p. 365) that the dreams "cannot be dismissed as a general technique to master anxiety." They thought that if that were all to them, the dreams "should disappear . . . gradually with time" and that their persistent repetition was due them symbolizing other deep-seated conflicts. According to their observations, interpreting this other meaning put an end to the repetition.

Despite Fayek's (1980) contrary opinion, most psychoanalysts bring transference repetitions under the pleasure principle just as readily by thinking of them as attempts to satisfy infantile wishes. Their characteristics are then no longer at variance with those attributed to them in other parts of the theory. For the moment, let us assume that the action that is repeated is one that substitutes for a memory; Boesky (1982) cites instances of patients who act out past events they have no trouble remembering. Why should this be so? And why is it said to recur in the context of the patient's nonacceptance of a reconstruction of an infantile past? Symons (1927) may well be right in holding that reproducing the old experience in action is less painful than recollecting it in clear consciousness, but that does not explain the context.

Several writers have suggested that what determines the regressive aspects of the transference neurosis is the clash between the patient's dependency needs and the analyst's frustratingly rigid emotional neutrality. Repetition-in-action, it is implied, is part of the patient's gradual adaptation to an infantile situation (Macalpine 1950; Marmor 1962; Kepecs 1966). Building on this idea only a little further, is it not plausible to suppose that patients, caught between unwillingness to accept a particular interpretative reconstruction and an equally strong desire to maintain the therapeutic relationship, evolve a compromise? Without having to acknowledge the correctness of the interpretation, they behave in a way that pleases the analyst and so maintains the relationship. Would this not be made all the easier because of the very general constellation of factors that are present in the examples Freud gives? Who has not felt scorned by parents, unable to accomplish big tasks in childhood, and so on? These feelings can be conceptualized more adequately outside the psychoanalytic framework than within it. Of course, rather than requiring minor peripheral modifications, this social-psychological conception cuts the ground from under a great deal of what is central to Freud's theory.[3]

Sadism and Masochism

Considering now the relevance of sadism and masochism to the death instinct, we note that Freud's explanation of how the death instinct generated sadism required him to give up his earlier assumption that there could not be a primary masochism. In *Beyond the Pleasure Principle* Freud said the death instinct was forced away from the self by narcissistic libido. Impressed into the service of the sexual function, it then manifested itself as a sadistic drive (Freud 1920a, pp. 53–55).

Three and a half years later, in "The Economic Problem of Masochism," he expanded this thesis by having sadism as an outward displacement from an original state of primary masochism. When redirected onto the self, the drive was observable clinically as secondary masochism. One portion of the death instinct was taken up in the ego "as an intensification of masochism," and another gave rise to conscience, thereby increasing the sadistic treatment of the ego. So supplementing each other, the two trends united "to produce the same effects" (Freud 1924b, p. 170). Sadism and masochism could be explained provided that one assumed a death instinct, a state of primary masochism, an equivalence between sadism and an outwardly directed death instinct, and some mechanism responsible for the redirection.

The alternative explanations of sadism and masochism are based on doubts about one or more of these assumptions. The variety of elements available for doubting is, I think, largely responsible for the disagreements, contradictions, and imprecise usage that Bieber (in Masserman 1959a), Salzman (1959), Spiegel (1978), Mollinger (1982), Maleson (1984), and Grossman (1986) have drawn attention to in the literature.

Masochism without the Death Instinct   One position completely denied the relevance of the death instinct. Given their very different attitudes about the reality of the instinct, one is surprised to find W. Reich, Symons, Alexander, and Federn sharing it. W. Reich (1926) claimed that sadistic behavior only followed sexual frustration, a fact that led him to conclude that "libido-obstruction is the visible individual source of destructive aggression and that sadism is due to this relation." Although he probably did not mean to use the word "source" quite in the same way as his translator, he added that "'primary masochism' is a purely hypothetical source of the death instinct." During a later attack on Alexander (1926, 1927/1928) and Reik (1925/1959) for what he considered to be their adoption of Freud's concept of primary masochism, he said that the perversion of masochism followed "*directly* from the pleasure principle" (W. Reich 1927/1928), a point already made by Symons (1927) when questioning whether masochism necessarily implied the reality of the death instinct. Alexander (1929) argued that one could speak of a death instinct only if there were clinical conditions in which primary masochism united with the sadistic impulses directed against the ego. Although he thought that that conjunction was observable in the melancholias of old age, he could not discern it in masochism or sadism.

Federn's (1932) vigorous defense of the death instinct was along similar lines. Even though he took the same view of melancholia as Alexander and was prepared to accept cruelty gratified solely through pain as one of the manifestations of the death instinct, he excluded sadism: "The death instinct is not necessary to explain sadism. The pleasure aim of gratification is a sufficient motive." Federn seems to have been just as doubtful about the relevance of the death instinct to masochism per se. Rado (in Masserman 1959a) went farther. He dismissed Freud's instinctually based approach altogether: "the theory of instincts has outlived its initial usefulness; for decades now, it has proved to be unfruitful." Mollinger (1982) also dismissed the instinctual drives completely. He sought support for this radical surgery in a "new trend," evident in "the last several decades," to remove sadism and masochism from "their instinctual bases." I will consider Rado's and Mollinger's theses shortly.

Masochism with the Death Instinct   Another position accepted and extended Freud's view. Fenichel (1928), for example, proposed that masochistic behavior resulted from a need for self-punishment to which the death instinct contributed directly. The unconscious guilt that created the need was "a unique, primitive, ruthless thing, which would not shrink from the destruction of the patient's own ego." Moreover, he emphasized, it was "the clinical representative of the mute death instincts." At first sight, Nunberg's (1926, 1932, pp. 140–156; cf. 1932/1955, pp. 157–171) account seems quite similar to Fenichel's until it is realized that his separation of unconscious guilt from the need for punishment assigned the death instinct only to the latter—the guilt came from unsatisfied libido. Because both W. Reich (1926) and Alexander (1929) also incorporated the sense of guilt into their explanations of masochism, the latter even after he ceased to believe in the death instinct (Alexander 1948, p. 120), these two positions have a certain independence of the role given the instinct.

Masochism and Observation   The independence of observation from belief brings us to the most important of the clinical issues, the observational status of Freud's new concept. Clearly it, too, is independent of belief. W. Reich, a nonbeliever, together with Alexander and Federn, both believers, took the position, best expressed by Alexander: "An unequivocal answer to this question as to the presence of a primary death-instinct cannot ... be obtained by the method of direct clinical observation" (Alexander 1929). The point is most tellingly illustrated by the bewildering array of causal mechanisms, developmental backgrounds, and psychodynamic factors that have been said to produce the typical masochist. Few of these alternative explanations draw on the death instinct, an oddity indeed, if its clinical manifestations are in any sense directly observable. It is to these other views that I now turn.

Beginning with Sadger (1926), one class of explanations of masochism drew on connections formed in infancy between sexual and painful sensations. Sadger implicated the frustration of childhood oral and genital needs after they had been deliberately aroused by the parents, an explanation that partly overlaps with that of Van Ophuijsen (1929). Both interpretations are reasonably consistent with M'Uzan's (1973) detailed description of the complex of feelings in his rather extravagant masochist. Sternbach (1975) proposed that during the oral and anal phases, heightened pleasurable and genital sensations became connected, and the child learned to tolerate visceral sensations that reached the point of physical pain. These quite different but *genitally* oriented views are all challenged by Friedenburg's (1956) thesis that unpleasure arising during *dentition*, just before the eruption of teeth, becomes associated with the infant's feelings of impotence at his inability to relieve his distress and feelings of hostility toward his mother for failing to help.

W. Reich (1932/1950) introduced a class of explanation centering on responses to castration anxiety. His had sexual tension caused by pain, tension, or threat relieved in a more or less peculiar but pleasurable way once the pain, tension, or threat was removed. As a child, Reich's patient so feared castration as a punishment that he experienced the beating he did receive from his father as a great relief. When he became an adult, the childhood fear of castration intervened each time he strove for sexual pleasure, but it was attenuated by a beating.

Gero (in Ostow 1957) proposed a variation: pain replaced the sexual pleasure that Oedipal guilt could not tolerate. Masochism and sadism were expressions of the sexual instinct, rather than results of a fusion of aggression and libido. Lewinsky (1944) took masochistic acts to be total denials of castration, and Spiegel (1978) saw them as providing a defensive means of escaping castration anxieties. On the other hand, Eissler (in M. H. Stein 1956) claimed that the masochist accepted castration, insisting that despite it he could still have erection and orgasm. Each one of these genital views is very different from its companions and from the role given castration anxiety by W. Reich.

More general variants of Reich's thesis are those of Bak, Rado, Romm, and Thompson. Bak (in M. H. Stein 1956) implicated the pleasurable relief of a simultaneously sexually exciting and unpleasant diffused tension. Later the unpleasure became a necessary condition for sexual excitement. Bak pointed out that his view was not unlike that of Loewenstein (in M. H. Stein 1956), who derived prototypal masochism from pleasure experienced by the child whose seductive behavior reunited him with a parent who had threatened him in a playful way. Only guilt needed to be added for true masochism to form. Rado's (in Masserman 1959a) alternative was based on learning: punishment and fear of punishment led to sexual inhibition, with the consequence that a painful experience had to be undergone to free "the inhibited organism for orgiastic release." Romm (1959) thought the patient did not as much wish to avoid an anxiety-free existence as much as "to create an over-all illusion of anxiety" in order to avoid overwhelming real anxiety: "It may represent his inadequate and futile attempt at mastery." Thompson (1959) proposed that the behavior allayed anxiety and gave the illusion of security.

Loewenstein's explanation went part way toward finding the origins of masochism in some peculiarity of the infant's love objects rather than in the pattern of stimulation. Berliner's explanation falls within a subgroup of this class. He concluded from his analyses that the infant experienced hatred quite directly from the mother. Because of its dependence, the infant had no choice but to submit and accept the suffering as a bid for maternal affection. Masochism was thus "the hate or the sadism of the object reflected in the libido of the subject" (Berliner 1947; cf. 1940, 1942, and in M. H. Stein 1956). A similar argument was put forward by Menaker (1953, 1956) who differed only by placing the experience of hostility earlier, at the oral level. Avery (1977) saw sadomasochism as "a type of object relationship which serves to defend against the threat of object loss," thus agreeing with Berliner and Menaker. He reinterprets earlier case material as showing primary loss in the pregenital phase rather than defense against Oedipal phase aggression. Bieber's (1953, 1966) explanation was also of this type, but placed more emphasis on masochistic self-injury as a means for avoiding harm from others, for evoking positive affection, and for maintaining a relation with the object. Mollinger (1982) also believed that sadism and masochism were best considered as modes of relation to love objects, and were best understood in terms of the stages of development of internal object relations hypothesized by Kernberg.

A further subclass of these object-love explanations is constituted by Thompson's (1959) theory in which the love object has definite positive qualities as well as negative ones. Masochistic behavior is an attempt to gain the attention, love, and dependency satisfactions that were lacking in childhood. Smirnoff's (1969) analysis of Sacher-Masoch's life and works is reasonably consistent with this view, even though he believed the masochist suffered to represent to himself his fusion with and separation from the love object, rather than to obtain pleasure. For the most part he implicated the mother's hostility. But, according to Grand's (1973) analyses, it was actually the father who hated or was indifferent to the child; the mother was detached, narcissistic, and dominant. As far as I can tell, among the explanations based on the relation to the object, only Parkin (1980) attributes the hatred solely to the subject. He derives it from the from the child's unsatisfactory relation to the mother.

The last group of explanations is based on very general childhood experiences that are supposed to have resulted in some distortion of ego or self. Masochistic behavior is thus an attempt to reestablish the ego's loss of the capacity for mastery (R.-J. Eisenbud 1967), or an effort "to restore and maintain the structural cohesiveness, temporal stability, and positive affective coloring of a precarious or crumbling self-representation" (Stolorow 1975b). They are broadly consistent with the object-love explanations, as well as with Stone's (1971) thesis that the basic connection between sexuality and aggressiveness arises "in the drive to master actual or threatened traumatic helplessness." Stolorow's view is also not very different from Eissler's (in M. H. Stein 1956), who claims that the masochist fears his ego will be overwhelmed during orgasm. It is also consistent with Keiser's (1949) report that his patients feared their sexual sensations, avoided unpleasure, and were unable to tolerate painful tension. Keiser felt that at heart the masochist could not manage the passive component of sexual activity.

All of these interpretations are very far removed from those based on a deliberately sought dissolution or isolation. For example, Horney (1937, pp. 259–280) contended that the masochist actively seeks out the dissolution of self. Salzman claimed that the masochist underwent degradation and humiliation in order to support the essential value system of "needing no one—a supreme isolation and separation without, however, the usual despair" (Salzman 1959). Thompson (1959) disagreed: for her the masochist's "deepest motive is the search for intimacy." Weiss (in Masserman 1959a) endorsed Salzman's discarding outdated mechanistic concepts but believed the masochist wished to eliminate the hated self by merging with another. Millet (1959), on the other hand, did not consider that Salzman's isolation motive had provided "a diagnostic concept of sufficiently clear differentiation" and looked to the initial experiences of disappointment of not obtaining absolute love from the mother in the symbiotic relationship as sowing the seeds of masochism.

These strikingly different explanations reveal a basic disagreement about the aim of masochistic activity. The key question was asked by Symons (1927): does the masochist seek pain as an end in itself or as a means to a pleasurable end? We may also ask, is the means determined through some relatively simple association or by some complex of psychodynamic factors from among unconscious guilt, need for punishment, castration anxiety, affirmation of self, and fear of object or of object loss? Almost all of the authors cited at least imply a complex means of achieving pleasure, but their usual scrutiny was of neurotic or psychotic conditions in which self-punitive *fantasies* predominated, rather than masochistic sexual *activity*. Because the latter ought to be more closely related to the death instinct or other aggressive tendencies, it is a more appropriate object for study than neuroses or psychoses.

When sexual masochism proper is examined, a somewhat different picture emerges. First, the actual tortures may be considerably more painful than those expressed in neurotic fantasies. Unlike the fantasied events, actual damage to the genitals may result, a fact that poses problems for most of the castration anxiety explanations

(M'Uzan 1973). Second, the masochist is bound to his torturer by what amounts to a formal contract specifying the amount of pain to be inflicted and the degree of humiliation to be undergone. Thus he retains complete control over the situation (Smirnoff 1969; cf. Lewinsky 1944; Eidelberg 1968). Third, the pain and suffering are primarily associated with orgiastic activity. Masochists do not have a heightened threshold for pain. As M'Uzan's (1973) patient put it: "it is the pain which releases the ejaculation." Outside of the sexual context he reacted to painful stimuli very much as others; in context, however, pain catalyzed and amplified his sexual excitement at the same time as destroying its specifically painful quality (cf. Bieber 1966).

How pleasure and pain become associated is the central question of masochism and, as Loewenstein (in Stein 1956) observes, the answer is not definitely known. Silverberg (1959), who took the view that masochism was "first and foremost" a sexual perversion, considered that until an answer was found to the question why an individual was able to gain pleasure through what he considers to be pain, "we will not be able to explain the more figurative types."

Masochism and the Need for Punishment   Finally we come to the unconscious sense of guilt and the need for punishment it supposedly creates. We have seen how these concepts are used both to support and oppose the death instinct interpretation, and that even the believers are not at all agreed how they contribute. Pretty obviously this is because all three concepts lack clear referents, a point well illustrated in comparing the early and late views of those who, like Alexander, Fenichel, and Eidelberg, slid from belief into unbelief. Late or early, their clinical observations are the same (Alexander 1926, 1929; Eidelberg 1968; Fenichel 1928, 1935/1954b, 1945b). And it is not at all surprising that Berliner (1947) was able to mount powerful arguments questioning the ultimate role of unconscious guilt and punishment in masochism; that Menaker (1956) and Spiegel (1978) denied the existence of those factors completely; that Salzman (1959) described the unconscious guilt as appearance; that Sternbach (1975) seriously proposed that sadism was neither necessarily connected with hate, nor masochism with self-hate, self-destructiveness, and self-punishment; and that, according to Spiegel (1978), the interpretation of moral masochism in terms of unconscious guilt "hardly ever generates more than mere intellectual agreement" among psychoanalysts.

It should now be clear that the problems that psychoanalysts have are partly a matter of what is to count as masochism or sadism. For Hoch, for example, the "fundamental question" is:

do we have a psychopathologic entity which can be explained dynamically in a similar way in all ... or merely phenomenologically similar features of which the causation is not the same? (Hoch 1959)

Sack and Miller (1975), who believed that "many and varied" mechanisms underlay masochism, even allowed there could be masochistic behavior without masochistic motivation. Much later, Maleson (1984) observed that although "it has often been noted that masochism is not simply or predominately a manifestation of a sexual instinct ... it remains a time-honored part of psychoanalytic instinct theory." Maleson makes the point that in the famous "A Child is Being Beaten" (Freud 1919a), Freud's attempt to maintain the relation of masochism with the instinctual drives led to a "strained and confusing labeling of the three phases of the beating fantasy." That is, the first phase was sadistic but, although the form of the third phase was also sadistic, the satisfaction in it was masochistic.

Within the fairly narrow confines of moral masochism, Spiegel (1978) distinguished four different but overlapping groups of ideas about its etiology and function. Maleson (1984) found ten different types of psychoanalytic explanations for masochism generally. They derived from three irreconcilable conceptualizations: masochism as a transformation of sadism, as an anal-sadistic fixation/regression, and as developing from masculinity or femininity. Maleson traces these confusions to Freud himself, who described any kind of suffering as well as frankly sexual behavior as masochistic. Masserman (1959b) was undoubtedly correct to remark that Sacher-Masoch would have been astounded at the use of his name to connote "a need for suffering" because his (and de Sade's) search was for "sexual pleasure-in-itself." Maleson also judges Freud's original descriptions of the nature and origin of the masochistic-sadistic component instincts to be "ambiguous" and "tentative," his basic argument to establish them "weak," and its outcome as creating terms with the dual meanings of instincts and behaviors that made it "particularly difficult to disentangle the clinical meanings ... whether broad or narrow ... from metapsychological formulations" (Maleson 1984).

Hoch (1959) favored a broad meaning. Masochism was much more than a specific sexual deviation. It occurred in almost all disorders. I take it he would even reject the once widely accepted advice, attributed to Brenner (Cooper, in N. Fischer 1981), to restrict the term to the seeking of unpleasure for the sake of *sexual* pleasure (Brenner 1959). And, although Grossman (1986) argues powerfully against extending the meaning, he actually goes beyond Brenner in wanting to restrict the term to *fantasies* in which there is an obligatory combination of pleasure with pain. Grossman, like Loewenstein (1957), even took out the sexual quality altogether, recognizing some forms of masochism as "desexualized." Maleson (1984) found, no surprise, that masochism could not "be explained by any consistent dynamic or metapsychological formula." He despaired at the possibility of a definitional solution at either the clinical-descriptive or theoretical-explanatory level (cf. Cooper, Glenn, and Fischer, in N. Fischer 1981). I would add that until the psychoanalytic couch produces basic facts about sadism and masochism, it is silly to pretend that what psychoanalysts like to call their observations have any bearing at all on any explanatory concepts, including those deriving from the death instinct.

Alternative Explanations for Aggression

Dissatisfaction with and disagreement over Freud's new explanation of aggressiveness were rarely more marked than with the explanation of sadism and masochism. The dissatisfaction was expressed almost immediately by the concept of the death instinct being denied clinical utility. For example, when discussing the usefulness of the new instinctual concepts in child psychology, Bernfeld observed that they made

certain aspects less clear; they are biological, philosophical ... they belong to metapsychology with which the present psychology of infants had better not concern itself yet. (Bernfeld 1925/1929, p. 99)

Spilling over into a footnote, Ernest Jones (1926) expostulated, "Freud's 'death instinct'. I find myself unable to operate with this philosophical concept in a purely clinical discussion." Many other analysts subsequently expressed similar opinions (e.g., Berliner 1940; Ostow 1958) or they at least noted that Thanatos and Eros were "largely left outside the mainstream of psychoanalytic theory and practice" (Valenstein, in N. Fischer 1981). More recently, Downey (1984) judged Freud's death instinct to have "placed a metaphorical obstruction in the path of psychoanalytic inquiry" and Werman (1985) said bluntly "there are few psychoanalysts today who support the concept of the death instinct." All this even though an externally directed aggressive-destructive drive is widely accepted (cf. M. I. Klein 1983). I now examine the alternative accounts of aggressiveness that developed out of this widespread dissatisfaction.

One of the most popular nondeath instinct explanations of aggressiveness derives it from some other biological drive that is not itself primarily aggressive, but has secondary destructive aims or a mode of action that generates aggressiveness as a side effect. For example, some type of self-preservative instinctual drive having its source wholly or partially in oral or gastrointestinal predatory, or devouring, or incorporative tendencies was postulated as the basis of aggressiveness by Loewenstein (1940, 1969, in Lussier 1972), Simmel (1944), and Ostow (1957, 1958). This kind of basis has been criticized, however, on the very good grounds that predatory aggression is not and probably never was a significant factor in interhuman conflict. Lantos (1958) therefore located what she called subjective aggression (which accompanied the affect of hate) in instinctually determined conflicts over territory, sexual rivalry, and the like. Somewhat similarly, Brunswick (1954) saw human aggression as manifestations of the innate defensive-aggressive responses that humans shared with animals. Although of this same general type, Winnicott's (1950–1955/1958) derivation has a quite different basis. For him, aggressiveness comes from infant motility drives having more fundamental determinants in a life force active in the very tissues themselves. Perhaps more debatably to be included in this class is Parens's (1973) thesis that motor activity resulting from some unknown physiological source generates *nondestructive aggression* (!) equivalent to the drive for mastery, as well as the more familiar destructive kind. A major stumbling block for all these conceptualizations is Werman's (1985) objection that there is a good deal of evidence from anthropology against the innateness of an aggressive drive independent of the death instinct, and no good evidence from biology for its having that origin.

Aggressiveness as a mode of instinctual operation, reflecting merely the way in which instincts seek their satisfaction, and therefore independent of any particular drive, was first proposed by Fenichel (1935/1954b). He adopted the very argument psychoanalysts first used against Adler's concept of an independent aggressive drive (E. Jones 1935–1936). Fenichel's suggestion seems to have been accepted by Szasz (1952) and explicitly endorsed by Gillespie (1971; cf. Fenichel 1935/1945b, p. 59).

Contributing to two other explanations is a distinction that was made between instinctual drives as Freud originally defined them, and the biological or philosophical forces they became in the new theory. Probably first made by Bernfeld (1925/1929, p. 99), the distinction eventually gave rise to distinct biological and psychological explanations. Bernfeld noted that "the life- and death-instincts are biological forces ... which extend beyond the domain of the individual" and later, in conjunction with Feitelberg, made the distinction more explicit (Bernfeld and Feitelberg 1931). However, it was Bibring who produced the most well-known formulation of the issue, the one we have already noted, in which he said that calling the life and death drives instincts had turned them into a vague "something" that gave direction to the life processes (E. Bibring 1936/1941). In his influential comments on the concept of instinctual drive, H. Hartmann (1948) claimed that the life and death instincts added little to the psychological understanding of drives. He fell in with the view that hypotheses deriving from them could only be tested biologically, and even suggested that Freud's earlier concept had to be extended "beyond the physiological substratum traceable today." A year later, he and his colleagues introduced the concept of a primary aggressive drive independent of the death instinct, that paralleled the sexual drive even though its source was unknown (H. Hartmann, Kris, and Loewenstein 1949).

Although not all ego-psychologists agreed with Hartmann's critique and particular solution (M. I. Klein 1983), the concept of a primary aggressive drive, not usually thought of as having any relation to Freud's death instinct (or at best an uncertain one), has been widely accepted (Waelder 1956a; Arlow 1959; Sandler, in Lussier 1972). Perhaps the most interesting recognitions, admittedly falling short of actual endorsement, are those of Segal and Anna Freud. As a member of the Kleinian School, which emphasizes the role of aggression and even looks kindly on Freud's revised theory, Segal (in Lussier 1972) moved considerably toward the Hartmann position in insisting that she had to use some concept of a primary aggressive drive and was prepared to think of it as separate from the death instinct. Although not moving as far as Segal, Anna Freud (1972) acknowledged the gap between clinical fact and biological speculation by accepting the kind of distinction made by Bernfeld and Bibring. To some extent the adoption of this distinction was aided by the argument of Lantos (1955, 1958) and Lampl-de Groot (1956). After recognizing the practical importance of the distinction, they both proposed terminological revisions that effectively restricted "instinctual drive" to Freud's first meaning and allowed Eros and the death instinct to be described only as "forces" or "tendencies." It was from this position that Lantos derived aggressiveness from conflicts over sexuality, territoriality, and the like.

H. Hartmann (1956) endorsed the Lantos–Lampl-de Groot proposal, dismissed Freud's revised theory as speculative and difficult of validation, and restated his thesis of primary aggression. Clearly the Bernfeld and Bibring distinction had allowed contemporary psychoanalysts to use the earlier concept of drive in a variety of ways, mostly inconsistent with one other, while comfortably ignoring Eros and Thanatos altogether. An exception is Downey (1984) who, recognizing the negative qualities of a death instinct-derived aggressive impulse, believes it to be "a *positive* force in psychological development and subsequent functioning" (!).

H. Hartmann's (1948) emphasis on the psychological inadequacies of Freud's life and death instincts led to the third method of dealing with the theory—that of removing its biological foundations completely. No doubt this may not have been intended, but it is an obvious influence in Pleune's (1961) thesis that drives "should be conceptualized as a psychological rather than a biological phenomenon." Pleune did not actually dispose of the somatic sources. That was left to Brenner. As Brenner (1979) said later, "it was Freud's need to anchor the aggressive drive in physiology, in the soma, that led him to relate it to a protoplasmic death drive," a concept he considered "neither useful nor defensible." Brenner (1971) began his argument by questioning the claim of H. Hartmann, Kris, and Loewenstein (1949) that the validity of the death instinct was a matter for biologists. Were not "psychoanalytical data by themselves ... sufficient evidence for the theory of aggression?" He defined a drive as "a theoretical construct which serves the purpose of explaining the nature of basic motivation," arguing further that psychological evidence provided "an acceptable basis for the concept of aggression as an instinctual drive" (Brenner 1971; cf. Brenner 1979).

One advantage of adopting Brenner's position is that disputes over sources, aims, and objects either disappear or are resolvable by psychoanalysts or psychologists rather than by biologists, or physiologists, or philosophers. From this psychological trend two quite different specific suggestions resulted, those of Stone and Holt. As we saw, Stone (1971) postulated that aggression arose from the drive to master traumatic helplessness. This was not a drive in an inborn, constantly acting, autochthonous sense, however, even though it had an *anlage* in the hostility, rage, and aggression of the prolonged helpless stage of infancy. Holt, on the other hand, wanted to do away with the concept of drive altogether, replacing it by the concept of "wish" found in much of Freud's early writing. Analysts would thereby avoid being committed "to a great deal of pseudoexplanatory mythology that does not have satisfactory grounding in fact" (Holt 1975a). Although having a different basis, a similarly monolithic position is seen in the trend, which Blanck and Blanck (1977) welcome, in which the very foundation of Freud's theory of instinctual drive—the ubiquitous bipolar contrast—is abandoned altogether.

Taken together these alternative explanations of aggression, of sadism and masochism, and of the compulsion to repeat show that the major problem, if not the central one, is that the death instinct has no characteristics that manifest themselves in unique ways. The very essence of the drive is that it is mute; unlike any other drive, its source is not located in a particular organ; it produces no tension of its own and acts solely by reducing the tensions introduced by other drives (cf. Fenichel 1935/1954b); and it reveals itself more or less openly, if at all, only after a complex series of transformations. It is true that at various times it was proposed to have clear or reasonably clear and unique manifestations (Fenichel 1928; Alexander 1926, 1929; Federn 1932; Nunberg 1932, pp. 62–66, 1932/1955, pp. 84–87; Heimann 1952; Garma 1971; M'Uzan 1973; Fayek 1980), but these claims were rejected fairly explicitly or implicitly by the vast majority of psychoanalytic writers. Among those who are reasonably direct in their rejection are W. Reich (1926, 1927/1928, 1932/1950), Fenichel (1932/1934, pp. 68–69, 272–273), E. Jones (1935–1936), E. Bibring (1936/1941), Berliner (1940, 1947), Reik (1941), Simmel (1944), Lewinsky (1944), H. Hartmann, Kris, and Loewenstein (1949), Flugel (1953), Lampl-de Groot (1956), Ostow (1958), Pratt (1958), Arlow (1959), K. Eissler (1969), Brenner (1971), Stone (1971), and Sandler, Segal, Loewenstein, and Rosenfeld (all in Lussier 1972). Those who reject it indirectly include Bernfeld and Feitelberg (1931), Loewenstein (1940), Kubie (1941a), Alexander (1948, p. 68), Waelder (1956a), Markovits (in Ostow 1957), Saul (1958), Pieper and Muslin (1961), Pleune (1961), Eidelberg (1962), Katan (1966), R.-J. Eisenbud (1967), Gillespie (1971), Lebovici and Diatkine (1972), and Sternbach (1975). The conceptual arm required to reach from a self-destructive tissue process and land a punch on someone's nose is far too long.

The weight of these opinions is consistent with the results of Cain's (1961) search for evidence of an aggressive drive in childhood being turned back upon the self prior to the formation of the superego. He believed he was successful, but he found no manifestations of the death instinct on which, in Freud's view, that drive rested.

Conclusion

Condensing our conclusions about Freud's concept of the death instinct, the clinical data from which it was inferred were capable of better and more familiar interpretations, the arguments adduced in its support were so riddled with faults they were not compelling, and the biological evidence was so defective or misinterpreted that a logically shoddy and empirically impervious prop had to be used to support its relevance. Neither the concept nor the explanations it generates are at all necessary.

Why then is the theory still taken seriously? Why has it not been discarded? First, the new theory does fill an explanatory hole. By providing an opponent for the sexual drive, the death instinct gives the theory symmetry. And, by explaining aggressiveness without recourse to the tortuous logic through which Freud previously derived the opposition between love and hate, the new theory also gains in simplicity. How much a simpler explanation of aggressiveness is valued can be seen in the fact that not one of the multitudinous critics of the new theory sought to revive the complex nonsense of "Instincts and Their Vicissitudes" as an alternative, even though it may be as Ikonen and Rechardt (1978) claim, that the current psychoanalytic theory of aggression rests more on that work than on *Beyond the Pleasure Principle*. Ironically, one of the few proposals to revive the concept of the ego instincts as a distinct class is based on their being needed to account for self-care and *counter* self-destructive tendencies (Khantzian and Mack 1983).

Second, none of the alternatives has any clear advantage over Freud's. Whether one considers aggression to be a drive in its own right, as do Hartmann, Kris, and Loewenstein, or as the side effect of another drive, as does Fenichel, the very difference of such constructs from the psychoanalytic concept of drive rules them out. Aggressiveness does not resemble the sexual and hunger drives subjectively or objectively. It is governed by neither tension reduction nor by the production of pleasure.

Objectively, there is an even greater difference. It has no definite source and its underlying processes cannot even be guessed at. Did the aggressive drive seem to possess characteristics described by Freud, Holt's objection that the physiological properties might not be the same as those sensed subjectively, would still have to be met.

A psychological concept of drive like that proposed by Brenner has other problems, mostly centering around the defining criteria. The problem was recognized by Plaut (1984). Part of his argument for reviving the concept of ego-instincts is that the only alternatives are "to abandon the concept of instincts altogether ... or to postulate an unlimited number." Plaut cites R. W. White (1959) and Kohut and Wolf (1978) as having already opted for the first and Yankelovich and Barrett (1970) for the second solution.[4] As the history of the concepts of instincts and drives in psychology shows, without strict criteria the number of essential or basic drives multiplies well beyond any reasonable necessity. I can do little better than cite Ikonen and Rechardt (1978) who say the "unsatisfactory state of psycho-analytic aggression theory is clearly revealed by recent publications, panels and congresses." Neither do they find support for the psychoanalytic theory of aggression in behavioral approaches, and the search in biology has been "equally fruitless."

Third, most of the alternatives provide only partial or fragmentary solutions. Presumably, this is because they are based on criticisms that for the most part deal with isolated, separate difficulties with Freud's concept. Nowhere does there seem to be a moderately comprehensive critique of Freud's revised theory. Consequently, there is nowhere a comprehensive alternative. Nor is it the case that any of the alternatives possesses the grandeur (or grandiosity) of Freud's tracing the basic tendencies governing mental activity to the cataclysmic events that brought life itself into being. Although this explanatory modesty is not at all a bad thing, it is the wider view that has the greater intellectual attraction. No less a critic of the death instinct and the compulsion to repeat than Waelder (in Gifford 1964) admitted that he accepted the general sense of the opposing tendencies of conservation and progress in human life being somehow related to life and death. Lowental (1983), who objects to the death instinct for its unsound conceptualization in drive theory, has a similar feeling. After separating it from aggression, he placed the death instinct in Freud's etiological equation (!) as a precondition for "death motivation." He also said he was "convinced of the driving momentum of the death instinct" as the motivator of a regressive striving for death (Lowental 1981). Freud's theory thus positively forces itself into the minds of psychoanalysts. I suggest it does so there and elsewhere because of the way it seems to mesh with a much larger intuition about life.

Although this last consideration may do for mythologists and literary critics, it is not to be taken too seriously. It is relevant only in the sense of the relevance of John Donne's striking anticipation of Freud's picture of death as an internal enemy:

Who then is this enemy? ... An enemie that is so well victualled against man as that he cannot want as long as there are men, for he feeds upon man himselfe.... he fights with our weapons, our own faculties, nay our calamities, yea our own pleasures are our death. (Donne, *Sermon*, preached at Whitehall, March 8, 1621)

Or as his better-known thought about the relation between birth and death that he preached just before his own death:

deliverance *from* ... the death of the *wombe*, is an *entrance*, a delivering over to *another death*, the manifold deathes of this *world*. Wee have a winding sheete in our Mothers wombe, which growes with us from our conception, and wee come into the world, wound up in that *winding sheet*, for wee come to *seeke a grave*. (Donne, *Sermon at White Hall*, the beginning of Lent, 1630)

The icy grip of Donne's words comes from the suddenness with which they reveal the central truth about our existence: our deaths begin with our lives. Freud's concept exercises command over us because it reveals the same truth. However, whereas Donne's thought aspires to no status other than that of theological poetry, Freud's version represents it as a scientific truth.

Freud's instinct theory also maintains its currency because of the intellectual torpidity of those who sleepily insist that it is better to have ideas that glow even feebly in the light of a thoroughly bad theory than admit complete ignorance.

Notes

1. The editors of the *Standard Edition* expand instincts here to ego instincts, so making the whole sentence refer to them. Apart from violating the direction of Freud's argument, which sought to demonstrate that all the instincts so far observed in psychoanalysis belonged to the class of life instincts, the interpolation makes nonsense of the next part of the argument in which Freud produced an example of an instinct belonging to the other class.

2. At least that is what I think they mean—*si ce n'est pas clair, c'est structuraliste*.

3. I am cautious about this speculative explanation because Boesky (1982) begins his review by observing that, despite the amount of literature on the subject, considerable confusion exists about the nature of acting out, and concludes that it "cannot be defined on empirical clinical grounds." After describing Freud's original examples of acting out as a substitute for remembering, Boesky asks his readers to notice "how different" they are "from the variety of behaviours we currently associate with the term." He believes problems with the concept of acting out are traceable to three sources: its link with memory, its placement in the topographic systems, and its connection with the instinctual definition of transference.

4. I am not sure that this plea would actually be endorsed by all of the authors Plaut cites.

13 The Structures of the Mind

... whenever she looked hard at any shelf, to make out exactly what it had on it, that particular shelf was always quite empty, though the others round it were crowded as full as they could hold.
—Lewis Carroll: *Through the Looking Glass*

In this chapter I consider how major alterations to Freud's theory of the mind were made necessary by his introducing the concept of a death instinct. An id, now containing destructive as well as sexual drives, was regulated by an ego and a superego. This new structural theory supplanted the old topographic theory, originally proposed in *The Interpretation of Dreams*, in which simple repressed sexual ideas imprisoned in *Ucs.* were controlled by *Cs./Pcs.*

The basic concepts of Freud's new structural theory can be briefly characterized as follows:

The *ego* controls the perceptual and motor apparatus, lays down memories, makes judgments, and selects possible courses of action. Only in the ego does consciousness arise and is anxiety experienced. The ego uses its functions to initiate repression or to control and delay instinctual discharge until realistic modes of need satisfaction have been found. Normally it is governed by the reality principle and operates according to the secondary process.

The *superego* is the vehicle of the ego-ideal, the repository of the individual's standards and values, the location of the conscience, the function that scrutinizes the person's behavior, forever measuring it against the standards of the ideal, and home of the mechanism that punishes violations of those standards.

The *id* is the reservoir of the psychic energy deriving from the twin drives of Thanatos, or death, and Eros, or life. Activity there is governed by the primary process, the tendency for instinctual drives to press for immediate discharge, and for their energies to be freely mobile, capable of condensation and displacement. The id is said to be timeless and to know nothing of logic, contradiction, or negation. This seething cauldron of instinctual drives is an original, inherited endowment of energy.

It may seem as if there is a simple isomorphism of the old with the new: *Ucs.* corresponding with the id and *Cs./Pcs.* with the ego and superego. But that overlooks the death instinct. What will be argued in this chapter is that the essential purpose of Freud's final theoretical revision was to incorporate the death instinct into the mind. It was precisely because that force could not be accommodated in the old that new structures had to be found to house it.

I begin chapter 13 with an examination of Freud's arguments in *The Ego and the Id* on replacing the topographic theory with the structural. After outlining how he found a place for the death instinct in the new structures, I show how this required him to stress the cognitive functions of the new ego, especially its capacity to sense and generate anxiety as a precursor to initiating repression, and how those functions had to be based on a neutral, disposable energy. I examine the relation among the id, *Ucs.*, and the death instinct, and Freud's toxic theory of neurosis and his changed view of primal repression as these relate to the anxiety that he now supposed to cause repression.

Why the Structural Theory?

Freud's explicit arguments for the structural theory did not include the difficulty of finding a place for the death instinct. His campaign was conducted on two seemingly different fronts. First, he adduced terminological difficulties with the words "conscious" and "unconscious" as one ground. Second, he announced two new discoveries—unconscious ego resistance and an unconscious need for punishment—that rendered the topographic theory obsolete and demanded its replacement. Both propositions must be challenged. The terminological difficulty, although real, was unimportant, whereas the discoveries were not made through uncomplicated observation, and at least one of them was definitely not new.

The Terminological Problem

Freud noted three ways in which the word unconscious was used in psychoanalysis: *descriptively*, *dynamically*, and *systematically*. A mental event, or idea, could be described as conscious if one were immediately and presently aware of it. In contrast, it might not be present in consciousness but be readily capable of becoming conscious. Such ideas could be described as *preconscious*, or latently conscious, and were unconscious only in the *descriptive* sense. Freud claimed psychoanalytic investigation showed that many ideas could not become conscious so easily, because an active force maintained them in a state of repression. Ideas unconscious in this way were so in the *dynamic* sense as well as descriptively. Freud had differentiated these two meanings before 1912, and in that year he added the third or *systematic* meaning when discussing the topographic theory originally set out in chapter 7 of *The Interpretation of Dreams* (Freud 1912c, p. 266). According to whether ideas belonged to the systems *Cs.*, *Pcs.*, or *Ucs.*, they were conscious, preconscious, or unconscious, respectively. Furthermore, those in *Cs.* or *Pcs.* were governed by the secondary process. They were rational, and the energy investing them was able to tolerate the postponement of immediate discharge. Contrariwise, ideas in *Ucs.* lacked structure, were illogical and contradictory, and their energy pressed for immediate discharge. In a word, they were ruled by the primary process. Thus the characteristics of ideas and their capacity for consciousness depended on the system to which they belonged.

Reduced to essentials, Freud's main argument in chapter 1 of *The Ego and the Id* was that it was necessary to describe both preconscious and repressed ideas as unconscious, but that only the repressed was unconscious in the dynamic sense. "In the descriptive sense there are two kinds of unconscious, but in the dynamic sense only one" (Freud 1923b, p. 15). Three things attest to the unimportance of confusion so created. First, when these different senses of the terms conscious and unconscious were formally delineated some eleven years earlier, these problems in usage were not even hinted at (Freud 1912c). Second, in 1915, when he did draw attention to them, he made no special case for abandoning the topographic theory; rather, he seems to have resigned himself to the ambiguity being inescapable (Freud 1915c, p. 172). Finally, in *The Ego and the Id* he indicated implicitly the degree of importance of the descriptive-dynamic distinction:

For purposes of exposition this distinction can in some cases be ignored, but in others it is of course indispensable. At the same time, we have become more or less accustomed to this ambiguity of the unconscious *and have managed pretty well with it.*   (Freud 1923b, p. 15. My emphasis)

By itself the ambiguity did not require a major theoretical revision. Something more was needed.

The First Discovery

At this point Freud revealed the first of his discoveries. "The further course of psycho-analytic work" had rendered the dynamic-descriptive distinction inadequate "in more ways than one." He claimed as "the decisive instance" his discovery of an unconscious resistance located in the ego (pp. 16–17). Each individual, he said, had a coherent organization of mental processes, called the ego, responsible for repression. During a psychoanalysis the resistance toward repressed mental contents had to be removed. But Freud found that

when we put certain tasks before the patient, he gets into difficulties; his associations fail when they should be coming near the repressed. We then tell him that he is dominated by a resistance; but he is quite unaware of the fact, and, even if he guesses from his unpleasurable feelings that a resistance is now at work in him, he does not know what it is or how to describe it.   (p. 17)

Because there was "no question" but that the resistance emanated from the ego,

We have come upon something in the ego itself which is also unconscious, which behaves exactly like the repressed—that is, which produces powerful effects without itself being conscious and which requires special work before it can be made conscious.   (p. 17)

For him the practical consequences of this recognition were momentous enough. Only after "endless obscurities and difficulties" could the neuroses be derived from a conflict between the conscious and unconscious. Now the neuroses reflected a different antithesis, that between "the coherent ego and the repressed" (p. 17). However, the theoretical implications were the most far-reaching. The unconscious portion of the ego, the part from which unconscious resistance arose, demanded the recognition of a third type of unconscious, one more than latently unconscious but not coextensive with the repressed.

The Second Discovery

What Freud claimed as his second discovery—an unconscious need for punishment—also required a theoretical emendation. It was best appreciated, he said, by reconsidering some well-established clinical facts:

There are certain people who behave in a quite peculiar fashion during the work of analysis. When one speaks hopefully to them or expresses satisfaction with the progress of the treatment ... their condition invariably becomes worse.   (p. 49)

This "negative therapeutic reaction" seemed to be determined by something over and above the usual forms of resistance such as defiance of the analyst, narcissistic inaccessibility, and the secondary gain from the illness itself:

In the end we come to see that we are dealing with what may be called a "moral" factor, a sense of guilt, which is finding its satisfaction in the illness and refuses to give up the punishment of suffering. We shall be right in regarding this disheartening explanation as final.   (p. 49)

For the patient, however:

this sense of guilt is dumb; it does not tell him he is guilty; he *does not feel guilty*, he feels ill. This sense of guilt expresses itself *only* as a resistance to recovery.   (pp. 49–50. My emphasis)

It was essentially in hysteria where the unconscious need for punishment (as this sense of guilt was more correctly called) remained so completely unconscious. Other disorders, especially melancholia and obsessional neuroses, exhibited conscious manifestations, sometimes quite strikingly so. As Freud saw it, this peculiar form of resistance was caused by the need for punishment powered by the death instinct operating unconsciously within the ego. There was thus another reason for recognizing an unconscious portion of the ego. Moreover, it was a part in direct communication with the instinct.

Recent? Discovery?

The idea of unconscious ego resistance was no more *recent*, as Freud implied, than it was a *discovery*. Notice the sequence of Freud's arguments: it is after having discussed the three meanings and the concepts of the topographic theory as if they were the usual currency of psychoanalytic discourse that he said it was "in the *further* course of psycho-analytic work" (My emphasis) that unconscious resistance had been "come upon" or "discovered" (Freud 1923b, pp. 16–17). An abstract, probably written by Freud himself, of a paper he gave some eight months earlier foreshadowed both claims: unconscious ego resistance was there also described as a new discovery (p. 4).

However, one of the cases reported in 1895 in *Studies on Hysteria* was the very first in which this kind of resistance was described. The behaviors from which it was then inferred were identical with those described in 1923. The patient was Elisabeth von R., and it was of her inability to produce ideas and visual images of etiological significance in response to the pressure of his hand that Freud first used the term resistance (Breuer and Freud 1895, pp. 153–154). Freud conceptualized the failures of his other patients to complete the associational trains he was following similarly (pp. 269–281, 287, 292–295, 301). In the model of the pathogenic memory structure outlined in the *Studies*, the closer memories were to the nucleus, the greater was the resistance to their recovery (pp. 288–289). Although perhaps put more succinctly in the *The Ego and the Id*, the behavior was the same: the closer the patient approached the repressed, the more the associations failed.

Freud's very earliest remarks about the patient's *consciousness* of resistance are not at all inconsistent with what he later said about *unconscious* resistance in *The Ego and the Id*. When he overcame resistance by repeated pressure, and a definite idea or memory emerged, the patient would frequently say something like, "I could have said it to you the first time" (Breuer and Freud 1895, p. 154; cf. pp. 269–270, 279). Some of the resistance was therefore a conscious unwillingness to report rather than an inability to recall. But this was not true of those breaks in the chains of associations that first caused Freud to use the pressure method repeatedly. What happened there was much more like what he later reported.

In the *Studies*, he briefly described a special series of five cases in which each link in the chain was recovered by separate, single pressures. These links appeared as isolated words, images, or ideas that the subject had little or no hesitation in reporting (pp. 273–278). These accounts read differently from those of conscious withholding, and the patients seem to have been quite unaware of any motive for the associational failure. Indeed, Freud described one of them as "quiet and co-operative" (p. 274) and another as putting up "only a remarkably small conscious resistance" (p. 275). At most, patients seemed to have experienced painful emotions, but not the specific feelings of aversion and repulsion supposed to motivate resistance (pp. 166, 269, 303–304). Other statements, including Freud's descriptions of his own mental state, clearly show the same kind of unawareness to be more usual (p. 117, n. 1.).

There was nothing new in 1923 in the idea of unconscious resistance—it had been so thought of, as H. Hartmann (1956) says, long before (cf. Freud 1896b, p. 162; Masson 1985, Draft N of May 31, 1897), and at neither time was it really a discovery. Although Freud had pictured repression as initiated by a conscious act, the process itself was unconscious. Once he combined that conceptualization with the view that both resistance and repression resulted from the same "aversion on the part of the ego" (Breuer and Freud, 1895, p. 269), it was logically necessary for resistance to be an unconscious ego process too. An unconscious portion of the ego, a portion responsible for resistance, is a simple logical outcome of locating repression there. Even if the idea is not to be dated as early as 1895, one cannot doubt that by 1923 it was neither new nor a discovery.

It is also difficult to accept the unconscious need for punishment as a discovery. First, what was observed was the negative therapeutic reaction. Complex interpretations were required before Freud could conclude that the reaction was a resistance or that it was due to an unconscious need for punishment. He had to weigh and eliminate the more usual forms of resistance in an intricately subjective manner before deciding there was a residual type. Attributing resistance to an unconscious need for punishment was also an interpretation, a point he emphasized himself, although in an odd way. Patients did not feel guilty, their guilt was manifest "only as a resistance to recovery" (Freud 1923b, p. 50). Indeed it was particularly difficult to convince them their behavior was motivated by a need for punishment.

Interpretations at least as complex are involved in Freud's claim that the unconscious need for punishment was also present in obsessional neuroses and melancholia. In them the sense of guilt was actually conscious, even "over-strongly" so (p. 51). Although a logical derivation of both conscious and unconscious senses of guilt from the same unconscious need for punishment might not be impossible, it seems to me very doubtful that these complex interpretations ought to be represented as discoveries. As to their novelty, the fact of guilt in obsessional neuroses and melancholia had been recognized from the time of their first description. Moreover, it is peculiar in the extreme that nowhere in Freud's earlier writing, or in the other psychoanalytic literature as far as I can ascertain, is there even a hint at a behavior as striking as the negative therapeutic reaction. Is one to believe it escaped the scrutiny of Freud and the whole of the first generation of psychoanalysts?

A Theoretical Motive?

At this point we have every right to be suspicious of Freud's motives. His argument rests on the twin pillars of an admittedly unimportant need for terminological clarification and two inferences paraded as discoveries. When one considers that he did not even allude to the really important criticisms of the topographic theory, including the crucial problem of structured fantasies in *Ucs.* he himself raised some eight years earlier, one is quite unable to avoid the suspicion that something else was hidden in the theoretical woodpile.

Let us assume Freud was really faced with the problem indicated at the beginning of this chapter, of fitting the death instinct into his theory of the mind. It would follow that under the pretense of pursuing a line of empirical inquiry he was really attempting a logical reorganization of some of his concepts. Only slightly, if at all, was he adjusting those concepts to newly discovered facts. My views here agree with Deigh's (1984) assessment that the structural theory resulted from Freud's reorganizing his views and bringing "to fruition several ideas the germs of which he had cultivated in earlier writings" rather than from new discoveries. I disagree with Deigh in seeing the structural theory precisely as a consequence of the introduction of a novel theoretical entity, a factor he dismisses. However, let us look at the theoretical needs from which I am certain the reconceptualization sprang.

Superficial consideration alone shows that Thanatos simply cannot be fitted into the old topographic theory. The death instinct cannot be located within *Cs./Pcs.*, as its manifestations would then have to be logical and rational, directly accessible to consciousness, and not subject to repression. These requirements are quite inconsistent with the instinct's projected role and in its having been so long overlooked. On the other hand, were it to be placed in *Ucs.*, dynamic considerations would require the existence of some other *Cs.* force to repress it. Further, the unstructured and primary process characterization of *Ucs.* would make it difficult for Thanatos to come into organized conflict with sexuality there. The very concept of a death instinct occasioned a new kind of unconscious, one more unconscious, than the merely latently unconscious, but not forming part of the repressed unconscious as that system was previously understood. A new kind of unconscious agency had to be invented that was inaccessible to *Cs./Pcs.*, but able to oppose the demands of Eros. The superego and the structural theory obviously met these requirements.

What basis do we have for supposing Freud was undertaking a theoretically based reorganization? We have two pieces of positive evidence. In July of 1922 Freud wrote to Ferenczi that he was "occupied with something speculative, a continuation of *Beyond the Pleasure Principle*" (cited in E. Jones 1953–1957, vol. 3, p. 99), and he repeated this thought in April 1923 in the preface to *The Ego and the Id*:

The present discussions are a further development of some trains of thought which I opened up in *Beyond the Pleasure Principle* and to which, as I remarked there, my attitude was one of a kind of benevolent curiosity.   (Freud 1923b, p. 12)

The speculations toward which he had then been so indulgent were precisely that there might be a death instinct and that it might conflict with the demands of Eros.

We can be sure that Freud envisaged the connection between the new mental structures outlined in *The Ego and the Id* and the instinctual theory of *Beyond the Pleasure Principle* as an especially intimate one, even though only a few writers— Schafer (1960, 1970) and Ricoeur (1970, pp. 281–309) among them—have remarked on it. I think Freud did not get beyond sensing the relation, and it may be that this implicitness is responsible for the connection being overlooked. Certainly he did not establish it as a logical necessity or an empirical finding. The new theory was justified neither by his terminological critique, which was weak, nor by his observations, for there were none.

Superego, Death Instinct, and Identification

The superego was the structure through which the death instinct controlled and sometimes punished the ego's expression of the sexual drive. Most of the materials from which Freud constructed his new concept are to be found in the older concepts of ego-ideal and conscience. However, in the new building the ego-ideal was almost totally reconstituted. Most important, the functions of the conscience were extended to include punishment.

Originally Freud thought the ego-ideal formed when children found it impossible to retain their early narcissistic perfection. They sought to recover a lost state of bliss by reviving in themselves the ideal ego originally belonging to the phase of primary narcissism:

What he projects before him as his [ego] ideal is the substitute for the lost narcissism of his childhood in which he was his own ideal.   (Freud 1914b, p. 94)

Critical admonitions first voiced by the parents prompted the formation of this ego-ideal. As the individual developed, the voices of others, especially teachers, peers, and public opinion were added to the individual's own critical judgments (pp. 94, 96). Conscience, which embodied the criticisms, ensured narcissistic satisfaction by constantly scrutinizing the actual ego and measuring its adequacy against the ideal (p. 95).

The superego[1] of the new theory included standards as well as a conscience. But there were two crucial differences: one in the functions of the new structure, the other in its mode of formation. The functions were extended beyond mere scrutiny. Freud now said the normal conscious sense of guilt or conscience was "the expression of a *condemnation* of the ego by its critical agency" (Freud 1923b, p. 51. My emphasis). In various pathological conditions the ego was described as being treated with "extraordinary harshness and severity" (p. 53). For example, in melancholia, "The whole of the sadism available in the person" raged against the ego (p. 53).

Ten years later, in the *New Introductory Lectures on Psycho-Analysis*, Freud clarified the functions of the superego by assigning each to a specific substructure within it. First, the standards were carried within the superego by the ego-ideal. Second, the scrutiny of the actual behavior of the ego, its measurement against the standards, was carried out by a special observing agency. Finally, punishment for infringements was meted out by the conscience. The term superego referred to the comprehensive structure covering these three distinct functions (Freud 1933b, p. 66; cf. pp. 58–65). The most novel, and the one differentiating the superego from any of its precursors, was the function of self-punishment. Through this punishment Freud gave the death instinct a place in mental life.

The Origins of the Superego

What were the origins of the new structure? Narcissism barely came into it. Freud now envisaged the superego forming during the demolition of the Oedipus complex. By a process he called *identification* a substructure based on the values and standards of the parents formed within the ego. Simultaneously, a process he termed *defusion* provided the energy of the death instinct to this altered part of the ego.

Defusion Considering defusion first, we note it was actually one of two related assumptions forced on Freud by his characterization of the death instinct. It will be recalled that the death instinct was initially directed at the very fabric of the organism; it sought to silence every sign of life and to return each cell to its original, inanimate condition. For the organism to survive for even a minimal period, this tendency to self-destruction had to be countered. As Freud saw it, instinctual drives such as sex and hunger interfered with this tendency. Eros neutralized the immediate self-destructive efforts of Thanatos by first gathering individual cells into colonies and then combining with Thanatos to create an externally directed impulse of aggressiveness or destructiveness.

Conceptually speaking, the first step in placing the death instinct within the organism had to be to find ways of mitigating its effects. Freud's conception of Thanatos fusing with Eros was an absolutely necessary consequence of the revised instinct theory. As he himself put it, the fusion of these instincts was "an *assumption* indispensable to our conception" (Freud 1923b, p. 41. My emphasis). But once the assumption had been made, a second became just as necessary: Thanatos had to be separated from Eros. Defusion had to be assumed if the superego were to be invested with a portion of the death instinct:

Once we have admitted the idea of a fusion of the two classes of instincts ... the possibility of a—more or less complete—"defusion" of them *forces itself upon us.* (p. 41. My emphasis).

As we will see, Freud further assumed relatively free communication between the ego and the id. Through that channel the defused portion of the death instinct was made available. Now charged with the might of Thanatos, the superego could oppose the tumultuous strivings of Eros.

Identifications How did identification bring about these consequences? Freud used the term identification to mean different things at different times, but his common meaning was that it was an alteration of the individual's behavior such that it became more like someone else's. At the level of interpretation, one ego became more like that of another. Freud initially made most use of this notion of identification as a change in the ego to explain some of the symptoms of disorders that, as in some depressions (or melancholias), were preceded by the loss of a sexual object. He believed libido was then detached from the mental representation of the object and returned to the ego, where it was used to establish an identification of the ego with the lost object. The self-reproaches of the melancholic, which might sometimes culminate "in a delusional expectation of punishment" (Freud 1917c, p. 244), were nothing more than the reproaches that the patient originally directed against the object. Now however, they were directed to his own ego:

Thus the shadow of the object fell upon the ego, and the latter could henceforth be judged by a special agency, as though it were an object, the foresaken object. In this way an object-loss was transformed into an ego-loss and the conflict between the ego and the loved person into a cleavage between the critical activity of the ego and the ego as altered by identification. (p. 249)

The "critical activity" was, of course, the conscience. In melancholia, the modifications produced in the ego by its incorporation of the lost object were sufficient to direct the reproaches of conscience against it.

It seemed to Freud that the lost object must have had two contradictory properties. First, the fixation to it had to have been very strong, otherwise it would not have become so important. On the other hand, it was given up relatively easily—its cathexis would not have had much power of resistance. Freud resolved the apparent contradiction by assuming the original basis for choosing the object was a narcissistic one. He proposed a mechanism of oral incorporation, a concept modeled on the act of eating:

The ego wants to incorporate this object into itself, and, in accordance with the oral or cannibalistic phase of libidinal development in which it is, it wants to do so by devouring it.   (pp. 249–250)

This identification "represents, of course, a *regression* from one type of object-choice to original narcissism" (p. 249). He assumed superego formation partly involved a similar regression to narcissism with a similar identification by incorporation.

Not every identification from which the superego formed incorporated an object. In *Group Psychology and the Analysis of the Ego*, Freud already recognized another kind of identification not based on object-choice at all. He declared that what may be called primary identification was "the earliest expression of an emotional tie with another person" (Freud 1921, p. 105; cf. p. 107). It was not at all the same thing as an object-choice:

It is easy to state in a formula the distinction between an identification with the father and the choice of the father as an object. In the first case one's father is what one would like to *be*, and in the second he is what one would like to *have*. . . . The former kind of tie is therefore already possible before any sexual object-choice has been made.   (p. 106)

Compared with this descriptive distinction, a meta-psychological or theoretical representation of it was, Freud wryly noted, "much more difficult" (p. 106).

In *The Ego and the Id* he brought both kinds of identification together in the following simplified account of the origins of the superego:

At a very early age the little boy develops an object-cathexis for his mother, which originally related to the mother's breast and is the prototype of an object-choice on the anaclitic model; the boy deals with his father by identifying himself with him.   (Freud 1923b, p. 31)

As the boy's sexual wishes for the mother grew more intense, the father was more frequently perceived as an obstacle to them, and the Oedipus complex developed. Thereupon the boy's identification with the father took on a hostile, aggressive coloring, and after that his relation to him was based on an ambivalent mixture of love and hate. With the demolition of the Oedipus complex, the object-cathexis of the mother was given up and its place taken by either an identification with her, an identification analogous with that in melancholia, or by an intensification of the identification with the father (pp. 31–32). This latter outcome was, said Freud, "the more normal" (p. 32).

Bisexuality   Outcomes were not usually simple. An omnipresent constitutional bisexuality caused the Oedipus complex to have a negative or inverted form as well as a positive. The positive complex in the boy, the one just discussed, is the combination of sexual desire for the mother with an ambivalent but basically hostile death wish toward the father. In it there is an object-choice of the mother and a primary identification with the father. The negative or inverted complex was based on the boy's *femininity*. It led him to choose his father as object and make a primary identification with his mother. When the Oedipus complex was dissolved, the four trends grouped themselves to produce

a father-identification and a mother-identification. The father-identification will preserve the object-relation to the mother which belonged to the positive complex and will at the same time replace the object-relation to the father which belonged to the inverted complex: and the same will be true, *mutatis mutandis*, of the mother-identification.   (p. 34)

He had his summary printed with emphasis:

The broad general outcome of the sexual phase dominated by the Oedipus complex may, therefore, be taken to be the forming of a precipitate in the ego, consisting of these two identifications in some way united with each other. This modification of the ego retains its special position; it confronts the other contents of the ego as [a] ... super-ego.   (p. 34)

Identification thus gave the superego its content as well as the energy necessary to execute its destructive functions.

The Ego and the Two Instincts

We have seen how the death instinct broke down the isomorphism of the structural with the topographic theory. It required, in essence, an unconscious portion of $Cs./Pcs.$ to be separated off and invested with the completely new function of punishment. Nor was there a match between what remained—the new ego operated in a fundamentally different manner from $Cs./Pcs.$ Again the difference was due to the death instinct. Because the basic conflict was now between Thanatos, housed in the superego, and Eros, located in the id, rather than between an active repressing force in $Cs./Pcs.$ and a sexual instinctual drive in $Ucs.$, the ego had to become a passive agency, almost a kind of arena on which the battle took place. As a consequence, the cognitive functions of perception, memory, judgment, and motor control were emphasized much more than they had been in $Cs./Pcs.$ They enabled an essentially cognitive basis for the decision to repress or not. And, although in one sense the ego's decision initiated repression, it was not the ego itself that carried it out, but the pleasure principle operating under the aegis of the death instinct in the superego.

In *The Ego and the Id*, Freud's proposals, although fragmentary, elucidate the changed role of the ego. First was the passivity of this new ego. It was a poor creature owing service to three masters and consequently menaced by three dangers: from the external world, from the libido of the id, and from the severity of the super-ego. (Freud 1923b, p. 56)

However, he gave this ego the power of apprehending anxieties arising from these sources. Where there was danger, the ego emitted anxiety and, if the danger came from the id, repression was initiated (p. 56). But the initiative was not the ego's:

as a rule the ego carries out repressions in the service and at the behest of its super-ego. (p. 52; cf. 1924a, p. 150)

Subordination was logically inevitable. If Freud were to continue asserting that repression derived from the individual's moral standards, and if he had transferred those standards to the superego, nothing remained in the ego from which repression could proceed. Very early he had made the ego's standards the point of departure for repression, and although that line of thinking seems to have been temporarily eclipsed by the stress he put on the organic theory of automatic repression in the period 1900–1912, the standards were reemphasized from 1912 onward (chapter 11). When, then, he reiterated that repression "took its stand on aesthetic and ethical motives," as he was to do in a historical account of psychoanalysis contemporaneous with *The Ego and the Id* (Freud 1924c, p. 197), it had to be the case that repression could really be instigated only by the structure housing those motives, namely, the superego.

There was a second respect in which the new ego was passive: it had no energy of its own that could be sensibly conceptualized as opposing and controlling the sexual instinctual drive. Freud gave it nothing corresponding to the energy of the self-preservation drive. All he provided was a form of libido so emasculated it could hardly be thought of as standing up to and directly denying the demands of its parent. But it was enough to allow the ego to perceive and evaluate instinctual danger and, if necessary, produce a signal of anxiety. Through the death instinct, the pleasure principle did the rest. Consequently, it was possible

to picture the id as under the domination of the mute but powerful death instincts, which desire to be at peace and (prompted by the pleasure principle) to put Eros, the mischief-maker, to rest.   (Freud 1923b, p. 59)

Meaning had been given to the otherwise peculiar conclusion of *Beyond the Pleasure Principle* that the pleasure principle seemed "actually to serve the death instincts" (Freud 1920a, p. 63).

Given its passive nature and its reliance on the superego, what the new ego required to carry out its tasks were functions that can broadly be referred to as cognitive. Given Freud's style of theorizing, it also had to be endowed with some energy enabling those functions to be exercised. It is to these two aspects of the new concept that I now turn.

The Ego's Cognitive Functions

Not all instinctual pressures necessitated repression, drives sometimes had to be satisfied. Nor did all danger arise from within. What came from outside required a choice between flight or active defense. The ego therefore had to be able to perceive stimuli, to assign an external or internal origin to them, to assess them for potential danger, and then to institute appropriate action. In his earlier theorizing Freud derived these judgmental and motor functions from the perceptual, motor, and memory systems. In *The Ego and the Id* and several other works from between 1923 and 1925, he synthesized the systems slightly differently. For the most part, he had already described or suggested the functions themselves in the *Project* of 1895, *The Interpretation of Dreams* of 1900, the papers on metapsychology of 1914, and *Beyond the Pleasure Principle* of 1920. What he now had to do was make them consistent with the new theory of repression, especially with the signal role given to anxiety.

Energy and Protection   Freud began the new synthesis by returning to his fictional primitive organism suspended in its world of potentially lethal energies. In the *Project* he contended that the sense organs protected the nervous system from intense quantities of excitation (Freud 1950/1954, *Project*, part I, sections 5–9 of 1895), and in *Beyond the Pleasure Principle* he developed this concept into one of a protective shield absorbing and attenuating most of the energy before passing it on (Freud 1920a, pp. 27–29; cf. 1940a, pp. 145–146). Five years later, in a short paper exploring an analogy with some of these concepts, he claimed he had *shown* that there was such a shield (Freud 1925b, p. 230). Although he may sometimes have given the impression that the shield was a mere passive membrane, a kind of baked crust, he clearly meant it to have active properties:

The protective shield is supplied with its own store of energy and must above all endeavour to preserve the special modes of transformation of energy operating in it against the effects threatened by the enormous energies at work in the external world.   (Freud 1920a, p. 27)

The first purpose for which Freud required the shield to have its own energy was to enable it to transform freely flowing energy into a bound or quiescent state. Binding reduced the intensity of potentially damaging external excitation or held it back altogether.

Energy and Perception   The second purpose for which energy was required was to give perception a protective function. Freud earlier supposed the sensory receptors—collectively the system *Pcpt.-Cs.*—to lie beneath the protective shield (Freud 1950/1954, *Project*, part I, sections 3, 5, and 9). He now went on to suppose they were supplied with energy:

cathectic innervations are sent out and withdrawn in rapid periodic impulses from within into the ... system *Pcpt.-Cs.* So long as that system is cathected in this manner, it receives perceptions (which are accompanied by consciousness) and passes the excitation on to the unconscious mnemic systems; but as soon as the cathexis is withdrawn, consciousness is extinguished and the functioning of the system comes to a standstill.   (Freud 1925b, p. 231; cf. 1920a, pp. 27–28, 1925d, p. 238)

As we saw in chapter 12, he believed the traumatic effects of excessive stimulation were reduced by the individual's expectation of danger or preparedness for it (Freud 1920a, pp. 13, 33). Because he believed preparedness to be an "increased sensory attention and motor tension" (Freud 1916–1917, pp. 394–395), and sensory attention to be a cathection of the sense organs, the periodic innervation of *Pcpt.-Cs.* had a protective function. This is what he seems to have meant when he said:

preparedness for anxiety and the hypercathexis of the receptive systems constitute the last line of defence of the shield against stimuli.   (Freud 1920a, p. 31)

And he probably was referring to the periodic sampling when he said the sense organs also included

special arrangements for further protection against excessive amounts of stimulation and for *excluding unsuitable kinds of stimuli.*   (p. 28)

Small amounts of cathexes periodically supplied to *Pcpt.-Cs.* allowed it to sample the external world, to take in specimens, as it were, to determine the nature and direction of any external stimulation, and, if necessary, to subdue it by binding (pp. 27–31; cf. 1925b, p. 231, 1925d, p. 238).

  Pcpt.-Cs. also received stimuli from within. Freud had always believed the most important internal stimuli were the feelings of unpleasure and pleasure caused by the pressure and discharge of instinctual drives (Freud 1950/1954, *Project*, part I, section 8; cf. 1900, pp. 598–603, 1915a, pp. 120–121). Building on an argument first advanced in "The Unconscious" (Freud 1915c, pp. 177–178) he reiterated that these feelings of pleasure and unpleasure became conscious directly (Freud 1923b, pp. 21–22; cf. 1940a, pp. 145–146).

Energy, Judgment, and Reality-Testing   Freud's coordination of this explicit sampling-protective view of *Pcpt.-Cs* with the motor functions hypothesized earlier allowed him to attribute judgmental functions to the new ego. In his earliest theorizing he assumed a direct connection between the motor and perceptual systems, and that the consequences of movement differentiated external sources of excitation from internal. Withdrawal, for example, caused external stimulation to cease but had no such effect on endogenous sources of excitation (Freud 1950/1954, *Project*, part I, section 1; cf. 1900, p. 565). As we saw in chapter 10, this differential result was incorporated into the definitions of stimulus and instinctual drive. The former could be "disposed of by a single expedient action" such as flight or withdrawal, but the latter could not (Freud 1915a, p. 118).

By these distinctions the organism also differentiated external from internal and the real or objective from the unreal or subjective. Freud argued that in what he termed "the efficacy of its muscular activity," the organism had "a basis for distinguishing between an 'outside' and an 'inside' ":

On the one hand, it will be aware of stimuli which can be avoided by muscular action (flight); these it ascribes to an external world. On the other hand, it will also be aware of stimuli against which such action is of no avail and whose character of constant pressure persists in spite of it; these stimuli are the signs of an internal world, the evidence of instinctual needs. (Freud 1915a, p. 119; cf. p. 134)

Slightly later, he made the additional point that this same movement made judgments of reality possible:

A perception which is made to disappear by an action is recognized as external, as reality; where such an action makes no difference, the perception originates within the subject's own body—it is not real.   (Freud 1917a, p. 232)

"Reality-testing," Freud's term for this judgmental function, was developed by him from the connection between the perceptual and the motor apparatus.

Note the active role that reality-testing imposed on the organism and the need it created for energy with which to carry it out. *Cs.*(*Pcpt.*), Freud said,

must have at its disposal a motor innervation which determines whether the perception can be made to disappear or whether it proves resistant.   (p. 233)

After stressing that "Reality-testing need be nothing more than this contrivance," he assigned that function squarely to his then concept of the ego (p. 233), although he later vacillated and placed it temporarily within the ego-ideal (Freud 1921, p. 114). When he reinstated reality testing as one of the major institutions of the new ego (Freud 1923b, p. 55), it was again through the connection of *Pcpt.-Cs.* with the motor system. That connection itself had to be placed within the new ego (Freud 1925d, pp. 237–238).

Connecting memory with *Pcpt.-Cs.* followed in a similar way from Freud's earlier theorizing. In both the *Project* and *The Interpretation of Dreams* the memory systems were placed immediately behind the perceptual, a proximity that seems to have been based on his twin beliefs that stimuli causing perceptions necessarily left traces of their passage, and that memory elements were of the same basic type as the perceptual (Breuer and Freud 1895, pp. 188, n. 1; Freud 1950/1954, *Project*, part I, section 3, 1900, pp. 538–540). Whatever the reasons, once memory was so situated, the ego was given a function enabling it to make ready comparisons between current stimulation and traces of previous experience.

Between them, these connections between the motor, the memory, and the perceptual systems gave the primitive organism the potential for perceiving stimuli, distinguishing them from instinctual drives, differentiating between its inner and outer worlds, testing the reality of its percepts, and remembering the effects of its actions. But its actions were very circumscribed. Really expedient action was limited—instinctual drives could be satisfied only in the hallucinatory mode and external stimuli could only be avoided. More was required. Freud reasoned that, if immediate primary process discharge could be delayed, earlier experiences could be scrutinized for appropriate courses of realistic action. He therefore gave the nucleus of the ego, the systems *Pcpt.-Cs.*, its own cathectic energy as well as the power to use it in any way at all. With these cathexes he gave the ego the ability to control what he variously termed the approaches to or access to motility, that is, to delay or initiate motor discharge.

The ego's power over its cathexes and its control of movement also enabled it to think. However, even that function was not new, nor was its attribution to an ego or egolike structure. From the time of the *Project*, Freud conceptualized thought as an experimental kind of *action*, an exploration of the mnemic traces of the movements that led to previous satisfactions (Freud 1950/1954, *Project*, part III, sections 1 and 4 of Oct. 5, 1895; cf. 1900, pp. 566–567, 598–599). He therefore retained this control over the motor system as one of the two essential characteristics of the new ego (Freud 1923b, p. 55; cf. 1925d, p. 238).

The other essential characteristic of the ego also derived from its omnipotent control of its own cathexes but, unlike the ego's control over the motor system, it was absolutely novel. Freud's sudden announcement in the concluding pages of *The Ego and the Id* that "The ego is the actual seat of anxiety" (Freud 1923b, p. 57) was quite unheralded. He meant two things. First, only the ego could generate anxiety, that is, emit it as a signal (p. 57). Second, as he added in a later clarification, only the ego could experience anxiety (Freud 1926a, p. 140). He later summarized the two functions by saying, "the ego alone can *produce* and *feel* anxiety" (Freud 1933b, p. 85. My emphasis). Disposable cathexes enabled the ego to judge whether an instinctual danger was present and to generate the anxiety, causing the superego to repress the drive.

The Ego's Energy

How did the ego acquire its displaceable store of energy, and precisely how did it use it? Taking the question of origins first, Freud argued that the energy was a special form of libido created during identification. Identification altered the ego so it resembled the parents and could be loved in the same way as they had been. The ego thus represented itself to the id as the original love objects and thereby attracted libido to itself (Freud 1923b, pp. 29–30). In doing so, Freud asserted, the libido became narcissistic and lost its sexual quality:

The transformation of object-libido into narcissistic libido which thus takes place obviously implies an abandonment of sexual aims, a desexualization—a kind of sublimation, therefore. (p. 30)

Desexualized, sublimated Eros was the ego's neutral and displaceable psychic energy. Despite its transformation, sublimated energy retained

the main purpose of Eros—that of uniting and binding—in so far as it helps towards establishing the unity, or tendency to unity, which is particularly characteristic of the ego. If thought-processes in the wider sense are to be included among these displacements, then the activity of thinking is also supplied from the sublimation of erotic motive forces.   (p. 45)

Consciousness itself was pictured as arising from displacements of energy. Freud here drew on some concepts he first outlined in *On Aphasia* (Freud 1891/1953, pp. 77–78; cf. *Standard Edition*, vol. 14, pp. 209–215) and expanded on in correspondence with Fliess (Masson 1985, Letters of May 30, 1896, Dec. 6, 1896, Dec. 22, 1897; Freud 1950/1954, *Project*, part III, section 1). In *The Ego and the Id* he proposed as a precondition for an unconscious idea becoming preconscious, and so acquiring the potentiality for consciousness, that it become connected with the words corresponding to it. An unconscious idea was a so-called "thing-representation," a direct mental representation of an earlier perception, particularly of its visual components. It was "the cathexis, if not of the direct memory-images of the thing, at least of remoter memory-traces derived from these" (Freud 1915c, p. 201). Verbal mnemic residues deriving primarily from the auditory perceptions corresponding to thing-representations formed what Freud called "word-representations." The ego raised unconscious ideas to preconsciousness by using its energy to link thing-representations with word-representations (Freud 1923b, pp. 19–23). An additional attentional hypercathexis then brought them to consciousness proper. Consequently, it was to the ego that consciousness was attached (p. 17).[2]

We can now appreciate Freud's summary propositions. The ego

starts out, as we see, from the system *Pcpt.*, which is its nucleus, and begins by embracing the *Pcs.*, which is adjacent to the mnemic residues. (Freud 1923b, p. 23; cf. 1926a, p. 92)

The motor connection was stressed because

the functional importance of the ego is manifested in the fact that normally control over the approaches to motility devolves upon it. (Freud 1923b, p. 25)

And the significance of what Freud called the important functions entrusted to the ego were

By virtue of its relation to the perceptual system it gives mental processes an order in time and submits them to "reality-testing". By interposing the processes of thinking, it secures a postponement of motor discharges and controls the access to motility. (p. 55)

Given its store of displaceable energy and its particular components, this ego could sense dangers, inhibit discharge, and act rationally. When it generated anxiety and called the pleasure principle into operation, instinctual drives were repressed. However, before examining how repression took place, we have to consider the forces the ego had to control.

Ucs., the Death Instinct, and the Id

To his revised concept of the ego Freud now opposed not simply the repository of repressed ideas constituting the topographic *Ucs.*, but a new structure containing the totality of those impersonal and uncontrollable forces that gave people the impression they were creatures of obscure powers, lived by alien drives and urges, and were acted upon as passive objects. He derived the name for this new structure from Georg Groddeck, a German physician of speculative persuasion and friend of psychoanalysis. Groddeck held the view that

man is animated by the Unknown, that there is within him an "Es", an "It", some wondrous force which directs both what he himself does, and what happens to him. The affirmation "I live" is only conditionally correct, it expresses only a small and superficial part of the fundamental principle, "Man is lived by the It". (Groddeck 1923/1949, p. 11)

His term *das Es* ("the It") has been rendered by the Latin *id* in English translations of Freud's works. Freud almost completely disregarded Groddeck's meaning in annexing the term. He made his id the repository of the death as well as the sexual instinctual drives, and attributed all the primary process characteristics of *Ucs.* to it. As he remarked some ten years later:

This impersonal pronoun seems particularly well suited for expressing the main characteristic of this province of the mind—*the fact of its being alien to the ego.* (Freud 1933b, p. 72. My emphasis)

Naïvely, "The ego represents what may be called reason and common sense, in contrast to the id, which contains the passions" (Freud 1923b, p. 25). The id was everything the ego was not.

If the ego was that part of the mind that started out from *Pcpt.*, the id was the unconscious part into which it extended. This idea of the ego merging with the id constitutes another of the main differences between the structural and topographic theories. Whereas the more or less absolute barrier of repression prevented contact between *Ucs.* and *Cs./Pcs.* in the earlier theory, direct communication between ego and id was possible. "The ego is not sharply separated from the id; its lower portion merges into it" (p. 24). He thus allowed for the effects of the third kind of unconscious, the nonrepressed kind. Moreover, this direct avenue was available to the repressed mental contents themselves; they also merged with the id, forming part of it and communicating with the ego through the id (p. 24).

The absence of a distinct barrier between the repressed and the id (and hence the ego) did not mean that repression and the storehouse of repressed ideas declined in importance. So drastic a modification would have required Freud to rewrite almost every page of his previous explanations of mental life. What was being allowed for was the retention of a part of the old in the context of the new. Repression separated the repressed contents only from the ego. As Freud's diagrams show, on one side of the storehouse of repressed ideas was the wall of repression, and on the other was an open archway leading to the id and from there directly to the ego (figure 13.1).

The idea that some unconscious processes might have direct access to higher structures was not new to Freud's thinking in 1923. As early as the metapsychological paper "The Unconscious," where the role of word-representations in bringing unconscious ideas to consciousness was stated most fully, he insisted there were no such things as unconscious affects (Freud 1915c, pp. 177–179). He repeated this argument in *The Ego and the Id*, adding that, when emotions and feelings became conscious, they did so directly, without requiring word-representation linkages at all. His reiteration came just before his description of the id, a description that emphasized the absence of a sharp division between it and the ego (Freud 1923b, pp. 22–23). Perhaps it was his purpose to suggest that what might be true of emotions in the unconscious

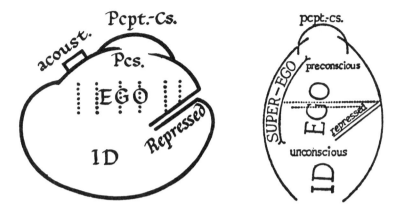

Figure 13.1
The structures of the structural theory (Freud 1923b, p. 24, 1933b, p. 78).

was true of the whole range of contents in the id. Although it is not a very plausible analogy, it does foreshadow part of Freud's explanation for the second of his claimed discoveries. An unconscious need for punishment positively demanded direct communication between the id and that part of the ego from which punishment proceeded. It also allowed for instinctually related anxieties to become conscious directly, and to serve as signals of danger and so precipitate repression.

Anxiety and Repression

A central proposition of the structural theory was that anxiety caused repression. Freud several times apologized for this about-face—in his earlier formula he had repression causing anxiety (Freud 1926a, pp. 93, 109; cf. 1933b, p. 89). More than a simple modification to the mechanism of repression was involved however. Freud had to abandon or drastically change his propositions about the essence of neuroses, to find a source of anxiety other than libido, and, to incorporate castration and superego anxieties, to rethink the distinction between primal repression and repression proper.

Toxicity and the Essence of Neuroses

Almost from the time he began writing about neuroses Freud stressed that their essence was a toxic state. Quite early he drew parallels between neuroses and conditions of what he called autointoxication such as the overactivity of the thyroid gland in Graves' disease or exophthalmic goiter (Freud 1888a, p. 41, 1892–1894, pp. 139–140, note to Charcot's p. 237). He cited this parallel frequently, usually as part of his argument that intoxication produced by accumulated sexual substances or their breakdown products were basic to both the actual and the psychoneuroses (Masson 1985, Draft I, undated, possibly of Oct. 8, 1895, Letter of Jan. 1, 1896; Freud 1950/1954, part I, section 12, 1905b, pp. 215–216 and 1920 modification, 1906a, pp. 278–279, 1908c, pp. 185–186, 1910e, p. 218, 1912b, p. 248, 1916–1917, pp. 388–391, 1925c, pp. 214–215, 1925a, pp. 25–26). We have seen how he believed anxiety in anxiety neurosis was caused by the deflection of the libido into the autonomic nervous system in an unsuccessful attempt to discharge sexual toxins (Masson 1985, Draft E, possibly June 6, 1894; Freud 1895a,b; 1916–1917, pp. 401–403). He believed he had discovered a similar process in the psychoneuroses:

Analyses of hysteria and obsessional neurosis yield the ... conclusion that a similar deflection with the same outcome may also be the result of a refusal on the part of the *psychical* agencies.   (Freud 1916–1917, p. 404)

Anxiety in the psychoneuroses could be seen as a similar attempt to discharge toxins. Repression could do away with neither libidinal energy nor the substances from which it derived.

Toxicity and Birth   Freud combined his toxic theory with the ego's signal function by searching for an original danger situation having toxic accompaniments the threatened recurrence of which could be signaled by the ego. He found this prototype of neurotic anxiety in the universal experience of being born. As early as 1908–1909 he drew attention to *anxiety* during birth:

the act of birth is the first experience of anxiety, and thus the source and prototype of the affect of anxiety.   (Freud 1900, pp. 400–401, n. 3 of 1909 written in 1908. Emphasis altered. Cf. Nunberg and Federn 1962–1975, vol. 2, Minute 87 of Nov. 17, 1909, pp. 323–324)

Two years later he connected this first anxiety with *danger*. Birth was

both the first of all dangers to life and the prototype of all the later ones that cause us to feel anxiety, and the experience of birth has probably left behind in us the expression of affect which we call anxiety.   (Freud 1910d, p. 173)

What was the danger? About six years later he specified it as the toxins that accumulated in the infant's blood stream between birth and independent respiration being established:

The immense increase of stimulation owing to the interruption of the renovation of the blood (internal respiration) was ... the cause of the experience of anxiety; the first anxiety was thus a toxic one. The name *Angst—angustiae, Enge* [Latin and German for "narrow place" and "straits"]—emphasizes the characteristic of restriction in breathing which was then present as a consequence of the real situation and is now almost invariably reinstated in the affect. (Freud 1916–1917, pp. 396–397; cf. Nunberg and Federn 1962–1975, vol. 2, Minute 60 of Nov. 25, 1908, pp. 71–72)

Neurotic anxiety could find its prototype in birth anxiety because both were reactions to toxins. For the same reason birth was the basis for the most common anxiety of childhood—separation from the mother or longing for her. During separation, libidinal desire for the mother led to toxicity and from thence to anxiety, just as in actual neuroses (Freud 1916–1917, pp. 405–408).

Toxicity and Normal Anxiety   If the ego's reaction to current threats could be put in toxic terms, a little juggling made it possible to link nonneurotic anxiety to being born. During 1916–1917, when Freud was still thinking in terms of an instinct theory that pitted libido against self-preservation, the only things that could be discharged in response to a current threat were the energy of the self-preservation instinct (more correctly, the egoism of the ego-instincts) or the narcissistic libido invested in the ego, the ego-libido. His choice then was monistically clear:

the state of anxiety is in every instance inexpedient, and its inexpedience becomes obvious if it reaches a fairly high pitch. In such cases it interferes with action, whether flight or defence, which alone is expedient and alone serves the cause of self-preservation. If, therefore, we attribute the affective portion of realistic anxiety to ego-libido and the accompanying action to the self-preservative instinct, we shall have got rid of the theoretical difficulty.   (p. 430; cf. p. 405)

Being the energy of the self-preservation drive, egoism could not be toxic. Ego-libido, on the other hand, had all the properties of sexual libido, including its toxicity. After all, it was only ordinary libido lodged in the ego. Normal anxiety could be given the same toxic source as neurotic anxiety if it resulted from the discharge of ego-libido.

Actually, whenever Freud discussed anxiety during the first ten to fifteen years of his work his references were always to neurotic anxiety. During the whole of that period he made only one mention of normal anxiety, and it is a quite unimportant, nontechnical, and passing one (Freud 1895a, p. 93). More or less suddenly in the *Introductory Lectures* he differentiated realistic from neurotic anxiety. Normal anxiety was the reaction of the ego to the perception of an external threat, and it was expedient to the extent that it was a signal to prepare for danger rather than being a massive and overwhelming trauma. On this ground, normal anxiety seemed rational and intelligible (Freud 1916–1917, pp. 393–394). But why were the discharge patterns identical? The only alternatives Freud seems to have considered were that the two kinds of anxiety might have a similar toxic basis or that they might be provoked by similar external conditions. He chose the first explanation. We have seen that he had a similar choice in accounting for the resemblance of birth to other anxieties. Was it because they were all reactions to toxins, or because they were provoked by similar dangers? Initially, Freud again chose toxicity—accumulated ego-libido caused realistic anxiety.

Toxic conceptualizations had to be given up in the structural theory. By then, Freud was not insisting on the special connection between anxiety and libido that was required by the thesis that repression caused anxiety. Nor, by then, was there any distinction between self-preservation and sexual drives—both were coalesced in Eros—and egoism could now no longer be distinguished from ego-libido or any other form of libido. Consequently, the revisions of the structural theory forced Freud to choose the second alternative: neurotic and objective anxiety now had in common the fact they were provoked by similar conditions of danger. Even birth anxiety, although still a reaction to toxicity, was not linked to other anxieties simply because of that fact. What anxiety situations had in common was excessive amounts of stimulation. What, then, was the source of the excess?

Sources of Anxiety

In *Inhibitions, Symptoms and Anxiety* (1926a) Freud rethought the problem of the sources of anxiety. There he proposed that certain very early traumatic experiences left behind memory traces that included traces of the affect. When the ego later compared new stimuli with its earlier records, it might judge that the same situation was about to recur. It would then inhibit the primary process discharge and revive an attenuated form of the earlier anxiety as a signal.

Defence and Flight   Freud's explicit model for defence against unwelcome internal stimuli was the organism's flight from external danger. At first the organism merely withdrew its cathexis from the dangerous perception; it made only a token attempt to flee. As the ego matured, the cathexis was used to produce a movement that took it away from the danger. Repression was

an equivalent at this attempt at flight. The ego withdraws its (preconscious) cathexis from the instinctual representative that is to be repressed and uses that cathexis for the purpose of releasing unpleasure (anxiety).   (Freud 1926a, pp. 92–93)

But the preconscious ego cathexis was not itself transformed into anxiety. Withdrawing it reduced the total cathexis, and according to our assumptions, unpleasure and anxiety can only arise as a result of an *increase* in cathexis.   (p. 93)

What the ego cathexis was used for was to reproduce the affect:

Anxiety is *not newly created* in repression; it is *reproduced* ... in accordance with an already existing mnemic image.   (p. 93. My emphasis)

Neither could Freud argue that this reproduced anxiety was explicable in economic terms. Reproduction required only a trivial increase in the total quantity of energy—just enough to generate the signal. He was therefore forced to propose that anxiety was generated in two different ways. Excessive stimulation breaking through the protective shield caused a profound economic disturbance experienced as a very intense anxiety. Freud termed the breakthrough a *traumatic situation* and the anxiety produced in it *automatic anxiety*. The impending recurrence of an original trauma placed the organism in a *danger situation* during which the original memory might be used to produce *signal anxiety* (pp. 137–138, 166; cf. 1933b, pp. 93–95).

The Components of Anxiety What then *was* anxiety? Freud thought it had three characteristics. First, there was the specific quality differentiating anxiety from other affects, especially from other unpleasant emotions. Second, there were the motor innervations of the various bodily organs, the processes of discharge, particularly those that increased the heart-rate and breathing. Third, there were the perceptions of the discharge. Of the connection between the characteristics, he said:

In accordance with our general views we should be inclined to think that anxiety is based upon an increase of excitation which on the one hand produces the character of unpleasure and on the other finds relief through the acts of discharge already mentioned. But a purely physiological account of this sort will scarcely satisfy us.   (Freud 1926a, p. 133)

Leaving aside the doubtful proposition that this account was a physiological one (excitation and discharge had ceased to be "purely physiological" as early as *The Interpretation of Dreams*), in what sense did it "scarcely satisfy" Freud? What he meant was that he could see no particular reason for the excitation, the unpleasure, and the pattern of discharge to occur together. He was therefore

tempted to assume the presence of a historical factor which binds the sensations of anxiety and its innervations firmly together. We assume, in other words, that an anxiety-state is the reproduction of some experience which contained the necessary conditions for such an increase of excitation and a discharge along particular paths, and that from this circumstance the unpleasure of anxiety receives its specific character. In man, birth provides a prototypic experience of this kind, and we are therefore inclined to regard anxiety-states as a reproduction of the trauma of birth.   (p. 133; cf. pp. 93–94)

Although this was not his original thought about birth at all, it was still the case that he could assert the innervations belonged to an action that had once been expedient:

at birth it is probable that the innervation, in being directed to the respiratory organs, is preparing the way for the activity of the lungs, and, in accelerating the heart-beat, is helping to keep the blood free from toxic substances.   (p. 134)

Toxins continued to constitute the specific traumatic situation at birth. But, according to Freud's new argument, being born was important primarily because the purposive reaction to the excessive stimulation it generated brought the three distinguishing characteristics of anxiety together. Later traumatic increases in stimulation resulted in similar feelings and the same perceptions of discharge even when toxins were not present. Irrespective of the physiology of the other traumatic situations, birth provided a prototypal, purposive, affective response for them. A complete recasting of his distinction between primal repression and repression proper now allowed Freud to link the various traumatic situations to one another and to relate them to signal anxiety.

Primal Repression and Repression Proper

Pretty clearly what signal anxiety caused was repression proper or after-pressure. What was signaled was the danger of an earlier traumatic situation recurring, and it was really that threat that caused the repression.

The Pathogenic Nucleus   It had always been a central point with Freud that later repressions had to be related to an earlier or primary and more pathogenic impression. In positing that Anna O.'s initial snake hallucination was "the root of her whole illness" Breuer pointed the way (Breuer and Freud 1895, p. 40). Independent of Breuer, the French school of psychopathologists proposed an elementary *condition seconde* as the core of all hysteria. The first experiences occurring in it formed a seed around which later symptoms precipitated. Similarly, it was crucial to Freud's view of his patients' pathology in *Studies on Hysteria*. At the center of the pathogenic memory structure was a "primary impression" in which the traumatic factor "found its purest manifestation" (pp. 75, n. 1, 288). At that time he believed that the impression had to have been "intentionally repressed," and he persevered until he found it (p. 116). A focus around which later pathogenic experiences crystallized was a sine qua non.

Freud never really dropped this notion of a central traumatic event as a focus from which later events derived their traumatic force. We find it again in the topographic theory as the repressed unconscious memory that attracted later expelled mental contents to itself. It is also recognizable during psychosexual development as the passive lagging behind or fixation of a libidinal component. Its final manifestation is as the concept of primal repression first introduced in the two-stage theory of repression described in "Repression" in 1915. Repression proper supplied an after-pressure linking later pathogenic experiences to those succumbing to the earlier primal repression. At that time Freud thought of primal repression as a psychosexual fixation (Freud 1915b, p. 148; cf. 1905b, p. 175, n. 2 of 1915, 1911a, pp. 61–62, 67–68).

Trauma and Primal Repression   Where in the structural theory were the parallels with traumatic and danger situations? After reiterating that a repression dealt with in therapy was an instance of after-pressure that presupposed a primal repression, he offered the brief speculation that it was "highly probable":

the immediate precipitating causes of primal repressions are quantitative factors such as an excessive degree of excitation and the breaking through of the protective shield against stimuli.   (Freud 1926a, p. 94)

Primal repression was the response to the automatic anxiety caused by the excessive stimulation arising from a trauma; after-pressure, or repression proper, was the response to the signal of its possible recurrence.

Although it might have been possible for the automatic anxiety of birth to cause *that* primal repression, none of the other traumatic situations had the slightest resemblance to birth in content. Nor was it the case that later signals necessarily conveyed messages that that particular danger or one like it was about to recur.

The structural theory also demanded a very specific place for castration anxiety. Otherwise there could be no superego and consequently no self-punishing tendency or moral anxiety. It would be an advantage in constructing a monolithic theory if birth were the first anxiety experience, if one of the early primal repressions were a response to castration threats, and if the superego, which then formed, was the sole agent of repression proper. But that conceptualization was clearly not viable. If his earlier case histories were to be believed, Freud had evidence of repression proper well before the superego formed. After-pressure presupposed

the operation of earlier, *primal repressions* which exert an attraction on the more recent situation. Far too little is known as yet about the background and preliminary stages of repression. There is a danger of over-estimating the part played in repression by the super-ego. We cannot at present say whether it is perhaps the emergence of the super-ego which provides the line of demarcation between primal repression and after-pressure. At any rate, the earliest outbreaks of anxiety, which are of a very intense kind, occur before the super-ego has become differentiated.   (Freud 1926a, p. 94)

Further, by itself the response to the threat of castration failed to explain how the three components of anxiety were joined.

In addition to birth, Freud eventually distinguished *four* traumatic situations: separation of the infant from its mother, threatened castration, losing the love of the chosen object, and threats from the superego (Freud 1926a, pp. 136–140, 1933b, pp. 87–88). In each situation the immature ego was especially helpless and readily overwhelmed by stimulation. Chronologically, the traumas matched the infant's development. Loss of the mother was most potent during the total dependence of infancy, castration during the phallic stage, and loss of the object and superego threats during latency. Being of such varied content and covering such a wide age range, the four traumatic situations generated enough foci to attract any ideas forced out of consciousness by repression proper. Female development could be accommodated by assuming that castration anxiety was replaced by anxiety over the loss of the object's love, a kind of prolongation of the infant's anxiety over the loss of the object itself (Freud 1926a, p. 143; cf. 1933b, pp. 87, 88).

Of the traumatic situations, birth was undoubtedly the most important. The response to its toxins was the prototype of the responses to the other excessive amounts of excitation. Without birth anxiety there could be no anxiety of any other kind. In the event of being discarded as a prototype, Freud's assumption that there always had to be an earlier core experience would require an equally central trauma as a substitute.

Evaluation of the Structural Theory

The structural theory is sometimes represented as resulting from Freud's resolving some of the minor problems of the topographic theory. My account shows there were more than just a few unimportant loose ends to be tied. The structural theory has considerable deficiencies, many of which it shares with the topographic theory (Gill 1963; Arlow 1975; Sandler, Dare, and Holder 1972, 1982; Sandler and Sandler 1983) and others peculiar to itself (Van der Waals 1952; Fayek 1980). My evaluation is organized around seven issues: anxiety; the prototype of the anxiety experience; anxiety as the cause of repression; the ego's acquisition of its energy and its objects; the role of identification; the Oedipus complex and the superego; and the formation of the female superego.

Anxiety

Freud insisted that the anxiety of signal anxiety was not newly *created* but *reproduced*. Because the difference seems to require two mutually exclusive sources of anxiety, it has provided the basis for a good deal of psychoanalytic criticism and evaluation. Would it not be better to find a single source for the automatic anxiety of the traumatic situations and the signal anxiety of the danger situations? Before considering whether a more parsimonious explanation is possible, I will consider the rather more important issue of whether any satisfactory explanation of the means by which the signal is generated can be given at all.

The Mechanism of Signal Anxiety

The anxiety signal was reproduced "in accordance with an already existing mnemic image" (Freud 1926a, p. 93). The problem with this apparently simple proposition is that it is not possible to derive the reproduction in a way consistent within itself or with the rest of psychoanalytic theory. I take up the three main aspects of the problem in turn: anxiety and the nature of affects, the reproduction of anxiety, and the attenuated form in which Freud supposed the signal to appear.

Anxiety and Affects   Freud saw two absolute differences between affects and ideas. Ideas existed at an unconscious level as actual structures, that is, as memory traces of things or events (thing-representations) and could become conscious only by being linked to words. An affect, on the other hand, was not a structure at all but a process of discharge having only a "potential beginning" (Freud 1915c, p. 178). Affects were "transmitted directly" (1923b, p. 23) to consciousness and became conscious as soon as the discharge commenced, without requiring linkage to word-representations. Even

when they are attached to word-presentations, their becoming conscious is not due to that circumstance, but they become so directly. (Freud 1923b, p. 23; cf. 1915c, pp. 177–178, 1916–1917, pp. 409–410)

Consequently,

there are no unconscious affects as there are unconscious ideas.... The whole difference arises from the fact that ideas are cathexes—basically of memory-traces—whilst affects and emotions correspond to processes of discharge, the final manifestations of which are perceived as feelings. (Freud 1915c, p. 178)

Until the end he maintained that affects were processes of discharge and that ideas were structures (Freud 1933b, p. 81). Nor did he deviate from his view that ideas became conscious by way of their verbal linkages, or give way on the directness with which affects became conscious. All of this had to be so. In the structural theory the difference between repressed and nonrepressed ideas was the difference between thing- and word-representations. And, for instinctual drives to communicate directly with ego and superego, there could be no impediment, certainly not a word-representation barrier, to even their slightest stirrings being sensed.

Nevertheless, several psychoanalytic writers have argued that affects can be unconscious (e.g., Pulver 1971; Brenner 1974). Their arguments are based on gross misunderstandings. For example, Pulver cites descriptions by Eissler (1953), G. S. Klein (1967), and Joffe and Sandler (1968) of what they say are unconscious affects, but it is clear, as those authors themselves indicate, that the affect is so only preconsciously. Freud did allow, of course, that the individual need not be conscious of the affective signal initiating repression. Because the absence of an attentional cathexis accounts sufficiently for this unconsciousness, I do not believe, as G. S. Klein (1967) seems to, that Freud was here being inconsistent. Pulver also bases his thesis explicitly on confusion between the descriptive and dynamic: "if an affect can be preconscious there is no theoretical reason why it should not be able to be unconscious" (Pulver 1971). But it is just the difference between the attentional cathexis, which raises preconscious ideas to consciousness, and the anticathexis, which denies consciousness to repressed ideas, that provides a very good theoretical counter to his proposition. Neither is Pulver's clinical evidence any more cogent—it is quite clear that what ordinarily passes for repression in psychoanalysis is not involved in any of his examples.

Schafer (1964) seems almost to fall victim to another terminological confusion in that he appears to allow that discharges could be barred from consciousness by being repressed rather than simply because they are processes. Siegal (1969) puts the matter correctly by saying that, as discharge processes, "it does not make sense" to speak of repression denying them access to consciousness. Brenner (1974) developed a rather more subtle argument by extending the definition of affect to include the idea associated with it. Since the ideational component can be repressed, ergo, so can the affective. Brenner's understanding of affect is, of course, quite at variance with Freud's and overlooks the point I previously stressed. That point, with which Green (1977) agrees, is that in many instances Freud says that repression *is* the stripping of the affect from its accompanying idea. Green (1977, and in Jaffe and Naiman 1978) also makes essentially the same criticism of Brenner's redefinition as I have, and Limentani (in Jaffe and Naiman 1978) supports him. Green grants that affects are "represented" in some way but, clearly consistent with Freud's usage, he restricts the term "repressed" to ideas and uses "suppressed" and "inhibited" to apply to affects. Like most of those who have written on the subject, Brenner also fails to treat the topic theoretically, and like everyone else, he does not consider affects in relation to the thing- and word-representation distinction.

Reproducing Anxiety   What then of the reproduction of anxiety? Even though it cannot be reproduced through the recathection of the trace of an earlier affect (there being no structural record to be revived), Freud himself sometimes seemed to suggest the traumatic situation did leave a trace of the affect behind, and the signal was produced by its recathection. Thus, although he was careful to speak of the reproduction of the affect *in accordance with* an existing memory image rather than *from* it, he did assert:

Affective *states* have become incorporated in the mind as precipitates of primaeval traumatic experiences, and when a similar situation occurs *they are revived* like mnemic symbols. (Freud 1926a, p. 93. My emphasis)

A *state* is hardly the same thing as a *process*. Two of Freud's later comments also seem to imply the revival of some kind of affective trace. After describing the ego noticing the recurrence of a situation similar to an earlier trauma, he went on to say it signaled danger

by an abbreviated repetition of *the impressions* one has experienced in connection with the trauma—by *an affect* of anxiety.   (Freud 1926b, p. 202. Emphasis altered)

Again, the ego brought about

the reproduction of *the unpleasurable feelings* at the beginning of the feared situation of danger.   (Freud 1933b, p. 90. My emphasis)

For a trace to be so revived and act like a mnemic symbol, it would have to have a rather more permanent structure than a *potential beginning*.

Consider now the possibility that the signal is somehow generated by the recathection of a memory trace of the event rather than of the affect. First, we note an essential vagueness about what Freud thought was recorded during the trauma. Second, we find him to be completely silent about how that record is related to the affect allegedly revived. In *The Ego and the Id* he referred only to "dangers" that threatened the ego and to "the menacing perception" or "the similarly regarded process in the id" from which the ego's cathexis was withdrawn (Freud 1923b, p. 57). In *Inhibitions, Symptoms and Anxiety* he was not much clearer. When discussing castration anxiety he said:

as soon as the ego recognizes the danger of castration it gives the signal of anxiety and inhibits ... the impending cathectic process in the id.   (Freud 1926a, p. 125)

An equivalent vagueness recurs in his discussion of separation anxiety:

It is the absence of the mother that is now the danger; and as soon as that danger arises the infant gives the signal of anxiety.   (p. 138)

Nor are his concluding remarks much more definite:

the ego subjects itself to anxiety as a sort of inoculation, submitting to a slight attack of the illness in order to escape its full strength. It vividly imagines the danger situation, as it were, with the unmistakable purpose of restricting that distressing experience to a mere indication, a signal. (p. 162)

Within his theory, one certainly imagined an event by reviving its memory through recathecting the memory trace of it. But he was vague about what the trace might be of and silent about the mechanism by which its recathection reproduced the associated affect.

In Freud's theory, the only alternative to producing the signal by recathecting an affective trace was to generate it through a partial discharge. That this was probably what Freud really had in mind (even though it also poses grave theoretical difficulties) is suggested by the parallel he frequently drew between affects and hysterical attacks (Freud 1926a, pp. 93–94, 133–134) and his treatment of pain in the *Project* (Freud 1950/1954).

According to the hypnoid state conceptualization of the mechanism of the hysterical attack, the intrusion of the *condition seconde* into the primary consciousness could occur spontaneously, as in the stage that Charcot described as *attitudes passionelles*, or it might be provoked

just as any memory can be aroused in accordance with the laws of association ... by stimulation of a hysterogenic zone or by a new experience which sets it going owing to a similarity with the pathogenic experience. (Breuer and Freud 1893, p. 16)

Hence Anna O.'s paralysis when the bent branch for which she was reaching reminded her unconsciously of the hallucinatory snake her temporary paralysis prevented her from warding off (Breuer and Freud 1895, pp. 38–39). Similarly, Freud supposed Emmy von N.'s attacks of arm and leg pains to be based on well-remembered rheumatic pains

originally associated only accidentally with those experiences, [but] were later repeated in her memory as *the somatic symbol* of the whole complex of associations. (p. 71, n. 1; cf. pp. 90–91. My emphasis)

Whatever the origins of the motor symptoms, Freud thought

they all have one thing in common. They can be shown to have an original or long standing connection with traumas, and *stand as symbols for them* in the activities of the memory. (p. 95. My emphasis)

Symbolism was sometimes achieved through words and ideas. Thus Frau Cäcilie's *penetrating* head pain was said to be based on a look of suspicion her grandmother gave her that was "so *piercing* that it had gone right into her brain" (p. 180. My emphasis). For physical and mental symptoms the "long standing connection" was provided by the facilitation created when the affect or sum of excitation of the original traumatic idea first discharged along an abnormal pathway. During any later attack, the affect of the provoking experience recreated the symptom by being directed along the same somatic or mental pathway.

Whether the symptom in the hysterical attack is *produced or reproduced* is a nice point. Clearly the motor or other innervation underlying the symptom can be described as being reproduced in accordance with the trace of the original traumatic idea. Just as clearly, each attack requires a fresh discharge of excitation; the symptom has no existence outside of the attack. It does not recur simply because a memory trace of the idea has been recathected (indeed it cannot), but because its recathection leads to another discharge along the original pathway and a subsequent reinnervation. So, I believe, with affects. The "potential beginning" of the process of discharge lies not in a trace but in the facilitatory pathway between the affective memory and the organs into which the discharge occurs. Just as with the symptom, it is a nice point as to which description is more correct: is the signal of anxiety reproduced in accordance with a memory, or is it produced by a fresh discharge?

Attenuating the Signal   Emphasizing the fresh discharge of excitation in this way immediately brings to the fore the third major problem: Freud's description of signal anxiety as an *attenuated* form of the original. Hysterical symptoms are not attenuated. An attack of paralysis is just as complete or a hallucination just as frightening on subsequent occasions as on the first. Some difference must therefore exist between a hypothesized discharge mechanism allowing a symptom to recur with its original intensity, and one that attenuates the level of anxiety to that of a signal. Freud does not say what this difference is but, as Compton (1972a) and Green (1977) have also noted, his discussion of pain in the *Project* suggests what it might be (cf. Glick 1966).

Freud thought that pain, like anxiety, was produced when excessively large quantities of excitation broke through the protective shield. The increase was felt as an unpleasure having the qualities peculiar to pain, an "inclination" to discharge, and a facilitation between that inclination and the memory image of the object causing the pain. Any subsequent perception cathecting the image caused a state to arise

which is not pain but which nevertheless has a resemblance to it. It includes unpleasure and the inclination to discharge which corresponds to the experience of pain. (Freud 1950/1954, *Project*, part I, section 12 of Sept. 1895)

It was impossible for this unpleasure to come from a simple recathection of the memory trace. To begin with, memory traces were without quality. Further, a recathection

is in the nature of any other perception and cannot have as a result a general raising of [quantities of excitation].   (Part I, section 12 of Sept. 1895)

Freud therefore assumed that, in addition to the motor neurons involved in the discharge of painful excitation, "key neurones" also were connected to the group of well-facilitated neurons constituting the ego. Stimulation of these hypothetical key neurons caused

the production of endogenous [quantities of excitation], and accordingly do not *discharge* [quantity] [by way of the musculature] but *supply* it in roundabout ways.... As a result of the experience of pain the mnemic image of the hostile object has acquired an excellent facilitation to these key neurones, in virtue of which [facilitation] unpleasure is now released in the affect.   (Part I, section 12 of Sept. 1895. My emphasis)

Allowing for the moment that roundabout ways actually refers to something fairly definite, a point reasonably disputed by Amacher (1965, pp. 71–72), the amount of *this* unpleasure could be readily attenuated. By disposing what he called a side cathexis on the facilitatory pathway, Freud pictured the ego as diverting the potential discharge to itself and binding it there. It was then easy

to imagine how, with the help of a mechanism which draws the ego's *attention* to the imminent fresh cathexis of the hostile mnemic image, the ego can succeed in inhibiting the passage [of quantity] from a mnemic image to a release of unpleasure by a copious side-cathexis, which can be strengthened according to need.   (Freud 1950/1954, *Project*, part I, section 14)

In this mechanism there is no doubt, as Compton (1972a) and Green (1977) would agree, that if the unpleasure occurs at all, it has to be generated anew by a minor excitation of the very key neurons involved in the original experience, and not simply by the reproduction of a memory.

At the time of the *Project* Freud had neither physiological nor clinical evidence for the existence of this mechanism (Amacher 1965, p. 72). Nor has any accumulated in the years that followed. After observing, not quite correctly, that Freud never referred to these supposed neurons again (cf. Freud 1900, pp. 468, 582, 1915c, p. 179, n. 1), Levin notes that Freud never offered an "alternative explanation of how a recathected memory might release unpleasure" (K. Levin 1978, pp. 176). Were it not for the generally low level of psychoanalytic writing, I would otherwise find it odd that in discussions of this most central point of the new theory, Freud's nonexplanation has not been picked up. But, because it is glossed over, we can be sure the problem has been identified. For example, Glover (1926) equated the revived memory with the affect itself, and H. Hartmann (1956) misrepresented the process by incorporating the signal into the *anticipation* rather than leaving it where Freud so clearly placed it, among the *consequences* of the sensed danger.

What is at issue here is nothing less than the psychoanalytic theory of affects. In relation to the concept of signal anxiety, Applegarth (1977a) remarked that "affect theory represents one of the most total failures" [of psychoanalytic theory]. Garza-Guerrero (1981a) went further and argued more generally that an adequate psychoanalytic theory of affects "is long overdue," noting as he does so the paradox that psychoanalytic work "has at its very heart the task of dealing with feeling states and emotions." The central issue is identified by Green in his comments on the notion of unconscious affect:

the whole question is to know how the "idea" which forms an integral part of the nature of affect differs from what is conventionally called an idea, the content.   (Green 1977)

Underlying this question is the broader one, discussed in chapter 11, of the essential lack of characterization of the concepts of instinct and instinctual representative. Consequently, even at the definitional level, almost anything can be said about affect. For example, although the three elements by which Kernberg (in Lester 1982) defines an affect seem to be the same as Freud's, what he calls an affect is a *structure* rather than a process.

Two other things should be especially noted about Freud's analysis. First, the emphasis is placed on a cognitive appreciation of the possible recurrence of the painful situation. It is an appreciation identical to that supposed to precede the generation of the signal of anxiety. Second, precisely because this mechanism inhibits discharge, it cannot be a device for generating a signal. What Freud describes in the *Project* is how an ego, *after already recognizing the imminence of another painful situation*, might attempt to control the amount of unpleasure to be released. But, had he tried to conceptualize signal anxiety in the same way he would have ended in an impasse. For the ego to produce a small amount of anxiety, it would have to inhibit partially the facilitatory pathway between the about-to-be-revived trace of the traumatic situation and the key neurons. To take that action its appreciation of the potential danger would have to have been concluded *before* the hypothesized key neurons could produce their small quantity of anxiety. Rangell makes the point forcefully in his colorful comparison of the ego to a water tap. What the ego/tap does:

controls the amount, but [the ego] does not and cannot know whether the water will come out hot or cold. If the water comes out hot, it experiences it, and acts further accordingly. (Rangell 1968)

The ego's appreciation cannot be other than cognitive, and that evaluation renders a subsequent signal quite unnecessary.

We now see clearly why the three choices of mechanisms open to Freud were equally unsatisfactory: first, recathection of the trace of a prior discharge could be brought about only at the expense of his theories of affect and repression; second, a recathected image of the event would not in itself reproduce the affect originally accompanying it; and third, the blocking of any facilitation between a recathected image and potential discharge would do away with the need for a signal at all. The description also contains more than a hint of inconsistency. How can imagining a situation "vividly" reproduce "a mere indication" of the original anxiety? (Freud 1926a, p. 162). Attractively simple as it may seem, the mechanism of signal anxiety has to be rejected. If it is not uncharacterized, it is, at the very least, so inadequately characterized that it can explain nothing.

Psychoanalytic Resolutions   From this vantage point we may now consider the issues raised by those psychoanalysts who have concerned themselves with Freud's theory of anxiety. Although almost all of them accept that anxiety occurs in traumatic situations and that it somehow acts as a signal of danger, very few accept Freud's toxicological theses, most are dissatisfied with the two sources he proposed, and practically none accept his view of the ego's signaling role.

One line of attack has centered on traumatic anxiety. Intimated earlier by others (e.g., Fenichel 1937/1945a; Oerlemans 1949), the main salvo was fired by Brenner (1953), with Schur (1953) providing close support and Flescher (1956) attempting the mopping up. Claiming the support of clinical observations, critics taking this line variously deny that anxiety is produced from libido, deny the existence of the entity Freud described as anxiety neurosis, and deny that an influx of excitation always precedes automatic anxiety or the traumatic neuroses. Each of these points has subsequently received wide endorsement (Compton 1972a,b). However, as there undoubtedly are traumatic situations as well as traumatic neuroses, some other characterization of them had to be made and, where anxiety does occur, another explanation found for it. Some form of instinctual energy has usually been proposed for anxiety. Aggression, either by itself or in a sadistic mix with libido and sublimated to some degree, is the candidate of Zetzel (1955a), Flescher (1956), H. Hartmann (1955), and possibly Brunswick (1954), but Rado (1933) favored an opposite, masochistic trend, and Ernest Jones (1929) derived it from the fear instinct. Melanie Klein (1932, pp. 182–185, 1948, 1952) prefers a fear of the death instinct but Rangell (1955) postulates a special defensive instinctual energy, as does Schur (1958, 1960). In complete opposition to these instinctual energy formulations, Brenner (1953, 1974) and Stewart (1967) proposed that experience gradually transmutes a purely psychological unpleasure, a conception requiring no energy at all. The evaluation of each of these alternatives goes beyond what I can reasonably undertake here. Most are so thoroughly embedded in larger revisionist frameworks they cannot readily be wrenched from them for separate scrutiny. But it can be said that, one way and another, they fail to maintain consistency with other parts of Freud's theory (and sometimes with their own).

No one seems to believe that the ego *produces* anxiety as a signal, not even those who believe anxiety has a signaling role or that some kind of smaller version of the trauma might be involved (Kubie 1941b; Fenichel 1937/1945a, 1941a; Oerlemans, 1949; Spitz 1950; Brenner 1953, 1974; Schur 1953, 1958; Rangell 1955, 1968; Pumpian-Mindlin 1958–1959; Benjamin 1961; Stewart 1967, pp. 173–174; Waelder 1967b; J. H. Smith 1977). Were it to do so, for the child at least, the signal might produce the same reaction as the trauma (Sandler 1967). Laplanche (1981) reaches a similar conclusion. He disputes the possibility that fear, considered as an adaptive reaction to danger, can be experienced before anxiety and, therefore, that anxiety develops from fear. He concludes that anxiety cannot be a signal of internal danger but is that danger itself.

Practically nothing remains of Freud's notion: the ego merely *experiences* anxiety or *uses* it in response to danger. Waelder aptly summarizes this whole trend:

The ego *anticipates* future events and samples the unpleasure of a future catastrophe in small doses—the anxiety signal- which then, through the pleasure-pain principle, sets the avoidance reaction into motion.   (Waelder 1967b)

This is, of course, exactly as Freud had it for pain in the *Project*. Waelder goes on to note that

the implicit ability of the ego to anticipate still contains the whole secret: how does the ego do the anticipating?   (op. cit.)

Consequently, "the idea of an 'anxiety signal' is in need of revision." It is hard to imagine a more thorough demolition of Freud's concept of signal anxiety than this one carried out by his loyal disciples and followers.

Even were it possible for the ego to produce its signal, the fatal inconsistencies that J. H. Smith (1977) and Bush (1978) remarked remain. If the primary processes eschew anything unpleasant, what accounts for the tendency of the id to either attract or propel into consciousness those unpleasant memories of danger situations that caused the ego to generate signal anxiety? And, if the ego's production of unpleasure in generating the signal is governed by the pleasure principle, how does that principle come into operation only after the unpleasure of the signal?

The Prototype of the Anxiety Experience

The question now to be asked is where Freud's theory of anxiety stands if birth anxiety is not the prototype of the later kinds. Clearly it is very seriously impaired. In the structural theory birth anxiety was much more than the starting point for symptom formation. Normal development also began there. Rejecting the prototypal role of birth anxiety therefore undermines the very foundations of Freud's personality theory.

Psychoanalytic Data on Birth Anxiety

Neither clinical nor observational data allow birth anxiety to be accorded the status Freud proposed. Greenacre (1941, 1945, 1967) concluded from her own psychoanalyses of adults and from direct observations of children that birth per se was not even an organic trauma. None of the studies of neonates confirm that early infantile anxieties are in any way based on birth. Direct observations, many of them conducted by psychoanalysts, as well as analytical interpretations of the observational studies of nonanalysts, show that infants experience physical distress or unpleasure rather than anxiety (Spitz 1950; Ramzy and Wallerstein 1958; Benjamin 1961, 1963; S. Brody and Axelrad 1966; Izzard, in Lester 1982). Even before most of that work was reported, Brenner (1953) concluded that infantile "anxiety experiences" were best described as unpleasurable. Furst later actually questioned whether acute psychophysiological stress situations in early infancy were "traumas in the psychoanalytic [i.e. Freud's] sense of the term." He went on,

A breach in an existing stimulus barrier, followed by a feeling of helplessness on the part of the ego, is a central feature of the psychoanalytic concept, while the early months of life are synonymous with *pre-ego* and *pre-stimulus* barrier.   (Furst 1967, My emphasis)

Because birth occurs "outside object relations," Neubauer (1967) judges the birth experience to have "limitations" as a model for understanding trauma. Or, as Compton (1972b) explains, there can be no content to the anxiety experience prior to the development of object cathexes.

Most psychoanalysts have concurred with the Neubauer-Compton position. The truly infantile ego is unable to experience anxiety of any kind. Although Benjamin (1961) was actually prepared to allow some usefulness to untestable propositions (!), he really delivered the coup de grace to Freud's by observing that the hypothesis of a prototypal birth experience was a universal proposition of just that kind. Greenacre (1941) saw the difference between herself and Freud over birth as revolving around phylogenesis. For her the importance of birth was as an individual experience; for

Freud the prototype of birth assimilated "the endless procession of the births of our forefathers." So, although Greenacre interpreted her observations as showing that birth organizes the anxiety pattern by bringing together the genetic and individually determined elements, it is little wonder she made no use of the concept of signal anxiety in relation to it (Greenacre 1941, 1945).

Even were birth as important as Freud supposed, he offered only a brief and general description of the primal repression it generated, and his discussion focused on demarcating primal repression from after-pressure. It would have been most convenient had Freud been able to argue that after-pressure appeared only subsequent to the formation of the superego. I have no doubt that in *Beyond the Pleasure Principle* and *The Ego and the Id* he was aiming at an all-embracing explanation of the neuroses, the origins of civilization, and the very beginnings of life. The elements of his explanation were the omnipotent trend to return to the inanimate state, the tendency of instincts to repeat previous experiences, a uniformly present prototype of anxiety, and a superego acquired after a prehistoric parricide. The individual's superego, created in response to a threat of castration, explained not only normal and neurotic development, but how civilization itself was maintained. But no development could take place without the universal trauma of birth to explain why anxiety was the reaction to the castration threat. Only birth anxiety provided the basis for the grandiose recapitulation Freud envisaged.

Primal Repression   Without necessarily endorsing the place Freud gave birth in his vision, primal repression is nevertheless granted extremely high status. Nunberg, for example, says all later repression is "but a repetition of the primal repression" (Nunberg 1932/1955, p. 234). In various ways Glover (1939, pp. 70–80, 153), Rapaport (1951, pp. 694–698), Lantos (1955), Eissler (1962), Whitman (1963), Anna Freud (1967), Loeb and Carroll (1966), and Grotstein (1977a,b) all attested to its importance. But, partly because Freud used the term in different ways at different times, the usual psychoanalytic confusions abound. Some comments are positively silly. For example, primal repression should not be taken to refer to time because "Freud was considering the mind of the adult when he wrote on repression" (!) (Pearson 1953, cited in Frank and Muslin 1967). Again, after reviewing and revising Freud's theory of repression, Cohen and Kinston claim they have given primal repression a precise place within repression theory. The "precise place" (Kinston and Cohen 1986) at which primal repression operates is "at any stage of life" and its basis is "an absence of structure" that is, metaphorically, "a hole in the mind" (Cohen and Kinston 1983). How is at "any" time to be equated with a "precise" place, and how is absence of "structure" also a process? They arrive at these spectacular self-contradictions by glossing Freud's almost self-evident point that no repression can take place until a sharp cleavage has developed between conscious and unconscious mental activity as meaning that that separation takes place *throughout* the life cycle. It would, on their gloss, possibly be excluded in conditions like the psychoses in which, they say, the separation has disappeared. Were it not for the grandiosity of their claim, what they have to say is, I think, best thought of as another example of the merely silly.

A number of substantial questions have nevertheless to be answered. As Madison put it:

the mechanism of "traumas" and "primal repression" is a puzzle. Seemingly Freud was saying that primal repression was a direct, automatic response to traumas ... apparently if a state of too intense stimulation occurs ... the infant's *automatic* response is to repress the impulses responsible.... How does this happen? What is the mechanism ...? Freud left the point undiscussed. (Madison 1961, p. 114)

In a partial answer, Parkin (1983) differentiated "developmental" from "defensive" primal repression. The former is, ad hoc, of relatively short duration, and occurs in response to trauma. The defensive variety opposes the entry into consciousness of wishful primary process impulses. But Parkin's case rests on a very arbitrary reading of Freud, which he places in a footnote, and has few consequences.

Frank and Muslin (1967) made the only substantial attempt at finding answers. They opened their paper with an acknowledgment that primal repression occupied "an uncertain niche in psychoanalytic psychology," before posing other equally significant questions:

How are we to understand primal repression as distinguished from repression proper? If we assume that primal denotes early repression, how early? When, how, and why does it begin? When, how, and why is it superseded by ... repression proper? And in what ways do the earlier ... and later ... forms ... differ? (Frank and Muslin 1967)

They went on to distinguish two kinds of primal repression. One was an early and passive form that caused fixations and had pathological consequences when it occurred in response to overwhelming stimulation. Passive primal repression was found, they thought, with the primary processes that "are in the foreground" up to age eighteen months (Frank 1969). The other form, the active process Freud described in his later works, was made possible only by the development of the ego and the secondary process. In this ahistorical solution, Frank and Muslin simply juxtaposed two of Freud's meanings without attempting to answer the question of how early primary repressions came about. They left their revision of Freud's developmental theory without a starting point.

Three other important consequences follow the removal of birth from its position as the first of the traumas. First, without birth, Freud had no explanation for the three components of anxiety being found together, and we have seen the emphasis he placed on that point. Second, none of the other traumas would *in themselves* generate anxiety. Their power came from their resemblance to birth in their toxicity or in their psychological content. Finally, none of them could provide the uniform cause for which Freud was searching—none was a truly *universal* experience. Even though it happened very frequently, not everybody underwent an actual separation or was really threatened with castration.

Castration and Phylogenesis

Even with birth as the starting point, anxiety over castration had to be universal. Otherwise no superego could form and no neurosis could develop, and there could be no perpetuation of civilization. But, if not every single individual were threatened, how could universal castration anxiety be accounted for? Freud proposed that individuals came into the world carrying the trace of a memory of an actual castration carried out on their forebears. Whether or not the individual was really threatened with castration, this phylogenetically inherited memory or archaic inheritance ensured that even the most gently expressed parental disapproval of childhood sexuality would be magnified:

When we study the reactions to early traumas, we are quite often surprised to find that they are not strictly limited to what the subject himself has really experienced but diverge from it in a way which fits in much better with the model of a phylogenetic event *and, in general, can only be explained by such an influence.* The behaviour of neurotic children towards their parents in the Oedipus and castration complex abounds in such reactions, which seem unjustified in the individual case and *only* become intelligible phylogenetically—by their connection with the experience of earlier generations.   (Freud 1939, p. 99. My emphasis. Cf. 1940a, pp. 190 and n.1, 200–201, 206–207)

The case of the patient known as the Wolf Man was paradigmatic:

the boy had to fit into a phylogenetic pattern, and he did so, although his personal experiences may not have agreed with it. Although the threats or hints of castration which had come his way had emanated from women, this could not hold up the final result for long. In spite of everything it was his father from whom in the end he came to fear castration. In this respect *heredity triumphed over accidental experience*; in man's prehistory it was unquestionably the father who practised castration as a punishment.   (Freud 1918, p. 86. My emphasis, MBM. Cf. pp. 97, 119)

Freud was quite explicit that what was passed on was much more than an innate, constitutional disposition. More was involved than even a tendency to develop or behave in a certain way (Freud 1918, p. 98). What was inherited was a subject matter: "memory traces of the experiences of earlier generations" (Freud 1939, p. 99). This must be so, of course. As Satinover (1986) observes, if there is any such thing as an "archaic heritage," it must be "undistorted" and not transmitted in symbolic form.

Freud also made it clear that the acquisition of individual moral standards and the perpetuation of the demands of civilization depended on the inheritance of this memory of a prehistoric castration. Castration anxiety, which brought the Oedipus complex to a close, coincided with

the most efficient way of mastering the archaic, animal heritage of humanity. . . . that heritage comprises all the forces that are required for the subsequent cultural development of the individual, but they must first be sorted out and worked over. (Freud 1919b, p. 262; cf. 1923b, pp. 37–38, 1925c, pp. 220–221, 1940a, pp. 205–207)

He was aware there was no evidence for the idea of the inheritance of acquired characteristics, especially for the inheritance of specific memories. He had, he said,

no stronger evidence for the presence of memory-traces in the archaic heritage than the residual phenomena of the work of analysis which call for a phylogenetic derivation, yet this evidence seems . . . strong enough to postulate that such is the fact. (Freud 1939, p. 100)

His "confession" (p. 100) that he could not do without a postulate for which there was no evidence other than the gaps in his speculative reconstructions is at once a measure of the weakness of the developmental schema and of the strength of the grip the uniformity assumption had on him. Both derive directly from the faulty causal assumptions he had made in his very earliest work on the actual neuroses, and from the concept of the pathogenic memory structure and the principles of inter-connection he devised in *Studies on Hysteria*.

Anxiety as the Cause of Repression

When Freud reversed his formulation of the relation between anxiety and repression, and announced that repression was caused by anxiety, he adduced his interpretations of the cases of Little Hans and the Wolf Man as evidence. The one thing that stands in the way of accepting these interpretations is that he previously construed these very cases as showing that anxiety was caused by repression. What was the real signi-ficance of the cases? Were Freud's reinterpretations justified?

The Cases and the Reinterpretations

Little Hans was a five-year-old boy with a fear of being bitten by a horse (Freud 1909a). He was the first child to be treated according to psychoanalytic principles, although most of his treatment was actually conducted by his father acting under Freud's direction. The phobia responded most markedly to a direct interpretation given by Freud, on the one occasion he saw the boy, that the child was actually afraid of his father (pp. 41–43). The Wolf Man was about twenty-five years old when Freud began treating him for an obsessional condition (Freud 1918). During his psychoanalysis it was found that some twenty years earlier he had feared that a wolf would devour him. Again, Freud's interpretation was that the patient had really been afraid of his father (p. 32). It is worth noting that Freud originally proposed the identification of the father with the wolf partly because of a *possibility* that the father *may* have playfully threatened to "gobble up" the boy (p. 32). In the second discussion, he represented this possibility as an *at least highly probable* component source of the phobia (Freud 1926a, p. 104).

In the reinterpretations he maintained that a hostile impulse directed at the father had been repressed, and that that repressed impulse was the basis of the phobias (Freud 1926a, p. 106). The motive for the repression was fear or anxiety over castration. In both cases the son feared the father would respond to the hostile impulse with an actual castration. The anxiety or unpleasure so created caused repression. The affect of anxiety came not from repressed or transformed libido but from the agency initiating repression—the ego itself. As Freud put it:

The anxiety belonging to the animal phobias was an untransformed fear of castration. It was therefore a realistic fear, a fear of a danger which was actually impending or was judged to be a real one. It was anxiety which produced repression and not, as I formerly believed, repression which produced anxiety.   (Freud 1926a, pp. 108–109)

But what was the sequence of events? Had castration anxiety really preceded and caused repression?

Little Hans   The boy experienced anxiety a few days before the phobia. At that time, however, his anxiety was about being separated from his mother (Freud 1909a, pp. 23–24). In fact, Freud initially adduced this very aspect of the sequence as evidence for repression having caused anxiety. He supposed that, when away from his mother, Little Hans's libidinal longing increased up to some level of intensity, after which it was repressed and then transformed into anxiety. True, a castration "threat" had been made some months earlier (pp. 7–8), but it had had such little effect at that time that Freud was driven to one of his characteristic assertions:

It would be the most completely typical procedure if the threat of castration were to have a *deferred* effect.   (pp. 7–8; cf. pp. 35–36)

Freud thought the phobia was of a horse because Little Hans had repressed his hostility to his father before the phobia developed (pp. 138–139). Although the hostility sought expression, it was caught up in the repression of the libidinal impulse toward the mother and provided the content of the phobia—the fear of the father-horse (pp. 138–139).

All that was directly observable was that Little Hans had been anxious over his mother's absence before the phobia developed, and that the interpretation of the fear as really being of his father preceded its disappearance. Little Hans's "repression" of his hostility toward his father was an obvious post hoc postulate accounting for, at most, the phobia being of a horse. Freud's reinterpretation commends itself even less. The history shows no anxiety about castration *before the onset of the phobia*. Thus what Schur (1953) called Rado's (1950) "mockery" of Freud's interpretation seems to have been based on Rado's explaining the fear without reference to castration at all!

The Wolf Man   The Wolf Man's phobia began when he was four years old and followed an anxiety dream in which he fancied a tree full of wolves outside his bedroom window. Freud assumed the dream was preceded by the boy hearing a fairy story in which a wolf had its tail pulled off. He then interpreted this assumed story as containing a castration theme that revived a much earlier memory of a time when, at the age of one and a half years, the boy had seen his parents having sexual intercourse and sensed that his mother was somehow being given pleasure by his father. Not only that, their *a tergo* position let him see that his mother lacked a penis (Freud 1918, pp. 29–47).

Freud believed the patient's reaction to this revived memory was interpretable in the context of a negative Oedipus complex. It was as if the scene meant that the boy would have to be deprived of his penis if he were to gratify his feminine libidinal wish by satisfying his father sexually. The result of this possibility of castration

was terror, horror of the fulfilment of the wish, [and] the repression of the impulse which had manifested itself by means of the wish.   (p. 36)

The fairy story merely provided the occasion for the repression to begin (pp. 41–42). The real "motive power" was the fear of castration (p. 36), although the phobic anxiety itself was transformed, repressed libido. Once again repression caused anxiety (pp. 46 112).

Evidence and Reconstruction

The history contains little direct evidence for either of Freud's interpretations. Perhaps this is not surprising. First of all, Freud's investigation of the Wolf Man's infantile past is "clearly anything but direct, since he reaches the infantile material through a very circuitous route." After noting that Freud judged the Wolf Man's story of having been seduced by his sister to be true because his elder cousin also recalled having been seduced by her, they say:

It is unclear what evidential value there is to the testimony of a relative in the form of a recollection by the patient.   (Jacobsen and Steele 1979)

They also question another of Freud's constructions, one based on the principle of deferred action, because "it appears impervious to any questioning or attack." Blum (in Isay 1978) contradicts Freud directly, claiming there was no evidence that these traumas served as the single shocklike events Freud supposed. A more detailed analysis by Jacobsen and Steele (1979) of the recollections of the castration threat (on which Freud relied so heavily) are shown by them to result from Freud *having added* the really important elements to the Wolf Man's limited recollection. Freud (1918, p. 92) should hardly have been as impressed as he was by the material fitting together "spontaneously" and filling "the gaps in the patients' memory." In the recapitulation he even staked a methodological claim on the reconstruction:

The gaps were filled ... in a fashion which must be regarded as unexceptional, if any value is to be placed on psycho-analytic work.   (p. 112)

One does not know whether to regard this claim as an exceptional one or merely rather quaint. Should we extend either of these appreciations to Little Hans? According to Schimek (1987), reconstruction plays the same role in his case as in the Wolf Man's: "the crucial early events (castration threat, primal scene) are never remembered but only reconstructed."

A second consideration is that the Wolf Man was, after all, recalling events from some twenty years earlier. What is surprising, however, is that while he recalled other direct castration "threats" from about the same time they had *not* produced any untoward reaction. By that age, of course, he had already observed his parents and also knew females lacked the penis (Freud 1918, pp. 24–26). Were it then to be argued that these other threats of castration could have no effect because they occurred before the Wolf Man's childish feminine genital impulses were directed toward his father, the problem then arises as to why those threats did not prevent those impulses from being directed toward his father in the first place. The Wolf Man first experienced anxiety during the dream about the wolves. It was, at best, *simultaneous* with the repression (p. 28). In both instances we see that the argument for repression being the cause of the anxiety required Freud to make the same very judicious use of the principles of deferred action and summation of traumas as he had in *Studies on Hysteria*.

In any case, both the first and the second explanations are tautological. As Compton said of Freud's explanation that the Wolf Man's repression was actuated by fear of castration:

But what is castration fear if not a form of anxiety? And, if so, what has been gained by "explaining" anxiety as a result of anxiety?   (Compton 1972a)

He makes the same objection to the second explanation (Compton 1972b) and it also applies, of course, to Little Hans. He notes further that in his first interpretation of Little Hans's case,

Freud does not allow his theory of anxiety [as caused by repressed libido] to interfere with the accumulation of observations that are not entirely convenient.   (Compton 1972a)

Overall, Compton concluded that Freud's theory of anxiety as transformed libido was

an illustration of how very far it is possible to go by making assumptions which cover without contradiction what cannot, at the given time, be understood—a successful exercise in ambiguity.   (Compton 1972b)

Nearly twenty years earlier Zetzel had asked some pertinent questions about anxiety. Because they had not been answered, Compton repeated them:

(1) To what extent is anxiety a response to a danger situation, internal or external? (2) To what extent is anxiety produced by the frustration of an instinct, again whether internal or external? (3) Should anxiety be regarded as a subjective awareness of instinctual tension, or, and to what extent, does anxiety represent a mode of instinctual discharge?   (Zetzel 1955a)

When Compton introduced this quotation from Zetzel he expressed doubt that "psychoanalysis has a working anxiety theory." And, in his concluding remarks, he does not seem to have classed Freud's revised theory as one of the contributions that had decreased "the areas of ambiguity" (Compton 1972b).

The Ego's Energy and Its Objects

Freud fails to account for five things about the ego and superego: why the ego rather than the superego acquires neutral energy and becomes masochistic, how sublimation is able to provide energy, where the superego's sexual characteristics come from, how identification produces a critical superego, and the contribution of narcissism to the superego.

Energy and Masochism in the Ego

It is not clear that sublimated energy should be lodged in the ego or, if it is, how that makes the ego masochistic.

Freud implied that the ego as a whole was altered by Oedipal identifications, but the change was really only to that part of the ego incorporating the essence of the parents—the superego-to-be. Consequently, sublimated energy should have been stored in it and not in the ego proper. Freud had to see it otherwise. The superego was "independent of the ego for its supply of energy" (Freud 1933b, p. 60). Having liberated Thanatos from Eros to make it available to the superego, he was not about to put the two instincts together again, and especially not in the superego. There they would again have to be fused and so unable to conduct their battle.

As to masochism in the ego, Spiegel (1978) drew attention to the contradiction of the destructive drive appearing as "an intensification of masochism in the ego and at the same time ... an increase of sadism in the superego." Brenner (1982) thought he had solved the problem by allowing both libidinal and aggressive drive derivatives into the superego, picturing the remorse and self-punishment deriving from the superego as providing a masochistic gratification. On the other hand, Arlow (1982) effectively drained the superego of Thanatos and filled it with neutralized energy instead. He was able to do this by saying nothing about fusion and defusion during identification. Laplanche (1981) attempted to resolve the issue by having "sexual-life drives" in the ego opposed to a sexual death-drive as "an extreme of sexuality ... working according to the principle of free energy and the primary process" in the id. Maleson (1984) therefore noted that it was "not at all clear why masochism was described as residing in the ego rather than the id." He traced much of the controversy to Freud's lack of clarity about the consequences of identification.

Sublimation and the Ego's Energy

Freud is also unable to explain how the ego acquires energy. He postulates that the ego is altered by identification to become like the parents and chosen as object by the defused portion of Eros that is also made available by identification. The new choice was "an abandonment of sexual aims, a desexualization—a kind of sublimation" (Freud 1923b, p. 30; cf. pp. 45–46, 54).

Three questions can be asked. How could the energy be nonsexual? What is the mechanism of sublimation? What does the ego operate with before the dissolution of the Oedipus complex?

Sexualization or Sublimation?   In every other one of Freud's descriptions of the sexual instinctual drive being directed to nonsexual objects, or to instinctual trends, or to various activities, the consequence is that that object, trend, or activity is *sexualized*. Thus, once it became admixed with libido, each one of the following was said to be sexualized: social instincts (Freud 1911a, p. 62), nonsexual instincts in general (Freud 1913d, p. 323); memories (Freud 1909b, p. 206, n. 1, 1918, p. 96); fantasies (Freud 1918, p. 103); thought (Freud 1909b, p. 245, 1910b, p. 80, 1912–1913, p. 89); actions such as looking, touching, and exploring (Freud 1916–1917, p. 309); and the ego itself during the secondary narcissism of megalomania (Freud 1911a, p. 72).

Ernest Jones (1926) observed that "narcissistic libido is still sexual." More recently Schafer noted that Freud's previous explanation of the "sexualization of ego functions" and "all the clinically observed varieties of sexualized secondary narcissism as well as the hypothesis of infantile primary libidinal narcissism" stood against transformation by sublimation. He was forced to reject desexualization so produced: "Taken on its own terms, Freud's proposition that desexualization occurs *through* Oedipal identification is untenable" (p. 205). It is no solution to shelter behind Ernest Jones's (1926) proposition of "degrees of desexualization" or H. Hartmann's (1955) that there is "a certain limit" beyond which sexualization of ego functions occurs and that implies sublimation to take place below that limit.

The Mechanism of Sublimation   What does the psychoanalytic literature have to say about sublimation? Since the concept of sublimation came under scrutiny, absolutely no agreement has been reached about the behavior to which the mechanism refers or the underlying processes on which it might be based. According to Glover (1931a), there had been "a good deal of confusion" about the concept before 1923, a confusion that had "increased rather than decreased" by the time he wrote (cf. Ernest Jones 1941). Nine years later Deri (1939) gave the impression that there was considerable agreement about the way in which the term was used, but Levey (1939), who applied what he took to be Freud's own standards, concluded his contemporaneous and influential analysis by saying that sublimation was "confused, obscure, incomplete, redundant, static, and lacking in objective verification." Eight to nine more years saw Brierely (1947) describe it as an "omnibus term" and H. H. Hart's (1948) opinion that "our notions of sublimation are none too clear." Seven years later again H. Hartmann said, "despite many efforts to free [sublimation] from ambiguities" there was no doubt there was "a certain amount of discontent" among psychoanalysts with the concept (H. Hartmann 1955; cf. Hartmann in Arlow 1955). Eleven years further on Kaywin (1966) opened his analysis by saying there were "still many ambiguities and disagreements" about the meaning "and even the usefulness" of the notion. After a lengthy analysis, one sympathetic to Freud's aims, Ricoeur (1970, pp. 483–492) concluded that sublimation was an empty concept.

The points especially singled out in the discussions include this doubt about the usefulness of the concept (R. W. White 1963), as well as whether an instinctual drive transformation per se can result in a socially valued activity (Bernfeld 1931, cited by Lantos 1955; Glover 1931a; Levey 1939; H. Hartmann 1955; Kubie 1962), whether the sublimated libido was genital or pregenital (Deri 1939), and the absence of characteristics defining sublimated activity and differentiating it from other mechanisms and processes (Levey 1939; Bergler 1945; Kubie 1962; Kaywin 1966; Hacker 1972). Even the question of whether only libido can be sublimated has also been raised and disputed (H. H. Hart 1948; H. Hartmann, Kris, and Loewenstein 1949; H. Hartmann 1955). The limitations of defining sublimation as mainly or fundamentally a change in the aim of the sexual drive were recognized early by Glover (1931a). He argued that the "permanent neutrality" of the desexualized energy supposedly formed during Oedipal identifications demanded that energy transformations had to be included in the definition. H. Hartmann (1955) later based his own approach to the essence of sublimation on Glover's point.

Many psychoanalytic theorists regard the energy transformation view as so inadequate or untenable that there must be serious doubt that sublimation can provide anything at all with which the ego can work (e.g., Colby 1955, pp. 1–36; Kubie 1962; Sandler and Joffe 1966; Kaywin 1966; Holt 1967/1968; Schafer 1968, chapter 3; Applegarth 1971). The most powerful line of criticism has been directed against the aphysiological notion of instinctual drive *energies* having different and variable aims. Begun by Colby (1955, pp. 30–35) and extended by Holt (1967/1968), the position was stated most succinctly by White:

an instinctual drive does not function with its own *kind* of energy, but with neural energies released in particular *places* (centers) and organized in particular *patterns*. Energy can be called sexual, for instance, only by virtue of the fact that certain somatic sources or hormonal conditions activate certain nerve centers which in their turn activate a characteristic pattern of excitations in skin, genitals, and elsewhere.... Aggressive energy is differentiated from sexual by the places and patterns that are central in the excitation. An ego interest, such as learning the skills necessary for an occupation, is neutral in the sense that its places and patterns are not those of either eroticism or aggression. (R. W. White 1963, pp. 178–179; cf. 1960)

Perhaps Freud's view was a hangover from Müller's and Helmholtz's theory that each sensory modality operated with its own kind of energy. But, given that that view was completely discredited by the latter part of the last century, it was an especially old-fashioned neurophysiology for even Freud to have adopted.

Early Ego Functions   If neutral energy is only created through Oedipal identifications, what does the ego operate with before the dissolution of the complex? Are we to believe one can have no realistic modes of thought and action before the age of five to seven years? Where the shield gets its energy, where perceptual and attentional cathexes come from, and the source of the anticathexes that bring about and maintain the very early primal repressions are also of more than a little importance.

In the absence of a satisfactory account of how it acquires its energy, the ego itself must remain, quite literally, an empty theoretical construct. Without desexualized energy it cannot judge incoming stimuli, bind traumatic excitation, think, or generate the signal of anxiety. The process of binding is crucial. In the words of Freud's last major work, it is the ego's *psychological* function. The ego's other main function, the *constructive* one of placing thinking between the instinctual demand and the satisfying act, was equally dependent on neutral energy. The ego,

after taking its bearings in the present and assessing earlier experiences, endeavours by means of experimental actions to calculate the consequences of the course of action proposed. (Freud 1940a, p. 199; cf. 1911b, p. 221, 1925d, p. 238, 1933b, p. 89, 1950/1954, part I, sections 16, 17, 18 of Sept. 1895, and part III, sections 1, 2, 3 of Oct. 1895)

Neutral energy is absolutely crucial to his conception of how the ego functions, and he is quite unable to give a consistent account of how it is obtained.

Sex and the Superego

One immediately obvious problem to which Freud himself drew attention was that the identifications from which the superego formed were

not what we should have expected, since they do not introduce *the abandoned object* into the ego.   (Freud 1923b, p. 32. My emphasis)

The analogy with melancholia leads to a superego of the wrong type. Having lost the maternal object, the boy should build his superego around his mother's qualities, and the girl, having lost the father, should have his masculine qualities reflected in her superego.

Freud's own attempt at filling the hiatus was embarrassingly inadequate:

Analysis very often shows that a little girl, after she has had to relinquish her father..., will bring her masculinity into prominence and identify herself with her father (that is, with the object which has been lost), instead of with her mother. This will clearly depend on whether the masculinity in her disposition—*whatever that may consist in*—is strong enough.   (p. 32. My emphasis)

Freud was silent about any such strengthening in the boy, merely remarking that the relative strengths of the two parts of the bisexual disposition determined which identification was the stronger (p. 33).

Bisexuality had another role. Each child chose both parents as objects, lost both, and incorporated both. The boy, for example, chose his mother because of the masculine component of his sexuality and his father because of the feminine (pp. 33–34). But while bisexuality made the choice of the same-sex parent possible, it did so at the cost of creating the paradox that the child's biological sexuality did not determine the essence of its psychological sexuality, but its opposite. For example, the boy's femininity led to the choice of the father and so determined one of the most essential of his male characteristics: the harsh, unforgiving, and law-ridden superego. The girl faced a further complication. Her masculine component determined the choice of the mother, but if it was strong enough, it caused her to identify with the father.

Few psychoanalytic writers have even remarked on the hiatus. Ernest Jones (1926), early on the scene, proposed a particularly tortuous resolution. Without mentioning primary identification at all, he based the superego on the replacement of an initial hostile rivalry with the father by homosexual love for him. As he later made explicit:

the super-ego is in all cases of predominantly homosexual origin, i.e. it arises from identification with the parent of the same sex as the child feels itself to be (not necessarily its actual sex).   (E. Jones 1928–1929)

Freud was unconvinced by Jones' ingenuity. He responded:

All the obscurities and difficulties you describe really exist. But they are not to be removed even with the points of view you emphasize. They need completely fresh investigations, accumulated impressions and experiences, and I know how hard it is to obtain these. Your essay is a dark beginning in a complicated matter.   (Freud to Jones, Letter of Nov. 20, 1926, cited in E. Jones 1953–1957, vol. 3, p. 285)

Etchegoyen (1985), apparently more easily satisfied, accepted Jones's suggestions as "more convincing" than Freud's. Relatively few psychoanalysts have even drawn attention to or alluded to the hiatus (e.g., Fenichel 1926/1954a; Fuchs 1937; Jacobson 1954; Koff 1961; Arlow 1982), and none has bridged it. The two explicit attempts I have found were based on combining identification with introjection. They are neither consistent nor successful. Widlöcher (1985) has primary identification alter the *ego*, with a narcissistic introjection-identification bringing the right-sexed parent into the superego, whereas Deigh (1984) has the child identify with both parents and then introject both. Nearly a quarter of a century after Freud introduced the structural theory, Fenichel noted, "The attempts at solving these problems have not yet advanced beyond Freud's formulation" of a bisexual involvement (Fenichel 1945b, p. 104). It is evident that no progress has been made since.

It is, of course, precisely because the terms "masculine disposition" and "feminine disposition" are so completely uncharacterized ("whatever that may consist in") that they can be put to such use. Even so, Freud was unable to explain how an erotic attachment to the mother was replaced by a strengthened identification with the father (Abend and Porder 1986). What must not be overlooked in these heroic theoretical endeavors of Freud's are that they are forced upon him because of the very untoward consequences of identification by incorporation. It is a quite inappropriate mechanism for explaining superego formation.

The Critical Function

In melancholia, the lost object reestablished in the ego was supposed to be *reproached by* an already existing critical agency, the conscience. But, when the superego formed, it was the lost *object* itself that *became* the critical agency, directing *its* complaints against the unaltered part of the ego. We may therefore ask about the adequacy of explanations based on identification by incorporation as well as about the nonpunitive functions that psychoanalysts (and perhaps Freud himself) believed the superego had.

The Critical Agency   Although it is obvious that the object incorporated in melancholia is *not* the critical ego, I have found Etchegoyen (1985) to be one of the few psychoanalytic writers to see this point. However, it is fairly widely recognized that during the formation of the superego, identification by incorporation has such different consequences from those in melancholia, if not opposite ones, it is difficult to reconcile the two mechanisms (Jacobson 1954; M. W. Brody and Mahoney 1964; Meissner 1970). Freud gives no hint about the conditions under which one rather than another consequence ensues. To this problem we should add the one that Deigh (1984) saw: why does identification lead to a part of the ego being split off rather than just being changed?

Superego v. Ego-Ideal   Many psychoanalysts have also found it difficult to reconcile the superego as a whole being harsh and punitive with its also containing the much less severe ego-ideal.

Freud first described the ego-ideal in "On Narcissism," and it is the ideal of narcissistic perfection described there that causes the theoretical difficulty. After being devalued by parental criticism, the infant's previous blissful narcissistic perfection was reestablished as an ego-ideal, an agency sharply differentiated from the critical agency of conscience. Conscience was the agency that *embodied* the parental criticisms and watched the actual ego, measuring its behavior against the standards of the ideal (Freud 1914b, p. 94; cf. 1916–1917, pp. 428–429). However, by 1921 Freud virtually claimed the opposite: the psychoanalyses of melancholia were now supposed to have shown that the ego-ideal itself was the critical agency (Freud 1921, pp. 132–133; cf. 1917c, pp. 247–248). He built on this reversed conception when he announced the structural theory two years later. There the ego-ideal was explicitly equated with the superego and given punitive functions in addition to the earlier ones of criticism, scrutiny, and standard bearing. In his very last formulation, in the *New Introductory Lectures*, only the names were changed. The superego exercised the function of conscience, it was "the vehicle" of the standards of the ego-ideal, and it was responsible for punishing behavior. As Holder (1982) observed, this ego-ideal was not only very different from that portrayed in "On Narcissism" but had little relation to narcissism at all.

By the time of the structural theory Freud had also pretty well inverted the source of the ideal's perfection:

There is no doubt that this ego-ideal is the precipitate of the old picture of the parents, the expression of admiration for the perfection which the child then *attributed to them*. (Freud 1933b, p. 65. My emphasis)

No longer is the child's own lost narcissistic perfection the model. The ego-ideal is clearly modeled on the parents.

Although the parental qualities Freud emphasized were harshness and severity (Freud 1923b, pp. 54–55, 1924b, p. 167, 1933b, p. 62), he also described the ego as seeking the love of its superego (Freud 1923b, p. 58, 1926a, pp. 139–140, 1930, p. 126, 1939, p. 117, 1940a, p. 206). For many psychoanalysts, this loving quality seemed to give the ego-ideal characteristics so different from the superego proper that they do not even accept it as "one of the functions of the super-ego" (H. Hartmann and Loewenstein 1962). According to Loewenstein, these theorists were unable to reconcile

the early formulations of Freud ... according to which the ego ideal is the substitute for the lost infantile narcissism, with his later proposition that the parents are taken as models for the child's ego ideal. (Loewenstein 1966b; cf. Blos 1974; Hammerman 1965).

From the difference was born the notion of the ego-ideal as a separate structure having benign properties balancing the superego's punitiveness. After outlining some of the history of this notion, Sandler, Holder, and Meers (1963) concluded, "There can be little doubt, on clinical and theoretical grounds, that some such step is necessary" (cf. Novey 1955; Loewenstein 1966b; Grunberger and Chasseguet-Smirgel, cited in Mancia and Meltzer 1981).

The proposal for separation is not new. Within ten years of Freud's new theory, Nunberg (1932/1955, p. 146) had differentiated the ego-ideal as "an image of the loved objects" from the superego as "an image of the hated and feared objects." Lampl-de Groot claimed the earlier work of Alexander and Flugel as support for her rather similar conceptualization in which a loving, wish-fulfilling ideal was contrasted with a prohibiting and punishing superego (Lampl-de Groot 1947, 1962). Murray put the issue in its most general form. The superego and ego-ideal were "distinct and separate elements ... each ... born in its own distinctly different manner" (J. M. Murray 1964). Even though Arlow (1982) called on Waelder's principle of multiple function to argue against separating the two agencies, saying that "the idealization 'ought to' was the other side of the coin 'must not,'" the division is now widely accepted.

There is little doubt that as well as these differences about the superego and ego-ideal, most of what has been referred to as "problems and inconsistencies" (Lampl-de Groot 1962), "loose ends" (Turiell 1967), "basic differences of opinion" (Steingart 1969), "vigorous discussion" (Furer 1972), "terminological confusion" (Kernberg 1982), and the four distinct meanings of the term "ego-ideal" that Sandler, Holder, and Meers (1963) distinguish among, result from the distinctly different functions ascribed to the two agencies (cf. Hägglund 1980).

Two variant resolutions of the separation position can be distinguished. In the one, the two structures are kept separate, with the ego-ideal usually seen as forming part of the ego (Piers and Singer 1953; A. Reich 1954; Bing, McLaughlin, and Marburg 1959; J. M. Murray 1964; Hendrick 1964; Bressler 1969; S. Ritvo 1971), but sometimes kept completely apart (Novey 1955). In the other, the ego-ideal eventually becomes part of the superego, but only after its relatively independent earlier development (Nunberg 1932/1955, pp. 137–147; Jacobson 1954, 1964, pp. 186–189; Schafer 1960; H. Hartmann and Loewenstein 1962; G. L. Bibring 1964; Deutsch 1964; Hammerman 1965; Loewenstein 1966b; Blos 1974). Other variants are also possible (Mancia and Meltzer 1981; Brickman 1983; Kramer 1986). Of these, the oddest must be that of Hägglund (1980) who considers the ego-ideal as a "developmental extension of the negative Oedipus complex" and the positive "based more on incest wishes" and "therefore the main *result* of the super-ego."

None of the resolutions is widely accepted and we must conclude that the differences in function remain unexplained. The problem is not, however, where the ego-ideal should be located or of any "intrinsic ambiguity" in the ideal being at once a component and a content of mind, as Blos (1974) contends. The problem is narcissism. Narcissism was "never ... adequately integrated with the later theoretical concepts" and no place at all could be found for it in the topographic theory (Spruiell 1979, 1981).

Narcissism and the Character of the Superego

Most theorists concerned with the differences between the superego and the ego-ideal took it that it had to have formed out of some kind of early narcissistic perfection. The problems that result from deriving it from narcissism are partly empirical and partly theoretical.

The Empirical Problems of Narcissism   Infantile forms of narcissism have doubtful empirical status in the psychoanalytic literature. Granting, as Loewenstein proposes, that the shift in the new theory to a secondary narcissism fits better with "the over-all concept of the mental apparatus," it remains the case that there is still an

extreme difficulty of stating clearly what happens in the mind of the child in the first few months of life. For that earliest period, *neither reconstructions* from later analyses *nor direct observations* will yield definite answers to questions regarding the interaction between primary and secondary narcissism.   (Loewenstein 1966b. My emphasis)

Balint (1960) showed, for example, that the observations supposedly supporting the concept of primary narcissism were relevant only to the secondary form, and a number of analysts have always taken a similar view (Wisdom 1968; B. E. Moore 1975; Pöstényi 1979). It is this issue that lies behind Laplanche's and Pontalis's (1967/1973, p. 338) conclusion that, empirically speaking, the existence of primary narcissism is "highly problematic," and Etchegoyen's (1985) more recent opinion that "the theory of primary narcissism is only a myth about origins." It was never the case, as Hartmann, Kris, and Loewenstein (1946) once asserted, that "Freud's theory of 'primary narcissism' seems still best to account for facts immediately observable after birth."

After 1923, Freud made only one mention of primary narcissism (Freud 1940a, p. 150) and none at all of the secondary form. But if neither form can be observed, it is

hardly possible to circumscribe the respective roles, at a given age, of narcissistic and object cathexes in the ontogenesis of the ego ideal.   (Loewenstein 1966b)

By speculating that the ideal formed from some kind of mix of parental and ego- or self-idealizations, psychoanalysts settled for a very poor second and did not reach a consensus about where the ingredients came from (Hägglund 1980). If we accept Loewenstein's point that observations are just as opaque as reconstructions, even those kinds of sources can never be known with any certainty.

The Theoretical Problems of Narcissism   It is agreed that Freud left the relation of his conceptualization of libido-narcissism to the ego-id-superego model far from clear (Compton 1981d; cf. 1981a,b,c) or "quite puzzling" (Jacobson 1954; cf. 1964).

Instinctual fusion, a concept absolutely demanded by the structural theory, means there cannot be a purely libidinal investment of a primitive ego or self. Narcissistic cathection can only mean "the relative predominance of libidinal over aggressive investment" (Kernberg 1975, p. 318; cf. 1982; Jacobson 1964, pp. 14–16; Mahler 1971). And, as Spruiell (1975) notes, the aggressive component "has never been satisfactorily included" in formulations of narcissism. Nevertheless, the authors of one of the main theoretical discussions of narcissism restricted their consideration to libidinal energy and indicated only in passing the need for studying aggressive drives (Bing, McLaughlin, and Marburg 1959). Even those of the few who note the importance of aggression or of the death instinct for understanding narcissism are unable to propose solutions (e.g., B. E. Moore 1975; Duruz 1981a,b).

A minimal theoretical solution comes from psychoanalysts who alter the target of libidinal investment and make structures and functions other than the ego, usually the self or the self-representation, the narcissistic focus (H. Hartmann 1950, 1955). It is, of course, hardly a solution; any resulting idealized qualities must still have aggressive characteristics. Consequently, as Furer (1972) observed, the shift to ego-psychology leaves the problems of superego formation unresolved. Another solution first separates libido from its aggressive companion before supposedly finding the essence of narcissism in an idealizing quality of the libido itself (Kohut 1971). Here one can only admire the sleight of mind that so cleverly disposes of both aggressive investment and primary narcissism.

Complex developmental schemas have also been constructed within which the interactive effects of aggressive and libidinal drives on ego, self, or self-representation are positioned. However, for the most part these schemas are inconsistent with each other and within themselves (e.g., Jacobson 1964, pp. 119–135; Kernberg 1975, 1976, 1982; Teicholz 1978; Tyson and Tyson 1984). Finally, and as might be expected, dissatisfaction of a more general kind with Freud's energy-investment concept led some to discard wholly or partially that mode of conceptualizing narcissism (Joffe and Sandler 1967). Some of the "functional" alternatives proposed move so far from the basic tenets of psychoanalysis that they can barely be considered extensions or amplifications of Freud's theses. An example is Stolorow's (1975a), which does away with ego to some extent and with drive altogether.

The core problem for the ego-ideal, then, is that once Freud incorporated a death instinct into his theory, his original notions of primary and secondary narcissism should have been done away with altogether. A death instinct or other primary aggressive drive necessarily ruled out the kind of narcissistic state or mode of existence required to produce a completely or even predominately positive ego-ideal.

The Role of Identification

Neither of the two kinds of identification from which the superego forms is based on assumptions consistent with other aspects of psychoanalytic theory. Primary identification ("being like") allowed the child to form emotional ties on a basis other than the satisfaction of its instinctual drives, and identification by incorporation ("having") took place when the childhood drive was supposed to be without objects.

Drives and Emotional Ties

Although it is true that Freud allowed for nonsexual feelings of affection, these are either aim-inhibited sexual drives (Freud 1923a, p. 258, 1925a, p. 39) or feelings arising as self-preservative needs are satisfied concurrently with sexual ones (Freud 1913e, pp. 180–181). Nowhere does he find a place for emotional bonds not deriving from instinctual drive satisfaction. In slightly different ways, Widlöcher (1985) and Abend and Porter (1986) drew attention to this aspect of the problem of identification. Padel (1985) noted that ego change through primary identification was inconsistent with the drive-satisfaction formulations required to explain introjection. He argued for a theory of ego formation built almost solely on a nondrive-satisfaction concept of primary identification. It would seem that Ricoeur's conclusion of there being "more questions than answers" in relating primary identification to an instinctual energetic view has been amply confirmed (Ricoeur 1970, p. 219).

Objects and Primary Identification

If primary identification were direct and quite different from object-choice, it seems very odd that Freud should so persistently describe it as based on the oral incorporation *of an object*. For example, after opening his discussion of the ego-ideal in *Group Psychology and the Analysis of the Ego* with the clear distinction between identification with an object (being like) and choosing it (having), Freud based what followed completely on identification through oral incorporation of the object, that is, on an oral object choice (Freud 1921, p. 105). Similarly in *The Ego and the Id* he wrote that the origin of the superego lay hidden in the individual's

first and most important identification, his identification with the father.... This is apparently *not* in the first instance the *consequence or outcome* of an *object cathexis*; it is a *direct and immediate* identification and takes place *earlier* than any *object-cathexis*. (Freud 1923b, p. 31. My emphasis)

Two pages earlier, however, he had expressed the opposite thought:

At the very beginning, in the individual's primitive oral phase, object-cathexis and identification *are no doubt indistinguishable.*   (p. 29. My emphasis)

No wonder Ricoeur (1970, p. 219) placed the supposed oral origin of identification as first among the many unanswered questions about it.

Identification as a Mechanism

In the psychoanalytic literature there is agreement that the core meaning of identification is simple—to be like or to become like another (Abend and Porder 1986). There is also agreement on its importance as a "nodal point in general psychoanalytic thinking and conceptualization" (Simenauer 1985; cf. Etchegoyen 1985). Yet as recently as 1984 Rangell judged identification to be "the most perplexing clinical-theoretical area" in psychoanalysis, an opinion that Carneiro Leao (1986) subsequently quoted and endorsed.

The fact is there are simply no agreed-upon definitions of identification or of the related concepts of incorporation, introjection, and internalization at either the theoretical or clinical level. Fuchs (1937), Knight (1940), Greenson (1954), Sandler (1960), H. Hartmann and Loewenstein (1962), and Meissner (1970, 1971, 1972) all drew attention to the "complications," "confusion," and "chaos" about identification, and advanced their own conceptual and terminological reforms. For example, Hartmann, Kris, and Loewenstein (1946) distinguished a pre-Oedipal identification that was both a defense mechanism and a means by which personality was formed from a second that contributed to the superego. Of the first they say its impact on ego development is not known in detail. The only explanation they offer for it, an obviously incorrect one, is that it is based on incorporation. Although the second is different, all they specify about it is the "concomitant change in the economy of psychic energy" they say it involves. But Etchegoyen (1985), among others, rejected the distinction between the two kinds of identification, and others, such as S. Ritvo and Solnit (1960), simply adopted one of the related terms (in their case internalization) as a blanket term.

Ferenczi (1909/1952a), who invented the concept of introjection, thought introjection was brought about by identification (Ferenczi 1912/1955a, 1913/1952c). Fenichel (1926/1954a) recognized Ferenczi's usage but treated introjection and identification as being the same, an "unjustified" identity according to Hendrick (1951). Fenichel also reluctantly accepted that incorporation could be equated with introjection, and this equation was adopted in whole or in part by Zilboorg (1938), Knight (1940), Nunberg (1955, pp. 141–142), M. W. Brody and Mahoney (1964), and Schafer (1973). What amounted to the converse of Ferenczi's hypothesis was also proposed:

incorporation resulted in identification (Knight 1940; H. H. Hart 1947; Greenson 1954). Incorporation was regarded as a physical process and introjection as psychological by Glover (1947) and Greenson (1954), but Schafer (1973) treated the terms as synonyms and saw both processes as psychological in that both referred to fantasy.

Fuchs (1937) held identification to be an ego-term and introjection an id-term. Meissner (1979b) similarly categorized identification as mature and introjection as immature. On the other hand, in Waelder's (1936) analysis, introjection was an ego mechanism and presumably mature.

Knight's (1940) solution was to restrict the various forms of identification to the result of some action or mechanism and not to allow the term to be used for the act itself, a suggestion partly anticipated by Fuchs (1937). Knight's proposal was substantially endorsed later by Greenson (1954), although Schafer (1968) argued against it and Sandler (1960) and H. Hartmann and Loewenstein (1962) kept the dual reference. Simenauer virtually put all the meanings together by making identification more than an assimilation and more than one mechanism among many. Indeed, for him, identification used "a whole series of cohorts of psychic mechanisms . . . [to] . . . integrate the individual with external objects" (Simenauer 1985).

Koff's (1961) original picture of a Humpty-Dumpty created confusion has not changed. Meissner (1970) also saw the looking-glass arbitrariness and similarly prefaced his lengthy evaluation with a reference to Carroll. But, whereas Koff (1961) had attributed the confusion to some of the terms having antithetical meanings, Widlöcher (1985) to its referring to "a complex of mental operations whose boundaries are indistinct," and Abend and Porder (1986) to identification being used to refer to both a process and a product, Meissner laid the responsibility on Freud himself. Freud had "used the term with considerable flexibility," having included under it "a variety" of ego alterations that really covered "a set of metapsychologically distinct processes" (Meissner 1972). Some even take the identificatory jumble to be a mark of progress. Widlöcher judged the confusion to reflect challenges to Freud's 1933 "explanatory theory and descriptions," and actually says that if they could not be challenged in this way, "what could be their scientific value fifty years later?" (Widlöcher 1985).

Primary Identification

By and large, psychoanalysts grant the importance and centrality of primary identification in psychoanalytic theory, even though they also grant that the concept varies "according to each author and his ideas, its meaning, in consequence, being far from precise" (Etchegoyen 1985). Actually, the problems associated with primary identification pretty well defeated the earlier critics. Fuchs (1937) gave up: primary identification did not involve introjection, the term should be dropped altogether and replaced with an (unspecified) description of what happened. Greenson (1954) simply accepted Freud's ambiguity, and it is not surprising that he admitted to knowing more about identifications that *resolved* the Oedipus complex than about "the earlier forms." Like Meissner, Sandler (1960) dismissed primary identification as not being "the sort which leads to superego formation." By then Jacobson (1954) had been able to describe superego formation by avoiding Freud's "somewhat vague" term altogether. Holder (1982) later outstripped even that feat by accounting for superego formation without drawing on identification of any kind (cf. McIntosh 1986), and Brenner (1982) failed to mention either the repression or dissolution of the Oedipus complex when he argued that the process of superego formation had not been understood.

Narcissism and Primary Identification   Primary identification is, Etchegoyen (1985) says, "anything but clear" and if attempts are made to relate it to the stage of primary narcissism, as he does, his caveat about the mythical nature of that origin must be recognized. There is another problem in that identification and narcissism are incompatible concepts that, as shown by Meissner's analyses, cannot be separated. Meissner (1970) found that identification had five different meanings—dream, hysterical, primary, narcissistic, and partial identification—and was based on as many processes. From Freud's descriptions of primary identification, he differentiated an "early objectless form," which was not based on introjection (presumably the "being like"), and one that was "a function of an object relation," which was (presumably "having"). Although both were narcissistic, he recommended the two were "better kept separate." Only the introjected object relation kind had, he said, "primary application to superego formation" but made no clear further reference to the very early form. Despite his critique, Meissner ended by accepting Freud's primary identification as a pre-object emotional attachment brought about by *oral incorporation*. He thus fell victim to the very ambiguity between identification "which required object loss" and other forms, which "did not depend upon object relation or object loss" he had himself discerned in Freud's conceptualization (Meissner 1972).

In this connection, Compton raises the possibility that the concept of primary identification was "perhaps a substitute" for that of narcissistic identification. He remarked that Freud "did not much explain" primary identification or its relation to later forms (Compton 1985a). Elsewhere he observes that the prior concept of primary narcissism "almost disappeared" from Freud's work after its introduction in "Mourning and Melancholia" (Compton 1986c). Perhaps Freud's coyness was deliberate. How could either concept be explained, especially the new one, when its characterization was so at variance with the rest of the theory? Compton (1985a) also described narcissistic identification as "cumbersome," as "unclear," and complained that it "did not make sense" when "put in terms of transposition of libido." In fact, as Abend and Porder (1986) suggest, Freud's original invention of narcissistic identification may have been because the Oedipal part of his theory had true object cathexes coming into existence only at that much later stage.

Much contemporary discussion continues to founder on the ambiguity. Parkin (1983), for example, says primary identification is a description of "the primary narcissistic union," but he does not see the contradiction that in that state any kind of emotional tie with another, even the most primitive, is an impossibility. The same objection applies to Simenauer (1985) and Widlöcher (1985), who both have primary identification occurring in a state of fusion, although Widlöcher clearly differentiates it from the oral incorporation of an object and insists it is not narcissistic, and Simenauer equates primary identification or "being" with narcissistic identification and object choice as "having." Even Carneiro Leao (1986), who in my view asks the most sensible questions about primary identification, ends by making it a form of narcissistic identification quite distinct from secondary identification. Defining all identifications as primary (the "to be like" kind), as does Deigh (1984), is of course not a solution. It immediately creates the problems of allowing no role for introjection and also making it difficult to differentiate permanent ego alterations from temporary ones. But it would allow some use for Kramer's (1986) uncharacterized—and ugly—term "dis-identification"!

Resolutions   Resolving the ambiguities and inconsistencies at least requires, as the analysis by Belmonte Lara and colleagues (cited in Etchegoyen 1985) shows, that primary identification be placed at the only place where it makes sense: at the beginning of the phallic phase. But even that is not enough. In concurring with Etchegoyen's negative judgment about primary identification, Blum (1986) not only concludes it is "so diffuse a concept that it has probably outlived its usefulness" but goes on to apply the criticisms of primary identification and primary narcissism to secondary identification. It "does not seem to make sense" to invoke an identification "when there is not yet an emotional tie to a differentiated object with which to identify." One cannot avoid Brenner's (1982) description of the current theory of the superego forming through identification as "inadequate." Even without my criticisms, disagreements about the meaning and usefulness of primary identification of the magnitude we have seen among psychoanalysts preclude accepting Freud's explanation of how the father comes to form the essence of the superego.

Why did Freud postulate a mechanism so confused as primary identification, one so lacking explanatory power, and one so at variance with the rest of his theory?

Because only through it could the superego be made sexually appropriate. Bisexuality had paradoxical consequences, and identification by incorporation provided an object of the wrong sex, ergo some other mechanism had to be found. Primary identification filled the bill nicely, perhaps all too nicely—it needed only to be "intensified" to give the superego sexually appropriate psychological characteristics. Thus the boy's superego was masculine because of a simple strengthening of the already existing resemblance of his ego to that of his father. Plausible as it is, this mechanism has to be rejected. Not only is primary identification inconsistent with the rest of the theory, but it is itself uncharacterized, its strengthening is unexplained, and its capacity to contribute more powerfully to the superego than the opposite-sex object positively mystifying.

The Oedipus Complex and the Superego

The strong trend among contemporary psychoanalysts to make the Oedipus complex less central than did Freud to development and to psychopathology may be an attempt to find solutions to some of the preceding problems. Although not brought out explicitly in these new wave discussions, it follows that the importance of the Oedipus complex to the development of the superego must be reduced.

Oedipus a "Shibboleth"

In his contribution to a recent panel discussion reevaluating the Oedipus complex, Basch (in Sacks 1985) represented psychoanalysis as defining itself as a science through the "particular construct" of the complex rather than through its method of investigation. He described the complex as a "shibboleth" that "limited what it was permissible to discover with the clinical method of psychoanalysis" and went so far as to identify and praise Ferenczi, Balint, Bowlby, Erikson, Fairbairn, Guntrip, Hendrick, Winnicott, and Kohut for being among the "distinguished psychoanalytic thinkers" who had freed themselves of its constraint and "uncovered new data which modified and expanded Freud's early conclusion that the Oedipus complex was central for all of development." Stressing that the reevaluation was a modification of Freud's position, Basch opined, "No one is challenging infantile sexuality and the oedipal phase as *one aspect* of human development" (my emphasis). Modell (in Sacks 1985) disagreed only slightly. He thought "the Oedipus complex is a universal biological predisposition of probable genetic origin" but did not consider it was necessarily "a universal contributor to psychopathology." Similarly Brenner (1982) granted Oedipal conflicts the largest role in superego formation while denying the superego was the heir to the Oedipus complex and asserting it to be one of many resulting compromise formations. According to Burgner (1985) in recent years many analysts "questioned a number of issues classically connected with the Oedipus complex, and sometimes even the centrality of the concept itself."

Oedipus and the Clinic   The matter is not only or even mainly a theoretical issue. Basch (in Sacks 1985) asked if it were not time to change psychoanalytic theories about the Oedipus complex "so that they are in keeping with our actual clinical experience (as opposed to the sanitized versions that appear in the literature)." However, Laufer (1982) endorsed Freud's view of the Oedipus complex as central, saying it remained "one of primary importance" to his own clinical work, and Lebovici (1982) claimed the Oedipus complex to be universal and at "the heart of the mental life of man."

Oedipus and the Clinical Facts   A 1985 panel discussion also showed that clinically obtained facts are too muddied to resolve the issue. Modell (in Sacks 1985) said the analyses of "many patients" were for years dominated by self and actualization issues "to the exclusion of oedipal conflicts." Despite this endorsement of the importance of self and actualization, Modell disagreed fundamentally with the conceptualization of them in Kohut's psychology of the self. On the other hand, Basch (in Sacks 1985) characterized Kohut's findings as challenging Freud's theory that "the Oedipus complex is focal and the universal gateway to normal maturation" and Simon (in Sacks 1985) described them as an "attack on the unique and privileged position of the Oedipus complex." In later general discussion Wolff (in Sacks 1985) described Kohut as having moved the Oedipus complex "from the center ... to a more peripheral position." Loewald (in Sacks 1985) disagreed, however, saying no dichotomy existed between Kohut's and Freud's views.

How Early Is the Oedipus Complex?

One of the major controversies about the Oedipus complex concerns its time of occurrence. For Laufer (1982) the controversy centers around the theories of Melanie Klein, who holds that the superego begins to develop in the first year of life through the mechanisms of projective identification and the introjection and projection of "good" and "bad" objects. In the phallic phase when, "according to classical theory," it becomes the heir of the Oedipus complex, it simply reaches its developmental climax (M. Klein 1952). Even with that qualification, Klein's concept of the superego and its formation is markedly different from Freud's.

Mancia and Meltzer (1981) note that Klein pays little attention to the ego-ideal, and where she does she seems to confuse it with the ideal ego. I have also noticed that she either does not use concepts such as identification, sublimation, neutralization, or repression at all or she uses them in ways very different from Freud. As to Klein's own notion of projective identification, Etchegoyen (1985) comments that it erases the essential distinction Freud made between "being like" and "having." Together with other commentators, Etchegoyen rejects its compatibility with the notion of a symbiotic union between mother and child. In that state, there is insufficient differentiation between ego and not-ego. In contrast, Silverman (1986) bases what he sometimes terms "primal" and at other times "primary" identification precisely on that union. He thinks the Kleinian mechanisms allow for the development of the separation. A further problem arises with the claim of compatibility, if it is true that the harshness of the superego can actually be derived from projective identification, as Mancia and Meltzer (1981) argue. Deigh (1984) makes the point that this is a different source from that proposed by Freud, who said that superego severity depended on the child's own aggressiveness. He also finds no evidence for Freud's endorsement of Melanie Klein's thesis that the severity of the superego reflects the child's view of how the parents treat it, as Wollheim claims.

Precursors to the Oedipus Complex?

Rangell (1978) claimed that psychoanalysts had pushed the frontier of the genital phase to the second year of life so that "genital"–"oedipal" and "pregenital"–"pre-oedipal" were no longer synonyms. If so, a major change is required to Freud's thesis that the development of and resolution of the Oedipus complex is a phenomenon of the phallic phase. The second of the controversies Laufer (1982) identified is this one over the relative contribution of pre-Oedipal components and that he associates with the views of Mahler, Kohut, Winnicott, and Jacobson.

A number of other clinicians also opted for early placement. Burgner (1985) reported that his group at the Hampstead Clinic, the center of anti-Kleinian thought, did not accept the classical concept of the superego forming only after Oedipal resolution. Although offered as an alternative to Melanie Klein's theses, Holder (1982) also describes the superego as forming before the phallic phase. He claims in addition that the resolution of the Oedipus complex is not an essential precondition for the superego's later autonomy.

There are probably even some clinicians who are silent on the issue. Gillman (1982) describes two fears among psychoanalysts who propose pre-Oedipal precursors to the superego: they might be construed as blurring the significance of the Oedipus complex or as endorsing Melanie Klein. The link was brought out clearly by Etchegoyen (1985) who, together with others whom he cited, viewed Klein's very early placement of the Oedipus complex as stripping the Oedipus complex of its nodular function in normal and pathological development. Etchegoyen prefers an early placement because it explained "the clinical facts better" and did away with "the *ad hoc* hypothesis of deferred revision" (i.e., deferred action).

Although Laufer (1982) noted that for Freud the Oedipus complex as a developmental landmark formed only in the phallic phase, he also represented Freud as believing that it was the culmination of a very long process. But not much that is specific is said about the precursors. Garza-Guerrero (1981a) found that although there are "allusions" to the effects of "biological roots," "constitutional endowments," "inherited potential," "instinctual givens," and "drives" on superego development in the psychoanalytic literature, these are mentioned "only in passing or in footnotes, or with the author's promising to elaborate later on." Holder (1982) is a good example. He speaks of phylogenetic contributions, but does not say what they are. The situation is similar with the nonphylogenetic components. Even though his paper is entitled "Problems of the Superego Concept" and he grants their existence, Arlow (1982) says practically nothing about them.

For the most part, Klein's theses are too deficient in other respects to provide strong precursors to the phallic phase. Gillman (1982), who does not accept the Kleinian view, cites Spitz, Furer, Gould, and Parens in support of his proposal that the precursors are the inhibitions and restraints of the child by its parents. On the other hand, Brickman (1983) sees them as the affective, cognitive, and behavioral differentiations that occur at the different stages of psychosexual development. It is then easy for him to incorporate Klein's ideas into the affective group of precursors. Loewald (in Sacks 1985) postulates the precursors as an initial transindividual phase that he discerns in the work of Mahler and Kohut.

What importance do psychoanalysts place on these pre-Oedipal events? Of the Kleinians, we might note that Garza-Guerrero (1981a) cites Winnicott as saying of analysts who claim too much for Klein's notion of the precursor of "depressive position" at six months of age: "what a pity to spoil a valuable concept by making it difficult to believe in." And, by themselves, without integration into a larger process, Laufer (1982) does not grant that any precursors provide answers to psychopathology. But that is the problem: psychoanalysts simply do not agree on the nature of that long process. Kramer (1986) and Kanzer (1985), among many, lump together, in the most superficial of ways, almost all the contradictory formulations into one or another spongelike developmental schemata, presumably in the hope that the differences will be soaked up. Garza-Guerrero (1981a) similarly observes that most of the discussions of the concept of the superego, including Flugel's (1945) encyclopedic contribution, are "additive" rather than "integrative." Nevertheless, he extends his own miniencyclopedia by merely adding Jacobson to Kernberg before placing the resulting hybrid within the most simplistic of frameworks, one generated from the list of the unresolved problems: the role of pre-Oedipal components, the relation of the ego-ideal to prohibitions, Oedipal resolution, and post-Oedipal development (Garza-Guerrero 1981b).

Without, I am sure, trying to be ironical, Simon (in Sacks 1985) refers to the "full elaboration" of the Oedipus complex as "a rich, elastic, and subtle theory with a great deal of explanatory power" before going on to say that however little it has to do with primordial history it is "definitely applicable" to explaining the schisms that mark the history of the psychoanalytic movement.

The Formation of the Female Superego

Freud's explanation of superego formation in the female, to which I have barely alluded so far, has the useful function of bringing together a number of issues arising from the various inadequacies of the concepts of identification and sublimation.

The Female as Sexually Masculine

For Freud the sharp distinction between male and female sexual characteristics was not established until puberty: until then clitoris and penis were both phallic in function, the vicissitudes of psychosexual development were the same, and the mother was the first sexual object for both sexes. Libido and sexuality were essentially masculine (Freud 1905b, pp. 219, 222). It was within the constraints posed by this conception that Freud had to explain how the female child came to be possessed by the twin desires of sexual love for the father and murderous hostility toward the mother, or how she developed a feminine superego.

When he began his theorizing about the female superego, Freud pictured the little girl as choosing the father, forming a primary identification with the mother, and emerging from the Oedipal situation in a way "precisely analogous" to the little boy (Freud 1923b, p. 32). The analogy has several problems. First, the girl could not choose the father as a sexual object anaclitically because he satisfied no self-preservation drives. Second, resolution of the Oedipus complex required that the father be identified with by incorporation; as a consequence, the girl's superego would have had masculine characteristics, a patently absurd result. Third, it was implicit in this description that the girl's sexuality was feminine, not masculine. Freud had no basis for his claim that the outcome of the Oedipus complex in the girl was precisely analogous.

Female Sexuality   Within essentially the same period that saw the completion of *The Ego and the Id*, Freud began the first of five works (four papers and a Lecture) that bore on the origins of female sexuality and over which he continued to worry during the next eight years. The works are as relevant to his attempt to complete the account of superego formation as they are to femininity as such.

Throughout the papers and the Lecture, Freud insisted that the female child's sexuality was initially masculine. In the first paper, "The Infantile Genital Organization," he implied that he had previously underestimated genital primacy. The dominance of the genitals in the infantile genital organization was not far removed from that of the mature form, but it was a primacy of the *phallus* rather than of the genitals (Freud 1923e, p. 142). Because only maleness existed, he had no doubt that the girl also went through the phallic phase (p. 145).

In the second paper, "The Dissolution of the Oedipus Complex," he noted that the girl could not experience the fear of castration that destroyed the boy's Oedipus complex and established his superego (Freud 1924d, pp. 175, 177). What essentially differentiated the girl from the boy was her acceptance of castration as "an accomplished fact." After becoming aware that a boy had a penis and she did not, she explained the deficiency by assuming that an earlier castration had robbed her of it. Without the fear of castration, "a powerful motive" dropped out for the formation of the female superego (p. 178). Nevertheless it was set up.

In the third paper, "Some Psychical Consequences of the Anatomical Distinction Between the Sexes," Freud described what turned the little girl away from the mother, and made her choose the father, as a passive "loosening" of the tie (Freud 1925f, p. 254). But, for the analogy to hold properly, she had to feel hostility toward her mother. Although in the fourth paper, "Female Sexuality," Freud described the attachment as being broken because of active feelings of hostility on the girl's part (Freud 1931, pp. 231–204, 240–242), it took him some time to propose the hatred was because the mother was responsible for the absence of a penis. Girls never forgave their mothers the lifelong disadvantage to which they had thus been put (Freud 1925f, p. 254, 1931, pp. 234–235; cf. 1916b). Freud could then argue in the Lecture, "Femininity," that the source of the superego, as with the boy, was the castration complex (Freud 1933b, p. 124).

The Choice of the Father   How was the father chosen? Freud drew on two of his much earlier notions: the male as a provider of the penis and the symbolic equivalence of penis with baby (Freud 1917d, p. 129; cf. 1913c, p. 282). He brought them together by describing the little girl as attempting to compensate for the assumed loss of her penis by symbolically transforming her wish for that organ into a wish for a baby and turning to her father for its gratification (Freud 1924d, pp. 178–179). What brought her female sexuality into being, then, was the stealing of her masculinity, and what consolidated it was her attempt at restitution.

Consequently, Freud's final resolution of the problem posed by the constraints retained the postulate of an initial male sexuality for the girl but supposed a developmental transformation that allowed her to enter the Oedipal situation with the right complement of feelings. Her situation was then truly analogous to that of the boy. She could choose the father and model her superego on his.

Femininity   The process by which Freud imagined the girl's Oedipus complex to be dissolved resulted in a superego that was less harsh and more forgiving than the boy's. Lacking castration anxiety, she had no real motive to surmount the Oedipus complex. She thus stayed in the Oedipal situation for an indeterminate length of time, the complex was demolished only incompletely, and the resulting superego was less like that of the male on which it was modeled (Freud 1925f, pp. 256–257, 1931, p. 230, 1933b, p. 129). In a word, she had acquired feminine characteristics. The female superego was less inexorable, less impersonal, and less independent of its emotional origins than the male's (Freud 1925f, p. 257). Related traits—woman's lesser sense of justice, her greater unwillingness "to submit to the great exigencies of life," and her being more readily swayed by feelings of affection and hostility—were all, Freud thought, "amply accounted for" by the incompleteness of the Oedipal situation (pp. 257–258). [But elsewhere he proposed a different explanation of the sense of justice (Freud 1933b, p. 134).]

Apart from peculiarities in the formation of the female superego, it seemed to him that feminine psychological characteristics were created in two other ways. Some appeared to be residuals from the pre-Oedipal phase: repeated alternations between masculinity and femininity, the failure of the libido of females to incorporate an aggressive component, the frequency of sexual frigidity, and the peculiarities in the choice of husband, and typical attitudes toward him and his male children (Freud 1933b, pp. 131–133). Other characteristics seemed to derive directly from penis envy, although Freud was rather less certain about them. He thought they included narcissism, vanity, and shame, as well as jealousy and envy itself (pp. 124, 131–132; cf. 1925f, p. 254 for jealousy).

Freud briefly summarized these various results of the girl remaining in the Oedipus situation for an indeterminate period and of her late and incomplete demolition of the complex:

In these circumstances the formation of the super-ego must suffer; it cannot attain the strength and independence which give it its cultural significance.   (Freud 1933b, p. 129)

I examine his claim of lesser cultural significance before concluding this discussion of the superego.

The Female and Cultural Development

In the remote prehistoric past, Freud proposed, some young members of the primal horde, in which people then lived, collectively killed the horde leader. The remorse that arose in the killers had two momentous and simultaneous consequences: a religion was established that centered around the worship of a totem animal ancestral figure representing the slain leader, and systems of taboos were set up forbidding the killing of the totem animal and denying sexual relations between the remaining members of the horde (Freud 1912–1913, pp. 140–146). The killing was the "great event with which civilization began" (p. 145) and he repeatedly emphasized its significance (Freud 1925a, p. 66; cf. Freud 1927a, p. 13, 1930, p. 101).

Because the leader of the horde was the father and his killers were his sons, civilization was solely a male creation. True, Freud did also assert that love, including woman's love, had to be recognized as one of the foundations of civilization (Freud 1912–1913, pp. 101, 103), but it was pretty obvious to him that woman's contribution could not be of the same magnitude as that of the man. Woman's love was fundamentally passive and narcissistic and led her to acquiesce in the desire of the male to keep his sexual objects near him. What contribution even that made was before the males had taken the really decisive action of killing their father (pp. 99–100).

However, for Freud there was a much more fundamental basis for woman's limited contribution to civilization. He believed her to have less capacity than man to sublimate her instinctual drives, that is, to have a slighter ability to redirect her libido onto cultural ends (Freud 1930, p. 103, 1933b, p. 134). She could not contribute to the growth of civilization to the same extent as man. The very limited sublimation also led her to make sexual demands on man that prevented him from deploying his libido for cultural purposes as fully as he might otherwise do. And, to the extent that he did not meet her sexual needs, she became hostile toward him, his civilizing mission, and its end product. Thus she doubly restrained and retarded the development of civilization (Freud 1930, pp. 103–104).

Woman's deficiencies came about during the formation of the superego. When the Oedipus complex was overcome, identifications replaced object cathexes and Eros and Thanatos were defused. Because the female surmounted the Oedipal situation only partially, the defusion also was only partial. Less sexual energy could therefore be liberated in her than in the male and less be made available to be sublimated. And if, as he also asserted, every identification was a sublimation (Freud 1923b, pp. 30, 45, 54), the incomplete identification meant that the female made less use of what was a smaller store of sublimated libido. Further, because less of the death instinct was freed, less of it was available to be taken up into the superego. Woman's superego was necessarily less harsh and less opposed to sexuality than man's (Freud 1924b, p. 167). A final consequence of the partial defusion was that more of the remaining alloy of Eros with Thanatos was left behind in the female than in the male. To the extent that it was internally directed, her erotogenic masochism—what Freud saw as the entire basis for feminine masochism—had therefore to be stronger.[3]

The female superego could not be other than as Freud described it, and woman's contribution to civilization could not be other than minor. So, after the killing of the primal father, when the superego formed, Freud could not allow that it was even through that agency that woman might have made one of her few contributions to civilization. Plaiting and weaving, which he grudgingly conceded that she "may have invented," sprang directly from genital deficiency; they were techniques based on an unconscious imitation of the way in which, at puberty, her matted pubic hair came to conceal her deficient genitals (Freud 1933b, p. 132).

Civilization was, it must be repeated, a *male* creation—woman had no part in it. Similarly, the remorse, and later the guilt that came to sustain it, was substantially a *male* feeling. What moral standards woman had, what capacity she had to resist instinctual demands, she acquired from the male by "cross-inheritance" (Freud 1923b, p. 37, 1925f, p. 258). When, then, in the course of her own development, Freud pictured the little girl as creating yet another incomplete superego, he was also picturing her as reaffirming the masculine foundation of civilization, her own relatively trivial later contributions, and the paucity of her moral standards.

Fundamentally, it is because Freud considers her to be a male, although an incomplete one, that he ends by representing the female so abjectly. We see, however, that her supposed inadequacies are much more a result of his postulate that her infantile sexuality is masculine than because of any supposed anatomical deficiency. Even were he correct, however, we also see that the mechanisms of identification and sublimation he proposes would be unable to bring about any change in her.

Structures and Functions

I think it is worth examining the uncertain status which Freud's structural formulations have been granted by psychoanalytic theorists and clinicians, rather than simply summarize my criticisms of them. Some accept Freud's 1923 theses and welcome the structural theory as resolving the ambiguities of the topographic theory. Others are no less enthusiastic in seeing it as a recasting of psychoanalytic concepts in a way that emphasizes conflict more and generally better fits the data of clinical observation (e.g., Arlow and Brenner 1964, pp. 43–55; Arlow 1975). Among those who have reacted in a generally positive way, some regard the theory as significantly incomplete and either extend it along lines they consider as essentially similar to Freud's (e.g., H. Hartmann 1939/1958) or argue that concurrent use should or has to be made of some parts or all of both theories (E. Kris 1950; Eissler 1962; Fayek 1980; Sandler, Dare, and Holder 1972, 1982; Sandler and Sandler 1983).

Negative responses are to be found beside the positive and, strangely enough, many of them are based on the opposite contentions. The structural theory is thus criticized for *not* being new, that is, for not really being different from the topographic, or as *sharing* the deficiencies of the earlier theory (e.g., Gill 1963). Others say the abstract systems of the structural theory are *too removed* from the realm of clinical experience and its emphasis on conflict (e.g., G. S. Klein 1976, pp. 7–8, chapter 4; Schafer 1976). In line with this, the Lacanists argue that the American housed ego-psychology adaptation of Freud's theory is also too removed from conflict. Still others, including some whose attitude is generally positive, attack it for it conserving too much of the topographic view, thereby perpetuating at least some of the original problems (Arlow 1975).

Anthropomorphic Structures?

Many critics join one or other of these arguments with the point that the structures are not real entities but mere groupings of psychological functions, if not unfortunate anthropomorphizations or reifications (Nacht 1952; Beres 1958, 1965, in Marcovitz 1963; Hayman 1969; Bieber 1972; Wiedeman 1972). H. Hartmann, Kris, and Loewenstein (1946) clearly were not successful in convincing other psychoanalysts that strict adherence to their functional definition of the structures effectively meets the charge that the structures are mere anthropomorphic metaphors for immediate experience. Pseudoentities such as these, the critics continue to say, should be purged from the theory. Opposing this demand, at least to some extent, are Laplanche and Pontalis (1967/1973, pp. 437–438, 452), Grossman and Simon (1969), and Kernberg (1982), who find some virtue, necessity even, in anthropomorphic formulations. Stolorow (1978) formulated a third point of view with anthropomorphism inherent in the conceptions of ego, superego, and id "as structures." Although he wants to do away with them even as groups of functions, he grants their usefulness as "a symbolic representation of the tripartite structuration of the subjective experiential world."

Ellman and Moskowitz (1980) pointed out that in the psychoanalytic criticisms of the structural theory the words anthropomorphic and reification tend to be defined inadequately or not at all. They show that whether or not a term is anthropomorphic is not a matter of the word itself. For an explanatory statement not to be anthropomorphic, they say the terms in it "must fit into a theoretical context that implicitly defines the explanatory terms and independently characterizes them." The real question is whether this can be done.

Realistic Structures?

It is as well to begin our consideration of this point by noting that Freud himself never spoke of the structural theory. According to Anna Freud, it was Ernst Kris who coined the phrase "structural theory" and it may have been through his use that others adopted it (Nagera 1967). Freud hardly ever even used the word "structure," usually speaking of the components of the "psychical apparatus" as "systems" or "agencies," or, less frequently, as "organizations," "formations," or "provinces."

My first point is that Freud's statements about the systems or agencies show him to have taken a realist stance—he clearly believed the structures to have a real existence. Thus, in introducing the 1923 "ego," he said:

We have formed the idea that in each individual there is a coherent *organization* of mental processes; and we call this his ego.   (Freud 1923b, p. 17. Emphasis altered)

As an organization, this ego was more than a set of functions. It was

the mental *agency* which supervises all its own constituent processes.   (p. 17. My emphasis)

And of the term "id":

I propose ... calling the *entity* which starts out from the system *Pcpt.* and begins by being *Pcs.* the "ego", and ... calling the other part of the mind, into which this *entity* extends and behaves as though it were *Ucs.*, the "id".   (p. 23. My emphasis on entity)

Later he expressed the hope that the readers of his *New Introductory Lectures*

will by now feel that in postulating the existence of a super-ego I have been describing a genuine *structural entity*, and have not been merely *personifying an abstraction*, such as conscience.   (Freud 1933c, p. 92. My emphasis)[4]

Ego, superego, and id, then, were organizations or entities as real as the systems *Pcpt.*, *Cs.*, *Pcs.*, and *Ucs.*

My second point is that Freud's realism has two consequences. On the one hand, by itself and without any further evaluation, it completely undermines the argument, prosecuted most vigorously by the ego-psychologists, that the structures should be defined by their functions. On the other, it provides the basis for circumventing the trivially silly criticism that the structures Freud described are mere reifications or anthropomorphizations.

Structures as Functions?

It seems to have been the ego-psychologists Hartmann and his collaborators who first adopted the nonrealist criterion of defining "psychic systems" such as the ego, superego, and id "by the functions attributed to them" (H. Hartmann, Kris, and Loewenstein 1946; H. Hartmann and Loewenstein 1962; cf. H. Hartmann 1939/1958). When they did this, Hartmann, Kris, and Loewenstein (1946) explicitly attributed the definition to Freud himself. I think it significant they did not produce any statement of Freud's in support. Neither in my reading of his works nor in the extensive psychoanalytic literature on psychic structures have I been able to find a single remark of Freud's that would remotely class him among those who define structures by their functions. Despite its non-Freudian origins, psychoanalysts have widely endorsed it (Rapaport 1951, 1959; Beres 1958, 1965; Rapaport and Gill 1959; Gill 1963; Marcovitz in Marcovitz 1963; Arlow and Brenner 1964; Hammerman 1965; Loewenstein 1966b; Moore and Fine 1967, cited in Wilson 1973; Hayman 1969; Arlow 1975).

What I will call this functional version of Freud's structural theory is associated with a number of problems. The criterion for assigning functions to structures is probabilistic, making "it difficult to maintain that explicit definition is involved," and the rules relating the structures to clinical data are "quite imprecise and loosely stated" (Wilson 1973). Possibly this is why even the same functions are sometimes defined differently by different authors, as for example, in the differences between Nacht and Hartmann about whether there are any ego functions that are not concerned with drive satisfaction (Nacht 1952). Nor is what is to count as a function, and therefore as a structure, agreed upon. Rapaport (1959), for example, considers affects and delayed discharge as structures, a proposition that Wiedeman (cited in Abrams 1971b; Wiedeman 1972) and Beres (1965) quite properly reject as self-contradictory or meaningless.

The functional theory has also been criticized from within (Beres 1958, 1965; cf. Schwartz 1981). According to Beres, those adopting the functional version have not been radical enough. Defining structures by a relative stability of functions (H. Hartmann 1964, p. xii), or by abiding patterns in the flux of processes (Rapaport and Gill 1959), or by recurrent patterns of functions, especially regulatory ones (Gill 1963, p. 113), is to define them too rigidly and inflexibly (Beres 1965). In Beres's view, even ideas and memories cannot be the *contents* of structures. Instead, they have to be *products* of functions.

The nub of the problem lies in the functionalist position itself. If functions are to be the criteria for defining structures, what are the rules that restrict them multiplying beyond necessity, that prevent arbitrariness in the ways in which they are grouped, and that guide their allocation to the correct structures? Not only are there no guiding principles, but the functionalist view has been interpreted to mean that one invents as many functions as are necessary to produce the behavior to be explained (Wilson 1973, citing Fodor). It is the lack of constraint on this inventive fertility that causes the significant differences in the different functional definitions of the three structures of ego, superego, and id. And they are irreconcilable.

It is all too easy to show there is no agreement about the functions supposedly defining any of the structures. For example, the often-expressed need for reevaluating the theory of the superego (e.g., M. H. Stein, cited in Goodman 1965) has been attributed to an overall problem of

analysts [finding] it difficult to distinguish conceptually between functions of the superego and those of ego or id when they attempted to apply the theory to clinical situations. (Loewenstein 1966b)

Loewenstein went on to raise issues such as whether anxiety, anticipation, and self-observation were solely ego functions or were in some measure shared with the superego. Sandler (1960) spoke of an "apparent "conceptual dissolution" of the superego" in the face of this reassignment of functions, and from the other end, so to speak, Modell (1975) noted a growing tendency to attribute id functions to the ego.

It has not been possible to arrive at a functional definition of any of the three structures. Beres (1958) found no conclusive list of functions defining the superego and many difficulties in assigning specific functions to it. The id has fared even worse. On the grounds that many ego tendencies were wrongly ascribed to it and that it drew attention away from the repressed unconscious, Van der Waals (1952) questioned "whether the introduction of the concept of the id has been profitable in every respect." Compared with the other structures,

The concept of the id has been perhaps the most consistently misused, misunderstood, and criticized of Freud's postulates. (V. H. Rosen 1968)

Examining the three main works devoted to the id show the misunderstandings result from basic ambiguities about its functions. Is it concerned only with energy pressing for immediate discharge, or does it "contain" real structures of primitive perceptions, memory traces, and repressed ideas? (Brierley 1951, cited by Hayman 1969; Schur 1966a). Does the id express instinctual drives as *needs* or does it press for the gratification of *wishes* stimulated by drives? (Beres v. Schur in Marcovitz 1963). Even after Schur's (1966a) massive reevaluation of the id, Hayman (1969) found it impossible to make a simple list of its functions. Central to her difficulty was the fact that id and ego are defined in terms of each other. Lack of specification of the functions of the one is necessarily associated with indeterminacy about the other.

The same points hold for one of the most resolutely functional approaches, the ego-psychology created by Hartmann and his collaborators. H. Hartmann (1939/1958) argued that the ego had its sources in processes other than conflicts over drive satisfaction, and that the impact of a harsh reality on the instinctual drives was only one of the bases of ego formation. In fact, he believed it was not possible to derive the ego from the conflict between drives and reality. Subsequently, he and his colleagues (H. Hartmann 1948; H. Hartmann, Kris, and Loewenstein 1946; H. Hartmann and Loewenstein 1962; Loewenstein 1966a) proposed that the ego differentiated itself from an original undifferentiated ego-id matrix, and that functions such as perception, thinking, memory, motor development, and the comprehension of objects—what they termed primary autonomous ego functions—developed outside of the sphere of conflict. These functions were thus autonomous and independent of drive satisfaction. They were fueled by a neutral and primary "mode of energy different from that of the drives" available from the very beginning of life. Instinctual needs thus activated but did not create "the apparatus serving perception, motility, and others that underlie ego functions" (H. Hartmann 1952). Ego-psychology has always drawn some fire on the very grounds of whether or not these so-called autonomous, conflict-free ego functions exist and in what ways they differ from the functions subserving conflict. In short, it is criticized for difficulties in the very matter it was partly designed to overcome: that of assigning functions to structures.

Structures as Structures?

The simple fact is that structures cannot be defined by their functions. Structures are different from functions. Structures are combinations of mutually connected and interdependent parts, elements, or components making up some whole. Functions are the activities proper to the structure or by which it fulfills its purpose (Rosenblatt and Thickstun 1977; McIntosh 1986). Structures thus *have* functions but they are clearly not the functions themselves. That is:

the structure of a thing determines its functions and, hence, the structural definition takes primacy over the functional definition. Without structure, function is impossible. (Berrien 1968, cited in Wiedeman 1972)

Wiedeman put it even more sharply: "Structure defined by its functions ... is a contradiction in terms" (cf. Eissler 1962; Nagera 1967). The contradiction is well illustrated in the misleading analogy Schwartz (1981) drew between a telephone and functional definition. He represented the communication transmission *functions* of the telephone as its *structure*, rather than seeing that those functions are the result of the way the component structures of the telephone—dialer chips, electret condenser microphones, and ceramic sounders—work, operate, or function.

In the case of physical or organic structures these elementary definitional points are almost self-evident. But they apply equally to other realms, including the mental. There we note it is not at all necessary for adequate definitions of psychological structures to have or include physical referents. One may speak as readily of simple mental structures, such as memories or ideas, or of complex ones such as ability, conscience, or self, without referring at all to either physical or organic elements or substrates (cf. Grossman and Simon 1969; Schwartz 1981).

If the essence of a structure is that it is a structure of something, then in psychoanalysis the prototype of a psychic structure is a mental representation. From my discussion of theoretical terms in chapter 6, it follows that the real question is how to characterize the structures of psychological theories. What are the components out of which the structures of the structural theory are built, and how do those structures give rise to the functions assigned them? The question is worth an answer. Freud was a realist in his theorizing and is done no service at all by those of his followers who have tried to turn him into a player of positivist functional pursuits.

Rapaport and Gill (1959) proposed the most widely adopted answer. For them, structures were "configurations of a slow rate of change," but apart from adding that they were "abiding patterns in the flux of processes" from which the structures were inferred, they did not mention what the configuration consisted of. W. C. Lewis (1965) endorsed Rapaport's innate discharge-regulating thresholds as the basis of psychic structures, at the same time defining a structure as "an ordered arrangement of elements, which may be perceptions, thoughts, reactions, et cetera of sufficient stability to give predictability." Rapaport's energic definitions of structures has several problems, as Schwartz (1981) pointed out. "Structure as process" leads to the ambiguity of the same concept being a structure controlling a process as well as process itself. For example, defense is an ego process as well as a structure that controls drive discharge. "Structure as energy" involves the use of a quite explicit and unacceptable analogy of psychic energy with physical energy. "Structure as internalization of environmental contingencies" leaves external events having no connection with the physical structure of the organism. "Structures as operations" lumps together elements that are too disparate, such as memories, which may be specific, and operations as general and abstract as cognitive skills.

Structures as Memory Traces?

What Freud meant by a structure in the *Project* was clear: the ego, for example, was a group of well-cathected neurons. The difference between the ego as that structure and its functions was no less clear: functions resulted from the movement of quantities of excitation within the neuronal network. Ego functions such as perceiving stimuli, making decisions about their origin, delaying motor responses to them, laying down memories of them, and preventing unpleasure from their attempted revival, result from the disposal of cathexes stored within the ego as a structure. After abandoning the pseudophysiological elements, Freud could have retained a realist meaning for the structures by rethinking the problem in psychological terms. But he did not do this, with the result that the relations between structure and function became implicit. Although it was clear that the structures of the structural theory were more than a group of functions, it was not at all clear what they consisted of.

At various earlier places I have argued that the implicit elements of many important structures in Freud's theory are memory traces. Entirely in accord with Freud's mode of thought Glover also noted:

The moment two sets of memory traces concerning experiences of gratification and frustration are linked (associated or merged) we have the makings of an ego nucleus.   (Glover 1961)

Similarly, Freud's account of the development of the reality-ego from the pleasure-ego through the incorporation of objects or their projection from it requires the formation or reorganization of the memory traces of objects with those making up the ego (chapter 11). Superego formation as we have described it in this chapter really only makes sense if thought of in the same way: primary identification reorganizes the existing ego traces to match the model of the person the child wishes to be like, and Oedipal identification links up existing traces in new ways. Despite Beres's (1965) reservations, there is no doubt that Glover was being perfectly consistent with Freud's own thinking when he identified groups of memory traces as the elements of structures (Glover 1943, 1947).

Of course, mounting a rescue operation for psychoanalytic theory forms no part of my intention. Psychoanalysts interested in structures must invest in that effort themselves. But should they try, they will almost certainly end in a cul-de-sac as barren as that in which we left the functionalists. Suppose they decided it was sensible to think of structures as being composed of something like memory traces. They will then have to face the fact that memory structures are just as inert as were Freud's neuronal structures. What explicit *psychological* meaning can be given to the quantities of excitation that once enlivened the neuronal net? Psychic energy? Yet, of all Freud's concepts, that of psychic energy must be the most severely criticized. No substitute for it has been proposed, and without it a trace-type structural theory is doomed.

Conclusion

Whether or not one agrees that the final version of Freud's personality theory is the consequence of the introduction of the concept of instinctual drive, one has to agree that components of the theory have grave deficiencies as Freud formulated them and as others have tried to correct them. First there is the totally unsatisfactory nature of Freud's concept of instinctual drive. Its inadequacies are already evident in the sexual instinctual drive, especially in its pseudophysiological referents and supposed infantile components. They become more striking in the ludicrous propositions about the ego drive, particularly as an opponent of sexuality and a source of hatred. The death instinct, both in itself and as a source of aggression, simply carries the original inadequacies, contradictions, and lack of characterization to a higher stage.

Second, the id, ego, and superego are completely empty theoretical structures. Even were it possible to establish other than in the broadest and most metaphorical manner what functions these structures perform, it is absolutely impossible find an intelligible account of how any of them function. Freud is also unable to give even a moderately coherent account of how the ego emerges from the id, how its functions are acquired, how it exercises those functions, and especially how it regulates the dangerous id drives. His description of the formation of the superego is, at best, the description of a process that gives the wrong properties to it.

Third, to the extent that mechanisms such as identification, repression, and sublimation are central to the formation and function of ego and superego, Freud does not explain the relation between primal repression and repression proper, the relation between anxiety (both the traumatic and the signal kind) and either kind of repression, or how the ego and superego acquire their stocks of neutral and destructive energy respectively.

If we ask what can be done to remedy this parlous situation, we are either fobbed off with reassurances that psychoanalysis is as yet too young to have developed a fully systematic account of its discoveries, or we are told that what is required is some new kind of framework within which those discoveries can be reinterpreted. We are never told that the so-called discoveries are dependent on methods of inquiry and interpretation so defective that even practitioners trained in their use are unable to reach vaguely congruent conclusions about such things as the interpretation of a dream or a symptom, let alone the basic clinical characteristics of infantile or perverse sexuality, the reconstruction of the early stages of an individual's development, or the functions that make up a given structure.

While the basic methodological deficiencies remain, it will not matter how great an effort is made or what perspective is adopted. There is no way in which either Freud's original form of psychoanalysis or any modern derivative will ever lead to a satisfactory personality theory. This is, of course, the quite explicit message of Schafer's proposal for the use of action language: after nearly one hundred years of psychoanalysis, psychoanalysts must begin all over again. They have to clarify what it is that requires explanation. Because psychoanalysts see only the need to reformulate the theory, the methodological point has been missed altogether by those who want a metapsychology something like that Freud proposed; they tamper with the structures or alter the nature and status of the drives, but their own concepts of drive and structure are inferred from facts gathered by a defective method. My point also holds for those like G. S. Klein and Holt who think it possible to save what they refer to as the clinical theory at the expense of the metapsychology. The psychoanalytic method is not capable of discovering clinical facts that can be agreed on.

I believe the conclusion I have just drawn is sufficiently documented from within psychoanalysis, so to speak. But it is, as we will see, also confirmed by those investigations made outside of that particular clinical setting. This additional evidence will be evaluated in chapters 14, 15, and 16, which constitute part IV.

Notes

1. In *The Ego and the Id* Freud used the term ego ideal as a synonym for superego (Freud 1923b, pp. 28, 34, 36). Only in his later writing did he differentiate the ego-ideal as a part of the superego, describing the superego as the vehicle or bearer of the ego-ideal (Freud 1933b, pp. 64–65 and n .1). The distinction involves more than the relatively minor semantic point it is sometimes represented as being (editor's note, *Standard Edition*, vol. 19, pp. 9–10; Laplanche and Pontalis, 1967/1973, pp. 144–145). For the present I write as if Freud had already made and meant something important by this finer differentiation, and discuss it more fully later.

2. Like Compton (1986a), I prefer "representation" to Strachey's "presentation," and will use that term as much as possible.

3. Despite the importance given erotogenic masochism, its basic weakness as a concept is that it accepts pain as the source rather than the condition of pleasure. Further, its theoretical underpinnings are said to be "strong but dubious" (!) and, although it was Deutsch who proposed it as the basis of feminine masochism, that relation has since been rejected by most writers (Maleson 1984).

4. Because it brings out Freud's thought so accurately, I have here quoted from the Sprott translation (cf. Wilson, 1973; Beres, 1965). The original German is "*Ich hoffe, Sie haben bereits den Eindruck empfangen, dass die Aufstellung des Über-Ichs wirklich ein Strukturverhätnis beschreibt und nicht einfach eine Abstraktion wie die des Gewissens personifiziert*" (Freud, 1933a, p. 71; cf. 1933b, p. 64). In the *Standard Edition*, *Aufstellung* is rendered as "hypothesis" rather than as "postulating the existence," and *Strukturverhätnis* as "structural relation" rather than "genuine structural entity." The accuracy of the latter translation is debatable, but there is no doubt that, albeit inadvertently, Strachey provided positivist fuel for the functional fire.

IV EVALUATION

14 Psychoanalysis as Theory and Therapy

Rosencrantz: Why don't you go and have a look?
Guildenstern: Pragmatism? Is that all you have to offer? You seem to have no conception of where
we stand.
—Stoppard: *Rosencrantz and Guildenstern are Dead*

In part IV I provide an evaluation of psychoanalysis that follows from the previous discussions. It is organized around the three components into which psychoanalysis is conventionally dismembered and which Freud's own writing warrants: a theory of personality, a method of investigation, and a type of psychotherapy (Freud 1913b, pp. 207, 210, 1924c, pp. 200, 205, 1925a, p. 30, 1926b, pp. 248, 252–253, 1927a, p. 36, 1933b, pp. 156–157). Chapters 14 and 15 deal with the three components. In chapter 16, which brings this book to a conclusion, I consider the senses in which psychoanalysis is a science.

Chapter 14 is devoted to evaluating psychoanalysis as a personality theory and as a type of psychotherapy, and begins with a discussion of the basis used for the evaluation. Whatever kind of theory one construes psychoanalysis to be—scientific, humanist, clinical, metapsychological, or hermeneutic—the explanations it generates must be deductive in form and adequately logical. This standard is applied to examine what I take to be the most central concepts of Freud's theory of personality. The most abstract—excitation, stimulus barrier, narcissism, and mental structures—are considered before the lower-level characteristics. Some new criticisms are advanced, with brief repetitions of a few of those made in earlier chapters. Where it is appropriate, data are cited relevant to the validity of the concepts. I conclude the chapter with an assessment of the effectiveness of psychoanalysis as a therapy and of the bearing of that effectiveness on its validity as a personality theory.

The Personality Theory

The core of Freud's theory of personality is about the transformation of an original inherited endowment—the id—into a set of mental structures that regulate the individual's relations with the surrounding world. Primary process gives way to secondary, ego and superego form out of the id, defense mechanisms begin operating, and character traits are laid down. This conglomerate of structures and processes constitutes the personality.

Personality results from a complex process in which the infant's original polymorphous sexual disposition is modified by having some of its libidinal aims changed and its autoerotic tendencies replaced by heterosexual object-love. Nonreproductive aims are brought under the sway of genital activities, and object-choices that do not lead in the direction of nonincestuous heterosexuality are abandoned. For the most part, personality development follows biologically determined pathways in which repression is the main agent of change.

The ego and superego develop from the id to play important roles in the two different kinds of repression. Some early traumas produce enough anxiety to bring about repression automatically. Usually this is when the ego is weak and before the superego has developed. At other times, usually later, a threatened reactivation of the memory traces of an earlier, even archaic, trauma or a threat to the individual's values and standards causes anxiety to be experienced by the ego. Repression as an after-pressure is then initiated at the behest of the superego.

Differences in personality result from variations in this complex developmental course. A normal outcome may come about despite peculiarities in the constitution and the effects of repression. Failure to complete some part of the process causes the development of fixations on particular libidinal aims or objects and on modes of ego and superego functioning. Depending on their strength, libidinal fixations result directly in perversions or in character traits. Fixated modes of libidinal satisfaction that are carried over into normal adult life as character traits are prolongations-continuations, sublimations, and reaction formations that developed during psychosexual development. Neuroses and psychoses result from later regressions to these fixation points when earlier libidinal aims and modes of satisfaction are revived, together with more primitive functioning of the mental structures.

The standard I adopt in evaluating Freud's personality theory is whether or not it allows for a deductive explanation of the facts with which it is concerned. As I argued in chapter 7, for an explanation to be genuine, it must be possible to deduce the facts to be explained from the propositions of the theory.

The Basis of Evaluation

Insisting that adequate explanations be deductive is not a demand unique to scientific explanations. Explanations in all domains are governed by it. Thus when I say that a particular narrative or case history provides a genuine explanation, I am saying that *if* the factors in the case or in the narrative are really as described, *then* the behavior to be explained can be deduced logically from them. Again, when I say that I can explain someone's behavior because of the empathic understanding I have of it, I mean that *if* I were in that person's situation, with his or her particular complement of feelings and experiences, *then* it would be logical for me to do the same, whether I was conscious of those feelings at the time or not. Thus the *if-then* structure of these explanations marks them as deductive. The structure requires they be evaluated in the same way as explanations that begin with the *if* assumptions of scientific theory and are followed by a *then* deduction of the facts to be explained. Naturally the point holds for explanations deriving from theories of high as well as low levels of abstraction. Consequently, my evaluation is not restricted to any particular type of explanation or level of theorizing.

It is necessary to stress this elementary point because in the past twenty-five to thirty years a number of attempts were made by psychoanalysts, for the most part those within psychoanalysis, to meet the demand to jettison Freud's theoretical assumptions and replace them with others. Two kinds of arguments can be distinguished. One is based on what is claimed to be a scientific standpoint. In it, concepts such as the instinctual drives and the structures on the mental apparatus are criticized for not being in line with contemporary knowledge of the physiology or psychology of drives or with current thinking about executive and controlling processes in the mind (e.g., Holt 1967/1968, 1975a). Depending on the critic, physical field theory, modern information-processing concepts, systems theory, or real contemporary neurophysiology or a purely psychological theory of drives is suggested as a substitute (e.g., Pumpian-Mindlin 1958–1959; Peterfreund 1975; Rosenblatt and Thickstun 1977; Reiser, summarized by Wallerstein 1985; G. S. Klein 1976). Basically this line of thought accepts Freud's scientific aims but says they have to be realized with different theoretical concepts. The second approach pretty well dismisses Freud's theorizing altogether: psychoanalysis is either not a science at all or, if it is one, it is not a science in the mold of the natural sciences. An implication is that the usual standards for evaluating theoretical explanations do not or should not apply.

Cutting across these two positions, although overlapping with them to some extent, are views about the level and function of Freud's theoretical statements. Because theoretical statements can often be arranged hierarchically, with the most abstract at the top and the most concrete at the bottom, it is held that the standards or techniques of evaluation should differ according to level. Some also maintain that explanations couched in the higher-level terms, such as psychic energy and cathexes, are too remote from what is experienced in the clinical or treatment situation to be useful. What these critics say is that psychoanalysis needs primarily or solely a *clinical* theory (e.g., G. S. Klein 1976). Some critics taking this line also imply that the standards for evaluating a new theory of this type have to be different from those used previously. Although both the level and function arguments may be made independent of the one about the correctness of the higher-level propositions, those making them tend to argue that almost all of Freud's theoretical statements are faulty as well as irrelevant (Schafer 1976).

Basic to these two kinds of criticisms is a confusing set of propositions about what is known as Freud's *metapsychology*. Unfortunately there is so much variation in the way this term is used that I have to clarify the term before estimating its relevance to my own evaluation of theories about metapsychology and the criticisms based on it.

Psychoanalytic Metapsychology

Freud gave his only formal definition of metapsychology in his 1915 paper "The Unconscious." After outlining how ideas were unconscious, either in the dynamic sense of being opposed by other forces or in the topographic sense of belonging to the system *Ucs.*, he discussed unconsciousness in terms of the withdrawal of cathexes of energy and the imposition of anticathexes. This explanation meant, he said, that he had adopted an economic point of view in addition to the dynamic and topographic. Consequently:

I propose that when we have succeeded in describing a psychical process in its dynamic, topographical and economic aspects, we should speak of it as a *metapsychological* presentation.   (Freud 1915c, p. 181)

A metapsychological description was therefore a comprehensive one that drew on three kinds of psychological concepts: forces, systems, and energy, respectively. In "A Metapsychological Supplement to the Theory of Dreams," written at the same time as "The Unconscious" but not published until two years later, he gave precisely such a comprehensive, three-fold description of dreams (Freud 1917a).

Three Viewpoints or Five?

Freud recognized only the three metapsychological viewpoints—dynamic, topographic (or systematic), and economic. By the early 1940s Glover distinguished an "adaptive" and a "genetic" viewpoint (Glover 1943), and by the late 1950s, mainly through the work of Rapaport and Gill, these two additional perspectives were accepted by a number of psychoanalysts. Not everyone approved of the extension, as Rapaport and Gill found when they attempted to systematize psychoanalytic theory. They were doubtful about the genetic perspective and reported that the least widely accepted of the five was the adaptive; "almost every reader" of the early drafts of their paper questioned its inclusion (Rapaport and Gill 1959). Years later, Warme (1981) continued to question the metapsychological status of the genetic and adaptive positions.

Reservations about a genetic and adaptive metapsychology are well founded. Although it is undoubtedly the case that all clinical practitioners, not only psychoanalysts, find it important to understand the adaptive function of behavior and the way it develops, neither of these perspectives is based on specific assumptions from which adaptive or genetic explanations can be derived. Rather, what exists are sets of principles against which the developmental or adaptive adequacy of the behavior can be judged. Consequently, descriptions based on these perspectives are different from the three Freud proposed, and explanations cannot be generated from them. I will therefore disregard them.

What Is beyond or Meta to Psychology

Freud clearly meant "metapsychology" to refer to something that went beyond the psychology of consciousness (Masson 1985, Letter of Mar. 10, 1898). The problem is to know what that something else is. In the correspondence with Fliess, he several times used the word explicitly, and many of his references to "psychology" are also really to it. One set of references is in the letters between 1895 and 1896, the other in those between 1898 and 1899. Although many of the remarks are impossible to interpret, there is no doubt that the overall context in which the first set occurs is that of Freud's difficulties with the *Project* and that of the second is the completion of what became the theoretical chapter of *The Interpretation of Dreams*. In both contexts, most of Freud's pre-1915 references or allusions are to explanations of conscious psychological phenomena through his economic, pseudophysiological concepts or through psychologically transformed versions of them (e.g., Masson 1895, Letters of Mar. 28, 1895, Apr. 27, 1895, May 25, 1895, Aug. 16, 1895, Sept. 23, 1895, Feb. 13, 1896, Apr. 2, 1896, June 4, 1896, Dec. 17, 1896, Feb. 9, 1898, Feb. 23, 1898, Mar. 10, 1898, Aug. 26, 1898, Aug. 31, 1898, July 22, 1899). In only one post-1915 paper does his use give clear meaning to metapsychology. There he classed quantitative variation in the strength of the instinctual drives as part of the economic approach (Freud 1937a, pp. 224–227, 234).

Psychoanalysts disagree about the meaning of "meta" in metapsychology. It does not seem to refer to phenomena that are simply not conscious (H. Hartmann 1959; Brenner 1980). And even allowing that Freud never really abandoned his pseudophysiology or his attempts to develop explanations consistent with it, his formal definition clearly rules out Pribram's and Gill's opinion that neurophysiology lay behind psychology (Pribram and Gill 1976; Gill 1977). But it is equally obvious that some metapsychological explanations of psychological phenomena could be based on purely psychological forces. Thus, a dynamic description or explanation may use propositions about drives, ego-interests, and conflict, for example, "without recourse to an organic substrate" (Rapaport and Gill 1959).

Neither can metapsychology be restricted to the assumptions on which the metapsychological viewpoints depend, as in the widely accepted definition of Rapaport and Gill (1959). Assumptions obviously underpin each of the viewpoints, but are themselves of interest only to the extent that valid descriptions or explanations can be generated from them. Nor can metapsychology be broadly defined as psychoanalytic theory in general or, as Brenner does, as "psychoanalytic psychology as a whole" (Brenner 1980; Reppen 1982; cf. Holt, in Chattah 1983). A metapsychological explanation or description is a comprehensive statement from three different viewpoints, each of which is based on a set of slightly different assumptions. For psychoanalysis, there can no more be a single metapsychology than a single theoretical explanation or description. Consequently, whereas Gill is correct to describe the broad definitions as the least defensible, one must also reject narrower definitions, like his own, in which metapsychology is the theory that explains the clinical theory (Gill 1977), or as the theory that "explains psychology in another universe of meaning than that of a person's aims," that is, biologically, neurophysiologically, or in terms of forces (Reppen 1982).

Metapsychology and the Levels of a Theory

The most persistent and pernicious definition of metapsychology is that of Waelder, who placed it at the highest level of abstraction in an hierarchy of theoretical statements. Brenner noted that Waelder's placement implied metapsychological propositions were the most speculative, the least useful, and the most difficult to prove, if provable at all. He also pointed out that many of the criticisms of metapsychology made by Gill and Holzman were of the same kind (Brenner 1980; cf. Waelder 1962; Gill and Holzman 1976). All three of Freud's metapsychological viewpoints are sufficiently abstract and "high" level to require complex deductive structures to link them to observations. In this respect there is little difference among a psychological force, an ego, and a quota of psychic energy. However, because the assumptions underlying each of the metapsychological points of view are different, the adequacy and validity of each requires its own evaluation.

These differences do cause some difficulties that are not evaded by defining metapsychology functionally, that is, as what metapsychology does rather than what it is (Modell 1981). Three different viewpoints generate three different descriptions or explanations and necessarily require three different evaluations.

Levels and Singularity

The error that metapsychology is singular is sometimes confounded with the error that it is the highest level of abstraction. Meissner's (1981b) placement of metapsychology at the highest of his six levels of generalization and conceptualization illustrates this. Meissner's levels are as follows:

1. Empirical observation. The analyst is a participant observer who uses empathy.

2. Empirical generalization. Regularities in the behavior of the single patient are established.

3. Clinical interpretation. Motivated and meaningful connections are postulated to account for the empirical generalizations.

4. Clinical generalization. The motives of the single patient are extended to groups of patients or phenomena.

5. Clinical theorizing. Explanations of the regularities of behavior are made in terms of mechanisms and processes such as conflict, repression, and developmental vicissitudes.

6. Metapsychology or the theory of psychoanalysis. This level includes a method, attitudes (!), and a set of resources for specifying relevant data, for establishing generalizations, for providing means of testing, for explaining, understanding, and predicting, and for elaborating concepts.

These levels are unremarkable in that they or something like them can be distinguished in the psychological sciences generally. But it is misleading to characterize metapsychology by a level, as can be seen by considering his levels 2 to 4. Only if the generalizations made there are purely descriptive can metapsychology be avoided. To go beyond them involves metapsychology. Consider level 3, for example. How are motivated and meaningful connections to be established without drawing on concepts such as the force of a motive or on the psychological processes that make connections meaningful? And, how do "conflict" and "repression" at level 5 avoid being *dynamic* metapsychological concepts?

What makes a theory useful and dependable is not how abstract or concrete it is but how well it is supported by its data (Brenner 1980). Tests of some psychoanalytic propositions, such as those about behavioral regularity and generality located at Meissner's levels 1 to 4, for example, might not have to draw on metapsychology at all. In line with these fairly obvious points, my evaluation will not be restricted to theoretical statements at any one level or to any particular metapsychological perspective. Although my main criticism is of the economic and structural viewpoints, it also includes material relevant to levels 4 and 5.

Where Personality Starts

What is the point from which Freud postulated that personality began? Here we are faced with the concept of the stimulus barrier and with Freud's confusions over narcissism and autoerotism.

The Stimulus Barrier

For a number of self-evident reasons, we should not be too critical of Freud's picture of the primitive organism surrounded by lethal energies. That immunity, however, cannot be extended to the concept of the protective shield or stimulus barrier, which has, or is supposed to have, important practical consequences. The objections are conceptual and evidential as well as practical.

Esman (1983) refers to the confusion surrounding the concept, a characteristic he derives from Freud's merging of the mental and physical levels of discourse (cf. Peterfreund 1978). Furst notes that most psychoanalysts see the shield in psychological terms, as "a complex *ego* function" (Furst 1978. My emphasis, MBM). That formulation is not accepted by all (e.g., Peterfreund 1978), and is, in any case, certainly not how Freud envisaged it. Esman (1983) also thought it was "unclear" whether Freud thought the shield was active or passive. To make it active, it had to have its own source of energy, and Freud could not provide it other than through some libido sublimated very much later in the individual's development. Possibly it was this difficulty that led him to hold simultaneously passive and active conceptualizations.

A number of psychoanalysts also concluded that, even though the shield obviously partly derives from Freud's neurophysiological ideas, the properties of the shield are not compatible with current knowledge of the nervous system (Benjamin 1965; Tennes, Emde, Kisley, and Metcalf 1972; Esman 1983). Actually, the shield was never consistent with any real nervous system. Both the stimulus seeking of the neonate (Tennes et al. 1972; D. Stern 1977; Spielman 1986; Furst 1978) and spontaneous activity in the nervous system and its receptors (Benjamin 1965) are strong evidence against the tendency to quiescence encapsulated in the notion of the shield. Nor have longitudinal studies beginning at birth and conducted for the most part within a psychoanalytical framework provided any evidence for it (Benjamin 1965; Wolff 1966; Tennes et al. 1972; D. Stern 1977; Lichtenberg 1981).

Psychoanalytically oriented studies of the infant's postnatal development show it to be triphasic. First, an initial passive insensitivity results from lack of functional connections in the nervous system. In the second phase there is marked sensitivity consequent on a maturational spurt. In the third phase the infant is able to regulate stimulus input actively. Within this sequence, Freud's stimulus barrier can be saved only if it is thought of as part of the *mother's* protective behavior in the second or sensitive phase (Esman 1983). If this interpretation of the evidence is consistent with the concept of a stimulus barrier at all, it makes for a barrier very different from the one Freud envisaged (Wolff, in Schafer 1965). The direct studies have been no more successful in confirming the existence of a protective shield than were Greenacre's earlier psychoanalytic reconstructions of the experience of trauma in childhood (Greenacre 1941, 1945).

Finally, the practical value of the concept of a protective shield has been impugned directly (Greenacre 1967; Neubauer 1967; Krystal 1978) and indirectly in the many discussions of trauma in which, if the concept is mentioned at all, it is to provide a background rather than a basis for explanations (Greenacre 1941, 1945; Rangell 1967; Sandler 1967; Solnit and Kris 1967). The point holds even for those who place the concept more centrally (A. Freud 1967; Furst 1967, 1978; Waelder 1967a). Nor do any of the writers mentioned discuss the role of the anticathexis, despite its importance in the barrier-based theory of trauma. Where solutions are proposed, they are often peculiar. For example, Ikonen and Rechardt (1978) provide the shield with energy and anticathexis deriving from Thanatos. They also represent the excitation that floods in through the stimulus barrier during a traumatic situation as narcissistic libido detached from its object!

Peterfreund (1978) wondered "why the concept should be retained at all," and after showing it was inconsistent with developmental data, Esman (1983) concluded it was "no longer tenable." Where it is retained, it refers to simple individual differences in thresholds for tolerating stimulation and tension (e.g., A. Freud 1967), or used as a mere metaphor, a kind of experiential equivalent of "indifference and 'thick-skinnedness'" (Ikonen and Rechardt 1978). A far cry indeed from the grandiose evolutionary significance Freud gave it.

Narcissism

Etchegoyen (1985) stressed that the basis of much of the confusion about autoerotism and narcissism, considered in chapters 10 and 11, respectively, lies in the consistency with which Freud adhered to the idea that autoerotism was the first stage of development and primary narcissism the second, while simultaneously asserting that sexual impulses remained autoerotic when they were discharged through objects.

The term narcissism was introduced into psychoanalysis by Sadger (Nunberg and Federn 1962–1975, vol. 2, p. 312) and we know that Freud first used it publicly in the 1910 alterations and additions to the *Three Essays*. For both Freud and Sadger the word meant "love of self," and Freud used it technically to describe a homosexual identification, although even then he foreshadowed his theory of a narcissistic developmental stage located between autoerotism and object-love.

In chapter 11 I set out the inconsistencies in Freud's formulations and cited psychoanalytic evaluations that supported my own. D. L. Smith draws similar conclusions. He notes, for example, that Freud put forward "three distinct and mutually exclusive" models for the development from narcissism to object-love (D. L. Smith

1985; cf. Teicholz 1978). Just as I did, Smith describes the motive of the first as economic—anxiety caused by the buildup of internal tension—and makes four crucial points about the model. The most important is that narcissism was never properly integrated with the theses about the psychosexual stages of development. Smith also observes that Freud does not really succeed in explaining the transformation of narcissism into object-love, that *only* in the Schreber analysis did he posit homosexual object-choice as a stage between narcissism and heterosexual choice, and that he could not adopt Ferenczi's account of omnipotence without abandoning his own anal-fixation/regression explanation (D. L. Smith 1985).

Together with Freud's failure to relate narcissism adequately to aggression in his instinct theories, the fact that he never "explicitly repudiated" the internal tension explanation is responsible, Smith says, for almost all of the confusion about narcissism so many writers have observed in the psychoanalytic literature (D. L. Smith 1985; cf. Pulver 1970; B. E. Moore 1975; Teicholz 1978; Meissner 1981a). In my view it is precisely the limitations, confusions, and internal contradictions of Freud's theses about narcissism that are also responsible for the evident confusions in more recent psychoanalytic literature about psychosexual development and the formation of the ego-ideal and superego (Teicholz 1978; Tyson and Tyson 1984). What is especially notable about that literature is how many contributors treat the mutually exclusive notions as noncontradictory, or use only one of Freud's three approaches without realizing that none of them is internally consistent (e.g., B. E. Moore 1975; Rothstein 1979a).

From Autoerotism to Object-Love

The movement from autoerotism to object-love poses the second major problem for the development of personality. Analyses of the problem by Compton (1985b) and Erlich and Blatt (1985) confirm the conclusions I set out in chapter 10. Compton shows that Freud's "apparently straightforward" distinction between the autoerotic and object-directedness of drives "proved difficult" to apply to the component drives of sadomasochism, scopophilia, and exhibitionism. Erlich and Blatt (1985) endorsed Balint's account of the pitfalls of primary narcissism and of the apparent contradictions among it, primary object-love, and autoerotism before making the more general point that what is "left obscure ... is the nature of the process" by which libido in both anaclitic and narcissistic object choices is remodeled into object relations. Compton (1985b) puts it slightly differently: within the theory of object-directedness the confused status of the mother's breast persists.

Compton also says that the difference between object-love, which is sexual, and the loving-affectionate current, which is not, "points to a considerable gap" in the 1905 theory. Neither are the determinants of the affectionate current "much pursued," apart from Freud's indicating modeling, or a derivation from the suckling relation. In summary, Freud "contradicted himself" on whether infantile drives were auto-erotic or directed toward objects, made "incompatible statements about whether or not object-choice occurs before puberty," and, by restricting himself to drive con-structs, used object-choice and object-directedness with an incomplete set of explana-tory constructs (Compton 1985b).

In a further analysis, Compton confirms that two separate developmental sche-mata can be distinguished in Freud's work. One is of stages of libidinal organization (oral, anal, genital) and the other of stages of object-directedness (autoerotic, narcis-sistic, homosexual object-directed, heterosexual object-directed). He observes that Freud "never quite resolved his equivocation about whether there is object-choice in infancy," emphasizing that the apparently unequivocal references Freud did make to the mother's breast as object, mainly in discussing the Oedipal situation, involved "*a different hypothesis altogether*." Compton also makes an absolutely overwhelming case for Freud holding to an objectless beginning, even after he formulated his final anxiety theory.

Development in the Female

In chapters 10 and 13 I brought out some of the difficulties Freud's theory of psycho-sexual development had in explaining female object-choice and superego formation. Basic to the theory is the assumption that at the very beginning of the developmental process the sex of the female child is masculine. The girl's sexual attachment to her mother weakens because of the hostility she feels at being deprived of a penis. Penis envy then develops. The father is chosen as an object because the symbolic equivalence of baby = penis means that he can supply both to her. Having already been castrated, both her entry into the Oedipal situation and her exit from it are less complete than for the male. As a consequence, her superego is less well formed and weaker. Important psychological characteristics of women, including femininity itself, form as a consequence of the peculiarities of this process.

What light does research throw on these aspects of Freud's theory? First, the assumed male starting point requires that the developmental stages through which females were supposed to pass have to be secondary to that starting point. Conse-quently, for the most part, what literature there is revolves around characteristics that are developmentally secondary, and the tests themselves are not direct tests of Freud's basic assumption. Second, when the assumption of masculine sexuality is sometimes questioned, it is only by being mentioned in a derogatory way. For exam-ple, by merely referring to it as "sexual phallic monism," Chasseguet-Smirgel (1976) fails to come to grips directly with the basic issue, and D. Bernstein (1983) and Cereijido (1983) do not come any closer. Avoidance is also true of earlier authors such as Horney (1923/1924, 1926, 1928), who questioned Freud's assumption, as well as those like Ernest Jones (1927, 1933, 1935), who assumed that the sexuality was feminine. Third, the clinical observations of psychoanalysts other than Freud fall broadly into two groups: those that confirm what Freud said he had seen and those that do not. Men and women are found in both camps, so the division does not seem to be related to the sex of the analyst.

To judge from the summary reviews of Fliegel (1982) and Chehrazi (1986), many of the differences over the secondary features have been settled. Whereas some modern psychoanalysts adhere strictly to Freud's original descriptions of the developmental consequences (J. Mitchell 1974; Nagera 1975), sometimes with a greater tenacity than he did (Lacan 1966/1982), most do not now believe girls masturbate only by rubbing the clitoris (Barnett 1968; Kestenberg 1975; Kleeman 1977), or enter the Oedipal situation through the formation of a negative Oedipus complex centered on the mother (Edgcumbe, Lundberg, Markowitz, and Salo 1976; Parens, Pollock, Stern, and Kramer 1977). Where the term "penis envy" is still used, it is taken to mean something other than what Freud described (Chasseguet-Smirgel 1976; Galenson and Roiphe 1976; Roiphe and Galenson 1972, 1981). The components of the developmental sequence seem to be very different from those that followed from Freud's assumed starting point.

As the discussions of Fliegel and Lampl-de Groot illustrate, however, the nature and paucity of the data make it difficult to know if analysts can (or wish to) reach agreement about either the starting point or how the development occurs (cf. Fliegel 1973; Lampl-de Groot 1982). Some who do have data believe the developmental sequence and outcome to be significantly different from those described by Freud. For example, Melanie Klein (1928, 1932), describes a quite different process, with a superego *more rigid* than the male's as its outcome. Others, such as Lacan have placed Freud's developmental sequence "out of reach of the 'absurdities of empirical refutation'" by reasserting it in metaphorical terms and elevating it "to the status of axiomatic truth" (Fliegel 1982; cf. Lacan 1966/1982).

The psychological characteristics have also been questioned. Again, very few data are reported, even of a clinical psychoanalytic kind, and what can be gleaned from the literature of either camp is limited. Thus, although Lowery (1985) introduced her remarks about women's supposed lesser capacity for sublimation, which she accepted, with the acknowledgment that the topic had received "little consideration," she discussed the supposed inferiority without mentioning any observations at all. Nor did Schafer (1974) cite any data in reaching his conclusion that "Freud's estimates of women's morality are logically and empirically indefensible," and none of the analyses subsequent to his is empirically any stronger (e.g., D. Bernstein 1983). Schafer believed he saw the influence of Freud's "traditional patriarchal and evolutionary values" on his "flawed" ideas about the development and psychological characteristics of the female in

> questionable presuppositions, logical errors and inconsistencies, suspensions of intensive inquiry, underemphasis on certain developmental variables, and confusions between observations, definitions and value preferences.   (Schafer 1974)

My impression of the literature is that most of these criticisms would be accepted by contemporary psychoanalysts. If so, explanations of female development cannot be derived from Freud's psychosexual theory.

The *goal* of Freud's explanations provides, I believe, a more fundamental ground for rejecting his theses. It seems to me obvious that he was not describing his female patients so much as putting forward the stereotyped view of women typically held by men of his time and social outlook. The "facts" he wanted to explain were certainly not clinical facts and were hardly facts at all. The secondary developmental transformation has a similar status. Given a "masculine" starting point, the changes were more or less demanded by the end point, and failure to confirm them was almost inevitable. Freud's account of the psychosexual development of the female is not so much wrong as totally unnecessary.[1]

What Develops

The ego and superego are the central components of Freud's personality theory. Because of my detailed examination of these structures in chapter 13, Here I summarize the developmental aspects of those criticisms and add such psychoanalytic opinion and argument as seems relevant. Issues about the development of functions such as realistic secondary process thinking are mentioned briefly.

The Structures

We have seen that two of the main problems with the structural theory are that psychoanalysts are not at all certain what constitutes a psychological structure and what the particular structures of the theory are. At the purely descriptive level they are not clear about which functions belong to which structure. For example, they cannot list which processes are appropriate to the id, or decide whether the ego-ideal's "goodness" allows it to be part of the superego or not. Nor can they explain *how* a given structure exercises its functions. In other words, the characterizations of the structures are at least uncertain, and it may be that they are not characterized at all.

Some of these problems are very old, as evidenced by the difficulties psychoanalysts had when they made their first attempts to bring order to the structural concepts. In 1947 Glover implicitly disregarded the metapsychological aspects of the superego, saying that it was "from first to last a clinical concept" (Glover 1947). Ten years later, Rapaport concluded his unpublished 1957 listing of the many unsolved theoretical problems about the superego with an outline of what he meant by metapsychology and a frank acceptance of defeat:

Clearly, I am not in a position today to give a metapsychological analysis of the superego concept and of the psychoanalytic propositions pertaining to it.   (Rapaport 1967)

Three years later he was still unable to include more than the ego in his ambitious attempt to systematize psychoanalytic theory:

the structural treatment of the id and superego is still so inadequate that the lengthy discussion it would require is beyond the scope of this presentation.   (Rapaport 1960, p. 54, n. 14)

As Beres (1958) found, there was not even a conclusive list of superego functions. More recent discussions show how little progress has been made over the past forty years. Metapsychological descriptions of the superego are either considered "less-than-well systematized" and not in keeping with clinical understanding (Garza-Guerrero 1981a), or are not even alluded to (e.g., Arlow 1982; Brenner 1982).

What Rapaport said about the metapsychology of the id in the late 1950s was confirmed throughout the 1960s, in the 1963 panel discussion of the American Psychoanalytical Association (Marcovitz 1963) and the attempted clarifications by Schur (1966a) and Hayman (1969). It seemed impossible to decide whether the id had any structure, to arrive at any consensus of its functions, to be certain whether all of it was unconscious in the descriptive sense, or to know what the relation between id and *Ucs.* was (Marcovitz 1963; Hayman 1969). Since then no further attempt has been made to clarify the concept either by describing its functions more adequately or resolving the theoretical problems associated with it (Shulman 1987). Until the functions are clarified, the concept can make only a pseudocontribution to Freud's personality theory, and its metapsychological explanation will continue to elude psychoanalysts.

The situation of the ego is similar. One searches in vain through the numerous papers celebrating the fiftieth anniversary of the publication of *The Ego and the Id* for anything definite about its functions (e.g., Arlow 1975; Holt 1975b; Modell 1975). Recent dissatisfaction about the uncertain functions led to calls to replace ego with other concepts, for example, the self (Kohut 1971, 1977) or schema (Slap and Saykin

1983; Slap 1986), or to modify the ego so substantially that it is included in the concept of self (Meissner 1986), or the self or some major function is included within it (Kernberg 1982) such as "representational world" (Rothstein 1981). Many of the proposed alterations are "subtly or not so subtly antithetical to Freudian psychoanalysis" (Spruiell 1981), a point also brought out by Patton and Sullivan (1980). All are based on the assumption that Freud's original definition of the ego had a reasonable basis in observation. Some time ago, however, Holt (1975b) concluded that neither the ego nor the id had ever fit the data of observation "in any usable way."

The Processes

I considered fairly fully in chapter 13 the generally unsatisfactory nature of Freud's account of how the main structures of the personality develop. One issue not raised there was how the ego developed its realistic, secondary process mode of thinking. In chapter 9 I did characterize what Freud said in *The Interpretation of Dreams* as a description (and an inadequate one) rather than an explanation. Nothing in the subsequent psychoanalytic literature attempts to transform the description into an explanation. Gill (1967) tried to avoid the problem altogether. After calling the primary process "an ingrained shibboleth of psychoanalytic thinking" he gave it secondary process characteristics from the beginning.

Deficiencies in Freud's theory of the development of the secondary process are very occasionally commented on in the psychoanalytic literature. In 1969 Noy had observed that Freud never really explored the theory of the primary process after he initially described it at the turn of the century, and that it had "remained frozen" in its original economic formulation. Nor did Freud revised the concept "to adjust it" to the new concepts of the structural theory, especially to the ego (Noy 1969). Noy commented that by 1956 two distinct arguments were being made about the primary process. One was that it should be restricted to the economic view and the other that it be widened to include the various chaotic processes Freud said he found in dream work. The opposition is a rather odd one. Chaos was inferred from the economic perspective, and it was supposed to be explained by the ways psychic energy was distributed.

Nevertheless, by gradually attributing more and more secondary process characteristics to the primary, the wideners pushed the two formulations even farther apart. For example, Holt (1967) argued that an economically defined primary process had to have a structural basis. It required structures within which to work and had to have them in the form of ideas on which to perform that work. Consequently, the primary process could not be a fixed, unchanging given but had to have a developmental history. Holt said thinking that had autistic, magical, and wishful properties was primary process thought and attempted to outline how it developed. On my reading of him, Holt seems to have thought of the history of the primary process as being part of what Freud probably would have described as the history of the secondary process.

Without referring to Holt, Steele and Jacobsen (1977) took a similar line; that is, the assumption of primary process functioning made it difficult to see how a hallucinated object could be formed during primary narcissism because "the perception of an actual object is an essential prerequisite for any subsequent hallucinating." They also showed it was precisely this prerequisite that forced Freud into the otherwise peculiar postulation of an "original reality-ego" that had to give way to a "pleasure-ego."

So fundamental are such differences that it is hard to accept the arguments of Gill (1967) that some degree of continuity exists between primary and secondary processes. The attempt by Zern (1968) to represent Freud's view of the mental processes as "an integrated and coherent whole" is based on a similar overlooking of the distinction between the imperative primary process and a delaying secondary. There is, of course, a relation between the polarities described by Freud (secondary-primary, conscious-unconscious, reality-pleasure, etc.) in that one member of the pair always derives from the other. But Zern turns those relations into similarities and bases an argument for integration on them. He simply leaves out the very differences that were postulated initially.

Steele and Jacobsen concluded that because of the contradiction that Freud created in having the secondary process function of binding located *prior* to the primary process one of discharge, and because of the "elegant, though implausible idea" of the presence of a pleasure-ego and a primary process at the beginning of life:

The problem of Freud's developmental explanation of mental functioning is not in *how* the primary process changes into the secondary process but in how *anything at all* emerges after the infantile primary process. (Steele and Jacobsen 1977. My emphasis)

They regard Freud as having treated "fact as fiction" and, like Holt, believe that secondary process thought must exist at the beginning of life. Perhaps it is the damaging nature of comments like these, brief as they are, that makes comprehensive discussion of the transformation of primary into secondary process unnecessary.

How Development Is Powered

The development of personality is powered by psychic energy provided from the instinctual drives. Several critical comments were made in chapters 11 and 12 about both concepts. The most important are that the sources of neither the ego nor the death drive can be specified, that an aggressive drive, however thought of, has no source or aim, that psychic energy is never consistently derived from an instinctual source, that psychic energy can not provide energy for the mental structures through sublimation, and that it can not exist in different forms, or if it can, those forms could not mix with or separate from one another.

So powerful are these criticisms of libido and the drives that Werman almost casually grants that

Contemporary psychoanalytic views of the instinctual drives ... are markedly heterogeneous. In regard to libido ... the opinions include considering libido as a purely neurophysiological phenomenon; accepting the drive but rejecting its energic qualities; conceptualizing libido as a wish, with or without a physical substrate; and rejecting libido, psychic energy, and all other related concepts as irrelevant, unverifiable, and of no explanatory value.   (Werman 1985)

Having acknowledged "more agreement" about libido than about aggression, he added there were "few ardent advocates of psychic economics today." I will neverthe-less take up some of the more basic features of these concepts.

The Limitations of an Excitatory Energy

We said in chapter 7 that Freud's conception of nervous system function lacks a genuine inhibitory component and is predominately excitatory (Mancia 1983). MacCarley and Hobson (1977) contrasted this aspect of the theory of the *Project* unfavorably with the theory proposed at about the same time by Exner, one of his colleagues. Weiner (1979) subsequently included in this unfavorable contrast Sher-rington's theory, which also incorporated an active inhibitory process. Instead of relying on the facts of the inhibition of neural function that were known at the time, Freud used an entirely speculative "lateral cathexis" to explain repression and, as Weiner (1979) also observes, the development of the secondary process.

Why did Freud not allow for an inhibitory process? Weiner (1979) writes as if Freud's concepts about neurons and connectivity "came from nowhere." However, at the time Freud began the *Project*, a good deal was known about both but, as I pointed out in chapter 7, Freud disregarded that knowledge. It is well known, as Kanzer (1973, 1981) confirms, that the neurological systems Freud invoked in the *Project* were drawn from clinical observation. Clinical observation required active *excitatory* processes to be repressed into the unconscious and maintained there by an equally active conscious *excitatory* process. An *inhibitory* repressive process would have involved a considerable self-contradiction. Attributing the limited usefulness of the theory in the *Project* to the neurophysiology of the day not being advanced enough, and describing it, as Applegarth (1971) does, as "too far removed from clinical material, too abstract to be useful" is only part of the explanation. The fact is, the conceptual nervous system Freud settled on was too simple to do the job (Solms and Saling 1986). The lack of a genuine inhibitory mechanism was part of that simplicity.

We might note in passing that Freud seems to have had a real ability for adopting out-dated conceptualizations of nervous system functioning. In addition, within about ten years of his first drafts of the *Project* and at about the same time as he was formulating his concept of instinctual drive, Sherrington saw that it was but a partial truth to group "all motor reflexes ... into those that tend to prolong the stimulus and those that tend to cut it short" (Sherrington 1906, p. 329). Consequently, even Freud's simple reality-testing function could not have the reflex basis he proposed.

There are some differences between the theory of the mental apparatus in chapter 7 of *The Interpretation of Dreams* and that of the *Project* (Bush 1978), but their basic properties are almost identical. MacCarley and Hobson (1977) and Weiner (1979) propose that the similarity derives from Freud's basing both on the same simple reflex model of tension reduction and using the same pseudophysiological constructs in both (cf. Swanson 1977). I would add that the resemblance each has to the structural theory has the same basis. Kanzer (1981) also observes that Freud's propositions about consciousness in his posthumously published "An Outline of Psycho-Analysis" (Freud 1940a) are "reminiscent of an updated *Project*."

The Concept of Psychic Energy

Commenting to psychologists in 1923 on mental energy, Adrian rightly concluded that it was an "impossible" concept. The facts of neural transmission made the notion of a nervous energy "unnecessary," and the less said about it and a mental energy "the better." He illustrated his point with a remark about "neurin," a hypothetical nervous "fluid" that McDougall proposed. He thought neurin was "more welcome" to psychologists than to physiologists for explaining phenomena such as fatigue, inhibition, and hypnosis (Adrian 1923). Just over twenty years later, in a paper delivered to psychoanalysts, Adrian stated that his early criticism of Freud's psychic energy concept had been based on the vagueness of its analogy with physical energy, and referred, rather prematurely, to those criticisms as "ancient history" (Adrian 1946).

There can, of course, be only limited objection to the concept of psychic energy on the grounds that no physical evidence can be found for it. Mental concepts lack extension, and the reality of psychic energy cannot be established in the same way as physical energy (Swanson 1976, 1977). But if psychic energy is considered as a neurophysiological concept, one that derives from neurophysiology, or a neurophysiological concept in disguise (Holt 1967/1968; Pribram 1962, 1965; Applegarth 1971, 1977a), the evidence is against it having the external source Freud and his predecessors seem to have supposed (Amacher 1965). Nor can a neurophysiological type of energy be limited in amount (Sherrington 1906, p. 325), function within a closed system (Pumpian-Mindlin 1958–1959; Rosenblatt and Thickstun 1977), or derive from an instinctual drive (Lashley and Colby 1957, cited in Holt 1968). And, of course, it can never exist in different forms such as sexual, aggressive, and neutral (R. W. White 1963), or vary quantitatively in ways consistent with the systems it energizes (McCulloch, cited in Kubie 1953; Holt 1967/1968).

The major conceptual problems with truly mentalistic concept of psychic energy proper are independent of its real existence. They include failure to find a measure of it independent of the phenomena it is meant to explain (Holt 1967/1968), the proposition that different amounts of it can be added or subtracted (Rosenblatt and Thickstun 1977), the indefiniteness of its relation to the instinctual drives and the obscurity of its relation to structures (Applegarth 1971), the inconsistent and largely descriptive characterization of its capacity for neutralization and binding (Holt 1962; Applegarth 1971), the contradiction of it being directionless but having aims (Apfelbaum 1965; Rosenblatt and Thickstun 1970, 1977), and the proposal that it exists in different forms (W. C. Lewis 1965), especially as the only change in it can be in its pathways (Sandler and Joffe 1966; Applegarth 1971). This postulate of a changing energy, so critical to so many psychoanalytic processes and explanations is, as W. C. Lewis (1965) noted, "something of a theoretical nightmare."

None of these conceptual problems is overcome in any alternative formulations, including those of the ego-psychologists (Apfelbaum 1965). Thus, although V. H. Rosen (1965) agrees that R. W. White's concept of a neutral and independent ego energy offers some theoretical advantages, there were no unambiguous criteria for its identification. Rosen also believes, with good reason, that those interested in retaining some concept of energy have not come to grips with the fact that the identification of different types of energy requires a social value judgment of their alleged aims, a problem logically identical to one I found earlier with sublimation.

Psychic Energy as a Metaphor   Adrian's reference to neurin highlights the metaphorical way in which the concept of psychic energy is so often used. As a metaphor it stands primarily for the subjective sense of effort or energy that mental work seems to entail, and in this respect it has the same origin as its physical counterpart (S. W. Jackson 1967, 1970; Kubie 1975). However, no concept of psychological energy has so far been realized through the experimental investigations and mathematical transformations that resulted in our modern conceptions of physical work and energy. Nor could it ever be; its reality is different (Shope 1971).

Rosenblatt and Thickstun (1970) observed that many psychoanalysts nevertheless seem happy to use the concept to translate subjective experience directly into what they feel are more meaningful terms, and in so doing to give it a physical "reality." Thus Shevrin (in Chattah 1983) described a patient whose experience of her own actions and thoughts in energic terms seemed to involve a real expenditure of energy. Shevrin also defined psychological work as the exercise of motive force over time, and explicitly equated it with the physical definition of work as energy expended over distance. The "physicalist" definitions of psychic energy given by Rapaport and Gill (1959) and Loewenstein (in Calder 1970) anticipated Shevrin almost exactly and illustrate how entrenched the habit of subjective translation is.

The applications made by psychoanalysts today are also similar to Freud's and, despite Adrian's optimism, metaphorical redescriptions posing as explanations are still invoked for fatigue-inhibition types of phenomena. For example, Lustman (1957) translated alterations in the neonate's responsiveness into changes in the distribution of energy between different processes, and a 1969 panel discussion revealed a similar abundance of metaphorical redescriptions (Calder 1970). Psychic energy was used to "explain" conflict (Treurniet), repression (Wexler), megalomania (Wexler, Garma), dreams and hallucinations (Garma), actual and/or traumatic neuroses (de M'Uzan, Mitscherlich-Nielsen), childhood autism (Greenson), momentary changes in a patient's state of consciousness (Rubinfine), the recovery of a patient who used his own psychological forces during analysis (Shor), and the neurotic absorption of a child in its own problems, as well as transference, free association, trauma, and displacement (Lustman). And although Schur warned the panel of the dangers of using economic explanations exclusively, his own list of candidates was as large as that of the rest of the panel put together (Calder 1970). Starke (1973, p. 39) subsequently extended its scope even farther, defending its usefulness "in elucidating the mental processes conditioned by the instincts."

The scope of these "explanations" illustrates what Nagel concluded nearly forty years ago:

in Freudian theory metaphors are employed without even half-way definite rules for expanding them ... in consequence ... metaphors such as "energy" or "level of excitation" have no specific content and can be filled in to suit one's fancy.   (Nagel 1959, p. 41)

A good illustration of Nagel's point is provided by Rapaport's two quite different explications of Freud's term binding. In 1951 he equated the binding of psychic energy with neutralization, but later, with the formation of structure (cited in Holt 1962; Applegarth 1971).

Almost all of the translations are also open to the more general objection made by Warme (1981) to metapsychological explanations in general: the movement from clinical data to inferred metapsychological process and to the use of clinical data to confirm the metapsychological process is circular.

Alternatives to Psychic Energy   Many psychoanalysts tacitly accept Nagel's criticism and are not enthusiastic about metaphorical energic explanations. Nor are they much keener about real energy. Over thirty years ago Apfelbaum (1965) commented, "it is mainly on the clinical level that the deficiencies of the quantitative approach are most serious." This was at about the time Holt (1967/1968) changed his view and began to wonder if the concept of psychic energy had been clinically more misleading than helpful. The convergence of opinion is of interest because Holt, unlike Apfelbaum, was then prepared to grant the potential usefulness of some as yet unknown but measurable kind of energy. The doubt they expressed was an influential one. Applegarth (1971) had concluded that it was a useful concept but wondered if it generated good explanations. Later she shifted her position: it was not whether it was useful but whether it was "indispensable" (Applegarth 1977a), a view with which Ellman and Moskowitz (1980) appear to agree.

During his attempt to justify a concept of psychic energy having neither physical nor metaphorical reference, Brenner (1980) pinpointed the explanatory problem. He contended that the effects of wishes led Freud to characterize an instinctual drive as something that drove or impelled the mind into action. That quality led in turn to the concept of psychic energy as the capacity of a drive to impel, a concept that contained "the idea that some wishes . . . are stronger than others." Hence:

Unless one is ready to assume that the drives never fluctuate in intensity, one must attribute a dimension of magnitude to psychic energy; there must be some quantitative or economic aspect.

Brenner made his plea for a concept of psychic energy because he believed it to be "a valid and useful generalization" about the variable capacity with which the mind is brought into activity.

Wallerstein (1977) asserted that, for Freud, as for most psychoanalysts, psychic energy had always been "a mental construct used metaphorically." It is true that it can be so interpreted. Years after Adrian's first critique, Apfelbaum (1965) proposed that, in addition to Freud's concept matching the common understanding of fatigue, exhaustion, and the running down of an energy store, it matched the common pseudoenergy view of relief from tension being obtained by working off tension by "direct energy expenditure." After remarking that "as commonsense notions often do, these metaphors mirror conscious experience," Apfelbaum also stressed how well "abreactive expression lends itself to physical explanations." As we saw in chapter 7, it was similar ordinary experiences from which Freud and Breuer drew their theoretical notions. And, we know Hughlings Jackson's quoting the common view may have contributed to Freud's energic concept of catharsis.

However, I would dispute that Freud's original concept of psychic energy was mental and its use metaphorical. In *Studies on Hysteria* he initiated the psychoanalytic tradition of directly translating subjective impressions and clinical phenomena into economic terms by translating his subjective response to resistance into an ego force. The opening sentences of the *Project* tell us that condensation, displacement, substitution, and stimulus "directly suggested the conception of neuronal excitation as quantity in a state of flow" and, consequently, that at that time Freud's fundamental economic propositions referred to a physical process (Freud 1950/1954, *Project*, part I). Stripped of their pseudophysiological referents they can equally well refer to psychical processes. Gill is absolutely correct that there is "no evidence" Freud intended psychic energy to be a mere metaphor or that he used it that way (Gill 1977).

One of the few things that is agreed among psychoanalytic theorists is that psychic energy readily allows for the explanation of the psychological processes of displacement and condensation. However, since it was from those very phenomena that the concept was inferred, any faith that contemporary psychoanalysts might have that the phenomena confirm the reality of the concept is only touching. The relation is, as Applegarth (1971) says, "not surprising." But Gill makes an even more fundamental objection: energy is not necessary to explain condensation and displacement (Gill 1977). What is left of Freud's concept if stripped of its conceptual usefulness and its evidentiary base?

Personality and Psychosexual Development

Because I have not previously discussed the means by which personality is formed, I now outline briefly Freud's theory of psychosexual development, and consider the mechanisms by which he thought personality characteristics were formed.

Stages of Psychosexual Development

We saw in chapter 10 that Freud believed infantile sexual behaviors were polymorphously perverse. Originally he referred to the oral, anal, and phallic (then called genital) *modes* of satisfaction of the sexual impulse, describing each as autoerotic. By this he meant that the object of the impulse was the subject's own body and that its aim was the stimulation of a given erotogenic zone (Freud 1905b, pp. 182–183).

These autoerotic modes of satisfaction originally were not considered to be sequentially related. Freud first thought of them as equally important in producing pleasure and in contributing to an overall autoerotic stage that preceded the stage of object-love (p. 207). Some time later he proposed narcissism as a developmental stage separating autoerotism and object-love. Autoerotic manifestations then underwent a metamorphosis, after which none were regarded as autoerotic.

Freud eventually termed the whole set of distinct patterns of infantile sexual behavior the *pregenital stages of libidinal organization*. They were the autoerotic, first described in the *Three Essays* (Freud 1905b), the narcissistic (Freud 1911a), the anal-sadistic (Freud 1913d), the oral (Freud 1915a), and the phallic (Freud 1923e). Each stage was one of a predominant mode of libidinal satisfaction and each necessarily involved the predominance of a particular relation of libido to objects.[2]

The Oral Stages

Two substages of the oral stage were eventually distinguished: oral-sucking and oral-sadistic (or oral-biting). In both, the object was the mother's breast, but in the first the aim was to suck at it and in the second it was to devour it. The second stage was referred to variously as oral-sadistic or oral-cannabalistic. Freud thought the destruction of the object derived from a fusion of sexual and destructive impulses; he therefore described the attitude toward the object as *ambivalent*.[3]

His original description of the oral mode of satisfaction drew heavily on the work of Lindner, of course (Freud 1905b, pp. 179–181), but it was Karl Abraham's clinical observations that provided the basis for differentiating the two substages. Abraham had described an adult schizophrenic patient who drank milk heated to body temperature with a pronounced sucking action and who tended to wake with strong sexual desires that were satisfied by drinking milk (K. Abraham 1916/1927b). However, if the patient was unable to find milk he would masturbate. He also had a number of fantasies with markedly cannibalistic themes. To Abraham, these and similar behaviors in other patients confirmed Freud's proposal of an infantile stage in which oral-sexual and aggressive impulses were fused. K. Abraham (1924/1927d) later stressed how ambivalent these behaviors and fantasies were, especially in depressed patients.

Abraham's evidence for the infantile oral-sadistic substage was not based on direct observation. Indeed, he disavowed the possibility that direct observations could supply evidence about it: "we are concerned with developmental processes which are hardly accessible to direct observation" (K. Abraham 1916/1927b). His evidence was a reconstruction of an infantile past based on a complex interpretation of disordered adult behavior. For the oral-sucking stage, the role of observation seemed more direct. Freud's picture of sucking as sexual did not include an aggressive tendency. Consequently, although Abraham's reconstruction only implied an initial nonambivalent stage, that implication was consistent with Freud's interpretation of Lindner's observations that early sucking gave unalloyed sexual pleasure.

The Anal Stages

Freud inferred the existence of anal erotism as a mode of libidinal satisfaction from the sexual pleasure in defecating he supposed children to experience (Freud 1905b, pp. 185–186). Eight years later he described a distinct stage with two discernible but not completely separate forms: a passive anal-erotism and an active anal-sadism, the latter being activated by the "instinct of mastery" (Freud 1913d).

Freud described no direct observations to support the existence of either form but, like Abraham, he offered a complex reconstruction based on the interpretation of a single patient. A woman developed an obsessional neurosis with a

compulsion for scrupulous washing and cleanliness and extremely energetic protective measures against severe injuries which she thought other people had reason to fear from her— that is to say, reaction-formations against her own *anal-erotic* and *sadistic* impulses. (Freud 1913d, p. 320)

The onset of the disorder was preceded her husband losing his potency. Freud linked that to the "well-known fact" that the character of women was often peculiarly altered after such a loss of sexual function:

They become quarrelsome, vexatious, and over-bearing, petty and stingy; that is to say, they exhibit typically sadistic and anal-erotic traits which they did not possess earlier, during their period of womanliness.... We can see this alteration of character corresponds to a regression of sexual life to the pregenital sadistic and anal-erotic stage. (pp. 323–324)

Freud's interpretation of these behaviors as reaction formations was a reconstruction that drew explicitly on the concept of regression. In the case of the sadistic component he assumed it was activated by an unspecified instinct for mastery.

K. Abraham (1924/1927d) differentiated two substages of the anal stage through some rather curious reasoning. He first proposed that the *similar* symptoms of melancholia and obsessional neuroses meant that both were based on a *similar* regression to an anal-sadistic stage (as it was then called). But, because the symptoms were *different*, the stage had to consist of different components. He then posited the existence of two different anal pleasures, fecal retention and fecal expulsion, as well as two different sadistic tendencies, control of the object and destruction of it. Then, drawing on parallels in speech, folklore, and mythology, as well as on symptom interpretation, he linked the two impulses together: anal expulsion and sadistic destruction marked the first anal substage, and anal retention and sadistic control the second. Once again, most of his evidence for these substages were reconstructions based on complex interpretations of symptoms rather than on direct observation.

The Phallic Stage

Genital erotism in children was described by Freud in the original edition of the *Three Essays* (Freud 1905b, pp. 187–189). That both boys and girls obtained pleasure from manipulating their sexual organs was directly observable and became the primary fact from which the stage was inferred. Differences between child and adult attitudes toward the organs led Freud later to rename the stage as phallic, a definition that reflected the childish belief that both sexes possessed a phallus and that it had primacy (Freud 1923e, p. 142).

His evidence that both boys and girls believed they had a penis appears to be based substantially on the beliefs of Little Hans. Certainly the phrases with which he described the belief have a striking correspondence with his account of that case.

Narcissism

Although the term narcissism was used by Freud in a 1910 footnote added to the *Three Essays*, at best, it only implied that a stage of sexual development was being referred to (Freud 1905b, p. 144, n. 1). Narcissism was proposed as a pregenital development stage as part of Freud's later endeavor to explain Schreber's delusionary psychosis (Freud 1911a, p. 72). The meaning of megalomania and delusions of persecutions were clarified by assuming that Schreber's own ego became grossly overvalued when it was chosen as the object of his own sexual instinctual drive. In the general context of Freud's thinking about regression, this required that the ego had had such a role previously. Again, the narcissistic stage was a reconstruction based on the interpretation of adult behavior, rather than on direct observation.

The Formation of Personality Characteristics

The three mechanisms by which Freud believed personality traits formed are prolongation or continuation, sublimation, and reaction formation.

The Mechanisms of Trait Formation

Freud recognized that there could be *prolongations* or *continuations* of component instinctual drives well before either of those words was used. In the *Three Essays* he remarked that if the erotogenic significance of the mouth persisted, these same children when they are grown up will become epicures, in kissing, will be inclined to perverse kissing, or, if males will have a powerful motive for drinking and smoking.   (Freud 1905b, p. 182)

Although he did not then mention any other prolongations, the essence of the process is clear. A prolongation or continuation carries over into adult life a largely unchanged version of an infantile mode of component drive satisfaction.

Freud first used the word *sublimation* to refer to a redirection of a component sexual instinctual drive. Thus, visual sexual curiosity

seeks to complete the sexual object by revealing its hidden parts. It can, however, be diverted ("sublimated") in the direction of art, if its interest can be shifted away from the genitals on to the shape of the body as a whole.   (p. 156)

He (1908b, p. 171) later made it explicit that the redirection was to a new aim and proposed a more formal definition. The sexual impulse

places extraordinarily large amounts of force at the disposal of civilized activity, and it does this in virtue of its especially marked characteristic of being able to displace its aim without materially diminishing in intensity. This capacity to exchange its originally sexual aim for another one, which is no longer sexual but which is psychically related to the first aim, is called the capacity for *sublimation*.   (Freud 1908c, p. 187)

The new activity was no longer sexual but the drive itself was unchanged.

His earliest uses of the term *reaction-formation* tend to confuse it with sublimation. However, reaction formation involves the replacement of the impulse itself by its opposite. Thus, in speaking of obsessional patients, Freud said that during the repression of the component

a special *conscientiousness* is created which is directed against the instinct's aims; but this psychical reaction-formation feels insecure and constantly threatened by the instinct which is lurking in the unconscious.   (Freud 1907b, p. 124)

Although the aim of a reaction-formation was the opposite of the original impulse, he also noted that the original component impulse could be satisfied. For example, cleaning and washing the anus satisfied the impulse without the satisfaction being conscious (Freud 1908b, p. 172).

In 1908 Freud also made an explicit but slightly ambiguous reference to feelings of shame, disgust and morality as "reaction formations, or counter-forces," an ambiguity he disposed of later by describing them explicitly as reaction-formations (Freud 1908b, p. 171, 1925a, p. 37; cf. 1913f, pp. 298–299). In none of these works did he propose a basis for identifying reaction-formations, nor did he explain how they were created.

The Traits by Stage

I now describe the typical personality characteristics Freud associated with each of the stages of libidinal development, emphasizing those considered responsible for the formation of character traits.

The Oral Stage Prolongation, sublimation, and reaction-formation produce similar results in both substages of the oral stage. The prolongations include eating, drinking, smoking, and oral sexuality. Sublimations from this stage take either socially acceptable forms of oral indulgence, such as food or wine tasting, or nonnutritive oral activities such as wind instrument playing, even including some without specific oral content, such as debating or public speaking. The reaction-formations include fads over foods and drink as well as, for example, concern with oral hygiene.

Important psychological characteristics supposedly deriving from the oral-sucking stage are passivity and dependence. The ambivalence and narcissism that develop in the oral-sadistic stage are sources of other important characteristics. Throughout this stage, the ego develops, and with it the reality principle commences. The beginnings of the superego are seen in the pre-Oedipal choice of the mother as sexual object by children of both sexes.

The Anal Stage The prolongations, sublimations, and reaction formations are again similar in both substages of the anal stage. Prolongations include all those behaviors related to the eliminative function, such as concerns with bowel regularity and constipation, and the actual attainment of pleasure through defecation or retention. All the graphic arts (painting, sculpture, photography), hobbies of collecting things (e.g., stamps, coins), and money making and its disbursement are seen as sublimations arising from the anal stage. Reaction-formations include a classic triad of cleanliness, orderliness, and parsimony and the traits related to them.

Emotional ambivalence becomes stronger, partly because aggression can now be expressed in a second way, and partly because of a growing awareness of the father as a possible rival for maternal affection. This latter factor is also responsible for the further development of the foundations of the superego.

The Phallic Stage Prolongations here include nonsocial and narcissistic forms of sexual behavior such as masturbating and petting. Sublimation gives rise to nongenital but erotic artistic endeavors: pornography, love poetry, themes of sacred love, and so on. Reaction-formations are directed against the obvious expression of sexuality and include excessive modesty and shame, and concern over standards of sexual behavior.

Castration anxiety, which begins developing in the latter part of the second anal stage, leads to the boy beginning to repress the Oedipus complex. The acceptance of castration causes the girl to choose the father as object. With these choices, the reality principle finally dominates the pleasure principle—the formation of the superego is completed for the boy, but for the girl a long period of renunciation of phallic sexuality commences.

Later Developments   After the repression of the phallic stage, Freud believed that a latency period sets in during which the expression of sexual impulses diminishes. Various character traits are strengthened, and the mechanism of sublimation becomes of particular importance for the development of social feelings. Puberty marks the onset of the genital stage with, at first, a revival of homosexual object-choices. These are brought about by the boy's identification with the father and the girl's with the mother, both identifications being determined by the castration complex. Adult normal heterosexuality develops gradually until, by the late teens, the personality with its structures, object choices, and characteristic modes of behavior is said to be complete.

Pathological Outcomes   Even though I am not primarily concerned with "abnormality," the three deviant behavioral outcomes that Freud linked to his theory of personality should be mentioned: psychoses and neuroses, sexual deviancies (perversions), and character defects. The psychoses and neuroses involve a libidinal and/or structural regression to an earlier, fixated stage. Fixation at and regression to the oral stage produce the schizophrenias as well as the manic and the depressive psychoses. At the anal stage the psychosis is paranoia, and the neuroses are the obsessive-compulsive disorders. Various forms of hysteria evolve from regression to the phallic stage.

Deviant sexual behavior results from particularly strong fixations at the various pregenital stages. Deviant oral and anal practices are fixations at their respective stages. Fixation at the phallic stage is substantially responsible for exhibitionism and voyeurism as well as for some disorders of sexual function (nymphomania, satyrisis, impotence, some types of frigidity). Other disorders, especially so-called character disorders, are related to the stages of psychosexual development but in a more complex way.

Freud hoped to associate particular disorders with particular modes of defense, for example, hysteria with repression and obsessions with reaction-formations. From this it might seem that certain types of defenses should be associated with certain developmental stages; repression with the phallic stage, for example. Whereas he did recognize some connections of this kind, the matter was much more complicated. However, he did think the modes of defense used by the individual were characteristic. Typical modes of defense, personality characteristics, and characteristics of the mental structures, especially the balance among them, constitute the main aspects of personality covered by Freud's theory.

The Bases of the Mechanisms

As to the determinants of the mechanisms, Freud left no room for doubt: they were constitutional. Thus, for prolongation, it was a "constitutional intensification" of the significance of a given erotogenic zone (Freud 1905b, p. 182) and it was "the innate constitution of each individual which decides in the first instance how large a part his sexual instinct it will be possible to sublimate" (Freud 1908c, p. 188). Although he did not say so explicitly, he certainly thought of the energy used by the reaction formation as desexualized libido. The neutral energy stored in the ego was appropriated by the trend to be reinforced and added to its own. Consequently, reaction-formation also had a constitutionally determined basis. Freud wrote as if development was determined jointly by these constitutional bases and environmental experiences, but he gave no guidelines for identifying the innate factors. His discussion of the interplay of accidental and constitutional factors is therefore almost totally devoid of meaning (Freud 1905b, pp. 239–240).

If we sense some vagueness in Freud's definition of sublimation, and if he only hints at the conditions under which it takes place, it is because of his belief that the capacity for sublimation was innately determined. He also granted that some direct sexual satisfaction of a sublimated impulse might be required (pp. 239–240), a qualification that raised the question of the nature of the change in the impulse. To account for apparent transformations of sexual impulses into aggressive ones and vice versa, Freud postulated the existence of a desexualized or sexually neutral psychic energy that could combine with either the sexual or aggressive impulses (Freud 1923b, p. 44). He extended this concept of desexualization by linking it with sublimation; adding desexualized energy changed not only the aim of the sexual impulse but its content. The intensity of the sublimated impulse was thus the intensity of a desexualized one.

As we saw in chapter 13, another of the major problems with sublimation was that Freud was unable to explain how the sexual impulse was emasculated and how its desexualized energy was supplied to the ego. Because the superego draws on the energy of the death instinct liberated at the same time as the libido is desexualized, the main structures of the personality have no fuel to drive them. Anxiety cannot be experienced and repression cannot take place. So great are the difficulties of the concept of a desexualized libido that a substantial body of psychoanalytic opinion favors abandoning it. There is a further and equally fatal difficulty in using sublimation to explain the formation of personality traits. Unless the content of the impulse changes, sexual satisfaction must result from the new activity, a consequence not at all what Freud wanted.

Apart from the theoretical difficulties the empirical problem is how sublimated behavior is to be identified. As discussed in chapter 13, its defining characteristics have never been described. If sublimated behavior cannot be identified, the conditions under which it occurs will be difficult to describe and a mechanism virtually impossible to formulate.

Freud attempted to clarify some aspects of reaction-formation when he formulated his last hypothesis of the relation between repression and anxiety. Reaction-formations arose out of situations of ambivalence, that is, when the individual had both positive and negative feelings toward an object. One trend, usually the affectionate one, would become intensified and repress the other. The one that remained was the reaction-formation. Although it was a permanent alteration in the ego and required a permanent expenditure of energy, it did avoid the need for the repression to be repeated (Freud 1926a, p. 102). Freud was able to characterize behavior motivated by reaction-formation by its exaggerated and compulsive quality.

Practical difficulties are present here, but the real difficulties are theoretical. Reaction-formation draws on desexualized or neutral energy in the ego and therefore rests on sublimation, instinctual defusion, and Oedipal identification. Further, if neutral energy creates new impulses in the ego directed against the original sexual impulse, how are sexual needs also satisfied through its discharge?

Evidence about the Characteristics

Evidence about the traits postulated by psychoanalytic personality theory comes from behavioral rather than clinical observations. The question is whether distinguishable constellations of adult personality traits are regularly associated with particular types of behavior at the different stages of psychosexual development. Do the traits cluster together, and are they related to the original dispositions, as postulated by the theory? For example, is there a constellation of traits defining the oral character, and is it associated with behavioral signs of fixation at the oral stage?

The procedure for answering these questions is essentially the one relied on originally by Freud (1908b) and by E. Jones (1918) and K. Abraham (1921/1927c) when they expanded Freud's initial formulations on the anal mode of satisfaction into the anal character. Although their observations were made during treatment, and the childhood behaviors they referred to were most frequently reconstructions based on patients' recollections, there is no reason to suppose that nonclinical methods of enquiry should not confirm their inferences. Factor and cluster analyses of data on traits collected by questionnaire and other methods ought to reveal the groupings of traits postulated by psychoanalysts, and direct inquiry ought to produce material on childhood fixations.

Much psychological energy has been expended in investigating trait clustering, but little or no support has been found for their grouping in the ways demanded by psychoanalytic personality theory (Sears 1942; P. Kline 1972, 1981; S. Fisher and Greenberg 1977; Fonagy 1981). However, for the results of these studies to be acceptable, the measures of the traits themselves must be reliable and valid. In most studies they are not. Nevertheless they are included in a number of reviews, for example, that of S. Fisher and Greenberg (1977). The only writer who insists that these methodological requirements be met is P. Kline (1972, 1981), and his analysis of the many studies on the clustering of character traits is really the only one worth considering.

In both editions of his book Kline summarizes the findings as showing there is "some" evidence to support the existence of a grouping of oral traits, "good" evidence for the anal, but "no evidence" for any other hypothesized psychosexual dimension, for example, the phallic (P. Kline 1972, p. 93, 1981, p. 128). These fairly guarded judgments are later transformed. In his summary conclusions Kline says that the evidence for *both* oral and anal characters is "good," and in a later reference describes both as being supported by a "considerable body of evidence" (P. Kline 1972, pp. 94, 335, 1981, pp. 129, 421; cf. 1984, pp. 64, 156).

Evidence on the relation of the personality characteristics to the original disposition is also a matter for direct nonpsychoanalytic investigation. Freud held that variations in the strength of the innate components of the sexual constitution were reflected in variations in the intensity of childhood oral, anal, and phallic behaviors. Although he has frequently been taken to mean that childhood experiences such as weaning and toilet training actually create fixations, his belief was that the experiences merely intensified existing tendencies for modes of libidinal satisfaction to become fixated. However, whichever of the interpretations is correct, a relation must exist between adult traits and childhood behaviors. Of all of the acceptable studies of the relation between adult personality characteristics and childhood behaviors (retrospective, cross-cultural, current, longitudinal, projective) that Kline found, he noted in the first edition of his review that only two, and in the second only four, gave "even slight support" to the relationship among personality, infant behaviors, and rearing practices (P. Kline 1972, p. 93, 1981, p. 128).

Kline's argument that the failure to relate the personality characteristics to childhood behaviors are due to technical difficulties is suspect, and it is ingenuous to conclude as he does that

The aetiological hypotheses may not ... be rejected until better techniques of investigation have been devised.   (P. Kline 1972, p. 94, 1981, p. 129)

The action is inappropriate. Given the suspect bases of the original hypotheses in the limited number of cases, the curious logic, and the reliance on reconstruction and interpretation, failure to find strong evidence for the personality characteristics to group together and for them to be associated with childhood behaviors is what might be expected. Because they were proposed without adequate supporting evidence, Freud's hypotheses deserve as much (or as little) consideration as any other idle speculation. They should be discarded.

Were one or other of Freud's hypotheses genuinely "aetiological," as Kline represents them, their confirmation would require rather more than the demonstration of a correlation between adult traits and childhood behaviors. What is hypothesized is that various mechanisms carry into adult life fixations that arise in childhood, largely from constitutional tendencies. All that confirming the association between the characteristics and the earlier behavior provides is a confirmation of the accuracy of the original observations. By themselves they throw no light on how the traits develop. The real question is what purpose the etiological hypotheses serve: are there any facts to be explained?

Part of the difference between psychoanalytical opinions about trait clustering and the very slight support provided by later work can be explained by the retrospective nature of the psychoanalytic observations. In samples of patients studied in this way, antecedent factors are often wrongly identified and estimates of their prevalence are usually inflated. Thus Stott's (1961) retrospective study of Down syndrome incorrectly identified maternal emotional shock as its cause. On the other hand, Pitt's (1961) prospective study of the prevalence of intellectual disability in children affected with rubella found normal rates rather than the much higher ones reported in retrospective studies of children with rubella-associated deafness seen at pediatric clinics. Similarly, the enuretics Lovibond (1964) recruited from a "normal" population showed few of the personality characteristics supposed to be associated with enuretics seen at child psychiatric clinics, and he was able to exclude a causal role for those that were present.

The errors to which retrospective studies of patients are prone arise independent of investigator bias. They reflect peculiarities of the method itself and of the samples of patients studied. The causal factors in the samples are different in kind and intensity, and they may operate differently than in the general population. Glover's (1955, pp. 43–46) response to Eysenck's (1952) evaluation of the evidence (some of which Kline also considered) suggests that these factors were present to some extent when the original psychoanalytic observations were made. At the very least the observations were unsystematic and sparse:

it is gratifying and not a little significant to find that *correlations* arrived at by two analysts round about 1922, *on the strength of a few uncontrolled observations of a few cases*, have been confirmed.   (Glover, 1955, p. 45. My emphasis)

Although Glover was wrong in saying that the original correlations had been confirmed, his comment about the early psychoanalytic work is consistent with my points regarding retrospective studies.

Finally, can fixation and the mechanisms of sublimation, reaction-formation, and prolongation-continuation explain how traits form? The answer has to be no. Freud left fixation without a definite place in his theory, and continuation or prolongation is based on an absolutely uncharacterized process of "normal repression." Sublimation is probably the least clear of all the mechanisms and, like reaction-formation, has few if any agreed-on behavioral correlates. Neither is there agreement about the economic and dynamic factors on which sublimation depends. It is not really surprising that the explanatory aspect of Freud's theory has so little support.

Some psychoanalytic writers dismiss the investigations of trait grouping and trait formation as being studies of concepts of personality that are outdated or not representative of psychoanalytic thought. There is no evidence that this is so. Discussions of the consequences for normal development of fixations are either central or of great importance in such texts as those of Hendrick (1934), Nunberg (1932/1955), Fenichel (1932/1934, 1945b), Fliess (1948), Brenner (1955, 1973), and Sterba (1968). R. E. Fischer and Juni (1981) emphasized the continuing importance given anal characteristics, and Baudry (1983) the concept of character itself. If Freud's trait theory is not representative or is outdated, we may reasonably ask what replaces it. Is it really being said that Freud's trait psychology or his theory of psychosexual development never had any substance? Part of the outdated response is quite silly. Take, for example, the irrelevant comment that the phrase "anal character" is so out of date that it is "restricted almost exclusively to a term of abuse between analysts"! (Fonagy 1982).

Phylogenesis

Many of the developmental aspects of Freud's theory of personality rest on the twin notions that species characteristics are acquired through individual experience and that individual development repeats or recapitulates the development of the species. Despite having no stronger evidence for them than "the residual phenomena of the work of analysis" (Freud 1939, p. 100), Freud strongly defended his need for these two ideas. In a letter to Groddeck he remarked of the inheritance of experiences that "a consistent continuation of Lamarck's theory of evolution coincides with the final outcome of psychoanalytic thinking" (cited in Satinover 1986). Sulloway subsequently demonstrated very impressively the centrality of the inheritance of acquired characteristics and the biogenetic law to all of Freud's explanatory schema (Sulloway 1979).

In the theory we are now considering, not only do recapitulation and acquired inheritance predetermine the stages of personality development, but the strength of the fixations is brought about by similar hereditary factors. Further, the disposition to react to a fixation by using one or another of the defense mechanisms is a matter of the archaic heritage.

It is not inappropriate to recall that one of the major points of difference between Janet on the one hand and Freud and Breuer on the other was over the role of hereditary factors in hysteria. Freud and Breuer both regarded them as being much less important than accidental environmental factors. By the time that one can speak of a psychoanalytic personality theory, Freud's thinking had been reversed. In fact, the farther one goes in studying the development of Freud's theory, one sees the greater the importance of innate, hereditary factors and the smaller the role of environment.

The dispositions Freud appeals to are inferred from the very behaviors they are said to explain. As we saw in relation to Mesmer's theory of animal magnetism and Beard's syndrome of neurasthenia, explanations of this kind fail because they are circular. In the case of a disposition to fixate a mode of satisfaction or to use a particular defense mechanism, the existence of the disposition cannot be established independent of the behavior or the use of the mechanism. In any case the prolongations are not clearly related to any events occurring within a stage, the concept of sublimation is almost devoid of meaning, and the tendency to reaction-formation is derived from another indistinctly defined dispositional concept. To the extent that Freud's personality theory rests on dispositions of these kinds, the essential determinants of personality cannot be identified or the personality characteristics explained.

Most psychoanalysts regard Freud's phylogenetic propositions as an embarrassment, flying as they do in the face of all fact and reason. When critically evaluating the use to which Freud put them in *Civilization and Its Discontents*, Werman (1985) judged them to be such "important weaknesses" that he passed over Freud's "untenable anthropological theories, his biologism, and his Lamarckism." This kind of criticism is not new. In his review of Wallace's *Freud and Anthropology*, Almansi

(1986) compares the ideas in Freud's *Totem and Taboo* that were favorably received when it was published with those that were not. The concepts accepted included those of the incest taboo, spirits as projection, magic as wish fulfillment and omnipotence of thought, and ambivalence toward the dead. On the other hand, "the tenets of cultural evolutionism" that were particularly psychoanalytical and more central to Freud's explanations were already strongly attacked by the turn of the century. Nor, Almansi adds, are Freud's ideas of "the hereditary transmissibility of culture, the recapitulation doctrine, the equation of primitive and prehistoric man and the concepts of parricide and the totemic meal" accepted today.

The structure of the personality most dependent on phylogenetic factors is the superego. What can be said about inheritance in relation to the Oedipus complex to which it is heir? As described in chapter 13, the majority view of contemporary analysts is that the contribution of the Oedipus complex to the superego is less central and less important than Freud proposed. A few traditionalists, such as Holder (1982), soldier on in Freud's footsteps by making the formation of the superego dependent on pre-Oedipal components supplied by the archaic heritage, and Rubenstein and Levitt (1959) use Freud's phylogenetic hypothesis to explain the fears their boy patients had of their nonthreatening fathers. The majority view is, however, more in accord with Almansi's summary of Wallace's opinion that Freud "went astray in his phylogenetic view" about the transmission of the Oedipus complex and its ubiquity (Almansi 1986).

Major problems remain with most of the alternative explanations psychoanalysts have put forward. For example, after implicitly rejecting Freud's phylogenetic explanation of the intensity of the boy's castration fear, H. Hartmann and Kris (1945) proposed that, although the child might not be threatened with castration, "the veiled intensity of the aggression of the adult against the child may still produce the same result." One sees very clearly that the problem of the residual Freud referred to is still present; something other than the child's own experience determines the anxiety. But an aggression of veiled intensity is no advance logically on his own explanation. The proposition is just as difficult or impossible to test as the phylogenetic original.

Psychoanalysis as a Psychotherapy

I turn now to the matter of whether psychoanalysis is effective as a therapy. Although the answer is undoubtedly important to the question of whether it can be recommended as a treatment for so-called mental illnesses or as a help with ordinary problems in day-to-day living, those practical matters are not the main reason for taking the issue up. The question is really the bearing of the effectiveness or ineffectiveness of psychoanalysis as a therapy on the validity of psychoanalysis as a theory of personality.

Eysenck's Critique

Until the publication of Eysenck's (1952) well-known review of the effects of psychological therapy, little attention was given to the effectiveness of psychoanalytic therapy. Among the studies Eysenck reviewed were reports of psychoanalytic treatment of neurotics from the Berlin Psycho-analytic Institute (Fenichel 1930, cited more fully in Bergin 1971), the London Institute for Psycho-analysis (E. Jones 1936, cited more fully in Bergin 1971), the Chicago Institute for Psychoanalysis (Alexander 1937, cited more fully in Bergin 1971), the Menninger Clinic (Knight 1941), and the study by Kessel and Hyman (1933). None included base data against which to judge the claimed effects. Eysenck therefore derived a baseline from studies of the effects of nonsystematic treatment. This had

some two-thirds of severe neurotics showing recovery or considerable improvement without the benefit of systematic psychotherapy.   (Eysenck 1952)

After drawing attention to various defects in the studies, including how outcome was assessed, Eysenck concluded that the comparison of outcome rates of systematic with nonsystematic treatment

fail to prove that psychotherapy, *Freudian or otherwise*, facilitates the recovery of neurotic patients.   (Eysenck 1952. My emphasis)

Depending on whether those who broke off psychoanalytic treatment were counted as "not improved" or excluded from the calculations altogether, the analytic recovery rates arrived at by Eysenck were either "44 percent" or "approximately 66 percent." The latter figure was not different from that for either the other forms of psychotherapy or from his baseline estimate. At best, psychoanalysis was the equal of other formal psychotherapies; at worst, it was less effective than nonsystematic treatment.

Eysenck's unpalatable conclusion stimulated a number of reanalyses of the data, the most notable of which was undertaken by Bergin (1971). After also emphasizing the inadequacies of the original data and implicitly agreeing with Eysenck about the difficulty of classifying outcomes, Bergin concluded that, depending on how the outcomes were classified, improvement rates as low as about 40 percent or as high as about 90 percent could be calculated for the five psychoanalytic reports.

Eysenck qualified his conclusion:

The figures ... do not necessarily disprove the possibility of therapeutic effectiveness.... Definite proof would require a special investigation, carefully planned and methodologically more adequate than these *ad hoc* comparisons.   (Eysenck 1952)

Although Bergin clearly distanced himself from Eysenck on other matters, I doubt that he would have disagreed with this characterization of the early work.

Post-Eysenck Critiques

None of the reasonably numerous post-1952 studies cited by Bergin (1971) met the criteria proposed by Eysenck, but even so, they generally returned rates below 50 percent. Lambert's (1976) analysis of waiting list remissions yielded a median rate of 43 percent, a baseline possibly closer to that of a true no-treatment control than Eysenck's. Lambert nevertheless regarded even that rate as misleading: depending on the disorder, remission rates as high as 70 percent were reported.[4]

Similarly, of the six studies they were able to find comparing psychoanalysis with no treatment, S. Fisher and Greenberg (1977, p. 321) noted all six had such "obvious methodological flaws or deficiencies" that the positive outcomes "could be as easily attributed to specific therapist characteristics as to the analytic treatment method employed." Compared with alternative therapies, psychoanalysis did not lead to markedly different outcomes. The authors concluded:

Our review of studies of the outcome of psychoanalysis seems to come down to two general conclusions: (1) psychoanalysis has been shown to be consistently more effective than no-treatment with chronic neurotic patients, and (2) psychoanalysis has not been shown to be significantly more effective than *other* forms of psychotherapy with any type of patient. (p. 341)

Kline's later review reached a similar conclusion:

Studies of the outcome of psychoanalytic therapy where even the minimum standards of methodology ... are satisfied simply do not exist.... Thus ... the net result of the studies ... of the outcome of psychoanalytic therapy is very small and little is yet known about its efficiency. (P. Kline 1981, p. 398)

In a more popular work, Kline repeated this assessment: "most studies" of the outcome of psychoanalytic therapy, "are too deficient in research design and measurement to stand rigorous scrutiny" (P. Kline 1984, p. 123). He concluded:

Sadly I have been unable to report any studies which clearly demonstrate the success or failure of psychoanalytic therapy.   (p. 131)

Justified melancholy indeed. Not only is it now about one hundred years since Freud pioneered his form of psychotherapy, but Kline is probably even more sympathetic to psychoanalysis than are Fisher and Greenberg! Neither do more recent reviews of psychotherapy research compel great dissent from Kline's conclusion (Bergin 1978; Strupp 1986; Stiles, Shapiro, and Elliott 1986). In fact, VandenBos indicates how tenuous our knowledge remains:

By about 1980 a consensus *of sorts* was reached that psychotherapy, as a generic treatment process, was demonstrably more effective than no treatment. (VandenBos 1986. My emphasis)

Adding, "some ... are less convinced that the controversy has yet to be fully resolved," he makes the qualification even more apparent.

Of course, to the extent the conclusion is warranted at all, it has been studies of nonanalytic therapy and, at best, psychoanalytic psychotherapy rather than *psychoanalysis* proper, that cleared away such doubts as have been resolved. Consequently, we still have no evidence to suppose that VandenBos's consensus includes psychoanalysis as therapy. Fonagy (1982), it seems to me, tried hard to bolster the claims of psychoanalysis to be effective, but even he cannot go beyond saying that it had "little to be ashamed of in the area of therapeutic outcome" or was "at least as successful as behaviour therapy," a conclusion at one with that of H. B. Lewis (1984). In addition, as Erwin (1980) shows, the fact that no alternative to the average improvement rate of two-thirds for patients treated nonsystematically has been determined does nothing to rebut Eysenck's conclusion that "there is no firm evidence that psychoanalysis is therapeutically effective."

The Columbia Center Studies

No controlled comparisons of the outcome of psychoanalytic therapy have appeared since the above reviews. However, data relevant to outcome is reported in the most important of the studies of psychoanalytic therapy which has been published since, that from the Columbia Psychoanalytic Center (Weber, Solomon, and Bachrach 1985; Weber, Bachrach, and Solomon 1985a; Weber, Bachrach, and Solomon 1985b; Bachrach, Weber, and Solomon 1985). At best, the improvement rates reported provide equivocal support for an effectiveness of psychoanalytic therapy greater than that of unsystematic treatment. Between 1945 and 1962, 9,000 patients were referred to the Center of whom 1,348 were accepted for treatment and who constituted the population from which sample 1 of the study was drawn. Patients were either treated wholly at the Center or transferred to private practice after beginning at the Center. Five hundred eighty-eight were seen four or five times per week in traditional psychoanalytic therapy, and 760 others were seen twice a week in the modified form of psychoanalysis known as psychoanalytically oriented psychotherapy. Complete data or data in which the evaluators had confidence was available for 295 of the 588 and 286 of the 760 who had completed treatment, that is, for slightly less than half of the total.

Considering first those of the 295 who completed a full psychoanalysis, of the 158 treated entirely at the Center, a "better" overall improvement rating was given to 56% and "no change" or "worse" to the other 44 percent. Of the 77 who became private patients after starting at the Center, 91 percent were "much improved" or "improved" (apparently equivalent to "better") and of 28 who began with a full analysis but were transferred to analytically oriented therapy, 86 percent were given the same ratings. Second, the 286 patients who were treated with only psychoanalytically oriented therapy where divided into two subgroups (the division need not concern us) and seen entirely at the Center. For them the "better" rates were 61 and 48 percent. There were virtually no differences between the findings from Sample 1 and those from Sample 2 of the same study. Sample 2 consisted of 77 cases drawn from an initial pool of 237 subjects seen at the Center between 1962 and 1971; 36 were treated with psychoanalysis and 41 with analytically oriented therapy. While there were some differences in the methods of investigation, the findings from Sample 2 confirmed those from Sample 1.

However, in Sample 1 of the Columbia Study, patient type, length of treatment, and independence of judgment of outcome are confounded. Before treatment even began, those patients eventually selected for a full psychoanalysis had been assessed as functioning at significantly higher levels than those allotted to analytically oriented therapy, and those who were eventually transferred to private practice showed a nonsignificant trend to be at the highest levels of all. Patients in psychoanalysis were also seen for longer than those treated with analytically oriented therapy. Those who were transferred and treated as private patients were seen for about twice as long (modal length of treatment 4+ years) as those who completed their analyses in the Center (1–2 years), but the modal time for those treated entirely with analytically oriented therapy was 6–12 months. For those seen entirely in the Center, whether treated with a full psychoanalysis or by analytically oriented therapy, the outcome was judged by psychoanalysts *not involved in the treatment*, but for those transferred to private practice, the outcome was assessed *by the analyst conducting the treatment*. A similar confounding exists in the data for Sample 2. Overall, then, the patients who did so exceptionally well were the less impaired private patients whose treatment took much longer and whose final status was judged by their therapists.

According to the Columbia investigators, there were no differences between their findings and the outcome of a number of smaller studies, reported since the middle 1970s, but not reviewed by Kline or Fisher and Greenberg. Nor were the results different from those of the small, intensively studied sample of the Menninger Foundation Psychotherapy Research Project (Wallerstein 1986c, ch. 23) It will be appreciated that the rates of "better" for the 56 percent of those treated with a full psychoanalysis in the Center and for the 61 and 48 percent of those seen in analytically oriented therapy are broadly consistent with Eysenck's original finding.

Therapeutic Outcome as the Test of a Theory

Even if psychoanalysis were an effective *therapy*, that fact has little bearing on the truth of psychoanalytic *theory*. Suppose that the positive changes that were supposed to take place in therapy could be strictly deduced from a given theory of psychopathology. Under those circumstances, the outcome could be thought of as like any other hypothesis that could be deduced from the theory: *if* the problem has the characteristics that the theory supposes it to have, *and* a particular kind of intervention that can change or modify those characteristics can be deduced from the theory, *then* the characteristics should be observed to change as the therapy is applied.

Four points must be made about the practical and logical consequences of the therapeutic test. First, the logic of testing any theory is such that a positive result does not *prove* the theory to be true but only possibly true. This is because the result may have come about for reasons entirely unrelated to the truth of the theory. Consequently, even if psychoanalysis were an effective therapy, that fact would not prove the truth of the theory of psychoanalysis. Processes might be at work in the therapeutic situation that have nothing whatever to do with psychoanalysis as such, for example, the relationship with the therapist, the possibility for the patient to learn new techniques for coping, or some change in the patient's ability to regain control of his or her life. Second, a therapy derived logically from a theory has to bring about its changes in a unique way if the theory is even to be confirmed. As far as one can tell, what effects psychoanalysis does have as therapy are not unique and do not confirm it as a theory.

The third point flows from the basic asymmetry of the logic of testing a theory. A positive result only confirms the theory, but a negative one may *disprove* it. However, a negative therapeutic outcome is not quite as unproblematic as it might seem from Scriven's argument that "negative results count heavily against [psychoanalytic] theory, positive ... count weakly, if at all for it" (Scriven 1959). A disorder or disease may be fully understood but be completely resistant to treatment. For example, many years elapsed between the identification of the causes of diseases such as tuberculosis and syphilis and the development of effective treatment for them. The lack of a therapy for AIDS is a modern example. Thus, it is perfectly possible to imagine psychoanalytic theory giving a correct etiological account of a disorder but having little or nothing to offer in the way of effective treatment. A negative therapeutic outcome would be irrelevant to the truth or falsity of psychoanalysis as a theory in that case.

The fourth point concerns the practical consequences of a positive outcome and is not germane to the logic of the test. Those who use, plan, or administer clinical-psychological and psychiatric services have to be able to choose among therapies on the grounds of their effectiveness and cost. Fisher and Greenberg (1977) summarized the practical evidence about psychoanalysis by concluding that "a patient suffering from chronic neurotic symptoms would do better with psychoanalysis than without." However, they continued,

> there is at present no justification for a patient to assume that he will achieve a greater degree of improvement in a therapy called psychoanalysis than in a therapy given another label such as analytically oriented, client-centered, or behavioral. There is virtually no evidence that psychoanalysis results in more long-lasting or profound patient change than other therapies. (p. 341)

There is no reason to choose psychoanalysis over other therapies, especially if its cost and duration are taken into account.

Whatever practical importance attaches to the question of the effectiveness of psychoanalysis as a therapy, the therapeutic arena is simply not the place on which to establish its truth as a theory.

Conclusion

Psychoanalysis as a theory of personality has little to recommend it. The formal deficiencies of much psychoanalytic explanation is fairly obvious, but we ought to ask what needs explaining. Do processes such as condensation and the summation of stimuli occur? Does a mechanism such as repression exist? Is there a transformation of the primary process into the secondary? Is there an Oedipus complex out of which a superego forms and from which the ego is provided with defused energy? Is the development of adult sexuality, character traits, and object-choice as Freud described them? Is female sexuality as Freud pictured it? From these points of view, psychoanalysis is not so much a bad theory, but a theory in search of some facts.

Neither does psychoanalysis have any particular positive advantages as a psychological treatment. Nor does it possess any quality marking it as a unique therapy. What, then, of its value as a method of enquiry into human behavior and mental processes? That question is taken up in chapter 15.

Notes

1. Being as curious as Schafer (1974) about "what sense, if any" Freud could have been making in his statements about women's lesser morality, I informally asked graduate students and acquaintances of both sexes who were unfamiliar with Freud's descriptions to characterize the typical differences between the moral standards and behavior of men and women. For what these data are worth, the question usually draws responses deeply uncomprehending of the question, and explanations do little to make it meaningful.

2. The changes in the concept of autoerotism, which cannot be detected in any of the editions of the *Three Essays* or the later footnotes to it, has a complex history that finds no explicit acknowledgement in either Freud's 1932 systematic account of the theoretical revisions of the previous sixteen years (Freud 1933b, pp. 99–102) or in the last major outline of his views written six years later (Freud 1940a).

3. Originally Freud used this term to refer to the active and passive forms of oral erotic activity (Freud 1915a, p.138).

4. In this literature, much is made of the need to use standards for assessing outcome that are more complex than simple ratings of symptomatic change. The demand is unwarranted. Mintz (1981) had two nonprofessional, naïve judges use precisely such simple ratings of symptom change ('maximum recovery' to 'no change' or 'worse') to assess outcome. He compared their ratings with those of the same patients made by Malan's (1976) experienced psychoanalytical Tavistock psychotherapist-judges who used complex psychodynamic standards. The correlations between the two measures were of the order of 0.8 to 0.9. Thus the symptom description contains the same information as the complex formulations that psychoanalysts and their friends urge should be adopted and that they insist, render Eysenck's studies of non-systematic and behavioral treatments irrelevant. Mintz's finding is so robust that I have confirmed it repeatedly in student practical exercises over the last seven or eight years. Well over half a class of second-year students of psychology, relatively naïve even as to the meaning of the word neurosis, can generate judgments of the amount of change shown by Malan's patients that correlate 0.70 or more with the Tavistock ratings. Yet the students base their judgments *only* on Malan's descriptions of the symptoms at presentation and follow-up. Wallerstein's conclusion that structural changes were not dependent on the mode of intervention is also consistent with Mintz's view (Wallerstein 1986b, pp. 720–721).

15 Psychoanalysis as a Method

Cecily: That certainly seems a satisfactory explanation, does it not?
Gwendolen: Yes, dear, if you can believe him.
Cecily: I don't. But that does not affect the wonderful beauty of his answer.
—Wilde: *The Importance of Being Earnest*, Act IV

The question I attempt to answer in this chapter is whether the psychoanalytic method is reliable and valid. That is, even if psychoanalysis has limitations as a theory of personality and a type of therapy, does it nevertheless provide us with an objective means for establishing facts about mental life?

Because the theoretical foundations of the basic method of psychoanalysis—free association—were examined in chapter 4, I begin here by considering how it is used and evaluating the evidence for its objectivity. Although the assumptions on which the method is based are extremely plausible, its results are too variable for it to be considered a reliable and valid means for collecting data. Free association evidently *creates* its data rather than *recovers* them. In addition, there are not and cannot be any guidelines to how these data should be interpreted or how they should be used in constructing or reconstructing the patient's past. Therefore, important differences among psychoanalysts about the basic characteristics of personality are inevitably irreconcilable. Psychoanalysis is not able to give us data to help us decide on different psychoanalytic conceptions of personality. Nor is it capable of providing us with real knowledge about the facts of human behavior and mental life.

Gathering the Data

Free association is the basic method of psychoanalysis. The patient focuses attention on an element of the dream, parapraxis, or symptom being analyzed, suspends his or her critical attitude, and reports all the ideas that force their way into consciousness. We know that Freud believed these ideas were not random. Gaps that occurred could be filled and broken causal connections restored. Trains of associations eventually led to the causes of the phenomenon being analyzed. When he spelled out the procedure in detail, he emphasized the role of the idea with which the patient began. He asked his patient "to surrender himself to free association *while keeping an idea in mind as a starting point*" (Freud 1916–1917, p. 106). Why was this? Freud believed that any thought chosen "quite freely" was determined and actually belonged to a connected whole. He argued that the same determinism was at work when a starting idea was given:

we shall no doubt be justified in concluding that things that occur to one with a single link—namely their link with the idea that serves as a starting point—cannot be any less determined.   (p. 108)

His investigations showed, he said, that apart from their connection with the starting point, the ideas so generated were also dependent on the patient's unconscious emotional thoughts and interests (p. 108).

For the train of associations to be influenced only by the patient's unconscious ideas, the psychoanalyst also had to adhere to a version of the fundamental rule, that is, maintain what Freud called "an evenly suspended attention." This meant attending to the patient's associations without paying attention to anything in particular and withholding his or her own conscious influences from them. Put purely in terms of technique, the psychoanalyst "should simply listen, and not bother about whether he is keeping anything in mind" (Freud 1912d, pp. 111–112, 115; cf. 1909a, p. 65, 1926b, p. 219). By analogy, the analyst had to

turn his own unconscious like a receptive organ toward the transmitting unconscious of the patient. He must adjust himself to the patient as a telephone receiver is adjusted to the transmitting microphone.... the doctor's unconscious is able, from the derivatives of the unconscious which are communicated to him, to reconstruct that unconscious, which has determined the patient's free associations.   (Freud 1912d, pp. 115–116)

As a receiver, the psychoanalyst was supposed to treat the patient with the coldness and detachment of a surgeon. It was important not even to take notes, since this would already be to select from the material being produced (Freud 1912d, p. 113). To reduce the influence of the analyst's facial expressions, Freud even went so far as to promote the virtues of sitting behind the patient during therapy (Freud 1913a, p. 134). The method had long-term applications. As long as analysts and patients gave up "their conscious purposive aims" and did not "dispute the guidance of the unconscious in establishing connecting links," a dream might be interpreted many days after it was dreamed (Freud 1911c, p. 94).

Three things should be emphasized. The first is that Freud did not ask his patients just to talk about anything that came to mind. Most of the contributors to the American Psychoanalytical Association's 1970 panel discussion of "the Basic Rule," as well as most of the experienced psychoanalysts surveyed much later by Lichtenberg and Galler, seem not to have realized this (Seidenberg 1971; Lichtenberg and Galler 1987). The theoretical underpinnings of the method, which I discussed in chapter 4, required Freud's patients to free associate to a starting idea. That beginning directed their thoughts toward the ideas that caused the dream, parapraxis, or symptom. The singularity of the method has also to be insisted on. It was never one of three techniques by which Freud believed the unconscious could be discovered, as Laplance and Pontalis mistakenly believe. They clearly confuse the three phenomena of symptoms, dreams, and faulty actions, which were all supposed to yield their secret causes to the method, with the method itself (Laplanche and Pontalis 1967/1973, pp. 178–179; cf. Freud 1910a, pp. 33–37). Finally, free association is a technique for investigating thinking, not a type of thought content. However, there is now such a basic lack of understanding about it among psychoanalysts that Gill stressed the obvious point that "free association should not be defined as chaotic 'deep' material —in fact not according to its content at all" (Reppen 1982).

The Validity of the Method

Freud thought his method of analyzing symptoms, based as it was on the way the fundamental rule was applied, was robust enough to guarantee "to a great extent ... that nothing will be introduced into it [the structure of the neurosis] by the expectations of the analyst" (Freud 1925a, p. 41). His claim was the development of an earlier one, first expressed in *Studies on Hysteria*, discussed in chapters 4 and 8, that he had never been able to force memories of traumatic events on to his patients (Breuer and Freud 1895, p. 295). What this view reflected was Freud's belief that psychological phenomena had internal determinants.

Does Freud's belief in psychic determinism hold for free association? Is it as objective a method as he thought? Not only is this issue not discussed in the psychoanalytic literature, most psychoanalytic authors show such slight comprehension of what Freud meant by psychic determinism that they couple it wholly or partly with what are, in this context, the quite irrelevant issues of free will, predeterminism, and questions of will, ethics, and morality (e.g., Oberndorf 1943 and Galdston's discussion; Knight 1946; Lipton 1955; Wheelis 1956; Angel 1959; Hoffman 1964; L. Friedman 1965; Waelder 1963; Kanzer 1968; Macklin 1976; Basch 1978; Phillips 1981). In the psychoanalytic literature to 1952 Zilboorg found only the two works by H. Hartmann and Anna Freud that dealt with "the whole problem of free associations and of the fundamental rule" at more than the practical and utilitarian level (Zilboorg 1952b; cf. 1952a). Neither Hartmann nor A. Freud took up the issue of objectivity. About ten years later Bellak (1961) could still describe the literature dealing with the rule as "scanty" and that "systematic metapsychological consideration is nonexistent."

Freud's concept has as little to do with free will and predetermination as it does with content. What it does have to do with is causality (Waelder 1963). Brill (1938–1939) stressed how "the psychoanalyst uses free association in order to find the origin of symptoms" and it was "equivalent to a search for the determinants" of traumatic episodes. In outlining how to use free association, Freud was consistent with Meynert. Recall the significance given the sound of the lamb by Meynert and Breuer-Freud: as one element of a previously experienced association, the sound allowed the logical inferences that a lamb was present and that it was the cause of the sound. Associations evoked by a starting idea were causes or links in a chain of causal associations that terminated in the causal idea.

The Evidence from the Clinic

Almost from the beginning some questioned both the rule and the claims based on it. Determinism per se was not at issue—most critics accepted a psychological form of determinism (e.g., Wells 1912). They did not doubt that parapraxes were caused but, like Roback, asked why it was necessary "to *create* a cause when the direct antecedent is in most cases apparent" (Roback 1919). Generally the critics contended that free associations were too affected by suggestion to be reliable sources of facts, and that psychoanalysts arbitrarily interpreted such facts as the method did provide.

Some of these doubters were never especially sympathetic to psychoanalysis (Ormerod 1910–1911; Woodworth 1917) but others once had a degree of fellow-feeling (Sidis 1906–1907, 1912, 1918; B. Hart 1916, 1929), some even to the extent of practicing analysis and defending the assumption before changing their view (Tannenbaum 1917, 1922, 1923a,b; Petersen, cited by Cioffi 1973). Others began with doubt but were won over (e.g., Putnam 1906–1907, 1910; cf. Vasile 1977, pp. x, 60, 74–75). I believe a major reason for these various positions, especially for the changes in them, was the paucity of facts about free association. From the earliest years most of what was said either for or against it was based solely on general logical considerations or clinical opinion (e.g., Schroeder 1919; B. Hart 1929, pp. 67–77).

Studies of Free Association

When questions about the validity of free association were raised, Freud sometimes referred to Jung's experiments using the word-association test (Freud 1900, pp. 531–532, and footnote of 1909, 1906b, 1910a, pp. 29–30; cf. E. Jones 1911b). Jung's work illustrated that associations given to stimulus words may have unconscious determinants, but is not relevant to the objectivity of free association as a method for gathering data. Jung nowhere discussed in any detail the associationist basis of his technique or the relation between his and Freud's methods (Jung 1906/1973a,b, 1910). Consequently, his studies tell us nothing about the degree to which free associations given by the patient *in the therapeutic situation* are determined *solely* by the patient's unconscious processes.

If Sears's reviews of studies of psychoanalytic concepts and phenomena can be taken as a guide, no investigation of any kind into the objectivity of the primary method of psychoanalytic data collection had been conducted by the end of the 1930s. Neither of his reviews even mentions the technique (Sears 1942, 1944). That situation seems not to have changed over the last fifty years. Not a single study of free association is reported by Hilgard (1952, 1968), Eysenck and Wilson (1973), or P. Kline (1981), and little of what Fisher and Greenberg have to say about it touches on the method's validity (S. Fisher and Greenberg 1977, pp. 386–388).

I found only two studies of free association per se. Both provide clear evidence that the content and number of associations is influenced by situational factors as simple as whether another person is present, and whether the verbal intervention of the experimenter is a question or a statement suggesting causality (Colby 1960, 1961). No studies at all have investigated how the method is actually used in therapy, there are only some as yet still unfulfilled methodological preliminaries to that topic (Bordin 1966a,b).

The Luria Technique

The only other claim of "experimental evidence for the validity of the technique of free association" seems to be that made in 1950 by Pumpian-Mindlin (1952, p. 141) for Luria's work on hypnotically produced conflict. What Luria did was gather chains of associations from his subjects before and after they were hypnotized. During hypnosis the suggestion was made that they had been involved in some traumatic incident, usually a crime. Words related to the suggested event were common among the free associations given after the suggestion, whereas those given before were all entirely normal. For example, Luria suggested to one subject that she had performed an abortion in a room at the top of a staircase. The posthypnosis associations included words such as wound, forceps, scalpel, operation, instruments, nurse, and staircase. The motor reactions accompanying the associations were also abnormal (Luria 1932, pp. 149–161). Free association seemed capable of leading back to the "trauma."

Modern hypnosis research gives three reasons for thinking that findings such as Luria's are not strong enough to bear the implication Pumpian-Mindlin and others want them to carry (Brickner and Kubie 1936; Huston, Shakow, and Erickson 1934). First, given that Luria's experiments were conducted in the middle 1920s, it is not surprising that they fail to meet present-day methodological criteria, particularly in lacking simulation controls. Luria's subjects, like those in most later experiments, could have "unconsciously" discerned the demand characteristics embedded in the experimental situation and behaved in accordance with them (Huston, Shakow, and Erickson 1934; M. H. Erickson 1935, 1944; J. Eisenbud 1937; Young 1941; Wolberg 1947; Bobbitt 1958; Counts and Mensh 1950; W. F. Moore 1964). In fact, appropriate controls in later experiments on hypnotically suggested trauma do show that most of the associated phenomena result from demand characteristics. The different positions on this topic are covered by several authors (Reyher 1962, 1967; Deckert and West 1963; J. E. Gordon 1967; Sheehan 1969).

Second, hypnotic amnesia is not as absolute as was once thought. Consequently, the parallel between amnesia for a suggested trauma and that supposed to be brought about by repression is not as close as Luria supposed and as Pumpian-Mindlin's inference requires (Sheehan and McConkey 1982, chapter 7; Kihlstrom 1985). Third, what would have happened had the subjects' expectations been systematically varied? Could subjects have been led to disregard the real trauma and produce evidence of a false one instead? This is the most important of the questions, and no investigations of it at all have been conducted.

Hypnotic Investigations of Dreams and Parapraxes

The methodological criticisms that can be made of the work on hypnotically implanted trauma also apply to most of the related work on hypnotically produced parapraxes and to dreams suggested or interpreted under hypnosis (Schroetter 1911/1951; Roffenstein 1924/1951; Nachmansohn 1925/1951; M. H. Erickson 1939; Farber and Fisher 1943; Mazer 1951; M. V. Kline 1963). Most authors, including psychoanalysts, now doubt that hypnotically produced dreams are equivalent to their nocturnal counterparts (Brenman 1949; Gill and Brenman 1959; Domhoff 1964; Tart 1965; Moss 1967; Witkin and Lewis 1967; Hilgard and Nowlis 1972; Levitt and Chapman 1979; Sheehan and Dolby 1979). When the dream experiments were repeated, it did not prove easy or even possible to duplicate the results (Kaywin, Hilger, and Finzer 1948, cited in Rapaport 1951, p. 252, n. 11; Gill and Brenman 1959, pp. 348–351; Barber 1962; Schneck 1963; Moss and Stachowiak 1963; C. Fisher 1966). The positive results were very probably due to a combination of the experimenter's enthusiasm and the subject's knowledge of the particular dream theory being investigated (Reis 1951, cited in Barber 1962; Rapaport 1951, pp. 240–241 and n. 13, p. 252 and n. 11, p. 268 and n. 29; Barber 1962; Tart 1965; C. Fisher 1966; Moss 1967; F. J. Evans 1972).

Determinants or Associations?

Since at least 1912 the objection has been made that the relation between associations and the unconscious ideas to which they seem to lead actually lacks the strict determination Freud hypothesized (e.g., Wells 1912, 1913). Associations to anything, even ideas selected at random, will lead, it was said, to a pressing problem whether or not the initial idea or the trains of thought are connected with it causally. Hence, Woodworth (1917) questioned how seriously it could be maintained that a thought B, to which associations from A led, was the cause of A rather than simply one of the subject's ideas. In rebuttal, Tannenbaum could only call on Freud's "Years of experience, corroborated by similar experiences of hundreds of other investigators" (Tannenbaum 1917). E. Jones (1911b) gave the same response together with some other equally irrelevant comments.

In a 1920 footnote to the *Psychopathology of Everyday Life* Freud seemed to grant that more than a call to experience was necessary. He had claimed that even associations to numbers chosen at random led back to determining ideas in the same way as those that were supposed to cause parapraxes and dreams. Schneider tested whether this might be only an apparent determinism by asking for associations to numbers chosen by others. Freud accepted that these associations "provided determinants just as abundant and full of meaning" as when subjects chose the numbers themselves. However, he asserted that Schneider had gone "too far" in concluding that numbers chosen spontaneously had not originated "from the thoughts discovered in the 'analysis' of them." He evaded Schneider's point by arguing that associations to numbers so presented said "nothing more" about the origin of spontaneously chosen numbers than was known before Schneider's experiment. Freud did allow that "a critical examination of the problem and with it a justification of the psychoanalytic technique" was needed, but said that topic lay "outside the scope" of his book (Freud 1901b, p. 250, n. 2).

Freud's concession, if concession it was, was much less generous than Flugel's about Wohlgemuth's similar investigation. Wohlgemuth generated his own associations to numbers chosen by Freud and said he was able to analyze them "with the same ease and elegance" as Freud (Wohlgemuth 1923, pp. 214–216; cf. Freud 1901b, pp. 242–243, 246–248). Flugel saw that if this were true, Freud's theory had to be "regarded as unproved," at least with regard to the evidence from associations. Because he thought they "might prove very useful and illuminating," Flugel urged that experiments on number determination be undertaken and extended to dream analysis. He mentioned Bleuler as "the only investigator to have realised the value of work along these lines" but dismissed Bleuler's findings as "too few and unsystematic" to be of value (Flugel 1924). But, as with the Schneider-type investigations Freud intimated, nothing was ever published. No counterattack was ever made to regain the position Flugel so quietly surrendered and, until Sand's (1982) paper, the matter seems not even to have been raised in psychoanalytic circles.

The tendency not to reply to the criticism that free association generates associations, not determinants, is well established in the psychoanalytic literature. Illustrating this point is the fate of Tannenbaum's criticism of Freud's use of free association to analyze one of his most commented-on parapraxes. After he moved away from psychoanalysis, Tannenbaum (1922) reexamined the "*aliquis* slip" that Freud described in *Psychopathology of Everyday Life* (Freud 1901b, pp. 8–14). The word had escaped the memory of a young man who was trying to recall Virgil's line *Exoriar(e)* *aliquis nostris ex ossibus ultor* [let someone (aliquis) arise from my bones as an avenger, or Let some avenger arise from my bones], so that what he produced was *Exoriar(e) ex nostris ossibus ultor*. From the association of "liquid" to "liquis" an indirect train of thought led to the young man's concern that he might have made a lady friend pregnant. As Stephen (1918–1919) had done before him, Tannenbaum pointed out that had any other word in the line been forgotten, the worry over the possible pregnancy would have been reached just as certainly. He then asked the further question why the anxiety did not cause "the forgetting of the word 'exoriare' (exorcism, expulsion, abortion) which can be so much more directly linked up with the presumably apprehended gestation" (Tannenbaum 1922). Because there was no answer after some fifty years, Timpanaro seems to have felt impelled to ask the same question. On the basis of a much deeper and detailed philological reanalysis of the slip, he showed that almost any of the elements in the line can be made to have links with the supposed causal idea, and not just *exoriare*. Like Tannenbaum, he pointed to the contradiction of Freud's explanation requiring an unconscious that was simultaneously primitive and linguistically sophisticated. Timpanaro also indicated that *aliquis* was part of an almost unique grammatical construction that would be strange and ambiguous even to a Latin speaker, and therefore the word in the line most likely not to be recalled. The error bears the hallmark of a "banalization," that is, of the kind made in the use of a language by one not completely familiar with it. *Aliquis* is also the one word least necessary to the meaning of the whole (Timpanaro 1974/1976, pp. 28–61, 219–220).

Using Free Associations

I now turn to four of the uses to which the data gained from free association are put: translating dream elements; interpreting dreams, symptoms, and parapraxes; constructing or reconstructing significant events in the patient's history; and building up a complete narrative of the patient. The topics are considered sequentially.

Psychoanalysis as Translation

Several times Freud drew an analogy between dreams and languages in which the differences between the manifest dream and the latent dream thoughts were supposed to parallel those between one language and another. Interpreting the dream was therefore like translating. We have to consider what Freud meant by translation and ask whether it is possible.

Well before Freud's systematic interest in interpreting dreams developed, he and Breuer used the language analogy to explain hysterical symptoms. His 1895 discussion of the hysterical vomiting of Katharina, whom Swales (1988) shows was seen by Freud in August 1893, indicates that they used it generally:

We had often compared the symptomatology of hysteria with a pictographic script which has become intelligible after the discovery of a few bilingual inscriptions. In that alphabet being sick means disgust. (Breuer and Freud 1895, p. 129)

When Freud applied the analogy to dreams he stated that they occupied "a far more unfavourable position than any of these ancient languages and scripts" (Freud 1916–1917, p. 231) and implied elsewhere this was also true of symptoms and parapraxes.

Problems with the Analogy   There are three reasons why the analogy between translation and the understanding of dreams, symptoms, and parapraxes breaks down. First, what Freud called primitive languages were

intended for communication: that is to say, they are always, by whatever method and with whatever assistance, meant to be understood. But precisely this characteristic is absent in dreams. A dream does not want to say anything to anyone. It is not a vehicle for communication; on the contrary, it is meant to remain ununderstood. (Freud 1916–1917, p. 231; cf. 1900, p. 341)

Although the patient's telling a dream was a communication, even then it was

a communication made by inappropriate means, for dreams are not in themselves social utterances, not a means of giving information. (Freud 1933b, p. 9)

Translation was supposed to transform the dream into a communication (ibid, p. 9). But if the manifest language is not one that communicates, is this really possible? (cf. Freud 1900, pp. 277–278, 1901b, p. 5, 1916–1917, pp. 175–177, 229–231, 1933b, p. 20).

Second, the would-be interpreter of dreams has no rules for semantic substitution. Freud described the process as resembling the decoding method in which fixed meanings set out in ancient dream books were substituted one at a time for each of the separate manifest elements. But, except for the act of substitution, what the psychoanalyst really does is not at all comparable.

To begin with, simple replacement of the elements produced by the dream work is not possible because, with the exception of a limited group of symbols, the elements do not have fixed meanings. That is precisely what made it necessary for the individual to provide associations to the elements of a dream (Freud 1901a, p. 684, 1916–1917, pp. 150–151). Not even the patient's dream thoughts were expressed through a lexicon of fixed meanings, and even the common symbols Freud claimed to have discovered, and that in dreams were used "almost exclusively" to express sexual objects and relations, sometimes functioned as symbols and sometimes as themselves (Freud 1900, pp. 345, 352, 1901a, p. 684).

Dream thoughts were so likely to be represented directly as by their opposites that Freud devised an "interpretative rule":

> every element in a dream can ... stand for its opposite just as easily as for itself. We can never tell beforehand whether it stands for the one or for the other; only the context can decide. (Freud 1900, p. 471; cf. p. 318)

He summed up these difficulties by saying that it was doubtful if any dream element should be taken in a positive or negative sense or interpreted as a symbol, as a historical recollection, or according to its wording (p. 341).

There is also what linguists term the many-to-many mapping problem, caused in this instance by condensation. Simply by omitting elements condensation prevented "a faithful translation or a point-for-point projection of the dream-thoughts" (p. 281). Manifest elements were determined "many times over" by latent thoughts, which were themselves represented in the dream several times over. That is:

> Associative paths lead from one element of the dream to several dream-thoughts, and from one dream-thought to several elements of the dream.   (p. 284)

Thus, a "manifest element may correspond simultaneously to several latent ones, and, contrariwise, a latent element may play a part in several manifest ones" (Freud 1916–1917, p. 173). No simple disentangling of dream thoughts from the condensed manifest elements was possible.

Third is the absence of syntactic rules. The production of manifest elements by the dream work is not governed by anything having the character of the grammatical rules of a language. True, there are rules, but they lack even the definiteness of those that enable ambiguous expressions to be deciphered. For example, because of the requirement of pictorial representability, none of the conjunctions necessary to understand speech or sentences could be represented at all. Thus, when the dreamer said that something in the dream was *either* one thing *or* another, the analyst had to take the expression to mean one thing *and* the other. Deciphering causal propositions presented a particular problem. The dream might be divided into two parts, one for the principal and the other for the dependent clause, or the dreamer might report having seen one image being transformed into another. But it did not follow that what came first was the cause rather than the effect, and in the case of the two-part dream, the division did not always represent a causal relation (Freud 1900, pp. 312–

318, 1901a, pp. 650, 661, 1913e, pp. 176–178, 1916–1917, pp. 178–180, 1933b, pp. 19–27).

Deciphering Ancient Scripts Despite Freud's suggestions to the contrary, the interpretation of dreams was by no means "completely analogous to the decipherment of an ancient pictographic script such as Egyptian hieroglyphics" (Freud 1913e, p. 177; cf. 1916–1917, pp. 229–232). Even with my minimal knowledge of how ancient language records have been deciphered, I know that in every case there was at least a partial parallel record in another already known script. For example, the beginning of our understanding of Egyptian hieroglyphs came from Young's alignment of eighty-six groups of demotic signs on the Rosetta stone with words of known meaning in the parallel Greek section. Young then demonstrated that the name of King Ptolemy, which occurred six times in the Greek and demotic scripts, was enclosed in each of the six otherwise incomprehensible cartouches in the hieroglyphic section. His study of this and other scripts led to his more or less correct deciphering the hieroglyphic equivalents of some eighty demotic words. The cuneiform alphabet similarly began to yield its secrets once it was conjectured that the names of known kings and known ritual phrases could be substituted at the beginnings and ends of the messages inscribed on the tablets. Similarly, Linear B was understood once Ventris correctly surmised that it was a form of ancient Greek. That so many ancient languages remain unknown is largely because dual scripts still have not been found.

Freud's comparison of the reliability of dream interpretation with that of cuneiform decipherment was also very wide of the mark (Freud 1916–1917, p. 232). He cited the experts who had been tested by the Royal Asiatic Society in 1857 and who were able to produce a good deal of agreement about the meaning of a cuneiform text given them as a test. What agreement they did reach was possible precisely because by then there were two scripts, and some of the semantic and syntactic rules were known. Similarly, when Freud earlier drew his famous parallel between archaeology and hysteria, he allowed his hypothetical explorer the luxury of obtaining his information about "the events of the remote past" through the successful deciphering of *bilingual* inscriptions (Freud 1896c, p. 192; cf. Breuer and Freud 1895, p. 129).

Solving a Rebus Freud's much commented-on comparison of the dream with a rebus is similarly misleading, or perhaps is construed in a misleading way. Both the manifest dream and the rebus are nonsensical of course, but Freud does not say that a dream *is* a rebus but that it is "a picture puzzle *of this sort*" (Freud 1900, p. 278. My emphasis). He could not have gone farther. A rebus is solved by replacing its pictorial elements with other elements (syllables and words) from a language already known to the reader. It is not a script in another language as much as a variant and peculiar orthography of the one language. So, when making the substitutions, the puzzle solver at least knows the rules governing the language into which the "translation" is to be made. The rules or conventions followed by the rebus maker can be discovered and may be known partly beforehand, as they often are to inveterate puzzle and cryptic crossword enthusiasts (cf. Wohlgemuth 1923, pp. 65–67).[1]

Little of what is done in solving a rebus can really be applied to dream translation. According to Freud, the dream translator has to compare "the original and the translation" to discover the "characters and syntactic laws" of the manifest content and so make the dream thoughts "immediately comprehensible" (Freud 1900, p. 277). But, it is precisely that comparison that cannot be made. There is no original. The second script of the dream thoughts does not exist in advance of the "translation."

A Second Script?   Fifty years after Freud's death the meaning of the second script, if it exists, remains elusive. Of the popularity of Lacan's formulation of the unconscious as a language, the Italian philologist Timpanaro remarked:

It is a matter for wonder that, for all the talk so little—if any—progress has been made in the formulation of the rules which must then govern the logic, grammar and lexis of the unconscious.   (Timpanaro 1974/1976, p. 221)

It would obviously be absurd, he went on,

to expect a kind of standardized grammar of the unconscious ... in which everything was rational and relied on a one-to-one correspondence between signifier and signified.... But however unencumbered and free-ranging, this language must still have its code.   (p. 221)

One cannot but agree. Again it follows that it would be ludicrous to try and test psychoanalytic translators in the same way as the Royal Asiatic Society tested the early translators of cuneiform. There is no other language to translate into.

Psychoanalysis as Interpretation

Under "interpretation" I evaluate the use to which psychoanalysts put the *sets* of elements already deciphered or translated after having been retrieved by free association.

Generally, psychoanalysts regard interpreted data as more relevant than observational data to testing psychoanalytic propositions. Two problems have to be considered. The first is the extent to which psychoanalysts can agree on the interpretation of a given behavior, a dream, or a symptom. That is, how reliably can interpretations be made? The second is whether the interpretation is valid: is it true or correct? Except for this second question, some of what I have considered as translation could just as easily have been discussed here.

The Reliability of Interpretations   We saw in chapter 9 no rules are available for interpreting dreams. From that fact alone we would not expect psychoanalysts to be very reliable in their other interpretations, an expectation confirmed in the variety of reinterpretations of Freud's and Dora's dreams reported in chapter 9 and in the various interpretations of masochistic behavior presented in chapter 12. More formal studies of reliability are also consistent with these expectations. Most of the studies to about 1969 were examined by Wallerstein and Sampson (1971) in the wider context of the difficulties of basing psychoanalytic research on the clinical situation, and Fonagy (1982) dealt more briefly with subsequent work. Whether the analysts who were studied considered dreams (Zane 1971), transference (Luborsky, Graff, Pulver, and Curtis 1973; Lower, Escoll, Little, and Otenberg 1973), or more general aspects of behavior in psychotherapy (Sargent 1961; Seitz 1966; Strupp, Chassan, and Ewing 1966), none was able to arrive at a system that ensured even minimal agreement among different interpreters. So recalcitrant is the problem that at least one research group, from the Chicago Institute for Psychoanalysis, gave up hope after three years and disbanded (Seitz 1966).

The Validity of Interpretations   Many analysts have stated or implied that the most appropriate place for testing the validity of psychoanalytic interpretations is the treatment setting itself (Isaacs 1939; Kubie 1952; Brenner 1955; Schmidl 1955). After the patient's behavior is interpreted, the person's subsequent behavior is examined to confirm or disconfirm the interpretation. The interpretation does not have to be told to the patient: the analyst may simply examine other aspects of the patient's more general behavior. When it is told, however, it is generally suggested that confirming or disconfirming signs be sought in some aspect of the patient's more or less immediate reaction. Psychoanalysts have discussed various problems of so using interpretation, sometimes suggesting refinements or additions, but the problems have not been resolved (Wisdom 1956, 1967; Ezriel 1951; Arlow 1959; H. Hartmann 1959; Lustman 1963; Sargent 1961; Wallerstein and Sampson 1971; Bowlby 1979, 1981; Rubinstein 1980; Edelson 1983, 1984).

The simplest way of establishing the validity of an interpretation might seem to be to take the subject's accepting it as confirmation. For example, a dream might suggest the hypothesis that a patient harbors unconscious sexual wishes for his mother. If he accepts the interpretation, it might be claimed he really has such feelings, that is, the interpretation is valid. The problem with this test is that it is indeterminate. Whether the hypothesis is true or false, it is not possible to state in advance, either from the hypothesis alone or in conjunction with other facts, whether the subject will accept or reject a given interpretation.

Consider the two bases for the subject rejecting an interpretation. Nonacceptance could mean *either* that it was incorrect *or* that it was correct but rejected because of, say, unconscious resistance. If these two reactions are difficult to distinguish, and we have reason to suppose they are, rejection is not clear evidence. On the other hand, if the subject accepts the interpretation it does not necessarily mean it is valid. It is not only possible to envisage a patient accepting an incorrect interpretation, but we have many notorious instances of agreement with false interpretations to show it is an actuality. For example, Freud's patients agreed they had been seduced, Rank's that the trauma of their births caused their present anxiety, and so on.

Wisdom (1967) pointed to the major problem of finding a way of ruling suggestion out from the confirmation. He formulated criteria that he thought would enable the analyst to do just that, but I believe their use would not have detected what happened in Mendel's "experiment." Mendel examined the effects of false interpretations in what appears to be the only investigation relating to this kind of suggestion. On each of six different days he offered four patients one of six different and spurious interpretations of their behavior. On any particular day the interpretation was the same for each patient and was made exactly ten minutes into the therapeutic session, irrespective of the content of the discussion at that time. On twenty of the twenty-four occasions, the patients experienced "enhancement of understanding ... and a forward movement in the therapeutic transaction" (Mendel 1964).

Mendel's "experiment" matches psychoanalytic practice. By the mid-1930s it became apparent that psychoanalysts varied considerably in the ways they used interpretation, including what and how they interpreted, but that outcomes depended only broadly on variation in this and other technical procedures (Glover 1937). Psychoanalysts now agree that interpretations may have positive effects whether they correspond to what is actually the case or not. Nor is suggestion excluded when interpretations are true: "truth is not even *necessary* for therapeutic efficiency" (Sherwood 1969, p. 250; cf. Glover 1931b, 1954, 1968; Schmideberg 1939; Ezriel 1951; Barratt 1976; Spence 1976, 1982a; Eagle 1980a; Reppen 1982; Wetzler 1985; Sass and Woolfolk 1988).

Reactions more complex than acceptance and rejection have also been proposed but the logical problems remain. True or false, an interpretation may be rejected or accepted, have no agreed-on effect, or produce a positive effect. It therefore is an uninformative test of psychoanalytic hypotheses.

Pseudoconfirmation Glover drew attention to the fact that because analysts did not apply to their observational data such controls as were appropriate:

a great deal of what passes as attested theory is little more than idle speculation, varying widely in plausibility.   (Glover 1952)

He stressed how "in any given case interpretation is an essential part of the process of psycho-analytical investigation" before adding

that nevertheless there is as yet no effective control of conclusions based on interpretation, is the Achilles heel of psycho-analytical research.   (op. cit.)

He pointed particularly to the way the uncertainties of the interpretive situation encouraged acceptance of the views of senior and prestigious psychoanalysts rather than the adoption of scientifically established propositions. Nearly twenty years later Wallerstein and Sampson (1971) said that appeal to authority was still common.

Adding to these problems, Rapaport reported that the absence of rules led to pseudoconfirmations:

We must be wary lest we smuggle in the confirmation (of the prediction) through the interpretation. Axiomatization and/or a canon of investigation protect other sciences from such circularity ... as things stand, there is no canon whereby valid interpretation can be distinguished from speculation, though *ex post facto* the experienced clinician can distinguish them well. (Rapaport 1960)

Not everyone would share Rapaport's faith in the virtue of experience.

Among the factors Glover discussed that militated against research in psychoanalysis was the undue neglect of criteria "to control the validity of interpretation" (Glover 1952). Such canons as have since been suggested, for example, the system Sargent, Horwitz, Wallerstein, and Sampson (1968) outlined for avoiding circularity, V. H. Rosen's (1969) ten criteria for helping to judge the validity of interpretations, and Rubinstein's (1980) more recent description of the kinds of behavior that could confirm an interpretation. Not only have they not been adopted, they have been widely criticized or resisted (Fonagy 1982; A. H. Kaplan 1981). Consequently, we do not know if any of those of the "findings" about personality that are based on interpreted data could meet any of them. Even when Freud's material is used, it is possible to provide a detailed reanalysis of a case like that of Little Hans—the first Oedipus—as not verifying "the classical theory of the Oedipus complex" (Garrison 1978, cf. Fromm 1970).

The Double Construction   What hardly anyone notices in discussions about rules for interpreting dreams and symptoms is that the latent content is actually *constructed* during interpretation, rather than *discovered* by it. No rules can be established for arriving at a correct interpretation because the absence of a second script prevents any from ever being formulated.

What Freud did when he interpreted a dream was to use *the same material*—the patient's (and his own) associations—to construct *both* the dream thoughts *and* the rules for transforming them. The latent dream is "not a dream at all but an interpretive construction" (Foulkes 1978, p. 45). Put another way, Freud's method of interpreting a dream is equivalent to attempting to solve "a single equation with two unknowns" (Spence 1986).

Weiss pointed out that when Freud made this dual use of associations he was "having his cake and eating it too" (Weiss 1974). The question is, is it possible to develop rules for revealing the meaning of a yet-to-exist second script when the meaning of the first also depends on them? In believing it can be done for dreams, Foulkes probably became a Micawber (Foulkes 1978, pp. 15–17, 45–46, 114–119). No one has suggested how it might be done for symptoms or parapraxes.

It is therefore inevitable, not just surprising, that psychoanalysts do so poorly on tests where they compare their interpretations of the same phenomenon. As simple in principle as that test might seem, success requires something that no one can have: knowledge of a second language that does not exist apart from the interpretation. Failures to agree on interpretations are therefore not matters to be explained away because of the complexities of human behavior, the obscurities of psychoanalytic propositions, or the poor quality of the analytic training in the interpretive arts. No matter how skilled the analyst, how simple the behavior, and how clear the theoretical proposition, without a second script existing independent of the interpretation, agreement can never be reached. Timpanaro's stark implication cannot be avoided: "not even the analyst" is able to interpret the "messages" conveyed from the unconscious by symptoms, dreams, and parapraxes (Timpanaro 1974/1976, p. 221).

Perhaps it is as well that psychoanalysts were, and have remained, "entirely ignorant of the attitude and knowledge with which a philologist would approach such a problem as that presented by dreams" (Freud 1913e, p. 177). Only by doing so have they been able to maintain their pose as guides along the royal road to the unconscious. For as long as no second script exists, not only can there be no rules for interpretation, but pseudoconfirmations and appeals to authority will prevent secure findings about personality functioning and development ever being established.[2]

Psychoanalysis as Construction

Freud used the word "construction" to refer to the picture he built of some incident he thought important in the patient's life but that the patient recollected not at all or only in part. Construction differs from translation and interpretation in that it necessarily draws on several sets of interpretations, each of which is based in turn on a large number of translated elements obtained by free association.[3]

Freud claimed that when a suppositional construction was put to a patient, the previously forgotten real event was sometimes recalled. This use of a construction can be illustrated from his own case of the Rat Man:

I ventured to put forward a construction to the effect that when he was a child of under six he had been guilty of some sexual misdemeanour connected with masturbation and had been soundly castigated for it by his father. This punishment, according to my hypothesis, had, it was true, put an end to his masturbating, but on the other hand it had left behind it an ineradicable grudge against his father and had established him for all time in his role of an interferer with the patient's sexual enjoyment. To my great astonishment the patient then informed me that his mother had repeatedly described to him an occurrence of this kind which dated from his earliest childhood and had evidently escaped being forgotten by her on account of its remarkable consequences. He himself, however, had no recollection of it whatever. (Freud 1909b, p. 205)

The actual event the patient described was similar to the suppositional one Freud had put to him: for the only time in his life, his father had beaten him. The similarity was taken as confirming those parts of psychoanalytic theory from which the construction derived, for example, that the Rat Man had unconscious feelings of hostility toward his father. Other analysts have observed similar effects from putting constructions to their patients, and those effects have been considered as going some way toward establishing the validity of free association.

Constructions, Truth, and Recall The significance of the reaction to constructions is only one of the issues involved in their use. Two others are the accuracy of what the patient recalls and the likely truth of the construction itself. Consider first whether the incident could really have happened in the way it is recalled, either wholly or partly. Psychoanalysts who discuss constructions are generally as skeptical of their veridicality as of the reality of the "recollections" they engender.

As early as 1956 E. Kris said it was hopeless to expect a construction to recreate exactly what happened in the patient's remote past. Memories were so modified by later experience that one could not say what the original incident actually was (E. Kris 1956). This opinion is shared by a large number of psychoanalysts (e.g., Klauber 1968; Arlow 1981; Spence and Geha, both cited in Messer 1986). As Gill told Reppen, reconstructions change during the relatively short period of analysis, and analysts usually made insufficient distinction between the recovery of the event and the patient's experience of it. He then observed, "The past cannot be revived as such but only in terms of the present" (Reppen 1982). These views of contemporary psychoanalysts are at one with the findings of experimental psychologists from Bartlett (1932) to Loftus and Loftus (1980). Memories are not like photographs that fade but do not really change. A personality theory cannot be made from them.

As to the likely truth of the constructions themselves, there is a good deal of psychoanalytic opinion against even the ones Freud suggested to his patients being veridical. Schimek (1987) found most of the seduction memories and all of the important early events in the cases of Little Hans and the Wolf Man to be constructions, and that all of the memories were in fact false. Most analysts would take a position on veridicality somewhere between Klauber and Spence or Skura. Klauber (1968) judged all constructions inevitably partial, but pointed only to "gaps" in the constructions Freud made about the Wolf Man. Decidedly more skeptical, Spence called Freud's constructions about the Wolf Man "invention" (Spence 1980; cf. Ahlskog 1980), and Skura seems to have dismissed them all as "delusive" (cited in Kermode 1985). Others vacillated. For example, Blum, who regards construction as "fundamental" in analysis, confidently constructed the pre-Oedipal events of *Freud's* own childhood at the same time as suggesting that important "corrections" were necessary to Freud's picture of the Wolf Man's childhood (Blum 1977, 1980, 1982).

The main issues regarding constructions are summarized by Laufer. A reconstruction is not the same as an infantile experience, transference experiences are not the same experiences as with the patient's parents, and fantasies obtained during treatment do not have the original content. To believe otherwise were pitfalls "which have more recently bedeviled and continued to weaken the use of our clinical data when formulating the nature and history of a specific psychopathology" (Laufer 1982).

What is really fundamental is a consequence of the paradox M. T. McGuire (1971, p. 3) outlines: the unconscious takes "once conscious perceptions, thoughts, and feelings" and changes them, often beyond recognition. That is, once again we have the absence of an independent second script, which in this case means there cannot be a true memory to be reconstructed.

Psychoanalysis as Narration

Sherwood (1969) argued that the core psychoanalytic explanation was a narrative account of behavior throughout an extended period of the individual's life. The narrative explanation is very different from explanations that were deductions from a covering law. It differs in its scope from a construction in that it is not restricted to a single incident, but usually covers a substantial part of the patient's life. Thus it may draw on more than one construction.

Criteria for Narratives   Because no criteria were available to assess narrative explanations, Sherwood (1969) examined Freud's account of the case of Paul Lorenz (the Rat Man) to see whether, and in what sense, its narrative characterization of causal factors constituted an explanation of the patient's behavior. In essence his conclusion was that the case narrative did constitute an explanation even though the deductive model of testing could not be applied to it.

Sherwood found it difficult to specify the positive explanatory properties of Freud's narrative but he did arrive at some criteria. He thought Freud's account of the Rat Man was adequate in the sense that it was self-consistent, coherent, and comprehensive, and he judged it to be accurate in the sense that Freud's suppositions about what must have happened were in some instances confirmed by the patient's recollection. The three criteria Sherwood therefore proposed for an acceptable narrative explanation were as follows:

Appropriateness—whether the explanation occurred within a relevant framework, whether the answers it gave to specific explanatory questions were apt, and whether it was at the proper level of complexity

Adequacy—whether it was self-consistent, coherent, and comprehensive

Accuracy—whether it was true

In one of the few psychoanalytic comments on these criteria, Eagle judged that there was usually no problem with appropriateness and adequacy, but that a real difficulty was associated with accuracy or truth. His conclusions are the same as those I drew independently at about the same time (Eagle 1973, 1980a; Macmillan 1974, chapter 17). He said it is precisely with respect to accuracy that Sherwood and other psychoanalytic writers are "ambiguous and unconvincing" (1980a). Accuracy must be at the core of a genuine narrative because it alone is concerned with the truth of what happened. To say this is not to demand absolute truth. Even with a level of truth less than absolute, the problem remains of how that degree of accuracy can be assessed, and how real can be differentiated from spurious accuracy.

The Strength of Causal Factors   One reason why it is all too easy for the psychoanalytic narrative to be given spurious accuracy was acknowledged by Freud, although not in those terms. In any given set of causal factors it is not possible to specify which are the weaker or the stronger. Only a post hoc inference can be made: the strongest factors are those that bring about the outcome. No inference can be made until that outcome is known.

The dependence of the measure on the result gives the reverse reading of a case history a quite different quality from the forward reading as Freud saw:

So long as we trace the development from its final outcome backwards, the chain of events appears continuous, and we feel we have gained an insight which is completely satisfactory or even exhaustive. But if we proceed the reverse way, if we start from the premises inferred from the analysis and try to follow these up to the final result, then we no longer get the impression of an inevitable sequence of events which could not have been otherwise determined. We notice at once that there might have been another result, and that we might have been just as well able to understand and explain the latter. The synthesis is thus not so satisfactory as the analysis; in other words, from a knowledge of the premises we could not have foretold the nature of the result.

It is very easy to account for this disturbing state of affairs. Even supposing that we have a complete knowledge of the aetiological factors that decide a given result, nevertheless what we know about them is only their quality, and not their relative strength. Some of them are suppressed by others because they are too weak, and they therefore do not affect the final result. But we never know beforehand which of the determining factors will prove the weaker or the stronger. We only say at the end that those which succeeded must have been the stronger. Hence the chain of causation can always be recognized with certainty if we follow the line of analysis, whereas to predict it along the line of synthesis is impossible.   (Freud 1920b, pp. 167–168)

Wallerstein and Sampson (1971) agreed that clinical retrospective studies have this kind of circularity built in to them, and the strength of the factors at work cannot be assessed adequately. The problem, however, is more general, not limited to the clinic. Even in the simplest of situations, where one wants to say that a particular outcome is dependent only on one of the two factors being stronger, one must have a measure of strength independent of outcome. Whether the situation involves the past, the present, or the future makes absolutely no difference. In psychoanalytic studies— current, prospective, or retrospective—it is unusual to find that even crude measures of the strengths of causal factors have been attempted.

The Flexibility of Narratives   More important than the inability to measure the strength of the factors are the points made by Cioffi and Spence about what Spence calls the "flexibility" of narratives. Cioffi, in his well-known seminar, "Why We Are still Arguing about Freud," delivered at Monash University in 1981, demonstrated that not only are there no criteria for judging the correctness of psychoanalytic explanations or interpretations, but that none can be formulated. As Cioffi had done, Spence also showed that narratives are almost infinitely flexible and anything can be fit to them. Farrell's comments on Freud's study of Leonardo da Vinci aptly illustrate the point. Despite Freud's massive errors of fact about Leonardo's childhood, about the bird of his fantasy, and about the content of some of Leonardo's paintings and drawings, "we must be grateful to him for giving us a simplified case history of Leonardo." The errors do not, therefore, basically undermine the force of Freud's interpretive narrative (Farrell 1963; cf. Freud 1910b).

Narratives can also be designed to fit or illustrate any principle (Spence 1980, 1982a). Blum's plausible reconstruction of Freud's pre-Oedipal development provides a good example. Without too much difficulty he fit the data about Freud to

Mahler's developmental theses rather than to Freud's own, but he could have fit them to any one of a number of similar theories (Blum 1977).[4]

Cioffi's and Spence's position are also well illustrated by comparing Freud's analysis of Michelangelo's statue *Moses* with the later one by Bremer, even though it is properly neither a narrative nor a psychoanalytic interpretation (Freud 1914a, 1927b; Bremer 1976).[5] After spending hours looking at the statue, it came to Freud that Michelangelo represented Moses full of anger at the very moment when, hearing his backsliding flock worshipping the Golden Calf, he was about to turn against them. Having just come down from the mountain with the tablets the Lord had given him with the Commandments already inscribed on them he, proceeded to break them.

Bremer argues that Freud was completely wrong. He believes Freud's interpretation was based "on several fundamental misconceptions," the most important of which was his use of the biblical account of Moses' *first* ascent of Mount Sinai rather than the *second*. Bremer concludes that the statue really depicts Moses in the presence of the Lord after this second ascent. All of the details of the statue are consistent with his interpretation, not Freud's. For example, the tablets under Moses' arm are blank, because this time Moses is to inscribe the Commandments at the Lord's dictation, rather than receiving them already written upon. The complex of emotions with which Moses' face is suffused is also appropriate to his being the only human being to have been allowed a glimpse of the glory of God's backside.

My point is not that I find Bremer's interpretation more convincing than Freud's (which I do) but, following Cioffi and Spence, that without external referents we can have no basis for judging any interpretation as better than another, let alone which is true. Consequently, the question of whether a psychoanalytic narrative gives a true account of what happened usually cannot be answered. We all have a sense of what constitutes an improbable or ridiculous interpretation or narrative explanation, but this does not help us decide which, if any, of a number of nonridiculous and more or less plausible interpretations or narratives is likely to be true.

A number of contemporary psychoanalysts think that asking about the truth of a narrative is as irrelevant as asking about the truth of a construction or interpretation. Kermode (1985) sums up this trend by saying an interpretation is never true or false but only something that contributes to "narrative intelligibility." One of the reasons why psychoanalysis has proved so impervious to criticism is precisely because it is impossible to make choices among different degrees of this intelligibility.

The question of the truth of a narrative does matter, of course. Take, for example, Freud's response to what the Rat Man told him about being punished by his father. His father had indeed beaten him, but not for masturbating or other sexual misdemeanor. What Freud then did was to invoke a phylogenetically inherited fear of castration to account for the Rat Man's current fear. Although narrative intelligibility was undoubtedly maintained, it was not only at the expense of replacing a hypothesis that might have been true with one about which it was impossible to know anything, it also considerably altered the psychoanalytic theory of child development, surely a matter of some real importance.[6] Fisher and Greenberg also warn against therapeutic consequences. The analyst's shift from establishing "what really happened" to the persuasive "this must have happened" reconstruction used by Freud is "an open acknowledgement of suggestion occurring in the treatment" (S. Fisher and Greenberg 1977, p. 366).

Free Association and the Creation of Data

In the early part of this century no evidence was available that data generated by patients in therapy matched the theoretical expectations of their analysts. Opinions that that might be so could be matched only by a contrary opinion. There were no facts about whether and to what extent the method of free association generated its data. Thus, when Woodworth proposed that it might be the case, Tannenbaum had "no hesitation" in saying Woodworth would not be able to verify his supposition (Woodworth 1917; Tannenbaum 1917). The exchange could only be of opinion. Now, of course, Woodworth's suspicion is a commonplace.

However, in the sparse later research literature, the few who questioned the objectivity of free association were not much better off for facts than Woodworth and Tannenbaum. Zubin (1964), for example, made only the general observation that Freudian patients dreamed Freudian dreams and Jungian Jungian, wittily adding that Rogerian patients had no dreams at all. Similarly, Marmor could call only on "clinical experience" to back his claim that patients' free associations were "strongly influenced by the values and expectations of the therapist." He did repeat his earlier observation that patients produced data that confirmed the interpretations and theories of their analysts, but the only hard evidence he cited was some of the marginally relevant nonanalytic literature on so-called verbal conditioning (Marmor 1970; cf. 1962; Crichton-Miller 1945, p. 117). The situation has not changed despite discussions of the objectivity of free association subsequent to Grünbaum's attack on psychoanalytic data as hopelessly contaminated by suggestion. All that has happened *after nearly one hundred years* is that psychoanalysts have finally put the need to study the method on the agenda (Grünbaum 1980, 1984; cf. Edelson 1984; Wallerstein 1986a, 1988; Arlow and Brenner 1988).

Selecting from Data

The implications drawn by observers like Zubin and Marmor are usually limited to discussions or warnings about selectively attending to and using data. For example, Zubin (1964) made his observation only to illustrate the selective effects of verbal reinforcement on affective statements in psychotherapy. Despite holding free association responsible for the self-validating data produced by patients, Marmor (1970) went only as far as recommending it not be relied on as the sole technique.

That psychoanalysts use their data selectively is widely recognized. For example, A. Kris almost casually granted that analysts impose their "personal proclivities and education" in selecting, interpreting, and using the data obtained by free association. He also seemed to have no doubts that personal factors were responsible for the variant forms of psychoanalysis (A. Kris 1983; cf. 1982). It actually was proposed that this kind of selection is inevitable and may be inherent in the therapeutic situation itself. According to Ahlskog (1980), the analyst cannot fully understand associations unless they fit into a context. Therefore a contradiction exists between the associations being generated freely by the patient and the analyst finding a context for them while maintaining an evenly suspended attention. This way of "fitting" seems to me to involve selection.

The Source of Variant Theories

More important than whether psychoanalysts selectively attend to and use the data gathered by free association for the foundations of their particular theories, is the question of whether free-association per se creates the data from which variant theories are built. Two questions about Rank's birth trauma theory provide an illustration: how did Rank's patients come to recollect the traumas of their own births, and how was it that Ferenczi was able to confirm Rank's "observations" but Freud was not? (Freud 1926a, pp. 135–136, 151–153, 161–162; E. Jones 1953–1957, vol. 3, pp. 58–77; H. C. Abraham and E. L. Freud 1965, Letter of March 4, 1924, Freud to Abraham).

One explanation of the Rank debacle is to say Rank and Ferenczi selectively retrieved particular ideas from an overall store. Another is that all the ideas were retrieved, but that Rank based his theory on only a subset of them and Ferenczi simply followed him. Mixtures of these explanations are possible, but note the basic assumption they share: all the material was there, waiting to be recovered or used. Consequently, if faulty theories were constructed, it must have been because the predilections of the analysts selectively influenced the material retrieved or that they made idiosyncratic use of it. In either view, free association could not have created the data on which Rank's theory was based. That method was as objective a device for collecting data as the microscope or telescope.

Constructions based on free association are central to many of the important modern variant theories of psychoanalysis, and it could also be argued that only personal influence in the retrieval or use of data was responsible for them. An implication of the opinions of a number of psychoanalysts must be counterpoised. In an extensive review of the main psychoanalytic theories of child development, S. Brody mentioned one result of the "primary technique" of psychoanalysis being "verbal and associative" was that too great a reliance was placed on reconstructions. She urged that they be drawn on sparingly and preferably only when direct observation was not possible. She concluded that the observational basis of all the developmental theories was questionable, and believed her conclusion was especially important for evaluating the imaginative constructive speculations of Balint, Kohut, and Kernberg (S. Brody 1982). Holder similarly dismissed Melanie Klein's view of superego functioning: it was "unfounded in the light of general developmental principles as well as observational and clinical data" (Holder 1982). Others similarly identified the questionable bases of Melanie Klein's theories as well as those of Margaret Mahler and the ego-psychologists (T. Shapiro 1981; Warme 1982; Wallerstein 1986b). Bowlby drew the more general conclusion that "Although psychoanalysis is avowedly a developmental discipline, it is nowhere weaker ... than in its concepts of development," a weakness he put down to the "pride of place" given reconstructions over what developmental psychology had established (Bowlby 1981).

Reconstruction had, of course, a central place in Freud's developmental theory. Although Freud (1914b, p. 90) admitted he had no direct evidence of primary narcissism, Steele and Jacobsen note how he

rests easy when everything has been traced back to the original objectless state of primary narcissism and the primary process, since for him this is the ultimate foundation. For the reader, though, it is the ultimate in speculation.   (Steele and Jacobsen 1977)

They call Freud's inferentially constructed narcissistic state "a purely theoretical [concept] ... without any direct link to observation."

What these criticisms amount to is that the basic data, that is, the basic facts of psychoanalysis, are at variance with reality. For the most part, these psychoanalysts are not proposing a check with some standard method for using free association or an agreed-on system of interpretation or construction, but a comparison with what actually takes place during development, with what exists. What they question is the objectivity of the method itself.

In recently placing the question of investigating psychoanalytic methods on the agenda, Arlow and Brenner revived the possibility that free association may create its data. After asking how the same observations could give rise to different theories, they comment:

It has been suggested more than once that the differences ... so apparent to every observer, may stem from the fact that the data of observation are not, in truth, the same. In fact, they are often very different.   (Arlow and Brenner 1988)

However, rather than biting this bullet, what they do is to advance what are in this context specious arguments about differences within disciplines being dependent on technique (e.g., astronomical theories based on the telescope versus those not, theories of infection using the microscope or not). All they can then plead for, but without being unduly optimistic about its realization, is the standardization of the psychoanalytic method of investigation. In one sense they have advanced little beyond Brenner's earlier critical remarks that the source of Melanie Klein's theory was the ease with which the analyst can find in a patient's associations anything that was postulated in advance. Nor is it much different from Scott's reply to similar methodological criticism: he proposed "more detailed observations of *memories* of infantile states" as a source of evidence (!) about primary narcissism (Scott 1952)

So considerable is the investment in the verbal and associative technique of free association, I would not expect Arlow and Brenner to do much more than they have, namely, confuse reliability with validity. Agreement on how the method is to be used or on how the material retrieved is to be translated and interpreted or fit into a construction, narrative, or causal explanation does nothing to establish its objectivity. The issue remains of whether or not the observations made with it are true.

Choosing among Variant Theories

Were only a personal selection of data involved in the construction of variant theories, that could be taken into account when evaluating them. To judge from the famous closed debate that took place in London during 1940 and 1950 between Melanie Klein and Anna Freud and their respective followers, the matter is more complex. In Steiner's (1985) otherwise comprehensive account of this debate, which must rank with the longest and most concentrated within any field, not a single reference is made to a psychoanalytical fact or observation that might have helped resolve the considerable differences between the two positions.

This failure to cite facts was probably because they were not thought important. In the discussions Home attended he observed that cases were presented "to confirm hypotheses rather than to test them." When there were disagreements, the appeal was "almost invariably to 'the literature' and not to the fact," a procedure having "no parallel ... in any other science." With this went the declaration that different views arose simply because different psychoanalysts spoke "different languages." To him, that attitude seemed "a monstrous abdication of intellectual responsibility" (Home 1966).

The failure may also have been connected with inability to use such facts as were available. Describing an address he gave to the British Psycho-Analytic Society during that time, Masserman recalled how

some members of opposing factions of the Society, neatly marshalled on opposite sides of an aisle that divided the room, insisted on indulging in polemics about various Freudian *versus* Kleinian dogmas by using my data almost completely out of context.   (Masserman 1959b)

Opinion was very polarized and the discussion period was, Masserman said, "far more memorable than the lecture."

Does this mean that controversy about differences between analytical theories is fundamentally different from scientific controversy? Holt (1982) seems to imply that Freud himself provided a positive answer. He says of Balmary's arguments in her book, *Freud and the Hidden Fault of the Father*, "Like Freud himself, she seems more concerned with rhetoric than science, aiming at convincing with persuasive words rather than refuting conjectures or testing hypotheses."

The present situation does not seem to be much different. For example, no facts can be adduced to allow a choice between Kohut and the traditional Freudians or between either of them and Kernberg.[7] When Simon expressed his pessimism as to the possibility of clinical data conclusively settling debates about the validity of psychoanalytic theory, he added he preferred it that way, and his preference was endorsed by Schafer (both in Sacks 1985). In the same discussion Sacks went so far as to praise the method of free association precisely because it was "a prime guarantor of freedom from the tyranny of any one theory" (Sacks 1985). Similarly, Breger denied Freud's claim of objectivity for the psychoanalytic method ("The process is not analogous to looking at cells under a microscope") and granted that only "in very general ways" would analytic observers agree about their observations (Breger 1981).

Some resist the appeal to facts even when they are available. Others reinterpret them, as Burgner's group did. Those analysts found evidence of what seemed to be Oedipal fears and desires as well as post-Oedipal latency in children raised in the absence of their fathers. They did not regard their findings as confirming Freud's view of the centrality of the Oedipus complex. They called what they saw "pseudo-Oedipal" and "pseudo-latency" behaviors (Burgner 1985). What also do we make of those who, like Wallerstein (1985), endorse the psychoanalytic method as providing "an immensely powerful method for the study of human memory" at the same time as having the resource (or effrontery) to cite Grünbaum's criticism of it in support? Reiser as well as Wallerstein seems to believe the method has "enormous heuristic value" for generating testable hypotheses, despite the centrality of Grünbaum's charge that the observations made with it are massively contaminated by suggestion! (Reiser, summarized in Wallerstein 1985).

Conclusion

For Freud to have faced the Rank affair squarely would have required him to question the laws that he thought determined psychological phenomena in the treatment situation, and to develop a more sophisticated understanding of how unconscious influences operated. The same consideration holds for the authors of the variant theories of psychoanalysis.

What experimental data we possess on verbal influence, what we know about the fabrication of memories under hypnosis, what we know about pseudosciences such as scientology, and what we glean from comparisons of different psychotherapies lead to the conclusion that each psychotherapy creates its own data. In this respect, psychoanalytic therapy seems no different from others. No evidence shows that only the patient's unconscious ideas guide the trains of associations in psychoanalytic treatment, and no evidence exists that the analyst's conscious purposive ideas, supposedly abandoned, play no role. Everything is consistent with the method of free association creating its own data, and nothing is consistent with those data being obtained by means of an objective method and then interpreted in a partial or biased way.

Notes

1. I owe this apt clarification of a rebus to Dr. D. C. Bradley. Recognizing that it is not a second language at all but only a variant form of writing has much deeper consequences than Jones's criticism that the rebus is consciously designed to dissemble. That criticism points only to the inconsistency of dream work that is logical (R. M. Jones 1965, 1970/1978, pp. 7–9).

2. Arlow and Brenner (1988) have recently voiced the heresy, "Experience has by now convinced the majority of analysts that dreams and their interpretations are not the high road to the unconscious mental life that Freud first thought them to be." However, their assertion seems not to be based on evidence or on recognition of the failure of the linguistic parallel.

3. The word "reconstruction" came into the psychoanalytic literature some time after Freud's term, but is usually regarded as a synonym for it (McGuire 1971). According to Greenacre (1980, 1981), neither term had much currency ten years ago.

4. The data about Freud are not very secure, and it says something about the standards of psychoanalytic judgment that Blum's paper was taken seriously enough to appear in a leading psychoanalytical journal.

5. As Ricoeur so strongly emphasizes, the method by which Freud analyzes the statue is exactly the same as the way he analyzes dreams. In view of Bremer's demonstration, it is perhaps unfortunate that Ricoeur also contends it is appropriately and genuinely analytic and that the psychoanalytic method is verified by it (Ricoeur 1970, pp. 167–169, 1969/1974, pp. 138–139, 201–202).

6. Glymour's argument that this incident demonstrates how oriented Freud was to empirical test has been endorsed by a number of analysts. What Freud did seems to me, however, a little different from that to be expected from someone genuinely interested in formulating testable hypotheses (Glymour 1974, 1980; cf. Edelson 1984; Schlessinger 1986).

7. Glassman's (1988) questionnaire-based attempt to provide just such evidence fails, in my view, because the questionnaires contain too many items of unknown validity. The differences he predicts may also not be specific enough.

16 Psychoanalysis as Science

When a truth becomes a fact it loses all its intellectual value.
—Wilde: *A Few Maxims for the Instruction of the Over-Educated*

It is easy to predict three of the responses to my criticism. They will begin in the following way:

What Macmillan says about psychoanalysis is old hat. Everyone, or at least those who matter, has known for a long time that Freud was no theorist. Since his time, psychoanalysis has developed into a theory very different from Freud's. Macmillan's criticisms are as irrelevant as those made by others before him because they miss this point.

To this I rejoin, what is this new theory and where is it set out? Where is the evidence that it has superseded Freud's? Where is the demonstration of its superiority over the original?

The simple facts are that no one has established an agreed-on comprehensive alternative to Freud's formulations. None of the many partial reformulations I considered earlier in passing command much assent. They are as flawed as Freud's, and the clinical and observational evidence relevant to them is just as weak.

Left as stated, this first response appeals to the traditionalist who wants only to develop or refine Freud's theory in the light of modern knowledge. Those who want psychoanalysis to be a different kind of science from Freud's expand it into the second of the probable responses:

Macmillan's criticisms miss the point because psychoanalysis is certainly not and probably was not even intended as a scientific discipline in the mold of the natural sciences. Rather than causal explanations of behavior, what psychoanalysis provides is understanding of how reasons or motives explain people's behavior. This kind of understanding gives an explanation, perhaps even a scientific one, but not a natural science one.

Expanding on my first rejoinder, the fact is that Freud treats motives and reasons as causes in his explanations, and those explanations are not different from natural science ones.

The third likely comment is a development of the first two: it denies scientific status to psychoanalysis altogether.

To treat psychoanalysis in the way Macmillan does misses the point that it is not a science at all. What psychoanalysis gives is an understanding of behavior and feelings, possibly an empathic understanding at that, rather than an explanation of them. Psychoanalysis is properly to be compared with literature, history, or the hermeneutic enterprises rather than with any of the sciences. Like them, it seeks to build a coherent picture through which the individual may understand his or her uniqueness. It is not at all concerned with general laws. Macmillan is irrelevant because he misunderstands its true nature.

Those who make this assessment do so from positions that are among the most modern of the contemporary versions of psychoanalysis. They also misunderstand the roles of reasons and motives in Freud's explanations, and they overlook the similarity between historical narratives and scientific explanations. Their representation of psychoanalysis as a historical or hermeneutic enterprise is based on restricting what Freud meant by "meaning," on glossing over problems in constructing coherent accounts of the patient's past, and on preventing psychoanalysis from having developmental significance.

What I want to do in this final chapter is develop these rejoinders and offer a more detailed rebuttal of the arguments of irrelevance and misconstrual. I begin by considering what Freud himself said about the status of psychoanalysis as a natural science before exploring some of the senses in which psychoanalysis is said not to be a science. I conclude with some brief speculations about the bases for the continuing appeal of a theory and a practice about which one can say so very little that is positive.

Psychoanalysis a Science?

Against the claim that psychoanalysis is not a natural science, what are we to make of Freud's belief that it was? Could he have been massively self-deluded, or did he simply misunderstand the nature of his life's work? These seem to me to be such important questions that I first examine Freud's own characterization of psychoanalysis. I do this in some detail, because those who believe that psychoanalysis is other than a natural science tend to cite one or two of Freud's remarks in isolation rather than to examine his position as a whole.

Freud's View of Psychoanalysis

Detailed documentation of Freud's insistence that psychoanalysis was a natural science hardly seems necessary. His earliest work on neuroses applied Pasteur's germ theory and Koch's postulates, albeit defectively, to a search for causes. When he turned to hysteria, he used the same methodological precepts for the same causal purpose. One of his arguments for the direct causal status of the memories of the hysteric came from the effects of abreaction supposedly reversing the Latin dictum *Cessante causa cessat effectus* [when the cause ceases, the effect ceases] (Breuer and Freud 1893, p. 7; Freud 1893a, p. 35). And what could put Freud's early allegiance to science more clearly than the opening sentence of his 1895 *Project* where he announced his intention of founding "a psychology that shall be a natural science" (Freud 1950/1954, *Project*, part 1, section 1). Later on, after psychoanalysis proper had developed, he spoke over and over again, without any qualification or doubt, of psychoanalysis as a science. Repeatedly he referred to it as our young science, our new science, or eventually simply as our science, and the brief definition he most often gave of psychoanalysis was that it was the science of unconscious mental processes.

Science and Psychoanalysis at Work   The details of Freud's descriptions of psychoanalytic work all match exactly what he said about the other natural sciences. Thus, psychoanalysis shared the empirical outlook of science, "like every other natural science, it is based on a patient and tireless elaboration of facts from the world of perception" (Freud 1925c, p. 217). In particular, there were no sources of knowledge "other than the intellectual working-over of carefully scrutinized observations ... and ... no knowledge derived from revelation, intuition or divination" (Freud 1933b, p. 159). Psychoanalysis did not have a *Weltanschauung* of its own and had no need to construct one. It was part of science and accepted science's *Weltanschauung* (Freud 1933b, pp. 158–159, 181).

Psychoanalysis had the same basic aim of physics in wanting to go behind the world of perceptual appearance and create a picture "which approximates more closely to what may be supposed to be the real state of affairs" (Freud 1940a, p. 196). It commended itself because of the truths it established about human nature (Freud 1933b, pp. 156–157). In many other places Freud put a similar stress on the empirical character of psychoanalysis and its natural-science realist aims (e.g., Freud 1914b, p. 77, 1915a, p. 117, 1926c, p. 266, 1940a, pp. 158, 196).

The uncertain way in which any science developed was also responsible for the uncertainties in the theoretical ideas of psychoanalysis (Freud 1915a, p. 117). Freud met the charge of uncertainty by comparing this with "all sciences," at various places specifically citing physics, chemistry, zoology, botany, and biology (Freud 1916–1917, p. 102, 1925a, pp. 57–58, 1940a, pp. 158–159, 196). Where basic psychoanalytic concepts were "nebulous, scarcely imaginable," he defended them by saying that they were not

the foundation of science, upon which everything rests: that foundation is observation alone. They are not the bottom but the top of the whole structure, and they can be replaced and discarded without damaging it. The same thing is happening in our day in the science of physics.   (Freud 1914b, p. 77; cf. 1925a, pp. 32–33, 58, 1926c, p. 266)

He complained that he had "always felt it as a gross injustice that people have refused to treat psychoanalysis like any other science" by demanding greater sufficiency and completeness from it than was possible (Freud 1925a, p. 58; cf. 1940a, pp. 158–159).

A Science of Mental Processes   Freud made a special point of arguing that psycho-analysis was not different from other sciences because it dealt with mental processes:

the intellect and the mind are objects for scientific research in exactly the same way as any non-human things.   (Freud 1933b, p. 159)

In studying the mind, psychoanalysts filled the gaps in their observations in the same way physicists did with their experiments: they inferred "a number of processes which are in themselves 'unknowable' and interpolate them in those that are conscious to us" (Freud 1940a, p. 196–197; cf. 1940b, p. 286). It was exactly those interpolations that gave psychoanalysis its understanding of symptoms, dreams, and parapraxes, and that established it a science (Freud 1925a, p. 47, 1940a, p. 158). It made a special contribution to science just because it approached unconscious mentation like any other scientific phenomenon: "Its contribution to science lies precisely in having extended research to the mental field" (Freud 1933b, p. 159).

In only one respect was the analogy with other sciences incomplete. Psychoanalytic observations on "the psychical apparatus" were made through "the medium of the same perceptual apparatus." Although important, the difference was not fundamental. It was precisely the breaks in the sequence of psychical events that enabled psychoanalysts to fill them in

by making plausible inferences and translating it into conscious material.... The relative certainty of our psychical science is based on the binding force of these inferences.   (Freud 1940a, p. 159)

The difference was trivial, "everyone ... has his opinion on psychological questions" (Freud 1940b, pp. 282–283).[1] Thus it was not necessary to find a special place for psychoanalysis: "Psychology, too, is a natural science. What else can it be?" (Freud 1940b, pp. 282).

Psychoanalysis and Scientific Achievement   When Freud publicly claimed a place for himself in the pantheon of the gods of science it was not merely because of vanity or because he wished to lay the foundation for a myth, although both of those motives undoubtedly contributed. Science, he said, delivered three blows to mankind's narcissism. Copernicus gave the cosmological blow when he removed the earth on which man stood from the center of the solar system. Darwin struck the biological blow when he toppled human beings from their position of domination over the other animals. Psychoanalysis delivered what was "probably the most wounding" blow of all, the psychological one, when it discovered the ego was not master of the sexual instinctual drives and the unconscious processes in its own house (Freud 1917b, pp. 139–144; cf. 1925c, p. 221). Of course Freud was not installed as the equal of

Copernicus and Darwin by some impersonal other; he conferred the honor himself. But, whatever else he may have done, he made what was probably his strongest claim for psychoanalysis being a natural science.

Freud matched his publicly declared beliefs with his private. We see this most strikingly in his reply to the wishes Albert Einstein extended to him on his ninetieth birthday. Einstein remarked that he had not been able to form a definite opinion about the amount of truth in Freud's ideas until he heard of some instances he thought could be explained only by repression. He was delighted, he told Freud, "since it is always delightful when a great and beautiful conception proves to be consonant with reality." Freud concurred with this realist interpretation of his theories in his reply: "I have often asked myself what indeed there is to be admired in them if they are not true, i.e. if they do not contain a large measure of truth" (Letters of Einstein to Freud of Apr. 21, 1936 and Freud to Einstein of May 3, 1936, cited in E. Jones, vol. 3, pp. 203–204).

At the time of his ninetieth birthday Freud was proposed for Corresponding Membership of the Royal Society, and some time after his election, the Secretaries brought the society's official Charter Book to him for him to sign (E. Jones, vol. 3, pp. 206, 234). In describing the visit to Arnold Zweig, Freud added:

They left a facsimile of the book with me and if you were here I could show you the signatures, from I. Newton to Charles Darwin. Good company! (Letter of Freud to A. Zweig of June 28, 1938, in E. L. Freud 1970)

Could he have been as wrong about psychoanalysis as his modern self-appointed interpreters would have us believe?

Alternatives to a Natural Science

Some psychoanalytic critics of Freud want to give up one or more of Freud's metapsychological viewpoints. Although a few want to maintain psychoanalysis as a natural science, many do not. In its place some offer science, but of a different kind, whereas others willingly abandon its scientific pretensions altogether. What opposes Freud's view of psychoanalysis as a natural science, then, is not a unitary argument but rather a number of separate arguments made up of different components. Most of the critics question the analyst's primary task. For some, that role is to understand mental processes rather than explain them in the ordinary way of science. Others wish to give meaning to the individual's thoughts, feelings, and behaviors by interpreting them or explicating the reasons, motives, or intentions underpinning them. Still others wish to generate narrative accounts of the individual more akin to those of the historian.

More than rejection of natural science standards is involved in most of these positions. All place an exceptional importance on subjectivity in one or more of the ways in which they define the area to be studied, the choice of methods by which it is to be investigated, or the standards by which their end product is to be evaluated. The emphasis is not accidental. We will see in our seriatim examination of the central components of these concerns that most feed off an avowed or disguised Cartesian dualism.

Understanding versus Explaining

Contrasting what we now term understanding with explaining goes back to at least renaissance times (Klauber 1968; Grolnick 1982). The contrast was introduced into psychology by Dilthey (1894/1977) and to psychiatry by Jaspers (1959/1962), and the two were first represented as opposites by Jaspers. He believed that the natural sciences contained rules, higher-level laws, and general causal connections that the sciences aimed to grasp. Psychology, on the other hand, had only rules and particular causal connections. Partly for that reason, it had to have a different aim that, Jaspers argued, was to understand empathically how one psychological event emerged out of another. He called this type of empathic understanding "genetic." He said the evidence for genetic understanding was of an ultimate kind. It carried

its own power of conviction and it is a pre-condition of the psychology of meaningful phenomena that we accept this kind of evidence just as acceptance of the reality and of causality is the pre-condition of the natural sciences.   (Jaspers 1959/1962, p. 302)

The sense of conviction was not acquired inductively through repeated experience, but "*on the occasion* of confronting human personality."

There are three parts to Jaspers's argument. First, he represents science as a completely inductive enterprise that arrives at its explanations purely through the study of particular instances. He then asserts that psychology is unable to move beyond the particular and has to use a different method. Finally, he jumps to the conclusion that that method has to be understanding. Each part can be disputed.

Hypotheses and Facts   Jaspers's version of scientific endeavor is a misleading high school one. Not even at the level of gathering data for the formulation of rules and laws has any science ever been purely empirical and based solely on inductive inquiry. Whether scientific or not, one's inquiry is always guided by concepts and hypotheses.

   What really seems to happen in scientific inquiry is that the scientist begins with a more or less clearly posed question and formulates some more or less clear and tentative hypotheses that might lead to answers. The hypotheses then guide a more or less clearly structured program for gathering and interpreting data. In the program, judgments are continuously made about the relevance of the data. Relevance here means that the fact or relation is logically related to the tentative hypothesis; that is, its occurrence or nonoccurrence may be deduced from the hypothesis. Consequently, in real scientific inquiry there is a continuous interplay between fact and hypothesis, between induction and deduction.

The inductive method also stops precisely at the point of most interest, that of formulating explanatory theoretical concepts. Consider Freud's mechanism of repression, for example, and the nonfactual notions of "unconscious wish," "disposition," and "libido" with which it was associated. Theoretical concepts such as these cannot be generated by induction. Their sources have to lie outside the realm of the factual because they refer to things and processes that cannot be observed directly.

Nor is the process by which theoretical ideas and hypotheses are formulated always completely logical and rational. Sometimes semirational processes play a part. For example, Kekulé's hypotheses about the arrangement of atoms in the molecules, which his structural theory of organic chemistry required, came to him during a reverie. Traveling across London on an omnibus late one evening he "saw" the atoms join together in chains while "whirling in a giddy dance" (cited in Japp 1898). In a second reverie on another occasion the idea of a possible structure for the benzene molecule came to him in the form of a dance of snakes.

After the hypothesis is arrived at, its logical implications have to be worked out and tested against the data of observation. As a consequence of his first reverie, Kekulé spent part of the rest of the night attempting to sketch the "dream forms"; once awakened from the dream of the snakes "as if by a flash of lightning," he spent "the rest of the night working out the consequences of the hypothesis." Then, to confirm the reality of the hypothesized structure, he had to work for months at experiments testing it (cited in Japp 1898; cf. Russell 1971). Nowhere are hypotheses generated purely by induction, although, as Gruber (1981) brings out so well in his discussion of Kekulé's and similar experiences, many facts have usually been collected and mulled over before the insight occurs.

The process by which hypotheses are arrived at is also socially and historically conditioned. At the time Charcot wrote, for example, expectations generally were not considered relevant, and it is not surprising that he did not collect data on them. Charcot studied only those facts such as reflex action and muscle contraction that were relevant to the physiological basis he attributed to hypnosis. By itself, collecting what appear to be relevant facts will not necessarily draw attention to incorrect hypotheses.

Empathic Comprehension   Jaspers represents the noninductive, direct, empathic comprehension of psychological phenomena as if it were the only road for psychology to follow, and he has no doubt about its validity:

When Nietzsche shows how an awareness of one's weakness, wretchedness, and suffering gives rise to moral demands and religions of redemption, because in this roundabout way the psyche can gratify its will to power in spite of its weakness, we experience the force of his argument and are convinced. It strikes us as something self-evident which cannot be broken down any further.   (Jaspers 1959/1963, p. 303)

It is clear that repeated experiences of the will to power mediating the connection between the human condition and redemptive religious experience cannot be responsible for any conviction Nietzsche's demonstration conveys. It is also clear that something is required. It may not be an inductive inference, but experience of some kind is necessary.

To begin with, how much conviction does this illustration produce in the present-day reader, especially one to whom the whole set of Nietzschian concepts is unfamiliar? To illustrate a point about the relation between consciousness and being, an English Marxist once wrote:

Suppose someone had performed the regrettable experiment of turning Bertrand Russell, at the age of nine months, over to a goat foster-mother, and leaving him to her care, in some remote spot, unvisited by human beings, to grow to manhood. When, say forty years later, men first visited Bertrand Russell would they find him with the manuscripts of the *Analysis of Mind* and the *Analysis of Matter* in his hands? Would they even find him in possession of his definition of number, as the class of all classes?   (Caudwell 1938, p. 214)

Of course, Caudwell's answer was no. Russell and his thought were, he maintained, essentially, if perhaps a little too simply, social products: "Society made him, just as it makes a hat" (p. 214).

Analogously, would we expect even a Jaspers raised by peasants in a remote village in the Black Forest, reading only books by the German equivalent of Enid Blyton, to be swayed immediately by Nietzsche's argument? Of course not. Without some minimal experience of wretchedness, moral demands, and redemption, and without some understanding of the causal connection between them and the will to power, Nietzsche's arguments are incomprehensible, even faintly absurd.

Empathic Conviction   We should nevertheless ask about the sources of the sense of conviction that empathy produces and about the status of the knowledge the feeling gives.

Although he is speaking of the basis for understanding the reasons for an action, M. S. Moore gives us a good indication of the conditions under which empathic understanding occurs. He says we understand an action because we understand that a rational agent would act that way, and that if we had a similar set of desires and beliefs we would act similarly:

As long as the object of the agent's desire is intelligible to us as something a person in our culture could conceivably want, and so long as the factual beliefs are not themselves irrational, we can empathize with the action ... because, knowing the belief/desire set, we perceive the activity to be the rational thing to do for an agent with such beliefs and desires.   (M. S. Moore 1980)

Even those philosophers who maintain that reasons are distinct from causes grant that reasons explain behavior to the extent that the observer comprehends the cultural context in which the reasons were acquired (e.g., Peters 1958/1960, pp. 5–7; Toulmin 1970a). Similarly, empathic understanding seems to derive from a set of beliefs and values shared with the person with whom we are empathizing, although we may not be consciously aware of its basis at the time.

Perhaps a lead to how empathic understanding comes about is found in the common "Eureka!" experience. We have all had the thought, often during a dream or on wakening, that we have found the solution to some problem. Although the experience is most frequently accompanied by an intense conviction that our solution is unassailably correct, as often as not we find it is hopelessly wrong. I believe "Eureka!" solutions are the conclusions of deductive arguments of which we are partly or completely unaware. When we have the experience, we are not aware of how the steps have led from the initial premises to the conclusion. Only after scrutinizing the argument, sometimes also semiconsciously, do we descry its deficiencies. When this happens, we realize we have shouted "Eureka!" too soon. From this experience we learn that no matter how certain this kind of knowledge seems to be or how much we would like to believe it, it cannot be taken on trust. Similarly, without further scrutiny, empathically based understanding has no status as knowledge. When it does survive our examination, what it gives us is an ordinary causal pattern or context for understanding and explaining that "explains the effect, in a sense of 'explain' that we understand as well as any" (Davidson 1963).

The issues involved in the debate over understanding are more complex than I have represented them. But there is no escaping the main point that the case for a sharp distinction between explanation and understanding is very much weaker than at first appears (Rangell 1979; Grünbaum 1984; Holzman 1985), a view consistent with the way the split developed and with earlier psychoanalytic opinion (H. Hartmann 1927/ 1964; Eissler 1968).

Further, the attempt to separate psychoanalysis from the natural sciences rests, as will be seen, on two paradoxes and a bad analogy. First, most of those who make it base their criticisms of psychoanalysis on the narrowest positivism and so join Jaspers in supping with the devil (e.g., D. M. Kaplan 1977; Ellman and Moskowitz 1980; Blight 1981). Second, the meaning of "meaning" is not at all clear (Shope 1973; Rubinstein 1975). Quite apart from the failure of the analogy between deciphering a text and psychoanalytic work (the centrality of which was discussed in chapter 15), there is the further problem of patients actively resisting attempts to understand their discourse in ways that texts never do (Holzman 1985). Freud was himself opposed to psychoanalysis being classed as an understanding discipline, and in what follows, I attempt to show that some of the efforts to class it otherwise are quite misleading.

What Do Motives Do?

Suppose we could obtain an understanding of another's motives or reasons, empathically or otherwise. What would that tell us about dreams, symptoms, faulty actions, or parapraxes like slips of the tongue?

Freud refers many times to desire, intention, motive, wish, purpose, and reason in connection with these phenomena (e.g., Freud 1900, pp. 570, 1901b, pp. 69, 80, 142, 143, 153, 239, 1916–1917, pp. 54, 56–57, 65). He has been read as if it is these very phenomena that are desired, intended, motivated, or wished for, or that result from purposes or reasons. It is contended that showing they are so intended, desired, etc., explains them or leads to our understanding of them (e.g., Balmuth, cited in Shope 1967; Kolenda 1964; Flew 1956; Siegler 1967). Is it as simple as this? Are motives to be so directly understood or explained? There are two reasons for supposing the answer is no.

First, Freud's basic position on symptoms and dreams was, as shown in chapter 9, that they were compromise formations expressing two mutually conflicting wishes. After her case was reported, Anna O.'s symptoms were also said to have arisen

in situations involving an impulse to an action which, however, had not been carried out but had for other reasons been suppressed. The symptoms had, in fact, appeared *in place of* the actions that were not performed. Thus, to explain the aetiology of hysterical symptoms, we were led to ... the interplay of mental forces (to dynamics).   (Freud 1924c, p. 193)

Similarly, to appear in the manifest dream, the wishful impulse had first

to submit to a distortion, which is the work of restrictive, censoring forces in the dreamer's ego. In this way the manifest dream ... comes about.... It is a compromise between two conflicting groups of mental trends, just as ... with hysterical symptoms.   (pp. 199–200)

Parapraxes also served definite purposes that,

owing to the prevailing psychological situation, cannot be expressed in any other way. These situations as a rule involve a psychical conflict which prevents the underlying intention from finding direct expression and diverts it along indirect paths.   (Freud 1913d, p. 167)

Thus, Freud did not describe the phenomena as intended, desired, or wished for. True, intentions and wishes did underlie them, but it was precisely because the phenomena were compromises that they could not have been intended or wished for.

Second, when Freud wrote of the meaning, the purpose, or the intention of the symptom, dream, or faulty act he was clearly referring only to one of the two intentions: the underlying suppressed or repressed one. For example, the secret meaning of the dream was in the latent dream thoughts. Its latent meaning

is always a wishful impulse which is represented as fulfilled at the moment of the dream. But, except in young children and under the pressure of imperative physical needs, this secret wish can never be expressed recognizably.   (Freud 1924c, p. 199)

Consequently, it was not the intention (if it can so be put) of the repressed wish or latent meaning of the dream to produce a distorted fulfillment. Left to itself, that intention would express itself directly, without distortion. The forces opposed to it acted with it to produce the distorted compromise.

Similarly, when Freud said that suppressed intentions were "responsible" for parapraxes, he clearly stated that those intentions had been prevented "from finding direct expression" and that the meanings and intentions served by the parapraxes could not "be expressed in any other way" (Freud 1913d, p. 167). His claim that "our blunders often turn out to be *a cover* for our secret intentions" clearly means, as my emphasis shows, that the blunders themselves are not intended (p. 169). Boudreaux (1977) cited some of Freud's examples in favor of the opposite view. To that extent he challenged Shope's rejection of the point that some slips are intended, at least in the form Shope put it (1967, 1970). I believe Boudreaux is wrong and that his error is clear in Freud's discussion of what Boudreaux supposes to be counterexamples. Take the slip made by a man who Freud described as having "intended his slip to express [a] view." Clear enough, one might think. But Boudreaux reads this literally and out of context; Freud actually discusses the slip in the context of "a thought-content which is at pains to remain concealed but which cannot nevertheless avoid *unintentionally* betraying its existence" (Freud 1901b, p. 80. My emphasis).

The same points hold for symptoms. Hysterical symptoms had "the meaning of fulfillments of secret and repressed wishes" but their "tormenting character" was due to the internal mental conflict occasioned by the need to combat the wishes.

Obsessional symptoms had a meaning given by "the proscribed wish," but the symptoms themselves reflected the conflict between the wish and "the punishment and atonement which that wish incurs." Even when Freud seemed to imply that "the ruling wish" could sometimes be expressed more or less directly, as in the stereotypes of the severe schizophrenias, those symptoms were the remains of an original compromise action or verbal symptom (Freud 1913d, p. 173).

Consequently, if psychoanalysts wish to understand or explain compromises, they must have a theory of mental dynamics showing how compromises are formed from the interaction between intention and counterintention. Understanding only what the intention and counterintention are is to know less than half of what one needs to know. Without a theory of compromise formation, understanding motives, empathically or otherwise, gives no understanding of mental life.

Causes, Interpretations, and Meaning

What did Freud think he was finding when he interpreted dreams, symptoms, and parapraxes? Was it an empathic or similar understanding of the motives of his patients? When he said the behaviors were not "senseless" but "had meaning," was he fitting them into a hermeneutic context rather than a scientifically causal framework? Both questions must be answered in the negative. As I explained in chapters 4 and 8, for Freud mental processes were continuous and governed by a psychic determinism in which associations, causal connections, and logical relations were identical. He did not have to differentiate between meanings and causes or between explanation and understanding.

Meaning

One of Freud's main criticisms of the scientific work on dreams that preceded his own was that it treated the dream as the product of a physiologically impaired condition in which associations were followed randomly. It could therefore have no meaning. What, then, did he mean by "meaning"? The most essential sense he gave to the word was that of replacing the unintelligible account of the symptom or the senseless and incoherent manifest dream with something that made as much sense as normal mental life. For him:

"interpreting" a dream implies assigning a "meaning" to it—that is, replacing it by something which fits into the chain of our mental acts as a link having a validity and importance equal to the rest.   (Freud 1900, p. 96)

He assumed dreams were

designed to take the place of some other process of thought, and that we have only to undo the substitution correctly in order to arrive at this hidden meaning. (p. 96)

Free association to the dream elements caused the "substitutive structures" to emerge. The "intermediate links" so brought out could be inserted between the manifest and latent dreams, the latent content reinstated, and the dream interpreted (Freud 1916–1917, p. 113, 1940a, p. 169).

Similarly, it was precisely the gaps in the patient's account of his or her symptoms that indicated the presence of secret motives; it was there that the psychoanalyst had to look for the connecting threads. Toward the end of treatment, the facts given by the patient enabled the analyst to construct an "intelligible, consistent, and unbroken case history" (Breuer and Freud 1895, p. 293; Freud 1905a, pp. 17–18).

Meaning and Context   Giving meaning by placing some psychological phenomenon into its context in this way requires the assumption that psychological processes are continuous. In chapter 4 we saw that Freud made precisely that assumption. The essence of his view was that gaps in a psychological process marked the points at which the process had become unconscious. After translating the material hidden in the gap into conscious material, a sequence of conscious events complementary to the unconscious psychical processes resulted (Freud 1940a, p. 159).

What he claimed to find at the end of the chain of events was the memory of some causal event. He took this view because of Meynert's associationism. To give meaning to some psychological phenomenon was to establish its causes. Symptoms, dreams, and parapraxes were given meaning by being placed in the context of the processes that produced them. This meaning of "meaning" is the one Freud most frequently drew on. It combines what Shope (1973) discerned as two of the connotations of meaning: the one just discussed, that for which a mental phenomenon substitutes, and its intention, purpose, and position in a causal sequence.[2]

Placing the symptom in the context of the circumstances in which it originates also allows for a somewhat different kind of explanation or understanding, one of why the symptom has the particular content it has. Take as an example Jackson's comments about recurrent utterances:

By considering (1) the external circumstances at the time of being taken ill; (2) the intensity of the emotional state under which the last attempt at speech was made; and (3) the gravity of the lesion, we may perhaps be able to show why this or that kind of recurring utterance remains in particular cases of speechlessness. (J. H. Jackson 1879–1880b)

Jackson explains two different things. The first is the utterance itself. In the sense that without the lesion there would be no recurrent utterance at all, the cause of the utterance is the lesion. The second thing he explains is the content of the utterance. The emotional state jumbles the elements of the words, and the external circumstances in which the victim was trying to articulate the particular proposition conspire to make the content "committymy" out of, "Come, pity me."

Meaning as Content   Meaning as content is something like the third of the connotations of meaning Shope (1973) differentiates—the symptom as a sign of something else.

It is pretty clear that those who would turn psychoanalysis into an interpretative discipline restrict Freud's meanings to just this one. Forrester (1980) went so far as to propose that Freud's explanation of symptoms was essentially the same as Jackson's. Both, he asserts, attempted to make sense of symptoms by putting them into context. Forrester uses this proposal as part of his argument against the ordinary view of Freud as a scientist. Giving meaning in this way is somehow supposed to run counter to scientific endeavor. Forrester seems not to be aware that Stengel (1954) drew the parallel before without feeling impelled to arrive at the same conclusion. Perhaps Stengel saw the obvious breakdown of the parallel in that the context explains only the content of the utterance and not that it is a symptom.[3]

Meaning and Development   Making psychoanalysis an interpretive search restricts its scope drastically. Freud did not confine the analyst to listening and interpreting. The purpose of the interaction was to place the verbal exchanges within a context that had to do with the origins of the symptoms.

The business of psychoanalysis was "to explain the striking symptoms by revealing their genesis" (Freud 1918, p. 105). As a therapy, it was unable to eliminate symptoms until their origins and development were traced. "From the very first" it was "directed towards tracing developmental processes" (Freud 1913d, p. 183). And, in addition "to discovering the genesis of symptoms," it had been led

to turn its attention to other psychical structures and to construct a genetic psychology which would apply to them too. Psychoanalysis has been obliged to derive the mental life of adults from that of children.   (p. 183)

The genetic psychology provided answers to "The many riddles of the sexual life of the adult" (p. 183), as well as demonstrating how infantile mental formations persisted and gave rise to the dreams of adults and to their dispositions to later illness (p. 184).

Psychoanalytic theoretical concepts about development still come mostly from working over data gathered during the analytic hour and are very different from the verbal exchanges themselves. Without the extratherapeutic context provided by the developmental processes, even the "understanding" of the patient would be very limited (cf. Eagle 1980a; Holzman 1985).

Freud's Causal Motives

Freud leaves us in no doubt of his view that interpreting dreams, parapraxes, and symptoms leads to their causes, that those causes are motives, intentions, and wishes, and that psychical forces like them do more than just speak through their mental products.

The Search for Causes

Throughout his life Freud maintained the position he adopted from the very beginning. He began his work on the actual neuroses and the psychoneuroses by placing the search for causes at the head of his endeavors, and brought to it the work of other scientists such as Pasteur and Koch. Those same considerations dominated *The Interpretation of Dreams, The Psychopathology of Everyday Life*, and the later works, including the very last ones. Throughout his quest he saw motives as a species of cause. Without that identity, his picture of a mental life caused by the interplay of psychical forces makes almost no sense.

As early as the *Preliminary Communication* we find that the search for causes was central. Breuer and Freud spoke of "the causal connection" or "the causal relation" between the determining or precipitating psychical trauma and the hysterical or other pathological phenomenon (Breuer and Freud 1893, pp. 3, 6). Breuer clearly saw that his first analyses of symptoms led to the experiences that caused the symptoms, and Freud himself spoke repeatedly of ideas, memories, recollections, impressions, psychical groups, and trains of thought as pathogenic. When Freud elaborated these expressions, he used words such as "causation," "determined," "explanation," and "understanding" as synonyms (Breuer and Freud 1895, pp. 209, 269, 282, 283, 287–288, 290; Freud 1896c, pp. 193–196).

An identical mode of thought characterizes his later work. For example, wherever there was a symptom there was a gap in the memory, and filling the gap implied removing the condition that produced the symptom (Freud 1910a, p. 20). Again, he claimed that in so far as analytic therapy did not make its first task the removal of symptoms, it was like a causal therapy (Freud 1916–1917, p. 436).

Formulations similar to these general ones are found in Freud's discussions of specific patients. Of Elisabeth von R.'s treatment he said, "I would carefully note the points at which some train of thought remained obscure or some link in the causal chain seemed to be missing" (Breuer and Freud 1895, p. 139). He described the whole work as "based on the expectation that it would be possible to establish a completely adequate set of determinants for the events concerned"; and as we know, he failed to trace "any psychical cause" for her first leg pains (p. 147). Of the Wolf Man, Freud wrote that a particular recollection provided "an important link between the primal scene and the later compulsive love which came to be of such decisive significance in his subsequent career" (Freud 1918, p. 92). Tracing the memories of childhood events and impressions that were supposed to cause perversions led to such "commonplace and unexciting" impressions, "without any traumatic force" that he was prepared only "to come to a provisional end ... in tracing back the train of causal connection" (Freud 1919a, p. 182).

Causes and Motives

Many times Freud uses motives and causes as synonyms. One of the earliest occurs when he discusses his own dreams:

since I am an excellent sleeper and obstinately refuse to allow anything to disturb my sleep, it very rarely happens that *external causes* of excitation find their way into my dreams; whereas *psychical motives* obviously *cause* me to dream very easily.   (Freud 1900, p. 229. My emphasis)

Here he explicitly equates psychical motives with causes and implicitly grants them the same status as external, physical causes of excitation (cf. p. 224).

Among other examples of his explicit identification of causes with motives, intentions, and wishes, we note the following:

A personal complex causes a name to be forgotten, an unconscious desire plays a part in causing a slip of the pen, the cause of a slip of the tongue is a motive other than the conscious intention, a rejected intention plays a part in causing a slip of the tongue, and (in one of his last works) it was when unconscious thoughts, wishes, and intentions became effective that they accounted for slips (Freud 1901b, pp. 22 128, 272, 1916–1917, p. 65, 1940b, p. 284).

A neurotic has a cause or motive for falling ill, the frustration of a wish or motive leads to the outbreak of a neurosis, the cause of psychical impotence is a masochistic attitude (Freud 1909b, p. 199; 1917d, p. 129; 1919a, p. 197).

Evil intentions cause a dream, unconscious wishful impulses combine with day residues to create or construct the latent dream-thought, and opposition to hidden impulses causes the basic feature of the dream, its distortion (Freud 1916–1917, pp. 218, 226, 1923d, pp. 262–263).

For all the phenomena he wanted to explain, Freud regarded motives as synonymous with causes.

Motives and Forces

Shope (1973) also pointed out that Freud treated causes and motives as the same partly because behind his use of the word motive lay the concept of a motive force. For example, consider his endorsement of Delage's opinion about the contribution made to the dream by thoughts interrupted or suppressed during the day:

The psychical energy which has been stored up during the daytime by being inhibited and suppressed becomes the motive force for dreams at night.   (Freud 1900, pp. 81–82)

In his own conceptualization he had the unconscious dream-wish supplying or providing the motive force for producing or making the dream (Freud 1900, pp. 541–542, 560–561).

A complex interplay of similarly conceived causal motive forces was the very basis of mental life. Not only did Freud speak of "the force ascribed by the patient to his motives" (Breuer and Freud 1895, p. 293), but he also conceptualized resistance and repression as motivated by a force having causal efficacy. What was the "kind of force," he asked, that caused resistance and "what motive could have put it into operation?" It was the same "repelling force of which the purpose was defence" that originally "forced" the idea "out of consciousness and out of memory." He had, he said:

attempted to sketch out the psychological hypotheses by the help of which this causal connection ... can be demonstrated.   (p. 269)

The motive for this repression was to be found in feelings of unpleasure (Freud 1904, p. 251; cf. 1913d, pp. 167, 171).

The most important consequence of giving meaning to a dream or symptom was that it identified the motive forces that caused it and allowed the repressing force to be modified. Hypnosis, the pressure method, and free association could all be described as aiming to fill the gaps in memory. Dynamically speaking, however, the aim was "to overcome resistances due to repression" (Freud 1914c, p. 148). The translation that replaced what had been unconscious with what was conscious had causal consequences:

we lift the repressions, we remove the preconditions for the formation of symptoms, we transform the pathogenic conflict into a normal one.   (Freud 1916–1917, p. 435)

A striking example of the use of the identity between causes and motives occurs in his interpretation of the meaning of the symptoms of two of his obsessional patients. He translated the ritual actions of both as having the meaning of wish-fulfilling re-enactments of earlier experiences. Each had a memory of the event, but neither connected it with her ritual. Of the first patient Freud said her memory "did not occur to her when she was asked directly to look for the *motives* of her obsessional action," and of the second that she failed to connect her "ceremonial and its *causes*" with her memory (Freud 1916–1917, p. 283). Here he not only explicitly equated motive with cause, but argued that the ritual stood for the cause. Wishes similarly provided the motive power or the motive force for the construction of dreams (Freud 1900, p. 598, 1901a, p. 682).

Motives and Causal Conditions

In concluding this section I stress that Freud does not accord psychic forces the status of causes just because they are instinctual or just because they draw on a somatic source of energy. He infers that status from the effects he supposes they bring about. How they achieve their ends through compromise formations and what energy they possess are only part of the issue of whether they are causes. All Freud's causal trappings are to be found in his discussions of parapraxes. For example, in *The Psychopathology of Everyday Life*, he placed the famous Signorelli error in the context of "conditions" that had to be fulfilled and in which "a motive" was added to the "factors" that brought about the forgetting. It was also a context in which he discussed his "explanations" in terms of "necessary" and "sufficient" conditions (Freud 1901b, pp. 5–6). Similarly, he reached an "explanation" of the distortion in recalling a line from "The Bride of Corinth," which was "sufficient" by tracing it to a thought-content that was "its cause" or the "source of the effect" (Freud 1901b, pp. 18, 21). Even without the idea of forces as ideas cathected or invested with psychic energy, he would have insisted on the causal status of motives and wishes (cf. Edelson 1977).

Consequently, Freud does not identify the ideas recovered by free association as the causes of dreams, parapraxes, and symptoms, simply because he made a *post hoc ergo propter hoc* confusion and neglected to consider suggestion, as Grünbaum proposed (Grünbaum 1980, 1984, pp. 58–59, 198–199). Freud was not quite so simple minded. Certainly, criticism of psychoanalysis must cover, as Grünbaum's does, Freud's misplaced reliance on the therapeutic touchstone and the contamination of free association by suggestion. But what seems to have escaped Grünbaum is that free association produced only a putative cause that Freud evaluated with his (deficient) adaptation of Koch's postulates. It was Freud's concept of determinism that contended that the ideas to which associations led were causes. A really penetrating excavation of the logical foundations of psychoanalysis has to get to the bedrock of Freud's view of psychic determinism and its relation to the fundamental rule of psychoanalysis. This Grünbaum fails to do.

Freud's belief that psychical forces had causal effects must be seen in the context of his general deterministic framework. The most general conclusion he drew from his analysis of parapraxes was that

certain shortcomings in our psychical functioning ... and certain seemingly unintentional performances prove ... to have valid motives and to be determined by motives unknown to consciousness.... If we give way to the view that a part of our psychical functioning cannot be explained by purposive ideas, we are failing to appreciate the extent of determination in mental life. (Freud 1901b, pp. 239–240)

Here as elsewhere, "determine" and its derivatives are synonyms for "cause" and its derivatives (cf. Freud 1910a, p. 14). Consequently, when he later said it was "quite unscientific" to think that there were "undetermined psychical events" and that that idea "must yield to the demand of a determinism whose rule extends over mental life," he was demanding recognition of motives and the like as causes (Freud 1916–1917, p. 106).

Can Motives Be Causes?

What about the arguments that motives are different from causes? Are they strong enough for us to reject Freud's equating them?

The Motive-Cause Distinction

Home is usually credited with having first raised the motive-cause distinction within psychoanalysis. He argued that Freud's "totally new principle of explanation" was that "the symptom could have meaning" and meaning was not the product of causes but "the creation of a subject" (Home 1966). The comprehension of meaning was a humanistic enterprise, not a scientific one. Home believed the distinction he was making was the same as that between interpretation and explanation or between reasons and causes. He thought psychoanalysts should ask the question of why things happen and look for answers "in terms of a subject's motives." He proposed a kind of Jaspers-like empathy, what he called cognition through identification, as the main way of understanding the motives and meaning of behavior.

By the time Home wrote, Davidson (1963) had already examined most of the following commonly held distinctions between reasons and causes:

Causes were events but reasons were not.

Unlike reasons, causes were logically distinct from their effects.

Cause-effect relations were law governed, but reason-action connections were not.

Causes were known inductively, but one's reasons were known directly.

Causes resulted in movements, not actions.

He concluded that the differences were not as absolute as was usually claimed, and that there were more similarities than differences (cf. Pears 1973; Davidson 1973; Dennett 1973). Most of the subsequent philosophical and psychoanalytic discussion has endorsed Davidson's conclusions.

Motives and Dualism

Actually, in the late 1940s, well before Home, the distinction between motives and causes began to be made (or was revived) in relation to psychoanalysis by Toulmin. At about the same time, in *The Concept of Mind*, Ryle also attempted to deal with the causal contribution of motives. Even at this point the conflict was never substantial enough to give comfort to those who believed psychoanalytic explanations apply to a domain separate from that of science.

Toulmin (1948) based his distinction between motives and causes on an explicit dualism, as Flew who developed it made clear. For Flew, motives were "quite intangible and insubstantial while efficient causes notoriously have to be substantial" (Flew 1949). Therefore the causes of "real and palpable" actions could only be the "substantial" physiological processes subserved by "solid, visible, tangible" neurones.

Toulmin differentiated among three types of factors used in explanations of behavior. Two were as intangible as they were motivational: the individual's stated reason for his or her behavior, and the reason reported for that behavior by someone else. Only the third factor was tangibly causal: the events that explained how the reasons had been acquired. Psychoanalytic explanations constituted a fourth type. They gave patients reasons for their behavior, the reasons were ones with which others familiar with the case would agree, and they necessarily drew on a causal history of facts from the patient's early life. Psychoanalytic explanations therefore combined causal and motivational factors (Toulmin 1948).

Ryle (1949) was not primarily interested in the motive-cause distinction as much as with overcoming the consequences of Descartes's rigid separation of mind from body. When he tried to bring motives under a nondualist but causal rubric, it was within his larger thesis. For him the word explain had two meanings. The first was the causal one used when explaining, for example, that a glass broke "because" a stone hit it. The second sense explained the breakage "because" the glass was brittle, that is, because it had a disposition to break. After showing the logical connection between the two kinds of causes, he defined motives as the dispositions or propensities for the individual to behave in certain ways (p. 89). Consequently, his theory was that explanations by motive were explanations of the dispositional type.

Just as with the brittle glass, a specific causal event had to be added to the motive if one wanted to know why a particular behavior occurred at a particular time. Politeness might be the motive from which a person, say, passed the salt when asked, but it was merely an inclination to be polite generally. What made the person pass the salt at that moment was hearing someone ask for it, a cause with which "we are perfectly familiar" (Ryle 1949, pp. 113–114). Such proof that actions had causes did not conflict with their having motives; a cause was already prescribed in the initial logical conditions that stated the motive (pp. 113–114). Hence, the question why a person acted in a certain way asked either for an explanation by requesting the specific cause of the action, or it asked about the motive, that is, the character or disposition. We knew quite well what caused someone to scowl and slam the door— he had been insulted (p. 325). In this "everyday sense" "we can all give 'causal explanations' for many of our actions and reactions" (p. 325).

Two things stand out in the comments that were made on the Ryle and Toulmin arguments. First are the different meanings of the word motive and the extremely limited scope of Ryle's concept of motive-as-disposition (Peters 1952, 1954, 1958/ 1960, pp. 32–33; cf. 1952; Urmson 1952; Pap 1959, pp. 288–289). Second, causal status of some type was granted directly to some or all of the terms to be considered as motives or reasons (Pap 1959; cf. Peters 1958/1960, pp. 12–16). Toulmin himself granted that dispositional motive-explanations did not differ "in any striking respect" from ordinary causal ones (Toulmin 1954), and Flew also softened his stance. Originally, he maintained that although a given behavior could be both motivated and caused, it was not possible to translate the language of causes into that of motives. Now he apologized for representing the difference "as an unbridged and unbridgeable gulf" (Flew 1954; cf. 1949). From his frankly dualist position even Toulmin (1970b) accepted that a compelling reason had causal efficacy and that reasons could be assimilated to causes.

Reconciling Motives and Causes

As early as the late 1950s, therefore, it was clear that some reconciliation of reasons and causes was possible. The most important step was taken when Davidson (1963) defended what he called the ancient and commonsense position that the reasons that explained actions by giving the agents' reasons for them—what he called rationalizations—were a species of ordinary causal explanation. For a reason to rationalize an action, the doer had to have some kind of positive attitude toward certain kinds of actions, together with a belief that his or her own action was of that kind. Davidson also observed that if causal explanations were wholly irrelevant to the understanding of actions, the connection between reasons and actions indicated by the word "because" in sentences like, "He did it because ..." could not be understood at all. Aristotle tried to close the gap through the causal concept of "wanting," but that concept was too narrow (cf. Brandt and Kim 1963). Rationalization was also wider in scope than disposition: the positive attitude included desires, wants, promptings, and all sorts of views, principles, prejudices, and the like. On Davidson's analysis, reasons were causes.

M. S. Moore (1980) developed Davidson's notion of rationalization by showing that beliefs and desires could function as a species of cause in Aristotle's "practical syllogism." To simplify, if X gave his desire to cool a room as his motive for opening a window, the motive was causal, provided that it really was his desire to cool the room (major premise) and that it was his belief that opening the window would in fact cool it (minor premise). The particular set of desires and beliefs causally explained X's action because, although he may have had any number of belief-desire sets, just that one caused him to act as he did. X's action was also rationalized by those same beliefs and desires because he portrayed the action as the rational thing to do. A true motivational explanation, Moore insisted, had to provide both rationalization and cause.

Subsequent to these discussions, Grünbaum made a very cogent point:

the causal relevance of an antecedent state X to an occurrence Y ... is a matter of whether X—be it physical, mental, or psychophysical—*makes a difference to the occurrence of Y, or affects the incidence of Y.* (Grünbaum 1984, p. 72. Emphasis altered)

He gives the example of someone who desires to read a book and believes it is available at a library:

If that combination of desire and belief actually prompts him/her to go there to borrow the book, then his reason (motive) M for doing so qualifies as explanatory *just because M makes a difference to going*: when the agent neither needs a book nor has any other business at the library, i.e., when he has no motive (reason) for going there, then he indeed refrains from going. (p. 73. My emphasis)

Grünbaum correctly concludes that his analysis vindicates Holt's assumption that "a reason is one kind of cause, a *psychological* cause" (Holt 1981). Of the many others who also made Holt's assumption, the most notable was Freud.

Freud's treatment of motives as causes poses a problem only to those who are not prepared to abandon Descartes's dualism and/or step outside the exceptionally restricted field within which Hume allowed causes to act. A rigid opposition between cause and reason is no more necessary than one between mind and body.

The Alternatives Proposed by the Critics

Having considered the components of the different kinds of criticism, I now try to relate what has been found to the critical positions themselves.

The Natural Science Critics

The natural science critics such as Pumpian-Mindlin (1958–1959), Peterfreund (1975), Rosenblatt and Thickstun (1977), and Reiser (cited in Wallerstein 1985) all welcome and foster attacks on Freud's metapsychology. They are not motivated by opposition to psychoanalysis as a natural science, however. Nor are they against abstract or higher-level theories per se—they may even emphasize, like Reiser, the importance of staying close to the clinical level. Their wish is to develop psychoanalysis on a different basis from Freud. They derive their explanations of what is *meta* to consciousness from physical field theory, information-processing theories, systems theory, and modern neurophysiology, respectively. In brief, the goal they share is to substitute a new metapsychology for Freud's.

These new natural science proposals have been little discussed in the psychoanalytic literature and have won practically no support. Actually, as Warme observes, the majority of psychoanalysts are "troubled, if not shocked" that metapsychology is even under attack (Warme 1981; cf. Ross 1980). Ellman and Moskowitz (1980), Meissner (1979c, 1981b), Ornstein (in Chattah 1983), and Erlich and Blatt (1985) believe that these analysts typically refer to one or other of Freud's theoretical perspectives, especially the economic and structural, as having immense value. Some add the fear that giving up the concept of instinctual drive would deprive psychoanalysis of the one concept that unified its basic concepts "into a coherent, interrelated whole" (Lotto 1982). Even though we saw in chapter 14 how the use of the metapsychological viewpoints was often wrong-headed in that metaphorical description was confused with explanation, it is equally clear that disquieted analysts have not been won over to any of the supposedly more modern positions.

A quite different kind of criticism, one of the kinds of bases chosen for the new natural sciences, was made by Gill. He proposed that psychoanalytic theories should be developed in the language used in the "common discourse of psychoanalysts" rather than, in his view, in other inappropriate and forced translations (Gill 1977). At best, his criticism is superficial and at worst it is irrelevant: what is important in a theory is its explanatory power, not its language.

The Different-Science Critics

Those seeking to establish psychoanalysis as a different kind of science usually make a sharp distinction between scientific-causal and personal-motive or -reason theories.

What most frequently results are the prototypal formulations of Schafer and G. S. Klein.

Schafer focuses on the purposively acting person and derives his explanations from reasons rather than from drives or motives. His alternative requires Freud's metapsychology to be jettisoned completely and a fresh start made by describing the behaviors to be explained in a new and, what he takes to be more theoretically neutral language (Schafer 1976). G. S. Klein, on the other hand, wants to explain behavior precisely in terms of motives, although, it is true, he also focuses on aims, reasons, and meanings. He wishes to save what he calls the clinical theory of psychoanalysis from metapsychology. Klein's central concept is that of a self-structure, rather than an ego. He places great importance on the role of the self in resolving incompatible motives, attributing this to a need for the self to maintain itself as a unified structure (G. S. Klein 1976).

The main point to be made about Schafer's and Klein's proposals is that the basic distinction on which their criticism rests does not hold. Motives and reasons both cause behavior, a fact generally not stressed sufficiently strongly in the otherwise extensive discussions of Schafer's proposals by Meissner (1979a,c), Rawn (1979), Calogeras and Alston (1980), Ellman and Moskowitz (1980), Anscombe (1981), Modell (1981), and Spence (1982b); and of Klein's by Ross (1980), Eagle (1980b), and L. Friedman (1980); or of both by Frank (1979).

Many psychoanalysts have accepted a good deal of Schafer's and Klein's criticisms along with other criticism from the different-science position. However, almost all turned away from the particular theoretical directions to which they point, or expressed considerable doubts about them. Among other things, by dismissing the concepts of drive and motive, Schafer places restrictions on what psychoanalysts are able to consider clinically important. Klein has a similar difficulty with sexual motives, and in addition, adopts a nebulous Rogers-like self and revives an almost Janet-like dissociation as a substitute for repression. There are also major logical inadequacies in Schafer's concept of person and in Klein's of self-structure. Perhaps of greatest significance is the inability of either to provide a coherent account of unconscious motivation.[4]

The Narrative-Science and Hermeneutic Critics

What we found about psychoanalytic narratives can be summarized briefly. Narrative explanations do not differ in their logical structure from explanations generally. Apart from the groundless distinction between cause and motive or reason, the main problem is the absence of standards for judging the validity of a narrative. For those not interested in truth, the problem of choosing from equally plausible narratives remains. These points are made clearly in the main published discussion of narratives, the symposium on Sherwood's analysis of narrative explanations (Rubinstein 1973; Eagle 1973; cf. Sherwood 1969, 1973).

A hermeneutic "reading" of the patient's discourse is supposed to lead the individual to a better understanding of the reasons and motives governing his or her life rather than to an explanation of it. Some of the difficulties with the narrative position overlap with those of the hermeneutic, even though the two may have essentially different aims (Sherwood 1973). Both share the problem of choosing between alternative readings. Obviously if one is interested only in the transformation of understanding, rather than in what it becomes or causes, the problem of different readings goes away.

The indeterminacy of hermeneutic readings has the same source as that of narratives: double construction in interpretation. The logical difficulties of these readings are much more profound than those of narratives, however. Sherwood thought it made sense to ask about the truth ("accuracy") of narratives, but the constructivist view of reality taken by hermeneuticists disallows that question. According to them there is no uninterpreted reality; reality comes into being through the act of interpretation. As Petocz stated in her examination, any coherent theory of symbolism requires three independently characterizable terms: signifier, signified, and subject. The constructivist assumptions of hermeneutics violate this requirement by collapsing signifier and signified into the one term (Petocz 1988a). She explains the consequence in her contemporaneous critique of the place of hermeneutics in psychology. Any reading or interpretation requires

some *thing* to be interpreted; and to a hermeneuticist who claims—"there is no reality, only an 'interpretation' of reality," the reply is: "an interpretation of . . . *what*?"   (Petocz 1988b)

Bringing a hermeneutic reading to a conclusion, if only temporarily, by what hermeneuticists term "closing the hermeneutic circle" is no solution. Closure is reached when the to-and-fro movement between the whole and the parts of the patient's story results in the emergence of some consistent pattern that allows all the details to be understood (e.g., Ricoeur 1970, 1974, 1977; Steele 1979). Emergence of pattern is little more than the notoriously faulty jigsaw puzzle Freud used to test childhood seduction memories and that underlies his equally doubtful analyses of Dora, Leonardo, the Rat Man, and Michelangelo's *Moses*, to name only the ones I have discussed.

Several commentators vigorously defend the scientific aspirations of psychology and psychoanalysis against hermeneutic criticism (e.g., Brenner 1980; Ellman and

Moskowitz 1980; Modell 1981). They especially dispute the analogy between interpreting passive and unresponsive text and interpreting the free associations of the
living patient with whom the analyst-reader interacts. Some of them grant the mean-
ing-cause distinction to be valid, but do not see the hermeneutic and scientific enterprises as being incompatible. The dilemma for most of these theorists is pithily
summed up in Meissner's contrast:

Hermeneutics without metapsychology gives us meaning without structure; metapsychology
without hermeneutics gives us structure without meaning.   (Meissner 1981b)

The contrast may not signal absolute opposition. Both Muslin and Holt (in Chattah
1983) asserted that Freud's empathic listening to his patients was influenced by his
metapsychological propositions. Muslin says "the data of the clinical encounters"
with Dora, the Rat Man, and the Wolf Man are "recognized in a fashion that is
reminiscent of the line of theorizing that has its roots in the 'Project.'" To this Holt
adds that metapsychology "actually directed Freud's observations" and is "intertwined with the clinical theory."

This may be true, but what Freud meant by meaning and the way he used his data
were rather different from contemporary hermeneuticists. Reducing the opposition
in this way does not answer the most telling of the criticisms, those by Grünbaum in
relation to psychoanalysis, and by Petocz in relation it and to psychology more
generally. Both rebut the by now familiar hermeneutic claims that there cannot be
such a thing as a scientific psychology because science is ahistorical, and is unable to
encompass human purposes or give causal explanations. Both also attack the test of
narrative coherence, Grünbaum in breadth and detail, Petocz with philosophical
depth. Petocz particularly clearly exposes the logical and conceptual confusions in the
consequences of the hermeneutic choice of a constructivist over a realist epistemology: the failure to grant ontological priority to existence over expression, particularly
linguistic expression, the hermeneutic rejection of language as a referential system,
and the promotion of what hermeneuticists term values above what they term facts.
Although much of Grünbaum's attack has been discussed, the limited response to
these particular rebuttals is inadequate (Grünbaum 1984; Petocz 1988b; cf. the commentary in *Behavioral and Brain Sciences* 1986, vol. 9, pp. 217–284; Ferguson 1985;
C. Evans 1986; Forrester 1986; Sharpe 1986; Spruiell 1986; Strenger 1986).

We know that choosing among different hermeneutic readings is as impossible as
choosing among traditional psychoanalytic interpretations, reconstructions, and narratives. It may be this that brings about the downfall of the hermeneutic position.
How can one judge the emotional, cognitive, or therapeutic value of a hermeneutic
reading? The main issue of interest to psychoanalysts which hermeneuticists exclude

is development. Not only does one have to forgo an understanding of how the patient comes to be as he or she is, but all theories of child development become impossible.

Being able to restrict psychoanalysis to a science of meaning, as Frank, Rosen, and Ricoeur did, or to a kind of religious exegeses as did such hermeneuticists as Lacan and Chabot, is also possible only, Brenner (1980) insists, by overlooking the similarities between the methods and data of psychoanalysis and those of the other sciences. These critics almost never refer to the psychoanalytic method, and prefer to concentrate on textual analyses rather than on the interactions that Freud believed led to an understanding of causes (Brenner 1980). As I interpret Brenner's point, it is that were they to accept Freud's view of the nature of the method, they would have no choice but to class psychoanalysis with the other natural sciences.

The Appeal of Psychoanalysis

Criticism of psychoanalysis is not new, and we should ask why Freud's theory continues to appeal. I believe it does for five main reasons. First, most lay people, as well as a large number of nonanalyst professionals, think of psychoanalysis as beyond substantial criticism and as not much changed from the ideas advanced by Freud. Second, the understanding that psychoanalysis gives of the determinants of behavior and personality seems to be especially extensive. Third is the attraction of the irrational, which appeals in and of itself. The psychoanalytic irrational also appeals because many aspects of it are like processes familiar from everyday life and not at all difficult to understand or apply. Fourth, psychoanalysis concentrates on precisely those things in which people have the greatest interest and about which no other discipline says much of anything. Fifth, most people take it for granted that the effectiveness of psychoanalysis as a therapy for a wide range of disorders and problems is well established and certainly not a matter of dispute.

Several aspects of these reasons are worth discussing, even though there are few hard data bearing on the contribution they and others make to the continuing appeal of psychoanalysis. I therefore apologize for abandoning my so far dull position of fact and take up the more exciting stance of speculation.

Criticism Is Not Known

First, the fact that none of the ideas Freud thought to be central to his theoretical perspectives has escaped attack, for the most part by psychoanalysts, is simply not known outside of psychoanalysis. People do not recognize how much of Freud's theory has been criticized, how profound that criticism has been, how little of the theory would remain if all the criticism were accepted, or how much of it has in fact been accepted within psychoanalysis. Who outside the field or related circles knows, for example, of the devastating criticisms by Holt, Bowlby, and S. Brody of the instinctual drives, the mental structures, or the developmental theses? Who has read Pumpian-Mindlin or Peterfreund or Rosenblatt and Thickstun or Reiser, for example, all of whom seek to explain what lies behind conscious mental processes with more powerful weapons than those in Freud's poorly equipped armory? Who is familiar with the proposals by G. S. Klein and others to do away with almost all of Freud's central theoretical concepts and found a purely clinical theory? Who is aware of the force of Schafer's case for completely discarding Freud's concepts and starting afresh at the most basic level, that of uncluttered observation, as if psychoanalytic theory had never existed?

Were these things known and their significance properly appreciated, I suggest psychoanalysis would lose a lot of its appeal. If to this were added knowledge of the inadequacy of the psychoanalytic method for inquiring into the human condition, the almost total disagreement among psychoanalysts on how to interpret the data gathered by it, and the lack of evidence for the effectiveness of the method as psychotherapy, the appeal would be even less, at least to rational beings.

Pseudoexplanatory Power

Second, on their first contact with psychoanalysis, few people escape the feeling that they have been introduced to an extremely powerful explanatory system, but they do not appreciate the paradox on which that conviction rests. Psychoanalytic explanations and interpretations are basically indeterminate, even though they have the appearance of being comprehensive and rigidly deterministic. Nothing seems to fall outside the explanatory net, but one cannot be too sure what has been caught.

The paradox comes about partly because there are no agreed-on rules for interpreting so-called products of the unconscious. The interpretations of Dora's symptoms and the dreams of Freud and Dora (examined in chapter 9) of supposedly perverse sexual behavior (chapter 10), and of aggressive behavior (chapter 12) show how phenomena such as these can be interpreted in almost any way at all. Because each presumed cause is also thought of as connected with every other, causes can be combined to make any number of plausible explanations. Consequently, any one psychoanalytic explanation of say, Schreber's psychosis (chapter 11) or the development of masochism (chapter 12) is, within broad limits, as good as any other.

The absence of rules for arriving at interpretations and evaluating explanations is only part of the problem. Much more basic is the use of the double construction in translating from the language of consciousness into the supposed language of the unconscious. Nothing is known or can possibly be known about this "language," which is independent of the act of interpretation. For the hermeneutic interpretation of psychoanalysis this indeterminacy poses an especially acute problem.

Nothing of this matters to those not concerned with how patients come to be the ways they are or what might be done to promote their healthy development. To judge from the welcome Kermode (1985) gave some interpretive revisions of Freud, psychoanalytic explanations appeal to those interested in history, philosophy, and the arts, and especially in literature and literary criticism, precisely because they already have a high degree of tolerance for other equally indeterminate endeavors (cf. Timpanaro 1974/1976, pp. 223–224; Chomsky, in Anonymous 1989).

For amateurs, the most important consequence of the absence of criteria for evaluating the adequacy of translations, interpretations, and explanations made by psychoanalysts is that they are at no disadvantage. They can arrive at explanations of their lives, their ideas, their feelings, or their behaviors that are just as plausible as those of the professionals.

The Appeal of the Irrational

Some of the appeal comes from the importance psychoanalysis attributes to irrational processes. At some time or another, most people have believed themselves to be at the mercy of forces they do not understand. Many are therefore ready to believe in the irrational. Few psychologists have not had at least one of their prosaic explanations of an unusual experience, say, a premonitory dream, rejected in favor of an irrational one. Similarly, many in the audience witnessing a magician demonstrating "extrasensory" powers will prefer an irrational explanation for what they have seen even after the magician assures them that only routine stage magic was involved. It is easy to accept the possibility that the unconscious and irrational processes underlying psychoanalytic explanations exist because they seem to reflect so much ordinary experience.

A further aspect of the appeal of the irrational is what Wittgenstein called the charm of psychoanalysis, which comes from the resemblance that Freud's unconscious motivational explanations have to ordinary ones. For all Freud's talk of a chaotic and irrational primary process, the unconscious wishes and motives with which he explains dreams or slips of the tongue seem just like ordinary ones, acting in exactly the same way as their conscious counterparts. Although the components from which psychoanalytic explanations are constructed may be irrational, they have the charm of familiarity that makes it relatively easy to grasp how they cause their effects. Nowadays, when so many of the concepts and technical terms of psychoanalysis are in common use, psychoanalytic ideas and the practice they engender are very easy to accept. Most of the films or television series dealing with psychological matters include a psychological miracle worker, often a psychoanalyst, or a psychiatrist or psychologist modeled on one. Quite young children may even become familiar with psychoanalytic theoretical concepts, as when the id of the main character (a kind of evil destructive double) was featured in an episode of *Dr. Who*, the BBC children's television program.

It is probably not an accident that the feeling of conviction generated by psychoanalytic explanations is greatest for dreams and parapraxes. There is no doubt these phenomena belong with the more irrational and puzzling aspects of our mental lives. It is for them that the analyst's explanations seem most complete, the unconscious processes most like conscious ones, and the motives uncovered the most reprehensible even when they are not sexual. Coming to Freud for the first time, we find we already understand the purely conscious instances of motivated forgetting and have little difficulty with the preconscious ones. It is then but a short step to accepting his examples of unconscious motives along with the rest of the theory. When, in turn, we come to supposed unconscious lusts and hatreds, we are prepared to find that they, too, resemble our conscious drives. Our self-applications, now easily made, produce a high level of conviction.

Freud may have been aware of the charm and power of his conceptualization of unconscious processes. Certainly he frequently capitalized on the postulated resemblance between them and conscious processes. Thus, he introduced his major work on parapraxes, *The Psychopathology of Everyday Life*, with what Shope (1970) shows to be a continuum of errors. As Freud set it out, slips of the tongue varied between those supposedly produced by counterintentions, of which we are aware at the time, and those produced by repressed unconscious impulses. In between are the ones caused by the preconscious motives or counterintentions that we can fairly readily bring back to consciousness. But, whatever their type and wherever they are located, these counterintentions act on the primary intention in exactly the same way. We also find Freud playing on the conscious-unconscious parallel extensively in the *Introductory Lectures*. The first four lectures are on the parapraxes and the next eleven on dreams. Only then does he begin the thirteen on neuroses (Freud 1916–1917). Certainly others recognize the power of the parallel. Timpanaro, for example, cites and endorses Musatti's view that after "understanding" the simple parapraxes, the reader of Freud's *The Psychopathology of Everyday Life* "is destined to become an adherent of analytic theory" (Timpanaro 1974/1976, pp. 15–17; cf. p. 105).

The appeal of Freud's parallel is inversely related to the strength of its logical foundations. Tannenbaum and Timpanaro cautioned that many of Freud's interpretations of parapraxes depend on a verbally competent unconscious, and so contradict his basic postulate that unconscious processes are irrational and nonverbal. The inconsistency is especially marked when the interpretation requires the supposition that there has been a complex translation between languages in which the speaker is not fully proficient (Tannenbaum 1922; Timpanaro 1974/1976, pp. 78–81). The point also applies to dreams. Progress from parapraxes and dreams to the farther reaches of Freud's theory is made easier if one does not know of these conceptual inconsistencies. But when Freud first proposes the conscious motive as model, there seems to be no difficulty about understanding the unconscious ones.

Sexuality

There is no doubt that the emphasis on sexuality was part of the attraction psychoanalysis exercised in its early days. Although it is alleged that a sexual revolution has occurred, that same emphasis seems to me to appeal to young people today (i.e., the undergraduate students I know) as strongly as it did to those two or three generations ago. Even among those who have some knowledge of the revolt of the object-relations theorists, such as Fairbairn or Winnicott, or perhaps just a dim understanding that Freud's sexual theories are out of date, psychoanalysis continues to license public interest in a matter in which almost everyone is still curious. Today when people derive explanations for their behavior from their own sexual unconscious motives, what they arrive at seems as valid as it did years ago.

The Appeal of Therapy

What of the appeal of psychoanalysis as therapy? Why are patients and psychoanalysts so convinced that what they do brings about change? We must start by reiterating that psychoanalysis is actually no more effective than other verbally based psychotherapies and marginally less effective than nontalking treatments. Equivalence in outcomes necessarily means, as Lakoff (1982) argued, that nothing in the content of the verbal interaction can be responsible for such effects as are produced.

I proposed elsewhere that we cannot go much beyond this confession of ignorance (Macmillan 1986). Some factors can be ruled out completely, however, particularly the personality characteristics of therapists and patients and the relation between them. What if anything about the relation that promotes change is unknown. It is certainly not the qualities determined by the therapist's genuineness, accurate empathy, and nonpossessive warmth, the conditions Rogers (1957) proposed as necessary and sufficient for therapeutic change (cf. K. M. Mitchell, Bozarth, and Krauft 1977). Even were they or the relationship with the patient or client critical, we lack concepts, psychoanalytic or otherwise, to bridge the gap between them and the consequences they are supposed to produce.

The Columbia study and the other studies of psychoanalytic therapy cited by its authors show psychoanalysts to be as ignorant as anyone else about the basis of therapeutic effects. First, analysts are unable to predict at much better than a chance level who will benefit from therapy. Even though the factors held by their "accepted clinical wisdom" to predict outcome can themselves be predicted to some degree, they have almost no relation to outcome. Observations made while the analysis is in progress do not help: "One must wait until an analysis is over before one knows what the final result will be" (Bachrach, Weber, and Solomon 1985). Therefore:

once a patient has been carefully selected as a suitable candidate for psychoanalysis ... the eventual fate of the treatment is only marginally predictable.   (Weber, Bachrach, and Solomon 1985b)

As with the psychotherapies generally, neither does any connection exist between outcome and the qualities of the analyst.

Second, patients in whom an "analytic process" will develop and who will be "analyzable" cannot be identified before treatment begins. That is, it cannot be foretold who will manifest transference, use their self-observations and dreams, and so on during therapy, or use insights gained from therapy in everyday life. Even if the analytic process were predictable, the damaging fact remains that when it does develop, little or no relation can be seen between it and whether the patient benefits from treatment. The Columbia investigators summarized a number of earlier studies as showing that in only about 50 percent of the improved patients were signs of an analytic process reported. They also found only a "modest" relation (correlations of 0.3 to 0.4) in their own investigation between its development and outcome.

If I am interpreting this finding correctly, it means that whether or not patients responded to therapy was largely independent of whether there were signs that a psychoanalysis had taken place! Whereas the highly selected nature of the patients and psychoanalysts did make prediction difficult, these findings are consistent with data on the other verbal therapies. In my view they are also consistent with the Menninger Foundation Psychotherapy Research Project finding that most of the change that did take place in their patients was due to "supportive" elements in treatment rather than to factors postulated in the classical psychoanalytical theory of therapy: insight through conflict resolution (Wallerstein 1986c, pp. 718–730).

What Does Happen in Therapy   The fact of the matter is that no one knows what brings psychotherapeutic effects about. Two important things have to be taken into consideration in trying to find out why therapists and patients think what they do causes such change as does occur. First, there is no evidence that psychoanalytic therapy produces changes over and above those brought about by nonsystematic treatment. Second, even the most effective of the psychological therapies, usually the behaviorally based ones, do not do that much better. A success rate of 85 percent is not, after all, a great deal higher than the 65 percent base rate. We ought therefore to be asking why the base rate is as high as it is, rather than simply using it as a standard for evaluating systematic treatments. The question would still be worth asking even if the rate were as low as the 40 percent some authors accept. In other words, what causes so-called spontaneous remission? Finding out why no therapy is necessary for so many patients requires us to turn away completely from current therapies. If this were done, I believe we would discover what factors really are at work.

My own belief is that patients or clients seek help precisely at the point when they have decided to try to regain control over some part of their life. For most of them, what happens in the psychological and behavioral therapies is that they learn to take responsibility for themselves. It may be that the content of the therapy does not matter (Macmillan 1986).

Some psychoanalytic opinion is consistent with my view. Of interpretation in psychoanalytic therapy Glover said:

Should the analyst's interpretations be consistently inaccurate then quite clearly he is practising a form of suggestion.... It follows then that when analysts differ radically as to the etiology or structure of a case ... one side or the other must be practising suggestion.   (Glover 1954)

My point is not that it is as logical to conclude that both sides are practicing suggestion, which they are, of course, but rather that the outcome of psychoanalysis is independent of interpretation. Glover also showed that it was independent of technique (Glover 1937), and the Columbia study indicates that it may be independent of whether psychoanalysis takes place or not.

What therapy provides is a framework within which the individual can come to understand and explain his or her behavior, and several analysts have said exactly that. According to Marmor, for example:

what we call insight is essentially the conceptual framework by means of which a therapist establishes ... a logical relationship between events, feelings, or experiences that seem unrelated in the mind of the patient.   (Marmor 1962)

And, even though he grants that what happens in therapy "is still mysterious," Klauber makes much the same point:

when the analyst gets a clear idea of what unifies the patient's associations and communicates it, something therapeutic happens in the patient.   (Klauber 1980)

Auerhahn's discussion of the research of Bieber and the observations of Anthony on the transcript of Dewald's sessions with a single patient bring out clearly that patients come to take over the style of speaking, the mode of thinking, and methods of analysis and interpretation used by their analysts. After an analysis has been completed, Auerhahn suggests that

> if the analysed patient is successfully to meet future trials and tribulations, then he must take away with him not only (static) content but a structure and mode of interpretation. Analysis is terminable *when the patient has internalized the process* and learned to self-reflect constructively. (Auerhahn 1979. My emphasis)

Similarly, Weiss concluded that dreams are used in therapy to build meaning for the dreamer. The inherent meaning *of* a dream and the meaning it might have *for* the dreamer are not the same. There are no criteria by which meaning-of can be evaluated or its congruity with meaning-for established, but meaning-for can be created even when the themes developed through the dreamer's associations are related "only very loosely or perfunctorily" to the dream report. Weiss implies that the real use Freud made of dream associations was to build up meaning-*for* (Weiss 1974). One might presume from the Columbia study finding of a modest relation between outcome and length of treatment that the longer a psychoanalysis lasts the more time patients have to build up a logical relationship between the different parts of their lives and to construct meanings for themselves.

In that many nonanalysts have *speculated* that the effective ingredient in therapy is the construction of meaning for the patient, none of this is particularly new. What is new is that some analysts now give credence to and extend what was originally a heretical opinion of Marmor's. For example, Basch (1981) outlined a theory explaining how interpretation could give rise to the cognitive transformations underlying changes in therapy. Should any significant numbers follow in these new directions, psychoanalysis may cease to be. Psychoanalysts will then come to grips with the fact that transformations need not involve truth. Widespread recognition that the truth of psychoanalytic theory is independent of the theory's plausibility and that its truth has no bearing at all on what little special effectiveness it does have as therapy, would completely undermine any claim of psychoanalysis to uniqueness. Apart from its roles as a belief system and a social movement, its status would revert to that of any of the other poorly understood psychotherapies.

Conclusion

When Brenner reiterated his characterization of psychoanalysis he did so in essentially the terms Freud used: psychoanalysis is different from other sciences only in the trivial sense of its different subject matter or field of inquiry. For Brenner, as for Freud, science is defined by its empirical approach and pragmatic and empirical attitudes. There was "no science other than natural science" and nothing to prevent psychoanalysis from being, or becoming, a branch of science. Although its data had meaning, what psychoanalysts did with their data was "no different in principle from what any other scientists do" (Brenner 1980, cf. 1968; Edelson 1977; Holt 1981; Wallerstein 1986a).

Should we therefore conclude that psychoanalysis is a science? My evaluation shows that at none of the different stages through which it evolved could Freud's theory generate adequate explanations. From the very beginning, much of what passed as theory was description, and poor description at that. The concepts of the *Project*, for example, were pseudophysiological and based on little more than a direct translations of Freud's ideas about condensation and summation of stimuli into neurophysiological concepts that were inadequate and out of date in their own day. His key psychological concept of repression was nothing but an objectification of his own sense of effort in overcoming resistance, and it had no greater explanatory power than realization, hypnoid isolation, or dissociation. In every one of the later key developmental theses, Freud assumed what had to be explained: in the transformation of the primary process into the secondary, in the resolution of the Oedipus complex and the formation of a superego having the right sexual qualities, in the fusion and defusion of instinctual drives providing the different kinds of energy to it and the ego, and in the development of adult libidinal sexuality, character traits, and object-choice.

What then of the potentiality of psychoanalysis to become a science? There are two related issues. First, no discipline exists apart from its practitioners. It is their attitudes that determine whether they use their methods to gather data and develop and test theories in an objective way. From the differences between chemistry and alchemy or between psychology and phrenology we see how much attitudes matter. The history of psychoanalysis records many occasions on which scientific attitudes were not noticeably manifest. They were almost completely absent in the evaluation of the Rank theory of birth trauma, and completely so in the attempt to resolve the Melanie Klein–Anna Freud differences. It is entirely in keeping with this tradition that discussions of contemporary variant theories of psychoanalysis are similarly deficient in those attitudes, and that the kinds of programs for methodological reform outlined by Wallerstein and his colleagues still have not been adopted (Wallerstein and Sampson 1971; Wallerstein 1975).

Second, at least until very recently, neither the defenders of Freud's psychoanalysis nor its psychoanalytic critics doubted the objectivity of the psychoanalytic method. For both, the method is supposed to have established certain basic facts reasonably securely. All that is or ever has been questioned are the sources of the theoretical constructs (e.g., in biological or cultural factors), the kinds of constructs (e.g., economic, structural, or dynamic), and the appropriateness of the type of theorizing (e.g., at the clinical or other level). The few who do have doubts about the method do not question it in any depth and never ask whether it creates its data (e.g., Brenner 1968; Arlow and Brenner 1988). Such questions demand a radical change in attitude and the explicit adoption of scientific skepticism. Until those questions are raised and answered, any potential that psychoanalysis might have to be a science must remain unrealized.

Over a hundred years ago the lesson psychoanalysts had to learn was given by the hysterical patient in Brouillet's painting. According to Charcot, her progression into the *arc-de-cercle* was as inevitable as it was physiologically lawful. As I observed in chapter 3, she could use the drawing of another patient who had already completed her arc as a model for her own. Charcot never accepted that the lawlike regularities in the behavior of patients at the Salpêtrière could result from unconscious influences of that and more subtle kinds. Nor did Freud after him.

When Collins examined Freud's defense of psychoanalysis against the charge that it was a version of suggestion therapy, he found it had three components. First, Freud dismissed the term "suggestion" as having no definite meaning; second, he said it could be kept under control by various technical stratagems including the emotional coldness of the analyst; and third, it had never occurred in his own practice. Collins finds the first "disingenuous," the second "scarcely satisfactory," and the third "astonishing" from someone whom he describes (incorrectly, of course) as "the first to describe the unawareness of behaviour" (Collins 1980). Freud did not believe in the importance of unconscious influences from expectations and demand characteristics and he did not guard against them. In fact, his particular beliefs about the internal determinants of psychological phenomena caused him to develop and use a method for gathering data that by its nature could not exclude them. None of his followers, including his revisionist critics who are themselves psychoanalysts, have probed any deeper than he did into the assumptions underlying their practice, particularly the assumptions underlying the basic method—free association. None has questioned whether those assumptions hold in the therapeutic situation; none has attempted to break out of the circle.

Notes

1. For reasons that I do not understand, Forrester (1986) thinks this is an important difference.
2. For Freud (and others), giving meaning by placing phenomena in a causal context was not restricted to

mental events: "Darwin taught us" that the innervations and motor activity underlying emotion and emotional responses "originally had a meaning and a purpose" (Breuer and Freud, 1895, p. 171).

3. One also wonders what Jackson would have made of the insinuation that he was not a scientist.

4. Klein and his supporters also imply that the clinical theory he foreshadowed is not metapsychology. The implication is quite misleading. Invoking the interplay of mental forces to explain symptoms was to turn, as Freud said, to "dynamics," that is to an explanation deriving from the dynamic metapsychological viewpoint (Freud, 1924c, p. 193).

Afterword

In this Afterword I wanted to reconsider the arguments and conclusions of *Freud Evaluated* in the light of the post-1989 literature, but a search of the *PsycLit* data base quickly showed that goal was unattainable. Between 1990 and 1995 some 3,500 journal articles or book chapters and 250 books appeared with "Freud" or "psychoanalysis" or both (or derivatives) in their titles, numbers that increase approximately three times if the search is based on those words in the content descriptions. The coverage in this Afterword is consequently less comprehensive than I would have liked. I have scanned the main serial publications available in Australia, asked my overseas colleagues to suggest works to include, considered what I found in the data base, and added some pre-1989 works originally unavailable or that I had overlooked or misunderstood.

What follows begins with the literature relevant to Freud's basic assumptions, mostly set out in part I and some of part II of *Freud Evaluated*, and then covers various theoretical concepts and issues from part III and the remainder of part II, such as those related to dreams, instinctual drives, narcissism, and the mental structures, before reconsidering the general issues raised in part IV.

From Charcot to the Traumatic Sexual Etiology of Hysteria

The assumptions I tried to bring out in parts I and II seemed to underlie Freud's understanding of hypnosis and hysteria, especially those about Charcot's work at the Salpêtrière, about Breuer's conceptualization and treatment of Anna O., the causes of the actual neuroses, and his method of investigating the psychoneuroses. I discuss the new literature in the same order.

Charcot

The considerable post-1989 literature on the history of hypnosis was brought together by Gauld (1992) and Crabtree (1993), and that on hysteria by Micale (1989, 1990a, 1995). Unfortunately, none of these surveys, or others of more limited scope (David-Ménard 1983/1989; M. N. Evans 1991), including those specifically devoted to hypnosis in therapy (Chertok and Stengers 1989/1992) or the work of Charcot (Micale 1990b), bears directly on my theses. Thus, although Gauld (1992, pp. 310–315) and Crabtree (1993, pp. 165–168), as well as Shorter (1992, pp. 181–185), bring out the errors in Charcot's delineation of hypnosis, none mentions the crucial role of Delboeuf's sceptical experiments in showing how the phenomena of transfer and the stages of hypnosis were caused by expectations and demand characteristics, rather than by the internally determined processes to which Freud attributed them.[1]

A similar consequence results from neglecting Charcot's traumatic hysteria in favor of major hysteria (*grande hysterie*) (David-Ménard 1983/1989; Micale 1990b, 1991, 1993; Evans 1991; Harris 1991; Shorter 1992, chapters 5 and 7). Where traumatic hysteria is discussed, it is classed as neurogenic and contrasted with Freud's psychogenic conceptualization (Micale 1995, pp. 24–27, 1990b, part IV, notes, pp. 112–120), and its causes are pictured as mere precipitators of symptoms in the predisposed (Gauld 1992, pp. 309–310). Consistent with this latter, Charcot's explanation of traumatic hysteria, on which Breuer and Freud based theirs, is dismissed as a pseudoscientific confabulation resulting from failure to recognize organic pathology (Webster 1995, pp. 96–99).

That Charcot's experiments producing an analogue of traumatic hysteria by indirect hypnotic suggestion are neglected is therefore not surprising. Charcot believed symptoms were caused by the unconscious "realization" of ideas, which is precisely what the ideas suggested in the experimental "trauma" seemed to do. Neglecting this aspect of his work obscures two significant connections of his thinking with Freud's (and Breuer's). First, although Charcot's concept of "realization" was characterized vaguely, it gave direction to Freud's later search for traumas having the same sensory content as the symptoms. Without this connection, Freud's concept of "determining quality" appears merely *ad hoc*, an arbitrary "formula" or "principle of similarity" (Scharnberg 1984, §132, 1993a, §§6, 11, 326), or link of "thematic affinity" or "thematic kinship" relating symptoms to alleged causes (Grünbaum 1984, 1993, pp. 127–141; cf. Erwin 1993, 1995, pp. 26–41). Second, the experimental analogue allows one to see particularly clearly how expectations and demand characteristics, rather than an internal deterministic process, produce the symptoms.

It is not at all necessary to appeal to neurology to explain anesthesias, catalepsies, or paralyses in hypnotized subjects, as Webster does (1995, pp. 63–65, 79–84), or losses of speech and hearing, for that matter. One can easily demonstrate that the symptoms produced by the ideas contained in a direct verbal suggestion have the same detailed characteristics as those Charcot produced by indirect suggestion and showed to be identical with the hysterical. This is true, for example, of the regularity of the hip boundary and the exclusion of the genitalia and soles of the feet in Le Log____'s anesthesia. Even had Le Log____ also incurred brain damage, as Webster insists and as may have been the case, the anesthesia is typically hysterical (and hypnotic) in corresponding to the popular idea of "the legs" rather than to a neurologically determined symptom (Webster 1995, pp. 74–77, and n. 5 and 6 on pp. 567–569; cf. my figures 3.4 and 3.5).

From an organic point of view, Charcot's work on hysteria and hypnosis was in error more because he misdiagnosed neurological disorders and symptoms rather than because he failed to rule out expectations and demand characteristics. Not recognizing the latter as the real source of Charcot's errors leads to their being overlooked in Freud's work.

Anna O.

Organicity is also directly relevant to Anna O. because much of the literature since 1989 continues to insist hers was a neurological disorder (Webster 1995, chapter 4, and n. 26–40 on pp. 576–579; cf. Micale 1993, Introduction and notes to Ellenberger's chapter 9 on Anna O., 1995, pp. 59–66; Wilcocks 1994, pp. 152–153, n. 32). Webster has made a case for a neurological condition most forcefully, but in my view it is neither convincing nor does it make any particular retrospective diagnosis more certain.

None of the neurological interpretations takes into account that one of the two main reasons for Breuer ruling out an organic condition and settling on a diagnosis of hysteria was the daily variation in Anna O.'s symptoms. Nor are Breuer's descriptions of many of her symptoms detailed enough for neurological alternatives to be explored. Thus, her contractures, paralyses, and anesthesias cannot be compared with their organic counterparts, as can be done with Charcot's patients. That she had an aphasia with a right hemiparesis is, of course, consistent with a left-sided brain lesion, but what do we make of the later concurrent left-sided paresis, and the way all three of these symptoms varied in ways unrelated to each another? Thus, while Webster's questioning of the diagnosis of hysterical aphasia is legitimate, Breuer's description of Anna O.'s spoken German is too sketchy, her command of written English too substantial, and the daily variation in it and the related paralyses too great for me to dissent from his diagnosis.[2]

Three other points should be made. First, Breuer's rapid evaluation of Anna O.'s cough as a tussis nervosa or tussis hysterica was not as off-hand as it might seem; that symptom had well defined and well accepted nonorganic characteristics (Hirschmüller 1989. pp. 108–109), Second, Webster draws attention to Thornton's argument that Anna O.'s squint could not be hysterical because the muscles involved are involuntary. That may be, but many people are able to learn to squint voluntarily, although no one seems to have induced a long-lasting squint under hypnosis. Third, Webster's parallel between neurological confusional states and Anna O.'s confusion during the stocking-wearing caprice overlooks the fact that dual consciousness gives explanation enough: she went to sleep in one state of consciousness and woke in another (Webster 1995, pp. 122–125). Gauld and Crabtree give compact but comprehensive accounts of pre-Breuer cases of dual personality showing that neither organic dementia nor confusional state need be postulated to account for behavior such as Anna O.'s.

Their accounts and Shorter's also require some modification of my claims for the historical and clinical priority of Mary Reynolds and Felida X, respectively (Gauld 1993, pp. 363–374; Crabtree 1993, pp. 283–306; Shorter 1992, chapter 6).

A point that escaped me about Thornton's neurologizing is her implying that Anna O. must have had neurological condition because she had one symptom sometimes found in that condition. Thus, Thornton speculates that a parietal lesion may have been present simply because something such as Anna O.'s seeing only one of the flowers in a bunch is sometimes reported in parietal disorders (Thornton 1986, p. 134; Webster 1995, pp. 114–115, and n. 26 on p. 576). Such comparisons seem plausible, but their superficiality contributes directly to contradictions among the rediagnoses. Here a hypothesized parietal lesion is put on a collision course with Orr-Andrawes's diagnosis of temporal lobe dysfunction. In chapter 1 I implicitly made the point that new diagnoses are always functions of whatever is currently fashionable; Micale explicitly illustrates that point by citing Merskey's rediagnosis of Anna O.'s disorder as depressive on the basis of the features Orr-Andrawes takes to be neurological (Merskey 1992; Micale 1995, pp. 62, 66, and n. 99). Fashion seems to override evidence, and there is more to her case than is conveyed by Weissberg's (1993) classification of it as iatrogenic.

My proposition that Breuer's original method was essentially verbal and the description of its emotional component added later has been accepted by those few writers who have commented on it (e.g. Chertok and Stengers 1982/1989, pp. 32–33, and n. 68. cf. p. 288; Esterson 1993, p. 3, n. 1; Webster 1995, pp. 106, and n. 8 on p. 574). Breuer's method was, quite literally, a talking cure in which removing the minor caprices was the essential step toward a verbal method for dealing with the more serious symptoms. That its developed form resulted from expectations shared between Breuer and Anna O. still seems to me to be its most likely source. I explicitly based the role of expectations on Ellenberger's thesis, but extended it after studying the case notes (Ellenberger 1972; cf. Macmillan 1977b, and my chapter 1).

Borch-Jacobsen recently pointed to a different source of shared expectations: Hansen's 1880 hypnotic stage demonstrations of such "symptoms" as were exhibited by Anna O. as anesthesias, contractures, positive and negative hallucinations, and aphasia; he believes these expectations more relevant and better documented than those I described (Borch-Jacobsen, 1995, Chapters 6–7; cf. Gauld, 1992, pp. 302ff and Shorter, 1992, pp. 150–154). Although Anna O. probably knew about these demonstrations and Breuer almost certainly did, I believe the details by which the talking cure evolved are not particularly well explained by them. However, both sets of expectations could have operated together. That Breuer's cure was neither permanent nor complete does not conflict with his reinstating Anna O.'s ability to speak, alleviating her fear and pity through story-telling, or removing her *caprices*. And, as slight a victory it may be, Breuer does seem to have removed her inability to drink.[3]

Were most of the changes due to spontaneous variation rather than to Breuer's therapy, his method would still be critically important for understanding two things that Freud never appreciated: first, it and his own affective version depended on shared expectations, and second, it did not provide a touchstone to differentiate the psychoneuroses from the actual neuroses.

Causality and Sexuality

I implicated Freud's faulty adaptation of Koch's postulates in his work on the actual neuroses as basic to his expectation that the causes of all neuroses would be sexual (my chapter 5). Glymour gave a different account of the origins of Freud's expectations, but otherwise only Scharnberg and Grünbaum seem to have considered the actual neuroses themselves.

From about the early 1880s the procedures enshrined in Koch's postulates were generally accepted as the way to determine whether a particular bacterium was the cause of a disease (Carter, 1980, 1987). In the ideal instance, the postulates required the suspect bacterium (i) to be present in every case of the disease, (ii) to stain differently from other bacteria, and (iii) to be able to produce the disease in susceptible animals infected with a pure culture from it. Requirement (i) established it as part of the necessary conditions, requirement (ii) showed its potential as specific cause, and (iii) showed it, together with susceptibility, to be part of the necessary and sufficient conditions. A bacterium meeting all three requirements was the specific cause of the given disease (e.g., of tuberculosis) and could not cause another (e.g., syphilis).

When Freud adapted Koch's postulates, he had first to show the ubiquity and specificity of the suspect cause by, ideally, finding it in the histories of all those suffering from the given neurosis (e.g., masturbation in every neurasthenic) and by being different from the cause of any other neurosis (e.g., not found in hysteria or anxiety neurosis). Although he could hardly deliberately cause the neurosis (requirement iii), he could easily have studied those who masturbated and those who practised coitus interruptus. He had then only to see if, when the other factors were also present, neurasthenia was confined to the first group and anxiety neurosis to the second. That is, he had to examine nonneurotics exposed to the combination of specific cause, hereditary precondition, and concurrent cause. Freud knew he needed these data but did not collect them, but by smuggling the word "suffices" into his description of the effect supposedly achieved by the combination of the specific and other causes, he explicitly claimed to have established the specific cause as part of the necessary and sufficient conditions (Macmillan 1976, my chapter 5).

The logical status of the causes proposed by Freud has been analyzed somewhat differently, and quite independent of me, by Grünbaum and Glymour (Grünbaum 1980, 1984, 1993; Glymour 1993, forthcoming, chapter 3). They believe Freud wanted to establish the specific cause as only a necessary condition. He therefore had to demonstrate its presence in every case of the given neurosis, and show its absence in others as well as in nonneurotics and not just susceptible ones. They contend that Freud, unable to show even this, had to settle for establishing the causal relevance of the specific cause by way of its relatively greater frequency in neurotics. In their opinion, Freud had to compare nonneurotics with neurotics or neurotics of different kinds; mine required the comparison with those in whom the specific factor plus the other factors could be assumed to be present. Thus, although the analyses differ over the status assigned to the causes, they agree that Freud's analysis was inadequate because he failed to make a critical noneurotic comparison.

Without the comparison, Freud's causal arguments reduce to little more than a simple enumeration of cases in which the cause is present (Macmillan 1976) or, more correctly, a post hoc ergo propter hoc assertion (Grünbaum 1984, pp. 120, 168–169, 253–255, 1993, pp. 317–321, 326–327; Glymour 1993, forthcoming, chapters 3 and 4). The same defect is found when Freud hypothesizes that some combination of conscious and unconscious determinants are the necessary and sufficient conditions for dreams, symptoms, and parapraxes. Because these causes do not have that status, these explanations also reduce to the same post hoc ergo propter hoc fallacy. Here I have to correct my mistaken judgment (my chapter 16) that Grünbaum did not see this point, especially as it is central to so much of his criticism of Freud.

On the empirical evidence for the specific causes, Scharnberg evaluated the relevance of Gattel's series of cases of actual neuroses. He notes major inadequacies in Gattel's data, and his rather generous judgment of the presence of the specific cause gives an estimate of only 69 percent of anxiety neurosis in which there was an interruption to sexual discharge, so that 20 percent of the cases are indeterminate and 10 percent are counterinstances. My calculation of the corresponding percentages for masturbation as the cause of neurasthenia are 54, 34, and 12 percent, respectively. Thus, the hypothesized specific factors are present too infrequently for even the necessary conditions to have been established, a conclusion also consistent with the small amount of Freud's data in the Fliess correspondence.[4] Scharnberg's estimates of hereditary influence in anxiety neurosis are so much lower than Freud's that he concludes that Freud's were "fabricated." My conclusion that Gattel's work "rather spectacularly" confirmed Freud's etiological theses therefore requires modification (Scharnberg 1993b, §§779–782, 788–791, 844–847; cf. Macmillan 1989a, 1990).

Scharnberg also scrutinizes Gattel's cases of hysteria for evidence of perverse sexual seduction. Although the number of patients with hysteria is small, and in all but one it is mixed with an actual neurosis, he found little evidence for seduction or other sexual factor. However, except in the one pure case (seen on nine occasions!), Gattel did not make detailed enquiries of his patients but, in this one exception the alleged cause was not trivial and had the same sensory content as the symptom. However, it also was not repressed as much as withheld by the patient (Scharnberg 1993b, §§801–802, 815–829, 838).

Glymour's purpose in examining Freud's work on actual neuroses was to trace the development of Freud's clinical methods. He placed their origins in the traditional Millian approach of real science, but contends that they became unreliable because of Freud's "strong prior disposition for sexual etiologies and a massive insensitivity to experimenter effects" (Glymour, forthcoming). For the disposition he provides only an 1888 passage in which Freud proposed a very general and quite widely held view that "conditions related functionally to sexual life play a great part in the aetiology of hysteria (as of all neuroses)" (Glymour 1993, forthcoming, chapters 3 and 4; cf. Gosling 1987, pp. 46–47, 52–55, 92–105; Oppenheim 1991, pp. 158–164, 201–206; my chapter 5). In emphasizing Mill, Glymour does not see that it was Koch's postulates with which Freud was best acquainted and that he adapted specifically, although defectively, for his causal search. To my mind, Glymour locates the determinants of Freud's expectations incorrectly, even adopting a distinctly anti-Koch (and anti-Freud) position in asserting that Freud could allow "several specific causes for an effect" (Glymour 1993, forthcoming, chapter 3, sections 1–4, chapter 4).

Although Freud's disposition and insensitivity are important, I believe the evidence shows a more complex sequence of factors. He had already shown "insensitivity" to experimenter effects as early as his work on the effects of cocaine on muscular endurance and reaction time, and his appreciation of the Salpêtrière work on hypnosis revealed complete insensitivity to the role of demand characteristics as well. But given his general assumptions about the uniformity of causes (my chapters 5 and 8), his defective adaptation of Koch's postulates was almost by itself able to result in a sexual etiology for the actual neuroses. Once established, Freud's incorrect causal thesis, together with his further assumptions about internal determinism and the identification of associations with causal connections and logical relations, was almost guaranteed to lead him to a sexual etiology for hysteria. And, contrasting with Glymour's documentation of only a very general expectation on Freud's part, are

Freud's previously suppressed letters to Fliess confirming that he began work on hysteria only after having "established" the sexual causes for the actual neuroses (Macmillan 1989a, 1989b, 1990).

Sexuality: Suggestion, Fantasy, and Fabrication

The post-1989 literature devoted to Freud's "abandoning" the seduction hypothesis is too extensive to cover more than a part of it, and I am unable to consider whether Freud was "correct" to give it up or his decision in relation to the recovered memory movement (the issues relating to the latter are well summed up in the interchanges recorded in Crews et al 1995 and Borch-Jacobsen 1996). Once there were only three explanations to consider: Freud's own, that the "memories" were based on internally generated fantasies, and the alternatives that the seductions had really happened, or had been created by suggestion during therapy. A fourth, previously hidden by the attention given the others, especially the first two, recently emerged: Freud's more or less complete fabrication of what was supposedly said or observed.

Freud gave four reasons for giving up the seduction theory: (i) failure to cure anyone, (ii) perverse seductions, especially those by fathers, would have to be very much more common than cases of hysteria, (iii) no indication of reality in the unconscious, and (iv) no evidence of seduction memories in psychotic deliria. This last reason is actually the least adequate but has still not been discussed. I will treat the others in the order of the attention given them in the post-1989 literature, namely, (iii), (ii), and (i).

Almost no one maintains that Freud adopted the fantasy explanation immediately. As Robinson says, the shift is not "adequately encompassed by the familiar image of an intellectual U-turn" (Robinson 1993, p. 166; cf. Masson 1984, pp. 119–122), and it was some time before Freud formulated a sexual theory from which the fantasies could be derived (my chapter 10). However, there are problems in dating the shift. As Esterson pointed out to me, as soon as Freud proposed that some memories were fantasies, the hypothesis that infantile seduction was the *exclusive* cause of hysteria had been abandoned. At the other end, no *single date* for the exclusive adoption of a fantasy explanation can be determined because, of course, Freud always allowed some role for real seduction (Izenberg 1991; Robinson 1993, pp. 168–169). Thus none of the dates suggested for Freud's completing the shift can be accepted: 1907, from a letter of Freud to Jung and made official in 1912 from the minutes of the Vienna Psychoanalytic Society (Powell and Boer 1995); 1909, from the Rat Man case (Glymour 1993, forthcoming, chapter 3, n. 19); or my nomination of 1914, the year the component instincts were finally given the independent bodily sources from which the fantasies could be generated.[5]

Freud's third reason, the lack of indications of reality in the unconscious, has been implicit in the many discussions of whether his patients reported memories of real events or fantasies. To judge from the papers in volume 42 (1994) of the *Journal of the American Psychoanalytic Association*, the clinic has been no more fruitful than the laboratory in arriving at criteria for distinguishing memories of real seduction and abuse from fantasies and false memories. In two instances reported there, one a memory of an alleged clitoridectomy (Good 1994) and the other of incest (Raphling 1994), the external evidence showed the memory was false, but most often in the clinical situation no such evidence exists. Not only are there are no criteria at all, but near insuperable difficulties arise in establishing any (Person and Klar 1994). Brenneis (1994) also concluded there was "no obvious way to differentiate" what he called the "belief" paradigm (i.e., that the memories were of real events) from the "suggestion" paradigm because both made the same predictions.

Reason (ii), as Esterson pointed out to me, really splits into two, one about seductions and the other about fathers, and the former continues to receive most attention through the allegation that Freud overlooked the role and prevalence of real sexual abuse. However, the effect of sexual abuse was not Freud's primary concern and its prevalence *in general* is quite irrelevant to the seduction theory. The specific sexual experience had to have a particular kind of sensory content (determining quality), and combine with susceptibility (my chapter 8). These seductions had to be more prevalent than hysteria, and the only relevant estimate of them available to Freud seems to be the improbably high one that Sulloway suggested could be derived from Gattel's cases: seduction half as prevalent as masturbation. Schröter and Hermanns (1992), who discuss Sulloway's thesis, seem to think it required Gattel to have examined *all* of his cases before the estimate could be derived. However, Gattel had only to have "compiled the bulk of his case histories" before discussing them with Freud (Sulloway 1979, p. 515), and there seems no doubt he had. Schröter and Hermanns seem equivocal in taking issue with Sulloway at the same time as agreeing with him.[6]

Freud's conclusion that the highest proportion of the seducers had to be fathers, although at variance with his published case material and his letters to Fliess, required him to acknowledge that his own father's perversity had caused his and his siblings' psychological difficulties. Balmary and Krüll proposed that Freud abandoned this part of his theory because he was defensive about his father, and Kupfersmid subsequently developed their proposal. But because we know Freud had no hesitation at all in acknowledging that role to Fliess, it could be a reason only were his "little hysteria" also well known publicly (Balmary 1979/1982; Krüll 1979/1986; Kupfersmid 1992). On the other hand, as Esterson, suggested to me, the growing discrepancy between Freud's later conviction that fathers were responsible, and his earlier one implicating a variety of seducers may have contributed to his giving up the theory.

Glymour and Borch-Jacobsen, among others, argued that Freud knew his suggestions had created the memories. Glymour notes that Freud specifically defended his clinical method against the charge that it resulted in unreliable data, but believes that Freud gradually came to have doubts. When these eventually became overwhelming, Glymour maintains Freud could not bring himself to question the methods publicly. After about nine years, when he did admit his mistake, he misrepresented both the content of the theory and the history of his claims (Glymour 1993, forthcoming, chapter 4). As I understand Glymour's position, it is the public misrepresentations themselves that persuade him "that Freud was principally concerned with concealing his doubts about his clinical methods." In contrast, Borch-Jacobsen showed that some of Freud's statements can be read as meaning that he knew the memories were created by "the hypnotic-suggestive" aspects of his method. However, that construction is possible only if Freud's claims for the independence of even this early method from suggestion are treated as "a big lie" (Borch-Jacobsen 1996). Both theses seem to me to be unsatisfactory in disregarding or downplaying Freud's sublime and unwavering faith in his method, whereas, as Cioffi pointed out some 20 years ago (and more recently, personally), even when Freud admits his own credulity about the seduction stories, he manages not to impugn it (Cioffi 1974). Glymour's case seems also to rest on a subjective judgment of intent.

In my view, the misrepresentations are better explained by Esterson, who contends they come from Freud's defending the reliability of his method in the context of particular shifts in his theorizing. Thus, until he began to stress the centrality of the Oedipus complex, Freud did not publicly mention fathers as seducers. Again, once he tried to include fantasies of primary seduction by the mother in his explanation of female sexuality, the fantasies of father seduction became secondary (Esterson 1993, pp. 21–25).

It is obvious that some memories were not recalled in any way, for example, those that Freud described as remaining unconscious even after the patient had been "overborne by the force of logic" about their occurrence (my chapter 8). However, possibly because of my almost daily attendance during the year in which the Victorian Board of Inquiry into Scientology sat, in which I heard scientology auditors and their preclear subjects testify to memories of traumatic experiences much more bizarre than seduction, that they had had in previous existences trillions of years earlier, I have always accepted that at least some were actually told to Freud by his patients, a view endorsed by Borch-Jacobsen (Macmillan 1977a; Borch-Jacobsen 1996). However, beginning with Schimek's (1987) reconsideration of Freud's descriptions, it has become clearer that many of even these latter "scenes" were, for the most part, not retailed as more or less complete "experiences" but reconstructed by Freud from fragmentary associations, somewhat in the way that Virginia Tighe's memory of a previous life as Bridey Murphy was built up. These seduction memories were not told to him in any ordinary sense of that word.

Some of those scholars who emphasized that the memories were reconstructions also suggested that on some occasions Freud may not have interpreted anything at all but fabricated the events without recourse to the patient's associations (Esterson 1993, pp. 110–114; Scharnberg 1993a, §§280–314). In the seduction theory papers, Freud fails to give enough detail of any of the "scenes," or other evidence, to test these hypotheses fully. Where detail appears in the Fliess letters, it is neither really confirmatory nor as strong as it seems. Evaluating the evidence on these arguments is too intricate a task to be done properly here, and all I can do is to refer the reader to the following works: D. L. Smith (1991, pp. 7–15), Simon (1992), Kupfersmid (1992), Schatzman (1992), Scharnberg (1993a, §§6, 219, 228, 280–314, 444–448, 505), Esterson (1993, pp. 5–31, 110–114), Israëls and Schatzman (1993), Powell and Boer (1994, 1995), and Borch-Jacobsen (1996).[7]

Discrepancies noted by Scharnberg and Salyard in Freud's account of how he accumulated his cases seem to point more directly to fabrication. At the beginning of February 1896 Freud sent off the manuscript of a paper in which he claimed to have successfully concluded thirteen of the seduction cases, but only seventy-six days later, when a second paper was completed, the number had grown to eighteen. From the number of hours he claimed to have spent with each patient, Schusdek (1966) calculated it was unlikely that he could have recovered any kinds of seduction memories or cured anyone in that time, a conclusion since endorsed by Kupfersmid (1992). Scharnberg subsequently questioned Schusdek's calculations on the grounds that the number was considerably less than either thirteen or eighteen. But, by calculating equivalently improbable figures for the number of hours required for all but two of the eighteen patients whom he assumes Freud commenced treating in November the previous year, Scharnberg raised even greater doubt. Originally I neglected Schusdek's calculations, but the questions posed by them and by Scharnberg's parallel work, clearly require answering (Scharnberg 1993a, §§14, 441–460, 504–511; Salyard 1994).

In 1970 Cioffi documented Freud's abuse of the term "observation" in arguing for his theory of infantile sexuality, a fact I would have acknowledged earlier explicitly but for my cryptamnesia. More recently Esterson drew attention to a similar issue in

Freud's saying that the seduction memories were obtained "by means of analysis." Sometimes the phrase seems to refer to what the patient retrieved, at others to what Freud constructed. Freud does not differentiate among "facts," "interpretations," and "constructions" because for him they all have the same evidential value. For his readers, ambiguity arises because they do not. Another problem Esterson identifies is that some of the constructions are distortions or fabrications of the very facts on which the interpretations are based (Esterson 1993, pp. 72, n. 24, 133–134).

Dreams, Symptoms, and the Reflex Apparatus

Chapter 9 of *Freud Evaluated* began with Freud's theory of dream and symptom formation and was followed by critical evaluations of his clinical application of it to the case of Dora, the theory of mind (the so-called topographic theory), and the clinical theory of wish fulfilment. I concluded by attempting to identify some of the sources of the problems and discussed more general issues of interpretation in chapter 15.

Although little seems to have been published recently on the dream theory as such, some striking parallels between Freud's understanding and use of dreams and those of Charcot, Janet, and Krafft-Ebing were described by Sand (1992). Not only did they use the dreams for diagnosis and for monitoring treatment, but many of the ideas thought to be peculiarly Freud's were not; for example, Krafft-Ebing's relating unconscious sexual wishes to symbols. Freud's concept of the dream tends to continue a well-established tradition.

Clinical Applications

The emphasis in recent discussions of the Dora case fell on the pressures from her family and from Freud rather than on those of her symptoms that I used as a pivot. In this context, Decker's (1991, 1992) undocumented claim that Dora was only thirteen years of age when Herr K., middle-aged and probably smelling of cigars, unexpectedly kissed her, provides an important new perspective. This younger age not only makes Freud's diagnosis of her reaction of disgust as hysterical even less reasonable, but it makes the whole story more than merely tawdry. Dora was "in her sixteenth year," that is, only fifteen, at the time of the second incident when Herr K. made a "proposal," either of marriage or to set her up as his mistress. Anthony Stadlen told me that at thirteen years (an age of which he is about 90% certain) Dora was under the Austrian legal age of consent. Strachey's representing her as sixteen the second time, rather than fifteen, also hides the fact that she was under the British age of consent both times.

Sulloway illustrated his description of a Freud who, as early as 1894, was "the prosecuting attorney in his own psychoanalytic court of law," with the therapeutic pressure on Dora. His characterization was taken further by Malcolm, Scharnberg, and Webster. The latter two liken Freud to a hyperauthoritarian and hyperbrutal police officer, reaching conclusions without evidence and extorting confessions from Dora. The characterization is not unfair, and Freud's use of his own associations rather than Dora's has to be seen within it (Sulloway 1979, pp. 95–96; Malcolm 1988, p. 97; Scharnberg 1993a, §§9, 30, 417; Webster 1995, p. 200; Esterson 1993, p. 48, and n. 13; Lakoff and Coyne 1993, pp. 81–82; Welsh 1994, pp. 36–37).

Emphasizing the pressure on Dora, as do Lakoff and Coyne (1993), Glymour (1993), and Robinson (1993, pp. 142–143), tends to focus attention on her "reactive" symptoms (e.g., her low spirits, her dissatisfaction with her family, her suicide threat) at the expense of those having a different basis (e.g., the "sensory hallucination" of Herr K's embrace and her avoidance behavior). Nonetheless, some of the points made in chapter 9 about Freud's lack of evidence for his explanations of these latter have been confirmed or extended, for example, about her starting masturbating (if she did), her stopping, and the role of masturbation in her symptoms (Esterson 1993, pp. 42–43, and n. 8; Scharnberg 1993a, §§9, 29, 50, 215, 411, 766; Webster 1995, pp. 199–200, 411). Freud's explanatory mechanisms of reversal of affect, displacement of genital excitation, and somatic compliance appear not to have been considered further.

Careful reading shows Freud's explanations of Dora's other symptoms to be similarly deficient. Of her difficult breathing, for example, Freud's "supposing" that, as an eight-year-old, she had heard her parents having intercourse, is next found as an "event" stored in her memory, which, as a later "recollection," caused her to cease masturbating (Scharnberg 1993a, §§17, 49, 198, 447; cf. Esterson 1993, p. 68, n. 20). Freud's alignment of Herr K.'s absences with Dora's aphonia and coughing contains too many gaps to infer anything from it, let alone that she loved him (Rubinstein 1983, pp. 185–186; Scharnberg 1993a, §30; Esterson pp. 38–40). Most of Dora's supposed fantasies either were fabricated by Freud (Scharnberg 1993a, §§299, 452) or were "constructions" based on his "customary practice" of justifying "conjectural notions" by tendentious interpretations (Esterson 1993, pp. 148, 191–192).

Interpreting Dreams

Freud's use of free association and interpretation continue to be commented on much as before 1989 (Glymour 1983, 1993; Sand 1993; Welsh 1994). Glymour (1993) argues that Freud attempted to establish the method of interpretation as reliable, and tried to infer intent "by a kind of extension of everyday psychology." But, he says Freud characterized the process of interpretation vaguely, did not seem to follow it, continually mixed association and commentary, and gave no rules for piecing the associations together or deciding when enough had been gathered. Hopkins (1991), who argues for Freud's using an extension of the commonsense understanding of motives in interpreting dreams, does not seem to be aware of these problems.

Welsh also notes how Freud consistently fails "to follow rules he set down himself." For example, because the context of a dream had to be known before it could be interpreted, Freud said he was restricted to using his own dreams in *The Interpretation of Dreams*, but in that work he interpreted a dream told him by a woman patient who had heard of it from someone else (Welsh 1994, pp. 19–26). Sand (1993) and Welsh agree with Glymour that the meaning of some of Freud's dreams, like that of Irma, seem obvious from the background detail Freud supplies. Sand allows that a therapist sensitive to these kinds of clues might be able to arrive at a correct understanding of an unconsciously motivated dream. But even when Freud's interpretation seems plausible, Glymour's question remains: is the method he used reliable?

Kitcher answers the question of whether dream contents are likely to be connected by associations with a yes, but that of whether free association reveals the connections with a no (Kitcher 1992, p. 125). Sand (1993) refers to the latter as "the free association fallacy." It consists of concluding that B is either the cause of, or a background thought to, A simply because associations from A lead to B. Sand allows that an interpretation might lead back to the cause where A depicts B, but the illustrations she provides do not have repressed, infantile, or sexual ideas or drives as their source. Welsh (1994, pp. 14–16) illustrates the same point with Wittgenstein's argument that *any* set of objects on a table can be connected in as coherent a way as the elements recovered by free association. To these considerations should be added the logical argument made by Grünbaum and Glymour that the content established by free association is not thereby warranted as the cause of the dream.

Because these criticisms of free association and interpretation are virtually identical with those made long ago (my chapters 9 and 15), it is especially dispiriting that they are still required.

Theory of Mind

Little of the literature appearing since 1989 has been concerned with Freud's theory of mind. As was noted in chapter 9, the reflex doctrine is the central core of the theory of the mental apparatus Freud described in *The Interpretation of Dreams*. He stressed it so explicitly and incorporated it so obviously into later models that

Kitcher's (1992) reaffirmation of its literal importance cannot be questioned by representing Freud's use of it as a mere metaphoric vehicle, as does Erdelyi (1994).

Freud's reflex model required the sequential activation of its components and in this respect, at least, Solms (1995b) raised the possibility that neuropsychology may provide some support for the dream theory. Solms concluded that the systematic variation in dreaming caused by systematic variations in types of brain damage was consistent with the sequential requirement of Freud's theory. Dreaming activity shifts from the frontal or the executive regions to the parieto-occipital or perceptual mnestic systems. Although Solms seems to grant that the retrogression is speculative, I doubt that Freud's theory can currently be confirmed by *any* particular sequence of neurophysiological events.

Confirmation of Solms's observation that destruction of the main structures responsible for rapid eye movement (REM) sleep has little or no effect on dreaming will require the neurophysiological theory proposed by MacCarley and Hobson to be questioned or even rejected. Psychoanalysts who adapted that theory to their purposes, despite its conflicting directly with Freud's, need not be discomfited. H. H. Stein (1995) already incorporated Solms's findings into his thesis that the dream is the guardian of sleep: although the structures producing REM may not be necessary for dreaming, dreams occur during REM because sleep is disturbed by their activation, just as it is by unconscious wishes and other disturbances.

The Wish-Fulfillment "Theory"

The extent to which Freud's theory was ever one of wish fulfilment was examined in the abstract by McLeod and questioned empirically by Medici de Steiner. McLeod (1992) traces the shift from the centrality and importance Freud originally gave the principle but neither attempts to resolve the differences, nor acknowledges the greater difficulties of testing the amended theory. Medici de Steiner (1993) also shows that Freud's later works describe some children's dreams as having all the characteristics of adult dreams, a feature at variance with what he has usually been taken to mean. The dreams reported by the child patients of Medici de Steiner and other analysts are also, she says, more complex than those Freud reported: not all children's dreams accomplish wishes, nor are they exceptions to the repetition compulsion. Nearly 100 years after *The Interpretation of Dreams* she stresses that what is needed is for analysts to collect, study, and discuss the different kinds of dreams children actually have.

Chapter 9 concluded with the not very original observation that *The Interpretation of Dreams* proposed two ways of explaining dreams: the first from a theory deriving explicitly from the reflex of physiology, and the other from repressed wishes. The latter is barely a theory (being based on fairly immediately apprehended psychological processes) in which repressed psychological wishes are opposed by a psychological censorship that insists they must be disguised through condensation, displacement, and symbolism.

Grünbaum proposed in 1984 that this second kind of dream theory was ill founded, although not necessarily false. To the objections made earlier by others about the failure of Freud's analyses to reveal the presence of repressed and/or infantile wishes (some of which are mentioned in my chapter 9), he also pointed out that Freud had failed to show they played a causal role in the Irma dream. He since proposed two independent clinical arguments (foreshadowed in 1984) that imply the wish-fulfillment theory is false.

First, only by postulating motives such as the wish to prove him wrong, or a masochistic wish for punishment, is Freud able to avoid counterwish dreams refuting the wish-fulfillment thesis. But he provides no independent evidence for either kind of wish. The second is that continued successful interpretation of dreams over the course of an analysis should reduce the frequency of dreaming. Analogously with the way interpretation supposedly removes symptoms, interpreting dreams should make the repressed wishes causing them to enter consciousness disappear. However, no reduction of dreaming during psychoanalysis is observed (Grünbaum 1993, pp. 357–384). Because Freud postulates the infantile wishful impulses to be *indestructible*, he might have met this objection by saying that interpretation provided only a more adequate means of coping with those dreams they did cause. Of course, any such evasion is hardly satisfactory logically.

Kitcher conjectured that the division between these wish-fulfillment propositions and the reflex-based model was due to Freud's wariness in tying the latter "too closely to specific neurological hypotheses," and to his deciding to derive "details about dream formation and interpretation" from the interrelated disciplines of psychology, psychiatry, and sexology on the one hand, and anthropology, philology, and literature on the other (Kitcher 1992, pp. 119–120). One should not be too harsh about a conjecture, but the 1900 reflex theory was deficient in depicting a *mental* apparatus lacking an organic body or core; at that time Freud had no theory of an infantile sexuality capable of fueling its operation (my chapter 9).

Mental Structures and Instinctual Drives

Since 1989 no one seems to have made a general assessment of Freud's concept of instinctual drive, either in itself or in relation to the structures the drives supposedly energize. What has been written is largely incidental to particular drives, and what emphasis there is on particular structures.

Structures in the Structural Theory

A number of the papers and panel presentations on psychic structure during the 75th anniversary meeting of the American Psychoanalytic Association in 1986 are published in book form (Shapiro 1991). In reviewing this collection, Perdigão (1994) expresses surprise over "the amount of disagreement among authors regarding the definition of the concept of structure." His surprise could not have been over the attention given to formal definitions of structure, because that was minuscule, but over the many different ways the concept has been and is still used (summarized by Meyer 1991; Boesky 1991). The oddest, surely, is that of Modell (1991) who uses the term "as if it were synonymous with characterologic change" (p. 225, n. 1). (A "structure" is a "change"? The slight logical difficulties of this equation were noted in chapter 13.) Similarly eccentric conceptions include Lichtenberg's notion of a structure as a "motivational-functional system" built around fundamental needs such as those that fulfilled physiological requirements and/or were directed toward attachment and affiliation (Lichtenberg 1991). Where fundamental questions about the nature of structures were remarked, as in the papers by Pulver (1991), Arlow (1991b), and Schafer (1991), the difficulties identified, and the means by which they might be overcome, were very like those considered in chapter 13.

Structural change is more than a theoretical issue; it is supposed to be central to therapeutic outcome. Wallerstein (1991) reported only limited success in defining and measuring it in the Psychotherapy Research Project of the Menninger Foundation, and that in the new Langley Porter Psychiatric Institute project the problem had been bypassed by measuring only the observable characteristics related to the structures, however the structures or structural change are conceptualized. Making almost the same points, Weinshel (1991) reiterated that ten years earlier he raised the possibility that "'Structural change' has become . . . a kind of slogan and shibboleth" and that it was "also difficult to demonstrate." Schafer (1991) showed there was a number of "minimalist" psychoanalytic theorists, including himself, for whom "psychic structure is pretty much an empty shell."

Is it surprising that disquiet continues (my chapter 13) with the functions attributed to the structures? Sandler and Sandler (1994) offer a completely new type of unconscious to make explicit the way the concept is actually used. Similarly, after asking if the term "id" had outlived its usefulness, Downey (1989) proposed replacing it with a "subego." Of the ego-ideal Milrod (1990) commented that there was little more understanding of it since Bibring's (1964) analysis twenty-five years earlier, a comment that actually applies to all three elements of the structural theory.

Sublimation, the mechanism by which the ego of the structural theory obtains its energy, remains in limbo. V. P. Gay (1992) reassessed the concept in the aesthetic field and, precisely because of that context, brought out very sharply the inadequacy of Freud's attempt to derive artistic and social qualities directly from the vicissitudes of the libido itself, that is, solely from biology. He also observed that the concept, which Sulloway (1979, pp. 175–178) showed gained its specific content from Freud's collaboration with Fliess, was required for theoretical rather than observational purposes. V. P. Gay joins the many others who say that it has no defining criteria.

Ego, Anxiety, and Repression

In the structural theory, repression was caused by anxiety rather than vice versa, and Freud cited the cases of Little Hans and the Wolf Man to support the change. Nothing further seems to have been published directly on how either case bears on the alteration. Three issues are involved: the chronology of the events, whether the feared animal represented the father, and the Oedipus-castration nexus. The castration events were, of course, originally cited by Freud as the occasions on which an arousal of libido had led to the repression that later caused anxiety (my chapter 13).

In the case of Little Hans, Esterson's scrutiny made apparent how the critical construction was an interpretation of a fabricated event: (i) the incident from which Freud infers the masturbatory fantasy and deferred castration anxiety is imaginary; (ii) what Freud calls his "proof" of the boy's repressing his hostile wish toward his father, which he had been able to "establish with certainty," turns out to be merely "a justified inference"; and (iii) the identification of the father with the feared horse, basic to the whole story, was "disclosed" to Little Hans by Freud himself. Esterson also points out that although Oedipal feelings and castration are discussed, neither element is related to the other and the complex itself is not mentioned (Esterson 1993, pp. 61–62, 150, n. 13, 151, 155, n. 2, 214, n. 6). Nearly forty years ago Wolpe and Rachman (1960) made Freud's evidence the basis of their criticism of the case, fifteen years ago Glymour (1980, p. 265) termed the evidence "appalling," and recently Grünbaum (1993, p. 314) endorsed that opinion.

Similar problems are evident with the evidence regarding the Wolf Man. Central to Freud's explanation is the famous infantile primal scene, the *coitus a tergo* allegedly observed by the Wolf Man in the parental bedroom when he was eighteen months old. According to Freud, during this thrice-repeated act the Wolf Man saw his mother's "wound" and her lack of a penis, and took both as evidence of castration. Anxiety was generated only later, at the time of a dream he had at age four.

In fact the primal scene was uncovered only through Freud's interpretation of the dream and is clearly a construction. Consistent with that fact, like the patients Freud described in the 1890s (my chapters 4 and 8), the Wolf Man, had no recollection of it. When one reads Freud carefully, as Fish (1989, pp. 545–546) does, one finds the scene is actually an *assumption* made necessary by the interpretation of the dream. However, Freud implies that the Wolf Man was able to recall real and extraordinary details, thinking that the coitus was violent, seeing the successive disappearance and reappearance of his father's penis, and judging the emotions his mother was feeling from the complex expression on her face. Citing a 1977 study by Vidermann of the inherent impossibility of the scene, Mahony notes that the Wolf Man's ability to see these elements, "would exceed the ingenious staging of any pornographic film producer" (Mahony 1984, p. 52).

Without a primal scene having just these characteristics, Freud's "laboriously constructed" story "falls apart" (Fish 1989, p. 531). Esterson argues that the near perfect fit of this central element to the others, which has impressed so many previous commentators, results from it being constructed for exactly that purpose. Freud makes plain that purpose included his need to place the importance of repressed infantile sexuality as centrally as possible in the face of the recent defections of Adler and Jung (Freud 1918, pp. 50–51; Mahony 1984, pp. 100–102; Esterson 1993, pp. 67–93, 231– 232).

Esterson adds that no evidence exists for the primal scene's being a fantasy based on observations of animal intercourse (1993, p. 202). And the Wolf Man himself said that although it was possible an exception had been made, he would not have been allowed to sleep in the parental bedroom. In Russia, in his social class, "children sleep in the nanny's bedroom, not in their parents'" (Obholzer 1980/1982, p. 36).[8] Even were the coitus memory that of a real event, Grünbaum makes the point that it is not possible to certify that fact intraclinically, and its causal status would not thereby be certified even had it been repressed. He also concludes that no independent evidence exists for the truth of Freud's accounts of various other scenes, for the Wolf Man's object-choices, or for the wish that he see his parents "in their love-making" (Grünbaum 1993, pp. 160–161, 202–204).

Compton brought out the inadequacy with which Freud reported both cases and stressed the problematic character of anxiety, including signal anxiety, in them. He does not believe that what initiates defence can, in general, be determined, and from his analyses it seems to follow that there is no connection at all between anxiety and repression (Compton 1992a,b,c,d). Beyond that, however, the collapse of the construction of the Wolf Man's primal scene brings repression down most heavily, because it is Freud's preconceived interpretation of the dream that renders his "explication of the process of repression bereft of substantive content" (Esterson 1993, p. 232). If the reported evidence in the case of Little Hans is too slight to support the postulated connection between repression and anxiety, in the case of the Wolf Man it is nonexistent.

Psychoanalysis as Theory and Therapy

After considering some of the very general issues examined in parts III and IV, I here take up sequentially a number of others important to Freud's theory of personality and its development.

The Metapsychology

The only substantial post-1989 examination of Freud's metapsychology is found in Kitcher's (1992) very clear chapter 3. She does not mention the adaptive and genetic viewpoints. For her, metapsychology has only three dimensions: dynamic, topographic, and economic. Kitcher explicitly rejects the notion of metapsychology as either metatheory or reductionist neurophysiology and speaks of it as an examination or description of mental or psychical phenomena from each perspective (pp. 39, 43) or, more generally, as "a complete theory of mental life, including its primeval origins, organic foundation, and proximate psychological causes" (p. 41). She makes an essential distinction between Freud's metapsychology as a set of "doctrines," or specific theories, and a set of "directives" for theorizing about psychology. The latter provides the perspectives and the former particular concepts such as the psychic energy of the economic doctrine.

In his review of Kitcher, Solms (1995a) claims that Kitcher equates "metapsychology" with "meta theory" and fails to realize it is not a set of directives. He departs from Freud in claiming that metapsychology is a framework for *any* theory wanting to go beyond conscious mental events, and that each new psychoanalytic conceptual model "represents *a* metapsychology, not *the* metapsychology." Solms also attacks Kitcher ad hominem—she is only a philosopher and not a trained analyst.

Freud's Conception of the Mind-Body Relation

Because he described the relation between mind and brain with the phrase "dependent concomitant" in *On Aphasia*, I noted that Freud held a materialist position (my chapter 4), and Wallace's (1992) more thorough consideration independently confirms it. Neither of us has been able to find that phrase in Hughlings Jackson, who is usually given as Freud's source. Nor have I found anyone familiar with Jackson's writings who has ever come across it. Jackson's position is well recognized to be psychophysical parallelism, and his use of just "concomitant" is consistent only with that position and not Freud's. On this point Solms and Saling's (1990) otherwise useful comments on Freud's philosophy, and Silverstein's (1989) more comprehensive attempt to demonstrate that Freud was a consistent dualist-interactionist, fail badly.

Rizutto's (1989, 1990a,b, 1992, 1993) recent demonstrations of how central elements from Freud's neurological conceptualizations of psychological processes in *On Aphasia* permeate his psychology are important for two reasons: first, for understanding his materialism and the connection of his ideas with Jackson's and second, for understanding difficult concepts such as cathexis, representation, and memory image. Her discussion of object representation does much to clarify the concept of object itself and, in confirming that the cathexis was of the mental representation (my chapter 11), she puts paid to McIntosh's (1993) view that Freud later made it a cathexis of the real object.

Phylogeny and Ontogeny

Although the importance of phylogeny in Freud's thinking was confirmed in a general way by Ritvo's (1990) examination of Darwin's influence on Freud, its centrality was most strikingly confirmed by Grubrich-Simitis' publication of the 1915 draft of Freud's previously lost metapsychological paper on the phylogenetic basis of repression (Freud 1985/1987). Both works fully support Sulloway's characterization of Freud as a cryptobiologist. Only in this respect is the promise of the title of L. B. Ritvo's book (*Darwin's Influence on Freud*) fulfilled because she shows that Freud shared with Darwin the version of Lamarckism that characteristics acquired through experience or use could be inherited (L. B. Ritvo 1990, pp. 74–98). However, Sulloway showed that topic to be the core of the ideas Freud shared with Fliess, and that it was precisely Freud's and Ferenczi's collaboration on it that fathered the lost metapsychological paper.

Published under the misleading primary title of *A Phylogenetic Fantasy* (Freud 1985/1987), rather than his own projected "Overview of the transference neuroses," Freud describes the influences of humankind's experiences during and immediately after the Ice Ages in creating the different disposition and fixation points on which repression acts. In his scenario, realistic anxiety first arose from the dangers experienced at the onset of the Ice Ages, hysteria from the strengthening of the tendencies to perversion then forced by life's exigencies, and obsessional neurosis from the forms of social organization generated during that time, together with the concurrent development of language and thinking. When life became easier and competition greater after the Ice Ages ended, the psychoses (termed here the "narcissistic neuroses") arose either from the complete loss of love objects caused by the castration of the sons by the leader of the primal horde (the schizophrenias), or from the sons' alternating states of elation and depression as they celebrated or were overcome by guilt at killing their father (the manic-depressive disorders). Freud's thesis here outstrips the grandiosity of the more narrowly constrained biological progression he shared with Fliess.

As Grubrich-Simitis (1985/1987) puts it, Sulloway's reconstruction of this Darwinian background "shimmers so noticeably" throughout this newfound draft. Although Freud seems to have completed the paper, he never published it. From Sulloway's convenient summarizing diagram, Ferenczi used it or the draft as the basis of *Thalassa*, his own phylogenetic speculation (Sulloway 1979, pp. 379–381; Ferenczi 1913/1952c, 1924/1968). In fact, Sulloway's summary is so presciently accurate that there is little in the *Fantasy* he had not already attributed to Freud. Note, however, that *Thalassa* projects farther back to include the dispositions created as life itself came into being—the basic grandiose biological theme of Freud's *Beyond the Pleasure Principle*.

The above considerations alone put paid to Erdelyi's (1994) and Robinson's (1993) weak and inaccurate objections to Sulloway's cryptobiologist thesis. Erdelyi (1994) rejects it because *The Interpretation of Dreams* is "a vast footnote" to the antithesis between beast and reason in Plato's *Republic*. This is certainly true, but he fails to consider that Freud was claiming to put that antithesis on a scientific base. Robinson's quoting Freud's reluctance "to seize on a phylogenetic explanation before the ontogenetic possibilities have been exhausted" (Robinson 1993, p. 85) is a legalistic defence. Alluding to some of Freud's phrases in which he expresses caution in drawing on phylogenesis simply overlooks the central part it played in the explanations of the neuroses of the Wolf Man and the Rat Man, to say nothing of the development of morality and human society.

The Oedipus Complex

Freud's Oedipal theory rests, as Daly and Wilson (1990) showed, on a reconstructed phylogeny and a hypothesised ontogeny for which the mere existence of sex-linked parent-offspring conflict is inadequate evidence. Daly and Wilson provide empirically supported, biologically based, non-Freudian explanations for the facts commonly taken as supporting the concept, for example, offspring choosing mates like their parents, male sexual rivalry, and male anxiety over genital injury. More important, they show that the supposed components of the Oedipus complex could not have been selected by the survival of the fittest. As to Freud's ontogenetic hypothesis, they indicate that it rests on the doubtful conjecture that "infantile filial affection is the precursor to mature sexuality as the caterpillar is to the butterfly." The metaphor is no more acceptable here than the similar gardening metaphor Freud used to relate infantile to adult sexuality (my chapter 10).

Daly's and Wilson's logic and data also tell against Friedman's and Downey's (1995) reframing of the Oedipus complex as a biologically determined "competitive-aggressive" relation with the father that combines with a fear of him. Nor are the major problems noted by Simon (1991) and Simon and Blass (1991), especially the complex as a basis for both male and female sexuality, resolvable by Friedman and Downey's proposal. Some idea of the complexities of the issues can be gauged from the negative answer Blass (1992) gives to the usually positively answered question, "Did Dora have an Oedipus complex?" Blass clearly shows that Freud's theorizing about her sexuality rested (as I maintained, but for different reasons) on a sexual theory transitional to one based on perverse infantile component drives generating Oedipal wishes and object-choices. Finally, the difficulty of there being no epistemological criteria for proving or disproving the complex, which Simon brings out, cannot be resolved by R. C. Friedman and Downey.

Narcissism

The major recent attempts to clarify Freud's concept of narcissism are those of Baranger (1991), Etchegoyen (1991), Grinberg (1991), and Treurniet (1991) in the volume on narcissism published by the International Psychoanalytical Association. They also identify most of the problems pointed out in my chapters 11 and 13, although in somewhat different terms. These are the contradictions involved in maintaining the two-instinct theory and autoerotism as both a stage and mode of satisfaction (Baranger, Etchegoyen), the contradictory relation with objects (Grinberg, Treurniet), the place of the ego-ideal (Etchegoyen), the contradictory postulations of ego and id as the sources of cathexes (Baranger), and the failure to account for or incorporate aggression and self-aggression (Baranger, Etchegoyen). Baranger elucidates more clearly than the other contributors the exceedingly complicated and sometimes self-contradictory nature of Freud's formulations. He not only differentiates nine ways in which Freud uses the term (only five of which seem important), but also reveals the problem of the contradictory developmental pathways and, with Grinberg, to the contradictions with the death instinct. Most contributors (including some not mentioned) outline the resolutions to these problems proposed in more modern psychoanalytic theories. However, none of the proposals is presented critically and almost all conflict with one another. Hansen's (1991) coverage is similar but also fails to arrive at a resolution.

Pointed criticisms of the developmental aspects of new psychoanalytic theories based on reconstructions have been made by Leichtman (1990), Parens (1990), Arlow

(1991a), and Zuriff (1992). Parens shows how direct observational studies fail to confirm female Oedipal theses; Leichtman foresees that these direct methods will generate a revolution in psychoanalytic developmental theories (presumably in the future); and Arlow proposes that because reconstructions are not of objective events, they cannot lead to adequate developmental theories. Quite separately, Zuriff made the absolutely central point that none of the new developmental theories really tests the old. There are still no empirical data bearing on them; indeed, in appealing as stubbornly as did Freud to reconstructions, most new theorists actually prevent any such data being collected. The looseness of the theoretical and observational aspects is illustrated by Greenberg's (1990) idiosyncratic developmental theses and his odd-sounding proposal to replace the death instinct with narcissism.

The Death Instinct, Aggression, and Masochism

Most psychoanalysts have been happy to leave the death instinct in obscurity, and Greenberg's (1990) paper is one of the exceptions. Another is I. A. Friedman's (1992) historically based analysis of *Todestrieb*. His positive suggestions are difficult to follow but he puts the binding function of the apparatus centrally and essentially as Freud pictured the response to pain in the *Project* (my chapters 12 and 13). However, he does not give the death instinct a biological opponent; the impulse is delivered to its object so allowing the aim to be realized for "the pleasure of discharge." Similarly, in the reconsideration of aggressive behaviors by Rizzuto, Sashin, Buie, and Meissner (1993), the death instinct is not involved. For them, aggression is not a constantly active biologically based drive so much as a drive capacity elicited by stimulus conditions.

An important correction to the history of Freud's concept of the death instinct comes from Kerr's tracing how the notion was actually used by Spielrein, from whom it is usually said to derive (Kerr 1994, pp. 367–372, 498–507). According to him, Spielrein in 1912 proposed death as a component of the sexual instinctual drive. When announcing his concept, Freud represented her as having proposed a hitherto unheard of primary masochism as well as anticipating a death instinct opposed to the life instinct. According to Kerr, neither notion is to be found in Spielrein or in the paper of Stärcke, the other source Freud cited. Both proposed that the sexual instinctual drive itself contained a destructive death-seeking component.

One wonders what clinical observational evidence could have told decisively for or against these or Freud's views. The question presages the two post-1989 surveys of masochism and sadism, the conclusions of which are in line with mine that those conditions lack an adequate observational base (my chapter 12). As Grossman (1991) says flatly, "many combinations of pleasure and pain, or unpleasure, in fantasy and behaviour … can be labelled 'sadomasochism'." Similarly, his recognition that a variety of developmental routes is possible and his proposal to refer to the condition as the sadomasochism*s*, shows that some psychoanalysts are beginning to realize they have to study the conditions directly, rather than through reconstructions.

One obtains a similar impression of a slow-growing recognition of the need for data, as opposed to reconstructions, from the set of papers on this topic in volume 39 (1991) of the *Journal of the American Psychoanalytic Association* (pp. 307–450), especially from Blum's summary. Doubtless, attempts such as Glenn's (1989) to combine reconstructive data will still be made. He proposes an erotogenic proto-masochism as a precursor that develops into masochism proper only during and after the Oedipal stage, when conscious and unconscious fantasies incorporating pain appear. Since some of his "precursors" are what others call the full condition, it is uncertain how a decision could be made about his proposal.

A striking illustration of the cavalier way in which data tends to be treated by psychoanalysts generally, and not just in arriving at reconstructions, is provided by Blum's (1991) study of Freud in relation to Moses. Blum cites Bremer's (1976) critique of Freud's interpretation of Michelangelo's statue of Moses as part of his panegyric to the thoroughness of Freud's analysis at the same time as characterising Bremer's fundamental undermining of Freud (my chapter 15) as a mere controversial inference. On the other hand, Yerushalmi (1991) discusses the statue as part of his extensive exploration of Freud's Jewishness without mentioning Bremer at all.

Personality Traits and Developmental Stages

Erwin (1996) examined much of the experimental and observational evidence supposedly consistent with Freud's hypotheses about the way personality traits group and develop. Although there are not many more studies than I considered in chapter 14, the philosophical and logical contexts Erwin provides for his detailed evaluation add considerable weight to his conclusion of the evidence being equivocal, weak, or irrelevant. In fact, I think he is overly generous in one respect, because he accepts the stronger summaries into which P. Kline transformed his weaker and earlier conclusions. From some 1,500 pre-1980 investigations of more general psychoanalytic concepts, Erwin also evaluates the best of the studies selected by proanalytic theorists. He concludes that this work has resulted in only "a massive failure at confirmation" (Erwin 1996, p. 193).

Similarly, the narrower, more experimental post-1989 investigations of the effects of postulated Freudian mechanisms on cognitive processes, "have yielded very little support, if any, for Freudian theory" (Erwin 1996, p. 236). These latter include the much quoted Silverman studies of the arousal of unconscious processes in subjects presented tachistoscopically with stimuli appropriate to their condition. For example, schizophrenics were said to show increases in thought disorder when the pictures expressed aggressive impulses toward their mothers. Scharnberg's analysis of the Silverman studies was similarly negative. He also noted that some of the processes that should have been affected were not, and that what passed for the elements of psychoanalytic theory being tested corresponded to commonplace nonpsychoanalytic knowledge (Scharnberg 1996a,b, §§924–929).

Psychoanalysis as Therapy

Except for its central importance to Grünbaum's arguments, the importance of the therapeutic effectiveness of psychoanalysis continues to be primarily practical rather than theoretical, and the recent summary of outcome and process studies of psychoanalytic therapy by Vaughan and Roose (1995) confirms the very loose relation between outcome and the content of therapy (my chapter 16). They found a consensus among analysts that the "psychoanalytic process" consisted of the four elements of free association, resistance, interpretation, and working through. However, a "process" so defined occurred in only about 40 percent of patients overall, and although maximum benefit was realized in about 90 percent of those in whom it did, it also was seen in about 50 percent of those in whom the process did not occur. Some of the convergence between Vaughan and Roose's conclusions and mine is explained by our both using the Columbia study. It will also be remembered that these figures come for the most part from the less impaired patients, who tended to be treated longer and more intensively. Wallerstein (1994, cf. 1991) makes similar points about what actually happened in the psychoanalyses examined in the Menninger Psychotherapy Project.

As to the efficacy of psychoanalysis, no more studies have been reported since 1989. Erwin evaluates what few data there are, including those summarized by Bachrach, Galatzer-Levy, Skolnikoff, and Waldron (1991), from which it is clear that the limitations of the Columbia study apply generally (my chapters 14 and 16). Patients who show marked improvement are usually only marginally impaired, and it is their therapists who make most of the judgments about improvement. Just as shown by Vaughan and Roose, the evidence is not strong for the effects being due to the characteristic features of psychoanalysis (Erwin 1996, p. 237).

Psychoanalysis as Science and as Method

The evidence I summarized in chapters 15 and 16 showed that Freud represented himself as a scientist, that he believed that psychoanalysis was itself a science, and that he thought free association was as scientific a method as any other. I therefore believed it was justifiable to judge his creation by the standards of the natural and experimental sciences. Two reviewers of the 1991 edition of *Freud Evaluated* took me to task over this conclusion. The objections of Leys (1992) can be disposed of shortly because her "review" is little more than a complaint that I did not adopt the fashionable ideological line of problematizing Freud's view of science, or take into account the social factors from which psychoanalysis was constructed. Because Leys does not support her blanket rejection of my unfashionable adherence to scientific values of truth with a single example of how this led me astray and, indeed, seems to have read only the introduction, my response matches hers in scholarly frivolity:

A Johns Hopkins professor, Ruth Leys,
Said "Reviewing Macmillan's a breys.
No problematic, no construction
in the whole introduction,
A pox on his sins." Leys majesteys?

Contrasting with Leys's review, Blomfield (1994) thoughtfully explicates a large number of objections to my theses, largely from a Ricoeurian position. My response to this critique appears together with his review, and can be examined there (Macmillan 1994). The problems posed by the hermeneutic approaches in general should also be judged through Strenger's (1991), Nussbaum's (1991), and Sachs's (1991) responses to Grünbaum's (1984) critique, and the respective replies of Eagle (1993b), Erwin (1993), and Grünbaum himself (1993).

Eagle's (1993a) review of *Freud Evaluated* is that of a psychologist fully cognizant of the problems posed by psychoanalytic theory, and he implies that practicing scientists do care about the truth of their theories. I would add that that can be so even when they are also fully aware of the contributions of social, political, and ideological factors to particular versions of that truth. The historians and philosophers of the "its-all-a-construction school" will be taken seriously by practicing scientists only when they are able give their reasons for preferring Galileo's construction over Ptolemy's without saying anything about the real state of the solar system.

Science and "Observations" in Psychoanalysis

In most instances in which I discussed Freud's case material originally I assumed that his observations were just that—things he had actually observed or thought he had—and that his interpretations and constructions were, even if mistaken, genuinely based on those observations. Thus I considered the construction he gave to the Rat Man (that he had been beaten by his father for masturbating) only in relation to its bearing on the veridicality of the beating itself. I did not know that Cioffi (1985) observed that the original case notes do not mention Freud's putting this conjecture to the patient at all. What they record is Freud's "constructing the material ... into an event" in which the Rat Man's father had forbidden him to masturbate, "using as a threat the phrase 'it will be the death of you' and perhaps also threatening to cut off his penis." His mother did recall a real beating from about this period of his life, but it was for *biting* his father, and he himself remembered being beaten, probably at a later age, for wetting the bed while in bed with his parents (Freud 1909b, pp. 263, 384). Starting from Cioffi, Esterson shows how Freud created the "fictionalized reconstruction" by fusing the episodes and transposing it to an earlier part of the published history (Esterson 1993, pp. 62–67; cf. Mahony 1986, pp. 72–74).

Many other "events," including the Rat Man's staring at his penis, sometimes in front of a mirror, were similarly fictionalized (Sulloway 1991). However, almost any repressed sexual activity would have served Freud's explanatory purpose, and whether they occurred or not, events such as these, or of the supposed unconscious processes on which they were based, would still be causally irrelevant (Grünbaum 1993, pp. 326–330).

A consequence of the fabrication of the "construction" is that considering whether the Rat Man's reaction validated the event is essentially a waste of time. But there is worse. A central part of Freud's analysis revolves around the Rat Man's fear at hearing a story in which live rats bored into the anus of a criminal. Drawing on Hawelka's 1974 complete edition of the original case notes, Scharnberg shows that several significant parts of the published story seem to have been added by Freud. These include changing the target of the rats from the buttocks to the anus, interpreting the patient's expression as one of fearing the pleasure the story gave him, and dramatizing the patient's distress by having him speak in incomplete sentences (Scharnberg 1993a, §§115, example 9, 135, 1993b, §§1103–1116). In both versions of the case history Freud also derived the Rat Man's homosexual object choices from his reaction to the story, although he had actually inferred them from things the patient told him earlier (Scharnberg 1993a, §§55, 119, example 8, 1993b, §1109). Much of the evaluation of Freud's arguments about the case, especially those drawing on notions such as "the principle of similarity" and "thematic affinity," depend to some degree on the veridicality of his descriptions (Scharnberg 1984, §§138–139, 1993a, §297; Grünbaum 1993, pp. 121–129, 137–138). Because we cannot know what Freud did, the importance of the case simply cannot be assessed.

How Did Freud Go Wrong?

I now turn to an important question bearing on the status of psychoanalysis as science and Freud as scientist. Asked in somewhat different ways by Kitcher, Glymour, and Webster, it is, how did Freud go wrong? Each answer emphasizes an aspect of Freud's personal judgment: Webster and Glymour give the role to his ambitious and devious nature, Kitcher to his unwillingness or inability to modify his theoretical views when he should have.

Webster's (1995) thesis is that Freud was driven by "huge and messianic ambitions" (p. 226). On the one hand the messianic component led to him disguising an essentially religious view of sexuality as a scientific theory, and it also caused him to fall under the spell of such disreputable theorists as Charcot, Breuer, Fliess, and Haeckel. On the other hand, his ambitions were responsible for his misdiagnosing neurological disorders as hysteria, for faking positive evidence, for disregarding counterinstances, and for claiming cures where there were none.

Kitcher's (1992) basic position is that Freud aimed at creating a psychology in a reciprocal harmony with the related disciplines of anthropology, linguistics, evolutionary biology, and brain anatomy and physiology. According to her, Freud later extended the fields with which psychoanalysis had these reciprocal relations, and took the fact that such harmony or "consilience" was possible as evidence for the value of his own work (pp. 109–112). Consequently, psychoanalysis was always "hostage to unfavorable developments in other fields" (p. 63). When the disciplines on which Freud drew failed to provide the kind of basis he sought, or when it was refuted, Kitcher maintains that he failed to change those aspects of his theory dependent on them. For example, when the limitations of the reflex doctrine became apparent, when neural energy could not be conceptualized as stored and transmitted in the way demanded by the *Project* and its psychological successors, and when there was definite refutation, as there was with the Lamarckian proposition of the inheritance of acquired characteristics, Freud made no real adjustment to his own theory. Although aiming at the goal of "a complete interdisciplinary science of mind," psychoanalysis ended in a cul-de-sac while the traffic of other scientific ideas continued along the highway.

A consequence of Kitcher's focus on the relations between psychoanalysis and the theories surrounding it is that her criticisms of Freud's own "doctrines" tend to be general, sometimes missing the point. Thus, in discussing Freud's neurophysiological doctrine she does not see that his is not a real neurophysiology but a speculative theoretical system brought into existence by translating behavioral and clinical observations such as "stimulus" and "condensation," directly into pseudophysiological terms of energy flow through neurons (my chapters 7 and 14).[9] Where there seems to be empirical content, she usually does not question it. Thus she does not notice that Freud's theses on childhood sexuality have their origins in doubtful interpretations of adult symptoms (e.g., Dora's) or misrepresentations of observational data (Lindner's)

(Macmillan 1980, chapter 10 this book). Nor does she scrutinize critically what Freud claimed to find as, for example, when she reports flatly that Freud's "researches into the neuroses implicated unconscious sexual wishes as the instigators of dreams" (Kitcher 1992, p. 130). To the extent that Freud arrived at a harmony or consilience of disciplines, it was because he used a filter that excluded theoretically discordant overtones.

Glymour (1983, 1993, forthcoming) argues that Freud "went wrong" and left science sometime between 1900 and 1910 when he gave up the conception of scientific method he had learned from the physiologists, with whom he worked until then, and was led astray by his strong preconception about the importance of sexuality and the unimportance of experimenter effects in developing his sexual etiologies. When the crisis developed over the seduction theory, Glymour says Freud resolved it by submerging his doubts about experimenter effects and claimed the extended powers of interpretation outlined in *The Interpretation of Dreams* of 1900. That work was designed to collect cases substantiating Freud's ability to detect the wishes hidden in dreams and to "provide the Millian instances for generalisations about dreams and their formation." Freud's adopting this "caricature" of the methods he had previously used, reveals, Glymour says, "a kind of failure of ... character, a weakness of intellectual will." It thus allegedly marked the beginning of Freud's departure from science. By 1909, when he said for the first time that childhood fantasies of sexual encounters could be etiological factors, it was complete (Glymour forthcoming, chapter 3, n. 19, chapter 4).

Glymour's thesis rests on there being a distinction between the scientific methods Freud used in his early and later work, a distinction that I do not believe can be made. Freud's early work was in disciplines—neurohistology and clinical neurology —that did not require active intervention by an experimenter. Before his work on the neuroses, his reputation rested on the use of well-established, constrained, and even passive methods of dissection and microscopy for studying various kinds of nervous tissue, and on the diagnostic procedures of clinical neurology. Constraint was provided by the more or less objective corroboration of other neurohistologists or from prognosticated diseases and/or postmortem examinations. Freud's use of experimental and quasi-experimental procedures did not go much beyond his undergraduate days. Jones concluded that when he did use them, he did not have much success, a judgment consistent with Glymour's (Jones 1953–1957, vol. I, pp. 52–55; Glymour 1993, forthcoming, chapter 3, section 9).

Freud was no more competent later in conducting experiments or entirely reliable in reporting their results. The methodological deficiencies of his (1885/1974) experiment on the effects of cocaine on muscular strength and reaction time are marked

(Bernfeld 1953), and he lied over the addictiveness of the cocaine with which he "experimentally" attempted to wean Fleischl from his morphine addiction during 1884–1885 (Jones 1953–1957, vol. I, pp. 78–97; Crews 1986, pp. 50–52; P. Gay 1988, pp. 44–45). His reports on this latter episode seem to presage his hiding his change of mind over the reality of the seduction memories.

There are parallels with his work on the causes of neurosis. It required a method best described as quasi-experimental, but his use of it violated the canons on which it was purportedly based, and Freud was less than truthful about what he actually found. He also claimed incorrectly that he had not been led to the sexual etiology of psychoneuroses by those quasi-experimental methods. We have seen that the post-1989 seduction theory literature provides strong evidence for doubting the accuracy with which he reported his observations and the numbers of his patients.[10]

Rather than confirming, as Glymour holds, a more or less definite period during which Freud left science, these data seem to me to be consistent with the view that in some significant respects he was never part of it.[11]

Science, Interpretation, and Free Association

Reliable interpretation is one of the preconditions for valid interpretation, but Rubovits-Seitz, who coordinated the 1950s Chicago Institute study of the consensus problem (Seitz 1966), observes that the literature on the interpretive methods central to psychoanalysis "is surprisingly meager" (Rubovits-Seitz 1992). His list of factors causing unreliability overlaps considerably with mine, but he believes that a specified and systematic method of "checking, revising, and selecting interpretive hypotheses" will help make interpretations more reliable. Because the process of error correction he describes is largely an "internal" one, I have the same doubt about it that he expresses about traveling the hermeneutic circle; that is, the evidence *for* a particular hypothesis actually derives *from* that same hypothesis. And, as he says, validation, the "most difficult, and least used step in the error correcting process" lies ahead.

Reliability as Agreement on Interpretations

An interesting method for studying the reliability of judgments about psychoanalytic propositions was recently described by Caston (1993). He had three groups judge propositions derived from verbatim transcripts of analytic therapy sessions. Two groups read the transcripts as well as the propositions (the "textwise" groups) but the other group saw only the propositions (the "mannequins"). Because they could produce only stereotypic psychoanalytic judgments, the mannequins were the controls. The correlation between the judgments made by the textwise judges was higher than that between either of them and the mannequins. Reliable judgments were therefore due to more than the use of stereotypes.

Differences between Caston's textwise judges tended to be over the relation of the propositions to historical conflictedness, present conflict, defense impulse configuration, and the historical links of early situations to current compromise formations. The exemplar propositions Caston cites are not particularly psychoanalytic, however. For example, what is the importance *to psychoanalysis* of analysts agreeing that a patient's present conflict about crying in front of her husband or asking what to do about being late for her appointment is, say, slight, but that conflict about telling the analyst how her mother had punched her or how she felt attracted to a supervisor is, say, marked? Caston's warning that the method cannot yet be used to validate psychoanalysis seems sensibly cautious.

The general factors Baudry (1994) isolated in the famous Freud-Klein controversies still operate to foster unresolvable disputes between psychoanalysts over their data. Two of the nine factors he identified are especially relevant: no clear separation between theory and the data required to substantiate it, and the difficulty of deciding what constitutes valid data to disprove a theory. Baudry notes that the latter is the most problematic for the preverbal period, that is, the one for which most present-day reconstructions are essayed.

All of these conceptualizations are light-years ahead of those mentioned in the recent report on the five-year study sponsored by the Psychoanalytic Research and Development Fund into the theory, concept, and technique of reconstruction. Nowhere in the rambling account of that project are criteria discussed for judging the reality of the events reconstructed. While it may come as a surprise to learn that at particular junctures the data nevertheless always strongly recommend "one specific reconstruction over many less 'fitting' alternatives" (Blum 1994, p. 153), is it a surprise that "no two analysts would necessarily offer identical reconstructions" (p. 167)? How can a fundamentally mysterious self-recommending process overcome disagreements about interpretations?

Validity and the Second Script

The validity of free association has still not been demonstrated and the topic seems to have been discussed by only Sacal, Bornstein, Edelson, Kitcher, Erwin, and Holt. Some of Sacal's (1990) more general conclusions are relevant to mine, but because of his context I can make only limited use of them. He appears to agree that the "variants of psychoanalysis" are produced by the different ways analysts use free association, although for him, those uses are in *self*-observation. Experimental studies of implicit perception and memory for recovering unconscious memories by free association are considered by Bornstein (1993) to have yielded mixed results, but I see them as inconsistent and not directed to *repressed* unconscious material.

Edelson (1984, 1988) makes out two cases for the validity of free association: one for associations not being contaminated by suggestion and the other for the validity of the causes they reveal. The first fails because it is at variance with the clinical and experimental evidence, and powerful answers to the second are provided by Erwin (1996, chapter 3). Erwin, together with Kitcher (1992, pp. 126–127), notes the irrelevance of Jung's word association experiments for establishing the validity of free association (my chapter 15), but neither examines the unlikely underlying deterministic assumptions of the method. Erwin also shows that experiments on the effects of hypnotically produced conflicts are irrelevant to the validity of free association, but does not consider experiments such as Luria's, which, if not contaminated by demand characteristics, apparently show free and word associations leading to the conflict.[12]

Holt's remarks on free association in his review of *Freud Evaluated* are necessarily brief but go to the heart of the matter. He says I am "asking (*inappropriately*, as well as in vain) for evidence of [free association's] reliability and validity" (Holt 1992. My emphasis). He also assumes that I believe "the free association *interview*" is like a psychological test, in being an attempt to measure something like a specific aspect of personality or ability (Holt 1995. My emphasis). However, I neither made the testlike assumption nor claimed free association was measuring things such as traits or abilities. Every psychologist would accept Holt's methodological point that freely created verbal data have to be recorded objectively and analyzed in disciplined ways. But my questions were different. First, are those data already so affected by the demand characteristics of the therapeutic situation that they cease to be reliable and valid guides to patients' thoughts, feelings, and memories? The only two enquiries into this matter show this not to be the case (my chapter 15). Second, assuming that the data are not so affected, where are the rules that allow different analysts to interpret them in the same way (i.e., reliably), and what methods allow analysts to show that what those interpretations reveal is true (i.e., valid)?

Discussions of psychoanalytic judgments and interpretations continue to ignore the fact that the problems of reliability and validity can have no solution. My point was that Freud's analogy between deciphering a language and interpreting a dream or a symptom is false. In the analogy, the unknown language or "first script" is the manifest content and the known language or "second script" the latent content. No unknown language has ever been deciphered without there being a partial parallel record in one that is known. But, in psychoanalytic deciphering, far from knowledge of the latent content (the second) assisting in understanding the manifest (the first), the second is actually a product of the first. Without an independent second script, agreement on interpretation is not merely difficult but impossible *in principle*.

Holt (1995) advanced what he takes to be a telling blow against this conclusion. He claims that all science begins with "insights, hunches, or hypotheses" for which there are "no complete rules" and which then have to be "checked against independent data." His example is the famous one (also used by me) of Kekulé's discovery of the benzene molecule, which Holt correctly says was made at a time when "there did not exist the chemical equivalent of a 'second script'—a direct method of seeing the carbon ring." Although Kekulé could not check his insight "against independent data" in any simple sense, he did carry out an intensive program of experimental work to test the consequences of his proposed structure against its competitors. What made that program possible was that chemistry had advanced to the point at which both the chemical elements forming the "vocabulary" of the second script and the "grammatical rules" governing their combinations were known.

In none of the other post-1989 literature is the weakness of Freud's language analogy even hinted at. Because he believes the lack of consensus may have other determinants, Rubovits-Seitz privately took issue with me over the emphasis I placed on the analogy as the source of the problem. He also sees flaws in my analysis. First, he cites C. Gordon's (1982) study of the deciphering of forgotten written languages to support his view that bilingual inscriptions have not always been used. Second, he quotes from Freud himself to suggest that conscious thought is the known script to which the "entirely rational" latent dream thoughts correspond.

First, although I was careless to imply that the second script had to be *written*, Rubovits-Seitz's appeal to Gordon's description of the use of "collateral information" where no second script was available fails. In every one of Gordon's instances the collateral information was equivalent to a second script or part of it: *written* Coptic in deciphering old Egyptian, *written* and *spoken* Zend-Avesta for Old Persian, and *written* and *spoken* Hebrew and Arabic for Akkadian, and so on (C. Gordon 1982, pp. 26–28, 44–45, 64–65). The Mayan glyphs were recently deciphered mainly by establishing their relation to records of ancient *spoken* Mayan, and confirming the connection with its contemporary equivalent. There was virtually no written second script at all (Coe 1992). In whatever way written words are represented, they are always, as Coe says, visible speech. True, in dreams we sometimes do discern the speech written in particular images but, even then, we can hardly ever apply that knowledge to translating the same picture in another dream, a restriction that rarely applies in deciphering an unknown language. Second, if, as Rubovits-Seitz suggested, conscious thought really were the known second script, there would be no problem, but it is not. Interpretive difficulties arise because of the inability of psychoanalysts to specify any consistent and defensible relation between conscious *visual* thoughts and unspoken dream thoughts.

By noting that reliability of interpretation can be established only with *independent* access to the "sense" of the dream, Glymour (1993) comes close to my position and Welsh (1994) closer still. After mentioning the language analogy, Welsh immediately states that when Freud introduces his observations on translation:

> he boldly treats inferences from the dream as evidentiary fact, part of the data on which his theory is based. Here and throughout the book the dream thoughts are, and can be nothing but, the narrative supplied by Freud ... The new narrative must be derived from the dream that became its expression. (Welsh 1994, pp. 17–18)

Although Welsh is distressed not only by these lapses or slides in Freud's argument but also "by his failure to follow rules he set down himself," the real point is that until the lexicon of the language of the unconscious is made visible and its grammar explicated, there can be no rules for anyone to follow.

Rhetoric and Method

In the face of its limited value as a therapy, its acknowledged weaknesses as a theory, and its reliance on a suspect method of enquiry, the continuing appeal of psychoanalysis requires explanation. Some writers believe they have enough data to explain it (e.g. Gellner 1985; Webster 1995), but I believe the only cogent data are like those recovered by Hale (1971, 1995) in his study of the response to and spread of psychoanalysis in the United States, and/or reports from individuals and institutions attracted to psychoanalysis, including short-term adherents. I continue to doubt that enough such data exist to establish reasonably definite conclusions.

Despite this lack, chapter 16 of the first edition of my book contained some speculations about the appeal. At that time, reading Freud had made me very sensitive to his use of assertions to cover those parts of his views in which the data or logic were weakest. For example, in establishing his concept of childhood sexuality, Freud misrepresented Lindner as having "clearly recognised" pleasure sucking as sexual, and merely asserted that delayed defecation was "no doubt" sexually enjoyable. In fact, I had become very wary about propositions containing phrases such as those or others such as "it would be absolutely typical if ..." or "it is a well-known fact that ..." and have since collected some empirical data justifying that caution. Scharnberg, among others, for example, Esterson and Wilcocks, is also struck by this peculiarity of Freud's style, and gives many examples of these phrases under the name of "superlatives" (Scharnberg 1993a, §§375, table 375.1; cf. Wilcocks 1994, pp. 127–128, n. 33, 153; Esterson 1993, pp. 212–215). But, not realizing the wider implications of these peculiarities, I missed the beginnings of what has become a major concern: the analysis of Freud's rhetoric.

Recent work on Freud's rhetoric, especially that by Sulloway and Welsh, demands attention. Sulloway (1991 1992) compared the technical methods, the literary devices, and the social context of the work of Robert Boyle with those of Freud. Boyle overcame the objections to the conclusions from his experiments with the then new and controversial air pumps in three ways: first, he described the pumps in such a way that others could repeat his observations; second, his literary style made the reader a virtual witness to the experiments; third, he conducted his experiments openly so that they could be observed at first hand.

By comparison, Freud's methods were never described fully. Others could not be sure whether they had understood symptoms correctly, or establish for themselves whether normal phenomena such as jokes, slips, and dreams resembled the abnormal. Second, Freud's case descriptions were incomplete, usually only "fragments" from or "notes" on patients, rather than whole histories. Third, there was nothing open about how his work was conducted. In the early years psychoanalysis could be learned during the regular meetings of Freud's Viennese followers or by an informal personal analysis. Later again there were congresses, the formal requirement of a personal analysis, and the Secret Committee (described by Grosskurth 1991). Here Sulloway insists that the Committee existed to guarantee that the *method* was passed on properly rather than to compel adherence to the true faith.

Scientific pioneers frequently attract bands of supporters who further their cause. For this reason, Thyer (1995) contended that Freud's Secret Committee was no different from the X Club, the semisecret society of Darwin's supporters. Thyer's interpretation has to be rejected. Nothing about Darwinism demanded the adoption of a privately defined, essentially mysterious method for studying a prescribed class of phenomena. As Barton's (1990) detailed study of the club shows, its members were devoted to advancing science in general. Their main campaign on Darwin's own behalf was to ensure his burial in Westminster Abbey (Desmond and Moore 1991, pp. 664–667). Most important, becoming a Darwinist required neither a personal initiation from a Darwinist nor the acquisition of other than publicly available knowledge.

There seems no escaping Sulloway's central point that the incompleteness of Freud's written histories was deliberate and the more narrowly rhetorical aspects mere devices to disguise the shortcomings of his method, especially that of interpretation. Without access to the details of Freud's method or its application, the reader of his works is left no option, Sulloway proposes, but to surrender to Freud's judgment.

Welsh's (1994) analysis complements Sulloway's thesis perfectly. In Welsh's view, the persuasiveness of *The Interpretation of Dreams*, the single work that he discusses, comes from its pretensions to science, its simulcrum of inductive procedures, the interest it shows Freud to have in detection (which his readers come to share), together with the way Freud's portrayal of his own politeness, modesty, restrained ambition, humor, and make-believe, including the manufacturing of evidence, stays within conventional bounds (pp. ix–x). Welsh brings out how the content and style of Freud's presentation forestalls the readers' criticism (pp. 116–117), carrying them "uncritically forward," even in the face of such contradictions as an irrational unconscious being "certain" its impulses will be opposed by censorship (pp. 111–114). What also contributes to the reader's momentum is what Welsh calls Freud's readiness not to confine himself strictly to facts, that is, to invent his data (p. 125).

If Welsh's analysis accounts for the reader's typically compliant response to *The Interpretation of Dreams*, the question remains of whether Freud's other writing appeals for similar reasons. Fish's (1989) scrutiny of the case of the Wolf Man and Wilcocks's (1994) of the main seduction theory paper and the Irma dream suggest that it does. Fish observes that Freud's witholding the critical information about the primal scene so immeasurably strengthens the grip of the narrative of the Wolf Man that the effect of its introduction is quite out of keeping with its being a mere assumption. In Wilcocks's analysis, a similar but cruder development characterises Freud's "Aetiology of Hysteria" paper (Freud, 1896c). There Freud also witholds the critical information that the trauma was always an especially revolting perverse sexual seduction, and again, even though little detail of any particular case is described, its production has maximum effect (Wilcocks 1994, pp. 134–135, 140–141). Wilcocks makes a more serious charge against the Irma dream. Like me, he argues that it could not have been dreamed on July 24–25, 1895; he also presents strong evidence that it was invented sometime after 1897, probably during 1899. In *The Interpretation of Dreams* it demonstrates the wish fulfilment thesis with maximum theatricality through Freud's "interpretation" of it as a self-exculpation (pp. 227–280).

Determinism, Development, and Appeal

Although these conclusions are important, Freud's rhetoric would mainly affect the readers of his works and would not explain the appeal of his ideas to those, probably the majority, who have not read him. In chapter 16 I suggested that part of the appeal of psychoanalysis was that it enabled individuals to construct plausible developmental histories of their own, and Welsh also gives some credence to this factor. Whether constructed by professionals or amateurs, psychoanalytic histories are like no others; not for the self-evident reason that each individual is unique, but because *every* aspect of the individual's life can be assigned a place in it. From Cassirer's observation that scientific explanations allow for accident but myths do not (in myths everything is strictly determined and nothing is accidental), Welsh concludes that Cassirer's characterization of myths applies "rather well to psychoanalysis" (Welsh 1994, p. 133). However, psychoanalysis is able to account for the individual's life history comprehensively only because of its pseudoexplanatory power and because it has no rules for evaluating the adequacy of the resulting narrative histories (my chapters 15 and 16).

Conclusion

The same pseudo-determinism that allows for the construction of personally satisfying but fundamentally indeterminate developmental histories is found almost everywhere in psychoanalysis: there are no rules for interpreting psychoanalytic data, and the determinants of those data are not internal, as psychoanalysts believe. The few indications in the pre-1991 literature that analysts were about to change their attitude toward the method basic to their discipline and investigate it remain indications only. There are still virtually no studies of the rules for reliable interpretation and none at all of the robustness and validity of the method itself. Post-1991 psychoanalytic thought remains imprisoned in the same circle that captured Freud.

Notes

1. Like many others, I attributed the first use of the word "hypnosis" to James Braid. I am glad to acknowledge Dr. Melvin Gravitz's correction of the historical record in his identification of the antifluidist, but splendidly named follower of Mesmer, Etienne Félix d'Hénin de Cuvillers, as the person through whose use the term became popular (Gravitz, 1993).

2. The accumulating literature on the absence of fixed relations between the comprehension and production of various written and spoken languages of multilingual aphasics, renders the differences in her language functioning less certain for the diagnosis of hysterical aphasia than I had thought. For providing opinions and guides to the literature that caused me to modify the weight I put on Breuer's interpretation of the difference, I am much in the debt of Professors Max Coltheart and Harry Whitaker. Equally, however, the lack of fixed relations is as problematic for a diagnosis of an organic aphasia.

3. Small errors are still found in the literature on Anna O. Thus Hopkins (1991) has Breuer treating the drinking *caprice* by hypnosis, and Grünbaum (1993, p. 137, 1990; cf. 1984, pp. 180–184) recently reiterated that it was not removed (cf. Hirschmüller 1978, 1989). Small errors are still found in the literature on Anna O. Thus Hopkins (1991) has Breuer treating the drinking *caprice* by hypnosis and Grünbaum (1993, p. 137, 1990. cf. 1984, pp. 180–184) recently reiterated that it was not removed (cf. Hirschmüller, 1978, 1989). It is also necessary to correct the impression I gave in the 1991 edition that Breuer was not especially knowledgeable about hypnosis. Somehow Hirschmüller's account of Breuer's familiarity with such human hypnotic phenomena as catalepsy, dating from 1868, and his experiments with so-called animal-hypnosis, published in 1874, slipped my mind (Hirschmüller, 1978, pp. 93–94 and n. 40, 48, 1989, pp. 129–130 and n. 40, 49).

4. Nor do recent discussions of neurasthenia as a diagnostic entity provide support for Freud's etiological hypotheses (e.g., in *Transcultural Psychiatric Research Review*, 1994, Vol. 31, and *Psychiatric Annals*, 1992, Vol. 22).

5. Izenberg (1991) concludes his summary of the stages through which Freud's thinking passed by making many of the same points I did, except he implies that the sexual theory was more developed in 1897 than it really was (my chapter 10).

6. Schröter and Hermanns's paper is really devoted to providing a wealth of interesting information about the otherwise shadowy Felix Gattel, but neither they nor Scharnberg sheds more light on the reasons for Freud's change in attitude to Gattel, on his charge of plagiarism, or on Gattel's "disgrace" (Scharnberg 1993b, §§844–847; Schröter and Hermanns 1992; cf. Macmillan 1989a, 1990b).

7. It is important to note that a number of those who judged the "memories" to be reconstructions, if not outright fabrications, made their judgments independent of other authors (Esterson 1993, p. 12, n. 2). Without giving discernible reason for his action, Schimek dissociated himself from the way Esterson and Crews used his conclusions and, by implication, from my use also. Consequently, however, the responses by Crews and Esterson to his charge seem more than adequate (Crews et al 1995; Esterson 1995; Schimek 1995).

8. Should it be thought that Dr. Pankejeff's nearly eighty-five-year-old memory was not to be trusted and/or that he denied the event because of dissatisfaction with the way Freud and the psychoanalytic movement treated him, it is worth pointing out that that what he says is accurate about Russian aristocratic child-rearing practice and not a personal memory. As I read Obholzer, Pankejeff did allow as a possibility—he said he could not know—that he may once have slept in the parental bedroom (Obholzer 1980/1982, p. 36). Although no one has so far impugned the accuracy of his recall on other points, Mikkel Borch-Jacobsen tells me that his as yet unpublished investigation of the accuracy of what Pankejeff told Obholzer does show some lapses (e.g., Pankejeff's denying he received certain letters that he was known to have received), there is otherwise little evidence of impairment in intellect or memory.

9. In the 1991 edition of *Freud Evaluated* I preferred to comment on particular aspects of the *Project* rather than to evaluate it as a whole, a decision that prevents fuller discussion here. Two interesting discussions are provided by Glymour (1991, forthcoming), who examines its relation to contemporary cognitive science, and Grünbaum (1995), who considers it in relation to the dream theory. In my view, neither author puts sufficient weight on the speculative nature of the neurophysiology.

10. Quinn (1992, 1993) has impugned Freud's honesty over his failed experiments in developing a method for staining neural tissue with gold chloride (Freud, 1884). Here the failure of the method is not at issue, for, at that time, new staining methods seem to have been announced almost as regularly as the old were declared failures. Freud claimed that, provided only that the specimen had not been overhardened, "unlike other gold methods it will never fail." Quinn's evidence is an indirect inference from Freud's letters to his fiancée (E. L. Freud 1970). Between August 23, 1883 and January 7, 1884 (possibly to January 16), Freud frequently mentions the "Method" to Martha always as something with which he is having difficulty, and in the last part of this period he also complains that he has nothing for publication. Suddenly, on January 28, he tells Martha that Fleischl is arranging publication and that he has "one to two weeks to work on it." Quinn takes the absence of a definite report of success during the period leading up to publication and his silence after it to indicate continuing difficulties with the "Method." What is really needed is more direct support from so far unpublished letters or other sources.

11. In the 1991 edition I did not take up the issue of whether psychoanalysis was a science or a pseudoscience and cannot do so now because the issues are too complex. The discussions on this topic that I have found most useful are the analyses by Laudan (1983), Cioffi (1985, 1988) and Grünbaum (1984, pp. 97–126, 279–285, 1993, pp. 49–68).

12. Before I sent the pages of the 1991 edition to the printer, John Kihlstrom pointed out a misunderstanding in my contrast of organic and posthypnotic amnesias that I did not correct. In both kinds of amnesia, "forgotten" material may influence behavior. Whether posthypnotic forgetting is as absolute as the organic variety, and neither is complete, is irrelevant to whether it resembles that produced by repression.

References

Note: The works by Sigmund Freud and by Josef Breuer and Sigmund Freud listed in these references come from the *Standard Edition of the Complete Psychological Works of Sigmund Freud*, edited and mainly translated by James Strachey, and published in 24 volumes in London between 1953 and 1974 by Hogarth Press and the Institute for Psycho-Analysis.

Abend, S. M., and Porder, M. S. (1986). Identification in the neuroses. *International Journal of Psycho-Analysis* 67: 201–208.

Ablon, S. L., and Mack, J. E. (1980). Children's dreams reconsidered. *Psychoanalytic Study of the Child* 35: 179–217.

Abraham, H. C., and Freud, E. L., eds. (1965). *A Psycho-Analytic Dialogue: The Letters of Sigmund Freud and Karl Abraham, 1907–1926.* New York: Basic Books.

Abraham, K. (1927a). The psycho-sexual differences between hysteria and dementia praecox. In K. Abraham, *Selected Papers on Psycho-Analysis* (pp. 64–79). London: Hogarth Press. (Original work published 1908.)

Abraham, K. (1927b). The first pregenital stage of the libido. In K. Abraham, *Selected Papers on Psycho-Analysis* (pp. 248–249). London: Hogarth Press. (Original work published 1916.)

Abraham, K. (1927c). Contributions to the theory of the anal character. In K. Abraham, *Selected Papers on Psycho-Analysis* (pp. 370–392). London: Hogarth Press. (Original work published 1921.)

Abraham, K. (1927d). A short study of the development of the libido, viewed in the light of mental disorders. In K. Abraham, *Selected Papers on Psycho-Analysis* (pp. 418–501). London: Hogarth Press. (Original work published 1924.)

Abrams, S. (1971a). The psychoanalytic unconsciouses. In M. Kanzer, ed., *The Unconscious Today* (pp. 196–210). New York: International Universities Press.

Abrams, S. (1971b). Models of the psychic apparatus. *Journal of the American Psychoanalytic Association* 19: 131–142.

Adrian, E. D. (1923). The conception of nervous and mental energy. *British Journal of Psychology* 14: 121–125.

Adrian, E. D. (1946). The mental and the physical origins of behaviour. *International Journal of Psycho-Analysis* 27: 1–6.

Ahlskog, G. (1980). Narrative truth and historical truth: Meaning and interpretation in psychoanalysis. *Psychoanalytic Review* 70: 290–294.

Alexander, F. (1925). A metapsychological description of the process of cure. *International Journal of Psycho-Analysis* 6: 13–34.

Alexander, F. (1926). Neurosis and the whole personality. *International Journal of Psycho-Analysis* 7: 340–352.

Alexander, F. (1928). Discussion on the need for punishment and the neurotic process. II. Reply to Reich's criticism. *International Journal of Psycho-Analysis* 9: 240–246. (Original work published 1927.)

Alexander, F. (1929). The need for punishment and the death-instinct. *International Journal of Psycho-Analysis* 10: 256–269.

Alexander, F. (1948). *Fundamentals of Psychoanalysis.* New York: Norton.

Almansi, R. J. (1986). Freud and anthropology. *Journal of the American Psychoanalytic Association* 34: 725–728.

Amacher, P. (1965). Freud's neurological education and its influence on psychoanalytic theory. *Psychological Issues* 4. Monograph 4.

Amacher, P. (1974). The concepts of the pleasure principle and infantile erogenous zones shaped by Freud's neurological education. *Psychoanalytic Quarterly* 43: 218–223.

Andersson, O. (1962). *Studies in the Prehistory of Psychoanalysis.* Stockholm: Srenska Bökforlaget.

Andersson, O. (1979). A supplement to Freud's case history "Frau Emmy v.N." in *Studies on Hysteria* 1895. *Scandinavian Psychoanalytical Review* 2: 5–16.

Angel, R. W. (1959). The concept of psychic determinism. *American Journal of Psychiatry* 16: 405–408.

Anonymous. (1989). Noam Chomsky: An interview. *Radical Philosophy* 53: 31–35.

Anscombe, R. (1981). Referring to the unconscious: A philosophical critique of Schafer's action language. *International Journal of Psycho-Analysis* 62: 225–241.

Apfelbaum, B. (1965). Ego psychology, psychic energy, and the hazards of quantitative explanation in psycho-analytic theory. *International Journal of Psycho-Analysis* 46: 168–182.

Apfelbaum, E., and McGuire, G. R. (1986). Models of suggestive influence and the disqualification of the social crowd. In C. F. Graumann and S. Moscovici, eds., *Changing Conceptions of Crowd Mind and Behavior* (pp. 27–50). New York: Springer-Verlag.

Applegarth, A. (1971). Comments on aspects of the theory of psychic energy. *Journal of the American Psychoanalytic Association* 19: 379–416.

Applegarth, A. (1977a). Psychic energy reconsidered. *Journal of the American Psychoanalytic Association* 25: 599–602.

Applegarth, A. (1977b). Review of H. Nagera, *Female Sexuality and the Oedipus Complex*. *Psychoanalytic Quarterly* 46: 693–695.

Arlow, J. A. (1955). Sublimation. *Journal of the American Psychoanalytic Association* 3: 515–527.

Arlow, J. A. (1958). The psychoanalytic theory of thinking. *Journal of the American Psychoanalytic Association* 6: 143–153.

Arlow, J. A. (1959). The theory of drives. In M. Levitt, ed., *Readings in Psychoanalytic Psychology* (pp. 197–212). London: Staples Press.

Arlow, J. A. (1975). The structural hypothesis—theoretical considerations. *Psychoanalytic Quarterly* 44: 509–525.

Arlow, J. A. (1980). Object concept and object choice. *Psychoanalytic Quarterly* 49: 109–133.

Arlow, J. A. (1981). Theories of pathogenesis. *Psychoanalytic Quarterly* 50: 488–514.

Arlow, J. A. (1982). Problems of the superego concept. *Psychoanalytic Study of the Child* 37: 229–244.

Arlow, J. A. (1991a). Methodology and reconstruction. *Psychoanalytic Quarterly* 60: 539–563.

Arlow, J. A. (1991b). Summary comments: Panels on psychic structure. In T. Shapiro, ed., *The Concept of Structure in Psychoanalysis* (pp. 283–294). Madison, CT: International Universities Press.

Arlow, J. A., and Brenner, C. (1964). *Psychoanalytic Concepts and the Structural Theory*. New York: International Universities Press.

Arlow, J. A., and Brenner, C. (1988). The future of psychoanalysis. *Psychoanalytic Quarterly* 57: 1–14.

Arndt, R. (1892a). Electricity, use of, in the treatment of the insane—Historical sketch. In D. H. Tuke, ed., *A Dictionary of Psychological Medicine* (pp. 426–431). London: Churchill.

Arndt, R. (1892b). Neurasthenia. In D. H. Tuke, ed., *A Dictionary of Psychological Medicine* (pp. 840–850). London: Churchill.

Arnoult, M. D. (1972). *Fundamentals of Scientific Method in Psychology*. Dubuque, Iowa: Brown.

Auerhahn, N. C. (1979). Interpretation in the psychoanalytic narrative: A literary framework for the analytic process. *International Review of Psycho-Analysis* 6: 423–436.

Avery, N. C. (1977). Sadomasochism: A defense against object loss. *Psychoanalytic Review* 64: 101–109.

Azam, E. (1876). Amnésie périodique, ou doublement de la vie. *Revue Scientifique* 10: 481–489.

Babcock, C. G. (1966). The manifest content of the dream. *Journal of the American Psychoanalytic Association* 14: 154–171.

Bachrach, H. R., Galatzer-Levy, R., Skolnikoff, A. and Waldron, S. (1991). On the efficacy of psycho-analysis. *Journal of the American Psychoanalytic Association* 39: 871–916.

Bachrach, H. M., Weber, J. J., and Solomon, M. (1985). Factors associated with the outcome of psycho-analysis (clinical and methodological considerations): Report of the Columbia Psychoanalytic Center Research Project (IV). *International Review of Psycho-Analysis* 12: 379–389.

Bailly, J. S., ed. (1784). *Rapport des Commissaires charges par le Roy de l'examen du magnétisme animal (Report of the Commissioners charged by the King to examine animal magnetism)*. Paris: Imprimerie Royale. (Tinterow, 1970, pp. 82–128; reprints the 1785 translation.)

Bair, J. H. (1901). Development of voluntary control. *Psychological Review* 8: 474–510.

Balint, M. (1938). Eros and Aphrodite. *International Journal of Psycho-Analysis* 19: 199–213. (Original work published 1936.)

Balint, M. (1956). Perversions and genitality. In S. Lorand and M. Balint, eds., *Perversions: Psychodynamics and Therapy* (pp. 16–27). New York: Random House.

Balint, M. (1960). Primary narcissism and primary love. *Psychoanalytic Quarterly* 29: 6–43.

Balmary, M. (1982). *Psychoanalyzing Psychoanalysis: Freud and the Hidden Fault of the Father* (N. Lukacher trans.). Baltimore: Johns Hopkins University Press. (Original work published 1979.)

Baranger, W. (1991). Narcissism in Freud. In J. Sandler, E. P. Person, and P. Fonagy, ed., *Freud's "On Narcissism: An Introduction"* (pp. 108–130). New Haven, CT: Yale University Press.

Barber, T. X. (1962). Toward a theory of "hypnotic" behavior: The "hypnotically induced dream." *Journal of Nervous and Mental Disease* 135: 206–221.

Barnett, M. C. (1968). "I Can't" versus "He Won't": Further considerations of the psychical consequences of the anatomic and physiological differences between the sexes. *Journal of the American Psychoanalytic Association* 16: 588–600.

Barratt, B. B. (1976). Freud's psychology as interpretation. *Psychoanalysis and Contemporary Science* 5: 445–478.

Bartlett, F. C. (1932). *Remembering: An Experimental and Social Study*. London: Cambridge University Press.

Barton, R. (1990). "An influential set of chaps." The X Club and Royal Society politics 1864–1865. *British Journal of the History of Science* 23: 53–81.

Basch, M. F. (1978). Psychic determinism and freedom of will. *International Review of Psycho-Analysis* 5: 257–264.

Basch, M. F. (1981). Psychoanalytic interpretation and cognitive transformation. *International Journal of Psycho-Analysis* 62: 151–175.

Baudry, F. (1983). The evolution of the concept of character in Freud's writings. *Journal of the American Psychoanalytic Association* 31: 3–31.

Baudry, F. (1994). Revisiting the Freud-Klein controversies fifty years later. *International Journal of Psycho-Analysis* 75: 367–374.

Beard, G. M. (1869). Neurasthenia, or nervous exhaustion. *Boston Medical and Surgical Journal* 3: 217–221.

Beard, G. M. (1880). *A Practical Treatise on Nervous Exhaustion (Neurasthenia), Its Symptoms, Nature, Sequences, Treatment*. New York: Wood.

Beard, G. M. (1881). *American Nervousness, Its Causes and Consequences, A Supplement to Nervous Exhaustion (Neurasthenia)*. New York: Putnam.

Beard, G. M. (1884). *Sexual Neurasthenia (Nervous Exhaustion), Its Hygiene, Causes, Symptoms, and Treatment*. New York: Treat.

Beard, G. M. (1894). *A Practical Treatise on Nervous Exhaustion (Neurasthenia), Its Symptoms, Nature, Sequences, Treatment* (3d ed., enlarged). New York: Treat. (Edited, with notes and additions by A. D. Rockwell.)

Beard, G. M., and Rockwell, A. D. (1867). *The Medical Use of Electricity, With Special Reference to General Electrization*. New York: Wood.

Beard, G. M., and Rockwell, A. D. (1891). *On the Medical and Surgical Uses of Electricity* (8th ed.). London: H. K. Lewis. (Prepared by A. D. Rockwell.)

Begel, D. M. (1982). Three examples of countertransference in Freud's Dora case. *American Journal of Psychoanalysis* 42: 163–169.

Bellak, L. (1959). The unconscious. *New York Academy of Sciences, Annals* 76: 1066–1097.

Bellak, L. (1961). Free association: The cornerstone of psychoanalytic technique. *International Journal of Psycho-Analysis* 42: 9–20.

Bellamy, E. (1969). *Dr. Heidenhoff's Process*. New York: AMS Press. (Original work published 1880.)

Bemporad, J. R. (1975). Sexual deviation: A critical review of psychoanalytic theory. In E. T. Adelson, ed., *Sexuality and Psychoanalysis* (pp. 267–290). New York: Brunner/Mazel.

Benjamin, J. D. (1961). Some developmental observations relating to the theory of anxiety. *Journal of the American Psychoanalytic Association* 9: 652–668.

Benjamin, J. D. (1963). Further comments on some developmental aspects of anxiety. In H. S. Gaskill, ed., *Counterpoint: Libidinal Object and Subject* (pp. 121–153). New York: International Universities Press.

Benjamin, J. D. (1965). Developmental biology and psychoanalysis. In N. S. Greenfield and W. C. Lewis, eds., *Psychoanalysis and Current Biological Thought* (pp. 57–80). Madison, Wis.: University of Wisconsin Press.

Beres, D. (1958). Vicissitudes of superego functions and superego precursors in childhood. *Psychoanalytic Study of the Child* 13: 324–351.

Beres, D. (1965). Structure and function in psycho-analysis. *International Journal of Psycho-Analysis* 46: 53–63.

Bergin, A. E. (1971). The evaluation of therapeutic outcomes. In A. E. Bergin and S. L. Garfield, eds., *Handbook of Psychotherapy and Behavior Change: An Empirical Analysis* (pp. 217–270). New York: Wiley.

Bergin, A. E. (1978). The evaluation of therapeutic outcomes. In S. L. Garfield and A. E. Bergin, eds., *Handbook of Psychotherapy and Behavior Change: An Empirical Analysis* (2d ed.) (pp. 139–189). New York: Wiley.

Bergler, E. (1945). On a five-layer structure in sublimation. *Psychoanalytic Quarterly* 14: 76–97.

Bérillon, E., ed. (1889). *Premier Congrés International de l'hypnotisme expérimental et thérapeutique*. Paris: Doin.

Berliner, B. (1940). Libido and reality in masochism. *Psychoanalytic Quarterly* 9: 322–333.

Berliner, B. (1942). The concept of masochism. *Psychoanalytic Review* 29: 386–400.

Berliner, B. (1947). On some psychodynamics of masochism. *Psychoanalytic Quarterly* 16: 459–471.

Bernard, L. L. (1924). *Instinct: A Study in Social Psychology*. London: Allen and Unwin.

Bernays, J. (1970). *Grundzüge der verlorenen Abhandlung des Aristoteles über Wirkung der Tragödie*. New York: Olms. (Original work published 1857.)

Bernfeld, S. (1929). *The Psychology of the Infant* (R. Hurwitz, trans.). London: Kegan Paul, Trench, Trubner. (Original work published 1925.)

Bernfeld, S. (1944). Freud's earliest theories and the school of Helmholtz. *Psychoanalytic Quarterly* 13: 341–362.

Bernfeld, S. (1951). Sigmund Freud, M.D., 1882–1885. *International Journal of Psycho-Analysis* 32: 204–217.

Bernfeld, S. (1953). Freud's studies on cocaine. *Journal of the American Psychoanalytical Association* 1: 581–613.

Bernfeld, S., and Feitelberg, S. (1931). The principle of entropy and the death instinct. *International Journal of Psycho-Analysis* 12: 61–81.

Bernheim, H. (1887). *De la suggestion et de ses applications a la thérapeutique* (2d ed.). Paris: Doin.

Bernheim, H. (1888–1889). Des hallucinations négatives suggérées. *Revue de L'hypnotisme* 3: 161–165.

Bernheim, H. (1888a). *Suggestive Therapeutics: A Treatise on the Nature and Uses of Hypnotism* (C. A. Herter, trans.). New York: Putnam. (Original work published 1887.)

Bernheim, H. (1888b). *Die Suggestion und Ihre Heilwirkung* (S. Freud, trans.). Leipzig: Deuticke. (Original work published 1887.)

Bernheim, H. (1891). *Hypnotisme, Suggestion, Psychotherapie: Etudes Nouvelles*. Paris: Doin.

Bernheim, H. (1892). *Neue Studien über Hypnotismus, Suggestion und Psychotherapie* (S. Freud, trans.). Leipzig: Deuticke. (Original work published 1891.)

Bernstein, D. (1983). The female superego: A different perspective. *International Journal of Psycho-Analysis* 64: 187–201.

Bernstein, I. (1980). Integrative summary: On the re-viewings of the Dora case. In M. Kanzer and J. Glenn, eds., *Freud and His Patients* (pp. 83–91). New York: Aronson.

Bernstein, M. (1956). *The Search for Bridey Murphy*. New York: Doubleday.

Bibring, E. (1941). The development and problems of the theory of the instincts. *International Journal of Psycho-Analysis* 22: 101–131. (Original work published 1936.)

Bibring, E. (1943). The conception of the repetition compulsion. *Psychoanalytic Quarterly* 12: 486–519.

Bibring, G. L. (1964). Some considerations regarding the ego ideal in the psychoanalytic process. *Journal of the American Psychoanalytic Association* 12: 517–521.

Bieber, I. (1953). The meaning of masochism. *American Journal of Psychotherapy* 7: 433–438.

Bieber, I. (1966). Sadism and masochism. In S. Arieti, ed., *American Handbook of Psychiatry* (vol. 3) (pp. 256–270). New York: Basic Books.

Bieber, I. (1972). Morality and Freud's concept of the superego. In S. C. Post, ed., *Moral Values and the Superego Concept in Psychoanalysis* (pp. 126–143). New York: International Universities Press.

Bieber, I. (1975). Biosocial roots of childhood sexuality. In E. T. Adelson, ed., *Sexuality and Psychoanalysis* (pp. 161–174). New York: Brunner/Mazel.

Binet, A. (1886). Les diverses écoles hypnotiques. *Revue Philosophique* 22: 532–533, 537.

Binet, A. (1889). Recherches sur les alterations de la conscience chez les hystériques. *Revue Philosophique* 27: 135–170.

Binet, A. (1889–1890). *On Double Consciousness: Experimental Psychological Studies*. Chicago: Open Court.

Binet, A. (1892). *Les Altérations de la Personnalité*. Paris: Alcan.

Binet, A. (1896). *Alterations of Personality* (H. G. Baldwin, trans.). London: Chapman and Hall. (Original work published 1892.)

Binet, A., and Féré, C. (1885a). L'hypnotisme chez les hystériques: Le transfert. *Revue Philosophique* 19: 1–25.

Binet, A., and Féré, C. (1885b). Hypnotisme et responsabilité. *Revue Philosophique* 19: 265–279.

Binet, A., and Féré, C. (1885c). La polarisation psychique. *Revue Philosophique* 19: 369–402.

Binet, A., and Féré, C. (1887a). *Animal Magnetism*. London: Kegan Paul and Trench. (Original work published 1887.)

Binet, A., and Féré, C. (1887b). Recherches expérimentales sur la physiologie des mouvements chez les hystériques. *Archives de Physiologie Normale et Pathologique* 10: 320–373.

Bing, J. F., McLaughlin, F., and Marburg, R. (1959). The metapsychology of narcissism. *Psychoanalytic Study of the Child* 14: 9–28.

Bird, B. (1972). Notes on transference: Universal phenomenon and hardest part of analysis. *Journal of the American Psychoanalytic Association* 20: 267–301.

Blanck, R., and Blanck, G. (1977). The transference object and the real object. *International Journal of Psycho-Analysis* 58: 33–44.

Blau, A. (1952). In support of Freud's syndrome of "actual" anxiety neurosis. *International Journal of Psycho-Analysis* 33: 363–372.

Blass, R. B. (1992). Did Dora have an Oedipus complex? A reexamination of the theoretical content of Freud's 'Fragment of an analysis.' *Psychoanalytic Study of the Child* 47: 151–187.

Blight, J. (1981). Must psychoanalysis retreat to hermeneutics: Psychoanalytic theory in the light of Popper's evolutionary epistemology. *Psychoanalysis and Contemporary Thought* 4: 147–205.

Bliss, E. L. (1980). Multiple personalities: A report of 14 cases with implications for schizophrenia and hysteria. *Archives of General Psychiatry* 37: 1388–1396.

Bloch, I. (1907). *Das Sexuallen unsurer Zeit in seinen Beziehungungen zur modernen Kultur* (6th ed.). Berlin: Marcus.

Bloch, I. (1908). *The Sexual Life of Our Time in Its Relations to Modern Civilization* (6th Ger. ed.) (M. Eden Paul, trans.). London: Rebman.

Blomfield, O. H. D. (1994). Special book review. *Australian and New Zealand Journal of Psychiatry* 28: 706–716.

Blos, P. (1973). The epigenesis of the adult neurosis. *Psychoanalytic Study of the Child* 27: 106–135.

Blos, P. (1974). The genealogy of the ego ideal. *Psychoanalytic Study of the Child* 29: 43–88.

Blum, H. P. (1966). Panel on working through. *Psychoanalytic Quarterly* 35: 633–635.

Blum, H. P. (1977). The prototype of preoedipal reconstruction. *Journal of the American Psychoanalytic Association* 25: 757–785.

Blum, H. P. (1980). The value of reconstruction in adult psychoanalysis. *International Journal of Psycho-Analysis* 61: 39–52.

Blum, H. P. (1981). The forbidden guest and the analytic ideal: The superego and insight. *Psychoanalytic Quarterly* 50: 535–556.

Blum, H. P. (1982). Theories of the self and psychoanalytic discussion. *Journal of the American Psychoanalytic Association* 30: 959–978.

Blum, H. P. (1986). On identification and its vicissitudes. *International Journal of Psycho-Analysis* 67: 267–276.

Blum, H. P. (1991). Freud and the figure of Moses: The Moses of Freud. *Journal of the American Psychoanalytical Association* 39: 513–535.

Blum, H. P. (1994). *Reconstruction in Psychoanalysis: Childhood Revisited and Recreated.* Madison, CT: International Universities Press.

Bobbitt, R. A. (1958). The repression hypothesis studied in a situation of hypnotically induced conflict. *Journal of Abnormal and Social Psychology* 56: 204–212.

Boesky, D. (1982). Acting out: A reconsideration of the concept. *International Journal of Psycho-Analysis* 63: 39–55.

Boesky, D. (1983). The problem of mental representation in self and object theory. *Psychoanalytic Quarterly* 52: 564–583.

Boesky, D. (1991). The concept of psychic structure. In T. Shapiro, ed., *The Concept of Structure in Psychoanalysis* (pp. 113–135). Madison, CT: International Universities Press.

Bolkosky, S. (1982). The alpha and omega of psychoanalysis: Reflections on Anna O., and Freud's Vienna. *Psychoanalytic Review* 69: 131–150.

Boor, M. (1982). The multiple personality epidemic: Additional cases and inferences regarding diagnosis, etiology, dynamics and treatment. *Journal of Nervous and Mental Disease* 170: 302–304.

Booth, D. S. (1906). Coitus interruptus and coitus reservatus as causes of profound neuroses and psychoses. *Alienist and Neurologist* 27: 397–406.

Bordin, E. S. (1966a). Free association: An experimental analogue of the psychoanalytic situation. In L. A. Gottschalk and A. H. Auerbach, eds., *Methods of Research in Psychotherapy* (pp. 189–208). New York: Appleton-Century-Crofts.

Bordin, E. S. (1966b). Personality and free association. *Journal of Consulting Psychology* 30: 30–38.

Borch-Jacobsen, M. (1995). *Souvenirs d'Anna O.: Une Mystification Centenaire*. Paris: Aubier. [Forthcoming, 1996, as *Remembering Anna O. A Century of Mystification* (M. Borch-Jacobsen, K. Olsen, and X. Callahan, trans.). New York: Routledge]

Borch-Jacobsen, M. (1996). Neurotica: Freud and the seduction theory. *October* 76: 15–43.

Bornstein, R. F. (1993). Implicit perception, implicit memory, and the recovery of unconscious material in psychotherapy. *Journal of Nervous and Mental Disease* 181: 337–344.

Boudreaux, G. (1977). Freud on the nature of unconscious mental processes. *Philosophy of the Social Sciences* 1: 1–32.

Bourneville, D. M. and Regnard, P. eds. (1879–1880). *Iconographie Photographique de la Salpêtrière* (vols. I–III). Paris: Bureaux du Progrès Médical.

Bourru, H., and Burot, P. (1885). De la multiplicité des états de conscience chez un hystéro-épileptique. *Revue Philosophique* 20: 411–416.

Bowlby, J. (1979). Psychoanalysis as art and science. *International Review of Psycho-Analysis* 6: 3–14.

Bowlby, J. (1981). Psychoanalysis as a natural science. *International Review of Psycho-Analysis* 8: 243–256.

Braid, J. (1846). The power of the mind over the body: An experimental inquiry into the nature and cause of the phenomena attributed by Baron Reichenbach and others to a "new imponderable." *Edinburgh Medical and Surgical Journal* 66: 286–312.

Braid, J. (1970a). *Satanic Agency and Mesmerism Reviewed*. Manchester: Simms, Denham, Gaet and Anderson. In M. M. Tinterow, ed., *Foundations of Hypnosis: From Mesmer to Freud* (pp. 318–330). Springfield, Ill.: Thomas. (Original work published 1842.)

Braid, J. (1970b). *Neurypnology, or the Rationale of Nervous Sleep*. London: Churchill. In M. M. Tinterow, ed., *Foundations of Hypnosis: From Mesmer to Freud* (pp. 269–316). Springfield, Ill.: Thomas. (Original work published 1843.)

Braithwaite, R. B. (1953). *Scientific Explanation: A Study of the Function of Theory, Probability and Law in Science*. Cambridge: Cambridge University Press.

Braithwaite, R. B. (1962). Models in the empirical sciences. In E. Nagel, P. Suppes, and A. Tarski, eds., *Logic, Methodology and Philosophy of Science* (pp. 224–231). Stanford, Calif.: Stanford University Press. (Original work published 1960.)

Bram, F. M. (1965). The gift of Anna O. *British Journal of Medical Psychology* 38: 53–58.

Bramwell, J. M. (1903). *Hypnotism; Its History, Practice, and Theory*. London: Richards. (New York: Julian Press reprint, 1956.)

Brandt, R., and Kim, J. (1963). Wants as explanations of actions. *Journal of Philosophy* 63: 425–435.

Breger, L. (1978). Daniel Paul Schreber: From male into female. *Journal of the American Academy of Psychoanalysis* 6: 123–156.

Breger, L. (1981). How psychoanalysis is a science—and how it is not. *Journal of the American Academy of Psychoanalysis* 9: 261–275.

Bremer, R. (1976). Freud and Michelangelo's Moses. *American Imago* 33: 60–75.

Brenman, M. (1949). Dreams and hypnosis. *Psychoanalytic Quarterly* 18: 455–465.

Brenneis, C. B. (1994). Belief and suggestion in the recovery of memories of sexual abuse. *Journal of the American Psychoanalytic Association* 42: 1027–1053.

Brenner, C. (1953). An addendum to Freud's theory of anxiety. *International Journal of Psycho-Analysis* 24: 18–24.

Brenner, C. (1955). *An Elementary Textbook of Psychoanalysis*. New York: International Universities Press.

Brenner, C. (1959). The masochistic character: Genesis and treatment. *Journal of the American Psychoanalytic Association* 7: 197–226.

Brenner, C. (1968). Psychoanalysis and science. *Journal of the American Psychoanalytic Association* 16: 675–696.

Brenner, C. (1971). The psychoanalytic concept of aggression. *International Journal of Psycho-Analysis* 52: 137–144.

Brenner, C. (1973). *An Elementary Textbook of Psychoanalysis* (2d ed.). New York: International Universities Press.

Brenner, C. (1974). On the nature and development of affects: A unified theory. *Psychoanalytic Quarterly* 43: 532–556.

Brenner, C. (1979). The components of psychic conflict and its consequences in mental life. *Psychoanalytic Quarterly* 48: 547–567.

Brenner, C. (1980). Metapsychology and psychoanalytic theory. *Psychoanalytic Quarterly* 49: 189–214.

Brenner, C. (1982). The concept of the superego: A reformulation. *Psychoanalytic Quarterly* 51: 501–525.

Bressler, B. (1969). The ego ideal. *Israeli Annals of Psychiatry and Related Disciplines* 7: 158–174.

Breuer, J. (1923). *Curriculum vitae Med. Drs. Josef Breuer*. Vienna: Weiner Akademie der Wissenschaften.

Breuer, J., and Freud, S. (1893). On the psychical mechanism of hysterical phenomena: Preliminary communication. *The Standard Edition of the Complete Psychological Works of Sigmund Freud* 2: 3–17.

Breuer, J., and Freud, S. (1895). *Studies on Hysteria. The Standard Edition of the Complete Psychological Works of Sigmund Freud* 2: 19–305.

Breznitz, S. (1971). A critical note on secondary revision. *International Journal of Psycho-Analysis* 52: 407–412.

Brickman, A. S. (1983). Pre-oedipal development of the superego. *International Journal of Psycho-Analysis* 64: 83–92.

Brickner, R. M., and Kubie, L. S. (1936). A miniature psychotic storm produced by a superego conflict over simple posthypnotic suggestion. *Psychoanalytic Quarterly* 5: 467–487.

Brierley, M. (1947). Notes on psycho-analysis and integrative living. *International Journal of Psycho-Analysis* 28: 57–105.

Brill, A. A. (1916). Masturbation, its causes and sequellae. *American Journal of Urology and Sexology* 12: 214–222.

Brill, A. A. (1938–1939). Determinism in psychiatry. *American Journal of Psychiatry* 95: 597–620.

Brody, M. W., and Mahoney, V. P. (1964). Introjection, identification and incorporation. *International Journal of Psycho-Analysis* 45: 57–63.

Brody, S. (1982). Psychoanalytic theories of infant development and its disturbances: A critical evaluation. *Psychoanalytic Quarterly* 51: 526–597.

Brody, S., and Axelrad, S. (1966). Anxiety, socialization, and ego formation in infancy. *International Journal of Psycho-Analysis* 47: 218–219.

Broughton, J. M. (1981). The genetic psychology of James Mark Baldwin. *American Psychologist* 36: 396–407.

Brown, W. (1920–1921a). The revival of emotional memories and its therapeutic value (I). *British Journal of Medical Psychology* 1: 16–19.

Brown, W. (1920–1921b). The revival of emotional memories and its therapeutic value (IV). *British Journal of Medical Psychology* 1: 30–33.

Brunswick, D. (1954). A revision of the classification of instincts or drives. *International Journal of Psycho-Analysis* 35: 224–228.

Brunswick, D. (1960). Discussion of "The metapsychology of pleasure." II. The physiological viewpoint. *International Journal of Psycho-Analysis* 41: 372–374.

Bunker, H. A. (1944). American psychiatric literature during the past one hundred years. In J. K. Hall, ed., *One Hundred Years of American Psychiatry* (pp. 195–271). New York: Columbia University Press.

Burgner, M. (1985). The oedipal experience: Effects on development of an absent father. *International Journal of Psycho-Analysis* 66: 311–320.

Burnham, J. C. (1974). The medical origins and cultural use of Freud's instinctual drive theory. *Psychoanalytic Quarterly* 43: 193–217.

Bush, M. (1978). Preliminary considerations for a psychoanalytic theory of insight: Historical perspective. *International Review of Psycho-Analysis* 5: 1–13.

Butcher, S. H. (1902). *Aristotle's Theory of Poetry and Fine Art*. London: Macmillan.

Bywater, I. (1909). *Aristotle on the Art of Poetry*. Oxford: Clarendon Press.

Cain, A. C. (1961). The presuperego "turning-inward" of aggression. *Psychoanalytic Quarterly* 30: 171–208.

Calder, K. T. (1970). Panel on "The use of the economic viewpoint in clinical psychoanalysis." *International Journal of Psycho-Analysis* 51: 245–249.

Calogeras, R. C., and Alston, T. M. (1980). On "Action language" in psychoanalysis. *Psychoanalytic Quarterly* 49: 663–696.

Camis, M. (1930). *The Physiology of the Vestibular Apparatus* (R. S. Creed, trans.). Oxford: Oxford University Press. (Original work published 1928.)

Camuset, L. (1882). Un cas de dédoublement de la personnalité. Période amnésique d'une année chez un homme hystérique. *Annales Medico-Psychologiques* 7: 75–86.

Carlson, E. T. (1970–1971). The nerve weakness of the 19th century. *International Journal of Psychiatry* 9: 50–54.

Carlson, E. T. (1984). The history of multiple personality in the United States: Mary Reynolds and her subsequent reputation. *Bulletin of the History of Medicine* 58: 72–82.

Carlson, E. T. (1989). Multiple personality and hypnosis: The first one hundred years. *Journal of the History of the Behavioral Sciences* 25: 315–322.

Carneiro Leao, I. (1986). Identification and its vicissitudes as observed in adolescence. *International Journal of Psycho-Analysis* 67: 65–75.

Carter, K. C. (1980). Germ theory, hysteria, and Freud's early work on psychopathology. *Medical History* 24: 259–274.

Carter, K. C. (1987). *Essays of Robert Koch* (K. C. Carter ed. and trans.). Westport, Conn.: Greenwood.

Cartwright, R. D. (1966). A comparison of the response to psychoanalytic and client-centered psychotherapy. In L. A. Gottschalk and A. H. Auerbach, eds., *Methods of Research in Psychotherapy* (pp. 517–529). New York: Appleton-Century-Crofts.

Caston, J. (1993). Can analysts agree? The problems of consensus and the psychoanalytic mannequin. I. A proposed solution. II. Empirical tests. *Journal of the American Psychoanalytic Association* 41: 493–511, 513–548.

Caudwell, C. (1938). *Studies in a Dying Culture*. London: John Lane the Bodley Head.

Cereijido, F. (1983). A study on feminine sexuality. *International Journal of Psycho-Analysis* 64: 93–104.

Cerminara, G. (1950). *Many Mansions*. New York: Sloane.

Chambard, E. (1881). *Du somnabulisme en général: Analogies, signification nosologique et étiologie*. Paris: Parent.

Charcot, J.-M. (1877). *Lectures on the Diseases of the Nervous System* (G. Siegerson, trans.). London: New Sydenham Society. (Original work published 1875–1877.)

Charcot, J.-M. (1879–1880). Procédés employés pour déterminer les phénomènes d'hypnotisme. In D. M. Bourneville and P. Regnard, eds., *Iconographie Photographique de la Salpêtrière* (vol. 3) (pp. 149–186). Paris: Bureaux du Progrès Médical.

Charcot, J.-M. (1883). *Lectures on the Localization of Cerebral and Spinal Diseases* (W. B. Haden, trans.). London: New Sydenham Society. (Original work published 1876–1880.)

Charcot, J.-M. (1886). *Neue Vorlesungen über die Krankheiten des Nervensystems insbesondere über Hysterie* (S. Freud, trans.). Leipzig and Vienna: Toeplitz und Deuticke. (Original work published 1887.)

Charcot, J.-M. (1887–1888). *Leçons du Mardi à la Salpêtrière*. Paris: Bureaux du Progrés Médical.

Charcot, J.-M. (1889). *Clinical Lectures on Diseases of the Nervous System* (T. Savill, trans.). London: New Sydenham Society. (Original work published 1887.)

Charcot, J.-M. (1894). *Poliklinische Vorträge, I* (S. Freud, trans.). Leipzig and Vienna: Franz Deuticke. (Original work published 1888.)

Charcot, J.-M., and Marie, P. (1892). Hysteria, mainly hystero-epilepsy. In D. H. Tuke, ed., *A Dictionary of Psychological Medicine* (pp. 627–641). London: Churchill.

Charcot, J.-M., and Richer, P. (1883). Note on certain facts of cerebral automatism observed in hysteria during the cataleptic period of hypnosis. *Journal of Nervous and Mental Disease* 10: 1–13.

Charcot, J.-M., and de la Tourette, G. (1892). Hypnotism in the hysterical. In D. H. Tuke, ed., *A Dictionary of Psychological Medicine* (pp. 606–610). London: Churchill.

Chasseguet-Smirgel, J. (1976). Freud and female sexuality: The consideration of some blind spots in the exploration of the "Dark Continent." *International Journal of Psycho-Analysis* 57: 275–286.

Chatel, J. C., and Peele, R. (1970–1971). The concept of neurasthenia. *International Journal of Psychiatry* 9: 36–49.

Chattah, L. (1983). Metapsychology: Its cultural and scientific roots. *Journal of the American Psychoanalytic Association* 31: 689–698.

Chehrazi, S. (1986). Female psychology: A review. *Journal of the American Psychoanalytic Association* 34: 141–161.

Chertok, L., and de Saussure, R. (1979). *The Therapeutic Revolution: From Mesmer to Freud* (R. H. Ahrenfelt, trans.). New York: Brunner/Mazel. (Original work published 1973.)

Chertok, L., and Stengers, I. (1992). *A Critique of Psychoanalytic Reason: Hypnosis as a Scientific Problem from Lavoisier to Lacan* (M. N. Evans trans.). Stanford, CA: Stanford University Press. (Original work published 1989.)

Chodoff, P. (1966). A critique of Freud's theory of infantile sexuality. *American Journal of Psychiatry* 123: 507–518.

Chrzanowski, G. (1970–1971). An obsolete diagnosis. *International Journal of Psychiatry* 9: 54–56.

Cioffi, F. (1970). Freud and the idea of a pseudo-science. In R. Borger and F. Cioffi, eds., *Explanation in the Behavioural Sciences* (pp. 471–499). Cambridge: Cambridge University Press.

Cioffi, F. (1972). Wollheim on Freud. *Inquiry* 15: 171–186.

Cioffi, F. (1973). Introduction. In F. Cioffi, ed., *Freud: Modern Judgements* (pp. 1–24). London: Macmillan.

Cioffi, F. (1974). Was Freud a liar? *The Listener* 91: 172–174.

Cioffi, F. (1985). Psychoanalysis, pseudo-science, and testability. In G. Currie and A. Musgrave, eds., *Popper and the Human Sciences* (pp. 13–44). Dordrecht: Nijhoff.

Cioffi, F. (1988). "Exegetical myth-making" in Grünbaum's indictment of Popper and exoneration of Freud. In P. Clark and C. Wright, eds., *Mind, Psychoanalysis, and Science* (pp. 61–87). Oxford: Blackwell.

Coe, M. D. (1992). *Breaking the Maya Code*. New York: Thames and Hudson.

Cohen, J. (1980). Structural consequences of psychic trauma: A new look at "Beyond the Pleasure Principle." *International Journal of Psycho-Analysis* 61: 421–432.

Cohen, J., and Kinston, W. (1983). Repression theory: A new look at the cornerstone. *International Journal of Psycho-Analysis* 65: 411–422.

Colby, K. M. (1955). *Energy and Structure in Psychoanalysis.* New York: Ronald Press.

Colby, K. M. (1960). Experiment on the effects of an observer's presence on the imago system during psychoanalytic free-association. *Behavioral Science* 15: 216–232.

Colby, K. M. (1961). On the greater amplifying power of causal-correlative over interrogative inputs on free association in an experimental psychoanalytic situation. *Journal of Nervous and Mental Disease* 133: 233–239.

Collins, S. (1980). Freud and "The riddle of suggestion." *International Review of Psycho-Analysis* 7: 429–437.

Colquhoun, J. C. (1970). Report on the magnetic experiments made by a committee of the Royal Academy of Medicine. In M. M. Tinterow, ed., *Foundations of Hypnosis: From Mesmer to Freud* (pp. 160–174). Springfield, Ill.: Thomas. (Original work published 1833.)

Compton, A. (1972a). A study of the psychoanalytic theory of anxiety I: The development of Freud's theory of anxiety. *Journal of the American Psychoanalytic Association* 20: 3–44.

Compton, A. (1972b). A study of the psychoanalytic theory of anxiety II: Developments in the theory of anxiety since 1926. *Journal of the American Psychoanalytic Association* 20: 341–394.

Compton, A. (1981a). On the psychoanalytic theory of instinctual drives I: The beginnings of Freud's drive theory. *Psychoanalytic Quarterly* 50: 190–218.

Compton, A. (1981b). On the psychoanalytic theory of instinctual drives II: The sexual drives and the ego-drives. *Psychoanalytic Quarterly* 50: 219–237.

Compton, A. (1981c). On the psychoanalytic theory of instinctual drives III: The complications of libido and narcissism. *Psychoanalytic Quarterly* 50: 345–362.

Compton, A. (1981d). On the psychoanalytic theory of instinctual drives IV: Instinctual drives and the ego-id-superego model. *Psychoanalytic Quarterly* 50: 363–392.

Compton, A. (1985a). The concept of identification in the work of Freud, Ferenczi, and Abraham: A review and commentary. *Psychoanalytic Quarterly* 54: 200–233.

Compton, A. (1985b). The development of the drive object concept in Freud's work: 1905–1915. *Journal of the American Psychoanalytic Association* 33: 93–115.

Compton, A. (1986a). Neglected classics: Hans Sachs's "On the genesis of perversions." *Psychoanalytic Quarterly* 55: 474–476.

Compton, A. (1986b). Discussion of Sachs's "On the genesis of perversions." *Psychoanalytic Quarterly* 55: 489–492.

Compton, A. (1986c). Freud: Objects and structure. *Journal of the American Psychoanalytic Association* 34: 561–590.

Compton, A. (1986d). The beginnings of the object concept in psychoanalysis. In A. D. Richards and M. S. Willick, eds., *The Science of Mental Conflict—Essays in Honor of Charles Brenner* (pp. 177–189). Hillsdale, N.J.: Analytic Press.

Compton, A. (1992a). The psychoanalytic view of phobias Part I. Freud's theories of phobias and anxiety. *Psychoanalytic Quarterly* 61: 206–229.

Compton, A. (1992b). The psychoanalytic view of phobias Part II. Infantile phobias. *Psychoanalytic Quarterly* 61: 230–253.

Compton, A. (1992c). The psychoanalytic view of phobias Part III. Agoraphobia and other phobias of adults. *Psychoanalytic Quarterly* 61: 400–425.

Compton, A. (1992d). The psychoanalytic view of phobias Part IV. General theory of phobias and anxiety. *Psychoanalytic Quarterly* 61: 426–446.

Counts, R. M., and Mensh, I. N. (1950). Personality characteristics in hypnotically-induced hostility. *Journal of Clinical Psychology* 6: 325–330.

Crabtree, A. (1993). *From Mesmer to Freud: Magnetic Sleep and the Roots of Psychological Healing*. New Haven, CT: Yale University Press.

Craig, W. (1918). Appetites and aversions as constituents of instincts. *Biological Bulletin of the Marine Biological Laboratory, Woods Hole, Mass.* 34: 91–107.

Cranefield, P. F. (1957). The organic physics of 1847 and the biophysics of today. *Journal of the History of Medicine and Allied Sciences* 12: 407–423.

Cranefield, P. F. (1958). Josef Breuer's evaluation of his contribution to psycho-analysis. *International Journal of Psycho-Analysis* 39: 319–322.

Cranefield, P. F. (1966). The philosophical and cultural interests of the biophysics movement of 1847. *Journal of the History of Medicine and Allied Sciences* 21: 1–7.

Crews, F. (1986). The Freudian way of knowledge. In F. Crews, *Skeptical Engagements* (pp. 43–87). New York: Oxford University Press. (Original work published 1984.)

Crews, F., et al. (1995). *The Memory Wars: Freud's Legacy in Dispute*. New York: New York Review of Books.

Crichton-Miller, H. (1945). *Psycho-analysis and Its Derivatives* (2d ed.). Oxford: Oxford University Press.

Dahl, H. (1968). Psychoanalytic theory of the instinctual drives in relation to recent developments (panel report). *Journal of the American Psychoanalytic Association* 16: 613–637.

Daly, M., and Wilson, M. (1990). Is parent-offspring conflict sex-linked? Freudian and Darwinian models. *Journal of Personality* 58: 163–189.

Darnton, R. (1968). *Mesmerism and the End of Enlightenment in France*. Cambridge: Harvard University Press.

Darwin, C. (1872). *The Expression of the Emotions in Man and Animals*. London: Murray.

David-Ménard, M. (1989). *Hysteria from Freud to Lacan: Body and Language in Psychoanalysis* (C. Porter trans.). Ithaca, NY: Cornell University Press. (Original work published 1983.)

Davidson, D. (1963). Actions, reasons, and causes. *Journal of Philosophy* 60: 685–700.

Davidson, D. (1973). Freedom to act. In T. Honderich, ed., *Essays in Freedom of Action* (pp. 137–156). London: Routledge and Kegan Paul.

Decker, H. S. (1977). *Freud in Germany*. New York: International Universities Press. (Original work published 1975.)

Decker, H. S. (1981). Freud and Dora: Constraints on medical progress. *Journal of Social History* 14: 445–464.

Decker, H. S. (1982). The choice of a name: "Dora" and Freud's relationship with Breuer. *Journal of the American Psychoanalytic Association* 30: 113–135.

Decker, H. S. (1991). *Freud, Dora, and Vienna 1900*. New York: Free Press.

Decker, H. S. (1992). Freud's "Dora's" case in perspective: The medical treatment of hysteria in Austria at the turn of the century. In T. Gelfand and J. Kerr, eds., *Freud and the History of Psychoanalysis* (pp. 271–288). Hillsdale, NJ: Analytic Press.

Deckert, G. H., and West, L. J. (1963). Hypnosis and experimental psychopathology. *American Journal of Clinical Hypnosis* 5: 256–276.

Deigh, J. (1984). Remarks on some difficulties in Freud's theory of moral development. *International Review of Psycho-Analysis* 11: 207–225.

Delboeuf, J. R. L. (1886a). La mémoire chez les hypnotisés. *Revue Philosophique* 21: 441–472.

Delboeuf, J. R. L. (1886b). De l'influence de l'éducation et de l'imitation dans le somnambulisme provoqué. *Revue Philosophique* 22: 146–171.

Delboeuf, J. R. L. (1886c). Les diverses écoles hypnotiques. *Revue Philosophique* 22: 533–538.

Delboeuf, J. R. L. (1886d). Une visite a la Salpêtrière. *Revue de Belgique* 54: 121–147, 258–275.

Delboeuf, J. R. L. (1888–1889). Le magnétisme animal: A propos d'une visite a l'école de Nancy. *Revue de Belgique* 60: 241–260, 386–408, 61: 5–33, 286–324.

Delboeuf, J. R. L. (1889). *Le Magnétisme Animal: A Propos d'une Visite a l'école de Nancy*. Paris: Alcan.

Delboeuf, J. R. L. (1891). Comme quoi il n'y pas d'hypnotisme. *Revue de L'hypnotisme* 5: 129–135.

Dennett, D. C. (1973). Mechanism and responsibility. In T. Honderich, ed., *Essays in Freedom of Action* (pp. 157–184). London: Routledge and Kegan Paul.

Deri, F. (1939). On sublimation. *Psychoanalytic Quarterly* 8: 325–334.

Desmond, A., and Moore, J. (1991). *Darwin*. London: Joseph.

Deutsch, H. (1964). Some clinical considerations of the ego ideal. *Journal of the American Psychoanalytic Association* 12: 512–516.

Dilthey, W. (1977). *Descriptive Psychology and Historical Understanding* (R. M. Zaner and K. L. Heiges, trans.). The Hague: Martinus Nijhoff. (Original work published 1894.)

Dingwall, E. J., ed. (1967). *Abnormal Hypnotic Phenomena* (Vol. 1: France). London: Churchill.

Domhoff, D. (1964). Night dreams and hypnotic dreams: Is there evidence that they are different? *International Journal of Clinical and Experimental Hypnosis* 12: 159–168.

Donkin, H. B. (1892). Hysteria. In D. H. Tuke, ed., *A Dictionary of Psychological Medicine* (pp. 618–627). London: Churchill.

Dorey, R. (1986). The relationship of mastery. *International Review of Psycho-Analysis* 13: 323–332.

Downey, T. W. (1984). Within the pleasure principle: Child analytic perspectives on aggression. *Psychoanalytic Study of the Child* 39: 101–136.

Downey, T. W. (1989). Id or subego? Some theoretical questions for clinicians. *Psychoanalytic Study of the Child* 44: 199–209.

Drever, J. (1917). *Instinct in Man: A Contribution to the Psychology of Education*. Cambridge: Cambridge University Press.

Du Potet de Sennovoy, Baron. (1970). *Course in Animal Magnetism*. Paris: Athenee Central. In M. M. Tinterow, ed., *Foundations of Hypnosis: From Mesmer to Freud* (pp. 175–189). Springfield, Ill.: Thomas. (Original work published 1834.)

Ducey, C., and Galinsky, M. D. (1973). The metapsychology of pleasure. *Journal of the American Psychoanalytic Association* 21: 495–525.

Dufay, J. (1876). Double memory (consciousness). *Revue Scientifique* (from *Mind* 1876 1: 552–553.)

Duruz, N. (1981a). The psychoanalytic concept of narcissism Part I. Some neglected aspects in Freud's work. *Psychoanalysis and Contemporary Thought* 4: 3–34.

Duruz, N. (1981b). The psychoanalytic concept of narcissism Part II. Toward a structural definition. *Psychoanalysis and Contemporary Thought* 4: 35–67.

Eagle, M. [N.] (1973). Sherwood on the logic of explanation in psychoanalysis. *Psychoanalysis and Contemporary Science* 2: 331–337.

Eagle, M. [N.] (1980a). A critical examination of motivational explanation in psychoanalysis. *Psychoanalysis and Contemporary Thought* 3: 329–380.

Eagle, M. [N.] (1980b). Symposium: George Klein's *Psychoanalytic Theory* in perspective. *Psychoanalytic Review* 67: 179–194.

Eagle, M. [N.] (1993a). Freud in historical context. *Contemporary Psychology* 38: 993–995.

Eagle, M. [N.] (1993b). The dynamics of theory change in psychoanalysis. In J. Earman, A. I. Janis, G. J. Massey, and N. Rescher, eds., *Philosophical Problems of the Internal and External Worlds: Essays on the Philosophy of Adolf Grünbaum* (pp. 373–408). Pittsburgh: University of Pittsburgh Press.

Eckardt, M. H. (1982). The structure of Freud's dream theory. In S. L. Gilman, ed., *Introducing Psychoanalytic Theory* (pp. 54–67). New York: Brunner/Mazel.

Edelson, M. (1977). Psychoanalysis as science. Its boundary problems, special status, relations to other sciences, and formalization. *Journal of Nervous and Mental Disease* 165: 1–28.

Edelson, M. (1983). Is testing psychoanalytic hypotheses in the psychoanalytic situation really impossible? *Psychoanalytic Study of the Child* 38: 61–109.

Edelson, M. (1984). *Hypothesis and Evidence in Psychoanalysis.* Chicago: University of Chicago Press.

Edelson, M. (1984). *Hypothesis and Evidence in Psychoanalysis.* Chicago: University of Chicago Press.

Edelson, M. (1988). *Psychoanalysis: A Theory in Crisis.* Chicago: University of Chicago Press.

Edes, R. T. (1904). The relation of some special causes to the development of neurasthenia. *Boston Medical and Surgical Journal* 150: 227–235.

Edgcumbe, R., Lundberg, S., Markowitz, R., and Salo, F. (1976). Some comments on the concept of the negative Oedipal phase in girls. *Psychoanalytic Study of the Child* 31: 35–61.

Eidelberg, L. (1960). A third contribution to the study of slips of the tongue. *International Journal of Psycho-Analysis* 41: 596–603.

Eidelberg, L. (1962). A contribution to the study of the unpleasure-pleasure principle. *Psychiatric Quarterly* 36: 312–316.

Eidelberg, L. (1968). Masochism. In L. Eidelberg, ed., *Encyclopedia of Psychoanalysis* (pp. 232–235). New York: Free Press.

Eisenbud, J. (1937). Psychology of headache: Case studied experimentally. *Psychiatric Quarterly* 11: 592–619.

Eisenbud, R.-J. (1967). Masochism revisited. *Psychoanalytic Review* 54: 561–582.

Eissler, K. R. (1953). Notes upon the emotionality of a schizophrenic patient and its relation to problems of technique. *Psychoanalytic Study of the Child* 8: 199–251.

Eissler, K. R. (1962). On the metapsychology of the preconscious: A tentative contribution to psychoanalytic morphology. *Psychoanalytic Study of the Child* 17: 9–41.

Eissler, K. R. (1968). The relation of explaining and understanding in psychoanalysis. *Psychoanalytic Study of the Child* 23: 141–177.

Eissler, K. [R.] (1969). Death and the pleasure principle. In H. M. Ruitenbeek, ed., *Death: Interpretations* (pp. 11–18). New York: Dell.

Eissler, K. R. (1977). Comments on penis envy and orgasm in women. *Psychoanalytic Study of the Child* 32: 29–88.

Ellenberger, H. F. (1956). Fechner and Freud. *Bulletin of the Menninger Clinic* 20: 201–214.

Ellenberger, H. F. (1965). Mesmer and Puységur: From magnetism to hypnotism. *Psychoanalytic Review* 52: 281–297.

Ellenberger, H. F. (1966). The pathogenic secret and its therapeutics. *Journal of the History of the Behavioral Sciences* 2: 29–42.

Ellenberger, H. F. (1970). *The Discovery of the Unconscious.* New York: Basic Books.

Ellenberger, H. F. (1972). The story of "Anna O.": A critical review with new data. *Journal of the History of the Behavioral Sciences* 8: 267–279.

Elliotson, J. (1843). *Numerous Cases of Surgical Operations Without Pain in the Mesmeric State.* London: Baillière.

Elliotson, J. (1970a). Mesmerism. *Zoist* 1: 58–94. In M. M. Tinterow, ed., *Foundations of Hypnosis: From Mesmer to Freud* (pp. 193–215). Springfield, Ill.: Thomas. (Original work published 1843.)

Elliotson, J. (1970b). Cases of cures by mesmerism. *Zoist* 1: 161–208. In M. M. Tinterow, ed., *Foundations of Hypnosis: From Mesmer to Freud* (pp. 216–241). Springfield, Ill.: Thomas. (Original work published 1843.)

Ellis, H. H. (1900–1901). *Studies in the Psychology of Sex* (2d ed.) (vols. 1–2). Philadelphia: Davis. (Original work published 1897–1899.)

Ellis, H. H. (1903). *Studies in the Psychology of Sex* (vol. 3). Philadelphia: Davis.

Ellman, S. J., and Moskowitz, M. B. (1980). An examination of some recent criticisms of psychoanalytic "metapsychology." *Psychoanalytic Quarterly* 49: 631–662.

Elms, A. C. (1980). Freud, Irma, Martha: Sex and marriage in the "Dream of Irma's injection." *Psychoanalytic Review* 67: 83–109.

Else, G. F. (1963). *Aristotle's Poetics: The Argument*. Cambridge: Harvard University Press.

Engels, F. (1947). *Herr Eugen Duhring's Revolution in Science* (F. Wattenberg, ed.). Moscow: Foreign Languages Publishing House. (Original work published 1894.)

Engels, F. (1982). Natural science in the spirit world (2d ed.). In F. Engels, *Dialectics of Nature* (pp. 50–61). Moscow: Progress Press. (Original work published 1898.)

Erdelyi, M. H. (1994). Freud and interdisciplinary cognitive science: A cautionary tale. *Contemporary Psychology* 39: 419–420.

Erickson, M. H. (1935). A study of an experimental neurosis hypnotically induced in a case of ejaculatio praecox. *British Journal of Medical Psychology* 15: 34–50.

Erickson, M. H. (1939). Experimental demonstrations of the psychopathology of everyday life. *Psychoanalytic Quarterly* 8: 338–353.

Erickson, M. H. (1944). The method employed to formulate a complex story for the induction of an experimental neurosis in a hypnotic subject. *Journal of General Psychology* 31: 67–84.

Erikson, E. H. (1954). The dream specimen of psychoanalysis. *Journal of the American Psychoanalytic Association* 2: 5–56.

Erikson, E. H. (1962). Reality and actuality. *Journal of the American Psychoanalytic Association* 10: 451–474.

Erlich, H. S., and Blatt, S. J. (1985). Narcissism and object love: The metapsychology of experience. *Psychoanalytic Study of the Child* 40: 57–79.

Erwin, E. (1980). Psychoanalytic therapy. The Eysenck argument. *American Psychologist* 35: 435–443.

Erwin, E. (1993). Philosophers on Freudianism: An examination of replies to Grünbaum's *Foundations*. In J. Earman, A. I. Janis, G. J. Massey, and N. Rescher, eds., *Philosophical Problems of the Internal and External Worlds: Essays on the Philosophy of Adolf Grünbaum* (pp. 409–460). Pittsburgh: University of Pittsburgh Press.

Erwin, E. (1996). *A Final Accounting: Philosophical and Empirical Issues in Freudian Psychology*. Cambridge: MIT Press.

Esdaile, J. (1846). *Mesmerism in India, and Its Practical Application in Surgery and Medicine*. London: Longmans.

Esman, A. H. (1983). The "stimulus barrier." A review and reconsideration. *Psychoanalytic Study of the Child* 38: 193–207.

Esterson, A. (1993). *Seductive Mirage: An Exploration of the Work of Sigmund Freud*. Chicago: Open Court.

Esterson, A. (1995). Letter to the editor, *New York Review of Books*. In F. Crews et al., *The Memory Wars: Freud's Legacy in Dispute* (pp. 147–150). New York: New York Review of Books. (Original work published April 21, 1994.)

Etchegoyen, R. H. (1985). Identification and its vicissitudes. *International Journal of Psycho-Analysis* 66: 3–18.

Etchegoyen, R. H. (1991). "On Narcissism: An Introduction": Text and context. In J. Sandler, E. P. Person, and P. Fonagy, eds., *Freud's "On Narcissism: An Introduction"* (pp. 54–74). New Haven, CT: Yale University Press.

Eulenberg, A. (1902). *Sadismus und Masochismus.* Weisbaden: Bergman.

Eulenberg, A. (1934). *Sadism and Masochism* (H. Kent, trans.). New York: New Era Press. (Original work published 1902.)

Evans, C. (1986). Book review: A. Grünbaum *The Foundations of Psychoanalysis: A Philosophical Critique. Psychoanalytic Review* 73: 223–226.

Evans, F. J. (1972). Hypnosis and sleep: Techniques for exploring cognitive activity during sleep. In E. Fromm and R. E. Shor, eds., *Hypnosis: Research Developments and Perspectives* (pp. 139–183). Chicago, Ill.: Aldine.

Evans, M. N. (1991). *Fits and Starts: A Genealogy of Hysteria in Modern France.* Ithaca, NY: Cornell University Press.

Exner, S. (1894). *Entwurf zu Einer Physiologischen Erklärung der Psychischen Erscheinungen.* Leipzig and Vienna: Deuticke.

Eysenck, H. J. (1952). The effects of psychotherapy: An evaluation. *Journal of Consulting Psychology* 16: 319–324.

Eysenck, H. J. (1986). *Decline and Fall of the Freudian Empire.* Harmondsworth, Middlesex: Penguin Books. (Original work published 1985.)

Eysenck, H. J., and Wilson, G. D., eds. (1973). *The Experimental Study of Freudian Theories.* London: Methuen.

Ezriel, H. (1951). The scientific testing of psycho-analytic findings and theory. *British Journal of Medical Psychology* 24: 30–34.

Fairbairn, W. R. D. (1939–1941). Is aggression an irreducible factor? *British Journal of Medical Psychology* 18: 163–170.

Fairbairn, W. R. D. (1941). A revised psychopathology of the psychoses and psychoneuroses. *International Journal of Psycho-Analysis* 22: 250–279.

Fairbairn, W. R. D. (1952). *Psychoanalytic Studies of the Personality.* London: Tavistock.

Fairbairn, W. R. D. (1956). A critical evaluation of certain basic psycho-analytical conceptions. *British Journal for the Philosophy of Science* 7: 49–60.

Fancher, R. E. (1971). The neurological origin of Freud's dream theory. *Journal of the History of the Behavioral Sciences* 7: 59–74.

Farber, L. H., and Fisher, C. (1943). An experimental approach to dream psychology through the use of hypnosis. *Psychoanalytic Quarterly* 12: 202–216.

Farrell, B. (1963). Introduction to S. Freud's *Leonardo da Vinci and a Memory of His Childhood.* Harmondsworth, Middlesex: Penguin Books.

Fayek, A. (1980). From interpretation to the death instinct. *International Review of Psycho-Analysis* 7: 447–457.

Federn, P. (1930). The neurasthenic core in hysteria. *Medical Review of Reviews* 36: 140–147.

Federn, P. (1932). The reality of the death instinct, especially in melancholia. *Psychoanalytic Review* 19: 129–151.

Feigl, H. (1970). The "orthodox" view of theories: Remarks in defense as well as a critique. In M. Radner and S. Winokur, eds., *Minnesota Studies in the Philosophy of Science* (vol. 4) (pp. 3–16). Minneapolis: University of Minnesota Press.

Feldman, S. S. (1956). On homosexuality. In S. Lorand and M. Balint, eds., *Perversions: Psychodynamics and Therapy* (pp. 71–96). New York: Random House.

Fenichel, O. (1928). The clinical aspect of the need for punishment. *International Journal of Psycho-Analysis* 9: 47–70.

Fenichel, O. (1934). *Outline of Clinical Psychoanalysis* (B. D. Lewin and G. Zilboorg, trans.). London: Kegan Paul, Trench, Trubner. (Original work published 1932.)

Fenichel, O. (1941a). The ego and the affects. *Psychoanalytic Review* 28: 47–60.

Fenichel, O. (1941b). *Problems of Psychoanalytic Technique* (D. Brunswick, trans.). New York: Psychoanalytic Quarterly. (Original work published 1938.)

Fenichel, O. (1945a). The concept of trauma in contemporary psycho-analytical theory. *International Journal of Psycho-Analysis* 26: 33–44. (Original work published 1937.)

Fenichel, O. (1945b). *The Psychoanalytic Theory of Neurosis.* London: Routledge and Kegan Paul.

Fenichel, O. (1954a). Identification. In H. Fenichel and D. Rapaport, eds., *Collected Papers of Otto Fenichel: First Series* (pp. 97–112). London: Routledge and Kegan Paul. (Original work published 1926.)

Fenichel, O. (1954b). A critique of the death instinct. In H. Fenichel and D. Rapaport, eds., *Collected Papers of Otto Fenichel: First Series* (pp. 363–371). London: Routledge and Kegan Paul. (Original work published 1935.)

Ferenczi, S. (1950). Actual- and psycho-neuroses in the light of Freud's investigations and psycho-analysis. In S. Ferenczi, *Further Contributions to the Theory and Technique of Psycho-Analysis* (2d ed.) (pp. 30–55). London: Hogarth Press. (Original work published 1908.)

Ferenczi, S. (1952a). Introjection and transference. In S. Ferenczi, *First Contributions to Psycho-Analysis* (pp. 35–93). London: Hutchinson. (Original work published 1909.)

Ferenczi, S. (1952b). On onanism. In S. Ferenczi, *First Contributions to Psycho-Analysis* (pp. 185–192). London: Hogarth Press. (Original work published 1912.)

Ferenczi, S. (1952c). Stages in the development of the sense of reality. In S. Ferenczi, ed., *First Contributions to Psycho-Analysis* (pp. 213–239). London: Hutchinson. (Original work published 1913.)

Ferenczi, S. (1955a). On the definition of introjection. In S. Ferenczi, *Final Contributions to the Problems and Methods of Psychoanalysis* (pp. 316–318). London: Hogarth Press. (Original work published 1912.)

Ferenczi, S. (1955b). Organ neuroses and their treatment. In S. Ferenczi, *Final Contributions to the Problems and Methods of Psychoanalysis* (pp. 22–28). London: Hogarth Press. (Original work published 1926.)

Ferenczi. S. (1968). *Thalassa: A Theory of Genitality* (H. A. Bunker trans.). New York: Norton. (Original work published 1924.)

Ferguson, M. (1985). A critique of Grünbaum on psychoanalysis. *Journal of the American Academy of Psychoanalysis* 13: 327–345.

Ferreira, A. J. (1965). On repetition compulsion. *Psychoanalytic Review* 52: 84–93.

Feyerabend, P. K. (1970). Against method: Outline of an anarchistic theory of knowledge. In M. Radner and S. Winokur, eds., *Minnesota Studies in the Philosophy of Science* (vol. 4) (pp. 17–130). Minneapolis: University of Minnesota Press.

Fish, S. (1989). Witholding the missing portion: Psychoanalysis and rhetoric. In S. Fish, *Doing what Comes Naturally: Change, Rhetoric, and the Practice of Theory in Literary and Legal Studies* (pp. 525–554). Oxford: Oxford University Press.

Fischer, N. (1981). Masochism: Current concepts. *Journal of the American Psychoanalytic Association* 29: 673–688.

Fischer, R. E., and Juni, S. (1981). Anality: A theory of erotism and characterology. *American Journal of Psychoanalysis* 41: 57–71.

Fisher, C. (1966). Commentary on "An experimental approach to dream psychology through the use of hypnosis." In C. S. Moss, ed., *The Hypnotic Investigation of Dreams* (pp. 125–126). New York: Wiley.

Fisher, S., and Greenberg, R. P. (1977). *The Scientific Credibility of Freud's Theories and Therapy*. New York: Basic Books.

Flescher, J. (1956). A dualistic viewpoint on anxiety. *Journal of the American Psychoanalytic Association* 3: 415–446.

Fletcher, R. (1957). *Instinct in Man*. London: Allen and Unwin.

Flew, A. (1949). Psychoanalytic explanation. *Analysis* 10: 8–15.

Flew, A. (1954). Psychoanalytic explanation. Foreword (1954). In M. Macdonald, ed., *Philosophy and Analysis* (pp. 139–140). Oxford: Blackwell.

Flew, A. (1956). Motives and the unconscious. In H. Feigl and M. Scriven, eds., *Minnesota Studies in the Philosophy of Science* (vol. 1) (pp. 155–173). Minneapolis: University of Minnesota Press.

Fliegel, Z. O. (1973). Feminine psychosexual development in Freudian theory. A historical reconstruction. *Psychoanalytic Quarterly* 42: 385–398.

Fliegel, Z. O. (1982). Half a century later: Current status of Freud's controversial views on women. *Psychoanalytic Review* 69: 7–28.

Fliess, F. (1948). *The Psycho-analytic Reader*. New York: International Universities Press.

Flowerman, S. H. (1954). Psychoanalytic theory and science. *American Journal of Psychotherapy* 8: 415–441.

Flugel, J. C. (1924). Critical notice of A. Wohlgemuth's *A Critical Examination of Psycho-Analysis*. *British Journal of Medical Psychology* 4: 50–58.

Flugel, J. C. (1945). *Man, Morals and Society*. London: Duckworth.

Flugel, J. C. (1953). The death instinct, homeostasis and allied concepts. *International Journal of Psycho-Analysis* 34: 43–73.

Fonagy, P. (1981). Research on psychoanalytic concepts. In F. Fransella, ed., *Personality, Theory and Measurement* (pp. 56–72). London: Methuen.

Fonagy, P. (1982). The integration of psychoanalysis and experimental science: A review. *International Review of Psycho-Analysis* 9: 125–145.

Forrester, J. (1980). *Language and the Origins of Psychoanalysis*. London: Macmillan.

Forrester, J. (1986). Essay review of Adolf Grünbaum *The Foundations of Psychoanalysis*. *Isis* 77: 670–674.

Fosshage, J. L., and Loew, C. L. (1978). *Dream Interpretation: A Comparative Study*. New York: Spectrum Publications.

Foulkes, D. (1978). *A Grammar of Dreams*. New York: Basic Books.

Foxe, A. N. (1943). Critique of Freud's concept of a death instinct. *Psychoanalytic Review* 30: 417–427.

Frank, A. (1969). The unrememberable and the unforgettable: Passive primal repression. *Psychoanalytic Study of the Child* 24: 48–75.

Frank, A. (1979). Two theories or one? Or none? *Journal of the American Psychoanalytic Association* 27: 169–207.

Frank, A., and Muslin, H. (1967). The development of Freud's concept of primal repression. *Psychoanalytic Study of the Child* 22: 55–76.

Frankley, G. (1950). Masturbation. In H. Herma and G. M. Kurth, eds., *Elements of Psychoanalysis* (pp. 221–226). New York: World.

Freeman, L. (1972). *The Story of Anna O*. New York: Walker.

Freeman, T. (1977). On Freud's theory of schizophrenia. *International Journal of Psycho-Analysis* 58: 383–388.

French, T. M. (1933). Interrelations between psychoanalysis and the experimental work of Pavlov. *American Journal of Psychiatry* 89: 1165–1203.

French, T. M. (1937). Reality and the unconscious. *Psychoanalytic Quarterly* 6: 23–61.

French, T. M. (1944). Clinical approach to the dynamics of behavior. In J. McV. Hunt, ed., *Personality and the Behavior Disorders* (vol. 1) (pp. 255–268). New York: Ronald Press.

Freud, A. (1967). Comments on trauma. In S. S. Furst, ed., *Psychic Trauma* (pp. 235–245). New York: Basic Books.

Freud, A. (1972). Comments on aggression. *International Journal of Psycho-Analysis* 53: 163–171.

Freud, E. L. (1970). *The Letters of Sigmund Freud and Arnold Zweig* (Prof. and Mrs. W. D. Robson-Scott, trans.). London: Hogarth Press.

Freud, S. (1884). A new histological method for the study of nerve-tracts in the brain and spinal-cord. *Brain* 7: 86–88.

Freud, S. (1886a). Report on my studies in Paris and Berlin. *The Standard Edition of the Complete Psychological Works of Sigmund Freud* 1: 5–15.

Freud, S. (1886b). Observation of a severe case of hemi-anaesthesia in a hysterical male. *The Standard Edition of the Complete Psychological Works of Sigmund Freud* 1: 25–31.

Freud, S. (1887). Review of Averbeck's *Die Akute Neurasthenie. The Standard Edition of the Complete Psychological Works of Sigmund Freud* 1: 35.

Freud, S. (1888a). Hysteria. *The Standard Edition of the Complete Psychological Works of Sigmund Freud* 1: 41–57.

Freud, S. (1888b). Aphasie. In A. Villaret, ed., *Handwörterbuch der Gesamten Medizin* (vol. 1) (pp. 88–90). Stuttgart: Enke.

Freud, S. (1888c). Preface to the translation of Bernheim's *Suggestion. The Standard Edition of the Complete Psychological Works of Sigmund Freud* 1: 75–85.

Freud, S. (1888d). Gehirn. In A. Villaret, ed., *Handwörterbuch der Gesamten Medizin* (vol. 1) (pp. 684–697). Stuttgart: Enke.

Freud, S. (1889). Review of August Forel's *Der Hypnotismus. The Standard Edition of the Complete Psychological Works of Sigmund Freud* 1: 91–102.

Freud, S. (1891). Hypnosis. *The Standard Edition of the Complete Psychological Works of Sigmund Freud* 1: 105–114.

Freud, S. (1892). Sketches for the "Preliminary Communication" of 1893. *The Standard Edition of the Complete Psychological Works of Sigmund Freud* 1: 147–154.

Freud, S. (1892–1893). A case of successful treatment by hypnotism. *The Standard Edition of the Complete Psychological Works of Sigmund Freud* 1: 117–128.

Freud, S. (1892–1894). Preface and footnotes to the translation of Charcot's *Tuesday Lectures. The Standard Edition of the Complete Psychological Works of Sigmund Freud* 1: 133–143.

Freud, S. (1893a). On the psychical mechanism of hysterical phenomena. *The Standard Edition of the Complete Psychological Works of Sigmund Freud* 3: 27–39.

Freud, S. (1893b). Some points for a comparative study of organic and hysterical motor paralyses. *The Standard Edition of the Complete Psychological Works of Sigmund Freud* 1: 160–172.

Freud, S. (1893c). Charcot. *The Standard Edition of the Complete Psychological Works of Sigmund Freud* 3: 11–23.

Freud, S. (1894). The neuro-psychoses of defence. *The Standard Edition of the Complete Psychological Works of Sigmund Freud* 3: 45–61.

Freud, S. (1895a). On the grounds for detaching a particular syndrome from neurasthenia under the description "anxiety neuroses." *The Standard Edition of the Complete Psychological Works of Sigmund Freud* 3: 90–117.

Freud, S. (1895b). A reply to criticisms of my paper on anxiety neurosis. *The Standard Edition of the Complete Psychological Works of Sigmund Freud* 3: 123–139.

Freud, S. (1895c). Obsessions and phobias: Their psychical mechanism and their aetiology. *The Standard Edition of the Complete Psychological Works of Sigmund Freud* 3: 74–82.

Freud, S. (1896a). Heredity and the aetiology of the neuroses. *The Standard Edition of the Complete Psychological Works of Sigmund Freud* 3: 143–156.

Freud, S. (1896b). Further remarks on the neuro-psychoses of defence. *The Standard Edition of the Complete Psychological Works of Sigmund Freud* 3: 162–185.

Freud, S. (1896c). The aetiology of hysteria. *The Standard Edition of the Complete Psychological Works of Sigmund Freud* 3: 191–221.

Freud, S. (1898a). Sexuality in the aetiology of the neuroses. *The Standard Edition of the Complete Psychological Works of Sigmund Freud* 3: 263–285.

Freud, S. (1898b). The psychical mechanism of forgetfulness. *The Standard Edition of the Complete Psychological Works of Sigmund Freud* 3: 289–297.

Freud, S. (1900). *The Interpretation of Dreams. The Standard Edition of the Complete Psychological Works of Sigmund Freud* 4–5: 1–621.

Freud, S. (1901a). *On Dreams. The Standard Edition of the Complete Psychological Works of Sigmund Freud* 5: 633–686.

Freud, S. (1901b). *The Psychopathology of Everyday Life. The Standard Edition of the Complete Psychological Works of Sigmund Freud* 6: 1–279.

Freud, S. (1904). Freud's psycho-analytic procedure. *The Standard Edition of the Complete Psychological Works of Sigmund Freud* 7: 249–254.

Freud, S. (1905a). Fragment of an analysis of a case of hysteria. *The Standard Edition of the Complete Psychological Works of Sigmund Freud* 7: 7–122.

Freud, S. (1905b). *Three Essays on the Theory of Sexuality. The Standard Edition of the Complete Psychological Works of Sigmund Freud* 7: 130–243.

Freud, S. (1905c). Psychical or (moral) treatment. *The Standard Edition of the Complete Psychological Works of Sigmund Freud* 7: 283–302. (Original work published 1890.)

Freud, S. (1906a). My views on the part played by sexuality in the aetiology of the neuroses. *The Standard Edition of the Complete Psychological Works of Sigmund Freud* 7: 271–279.

Freud, S. (1906b). Psycho-analysis and the establishment of the facts in legal proceedings. *The Standard Edition of the Complete Psychological Works of Sigmund Freud* 9: 103–114.

Freud, S. (1907a). Delusions and dreams in Jensen's Gradiva. *The Standard Edition of the Complete Psychological Works of Sigmund Freud* 9: 7–95.

Freud, S. (1907b). Obsessive actions and religious practices. *The Standard Edition of the Complete Psychological Works of Sigmund Freud* 9: 117–127.

Freud, S. (1908a). Hysterical phantasies and their relation to bisexuality. *The Standard Edition of the Complete Psychological Works of Sigmund Freud* 9: 159–166.

Freud, S. (1908b). Character and anal erotism. *The Standard Edition of the Complete Psychological Works of Sigmund Freud* 9: 169–175.

Freud, S. (1908c). "Civilized" sexual morality and modern nervous illness. *The Standard Edition of the Complete Psychological Works of Sigmund Freud* 9: 181–204.

Freud, S. (1908d). On the sexual theories of children. *The Standard Edition of the Complete Psychological Works of Sigmund Freud* 9: 209–226.

Freud, S. (1909a). Analysis of a phobia in a five-year-old boy. *The Standard Edition of the Complete Psychological Works of Sigmund Freud* 10: 5–149.

Freud, S. (1909b). Notes upon a case of obsessional neurosis. *The Standard Edition of the Complete Psychological Works of Sigmund Freud* 10: 155–318.

Freud, S. (1910a). Five lectures on psycho-analysis. *The Standard Edition of the Complete Psychological Works of Sigmund Freud* 2: 9–55.

Freud, S. (1910b). Leonardo da Vinci and a memory of his childhood. *The Standard Edition of the Complete Psychological Works of Sigmund Freud* 11: 63–137.

Freud, S. (1910c). The future prospects of psycho-analytic therapy. *The Standard Edition of the Complete Psychological Works of Sigmund Freud* 11: 141–151.

Freud, S. (1910d). A special type of choice of object made by men. *The Standard Edition of the Complete Psychological Works of Sigmund Freud* 11: 165–175.

Freud, S. (1910e). The psycho-analytic view of psychogenic disturbance of vision. *The Standard Edition of the Complete Psychological Works of Sigmund Freud* 11: 211–218.

Freud, S. (1911a). Psycho-analytic notes on an autobiographical account of a case of paranoia (dementia paranoides). *The Standard Edition of the Complete Psychological Works of Sigmund Freud* 12: 9–82.

Freud, S. (1911b). Formulations on the two principles of mental functioning. *The Standard Edition of the Complete Psychological Works of Sigmund Freud* 12: 218–226.

Freud, S. (1911c). The handling of dream interpretation in psycho-analysis. *The Standard Edition of the Complete Psychological Works of Sigmund Freud* 12: 91–96.

Freud, S. (1912a). The dynamics of transference. *The Standard Edition of the Complete Psychological Works of Sigmund Freud* 12: 99–108.

Freud, S. (1912b). Contributions to a discussion on masturbation. *The Standard Edition of the Complete Psychological Works of Sigmund Freud* 12: 243–254.

Freud, S. (1912c). A note on the unconscious in psycho-analysis. *The Standard Edition of the Complete Psychological Works of Sigmund Freud* 12: 260–266.

Freud, S. (1912d). Recommendations to physicians practising psycho-analysis. *The Standard Edition of the Complete Psychological Works of Sigmund Freud* 12: 111–120.

Freud, S. (1912–1913). *Totem and Taboo. The Standard Edition of the Complete Psychological Works of Sigmund Freud* 13: 1–161.

Freud, S. (1913a). On beginning the treatment. *The Standard Edition of the Complete Psychological Works of Sigmund Freud* 12: 123–156.

Freud, S. (1913b). On psycho-analysis. *The Standard Edition of the Complete Psychological Works of Sigmund Freud* 12: 207–211.

Freud, S. (1913c). The occurrence in dreams of material from fairy tales. *The Standard Edition of the Complete Psychological Works of Sigmund Freud* 12: 281–287.

Freud, S. (1913d). The disposition to obsessional neurosis. *The Standard Edition of the Complete Psychological Works of Sigmund Freud* 12: 317–326.

Freud, S. (1913e). The claims of psycho-analysis to scientific interest. *The Standard Edition of the Complete Psychological Works of Sigmund Freud* 13: 165–190.

Freud, S. (1913f). The theme of the three caskets. *The Standard Edition of the Complete Psychological Works of Sigmund Freud* 12: 291–301.

Freud, S. (1914a). The Moses of Michelangelo. *The Standard Edition of the Complete Psychological Works of Sigmund Freud* 13: 211–238.

Freud, S. (1914b). On narcissism: An introduction. *The Standard Edition of the Complete Psychological Works of Sigmund Freud* 14: 73–102.

Freud, S. (1914c). Remembering, repeating and working-through. *The Standard Edition of the Complete Psychological Works of Sigmund Freud* 12: 147–156.

Freud, S. (1915a). Instincts and their vicissitudes. *The Standard Edition of the Complete Psychological Works of Sigmund Freud* 14: 117–140.

Freud, S. (1915b). Repression. *The Standard Edition of the Complete Psychological Works of Sigmund Freud* 14: 146–158.

Freud, S. (1915c). The unconscious. *The Standard Edition of the Complete Psychological Works of Sigmund Freud* 14: 166–215.

Freud, S. (1915d). Thoughts for the times on war and death. *The Standard Edition of the Complete Psychological Works of Sigmund Freud* 14: 275–302.

Freud, S. (1916a). On transience. *The Standard Edition of the Complete Psychological Works of Sigmund Freud* 14: 305–307.

Freud, S. (1916b). Some character-types met with in psycho-analytic work. *The Standard Edition of the Complete Psychological Works of Sigmund Freud* 14: 311–333.

Freud, S. (1916–1917). *Introductory Lectures on Psycho-Analysis. The Standard Edition of the Complete Psychological Works of Sigmund Freud* 15–16: 9–496.

Freud, S. (1917a). A metapsychological supplement to the theory of dreams. *The Standard Edition of the Complete Psychological Works of Sigmund Freud* 14: 222–235.

Freud, S. (1917b). A difficulty in the path of psycho-analysis. *The Standard Edition of the Complete Psychological Works of Sigmund Freud* 17: 137–144.

Freud, S. (1917c). Mourning and melancholia. *The Standard Edition of the Complete Psychological Works of Sigmund Freud* 14: 243–260.

Freud, S. (1917d). On transformations of instinct as exemplified in anal erotism. *The Standard Edition of the Complete Psychological Works of Sigmund Freud* 17: 127–133.

Freud, S. (1918). From the history of infantile neurosis. *The Standard Edition of the Complete Psychological Works of Sigmund Freud* 17: 7–123.

Freud, S. (1919a). A child is being beaten. A contribution to the study of the origin of sexual perversions. *The Standard Edition of the Complete Psychological Works of Sigmund Freud* 17: 179–204.

Freud, S. (1919b). Preface to Reik's *Ritual: Psycho-Analytic Studies. The Standard Edition of the Complete Psychological Works of Sigmund Freud* 17: 259–263.

Freud, S. (1919c). Introduction to *Psycho-Analysis and the War Neuroses. The Standard Edition of the Complete Psychological Works of Sigmund Freud* 17: 207–215.

Freud, S. (1919d). The "uncanny." *The Standard Edition of the Complete Psychological Works of Sigmund Freud* 17: 219–256.

Freud, S. (1920a). *Beyond the Pleasure Principle. The Standard Edition of the Complete Psychological Works of Sigmund Freud* 18: 7–64.

Freud, S. (1920b). The psychogenesis of a case of homosexuality in a woman. *The Standard Edition of the Complete Psychological Works of Sigmund Freud* 18: 147–172.

Freud, S. (1921). *Group Psychology and the Analysis of the Ego. The Standard Edition of the Complete Psychological Works of Sigmund Freud* 18: 69–143.

Freud, S. (1923a). Two encyclopaedia articles: (A) Psycho-analysis and (B) The libido theory. *The Standard Edition of the Complete Psychological Works of Sigmund Freud* 18: 235–259.

Freud, S. (1923b). *The Ego and the Id. The Standard Edition of the Complete Psychological Works of Sigmund Freud* 19: 12–59.

Freud, S. (1923c). Remarks on the theory and practice of dream-interpretation. *The Standard Edition of the Complete Psychological Works of Sigmund Freud* 19: 109–121.

Freud, S. (1923d). Josef Popper-Lynkeus and the theory of dreams. *The Standard Edition of the Complete Psychological Works of Sigmund Freud* 19: 261–263.

Freud, S. (1923e). The infantile genital organization (an interpolation into the theory of sexuality). *The Standard Edition of the Complete Psychological Works of Sigmund Freud* 19: 141–145.

Freud, S. (1924a). Neurosis and psychosis. *The Standard Edition of the Complete Psychological Works of Sigmund Freud* 19: 149–153.

Freud, S. (1924b). The economic problem of masochism. *The Standard Edition of the Complete Psychological Works of Sigmund Freud* 19: 159–170.

Freud, S. (1924c). A short account of psycho-analysis. *The Standard Edition of the Complete Psychological Works of Sigmund Freud* 19: 191–209.

Freud, S. (1924d). The dissolution of the Oedipus complex. *The Standard Edition of the Complete Psychological Works of Sigmund Freud* 19: 173–179.

Freud, S. (1925a). *An Autobiographical Study. The Standard Edition of the Complete Psychological Works of Sigmund Freud* 20: 7–74.

Freud, S. (1925b). A Note upon the "Mystic Writing-Pad." *The Standard Edition of the Complete Psychological Works of Sigmund Freud* 19: 227–232.

Freud, S. (1925c). The resistances to psycho-analysis. *The Standard Edition of the Complete Psychological Works of Sigmund Freud* 19: 213–222.

Freud, S. (1925d). Negation. *The Standard Edition of the Complete Psychological Works of Sigmund Freud* 19: 235–239.

Freud, S. (1925e). Josef Breuer. *The Standard Edition of the Complete Psychological Works of Sigmund Freud* 19: 279–280.

Freud, S. (1925f). Some psychical consequences of the anatomical distinction between the sexes. *The Standard Edition of the Complete Psychological Works of Sigmund Freud* 19: 248–258.

Freud, S. (1926a). *Inhibitions, Symptoms and Anxiety. The Standard Edition of the Complete Psychological Works of Sigmund Freud* 20: 87–172.

Freud, S. (1926b). *The Question of Lay Analysis. The Standard Edition of the Complete Psychological Works of Sigmund Freud* 20: 183–258.

Freud, S. (1926c). Psycho-analysis. *The Standard Edition of the Complete Psychological Works of Sigmund Freud* 20: 263–270.

Freud, S. (1927a). *The Future of an Illusion. The Standard Edition of the Complete Psychological Works of Sigmund Freud* 21: 5–56.

Freud, S. (1927b). Postscript to my paper on the Moses of Michelangelo. *The Standard Edition of the Complete Psychological Works of Sigmund Freud* 13: 237–238.

Freud, S. (1930). *Civilization and Its Discontents. The Standard Edition of the Complete Psychological Works of Sigmund Freud* 21: 64–145.

Freud, S. (1931). Female sexuality. *The Standard Edition of the Complete Psychological Works of Sigmund Freud* 21: 225–243.

Freud, S. (1932). My contact with Josef Popper-Lynkeus. *The Standard Edition of the Complete Psychological Works of Sigmund Freud* 22: 219–224.

Freud, S. (1933a). *Neue Folge der Vorlesungen zur Einführung in die Psychoanalyse. Gesammelte Werke* 15: 1–208.

Freud, S. (1933b). *New Introductory Lectures on Psycho-Analysis. The Standard Edition of the Complete Psychological Works of Sigmund Freud* 22: 5–185.

Freud, S. (1933c). *New Introductory Lectures on Psycho-Analysis* (W. J. H. Sprott, trans.). London: Hogarth Press.

Freud, S. (1937a). Analysis terminable and interminable. *The Standard Edition of the Complete Psychological Works of Sigmund Freud* 23: 216–253.

Freud, S. (1937b). Constructions in analysis. *The Standard Edition of the Complete Psychological Works of Sigmund Freud* 23: 257–269.

Freud, S. (1939). *Moses and Monotheism: Three Essays. The Standard Edition of the Complete Psychological Works of Sigmund Freud* 23: 7–137.

Freud, S. (1940a). *An Outline of Psycho-analysis. The Standard Edition of the Complete Psychological Works of Sigmund Freud* 23: 144–207.

Freud, S. (1940b). Some elementary lessons in psycho-analysis. *The Standard Edition of the Complete Psychological Works of Sigmund Freud* 23: 281–286.

Freud, S. (1953). *On Aphasia: A Critical Study* (E. Stengel, trans.). New York: International Universities Press. (Original work published 1891.)

Freud, S. (1954). *The Origins of Psycho-Analysis.* New York: Basic Books. (Original work published 1950.)

Freud, S. (1974). Contribution to the knowledge of the effect of cocaine. In R. Byck, ed., *Cocaine Papers by Sigmund Freud* (pp. 97–104). New York: Meridian. (Original work published 1885.)

Freud, S. (1987). *A Phylogenetic Fantasy: Overview of the Transference Neuroses,* (I. Grubrich-Simitis, ed., and A. and P. T. Hoffer, trans.). Cambridge: Harvard University Press. (Original manuscript 1915; original work published 1985.)

Friedenberg, F. S. (1956). A contribution to the problem of sado-masochism. Psychoanalytic Review 43: 91–96.

Friedman, J. A. (1992). Freud's *Todestrieb*: An introduction. Parts 1 and 2. *International Review of Psycho-Analysis* 19: 189–196, 309–322.

Friedman, L. (1965). The significance of determinism and free will. *International Journal of Psycho-Analysis* 46: 515–520.

Friedman, L. (1977). Reasons for the Freudian revolution. *Psychoanalytic Quarterly* 46: 623–649.

Friedman, L. (1980). Symposium: George Klein's *Psychoanalytic Theory* in perspective. *Psychoanalytic Review* 67: 195–216.

Friedman, R. C., and Downey, J. I. (1995). Biology and the Oedipus complex. *Psychoanalytic Quarterly* 64: 234–264.

Fromm, E. (1970). The Oedipus complex: Comments on the case of Little Hans. In E. Fromm, *The Crisis of Psychoanalysis* (pp. 69–78). New York: Holt, Rhinehart and Winston. (Original work published 1968.)

Frosch, J. (1981). The role of unconscious homosexuality in the paranoid constellation. *Psychoanalytic Quarterly* 50: 587–613.

Fuchs, S. H. (1937). On introjection. *International Journal of Psycho-Analysis* 18: 269–293.

Furer, M. (1972). The history of the superego concept in psychoanalysis: A review of the literature. In S. C. Post, ed., *Moral Values and the Superego Concept in Psychoanalysis* (pp. 11–59). New York: International Universities Press.

Furst, S. S. (1967). Psychic trauma: A survey. In S. S. Furst, ed., *Psychic Trauma* (pp. 3–50). New York: Basic Books.

Furst, S. S. (1978). The stimulus barrier and the pathogenicity of trauma. *International Journal of Psycho-Analysis* 59: 345–352.

Galaty, D. H. (1974). The philosophical basis of mid-nineteenth century German reductionism. *Journal of the History of Medicine and Allied Sciences* 29: 295–316.

Galenson, E., and Roiphe, H. (1976). Some suggested revisions concerning early female development. *Journal of the American Psychoanalytic Association* 24: 29–57.

Garma, A. (1969). Present thoughts on Freud's theory of dream hallucination. *International Journal of Psycho-Analysis* 50: 485–494.

Garma, A. (1971). Within the realm of the death instinct. *International Journal of Psycho-Analysis* 52: 145–154.

Garrison, M. (1978). A new look at Little Hans. *Psychoanalytic Review* 65: 523–532.

Garza-Guerrero, A. C. (1981a). The superego concept. Part I: Historical review; object relations approach. *Psychoanalytic Review* 68: 321–342.

Garza-Guerrero, A. C. (1981b). The superego concept. Part II: Superego development, superego pathology, summary. *Psychoanalytic Review* 68: 513–546.

Gattel, F. (1898). *Ueber die sexuellen Ursachen der Neurasthenie und Angstneurose.* Berlin: Hirschwald.

Gauld, A. (1992). *A History of Hypnotism.* Cambridge: Cambridge University Press.

Gay, P. (1988). *Freud: A Life for Our Time.* New York: Norton.

Gay, V. P. (1992). *Freud on Sublimation: Reconsiderations.* Albany, NY: State University of New York Press.

Gediman, H. K. (1984). Actual neurosis and psychoneurosis. *International Journal of Psycho-Analysis* 65: 191–202.

Gedo, J. E., and Goldberg, A. (1973). *Models of the Mind: A Psychoanalytic Theory.* Chicago: University of Chicago Press.

Gedo, J. E., Sabshin, M., Sadow, L., and Schlessinger, N. (1964). "Studies on Hysteria": A methodological evaluation. *Journal of the American Psychoanalytic Association* 12: 734–751.

Gellner, E. (1985). *The Psychoanalytic Movement or the Coming of Unreason.* London: Paladin.

Gifford, S. (1964). Repetition compulsion. *Journal of the American Psychoanalytic Association* 12: 632–649.

Gifford, S. (1986). Review of D. Stern *The First Relationship, Journal of the American Psychoanalytic Association* 34: 225–227.

Gill, M. M. (1963). Topography and systems in psychoanalytic theory. *Psychological Issues* 3. Monograph 10.

Gill, M. M. (1967). The primary process. *Psychological Issues* 5: 260–298. Monograph 18/19.

Gill, M. M. (1977). Psychic energy reconsidered. *Journal of the American Psychoanalytic Association* 25: 581–597.

Gill, M. M., and Brenman, M. (1959). *Hypnosis and Related States: Psychoanalytic Studies in Regression.* New York: International Universities Press.

Gill, M. M., and Holzman, P. S., eds. (1976). *Psychology versus Metapsychology: Psychoanalytic Essays in Memory of George S. Klein.* New York: International Universities Press.

Gillespie, W. H. (1952). Notes on the analysis of sexual perversions. *International Journal of Psycho-Analysis* 33: 397–402.

Gillespie, W. H. (1956a). The general theory of sexual perversion. *International Journal of Psycho-Analysis* 37: 396–403.

Gillespie, W. H. (1956b). The structure and aetiology of sexual perversion. In S. Lorand and M. Balint, eds., *Perversions: Psychodynamics and Therapy* (pp. 28–41). New York: Random House. (Original work published 1965.)

Gillespie, W. H. (1964). The psycho-analytic theory of sexual deviation with special reference to fetishism. In I. Rosen, ed., *The Pathology and Treatment of Sexual Deviation* (pp. 123–145). London: Oxford University Press.

Gillespie, W. H. (1971). Aggression and instinct theory. *International Journal of Psycho-Analysis* 52: 155–160.

Gillman, R. D. (1982). Preoedipal and early oedipal components of the superego. *Psychoanalytic Study of the Child* 37: 273–281.

Gilman, S. L. (1981). Freud and the prostitute: Male stereotypes of female sexuality in fin-de-siècle Vienna. *Journal of the American Academy of Psychoanalysis* 9: 337–360.

Glassman, M. (1988). Kernberg and Kohut: A test of competing psychoanalytic models of narcissism. *Journal of the American Psychoanalytic Association* 36: 597–625.

Glenn, J. (1980). Freud's adolescent patients: Katharina, Dora and the "homosexual woman." In M. Kanzer and J. Glenn, eds., *Freud and His Patients* (pp. 23–47). New York: Aronson.

Glenn, J. (1986). Freud, Dora, and the maid: A study of countertransference. *Journal of the American Psychoanalytic Association* 34: 591–606.

Glenn, J. (1989). From protomasochism to masochism: A developmental view. *Psychoanalytic Study of the Child* 44: 73–86.

Glick, B. S. (1966). Freud, the problem of quality and the "secretory neurone." *Psychoanalytic Quarterly* 35: 84–97.

Glover, E. (1926). Descriptive notice: *Hemmung, Symptom und Angst. British Journal of Medical Psychology* 6: 121–136.

Glover, E. (1931a). Sublimation, substitution and social anxiety. *International Journal of Psycho-Analysis* 12: 263–297.

Glover, E. (1931b). The therapeutic effect of inexact interpretation: A contribution to the theory of suggestion. *International Journal of Psycho-Analysis* 12: 397–411.

Glover, E. (1937). Symposium on the theory of the therapeutic results of psycho-analysis. *International Journal of Psycho-Analysis* 18: 125–132.

Glover, E. (1939). *Psycho-Analysis: A Handbook for Medical Practitioners and Students of Comparative Psychology* (2d ed.). London: Staples Press.

Glover, E. (1943). The concept of dissociation. *International Journal of Psycho-Analysis* 24: 7–13.

Glover, E. (1947). Basic mental concepts: Their clinical and theoretical value. *Psychoanalytic Quarterly* 16: 482–506.

Glover, E. (1952). Research methods in psychoanalysis. *International Journal of Psycho-Analysis* 33: 404–409.

Glover, E. (1954). Therapeutic criteria of psycho-analysis. *International Journal of Psycho-Analysis* 35: 95–101.

Glover, E. (1955). Note of 1955 to "Notes on oral character formation" (1924). In E. Glover, ed., *Selected Papers on Psycho-Analysis.* (vol. I). *On the Early Development of Mind* (pp. 43–46). London: Imago.

Glover, E. (1961). Some recent trends in psychoanalytic theory. *Psychoanalytic Quarterly* 30: 86–107.

Glover, E. (1968). *The Birth of the Ego.* London: Allen and Unwin.

Glymour, C. (1974). Freud, Kepler, and the clinical evidence. In R. Wollheim, ed., *Freud: A Collection of Critical Essays* (pp. 285–304). New York: Anchor Books. (Original work published 1974.)

Glymour, C. (1980). *Theory and Evidence.* Princeton, N.J.: Princeton University Press.

Glymour, C. (1983). The theory of your dreams. In R. S. Cohen and L. Laudan, eds., *Physics, Philosophy and Psychoanalysis: Essays in Honour of Adolf Grünbaum* (pp. 57–71). Dordrecht: Reidel.

Glymour, C. (1991). Freud's androids. In J. Neu, ed., *The Cambridge Companion to Freud* (pp. 44–85). Cambridge: Cambridge University Press.

Glymour, C. (1993). How Freud left science. In J. Earman, A. I. Janis, G. J. Massey, and N. Rescher, eds., *Philosophical Problems of the Internal and External World: Essays on the Philosophy of Adolf Grünbaum* (pp. 461–487). Pittsburgh: University of Pittsburgh Press.

Glymour, C. (forthcoming). *Freud's Androids: Essays on Psychology and Scientific Inference.*

Goldberg, D. A. (1985). A reexamination of the concept "object" in psychoanalysis. *Journal of the American Psychoanalytic Association* 33: 167–185.

Goldsmith, M. (1934). *Franz Anton Mesmer; a History of Mesmerism.* New York: Doubleday, Doran.

Good, M. I. (1994). The reconstruction of early childhood trauma: Fantasy, reality, and verification. *Journal of the American Psychoanalytic Association* 42: 79–101.

Goodman, S. (1965). Current status of the theory of the superego. *Journal of the American Psychoanalytic Association* 13: 172–180.

Gordon, C. (1982). *Forgotten Scripts: Their Ongoing Discovery and Decipherment* (rev. and enlarged). New York: Basic Books.

Gordon, J. E. (1967). Hypnosis in research on psychotherapy. In J. E. Gordon, ed., *Handbook of Clinical and Experimental Hypnosis* (pp. 148–200). New York: Macmillan.

Goshen, C. E. (1952). The original case material of psychoanalysis. *American Journal of Psychiatry* 108: 829–834.

Gosling, F. G. (1987). *Before Freud: Neurasthenia and the American Medical Community*. Chicago: University of Chicago Press.

Grand, H. G. (1973). The masochistic defence of the "double mask": Its relationship to imposture. *International Journal of Psycho-Analysis* 54: 445–454.

Gravitz, M. A. (1993). Etienne Félix d'Hénin de Cuvillers: A founder of hypnosis. *American Journal of Clinical Hypnosis* 36: 7–11.

Greaves, G. B. (1980). Multiple personality: 165 years after Mary Reynolds. *Journal of Nervous and Mental Disease* 168: 577–596.

Green, A. (1977). Conceptions of affect. *International Journal of Psycho-Analysis* 58: 129–156.

Greenacre, P. (1941). The predisposition to anxiety. *Psychoanalytic Quarterly* 10: 66–94.

Greenacre, P. (1945). The biological economy of birth. *Psychoanalytic Study of the Child* 1: 31–51.

Greenacre, P. (1967). The influence of infantile trauma on genetic patterns. In S. S. Furst, ed., *Psychic Trauma* (pp. 108–153). New York: Basic Books.

Greenacre, P. (1980). A historical sketch of the use and disuse of reconstruction. *Psychoanalytic Study of the Child* 35: 35–40.

Greenacre, P. (1981). Reconstruction: Its nature and therapeutic value. *Journal of the American Psychoanalytic Association* 29: 27–46.

Greenberg, D. E. (1990). Instinct and primary narcissism in Freud's later theory: An interpretation and reformulation of "Beyond the pleasure principle." *International Journal of Psycho-Analysis* 71: 271–283.

Greenberg, R., and Pearlman, C. (1978). If Freud only knew: A reconsideration of psychoanalytic dream theory. *International Review of Psycho-Analysis* 5: 71–75.

Greenson, R. R. (1954). Problems of identification. *Journal of the American Psychoanalytic Association* 2: 197–217.

Greenspoon, J. (1955). The reinforcing effect of two spoken sounds on the frequency of two responses. *American Journal of Psychology* 68: 409–416.

Greenspoon, J. (1962). Verbal conditioning and clinical psychology. In A. J. Bachrach, ed., *Experimental Foundations of Clinical Psychology* (pp. 510–553). New York: Basic Books.

Grenell, R. G. (1977). The mind-body problem revisited. Commentaries on Freud's *"Project" Re-assessed.* Commentary from psychobiology. *Journal of Nervous and Mental Disease* 165: 427–441.

Grinberg, L. (1991). Letter to Sigmund Freud. In J. Sandler, E. P. Person, and P. Fonagy, eds., *Freud's "On Narcissism: An Introduction"* (pp. 95–107). New Haven. CT: Yale University Press.

Grinker, R. R., and Spiegel, J. P. (1943). *War Neuroses in North Africa*. No place: Air Surgeon Army Air Force.

Grinker, R. R., and Spiegel, J. P. (1945). *Men Under Stress*. Philadelphia: Blakiston.

Grinstein, A. (1968). *Sigmund Freud's Dreams*. Detroit: Wayne State University Press.

Grinstein, A. (1971). Freud's first publications in America. *Journal of the American Psychoanalytic Association* 19: 241–264.

Grinstein, A. (1983). *Freud's Rules of Dream Interpretation*. New York: International Universities Press.

Groddeck, G. (1949). *The Book of the It* (V. M. E. Collins, trans.). London: Vision. (Original work published 1923.)

Grolnick, S. A. (1982). The current psychoanalytic dialogue: Its counterpart in renaissance philosophy. *Journal of the American Psychoanalytic Association* 30: 679–699.

Groos, K. (1899). *Die Spiele der Menschen*. Jena: Fischer.

Groos, K. (1901). *The Play of Man* (E. L. Baldwin, trans.). New York: Appleton.

Grosskurth, P. (1991). *The Secret Ring: Freud's Inner Circle and the Politics of Psychoanalysis*. London: Cape.

Grossman, W. I. (1986). Notes on masochism: A discussion of the history and development of a psychoanalytic concept. *Psychoanalytic Quarterly* 55: 379–413.

Grossman W. I. (1991). Pain, aggression, fantasy, and concepts of sado-masochism. *Psychoanalytic Quarterly* 60: 22–52.

Grossman, W. I., and Simon, B. (1969). Anthropomorphism: Motive, meaning, and causality in psychoanalytic theory. *Psychoanalytic Study of the Child* 24: 78–111.

Grotstein, J. S. (1977a). The psychoanalytic concept of schizophrenia: I. The dilemma. *International Journal of Psycho-Analysis* 58: 403–425.

Grotstein, J. S. (1977b). The psychoanalytic concept of schizophrenia: II. Reconciliation. *International Journal of Psycho-Analysis* 58: 427–502.

Gruber, H. E. (1981). On the relation between "aha experiences" and the construction of ideas. *History of Science* 19: 41–59.

Grubrich-Simitis, I. (1987). Metapsychology and metabiology. In S. Freud, *A Phylogenetic Fantasy: Overview of the Transference Neuroses* (I. Grubrich-Simitis, ed., and A. and P. T. Hoffer, trans.) (pp. 73–107). Cambridge: Harvard University Press.

Grünbaum, A. (1980). Epistemological liabilities of the clinical appraisal of psychoanalytic theory. *Nous* 14: 307–385.

Grünbaum, A. (1984). *The Foundations of Psychoanalysis: A Philosophical Critique*. Berkeley, Calif.: University of California Press.

Grünbaum, A. (1990). Meaning and connections in the human sciences: The poverty of hermeneutic philosophy. *Journal of the American Psychoanalytic Association* 38: 559–577.

Grünbaum, A. (1993). *Validation in the Clinical Theory of Psychoanalysis: A Study in the Philosophy of Psychoanalysis*. Madison, Conn.: International Universities Press.

Grünbaum, A. (1995, May) . *Is Manifest Dream-Content a Compromise Formation with Repressed Wishes? A Critique of Freud's Pre-analytic and Psychoanalytic Dream Theory*. Paper presented at the International Congress on Freud's Pre-Analytical Writings (1877–1900), University of Ghent, Belgium.

Guillain, G. (1959). *J. M. Charcot, 1825–1893: His Life, His Work* (P. Bailey, ed. and trans.). New York: Hoeber. (Original work published 1955.)

Guttman, S. A. (1985). The psychoanalytic point of view: Basic concepts and deviant theories. A brief communication. *International Journal of Psycho-Analysis* 66: 167–170.

Hacker, F. J. (1972). Sublimation revisited. *International Journal of Psycho-Analysis* 53: 219–223.

Hägglund, T.-B. (1980). Some viewpoints on the ego ideal. *International Review of Psycho-Analysis* 7: 207–218.

Hale, N. G. (1971). *The Beginnings of Psychoanalysis in the United States*. New York: Oxford University Press.

Hale, N. G. (1995). *The Rise and Crisis of Psychoanalysis in the United States: Freud and the Americans, 1917–1985*. New York: Oxford University Press.

Hammerman, S. (1965). Conceptions of superego development. *Journal of the American Psychoanalytic Association* 13: 320–355.

Hanly, C. (1978). Instincts and hostile affects. *International Journal of Psycho-Analysis* 59: 149–156.

Hansen, J. T. (1991). Autoerotism to secondary narcissism. *Psychoanalytic Review* 78: 225–236.

Hardison, O. B. (1968). *Aristotle's Poetics: A Translation and Commentary for Students of Literature* (L. Golden, trans.). Englewood Cliffs, N.J.: Prentice-Hall.

Harrington, A. (1988). Metals and magnets in medicine: Hysteria, hypnosis and medical culture in *fin-de-siècle* Paris. *Psychological Medicine* 18: 21–38.

Harris, R., ed. (1991). Introduction to J-M. Charcot, *Clinical Lectures on Diseases of the Nervous System* (T. Savill, trans.). London: Tavistock/Routledge. (Original French published 1887, English translation originally published 1889.)

Hart, B. (1916). *The Psychology of Insanity* (3d ed.). Cambridge: Cambridge University Press.

Hart, B. (1929). *Psychopathology: Its Development and Its Place in Medicine* (2d ed.). Cambridge: Cambridge University Press.

Hart, H. H. (1947). Problems of identification. *Psychiatric Quarterly* 21: 274–293.

Hart, H. H. (1948). Sublimation and aggression. *Psychiatric Quarterly* 22: 389–412.

Hart, H. L. A., and Honoré, T. (1985). *Causation in the Law* (2d ed.). Oxford: Clarendon Press.

Hartman, F. R. (1983). A reappraisal of the Emma episode and the specimen dream. *Journal of the American Psychoanalytic Association* 31: 555–585.

Hartmann, E. von (1931). *Philosophy of the Unconscious* (9th ed.) (W. C. Coupland, trans.). London: Kegan Paul, Trench, Trubner. (Original work published 1882.)

Hartmann, H. (1948). Comments on the psychoanalytic theory of instinctual drives. *Psychoanalytic Quarterly* 17: 368–388.

Hartmann, H. (1950). Comments on the psychoanalytic theory of the ego. *Psychoanalytic Study of the Child* 5: 74–97.

Hartmann, H. (1952). The mutual influences in the development of ego and id. *Psychoanalytic Study of the Child* 7: 9–30.

Hartmann, H. (1955). Notes on the theory of sublimation. *Psychoanalytic Study of the Child* 10: 9–29.

Hartmann, H. (1956). The development of the ego concept in Freud's work. *International Journal of Psycho-Analysis* 37: 425–438.

Hartmann, H. (1958). *Ego Psychology and the Problem of Adaptation* (D. Rapaport, trans.). New York: International Universities Press. (Original work published 1939.)

Hartmann, H. (1959). Psychoanalysis as a scientific theory. In S. Hook, ed., *Psychoanalysis, Scientific Method, and Philosophy* (pp. 3–37). New York: New York University Press.

Hartmann, H. (1964). *Essays in Ego Psychology*. London: Hogarth Press.

Hartmann, H. (1964). Understanding and explanation. In H. Hartmann, *Essays in Ego Psychology* (pp. 369–403). New York: International Universities Press. (Original work published 1927.)

Hartmann, H., and Kris, E. (1945). The genetic approach in psychoanalysis. *Psychoanalytic Study of the Child* 1: 11–30.

Hartmann, H., and Loewenstein, R. M. (1962). Notes on the superego. *Psychoanalytic Study of the Child* 17: 42–81.

Hartmann, H., Kris, E., and Loewenstein, R. M. (1946). Comments on the formation of psychic structure. *Psychoanalytic Study of the Child* 2: 11–38.

Hartmann, H., Kris, E., and Loewenstein, R. M. (1949). Notes on the theory of aggression. *Psychoanalytic Study of the Child*, 9–36.

Havens, L. L. (1966). Charcot and hysteria. *Journal of Nervous and Mental Disease* 141: 505–516.

Havens, L. L. (1973). *Approaches to the Mind: Movement of the Psychiatric Schools from Sects Toward Science*. Boston: Little, Brown.

Hayman, A. (1969). What do we mean by "id"? *Journal of the American Psychoanalytic Association* 17: 353–380.

Heimann, P. (1952). Notes on the theory of the life and death instincts. In M. Klein, P. Heimann, S. Isaacs, and J. Riviere, eds., *Developments in Psycho-Analysis* (pp. 321–337). London: Hogarth Press.

Heimann, P. (1962). Notes on the anal stage. *International Journal of Psycho-Analysis* 43: 406–414.

Heine, R. W. (1953). A comparison of patient's reports on psychotherapeutic experience with psycho-analytic, nondirective and Adlerian therapists. *American Journal of Psychotherapy* 7: 16–23.

Hendrick, I. (1934). *Facts and Theories of Psychoanalysis.* New York: Knopf.

Hendrick, I. (1942). Instinct and the ego during infancy. *Psychoanalytic Quarterly* 11: 33–58.

Hendrick, I. (1943a). Work and the pleasure principle. *Psychoanalytic Quarterly* 12: 311–329.

Hendrick, I. (1943b). The discussion of the "instinct to master." *Psychoanalytic Quarterly* 12: 561–565.

Hendrick, I. (1951). Early development of the ego: Identification in infancy. *Psychoanalytic Quarterly* 20: 44–61.

Hendrick, I. (1964). Narcissism and the prepuberty ego ideal. *Journal of the American Psychoanalytic Association* 12: 522–528.

Hering, E. (1913). *Memory: Lectures on the Specific Energies of the Nervous System.* Chicago: Open Court. (Original work published 1870.)

Heynick, F. (1981). Linguistic aspects of Freud's dream model. *International Review of Psycho-Analysis* 8: 299–314.

Hilgard, E. R. (1952). Experimental approaches to psychoanalysis. In E. Pumpian-Mindlin, ed., *Psycho-analysis as Science* (pp. 3–45). Stanford, Calif.: Stanford University Press.

Hilgard, E. R. (1968). Psychoanalysis: Experimental studies. In *International Encyclopedia of the Social Sciences* (vol. 13) (pp. 13–45). New York: Macmillan and Free Press.

Hilgard, E. R. (1977). *Divided Consciousness: Multiple Controls in Human Thought and Action.* New York: Wiley.

Hilgard, E. R., and Nowlis, D. P. (1972). The contents of hypnotic dreams and night dreams: An exercise in method. In E. Fromm and R. E. Shor, eds., *Hypnosis: Research Developments and Perspectives* (pp. 511–524). Chicago: Aldine.

Hillman, R. G. (1965). A scientific study of mystery: The role of the medical and popular press in the Nancy-Salpêtrière controversy on hypnotism. *Bulletin of the History of Medicine* 39: 163–182.

Hirschmüller, A. (1978). *Physiologie und Psychoanalyse in Leben und Werk Josef Breuers.* Bern: Huber.

Hirschmüller, A. (1989). *The Life and Work of Josef Breuer: Physiology and Psychoanalysis.* New York: New York University Press.

Hobson, J. A., and MacCarley, R. W. (1977). The brain as a dream state generator: An activation-synthesis hypothesis of the dream process. *American Journal of Psychiatry* 134: 1335–1348.

Hoch, P. H. (1959). Masochism: Clinical considerations. In J. H. Masserman, ed., *Individual and Familial Dynamics* (pp. 42–43). New York: Grune and Stratton.

Hoenig, J. (1976). Sigmund Freud's views on the sexual disorders in historical perspective. *British Journal of Psychiatry* 129: 193–200.

Hoffman, M. (1964). The idea of freedom in psychoanalysis. *International Journal of Psycho-Analysis* 45: 579–583.

Hojer-Pedersen, W. (1956). An attempt at evaluating the contents of the concept of actual neurosis. *Acta Psychiatrica et Neurologica Scandinavika* 31: 447–457.

Holbrook, D. (1971). *Human Hope and the Death Instinct.* Oxford: Pergamon Press.

Holder, A. (1982). Preoedipal contributions to the formation of the superego. *Psychoanalytic Study of the Child* 37: 245–272.

Hollender, M. H. (1980). The case of Anna O.: A reformulation. *American Journal of Psychiatry* 137: 797–800.

Holt, R. R. (1962). A critical examination of Freud's concept of bound vs. free cathexis. *Journal of the American Psychoanalytic Association* 10: 475–525.

Holt, R. R. (1965). A review of some of Freud's biological assumptions and their influence on his theories. In N. S. Greenfield and W. C. Lewis, eds., *Psychoanalysis and Current Biological Thought* (pp. 93–124). Madison, WI: University of Wisconsin Press.

Holt, R. R. (1967). The development of the primary process: A structural view. *Psychological Issues* 5: 345–400. Monograph 18/19.

Holt, R. R. (1968). Beyond vitalism and mechanism: Freud's concept of psychic energy. In B. B. Wolman, ed., *Historical Roots of Contemporary Psychology* (pp. 196–226). New York: Harper and Row. (Original work published 1967.)

Holt, R. R. (1975a). Drive or wish? A reconsideration of the psychoanalytic theory of motivation. *Psychological Issues* 9: 158–197. Monograph 36.

Holt, R. R. (1975b). The past and future of ego psychology. *Psychoanalytic Quarterly* 44: 550–576.

Holt, R. R. (1981). The death and transfiguration of metapsychology. *International Review of Psycho-Analysis* 8: 129–143.

Holt, R. R. (1982). Family secrets. *Sciences* 22: 26–28.

Holt, R. R. (1992). Review of Malcolm Macmillan, *Freud Evaluated: The Completed Arc. Isis* 83: 698.

Holt, R. R. (1995). Letter to the editor, *New York Review of Books*. In F. Crews et al, *The Memory Wars: Freud's Legacy in Dispute* (pp. 140–144). New York: New York Review of Books. (Original work published April 21, 1994.)

Holzman, P. (1985). Psychoanalysis: Is the therapy destroying the science? *Journal of the American Psychoanalytic Association* 33: 725–770.

Home, H. J. (1966). The concept of mind. *International Journal of Psycho-Analysis* 47: 42–49.

Hopkins, J. (1991). The interpretation of dreams. In J. Neu, ed., *The Cambridge Companion to Freud* (pp. 86–135). Cambridge: Cambridge University Press.

Horney, K. (1924). On the genesis of the castration complex in women. *International Journal of Psycho-Analysis* 5: 50–65. (Original work published 1923.)

Horney, K. (1926). The flight from womanhood. *International Journal of Psycho-Analysis* 7: 324–339.

Horney, K. (1928). The problem of the monogamous ideal. *International Journal of Psycho-Analysis* 9: 318–331.

Horney, K. (1937). *The Neurotic Personality of Our Time*. New York: Norton.

Hubbard, L. R. (1952a). *Scientology: A History of Man*. Silver Springs, Md.: Distribution Center.

Hubbard, L. R. (1952b). *Scientology: 8–80*. Silver Springs, Md.: Distribution Center.

Hull, C. L. (1943). *Principles of Behavior: An Introduction to Behavior Theory*. New York: Appleton-Century-Crofts.

Hurst, A. F. (1920). *The Psychology of the Special Senses and their Functional Disorders*. London: Frowde.

Huston, P. E., Shakow, D., and Erickson, M. H. (1934). A study of hypnotically induced complexes by means of the Luria technique. *Journal of General Psychology* 11: 65–97.

Ikonen, P., and Rechardt, E. (1978). The vicissitudes of Thanatos: On the place of aggression and destructiveness in psychoanalytic interpretation. *Scandinavian Psychoanalytical Review* 1: 79–114.

Isaacs, K. S., and Haggard, E. A. (1966). Some methods used in the study of affect in psychotherapy. In L. A. Gottschalk and A. H. Auerbach, eds., *Methods of Research in Psychotherapy* (pp. 226–239). New York: Appleton-Century-Crofts.

Isaacs, S. (1939). Criteria for interpretation. *International Journal of Psycho-Analysis* 20: 148–160.

Isay, R. A. (1978). The pathogenicity of the primal scene: Panel report. *Journal of the American Psychoanalytic Association* 26: 131–142.

Israëls, H., and Schatzman, M. (1993). The seduction theory. *History of Psychiatry*, 4: 23–59.

Izenberg, G. N. (1991). Seduced and abandoned: The rise and fall of Freud's seduction theory. In J. Neu, ed., *The Cambridge Companion to Freud* (pp. 25–43). Cambridge: Cambridge University Press.

Jackson, J. H. (1878–1879). On affections of speech from disease of the brain. *Brain* i: 304–330.

Jackson, J. H. (1879–1880a). On affections of speech from disease of the brain. *Brain* ii: 203–222.

Jackson, J. H. (1879–1880b). On affections of speech from disease of the brain. *Brain* ii: 323–356.

Jackson, J. H. (1889). On the comparative study of diseases of the nervous system. *British Medical Journal* ii: 355–362.

Jackson, S. W. (1967). Subjective experiences and the concept of energy. *Perspectives in Biology and Medicine* 10: 602–626.

Jackson, S. W. (1970). Force and kindred notions in eighteenth-century neurophysiology and medical psychology. *Bulletin of the History of Medicine* 44: 397–410, 539–554.

Jacobsen, P. B., and Steele, R. S. (1979). From present to past: Freudian archaeology. *International Review of Psycho-Analysis* 6: 349–362.

Jacobson, E. (1953). The affects and their pleasure-unpleasure qualities, in relation to the psychic discharge processes. In R. M. Loewenstein, ed., *Drives, Affects, Behavior* (pp. 38–66). New York: International Universities Press.

Jacobson, E. (1954). The self and the object world: Vicissitudes of their infantile cathexes and their influence on ideational and affective development. *Psychoanalytic Study of the Child* 9: 75–127.

Jacobson, E. (1964). *The Self and the Object World*. New York: International Universities Press.

Jaffe, D. S., and Naiman, J. (1978). Plenary session on "affects and the psychoanalytic situation." *International Journal of Psycho-Analysis* 59: 7–18.

James, W. (1890a). The hidden self. *Scribner's Magazine* 7: 361–373.

James, W. (1890b). *The Principles of Psychology* (vols. 1–2). New York: Holt.

Janet, J. (1888). L'hystérie et l'hypnotisme, d'après la théorie de la double personnalité. *Revue Scientifique* 41: 616–623.

Janet, P. (1886). Les actes inconscients et le dédoublement de la personnalité pendant le somnambulisme provoqué. *Revue Philosophique* 22: 577–592.

Janet, P. (1887). L'anesthésie systématisée et la dissociation des phénomènes psychologiques. *Revue Philosophique* 23: 449–472.

Janet, P. (1888). Les actes inconscients et la mémoire pendant le somnambulisme. *Revue Philosophique* 25: 238–279.

Janet, P. (1889). *L'Automatisme Psychologique*. Paris: Alcan.

Janet, P. (1892a). L'anesthésie hystérique. *Archives de Neurologie* 23: 323–352.

Janet, P. (1892b). L'amnésie hystérique. *Archives de Neurologie* 24: 29–55.

Janet, P. (1892c). La suggestion chez les hystériques. *Archives de Neurologie* 24: 448–469.

Janet, P. (1892d). *L'etat Mental Hystériques*. Paris: Rueff et Fils.

Janet, P. (1895). J.-M. Charcot, son oeuvre psychologique. *Revue Philosophique* 39: 569–604.

Janet, P. (1920). *The Major Symptoms of Hysteria* (2d ed.). New York: Macmillan. (New York: Hafner reprint, 1965.)

Janet, P. (1925). *Psychological Healing* (vols. 1–2) (E. and C. Paul, trans.). London: Allen and Unwin. (Original work published 1919.)

Japp, F. R. (1898). Kekulé memorial lecture. *Journal of the Chemical Society* 73: 97–138.

Jaspers, K. (1963). *General Psychopathology* (7th ed.) (J. Hoenig and M. W. Hamilton, trans.). Manchester: Manchester University Press. (Original work published 1959.)

Jennings, H. S. (1906). *Behavior of the Lower Organisms*. New York: Columbia University Press. (Indiana University Press reprint, 1962.)

Jennings, J. L. (1986). The revival of "Dora": Advances in psychoanalytic theory and technique. *Journal of the American Psychoanalytic Association* 34: 607–635.

Jensen, E. M. (1970). Anna O—A study of her later life. *Psychoanalytic Quarterly* 39: 269–293.

Joffe, W. G., and Sandler, J. (1967). Some conceptual problems involved in the consideration of disorders of narcissism. *Journal of Child Psychotherapy* 2: 56–66.

Joffe, W. G., and Sandler, J. (1968). Comments on the psychoanalytic psychology of adaptation, with special reference to the role of affects and the representational world. *International Journal of Psycho-Analysis* 49: 445–454.

Jones, E. (1910). Remarks on Dr. Morton Prince's article: "The mechanism and interpretation of dreams." *Journal of Abnormal Psychology* 5: 328–336.

Jones, E. (1911a). The pathology of morbid anxiety. *Journal of Abnormal Psychology* 6: 81–106.

Jones, E. (1911b). The psychopathology of everyday life. *American Journal of Psychology* 22: 477–527.

Jones, E. (1918). Anal-erotic character traits. *Journal of Abnormal Psychology* 13: 261–284.

Jones, E. (1926). The origin and structure of the super-ego. *International Journal of Psycho-Analysis* 7: 303–311.

Jones, E. (1927). The early development of female sexuality. *International Journal of Psycho-Analysis* 8: 459–472.

Jones, E. (1928–1929). The development of the concept of the super-ego. *Journal of Abnormal and Social Psychology* 23: 276–285.

Jones, E. (1929). The psychopathology of anxiety. *British Journal of Medical Psychology* 9: 17–25.

Jones, E. (1933). The phallic phase. *International Journal of Psycho-Analysis* 14: 1–32.

Jones, E. (1935). Early female sexuality. *International Journal of Psycho-Analysis* 16: 263–273.

Jones, E. (1935–1936). Psycho-analysis and the instincts. *British Journal of Psychology* 26: 273–288.

Jones, E. (1941). Evolution and revolution. *International Journal of Psycho-Analysis* 22: 193–208.

Jones, E. (1953–1957). *The Life and Work of Sigmund Freud* (vols. 1–3). New York: Basic Books.

Jones, R. M. (1965). Dream interpretation and the psychology of dreaming. *Journal of the American Psychoanalytic Association* 13: 304–319.

Jones, R. M. (1978). *The New Psychology of Dreaming*. Harmondsworth, Middlesex: Penguin Books. (Original work published 1970.)

Joseph, B. (1959). An aspect of the repetition compulsion. *International Journal of Psycho-Analysis* 40: 213–222.

Juda, D. P. (1983). Exorcising Freud's "daemonic" compulsion to repeat: Repetition compulsion as part of the adaptational/maturational process. *Journal of the American Academy of Psychoanalysis* 11: 353–375.

Jung, C. G. (1910). The association method. *American Journal of Psychology* 21: 216–269.

Jung, C. G. (1973a). Psychoanalysis and association experiments. In H. Read, M. Fordham, G. Adler, and W. McGuire, eds., *The Collected Works of C. G. Jung* (vol. 2) (pp. 288–317). London: Routledge and Kegan Paul. (Original work published 1906.)

Jung, C. G. (1973b). The psychopathological significance of the association experiment. In H. Read, M. Fordham, G. Adler, and W. McGuire, eds., *The Collected Works of C. G. Jung* (vol. 2) (pp. 408–425). London: Routledge and Kegan Paul. (Original work published 1906.)

Juni, S. (1979). Theoretical foundations of projection as a defence mechanism. *International Review of Psycho-Analysis* 6: 115–130.

Kampman, R., and Hirvenoja, R. (1978). Dynamic relation of the secondary personality induced by hypnosis to the present personality. In F. H. Frankel and H. S. Zamansky, eds., *Hypnosis at Its Bicentennial* (pp. 183–188). New York: Plenum Press.

Kanfer, F. H. (1968). Verbal conditioning: A review of its current status. In T. R. Dixon and D. L. Horton, eds., *Verbal Behavior and General Behavior Theory* (pp. 254–290). Englewood Cliffs, N.J.: Prentice-Hall.

Kanzer, M. (1964). Freud's uses of the terms "autoerotism" and "narcissism." *Journal of the American Psychoanalytic Association* 12: 529–539.

Kanzer, M. (1968). Psychic determinism: Freud's specific propositions. *Psychoanalytic Quarterly* 37: 485–486.

Kanzer, M. (1973). Two prevalent misconceptions about Freud's "Project" (1895). *Annual of Psychoanalysis* 1: 88–103.

Kanzer, M. (1980). Dora's imagery: The flight from a burning house. In M. Kanzer and J. Glenn, eds., *Freud and His Patients* (pp. 72–82). New York: Aronson.

Kanzer, M. (1981). Freud, Theodor Lipps, and "scientific psychology." *Psychoanalytic Quarterly* 50: 393–410.

Kanzer, M. (1985). Identification and its vicissitudes. *International Journal of Psycho-Analysis* 66: 19–30.

Kanzer, M., and Eidelberg, L. (1960). Discussion of "The metapsychology of pleasure." I. The structural description of pleasure. *International Journal of Psycho-Analysis* 41: 368–371.

Kaplan, A. H. (1981). From discovery to validation: A basic challenge to psychoanalysis. *Journal of the American Psychoanalytic Association* 29: 3–26.

Kaplan, D. M. (1977). Differences in the clinical and academic points of view on metapsychology. *Bulletin of the Menninger Clinic* 41: 207–228.

Kaplan, D. M. (1984). Some conceptual and technical aspects of the actual neurosis. *International Journal of Psycho-Analysis* 65: 295–305.

Kapp, R. O. (1931). Comments on Bernfeld and Feitelberg's "The principle of entropy and the death instinct." *International Journal of Psycho-Analysis* 12: 82–86.

Karpe, R. (1961). The rescue complex in Anna O's final identity. *Psychoanalytic Quarterly* 30: 1–27.

Kasanin, J. S. (1944). Neurotic "acting out" as a basis for sexual promiscuity in women. *Psychoanalytic Review* 31: 221–232.

Katan, M. (1966). Precursors of the concept of the death instinct. In R. M. Lowenstein, L. M. Newman, M. Schur, and A. J. Solnit, eds., *Psychoanalysis—A General Psychology* (pp. 86–103). New York: International Universities Press.

Katan, M. (1979). Further exploration of the schizophrenic regression to the undifferentiated state. *International Journal of Psycho-Analysis* 60: 145–175.

Kaywin, L. (1966). Problems of sublimation. *Journal of the American Psychoanalytic Association* 14: 313–334.

Keiser, S. (1949). The fear of sexual passivity in the masochist. *International Journal of Psycho-Analysis* 30: 162–171.

Kepecs, J. G. (1966). Theories of transference neurosis. *Psychoanalytic Quarterly* 35: 497–521.

Kermode, F. (1985). Freud and interpretation. *International Journal of Psycho-Analysis* 12: 3–12.

Kernberg, O. (1975). *Borderline Conditions and Pathological Narcissism.* New York: Aronson.

Kernberg, O. (1976). *Object Relations Theory and Clinical Psychoanalysis.* New York: Aronson.

Kernberg, O. F. (1982). Self, ego, affects, and drives. *Journal of the American Psychoanalytic Association* 30: 893–917.

Kerr, J. (1994). *A Most Dangerous Method: The Story of Jung, Freud, and Sabina Spielrein.* London: Sinclair-Stevenson. (U.S. edition 1993, New York: Knopf.)

Kessel, L., and Hyman, H. T. (1933). The value of psychoanalysis as a therapeutic procedure. *Journal of the American Medical Association* 101: 1612–1615.

Kestenberg, J. (1975). Children and Parents: *Psychoanalytic Studies in Development.* New York: Aronson.

Khantzian, E. J., and Mack, J. E. (1983). Self-preservation and the care of the self: Ego instincts reconsidered. *Psychoanalytic Study of the Child* 38: 209–232.

Kihlstrom, J. F. (1985). Posthypnotic amnesia and the dissociation of memory. *The Psychology of Learning and Motivation* 19: 131–178.

Kinston, W. (1983). A theoretical context for shame. *International Journal of Psycho-Analysis* 64: 213–226.

Kinston, W., and Cohen, J. (1986). Primal repression: Clinical and theoretical aspects. *International Journal of Psycho-Analysis* 67: 337–355.

Kitcher, P. (1992). *Freud's Dream: A Complete Interdisciplinary Science of Mind.* Cambridge: MIT Press.

Klauber, J. (1968). On the dual use of historical and scientific method in psychoanalysis. *International Journal of Psycho-Analysis* 49: 80–88.

Klauber, J. (1980). Formulating interpretations in clinical psychoanalysis. *International Journal of Psycho-Analysis* 61: 195–201.

Kleeman, J. (1965). A boy discovers his penis. *Psychoanalytic Study of the Child* 20: 239–266.

Kleeman, J. (1977). Freud's views on female sexuality in the light of direct child observation. In H. P. Blum, ed., *Female Psychology. Contemporary Psychoanalytic Views* (pp. 3–28). New York: International Universities Press.

Klein, G. S. (1967). Peremptory ideation: Structure and force in motivated ideas. *Psychological Issues* 5: 80–130. Monograph 18/19.

Klein, G. S. (1975). Freud's two theories of sexuality. *Psychological Issues* 9: 14–70. Monograph 36.

Klein, G. S. (1976). *Psychoanalytic Theory: An Exploration of Essentials.* New York: International Universities Press.

Klein, M. (1928). Early stages of the Oedipus complex. *International Journal of Psycho-Analysis* 9: 167–180.

Klein, M. (1932). *The Psycho-Analysis of Children* (A. Strachey, trans.). London: Hogarth Press.

Klein, M. (1948). A contribution to the theory of anxiety and guilt. *International Journal of Psycho-Analysis* 29: 114–123.

Klein, M. (1952). The mutual influences in the development of ego and id. *Psychoanalytic Study of the Child* 7: 51–55.

Klein, M. I. (1981). Freud's seduction theory: Its implications for fantasy and memory in psychoanalytic theory. *Bulletin of the Menninger Clinic* 45: 185–208.

Klein, M. I. (1983). Freud's drive theory and ego psychology: A critical evaluation of the Blancks. *Psychoanalytic Review* 70: 505–517.

Klein, M. I., and Tribich, D. (1982a). *The short life and curious death of Sigmund Freud's seduction theory.* Unpublished manuscript.

Klein, M. I., and Tribich, D. (1982b). Blame the child. *Sciences* 22: 14–20.

Kline, M. V., ed., (1963). *Clinical Correlations of Experimental Hypnosis.* Springfield, Ill.: Thomas.

Kline, P. (1972). *Fact and Fantasy in Freudian Theory.* London: Methuen.

Kline, P. (1981). *Fact and Fantasy in Freudian Theory* (2d ed.). London: Methuen.

Kline, P. (1984). *Psychology and Freudian Theory. An Introduction.* London: Methuen.

Knight, R. P. (1940). Introjection, projection and identification. *Psychoanalytic Quarterly* 9: 334–341.

Knight, R. P. (1941). Evaluation of the results of psychoanalytic therapy. *American Journal of Psychiatry* 98: 434–446.

Knight, R. P. (1946). Determinism, "freedom" and psychotherapy. *Psychiatry* 9: 251–262.

Koff, R. H. (1961). A definition of identification: A review of the literature. *International Journal of Psycho-Analysis* 42: 362–370.

Kohon, G. (1984). Reflections on Dora: The case of hysteria. *International Journal of Psycho-Analysis* 65: 73–84.

Kohut, H. (1971). *The Analysis of the Self*. New York: International Universities Press.

Kohut, H. (1977). *The Restoration of the Self*. New York: International Universities Press.

Kohut, H., and Wolf, E. S. (1978). The disorders of the self and their treatment: An outline. *International Journal of Psycho-Analysis* 59: 413–425.

Kolenda, K. (1964). Unconscious motives and human action. *Inquiry* 7: 3–36.

Koppe, S. (1983). The psychology of the neuron: Freud, Cajal and Golgi. *Scandinavian Journal of Psychology* 24: 1–12.

Kraepelin, E. (1889). *Psychiatrie* (3d ed.). Leipzig: Abel.

Kraepelin, E. (1899). *Psychiatrie*. Leipzig: Barth.

Kraepelin, E. (1904). *Lectures on Clinical Psychiatry* (T. Johnstone, rev. and ed.). London: Baillière, Tindall, and Cox.

Kraepelin, E. (1907). *Clinical Pychiatry* (A. R. Diefendorf, rev. and ed.). New York: Macmillan. (Original work published 1903.)

Krafft-Ebing, R. von (1879–1880). *Lehrbuch der Psychiatrie auf klinischer Grundlage für practische Artze und Studirende*. Stuttgart: Ferdinand Enke.

Krafft-Ebing, R. von (1898). *Psychopathia sexualis, mit besonderer Berückrichtigung der conträren Sexualempfindung* (7th ed.). Stuttgart: Ferdinand Enke.

Krafft-Ebing, R. von (1904). *A Textbook of Insanity Based on Clinical Observations for Practitioners and Students of Medicine* (G. C. Chaddock, trans.). Philadelpia: Davis.

Krafft-Ebing, R. von (1965). *Psychopathia Sexualis: With Special Reference to the Antipathic Sexual Instinct* (12th Ger. ed.) (F. S. Klaf, trans.). New York: Stein and Day.

Kramer, S. (1986). Identification and its vicissitudes as observed in children: A developmental approach. *International Journal of Psycho-Analysis* 67: 161–172.

Krasner, L. (1958). Studies of the conditioning of verbal behavior. *Psychological Bulletin* 55: 148–170.

Kris, A. (1982). *Free Association: Method and Process*. New Haven, Conn.: Yale University Press.

Kris, A. (1983). The analyst's conceptual freedom in the method of free association. *International Journal of Psycho-Analysis* 64: 407–411.

Kris, E. (1950). On preconscious mental processes. *Psychoanalytic Quarterly* 19: 540–560.

Kris, E. (1956). The recovery of childhood memories in psychoanalysis. *Psychoanalytic Study of the Child* 11: 54–88.

Krohn, A., and Krohn, J. (1982). The nature of the oedipus complex in the Dora case. *Journal of the American Psychoanalytic Association* 30: 555–578.

Krüll, M (1986). *Freud and His Father* (A. J. Pomerans, trans.). New York: Norton. (Original work published 1979.)

Krystal, H. (1978). Trauma and affects. *Psychoanalytic Study of the Child* 33: 81–116.

Kubie, L. S. (1939). A critical analysis of the concept of a repetition compulsion. *International Journal of Psycho-Analysis* 20: 390–402.

Kubie, L. S. (1941a). The repetitive core of neurosis. *Psychoanalytic Quarterly* 10: 23–43.

Kubie, L. S. (1941b). The ontogeny of anxiety. *Psychoanalytic Review* 28: 78–85.

Kubie, L. S. (1952). Problem and techniques of psychoanalytic validation and progress. In E. Pumpian-Mindlin, ed., *Psychoanalysis as Science* (pp. 46–124). Stanford, Calif.: Stanford University Press.

Kubie, L. S. (1962). The fallacious misuse of the concept of sublimation. *Psychoanalytic Quarterly* 31: 73–79.

Kubie, L. S. (1975). The language tools of psychoanalysis: A search for better tools drawn from better models. *International Review of Psycho-Analysis* 2: 11–24.

Kuhn, T. S. (1962). *The Structure of Scientific Revolutions*. Chicago: University of Chicago Press.

Kuper, A., and Stone, A. A. (1982). The dream of Irma's injection: A structural analysis. *American Journal of Psychiatry* 139: 1225–1234.

Kupfersmid, J. (1992). The "defense" of Sigmund Freud. *Psychotherapy* 29: 297–309.

Lacan, J. (1982). The meaning of the phallus. In J. Mitchell and J. Rose, ed., *Feminine Sexuality. Jacques Lacan and the ecole freudienne* (pp. 74–85). (Original work published 1966.)

Lagache, D. (1953). Some aspects of transference. *International Journal of Psycho-Analysis* 34: 1–10.

Lain Entralgo, P. (1970). *The Therapy of the Word in Classical Antiquity* (L. J. Rather and J. M. Sharp, trans.). New Haven, Conn.: Yale University Press. (Original work published 1958.)

Lakatos, I. (1970). Falsification and the methodology of scientific research programmes. In I. Lakatos and A. Musgrave, eds., *Criticism and the Growth of Knowledge* (pp. 91–196). Cambridge: Cambridge University Press.

Lakoff, R. (1982). The rationale of psychotherapeutic discourse. In J. C. Anchin and D. J. Kiesler, eds., *Handbook of Interpersonal Psychotherapy* (pp. 132–146). New York: Plenum Press.

Lakoff, R. T., and Coyne, J. C. (1993). *Father Knows Best: The Use and Abuse of Power in Freud's Case of "Dora."* New York: Teachers College Press.

Lambert, R. T. (1976). Spontaneous remission in adult neurotic disorders. *Psychological Bulletin* 83: 107–119.

Lampl-de Groot, J. (1947). On the development of the ego and super-ego. *International Journal of Psycho-Analysis* 28: 7–11.

Lampl-de Groot, J. (1950). On masturbation and its influence on general development. *Psychoanalytic Study of the Child* 5: 153–174.

Lampl-de Groot, J. (1956). The theory of instinctual drives. *International Journal of Psycho-Analysis* 37: 354–359.

Lampl-de Groot, J. (1962). Ego ideal and superego. *Psychoanalytic Study of the Child* 17: 94–106.

Lampl-de Groot, J. (1982). Thoughts on psychoanalytic views of female psychology 1927–1977. *Psychoanalytic Quarterly* 51: 1–18.

Langs, R. (1980). The misalliance dimension in the case of Dora. In M. Kanzer and J. Glenn, eds., *Freud and His Patients* (pp. 58–71). New York: Aronson.

Langs, R. (1984). Freud's Irma dream and the origins of psychoanalysis. *Psychoanalytic Review* 71: 591–617.

Lantos, B. (1955). On the motivation of human relationships: A preliminary study based on the concept of sublimation. *International Journal of Psycho-Analysis* 36: 267–288.

Lantos, B. (1958). The two genetic derivations of aggression with reference to sublimation and neutralization. *International Journal of Psycho-Analysis* 39: 116–120.

Laplanche, J. (1976). *Life and Death in Psychoanalysis* (J. Mehlman, trans.). Baltimore, Md.: Johns Hopkins University Press. (Original work published 1970.)

Laplanche, J. (1981). A metapsychology put to the test of anxiety. *International Journal of Psycho-Analysis* 62: 81–89.

Laplanche, J., and Pontalis, J.-B. (1968). Fantasy and the origins of sexuality. *International Journal of Psycho-Analysis* 49: 1–18. (Original work published 1964.)

Laplanche, J., and Pontalis, J.-B. (1973). *The Language of Psycho-Analysis* (D. Nicholson-Smith, trans.). London: Hutchinson. (Original work published 1967.)

Laudan, L. (1983). The demise of the demarcation problem. In R. S. Cohen and L. Laudan, eds., *Physics, Philosophy and Psychoanalysis: Essays in Honour of Adolf Grünbaum* (pp. 111–127). Dordrecht: Reidel.

Laufer, M. (1982). The formation and shaping of the Oedipus complex: Clinical observations and assumptions. *International Journal of Psycho-Analysis* 63: 217–227.

Laycock, T. (1845). On the reflex function of the brain. *British and Foreign Medical Review* 19: 298–311.

Lebovici, S. (1982). The origins and development of the Oedipus complex. *International Journal of Psycho-Analysis* 63: 201–215.

Lebovici, S., and Diatkine, R. (1972). Discussion on aggression: Is it a question of a metapsychological concept? *International Journal of Psycho-Analysis* 53: 231–236.

Leichtman, M. (1990). Developmental psychology and psychoanalysis. I. The context for a revolution in psychoanalysis. *Journal of the American Psychoanalytic Association* 38: 915–950.

Lennard, H. L., and Bernstein, A. (1960). *The Anatomy of Psychotherapy: Systems of Communication and Expectation*. New York: Columbia University Press.

Lester, E. P. (1982). New directions in affect theory. *Journal of the American Psychoanalytic Association* 30: 197–211.

Levey, H. B. (1939). A critique of the theory of sublimation. *Psychiatry* 2: 239–270.

Levin, A. J. (1951). The fiction of the death instinct. *Psychoanalytic Quarterly* 25: 257–281.

Levin, K. (1978). *Freud's Early Psychology of the Neuroses*. Pittsburgh: University of Pittsburgh Press.

Levitt, E. E., and Chapman, P. H. (1979). Hypnosis as a research method. In E. Fromm and R. E. Shor, eds., *Hypnosis: Developments in Research and New Perspectives* (2d ed.) (pp. 185–215). New York: Aldine.

Levy, D. M. (1927). Finger sucking and accessory movements in early infancy. *American Journal of Psychiatry* 7: 881–918.

Lewin, K. K. (1973–1974). Dora revisited. *Psychoanalytic Review* 60: 519–532.

Lewinsky, H. (1944). On some aspects of masochism. *International Journal of Psycho-Analysis* 25: 150–155.

Lewis, H. B. (1984). Freud and modern psychology: The social nature of humanity. *Psychoanalytic Review* 71: 7–26.

Lewis, W. C. (1965). Structural aspects of the psychoanalytic theory of instinctual drives, affects, and time. In N. S. Greenfield and W. C. Lewis, eds., *Psychoanalysis and Current Biological Thought* (pp. 151–179). Madison, Wis.: University of Wisconsin Press.

Leys, R. (1992). Review of *Freud Evaluated. Bulletin of the History of Medicine* 66: 673–674.

Lichtenberg, J. D. (1981). Implications for psychoanalytic theory of research on the neonate. *International Review of Psycho-Analysis* 8: 35–52.

Lichtenberg, J. D. (1991). A theory of motivational-functional systems as psychic structures. In T. Shapiro, ed., *The Concept of Structure in Psychoanalysis* (pp. 57–72). Madison, CT: International Universities Press.

Lichtenberg, J. D., and Galler, F. B. (1987). The fundamental rule: A study of current usage. *Journal of the American Psychoanalytic Association* 35: 47–76.

Lindner, S. (1879–1880). Das Saugen an den Fingern, Lippen etc. bei den Kindern (Ludeln). *Jarbuch für Kinderheilkunde* 14: 68–91.

Lindner, S. (1975). Ludeln. In E. T. Adelson, ed., *Sexuality and Psychoanalysis* (pp. 175–188). New York: Brunner/Mazel. (Original work published 1879–1880.)

Lindner, S. (1980). The sucking of the fingers, lips etc. by children (pleasure-sucking). *Storia e Critica della Psicologia* 1: 117–143. (Original work published 1879–1880.)

Lipin, T. (1963). The repetition compulsion and "maturational" drive-representatives. *International Journal of Psycho-Analysis* 44: 389–406.

Lipton, S. D. (1955). A note on the compatibility of psychic determinism and freedom of will. *International Journal of Psycho-Analysis* 36: 355–356.

Loeb, F. F., and Carroll E. J. (1966). General systems theory and psychoanalysis. II. Application to psychoanalytic case material (Little Hans). *Psychoanalytic Quarterly* 35: 388–398.

Loewald, H. W. (1971). Some considerations on repetition and repetition compulsion. *International Journal of Psycho-Analysis* 52: 59–66.

Loewenstein, R. [M.] (1940). The vital or somatic instincts. *International Journal of Psycho-Analysis* 21: 377–400.

Loewenstein, R. M. (1957). A contribution to the psychoanalytic theory of masochism. *Journal of the American Psychoanalytic Association* 5: 197–234.

Loewenstein, R. M. (1965). Observational data and theory in psychoanalysis. In M. Schur, ed., *Drives, Affects, Behavior* (vol. 2) (pp. 38–59). New York: International Universities Press.

Loewenstein, R. M. (1966a). Heinz Hartmann b. 1894. Psychology of the ego. In F. Alexander, S. Eisenstein, and M. Grotjahn, eds., *Psychoanalytic Pioneers* (pp. 469–483). New York: Basic Books.

Loewenstein, R. M. (1966b). On the theory of the superego: A discussion. In R. M. Lowenstein, L. M. Newman, M. Schur, and A. J. Solnit, eds., *Psychoanalysis—A General Psychology* (pp. 298–314). New York: International Universities Press.

Loewenstein, R. M. (1969). Developments in the theory of transference in the last fifty years. *International Journal of Psycho-Analysis* 50: 583–588.

Loftus, E. F., and Loftus, G. R. (1980). On the permanence of stored information in the human brain. *American Psychologist* 35: 409–420.

López Piñero, J. M. (1983). *Historical Origins of the Concept of Neurosis* (D. Berrios, trans.). Cambridge: Cambridge University Press. (Original work published 1963.)

Lorenz, K. Z. (1957). The conception of instinctive behaviour. In C. H. Schiller, ed., *Instinctive Behaviour* (pp. 129–175). London: Methuen. (Original work published 1937.)

Lotto, D. J. (1982). Another point of view on Freud's metapsychology. *Journal of the American Academy of Psychoanalysis* 10: 457–481.

Lovibond, S. H. (1964). *Conditioning and Enuresis*. Oxford: Pergamon Press.

Low, B. (1920). *Psycho-Analysis: A Brief Account of the Freudian Theory*. New York: Harcourt, Brace and Howe.

Lowenfeld, H. (1941). Psychic trauma and productive experience in the artist. *Psychoanalytic Quarterly* 10: 116–129.

Lowental, U. (1981). Dying, regression, and the death instinct. *Psychoanalytic Review* 68: 363–370.

Lowental, U. (1983). The death instinct. *Psychoanalytic Review* 70: 559–570.

Lower, R. B., Escoll, P. J., Little, R. B., and Ottenberg, B. P. (1973). An experimental examination of transference. *Archives of General Psychiatry* 29: 738–741.

Lowery, E. F. (1985). Sublimation and female identity. *Psychoanalytic Review* 72: 441–455.

Luborsky, L., Graff, H., Pulver, S., and Curtis, H. (1973). A clinical-quantitative examination of consensus on the concept of transference. *Archives of General Psychiatry* 29: 69–75.

Luria, A. R. (1932). *The Nature of Human Conflicts or Emotion, Conflict and Will* (W. H. Gantt, trans.). New York: Liveright. (Original work published 1932.)

Lussier, A. (1972). Panel on "aggression." *International Journal of Psycho-Analysis* 53: 13–19.

Lustman, S. L. (1957). Psychic energy and mechanisms of defense. *Psychoanalytic Study of the Child* 12: 151–163.

Lustman, S. L. (1963). Some issues in contemporary psychoanalytic research. *Psychoanalytic Study of the Child* 18: 51–74.

Lyons, J. (1982). Schreber and Freud: The colonizing of taboo. *American Journal of Psychoanalysis* 42: 335–347.

M'Uzan, M. de (1973). A case of masochistic perversion and an outline of a theory. *International Journal of Psycho-Analysis* 54: 455–467.

Macalpine, I. (1950). The development of the transference. *Psychoanalytic Quarterly* 19: 501–539.

MacCarley, R. W., and Hobson, J. A. (1977). The neurobiological origins of psychoanalytic dream theory. *American Journal of Psychiatry* 134: 1211–1221.

MacCorquodale, K., and Meehl, P. E. (1948). On a distinction between hypothetical constructs and intervening variables. *Psychological Review* 55: 95–107.

MacCurdy, J. T. (1918). *War Neuroses*. Cambridge: Cambridge University Press.

MacCurdy, J. T. (1923). *Problems in Dynamic Psychology*. New York: Macmillan.

McDougall, W. (1905). *Physiological Psychology*. London: Dent.

McDougall, W. (1908). *An Introduction to Social Psychology*. London: Methuen.

McDougall, W. (1920–1921). The revival of emotional memories and its therapeutic value (III). *British Journal of Medical Psychology* 1: 23–29.

McGuire, G. R. (1986a). *Forgotten frontiers and the history of psychology: Psychical research and the development of psychopathology in France*. Unpublished manuscript.

McGuire, G. R. (1986b, June). *Psychopathology, hypnosis, and Pierre Janet's conception of the organic subconscious*. Paper presented at the 18th annual meeting of Cheiron: International Society for the History of the Behavioral Sciences, University of Guelph, Canada.

McGuire, M. T. (1971). *Reconstructions in Psychoanalysis*. London: Butterworths.

McGuire, W., ed. (1974). *The Freud/Jung Letters: The Correspondence Between Sigmund Freud and C. G. Jung*. Princeton, N.J.: Princeton University Press.

McHenry, L. C. (1969). *Garrison's History of Neurology*. Springfield, Ill.: Thomas.

McIntosh, D. (1986). The ego and the self in the thought of Sigmund Freud. *International Journal of Psycho-Analysis* 67: 429–448.

McIntosh, D. (1993). Cathexes and their objects in the thought of Sigmund Freud. *Journal of the American Psychoanalytic Association* 41: 679–709.

MacIntyre, A. C. (1958). *The Unconscious: A Conceptual Analysis*. London: Routledge and Kegan Paul.

Macklin, R. (1976). A psychoanalytic model for human freedom and rationality. *Psychoanalytic Quarterly* 458: 430–454.

McLaughlin, J. T. (1981). Transference, psychic reality, and countertransference. *Psychoanalytic Quarterly* 50: 639–664.

McLeod, M. N. (1992). The evolution of Freud's theory of dreaming. *Psychoanalytic Quarterly* 61: 37–64.

Macmillan, M. B. (1974). *The Historical and Scientific Evaluation of Psychoanalytic Personality Theory*. Melbourne: Monash University, Department of Psychology.

Macmillan, M. B. (1976). Beard's concept of neurasthenia and Freud's concept of the actual neuroses. *Journal of the History of the Behavioral Sciences* 12: 376–390.

Macmillan, M. B. (1977a). Freud's expectations and the childhood seduction theory. *Australian Journal of Psychology* 29: 223–236.

Macmillan, M. B. (1977b). The cathartic method and the expectancies of Breuer and Anna O. *International Journal of Clinical and Experimental Hypnosis* 25: 106–118.

Macmillan, M. B. (1980). Introduction: Freud and Lindner on pleasure sucking. *Storia e Critica della Psicologia* 1: 111–116. (Original work published 1879–1880.)

Macmillan, M. B. (1986). Souvenir de la Salpêtrière: M. le Dr. Freud à Paris, 1885. *Australian Psychologist* 21: 3–29.

Macmillan, M. B. (1989a). New answers to old questions: What the complete Freud-Fliess correspondence tells us. In J. A. Keats, R. Taft, R. A. Heath, and S. H. Lovibond, eds., *Proceedings of the XXIV International Congress of Psychology* (vol. 4) (pp. 303–314). Amsterdam: North-Holland.

Macmillan, M. B. (1989b). Freud's expectations and the childhood seduction theory. In L. Spurling, ed., *Sigmund Freud, Critical Assessmentst* (vol. 1) (pp. 366–383). London: Routledge.

Macmillan, M. B. (1990). New answers to old questions: What the complete Freud-Fliess correspondence tells us. *Psychoanalytic Review* 77: 555–572.

Macmillan, M. B. (1994). Author's response [to O. H. D. Bloomfield's review of *Freud Evaluated*]. *Australian and New Zealand Journal of Psychiatry* 28: 716–720.

Maddi, S. R. (1974). The victimization of Dora. *Psychology Today* 8: 91–100.

Madison, P. (1961). *Freud's Concept of Repression and Defense, Its Theoretical and Observational Language*. Minneapolis: University of Minnesota Press.

Mahler, M. S. (1971). A study of the separation-individuation process and its possible application to borderline phenomena in the psychoanalytic situation. *Psychoanalytic Study of the Child* 26: 403–424.

Mahony, P. J. (1984). *Cries of the Wolf Man*. New York: International Universities Press.

Mahony, P. J. (1986). *Freud and the Rat Man*. New Haven, CT: Yale University Press.

Malan, D. H. (1976). *The Frontiers of Brief Psychotherapy*. New York: Plenum Press.

Malcolm, J. (1982). *Psychoanalysis: The Impossible Profession*. New York: Random House.

Maleson, F. G. (1984). The multiple meanings of masochism in psychoanalytic discourse. *Journal of the American Psychoanalytic Association* 32: 325–356.

Malev, M. (1969). Use of the repetition compulsion by the ego. *Psychoanalytic Quarterly* 38: 52–71.

Mancia, M. (1983). Archaeology of Freudian thought and the history of neurophysiology. *International Review of Psycho-Analysis* 10: 185–192.

Mancia, M., and Meltzer, D. (1981). Ego ideal functions and the psychoanalytical process. *International Journal of Psycho-Analysis* 62: 243–249.

Marcovitz, E. (1963). The concept of the id. *Journal of the American Psychoanalytic Association* 11: 151–160.

Marcus, S. (1984). Freud and Dora: Story, history, case history. In S. Marcus *Freud and the Culture of Psychoanalysis* (pp. 42–86). London: Allen and Unwin. (Original work published 1974.)

Marmer, S. S. (1980). Psychoanalysis of multiple personality. *International Journal of Psycho-Analysis* 61: 439–459.

Marmor, J. (1962). Psychoanalytic therapy as an educational process. In J. H. Masserman, ed., *Science and Psychoanalysis* (vol. 5) (pp. 286–299). New York: Grune and Stratton.

Marmor, J. (1970). Limitations of free association. *Archives of General Psychiatry* 22: 160–165.

Martorano, J. T. (1984). The psychopharmacological treatment of Anna O. In M. Rosenbaum and M. Muroff, eds., *Anna O. Fourteen Contemporary Reinterpretations* (pp. 85–100). New York: Free Press.

Masserman, J. H., ed. (1959a). *Individual and Familial Dynamics*. New York: Grune and Stratton.

Masserman, J. H. (1959b). Masochism: A biodynamic summary. In J. H. Masserman, ed., *Individual and Familial Dynamics* (pp. 73–84). New York: Grune and Stratton.

Masson, J. M. (1984). *The Assault on Truth: Freud's Suppression of the Seduction Theory*. New York: Farrar, Straus and Giroux.

Masson, J. M. (1985). *The Complete Letters of Sigmund Freud to Wilhelm Fliess 1887–1904*. Cambridge: Harvard University Press.

Masterson, J. F. (1984). Reflections on Anna O. In M. Rosenbaum and M. Muroff, eds., *Anna O. Fourteen Contemporary Reinterpretations* (pp. 42–46). New York: Free Press.

Matarazzo, J. D. (1962). Prescribed behavior therapy: Suggestions from interview research. In A. J. Bachrach, ed., *Experimental Foundations of Clinical Psychology* (pp. 471–509). New York: Basic Books.

Maudsley, H. (1867). *The Physiology and Pathology of Mind*. New York: Appleton.

Maze, J. R. (1954). Do intervening variables intervene? *Psychological Review* 61: 226–234.

Mazer, M. (1951). An experimental study of the hypnotic dream. *Psychiatry* 14: 265–277.

Meagher, J. F. W. (1924). *A Study of Masturbation and Its Reputed Sequelae*. New York: Wood.

Meagher, J. F. W. (1936). *A Study of Masturbation and the Psychosexual Life* (3d ed.). Baltimore: Wood.

Medici de Steiner, C. (1993). Children and their dreams. *International Journal of Psychoanalysis* 74: 359–370.

Meissner, W. W. (1970). Notes on identification I. Origins in Freud. *Psychoanalytic Quarterly* 39: 563–589.

Meissner, W. W. (1971). Notes on identification II. Clarification of related concepts. *Psychoanalytic Quarterly* 40: 277–302.

Meissner, W. W. (1972). Notes on identification III. The concept of identification. *Psychoanalytic Quarterly* 41: 224–260.

Meissner, W. W. (1979a). Methodological critique of the action language in psychoanalysis. *Journal of the American Psychoanalytic Association* 27: 79–105.

Meissner, W. W. (1979b). Internalization and object relations. *Journal of the American Psychoanalytic Association* 27: 345–360.

Meissner, W. W. (1979c). Critique of concepts and therapy in the action language approach to psychoanalysis. *International Journal of Psycho-Analysis* 60: 291–310.

Meissner, W. W. (1980). The problem of internalization and structure formation. *International Journal of Psycho-Analysis* 61: 237–248.

Meissner, W. W. (1981a). A note on narcissism. *Psychoanalytic Quarterly* 50: 77–89.

Meissner, W. W. (1981b). Metapsychology—Who needs it? *Journal of the American Psychoanalytic Association* 29: 921–938.

Meissner, W. W. (1986). Can psychoanalysis find its self? *Journal of the American Psychoanalytic Association* 34: 379–400.

Menaker, E. (1953). Masochism—A defense reaction of the ego. *Psychoanalytic Quarterly* 22: 205–220.

Menaker, E. (1956). A note on some biologic parallels between certain innate animal behavior and moral masochism. *Psychoanalytic Review* 43: 31–41.

Mendel, W. M. (1964). The phenomena of interpretation. *American Journal of Psychoanalysis* 24: 184–189.

Merskey, H. (1992). Anna O. had depressive illness. *British Journal of Psychiatry* 161: 185–194.

Mesmer, F. A. (1970). *Dissertations on the Discovery of Animal Magnetism* In M. M. Tinterow, ed., *Foundations of Hypnosis: From Mesmer to Freud* (pp. 31–57). Springfield, Ill.: Thomas. (Original work published 1779.)

Messer, S. B. (1986). Behavioural and psychoanalytic perspectives at therapeutic choice points. *American Psychologist* 41: 1261–1272.

Meyer, H. H. (1928). Josef Breuer 1842–1925. In *Neue Österreichische Biographie AB 1815* (pp. 30–47) (band 5). Vienna: Amalthea. (Nendeln: Kraus reprint, 1970.)

Meyer, J. K. (1991). The concept of adult psychic structure. In T. Shapiro, ed., *The Concept of Structure in Psychoanalysis* (pp. 101–112). Madison, CT: International Universities Press.

Meynert, T. (1885). *Psychiatry* (B. Sachs, trans.). New York: Putnam. (Original work published 1884.)

Micale, M. S. (1989). Hysteria and its historiography—A review of past and present writings (I) and (II). *History of Science* 27: 223–261, 319–351.

Micale, M. S. (1990a). Hysteria and its historiography: The future perspective. *History of Psychiatry* 1: 33–124.

Micale, M. S. (1990b). Charcot and the idea of hysteria in the male: Gender, mental science, and medical diagnosis in late nineteenth-century France. *Medical History* 34: 363–411.

Micale, M. S. (1991). Hysteria male/hysteria female: Reflections on comparative gender construction in nineteenth-century France and Britain. In M. Benjamin, ed., *Science and Sensibility: Essays on Gender and Scientific Enquiry 1780–1945*. London: Blackwell.

Micale, M. S., ed. (1993). *Beyond the Unconscious: Essays of Henri F. Ellenberger in the History of Psychiatry*. Princeton, NJ: Princeton University Press.

Micale, M. S. (1995). *Approaching Hysteria: Disease and Its Interpretations*. Princeton, NJ: Princeton University Press.

Mill, J. S. (1878). *An Examination of Sir William Hamilton's Philosophy* (5th ed.). London: Longmans, Green, Ryder, and Dyer.

Miller, J. A., Sabshin, M., Gedo, J. E., Pollock, G. H., Sadow, L., and Schlessinger, N. (1969). Some aspects of Charcot's influence on Freud. *Journal of the American Psychoanalytic Association* 17: 608–623.

Miller, S. B. (1986). Disgust: Conceptualization, development, dynamics. *International Review of Psycho-Analysis* 13: 295–307.

Millet, J. A. P. (1959). Masochism: Psychogenesis and therapeutic principles. In J. H. Masserman, ed., *Individual and Familial Dynamics* (pp. 44–52). New York: Grune and Stratton.

Milrod, D. (1990). The ego ideal. *Psychoanalytic Study of the Child* 45: 43–60.

Milton, J. (1671). *Samson Agonistes, a Dramatic Poem*. London: Starkey.

Mintz, J. (1981). Measuring outcome in psychodynamic psychotherapy. Psychodynamic vs. symptomatic assessment. *Archives of General Psychiatry* 38: 503–506.

Mitchell, J. (1974). *Psychoanalysis and Feminism*. London: Lane.

Mitchell, K. M., Bozarth, J. D., and Krauft, C. C. (1977). A reappraisal of the therapeutic effectiveness of accurate empathy, non-possessive warmth, and genuineness. In A. S. Gurman and A. M. Razin, eds., *Effective Psychotherapy: A Handbook of Research* (pp. 482–502). New York: Pergamon Press.

Mitchill, S. L. (1816). A double consciousness, or a duality of person in the one individual. *Medical Repository* 3: 185–186.

Modell, A. H. (1975). The ego and the id: Fifty years later. *International Journal of Psycho-Analysis* 56: 57–68.

Modell, A. H. (1981). Does metapsychology still exist? *International Journal of Psycho-Analysis* 62: 391–402.

Modell, A. H. (1991). Changing psychic structure through treatment: Preconditions for the resolution of transference. In T. Shapir, ed., *The Concept of Structure in Psychoanalysis* (pp. 225–239). Madison, CT: International Universities Press.

Moll, A. (1897). *Untersuchungen über die Libido sexualis*. Berlin: Fischer.

Moll, A. (1912). *The Sexual Life of the Child* (E. Paul, trans.). London: Allen and Unwin. (Original work published 1909.)

Moll, A. (1933). *Libido Sexualis* (D. Berger, trans.). New York: New Era Press.

Mollinger, R. N. (1982). Sadomasochism and developmental stages. *Psychoanalytic Review* 69: 379–389.

Montgrain, N. (1983). On the vicissitudes of female sexuality. The difficult path from "anatomical destiny" to psychic representation. *International Journal of Psycho-Analysis* 64: 169–186.

Moore, B. E. (1975). Toward a clarification of narcissism. *Psychoanalytic Study of the Child* 30: 243–276.

Moore, M. S. (1980). The nature of psychoanalytic explanation. *Psychoanalysis and Contemporary Thought* 3: 459–543.

Moore, W. F. (1964). Effects of posthypnotic stimulation of hostility upon motivation. *American Journal of Clinical Hypnosis* 7: 130–135.

Mora, G. (1970–1971). Antecedent to neurosis. *International Journal of Psychiatry* 9: 57–60.

Morgan, C. L. (1896). *Habit and Instinct.* London: Arnold.

Morton, W. J. (1883). Obituary: George Miller Beard. *Journal of Nervous and Mental Disease* 10: 130–134.

Moses, R. (1978). Adult psychic trauma: The question of early predisposition and some detailed mechanisms. *International Journal of Psycho-Analysis* 59: 353–363.

Moss, C. S. (1967). *The Hypnotic Investigation of Dreams.* New York: Wiley.

Moss, C. S., and Stachowiak, J. G. (1963). The ability of hypnotic subjects to interpret symbols. *Journal of Projective Techniques* 27: 92–97.

Müller, J. (1833–1842). *Elements of Physiology* (W. Baly, trans.). London: Taylor and Walton. (Original work published 1833–1840.)

Munthe, A. (1945). *The Story of San Michele.* London: Methuen. (Original work published 1929.)

Murray, E. J. (1956). A content-analysis method for studying psychotherapy. *Psychological Monographs* 70: 1–31.

Murray, J. M. (1964). Narcissism and the ego ideal. *Journal of the American Psychoanalytic Association* 12: 477–511.

Muslin, H., and Gill, M. (1978). Transference in the Dora case. *Journal of the American Psychoanalytic Association* 26: 311–328.

Myers, C. S. (1920–1921). The revival of emotional memories and its therapeutic value (II). *British Journal of Medical Psychology* 1: 20–22.

Myers, F. W. H. (1886–1887). Automatic writing. 3. Physiological and pathological analysis. *Proceedings of the Society for Psychical Research* 4: 209–261.

Myers, F. W. H. (1889–1890). A letter to the editor. *Journal of the Society for Psychical Research* 4: 60–63.

Nachmansohn, M. (1951). Concerning experimentally produced dreams. In D. Rapaport, ed., *Organization and Pathology of Thought* (pp. 257–287). New York: Columbia University Press. (Original work published 1925.)

Nacht, S. (1952). The mutual influences in the development of ego and id. *Psychoanalytic Study of the Child* 7: 54–59.

Nagel, E. (1959). Methodological issues in psychoanalytic theory. In S. Hook, ed., *Psychoanalysis, Scientific Method, and Philosophy* (pp. 38–56). New York: New York University Press.

Nagera, H. (1967). The concepts of structure and structuralization: Psychoanalytic usage and implications for a theory of learning and creativity. *Psychoanalytic Study of the Child* 22: 77–102.

Nagera, H. (1975). *Female Sexuality and the Oedipus Complex.* New York: Aronson.

Needles, W. (1962). Eros and the repetition compulsion. *Psychoanalytic Quarterly* 31: 505–513.

Needles, W. (1964). Comments on the pleasure-unpleasure experience. *Journal of the American Psychoanalytic Association* 12: 300–314.

Needles, W. (1969). The pleasure principle, the constancy principle, and the primary autonomous ego. *Journal of the American Psychoanalytic Association* 17: 808–825.

Nemiah, J. C. (1974). Conversion: Fact or chimera. *International Journal of Psychiatry in Medicine* 5: 443–448.

Nemiah, J. C. (1985). Review of A. Roy (ed.) "Hysteria." *Psychosomatic Medicine* 47: 303–305.

Neubauer, P. B. (1967). Trauma and psychopathology. In S. S. Furst, ed., *Psychic Trauma* (pp. 85–107). New York: Basic Books.

Nichols, M. P., and Zax, M. (1977). *Catharsis in Psychotherapy*. New York: Gardner Press.

Niederland, W. G. (1951). Three notes on the Schreber case. *Psychoanalytic Quarterly* 20: 579–591.

Niederland, W. G. (1959a). Schreber: Father and son. *Psychoanalytic Quarterly* 28: 151–169.

Niederland, W. G. (1959b). The "miracled-up" world of Schreber's childhood. *Psychoanalytic Study of the Child* 14: 383–413.

Niederland, W. G. (1960). Schreber's father. *Journal of the American Psychoanalytic Association* 8: 492–499.

Niederland, W. G. (1974). *The Schreber Case: Psychoanalytic Profile of a Paranoid Personality*. New York: Quadrangle Books.

Noshpitz, J. D. (1984). Anna O. as seen by a child psychiatrist. In M. Rosenbaum and M. Muroff, eds., *Anna O. Fourteen Contemporary Reinterpretations* (pp. 59–70). New York: Free Press.

Novey, S. (1955). The rôle of the superego and ego-ideal in character formation. *International Journal of Psycho-Analysis* 36: 254–259.

Novey, S. (1957). A re-evaluation of certain aspects of the theory of instinctual drives in the light of modern ego psychology. *International Journal of Psycho-Analysis* 38: 137–145.

Noy, P. (1969). A revision of the psychoanalytic theory of the primary process. *International Journal of Psycho-Analysis* 50: 155–178.

Nunberg, H. (1926). The sense of guilt and the need for punishment. *International Journal of Psycho-Analysis* 7: 420–433.

Nunberg, H. (1932). *Allgemeine Neurosenlehre auf psychoanalytisches Grundlage*. Bern: Huber.

Nunberg, H. (1951). Transference and reality. *International Journal of Psycho-Analysis* 32: 1–9.

Nunberg, H. (1955). *Principles of Psycho-Analysis: Their Application to the Neuroses* (M. Kahr and S. Kahr, trans.). New York: International Universities Press. (Original work published 1932.)

Nunberg, H., and Federn, E. (1962–1975). *Minutes of the Vienna Psychoanalytic Society* (vols. 1–4) (H. Nunberg trans.). New York: International Universities Press.

Nussbaum, C. (1991). Habermas and Grünbaum on the logic of psychoanalytic explanations. *Philosophy and Social Criticism* 17: 193–216.

Nuttin, J. (1956). Human motivation and Freud's theory of energy discharge. *Canadian Journal of Psychology* 10: 167–178.

O'Neil, W. M. (1953). Hypothetical terms and relations in psychological theorizing. *British Journal of Psychology* 44: 211–220.

O'Neil, W. M. (1962). *An Introduction to Method in Psychology* (2d ed.). Melbourne: Melbourne University Press.

O'Neil, W. M. (1969). *Fact and Theory: An Aspect of the Philosophy of Science*. Sydney: Sydney University Press.

Oberndorf, C. P. (1943). Psychic determinism in Holmes and Freud. *Journal of Nervous and Mental Disease* 98: 184–188.

Obholzer, K. (1982). *The Wolf-Man: Conversations with Freud's Patient—Sixty Years Later* (M. Shaw, trans.). New York: Continuum Publishing. (Original work published 1980.)

Oerlemans, A. C. (1949). *Development of Freud's Conception of Anxiety*. Amsterdam: N.V. Noord-Hollandshe Uitgeuers Maatschappij.

Ogden, T. H. (1980). On the nature of schizophrenic conflict. *International Journal of Psycho-Analysis* 61: 513–533.

Oppenheim, J. (1991). *"Shattered Nerves": Doctors, Patients, and Depression in Victorian England.* New York: Oxford University Press.

Ormerod, J. A. (1910–1911). Two theories of hysteria. *Brain* 33: 269–287.

Ornston, D. (1978). On projection: A study of Freud's usage. *Psychoanalytic Study of the Child* 33: 117–166.

Orr-Andrawes, A. (1987). The case of Anna O.: A neuropsychiatric perspective. *Journal of the American Psychoanalytic Association* 35: 387–419.

Ostow, M. (1957). Theory of aggression. *Journal of the American Psychoanalytic Association* 5: 556–563.

Ostow, M. (1958). The death instincts—A contribution to the study of instincts. *International Journal of Psycho-Analysis* 39: 5–16.

Ostow, M., ed., (1974). *Sexual Deviation: Psychoanalytic Insights.* New York: Quadrangle/New York Times.

Owen, A. R. G. (1971). *Hysteria, Hypnosis and Healing: The Work of J.-M. Charcot.* London: Dobson.

Ozturk, M., and Ozturk, O. M. (1977). Thumbsucking and falling asleep. *British Journal of Medical Psychology* 50: 95–103.

Padel, J. (1985). Ego in current thinking. *International Review of Psycho-Analysis* 12: 273–283.

Palombo, S. R. (1984). Deconstructing the manifest dream. *Journal of the American Psychoanalytic Association* 32: 405–420.

Pao, P.-N. (1977). On the formation of schizophrenic symptoms. *International Journal of Psycho-Analysis* 58: 389–401.

Pap, A. (1959). On the empirical interpretation of psychoanalytic concepts. In S. Hook, ed., *Psychoanalysis, Scientific Method, and Philosophy* (pp. 283–297). New York: New York University Press.

Pappenheim, E. (1980). Freud and Gilles de la Tourette. Diagnostic speculations on "Frau Emmy von N." *International Review of Psycho-Analysis* 7: 265–277.

Parens, H. (1973). Aggression: A reconsideration. *Journal of the American Psychoanalytic Association* 21: 34–60.

Parens, H. (1990). On the girls' psychosexual development: Reconsiderations suggested from direct observation. *Journal of the American Psychoanaletic Association* 38: 743–772.

Parens, H., Pollock, L., Stern, J., and Kramer, S. (1977). On the girl's entry into the Oedipus complex. In H. P. Blum, ed., *Female Psychology. Contemporary Psychoanalytic Views* (pp. 79–107). New York: International Universities Press.

Parkin, A. (1980). On masochistic enthrallment. A contribution to the study of moral masochism. *International Journal of Psycho-Analysis* 61: 307–314.

Parkin, A. (1983). On structure formation and the processes of alteration. *International Journal of Psycho-Analysis* 64: 333–351.

Pattie, F. A. (1956). Mesmer's medical dissertation and its debt to Mead's *De Imperio Solis ac Lunae. Journal of the History of Medicine and Allied Sciences* 11: 275–287.

Patton, M. J., and Sullivan, J. J. (1980). Heinz Kohut and the classical psychoanalytic tradition. *Psychoanalytic Review* 67: 365–388.

Pears, D. (1973). Rational explanation of actions and psychological determinism. In T. Honderich, ed., *Essays in Freedom of Action* (pp. 105–136). London: Routledge and Kegan Paul.

Penrose, L. S. (1931). Freud's theory of instinct and other psycho-biological theories. *International Journal of Psycho-Analysis* 12: 87–97.

Perdigão, H. G. (1994). Review of T. Shapiro's *The Concept of Structure in Psychoanalysis. Psychoanalytic Quarterly* 63: 357–359.

Person, E. S., and Klar, H. (1994). Establishing trauma: The difficulty of distinguishing between memories and fantasies. *Journal of the American Psychoanalytic Association* 42: 1055–1081.

Peterfreund, E. (1975). The need for a new theoretical frame of reference for psychoanalysis. *Psychoanalytic Quarterly* 44: 534–549.

Peterfreund, E. (1978). Some critical comments on psychoanalytic conceptualizations of infancy. *International Journal of Psycho-Analysis* 59: 427–441.

Peters, R. S. (1949). Cure, cause and motive. Two brief comments. *Analysis* 10: 103–109.

Peters, R. S. (1952). Symposium: "Motives and causes." *Proceedings of the Aristotelian Society. Supplementary Volume* 26: 139–162.

Peters, R. S. (1954). Footnote to Peters (1949). In M. Macdonald, ed., *Philosophy and Analysis* (p. 154, n. 2). Oxford: Blackwell.

Peters, R. S. (1960). *The Concept of Motivation* (2d ed.). London: Routledge and Kegan Paul. (Original work published 1958.)

Peters, R. S. (1970). Comment on Toulmin's "Reasons and causes." In R. Borger and F. Cioffi, eds., *Explanation in the Behavioural Sciences* (pp. 27–41). Cambridge: Cambridge University Press.

Petocz, A. (1988a, August). *Theories of the symbol: Freud's contribution.* Paper presented at the 24th International Congress of Psychology, Sydney, N.S.W.

Petocz, A. (1988b, August). *The place of hermeneutics in contemporary psychological theory.* Paper presented at the 24th International Congress of Psychology, Sydney, N.S.W.

Philips, J. P. (1970). *A Theoretical and Practical Course on Nervous Hypnotism.* Paris: Baillière. In M. M. Tinterow, ed., *Foundations of Hypnosis: From Mesmer to Freud* (pp. 391–405). Springfield, Ill.: Thomas. (Original work published 1860.)

Phillips, M. A. (1981). Freud, psychic determinism and freedom. *International Review of Psycho-Analysis* 8: 449–455.

Pieper, W. J., and Muslin, H. L. (1961). A further note on the primal instinct theory. *American Imago* 18: 383–390.

Piers, G., and Singer, M. B. (1953). *Shame and Guilt: A Psychoanalytic and a Cultural Study.* Springfield, Ill.: Thomas.

Pitt, D. B. (1961). Congenital malformations and maternal rubella: Progress report. *Medical Journal of Australia* 1: 881–890.

Plaut, E. A. (1984). Ego instincts: A concept whose time has come. *Psychoanalytic Study of the Child* 39: 235–258.

Pleune, F. G. (1961). Aggression and the concept of aim in psycho-analytic drive theory. *International Journal of Psycho-Analysis* 42: 479–485.

Podmore, F. (1909). *Mesmerism and Christian Science, a Short History of Mental Healing.* London: Methuen.

Pollock, G. H. (1972). Bertha Pappenheim's mourning: Possible effects of childhood sibling loss. *Journal of the American Psychoanalytic Association* 20: 476–483.

Pollock, G. H. (1973). Bertha Pappenheim: Addenda to her case history. *Journal of the American Psychoanalytic Association* 21: 328–332.

Popper, K. (1959). *The Logic of Scientific Discovery.* London: Hutchinson.

Possick, S. (1984). Termination in the Dora case. *Journal of the American Academy of Psychoanalysis* 12: 1–11.

Pöstényi, A. (1979). Ricoeur's philosophy and its implications for psychoanalysis. *Scandinavian Psychoanalytical Review* 2: 35–48.

Powell, R. A., and Boer, D. P. (1994). Did Freud mislead patients to confabulate memories of abuse? *Psychological Reports* 74: 1283–1298.

Powell, R. A., and Boer, D. P. (1995). Did Freud misinterpret reported memories of sexual abuse as fantasies? *Psychological Reports* 77: 563–570.

Pratt, J. S. (1958). Epilegomena to the study of Freudian instinct theory. *International Journal of Psycho-Analysis* 39: 17–24.

Preyer, W. (1882). *Die Seele Des Kindes*. Leipzig: Grieben.

Preyer, W. (1893a). *The Mind of the Child. Part I: The Senses and the Will* (2d Ger. ed.) (H. W. Brown, trans.). New York: Appleton.

Preyer, W. (1893ba). *The Mind of the Child. Part II: The Development of the Intellect* (2d Ger. ed.) (H. W. Brown, trans.). New York: Appleton.

Pribram, K. H. (1962). The neuropsychology of Sigmund Freud. In A. J. Bachrach, ed., *Experimental Foundations of Clinical Psychology* (pp. 442–468). New York: Basic Books.

Pribram, K. H. (1965). Freud's *Project*: An open, biologically based model for psychoanalysis. In N. S. Greenfield and W. C. Lewis, eds., *Psychoanalysis and Current Biological Thought* (pp. 81–92). Madison, Wis.: University of Wisconsin Press.

Pribram, K. H., and Gill, M. M. (1976). *Freud's "Project" Re-assessed: Preface to Contemporary Cognitive Theory and Neuropsychology*. London: Hutchinson.

Prince, M. (1910a). The mechanism and interpretation of dreams. *Journal of Abnormal Psychology* 5: 139–195.

Prince, M. (1910b). The mechanism and interpretation of dreams—A reply to Dr. Jones. *Journal of Abnormal Psychology* 5: 337–353.

Pulver, S. E. (1970). Narcissism: The term and the concept. *Journal of the American Psychoanalytic Association* 18: 319–341.

Pulver, S. E. (1971). Can affects be unconscious? *International Journal of Psycho-Analysis* 52: 347–354.

Pulver, S. E. (1987). The manifest dream in psychoanalysis: A clarification. *Journal of the American Psychoanalytic Association* 35: 99–118.

Pulver, S. E. (1991). Psychic structure, function, process, and content: Toward a definition. In T. Shapiro, ed., *The Concept of Structure in Psychoanalysis* (pp. 165–189). Madison, CT: International Universities Press.

Pumpian-Mindlin, E. (1952). The position of psychoanalysis in relation to the biological and social sciences. In E. Pumpian-Mindlin, ed., *Psychoanalysis as Science* (pp. 125–158). Stanford, Calif.: Stanford University Press.

Pumpian-Mindlin, E. (1958–1959). An attempt at the systematic restatement of the libido theory. 3. Propositions concerning energetic-economic aspects of libido theory: Conceptual models of energy and structure in psychoanalysis. *New York Academy of Sciences, Annals* 76: 1038–1052.

Putnam, J. J. (1906–1907). Recent experiences in the study and treatment of hysteria at the Massachusetts General Hospital: With remarks on Freud's method of treatment by psychoanalysis. *Journal of Abnormal Psychology* 1: 26–41.

Putnam, J. J. (1910). Personal impressions of Sigmund Freud and his work. *Journal of Abnormal Psychology* 5: 1–26.

Quay, H. (1959). The effect of verbal reinforcement on the recall of early memories. *Journal of Abnormal and Social Psychology* 59: 254–257.

Quinn, B. (1992). Sigmund Freud and the history of neurotechnique: The "lost" year. *Society for Neuroscience Abstracts* 18: 181.

Quinn, B. (1993). Freud's gold chloride myelin stain: A vignette in the history of neurologic science in Vienna. *Neurology* 43(S2): A377.

Rado, S. (1933). Fear of castration in women. *Psychoanalytic Quarterly* 2: 454–458.

Rado, S. (1950). Emergency behavior: With an introduction to the dynamics of conscience. In P. H. Hoch and J. Zubin, eds., *Anxiety* (pp. 150–175). New York: Hafner.

Ramzy, I., and Wallerstein, R. S. (1958). Pain, fear and anxiety: A study in their interrelationships. *Psychoanalytic Study of the Child* 13: 147–189.

Rangell, L. (1955). On the psychoanalytic theory of anxiety: A statement of a unitary theory. *Journal of the American Psychoanalytic Association* 3: 389–414.

Rangell, L. (1967). The metapsychology of psychic trauma. In S. S. Furst, ed., *Psychic Trauma* (pp. 51–84). New York: Basic Books.

Rangell, L. (1968). A further attempt to resolve the "problem of anxiety." *Journal of the American Psychoanalytic Association* 16: 371–404.

Rangell, L. (1978). On understanding and treating anxiety and its derivatives. *International Journal of Psycho-Analysis* 59: 229–236.

Rangell, L. (1979). Contemporary issues in the theory of therapy. *Journal of the American Psychoanalytic Association* 27: 81–112 .

Rangell, L. (1985). The object in psychoanalytic theory. *Journal of the American Psychoanalytic Association* 33: 301–334.

Rapaport, D. (1951). *Organization and Pathology of Thought: Selected Sources* (D. Rapaport, trans.). New York: Columbia University Press.

Rapaport, D. (1959). A historical survey of psychoanalytic ego psychology. *Psychological Issues* 1: 15–17. Monograph 1.

Rapaport, D. (1960). The structure of psychoanalytic theory: A systematizing attempt. *Psychological Issues* 2. Monograph 6.

Rapaport, D. (1967). A theoretical analysis of the superego concept. In M. M. Gill, ed., *The Collected Papers of David Rapaport* (pp. 685–709). New York: Basic Books.

Rapaport, D., and Gill, M. M. (1959). The points of view and assumptions of metapsychology. *International Journal of Psycho-Analysis* 40: 153–162.

Raphling, D. L. (1994). A patient who was not sexually abused. *Journal of the American Psychoanalytical Association* 42: 65–78.

Rawn, M. L. (1979). Schafer's "action language": A questionable alternative to metapsychology. *International Journal of Psycho-Analysis* 60: 455–465.

Reich, A. (1951). The discussion of 1912 on masturbation and our present-day views. *Psychoanalytic Study of the Child* 6: 80–94.

Reich, A. (1954). Early identifications as archaic elements in the superego. *Journal of the American Psychoanalytic Association* 2: 218–238.

Reich, W. (1926). The sources of neurotic anxiety: A contribution to the theory of psycho-analytic therapy. *International Journal of Psycho-Analysis* 7: 381–391.

Reich, W. (1928). Discussion on the need for punishment and the neurotic process I. A criticism of recent theories of the problem of neurosis. *International Journal of Psycho-Analysis* 9: 227–240. (Original work published 1927.)

Reich, W. (1950). The masochistic character. In W. Reich, *Character Analysis* (3d ed.) (T. P. Wolfe, trans.) (pp. 208–247). London: Vision. (Original work published 1932.)

Reichard, S. (1956). A re-examination of "Studies in Hysteria." *Psychoanalytic Quarterly* 25: 155–177.

Reik, T. (1941). *Masochism in Modern Man.* New York: Farrar, Straus and Cudahy.

Reik, T. (1959). The compulsion to confess (N. Rie, trans.). In T. Reik, *The Compulsion to Confess* (pp. 175–356). New York: Farrar, Straus and Cudahy. (Original work published 1925.)

Reppen, J. (1982). Merton Gill: An interview. *Psychoanalytic Review* 69: 166–190.

Reyher, J. (1962). A paradigm for determining the clinical relevance of hypnotically induced psychopathology. *Psychological Bulletin* 59: 344–352.

Reyher, J. (1967). Hypnosis in research on psychopathology. In J. E. Gordon, ed., *Handbook of Clinical and Experimental Hypnosis* (pp. 110–147). New York: Macmillan.

Reynolds, J. R. (1869). Remarks on paralysis and other disorders of motion and sensation dependent upon idea. *British Medical Journal* ii: 483–485.

Ribot, T. H. (1910). *The Diseases of Personality* (4th ed.). Chicago: Open Court. (Original work published 1884.)

Ricoeur, P. (1970). *Freud and Philosophy: An Essay on Interpretation* (D. Savage, trans.). New Haven, Conn.: Yale University Press.

Ricoeur, P. (1974). *The Conflict of Interpretations* (D. Ihde, ed.). New Haven, Conn.: Yale University Press. (Original work published 1969.)

Ricoeur, P. (1977). The question of proof in Freud's psychoanalytic writings. *Journal of the American Psychoanalytic Association* 25: 835–871.

Rieff, P. (1959). *Freud the Mind of the Moralist*. London: Gollancz.

Ritvo, L. B. (1972). Darwin's influence on Freud. *Dissertation Abstracts International* 34: 685A. (University Microfilms No. 73–18: 532.)

Ritvo, L. B. (1990). *Darwin's Influence on Freud: A Tale of Two Sciences*. New Haven, CT: Yale University Press.

Ritvo, S. (1971). Late adolescence developmental and clinical considerations. *Psychoanalytic Study of the Child* 26: 241–263.

Ritvo, S., and Solnit, A. J. (1960). The relationship of early ego identifications to superego formation. *International Journal of Psycho-Analysis* 41: 295–300.

Rivers, W. H. R. (1918). The repression of war experience. *Proceedings of the Royal Society of Medicine, Section of Psychiatry* 11: 1–17.

Rivers, W. H. R. (1923). *Conflict and Dream*. London: Kegan Paul, Trench, Trubner.

Rizzuto, A-M. (1989). A hypothesis about Freud's motive for writing the monograph "On Aphasia." *International Review of Psycho-Analysis* 16: 111–117.

Rizzuto, A-M. (1990a). The origins of Freud's concept of object representation ("Objektvorstellung") in his monograph "On Aphasia": Its theoretical and technical importance. *International Journal of Psycho-Analysis* 71: 241–248.

Rizzuto, A-M. (1990b). A protodictionary of psychoanalysis. *International Journal of Psycho-Analesis* 71: 261–270.

Rizzuto, A-M. (1992). Freud's theoretical and technical models in *Studies on Hysteria*. *International Review of Psycho-Analysis* 19: 169–177.

Rizzuto, A-M. (1993). Freud's speech apparatus and spontaneous speech. *International Journal of Psycho-Analysis* 74: 113–127.

Rizzuto, A-M., Sashin, J. I., Buie, D. H., and Meissner, W. W. (1993). A revised theory of aggression. *Psychoanalytic Review* 80: 29–54.

Roback, A. A. (1919). The Freudian doctrine of lapses and its failings. *American Journal of Psychology* 30: 274–290.

Robertson, G. C. (1889). Prof. Delboeuf on hypnotism and the Nancy school. *Mind* 14: 470–471.

Robertson, G. M. (1892). Hypnotism at Paris and Nancy. Notes of a visit. *Journal of Mental Science* 38: 494–531.

Robinson, P. (1993). *Freud and His Critics*. Berkeley, Calif.: University of California Press.

Roffenstein, G. (1951). Experiments on symbolization in dreams. In D. Rapaport, ed., *Organization and Pathology of Thought* (pp. 249–256). New York: Columbia University Press. (Original work published 1924.)

Rogers, C. R. (1957). The necessary and sufficient conditions of therapeutic personality change. *Journal of Consulting Psychology* 21: 95–103.

Rogow, A. A. (1978). A further footnote to Freud's "Fragment of an analysis of a case of hysteria." *Journal of the American Psychoanalytic Association* 26: 331–356.

Rogow, A. A. (1979). Dora's brother. *International Review of Psycho-Analysis* 6: 239–259.

Roiphe, H., and Galenson, E. (1972). Early genital activity and the castration complex. *Psychoanalytic Quarterly* 41: 334–347.

Roiphe, H., and Galenson, E. (1981). *Infantile Origins of Sexual Identity.* New York: International Universities Press.

Romm, M. E. (1959). The roots of masochism. In J. H. Masserman, ed., *Individual and Familial Dynamics* (pp. 38–41). New York: Grune and Stratton.

Rosen, G. (1946). Mesmerism and surgery: A strange chapter in the history of anesthesia. *Journal of the History of Medicine and Allied Sciences* 1: 527–550.

Rosen, V. H. (1965). Review of R. W. White *Ego and Reality in Psychoanalytic Theory. International Journal of Psycho-Analysis* 46: 256–258.

Rosen, V. H. (1968). Review of M. Schur's "The Id and the Regulatory Principles of Mental Functioning." *International Journal of Psycho-Analysis* 49: 100–101.

Rosen, V. H. (1969). Sign phenomena and their relationship to unconscious meaning. *International Journal of Psycho-Analysis* 50: 197–207.

Rosenbaum, A. L. (1983). Reanalysis of child analytic patients. *Journal of the American Psychoanalytic Association* 31: 677–688.

Rosenbaum, M. (1980). The role of the term schizophrenia in the decline of diagnoses of multiple personality. *Archives of General Psychiatry* 37: 1380–1385.

Rosenberg, C. E. (1962). The place of George M. Beard in nineteenth-century psychiatry. *Bulletin of the History of Medicine* 36: 245–259.

Rosenblatt, A. D., and Thickstun, J. T. (1970). A study of the concept of psychic energy. *International Journal of Psycho-Analysis* 51: 265–278.

Rosenblatt, A. D., and Thickstun, J. T. (1977). Energy, information, and motivation: A revision of psychoanalytic theory. *Journal of the American Psychoanalytic Association* 25: 537–558.

Ross, J. M. (1980). Symposium: George Klein's *Psychoanalytic Theory in perspective. Psychoanalytic Review* 67: 161–167.

Rothstein, A. (1979a). The theory of narcissism: An object-relations perspective. *Psychoanalytic Review* 66: 35–47.

Rothstein, A. (1979b). An exploration of the diagnostic term "narcissistic personality disorder." *Journal of the American Psychoanalytic Association* 27: 893–912.

Rothstein, A. (1981). The ego: An evolving construct. *International Journal of Psycho-Analysis* 62: 435–445.

Rubinstein, B. B. (1973). On the logic of explanation in psychoanalysis. *Psychoanalysis and Contemporary Science* 2: 338–358.

Rubinstein, B. B. (1975). On the possibility of a strictly psychoanalytic theory: An essay in the philosophy of psychoanalysis. *Psychological Issues* 9: 229–264. Monograph 36.

Rubinstein, B. B. (1980). The problem of confirmation in clinical psychoanalysis. *Journal of the American Psychoanalytic Association* 28: 397–417.

Rubinstein, B. B. (1983). Freud's early theories of hysteria. In R. S. Cohen and L. Laudan, eds., *Physics, Philosophy and Psychoanalysis: Essays in Honour of Adolf Grünbaum* (pp. 169–190). Dordrecht: Reidel.

Rubenstein, B. O., and Levitt, M. (1959). Some observations regarding the role of fathers in child analysis. In M. Levitt, ed., *Readings in Psychoanalytic Psychology* (pp. 375–387). New York: Appleton-Century.

Rubovits-Seitz, P. (1992). Interpretive methodology: Some problems, limitations, and remedial strategies. *Journal of the American Psychoanalytical Association* 40: 139–168.

Russell, C. A. (1971). *The History of Valency*. Leicester: Leicester University Press.

Ryle, G. (1949). *The Concept of Mind*. London: Hutchinson.

Sacal, S. (1990). Free association as a method of self-observation in relation to other principles of psychoanalysis. *Psychoanalytic Quarterly* 59: 420–436.

Sachs, D. (1991). In fairness to Freud: A critical notice of *The Foundations of Psychoanalysis*, by Adolf Grünbaum. In J. Neu, ed., *The Cambridge Companion to Freud* (pp. 309–338). Cambridge: Cambridge University Press.

Sachs, H. (1986). On the genesis of perversions. *Psychoanalytic Quarterly* 55: 477–488. (Original work published 1923.)

Sack, R. L., and Miller, W. (1975). Masochism: A clinical and theoretical overview. *Psychiatry* 38: 244–257.

Sacks, M. H. (1985). The oedipus complex: A reevaluation. *Journal of the American Psychoanalytic Association* 33: 201–216.

Sadger, J. (1926). A contribution to the understanding of sado-masochism. *International Journal of Psycho-Analysis* 7: 484–491.

Salyard, A. (1994). On knowing what you know: Object-coercive doubting and Freud's announcement of the seduction theory. *Psychoanalytic Review* 81: 659–676.

Salzinger, K. (1959). Experimental manipulation of verbal behavior: A review. *Journal of General Psychology* 61: 65–94.

Salzman, L. (1959). Masochism: A review of theory and therapy. In J. H. Masserman, ed., *Individual and Familial Dynamics* (pp. 1–20). New York: Grune and Stratton.

Sand, R. (1982). *A systematic error in the use of free association*. Unpublished manuscript.

Sand, R. (1983). Confirmation in the Dora case. *International Review of Psycho-Analysis* 10: 333–357.

Sand, R. (1992). Pre-Freudian discoveries of dream meaning: The achievements of Charcot, Janet, and Krafft-Ebing. In T. Gelfand and J. Kerr, eds., *Freud and the History of Psychoanalysis* (pp. 215–229). Hillsdale, NJ: Analytic Press.

Sand, R. (1993). On a contribution to a future scientific study of dream interpretation. In J. Earman, A. I. Janis, G. J. Massey, and N. Rescher, eds., *Philosophical Problems of the Internal and External Worlds: Essays on the Philosophy of Adolf Grünbaum* (pp. 527–547). Pittsburgh: University of Pittsburgh Press.

Sandler, J. (1960). On the concept of superego. *Psychoanalytic Study of the Child* 15: 128–162.

Sandler, J. (1967). Trauma, strain, and development. In S. S. Furst, ed., *Psychic Trauma* (pp. 154–174). New York: Basic Books.

Sandler, J. (1983). Reflections on some relations between psychoanalytic concepts and psychoanalytic practice. *International Journal of Psycho-Analysis* 64: 35–45.

Sandler, J., and Joffe, W. G. (1966). On skill and sublimation. *Journal of the American Psychoanalytic Association* 14: 335–355.

Sandler, J., and Sandler, A.-M. (1983). The "second censorship" the "three box model" and some technical implications. *International Journal of Psycho-Analysis* 64: 413–425.

Sandler, J., and Sandler, A.-M. (1994). The past unconscious and the present unconscious: A contribution to a theoretical frame of reference. *Psychoanalytic Study of the Child* 49: 278–292.

Sandler, J., Dare, C., and Holder, A. (1972). Frames of reference in psychoanalytic psychology: I. Introduction. *British Journal of Medical Psychology* 45: 127–132.

Sandler, J., Dare, C., and Holder, A. (1982). Frames of reference in psychoanalytic psychology: XII. The characteristics of the structural frame of reference. *British Journal of Medical Psychology* 55: 203–207.

Sandler, J., Holder, A., and Meers, D. (1963). The ego ideal. *Psychoanalytic Study of the Child* 18: 139–158.

Sargent, H. D. (1961). Intrapsychic change: Methodological problems in psychotherapy research. *Psychiatry* 24: 93–108.

Sargent, H. D., Horwitz, L., Wallerstein, R. S., and Sampson, P. S. (1968). Prediction in psychotherapy research: A method for the transformation of clinical judgements into testable hypotheses. *Psychological Issues* 6. Monograph 2.

Sarton, G. (1944). Vindication of Father Hell. *Isis* 35: 97–105.

Sass, L. A., and Woolfolk, R. L. (1988). Psychoanalysis and the hermeneutic turn: A critique of *Narrative Truth and Historical Truth*. *Journal of the American Psychoanalytic Association* 36: 429–454.

Satinover, J. (1986). Jung's lost contribution to the dilemma of narcissism. *Journal of the American Psychoanalytic Association* 34: 401–438.

Saul, L. J. (1958). Freud's death instinct and the second law of thermodynamics. *International Journal of Psycho-Analysis* 39: 323–325.

Schafer, R. (1960). The loving and beloved superego in Freud's structural theory. *Psychoanalytic Study of the Child* 15: 163–188.

Schafer, R. (1964). The clinical analysis of affects. *Journal of the American Psychoanalytic Association* 12: 275–299.

Schafer, R. (1965). Contributions of longitudinal studies to psychoanalytic theory. *Journal of the American Psychoanalytic Association* 13: 605–618.

Schafer, R. (1968). *Aspects of Internalization*. New York: International Universities Press.

Schafer, R. (1970). An overview of Heinz Hartmann's contributions to psychoanalysis. *International Journal of Psycho-Analysis* 51: 425–446.

Schafer, R. (1973). Internalization: Process or fantasy? *Psychoanalytic Study of the Child* 27: 411–436.

Schafer, R. (1974). Problems in Freud's psychology of women. *Journal of the American Psychoanalytic Association* 22: 459–485.

Schafer, R. (1976). *A New Language for Psychoanalysis*. New Haven, Conn.: Yale University Press.

Schafer, R. (1991). Discussion of panel presentations on psychic structure. In T. Shapiro, ed., *The Concept of Structure in Psychoanalysis* (pp. 295–312). Madison, CT: International Universities Press.

Scharfman, M. A. (1980). Further reflections on Dora. In M. Kanzer and J. Glenn, eds., *Freud and His Patients* (pp. 48–57). New York: Aronson.

Scharnberg, M. (1984). *The Myth of Paradigm Shift, or How to Lie with Methodology*. (Acta Universitatis Upsaliensis Uppsala Studies in Education 20.) Stockholm: Almqvist & Wiksell International.

Scharnberg, M. (1993a). *The Non-Authentic Nature of Freud's Observations*. Vol. I. *The Seduction Theory*. (Acta Universitatis Upsaliensis Uppsala Studies in Education 47.) Stockholm: Almqvist & Wiksell International.

Scharnberg, M. (1993b). *The Non-Authentic Nature of Freud's Observations*. Vol. II. *Felix Gattel's Early Freudian Cases and the Astrological Origin of the Anal Theory*. (Acta Universitatis Upsaliensis Uppsala Studies in Education 48.) Stockholm: Almqvist & Wiksell International.

Scharnberg, M. (1996a). *Textual Analysis: A Scientific Approach for Assessing Cases of Sexual Abuse*. Vol I. *The Theoretical Framework, the Psychology of Lying, and Cases of Older Children* (Acta Universitatis Upsaliensis Uppsala Studies in Education 64.) Stockholm: Imqvist & Wiksell International.

Scharnberg, M. (1996b). *Textual Analysis: A Scientific Approach for Assessing Cases of Sexual Abuse*. Vol II. *Cases of Younger Children, Including a Case of Alleged Necrophilia, and the Shortcomings of Judicial Logic* (Acta Universitatis Upsaliensis Uppsala Studies in Education 65.) Stockholm: Almqvist & Wiksell International.

Schatzman, M. (1971). Paranoia or persecution: The case of Schreber. *Family Process* 10: 177–212.

Schatzman, M. (1973). *Soul Murder: Persecution in the Family*. New York: Random House.

Schatzman, M. (1992). Freud: Who seduced whom? *New Scientist* 133: 34–37.

Schilder, P. (1938). *Psychotherapy*. London: Kegan Paul, Trench, Trubner.

Schimek, J. G. (1987). Fact and fantasy in the seduction theory: A historical review. *Journal of the American Psychoanalytic Association* 35: 937–965.

Schimek, J. (1995). Letter to the editor, *New York Review of Books*. In F. Crews et al, *The Memory Wars: Freud's Legacy in Dispute* (p. 77) New York: New York Review of Books. (Original work published February 3, 1994.)

Schlessinger, N., Gedo, J. E., Miller, J., Pollock, G. H., Sabshin, M., and Sadow, L. (1967). The scientific style of Breuer and Freud in the origins of psychoanalysis. *Journal of the American Psychoanalytic Association* 15: 404–422.

Schmideberg, M. (1939). The role of suggestion in analytic therapy. *Psychoanalytic Review* 26: 219–229.

Schmidl, F. (1955). The problem of scientific validation in psycho-analytic interpretation. *International Journal of Psycho-Analysis* 36: 105–113.

Schneck, J. M. (1961). Jean-Martin Charcot and the history of experimental hypnosis. *Journal of the History of Medicine* 16: 297–305.

Schneck, J. M. (1963). Clinical and experimental aspects of hypnotic dreams. In M. V. Kline ed., *Clinical correlations of experimental hypnosis* (pp. 75–100). Springfield, Ill.: Charles C Thomas.

Schorske, C. E. (1975). Politics and patricide in Freud's *Interpretation of Dreams*. *Annual of Psychoanalysis* 2: 40–60.

Schreber, D. P. (1955). *Memoirs of My Mental Illness* (I. Macalpine and R. A. Hunter, trans.). London: Dawson. (Original work published 1903.)

Schroeder, T. (1919). The psychologic aspect of free association. *American Journal of Psychology* 30: 260–273.

Schröter, M., and Hermanns, L. M. (1992). Felix Gattel (1870–1904): Freud's first pupil. Parts I and II. *International Review of Psycho-Analysis* 19: 91–104, 197–208.

Schroetter, K. (1951). Experimental dreams. In D. Rapaport, ed., *Organization and Pathology of Thought* (pp. 234–248). New York: Columbia University Press. (Original work published 1911.)

Schur, M. (1953). The ego in anxiety. In R. M. Loewenstein, ed., *Drives, Affects, Behavior* (pp. 67–105). New York: International Universities Press.

Schur, M. (1958). The ego and the id in anxiety. *Psychoanalytic Study of the Child* 13: 190–220.

Schur, M. (1960). Phylogenesis and ontogenesis of affect- and structure-formation and the phenomenon of repetition compulsion. *International Journal of Psycho-Analysis* 41: 275–287.

Schur, M. (1966a). *The Id and the Regulatory Principles of Mental Functioning*. New York: International Universities Press.

Schur, M. (1966b). Some additional "day residues" of "the specimen dream of psychoanalysis." In R. M. Lowenstein, L. M. Newman, M. Schur, and A. J. Solnit, eds., *Psychoanalysis—A General Psychology* (pp. 45–85). New York: International Universities Press.

Schur, M. (1972). *Freud: Living and Dying*. New York: International Universities Press.

Schur, M., and Ritvo, L. B. (1970). A principle of evolutionary biology for psychoanalysis. *Journal of the American Psychoanalytic Association* 18: 422–439.

Schusdek, A. (1966). Freud's "seduction theory": A reconstruction. *Journal of the History of the Behavioral Sciences* 2: 159–166.

Schwartz, F. (1981). Psychic structure. *International Journal of Psycho-Analysis* 62: 61–72.

Scott, W. C. M. (1952). The mutual influences in the development of ego and id. *Psychoanalytic Study of the Child* 7: 60–65.

Scriven, M. (1959). The experimental investigation of psychoanalysis. In S. Hook, ed., *Psychoanalysis, Scientific Method, and Philosophy* (pp. 226–251). New York: New York University Press.

Sears, R. R. (1942). *Survey of Objective Studies of Psychoanalytic Concepts*. New York: Social Sciences Research Council.

Sears, R. R. (1944). Experimental analysis of psychoanalytic phenomena. In J. McV. Hunt, ed., *Personality and the Behavior Disorders* (vol. 1) (pp. 306–332). New York: Ronald Press.

Sechenov, I. M. (1863). Reflexes of the brain. In K. Koshtoyants, ed., *I. Sechenov: Selected Physiological and Psychological Works* (pp. 31–139) (S. Belsky, trans.). Moscow: Foreign Languages Publishing House.

Segel, N. P. (1969). Repetition compulsion, acting out, and identification with the doer. *Journal of the American Psychoanalytic Association* 17: 474–488.

Seidenberg, H. (1971). The basic rule: Free association—A reconsideration. *Journal of the American Psychoanalytic Association* 19: 98–109.

Seitz, P. F. D. (1966). The consensus problem in psychoanalytic research. In L. A. Gottschalk and A. H. Auerbach, eds., *Methods of Research in Psychotherapy* (pp. 209–225). New York: Appleton-Century-Crofts.

Shapiro, A. K. (1960). A contribution to the history of the placebo effect. *Behavioral Science* 5: 109–135.

Shapiro, A. K., and Morris, L. A. (1978). The placebo effect in medical and psychological therapies. In S. L. Garfield and A. E. Bergin, eds., *Handbook of Psychotherapy and Behavior Change* (2d ed.) (pp. 369–410). New York: Wiley.

Shapiro, T. (1981). On the quest for the origins of conflict. *Psychoanalytic Quarterly* 50: 1–21.

Shapiro, T., ed. (1991). *The Concept of Structure in Psychoanalysis*. Madison, CT: International Universities Press.

Sharpe, R. A. (1986). Review discussion. Psychoanalysis, science or insight? Adolf Grünbaum: *The Foundations of Psychoanalysis*. *Inquiry* 29: 121–132.

Sheehan, P. W. (1969). Artificial induction of posthypnotic conflict. *Journal of Abnormal Psychology* 74: 16–25.

Sheehan, P. W., and Dolby, R. M. (1979). Motivated involvement in hypnosis: The illustration of clinical rapport through hypnotic dreams. *Journal of Abnormal Psychology* 88: 573–583.

Sheehan, P. W., and McConkey, K. M. (1982). *Hypnosis and Experience: The Exploration of Phenomena and Process*. Hillsdale, N.J.: Erlbaum.

Sherrington, C. (1906). *The Integrative Action of the Nervous System*. New Haven, Conn.: Yale University Press.

Sherwood, M. (1969). *The Logic of Explanation in Psychoanalysis*. New York: Academic Press.

Sherwood, M. (1973). Another look at the logic of explanation in psychoanalysis. *Psychoanalysis and Contemporary Science* 2: 359–366.

Shope, R. K. (1967). The psychoanalytic theories of wish-fulfilment and meaning. *Inquiry* 10: 421–438.

Shope, R. K. (1970). Freud on conscious and unconscious intention. *Inquiry* 13: 149–159.

Shope, R. K. (1971). Physical and psychic energy. *Philosophy of Science* 38: 1–12.

Shope, R. K. (1973). Freud's concepts of meaning. *Psychoanalysis and Contemporary Science* 2: 276–303.

Shorter, E. (1992). *From Paralysis to Fatigue: A History of Psychosomatic Illness in the Modern Era*. New York: Macmillan.

Shulman, M. E. (1987). On the problem of the id in psychoanalytic theory. *International Journal of Psycho-Analysis* 68: 161–173.

Sidis, B. (1906–1907). Review of *The Psychopathology of Everyday Life*. *Journal of Abnormal Psychology* 1: 101–103.

Sidis, B. (1912). Dreams. *Psychological Bulletin* 9: 36–40.

Sidis, B. (1918). A clinical study of a dream personality. *Journal of Abnormal Psychology* 13: 137–157.

Siegal, R. S. (1969). What are defense mechanisms? *Journal of the American Psychoanalytic Association* 17: 785–807.

Siegler, F. A. (1967). Unconscious intentions. *Inquiry* 10: 251–267.

Silberer, H. (1921). Beyond psychoanalysis. *Psyche and Eros* 2: 142–151.

Silverberg, W. V. (1959). Masochism: Semantics and transference. In J. H. Masserman, ed., *Individual and Familial Dynamics* (pp. 70–72). New York: Grune and Stratton.

Silverman, M. A. (1986). Identification in healthy and pathological character formation. *International Journal of Psycho-Analysis* 67: 181–191.

Silverstein, B. (1989). Contributions to the history of psychology. LVII. Freud's dualistie mind-body interactionism: Implications for the development of his psychology. *Psychological Reports* 64: 1091–1097.

Simenauer, E. (1985). Identification in the theory and technique of psychoanalysis. Some thoughts on its farther reaches and functions. *International Journal of Psycho-Analysis* 66: 171–184.

Simmel, E. (1944). Self-preservation and the death instinct. *Psychoanalytic Quarterly* 13: 160–185.

Simon, B. (1991). Is the Oedipus complex still the cornerstone of psychoanalysis? Three way obstacles to answering the question. *Journal of the American Psychoanalytic Association* 39: 641–668.

Simon, B. (1992). "Incest—See under Oedipus complex": The history of an error in psychoanalysis. *Journal of the American Psychoanalytic Association* 40: 955–988.

Simon, B., and Blass, R. B. (1991). The development and vicissitudes of Freud's ideas on the Oedipus complex. In J. Neu, ed., *The Cambridge Companion to Freud* (pp. 161–174). Cambridge: Cambridge University Press.

Sjoback, H. (1973). *The Psychoanalytic Theory of Defensive Processes.* New York: Wiley.

Slap, J. W. (1967). Freud's view on pleasure and aggression. *Journal of the American Psychoanalytic Association* 15: 370–375.

Slap, J. W. (1986). Some problems with the structural model and a remedy. *Psychoanalytic Psychology* 3: 47–58.

Slap, J. W., and Slaykin, A. J. (1983). The Schema: Basic concept in a non-metapsychological model of the mind. *Psychoanalysis and Contemporary Thought* 6: 305–325.

Slipp, S. (1977). Interpersonal factors in hysteria: Freud's seduction theory and the case of Dora. *Journal of the American Academy of Psychoanalysis* 5: 359–376.

Smirnoff, V. N. (1969). The masochistic contract. *International Journal of Psycho-Analysis* 50: 665–671.

Smith, D. L. (1985). Freud's developmental approach to narcissism: A concise review. *International Journal of Psycho-Analysis* 66: 489–497.

Smith, D. L. (1991). *Hidden Conversations: An Introduction to Communicative Psychoanalysis.* London: Tavistock/Routledge.

Smith, J. H. (1977). The pleasure principle. *International Journal of Psycho-Analysis* 58: 1–10.

Solms, M. (1995a). Book review of Kitcher's *Freud's Dream: A Complete Interdisciplinary Science of Mind* (1992). *Isis* 86: 133.

Solms, M. (1995b). New findings on the neurological organisation of dreaming: Implications for psychoanalysis. *Psychoanalytic Quarterly* 64: 43–67.

Solms, M., and Saling, M. (1986). On psychoanalysis and neuroscience: Freud's attitude to the localizationist tradition. *International Journal of Psycho-Analysis* 67: 397–416.

Solms, M., and Saling, M. (eds. and trans.). (1990). *A Moment of Transition: Two Neuroscientific Articles by Sigmund Freud.* London: Institute of Psycho-Analysis.

Solnit, A. J., and Kris, M. (1967). Trauma and infantile experiences: A longitudinal perspective. In S. S. Furst, ed., *Psychic Trauma* (pp. 175–220). New York: Basic Books.

Solomon, R. C. (1974). Freud's neurological theory of mind. In R. Wollheim, ed., *Freud: A Collection of Critical Essays* (pp. 25–52). New York: Anchor Books.

Spanjaard, J. (1969). The manifest dream content and its significance for the interpretation of dreams. *International Journal of Psycho-Analysis* 50: 221–235.

Spence, D. P. (1976). Clinical interpretation: Some comments on the nature of the evidence. *Psychoanalysis and Contemporary Science* 5: 367–388.

Spence, D. P. (1980). *Narrative Truth and Historical Truth: Meaning and Interpretation in Psychoanalysis.* New York: Norton.

Spence, D. P. (1981). Toward a theory of dream interpretation. *Psychoanalysis and Contemporary Thought* 4: 383–405.

Spence, D. P. (1982a). Narrative truth and theoretical truth. *Psychoanalytic Quarterly* 51: 43–69.

Spence, D. P. (1982b). On some clinical implications of action language. *Journal of the American Psycho-analytic Association* 30: 169–184.

Spence, D. P. (1986). When interpretation masquerades as explanation. *Journal of the American Psycho-analytic Association* 34: 3–22.

Spencer, H. (1860). The physiology of laughter. *Macmillan's Magazine* 1: 395–402.

Spencer, H. (1873). *The Principles of Psychology* (vol. 1). New York: Appleton.

Spero, M. H. (1984). Shame: An object-relational formulation. *Psychoanalytic Study of the Child* 39: 259–282.

Spiegel, L. A. (1978). Moral masochism. *Psychoanalytic Quarterly* 47: 209–236.

Spielman, P. (1986). Psychoanalysis and infant research. *Journal of the American Psychoanalytic Association* 34: 215–219.

Spitz, R. A. (1950). Anxiety in infancy: A study of its manifestations in the first year of life. *International Journal of Psycho-Analysis* 31: 138–143.

Spitz, R. A., and Wolf, K. M. (1949). Autoerotism: Some empirical findings and hypotheses on three of its manifestations in the first year of life. *Psychoanalytic Study of the Child* 3–4: 85–120.

Spotnitz, H. (1984). The case of Anna O.: Aggression and the narcissistic transference. In M. Rosenbaum and M. Muroff, eds., *Anna O. Fourteen Contemporary Reinterpretations* (pp. 132–140). New York: Free Press.

Spring, W. J. (1934). A critical consideration of Bernfeld and Feitelberg's theory of psychic energy. *Psychoanalytic Quarterly* 3: 445–473.

Spruiell, V. (1975). Three strands of narcissism. *Psychoanalytic Quarterly* 44: 577–595.

Spruiell, V. (1979). Freud's concepts of idealization. *Journal of the American Psychoanalytic Association* 27: 777–791.

Spruiell, V. (1981). The self and the ego. *Psychoanalytic Quarterly* 50: 319–344.

Spruiell, V. (1986). The foundations of psychoanalysis: An essay review on a philosophical book by Adolf Grünbaum. *International Review of Psycho-Analysis* 14: 169–183.

Stainbrook, E. (1948). The use of electricity in psychiatric treatment during the nineteenth century. *Bulletin of the History of Medicine* 22: 156–177.

Starke, J. G. (1973). *The Validity of Psycho-Analysis.* Sydney: Angus and Robertson.

Steele, R. S. (1979). Psychoanalysis and hermeneutics. *International Review of Psycho-Analysis* 6: 389–411.

Steele, R. S., and Jacobsen, P. B. (1977). From present to past: The development of Freudian theory. *International Review of Psycho-Analysis* 5: 393–411.

Stein, H. H. (1995). The dream is the guardian of sleep. *Psychoanalytic Quarterly* 64: 533–550.

Stein, M. H. (1956). The problem of masochism in the theory and technique of psychoanalysis. *Journal of the American Psychoanalytic Association* 4: 526–538.

Stein, M. H. (1965). States of consciousness in the analytic situation. In M. Schur, ed., *Drives, Affects, Behavior* (vol. 2) (pp. 60–86). New York: International Universities Press.

Steiner, R. (1985). Some thoughts about tradition and change arising from an examination of the British Psycho-Analytical Society's controversial discussions (1943–1944). *International Review of Psycho-Analysis* 12: 27–71.

Steingart, I. (1969). On self, character, and the development of a psychic apparatus. *Psychoanalytic Study of the Child* 24: 271–303.

Stengel, E. (1954). A re-evaluation of Freud's book "On Aphasia." Its significance for psycho-analysis. *International Journal of Psycho-Analysis* 35: 85–89.

Stephen, A. (1918–1919). On the assumptions of psychoanalysts. *Journal of Abnormal Psychology* 13: 17–22.

Sterba, R. F. (1968). *Introduction to the Psychoanalytic Theory of the Libido* (3d ed.). New York: Robert Brunner.

Stern, A. (1930). Masturbation: Its rôle in the neuroses. *American Journal of Psychiatry* 9: 1081–1092.

Stern, D. N. (1977). *The First Relationship: Infant and Mother*. London: Fontana.

Stern, M. M. (1957). The ego aspect of transference. *International Journal of Psycho-Analysis* 38: 146–147.

Sternbach, O. (1975). Aggression, the death drive and the problem of sadomasochism. A reinterpretation of Freud's second drive theory. *International Journal of Psycho-Analysis* 56: 321–333.

Stewart, W. A. (1967). *Psychoanalysis: The First Ten Years*. New York: Macmillan.

Stiles, W. B., Shapiro, D. A., and Eliott, R. (1986). "Are all psychotherapies equivalent?" *American Psychologist* 41: 165–180.

Stolorow, R. D. (1975a). Toward a functional definition of narcissism. *International Journal of Psycho-Analysis* 56: 179–185.

Stolorow, R. D. (1975b). The narcissistic formation of masochism (and sadism). *International Journal of Psycho-Analysis* 56: 441–448.

Stolorow, R. D. (1978). The concept of psychic structure: Its metapsychological and clinical psychoanalytic meanings. *International Review of Psycho-Analysis* 5: 313–320.

Stolorow, R. D., and Atwood, G. E. (1982). Psychoanalytic phenomenology of the dream. *Annual of Psychoanalysis* 10: 205–220.

Stone, L. (1971). Reflections on the psychoanalytic concept of aggression. *Psychoanalytic Quarterly* 40: 195–244.

Stott, D. H. (1961). Mongolism related to shock in early pregnancy. *Vita Humana* 4: 57–76.

Strenger, C. (1986). Book review: A. Grünbaum *The Foundations of Psychoanalysis*. *International Journal of Psycho-Analysis* 67: 255–260.

Strenger, C. (1991). *Between Hermeneutics and Science: An Essay in the Epistemology of Psychoanalysis*. Madison, CT: International Universities Press.

Strupp, H. H. (1986). Psychotherapy: Research, practice, and public policy (how to avoid dead ends). *American Psychologist* 41: 120–130.

Strupp, H. H., Chassan, J. B., and Ewing, J. A. (1966). Toward the longitudinal study of the psychotherapeutic process. In L. A. Gottschalk and A. H. Auerbach, eds., *Methods of Research in Psychotherapy* (pp. 361–400). New York: Appleton-Century-Crofts.

Sulloway, F. J. (1979). *Freud, Biologist of the Mind*. New York: Basic Books.

Sulloway, F. (1991). Reassessing Freud's case histories: The social construction of psychoanalysis. *Isis* 82: 245–275.

Sulloway, F. (1992). Reassessing Freud's case histories: The social construction of psychoanalysis. In T. Gelfand and J. Kerr, eds., *Freud and the History of Psychoanalysis* (pp. 153–192). Hillsdale, NJ: Analytic Press.

Sully, J. (1892). *Outlines of Psychology with Special Reference to the Theory of Education* (8th ed.). London: Longmans, Green.

Susemihl, F. F. C. E., and Hicks, R. D. (1894). *The Politics of Aristotle*. London: Macmillan.

Sutcliffe, J. P. (1960). "Credulous" and "sceptical" views of hypnotic phenomena: A review of certain evidence and methodology. *International Journal of Clinical and Experimental Hypnosis* 8: 73–101.

Sutcliffe, J. P., and Jones, J. (1962). Personal identity, multiple personality, and hypnosis. *International Journal of Clinical and Experimental Hypnosis* 10: 231–269.

Swales, P. J. (1986a). *Freud, Breuer, and the Blessed Virgin*. Paper presented at the Seminars on the History of Psychiatry and the Behavioral Sciences, New York Hospital-Cornell Medical Center.

Swales, P. J. (1986b). Freud, his teacher, and the birth of psychoanalysis. In P. E. Stepansky, ed., *Freud: Appraisals and Reappraisals* (vol. 1) (pp. 3–82). Hillsdale, N.J.: Analytic Press.

Swales, P. J. (1988). Freud, Katharina, and the first "wild analysis." In P. E. Stepansky, ed., *Freud: Appraisals and Reappraisals* (vol. 3) (pp. 80–164). Hillsdale, N.J.: Analytic Press.

Swanson, D. R. (1976). On force, energy, entropy, and the assumptions of metapsychology. *Psychoanalysis and Contemporary Science* 5: 137–153.

Swanson, D. R. (1977). A critique of psychic energy as an explanatory concept. *Journal of the American Psychoanalytic Association* 25: 603–633.

Symons, N. J. (1927). Does masochism necessarily imply the existence of a death-instinct? *International Journal of Psycho-Analysis* 8: 38–46.

Szasz, T. M. (1952). On the psychoanalytic theory of instincts. *Psychoanalytic Quarterly* 21: 25–48.

Taine, H. (1873). *De l'intelligence* (Tom. I) [*On intelligence* (vol. 1)] (3d ed.). Paris: Hachette.

Tannenbaum, S. A. (1917). Some current misconceptions of psychoanalysis. *Journal of Abnormal Psychology* 12: 390–422.

Tannenbaum, S. A. (1922). Analyzing a Freudian analysis. *Journal of Abnormal and Social Psychology* 17: 194–205.

Tannenbaum, S. A. (1923a). Commonplace mistakes in psychic functioning. *Journal of Abnormal and Social Psychology* 18: 246–257.

Tannenbaum, S. A. (1923b). Psychic determinism and "accidents." *Journal of Sexology and Psychoanalysis* 1: 305–309.

Tart, C. T. (1965). The hypnotic dream: Methodological problems and a review of the literature. *Psychological Bulletin* 63: 87–99.

Tausk, V. (1951). On masturbation. *Psychoanalytic Study of the Child* 6: 61–79. (Original work published 1912.)

Taylor, W. S., and Martin, M. F. (1944). Multiple personality. *Journal of Abnormal and Social Psychology* 39: 281–300.

Teicholz, J. G. (1978). A selective review of the psychoanalytic literature on theoretical conceptualizations of narcissism. *Journal of the American Psychoanalytic Association* 26: 831–861.

Tennes, K., Emde, R., Kisley, A., and Metcalf, D. (1972). The stimulus barrier in early infancy: An exploration of some formulations of John Benjamin. *Psychoanalysis and Contemporary Science* 1: 206–234.

Thompson, C. (1957). *Psychoanalysis: Evolution and Development*. New York: Grove Press.

Thompson, C. (1959). The interpersonal approach to the clinical problems of masochism. In J. H. Masserman, ed., *Individual and Familial Dynamics* (pp. 31–37). New York: Grune and Stratton.

Thornton, E. M. (1986). *The Freudian Fallacy: Freud and Cocaine*. London: Paladin.

Thyer, B. A. (1995). The X Club and the Secret Ring—Lessons on how behavior analysis can take over psychology. *Behavior Analyst* 18: 23–31.

Timpanaro, S. (1976). *The Freudian Slip: Psychoanalysis and Textual Criticism* (K. Soper, trans.). London: NLB. (Original work published 1974.)

Tinterow, M. M. (1970). *Foundations of Hypnosis: From Mesmer to Freud.* Springfield, Ill.: Thomas.

Toulmin, S. (1948). The logical status of psycho-analysis. *Analysis* 9: 23–29.

Toulmin, S. (1954). Postscript (1954). In M. Macdonald, ed., *Philosophy and Analysis* (pp. 155–156). Oxford: Blackwell.

Toulmin, S. (1970a). Reasons and causes. In R. Borger and F. Cioffi, eds., *Explanation in the Behavioural Sciences* (pp. 1–26). Cambridge: Cambridge University Press.

Toulmin, S. (1970b). Reply to Peters. In R. Borger and F. Cioffi, eds., *Explanation in the Behavioural Sciences* (pp. 42–48). Cambridge: Cambridge University Press.

Treurniet, N. (1991). Introduction to "On narcissism." In J. Sandler, E. P. Person, and P. Fonagy, eds., *Freud's "On Narcissism: An Introduction"* (pp. 75–94). New Haven, CT: Yale University Press.

Truax, C. B. (1966). Reinforcement and nonreinforcement in Rogerian psychotherapy. *Journal of Abnormal Psychology* 71: 1–9.

Truax, C. B. (1968). Therapist interpersonal reinforcement of client self-exploration and therapeutic outcome in group psychotherapy. *Journal of Counseling Psychology* 15: 225–231.

Truax, C. B., and Carkhuff, R. R. (1965). Experimental manipulation of therapeutic conditions. *Journal of Consulting Psychology* 29: 119–124.

Truax, C. B., and Mitchell, K. M. (1971). Research on certain therapist interpersonal skills in relation to process and outcome. In A. E. Bergin and S. L. Garfield, eds., *Handbook of Psychotherapy and Behavior Change: An Empirical Analysis* (pp. 299–334). New York: Wiley.

Turiell, E. (1967). An historical analysis of the Freudian conception of the superego. *Psychoanalytic Review* 54: 118–140.

Tyson, P., and Tyson, R. L. (1984). Narcissism and the superego development. *Journal of the American Psychoanalytic Association* 32: 75–98.

Ullman, E. (1970). About Hering and Breuer. In R. Porter, ed., *Breathing: Hering-Breuer Centenary Symposium* (pp. 3–15). London: Churchill.

Urmson, J. O. (1952). Symposium: "Motives and causes." *Proceedings of the Aristotelian Society. Supplementary Volume* 26: 179–194.

van der Hart, O., and Braun, B. G. (1986, September). *The hypnotic techniques of Pierre Janet in the treatment of dissociative disorders.* Paper presented at the third International Conference on Multiple Personality/Dissociative States, Chicago, Illinois.

van der Hart, O., and Horst, R. (1986, September). *The dissociation theory of Pierre Janet.* Paper presented at the third International Conference on Multiple Personality/Dissociative States, Chicago. Illinois.

van der Hart, O., and van der Velden, K. (1987). The hypnotherapy of Dr. Andries Hoek: Uncovering hypnotherapy before Janet, Breuer and Freud. *American Journal of Clinical Hypnosis* 29: 264–271.

Van der Waals, H. G. (1952). The mutual influences in the development of ego and id. *Psychoanalytic Study of the Child* 7: 66–68.

Van Deusen, E. H. (1868–1869). Observations on a form of nervous prostration, (neurasthenia,) culminating in insanity. *American Journal of Insanity* 25: 445–461.

Van Ophuijsen, J. H. W. (1929). The sexual aim of sadism as manifested in acts of violence. *International Journal of Psycho-Analysis* 10: 139–144.

VandenBos, G. R. (1986). Psychotherapy research: A special issue. *American Psychologist* 41: 111–112.

Vaughan, S. C., and Roose, S. P. (1995). The analytic process: Clinical and research definitions. *International Journal of Psycho-Analysis* 76: 343–356.

Vasile, R. G. (1977). *James Jackson Putnam: From Neurology to Psychoanalysis.* Oceanside, N. Y.: Dabor Science Publications.

Veith, I. (1965). *Hysteria: The History of a Disease*. Chicago: University of Chicago Press.

Vetter, I. (1988). *Die Kontroverse um Sigmund Freuds Sogenannte Verführungstheorie*. Unpublished manuscript.

Waelder, R. (1933). The psychoanalytic theory of play. *Psychoanalytic Quarterly* 2: 208–224. (Original work published 1932.)

Waelder, R. (1936). The principle of multiple function: Observations on over-determination. *Psychoanalytic Quarterly* 5: 45–62. (Original work published 1930.)

Waelder, R. (1956a). Critical discussion of the concept of an instinct of destruction. *Bulletin of the Philadelphia Association for Psycho-Analysis* 6: 97–109.

Waelder, R. (1956b). Freud and the history of science. *Journal of the American Psychoanalytic Association* 4: 602–613.

Waelder, R. (1962). Psychoanalysis, scientific method and philosophy. *Journal of the American Psychoanalytic Association* 10: 617–637.

Waelder, R. (1963). Psychic determinism and the possibility of predictions. *Psychoanalytic Quarterly* 32: 15–42.

Waelder, R. (1967a). Trauma and the variety of extraordinary challenges. In S. S. Furst, ed., *Psychic Trauma* (pp. 221–234). New York: Basic Books.

Waelder, R. (1967b). Inhibitions, symptoms and anxiety: Forty years later. *Psychoanalytic Quarterly* 36: 1–36.

Waite, A. E. (1899). *Braid on Hypnotism: The Beginnings of Modern Hypnosis by James Braid, M.D.* London: Redway. (New York: Julian Press reprint, 1960)

Wallace, E. R. (1982). The repetition compulsion. *Psychoanalytic Review* 69: 455–469.

Wallace, E. R. (1992). Freud and the mind-body problem. In T. Gelfand and J. Kerr, eds., *Freud and the History of Psychoanalysis* (pp. 231–267). Hillsdale, NJ: Analytic Press.

Wallerstein, R. S. (1975). Psychoanalysis as a science: Its present status and its future prospects. *Psychological Issues* 9: 198–228. Monograph 36.

Wallerstein, R. S. (1977). Psychic energy reconsidered. *Journal of the American Psychoanalytic Association* 25: 529–535.

Wallerstein, R. S. (1985). Book review: M. F. Reiser *Mind, brain, body: Toward a convergence of psychoanalysis and neurobiology*. *International Journal of Psycho-Analysis* 66: 518–521.

Wallerstein, R. S. (1986a). Psychoanalysis as a science: A response to the new challenges. *Psychoanalytic Quarterly* 55: 414–451.

Wallerstein, R. S. (1986b). Psychoanalysis and its discontents. *Psychoanalytic Quarterly* 55: 323–334.

Wallerstein, R. S. (1986c). *Forty-Two Lives in Treatment: A Study of Psychoanalysis and Psychotherapy*. New York: Guilford Press.

Wallerstein, R. S. (1988). Psychoanalysis, psychoanalytic science, and psychoanalytic research—1986. *Journal of the American Psychoanalytic Association* 36: 3–30.

Wallerstein, R. S. (1991). Assessment of structural change in psychoanalytic therapy and research. In T. Shapiro, ed., *The Concept of Structure in Psychoanalysis* (pp. 241–261). Madison, CT: International Universities Press.

Wallerstein, R. S. (1994). Psychotherapy research and its implications for a theory of therapeutic change: A forty year overview. *Psychoanalytic Study of the Child* 49: 120–141.

Wallerstein, R. S., and Sampson, H. (1971). Issues in research in the psychoanalytic process. *International Journal of Psycho-Analysis* 52: 11–50.

Walmsley, D. M. (1967). *Anton Mesmer*. London: Hale.

Warme, G. E. (1981). The denouement of metapsychology. *American Journal of Psychoanalysis* 41: 249–259.

Warme, G. E. (1982). The methodology of psychoanalytic theorizing: A natural science or personal agency model? *International Review of Psycho-Analysis* 9: 343–354.

Weber, J. J., Bachrach, H. M., and Solomon, M. (1985a). Factors associated with the outcome of psychoanalysis: Report of the Columbia Psychoanalytic Center Research Project (II). *International Review of Psycho-Analysis* 12: 127–141.

Weber, J. J., Bachrach, H. M., and Solomon, M. (1985b). Factors associated with the outcome of psychoanalysis: Report of the Columbia Psychoanalytic Center Research Project (III). *International Review of Psycho-Analysis* 12: 251–262.

Weber, J. J., Solomon, M., and Bachrach, H. M. (1985). Characteristics of psychoanalytic patients: Report of the Columbia Psychoanalytic Center Research Project (I). *International Review of Psycho-Analysis* 12: 13–26.

Webster, R. (1995). *Why Freud Was Wrong: Sin, Science and Psychoanalysis*. London: HarperCollins.

Weiner, H. (1979). Review of *Freud's Project Reassessed* by K. H. Pribram and M. M. Gill. *Journal of the American Psychoanalytic Association* 27: 215–223.

Weininger, O. (1906). *Sex and Character* (translation of 6th Ger. ed.). New York: Putnam. (Original work published 1903.)

Weinshel, E. M. (1991). Structural change in psychoanalysis. In T. Shapiro, ed., *The Concept of Structure in Psychoanalysis* (pp. 263–280). Madison, CT: International Universities Press.

Weiss, F. (1974). Meaning and dream interpretation. In R. Wollheim, ed., *Freud: A Collection of Critical Essays* (pp. 53–69). New York: Doubleday/Anchor.

Weissberg, M. (1993). Multiple personality disorder and iatrogenesis—The cautionary tale of Anna O. *International Journal of Clinical and Experimental Hypnosis* 41: 15–34.

Weissman, P. (1956). On pregenital compulsive phenomena and the repetition compulsion. *Journal of the American Psychoanalytic Association* 4: 503–510.

Welsh, A. (1994). *Freud's Wishful Dream Book*. Princeton, NJ: Princeton University Press.

Wells, F. L. (1912). Critique of impure reason. *Journal of Abnormal Psychology* 7: 89–93.

Wells, F. L. (1913). On formulation in psychoanalysis. *Journal of Abnormal Psychology* 8: 217–227.

Werman, D. S. (1985). Freud's *Civilization and Its Discontents*—A reappraisal. *Psychoanalytic Review* 72: 239–254.

Wetzler, S. (1985). The historical truth of psychoanalytic reconstructions. *International Review of Psycho-Analysis* 12: 187–197.

Wheelis, A. (1956). Will and psychoanalysis. *Journal of the American Psychoanalytic Association* 4: 285–303.

White, R. B. (1961). The mother-conflict in Schreber's psychosis. *International Journal of Psycho-Analysis* 42: 55–73.

White, R. W. (1959). Motivation reconsidered. *Psychological Review* 66: 297–333.

White, R. W. (1960). Competence and the psychosexual stages of development. In M. R. Jones, ed., *The Nebraska Symposium on Motivation, 1960* (pp. 97–144). Lincoln: University of Nebraska Press.

White, R. W. (1963). Ego and reality in psychoanalytic theory: A proposal regarding independent ego energies. *Psychological Issues* 3. Monograph 11.

White, W., Hartzell, W., and Smith, B. (1956). The Bridey Murphy controversy. *Chicago American*, May 27–June 7, various pages.

Whitman, R. M. (1963). Remembering and forgetting dreams in psychoanalysis. *Journal of the American Psychoanalytic Association* 11: 752–774.

Whyte, L. L. (1960). *The Unconscious Before Freud*. New York: Basic Books.

Widlöcher, D. (1985). The wish for identification and structural effects in the work of Freud. *International Journal of Psycho-Analysis* 66: 31–46.

Wiedeman, G. H. (1972). Comments on the structural theory of personality. *International Journal of Psycho-Analysis* 53: 307–314.

Wiener, P. P. (1956). G. M. Beard and Freud on "American nervousness." *Journal of the History of Ideas* 17: 269–274.

Wilcocks, R. (1994). *Maelzel's Chess Player: Sigmund Freud and the Rhetoric of Deceit.* Lanham, MD: Rowan and Littlefield.

Wilbur, G. B. (1941). Some problems presented by Freud's death instinct theory. *American Imago* 2: 134–196.

Williams, L. P. (1989). André-Marie Ampère. *Scientific American* 260: 72–79.

Wilm, E. C. (1925). *The Theories of Instinct.* New Haven, Conn.: Yale University Press.

Wilson, E. (1973). The structural hypothesis and psychoanalytic metatheory: An essay on psychoanalysis and contemporary philosophy of science. *Psychoanalysis and Contemporary Science* 2: 304–328.

Winnicott, D. W. (1958). Aggression in relation to emotional development. In D. W. Winnicott, *Collected Papers: Through Paediatrics to Psycho-Analysis* (pp. 204–218). London: Tavistock. (Original work published 1950–1955.)

Wisdom, J. O. (1956–1957). Psycho-analytic technology. *British Journal for the Philosophy of Science* 7: 13–28.

Wisdom, J. O. (1967). Testing an interpretation within a session. *International Journal of Psycho-Analysis* 48: 44–52.

Wisdom, J. O. (1968). What sort of ego has an infant? A methodological approach. In E. Miller, ed., *Foundations of Child Psychiatry* (pp. 233–249). Oxford: Pergamon Press.

Witkin, H. A., and Lewis, H. B. (1967). Presleep experiences and dreams. In H. A. Witkin and H. B. Lewis, eds., *Experimental Studies of Dreaming* (pp. 148–201). New York: Random House.

Wohlgemuth, A. (1923). *A Critical Examination of Psycho-Analysis.* London: Allen and Unwin.

Wolberg, L. R. (1947). Hypnotic experiments in psychosomatic medicine. *Psychosomatic Medicine* 9: 337–342.

Wolf, T. H. (1973). *Alfred Binet.* Chicago: University of Chicago Press.

Wolfenstein, E. V. (1985). Three principles of mental functioning in psychoanalytic theory and practice. *International Journal of Psycho-Analysis* 66: 77–94.

Wolff, P. H. (1966). The causes controls and organization of behavior in the neonate. *Psychological Issues* 5. Monograph 17.

Wolff, P. H. (1967). Psychoanalytic research and infantile sexuality. *International Journal of Psychiatry* 4: 61–64.

Wollheim, R. (1971). *Freud.* London: Fontana.

Wolpe, J., and Rachman, S. (1960). Psychoanalytic "evidence": A critique based on Freud's case of Little Hans. *Journal of Nervous and Mental Disease* 131: 135–148.

Woodworth, R. S. (1903). *Le Mouvement.* Paris: Doin.

Woodworth, R. S. (1906). The cause of a voluntary movement. In *Studies in Philosophy and Psychology by Former Students of Charles Edward Garman* (pp. 351–392). Boston: Houghton Mifflin.

Woodworth, R. S. (1917). Some criticisms of the Freudian psychology. *Journal of Abnormal Psychology* 12: 174–194.

Yankelovich, D., and Barrett, W. (1970). *Ego and Instinct: The Psychoanalytic View of Human Nature—Revised.* New York: Random House.

Yerushalmi, Y. H. (1991). *Freud's Moses: Judaism Terminable and Interminable.* New Haven, CT: Yale University Press.

Young, P. C. (1941). Experimental hypnotism: A review. *Psychological Bulletin* 38: 92–104.

Zane, M. D. (1971). Significance of differing responses among psychoanalysts to the same dream. In J. Masserman, ed., *Science and Psychoanalysis* (pp. 174–177). New York: Grune and Stratton.

Zern, D. (1968). Freud's considerations of the mental processes. *Journal of the American Psychoanalytic Association* 16: 749–782.

Zetzel, E. R. (1955a). The concept of anxiety in relation to the development of psychoanalysis. *Journal of the American Psychoanalytic Association* 3: 369–388.

Zetzel, E. R. (1955b). Recent British approaches to problems of early mental development. *Journal of the American Psychoanalytic Association* 3: 534–543.

Zetzel, E. R. (1956). Current concepts of transference. *International Journal of Psycho-Analysis* 37: 369–376.

Zilboorg, G. (1938). Some observations on the transformations of instinct. *Psychoanalytic Quarterly* 7: 1–24.

Zilboorg, G. (1952a). Clinical and technical aspects of free associations in the light of five decades of psycho-analysis. *International Journal of Psycho-Analysis* 33: 272.

Zilboorg, G. (1952b). Some sidelights on free associations. *International Journal of Psycho-Analysis* 33: 489–495.

Zubin, J. (1964). Criteria for the evaluation of the results of psychotherapy. *American Journal of Psychotherapy* 18, Supplement 1: 138–144.

Zuriff, G. E. (1992). Theoretical inference and the new psychoanalytic theories of infancy. *Psychoanalytic Quarterly* 61: 206–229.

Index

Multiple personality. *See* Cases, Anna O., Felida
  X., Mary Reynolds
Munthe, 42
Murray, E. J., 212
Murray, J. M., 492
Musatti and parapraxes, 620
Muslin, 262, 616
Mutton, Breuer's and Freud's, 106, 108
M'Uzan de, 427, 430, 435, 540
Myers, C. S., 23
Myers, F. W. H., 79, 80

Nachmansohn, 568
Nacht, 509, 511
Nacke, 358
Nagel, 195, 540, 541
Nagera, 510, 513, 532
Narcissism
  autoerotic mode vs. developmental stage,
    339–343, 348–349, 359–363, 368, 529–530, 545
  contradictory development from, 364, 529–531,
    535–536, 651
  conflict of ego and sexuality, 333–334, 348–357,
    363–372
  fixation-disposition-regression hypothesis,
    339–342, 359–361, 363, 372–373
  Freud's blow to mankind's, 594
  homosexuality, 339–342, 357–358
  megalomania, 341–342
  object-choice, 338–340
  primal state, 337–338, 349, 535–536
  primary identification, 498–499
  reconstructions vs. observations, 357–358, 493,
    545
  revised instinct theory, 376–377
  self/ego as object, 338–343, 348–351, 361–363,
    364, 376, 490–491, 493–495
  sexualization and omnipotence of thought,
    342–343, 371
  superego and, 490–494
  theoretical problems, 493–494
  topographic and structural theories and, 492–494
Natural-science alternatives to Freud, 591–592,
  613
Need for punishment (unconscious), 426, 430–432,
  440, 442–444, 459
Needles, 400, 413, 414, 416
Negative therapeutic reaction. *See* Need for
  punishment (unconscious)
Nemiah, 153
Neo-dissociation theory, 153, 333, 614
Nerve force as pseudophysiological concept, 125,
  180–181

Nervous system. *See also* Principles
  Breuer's self-regulating view, 172, 407–408,
  Freud's anachronous concepts, xxii, 180–181,
    192, 196n1, 487, 527–528
  Freud's translations from psychology, 408, 415,
    540, 542
  neural transmission, 123–125, 170, 178–181, 192
Neubauer, 479, 529
Neurasthenia
  history and demise of, 121–122, 125–126,
    197–201, 634, 666n4
  Beard and Freud, 126–131, 137, 554
  Beard's theses, 121–126, 554
  Freud's theses, 117–118, 126–131, 135, 197–201
  sexual causal factors, 117–118, 127, 128–131,
    138n1, 197–199
Neurons, key or "secretory," 472–474
Neuroses. *See also* Actual neuroses; Anxiety
  neurosis; Hysteria; Neurasthenia; Obsessional
  neuroses; Traumatic neuroses
  choice of, 359, 548
  perversions and, 285–289, 293–294, 315–316,
    326–327
  repression and, 293, 302, 326–327
  sexuality and, 117–118, 127, 128–132, 134–137,
    202–205, 293–294
  specific causes of, 119–121, 132–138, 633–636
  structure of, 99–105, 208–210, 217–222,
    227–228, 257, 327–328
  toxicity and, 159, 202–204, 459–462
Newton, 328, 399, 595
Nichols and Zax, 12, 22, 82
Niederland, 360
Nietzsche and moral demands, 598
Normal and pathological repression, 302,
  326–327, 553
Noshpitz, 10
Novey, 354, 362, 491, 492
Noy, 535
Nunberg, 356, 419, 426, 435, 477, 491, 492, 496,
  553
Nunberg and Federn, 369, 460, 461, 529
Nussbaum, 655
Nuttin, 416

Oberndorf, 565
Obholtzer, 647, 667n8
Object and Object-love. *See also* Narcissism
  affectionate current, 299–301, 302, 495, 530–531
  ambiguity of concept, 302, 304, 366–368,
    514–515
  autoerotism and, 317–318, 339–340, 530–531
  cathexis and representation, 366–368